This Is Who We Were: In The 1920s

This Is Who We Were: In The 1920s

Based on material from Grey House Publishing's
Working Americans Series by Scott Derks

Grey House
Publishing

PUBLISHER: Leslie Mackenzie
EDITORIAL DIRECTOR: Laura Mars
ASSOCIATE EDITORS: Diana Delgado; Sandy Towers
PRODUCTION MANAGER: Kristen Thatcher
MARKETING DIRECTOR: Jessica Moody
COMPOSITION: David Garoogian

Grey House Publishing, Inc.
4919 Route 22
Amenia, NY 12501
518.789.8700
FAX 845.373.6390
www.greyhouse.com
e-mail: books @greyhouse.com

Publisher's Cataloging-In-Publication Data
(Prepared by The Donohue Group, Inc.)

This is who we were. In the 1920s / [edited by] Grey House Publishing. — [First edition].

   612 pages : illustrations ; cm

   Edition statement supplied by publisher.
   "Based on material from Grey House Publishing's Working American Series by Scott Derks."
   Includes bibliographical references and index.
   ISBN: 978-1-61925-284-4

1. United States—Economic conditions—1918-1945. 2. United States—Social conditions—1918-1932.
3. United States—Civilization—1918-1945. 4. United States—History—1919-1933. 5. Nineteen twenties.
I. Based on (work) Derks, Scott. Working Americans. II. Grey House Publishing, Inc. III. Title: In the 1920s

HC106.3 .T45 2014
330.973

TABLE OF CONTENTS

Section One: Profiles

This section contains 28 profiles of individuals and families living and working in the 1920s. It examines their lives at home, at work, and in their neighborhoods. Based upon historic materials, personal interviews, and diaries, the profiles give a sense of what it was like to live in the years 1920 to 1929.

Section Two: Historical Snapshots

This section includes lists of important "firsts" for America, from technical advances and political events to new products and top selling books. Combining serious American history with fun facts, these snapshots present, in chronological categories, an easy-to-read overview of what happened in the 1920s.

Section Three: Economy of the Times

This section looks at a wide range of economic data, including food, clothing, transportation, housing and other selected prices, with reprints of actual advertisements for products and services of the time. It includes figures for the following categories, plus a valuable year-by-year listing of the value of a dollar.

Section Four: All Around Us—What We Saw, Wrote, Read & Listened To

This section includes reprints of newspaper and magazine articles, speeches, and other items designed to help readers focus on what was on the minds of Americans in the 1920s. These printed pieces show how popular opinion was formed, and how American life was affected.

Section Five: Census Data

This section includes state-by-state comparative tables and demographic trends for metropolitan areas from 1920 to 1930.

ESSAY ON THE 1920s

In the decade following the Great War, America was dividing itself into a society that embraced change and consumerism versus a society resistant to new freedoms for women, new inventions, and shifting social ethics. *This Is Who We Were: In the 1920s* profiles Americans who were at the center of a variety of social issues. Here is where the country stood nearly 100 years ago:

Consumerism

The 1920s were marked by a new nationalism symbolized by frenzied consumerism. At the beginning of the decade, urban Americans began to define themselves—for their neighbors and for the world—in terms of what they consumed. The car was becoming universal—at least in its appeal. The 4,192 automobiles that were registered nationwide in 1900 jumped to 1.9 million by 1920. Simultaneously, aggressive new advertising methods began appearing, designed to fuel the new consumer needs of the buying public. And buy, they did. The sale of electrical appliances from radios to refrigerators skyrocketed. Increased use of electric lights, telephones, and powered vacuum cleaners made them essential household items. From 1921 to 1929, Americans bought and America boomed, although debt was growing due to the extended use of credit.

Leisure

With expanded wages and buying power, and the 48-hour work week, came increased leisure time for recreation, travel, and even self-improvement. Advertising reinforced the idea that the conveniences and status symbols of the wealthy were attainable for everyone. The well-to-do and the wage earner began to look a lot more alike. Travel became more commonplace. At least 40 million people went to the movies each week, and college football became a national obsession.

Manufacturing

Industrial production rose 50 percent during the decade as the concept of mass production was refined and broadly applied. U.S. goods and services reached all-time highs.

Following the Great War, the attitude of many Americans was expressed in President Calvin Coolidge's famous remark, "The chief business of the American people is business." The availability of electricity expanded the universe of goods that could be manufactured and sold. Construction boomed as half of all Americans now lived in urban areas. With increasing sophistication came higher costs, and wages for skilled workers continued to rise during the 1920s. Unlike in previous decades, national prosperity was not fueled by the cheap labor of new immigrants, but by increased factory efficiencies, innovation, and more sophisticated methods of managing time and materials. American exports more than doubled during the decade, and heavy imports of European goods virtually halted.

Education

Parents in the 1920s demanded that progressive educational efforts be branded "fads" and tossed aside in favor of teaching basic skills, and the IQ test—the forerunner to standardized testing that would later shape America's educational curriculum—was firmly entrenched in educational philosophy. Two interesting facts: new concerns were raised that too many men were attending college unnecessarily; and the threat of expulsion from college hovered over students if caught smoking, which was illegal in 14 states.

Move to the City

Harry Donaldson's song "How Ya Gonna Keep 'Em Down on the Farm after They've Seen Paree?" described another basic shift in American society. The 1920 Census reported that more than 50 percent of the population—54 million people—lived in urban areas. The move to the cities was the result of raised expectations, increased industrialization, and the migration of millions of Southern blacks to the urban North.

Women

Following the war years, many women who had worked in men's jobs in the late teens remained in the work force, although at lower wages. Women, now allowed to vote nationally, were also encouraged to consider college and options other than marriage. On the other hand, a bill was proposed in Utah to imprison any woman who wore her skirt higher than three inches above the ankle.

Immigration

Starting in the teens, the flow of new immigrants began to slow, culminating in the restrictive immigration legislation of 1924, when the number of new workers from Europe reduced to a trickle. The efforts were largely designed to protect the wages of American workers—many of whom were only one generation from their native land. As a result, wages for unskilled labor remained stable, union membership declined, and strikes, on average, decreased. The effort to halt immigration also reduced the number of new students from foreign lands.

Poverty and Protest

Despite a growing middle class, the share of disposable income going to the top five percent of the population continued to increase. While 50 percent of Americans appeared to be in an era of unending prosperity, the other 50 percent, by one estimate, still lived in poverty. Coal and textile workers, Southern farmers, unorganized labor, single women, the elderly, and most blacks were excluded from the economic giddiness of the period. Poor or not, not all Americans relished the changes that roared in with this decade—a film code limiting sexual material in silent films was created to prevent "loose" morals, and expanded membership of the Ku Klux Klan sought to repress Catholics, Jews, open immigration, make-up on women, and the prospect of unrelenting change.

The nightmare on Wall Street in November 1929 brought an end to the economic festivities, setting the stage for a more proactive government and an increasingly cautious worker.

INTRODUCTION

This Is Who We Were: In The 1920s is an offspring of our 13-volume *Working Americans* series, which was devoted, volume by volume, to Americans by class, occupation, or social cause. This new edition is devoted to one decade—the 1920s. It represents all classes, dozens of occupations, and all regions of the country. This comprehensive look at the decade when consumerism, new freedoms for women, new inventions, and shifting social ethics were introduced presents American history through the eyes and ears of everyday Americans, not the words of historians or politicians.

This Is Who We Were: In The 1920s presents 28 profiles of individuals and families—their life at home, on the job, and in their neighborhood—with lots of photos and historical images of the time. These stories are told through the eyes and ears of everyday Americans, some struggling and some successful, but all authentic.

Together, the profiles, with the other sections outlined below, present a complete picture of what it was like to live in America in the 1920s, from the doctor who started an uproar by distributing birth control literature to his patients, to the inventor of the zipper, to the Kansas woman who advocated for the censorship of silent films.

Section One: Profiles

Each of 28 profiles in Section One begins with a brief introduction that anchors the text to the decade. Then, each profile is arranged in three categories: Life at Home; Life at Work; Life in the Community.

Section Two: Historical Snapshots

Section Two is made up of three long, bulleted lists of significant events and milestones. In chronological order—Early 1920s, Mid 1920s and Late 1920s—these offer an amazing range of firsts and turning points in American history, including:
- Thousands of gallons of milk dumped into NYC streets by striking milk truck drivers
- Race riots in Tulsa
- First commercially prepared baby food
- First female governor (Wyoming)
- Babe Ruth's 500th home run
- First successful treatment of a skin infection with penicillin
- NYC Mayor Walker urging the showing of cheerful movies after the market crashed

Section Three: Economy of the Times

One of the most interesting things about researching an earlier time is learning how much things cost and what people earned. This section offers this information in spades. Each of three categories—Consumer Expenditures, Annual Income of Standard Jobs, and Selected Prices—offers actual figures from three years—1923, 1925, and 1929—for easy comparison and study.

At the end of Section Three is a Value of a Dollar Index that compares the buying power of $1.00 in 2013 to the buying power of $1.00 in every year prior, back to 1860, helping to put the economic data in *This Is Who We Were: In The 1920s* into context.

Section Four: All Around Us

There is no better way to put your finger on the pulse of a country than to read its magazines and newspapers. This section offers 60 original pieces—articles, book excerpts and speeches—that influenced American thought in the 1920s. With articles declaring "Code of Conduct for Teachers," "Church and Politics," and "Financial Questions That Women Ask Me," this section is the eyes and ears of America in the 1920s.

Section Five: Census Data

This section includes two elements, both invaluable in helping to define the decade of the 1920s. First, 10 State-by-State comparative tables that rank data from the 1920, 1930, and 2010 Census. Topics include Population, Foreign-born, and Homeownership. Second, reprints from the 1930 Census of Population, including a United States Summary and detailed statistics on various topics.

This Is Who We Were: In The 1920s ends with a comprehensive Bibliography, arranged by topic, and a detailed Index.

Doctor Who Supported Women's Reproductive Rights in 1921

The issue of reproductive health became critically important for Dr. Henry Boekholt, a physician in Hopatcong, New Jersey, whose frightened patients begged him to teach them about birth control.

Life at Home

- Henry Boekholt never viewed himself as a radical or an activist.
- He didn't even like to speak in public.
- He was what he was—a simple country doctor who loved to care for the people of his community.
- Even as a small boy, he had known that he would follow in his father's—and grandfather's footsteps and become a doctor.
- In Hopatcong, New Jersey, there had been a Dr. Boekholt as far back as anyone could remember.
- Henry's Dutch ancestors helped settle the area and establish the Dutch Reformed Church there.
- Twenty-three years ago, when Henry Boekholt married Hanne Müller, a fourth-generation German, Hanne had become the first non-Dutch member of the family since the Boekholts immigrated to America in 1755.
- After the first three years of his marriage, Henry knew his wife had won family approval when his grandmother pulled him aside and said, "She works like a Dutch woman."
- Everyone in the community had sought help from him at some stage of their lives.
- Yet lately his place in the community seemed to be becoming insecure.
- Now the town was divided concerning his fitness as a doctor.
- The trouble had begun when he started talking about birth control to some of his patients, mostly farm women who begged for contraception information.
- At age 48, Henry had seen it all, but increasingly he was troubled by tragedies he could not even describe to his father.
- The women under his care who died in childbirth haunted his sleep, especially those who were ill-prepared or simply exhausted by too many births.
- He knew that in a country community, birth control was considered to be unnatural.
- Some others believed birth control to be degrading to mental health and injurious to both the husband and wife in their physical interactions.
- In medical school he had been taught that married couples who used birth control were being selfish in choosing to limit their family size.
- Moreover, they were choosing to enjoy sexual pleasure over domestic fulfillment.

Dr. Henry Boekholt (Library of Congress)

- Yet for nearly 25 years, he had lived by the doctrine that it was his job to treat his patients' illnesses, not to tell them how to live their lives.
- It was hard enough to get his wife and three children to pay attention to his wishes, especially his headstrong 20-year-old daughter, Clara, who was striving to be a "modern" woman.
- Henry no longer believed that birth control was a straight path to sterility, amnesia, and insanity.
- He had to admit that the American Birth Control League's pamphlet on the female contraceptive method was the best he had ever seen, even if the league's founder, Margaret Sanger, was a radical.
- But jumping into the complex world of women's reproductive rights meant wallowing in the nonprofessional world of the lower classes, a place he did not wish to go.
- And intuitively he knew that once he opened the door to birth control, its neighbor was sure to be abortion, a topic he did not wish to broach.

Clara Boekholt had a mind of her own

Life at Work

- When a 33-year-old woman who had almost died during the birth of her fifth child begged for help, Henry Boekholt had listened.
- She was terrified of becoming pregnant again, but she knew that her husband would not agree to using male contraceptives.
- For days Henry wondered if teaching her preventive, self-help techniques was acceptable.
- From hard-earned experience, his father and grandfather had advised him that self-help medicine was not the mission of doctors.
- Besides, Henry was still unsure that birth control was an appropriate topic to discuss; who was he to tell women when they had borne "enough" children?
- Since 1873 a federal law known as the Comstock Act had forbidden the distribution of birth control information, labeling distribution an "obscene" act.
- Dozens of arrests had been made in enforcing the law—Margaret Sanger was a regular offender—although the courts appeared to say that the distribution of birth control information was permitted for professionals such as doctors.
- To make matters more confusing, the world of birth control was dominated by social rebels like Sanger—who at least was an experienced public health nurse—and by self-taught midwives who preached practices straight out of the Middle Ages.
- Moreover, the Catholic Church vociferously condemned any limitation on the size of the family.
- His 33-year-old patient, Hilda, was exhausted from raising stair-step children and was convinced she would die in childbirth if she became pregnant again.
- Complications had made childbirth difficult for her the last time, resulting in hemorrhaging, swelling, and depression.

Clara as a toddler

- Too little money for food and too little time to care for the other children had not helped Hilda's state of mind.
- Henry Boekholt was not convinced that this anemic, frightened mother of five would survive another pregnancy, either.
- The question became very personal when Hilda said, "Your wife knows how to stop the babies; why can't I?"
- And he knew she was not alone in her fears.
- Henry earnestly believed that half of the women he had lost could have been helped with birth control information, better prenatal care, and more family support.

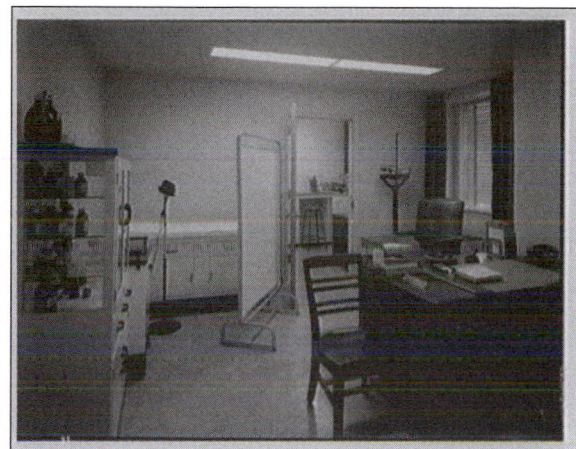

Doctor's office (Library of Congress)

- Apparently, among many of his patients, the creating of a child took two, but the raising fell to only one.
- Studies showed that up to 80 percent of the women in rural areas like his received no training or care before the birth of a child.
- Many did not have trained care, or even any care at all, during the period of confinement following childbirth.
- Yet every time a local or national politician approached the subject of increased funding for maternity care, he was branded as a socialist.
- The real problem, Henry thought, was that many physicians still believed birth control to be unnatural and possibly a threat to the human race, and that populating the world was an obligation, not a choice.
- So Henry invited Hilda back to his office and explained the reproductive cycle of women and when sexual relations with her husband were safest.
- He told her that female contraceptive devices existed, and he gave her a booklet published by a birth control information group.
- He did not anticipate that Hilda would tell everyone in her neighborhood about the lifesaving information he had provided to her.
- Within days, dozens of women of child-bearing age wanted the information, too.
- Within a month, Henry was visited by the town leaders, who demanded that he stop "promoting birth control."
- The community did not want the reputation of harboring a radical doctor; that might keep people from locating in Hopatcong, and families with daughters approaching marriageable age might not chose Lake Hopatcong as their holiday destination.
- Henry was stunned by their reaction.
- Then he became angry that the men of Hopatcong, New Jersey, intended to decide for him and his female patients how he should practice medicine.
- Henry only grew more determined when he was denounced by name from the pulpit.
- Truly he had crossed a line; there was no going back.

Life in the Community: Hopatcong, New Jersey

- Hopatcong, New Jersey, was settled by Europeans on land traditionally occupied by the Nariticong clan of the Delaware nation, who lived on the shores of Lake Hopatcong.
- In the 1820s the Morris Company dug a canal that linked the inland community to the Delaware River and thus to prosperity.

- By 1866 the Morris Canal carried almost a million tons of freight per year, including coal and iron ore.
- In the 1880s the Central Railroad of New Jersey doomed the slower canal business.
- Hundreds of residents took jobs in the Lake Hopatcong ice industry, providing ice blocks to homes as far away as New York City.
- In the 1890s the community saw the blossoming of Lake Hopatcong as a summer resort, where the wealthy would rent large furnished houses—called cottages—on the water's edge.
- Over time 40 hotels—some of them grand and regionally, even nationally, known— and less expensive rooming houses became clustered around the lake. The grand hotels lured the wealthy of New York and dozens of vaudeville stars in the summer, when most theaters were closed.
- But change hovered over the community following the Great War.
- Agricultural prices were depressed; the Morris Canal was being shut down, and every day more women were wearing makeup and skirts that didn't reach the floor.
- At the same time, the post-suffrage women's movement was transitioning to its next phase, from voting rights to reproductive rights.
- The idea of a woman's right to control her own body, and especially to control her own reproduction and sexuality, had been a radical concept when introduced half a decade earlier.
- Many critics interpreted sexual control to include sexual freedom, which would, they said, result in both promiscuity and the destruction of morality.
- The women's movement not only worked to educate women about existing birth control methods but also popularized the

Bathing beauties of Lake Hopatcong

belief that meaningful freedom for modern women included the right to decide whether they would become mothers, and when.
- During the 1920s the movement became more professionally directed and less political as the issues of medical health and population control took precedence.
- This transition legitimized the movement while relegating sex education and birth control to the background.
- Statistically, the United States ranked seventeenth in the world in the care and treatment it provided to women in childbirth, according to a May 8, 1921, article in the *New York Times* reporting on President Harding's endorsement of the Sheppard-Towner maternity bill.

The New Breslin Hotel, Lake Hopatcong (Library of Congress)

- According to the Children's Bureau of the Department of Labor, the *Times* writer continued, 23,000 women had died in childbirth in the United States the year before, and every year, 250,000 babies under the age of one year died in the United States.
- This level of mortality for both mothers and babies was called "startling and disgraceful" by the U.S. House Committee on Interstate and Foreign Commerce, which investigated the issue.
- The committee's report said that the great majority of women could be saved if the federal government would aid the state and local authorities in giving instruction and treatment to these women before and after the birth of their babies.
- The *Times* article reported that Dr. J. Whitridge Williams, obstetrician in chief at John Hopkins University, Baltimore, had asserted that at least 75 percent of the women who died in childbirth could be saved.
- In its report to Congress, the House Interstate and Foreign Commerce Committee noted that, "During the past 20 years, the typhoid rate has been reduced more than 50 percent, the tuberculosis rate has been remarkably reduced, the diphtheria rate has been reduced more than one-half, smallpox has been nearly wiped out, but there has been no reduction in maternal deaths."
- According to the report, "nearly one-half of infant deaths occur within six weeks of birth and are due chiefly to the condition of the mother and lack of proper care and attention during and following confinement."
- During 1921 Congress took the first steps toward better care of women of child-bearing age, with a $1.48 million allocation to work with individual states to promote the "care of maternity and infancy," including infant hygiene.
- The original request, from the Children's Bureau, had been for $4 million.
- National organizations such as the General Federation of Women's Clubs, the Council of Jewish Women, the Continental Congress of the Daughters of the American Revolution, and the National Organization for Public Health Nurses, as well as the governors of 34 states, had endorsed the educational effort for women and their children.
- The May 1921 *New York Times* article noted that "Almost every important religious denomination in America has endorsed the bill," which the House committee's report deemed "necessary and of an emergency character."
- "In this prosperous country," the House report said, "more women between the ages of 15 and 45 lose their lives from conditions connected with childbirth than from any other cause except tuberculosis. ...It must be apparent that some action is necessary to remedy these shocking conditions."

The Lake Hopatcong train station, 1911; Delaware, Lackawanna & Western Railroad Co.
Photo: William B. Bunnel

Women's Rights Timeline

1873　To prohibit the distribution of birth control literature, Congress passed the Comstock Law, officially called the *Act for the Suppression of Trade in, and Circulation of, Obscene Literature and Articles of Immoral Use.*

1900　Two-thirds of all divorce cases were initiated by the wife.

1903　The National Women's Trade Union League was established to advocate for improved wages and working conditions for women.

　　　Marie Curie was awarded the Nobel Prize for physics for her discovery of radioactivity.

1908　The Portia Law School in Boston offered women the opportunity to attend classes in the evening.

1909　Twenty thousand women garment workers struck in New York for better wages and working conditions, forcing over 300 shops to eventually sign union contracts.

1911　American mountain climber Annie Smith Peck ascended Mount Coropuna in Peru at the age of 61; at the summit, she unfurled a banner reading "Votes for Women."

1912　In Atlanta, Georgia, Juliette Gordon Low founded the first American group of Girl Guides, later renamed the Girl Scouts of the USA, to promote self-reliance and resourcefulness.

1913　Alice Paul and Lucy Burns formed the Congressional Union to work toward the passage of a federal amendment to give women the vote.

1914　Margaret Sanger was arrested for publishing information about birth control in her new magazine *Woman Rebel,* which the Post Office banned from the mails.

　　　The Amateur Athletic Union in the United States allowed women for the first time to register for swimming events.

1915　Radical Emma Goldman lectured on "the right of the child not to be born."

1916　Margaret Sanger opened the first U.S. birth control clinic in Brooklyn, New York, which was shut down after 10 days.

1917　Margaret Sanger was tried for disseminating birth control information.

　　　As part of the war effort, women moved into heavy industry jobs in mining, chemical manufacturing, automobile and railway plants, as well as running street cars, conducting trains, directing traffic, and delivering the mail.

　　　Jeannette Rankin of Montana became the first woman elected to the U.S. Congress.

1919　Congress passed the federal woman suffrage amendment, originally proposed in 1878, and sent it to the states for ratification.

　　　Barbara Armstrong became the first woman appointed to a tenure-track position at an accredited law school at the University of California at Berkeley.

1920　The Women's Bureau of the Department of Labor was formed to collect information about women in the workforce and safeguard good working conditions for women.

　　　The Nineteenth Amendment to the Constitution granting women the right to vote was signed into law by Secretary of State Bainbridge Colby.

　　　Margaret Sanger published *Woman and the New Race.*

1921　Margaret Sanger organized the American Birth Control League.

　　　Writer Edith Wharton won the Pulitzer Prize for fiction.

Birth control activist Margaret Sanger, 1922 (Library of Congress)

"First Birth Control Clinic to Open Here"
The New York Times, November 13, 1921

A birth control clinic, the first in the United States, will be opened in the city next Wednesday, according to an announcement made last night by Mrs. Margaret Sanger at a dinner at the Hotel Plaza in connection with the first American Birth Control Conference, of which Mrs. Sanger is Chairman...

The clinic is at 317 East Tenth Street, where four rooms on the ground floor have been leased for a year. A staff of 40 physicians has been selected, of whom 30 will be in regular attendance and 10 who will act in an advisory capacity. "The little clinic is practically ready to open within the next few days," said Mrs. Sanger.

"The next question will be that of establishing similar clinics in the cities of the various other states of the nation..."

Mrs. Sanger did not give further details in regard to the new clinic, but from Mrs. Anne Kennedy, a member of the committee that arranged the conference, it was learned that the backers of the institution have no fear of the police. "Under a decision of the Court of Appeals," explained Mrs. Kennedy, "Mrs. Sanger was found to have been entirely within the law. The clinic will afford an opportunity to women suffering from a disease, such as tuberculosis, to inform themselves." Mrs. Kennedy further explained that a large staff of doctors was necessary because the plan of those backing the project is to make the clinic immediately a first-class institution for research.

$\approx$ ᙣ ᙣ ᙣ ᙣ ᙣ

"Eugenics Uphold Control of Birth"
The New York Times, September 27, 1921

Birth control to prevent the transmission of disease and constitutional defects and the birth of too many children in families of small income where the latest-born are likely to be neglected, was urged by speakers yesterday at the Second International Congress of Eugenics in the American Museum of Natural History. Others deplored the failure of college-bred women to raise more children.

The subject of birth control has been kept in the background, but among the scientists who met yesterday, speaker after speaker attacked the laws forbidding physicians to impart information on this subject, and urged family limitation where economic or other circumstances meant that additional children would have to grow up in sickness or squalor.

Dr. Harriette A. Dilla of Smith College was applauded when she mildly reproached the medical profession for submitting passively to laws of this kind. She said that the denial of scientific information resulted in crimes and tragedies where women, turned away by medical men, resorted to expenditures suggested by despair.

Dr. Irving Fisher of Yale, who was presiding, said that care had been taken to avoid identifying the congress with "protagonists of birth control," but that the subject was one which could not be ignored.

"I think that without question," he said, "birth control is today the great new factor affecting the future character of the human race. Birth control has in its power the determination of the human race."

Elementary School Teacher of Immigrant Children in 1921

Mildred Gambon, a widow who taught in the Minneapolis public school system, decided that if her immigrant students were going to learn how to be Americans, it was her job to teach them English—in English only.

Life at Home

- Mildred Gambon knew that the time of reckoning had finally arrived.
- Thirty-four states had passed, or were considering, legislation mandating instruction in English.
- After years of having to listen to her students jabbering in a foreign language, she was relieved that English-only instruction was going to be the law of the land.
- Many of the students were second- and third-generation immigrants, she knew, and without English, they would never be real Americans.
- Why in the world would they cling to something so foreign to the American way?
- Well, it was out of their hands now: English-only instruction was on the horizon, and they couldn't do a thing about it.
- Mildred had lost count of the number of children who had arrived at her first-grade class without a word of English.
- Their parents had not bothered to Americanize them properly and proudly spoke only German at home.
- She would never have handicapped her own three children in that way.
- She never ceased to be amazed at the way some parents treated their children.
- Mildred had been a schoolteacher before her marriage, and after her husband died, she returned to teaching.
- Thanks to her husband's good business sense, she did not have to worry about losing her home, but she had to watch her expenses carefully.
- Mildred made sure that her children did not want for necessities, but luxuries were another matter.
- Still, now that they were older, she could see that her children appreciated the sacrifices she had made for them.
- Mildred's eldest son, Andrew, had returned with scarred lungs from fighting in the trenches in France during World War I—the result of German mustard gas.

Mildred Gambon

- It had caused horrible blisters and internal bleeding, temporary blindness, and excruciating pain.
- Fortunately James, the younger of her two boys, was too young to fight.
- When their sister, Anna, Mildred's middle child, was about to graduate from high school, she had spoken of volunteering as a nurse's aide, but Mildred had insisted that she was too young and was needed at home.
- Mildred had encouraged Anna to enroll in secretarial school and volunteer to work with the Red Cross in Minneapolis instead.
- Anna became involved in making a memorial quilt to be raffled off to raise money for the Red Cross. According to the December 1917 *Modern Priscilla Magazine,* in which her group found their pattern, each memorial quilt could raise up to $1,000 for purchasing ambulances and medical supplies.
- Along with many of her fellow teachers and other people throughout the city, Mildred paid ten cents to have her name embroidered on the quilt, and she also bought two quilt raffle tickets.
- Mildred was proud of Anna for putting the sewing skills she had been taught to such good use, and she herself knitted a number of pairs of socks to help the war effort, as the Red Cross requested.
- Mildred also knew exactly how important those medical supplies were.
- Mildred could have little sympathy for German Americans after Germany's aggression caused so much tragedy: she knew her son could easily have died on foreign soil, far from his home and family.
- Even now Andrew's lungs were weak.
- It seemed appropriate to her when, at the outset of the war years, "frankfurters" were renamed "hot dogs," and works by German composers—living and dead—were erased from upcoming seasons of classical music.
- Like everyone she knew, except possibly some boys around James's age who thought that they had missed their chance to be heroes, Mildred was relieved when the war ended.
- She knew, though, that the end of the war did not mean the end of her elder son's physical or emotional pain.
- Mildred was anxious about Andrew's adjustment back to civilian life.
- As a veteran he was respected, but he had needed time to recuperate, and now he was restless and having trouble staying in a job for very long.
- Mildred did everything she could to keep life at home quiet and predictable to avoid causing Andrew stress.

Life at Work

- While some states mandated English as the exclusive language of instruction in the public schools, Pennsylvania and Ohio in 1839 became the first to permit German to be used as an official alternative.
- Some public and many private parochial schools, primarily in rural areas, taught exclusively in German throughout the 1800s.
- According to the 1910 census, in a total U.S. population of 92 million, fully 9 million people in the country spoke German as their dominant language.
- Following the onset of the First World War in Europe, German American influence waned, especially once the United States entered the war in 1917.
- German Americans, especially immigrants, were scapegoated for the aggression of the German Empire; in many places, speaking German came to be seen as unpatriotic.
- Mildred Gambon had to admit that many German families she encountered were trying harder to

become Americans now that the American doughboys had halted Germany's drive toward world domination.

- Some families Anglicized their surnames; in her own classes, the Schmidts became the Smiths, the Schneiders became the Taylors, and the Müllers became the Millers.
- German disappeared nearly everywhere from the public arena, the schools included.
- During World War I, local library boards even removed books in the German language from their library shelves.

"Americanizing" immigrant children in Mildred's school

- Mildred was now able to fully implement her "sink or swim" program—total submersion, she called it privately—requiring her German-speaking first- and second-graders to learn English and how to read simultaneously.
- Her first-grade class of 27 included 5 German-speaking-only students, four boys and one girl.
- On day one, she had placed the five in the back corner, near the punishment stick, and told them to be silent.

Americanization class for adults (Library of Congress)

- It was their job to learn English, and she was not about to hold the rest of the class back.
- She had an obligation to her other students and saw no reason to penalize the majority for the problems of the few.
- For two weeks the terrified girl cried quietly, and then she disappeared.
- The quietest boy was moved to the slow class, but the other three boys learned enough to pass their tests.
- Mildred wondered what had become of the girl, but now maybe her parents would realize what they had to do to help her.

Life in the Community: Minneapolis, Minnesota

- Minneapolis and Saint Paul are collectively known as the "Twin Cities," and fostered a rivalry during their early years, with Saint Paul being the capital city and Minneapolis becoming prominent through industry.
- Minnesota, with its good farmland, became an attractive region for European immigration and settlement.
- In 1870 Minnesota's population was 439,000; this number tripled during the two subsequent decades.
- The railroad industry, led by the Northern Pacific Railway and the Saint Paul and Pacific Railroad, advertised the many opportunities in the state and worked to get German immigrants to settle in Minnesota.
- The power of the Saint Anthony Falls first fueled sawmills, but later it was tapped to serve flour mills.

- In 1870 there were only a small number of flour mills in the Minneapolis area, but by 1900 Minnesota mills were grinding 14 percent of the nation's grain. Minneapolis and the town of Saint Anthony merged in 1872.
- Advances in transportation, milling technology, and harnessing water power combined to give Minneapolis dominance in the milling industry.
- Technological improvements led to the production of "patent" flour, which commanded almost double the price of "baker's" or "clear" flour, which it replaced.
- Pillsbury and the Washburn-Crosby Company became the leaders in the Minneapolis milling industry.

The Pillsbury Mill at St. Anthony's Falls (Library of Congress)

- Until 1905 the majority of immigrants to Minnesota came from Germany, but thereafter more came from Scandinavia, mostly from Sweden and Norway.
- During the century preceding the First World War, a well-established German-language culture existed in the United States, supported by a vast array of German-language newspapers and publications.
- In the Minneapolis area, New Ulm, to the southwest of Minneapolis in central Minnesota, had a particularly strong German identity.
- World War I-era bans on the German language hit some groups particularly hard.
- Among the Missouri Synod Lutherans, the war and postwar hysteria discouraged the teaching of Lutheran Bible exegesis in German, its original language.
- "Americanization" classes were organized by educators and community leaders throughout the nation to teach adult immigrants English, American history, and civics; in some cities, women were even taught a variety of domestic subjects. The U.S. Department of State distributed pamphlets with advice for publicizing such classes, and in areas with large immigrant communities, it also sponsored teacher training.
- In the World War I era, more than 30 states instituted Americanization programs.
- Although some officials regarded naturalization and Americanization as essentially separate, with education authorities firmly in charge of the latter, many American "nativists" did not agree.
- They thought immigrants should commit to the United States by learning English and becoming citizens in short order, and that the government should essentially enforce assimilation.
- In April 1919 the state legislature of Nebraska declared: "No person, individually or as a teacher, shall, in any private, denominational, parochial or public school teach any subject to any person in any language other than the English language."
- One state representative spoke for many when he said, "If these people are Americans, let them speak our language. If they don't know it, let them learn it. If they don't like it, let them move."
- The issue of multiple languages had ricocheted across public opinion throughout American history.
- As a result of the Louisiana Purchase in 1803, the United States acquired French-speaking populations in Louisiana.
- Following the Mexican-American War, the United States acquired about 75,000 Spanish speakers in addition to several indigenous language-speaking populations.
- In 1868 the Indian Peace Commission recommended English-only schooling for Native Americans.
- In 1849 the California state constitution had recognized Spanish-language rights, but the 1878-1879 constitution required that all official business "shall be conducted, preserved, and published in no other than the English language."

- In the late 1880s, Wisconsin and Illinois passed English-only instruction laws for both public and parochial schools.
- In a few large cities, however, such as Baltimore, Cleveland, and Cincinnati, bilingual public schools were available.
- Most states enacted laws that required the use of English in specific situations, such as in testing for occupational licenses.
- During World War I, the idea of expulsion as an alternative to assimilation was frequently discussed. Believing that many immigrants' loyalties lay with their home country rather than with the United States, American nativists feared that immigrants would foment sabotage and sedition.
- Private interest groups such as the National Americanization Committee and the Foreign Language Information Service sprang up alongside public bureaus and committees to influence legislation and shape public opinion on the Americanization issue.
- In 1916 the National Americanization Committee sponsored a bill in Congress to deport all aliens who did not apply for citizenship within three years.
- The National Americanization Committee represented business and industry; its leadership largely overlapped that of the U.S. Chamber of Commerce's Immigration Committee.
- It had such close ties to the Federal Bureau of Education that until June 1919, it paid for the bureau's Americanization work, which Congress had neglected to fund. This arrangement continued until, at the end of fiscal year 1919, federal agencies could no longer accept private funding.

Daniel Webster Flour was produced by the Eagle Roller Mill Company in New Ulm, Minnesota

"Courses Offered in the Second Term, State Normal School"
Virginia Teacher, **March 1921**

113. Elementary Education

The first 25 days of the course will be based on LaRue's *The Science and Art of Teaching.* Topics: nature teaching; method as determined by the nature of the child; method as related to the teacher; teaching as conditioned by subject matter; administrative organization of schools; specific school problems, the first day, the daily program, children's textbooks, attendance, grading, children's monthly reports, promotion; how to get acquainted with school and regulations; how to get needed repairs and equipment; how to get a school library; monthly and term reports to superintendents; duties of teachers to children, the community, politicians, to fellow teachers, to superior officers, to profession.

116. Methods in Reading for Primary Grades, First Year

General topic for term, the introduction of the child to reading. Topics: meaning of reading; elements in reading, problems in beginning reading, the best approach, units of reading, material. (A.) children's poems, (D.) stories, (C.) nature, (D.) plays and games, (E.) school activities; mechanical elements, essentials in phonic study, drill, devices; relationship between oral and silent reading in first grade; critical study of primers and first readers, including those which are on the State list.

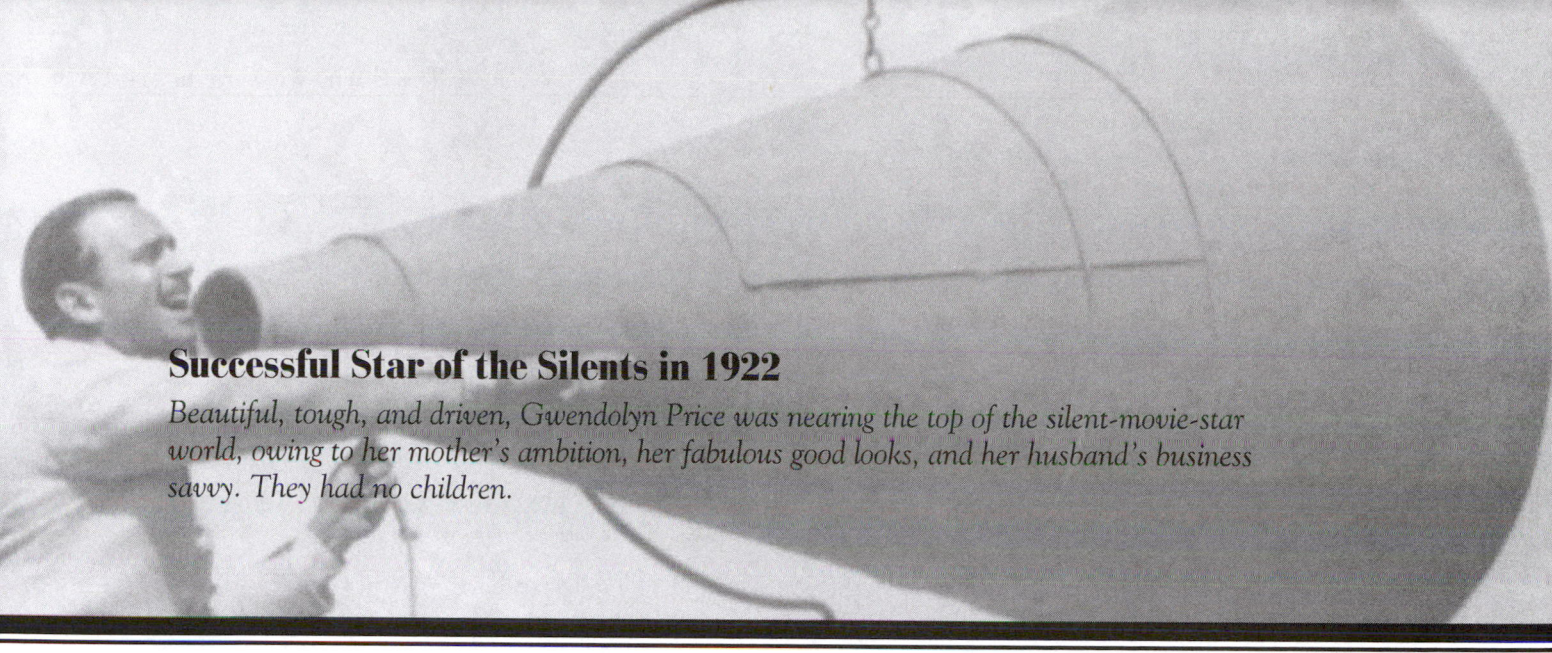

Successful Star of the Silents in 1922

Beautiful, tough, and driven, Gwendolyn Price was nearing the top of the silent-movie-star world, owing to her mother's ambition, her fabulous good looks, and her husband's business savvy. They had no children.

Life at Home

- Gwendolyn and her husband, Walter Zarnov, lived west of Los Angeles in a sprawling 3,800-square-foot home complete with an Olympic-size pool, where Walter exercised; since they both worked in the movie industry, they lived near the studio, but they still enjoyed a mountain view.

- Recently, they had purchased a Daniels automobile from "back East" that gave them the look they both desired, since the car was not only expensive—something he liked—but also very sexy—something she liked.

- Gwendolyn began appearing in movies in 1910, when she was only 14 years old, driven by a very determined mother and her own desire to be famous.

- One of three daughters, she soon began to gain fame, along with her elder sister, in the movie industry; their mother took the three girls to Hollywood with the express purpose of getting them into the movies.

- The girls knew little of their father, who had left them and their mother long before the sisters made their first movie.

- Like many of her contemporaries, Gwendolyn "came from nowhere and nothing," according to the movie magazines.

- For many young actresses, movies were viewed as a way out of poverty.

- When she was featured in the 1911 hit *An Old Man's Love Story*, Gwendolyn's head of thick, black hair and her seductive beauty launched her career. By 1914 movie scripts were being written around her talent and name.

- That same year, at 18 years old, she married Walter, a Russian immigrant who had created a fortune in movies, first as the owner of a chain of movie houses and later as a movie producer. Walter was 19 years Gwendolyn's senior, and she called him Daddy.

Gwendolyn Price

- After their marriage, her husband established a Hollywood-based production company to feature his wife's skills and those of her sister.
- For the past several years, her movies had featured not only her natural beauty but dozens and dozens of fabulous outfits; women often went to her movies to marvel at the latest fashions she displayed on the screen.
- Her roles ranged from traditional women to exotic, ethnic characters; lately she had played an Asian maiden; the daughter of one of the

Gwendolyn and Walter's lavish home west of Los Angeles

first families of Virginia, fated to marry the wrong man; and a self-sacrificing Russian princess, in a movie entitled *New Moon*. In *Isle of Conquest*, soon to be released, she was shipwrecked with a man who hated women.
- Her elder sister often played in comedies; they had found that their parallel careers were complementary, and they very rarely competed with one another for attention.
- Their younger sister, who only managed to land small parts in a handful of moving pictures, had recently married movie star Buster Keaton.

Life at Work

- Gwendolyn belonged to a tiny group of highly celebrated movie actresses who came to symbolize the romantic ideals of the nation. She was flooded with fan letters; girls across the nation emulated her clothing and hairstyles and her "way with men."
- Although, during the early years, she worked an arduous dawn-to-dusk schedule to get parts, Gwendolyn's fame was now said to rival that of "America's Sweetheart," Mary Pickford, who was earning more than $100,000 per picture.
- Like many of her fellow movie stars, Gwendolyn was small, at only five feet tall, and she often performed with leading men who were only six- to eight inches taller.
- Gwendolyn's adoring fans saw her as a woman with one foot in the 1890s and the other in the 1920s. In one movie she was shown driving her roadster at top speed while planning her "radiophone" dance for the coming evening—a scene displaying both her "old" persona of wife and hostess, focusing her attention on social events, and her "new woman" persona as the driver of a powerful—and fast—automobile.

The Daniels, the epitome of automobile luxury

- By early 1922 she had appeared in more than 200 movies; she could now name her price, often up to $100,000 per picture, and she was able to make four or five movies a year.
- For his part, Walter generally made $350,000 a year through movie productions and the management of several movie stars, including Gwendolyn.
- Silent movies were about emotion and action, and Gwendolyn had a talent for displaying both without speaking; title cards displayed throughout the movies provided the viewers with an ongoing conversation, relaying historical information, mood, dialogue, and, often, wit.
- Gwendolyn loved her job, and she worshipped the money she made as a movie star; having money and power had made her wonder why so many movie directors demanded that female actors appear so childlike, helpless, and frightened while waiting for heroic men to save them.

- One reason Gwendolyn could command such high salaries was the creation of the star system, which began in 1913 when actors began demanding screen credits for their work. They could negotiate for higher and higher wages as the public demanded to see their favorite stars.

Life in the Community: Hollywood, California

- In 1910 Hollywood, California, was a quiet, country town near Los Angeles, dominated by lemon groves, churches, and a few sprawling estates.
- Four years later, Hollywood claimed 52 moviemaking companies, which together spent $5.7 million a year to crank out more than a thousand miles of developed film annually.
- The area also offered scenic lands for the shooting of cowboy movies; majestic backdrops, such as the Pacific Ocean; and mountains and deserts only a day away.
- The ability to concentrate production in factorylike studios and to integrate virtually all aspects of

Gwendolyn was famous for her exotic roles and their exotic fashions

production allowed Hollywood-produced movies to be shot more quickly, at less cost, with more control.
- The Hollywood system became the model worldwide. Its products and its stars, such as Charlie Chaplin and Mary Pickford, became international cultural icons.
- By the early 1920s Hollywood-produced movies were dominant worldwide; World War I had dramatically reduced the ability of many European producers to compete with American films.
- Nationwide Americans enjoyed a great variety of entertainment—motion pictures, baseball, and boxing all regularly drew record crowds.
- Everyone wanted to be in the movies and in Hollywood, to the point that the Chamber of

Escape artist Harry Houdini about to demonstrate his remarkable skills

Commerce bought newspaper ads to discourage young women from coming to Hollywood—the "land of broken dreams," as they called it. The advertisements pleaded, "Please don't try to break into the movies."
- Even the great escapologist Harry Houdini made films to display his greatest stunts; unfortunately, his astonishing ability to escape from impossible situations proved irrelevant on the screen, where, audiences knew, stunts could easily be faked.
- Nationwide, by early 1922, more than twenty thousand cinemas had opened, two thousand of which were picture palaces for the showing of exclusive, first-run movies of "feature length"—that is, running about 90 minutes.
- Picture palaces were architectural marvels, designed to capture attention; many featured colossal electric signs that could be seen for miles, while their interior decoration often showcased opulent chandeliers, classical drapery on walls and entrances, and elegant furniture. Many offered patrons free child care.

Film Industry Timeline

1889 Thomas Edison was commissioned to build the first motion-picture camera, named Kinetograph.

1894 The Edison Corporation established the first motion picture studio, nicknamed the Black Maria, a slang expression for a police van.

The first Kinetoscope parlor opened at 1155 Broadway in New York City, where spectators were charged $0.25 to watch films.

1895 In France, Auguste and Louis Lumière invented the Cinématograph, a combination camera and projector.

1896 The Edison Corporation produced *The Kiss,* the first film ever made of a couple kissing; the short 20-second film, with a close-up of a kiss, was denounced as shocking and pornographic by some early moviegoers and caused the Roman Catholic Church to call for censorship.

1901 With the arrival of electricity, Broadway set out white lights stretching from 13th to 46th Streets in New York City, inspiring the nickname "the Great White Way."

1903 Edison Corporation's Edwin S. Porter directed the first Western, *The Great Train Robbery,* which lasted 12 minutes.

The courts ruled that a film did not have to be copyrighted frame-by-frame, but rather that it could be covered in its entirety by one copyright submission.

1904 The 35 mm film width, and a projection speed of 16 frames per second, were accepted as an industry standard.

1905 In Pittsburgh, the first movie theater opened, named a nickelodeon after the cost of admission, a nickel, and the Greek word for theater, "odeon."

1906 The Keith organization began converting vaudeville theatres into motion picture houses and encouraged parents to send their children there after school was over.

1907 *The Saturday Evening Post* reported that daily attendance at nickelodeons exceeded two million nationwide.

The Chicago Daily Tribune denounced nickelodeons as firetraps and tawdry corrupters of children.

The first film makers arrived in Los Angeles, which offered a favorable climate and a variety of natural scenery.

Bell and Howell developed a film projection system.

1908 About 9,000 nickelodeons were open across the country.

1909 *The New York Times* published the first movie review, a report on D. W. Griffith's *Pippa Passes.*

The New York Times coined the term "stars" for prominent movie actors.

The Motion Picture Patents Company (MPPC) was formed and became a holding company for all of the patents belonging to the film producers who were members.

The MPPC agreed to submit its films to the Board of Censorship, which had been established by the People's Institute of New York City to head off state and local censorship efforts.

1910   Thomas Edison introduced his kinetophone, which made talkies a reality more than a decade later.

      The first movie stunt featured a man jumping from a burning balloon into the Hudson River.

1911   Pennsylvania became the first state to pass a film censorship law.

      Credits began to appear at the beginning of motion pictures.

1912   *Photoplay* debuted, the first magazine for movie fans.

      Motion pictures began to move out of nickelodeons and into real theaters as movies became longer, more expensive and featured more stars.

1913   America's first feature-length film dealing with sex was *Traffic in Souls,* a "photo-drama" exposé of white slavery at the turn of the century in New York City.

1914   Charlie Chaplin played the role of the Little Tramp, his most famous character.

      Winsor McCay released *Gertie the Dinosaur,* the first animated cartoon.

1915   D. W. Griffith released *The Birth of a Nation,* which introduced the movie techniques of the narrative close-up and the flashback; the film ignited controversy over its depiction of the Civil War and Reconstruction era.

      The Bell & Howell 2709 movie camera allowed directors to film close-ups without physically moving the camera.

      The Board of Censorship became The National Board of Review.

      Movie sex goddess Theda Bara's role as a worldly, predatory woman who stole a married man away from his wife and child in *A Fool There Was* earned her the title of "the wickedest woman in the world."

      A Free Ride, the earliest-known silent stag or pornographic film, was released.

1916   Charlie Chaplin signed on with Mutual Studios for an unprecedented $10,000 a week.

1917   The Lincoln Motion Picture Company, the first African-American-owned studio, was founded.

1919   Charlie Chaplin, D. W. Griffith, Douglas Fairbanks Sr., and Mary Pickford established United Artists in an attempt to control their own work.

      Felix the Cat first appeared.

      Cecil B. DeMille's film *Male and Female* included a semi-nude scene of actress Gloria Swanson disrobing in preparation for a lavish bath in a sunken tub.

1920   Actress Yvonne Gardelle appeared naked during a Garden of Eden prologue sequence in *The Tree of Knowledge.*

1921   *The Sheik,* starring Rudolph Valentino, was released.

      Charlie Chaplin produced *The Kid,* which featured Jackie Coogan.

      Comedian Roscoe "Fatty" Arbuckle was arrested for the alleged rape and murder of 25-year-old actress Virginia Rappe during a wild party in San Francisco, reinforcing the public's image of Hollywood as scandalous.

1922   Hollywood censored itself by creating the Motion Picture Producers and Distributors of America (MPPDA).

Movie director William Desmond Taylor was found murdered in Los Angeles with a bullet in his back; dozens of potential starlets were suspects.

1923 German shepherd Rin Tin Tin became film's first canine star.

Cecil B. DeMille's first version of *The Ten Commandments* featured the largest set ever constructed in movie history up to that time; the "City of the Pharoah" was 120 feet tall and 720 feet wide, with massive Egyptian statuary weighing one million pounds.

The Hollywood sign, spelled HOLLYWOODLAND, was built for $21,000.

1924 Walt Disney created his first cartoon, *Alice's Wonderland.*

1925 *Ben-Hur,* which cost a record-setting $3.95 million to produce, included a segment featuring rows of bare-breasted flower girls dancing in a pageant procession as they tossed flowers to the crowd lining the street.

The first in-flight movie, a black-and-white silent film titled *The Lost World,* was shown in a WWI converted bomber during a 30-minute flight near London.

1926 Leading man John Barrymore starred in *Don Juan* with Mary Astor and Estelle Taylor, a film that included 127 kisses.

1927 Popular vaudevillian Al Jolson marked the end of the silent movie era when he spoke the line: "Wait a minute. Wait a minute. You ain't heard nothing yet!" in *The Jazz Singer.*

A sound-on-film system called Movietone was developed in which the sound track was placed onto the actual film next to the picture frames, rather than on a separate synchronized disc, as in Vitaphone.

Motion picture film became standardized at 24 frames per second.

The Hays Office issued a memorandum, "Don'ts and Be Carefuls," a code of decency telling the studios 11 taboos to avoid, including profanity, "licentious or suggestive nudity," illegal traffic in drugs, any inference of sex perversion, white slavery, miscegenation, sex hygiene and venereal diseases, scenes of actual childbirth, children's sex organs, ridicule of the clergy, and willful offense to any nation, race or creed.

Paramount released a film titled *It* featuring sexy starlet Clara Bow as a lingerie salesgirl, who soon became known as the "It Girl."

1928 Walt Disney introduced *Galloping Gaucho* and *Steamboat Willie,* the first cartoons with sound.

The Academy Awards were awarded for the first time; *Wings* won Best Picture.

"Film Men Attack Morality Drives"
***The New York Times*, January 28, 1928**

Various suggestions to improve the motion picture and means to overcome the exhibitor's difficulties in obtaining desirable films were discussed yesterday at the fourth annual Conference of the National Board of Review of Motion Pictures at the Waldorf. Delegates representing Better Film Committees condemned morality drives and the like and urged intelligent selection of pictures as opposed to the methods of reform groups.

Discussing a community plan to encourage the high type of motion picture, Professor Leroy E. Bowman of the Department of Social Science at Columbia [said] that the best pictures "can be evolved only through intelligent selection by the interested public and not through censorship, moralism or monopoly. It is the plan of common effort and of common sense as opposed to the narrow, moralistic and monopolistic plans that have been proposed in various quarters."

Professor Bowman praised the National Board of Review as the only extensive agency in the country on which reliance can be placed to express the interest and wishes of the public "because it approaches the problem from a natural, human point of view without bureaucratic censorship."

"The only thing the matter with movies is the audience," Ida Clyde Clarke, lecturer and author, told the delegates.

"The American public is tabloid-minded and has the tabloid soul," she said. "It wants a stimulant for its atrophied or undeveloped emotions and prefers to take it undiluted and unrefined."

Dr. Horace M. Kallen of the New School for Social Research traced the history of censorship, the psychological foundation of which, he said, is based on the three emotions-"fear, greed and a sense of shame."

Morality drives, he declared, originate in the emotions of persons who feel certain that the evils they would correct will not hurt them but might have a harmful influence on others.

Dr. Kallen warned the audience "to make sure that the vague and uncertain rules laid down are not used as instruments of competitive oppression within the industry.

"Certain types of prohibitions," he said, "have been recently adopted by the picture industry which involve affecting the sense of shame with respect to sex. It is necessary to make sure that there is not some psychopathic influence in the work of censorship within the industry."

D. W. Griffith, Mary Pickford, Charlie Chaplin, and Douglas Fairbanks Jr. (front, left to right) create United Artists studio, 1919 (New York World-Telegram and the Sun Newspaper Collection, Library of Congress)

Welsh Immigrant Printing Plant Worker in 1923

Enid Gaskell, a 30-year-old Welsh immigrant who worked at a printing plant in Tulsa, Oklahoma, supported her family of four. Her husband, Henry, was an unemployed coal miner in his mid-thirties. In 1923 the Gaskells had two children, Edward and Anna, under the age of 12. Anna was barely out of diapers.

Life at Home

- Living on the outskirts of Tulsa, Henry and Enid were preoccupied with making ends meet.
- Enid had more job mobility than Henry, but naturally the jobs open to her paid considerably less than Henry could make at the mine.
- Henry was a veteran of World War I. He had seen little action during the war but loved traveling across country by train. He had especially enjoyed seeing France.
- When he returned to Tulsa, Henry was amazed at how the city had grown. There was a new city hall, and tall new office buildings were everywhere.
- There was even a new daily afternoon newspaper, the *Tulsa Tribune*.
- Henry came home expecting to go back to steady work at the coal mine, and he was rehired by his old company.
- Henry knew that a number of Negro men from Tulsa had enlisted in the army; some had even fought in France, including the popular football coach at the high school in Tulsa's Greenwood district, also called Little Africa.
- But Negro soldiers had their own units, and Henry rarely encountered them during his wartime service.
- Back home in Tulsa, whites and blacks mostly stayed separate.
- Some men Henry knew considered that Negro business owners in Greenwood had too much money.
- When Greenwood was burnt out during a ferocious race riot on May 31 and June 1, 1921, Henry and Enid learned about it mostly from the neighbors, at church, and in the pages of the *Tulsa World*, the city's older newspaper.
- Henry was troubled that some of the victims of the riot—no one knew exactly how many there were—were veterans like himself.
- But people talked mostly about crime and bad morals in Tulsa, and some men Henry worked with were joining the Ku Klux Klan to punish bootleggers, automobile thieves, and others that official law enforcement never seemed to touch.

Enid Gaskell

23

- In 1922, when the coal industry fell on hard times, Henry was laid off, as were more than half of all coal industry workers.
- Henry grew resentful that the government that had asked him to fight didn't care that he had lost his job.
- Henry even lost the War Risk Insurance he had earned because he could not keep up with the payments.
- Desperate for work, Henry traveled as far as Oklahoma City in search of a job.
- Prohibition had begun in 1920, and Henry considered operating an illegal liquor still, as many unemployed miners did.
- Even though her husband was unemployed, Enid was still responsible for cooking all meals and caring for the children.
- Edward was enrolled in school, but his attendance seemed to be slipping, and Enid worried that in a few years, he would drop out and lie about his age to get work.
- Enid firmly believed in the importance of education.
- Once Enid returned to work after Anna was born, she arranged for a neighbor to look after the baby during the day.

Henry Gaskell searching for work

- Enid prepared her own baby formula at home, always using fresh whole milk, or—when she could get it— "top milk," which she knew was easier for Anna to digest. Enid's doctor told her to add some Karo syrup for energy and to give Anna some vegetable juice as well.
- The newest recommendation was to feed babies cod liver oil to prevent scurvy and rickets, but Anna did not like its taste.
- Enid instructed her neighbor to sterilize the rubber bottle nipple each time before feeding the baby.
- The new rubber nipples were much easier to clean properly than the old type she had used with Edward.
- Feeding Anna was much easier once the baby could eat strained vegetables and cereal.
- At lunchtime Enid sometimes managed to take a trolley home to check on Anna and play with her for a few minutes.

- There was a day nursery nearer the printing plant, but Enid had read that the care at day nurseries sometimes wasn't very good.
- The neighbors considered day nurseries to be for poverty-stricken families, not working mothers.
- Enid's coal stove was hard to regulate, and she was trying to save enough money to make a down payment on a new stove. A Kalamazoo gas range, which could be purchased on the installment plan, was a likely choice. The cash price was $47.90; the credit price was $52.70.

Life at Work

- At a printing plant located outside Tulsa, Enid made $12.15 a week.
- Enid was hired to package and ship print jobs, but because she had an eleventh-grade education, she also worked as a proofreader of copy, catching spelling and grammatical errors.
- Occasionally Enid also hand-set type, especially for the headlines of short-run fliers that had to be produced quickly.
- She was a valuable employee who worked hard to make sure her work did not pile up and was completed on schedule.
- Although the state limited a working woman's hours to 9, an 8-hour day was standard. The 6-day week was more common than a 5 1/2-day week. Enid's 48-hour week was shorter than the state-mandated maximum of 54 hours per week.

Printing plant workers monitoring the presses (Harris & Ewing Collection, Library of Congress)

- Most of the printing plants in the state operated on an eight-hour schedule rather than requiring nine-hour days.
- Most of the women working in laundries and food manufacturing worked a full nine-hour day.
- Enid was allowed an hour for lunch, a practice common in the manufacturing industry.
- Lighting was good at the printing plant, since it was a necessity for the printing facility.
- State law required that "establishments employing females shall provide suitable seats," and the printing facility complied with this regulation.
- Enid had previously worked in a factory that made overalls. There she was paid on a piecemeal basis. Nearly all of Oklahoma's shirt- and overall workers were female.
- Although she had made as much as $14.50 a week stitching overalls, Enid preferred working at the printing plant because the work was more interesting and she was paid on a time-work basis. She liked knowing what she would make every week.

Women and men operating presses on the plant floor (National Photo Company Collection, Library of Congress)

- In addition, the working conditions at the overall plant were poor. An inspection showed that the factory had no lunchroom, cloakroom, or restroom; light bulbs were unshaded and caused glare; a common drinking cup and common towel were shared by all workers; and most workers were not provided with seats but had to stand throughout the day.

Life in the Community: Tulsa, Oklahoma

- In 1870 unemployment in the eastern United States had persuaded many miners to accept the railroad's offer of free transportation to Indian Territory. Scores of skilled immigrants from the British Isles were among those who went to the Tulsa area.
- A generation later Irish, Scottish, and Welsh surnames were common in the region.
- Coal seams were concentrated in the northeastern portion of Indian Territory.
- The Cedar Bluff, Checkerboard, Tulsa, and Upper- and Lower Dawson seams were all located in what became Tulsa County.
- At the Dawson seams both strip mining and shaft mining were employed.

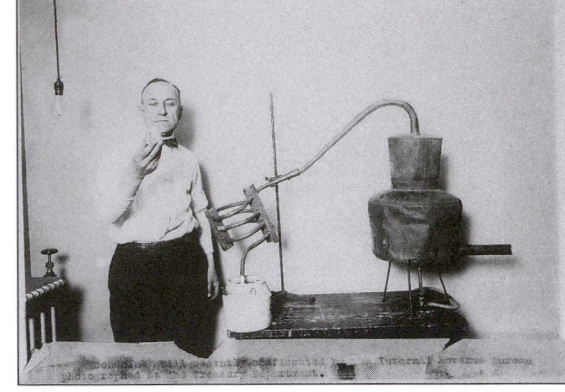

An Internal Revenue Bureau agent examines a confiscated moonshine still (Library of Congress)

- In 1889 Congress opened up to white settlement some two million acres of what in 1890 became the Oklahoma Territory.
- In 1903 an Oklahoma miner's base wage was $2.45 per day; little machinery was used because labor was so plentiful.
- Workers often worked in knee-deep water or crawled on all fours during their 12-hour shifts.
- Once the coal mines were unionized in 1903, hours were reduced to eight per day.
- In 1905 the Indian Territory—where the Five Civilized Tribes (Cherokee, Choctaw, Chickasaw, Muscogee (Creek), and Seminole) had been resettled from the southeastern United States in the 1830s—unsuccessfully attempted to gain statehood.

Texaco built its refinery headquarters in west Tulsa in 1921

- Oil was first drilled for in Oklahoma in 1897; by 1905, there were 255 producing wells in Indian Territory.
- Oklahoma became the Southwest's leading producer of crude oil. The oil wells produced fabulous wealth for a few.
- In November 1907 Oklahoma Territory and Indian Territory were joined together as the State of Oklahoma, the forty-sixth state.
- The state's oil- and gas-producing fields increased from 39 in 1908 to 110 in 1915; the flood of crude into the market over the same period pushed prices down from $1.05 per barrel to $0.35 a barrel.
- The outbreak of war in Europe and the rising sales of automobiles drove prices back up. Farmers anxious to take advantage of wartime agricultural prices purchased gasoline-driven equipment in large numbers.
- By the mid-1920s, the Greater Seminole Field, which encompassed five counties and seven major pools of oil, pumped 10 percent of all the oil produced in the United States.
- Although many of the discoveries were made on what had been Indian Territory lands, by the time of the

great oil booms, many Native American allotments had passed to white owners through embezzlement, forgery, or the deliberate mismanagement of the probate courts.

- Only among the Osage were mineral rights reserved to the tribe as a group; the discovery of the Burbank field in the 1920s made the tribe the richest tribe of Native peoples in the world.
- Between 1910 and 1920, the nation's urban population increased 29 percent; in Oklahoma the growth rate was 69 percent.
- Oil made Tulsa a boom town. By 1920 the population of greater Tulsa was more than 100,000.
- Beginning in 1918 a number of Western movies were produced in Tulsa.
- As a result of the oil strikes and the enormous wealth they generated, Tulsa attracted not only entrepreneurs and enterprising workers but also gamblers, bootleggers, and prostitutes. Tulsa gained a national reputation as a city where crime flourished and law enforcement was lax.
- The Oklahoma coal industry, which paid operators $6.00 a day during World War I, peaked in 1920.
- The discovery of rich oil and gas fields in the mid-1920s transformed the economy of the state and reduced the competitiveness of coal. Many coal miners lost their jobs.
- At the same time, social change swept the country, raising issues about morality and ethics.
- Even a deck of "Old Maid" playing cards reflected the changing times, featuring Rudolf Sheik, Mandy Lou, Sailor Al K. Hall, Hiram Squash, and Doughboy Dolph.
- Much of the anger over bad times and shifting mores was directed at African Americans and Catholics, and many saw the Ku Klux Klan as the answer to their problems. Anti-Catholic newspapers gained wide circulation.
- The Women's Auxiliary of the Episcopal Church launched a nationwide morality campaign, conducting a series of meetings for girls to discuss the problem of "upholding standards."
- In Tulsa the new afternoon daily newspaper, the *Tulsa Tribune,* conducted an inflammatory campaign against crime and corruption.
- The tinder was already in place, but in late May 1921, the *Tribune*'s story and editorial about a black man's alleged assault on a white woman evidently set off the Tulsa race riot of May 31-June 1, considered to be the worst in the nation's history.
- Official estimates placed the death toll in the thirties; unofficial estimates ran some ten times higher, with millions of dollars in property losses.
- The victims of the riot were overwhelmingly African Americans, many of whom perished after shockingly brutal attacks. Many of the black victims were buried in unmarked graves, their fate unknown to their families.
- Property damage was almost entirely confined to the black enclave known as Greenwood or Little Africa, which was completely destroyed. Churches, schools, and hospitals were torched.
- Almost immediately after the riot, a fire ordinance was passed that was intended to ensure that Greenwood would be not be rebuilt.
- Many black Tulsans spent the winter of 1921-1922 living in tents.
- African American attorneys, notably B. C. Franklin, later succeeded in persuading the Oklahoma Supreme Court to declare the ordinance unconstitutional.
- After the riot Tulsa became an active center of Klan activity. Prominent Tulsa citizens and politicians openly were members; Tulsa had not only a chapter of the Klan's women's auxiliary but an affiliate chapter for youth, the Junior Ku Klux Klan.

"EVERYTHING BUT THE KITCHEN STOVE"

Is what Will Rogers says we promised the soldiers, when they went away, but now: "You didn't tell him he had to come home on a stretcher before you would give him anything, did you?"

High School Junior in 1923

A native of Seaman, Ohio, Jervey Steffens dreamed of becoming a famous jazz saxophone player or writing a controversial book that would rile the censors, although she also thought she might settle on a few years in college first.

Life at Home

- Even though her real name was Eleanor, her father had called her by her middle name, Jervey, since she was a little girl; now everyone did.
- She loved having a name different from everyone else's.
- Once she turned 16, having read about what Napoleon and Mozart did as teens, Jervey believed it was time for her to think important thoughts and make big discoveries.
- She felt that greatness was her destiny, too, and that she would make her mark on the world through music or literature.
- To play saxophone with Fletcher Henderson's jazz band or write a great novel that would make the censors cringe—now, that would be grand.
- The previous year, when she was much younger, she had often spent time wondering about her neighbors' real occupations: Was the debonair man who lived down the street really a desperate criminal? Could the lady next door actually be a world-famous dancer or a World War I spy, or both? Did the Wilkersons have countless millions buried in their backyard?
- As a junior in high school, she put those fantastic notions behind her, although she still sometimes wondered about the past of the debonair man down the street.
- Jervey's family attended the Methodist church; her mother was a committed advocate for the Epworth League, often urging Jervey to convince her friends of all the good they could do as members of that church organization for young people.
- Jervey always knew when *The Epworth Herald* had arrived; after reading it, her mother could be relied on to talk about going to a devotional, inspiring young people, or helping others—sometimes all at the same time.
- Lately her mother had been preoccupied by the campaign to eliminate child labor across America, telling everyone she knew, "Children should have a childhood."
- Jervey and her family lived in a turn-of-the-century Queen Anne-style house that had a dining room, living

Jervey Steffens with her friend Dorothy

room, and sitting room on the first floor, in addition to a bathroom, pantry, and kitchen.

- The front- and rear staircases led to a 790-square-foot second floor with four bedrooms—one of which was Jervey's—and a bath, shared by the family.

- Jervey considered her father impossible to figure out; all he ever seemed to say to her was, "Turn off the lights when you leave the room; I'm not made of money," yet he had spent $112 to install a new coal-burning central heating system so that he would not have to tend to the fire so much.

- For reasons that were beyond Jervey, all of her friends seemed to like her mother and even her two pesky younger brothers, and the girls came over to the house often—especially once the Steffenses bought an electric mixer, which made cookie- and cake-baking a breeze.

The comfortable Steffens family home

- Jervey's mother said her favorite time of the week was when the two of them sat down in the kitchen together to snap string beans; Jervey was rather less enamoured of this ritual.

- The entire family—even her father, who worked at the bank and was very serious—went to the cinema to see Cecil B. DeMille's *The Ten Commandments*, which, they agreed, was wonderful.

- Seaman's moving picture theater came into being after local businessmen banded together and bought one or two shares each in the Star Moving Picture Company, so that the town could enjoy the movie boom sweeping America.

- Jervey was waiting impatiently to see *The Pilgrim*, starring Charlie Chaplin, and the thrilling *Hunchback of Notre Dame*, with Lon Chaney, when they came to town.

- Jervey's grandfather operated the town's biggest produce house, dealing in eggs, poultry, cream and veal calves.

- Business was so good that he now owned two trucks and took local produce to Cincinnati twice a week.

- Sometimes he returned with small gifts for Jervey and her brothers.

- Jervey was very pleased that she now had a school dress that included a clasp-locker, or what some magazines were calling a zipper.

Dorothy Lancaster, Jervey's best friend

- Ever since World War I, the zipper had been becoming more popular.

- Jervey had been convinced that her friend Dorothy Lancaster would have a dress with a zipper first, but Jervey's birthday came before Dorothy's, so it did not turn out that way.

- Jervey decided she would even wear the dress to the circus that was planning a stop near her home in Seaman.

- Featured acts advertised in fliers include John Zellnerino Batistichiski, the Italian knife thrower; Clark Brooks Martinique, the cigarette fiend; Helene Foxe, the graceful tight rope walker; Clara Beard Evans, the bearded lady; and Maurice Bair Valintino, the cowpuncher who courted death and laughed at disaster.

- The family had just purchased a radio, and many evenings were spent listening to the glorious sounds of the Lyric Quartet or to the Lucky Strike show.
- Jervey loved listening to jazz and pretending that she was on stage right in the midst of the orchestra.

Life at School

- In class Jervey was known as a reader and a dreamer.
- On more than one occasion, she was caught reading a book other than the assigned text.
- Jervey's favorite teacher, Miss Bertha Patterson, a graduate of Cornell University, understood Jervey's need to read.
- Jervey still enjoyed adventure stories—with girls as the heroines, of course, as in *The Radio Girls on Station Island,* by Margaret Penrose.
- But after class Miss Patterson often challenged Jervey to move on from series books and read current literature.
- Wanting to be like Miss Patterson, Jervey had managed to get a copy of F. Scott Fitzgerald's *Tales of the Jazz Age;* Jervey found it daring, and she loved Fitzgerald's style, but she found it hard to relate to the young women in the stories.

Miss Patterson, Jervey's role model

- Jervey was on the girls' basketball team and was the only girl in her school's Saxophone Club.
- Her basketball team only played five games during the season, because traveling long distances during Ohio winters could be treacherous.
- The team lost four of its five games, beginning with a 23-to-6 defeat in the first game of the season, but it improved as the season went on.
- Jervey loved being able to play the saxophone just as well as the five boys in the club.
- Some of Jervey's neighbors were concerned that a group composed of five boys and one girl did not seem proper, so the club held most of its practices in the Steffenses' front parlor, where, obviously, everyone would be properly supervised.
- Jervey snickered when she read the line in her high school Annual announcing that the Saxophone

Jervey's basketball team and its mascot

Club was "the first organization of its type" and was "proving to be a popular organization which has been very acceptable to the public and the pupils of the high school."
- Everyone knew that the club would never have been formed if Jimmy Epting's father hadn't gone to the superintendent's office and threatened to sue if the group wasn't sanctioned.
- Jervey couldn't wait to be a senior, when she and her friends would be the oldest and in charge.
- Jervey had always thought she would go to secretarial school, but she and Dorothy were both now thinking about college.

- Last year nearly half of the class had gone on to college, most to Ohio State and Miami University; a few went to Oberlin and Wooster.
- Jervey thought that going to Cornell, like Miss Patterson, would be keen.

Life in the Community: Seaman, Ohio

- The community of Seaman was named for Frank Seaman, a wealthy farmer who bought a 180-acre farm in 1880 at a sheriff's sale on the courthouse steps to settle the Hamilton estate.
- Much of the village was located on that original property.
- Two years later, in 1882, Frank Seaman donated two acres to the Cincinnati and Eastern Railway for a railway station on the condition that they named the station Seaman.

Seaman, a small but prosperous Midwestern town

- To encourage the construction of a railway to their land, local farmers donated fine oak logs to the railway company and hauled them to a sawmill to be cut into lumber for the station.
- The invention of small electric motors made possible a revolution in household appliances, including vacuum cleaners, and reliable refrigerators and washing machines, all of which were becoming common in Seaman.
- Many appliances could be bought on the installment plan, which allowed payments for a new appliance to be spread over 12 months.
- Seaman businesses generally were doing very well.
- The streets of Seaman were dramatically improved when the State Highway Department—thanks to considerable lobbying—scraped the roads and covered them with crushed rock.
- The current high school, constructed of brick and stone, sat on a five-acre tract west of the village.
- The high school had an auditorium-gymnasium, in which were held sporting events, concerts, and theatricals.
- Seaman prided itself on being a respectable, well-mannered town.

The Methodist Church in Seaman

- To keep stray dogs under control in Seaman, "Stringer" Barnes, the railway freight conductor, paid young boys to gather up all the unclaimed dogs and haul them to the station; Barnes then transported them on the train to the neighboring community of Portsmouth and turned them loose.
- After the Nelson brothers escorted a cow into the office of the cinema, the city fathers attempted to establish a 9:00 p.m. curfew for teenagers.
- The matter was dropped after Mr. Nelson made his two boys clean the theater for four weeks and paid for the ledger book and tickets destroyed by the cow.

Businessman and Anti-Immigration Activist in 1923

Joseph Stellini was certain that if immigration to the United States were not curtailed, Americans like him would be put out of business. His major concern was that immigrants entering the United States could not communicate in English.

Life at Home

- Ever since the Great War ended five years earlier, Joseph Stellini had been on constant alert.
- He knew from experience that the anarchists of Europe and their allies everywhere would never sleep until America was destroyed.
- Men like him—a small businessman and Rotarian—would be driven out of their businesses at best and maybe even killed by an anarchist bomb.
- The rule of law would be overthrown, and society would become disorderly and violent.
- He would lose everything he had spent his life working for.
- Joseph understood that he had a responsibility to protect America from attack by foreigners.
- He was especially alarmed about immigrants who refused to learn the English language.
- If they had no interest in learning English, Joseph thought, they had no interest in becoming good American citizens.
- Joseph believed that most immigrants had done a poor job of joining in the political life of the democracy that nurtured them.
- The problem in his own state of New Mexico was bad enough; a recent story in a national magazine said the New Mexico House spent one-fifth of its $7,287.50 personnel budget on translators and interpreters.
- That meant that some of the duly elected members of the Lower House in New Mexico could not transact their legislative business in English.
- The compact under which New Mexico was admitted to the Union specifically required that elected officials "read, write, speak and understand the English language sufficiently well to conduct the duties of the office without the aid of an interpreter."
- Joseph knew that if he had to hire interpreters to sell tires at his garage, he would go broke.
- His Italian father came to America as a merchant, worked hard and bought a horse stable when carriages were fashionable.

Joseph Stellini

- He was successful because he learned English and became a real American, moving west and creating a business that could put shoes on horses and tires on cars.
- His tire supply store became one the largest in Santa Fe, serving customers as far away as Farmington, New Mexico.
- When Joseph took over the business, he worked conscientiously to live up to his father's achievements.
- He saw that maintaining his business required of him discipline and diligence, and also that economic success—his and others'—depended on social stability and order, which only government could provide.
- A lifelong bachelor, Joseph allowed himself two drinks with friends at the end of the workday, after which he went straight home to handle business paperwork such as inventory, bookkeeping, and payroll.
- Employing nine men was a big responsibility.
- "A man is not a man," he liked to tell friends, "until he has met the pressure of making a payroll week after week."

Life at Work

- Two years earlier, Joseph had embarked on a crusade to protect the United States from anarchists and to make sure the country was preserved for Americans.
- That kind of goal required organization, cooperation, and commitment.
- With a small group of like-minded businessmen, he formed what he thought of as a core of "right-thinking" citizens prepared to speak out against unfettered immigration.
- The first step was to organize the store owners of Santa Fe based around something simple: No service to anyone who didn't speak English well enough to be understood.
- At Eve's Eats, where the successful merchants of the downtown district gathered six days a week, Joseph threw the idea on the table.
- There was an immediate response: For long enough, America had accepted the world's "tired and poor yearning to be free."
- Maybe now that the United States had fought the Great War and saved Europe from German domination, it was time to take care of Americans.
- After all, they couldn't just let everyone in, or soon there would be no jobs for Americans, especially since the immigrants were willing to work for hardly anything.
- So everyone, except Bill Hammond, who had married a Mexican girl, agreed to put up "Only English Spoken Here" signs in their places of business.
- Joseph told his fellow businessmen they would not lose any business because good Americans would buy more and foreign-speaking immigrants would have a powerful incentive to learn English faster.

Aftermath of an Anarchist bombing, New York City, 1920 (G. G. Bain Collection, Library of Congress)

- Step two was to organize Santa Fe's service clubs into a single voice dedicated to keeping anarchists away from America's shores.
- Nearly everyone agreed that immigration restrictions were necessary.
- After Joseph made an impassioned plea for help during a regular luncheon meeting of the city's five key civic clubs, they all agreed to appoint someone to write a letter to their U.S. senators and representatives, demanding stricter immigration laws.
- As a third step, Joseph wanted to put real teeth into the enforcement of immigration laws.

- He had an enormous fear that the 14 million foreign whites who now lived in the United States could easily threaten his way of life.
- Moreover, he knew that Mexican anarchists like Ricardo Flores Magón advocated for social revolution, and they were prepared to resort to violence to achieve it.
- Fortunately Flores Magón was in prison at Fort Leavenworth, but others who shared his ideas were ready to act and moving back and forth between Mexico and the United States.
- America needed to protect its borders with manned patrols if unwanted foreigners, anarchists, communists and illegal immigrants were to be stopped from entering the country.
- Laws alone, Joseph believed, were only a first step; an enlightened, English-speaking citizenry willing to accept responsibility for the implementation of those laws was what made a democracy function.

Librado Rivera and Enrique Flores Magon, Mexican Anarchists, circa 1915 (G. G. Bain Collection, Library of Congress)

Life in the Community: Santa Fe, New Mexico

- During the first 15 years of the twentieth century, more than 13 million people had come to the United States before America's open door was closed by the dangers and conflicts associated with World War I.
- For some time, public sentiment against unrestricted immigration had been growing.
- Americans, especially those belonging to the emerging urban middle class, no longer thought of America as having a great internal empire to settle.
- This sentiment expressed itself in a series of measures aimed at limiting the number of immigrants and restricting them by countries of origin to proportions based on the number of immigrants of their nationality already in the United States in 1920.
- By drastically limiting immigrant numbers, America curbed one of the great population movements of world history, a process at least two centuries old.
- The U.S. Census in 1920 placed New Mexico's population at 350,000, of whom half were of Mexican-Spanish stock.
- New Mexico had entered the Union as the forty-seventh state less than a decade before, in 1912.
- Complex questions of land title that had been simmering since the Treaty of Guadalupe Hidalgo in 1854 became acute as longstanding Hispanic and Native conceptions of common land tenure clashed with Anglo American practices.
- In 1876 the U.S. Supreme Court had ruled that the Pueblo were culturally advanced enough to not to be dependents of the U.S. government, giving the Pueblo the right to sell their lands as they saw fit.
- But the Supreme Court reversed this decision in 1913, thereby negating the land titles of people who had purchased Pueblo lands in the interim.
- The Bursum Land Bill drafted in 1921 was intended to restore non-Pueblo ownership of lands acquired before 1920 and give the state courts jurisdiction over all future land title disputes.
- The state courts were notoriously disinclined to support Native American land claims, and the Pueblo stood to lose title to great expanses of their best lands.

- Artists and writers who had settled in Taos helped rouse Pueblo leaders, who had not even been informed of the imminent threat of the Bursum Bill, to organize in opposition to it.
- The Pueblo successfully made their case to Congress, and the Bursum Bill was defeated.
- Meanwhile Santa Fe had developed a tourism industry largely based on Native American history and culture.
- The Atchison Topeka and Santa Fe Railway heavily promoted the tourism economy of the Southwest.
- Beginning in 1911, Santa Fe held an annual Santa Fe Fiesta, which became a major regional cultural event.
- The fiesta was designed to celebrate New Mexico's Hispanic, Native, and Anglo heritage.
- Native peoples were persuaded to participate in the fiesta after long negotiations, and in 1923 some 200 Indians made the journey to Santa Fe for the three-day event.
- A platform erected in front of the Palace of the Governors served as the main fiesta performance venue for Native dancers.
- In September 1922, in conjunction with the fiesta, the First Annual Southwest Indian Fair and Industrial Arts and Crafts Exhibition—a juried exhibition of traditional Native arts—opened behind the Palace of the Governors in the National Guard Armory Building.
- The Indian market, as it became known, was founded in part to preserve and foster traditional Native arts.
- In the view of some observers, including museum curators, standards had begun to erode under the pressure of the tourism economy.
- The market produced income for Native artists, and its competitions in various categories rewarded the finest work.

El Palacio Real de Santa Fe (Royal Palace of Santa Fe), Palace Avenue (Historic American Buildings Survey, Library of Congress)

New Mexico Timeline

1841   Soldiers from Texas invaded New Mexico and claimed all land east of the Rio Grande.

1846   The Mexican-American War began; the United States annexed New Mexico.

1848   The Treaty of Guadalupe Hidalgo ended the Mexican-American War.

1850   New Mexico (which included present-day Arizona, southern Colorado, southern Utah, and southern Nevada) was designated a territory but was denied statehood.

1854   The Gadsden Purchase from Mexico added 45,000 square miles to the territory.

1861   Confederate soldiers invaded New Mexico from Texas.

The Territory of Colorado was created; New Mexico lost its extreme northernmost section to the new territory.

1862   After the Battles of Velarde and Glorieta Pass were fought, the Confederate occupation of New Mexico ended.

1863-1868 Navajo and Apache tribes were relocated to Bosque Redondo; thousands died of disease and starvation.

1863   New Mexico was partitioned in half, and the territory of Arizona was created.

1878   The railroad arrived in New Mexico, opening full-scale trade and migration from the East and Midwest.

1881   Sheriff Pat Garrett shot Billy the Kid in Fort Sumner, New Mexico.

1886   Geronimo surrendered, ending Indian hostilities in the Southwest.

1898   Thomas Edison created the first movie filmed in New Mexico: *Indian Day School*.

1906   The people of New Mexico and Arizona voted on joint statehood; New Mexico voted in favor, Arizona against.

1912   New Mexico was admitted to the Union as the forty-seventh state.

1922   Secretary of State Soledad Chacon and Superintendent of Public Instruction Isabel Eckles were elected as the first women to hold statewide office.

1923   Oil was discovered on the Navajo Reservation.

ॐॐॐॐॐॐॐ

"The Immigration Peril" Gino Speranza
The World's Work, December 1923

...The basis of the tragedy has its roots in the popular notion or assumption that American institutions are so inherently excellent they fit all peoples. This assumption has been industriously, and at times insidiously encouraged by New Stock "intellectuals." These blatant "friends of freedom" lightly preach that government of and by the people is something that anyone can have and enjoy irrespective of character, intelligence, or special political training and antecedents. These theorists utterly forget that the Constitution of the United States was framed by men of Anglo-Saxon origin for their own government, and it presupposes the long political evolution to which that race has been subjected in the motherland during eight or nine centuries. It presupposes the Anglo-Saxon virtues of fair play. To impose free institutions upon a people which does not possess them is to endanger the social order and bring free institutions into unmerited reproach.

Try to visualize the invasion of "potential American citizens" in a *single year* of "liberal" immigration policy; there rushed in enough Austro-Hungarians to populate 27 towns the size of Portsmouth, N.H.; enough Poles and Jews from Old Russia to fill 18 more towns the size of Lawrence, Kansas; enough Italians to give us a new city of the size of Indianapolis, Indiana, besides four German cities of 10,000 each, six of Scandinavians, one of French, one of Greeks, six of English, five of Irish and nearly two of Scotch and Welch. The balance of that single year's inpouring (merely considering Europe) gave us Belgians, Dutch, Portuguese, Romanians, Swiss, and European Turks to populate six cities of the size of the New Mexican town of Raton, without counting the Serbians, Bulgarians, Montenegrins, and Spaniards. Even under the "Quota Immigration Law," which some assail as being too drastic, there were injected into the fabric of the Republic in 1922 twice as many non-American-minded potential citizens as there are "natives" in New Mexico today, with the added handicap that this mass of cultural alienage represented not one, but *39 different races, nations, and cultures!*

Is it unfair to stigmatize as "unreasoning" even a sincere faith which believes that by a mere legal formality after a five-year residence and the simplest of tests, these racial blocks can be transmuted into reliable and useful forces of American democratic self-government? Is it unfair to charge as thoughtless an optimism which assumes that the children of these heterogeneous invaders, born this side of Ellis Island (some, perhaps a week after parents' landing!) can be, on attaining maturity, politically minded as American democrats in any but the most narrow, legalistic sense? Is it an incitement to "race-hatred," as the demagogic race-vote-getters tell you? Or is it not rather an appeal to reason to urge upon the American people the necessity for the serious study of the effects of these huge blocks of racial votes upon American political life?

The Immigration Peril was a six-part series in the xenophobic World's Work *branding Greek, Italian, and Slavic immigrants a "menace to American ideals"*

"The March of Events"
The World's Work, **December 1923**

In order properly to appreciate the immigration situation, which promises to occupy a prominent place in the discussions of the new Congress, Americans should let their minds go back 40 or 50 years, when a threatened inundation of the Pacific Coast called for dramatic remedy. At that time Chinese and other Mongolians were landing in California at a rate that, if unchecked, would make this part of the United States, in one or two generations, little better than an Asiatic domain. There was no objection to these immigrants on the ground of industry or good behavior. As a mass they were hard-working, law-abiding, in an economic sense they unquestionably possessed great value. They were found useful in building the Pacific railroads, in cultivating farms, in creating wealth in many ways. Nor were they lacking in intelligence; they were the children of a very ancient civilization, a civilization that was old when Greece and Rome were young and when the continent of Europe was the abiding place of naked savages. There was only one objection to these incomers. Mentally and physically they were absolutely alien to the races that founded the American Nation. The idea of ever incorporating them into the body politic could not be entertained. Intermarriage with Northwestern Europeans could produce only hybrid descendants, and introduce another insoluble race problem. The only possible future for these Mongolians would be existence as a people apart, a bloc of suspicious and hostile unassimilables, something which is a public evil in any nation, but which is especially hateful in a nation founded upon American principles. The statesmen of 40 years ago solved this problem in the wisest way. They abruptly stopped Asiatic immigration. There were plenty of "liberals" of that date who denounced the Chinese exclusion laws, as there are plenty subsequently who denounced the anti-Japanese measures, but the result of this foresight is now apparent. California is today a beautiful and flourishing community of Northwestern Europeans, one of the parts of the United States of which Americans are chiefly proud, instead of being, as it would have become except for the exclusion laws, a great expanse devoted largely to an Asiatic civilization.

What the country and Congress should understand is that the Atlantic Coast is now living in the shadow of a similar peril. What are the races that have poured into the great Eastern cities in the last 15 years and which are now clamoring for admission? Greeks, Armenians, Bulgars, Rumanians, Croats, Southern Italians, Eastern Jews. The folly of attempting to transform these races into American citizens, now or centuries from now, is clear to all students of history. On this point there's practically no disagreement; discussion or argument are unnecessary. Unless the flood is checked, however, and abruptly checked, the Atlantic Coast, in a few generations, will be largely peopled with this kind of human material.

Father and Son (1921), painting by Bror Julius Olsson Nordfeldt

Ice Delivery Company Owner in 1923

Since his earliest days growing up outside Chicago, Illinois, Allan Kusse had loved the process of harvesting, shaping, and distributing ice.

Life at Home

- Allan Kusse saw gold when he handled a block of ice.
- The advent of electricity in homes had only increased consumer demand for the precious resource.
- Some people—including Allan's eldest son, Joseph—were predicting that the refrigeration of food would one day be accomplished without an ice delivery.
- But people were also predicting that humans would one day walk on the moon, leading Allan to believe that "some people" would forecast anything to get attention.
- Allan was convinced that the ice business was limitless.
- Rumors of workable artificial refrigeration had been around since American inventor Oliver Evans designed the first refrigeration machine in 1805.
- His design was followed in 1834 by that of Jacob Perkins, who used ether in a vapor compression cycle.
- Yet here the American consumer stood, two decades into the twentieth century—the most progressive era in the history of humanity—without a reliable cooling machine.
- In fact, the use of toxic gases such as ammonia, methyl chloride, and sulfur dioxide as refrigerants had led to several fatal accidents when gases leaked out of refrigerators.
- Meanwhile the growing city of Chicago was supporting 16 separate ice delivery companies—all eager to take his business if he stumbled.
- Joseph was less confident and wanted to diversify the business, or at least abandon horse-drawn delivery wagons for speedier—and much more expensive—delivery trucks.
- Allan thought that trucks were unnecessary but that employing the new scientific methods of business would allow his company to compete more profitably.
- Allan was sure his son should work harder and carp less; once- or twice-weekly ice delivery to every respectable home in Chicago was here to stay.

Allan Kusse

41

- Born just downwind from his grandfather's 54-acre lake, Allan grew up on the ice, helping his father and grandfather cut, store, and deliver the highly perishable product.
- Allan learned from his father the special methods and various tools needed for cutting and removing the ice, including large saws and horse-drawn cutters.
- Allan stayed in school until the ninth grade, when his father's back injury threatened the family's livelihood.
- As clear as day, Allan remembered his father, mother, and two sisters coming together to ask him to quit school and run the family business.
- His mother, who spoke English in her native Dutch accent, said simply: "You are a man now, and we need you."
- His father died 16 months later of a massive heart attack while sawing a huge block of newborn ice.
- Fifteen years later, in 1900, when Allan was 31 and Joseph still an infant, motor-driven saws came into popular use, speeding the harvesting process.

Life at Work

- Seasonal ice harvesting began around the first of January.
- The ice harvested then was taken to the ice house to be stored until summer.
- The ice house was a double-walled brick or wooden building where the ice was covered with layers of hay or sawdust to keep it from melting.
- When the weather turned warm, the demand for ice began.
- The ice wagon, delivering ice door to door, was a common sight around every town.
- The large demand for ice made it one of the top commodities handled by the shipping industry.
- While ice harvesting was a very profitable business, it was also risky.
- In addition to the potential for physical danger to employees, there was the chance that a warm winter might produce a limited supply—or that not enough ice would be stored to meet the summertime demand.

Cutting grooves after marking the ice for harvesting (stereograph; Library of Congress)

- Allan Kusse was very proud the day he announced to his son the reorganization of the company.
- After months of study, Allan had decided Joseph would be in charge of harvesting, storage, bookkeeping, and wholesale sales to saloons, grocery stores, and restaurants.
- Allan would take charge of delivery.
- For years the company had functioned under the implied threat that unhappy ice delivery drivers would quit and take their customers to a competitor.
- From then on, all customers of Kusse Ice were going to stay customers of the company, not the deliverymen.
- As at most ice companies, it had been the custom at Kusse Ice to split up routes in the early spring and give a new man 30 to 40 customers with the expectation that he would increase that number to 250 customers.
- In the process the company which was taking all the financial risks of harvesting and storing the ice, seldom came into direct contact with the customer, who saw only the driver.
- Consequently, that was where the customer's loyalty lay.

- That needed to change.
- Allan knew the biggest drawback to installing modern management methods was the opposition of the employees, especially the drivers, to anything new.
- Most resistant were the drivers who ran their routes in a sloppy manner, allowing more ice to melt than necessary—and, Allan was certain, drivers who regularly pocketed some of the customers' payments, lowering company profits.
- For one reason or another, Allan was convinced, 90 percent of the drivers had no desire for direct supervision.
- But the scientific management of a company demanded that all work patterns become standardized, all processes be measured, and every employee be supervised.

Separating sections of ice and floating them toward the ice house (stereograph; Library of Congress)

- Allan knew that his new organizational plan—with three new supervisors and two checkers—would be unpopular, and he was prepared for dissent.
- When one driver with 17 years of experience immediately refused to cooperate, Allan fired him and assigned his route to a new man.
- For weeks afterwards, the fired driver solicited his old customers on behalf of his new employer, yet 297 stayed and only 14 left.
- Allan figured that was a fair price to pay to stop the man's complaining and prove a point to the company's other 66 employees.
- It was time for Kusse Ice to be modern.
- The object of scientific management was to limit waste and increase efficiency, thereby increasing productivity, which meant lowering the cost per article produced.
- The company would benefit, and the customers would, too.
- Just a dozen years before, in 1911, Frederick Winslow Taylor, the father of scientific management, had pioneered standardization and best practice deployment in his book *Principles of Scientific Management*.
- According to Taylor: "Whenever a workman proposes an improvement, it should be the policy of the management to make a careful analysis of the new method, and if necessary conduct a series of experiments to determine accurately the relative merit of the new suggestion and of the old standard.

Shooting the ice cakes toward the wagons (stereograph; Library of Congress)

- "And whenever the new method is found to be markedly superior to the old, it should be adopted as the standard for the whole establishment."
- Automobile manufacturer Henry Ford popularized Taylor's obsession with wasted movement with an improved mass assembly manufacturing system that dramatically improved production, lowered costs and improved profits.

- In fact, Allan was inspired to transform Kusse Ice based on the scientific method after reading Henry Ford's book *My Life and Work*.
- Ford wrote, "I believe that the average farmer puts to a really useful purpose only about 5 percent of the energy he expends. ... Not only is everything done by hand, but seldom is a thought given to a logical arrangement. A farmer doing his chores will walk up and down a rickety ladder a dozen times. He will carry water for years instead of putting in a few lengths of pipe. His whole idea, when there is extra work to do, is to hire extra men. He thinks of putting money into improvements as an expense. ... It is waste motion—waste effort—that makes farm prices high and profits low."
- Allan knew from experience that similar waste and inefficiency characterized the delivery department of most ice companies.
- He was determined to cut out the unnecessary motions that drivers performed from the time they commenced to cut a piece of ice to when it was delivered.
- While riding the routes with his drivers—something he hadn't done in years—he heard one driver say to his helper, "I think she needs a 10-pounder today."
- The helper then walked, empty-handed, to the house to confirm that the housewife needed 10 pounds of ice to stock her icebox. He returned to tell the driver to saw a 10-pound block of ice, which he then took to the kitchen, another round-trip to the customer's house.
- The entire operation could have been handled much more efficiently, Allan believed, and he was prepared to make changes.
- Improper routing was also high on his list of scientific management issues.
- Since most of the ice was sold for cash, only the drivers really knew how many customers were on a route and who paid what amount for how much ice.
- Allan believed an exact routing pattern would give the company more control and the ability to make each route more precise.

An ice delivery

- Efficient routes and efficient operations would make it possible to load more tonnage per wagon, which would mean a decreased cost per ton of delivered ice.
- Logically improved efficiency would lead to more ice being delivered in a shorter time, producing better revenues per wagon and possibly less melted ice—which was purely lost income.
- The application of scientific management would allow managers to measure the exact time required for various operations and establish routes that were more efficient.
- Next Allan wanted to focus on an efficient accounting system capable of tracking the daily transactions that also could be used to summarize the entire operation on a weekly or monthly basis.
- The scientific management system dictated that an organization was only as strong as its leaders.
- Special attention must be paid to the work of superintendents and foremen; checkers should be hired to review the work of even the most experienced supervisors.
- The book *Ice Delivery* advised, "The work of superintendents and foremen should be constantly checked. Daily visits and inspection by the Superintendent of Delivery will keep station superintendents on edge."
- The book even broke down the finances: "As an illustration of the cost and the increase in income as a result of the proper supervision of routes, we will assume a company operates 36 single wagons and has two foremen in charge of them at $7 per day; drivers are paid $5 per day. It will require 40 horses

Girls delivering ice from an ice truck, New York City (Library of Congress)

to operate the 36 wagons. With feed and stable expenses of, say, $0.97 a day per horse, the expense will be $38.80; 36 drivers at $5, $180; a total of $232.80.

- "Assume these wagons average 2.3 tons per day, for a total of 83.0 tons, but this will give an average cost of $2.805 per ton. Suppose we change to the more efficient plan of having a foreman for each six wagons, which will increase the total cost to $260.80. As a result of this closer supervision we increase tonnage per wagon to 2.8 tons, or a total of 101 tons a day, which reduces the cost per ton to $2.584.
- "With two foremen above, the cost per ton for a foreman's wage is 16.8 cents per ton; with six foremen it is increased to 41.6 cents, a

difference of 24.8 cents per ton. Assume that the average price received per ton is $9.50. On a daily output of 83 tons ,it would amount to $788.50; on a daily output of 101 tons the amount is $959.50, an increase in income of $171. The only additional expense for this increased revenue is the cost of 18 tons of ice at $4 a ton, $72; and the wages of the four additional foremen, $28; a total of $100, leaving the net gain of $71 daily."

- Allan told his son about his plans. Allan added that before he imposed the scientific management system on Kusse Ice, Joseph needed to finish high school.
- And there was a thundering silence.
- The typically talkative boy, who had been known to chide his father for his old-fashioned ways, finally said, "We are not Ford Motor Company."

Life in the Community: Chicago, Illinois

- Allan Kusse had every reason to be optimistic about the ice business in a city growing as rapidly as was Chicago.
- Incorporated in 1833, Chicago grew at a rate that ranked among the fastest growing in the world during its first 90 years.
- By the close of the nineteenth century, Chicago was the fifth-largest city in the world and the largest city that had not existed at the dawn of the century.
- Within 50 years of the Great Chicago Fire of 1871, the population had nearly tripled, to over 2.7 million.
- Chicago's flourishing economy attracted new residents from rural communities and immigrants from Europe.

World War I-era government- and industry-sponsored propaganda poster promoting the ice industry (Library of Congress)

- Almost one-third of Chicago's residents were foreign-born; more than one million were Catholics and another 125,000 were Jews.
- Immigrant groups consistently clustered to preserve the Old World culture of their patrimony while learning to become Americans.
- Polish, Greek, German and Russian neighborhoods were clearly defined.
- The growth in Chicago's manufacturing and retail sectors flourished in the Midwest and greatly influenced the nation's economy.
- The Chicago Union Stock Yards dominated the packing trade.
- Chicago had become the world's largest rail hub and one of its busiest ports.
- The thriving economy helped Chicago attract thousands of African-Americans coming north in the Great Migration, starting in 1910.

The vast Chicago Great Union Stockyards (stereograph; Library of Congress)

- With new populations competing for limited housing and for jobs, especially on the South Side, social tensions rose in the city.
- The post-World War I years were ripe with unrest; black veterans demanded more respect for having served their nation, and some whites resented that.
- In 1919 the Chicago Race Riot, led by members of Irish athletic clubs determined to defend their "territory" against the growing presence of African Americans, resulted in the death of 23 blacks and 15 whites; 537 people were injured.
- The 1920s brought international notoriety to Chicago as gangsters such as Al Capone and Bugs Moran battled each other and the law during the Prohibition era.

African American family, protected by police, abandoning their damaged home in the aftermath of the 1919 Chicago race riot (Schomburg Center for Research in Black Culture, New York Public Library)

Dentist in 1924

William Nash, a 34-year-old dentist living in Columbia, South Carolina, had been in practice a dozen years. After the second of their two sons was born, William and his wife, Martha, bought a new home on the edge of the city for their growing family.

Life at Home

- William and Martha met through their church, the Associate Reform Presbyterian Church in Columbia, South Carolina.
- Their first house in Columbia was located downtown on a small 60 foot-by-80 foot lot—a two-story home with a front porch, living room, kitchen, and dining room downstairs, and bedrooms upstairs.
- In 1920, when their second child, George, was born, the Nashes moved to a larger home on the city limits.
- They were attracted to their new red-brick home by its four bedrooms, wide porch, and carport and garage as well as its large landscaped lot; the surrounding countryside seemed to stretch outward from their garden.
- William had a passion for plants and often drove as far as Charleston to obtain a new specimen; one of his hobbies was grafting camellia bushes to create different flower combinations.
- William planted peach trees, cherry trees, and small apple trees in the yard. He liked to experiment with vegetables; this year a late frost once again burned his English peas.
- William and Martha's house had fireplaces in every major room, and the back rooms were heated by a coal stove in the kitchen.
- The family spent considerable time in a large, bright breakfast room.
- William loved fresh air, and it was important to him that the bedrooms had the best ventilation possible.
- In Columbia the temperature often reached the high 90s in the summertime.
- The Nashes found that they would have to pay extra for their elder son, also named William, to attend a Columbia city school because their house was on the "country" side of the city school district limits.
- Martha did all the cooking and took great pride in this skill; the family did not employ a maid for cooking or routine housekeeping.
- Martha freely called her husband by his first name; her mother always referred to her own husband, Martha's father, as "Mister," never using his first name.

William Nash, DDS

- When they made large purchases, such as their automobile and the house, the Nash family avoided going into debt; William and Martha did not believe in installment loan debt for cars or appliances, even though the practice was becoming widely accepted.
- Martha wore dresses every day, often changing at midday into "visiting clothes" following her morning cooking and cleaning.
- During the summertime the children took baths at lunchtime and changed their clothes.
- The local dry-cleaning service came to their home to pick up and deliver clothes; occasionally the dry-cleaner would come on Saturday night to ensure that Martha had the dress she needed for Sunday morning.

The Nash family's first home, an American Foursquare

- Neither William nor his wife drank or smoked; most of their socializing was with the extended family or within their church circle.
- Social gatherings often included singing around the piano.
- Martha was an accomplished pianist, and the family owned dozens of pieces of sheet music, ranging from "Love's Golden Star" to "My Melancholy Baby," a popular "fox-trot ballad."
- The family was active in church, often attending morning, afternoon, and evening services on Sunday; in between they visited the homes of friends who belonged to the same church.
- Martha carefully oversaw the children's activities; especially on Sundays, both at church and at friends' homes, the boys were expected to be quiet, polite, and well behaved.
- The family's Sunday meal often consisted of chicken or roast beef with rice or macaroni pie, and it always included fresh vegetables. Everyone also enjoyed Martha's homemade blackberry jam, a year-round treat.
- The family's food was cooled in an icebox; the iceman came to the house three times a week, cutting 25-pound sections from his 300-pound block, carrying the ice to the door and even setting it into the icebox.
- The Nash house was wired for electricity.
- Nationwide in 1912, only 16 percent of the U.S. population lived in houses with electric lights; by 1924 more than 50 percent of houses had been wired for electricity.

The Associate Reform Presbyterian Church (Historic American Buildings Survey, Library of Congress)

- The family owned an electric-motor-driven vacuum cleaner, which William purchased to please Martha.
- The family took a two-week vacation each year—always in August, when Columbia was hottest.
- The family vacationed near Asheville in the North Carolina mountains; William liked hiking the steep terrain and occasionally encountering the rare flora fostered by the region's special climate, while Martha and the boys explored Asheville's resort amusements.

- The whole family enjoyed horse-drawn carriage rides on Asheville-area carriage trails, and young William was learning to ride a pony.
- William and Martha liked the independence their automobile gave them, agreeing completely with the Chevrolet advertisement that declared, "Every owner is in effect a railroad president, operating individually on an elective schedule."

Life at Work

- William and one of his brothers opened a joint dental office on Main Street in Columbia in 1912 following their graduation from Atlanta-Southern Dental College.
- Their elder sisters had helped each of them fund a three-year course in dentistry at the dental college, which the brothers found through a magazine advertisement.
- Atlanta-Southern was a proprietary school with private owners; no state or regional governing body accredited dental schools or established their curricula.
- Most dentists in North Carolina, South Carolina, Georgia, and Tennessee were trained in Atlanta.
- At school William and his brother watched seniors work and learned the basics of dentistry, such as how to make amalgam fillings composed of silver, tin, zinc, and mercury.
- They also learned how to create and install gold fillings.
- The brothers' office was on the second floor of their building; a ladies' apparel shop occupied the first floor.

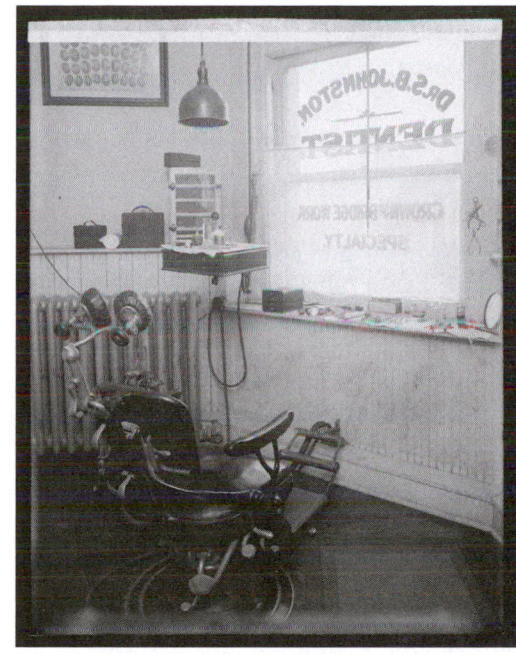

While in dental college, William apprenticed in Dr. Johnston's Atlanta office, above (Library of Congress)

- A year after opening for business, they decided that two offices would allow them to serve more patients; William then rented a second-floor office just off Main Street, over Malone's Piano Store.
- William missed working alongside his brother, but from the business standpoint, moving proved to be a wise decision.
- William remained satisfied with his office, which he took pride in furnishing with the most up-to-date equipment.
- The brothers agreed that their patients noticed and appreciated their efforts to keep up with modern dentistry, and that was good for business.
- William wore a hat and business suit to work every day; once at the office, he removed his suit jacket—but not his necktie—and donned a lab coat.
- Martha drove him to work each morning in the family Buick, which they purchased from Roddy's, a local dealership.
- The office opened at 8:45 a.m.; William worked until 1 p.m., when Martha picked him up and took him home for the lunch she had prepared.

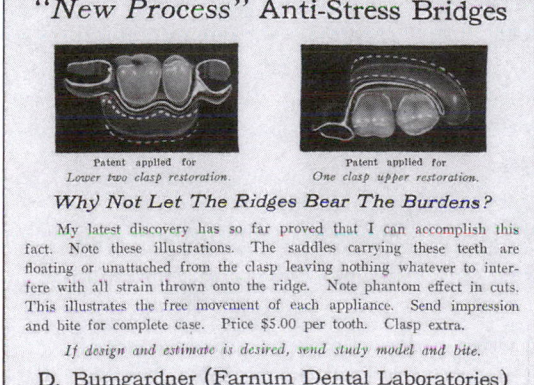

- She drove him back to the office by 2:30 p.m., and William saw patients until 5:45 p.m., when the office closed; Martha picked him up again and brought him home for dinner.
- William typically saw 20 scheduled patients a day; most appointments took no longer than 30 minutes.
- He also accepted walk-in patients when time permitted.
- William's regular patients preferred to make appointments, but he always managed to make time for emergency visits.
- William did not employ a chairside assistant or bookkeeper, attending to the accounting side of his business himself.
- Frugal by temperament, William wanted to know at all times how his practice was doing financially; he kept close track of expenditures and planned carefully for his investments in new equipment.
- Once his practice was well established, William hired a receptionist to answer the telephone, schedule appointments, and manage the office.
- Typically William charged $1.00 for an extraction; fillings normally cost $0.50 but occasionally a bit more, depending on size and difficulty.

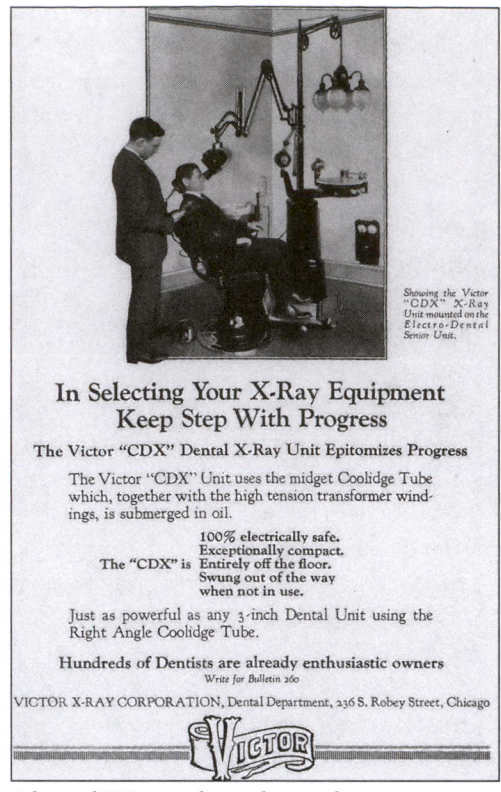

Advanced X-Ray machine, a boon to dentistry

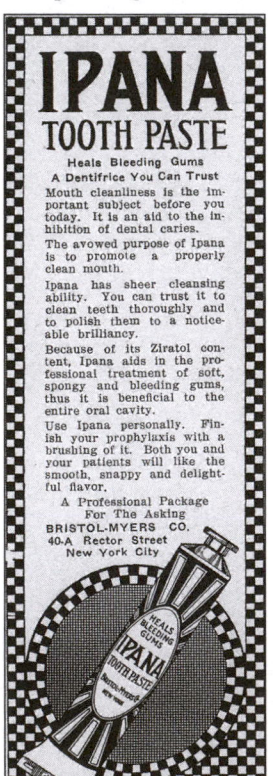

- He expected payment at the time of service; he did not use credit himself, and he did not encourage others to use it. Nevertheless, William sometimes accepted payment in the form of fresh produce or even live chickens if that was all his patient could manage.
- William's operatory had two chairs, both of which faced the windows looking out over Main Street.
- The office also had a darkroom for developing X-rays, a lavatory accessible to patients, and a dental sink.
- William did his own gold-casting, occasionally assisted by a black man who was highly skilled at this exacting work and was employed by a doctor nearby.
- The office was equipped with an X-ray machine, considered the finest invention in dentistry; when the machine was turned on, its light arced across the room, and neither patient nor dentist wore any protective covering.
- For most dentists, the preferred anesthesia was cocaine, although some patients elected to forgo a painkiller rather than take the drug.
- William had a telephone at the office and another telephone at home.
- The residential phone was a two-party line shared with his neighbor; a local operator connected most callers from a central switchboard.
- The office telephone number, when dialed at home, was four digits long.
- Some businesses were using postcard mailers to attract new customers, but William was not convinced that it was prudent to spend money on advertising with no certain return.

- He and his brother both preferred to gain new patients by word of mouth; each had a good professional reputation and almost as many patients as he could handle.
- William worked six days a week, caring for patients all day Saturday; he closed the office at lunchtime on Fridays.
- He usually spent Friday afternoons with his family, often driving the family to an amusement spot in the country or to a lake where they could picnic and swim.

Life in the Community

- Located in the center of South Carolina at the confluence of three rivers, the city of Columbia was the state capital; a planned city, it was carved from a plantation in the late 1700s.
- Columbia was one of the hottest locations in the state, with temperatures often brushing 100 degrees Fahrenheit in the summer.
- The city was the home of the University of South Carolina, where tuition was $20 per semester plus $20 per semester for a dorm room shared with a roommate; law school tuition was $32.50.

Trolley lines serving downtown Columbia

- The city was prospering; the steady government payroll and the dozens of textile plants on the outskirts of the city supported a stable, vibrant economy.
- Nine rail lines linked the capital with numerous other cities and towns, making Columbia a major shopping destination for the whole state.
- Between 1910 and 1920, the city's population increased 42 percent, from 26,300 to 37,600; as the mid-1920s approached, growth continued at the same pace.
- The rural economy was doing less well; falling cotton prices and the ravages of the boll weevil forced thousands of farm bankruptcies, and between 1922 and 1924 some 90 South Carolina banks failed. Four of these institutions were in Columbia.
- Public education for white children gained momentum in the years following World War I; in 1922 Columbia voters approved a bond issue for the construction of a new high school, and in 1923 they approved a $300,000 bond for general school improvements.

University of South Carolina Library on South Sumter Street (M. B. Paine, Historic American Buildings Survey, Library of Congress)

- School days were made longer; the high school day ended at 3:00 p.m. instead of 2:00 p.m., and grade schools were dismissed at 2:15 p.m. instead of 2:00 p.m.
- A special school was organized for "problem" children and children regarded as being mentally retarded.
- The *State Newspaper*, the largest newspaper in the state, was currently crusading against lynching, for compulsory education, and for child labor laws.
- Segregation of races was a largely unquestioned way of life throughout South Carolina and the nation at large.

- Columbia had three motion picture theaters: the Grand and Lyric for white customers and the Majestic for blacks.
- Also popular was the Town Theatre, which was constructing a new building in response to public demand.
- Many of the white men in the community belonged to the newly formed Columbia Club, with a membership composed of influential citizens; their wives were members of the Assembly, which organized fancy balls designed to maintain a standard of graciousness and dignity in Columbia. By custom, the balls were always card dances.
- The Century Club had been formed "to promote social life among our women, to encourage among us diligent literary work, and to foster public spirit among our citizens."
- With a membership of approximately four hundred, the Associate Reformed Presbyterian Church of Columbia was also known as the Centennial Church, because it was erected to mark the centennial of the Associate Reformed Synod of the South.
- The number of streetcar riders nationwide peaked in 1923 at 15.7 billion, but automobile use was increasing. General Motors bought up bankrupt streetcar lines, tore up the tracks, and introduced buses.
- When the first State Highway Commission came into begin in 1917, South Carolina claimed forty thousand automobiles; by 1922, the state was levying its first gasoline tax.
- Women's suffrage, which was vigorously debated nationwide, was not generally well received in South Carolina; in 1919 the General Assembly refused to ratify the nineteenth amendment, which became U.S. law without the state's approbation.

In segregated Columbia, this young girl likely got her doll because her mother was a maid in a white home

Columbia residents buying local produce in a city market

Civic Leader and Entrepreneur in 1924

Seventy-year-old Garrett Cooper invested so much of his money, energy, and life in guiding the growth of Tulsa, Oklahoma, that he was considered the unelected mayor of this oil boom community. A millionaire thanks to the boom, he devoted his time to civic projects on behalf of Tulsa.

Life at Home

- Over his long career in Tulsa, Garrett Cooper operated a mercantile store, was appointed postmaster, founded a bank, and served as a board of education member and as a Sunday School superintendent. He also was president of the old Commercial Club.
- The love of his life, his wife Nell, whom he met during a trip to Atlanta, Georgia, kept her job as a third-grade schoolteacher for years after he had made his first million.
- After her death in 1921, Garrett turned her bedroom into a shrine to her memory, cherishing pictures of Nell as a young woman, when they first fell in love.
- Although the couple had no children, they jointly reveled in the potential of Tulsa to be a great city.
- Garrett attended Tulsa's First Presbyterian Church, which he had helped organize. In 1924, after 30 years, he was still the Presbyterian Sunday School superintendent; even before the church came into being, he had founded the Union Sunday School with Baptist and Congregationalist partners.

Garrett Cooper

- Many called Garrett "Mayor," and even though he never officially held the position, few civic leaders would attempt a project without getting his support in advance.
- Garrett and Nell came to Tulsa with little money when the community was still small and struggling.
- Drawing on his shopkeeping experience, Garrett opened a small general store catering to the largely male population, especially the oilmen continually drilling in the area.
- Oil had become precious owing to dramatic increases in the sales of automobiles and gasoline engines.
- Even when money was scarce, Nell backed Garrett's decision to give certain oil wildcatters store supplies on credit in exchange for a portion of their drilling discoveries.
- This decision and his natural leadership abilities eventually made Garrett millions.
- Garrett Cooper lived in an old section of town, in a house he and Nell had built at the turn of the century;

most of the homes around his were built later and were much larger, owned by men who had made their fortunes in the oilfields.

- Last year had been particularly gratifying for his neighbors: oilman Harry Sinclair's horse Zev won the Kentucky Derby, and oilman Josh Cosden's horse Martingale came in second.
- Cosden was mildly disappointed with second place, having won the Derby in 1921 with his horse Paul Jones.
- Garrett and Josh Cosden had been friends from the time Josh came from Baltimore, around 1912, with the dream of supplying the emerging automobile market with lubricants and cheaper gasoline.
- Josh Cosden arrived with little money and borrowed a lot from Garrett's mercantile store.
- Four years later, when Josh acquired $12 million from Wall Street to build a refinery, Garrett was handsomely repaid for his generosity and patience.

Nell Cooper

- Newspaper reporters speculated that Josh Cosden was worth more than $50 million; his home became known throughout the state as a showplace, featuring an indoor swimming pool and garden braced by two clay tennis courts built with soil imported from France—at a cost of $10,000.
- Always careful with his money, Garrett would never have considered building a home on the scale of his friend's.
- Garrett and Nell had always said that education was a key to Tulsa's future.
- In 1898 Garrett and three partners had borrowed money to purchase the Presbyterian mission school in Tulsa; the church's mission board no longer wanted to support the school, since most of its students were white children. Garrett and his partners held the property until the town could pay for it, and it became Tulsa's first public school.

The Skelly Building, headquarters of the Skelly Oil Company, built in 1921 (Beryl Ford Collection, Tulsa City-County Library)

- Nearly a decade later, as a member of the Commercial Club, Garrett helped draw up Tulsa's successful bid to bring Henry Kendall College from Muskogee to Tulsa when the opportunity arose.
- To attract upstanding citizens and to prosper, Garrett thought, Tulsa needed a college.
- The college had begun as a missionary school for Indian girls, but it had always struggled financially, and the Oklahoma Synod of the Presbyterian Church had been instructed to sell its Muskogee site and relocate the college if possible.
- Garrett approved of the college's resolution to maintain its Presbyterian roots even when the college passed out of the church's control.
- Tulsa offered a 20-acre campus and a trust fund of $100,000, to be disbursed over time, for the purpose of erecting buildings and purchasing equipment; the

Commercial Club also undertook to subsidize the college's fuel and energy costs and to run a trolley line to the college.

- The synod's College Commission gratefully accepted, and it named Garrett to the original board of trustees. He was also a member of the executive committee that nominated that college's faculty members.
- Garrett remained on the board for many years, helping to oversee the college's growth.
- Garrett loved to attend University of Tulsa football games and especially enjoyed the 1922-1923 season, when the Golden Hurricane went undefeated.

Life at Work

- Garrett Cooper opened one of the first mercantile stores in Tulsa.
- Like many Tulsa merchants, he preached a simple motto: "A dollar's worth of honest goods for a dollar in money."
- Honest and hardworking by nature, he was trusted by the community's citizens as a shopkeeper and even with their cash when he helped establish one of the first banks in the area.
- A founding member of the Tulsa Commercial Club, begun in 1902, Garrett was involved in the city's most critical decisions from the time the oil boom began.
- That development could be dated precisely to June 25, 1901, with the eruption of the Sue Bland No. 1 well at Red Fork, just across the Arkansas River from Tulsa.
- Almost overnight the area was teeming with adventurous oilmen, investors, speculators, gamblers, wildcatters, geologists and lease hounds, all eager to wrest wealth from "black gold."
- So much oil was produced so rapidly that for a short period, crude oil dropped to an all-time low price of $0.03 per barrel.

An oil derrick in west Tulsa

- Oil companies worked off the surplus by marketing their products to railroad companies, shipping concerns, sugar refineries, breweries and other businesses as a cheap alternative to coal.
- They also began selling gasoline to automobile owners—then just a small, wealthy niche market.
- The Commercial Club played a key role in creating the additional infrastructure needed to cope with the oil boom: railroad facilities, bridges, hotels, banks and housing.
- In 1902, in one of the club's first steps, 50 of the member businessmen—including Garrett—collectively pledged $12,000 plus several miles of free land to persuade the railroad to include Tulsa on its planned route from Muskogee to Pawhuska.
- Although many of the businessmen pledged individual amounts in excess of their personal assets, once the railroad traffic arrived, the payoff was tremendous.
- This unified "Tulsa Spirit" was invoked repeatedly over succeeding decades to encourage and guide growth.
- In 1904, for example, after a city-wide bond effort failed, Garrett invested in a similar private effort—colloquially called a stud horse note—to build a bridge from Tulsa to the Red Fork oil development.

- The impact of the bridge on the city was immediate; Garrett and his fellow investors not only improved Tulsa's access to the oil fields but saw the value of their personal real estate and oil holdings dramatically escalate.
- When proposals began to circulate for a new college in Tulsa to be named for oilman Robert M. McFarlin, Garrett helped persuade the Henry Kendall College trustees to reconstitute Henry Kendall College, together with the new McFarlin College, as the University of Tulsa. A charter for the university was approved in 1920.
- Meanwhile, forward-looking Tulsa businessmen talked about giving the city a municipal airport using the familiar stud horse note procedure; oil and aviation seemed to go together for men who loved risk and were always in a hurry.

Garrett's partners in the 1904 "stud horse note"

- Garrett saw the potential of air travel for the city and also for his own business interests, and he enthusiastically supported an aviation land-site committee formed in 1917 by the Tulsa Chamber of Commerce, which had succeeded the Commercial Club.
- As a result, within two years Tulsa bought land four miles east of the city and developed its first airfield, operated by barnstormer Duncan A. McIntyre.
- By 1919 McIntyre Airport was the second largest commercial airfield in the United States and the only one with runways both lit for night flights and long enough for two passenger airplanes.
- It was a grand moment for Garrett and Nell to watch America's first air shipment of goods over an interstate route—from Tulsa to a factory in Kansas City, Missouri—leave McIntyre Airport.
- The Chamber's Aviation Committee produced a report indicating that a "great public airport" was needed to keep the city at the forefront of aviation.
- Garrett and his friends, not entirely satisfied with the speed and urgency shown by the Chamber, began raising money to buy the necessary land for an enlarged airport.
- Garrett had a strong interest in aviation, but he was chiefly engaged in trying to repair the most recent damage done to Tulsa's reputation: in 1923 Governor Jack C. Walton had declared martial law in Tulsa County after Ku Klux Klan mob violence, including numerous whippings.
- Along with its booming economy, Tulsa had developed an underworld of crime and vice, and after World War I, unemployment and lawlessness became more pronounced. There were labor fights, clashes between racial groups, bank robberies, and mob whippings.
- Governor Walton later extended martial law to the whole state, but Tulsa (along with Oklahoma City) had been singled out, and Walton had assigned 150 National Guardsmen to the city.
- Walton suspended the writ of habeas corpus in Tulsa County, an action expressly forbidden by the state constitution, and partly as a result, he was impeached after serving as governor for less than a year.
- The continuing vigilante violence kept fresh the tragic events of the Tulsa race riot of May 31-June 1, 1921, when Little Africa, Tulsa's prosperous African American district along Greenwood Avenue —known nationally as the Negro Wall Street—was completely destroyed, at horrific loss of life.
- Despite the devastation in Greenwood, many whites blamed the blacks for the riot; to Garrett's dismay, in the aftermath the Klan took firm root in Tulsa, with organizers cheering the riot and conducting mass membership drives extending even to women and youth.
- In fact, many business and political leaders in the state were members of the KKK; Garrett visited them privately to ask that they control the Klan for the sake of Tulsa.

- Klan violence became common against women who wore their hair or skirts short; Jewish merchants who opened on Sundays; foreigners, especially Catholics, who did not speak English; and students who spoke out.

Life in the Community: Tulsa, Oklahoma

- The Tulsa Regional Commission was organized to devise a city plan for promoting future expansion.
- The commission attempted to eliminate serious obstacles to future expansion, such as the haphazard growth of subdivisions outside the city limits.
- The plan provided for railroad terminals, parks, a civic center and control of subdivisions both within the city and those extending three miles beyond the city limits in all directions.
- In August 1919 Horace M. Hickam, Director of the National Air Service in Washington, D.C., added Tulsa as a regular stop for all transcontinental mail and military flights, securing the future role of air travel in Tulsa.
- Air travel also helped Tulsa become the unchallenged leader of the oil industry; after World War I, executives from all parts of the world traveled to northeastern Oklahoma for training in the latest techniques of producing and marketing petroleum.
- In 1923, while serving as president of the Tulsa Chamber of Commerce, W. G. Skelly, founder of Skelly Oil Company, helped organize the first International Petroleum Exposition (IPE) at Tulsa.
- The IPE was becoming known as the home of the "World's Fair of the Oil Industry."
- The community had come a long way in a short time; at the end of 1882, Tulsa's entire commercial district consisted only of Hall's General Store, Bullette Brothers' Store, Perryman Brothers' Store, Archer's Furniture and Hardware, Chauncey Owen's boarding house, and the office of one physician, Dr. W. P. Booker.
- When Tulsa was officially incorporated as a City of the Creek Nation on January 18, 1898, the population totaled 1,100.
- The citizenry was almost entirely white as a result of the 1889, 1891 and 1893 land runs.
- In 1900, this former Indian meeting place, still known as Tulsey Town, consisted of a single dirt street lined with buildings; the population was 1,340.
- The community's entire freight business for the first week of 1900 was listed as, "Receipts: One car—bran; Shipments: Two cars—hogs; One car—sand; One car—mules."
- Then in 1902, oil was discovered, and by 1910, the population had reached 18,182; agrarian Tulsa quickly evolved into oil-town Tulsa.
- Within a decade, more than 100 oil and gas companies were established, employing 15,000 field workers and averaging $15,000 in royalty payments per month.
- In the single year of 1911, nationally and locally based firms drilled 4,986 wells at a combined cost of $11 million, losing only $800,000 on 675 speculative sites that produced dry holes; of the 114 petroleum companies in the state, 95 located their home offices in Tulsa.

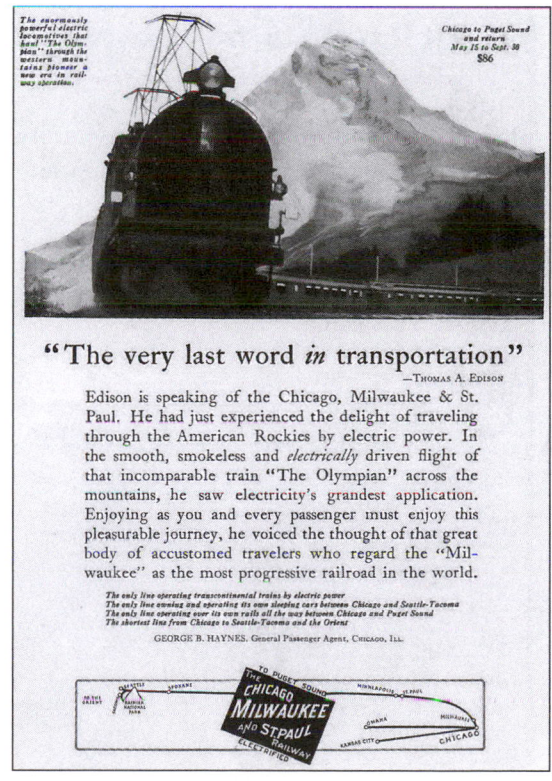

"The very last word *in* transportation"
—Thomas A. Edison

Edison is speaking of the Chicago, Milwaukee & St. Paul. He had just experienced the delight of traveling through the American Rockies by electric power. In the smooth, smokeless and *electrically* driven flight of that incomparable train "The Olympian" across the mountains, he saw electricity's grandest application. Enjoying as you and every passenger must enjoy this pleasurable journey, he voiced the thought of that great body of accustomed travelers who regard the "Milwaukee" as the most progressive railroad in the world.

- At the same time, the Mayo Brothers constructed a five-story building downtown—widely considered the "finest building in Tulsa"—setting a standard for others to follow. The Mayo brothers doubled the height of their building in 1914 and added additional stories in 1917.
- By the beginning of World War I, the city boasted 72 miles of paved streets; 32 passenger and freight trains arrived and departed daily, and tourists had the choice of 20 hotels—two of which were six stories high.
- Thanks to the oil money, everything was new; in the year 1920 alone, Tulsa spent $3 million paving 110,243 square miles of streets.
- Not everyone prospered, however, and the Ku Klux Klan found a receptive audience in some quarters, among both the unemployed and those who felt threatened by the accelerating social and economic changes of the 1910s and 1920s.
- The Tulsa race riot of May 31-June 1, 1921, possibly the worst in American history, was set off by reports in Richard Lloyd Jones's *Tulsa Tribune* of an alleged assault by a black man against a white woman; the riot was fueled by rumors of a black insurrection emanating from Tulsa's prosperous African American district along Greenwood Avenue.
- Known nationally as the "Negro Wall Street," Greenwood, also called Little Africa, was looted and completely burnt out. The official death toll was 39, mostly African Americans; other estimated ran up to some 300, with $1.5 million (in 1921 dollars) in property damage.
- In the 35-block area, black churches, schools, and a hospital were set alight by arsonists, and more than 1,200 homes were destroyed. Many African American victims were buried in unmarked graves.
- Those residents who had not fled or been killed or seriously injured were mostly held by the authorities for up to a week, effectively under arrest, before being allowed to make their way back to their homes and businesses, only to find that they had lost everything.
- Some white Tulsans rejoiced in the misery of their black fellow citizens; others opened their homes to the dispossessed or donated food, clothing, and money for their relief.
- Klan organizers (who were paid on a commission basis) promptly capitalized on the riot and the fears that had incited it. They enrolled thousands of members in the Tulsa area. Many were from disaffected groups, but others were business and civic leaders, politicians, newspaper editors, even ministers.
- The Klan became politically very active in Tulsa, and candidates sought Klan support.
- Despite the passage just days after the riot of a fire ordinance intended to prevent the rebuilding of Greenwood as a commercial district, African American attorneys succeeded in having the ordinance declared unconstitutional by the Oklahoma Supreme Court. Eventually Greenwood was rebuilt on its original site.
- Throughout the city construction proceeded at a torrid pace; the residence of Richard Lloyd Jones raised a few eyebrows with its modern lines and a "strange and startling beauty that fits naturally into a setting unconscious of a past."
- In 1924 the city finally secured a satisfactory water system, solving this longstanding problem thanks to a $7.5 million project to bring water from the Spavinaw Hills, 65 miles to the northeast.
- At the same time, Tulsa purchased the land surrounding Lake Spavinaw, which had been created by damming Spavinaw Creek, to protect the water from pollution. The city then began building public recreational facilities, including picnic tables and cabins, and providing boats for hire.
- The availability of water also meant that ice could be provided for the Tulsa Ice Oilers, the city's professional hockey club.
- When the 400-plus students returned to the University of Tulsa campus in the fall of 1921, they found that the wooden gymnasium had been removed and its lumber used to erect four temporary buildings—two for classrooms, one for music and the fourth for storage.
- In 1923 a special technical department was formally launched at the public Carnegie Library, creating a comprehensive collection of information on the petroleum industry.
- In 1924 Tulsa's population stood at 110,000, enough both to rival Oklahoma City and to be listed nationally with other cities that claimed more than 100,000 people.

WHO has not sailed a pirate ship or looked for treasure lands! · · · Those boyhood dreams return once more to the man who sits at the wheel of his LaFayette · · · His is the sense of command of every situation · · · He may lay his course to match his mood and whim. Doors to new motoring pleasures are opened to him. Trails once forbidden are easily mastered. Travel is glorious and secure.

Steadily the conviction that the LaFayette is one of the world's finest motor cars is finding wider and wider acceptance as the experience of LaFayette owners becomes known

LaFayette Motors Corporation, Milwaukee, Wisconsin

LaFAYETTE

Automobile ad pitching motoring as the route to adventure

National Guard troops taking the wounded to the Brady Theater, June 1, 1921 (Tulsa World)

Textile Mill Worker in 1925

Dorothy Urbig lived in a mill village created by the Saxon Mill textile company in Spartanburg, South Carolina. Her parents and two of her four siblings also worked at the mill.

Life at Home

- The original Saxon Mill village consisted of 40 houses in four different styles, all built near the mill; it also included several churches, a barbershop, and a general store.
- By the time the Urbig family moved there, the community included 168 homes, 23 of which were new bungalows.
- The Urbigs paid $0.25 a week per room, or $1.50 a week, in rent.
- Dorothy, the second child and oldest girl in the family, left high school after tenth grade to take a job at the mill.
- She was a good student but knew that she would not need to graduate to get a steady job at the mill.
- Her parents, and especially her mother, were glad that she had stayed in school longer than many of village children, but they agreed with her decision.
- Dorothy hoped to get married and move into one of the bungalettes in the community, which cost $1.25 a week. The bungalettes were built along an attractive street known as Honeymoon Lane.
- Dorothy's 22-year-old boyfriend also worked in the mill, and he earned a bit extra by serving as a swimming instructor at the community pool.
- Dorothy had her own bank account at the mill's bank and was able to accumulate some savings; the mill ran its own bank to assist the workers in saving, and it paid interest on funds undisturbed for six months.
- Many of Dorothy's coworkers who would not open an account at a regular bank made regular deposits at the mill bank.
- The Urbigs' house had electricity, as did all the houses in the Saxon Mill village.
- The family had a percolator to make coffee, and Dorothy had splurged on a curling iron; these were the only electrical appliances in the Urbig house.
- Radio set ownership had reached three million nationwide; the Urbig family was saving for a set. Several neighbors already had a radio.
- Every house had running water. The water was not metered, measured, or restricted as to use; its cost was included in the mill-controlled rent.

Dorothy Urbig

- All the houses had bathrooms in which toilets were installed. Sixty of the 168 homes now had bathtubs, including the Urbigs' house.
- A sewerage system had begun operation in 1910.
- Three wet-wash laundries competed for the dirty clothing of Saxon Mill residents, freeing the women for other duties.
- In 1925 no house in the mill village was more than a five-minute walk from the mill; 50 more homes were under construction.
- The mill village had streetlights, streetcar service to town, and a Piedmont & Northern Railway station in the village.

Textile mill workers with a company floor manager

- The Urbigs took the daily newspaper, as did the majority of their neighbors.
- The family had a Bible but few other books.
- Most of the books they read were borrowed from the mill library; light fiction was a favorite.
- Dorothy sometimes used to buy confession magazines, available at the bookstore, but, with the bungalettes in mind, she had decided not to spend her money on them anymore and usually managed to stick to her decision.
- Her brother Henry, who had begun working at the mill two years after Dorothy, was participating in a work-study program at the Technical Industrial Institute in Spartanburg; the mill allowed him to alternate weeks of work at Saxon Mill with weeks studying at the institute.
- Dorothy and Henry had always been close, but now Dorothy saw Henry striving for something—she was not sure what—that seemed beyond her reach.
- Among the families in Saxon Mills, 5 percent had pianos, 16 percent had a Victrola or phonograph machine, 1 percent had radios, and 31 percent had automobiles.
- The children of 18 of the village's 168 families were attending college; Henry was one of them.
- When the children were young, Dorothy's mother, Edith, sewed most of their clothing as well as shirts for her husband, Earl.
- Work dresses were made by a village seamstress, and dressup, or Sunday clothes, were bought "ready-made."
- This suited Dorothy, who did not especially enjoy sewing.
- Dorothy's younger sister Mildred worked part-time at the mill, but Mildred dreamed of getting a "city" job, as her oldest brother, Jonathan, had after returning from the Great War.

Family members often worked together at the mill (Lewis W. Hine, Library of Congress)

- Jonathan had been hired for a minor job at the local bank and was recognized for his conscientious work; even though he had only a seventh-grade education, he was promoted to bookkeeper.
- Dorothy was old enough to vote, a right finally gained by women in 1920, and she felt very modern when she voted for the first time in the 1924 presidential election.
- Her mother, however, was still hesitant, believing that politics was outside a woman's sphere.
- For now, at least, Dorothy was content to be a mill girl; she enjoyed having some economic

independence, and except for a few traditionally female occupations such as schoolteacher or nurse, there were not very many respectable jobs available for young women.

- She wondered if this was changing; a friend of hers had just found a job as a secretary at an insurance company.
- Dorothy knew that if she took a city job, she would miss the sense of community at Saxon Mill.

Life at Work

- Saxon Mill was built at the turn of the century for $200,000.
- The city of Spartanburg supplied half of the capital needed to build the plant.
- The mill had been built with local money, and management of the mill was in the hands of local men.
- The new factory comprised more than 10,000 spindles, a measure used in mills to determine size.
- Saxon Mill was considered more progressive than most in its treatment of its workers, providing a school and some medical services and allowing the workers to participate in the Technical Industrial Institute's work-study program in Spartanburg.
- The company sponsored picnics and other community events, and it even gave the villagers a ham or turkey at Christmas.
- Some observers noted that despite this "welfare capitalism," the mill operators controlled almost every aspect of their workers' lives.
- Some of the more politically minded villagers were of the opinion that Saxon Mill operators were as interested in dissuading workers from unionizing or protesting their working conditions as in the workers' well-being.
- For more than two decades, entire families had migrated between the mill and the farm, an indication that for some—but not the Urbigs—agriculture was often being supplemented rather than supplanted by the textile industry.
- Dorothy's father had struggled for many years to make a living on the family farm; despite the long hours and unrelenting noise at Saxon Mill, he was happy to receive a steady paycheck.

The sprawling mill community was controlled by mill management

- The house in the mill village, with its indoor plumbing and electricity, was much better than the farmhouse he had left behind, and as a renter, he was not responsible for making repairs.
- He missed the farm, but not the ever-present economic insecurity farming brought with it.
- Like the Urbigs, members of many Saxon Mill village families worked alongside one another at the mill.
- Dorothy was a "winder"; she tended rows, or "sides," of spinning machines, working in the broken thread ends on the spools.
- Lint and dust were constant problems in the mill.
- Recent improvements in the Saxon Mill village encompassed the construction of a community educational and social center and the expansion of a playground, including the transformation of one millpond into a lake for swimming and recreation purposes.
- Closely identified with village life was the Saxon Mills vacation camp, located on Lake Summit, 40 miles away in the Blue Ridge Mountains.
- Ninety percent of the mill village families carried life insurance; paid weekly, it normally cost $0.10 to $0.25. The purpose invariably was to provide for a "good burying."

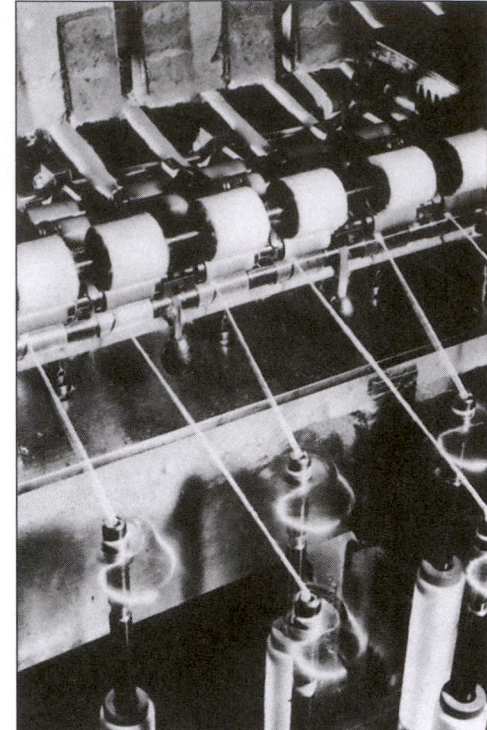

Spindle count was an informal measure of mill size

- The Urbigs carried $500 in life insurance. Every member of the family was covered except Evelyn, the youngest child, who was not yet working.
- Typhoid fever and measles often drained a family of all savings, putting them in debt at the mill store.
- Several children in the mill died of measles during the 1922 and 1923 epidemic.
- Some of the mill village's residents worked in the city, and other workers commuted from the city or the countryside to work at the mill, a trend that was increasing.
- The American Cotton Manufacturer's Association had reported that the low cost of mill house rents, "free" light and water, and coal and wood at cost added the equivalent of $4.36 to the weekly wage of each worker. "Where there are three or four workers in a family, as is often the case, this mounts up."

Life in the Community: Spartanburg, South Carolina

- Spartanburg County was the home of two colleges and 37 textile mills.
- The builders of the cotton mills did not see themselves as primarily manufacturers but rather as the empire builders of a new, industrialized South.
- Spartanburg, with 22,638 residents as of the 1920 U.S. census, was one of only 13 cities in South Carolina exceeding 10,000 in population.
- During a typical month, the county bookstore sold 25 copies of *Harpers*, but it also sold 750 copies of confession and adventure magazines—from under the counter.
- In August 1923 the *Spartanburg Herald* announced construction of the city's first major office building with a headline that read, "Ten-Story Skyscraper Will Cost Over Million Dollars."
- A small headline that same day announced that President Warren G. Harding had died.

- While in other parts of the United States, men rolled over Niagara Falls in barrels or walked across the falls on tightropes, in Spartanburg a daredevil human fly scaled the outside of the eight-story Chapman Building as hundreds of spectators gawked on the sidewalk below.

- In 1925 the Interstate Commerce Commission granted Spartanburg the same preferential freight rates already in effect in Atlanta, Georgia, and in Norfolk, Virginia, adding to Spartanburg's importance as a trade center.

The Saxon Mills W.O.W [Woodmen of the World fraternal organization] Band

- Spartanburg was the only city in South Carolina with a commercial airport—the principal reason that the city was Col. Charles A. Lindbergh's only stop in the state following his famous transatlantic flight.

- Although Prohibition was under way in 1925 and many Southern counties had been "dry" prior to the constitutional change, illegal liquor traffic continued, mostly in the form of moonshine whiskey: "A touring car brings it in from the country and sells it on the quiet at the picture show."

- The first regularly licensed radio broadcasts in America began on August 20, 1920, but radio was not a part of most people's daily life in Spartanburg; in 1925 not a single commercial radio station operated in South Carolina.

- The average wage paid to textile workers in four Southern states was $644.00 a year.

- "The individual wage is small but a father and mother with six children, two of whom are of working age, can earn about $25.00 to $30.00 a month," reported Richard Woods Edmunds in *Cotton Mill Labor Conditions in the South and New England* (1925).

- Textile mill recruiters, who visited farms seeking employees, favored large families, since father, mother, and children could all be employed.

- The small children of such working families were cared for by older children for one-third of the time, by a nurse for another third of the time, and by grandparents for 23 percent of the time.

- Black nurses were hired to care for children when a mother could negotiate a nurse's wage low enough to allow a margin of profit for the working mother; widowed mothers with young children often attempted this form of child care.

- The average mill family had 3.5 children in the home. The children usually were encouraged to attend school until age 14 so that they could learn more than their parents, most of whom could not read.

- Some parents moved from mill to mill to obtain a better education for their children.

- Night school was also available in the community for adults; programs usually provided elementary schoolwork.

- For advanced work, the International Correspondence School Textile Courses were used.

- On average, two children of every family worked in the mill. Often the mother left mill work once her children were old enough to take her place.

- Textile mill workers were known as a "moving population," often changing jobs or moving from town to town every few years.
- Approximately 90 percent of the mill workers formerly were farmers; 64 percent had left jobs as farm tenants, and 26 percent were former farm owners.
- Some of the workers could not resist the call of the land; every spring they returned to the farm, where they tended cotton. They returned to the mill in the fall.
- Many put their children, restricted from mill work by child labor regulations, to work on the farm. The children routinely were taken out of school several weeks before the school year ended, and they returned weeks after the fall session had begun.

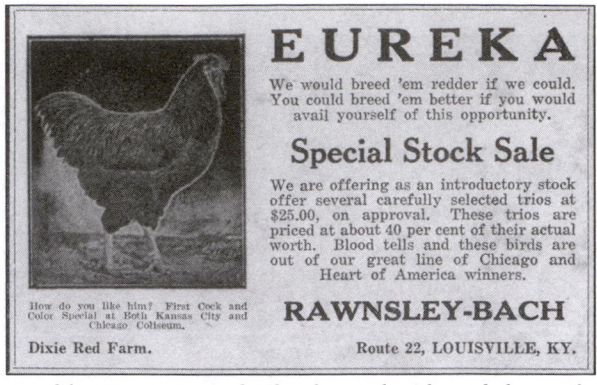

An ad for prizewinning poultry breeding stock might catch the eye of a mill worker still attached to farming

- About 30 percent of the mill workers were Baptists, 16 percent were Methodists, and slightly less than half claimed no organized religion or faith. Approximately 50 percent of the children attended Sunday School.
- A local religious leader commanded his followers not to work on the night shift because in the Bible it was written that Christ said, "The night cometh, when no man can work" (John 9:4). Little came of the edict.
- Many people still talked about the six-week-long revival held by the Rev. William Ashley "Billy" Sunday, the world's most widely known evangelist, in Spartanburg in January 1922.
- Services were held in a huge frame "tabernacle" built to the evangelist's specifications and seating 7,000 people. Situated on Magnolia Street, it was by far the largest auditorium in South Carolina at the time.
- Sunday had his photograph taken with members of the Spartanburg Fire Department; the picture was published in the *Herald.*
- In 1925 many South Carolina-based banks, which were agriculturally oriented, were already on shaky ground.
- After cotton prices dropped from the World War I levels of $0.50 or more per pound to $0.05 per pound by the mid-1920s, the farmer was also harmed by the invasion of the boll weevil, a highly destructive pest.
- Cotton farming became a highly speculative venture, at best, and many more farms failed, driving even more farmers to the cities and the mills.

Miner and Professional Football Player in 1925

Allen Flannery worked six days a week in the depths of the Pennsylvania anthracite coal mines and gloried in the opportunity to play professional football on the seventh day.

Life at Home

- Allen Flannery was named after Necho Allen, a hunter who supposedly discovered the anthracite coal in the region; anthracite gave Pottsville, Pennsylvania, its considerable early-twentieth-century economic importance.
- A star player on his high school football team, Allen played several positions but especially excelled on the defensive line, crashing through to stop the run.
- Allen used to go with his father on Sundays to watch the new local independent professional football team, the Pottsville Maroons.
- He had hopes of playing football at Lafayette College in Easton, Pennsylvania.
- But Allen's father died of pneumoconiosis, or "miner's asthma," when Allen was only 17.
- As the oldest boy in the family, Allen had to quit school and go to work.
- The mines were the best option; Pennsylvania law forbade underage miners from working, but Allen's uncle vouched for him as 18, and he went to work.
- When Allen left school, he left behind his football and baseball playing as well.
- He rose at 5:30 every morning, Monday through Saturday, to work underground—sometimes for as long as ten hours per day.
- Each morning Allen would walk deep into the mine, inspecting the buttresses lit by his lamp in the labyrinthine tunnels, recalling the death of an older cousin who was just one of the more than 2,000 fatalities every year in U.S. mines.
- Laboring in the mines gave Allen arms of steel, and he was in the best physical condition of his life.
- On Sunday came Allen's only day not committed to work.
- One Sunday afternoon, at a community picnic, Allen became involved in a football game.
- Allen was thrilled to have the opportunity to play the game he loved so much.
- His skills impressed three players participating in the game; Allen thought they were the best he had ever played against.
- They approached him after the game, saying they were on the Pottsville Maroons team. They encouraged him to try out for a vacant reserve spot on the team's 16-man roster.
- Allen made the club; he was one of only two Maroons players who had not attended college.

Allen Flannery

- Allen earned $100 a game; at the mine, he earned $0.78 an hour for a 48-hour work week.
- The extra money allowed him not only to support his family but also to propose to his girlfriend, Ethel.
- Allen could even afford some luxuries, such as taking Ethel to see movies at the Majestic Theater.
- They especially enjoyed seeing Harold Lloyd play a human tackling dummy in *The Freshman*.
- The laughter was good for Allen.
- Three years in the mines had aged him, making him appear years older than he actually was.

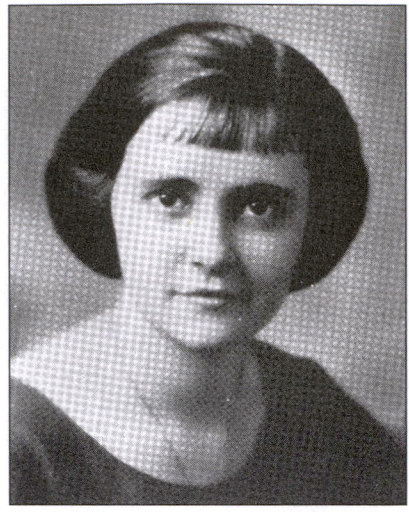

Allen's girlfriend Ethel, a high school graduate

Life at Work

- Allen Flannery had been a fan of the Pottsville Maroons, a Pennsylvania Anthracite League football team, since the team's formation in 1920.
- Dr. John C. Striegel, the Maroons's manager, purchased the franchise in 1924 for $1,500.
- In the summer of 1925, Striegel applied for membership in the budding National Football League.
- The original eight teams each had paid $100 to join the league, but by 1925 expansion costs had risen to $500.
- Pottsville was granted an NFL team because the Maroons enjoyed one of the most faithful followings in all of professional football, and because the nearest NFL team, the Frankford Yellow Jackets of northeastern Philadelphia, played their games on Saturdays.
- Logistically it would be lucrative for clubs already in the area to play Pottsville on Sundays.
- County "blue laws" forbade organized sporting events on Sundays, but the scheduled games were played without interference; spectators sometimes included police officers, council members, and—rumor had it—even the mayor, in disguise.
- While the league was excited about the New York Giants bringing the NFL to America's biggest city, on the field it was Pottsville that garnered the excitement.
- The Maroons boasted several of the league's early stars, whom Striegel had lured away from the three-time champion Canton Bulldogs.
- Coach Dick Rauch, a Penn State football legend who was assisting at Colgate University, had been hired to lead the team.
- As a substitute player, Allen was always ready to play any one of six positions on offense or defense.

Young "nippers" (miner's assistants) working in a Pennsylvania mine (Lewis W. Hine, Library of Congress)

- Allen particularly liked teammate Tony Latone, who, like Allen, had entered the mines after the death of his father.
- Tony had worked as a slate picker in the mines, developing powerful leg muscles pushing shuttle cars up the slope.
- On the football field Tony was physical, powerful, and unrelenting; his teammates considered him to be a "one-man gang."
- During the memorable 1925 season, Tony contributed eight touchdowns, leading up to the NFL championship game in Chicago.
- For budget reasons, Striegel required players to live locally, which gave Rauch a luxury

that no other NFL coach had at the time—scheduled team practices with everyone available to participate.

- Allen was able to make the daily practices once it was established that he would not work in the mine longer than his regular eight-hour shift.
- After practice Allen and the team would sometimes meet at the fire department hall to play cards and drink bottles of locally made Yuengling, from the nation's oldest brewery—headquartered right in Pottsville, on Mahantongo Street.
- Owing to Prohibition, the product was called "near beer."
- The regular football practices paid off as Pottsville became one of the best teams in the league, with a 9-2 record heading into the last week of the season.

An exciting punt return on the field (National Photo Company Collection, Library of Congress)

- The Maroons played the Chicago Bears, led by rookie sensation Harold "Red" Grange, the "Galloping Ghost"; Pottsville knocked Grange out of the game twice.
- After getting knocked out for the second time, Grange said, "The hell with $500 (his pay for the game), it ain't worth it," and walked off the field.
- The Maroons's final game was on December 6, at Comiskey Park in Chicago, against the 8-2-1 Cardinals. It was billed as "for the championship."
- The swirling snowstorm didn't bother Allen or the Maroons, who dominated the game, winning 21-7.
- The Maroons thought that they had won the championship.
- In accordance with a new NFL rule, the Maroons scheduled an additional game against a Notre Dame alumni team including the famed "Four Horsemen" of the Notre Dame backfield; players on the Notre Dame alumni team had boasted before the Pottsville–Chicago game that they could beat the NFL champion, whichever team it proved to be.
- An extra game with a big draw such as the Notre Dame players meant money in everyone's pocket, including Allen's.
- Meanwhile, the Chicago Cardinals wanted to cash in on the popularity of the Bears's Red Grange; two games were scheduled against lesser opponents in order to entice the Bears to play a game against them.

A tough defensive line at work (National Photo Company Collection, Library of Congress)

- The Cardinals won the two games with ease, in large part because both teams had already disbanded for the season; Milwaukee struggled to field enough players to play the game, which was in danger of being canceled.
- In order to field a Milwaukee team, Chicago halfback Art Folz helped Milwaukee recruit four high school players—ineligible players, under league rules.
- The game was a 58-0 slaughter, and when NFL commissioner Joseph Carr found out what had transpired, he not only fined Milwaukee owner Ambrose L. McGurk but

forced him to sell the franchise within 90 days and banned him for life from the NFL.

- For his part in the drama, Art Folz was banned from the league as well.
- Meanwhile Red Grange was injured in an exhibition game; following doctor's orders, he ended his season and the hope of an all-Chicago match.
- At the same time, Striegel decided to move the highly hyped Pottsville-Notre Dame game to Philadelphia to accommodate the anticipated larger crowd.
- The Frankford Yellow Jackets ownership cried foul, claiming that Pottsville was infringing on their territory.
- Protection of territory was one of the chief inducements for teams to join the league.

Rookie sensation Harold "Red" Grange (National Photo Company Collection)

- Commissioner Carr agreed with Frankford, and he telegraphed a warning to Striegel that if the Maroons played the game in Philadelphia, the Pottsville team could expect suspension.
- The Maroons ignored the warning and played at Shibe Park in front of 10,000 screaming fans who had paid an average of $1 per ticket; still, the crowd was smaller than anticipated.
- The game was hard fought, with Notre Dame dominating, but Allen made a critical tackle late in the game that gave the Maroons one last chance.
- The contest was won with a dramatic last-second field goal, 9-7.
- As threatened, however, Carr suspended the Maroons. The suspension left the Chicago Cardinals with the league's best winning percentage; therefore the Cardinals were the 1925 NFL champions, by default.
- In all the confusion, no actual vote was taken to declare a champion.
- Pottsville was outraged at having its championship taken away; Allen was confused when he heard the news.

Life in the Community: Pottsville, Pennsylvania

- Pottsville, 97 miles northwest of Philadelphia, was an unlikely place for a professional football team.
- In all of the United States, only northeastern Pennsylvania had significant anthracite deposits; Pottsville, in Schuykill County, was one of the "six principal anthracite cities."
- The first attempt to organize mine workers for collective bargaining took place in the anthracite coal region in 1849; the short-lived Miners and Laborers Benevolent Association, under the leadership of John Bates, called a strike but failed to win concessions from mine operators.
- The Workmen's Benevolent Association (later chartered as the Miners' and Laborers' Benevolent Association) was organized in 1867 to press for an eight-hour work day.
- Its president, John Siney Sr., of Saint Clair—just two miles north of Pottsville—called a series of strikes and in 1869 negotiated the first annual agreement between miners and operators establishing a wage scale.
- In 1873, after reverses in the anthracite (hard coal) region, Siney moved to the bituminous (soft) coal mining region to the west; he became president of the Youngstown, Ohio-based Miners National Association, the second national organization of coal miners.
- By 1876 the Miners National Association had failed.
- In 1890 the United Mine Workers of America union (UMWA) was founded in Ohio.

- In August 1900 UMWA president John Mitchell, convened a conference in Hazleton, Pennsylvania, to call for a 10-percent increase in wages and union recognition.
- Having received no constructive response from the operators, Mitchell called a strike on September 17, although the union had only 9,000 dues-paying members among the 145,000 miners working in the anthracite fields.
- The strike started slowly, but within two weeks, approximately 112,000 miners were on strike.
- The operators decided to settle, and the strike ended on October 29, leaving the UMW firmly established in the anthracite region.
- By February 1902, however, operators refused to renew the wage agreement.
- This time the operators were determined to break the union, and they rejected an arbitration process.
- By mid-May 147,000 coal miners were on strike.
- In Shenandoah, where the 1900 strike had seen a violent clash that left one man dead and 20 injured, 2,000 National Guardsmen were called out to keep the peace. Nevertheless, one man was killed and others were injured in a riot.
- Sporadic violence continued as no progress was made to settle the strike.
- On September 6 President Theodore Roosevelt called for an end to the strike; at the beginning of October he summoned John Mitchell and representatives of the coal operators to meet with him.
- Roosevelt proposed an arbitration plan, which operators accepted. With their grievances now submitted to arbitration, the miners gradually returned to work, and the strike ended after 164 days.
- The miners won a 10-percent pay increase and a nine-hour work day.
- The mines remained very dangerous workplaces, and the struggle between miners and operators simmered, reviving each time the contract came up for renewal.
- When the contract negotiated in 1919 expired in March 1922, the coal operators again attempted to roll back union-negotiated gains. After the inevitable breakdown of negotiations, the UMWA launched the first national strike by both anthracite and bituminous coal miners, some 610,000 workers in all.
- Pottsville mayor J. O. Bearstler of Pottsville, along with the mayors of Scranton, Wilkes-Barre, Carbondale, Pittston, and Hazleton, attempted to mediate the anthracite dispute, meeting first with President Harding and UMWA president John L. Lewis and then, on August 1 in Philadelphia, with S. D. Warriner and other representatives of the operators.
- The UMWA declared itself willing to meet with the operators for direct negotiations; the operators said they would agree to direct negotiations or submission to arbitration.
- The union rejected arbitration as an acceptable alternative to collective bargaining.
- The Harding administration, especially Commerce Secretary Herbert Hoover, wished to end the disorder and ensure that there would not be a coal shortage in the coming winter.
- In June Harding himself unsuccessfully tried to intervene in the strike, but his support for binding arbitration doomed this effort.
- With the backing of the president and his administration, however, Pennsylvania's senators, George W. Pepper and David A. Reed, brokered an agreement.
- The Pepper-Reed proposal called for extension of the terms of the

"View of Pottsville Taken from Sharp Mountain & respectfully dedicated to the enterprising citizens of the Coal Region," by J.R. Smith, c. 1833. (Marian S. Carson Collection, Library of Congress)

contract in force on March 31, 1922, until August 31, 1923, or March 31, 1924, and the creation of a federal coal commission to investigate industry conditions and ensure continued coal production after the extension date.

- The operators agreed to the August 31, 1923, extension date, and the new contract was signed on September 3, 1922, ending the strike after 163 days.
- The UMWA proclaimed victory for the miners, but the 70,000 nonunion workers who had supported the strike were essentially abandoned, and in fact the competition from nonunion mines put strong pressure on the union to settle.
- In 1922 Minersville was a center of unrest among the miners, many of whom distrusted not only the operators but the national union leadership; they instead supported dissident labor organizers.
- By the time the contract came up for renewal, all parties preferred to avoid economic instability; a three-year contract was signed in 1924 that preserved the status quo.
- When the U.S. Coal Commission submitted its report in 1925, it did little more than deem acceptable the operators' desire for local rather than national labor contracts and support nonunion mines as a check on union power.
- Meanwhile, football became a popular sport in the coal mine region of Pennsylvania; residents loved the quick pace and simple, rough and tough game.
- Up to 1920, "football" largely meant "college football," but that perception was about to change.
- Professional football began in Pennsylvania in the 1890s.
- By 1896 the Allegheny Athletic Association of Allegheny City, Pennsylvania (later annexed to Pittsburgh), had become the sport's first entirely professional team; soon professional and semiprofessional teams were being organized nationwide.
- The National Football League was founded in 1922 at a Canton, Ohio, Hupmobile dealership; the Hupmobile was an automobile built by the Hupp Motor Co. of Detroit, Michigan, beginning in 1909.
- Pottsville's professional football team, the Pottsville Eleven, became the Maroons in 1924.
- The name change followed delivery of the uniforms, which were an eye-catching maroon color.
- The Maroons quickly became the talk of the town after opening the season with a 28–0 drubbing of Buffalo.
- In the Pottsville barbershops, the usual talk of hunting was cast aside in favor of football.
- Dr. Striegel billed the team as a blue-collar club, emphasizing the miners on the team, but in fact many players had been college stars or were signed away from other pro teams with lucrative offers.
- Minersville Park, the high school field used by the Maroons, could seat only 5,000, but the devoted fans made the club a financial success.

శ్రీశ్రీశ్రీశ్రీశ్రీ

"Pro Football Here to Stay, Experts Admit"
Edward Derr, *San Mateo Times* (CA), December 1, 1925

Professional football has become so strong that the colleges and universities are powerless to check its advances, according to Maj. John L. Griffith, Commissioner of Big Ten athletics. He predicted that the Western conference athletic directors in their annual meeting here in Chicago Thursday, Friday, and Saturday "will adopt no definite rules against pro football because there is nothing that we can do to stop it."

"We are opposed to professional football, of course," Griffith told United Press in an interview. "But we realize that our hands are tied. About all we can do is to discourage it among the college players. If we could adopt some rules or regulations that would curb it, we probably would do it, but I cannot see how that would be possible."

Phonograph Salesman in Chicago in 1925

Leo Kunstadt, a Chicago native, was immersed in the evolving technology of machines that reproduced sounds.

Life at Home

- Leo Kunstadt was enthralled by the phonograph from the first time his father played him a recorded marching tune in the Kunstadt hardware store in downtown Chicago's Loop area.
- Leo was mesmerized, despite the hissing sounds and chorus of pops and burps.
- Thomas Edison had first developed the phonograph in 1877, ten years before Leo was born, during an era of innovations in the communications industry; the cavalcade of inventions of the day included the telegraph, typewriter, and telephone.
- As conceived by Edison, the phonograph translated the air vibrations created by the human voice into minute indentations on a sheet of tinfoil placed over a metallic cylinder, which could then reproduce the sounds.
- When Leo was a child, the wax-cylinder phonograph dominated the recorded sound market; its scratchy sound and high-pitched tones could be ignored for the glory of hearing music in your own home.
- It was simply magical to be able to listen to music whenever you wanted to, even if one critic described the cylinder's sound as resembling a "partially educated parrot with a sore throat and a cold."
- These problems were in part solved by the development of the phonograph record, a flat disc with an inscribed, modulated spiral groove, which brought sound recordings to a new level of quality.
- For 22 years Leo Kunstadt and his father, Wilhelm, had been on the leading edge of phonograph, or "talking machine," sales.
- Wilhelm and Leo followed the technological improvements in phonographs carefully.
- Wilhelm considered the Victor Records recording made of opera singer Enrico Caruso to be a masterpiece.
- In Wilhelm's opinion Caruso's rich, powerful low tenor voice highlighted the phonograph's best range of audio fidelity, and he used Caruso's voice to demonstrate his Victor phonographs for sale.

Leo Kunstadt with his wife, Harriet

- By 1925, however, sales of Victor phonographs had been declining for two years, and Leo—whom Wilhelm had made co-owner of Kunstadt Hardware just two years before—was ready for the next big change.
- Now Victor Records had announced revolutionary plans to upgrade their discs even more.
- Leo's best customers were buzzing with excitement; with all the technological changes under way, this was a great time to be alive.
- Leo and his wife, Harriet, were just as excited as the customers.

The Zez Confrey Band (G. G. Bain Collection, Library of Congress)

- Harriet sang in a women's choir; she loved music and shared Leo's fascination with the phonograph.
- Harriet also understood that her family's livelihood largely depended on the success of the machine.
- Leo and Harriet's younger children, Anna and Peter, had agreed that their fox terrier could pretend to be the Victor logo dog, Nipper, listening to "his master's voice."
- After all, Nipper was a fox terrier.
- Once the manufacturers began to produce attractive phonograph cabinets, the phonograph moved into the parlor.
- That allowed middle-class families to embrace the idea of a "musical library."
- Despite an obsession within the industry with preventing the "lower classes" from cheapening the instrument, "vaudeville trash" was easily recorded and sold extremely well.
- Leo kept some of the more risqué recordings behind the counter for special customers.
- He also carried some "race records," which were becoming very popular with both blacks and whites; Victor had a whole catalog of race records for sale.
- Industry spokesmen liked to rhapsodize about the various ways the talking machine could serve as an "active agent in the spread of civilization."
- But Leo knew from experience that most households wanted a little vaudeville or at least the sounds of a popular orchestra like Zez Confrey's to mix with their opera.
- Leo was of the opinion that the need (mentioned in phonograph advertisements) to create an "oasis of calm" within the home was a figment of the advertising imagination, clearly conceived by someone with no children or at least a nanny and a housekeeper.

Music at home, courtesy of the phonograph

- His teenaged son, Martin, was happy not only to play popular recordings but to invite his friends to the Kunstadt house on the city's North Side to hear the latest vaudeville tunes and dance bands.
- An "oasis of calm" it was not, but to Leo's astonishment, Harriet seemed to encourage these gatherings.
- Leo figured the manufacturers could talk "highbrow" while he made a living helping regular customers every day.
- Several advertisements depicted the great recording stars as specially selected "after-dinner guests personally invited to entertain you."

- Another read, "Measured by every standard, what could be more valuable, more concretely useful, as well as delightfully entertaining than the Victrola? Second only to the actual physical needs of the body is the imperative hunger of the mind and spirit…music, literature, inspiration, education, comfort and laughter…"

Life at Work

- For two decades Kunstadt Hardware had been following a national trend in shifting from general to specialty products.
- The phonograph display in the big picture window never failed to attract attention, and now that Victor was planning a recording revolution, Leo wanted to take full advantage of the opportunity.
- *The Voice*, a publication issued by the Victor Company, included instructions, pictures, and scale drawings of display windows that produced high sales because they told a story.
- For a while, at least, Leo was even ready to shift the store's second window from a radio cabinet montage to a second display entirely of phonographs and phonograph records.
- He even planned to include a few of the early phonographs and discs to show how far phonograph technology had come.
- Early disc recordings were produced in a variety of speeds ranging from 60 to 130 revolutions per minute, and a variety of sizes, from 5 to 7 to 12 inches.

VOCAL BLUES
RELIGIOUS   SPIRITUALS
RED HOT DANCE TUNES
SERMONS   NOVELTIES

Victor's catalog of "race records"

A Victor recording of Enrico Caruso (G. G. Bain Collection, Library of Congress)

- By 1894, Emile Berliner's United States Gramophone Company was selling single-sided seven-inch discs with an advertised standard speed of "about 70 rpm" (revolutions per minute).
- Soon 78 rpm became the standard for the phonograph industry, because it was the speed created by one of the early hand-cranked machines.
- Leo remembered how excited he had been when Victor added a spring-loaded motor to its talking machines to ensure a constant turntable speed.
- There were still plenty of technological challenges; Leo, who shared Wilhelm's interest in sound technology, liked nothing better than discussing the technical issues with knowledgeable customers.
- Since the introduction of talking machines, large orchestras had been at a disadvantage in acoustical recordings; musicians had to gather as closely as possible around the recording horn, and sometimes percussion instruments could not be heard on recordings at all.
- Under pressure from the industry, Victor had agreed in 1924 to shift from the acoustical, or mechanical,

method of recording sound to the new microphone-based electrical system developed by Western Electric.

- Victor decided to name its version of the improved-fidelity recording process "Orthophonic," and it sold a line of new designs of phonographs to play these improved records, called "Orthophonic Victrolas."
- The highest-quality models of Orthophonic Victrolas had a six-foot-long horn coiled inside the cabinet and achieved audio fidelity unmatched by most home electric phonographs until some 30 years later.

The all-girl Melody Belles band, one of the first bands heard over the airwaves in Pittsburgh, 1920

- With a large advertising campaign, Victor introduced its Orthophonic records on "Victor Day," November 2, 1925.
- Kunstadt Hardware was flooded with customers eager to hear the new sound recordings.
- Leo believed Victor was the best in the business at advertising its products in a way that drove customers into his store.
- He heartily agreed with the assessment of his favorite trade magazine, *Talking Machine World,* that "instead of losing time and waiting for the people to become acquainted with the charms of the talking machine in the ordinary way, the creative forces have accomplished in 10 years what would have taken half a century."
- Thanks to the quality of the advertisements in upscale magazines, even the most sophisticated customers were eager to show off their expensive Orthophonic phonographs in handsome cabinet furniture.

A songbook for the "progressive music teacher"

- Victor also provided customer financing; by the mid-1920s, 90 percent of phonographs—ranging in price from $15 to $250—were bought on installment credit.
- The purchase of phonographs totaled 15 percent of all consumer debt; automobiles represented 50 percent.
- Leo often went to a Victrola purchaser's house personally to collect his or her monthly payment so that he could then demonstrate a generous handful of the newest records.
- After all, a family only needed one talking machine, but to fully use their asset, they needed to keep up with the newest musical trends.
- Leo had also enthusiastically taken up the idea of loaning a phonograph player to the neighborhood school under a Victor-sponsored program to put a "great army of music educators" into the classroom.

- The professed aim of the program was to "foster a love of music," but it was not lost on Leo or on Victor Records that the students and their families were promising potential customers.
- Schoolchildren were encouraged to enter music memory contests, which motivated proud parents to invest in a phonograph and records "for the children's sake."
- A 1924 survey of 36 American cities determined that 59 percent of households owned a hand-cranked or electric phonograph.
- Radio set sales were in their infancy but growing exponentially following their commercial introduction in 1922; Leo had convinced Wilhelm that it was time for Kunstadt Hardware to carry a broader selection of radio sets.
- Initially, radio stations were created to support radio sales; "We broadcast primarily so that those who purchase RCA radios may have something to feed those receiving instruments," said David Sarnoff, vice president of Radio Corporation of America.

Bandleader Zez Confrey with a portable Victor phonograph (G. G. Bain Collection, Library of Congress)

- It was becoming clear that radio and the phonograph industry were symbiotic: radio helped build an audience for recording artists, and records reinforced the audience's interest in keeping up with their favorite stars.
- *Talking Machine World* noted that two of the three major record companies—Brunswick, Columbia, and Victor—already had affiliations with Radio Corporation of America.

Life in the Community: Chicago, Illinois

- Chicago was a city that understood business.
- Starting in the 1830s, entrepreneurs saw the potential of Chicago, Illinois, as a transportation hub and engaged in land speculation to obtain the choicest lots; by 1840, the boomtown had a population of more than 4,000.
- To open the surrounding farmlands to trade, the Cook County commissioners built roads south and west, which enabled hundreds of wagons per day of farm produce to be shipped to the East through the Great Lakes.

Lobby of the Chicago and North Western Terminal, built in Renaissance Revival style in 1911 (Library of Congress)

- By the 1850s more than 30 railroad lines entered the city.
- Factories were built, including the Harvester Factory, which was opened in 1847 by Cyrus Hall McCormick.
- Chicago became a processing center for natural-resource commodities extracted in the West.
- Hundreds of thousands of hogs and cattle were shipped to Chicago's stockyards and processed in its meatpacking plants.
- In 1883 the standardized system of North American Time Zones was adopted by the general time convention of railway managers in Chicago, giving the continent a uniform system for telling time.

- With its road, rail, and water connections, Chicago was ideally positioned to become home to several national retailers offering catalog shopping, including giants Montgomery Ward and Sears, Roebuck and Company.
- This growth allowed Chicago to surpass St. Louis and Cincinnati as the major city in the Midwest.
- Economic opportunity drew immigrants to the city; the immigrants tended to cluster together in neighborhoods, with new immigrants joining their predecessors.
- In the mid-nineteenth century, most of the newcomers were Irish and German.
- In 1871 the center of the city burned: in the Great Chicago Fire, 300 people died, 18,000 buildings were destroyed, and nearly 100,000 of the city's 300,000 residents were left homeless.
- The outlying industrial districts were unharmed, including the Union Stock Yard, the grain elevators, and the railroad freight terminals.
- A building boom followed, and between 1870 and 1900, Chicago's population grew from 299,000 residents to nearly 1.7 million.
- After the turn of the twentieth century, immigrants from eastern and southern Europe— including Poles, Lithuanians, Ukrainians, Hungarians, Czechs, Slovaks, Greeks, and Italians flocked to the city, as did Jews from throughout Eastern Europe.
- Then, after 1914, the First World War cut off immigration from Europe.
- After the war's end, federal immigration legislation instituted in 1924 restricted populations from eastern and southern Europe.
- As the First World War cut off immigration, tens of thousands of African Americans came north in the "Great Migration" out of the rural South.
- Between 1916 and 1918, Chicago's black population more than doubled.
- The city's so-called Black Belt—a neighborhood where most blacks in Chicago lived, more or less by necessity—could not absorb the huge influx of African Americans into the city.
- Located along State Street, the Black Belt originally was a narrow strip some 21 blocks long, bounded on the east, south, and west by what was called the South Side.

A crowded beach on Chicago's Lake Michigan waterfront (National Archives)

- By necessity black migrants began to move into South Side neighborhoods bordering the Black Belt.
- Already established on the South Side were European immigrants—chiefly the long-resident Irish but also Italians, Poles, and Lithuanians—who formed neighborhood covenants to keep African Americans out.
- Each group had its own recognized turf and its own social and athletic clubs; in the case of the Irish in particular, these clubs had come to be closely tied to the political structure of the city and to the police force.
- Relations between the European immigrant groups were often antagonistic; the Poles and Lithuanians detested one another, and the lighter-skinned northern European groups frequently clashed with the darker-skinned southern Europeans.
- Tensions festered in Chicago as the black newcomers competed against the earlier groups not only for housing but for relatively low-paid, low-skill jobs in the South Side's stockyards, meatpacking plants, and industrial facilities.
- African Americans were sometimes hired as strikebreakers, further inflaming white workers.
- The need to reintegrate World War I veterans into the community exacerbated the situation. Some returning white veterans found that their jobs had gone to newly arrived blacks; for their part, black veterans were reluctant to accept inferior status after fighting for democracy and others' freedom during the war.
- In late July 1919 the Chicago Race Riots erupted; the riots proved to be one of the worst occurrences in a nationwide string of violent outbreaks over what became known as the "Red Summer."
- The violence was set off when a black teenager swimming with a makeshift raft in Lake Michigan drifted past an unmarked but ironclad boundary between the waters of the 25th Street beach, which was known to be used only by blacks, and the 29th Street beach, which was known to be used only by whites.
- A white male threw stones at the teenager, who was struck by a stone and either was killed outright or lost his grip on his raft and drowned.
- When police failed to arrest any whites in the incident but instead arrested a black man, the violence began.
- Between July 27 and August 3, 38 people—23 blacks and 15 whites—died in a paroxysm of arson, looting, and murder; more than 500 people were injured, and more than a thousand blacks lost their homes.
- The police proved ineffective, and the state's National Guard had to be deployed in Chicago to restore order.
- By 1920 a third of Chicago's 2.7 million residents were foreign-born; more than a million were Catholic, and another 125,000 were Jewish.
- Increasingly, new white immigrants settled in the suburbs, which also saw growth as white residents moved out from the city, particularly the South Side; after 1920 growth in the suburbs outpaced growth in the city.
- Cars and trucks enabled both people and industries to relocate to the suburbs.

"Victor Co. Produces a New Record, Officials Say Invention for Phonograph Will Revolutionize the Industry"
The New York Times, August 14, 1925

The Victor Talking Machine Company announced yesterday that it will soon place on the market an improved music-producing instrument which "will revolutionize the entire industry."

This statement came less than 24 hours after the announcement of the Brunswick-Balollender of the Panatrome substitute for the phonograph, which has been developed by the Radio Corporation of America, the General Electric Company, the Westinghouse Electric Company, and the Brunswick Company.

Both the Victor and the Brunswick companies say that there is no reason for scrapping the existing instruments. The new records which they are issuing can be played on the existing phonographs and Victrolas. They are said to be an improvement over the old records when played on the ordinary machines, but it is asserted that the new reproducing instruments are needed to bring our their full values.

E. K. McEwan, secretary of the Victor Talking Machine Company, described the new Victor invention as "a knockout." He said it would be placed on the market very soon.

E. R. Fenimore Johnson, president of Victor Co., said that he was not ready to describe the invention in detail, but he called it "the ultimate sound reproduction." He said that it gave complete mechanical reproduction for the entire range of audible sound.

The New Brunswick machine, called the Panatrome, is equipped with vacuum tube amplifiers and disc resonators run either by batteries or by connection with an electrical system. The new Victor machine, it was said, is nonelectrical.

While both inventions are intended as an answer to the competition of radio, which has cut heavily into the music reproduction businesses, both are indebted to radio. The Brunswick instrument is almost a byproduct of radio. Many of its features are adapted from inventions and developments resulting from radio research. It is asserted that the Brunswick instrument makes it possible to put eight or nine times as much music on a 12-inch record as at present, or, in other words, to make a 12-inch record that will play 40 or 45 minutes. This development, however, is so far only in the laboratory stage. Practical difficulties, it was said, would make it a year or two before 45-minute records can be marketed.

Victor officials declined to say whether the new product would make possible records which could play a great length of time without change.

Discussing the statement that the New Brunswick music reproduced partly on principle that used in the talking film, Dr. Lee De Forest, inventor of the Phonofilm, said yesterday his patents were not in any way infringed.

"I welcome this invention. I believe it will save the phonograph. I am very fond of the phonograph, I haven't played mine for months, simply because I am tired of changing the records every few minutes. If they are successful in getting out a record which will play for half an hour without interruption, it will certainly be a remarkable achievement which the public would greatly appreciate."

Timeline of the Victor Phonograph Company

1900 Eldridge Johnson purchased the Berliner Gramophone Company after Berliner lost a legal battle over rights to manufacture flat-disc gramophones; Johnson formed the Consolidated Talking Machine Company.

1901 Johnson reorganized Consolidated Talking Machine and called the new venture The Victor Talking Machine Company.

Victor $3, Type A, Type B, Type C, Monarch, and Monarch Deluxe models were introduced.

Victor sold 7,570 phonographs during the year.

1902 Victor introduced the "Rigid Arm" tone arm concept, which allowed the arm to pivot independently from the horn.

Victor Monarch Jr., Monarch Special, Type P, Royal, Victor II, Victor III and Victor IV models were introduced.

1903 Victor introduced Type D, Type Z, Victor I models.

Initial sketches of an internal horn phonograph design appeared, eventually leading to production of the Victrola.

1904 Victor introduced the deluxe gold-trimmed Victor VI model, selling for $100.

A tapering tone arm debuted on certain models.

1905 Victor sold 65,591 phonographs during the year.

1906 The pneumatic-powered Victor Auxetophone, introduced in May, sold for $500.

The Victrola, the first internal horn phonograph, was introduced and became an instant success.

1907 Victor began transitioning manufacture of Victrola cabinets to its Camden plant.

The "domed lid" was introduced on the Victrola.

1908 Victor sold a record 107,000 phonographs.

1909 Victor introduced the first tabletop internal horn phonograph, the Victrola XII, which sold for $125, and the economy Monarch Jr. external horn phonograph, priced at $10.00.

Victor sales plummeted over 50 percent during the year due to the economic downturn.

1910 Victor focused design and production efforts on the internal horn phonograph and away from the external horn models.

1911 Victor introduced the Victrola IX, the first truly low-cost internal horn tabletop model, selling for $50.

Internal horn Victrola sales exceeded those of the external horn Victor phonographs for the first time.

Victor sales were at a record 125,000 for the year.

1912 Victor sales nearly doubled from the previous year, passing 252,000.

1913 Victor introduced the automatic brake feature on many models.

The Victor XXV "Schoolhouse" model was introduced.

1914 Victor introduced brown mahogany as a finish option.

1915 The elegant Victrola XVIII was introduced, selling for $300 in basic mahogany.

1917 Victor reached an all-time production high of 573,000 phonographs during the year.

1918 Wartime inflation resulted in a series of price increases for all Victor products.

Victor production partially converted to rifle components and biplane wings; phonograph production dropped over 40 percent from the previous year.

1919 Victor production converted back to phonographs, with annual production rising to 474,000 units.

Additional price increases were implemented due to inflation.

1920 Annual sales of Victor phonographs topped 560,000, the second-best year ever.

1921 Intense competition reduced sales by 30 percent for the year.

Victor offered its first "suitcase portable" model, the Victrola No. 50.

1922 Victor introduced a low-priced line of "flat-top" consoles, selling for $100, that were immediately successful.

New phonograph competitors and the rise of radio sales increased to five percent.

1923 Victor launched a series of upper-medium-priced consoles; total Victor production levels remained stagnant at around 400,000 units per year.

1924 Victor sales continued to slide during the year, deteriorating to a low point during the usually busy Christmas season.

Radios were now the dominant Christmas entertainment gift.

1925 Victor licensed the electric recording process.

During the summer, Victor launched a "half-price" sale to unload its stock of old-style Victrolas in anticipation of the Orthophonic debut.

Four new Orthophonic Victrolas were introduced on November 2; the products were highly successful, since the fidelity and volume were many times greater than the earlier Victrolas, and costs ranged from $85 to $275.

Victor offered its first radio/phono combination console, the Alhambra I, selling for $350.00.

Victor sales dropped nearly 40 percent to an annual rate of 262,000 units.

Elementary School Teacher in 1926

Jean Williams taught elementary school children in Syracuse, New York, where she lived by herself in a boardinghouse, sharing a bathroom with three other women.

Life at Home

- Jean Williams was a new graduate of the Brockport State Normal School, one of four New York State public institutions where teachers were trained.
- Like other "normal school" graduates, Jean had received a certificate of study qualifying her to teach in the New York schools, but normal schools did not grant bachelor's degrees.
- When she did her "practice" teaching at the demonstration school attached to Brockport, Jean knew she had made the right career choice.
- She had received free tuition, including the use of textbooks, and was now determined to fulfill her commitment to teach public-school students in the state.
- Brockport was an attractive, Victorian-looking village, but Jean jumped at the chance to take a teaching job in bustling Syracuse.
- It was generally agreed that Syracuse had one of the best school systems in the country.
- She considered herself lucky to have found a room at a clean and respectable small boardinghouse for $7.50 a week.
- Rooms in Syracuse for single women ranged from $6.00 per week to $11.00 a week.
- Jean chose her residence carefully, using a set of standards compiled by the Young Women's Christian Association (YWCA) for teachers who were living away from home.
- As advised by the YWCA's guidelines, she rejected two boardinghouses out of hand because they did not ask her for character references.
- She looked especially for bathroom facilities "completely equipped with superior sanitary equipment (toilet, porcelain bowl, porcelain or enameled iron tub, hot and cold water, mirror)," also ensuring that the bathroom she would use was not "located on a hall to which the general public has access."
- The YWCA stressed that no more than six people should be expected to share one bathroom.

Jean Williams (right) with a fellow first-year teacher

- Jean shared the bathroom down the hall with three other tenants—all female, and all, fortunately, neat and orderly, and inclined to keep the bathroom clean.
- Jean knew that in boardinghouse rooms, "There should be good provision for natural as well as artificial lighting," as the YWCA put it; her room was not quite ideal in this respect, but Jean was willing to compromise on this point.
- Her boardinghouse catered to single female teachers; Jean's parents were more comfortable with this than they would have been with a large boardinghouse with male as well as female tenants.
- Jean—and her parents—had been pleased to find that her boardinghouse had a parlor, thus satisfying the YWCA recommendation that teachers look for a residence "in which the roomer may receive men guests."
- Jean saved money by being her own washwoman whenever possible.
- She spent money on both a local newspaper and an out-of-town newspaper, usually from New York City, on Sundays.
- She delighted in Syracuse's many cultural offerings and general atmosphere of innovation.
- Jean found it very satisfying to open the door to the wide world for her young charges by teaching them to read.
- Jean's salary might be lower than that of a skilled factory worker, but her occupation brought her solidly middle-class status.
- It also afforded her considerable independence; she lived away from her family, yet her situation was eminently respectable, as even her parents agreed.

Life at Work

- Teachers' salaries accounted for about 75 percent of the total expenses of the schools in New York State.
- As was overwhelmingly the case in the northeastern United States, most of the teachers at Jean's school were female, while the school administrators were predominately male. Salaries varied accordingly.
- Jean had already begun to make friends among the teachers; a considerable number of them were new to the profession, and they had quickly discovered that they had a lot in common.
- She had been told that within four or five years, many of her new female colleagues would marry and leave teaching, but at the moment she thought that seemed unlikely.
- It was an exciting time to be a teacher, particularly if one was open to new ideas.
- At Brockport Jean had been introduced to new notions about curriculum that were sweeping the profession.
- Frederick Bobbitt's ideas about what he called Social Efficiency had been introduced a dozen years before, and for the first time, it seemed, the school curriculum was being put on a truly scientific basis.
- Bobbitt held that, "It is the need of the world of affairs that determines the standard specification for the educational product. A school system can no more find standards of performance within itself than a steel plant can find the proper height or weight per yard for steel rails from the activities within the plant. ... The standards must of necessity be

First graders at work (stereograph; Library of Congress)

84

determined by those that use the product, not by those who produce it. ... Standards are to be found in the world of affairs, not in the schools."

- While the marketplace—the "world of affairs"—was to provide the objectives for schools in terms of what educated students needed to achieve, educators, like industrial managers, needed to determine how to reach those objectives.
- At times it seemed to Jean that the big ideas of Social Efficiency lay rather beyond the immediate concerns of her classroom, but as long as the "how" remained with teachers and she could teach her first-graders as she thought best, she found the grand concept exhilarating.
- During the school day Jean interacted almost exclusively with her students, but after school and on weekends, she loved debating the merits of educational theories with her new colleagues, some of whom were fast becoming friends.
- She thought of herself as a modern teacher, attuned to the social and economic progress she saw all around her, and she wanted to help her students become a part of it from the very beginning of their school years.
- Probably more directly relevant to her everyday work was the presence in her school of a school nurse; that was a very useful innovation indeed.
- Teachers College in New York City had offered a course in school nursing as early as 1910.
- Only now was it becoming common for a school to have a nurse available—although the nurse was employed by a community health agency, not the school district itself.
- Physical education was another important development—not entirely new, to be sure, but the more systematic approach benefitted all the students, making them healthier and, Jean was convinced, happier.
- Phys Ed also helped the students channel all their pent-up energy.
- Public school teachers used a variety of books, or "readers," to instruct children.
- Jean found it hard to believe that anyone still used the *McGuffey's* readers, which worshipped the rural lifestyle of the past and viewed urbanization with caution, but she knew that in some classrooms, *McGuffey's* could still be found.
- From her correspondence with her former Brockport classmates, she learned that inadequate books and classroom materials were a serious problem for many teachers; some even bought classroom necessities with their own money rather than struggle with uncooperative school boards and administrators.
- The new Social Efficiency curriculum promoted "democratic" social cohesion and "social hygiene," which included personal habits tending to cleanliness and good health.
- In Jean's own small upstate town, these matters were generally enforced by the community: if children were dirty and ill-kempt, people noticed.
- But in larger towns and cities, where immigration was significant and there was a steady movement of poorer people from rural areas into the cities, this could not be the case.
- Naturally it fell to the schools to deal with such problems.
- In her classroom Jean was vigilant about how her students interacted, and she constantly enforced the idea that the children had to respect one another, whatever their differences of ethnic origin and class.
- Every morning she and her students saluted the flag and said the Pledge of Allegiance. The pledge obviously was intended to instill patriotism, and that was a goal of which Jean approved.
- Just two years before, the words "flag of the United States of America" had been prescribed, so all of the children, native-born or immigrant, would learn that they were all Americans, and all equal.
- Reciting the pledge also brought her rambunctious first-graders to order and signaled to the children that it was time for the school day to begin.

Masthead of the Syracuse American *(also called the* Syracuse Sunday American*), the Sunday edition of the* Syracuse Telegram *and later the* Syracuse Journal-Telegram

Life in the Community: Syracuse, New York

- Located near the center of the state, in the Great Lakes Plain, Syracuse got its start from salt manufacturing, especially after the construction of the Erie Canal.
- Syracuse became known for the manufacture of plows, shoes, hardware, and other farm products.
- The city also manufactured church and ornamental candles, following a tradition started by German immigrant Anthony Will in 1855.
- Syracuse University was founded in 1870, "crowning one of Syracuse's many hills"; as it grew, the university did much to change the face of the city. Its School of Education opened in 1906.
- Onandaga Pottery Company was founded in 1871 and became renowned for its Syracuse China.
- Gustav Stickley built his furniture making business in the Eastwood suburb of Syracuse from 1898; he rented the Crouse stables in Syracuse for his showroom and executive offices, calling the space the Craftsman Building.
- Even after Stickley moved the company headquarters to New York, he kept his factory in Syracuse. After his firm failed in 1915, Stickley returned to Syracuse, where he spent the remainder of his life.
- Over time, industry had shifted from the downtown area to the north and west. The city center was given over to commercial activities and municipal government.
- Syracuse attracted a number of well-known architects, including Horatio N. White, J. Lyman Silsbee, and Archimedes Russell; they built in the Neo-Gothic and Beaux Arts styles, giving Syracuse a solidly handsome city core.
- Henry Keck, trained in the workshops of Louis Comfort Tiffany, settled in Syracuse in 1913 and worked extensively with Arts and Crafts architect Ward Wellington Ward. Keck's high reputation as a craftsman rested, however, mostly on his windows for Gothic Revival churches.

Ad for Onondaga Pottery Company, which introduced its first colored-clay body, Old Ivory, in 1926

- Parks and squares had been incorporated into the city as it grew; in 1911 alone, Onondaga Park was created when Wilkinson Reservoir was scaled down and renamed Hiawatha Lake, and Schiller Park was opened, with a monument dedicated to the German poets Goethe and Schiller.
- By the mid-1920s, Syracuse was the fourth largest city in the state and was well known for the manufacture of high-grade steel and automobile parts.

- Clinton Square was the heart of the city, located alongside the Erie Canal; in the 1920s the Syracuse section of the canal was filled in.
- The Franklin automobile, which boasted an air-cooled rather than a water-cooled engine, established the region as an automobile manufacturer.
- By the mid-1920s, Franklin produced nearly 15,000 cars a year; it employed 3,500 people, making it Syracuse's leading company.
- Syracuse had become known as the "typewriter city." In 1887 Lyman C. Smith and his brother Wilbert began manufacturing a typewriter invented by Alexander Brown, an employee in their Syracuse shotgun factory; the brothers soon got out of the shotgun business and formed the Smith-Premier Typewriter Company.

The 1922 Franklin sedan (National Photo Company Collection, Library of Congress)

- The Smith Corona company was created in 1926 when L. C. Smith & Bros. was merged with Corona Typewriter; L. C. Smith & Bros. made office typewriters, and Corona Typewriter made portables.
- In 1926 Syracuse University had approximately 7,000 students and a faculty of 500.
- Just two years before, Syracuse University's Maxwell School of Citizenship and Public Affairs had been dedicated; it was the first institution to offer a graduate professional degree in public administration, a subject of consuming interest to the city's leading citizens.

THESE ARE BUSY TIMES FOR MANUFACTURERS—VIEW OF THE FRANKLIN COMPANY FACTORY YARD AT SYRACUSE, N. Y.

The "factory yard" for the H. H. Franklin Automobile Company, 1906

- By the 1920s, in order to eliminate dangerous street crossings and traffic delays, the at-grade railroad tracks that crossed the city were to be torn up; controversy raged over whether to construct elevated tracks, put the rail system underground (as had been done in New York City), or re-route the tracks to the north.
- The city was held up as model for public health. Beginning in 1923, the Milbank Memorial Fund provided approximately $450,000 in grants for public health projects. As a result of public and private investment in health care, Syracuse had one of the nation's lowest infant mortality rates.
- Syracuse billed itself as the "most centrally located city of the great Empire State."
- In 1926 a 16-page booklet called *Syracuse Convention City* boasted of the city's "two modern, first-class hotels, The Onondaga and the Hotel Syracuse, which have every appurtenance for the successful handling of conventions." There were also, it was noted, a number of excellent smaller facilities.
- The city was a transportation hub, the booklet announced, "being served by the New York Central, the Delaware, Lackawanna and Western, and the West Shore Railroads. Branches of the Pennsylvania, Lehigh Valley, and Ontario and Western connect within fifty miles with lines running into Syracuse."
- "Both the New York Central and the Lackawanna furnish excellent through Pullman service," the booklet continued, and "One hundred and eighty-one passenger trains arrive and depart daily."
- "Those far-sighted engineers and city builders," the founders of Syracuse, "included in the plans of Syracuse, the City Beautiful, hundreds of acres of the city's most valuable property to be used for recreation purposes." Syracuse truly was a "city of trees."
- The booklet noted that Syracuse in 1926 had three national banks, four trust companies, and two savings banks.
- There were three daily newspapers.
- Within the city's 25.31 square miles, there were 40 public schools, 106 churches, and 38 theaters.

Jewish Cartoonist in 1926

Saul Bloomfield, an ambitious 28-year-old Jewish cartoonist, worked for a newspaper in San Francisco, drawing editorial, sports, and event cartoons on demand. Newly married, he was considering moving to New York City, the center of the cartooning world.

Life at Home

- Saul grew up in Chicago and was an errand boy for a wholesale jewelry concern; he became a salesman at an early age.
- He dropped out of school to sell jewelry; his job allowed him to travel extensively throughout the West.
- He earned so much in commissions that he started his own jewelry business with his brother.
- Back in Chicago, he became friends with many of the city's best-known writers and artists, often meeting them in the bars after work.
- They loved his jokes and ideas so much that the established cartoonists encouraged him to begin drawing and cartooning.
- Saul began by collaborating with an artist who drew his ideas for him, but Saul soon developed his own style and did his own artwork.
- When Saul decided to pursue a career as a cartoonist, his father was dismayed, since drawing pictures for newspapers was not a "respectable living."
- Saul left his jewelry business to the management of his brother, but he remained a co-owner.
- Thanks to hard work and the prosperity of the 1920s, many of Saul's friends, mostly the children of Jewish immigrants, were entering law, medicine, dentistry, and teaching.
- The rapid rise of Jews into professional jobs created controversy; Harvard University debated the use of a quota system for Jewish students to "preserve the representative character" of the school.
- He experienced less discrimination in his work than did his Jewish friends who went into medicine; newspaper cartooning was an open field.
- He laughed at his father's suggestion that he "at least work for a Jewish paper."
- Across the United States, the Jewish press consists of 111 periodicals, including 9 dailies and

Saul Bloomfield

68 weeklies; 44 were in New York City, where Saul longed to live, and 12 were in Chicago, where he grew up.

- Just one Jewish newspaper existed in San Francisco; it had a circulation only a fraction of the size of that of the San Francisco paper in which Saul's work was published.
- In 1926 San Francisco had a Jewish population of 35,000; of the 13 congregations, 7 had their own rabbi.
- Saul's new wife, Heddy, was a native of San Francisco, but she, too, dreamed of going to New York to live.
- Despite their intention to "save every dime," Saul and Heddy had recently visited Mexico to see firsthand the Mayan forms and pre-Columbian art that were having such a big influence on the art scene.

Life at Work

- Cartoons were showing up throughout the newspapers—on the front page, editorial page, and sports pages, and in the classified section and, of course, the funny pages.
- Many of Saul's days were spent at sporting events, getting ideas for the edgy cartoons that his sports editor demanded.
- Boxing was a particular focus; bouts attracted enormous interest.
- Once he got an idea, Saul made a rough sketch, normally in a matter of minutes; then he spent several hours creating the final cartoon.
- Frequently an editor was standing over his shoulder, telling him to hurry up.
- Saul was known for his sharp ideas and speed; recently he had also been receiving compliments for his shading and perspective.
- As the drawing was getting easier, coming up with great ideas was getting harder.

Work of famed cartoonist Jack Lustig depicting "San Francisco's expert club makers" George Brian and Joe Cuneo

- The competition was intense; within San Francisco alone, six other cartoonists were producing cartoon drawings for newspapers.
- The demand was high for cartoons, and wages were excellent even for beginning artists.
- Veteran cartoonist Sidney Smith, creator of the *Gumps* cartoon strip, had recently signed a $100,000-a-year contract.
- The national demand for new cartoon characters likewise was high; Saul had held some conversations with the Bell Newspaper Syndicate about a regular strip, but nothing had yet come of it.
- Using his well-established sales skills, he proposed that he be allowed to market his new strip directly to newspapers across the country.
- Saul's role model was the great Reuben "Rube" Goldberg, who had worked as a sports cartoonist for the *San Francisco Chronicle* and the *San Francisco Bulletin* before departing for New York City in 1907.
- In 1916 Pathé distributed Goldberg's animated cartoons; Goldberg wrote and directed these, but they were illustrated by another cartoonist.
- By 1921 Goldberg's work was syndicated; since 1922 he had been with the McNaught Syndicate.

- When, in the estimation of his editor, Saul's work was particularly good, the entire sports page was built around his drawings.
- Saul was also called on to do editorial cartoons and events-of-the-day drawings, but his first love was sports.
- Nevertheless, at the urging of his friends, Saul had submitted his work to *Argosy*, the all-story weekly; he thought that an *Argosy* cover illustration might be the break he needed.
- Nationwide 2,001 daily newspapers existed, with a total circulation of 36 million; Sunday circulation nationwide was 24 million.
- Advertisements were everywhere, many promoting ways a product could make people more successful.
- Many products provided "cures" for newly defined diseases such as halitosis (bad breath), bromodosis (smelly feet), and acidosis (sour stomach).
- An army of "personal" homemaking advisers was created to assist insecure housewives: Betty Crocker and Mary Hale Martin for Libby, Ruth Miller for Odo-ro-no, Dorothy Dix for Lux Soap, and Mary Pauline Callender for Kotex.

Argosy, a men's adventure magazine

- In 1914 American firms had spent $682 million on advertising; by 1926 the total was nearly $3 billion.
- Saul saw the advertising field as another potentially lucrative avenue for his talents.

Life in the Community: San Francisco, California

- Saul regularly used the trolley cars to get to work and sporting events; nearly everyone he knew used the streetcars, and few people drove cars to work.
- Nevertheless automobile traffic was increasing; recently Chief of Police Daniel J. O'Brien had ordered that on Sundays and holidays, traffic controls would be stationed on Market Street from First to Sixth Streets.
- Residents along Pacific Avenue from Van Ness to Fillmore were organizing a protest; they believed the area was losing its scenic beauty because of too many telephone wires, which they wanted installed underground.
- San Francisco's city engineer had begun having the city's garbage disposal plants inspected regularly, suspecting that illegal stills were operating in the plants, tucked in amidst the garbage.
- Despite Prohibition there were speakeasies everywhere.

The Golden Gate Park Music Stand, rebuilt after the 1906 earthquake

- In July 1926 the federal Prohibition administrator for Northern California and Nevada actually confessed to a variety of charges, including protecting bootleggers, socializing with rum runners, associating with women of the criminal class, and appropriating seized liquor for himself.
- Before the end of the year, having testified in his own defense to the effect that he had done nothing illegal, he was acquitted of embezzlement and restored to his position.
- The city's population increased by 20 percent between 1910 and 1920; newcomers were drawn by the economic opportunities the city offered.
- It was widely acknowledged that San Francisco had one of the best natural harbors in the world.
- In April 1926 the Port of San Francisco recorded the arrival of a total of 505 ships, with a tonnage estimated at 1.3 million—an increase of 452 tons over the same month in 1925.
- Relatively recent municipal improvements included sewer, aqueduct, and streetcar systems.
- Fueled by an economic boom, the city continued to build at a furious pace.

Idle incinerators were not the only ones suspected of harboring illegal stills

- In addition to the grand buildings housing banks, courts, municipal offices, major retail concerns, and more, the cityscape now included a number of theaters, including the Alhambra Theatre, on Polk Street; the Harding, at Alamo Square; the Balboa, in the Richmond area; and the Roosevelt Theater on 16th, which started as a vaudeville house but soon became a movie theater instead.
- The jewel of the San Francisco park system, the three-mile-long Golden Gate Park, had been open since the 1870s and remained one of the nation's most-visited public parks.
- San Francisco took its amusements seriously; the city was dubbed the Playground of the West Coast.
- By the 1880s there were amusement park concessions at Ocean Beach, and from 1913 Arthur Looff's Chutes-at-the-Beach offered the Hippodrome, an elegant carousel with a $5,000 organ. In 1926 George Whitney became the park's manager and changed its name to Playland-at-the-Beach.

A rollercoaster at Playland at the Beach

- San Franscisco was overflowing its narrow peninsula; since 1916 serious planning had been under way for the construction of a bridge spanning the Golden Gate, the turbulent strait at the entrance to San Francisco Bay.
- The bridge would link the city to Marin County; currently, except to its south toward San Mateo, San Francisco's connections with surrounding communities depended on ferry service.
- In May 1923 the state legislature passed the Golden Gate Bridge and Highway

District Act approving creation of a special district to oversee the financing, design, and construction of the bridge.

- The district was also intended to give all of the surrounding counties representation on the decision-making body.
- Opponents naturally included the Southern Pacific Railroad, which operated the ferries. At first, the War Department thought the bridge might obstruct ship traffic; the Navy feared that sabotage to the bridge could block access to its installations, and the unions wanted assurances that local workers would be hired for the construction.
- In December 1924 the War Department, which owned the land on both sides of the proposed structure and also had jurisdiction over all harbor construction, granted a provisional permit for the project.
- Now the formation of the special district was being challenged in the courts of all the counties involved.

Poet Miles Overholt produced a series of illustrated poems for the San Francisco Examiner "celebrating the distinctive places of San Francisco"

16   B. ALTMAN & CO., *Fifth Avenue*, NEW YORK

Women's Frocks of Desirable Summer Fabrics

Sizes 36 to 44; lengths (in all sizes) are fifty inches, measured from the centre back of neckline

34S20
$6.00

34S21
$6.00

71S30
$14.00

71S33
$13.50

71S34
$9.75

71S32
$11.50

71S31
$10.85

71S30 Frock of linen, the skirt semi-tailored, and made with side panels, with hand-drawn stitching introduced throughout. The embroidered band at the neck and sleeves is in the Persian colorings. The frock is in orchid, white or copen . . . **$14.00**

71S31 Frock of checked gingham, in black-and-white, brown-and-white or blue-and-white. A most attractive model, with its modish pockets, collar and cuff effect of white embroidered organdie, and its button-trimmed straps of the gingham; tie sash of the material. **$10.85**

71S32 Cretonne in blue and rose colorings—a charming spring-like pattern forms the lower section of this one-piece frock, the upper part being of tan poplin. It is made on the long-waisted lines, a slip-on model, closing with a Peter Pan collar, and having slashed cuffs that correspond, both being fashioned of the cretonne, bound with the tan poplin. The skirt section is made with an inverted plait at each side **$11.50**

71S33 Frock of blue, gray or maize linen, a tailored model on long straight lines, in paneled effect accentuated by the hemstitching and the briar stitching which form the long slender inserts. Pearl buttons, both large sized and smaller, are used smartly, and the vestee and rever collar give especially good lines **$13.50**

71S34 This model of checked gingham uses white pique by way of interesting contrast, and the touch of colored embroidery lends a decided charm. White pearl buttons appear on the inserts of pique. The gingham is in blue-and-white or orchid-and-white checks **$9.75**

Spring Hats

34S20 Hat of visca straw cloth, mushroom shape with silk facing, trimmed with a fan-shape of plaited ribbon, with jet button; in havana-brown, black or navy blue **$6.00**

34S21 Turban of visca straw cloth, draped with two-toned silk, and finished with two fancy pins at the front; in black straw, trimmed with copen and pheasant-color silk **$6.00**

Young Stickball Player in 1926

Nine-year-old Ivo Novajovsky was born in the United States shortly after his family immigrated to New York City from Croatia. The family lived in Brooklyn, in the new East Flatbush section, where Ivo belonged to a champion stickball team.

Life at Home

- Ivo Novajovsky loved the New York Yankees, his dog, his mother, his sister, his little brother, and sometimes his father—roughly in that order.
- Until Ivo was five years old, the family had lived on the East Side of New York City, where 200,000 people were packed into a territory measuring less than one square mile.
- A miniature Europe could be found there, with dozens of languages spoken, every faith professed, and as many as 15 people living in a four-room flat; 300 people often crowded into tenements originally built to house 50.
- On Ivo's East Side block alone, there were people of 27 nationalities.
- Having come to New York to work for his uncle as a shopkeeper, Ivo's father now owned his own street-front grocery in East Flatbush.
- Ivo loved his new home and school, and he even loved helping his father at the grocery, where the entire family worked.
- Ivo's mother spoke English but had trouble reading it; she could manage the calculations needed to run the store but tended to leave direct dealings with non-Croatian customers to her husband and son.
- Ivo was proud that he spoke English well and that his father often asked him to help read items in the newspaper.
- As a third-grader Ivo could read the magazines at school, even the ones with long sentences.
- Recently he had read a wonderful story called "A Blooded Dog" in John Martin's *The Magazine for Young People*.
- Ivo loved dogs of all kinds, especially his own dog, Jake; Ivo regarded Jake as a "blooded dog," like the dog in the story.
- Now this son of immigrant parents was about to live his dream; with his entire champion stickball team, Ivo had been chosen to attend a game between the New York Yankees and the Philadelphia Phillies.

Ivo Novajovsky (far right) and his family

- The New York Yankees had invited dozens of baseball and stickball teams from across New York City to Yankee Stadium to be the guests of the Yankees's owner, Col. Jacob Ruppert, at the game.
- The invitation gave Ivo a chance to fulfill his dream of meeting his hero, Babe Ruth, the Sultan of Swat.
- For Ivo and his buddies, following the Yankees's progress on a radio outside the pharmacy just down the street was the number one priority.
- Following closely on that was playing stickball every day; Ivo relished the chance to drive a rubber ball deep into a brownstone alley—a hit guaranteed to produce at least a double every time.

Life at Play

- For years Ivo's secret wish had been to attend a Yankees baseball game and see his hero—Babe Ruth.
- Now that wish had been granted: Thanks to the generosity of Colonel Ruppert, 50 kids from Ivo's neighborhood sat in the bleachers for an afternoon game.
- No one was sure who generated the idea of opening Yankee Stadium up to poor kids, but Ivo was convinced it was the great Babe Ruth himself.
- The Babe was the kind of guy who would think of it, even if it meant spending some of his own money.
- After all, wasn't the Babe the man who made three-year-old Ray Kelly his personal mascot, gave him a uniform, and let him sit with him during games?
- The Yankees planned everything for this big day, including the money that each boy needed to make the round trip by subway to the stadium.
- All the guys on Ivo's stickball team decided to take their gloves—in case the Yankees needed some help during the late innings.
- Going to the game was an experience in itself, but emerging from the subway station and seeing Yankee Stadium looming like a skyscraper overhead was breathtaking.

"A Blooded Dog," by Frances Dickerson Pinder,
The Magazine for Young People, **August 1927:**

If one saw him trot round the corner, one knew that there would be a boy right behind him. Pete was that kind of dog. At least, that was what Mrs. Pettis told Jimmie, on his first trip on his new paper route.

"Yes'm, he's an A-1 dog, all right," said Jimmie politely, while Mrs. Pettis hunted in her pocketbook for the change.

Pete wagged his tail and swallowed his tongue and stuck it out again.

"What sort of dog is he?" asked Mrs. Pettis, looking at Pete, very friendly.

Pete cocked his ear and looked at Jimmie.

"Pete?—he's a blooded dog, he is," said Jimmie, dropping the change in his pocket. "All set, Pete."

At the newspaper office, Jimmy had heard a reporter telling about a dog show he had been to, at a place—Jimmie didn't remember the name—but anyway, from all Jimmie had heard, a blooded dog was the cat's cuff and all the rest of it, and the more blood the better.

There were a good many reasons why Jimmie was sure that Pete was a blooded dog. For one thing, he never forgot that business is business. Some dogs, just common dogs—nothing much, that is—run off, all over, nosing into other people's garbage pails and making trouble. And they bark at the wrong thing, without any sense at all. Pete, he could be depended on in all these matters, and in a great many more.

Yankee Stadium, in the Bronx, New York, opened in 1923

- The stadium had opened just three years before, on April 18, 1923.
- It sat 60,000 fans on that first day, while 10,000 more stood outside.
- The grand opening music was provided by the Seventh Regiment Band under the baton of John Philip Sousa.
- The structure was hailed as the first true baseball stadium, designed to accommodate massive crowds and make a progressive and confident statement about the future of the game.
- When Ivo's team arrived and sat down, they couldn't believe they were really looking at Babe Ruth himself; throughout the entire game, Ivo couldn't quit smiling.
- In the very first inning, with his buddies at his side, Ivo saw Lou Gehrig step up to the plate and deliver a two-run homer to put the Yankees ahead.
- Ivo immediately knew that this was going to be the greatest day of his life.
- Then, in the seventh inning, the Babe, on a count of three and two and with no one on, drove a line-drive homer into the right-field stands, delivering his thirty-eighth homer of the year.
- The Yankees went up, three runs to zero.
- It was a packed house, and all 40,000 fans must have cheered at once: a home run by Babe Ruth himself!
- With his buddies screaming and the popcorn guy shouting, Ivo couldn't believe this was happening to him.
- The newspapers call Babe Ruth the Sultan of Swat, the Behemoth of Swing and the Colossus of Clout, and every word was true, Ivo believed.
- Ruth, a former reform-school boy who rose to riches hitting home runs, had changed baseball from a game based on strategy, base running and precise bunts into a power game; one swing and the game could be over.
- When Ruth hit 29 home runs for the Boston Red Sox in 1919, historians had to pore over the records to discover that the next-closest man in history was Buck Freeman, who had hit 25 homers in 1899.

Babe Ruth and his personal mascot, "Little Ray" Kelly

At Times Square, an enormous crowd gathered around the New York Times *building to hear the play-by-play of the 1920 World Series*

- In 1920, when Ruth hit 54 home runs, the baseball world watched in astonishment, and the Yankees's home attendance soared to a record 1.3 million fans.
- By 1923 the Yankees had won three pennants in a row; that year Ruth batted .393, with 41 home runs.
- The Yankees went on to win their first World Series victory and surpass the Giants as New York's—and arguable the country's— most popular team.
- In 1924 the Yankees did not win the American league race, although Ruth still led the league with a batting average of .378 and 46 home runs.
- Last year, 1925, had been a disappointment for Ivo and the Yankees; Ruth had collapsed during spring training and been out until June.
- But 1926 would be the Yankees's year, Ivo was sure, and he was seeing it happen.
- The game was so exciting—and the Yankees won, beating the Phillies 4-2.
- To stave off hunger, Ivo and his buddies pooled their money and bought three hot dogs among them—everyone got at least one good-sized bite.
- When he got home, his mother was eager to hear every word, but, exhausted with excitement, Ivo said little.

Life in the Community: New York City

- Enrollment in New York City public schools exceeded one million students, of whom 863,232 were in elementary, junior high, or truant schools and 131,685 were in high school. The rest were training to be teachers or attending vocational schools.

Elementary school students in New York City's public school system

- The school population of New York had begun a shift toward outlying sections; a report in the *New York Sun* read: "Older sections of the city, not only in Manhattan, but in the Bronx and Brooklyn as well, are losing residents to Queens, Staten Island, and to those sections of Brooklyn and the Bronx which a few years ago were sparsely settled."
- According to the report, School District 2 on the Lower East Side had lost 11.79 percent of its students in 1925, and more than 7 percent in each of the two preceding years.
- Meanwhile, areas that gained included South Brooklyn, Flatbush, the new East Flatbush section, Midwood, and East New York.
- Governor Al Smith, a graduate of New York City's tough East Side, was battling the city's poor housing conditions, especially the dark, airless apartments.
- Smith proposed that loans be provided at low interest rates so more people could buy their own homes; he was aggressively using property condemnation to open up large parcels of land at reasonable prices for more quality housing, parks, and playgrounds in the inner city.
- Smith said, "Someday, the test of a city's merit will be not 'How many inhabitants have you?' but 'How do those inhabitants live?'"
- The average male worker in New York City earned $31.94 a week, while the average female worker made $19.45.
- The building of the world's largest suspension bridge, and the first of any kind to cross the Hudson River, would soon begin.
- It was being called the Hudson River Bridge and was expected to be two and a half times as large as the Brooklyn Bridge and twice the size of the recently opened Philadelphia-Camden Bridge over the Delaware.
- The first vehicle was expected to cross the structure in 1932.
- Construction on the Clifford Milburn Holland tunnel under the Hudson River, between lower Manhattan and Jersey City, New Jersey, had begun in March 1922.
- Originally named the Hudson River Vehicular Tunnel, it was renamed for its first chief engineer in 1924.
- Even Thomas Edison had proclaimed that it would be impossible to ventilate the tunnel effectively, but a later chief engineer, Ole Singstad, devised a system mechanically ventilating the tunnel with 84 fans in four ventilation buildings.
- Using Singstad's design it was possible completely to change the air within the tunnel every 90 seconds.

- The tunnel was nearing completion.
- Meanwhile an army of six thousand men was employed building a new subway beneath New York City; thanks to more advanced shovels and derricks, the work was going faster and more safely than ever before.
- A single steam shovel could do the work of 12 men, while the Caterpillar tractor, used in the war on uneven, muddy ground, had been adapted for use in expanding the subway system.
- Like so many other American cities, New York City was a baseball town; its three teams naturally were fierce rivals.
- In addition to the New York Yankees and John McGraw's New York Giants, who played at the Polo Grounds in upper Manhattan—a field shared by the Yankees in the years before the opening of Yankee Stadium in 1923—Brooklyn had its own team, the Brooklyn Dodgers, who played at Ebbets Field in Flatbush.
- Besting the Giants, the Dodgers had won the National League pennant in 1920, but over the following years, they compiled a dismal record.
- Beginning in 1926 the Dodgers had their own "Babe," Floyd Caves "Babe" Herman, an outfielder who batted over .300 that year.
- Various Dodgers players put up strong statistics—Arthur "Dazzy" Vance pitched a no-hitter in 1925 and led the National League in strikeouts in 1926—but the error-prone team was plagued with mishaps and became known as a zany club.
- The most spectacular of the flubs was a "three men on third" pileup in a game played on August 15, 1926, involving Dazzy Vance, Chick Fewster, and Babe Herman, owing to flat-out inattention and a misunderstood call from the third base coach.
- At World Series time, New Yorkers piled into the streets around Times Square to hear the play-by-play from the *New York Times*.

Gideon Sundback and the "Zipper" in 1926

Gideon Sundback, who had immigrated to the United States from Sweden, was working as an engineer at the Westinghouse Electric and Manufacturing Company when he was persuaded to join Automatic Hook and Eye to work on a revolutionary invention. Two decades later the "zipper" made his fortune.

Life at Home

- Otto Frederick Gideon Sundback had never heard of the Automatic Hook and Eye Company or its product when he immigrated to the United States from Sweden in 1905.
- The 24-year-old German-trained engineer quickly made his way to East Pittsburgh, Pennsylvania, where a job as a tracer of engineering drawings awaited him in George Westinghouse's thriving electrical works.
- For a young electrical engineer, Westinghouse was the place to be in the winter of 1905.
- The Westinghouse Electric and Manufacturing Company had been responsible for building the gigantic dynamos installed in the electric power project at Niagara Falls.
- The project and the accompanying publicity placed Westinghouse on the cutting edge of new technology; the world's brightest minds wanted to be a part of the excitement.
- Gideon was well trained for the opportunity before him.
- The son of a prosperous family in southern Sweden, Gideon had completed a thorough technical education in Germany and had received a certificate of electrical engineering from the Polytechnic in Bingen in 1903.
- Wealthy and ambitious, Gideon was drawn to America by opportunity and the glowing stories sent back by friends who had preceded him.
- After six months with Westinghouse, Gideon was promoted to draftsman, a job he held for another year.
- During that time, through Swedish social contacts, Gideon was introduced to Automatic Hook and Eye president Frank Russell, who persuaded him to visit the company headquarters in Hoboken, New Jersey.
- There Gideon was offered the opportunity to join a struggling little company with an uncertain future that needed his expertise.
- The company's sliding fasteners were bulky, unreliable, and difficult to make.
- Gideon saw a challenge before him.

Gideon Sundback

- It didn't hurt that he was attracted to—and would eventually marry—the daughter of Automatic's chief mechanic and plant manager, Peter Aronson, who, like Gideon, had immigrated to the United States from Sweden.
- Elvira Aronson worked at the plant and even modeled its products in the company's early advertisements.
- Gideon joined Automatic Hook and Eye in 1906, at a critical point in its transition; its founders and discouraged financiers were moving on and a refocusing was under way.
- The company's newest fastener product was less than a year old.
- But major changes were underway when Gideon came aboard.
- His marriage to Elvira Aronson in June 1909 cemented Gideon's desire to make the fastener ubiquitous.
- When his father died in the summer of 1910, Gideon was able to travel to Sweden to see his family.
- Then tragedy struck: Gideon's young wife died in 1911 shortly after giving birth to a daughter, Ruth Margit.
- The grief-stricken young father sent his baby to be raised by his mother in Sweden and then threw himself into his work.
- Ruth did not return to the United States until she was nearly grown.

Life at Work

- The mechanically clever fastener, later called the zipper, had a vexed history.
- Elias Howe, who invented the sewing machine, received a patent in 1851 for an "Automatic, Continuous Clothing Closure."
- Perhaps because of the overwhelming success of his sewing machine, Howe did not pursue marketing his clothing closure.
- Forty years later, Whitcomb Judson invented the "Clasp Locker," one of 30 patents Judson would earn during the last 20 years of his life.
- The Chicago inventor's "clasp" was a complicated hook-and-eye fastener that was described as a "locker or unlocker" for shoes.
- Together with businessman Colonel Lewis Walker, Whitcomb launched the Universal Fastener Company to manufacture the new device.
- The clasp locker made its public debut at the 1893 Chicago World's Fair and met with little commercial success.
- Additional patents followed, each seeking to improve the mechanism and make the invention suitable for fastening everything from ladies' fine gloves and corsets to work shoes and heavy-duty mailbags.
- The patent improvements submitted by Universal were among the more than 40,000 applications received by the patent office each year during the 1890s.
- Undeterred by its limited applicability, its technical uncertainty and the dismal business climate, the company sent salesmen out to sell the new technology to shoe manufacturers and housewives who sewed their own clothing.
- Early on, the device worked so sporadically that salesmen learned to avoid towns where they had been successful the previous year.

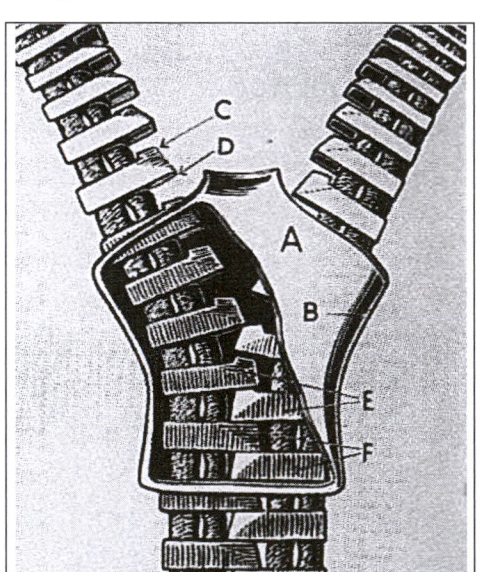

The oblong shape of the fastener elements proved to be essential to the success of Sundback's design

- Every time a new investor could be found, improvements were made and a new sales effort launched.
- It was believed that no machine was adequate to the task of making the fastener.
- Punch presses were used to cut and shape small pieces of tin sheets of metal and form the hooks and eyes; these tiny pieces were then finished off by smoothing rough edges and applying a protective coating.
- Workers then put them into steel racks and fed them into assembling machines which brought cloth tape to the hooks and eyes that allowed workers to clamp them together with the right spacing.
- The device was promoted as a novelty and sold door-to-door by salesmen.
- Gideon Sundback was hired just one year after Whitcomb Judson's C-curity fastener was brought to market.
- The sales team emphasized the C-curity's ability to prevent skirts from embarrassingly gapping out, and customers received a personal instruction book on how to install and use the innovative device.
- The instructions noted the necessity to remove the fastener before the clothing was washed to prevent rusting.
- Price, too, was an issue in 1906.
- At the time, Sears, Roebuck & Company advertised skirts as cheaply as $0.77 each, and top-of-the-line skirts were less than $2.50.

Early clasp fasteners had to be removed by the consumer before the garment could be washed

- Buttons for the skirts were priced at $0.05 a gross, while each fastener cost $0.35 each.
- Gideon Sundback was hired to bring those costs down.
- The Plako fastener was Gideon's first substantial contribution and was useful in keeping the company's doors open, but its hook-and-eye design suffered from the basic flaws of the past: it was inefficient, stubborn, and unreliable.
- At one point, to keep the company's metal supplies from being shut off, Gideon took in outside work to keep the company afloat.
- In exchange, the company gave Gideon patent rights to non-American markets, igniting a short-lived effort to peddle the slide fastener to the fashion salons of Paris.
- Eventually Gideon rejected the hook-and-eye design that he had inherited and improved.
- He explored a new idea that was more flexible and avoided the metallic appearance.
- "One side of the fastener has spring jaw members which clamp around the corded edge of the tape on the opposite side; the slider opens up the jaw members and carries the corded edge in under the jaws.
- "One can see how the cord is inside of the jaw members and held against the crosswise strain which is put on the fastener when it is in active use."
- Gideon referred to his new invention as a "hookless fastener."
- He soon realized, however, that the design for a truly effective fastener was still eluding him; the corded fabric edge of his hookless fastener could not long withstand the abrasion caused by the jaw members.

- On the strength of this promising new design, however, Colonel Lewis Walker reorganized Automatic as the Hookless Fastener Company and in July 1913 moved it from Hoboken to Meadville, Pennsylvania.
- New life was pumped into the old company and new capital was attracted from old investors.
- A newspaper story covering the factory opening said the company would manufacture "a mechanical fastener for garments, corsets, shoes, curtains, mail patches, partial post packaging, etc."
- Reality at this point did not quite match expectations.
- Gideon was driven to try again. He did not keep a careful record of his attempts but worked feverishly to come up with a better concept, meanwhile putting effort into the improvement and production of the Plako.
- By December 1913 Gideon finally had his solution. This time he increased the number of fastening elements from 4 per inch to 10 or 11, used two facing-rows of teeth that were pulled into a single piece by the slider, and enlarged the opening for the teeth guided by the slider.
- The patent for the "Separable Fastener" was applied for in 1916.
- The patent was not immediately granted, however; Gideon had to convince the examiners that his design for a flexible fastener was indeed unique, and eventually he succeeded.
- For the new fastener, Gideon Sundback also created the manufacturing machine, which required no hand work.
- The " S-L," or "scrapless machine," took a special Y-shaped wire and cut scoops from it, then punched the scoop dimple and nib, and finally clamped each scoop on a cloth tape to produce a continuous fastener chain.
- Within the first year of operation, Sundback's machinery was producing a few hundred feet of fastener per day.
- The company particularly wanted to capture the business of the New York garment industry; three-quarters of manufactured women's dresses—employing only buttons or clasps—were made in the city every year.
- The company's sales force made little progress, however, with the largely German-Jewish garment industry owners, who were not eager to change.
- Workers unfamiliar with the fasteners wanted more money for putting the new article into dresses, and the unions wanted a say in this change in procedure.
- The Hookless Fastener Company's biggest impediment, however, was the abysmal reputation of their previous products; a track record of ten years of various unreliable fasteners made new customers hesitant and old customers hostile.
- Then came America's entry into World War I in 1917.
- At first, it appeared to be the beginning of the end; wartime restrictions prohibited new products and limited the availability of metals needed for the fastener's manufacture.
- The War Industries Board worked hard to diminish what it saw as wasteful competition in many industries; manufacturers of shoes, for example, were forbidden to introduce new styles.

Whitcomb Judson's patent drawings for his "Clasp Locker"

- But aviators had unique needs in their open cockpits, and sailors, who had no pockets in their uniforms, wanted a place to carry cash.
- So at the suggestion of a veteran New York tailor, Gideon and his team created a waistcoat for aviators that incorporated a hookless fastener and a money belt with the unique fastener included.
- The waistcoat languished, but the major New York stores that stocked the money belt sold out immediately.
- From Abercrombie and Fitch to the neighborhood drugstore, the functional virtues of the new product overcame concerns about price.

World War I-era aviators flying planes with open cockpits created the breakthrough market for Gideon's hookless fastener

- The New York tailor became Hookless's biggest customer, and other military applications for the fastener were soon found.
- Gideon was called upon to create a heavier and longer version of the fastener that could be used in sleeping bags, overalls and garment bags.
- Quality control became essential for sliding fasteners in sleeping bags as long as 70 inches; however, this specially created heavier version allowed the fastener to be operated with one hand—another customer selling point.
- Orders came in from the Everfloat Life Preserver Company and the NuBone Corset Company; hookless tennis racket covers and bathing suit bags were also made.
- But it was the Locktite tobacco pouch and B. F. Goodrich galoshes that truly made the hookless fastener a necessity.
- Locktite promoted their product by claiming, "Once closed, no tobacco will leak out in your pocket. No buttons or strings to fasten."
- By 1922 Gideon's factory was producing 25 gross per week to meet the needs of the Locktite tobacco pouches alone, for a total of 187,200 fasteners per year.
- To meet these needs, the factory used Gideon's scrapless machine, which used a pre-formed wire rather than a flat metal tape as the feed.
- With patents on both the scrapless machine and fastener it produced, Hookless could restrain emerging competitors.
- By 1923 the Hookless Fastener Company's tiny Meadville factory created more than two million units, but their biggest order was just around the corner.
- The B. F. Goodrich Rubber Company in Akron, Ohio, first ordered $5.00 worth of fasteners in April 1921; they wanted to look over the novel closure.
- Serious negotiations followed, including a demonstration that the fastener could withstand the stress generated by rubber galoshes.
- There was also discussion of the right of exclusivity.
- In 1922 a satisfied Goodrich Rubber Company unveiled plans for rubber galoshes featuring the sliding fastener, which they dubbed the "zipper" in major magazine ads.
- The galoshes were a huge hit, and thanks to their exclusive arrangement with Hookless, Goodrich dominated foul-weather shoe sales.
- Goodrich's share of the galoshes market went from 5 percent to 16 percent in two years, often at the expense of other companies that could not obtain reliable zippers.

- Hookless aggressively pursued imitators in the courts, suing for patent infringement in both America and Canada.
- To balance the impact of the Goodrich account, which consumed 70 percent of the zipper factory's output, Hookless sought new customers in 1926.
- The H. D. Lee Mercantile Company of Kansas City purchased more than a million zippers for use in firefighters' clothing—five zippers in each jacket.
- The Hookless Fastener Company began advertising in the *Saturday Evening Post*, featuring its products in quarter-page ads with black-and-white depictions of luggage, sweaters, and children's pencil cases, all employing the dependable zipper.
- After 21 years, Gideon was an "overnight" success.

Life in the Community: Meadville, Pennsylvania

- Meadville was founded on May 12, 1788, by a party of settlers led by David Mead, at the confluence of Cussewago Creek and French Creek.
- Around the year 1800, settlers began flocking to the Meadville area after receiving land bounties for service in the Revolutionary War.
- Allegheny College, the second-oldest college west of the Allegheny Mountains, was founded in Meadville in 1815.
- Meadville became an important transportation center after construction of the French Creek Feeder Canal in 1837, and of the Beaver and Erie Canal it connected to at Conneaut Lake, as well as subsequent railroad development.
- The Meadville Theological School was established in 1844 by a wealthy businessman, a Unitarian named Harm Jan Huidekoper.

The Independent Congregational Church, Meadville (William J. Bulger, Historic American Buildings Survey, Library of Congress)

Allegheny College, Meadville (Library of Congress)

- The theological school operated in Meadville until it was moved to Chicago and became affiliated with the University of Chicago in 1926.
- In the late 1700s and early 1800s, Meadville played a small part in the Underground Railroad, helping escaping slaves to freedom.
- An event in Meadville in September 1880 led to the end of segregation by race in Pennsylvania's public schools.
- Meadville was divided into two wards, the North Ward and the South Ward; each ward had its own school board.
- Elias Allen, a black carpenter, tried unsuccessfully to enroll his two children in the South Ward schools near his home; he was denied on the basis of the state education act, which mandated separate schools for black children if there were more than 20 in a given locality.
- Allen appealed to the Crawford County Court of Common Pleas. Judge Pearson Church declared unconstitutional the 1854 state law mandating separate schools for Negro children.
- In 1892 the Keystone View Company was founded in Meadville by Benneville Lloyd Singley, a former Allegheny College student; its first big success was a view of French Creek floodwaters inundating Meadville.
- Eventually Keystone was housed in the former Centennial High School.
- Singley was interested in the educational market and later in the medical market, for which the company produced slides used by opthalmologists, safety engineers, and psychologists.
- The company sold stereoscopes as well as stereo views and lantern slides, making Meadville the headquarters of the world's largest producer of stereo photographic views.
- By the late nineteenth century, Meadville's economy was also driven by logging, agriculture in the rich French Creek Valley, and iron production.
- The Erie Railroad Company's locomotive and railroad car repair yards were located in Meadville.

Atlantic & Great Western Railroad repair shops (Historic American Building Survey/Historical American Engineering Record, Library of Congress)

Successful Small Farmer in 1927

Edgar Rutherford inherited his family farm in Culpeper County, Virginia, in 1920. He kept up with advances in farming with the help of his county demonstration agent, and the farm thrived. Now Edgar and his wife Edith had an automobile and electricity, a rarity in rural America. Their four children ranged in age from 3 to 16.

Life at Home

- Edgar and Edith had been married for 19 years.
- For most of that time they lived with Edgar's parents on the Rutherford family farm.
- The farm consisted of 200 acres, more than half of which were under cultivation; the Rutherfords produced corn, oats, and legumes as field crops, and they raised livestock for sale as well as for their own use.
- Until 1925 there was no running water in their substantial wood-frame house, and it was still heated entirely by burning wood in two fireplaces.
- Doing some of the work himself, Edgar had recently had part of the house wired for electricity.
- Both Edgar and Edith graduated from elementary school, and Edgar attended high school for two years as well.
- Their eldest child, John, had just finished tenth grade and planned to leave school to work on the farm.
- The second boy, Arthur, would graduate from elementary school in two years; he wanted to finish high school and then go on to college to study engineering.
- Alice, the elder of the Rutherfords' two girls, had started elementary school the previous September; she had missed her mother and playing with her younger sister, Sarah, at home.
- The Virginia compulsory school law required that children from ages 8 to 16 attend school.
- In many rural areas, school did not start until September 15 and it ended on April 15, to accommodate harvest and planting seasons.
- Edgar, like most farmers, worked between 12 and 13 hours per day during the summer and about 10 hours per day during the remainder of the year; Edith's domestic tasks occupied almost as many hours, and she helped out on the farm as well.
- Edgar hired help at the busiest times of the year, for sowing and harvesting.
- The family mostly ate in the kitchen, where the cooking was done, and during the winter everyone tended to stay in the three rooms that were heated—the living room, the kitchen, and one bedroom.

Alice, Edith, and Edgar Rutherford

- Few of the Rutherfords' neighbors had electricity or gas; even among the wealthiest farm families in the county, only 25 percent had electricity.
- The family still used oil lamps in all bedrooms.
- Edgar had decided to buy a washing machine, now that electricity was available and used for some lights.
- The family has seen a Minnesota washing machine with console advertised in the Sears Roebuck Catalog, for $33.95. In Frederickburg they saw a Cork Wall, Top-Icer "Alaska" Refrigerator for $16.95 that could be purchased with "deferred payments."
- The Rutherford family was cautious about the use of "installment credit," advertised as "exercising your credit." A salesman had told Edgar that 15 percent of all retail purchases were now made on deferred payments.
- But Edgar and Edith are hesitant; they had seen more than one family go bankrupt following the war when prices fell and farm equipment purchased on credit to meet the increased wartime demand remained unpaid for.
- Temptation to buy was everywhere, from the Sears catalog to the advertisements in popular magazines.
- Photographs in advertisements were becoming more realistic and more frank; in popular magazines products such as Odo-ro-no deodorant and Kotex were advertised openly.
- Most food of the family's food was grown on the farm; only 15 percent was purchased.
- Edgar and Edith contributed about four percent of their income, or $68.00 a year, to their church.
- Approximately $60.00 went to doctors and dentists. A county health unit was available and emphasized preventive medicine to reduce communicable diseases.
- The Rutherfords spent $25.00 annually for insurance; 38 percent of neighbors in a similar financial situation had insurance, mostly life insurance on the head of household.

The local elementary school Arthur and Alice attended

- In general families had little money set aside for this type of tragedy; most insurance money was used to cover burial costs, not to provide future income for the family.
- The average cost of a funeral for families that carried insurance was $432.00. Among the Irish, the average bill was $452.00, among Italians, $421.00, and among Jews, because of simpler ceremonies, $247.00.
- This year the Rutherfords had bought a telephone; half of the neighbors now had telephones.
- Six families shared the Rutherfords' party line, and the Rutherfords had to wait to make a call if any member of the other families was already using the line.
- The family spent $21.00 a year on recreation and entertainment, including newspapers and magazines and even, very occasionally, a movie.
- *Time*, the weekly news magazine published since 1923, cost $0.15 per issue.
- On average the Rutherfords drove into the town of Culpeper six times a month; the drive went fairly quickly in their automobile, but Edgar was reluctant to expend the time and money unless he had a good reason to make the trip.
- Three years earlier Edgar had paid for the family's Model T Ford by selling more of his cattle than he usually did, because he got a good price.
- The newspaper carried the news that the first "synchronized sound" movie, *The Jazz Singer*, featuring Al Jolson, had opened in New York; the movie was expected to revolutionize the motion picture industry.
- The Rutherfords decided to make a trip to see the movie in a grand Richmond theater; they would make a short vacation of it and probably see the movie weeks before it reached the small theater in Culpeper.
- Over the past five years, the family had left Culpeper County just three times: they traveled to Fredericksburg and Richmond, once to Washington, D.C., and once to a funeral in Norfolk.

Life at Work

- Many farmers in the community still grew tobacco and cotton; these were cash crops with established markets that could withstand rough handling and the crudest form of processing for marketing and storing.
- Growing perishable crops for sale was risky because of the transportation hurdles farmers faced.

The Rutherford farmhouse—roomy and comfortable, and wired for electricity (Historic American Buildings Survey, Library of Congress)

- Nevertheless, dependency on a single crop carried its own risks; as prices dropped, crop liens increased, and often crop liens could be obtained only by continuing to grow the products (such as cotton) on which merchants were willing to make advances.
- Cotton did not ripen all at once, requiring three pickings to completely harvest the crop.
- International Harvester Company introduced cotton-picking machines in 1924; they failed to become popular in the cash-poor and sometimes labor-rich South because mechanically picked cotton contained trash and unripe cotton, which many cotton gins could not handle.

The County Farm Bureau gave Arthur a calf to raise on credit, on the condition that he exhibit the calf at the annual agricultural show (Lewis W. Hine, National Child Labor Committee Collection, Library of Congress)

- The farms of the United States, particularly in the South, were becoming depopulated as young workers rushed to the cities to take manufacturing jobs.
- The Great War had drawn a half-million blacks out of the rural South, some into the army but most into the factories of the North.
- By the end of the decade, another million African Americans had left the Deep South to look for employment in the Northeast and Midwest.
- The severe depression that followed World War I fostered the idea that economic forces were conspiring against the farmer. Farm prices dropped dramatically in 1921; by 1927 they still had not returned to the inflated prices of 1914-1919.
- By 1927 the producers of staple crops in Virginia were feeling the competition from the lower-cost producing areas farther west.

Life in the Community: Culpeper County and Richmond, Virginia

- Culpeper County, in the northern part of the state, was close to the Blue Ridge Mountains in the Piedmont region of Virginia.
- The topography was less rugged than in many Piedmont counties; several detached spurs or mountains gave the southwestern portion of the county a more broken and picturesque appearance.
- The soil was red clay, chocolate, and black silk, sometimes sandy, and it was well adapted to white corn, rye, oats, hay, and legumes; wheat, corn, and legumes were the leading crops.

John with his friends in Culpeper

- The region was suitable for growing fruit, and apples did well, especially along the mountainsides.
- Cattle, hogs, and the dairy industry were also important. Forest products included railroad ties, tan bark, and pulpwood.
- Culpeper, the county seat, was incorporated, and in 1920 it had a population of 1,118.
- Organization among the farmers had grown in recent years.

- The services of a farm demonstration agent were available to the people of the county. In progressive agricultural development, Culpeper was among the leading counties of Virginia.
- The South in the 1920s was the nation's most rural region. Not a single Southern state met the superintendent of the census's modest definition of "urban" in 1920: having a majority of its population in cities of 2,500 or more souls.
- Richmond was the "big city" where Culpeper County farmers occasionally traveled for supplies and entertainment.
- Chosen as the site of the Fifth Federal Reserve Bank in 1914, Richmond was becoming a financial center, with strong banks and a strong manufacturing base.
- The city was home to the world's largest cigarette factory, baking powder factory, and furniture company.
- Richmond built its first free library in 1924, the last city of its size to do so.
- U.S. Customs receipts at Richmond surpassed $2 million in 1926, up from $20,000 in 1897.
- Between 1910 and 1920, Richmond's population increased by 35 percent, topping 171,000 in 1920.
- Nevertheless, the percentage of blacks in the city's population substantially declined, from 45 percent in 1870 to 29 percent in 1927, as immigration to Northern cities accelerated after World War I.
- The average weekly pay rate for white workers in the paper products industry was $18.54; in the tobacco industry, the pay was $12.87 weekly.

Where cleanliness is most considered, paint and varnish are indispensable

"Save the surface and you save all" – *Paint & Varnish*

PAINT makes dirt noticeable and easier to remove. Paint brings light into dark places. And where are cleanliness and light more needed than where milk starts its journey from cow to cup?

In cow barns, milk house, testing laboratory—paint and varnish assist in the business of making milk safe for infants and adults. Walker-Gordon plants are models of what surface protection means to all who produce or use milk. Painting is as regular a part of the program as milking.

The magic of paint and varnish is to give the user what he needs, be it sanitation, light, better appearance, preservation, alone or in combination. "Save the surface and you save all" states a very practical truth. The benefits are great—and open to everyone.

SAVE THE SURFACE CAMPAIGN
18 East 41st Street, New York

A cooperative movement by Paint, Varnish and Allied Interests whose products and services conserve, protect and beautify practically every kind of property.

- Blacks were largely confined to lower-paying jobs; the average wage of domestics in one-servant homes was $8.00 per week and in two-servant homes, $12.00 a week. Most were furnished with meals and uniforms.
- A survey of single women living in Richmond showed that female clerical workers made an average $1,082.00 per year; female factory workers averaged $667.00.
- In those days before radio broadcasts of baseball games, fans gathered at the *Richmond Times-Dispatch* to "watch" the game on a baseball diamond rigged up on the wall of the newspaper.
- As events took place, the reporter telephoned his editor, who moved figures representing the players around the bases; when the batter made a base hit, a bell rang and the figure "at bat" was moved to the proper base.
- Excited crowds jam the street to follow the heroic feats of Roger Hornsby or Walter Johnson.

"CRAYOLA" in Eskimo Land

WHEN David Binney Putnam, the 13-year old explorer, went to Greenland last summer, he took some "CRAYOLA" Crayons with him.

In the picture above you see Kakutia, the Eskimo artist, with two happy little Eskimos. Kakutia used the "CRAYOLA" Crayons to draw pictures for David's book, which is called "David Goes to Greenland."

It will be fun for you to get some "CRAYOLA" Crayons, and after you have read David's book, to see whether you can draw a polar bear the way Kakutia did.

"CRAYOLA" Crayons, Eight colors, 10c.

BINNEY & SMITH CO.
41 East 42nd Street   New York, N.Y.

Socialite in 1927

The Ormsby family divided its time between Palm Beach, Florida, and a Main Line suburb of Philadelphia, Pennsylvania, where Harriet Ormsby was a prominent socialite.

Life at Home

- The daughter of wealthy parents, Harriet, née Evans, married well and was widowed at age 40 when her husband died of a heart attack while participating in a polo match.
- The next year, while crossing the Atlantic on a cruise with her daughter, Marie, Harriet met Martin Ormsby, a handsome widower, and the two immediately fell in love.
- Originally from New York City, Martin moved to Philadelphia following the wedding, which was attended by former president William Howard Taft.
- Martin took riding lessons and soon joined the Rose Tree Hunt.
- An investment banker by profession, Martin handled the family's affairs, as had Harriet's first husband, who was very active in commercial development.
- Even though some wealthy Main Line Philadelphia matrons shunned the Ormsbys' partygiving and attendant display of wealth, Harriet was determined to become the Main Line's reigning hostess.
- Harriet kept detailed scrapbooks of every event, including seating charts and menus.
- Her jewelry collection could pass for the contents of a jewelry store.
- Her favorite necklaces were displayed on mannequins on a dressing table, and her diamond tiara was so heavy that she occasionally complained that it gave her a sore neck.
- Built at a cost of $1 million, the Ormsby home in Palm Beach, Florida, was a 75-room neo-Georgian mansion with quarters for 30 servants and a garden room in which Harriet had often received 200 guests.
- A recent party there had featured two orchestras, a Champagne fountain, and 25 pounds of beluga caviar.
- The Ormsbys' three-story, 50-room, 38,000-square-foot Main Line home, set on nearly 1,000 rolling acres, cost $3 million to construct over a three-year period before the War.
- There were a few larger houses in the Philadelphia area, but very few that could match the Ormsbys' for both comfort and glamour.

Harriet Ormsby

The Ormsbys' lavish Main Line home

- The living room, or hall, often used for receptions, measured 1,200 square feet, and the dining room could easily accommodate 40 dinner guests.
- Of course the house had a library, billiards room, and a ballroom with a grand piano.
- There were three elevators and a men's dressing room for the convenience of the Hunt, which always met at the Ormsbys'; after dinner the gentlemen would repair to Martin's study for brandy and cigars.
- Four wine cellars ensured that guests could be served any wine they cared to name; before Prohibition went into effect, the Ormsbys had taken care that the wine cellars were completely stocked.

Recently divorced, Geoffrey Ormsby thought about speculating in Florida real estate

- A rear staircase led to the butler's pantry, the kitchen, the servants' dining room, and the rest of the service wing.
- An imposing stone balustrade surrounded the front courtyard.
- The house was staffed by 16 servants and included its own telephone switchboard and operator.
- Twenty gardeners and groundskeepers, some of whom lived on the property, tended the landscaped and wooded grounds; two chauffeurs cared for the family's four Packards.
- The Ormsby family also had a house at Bar Harbor, Maine, where they vacationed and entertained in the summertime.
- When Maria made her début at age 18, the 600 invited guests were entertained by four orchestras.
- That night Harriet presented her daughter with a $1.5 million pearl necklace once owned by Catherine the Great of Russia.
- The necklace had been a gift to Harriet from her first husband, bought from Cartier's in New York; Harriet had worn it only twice.

- Harriet's 36-year-old son Geoffrey was currently living with Harriet and Martin, following his divorce from an automobile heiress.
- Married after a two-month courtship, he and his bride had entertained more than 2,000 guests at a reception at the palatial Grosse Pointe, Michigan, home of her parents as guards watched over the $100,000 pearl necklace worn by the bride, a wedding gift from her father.
- The bride's mother gave the couple a wedding present of $100,000 in silver.
- Following the wedding, the couple took a year-long honeymoon, visiting Europe and Asia and sailing around the tips of both South America and Africa during the year.
- Geoffrey's taste for liquor, gambling, and other women was overlooked until he lost millions of his wife's money attempting to control the Florida resort market; then a quiet divorce was arranged by her father.

Life at Work

- Harriet convinced her husband Martin that they should begin to make some significant donations to charities; she had seen what philanthropy did for the social standing of the Belmont family, especially for August Belmont's second wife, Eleanor.
- Harriet also thought that once their donations and appearances at charity balls hit the society pages, it would permanently divert attention from Geoffrey's divorce, word of which naturally had spread among Philadelphia society matrons.
- Harriet was stung by a snub from the aristocratic Mrs. Alexander Williams Biddle, who was very adept at slighting those she did not believe to be in her class—no matter how much money they had.
- Several important parties had come and gone without an invitation to the Ormsbys.

Tennis was popular with the wealthy elite

As a college junior, Geoffrey took up golf

- Martin was untroubled by this; he was always happy to indulge his wife's interests but did not especially like parties himself.
- In season, he had the Hunt to look forward to, and he knew that the Hunt crowd took such things in stride.
- Martin enjoyed golf, and he had become interested in the potential for building golf courses near every major city.
- Having recently toured golf courses in three states to learn more about proper design, Martin was particularly impressed with a course he had seen in Augusta, Georgia.
- He also visited courses in Florida, but for the moment he was avoiding the Palm Beach scene; during a party at the home of Marjorie Merriweather Post, which featured animals loaned by the Ringling Brothers and Barnum and Bailey Circus, Geoffrey had become intoxicated and caused a scene when he attempted to ride one of the elephants.

The Cunard line catered to wealthy Americans, promising the "fastest steamers in the world"

- Geoffrey was asked to leave and did not expect to be invited back; on reflection, he decided that there was room for a "second Palm Beach" for people who were more fun-loving and uninhibited.
- When the time was right, Geoffrey planned to invest in Florida again; he believed that his losses in land development there were simply bad luck, and he was sure he had learned from his mistakes.
- No one could have predicted that the Northern press would attack the Florida land boom and a railroad strike would stop the flow of materials just at the same time that a hurricane struck, killing 400 people and making everyone skittish.
- Now that Geoffrey was again unattached, he was planning a trip to Paris to see "what was new" in the way of show girls, café society, and heiresses.
- Rarely did a day go by that Geoffrey did not place a bet on a baseball game or boxing match; convinced that the American League was more corrupt, he placed most of his money on National League teams.
- Meanwhile Harriet and Martin's friend Albert Coombs Barnes was gaining considerable, if controversial, fame for his collection of modern art.
- Barnes despised society and elites, but for some reason he had taken a liking to Harriet and Martin; perhaps it was Martin's calm demeanor and near-total disinterest in achieving social distinction.
- Barnes had more than a thousand paintings, precisely hung according to his own principles, displayed in his new art school, set in a 12-acre park in Merion, a Philadelphia suburb.
- Harriet had told Barnes that she admired his art, although secretly she agreed with Philadelphia's cultural elite that her

The Barnes Foundation's Renoir Room (Library of Congress)

eccentric friend's extensive collection of Renoirs, Van Goghs, Matisses, and Pascins was not art of a high order.

- Barnes had allowed his collection to be displayed at the Philadelphia Academy of Fine Art, but the harsh critical reaction had prompted him to withdraw from the established art world, which he now generally regarded with disgust.
- In addition to the students, he now admitted only those he considered worthy to see his collection, pointedly excluding anyone connected with the Philadelphia art establishment.
- He particularly disdained patrons and employees of the Philadelphia Academy and the Philadelphia Museum of Art.

Built in 1917, the McAllister Hotel was one of Miami's first skyscrapers (State Archives of Florida)

- It was possible, Harriet thought, that the elite snubbed Barnes lest he snub them.

Life in the Community: Palm Beach, Florida, and Philadelphia, Pennsylvania

- Movie theaters in both Palm Beach and Philadelphia were installing air conditioning, which required an apparatus taking up the entire basement to house more than 15,000 feet of heavy-duty pipe, giant 240-horsepower electric motors, and two 1,000-pound flywheels.
- Though in the past the theaters simply closed during the summertime because of the heat, summer was becoming the peak movie going season nationwide, thanks to the advent of air conditioning and the construction of elaborate movie palaces.
- In Florida increased railroad construction dramatically increased the number of people visiting Florida each year, even in the face of the collapse of the real estate boom.

The New Public Buildings at Penn Square in Philadelphia, c. 1927 (Historic American Buildings Survey, Library of Congress)

- Last year alone, 2.5 million tourists had visited Florida; some came by airplane, since the state now had nine airports.
- Jacksonville remained Florida's largest city, but Miami had moved from fourth in 1920 to second place.
- During the land boom, which had just peaked in 1925-1926, the *Miami Herald* was the world's largest newspaper in terms of advertising space, with one issue setting a record by publishing 22 sections containing 504 pages.
- Meanwhile, the state of Pennsylvania was debating the merits of erecting a statue to the memory of Boies Penrose, the city boss who became one of the nation's most powerful U.S. senators.
- Penrose, who died in 1921, was frank about the reciprocal relationship between politics and business, which he supported, encouraged, and benefitted by in Philadelphia.
- Known as a wit, he also said, "Public office is the last refuge of a scoundrel."

- Scoundrels of that stripe abounded in Philadelphia.
- Prohibition was very unpopular in the city, and many public officials were content with its lax enforcement.
- Early in 1926, after two frustrating years of trying to crack down on bars, speakeasies, and police corruption, Smedley Butler the former brigadier general of the U.S. Marine Corps who was director of public safety—had resigned.
- After a period of stagnation, however, Philadelphia had begun to modernize; steel and concrete skyscrapers were being constructed and older buildings renovated.
- The new Philadelphia Museum of Art building was nearing completion; the wings were built first, ensuring that the main building would be completed.
- At the same time, the automobile was changing the face of the city; roads were widened and parkways built, and in 1926 the Delaware River Bridge opened, connecting Philadelphia and New Jersey.
- The automobile was also encouraging commercial development in the suburbs, especially in the direction of the Main Line.
- New shopping districts outside the city core were designed for convenient access by automobile.
- Main Line suburban towns to the west of Philadelphia, ranged around the main line of the Pennsylvania Railroad, attracted the wealthy and exclusive Philadelphia elite; many kept homes in the city and built palatial estates on the Main Line, where social reputations were made and lost.

One of the first planned golf course communities in the United States was in Florida

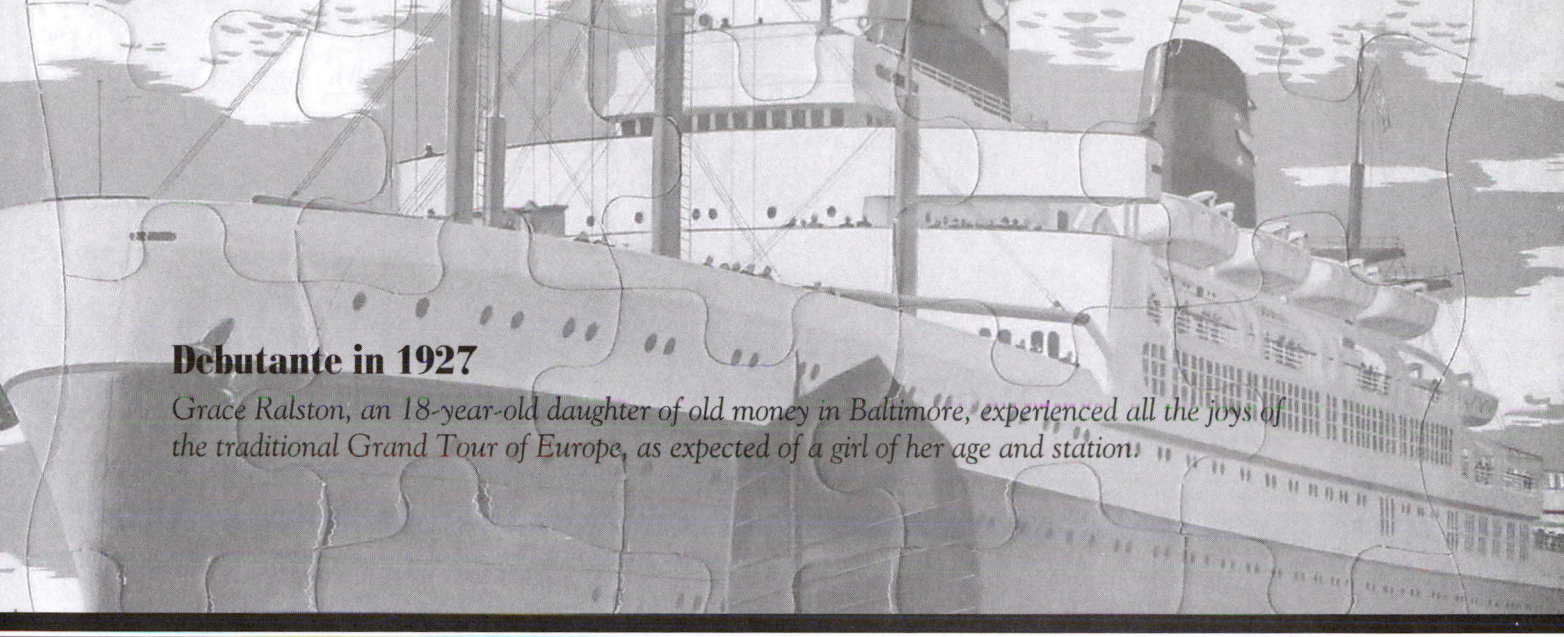

Debutante in 1927

Grace Ralston, an 18-year-old daughter of old money in Baltimore, experienced all the joys of the traditional Grand Tour of Europe, as expected of a girl of her age and station.

Life at Home

- Grace Ralston's family had long been considered "old Baltimore money"; her father, grandfather and great-grandfather all made their fortunes in the shipping business.
- Her place in Baltimore society had been carefully planned since she was tiny: the right dance school at age six, followed by private school in the city, dinners at the right homes, and then an invitation to the Bachelor's Cotillion, an event that predated the Civil War.
- When Grace turned 13, her mother marked the date of the cotillion, the first Monday in December—five years in the future—on her calendar.
- The hall where the cotillion was held limited the selection of Baltimore 18-year-olds to only 60 to 80 girls each year, but Grace's mother never doubted that Grace would be among those chosen.
- Arriving for the ball and presentation, dressed in the traditional white gown, Grace was overwhelmed by the profusion of flowers sent to each of the debutantes by escorts, relatives, and family friends.
- In all, she received 53 bouquets, an outpouring comparable to that bestowed on all of the other girls.
- Her father, older brother, and uncle served as her primary escorts for the evening.
- Promptly at 11 p.m., the orchestra stopped, a whistle was blown, and the debutante figure, or march, was announced.
- The floor was cleared except for the debutantes and their partners, after which one of the governors led the couples through a simple figure, a tradition that allowed everyone to see all the debutantes.
- With everyone staring at her at once, Grace felt like a show horse prancing for a judge—and she loved it.
- This simple, dignified ceremony lasted less than 10 minutes and was followed by more champagne, more food, and more dancing.
- Everyone told her she was a marvelous dancer; by 3 a.m., when it all ended, Grace was exhausted.
- Once the cotillion was over, Grace was able to turn her full attention to the Grand Tour of Europe.

Grace Ralston

- If all went well on the trip, she would find a rich, exotic, exciting husband and live forever in a place where her mother couldn't watch her every move.
- Besides, that way she wouldn't have to attend college, pretending to earn a B.A. in English when everyone knew her only real interest was in getting an MRS.
- Many magazine articles suggest that a trip to the capitals of Europe could be made for $500, but $2,000 had been set aside just for her spending money.
- Her biggest fear was not the trip but what she would do when she returned; she knew she was supposed to do "something" but was unsure of what that might be.
- At least she had Christmas planned: she hoped to receive one of the new phonograph players with an automatic record changer—what a joy when she did!
- Christmas had always been a time to see her cousins, who all grew up in the same area.
- As children they had done everything together, but now many had moved away, married or gone to college.

Debutantes playing horseshoes (Library of Congress)

Life on the Grand Tour

- For two years, Grace's family had meticulously planned her Grand Tour of Europe.
- After the cotillion, in preparation, Grace had her long hair cut very short and styled.
- She was delighted to discover that this horrified her mother.
- Grace was sure the new look set off her dimples perfectly; besides, her bob complemented the cocktail dresses she had bought for the trip.

Paris was known to have its risqué side

- The entire smart set was just mad for the new dresses.
- As soon as the ship was under way, Grace delighted in tossing off the latest slang: "rug jumper" for dancer; "sash weight" for doughnut, "hog hips" for bacon, and even "dogs" for feet.
- Her aunt Mary, who, years before, had agreed to chaperon Grace on the two-month-long trip, hated the new obsession with slang; it sounded so common.
- Aunt Mary also disliked the popular novels her niece was reading; only bad ideas could arise from a story entitled A *Rooftop Romance*.
- When her aunt was not around, Grace practiced walking with her hips thrown forward and a cigarette holder between her teeth—a look becoming known as the "debutante slouch."
- On deck she would watch people carefully, torn between being a participant and an observer.
- Her fellow travelers included a bachelor bookkeeper, who was spending ten years' savings on one delirious trip; a German violinist, who seemed to be romancing a drab but very excitable girl; and a college couple, who

felt so free about actually kissing in front of people that it made Grace's heart pound.

- She was sure it was time for her to get into the flow, but leading an exciting life had seemed so much easier when she was surrounded by brochures instead of people.
- Grace was also fascinated by several older men—professors, she thought—who held impromptu talks with small flocks of young women eager to hear their every word.
- She wondered if college was like this, and whether she ought to reconsider the idea of college after all.
- Her first stop on the Grand Tour was, of course, France; she stepped ashore at Cherbourg and was promptly whisked by rail into Paris.
- She was a bundle of nerves, but she marveled that she was holding a European train menu, seeing the light on the city at dusk, and reading signs in French: "Chocolat Menier," "Avenue de l'Opéra."

French Line steamer ad promising visitors a "thousand years of daring"

- She couldn't wait to see Sainte-Chapelle when the sun shone through its multicolored windows, attend a service at the cathedral of Nôtre Dame de Paris, stroll in the Jardin du Luxembourg.
- During the first few days in France, Grace and Aunt Mary visited Versailles and Belleau Wood; they shopped for gloves, handkerchiefs, frocks, lingerie, and perfume.
- A whole day was set aside to see the Louvre; Grace and her aunt were two eager pilgrims among the millions who passed through the museum's gates each year.
- Then, Grace thought, it was time to see the real France; she desperately wanted to go dancing and meet some French boys.
- That did not quite happen, however.
- Next on the schedule was Marseilles and Nice, with a short stop at Monte Carlo; no gambling, of course, Aunt Mary said repeatedly, but just a quick look around would be interesting.
- Then it was on to Italy: first Genoa, where, Grace was amazed to see, the streets were so narrow that the houses almost met across them; then Rome and the Sistine Chapel and the Forum—both disappointments for Grace, who found them remote and rather fusty.
- In Rome rumors bubbled about problems with the drinking water, so they pressed on to Naples, where the glass-bottomed boats were adorable, and then to Vesuvius, where Grace was overcome by a sense of drama and tragedy.
- She and Aunt Mary dined in a scarlet sunset, debating who wrote *The Last Days of Pompeii.*
- Next on their itinerary were Florence, Venice, and Milan, which passed as something of a blur; there was so much to do and see, Grace could hardly take it all in.

PARIS. -- L'Hôtel de Ville.

Grace had never seen anything like the Hôtel de Ville in Paris

The Duomo in Florence gave Grace a new definition of magnificence

- She was shocked to realize that her two-month cultural adventure was already half over.
- Arriving in Switzerland, Grace and her aunt collapsed into a deep rest; for two days they did little except to take long walks in the evenings before meals.
- In Amsterdam, while Aunt Mary aunt was off buying cheese and wooden shoes, Grace was bold enough to take pictures of the men smoking long pipes in the doorways.
- She enjoyed the sense of intrigue and mystery in Amsterdam, but there was still no time to meet young men, it seemed.
- The Hague, home of the World Court, did not much interest Grace; Antwerp was little better.
- She began to anticipate going home.
- At last the white cliffs of Dover came into view; merry England was the last leg of the trip.

In London Grace and Aunt Mary were comfortably situated

- The week in London passed like a confusing but pleasant dream; Grace delighted in hearing the English language again and having eggs for breakfast.
- These were familiar comforts, but at home she did not hear hand organs playing jazz tunes underneath her window.
- Grace bought a pipe for her father and scarves for her mother, cashing the last of her traveler's checks.
- She couldn't believe that she had spent $2,000 during the trip; it must have been the dozens and dozens of postcards she purchased and mailed home.

- While in London, Grace and Aunt Mary attended a performance of Shakespeare's *Merry Wives of Windsor* at the Criterion Theatre, starring James K. Hackett as the "fat knight" Sir John Falstaff and Viola Allen as clever Mistress Ford.
- It dawned on Grace that Sir John had intentions that could be called impure, but, strangely, Aunt Mary did not seem troubled by this.
- Grace was delighted to read in the program that in this, the age of automobiles, "The curtain will rise promptly at 8 o'clock; carriages may be called at 10:50."
- During a side trip, Grace and her aunt visited Kenilworth Castle; then they squeezed in a bit more shopping before embarking for home.
- Once Grace was fully rested and on the steamship back to the United States, she was, she thought, determined to be bolder about meeting men, drinking wine, and dancing until dawn—all of which, except a bit of wine, had eluded her on this dizzying, wonderful trip.

Kenilworth Castle was Grace's last tour destination in England

Life in the Community: Baltimore, Maryland

- The port city of Baltimore had long been a transportation hub, both by water and rail.
- Supplementing the area's longstanding dominance as a port, Baltimore's railroads traveled the Atlantic coast, hauling merchandise and farm produce to the city.
- At the beginning of the Great War, 12 shipping lines, all under foreign flags, operated out of Baltimore.

The grand Masonic Temple in Baltimore

- A steel mill and shipyard constructed by the Pennsylvania Steel Company in 1893 was acquired by Bethlehem Steel in 1916; thereafter steel production dominated the Baltimore economy.
- The prospect of employment in Baltimore's industrial economy, especially the steel industry, drew workers from rural Maryland, Pennsylvania, and the southern states as well as Irish, German, Welsh, Hungarian, Polish and Russian immigrants.
- Baltimore was an important point of entry for European immigrants to the United States; between 1821 and 1914, it ranked third in the number of immigrants admitted, behind only New York City and Boston.
- The peak year of immigration through Baltimore's port was 1907, with almost a million arrivals; 60 steamers with 66,000 immigrants docked at Locust Point.
- The steamers departed from Bremen, Germany, but carried immigrants from all over Europe.

- Immigration via Baltimore virtually ended in 1914 with the onset of World War I; thereafter most immigrants went through New York.
- After the National Origins Quota Act of 1924 was passed by Congress, each source country was assigned a quota for immigration according to the ethnic distribution of the U.S. population in 1920, severely restricting the number of immigrants admitted from eastern and southern Europe.
- Entering the 1920s, Baltimore's population was some 20 percent African American; the city was rigidly segregated.
- Around the turn of the century, West Baltimore had replaced East Baltimore's Fells Point area as the heart of the city's black community.
- In the 1920s Baltimore's African American population began to grow more rapidly that the city's population as a whole, chiefly owing to the migration of rural blacks to the Baltimore.
- In 1927 Bethlehem Steel Company was augmenting the capacity of its plant and hauling ore from Chile and Peru.
- Tankers were bringing crude oil from the Gulf ports and Mexico to the refineries on the south shore of the Patapsco River.
- New fertilizer and chemical plants were belching smoke and vapors over Curtis Bay.
- Spurred by the excitement generated by Charles Lindbergh's transatlantic flight, Baltimore's leaders were talking about building the nation's biggest airport.
- Although President Woodrow Wilson had vetoed the Volstead Act, his veto was overridden by Congress in October 1919, and Prohibition went into effect in January 1920.
- Maryland was the only state that never passed a state enforcement act, viewing Prohibition as an infringement on a state's right to regulate liquor traffic within its borders as it saw fit.
- Baltimore was a defiant center of resistance to Prohibition.
- Iconoclastic *Baltimore Sun* journalist H. L. Mencken lived almost all of his life in a brick rowhouse on Baltimore's middle- and upper-middle-class Union Square.
- A vociferous opponent of Prohibition, he frequented the Owl Bar at the Belvedere Hotel on East Chase Street.
- Mencken was a regular at Haussner's Restaurant, which opened on Eastern Avenue in 1926; the "Sage of Baltimore" also held court at Maison Marconi's on Saratoga Street.
- Mencken's *The American Language,* a book about how English as spoken and written in the United States had diverged from British English, was partly inspired by his curiosity about the English he heard spoken on the streets of Baltimore.
- The book met with near-universal acclaim when it was published in 1919.
- It was Mencken who first suggested to Clarence Darrow that Darrow defend teacher John Scopes in the famous "monkey trial" (as Mencken himself dubbed it) over the teaching of evolution in public schools.
- Mencken's caustic reports from the eight-day trial in Dayton, Tennessee, in July 1925, were nationally syndicated.

Heavyweight Prizefighter in 1927

William Lawrence "Young" Stribling spent most of his childhood in vaudeville with his parents and a younger brother, but in his teenage years, he became a formidable boxer.

Life at Home

- William Lawrence "Young" Stribling was born to be a prizefighter.
- His birth announcement, composed in 1904, read: "Born to Mr. and Mrs. W. L. Stribling Sr, a future heavyweight champion of the world, the day after Christmas, to be called William Lawrence Stribling Jr."
- As one of a traveling vaudeville act, "Four Novelty Grahams" (the other members were his parents and younger brother Herbert, called "Babe"), Young Stribling grew up on the road.
- The family's repertoire consisted of gymnastics and balancing acts, culminating in a boxing match between Young and Babe, who wore oversized gloves.
- It was an enormous hit and never failed to bring the house down.
- Ma and Pa Stribling, both trained acrobats, spearheaded their son's boxing career, including maintaining his physical condition and performance level.
- Pa served as his manager and promoter, while Ma actually donned gloves and sparred with Young up until he was 14 years old.
- The Striblings were not a typical hard-living vaudeville family.
- They prayed and read the Bible together before each show, and they attended church every Sunday, no matter where they were performing.
- The Four Novelty Grahams were so popular that the Stribling family was paid to perform in 38 countries over several years.
- They settled down in Macon, Georgia, just before World War I.
- Young fought his first professional bout in 1921, as a 16-year-old bantamweight in Atlanta, Georgia.
- He fought 75 professional bouts while still in high school and gained a reputation as an up-and-coming pugilist.
- Led by Young as forward, Macon's Lanier High School won the state basketball championship in 1922.
- Yet when the team was invited to the National Interscholastic Tournament in Chicago, Young was

William Lawrence "Young" Stribling

ineligible to play because of his status as a professional boxer.

- On his twenty-first birthday, Young Stribling married his high-school sweetheart, Brenau College student Clara Virginia Kinney.
- She was high society and he was a prizefighter.
- The couple met at Lanier High School; their romance blossomed quickly, from love notes to walking home from school, with Young carrying her books.
- Clara's father was a successful Macon businessman in the cotton industry, and her mother was the first woman elected to the City Council.
- When he was not in serious training for a fight, Young and Clara spent considerable time together, often listening to the Crosby radio, like so many other Americans.
- In 1922 the Crosby Radio Corporation had created a radio that relied on simpler vacuum tubes instead of crystals; it was the first radio with dials to adjust the volume and tune in to stations.
- Just as important, it was packaged and sold in an attractive wooden case, a respectable-looking piece of furniture that fit in any parlor.

Clara Kinney

- Clara and Young listened to the *Maxwell House Hour* and the *Midweek Hymn Sing*, both sponsored by Maxwell House Coffee, and the *Goodrich Zippers Banjo Ensemble*, sponsored by B. F. Goodrich.
- By the time Young was 21, he had earned more than a million dollars from his boxing purses.
- He and Clara could afford the best of everything.
- The nation, too, had the appearance of prosperity.
- About 80 percent of American homes had a yearly income of $3,000 and could afford electric vacuum cleaners, washing machines, refrigerators, and electric ranges.

Stribling with Ma and Pa, 1925 (Library of Congress)

- A frequent guest in the Stribling household was golfer Bobby Jones, who was born in Atlanta.
- In 1926 Jones became the first golfer to win the British Open and the U.S. Open in the same year, earning him a ticker-tape parade.
- Bobby Jones and Young Stribling often walked around Macon wearing their "plus fours," knickers made with four extra inches of fabric, widely worn by men during sporting activities such as golf.
- Young drove fast cars and motorcycles, and he often flew his own airplane to boxing matches across the country.
- Most barnstorming pilots in the 1920s flew Jenny's surplus Curtis JN 4D trainers; thousands had been manufactured too late for World War I and therefore could be bought for $300 each.
- Young loved flying, and he longed for one of Henry Ford's tri-motor 4-AT airliners; the 4-ATs were closely patterned on the German Fokker and were considered safe and dependable.
- Young liked the enclosed cockpit.

- He always preferred to travel with his family, and since 4-ATs could carry 11- to 14 passengers, the carrier would make it possible to fly everyone cross-country to his bouts.

Life at Work

- Young Stribling was a poster boy for clean living; he never drank, never smoked, and was discriminating in his eating habits.
- The handsome, charismatic Young Stribling was considered a scientific boxer who preferred to win on points rather than rely on the knockout.
- Nevertheless, Stribling possessed a mean knockout punch and sent half his opponents to the canvas.
- He despised what he considered to be pointless violence in the sport and spoke out against it.
- He took his first shot at a championship title fight when he challenged Irishman Mike McTigue for the light heavyweight championship of the world on October 4, 1923, in Columbus, Georgia.
- Young was 18 years old.
- Once he saw Stribling in person, McTigue, a hardened veteran, realized that he had seriously underestimated his opponent.
- McTigue had been led to believe by his manager, Joe Jacobs, that Stribling would give him no problems.
- On the morning of the scheduled championship fight, McTigue attempted to use a hand injury to back out, but X-rays showed it to be an old injury, despite the champion's protests.
- Supported by a hometown crowd, Young dominated the ten-round light heavyweight championship fight, only to have the referee declare a draw.
- When the 8,000 spectators boisterously challenged his decision, the referee declared Young the winner.
- Three hours later, the referee, hiding out in a secret location, reversed himself again and declared the fight a draw.
- Young had been a champion for three hours.

MIKE McTIGUE "The Cyclonic Celt"
WHO MADE PUGILISTIC HISTORY OVER NIGHT

Crowd waiting for boxer Jack Johnson (G. G. Bain Collection, Library of Congress)

- Great controversy ensued nationwide.
- After the fight McTigue issued a statement to the press: "I was really surprised this morning when they forced me to go in the ring with only one hand to defend my title. I went into the ring with one hand and I believe I scored more points with that one hand than Stribling did with both of his."
- Four years later, despite having fought hundreds of opponents and having vanquished almost all of them, Young was still in pursuit of an official title.
- Writer Damon Runyon dubbed Young "King of the Canebrakes" after Young's 18,000-mile barnstorming tour across the

country in 1925, referring to Stribling's popularity in rural areas.

- For the tour the family had purchased a bus to give fans in smaller towns an opportunity to see the popular boxer in exhibition bouts.
- Pa Stribling pitted Young against the local champion at each stop, offering $10 to anyone who could beat his son.
- Young fought 33 matches that year and did much to popularize the sport with his reputation for clean sportsmanship and wholesome living.
- Another cross-country tour in 1927 resulted in 57 straight wins with only one draw and one loss.
- A careful fighter, possessing superb defensive skills, Young had never yet picked up a scar to mar his movie-star looks.
- Many observers, however, thought that he had yet to fulfill his potential as a prizefighter, despite his lopsided record of victories in the ring.
- Young Stribling, a lieutenant in the Army Air Reserve Corps, was beloved across Georgia.
- Black Georgians, though, generally were less enthralled, because Young refused to face black fighters.

Jack Dempsey in the ring (G. G. Bain Collection, Library of Congress)

Life in the Community: Macon, Georgia

- Macon was called the "Heart of Georgia" because of its location near the Ocmulgee River in central Georgia, home of some of the most impressive Indian mounds in the southeastern United States.
- The region was first inhabited by Creeks and their predecessors 12,000 years before white people arrived.
- In 1806, President Thomas Jefferson had a trading post established there as a peacekeeping and trading site after the Creeks ceded their lands east of the Ocmulgee River.
- Chartered in 1823, Macon was named for Nathaniel Macon, a North Carolina Congressman.
- When surveyor James Webb laid out the downtown streets of Macon, Georgia, in 1832, he incorporated parks, including 250 acres for Central City Park.
- Citizens were required by ordinances to plant shade trees in their front yards, giving the city a gracious appearance.
- Cotton became the mainstay of Macon's early economy as boats, stagecoaches, and, in 1843, a railroad all brought prosperity to Macon.

Downtown Macon (Walker Evans, Library of Congress)

- During the Civil War, Macon was spared destruction during the Union Army's march to the sea.
- Following the war and into the twentieth century, Macon continued to build on its agricultural base and its location on the "fall line" where the Piedmont rises from the coastal plain; the city became a transportation hub for the entire state.
- Henry Ford's Model T was helping to end the isolation of rural people; America was becoming a nation constantly on the move.
- The ubiquitous car was known by a variety of names, including the Tin Lizzie, Flivver,

Detroit Disaster, Michigan Mistake, Tacks Collector, Nagivatin' Nancy, and Old Faithful.

- With a production run of 15 million over 1908-1927, the Model T arguably had more impact on the nation than the telegraph, telephone, phonograph, radio, electric light and power, or rural free delivery.
- It could run on anything from gasoline to good-grade kerosene.
- The car's 10-gallon fuel tank was mounted in the car frame beneath the front seat.
- It relied on gravity, and consequently the Model T could not climb a steep hill when fuel was low; some drivers solved this problem by driving up steep hills in reverse.
- The Model T runabout sold for $260; the touring model was $290.

The prosperity of the 1920s enabled many Americans to own cars

- The Model A was the second huge success for the Ford Motor Company, starting in 1927.
- The 40-horsepower engine gave the car a top speed of 65 miles per hour.
- The Model A was the first Ford to use the standard set of driver controls, with conventional clutch and brake pedals, throttle, and gearshift, and it was the first car to have safety glass in the windshield.
- The general prosperity of the Roaring Twenties put the Model T within reach of the American middle class, as Ford had intended.
- Georgia's economy, however, remained tied to cotton.
- While other parts of the country were experiencing a manufacturing boom, the South, including

Randolph House, Macon (Frances Benjamin Johnston, Library of Congress)

Georgia, was in the midst of an agricultural crisis, owing to the devastation of the cotton crop by the boll weevil.

- The boll weevil was known in Texas by the early 1890s; in Georgia it first appeared in Thomasville in 1915.
- By 1917 the boll weevil was present in every cotton-producing county in Georgia.
- The state's cotton production began declining rapidly, from a historical high of 2.8 million bales in 1914 to 600,000 bales in 1923.
- By 1926 airplanes were being used to dust the cotton fields with pesticides.
- Nevertheless, in 1927 cotton remained the number one cash crop in Georgia, exceeding the value of all the other crops grown in the state.
- In Georgia, as elsewhere, newspapers were replete with stories about America's youth, their daring clothes, their scandalous dancing, sensual jazz, late-night parties and cynical opinions.

- In most of rural America, however, where Young was a hero, few had come in contact with this kind of lifestyle.
- According to popular evangelist Billy Sunday, the world was a "battleground between the children possessed by Satan and the children of God."
- Sunday's son, Billy Jr., had been caught frequenting big-city speakeasies, where he danced the night away with women of questionable repute.
- To most country dwellers, it seemed clear that the Devil lived in the big cities, where he was eager to test one's faith.

᚛ᚉ᚛ᚉ᚛ᚉ᚛ᚉ᚛ᚉ᚛ᚉ

"Society Fiancé of Stribling Proud of Him"
Malcolm Ellis, *Davenport Democrat and Leader* (IA), January 1, 1926

If the graying ladies with their memories of the days when Sherman cut a swath through Georgia cotton fields, and when Uncle Remus played as a boy in these neighborhood woods, are somewhat shocked over the marriage of the daughter of the Davenports and the Guerrys and the Kinneys to a prizefighter, the younger generation is not the least perturbed.

Truth to tell, there is not among the younger set of this giddy generation enough agitation over the marriage of Young Stribling, contender for the light heavyweight championship of the world, and Miss Clara Virginia Kinney, to make it interesting. The younger set takes it along with the less flamboyant romances. Indeed, to them it is the natural denouncement since the romance has budded and bloomed under the eyes of the town.

Five years ago, Young Stribling was better known as just one of the growing-up kids around town than as a prizefighter. As a basketball player on the high school team he was bidding for stardom, and to the youth of the high school that was far more thrilling than his occasional fights. He came to be the star player on the championship prep and high school basketball team of that state.

It was out of the classroom that this romance emerged, aided by the notes that were slipped surreptitiously while the geometry teacher had his attention centered on proving a theorem. Stribling walked home with Miss Kinney, carrying her books. When influence came he was paying an income tax well up in the five figures, it was in a fast motorcar that they went to the handsome Kinney home in the fashionable Cherokee Heights.

Miss Kinney had dates with other boys, but never eyes for them. She was popular in high school and in college she became the sponsor of a college fraternity and was starred in amateur theatricals.

Of French extraction, from the DuPonts, the same line as the DuPonts of Delaware and the Guerrys, she is dainty and petite, the exemplification of breeding and culture that has existed for multiple generations. Her maternal ancestors were among those French Huguenot settlers who peopled Charleston and made it the South's most aristocratic city. Her paternal ancestors were among the English cavaliers who made Virginia the richest colony...

How will her mother take the match? "I'm glad Clara is going to have Strib," she said. "He is one of the finest boys I've ever known. I have known him and watched him for years almost as closely as his own mother would. I know they will be happy together. They've been sweethearts since high school days. My daughter could not have picked a better man."

Blues Singer Florence Mills in 1927

The voice of blues singer Florence Mills was described as being "bell-like" with "bird-like tones," characteristics that helped make her one of the most prominent entertainers of the 1920s.

Life at Home

- Known as the "Queen of Happiness," Florence Mills, born Florence Winfrey, captivated the public with her enchanting song "I'm a Little Blackbird Looking for a Bluebird" and with her stage performances.
- The youngest of three daughters of John and Nellie Winfrey, Florence was born into extreme poverty on January 25, 1895, probably in Washington, D.C., or in the vicinity of the city.
- Both her parents were born in slavery in Amherst County, Virginia, and worked in the tobacco industry.
- When tobacco farming tanked, the family moved from Lynchburg, Virginia, to Washington, D.C., where her father worked as a day laborer and her mother took in laundry.
- Both parents were illiterate.
- Florence grew up in the streets of Goat Alley, Washington, DC's infamous slum, where she first demonstrated the natural gifts as a singer and dancer that would bring her to the attention of an international audience.
- At age five, Florence won prizes for cakewalking and buck dancing, and she was awarded a bracelet by the wife of the British ambassador for entertaining her international guests from the diplomatic corps.
- The family moved to Harlem, in upper Manhattan, in 1903.
- By age seven, Florence was a regular performer in theaters and private homes, and she rapidly developed a name for herself on the vaudeville and burlesque circuits.
- Some of her earliest roles were as a "pickaninny," or "pick," in white vaudeville, and she performed as part of a sister act on the black popular entertainment circuit.
- It was a tough life for a young girl, playing small venues all over the country, putting in endless hours rehearsing and traveling.

Florence Mills

- The high point of her childhood was her appearance in the road company production of Bert Williams and George Walker's *Sons of Ham,* in which she sang "Miss Hannah from Savannah."
- As a result, the traveling white vaudeville team of Bonita and Hearn hired her.
- By age 14 Florence had organized a traveling song-and dance act with her sisters known as the Mills Sisters.
- From then on, Florence Mills was the name she used, instead of Florence Winfrey.
- Florence was innovative: skilled in all varieties of jazz and tap dance, she was especially renowned for her "acrobatic" and "eccentric" dancing.

Tobacco farm

- Her lessons in tap came from her close personal friend Bill "Bojangles" Robinson when she was living in Chicago in 1916-1917.
- Florence also learned much from her husband, Ulysses S. "Slow Kid" Thompson, the originator of "slow motion dancing" and one of the earliest practitioners of "Russian dancing," or "legomania."
- Thompson was a fine dancer, and he conducted the orchestra for a traveling act called the Tennessee Ten, which Florence was invited to join in 1915.
- In 1917 the vaudeville star Nora Bayes brought the Tennessee Ten to New York to perform with her in a new show.
- After the United States entered World War I, however, Thompson was drafted; he was given military training and was sent to France in 1918.
- After his return in 1919, Slow Kid and Florence performed with the Tennessee Ten in *Folly Town,* a very successful burlesque revue with an integrated cast that starred the white vaudevillian Bert Lahr.
- Florence's big break came soon afterward in *Shuffle Along,* which had music and lyrics by black songwriters Noble Sissle and Eubie Blake.
- By the time *Shuffle Along* opened in 1921, Florence and Slow Kid had married.

Life at Work

- *Shuffle Along* was the off-Broadway hit show that introduced syncopated song and dance to white America.
- When the show opened in New York, it was an immediate hit. The star originally was Gertrude Saunders, but when Saunders departed, Florence replaced her.

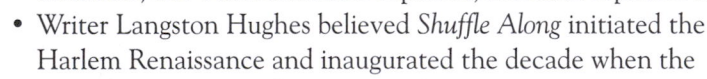

- Writer Langston Hughes believed *Shuffle Along* initiated the Harlem Renaissance and inaugurated the decade when the "Negro was in vogue."
- Florence's uninhibited singing and dancing stunned the audiences.
- She was paid $125 per week.
- "We were afraid people would think it was a freak show and it wouldn't appeal to white people," said Eubie Blake. "Others thought that if it was a colored show, it might be dirty."
- Sissle and Blake had first joined forces as members of the World War I "Hell Fighters" Jazz Band of the 369th Infantry, led by James Reese Europe.

Alberta Hunter on the Black Swan record label

- They transformed an old sketch named "The Mayor of Jimtown" into a lively musical featuring hit songs such as "I'm Just Wild about Harry" and "Love Will Find a Way," combined with energetic dancing.
- After a while, concurrently with *Shuffle Along*, Florence appeared after theater hours at the Plantation Room, a club on the rooftop of the Winter Garden Theater, in an act that also featured a wide range of black talent, including visiting performers such as Paul Robeson.
- Florence was convinced to do the show by Lew Leslie, a white promoter, who built the show around her.

Florence Mills and Johnny Hudgins rehearsing Blackbirds on a London rooftop, 1926

- The show—which charged $3 admission—entranced white audiences with the ebullient, fast-paced rhythms of black music.
- Edith Wilson and the Jazz Hounds served as Florence's house orchestra.
- Florence was paid $200 per week.
- In 1922 the nightclub act was converted into a Broadway show called *The Plantation Revue*; Slow Kid Thompson joined Florence in the cast.
- Florence was positioned to become one of the first black female performers to break into the racially restricted show business establishment.
- She was paid $500 per week, for no fewer than 35 weeks a year.
- Civil rights crusader Bert Williams, of the Bert Williams-George Walker duo, believed that Florence would accomplish more than he had: "This is once where the pint is better than the quart."
- Florence did it all: she sang blues, "hot jazz" and ballads, plus she danced, acted, and was an accomplished comedian and mime.
- Luminaries such as Jelly Roll Morton, James P. Johnson, and Willie "The Lion" Smith helped dub her the "Queen of Jazz."
- Composer Irving Berlin said that if he could find a white woman who could sing like Florence, he would be inspired to write a hit a week.
- Writer James Weldon Johnson wrote, "The upper range of her voice was full of bubbling, bell-like, bird-like tones.
- "It was a rather magical thing Florence Mills used to do with that small voice in her favorite song, 'I'm a Little Blackbird Looking for a Bluebird,' and she did it with such exquisite poignancy as always to raise a lump in your throat."
- But that did not change the fact that the set where she performed was fashioned like a pre-Civil War southern plantation featuring a large watermelon slice, whose seeds were electric lights, and a bandanna-coifed black woman flipping pancakes.
- Nonetheless, Florence brought the house down with the naughty song, "I've Got What It Takes But It Breaks My Heart to Give It Away"; Edith Wilson performed her showstopper in the same revue: "He May Be Your Man, But He Comes to See Me Sometimes."
- Florence was reported to be the "highest-salaried colored actress on the American stage."
- The Great White Way was not solely white anymore.
- On opening night for the second, 1922-1923 season, the audience included Charlie Chaplin, Irving Berlin and Irene Bordoni.

- One of the new songs added to the second season, "Aggravatin' Pappa," became a radio hit—by Sophie Tucker; by the end of the year, a dozen female singers had recorded Florence's new song.
- When Sir Charles B. Cochran began looking for attractions for the London stage, he invited the Plantation Company to the Pavilion in the spring of 1923, despite a newspaper headline reading, "Nigger Problem Brought to London."
- The show that Cochran devised was called *Dover Street to Dixie*; it was staged with an all-English cast in the first half and featured Florence and the Plantation cast in the second half.

King and Carter Jazzing Orchestra, 1921 (Robert Runyon Photograph Collection)

- It proved so successful that issues of race were soon forgotten.
- The Prince of Wales was said to have seen the show numerous times; Florence became so popular that she was to London what Josephine Baker was to Paris.
- Composer Duke Ellington wrote a musical portrait for Florence called "Black Beauty"; she was featured in *Vogue* and *Vanity Fair* and photographed by Bassano and Edward Steichen.
- In 1923, on her return to New York, Florence received an invitation to appear in the Greenwich Village Follies annual production—the first time a black woman was offered a part in the major white production.
- She was also offered a contract to join the Ziegfeld Follies, but she turned it down.
- She elected to stay with Lew Leslie to create a rival show with an all-black cast.
- Florence felt she could best serve her race by providing a venue for an entire company of actors and singers; "If in any way I have done anything to lift the profession, I am unconscious of it, and it was done only for love of my art and for my people."
- Florence enjoyed a triumphant return.
- Her popularity knew no bounds—she was now an international star.

Mamie Smith on the Okeh record label

- Florence and her husband bought a new house—a five-story brownstone in the middle of Harlem—and furnished it with carpets imported from China and a music box that played records without rewinding.
- *Dover Street to Dixie*, which had thrilled in London, became *Dixie to Broadway* when it opened in New York on October 29, 1924, with a brand-new slate of songs.
- Advertisements proclaimed Florence to be the "World's Greatest Colored Entertainer: The Sensation of Two Continents."
- One critic said, "The vital force of the revue proceeds from the personality of Miss Mills."

- In 1926, when Leslie produced *Blackbirds*, Florence achieved her goal of creating a major all-black revue with the opening of this show at the Alhambra Theatre in Harlem.
- The show moved in September to London's Pavilion Theatre and enjoyed 276 performances.
- Exhausted from so many successive performances, Florence went to Germany to rest, but her condition did not improve.
- In 1927 she returned to New York to a royal welcome.
- Finally compelled to deal with her health problems, she was diagnosed with "pelvic tuberculosis," and it was decided that she needed surgery.
- On October 24, 1927, she entered the hospital.
- One week later, on November 1, 1927, after two operations, Florence Mills died, at age 31.
- Some 3,000 people attended her funeral at the Mother AME Zion Church; kings sent flowers, Americans—black and white—mourned.
- Harlem came to a standstill as 150,000 people—the largest such gathering in Harlem's history—lined the streets during the funeral procession.

Life in the Community: Harlem, New York City, New York

- Harlem's history was defined by a series of boom-and-bust cycles, with significant ethnic shifts accompanying each one.
- A housing boom in the 1890s produced an overabundance of houses, and by 1903, builders had opened their doors to tenants of all colors and races.
- Entrepreneur Philip Payton and his Afro-American Realty Company actively recruited black families already living in the city, almost single-handedly igniting the migration of blacks from their previous New York neighborhoods, the Tenderloin, San Juan Hill and Hell's Kitchen.
- The move by black residents to northern Manhattan was partially driven by fears of anti-black riots, which occurred in the Tenderloin in 1900 and in San Juan Hill in 1905.
- New black residents began to arrive from elsewhere en masse in 1904, the year of the beginning of the Great Migration by Southern blacks fleeing poverty, lack of opportunity, and aggressive enforcement of discriminatory Jim Crow laws.
- By 1910 Harlem had a population of approximately 500,000, of whom 50,000 were African-American and 75,000 were native-born whites; the rest were immigrants from Ireland, Germany, Hungary, Russia, England, Italy and Scandinavia.
- In the 1920s the district was the setting of the "Harlem Renaissance," an unprecedented outpouring of artistic and professional work by African Americans.

A view of Harlem north of Columbia University

- By this time new opportunities were developing for the black artistic community, which had long been subject to humiliating discrimination and Jim Crow laws.
- White promoter Otto Heinemann and his company OKeh Records were struggling to get established; Heinemann was willing to try anything when he asked Cincinnati's young black singer Mamie Smith to cut a record.
- For the premiere recording, Smith sang "That Thing Called Love" and "You Can't Keep a Good Man Down," backed by the house orchestra—to keep the record from sounding "too colored."
- This was quickly followed by the recording of "Crazy Blues" and "It's Right Here for You (If You Don't Come Get It, 'Taint No Fault of Mine)," this time accompanied by a five-piece black band known as the Jazz Hounds.
- The result was impressive and possibly the first actual blues recording by a black artist with black accompaniment.
- Within a month, 75,000 copies of "Crazy Blues" had been sold in Harlem record shops; in only seven months, national sales topped one million copies.
- Mamie Smith and her band were pure gold; everything they recorded sold immediately.
- Smith made more than $100,000 in recording royalties alone; in addition, she was making between $1,000 and $1,500 a week in the large theaters of New York and Chicago.
- As a result, record companies scrambled to sign new blues singers; Columbia Records even bragged that it had "more colored artists under exclusive contract than any company today."
- Black Swan Records, produced for Pace Phonograph Company of New York, advertised itself as the "only genuine colored record. Others are only passing for colored."
- In this period Harlem earned a reputation as the Mecca for jazz and blues.
- Venues such as the Cotton Club and the Apollo Theater made stars out of many entertainers, including Fletcher Henderson and Duke Ellington.
- During World War I, expanding industries recruited black laborers to fill new jobs.
- By 1920 central Harlem was 32.43 percent black; between 1920 and 1930, according to census figures, 118,792 white people left the neighborhood and 87,417 blacks arrived.

School band in Harlem

IQ Test Salesman in 1927

When Scott Kelly took a deep breath and reflected on the future—his future—he envisioned a world with more order and a more efficient workforce, brought about by a scientific approach to the pressing problems of the day.

Life at Home

- Scott Kelly was sure that in the modern world of 1927, with automobiles, telephones, and radios virtually everywhere, testing schoolchildren would produce scientific efficiency in the nation's classrooms, better workers for America's factories, and early identification of students with high IQ potential.
- Scott believed that, once people understood that IQ testing was for their own good, all the barriers would fall.
- That, he thought, would make him a millionaire.
- The 29-year-old super-salesman had just been awarded the right to sell the Cooperative Test Service, a sophisticated form of IQ testing, in southern California.
- He already had his eye on a wonderful stretch of beach to buy and develop—once he hit a home run in school sales.
- Scott had never considered the education market as one to which he was especially attuned, having achieved his success thus far by pitching the modern conveniences that had so transformed most American homes.
- There was always sales work of that kind of available, but Scott preferred to stay ahead of the curve, where the work was more challenging, the stakes higher, and the rewards more satisfying.
- The key to Scott's success in sales was his ability to diagnose a prospective customer's needs and then to demonstrate, in persuasive detail, exactly how his product would meet those needs.
- Now it appeared that the future of education was grouping, or tracking, students based on their IQ score, and he had the right product for the task.
- With the Co-operative Test Service, Scott would be in the vanguard of that movement.
- During the war years, the military had worked intensively on developing such tests; the concept was widely accepted.

Scott Kelly

- The established market included both elementary schools and colleges—and that was just the beginning: the commercial sector had already taken an interest in testing.
- Scott saw numerous applications for the product.
- After all, the Co-operative Test Service was an American Council on Education venture, giving it instant credibility.
- Scott figured that before too long, a lot of people would want to know their IQ—a number at least as integral to their lives as the number of their favorite radio show on the dial.
- Scott Kelly paid little attention to the critics who charged that the IQ tests subscribed to the "cult of efficiency," which tended to disregard individuality and creativity.

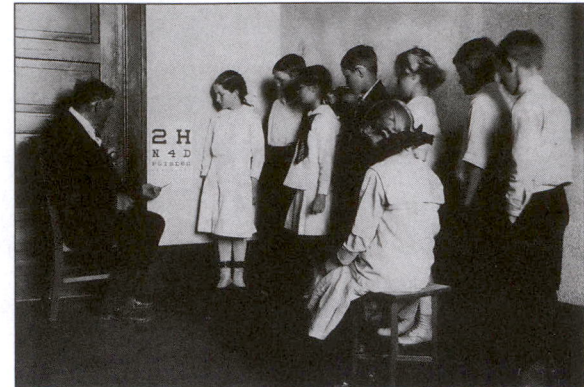

Students lined up for medical testing (Lewis W. Hine, Library of Congress)

- The cult of efficiency was as "American as the assembly line, and perhaps as alienating," one critic charged.
- By 1927 the assembly line had proved its worth, Scott insisted, and the tests had shown their value.
- The economy was thriving, keeping Scott's own prospects bright, but he had come to understand that America's future depended on the application of sound scientific principles and efficient management standards not only in the workplace but in all aspects of life.
- It stood to reason that the earlier such principles and standards were applied, the more effective they would be.
- Scott was a bachelor, but if this testing venture paid off, it might be time for him to consider settling down—or perhaps he might wait until he saw how the beach development panned out.

Life at Work

- American educators became increasingly convinced of the need for universal intelligence testing—and believers in the efficiency it could contribute to school programming—based on the notion that intelligence tests were accurate and scientific.

Alfred Binet

- Intelligence testing received its initial boost in 1905 when the French government commissioned psychologist Alfred Binet to find a method of differentiating between children who were intellectually normal and those who were inferior.
- The purpose was to put the slow students into special schools, where they would receive more individual attention; not incidentally, the disruption they caused in the education of intellectually normal children would be avoided.
- This led to the development of the Binet Scale, which tested children by asking them to follow commands, copy patterns, name objects, and put things in order or arrange them properly.
- Since Parisian schoolchildren were used to initiate the program, their scores became the standard, or norm; if, for example, 70 percent of the Parisian eight-year-olds passed a particular test, then success on the test represented the eight-year-old level of intelligence.

Yawning and stretching in the classroom (Frances Benjamin Johnston, Library of Congress)

- After Binet's work was adopted by American promoter Lewis Terman of Stanford University, the phrase "intelligence quotient," or "IQ," entered the vocabulary.
- The IQ was defined as the ratio of "mental age" to chronological age, with 100 being average. So an eight-year-old who passed the ten-year-old's test would have an IQ of 10/8 x 100, or 125.
- Although his scale constituted a revolutionary approach to the assessment of individual mental ability, Binet himself cautioned against misuse of the scale and misunderstanding of its implications.
- According to Binet, the scale was designed with a single purpose in mind; it was to serve as a guide for identifying students who could benefit from extra help in school.
- His assumption was that a lower IQ indicated the need for more teaching, not an inability to learn; the test was emphatically not intended to be used as "a general device for ranking all pupils according to mental worth."
- Binet himself complained that some researchers had begun falsely claiming that an individual's intelligence was a fixed quantity that could not be increased: "We must protest and react against this brutal pessimism; we must try to demonstrate that it is founded on nothing."
- Binet's scale had a profound impact on educational development in the United States and elsewhere.
- Yet the American educators and psychologists who championed the scale and its revisions ignored Binet's caveats concerning its limitations.
- Soon, according to its critics, intelligence testing assumed an importance and respectability out of proportion to its actual value.
- Private industry gave the IQ test a tentative tryout in a hunt for the best workers, but the first major test was entry of the United States into the Great War.
- In 1917, with the war in Europe well under way, the military was being asked to sort through the skills of the 24 million men registered by the nation's draft boards, of whom almost 3 million were to be inducted into the armed forces.
- To assign them to appropriate army units was a daunting task.

- Psychologists, especially those with prewar applied personnel management experience, thought they had the answer: intelligence testing.
- A specially formed Committee on the Classification of Personnel in the Army (CCPA) applied a prewar Rating Scale for Selecting Salesmen with minimal modification—as a Rating Scale for Selecting Captains, and also constructed proficiency tests for 83 military jobs.
- Character, not just intelligence, loomed large in official army documents regarding the acceptability of recruits.
- The Vineland Training School for Feebleminded Girls and Boys in New Jersey, directed by Henry Goddard from 1906 until 1918, became a site where the Army "Alpha and Beta" mental test was worked out.
- The main issue under consideration was simply one of determining which technical and statistical devices could be employed to best allocate resources and balance the needs of the Army.

- Researchers found a way to transform examinees' answers from highly variable, time-consuming oral or written responses into easily marked choices among fixed alternatives, quickly scored by clerical workers with the aid of superimposed stencils.
- The Army tests then were marketed as a means to root out those who could not understand or follow orders; to assess the trainability potential of recruits and predict what rank a soldier might be expected to attain; and to administratively balance the average intellectual quality of military units.
- As a result, the assigning of an IQ score took on an exalted position as a primary, definitive, and permanent representation of the quality of an individual, and it became entrenched in the schools over the next several decades.
- Henry Goddard preached his belief in the inalterability of intelligence levels: "It is quite possible to restate practically all of our social problems in terms of mental level. ... Testing intelligence is no longer an experiment or of doubted value. It is fast becoming an exact science. ... Can these new facts be used to increase our efficiency? No question! We only await the Human Engineer who will undertake the work."
- Goddard was a believer in eugenics: improving the human race by promoting (or enforcing) "selective breeding" or "human engineering," that is, choosing which people become parents.
- In 1913 Goddard had instituted an intelligence testing program at the Ellis Island immigration center, with the intention of improving on the subjective judgment of immigration officers as to identifying "feeble-minded" persons.
- He examined "representative" Jewish, Hungarian, Italian, and Russian immigrants, 152 in all, of whom on average 80 percent were found to be feeble-minded.
- Goddard had "discovered" that all immigrants except those from Northern Europe were of "surprisingly low intelligence."
- Little notice was taken of the fact that Goddard's conclusions were based on the results of tests—given in English and with questions based on American cultural assumptions—administered to people who scarcely knew the language and who may never before have taken a test.
- By the 1920s, however, mass use of the Stanford-Binet Scale and other tests had created a multimillion-dollar testing industry.

- And the debate concerning the area of education was wide open.
- Comprehensive schools were being advocated as a way of safeguarding the U.S. economy, while two-thirds of those entering high school were still failing to graduate.
- Within the context of the classroom, blame was plentiful and free flowing.
- Academics viewed the high failure rates—especially in mathematics, science, and language arts—as the result of the personal shortcomings of students, disregarding factors such as institutional structure or the curricula of progressive public schooling.
- Once again, testing seemed to be the answer.
- Standards evolved that called for a formal multiple-track plan made up of five psychometrically defined groups: gifted, bright, average, slow, and "special."

Mexican children were often behind at school

- While the "road for transfer" between tracks must be left open, the abilities measured by the tests were considered largely constant and determined by heredity.
- Scott didn't hesitate to tell school-based prospects about the importance of testing as an "instrument for further research" into important psychological questions such as mental growth, potential for re-education, and individual differences.
- Scott also played up the fact that California had been a proving ground for the IQ tests; as he would always mention to an elementary school principal, these student evaluations and predictors of success were homegrown.
- Scott's sales pitch included a new opportunity for the state's school administrators to deal with the ongoing issue of immigrant Mexican schoolchildren.
- According to the tests on 12-year-old pupils of Hispanic ancestry, 42 percent of these students were behind their grade level; such "retardation" was nearly twice as high in schools in which Hispanic pupils predominated as it was in other schools.
- In order to avoid a rise in failure rates of these students, it was decided to put into place a program of "vocational guidance" at the beginning of the seventh grade.
- Scott could then argue that tests would provide a means by which educators could guide students toward appropriate paths based on their skills, helping them negotiate the increasingly complex nature of society and its occupational structure.

Life in the Community: San Diego, California

- When the Alta Territory in California became part of the United States in 1850, following the U.S. victory in the Mexican-American War, it included the small village of San Diego.
- The U.S. Census reported the population of the town as 650 in 1850 and 731 in 1860.
- Thousands stopped briefly in San Diego on their way to the San Francisco Gold Rush, but few stayed.
- William Heath Davis was one of a small group of investors who saw the potential of San Diego; he spent $60,000 constructing a wharf near the property he had purchased near the foot of Market Street, but it was a financial disaster.
- By 1860 many of the enterprises that had been established during the early 1850s had closed.
- The remaining businesses that survived suffered from water shortages, high costs of shipping, and a declining population.
- Fifty-three-year-old Alonzo Horton was the visionary San Diego needed in 1867.

- Although his first view was of barren, mesquite-covered land with a few decaying structures, he was awed, saying, "I have been nearly all over the world and it seemed to me to be the best spot for building a city I ever saw."
- Less than a month after his arrival, he had purchased more than 900 acres for only $265, an average of 27.5 cents an acre.
- He began promoting San Diego by enticing entrepreneurs and residents alike; he built a wharf and promoted development there.

San Diego Parade Grounds, 1920 (National Archives)

- By 1878, San Diego was staking a claim as a rival of San Francisco's trading ports.
- In 1885, a transcontinental railroad transfer route came to San Diego, and the population boomed, reaching 16,159 by 1890.
- In 1906, the San Diego and Arizona Railway of John D. Spreckels was built to provide San Diego with a direct transcontinental rail link to the East by connecting with the Southern Pacific Railroad lines in El Centro, California.
- San Diego hosted the Panama-California Exposition in 1915, celebrating the opening of the Panama Canal.
- San Diego was to be the first American port of call on the Pacific coast for northbound canal-going ships.
- The exposition successfully promoted the city and left a lasting legacy in the form of Balboa Park.
- In 1921 land within the park was allocated for the San Diego Zoo, which gave a permanent home to the animals of the exotic animal exhibitions abandoned after the exposition.
- The zoo also acquired the menagerie of the Wonderland beachfront amusement park in Ocean Beach, which closed in 1916; the animals had been rented to the exposition in 1915-1916.
- A significant U.S. Navy presence began in 1901, with the establishment of the Navy Coaling Station in Point Loma, and expanded greatly during the 1920s.
- Camp Kearny was opened in 1917 on a mesa north of the city; it served as a mobilization and training site for troops soon to be deployed in World War I, and later as a demobilization center.
- The site was largely shuttered by 1920, but the government continued to hold it as a military and civilian airfield.
- In early 1927 the San Diego-based Ryan Aircraft Company used the airfield to weight-test *the Spirit of St Louis*, the custom-built monoplane commissioned by famed aviator Charles A. Lindbergh.
- Lindbergh was competing for the $25,000 Orteig Prize for the first non-stop flight between New York and Paris.
- Time was of the essence; working closely with Lindbergh, Ryan Aircraft designed and built the plane in just 60 days.
- Embarking from Roosevelt Field in Long Island, New York, the previously little-known Lindbergh garnered worldwide adulation when he completed this first nonstop transatlantic flight on May 20-May 21, 1927.

San Diego's Union Station passenger terminal, December 1, 1919

WCTU Movie Monitor in 1928

Carla Mufson liked the movies but was convinced that impressionable young people should be shielded from the more vile thoughts that emanated from Hollywood. So she offered to monitor movies for the Topeka, Kansas, chapter of the Woman's Christian Temperance Union.

Life at Home

- The last of 11 children, Carla Mufson almost died at birth.
- Barely breathing at birth, she was set aside while the doctors concentrated on saving the life of her 38-year-old mother.
- From that day forward, everyone agreed, Carla was serious, determined, and headstrong.
- Early on she decided that a quality education would be more valuable to her than a farmer-husband who might harbor a love of intoxicating drink, like her father.
- Despite much discouragement and little support at home, Carla finished 11 years of school and then one year in a secretarial school.
- She wanted to go to college and hoped to attend Washburn College in southwestern Topeka; founded in 1865, Washburn had been named Lincoln College originally but was renamed for a Massachusetts benefactor who approved of the college's commitment to educating women and African Americans.
- Carla had to support herself, however, and at age 48, she knew that college had long been an opportunity that passed her by.
- Although she had never accomplished, or entirely relinquished, her secret dream of holding a four-year degree, she remained wistful rather than bitter about it.
- There were days when she was convinced that she was smarter than most of the men at the County Bank, where she had worked for 20 years.
- Yet she was a cheerful as well as a competent colleague and was well liked at the bank.
- She spent several afternoons each week counseling scores of promising young girls to stay in school and even pursue a degree.
- She observed that even in the liberated 1920s, men still sang most of the songs and women were still expected to hum along in unison.
- It was while working with the smartest girls in Topeka, Kansas, that she discovered the power of moving picture shows for good and for evil.

Carla Mufson

- Several well-raised, very bright young ladies had skipped their appointed tea and conversation to view the latest movie.
- Carla was disappointed and at first even a bit offended, but then she became curious.
- Taking her usual straightforward approach, she decided to attend a movie to find out why her young charges had put going to a movie ahead of having a conversation about their future.
- After all, the girls clearly enjoyed their weekly sessions and appreciated her help.
- Carla's first film experience was *Safety Last*, a wild comedy featuring Harold Lloyd playing Harold Lloyd, a lovable country hick with an ingratiating smile and large black glasses.

Committee on Arrangements for National WCTU Convention, 1924

- Because the film was a six-reeler, Carla had time to calm her nerves: it was very unsettling to be in a darkened room full of strangers.
- She quickly grew accustomed to the flashing titles and organ music, and then she was drawn into the comical plot.
- Halfway through, she realized that she had laughed herself silly.
- What a marvelous experience, she thought. How intoxicating an influence on the souls of impressionable girls!
- That was in 1925.
- Since then she had feasted on the *Hunchback of Notre Dame*, been horrified by the murder of Trina in the movie *Greed*, reveled in Charlie Chaplin's *The Gold Rush*— and walked indignantly out of a dozen other films.
- Melodrama had its limits, and Carla grew convinced that immoral content in movies should be edited out before young people saw it.
- Sometimes it also seemed to her that too many movies romanticized a thirst for blood and revenge.
- Many of the patrons she saw in the movies were working-class people whose emotions, she felt, were easily inflamed.
- Most of all, of course, she wanted to protect her impressionable girls: there were already so many pressures on them to abandon their educational dreams.
- Men and women—young men and young women—sat together in the audience at the darkened theater.
- As was typical of Carla, when she saw a problem, she became determined to do something about it.
- She presented herself to the Topeka branch of the Woman's Christian Temperance Union and offered to monitor movies that came to town.
- By herself, she had realized, she could do little to influence the situation, but the WCTU was widely respected in Topeka.
- It had the resources of a national network, and Topeka newspapers and politicians paid attention to it.
- Carla tentatively began to discuss the good and bad things about films at her weekly counseling teas.
- Everyone knew, thanks to the new science, that film images moved straight from the eyes to the brain without interpretation or conscious reflection.
- People simply couldn't help their reactions to movies.
- This was why, in addition to her monitoring activities, she sought out the movie house managers when they came to the bank.
- Someone needed to tell them that morality was more important than money.

Life at Work

- The WCTU members welcomed Carla's offer of help and gave her a list of movie guidelines—issued by the movie industry—knowing that right-thinking people understood that these rules were just the beginning.
- As a result, Carla began to watch three movies each week—but never with the young ladies she was mentoring.
- She couldn't monitor the films and at the same time cope with the reactions of her girls to scenes such as an unmarried couple engaged in a passionate embrace.
- Carla had seen enough movies to know that the alarm bells could not be rung loudly enough.

Gilbert Roland, Norma Talmadge, and Arnold Kent in The Woman Disputed, *1928*

- *The Wind* was a case in point: Lillian Gish stirring Texas ranch hands and a more sophisticated stranger to a fevered pitch; Carla was astonished that Lillian Gish, who looked so delicate, would act that kind of role.
- Not only was Gish's character violated in the film but she committed the sin of murder; in the harsh landscape of Texas, her action was presented as justifiable, even heroic.
- Without a doubt, the film was capable of unleashing ungovernable emotions among young people; Carla thought it must be edited—especially that murder scene with the stranger—if it was to be shown in Kansas again.
- Carla still loved the movies and thought they offered wonderful entertainment; she saw that they had great potential for good, and she wanted young people to enjoy films without being harmed by them.
- The WCTU worked community by community in an attempt to convince theater owners not to show unwholesome movies, especially on Sundays, when children were especially likely to be in the theater.
- Although at first Carla, uncharacteristically, found it intimidating to say a movie needed changes, she knew that her work had an impact in both Topeka and a five-state region.
- Because of the high cost of changing movie prints, one state's demand for change often resulted in the distribution of the edited version throughout the entire region.

Carla counseled girls who showed energy and leadership potential (National Photo Collection, Library of Congress)

- Carla had read that president-elect Herbert Hoover had expressed the opinion that movies filled with debauchery were destroying America's image abroad.
- A Uruguayan editor had told him that American movies were a "main obstacle to the proper understanding and esteem between the United States and the South American countries" because the films showed only "cabaret life, the sins of society and crime."
- This was an argument Carla had not thought of. The horrors of World War I, she thought, had proved that every tool, including movies, should be marshaled toward the cause of international understanding so as to prevent another devastating war.

Life in the Community: Topeka, Kansas

- The Woman's Christian Temperance Union had become interested in the monitoring of movies as far back as the 1890s, at the dawn of the fledgling industry.
- The WCTU's first goal was the creation of motion pictures useful for educational and moral reform, followed quickly by the establishment of an environment appropriate for young people within the nickelodeons and picture palaces.
- They even got an agreement from Thomas Edison that his movie studio would not promote drinking scenes.
- Mostly they had to settle for modification of the content of films distributed in their region that they regarded as immoral or wrongheaded.
- Many fretted that movies were taking the place of parents as the primary teacher of young children, and this was an issue that should resonate especially with mothers.
- Their fear that films could have a strong negative influence had been vindicated many times.
- For example, after the 1910 Johnson-Jeffries heavyweight fight in which black boxer Jack Johnson defeated the "Great White Hope," champion Jim Jeffries, race riots erupted all over the United States.
- Noting that "unwonted elation among the more ignorant negroes" caused poor whites to become violent, the WCTU petitioned Congress to ban films of prize fights.
- Officials in nine states and in scores of racially mixed cities quickly moved to bar prize-fight films, and by 1912 a federal law banned films featuring a prize fight.
- Since 1912 alone, nearly 10,000 films had been produced.

Pie-eating contest (Omar F. Hawkins)

- In 1915 the U.S. Supreme Court ruled that motion pictures could be regulated because they were not art but instead were created only to make money; thus, the First Amendment did not apply.
- Kansas created a Board of Review shortly thereafter.
- Nationally the WCTU was focused on federal regulation, especially once movies with sound were being advertised.
- Without a doubt, every decent woman in America knew that the movie moguls would try to make more money by adding dirty words to their films.
- In 1922, as a direct result of the reformers' work, the Motion Picture Producers and Distributors Association hired Will Hays, a former Postmaster General, to regulate the industry itself.

Firestone tires being loaded onto a railcar (Omar F. Hawkins)

- After a short period of elation, the WCTU soon grew disappointed because Hays would not compel filmmakers to meet the WCTU's standards of purity.
- Many came to believe that the $150,000 annual salary paid to Will Hays was a down payment on his soul.
- In 1925 the national WCTU disbanded its Department of Purity in Literature and Art and instead formed a Motion Picture Department to advocate for censorship laws.
- In Kansas the film reviewers often deleted drinking scenes from movies, making the Kansas WCTU a powerful voice for censorship.
- Their deletions also included scenes of white women in physical danger at the hands of villainous, leering Chinamen, German spies, and Mexican assaulters.
- Chastity was paramount, and depictions and suggestions of blacks and whites "mixing" were to be avoided, including scenes of black men looking at a woman's figure.
- After watching the 1920 film *The House of Blindness*, the Kansas board of review demanded that the pivotal scene in which Dora was forced to drink poison be removed.
- As a result, that section of the film wound up on the cutting room floor, although it was untouched in other states.
- Kansas was not alone in its attempt to control the potentially "debasing" new medium.
- Virginia, Maryland, New York, Pennsylvania, and Ohio—as well as approximately 50 cities—had also created boards to review and censor movies.
- Since the review boards took an active role in monitoring the moral content of films, movie makers were forced to adapt the film state by state, based on the state boards' sensitivities.
- Approval guidelines included the review of subtitles, spoken dialogue, songs, other words or sounds, and advertising materials such as folders and posters to make sure they were "moral and proper."
- When the board viewed films, it was looking for moving picture shows that were "cruel, obscene, indecent or immoral, or such as tend to debase and corrupt morals."
- In Kansas all films to be shown had to be first passed by a board of three censors.
- This board not only had the power to remove any scenes that corrupted morals but could ban films completely.
- After being reviewed and edited, the film was tagged with a unique serial number that allowed it to be distributed for public showing.
- Penalties for showing unauthorized films ranged from a substantial fine to 30 days in the county jail.

- The state review boards met with substantial resistance from the motion picture industry, which was forced to pay for both the initial review and any subsequent edits.
- Motion picture companies spent significant sums lobbying legislators and trying to influence local elections.
- Some movie houses even recruited and then promoted anti-censorship candidates on the big screen itself.
- The first rating system was started in Chicago in 1914, when an official restricted attendance to the movie *The Scarlet Letter* to persons over the age of 21.
- Even though women in the community supported showing the film, the official frankly admitted that he did not know how to explain to his 15-year-old daughter the meaning of the scarlet "A," which was so central to the plot.
- Afterward, movies restricted to those over 21 were issued "pink permits."

Memorial Hall, Topeka

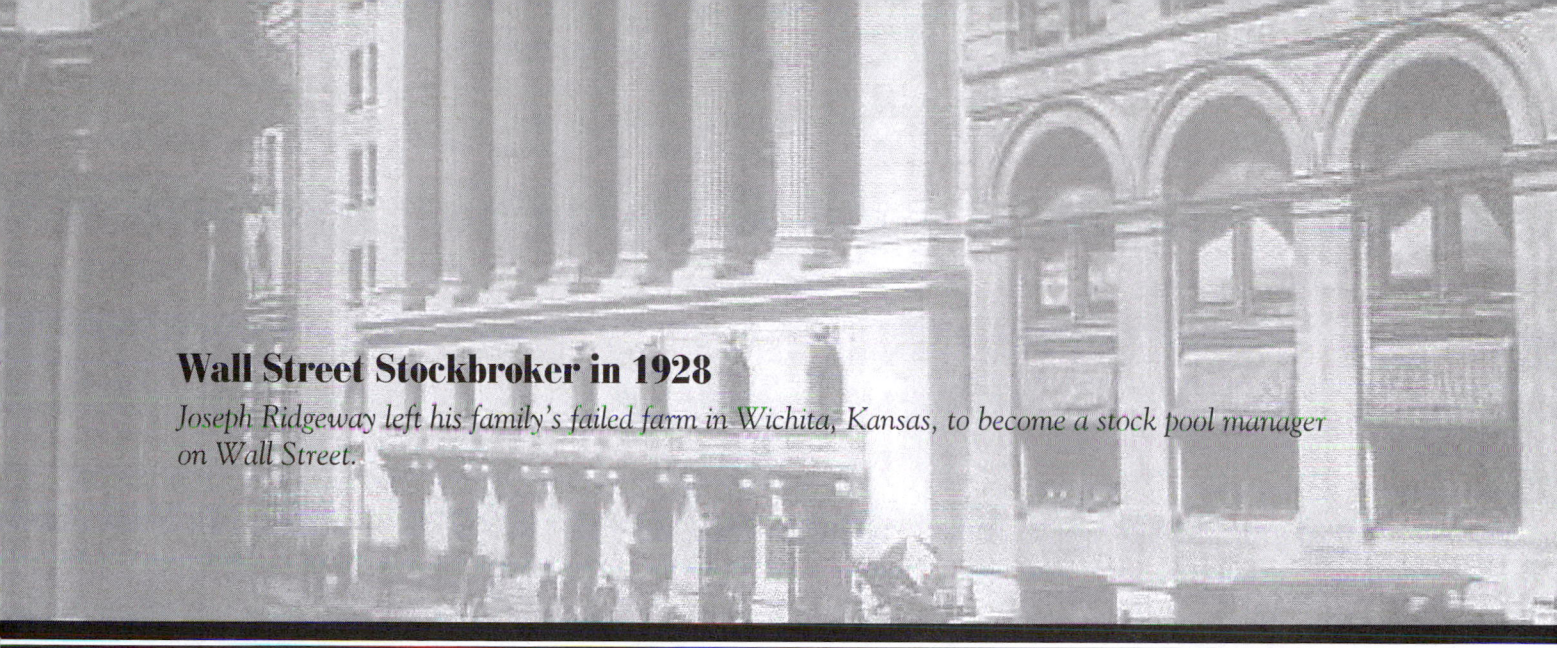

Wall Street Stockbroker in 1928

Joseph Ridgeway left his family's failed farm in Wichita, Kansas, to become a stock pool manager on Wall Street.

Life at Home

- Joseph Ridgeway didn't mind being condemned in the press for being rich.
- He loved being so rich he didn't always remember what he owned.
- Once, vacationing in Cuba, he bought a car and then left it behind when he returned to New York; one night he picked up the tab for an entire restaurant.
- Joseph had known poor, and he had no desire to make its acquaintance again.
- Born during the Panic of 1893, Joseph grew up hearing stories of how his parents lost the farm in Wichita, Kansas, to the bankers and the railroad barons.
- First they had been victims of the railroads, which squeezed the profit out of the wheat crop every year when it came time to ship the harvest eastward.
- Then the bankers, all dressed in clean suits, used a piece of legal paper to take away three generations of hope and hard work.
- Joseph's grandfather, using his Civil War-issue Springfield rifle, committed suicide beneath a cottonwood tree after one particularly devastating harvest.
- His father grew more and more bitter every year, and he didn't object when his eldest son announced one day that farming was not part of his future.
- His goal, Joseph announced that same day, was to go East and see where the money was hiding.
- Obviously it wasn't being allowed to travel westward to Kansas.
- Educated in the public schools, in which hunting season routinely took precedence over a history test, Joseph possessed enough charm and mathematical ability to catch the attention of a well-established local rancher, Kevin Hatcher.
- When Hatcher was a young man, cattle ranching had paid well for those who worked hard and were fortunate enough to have inherited vast stretches of land.

Joseph Ridgeway

- The railroads were the key to economic growth in the second half of the nineteenth century, and at first everyone prospered.
- For the first time in U.S. history, agricultural and manufactured goods could be shipped cheaply and efficiently throughout the country.
- Entrepreneurialism flourished until the railroad began fixing prices for the regular farmer and dropping prices for the few.
- Total rail mileage in the United States grew from 53,000 miles in 1870 to just under 200,000 miles at the turn of the twentieth century.
- Along with the railroad boom came solutions to problems that had plagued the industry in the past.

Deluxe overland limited train: Atchison, Topeka and Santa Fe Railroad (Library of Congress)

- Cross-country scheduling became easier in 1883 when the railroads established the Eastern, Central, Mountain, and Pacific time zones across the United States.
- Shipping delays caused by railroads using tracks of different gauges were resolved in 1886, when almost all the companies adopted a 4-foot, 8-11/42 inch standard.
- But intense competition among railroads led some into bankruptcy, sank others heavily into debt, and ignited ruinous rate wars.
- To limit competition, lines operating in the same region sometimes worked out an agreement to share the territory or divide the profit equally at the end of the year.
- Known as pooling, this process kept rates artificially high, and it enraged ranchers like Kevin Hatcher.
- The railroad companies competed against each other by paying kickbacks or rebates to large customers while making up losses by charging small shippers more.
- Because of such practices, rates were often lower for a long haul than for a short one; shipping goods from Chicago to New York, for example, where several companies had routes, was cheaper than sending the same shipment from Buffalo to Pittsburgh, where only one railroad had a monopoly.
- The unfairness of such rate-setting practices led to passage of the Interstate Commerce Act of 1887, which required that rates must be "reasonable" and prohibited pooling, rebates, and long/short haul rate differentials.
- To Hatcher's way of thinking—law or no law—the railroad men got fatter every year while the farmers got leaner.
- Hatcher had long harbored a need to control his own destiny, and he had come to the conclusion that that meant controlling a piece of Wall Street.
- Hatcher understood that he was too old to learn the ways of the big city, but the combination of his money and Joseph's abilities might give them both a chance.
- If pooling had worked for the railroads, maybe it could be made to work in the stock market as well.
- In 1911, when he turned 18, Joseph became Hatcher's willing apprentice.

Real Wild West Show, 1927 (Library of Congress)

- Together they worked out how to legally manipulate the stock market so that America's wealth could start flowing westward again.
- To finance his scheme, Hatcher sold some of his best land—to the railroad men, ironically—and leveraged the rest of his ranch to borrow more.
- When Joseph was 24, Hatcher decided that the younger man's education was complete and financed his trip to New York City.
- It was time to challenge the big boys at their own game.

Life at Work

- Joseph Ridgway started out as a ticket broker, scalping aisle seats to Broadway hits for partners and executives with the big banks, such as Morgan, Lehman, and Goldman Sachs.
- The men of Wall Street loved Joseph's eagerness and soon helped him set himself up as a curb broker.
- The New York Curb Market operated outdoors for decades after the New York Stock Exchange Board moved indoors.
- At first the independent curb brokers continued to operate literally at the curb of the Stock Exchange's New Street entrance.
- The Curb Market, still outdoors, later moved to Broad Street but retained its raucous, unregulated, and allegedly unscrupulous ways; in 1920 an assistant attorney general characterized the curb market as a "public nuisance."

Stock Exchange and Bankers Trust building, Wall Street, New York (Irving Underhill, Library of Congress)

- It was also something of a tourist attraction, and Joseph immediately took to its theatrical side.
- Meanwhile, it had become clear that the market would soon lose its outdoor venue (transactions in which actually depended on the activity of clerks in some of the surrounding buildings, now being eyed by the likes of J. P. Morgan), and in June 1921 the New York Curb Market moved indoors to a new building at Trinity Place.
- Joseph had fared well as a curb broker, sharpening his skills as a bold and agile trader; before the new Curb Market building opened, however, he had moved to the Stock Exchange—the seat of wealth and power worldwide.

Curb brokers on Wall Street

- Wall Street had become the world's money center only recently—in 1914—and by default; until then, London, England, had ruled the world financial markets for decades.
- But when London money managers suspended gold payments against the pound sterling in the opening weeks of World War I, the financial center of the world quickly shifted to New York.
- When Joseph began trading, the market was highly vulnerable.

- The aftermath of World War I had caused uncertainty, inflation, shifting alliances, and overproduction.
- In 1921, when the average price of all farm products was cut in half, Joseph learned the fine art of the bear raid: making money in a falling market.
- Then, in 1922, he learned to be a bull when it came to hot automobile products.
- After all, between 1921 and 1923, the annual factory sales of passenger cars rose from $1.5 million to $3.6 million, and the total number of motor vehicles on American roads increased from 10.5 million to 15.1 million.
- Most of all, Joseph learned the art of market volatility; there was money to be made within huge swings in the market.

Dairy farmer tuning in to radio at milking time (Library of Congress)

- But the real money was waiting to be made in legal stock manipulation—the engineering of a rapid rise in a specific stock followed by a rapid, controlled decline.
- That was the business Joseph for which had been trained; that's how Eastern money was going to move West.
- Joseph Ridgeway was elated when he was invited to be part of a small group prepared to manipulate the price of Radio Corporation, one of the hottest issues on the market.
- Under a formal partnership agreement approved by their lawyers, the nine men in the room agreed to purchase one million shares, with a value of $90 million.
- They had also engaged the services of the stock exchange member who acted as the floor specialist for radio stock.
- At the start of the manipulation, the price of the stock was $90.
- Using a series of carefully contrived maneuvers, deliberately calculated to deceive the investing public, the stock pool manager quickly drove the price to $109 a share.
- The rapid rise caught the attention of the regular investors, who jumped at the chance to ride the wave of this new hot stock, not understanding that the price rise was artificial and controlled by nine wealthy men.
- That's when Joseph and his partners began unloading the stock, taking a profit on every share.
- The entire operation took a little over a week; the stock specialist received a $500,000 fee and the nine men split $5 million.
- Joseph kept $150,000 and banked $400,000 for his backer, Kevin Hatcher.
- It was all a perfectly legal and even common practice on Wall Street; often, the directors of the companies whose stock was being manipulated themselves participated in the profit-taking.
- Only the "rubes" from the street, many of whom bought on margin, took a loss, having borrowed most of the money to buy a hot stock in expectation of a big payout.
- But when the hot stock lost too much value, the broker would have to sell it; thus, the stock investor would be without the stock but would still owe money for it.
- The radio was the perfect vehicle for creating a hot stock: the medium was new and mysterious, and it was difficult to fathom its real money-making potential.
- By the end of 1923, an estimated 400,000 households had a radio, a jump from 60,000 just the year before, and in that year's spring catalog, the Sears, Roebuck Company offered its first line of radios, while Montgomery Ward was preparing a special 52-page catalog of radio sets and parts.

- Overnight, it seemed, everyone went into broadcasting: newspapers, banks, public utilities, department stores, universities and colleges, cities and towns, pharmacies, creameries, and hospitals.
- Broadcasters decided to give listeners a mix of culture, education, information, and some entertainment.
- The information included financial news; Joseph privately thought that some of what he heard on the airwaves should have been classed as entertainment.
- To Joseph running a stock pool was simplicity itself—using the stock exchange ticker tape to tell a story that was

Radio operator

essentially false, he could lure an all-volunteer army of investors into the pool just as the price was peaking.
- The first time Joseph ran his own pool, he spent almost 60 days quietly acquiring a large block of shares of Hudson Motor Car Company for himself and three other investors.
- This was made easier when the company agreed to participate in the pool manipulation and gave Joseph an option to buy company shares at a fixed price.
- On behalf of the pool, Joseph as pool manager began buying and selling shares of the stock at frequent intervals in no apparent pattern.
- Sometimes he would even buy and sell stock between members of the pool to generate activity for tape watchers eager to run with the next wave.
- The constant appearance of the stock symbol on the tape as each transaction was recorded served as an advertisement, drawing in more investors.
- At some point, the manipulation became self-sustaining as public buying pushed the price higher and higher with no help from the pool manager.
- That's when Joseph's skills were tested: how and when he "pulled the plug" would determine his investors' profits.
- Cautiously he fed stock into the market, attempting to keep the price high as long as possible before dumping thousands of shares.
- During the roller coaster ride, his investors who bought at the bottom and sold at the top experienced a rise of $41 per share, while the investing public received everything from small profits to large losses.
- Joseph managed to make $1.2 million; America's money was flowing westward.
- Everyone on Wall Street considered the work of a pool manager a high art; even the investing public did not object because they thought that one day they, too, would hit the big time.
- Newspaper and radio reporters and editors played the market alongside everyone else, but often they had the advantage of inside information.
- Some accepted payoffs for stock tips; others were bribed to tout certain stocks, receiving cash or information.
- The word was that reporters on all of the big newspapers could be bought.
- But some of the New York newspapers were less obliging; they began publishing Joseph's activities when a pool buy was first developing, robbing it of its secrecy.
- They even called it fraud and Joseph a scoundrel.
- Early in 1928, Joseph solved most of his publicity problems by allowing certain reporters to participate in the pool.

- Only the *Wall Street Journal* declined the opportunity and managed to provide a day-to-day accounting of Joseph's current stock pool.
- Thanks to the publicity and the eagerness of the public to win on the rise of stock, the pool was a huge success, but Joseph's reputation was tarnished.
- After an exchange of letters with Kevin Hatcher, Joseph decided that his Wall Street career had run its course; he sold all of his stock on Wall Street and prepared to return home a multimillionaire.
- As Joseph boarded the train back to Kansas, he couldn't help but wonder what excitement he would be missing in 1929.

Life in the Community: Wall Street, New York City

- Located in Lower Manhattan, Wall Street runs east from Broadway to South Street on the East River, through the historical center of the financial district.
- The name of the street was handed down from the seventeenth century, when Wall Street formed the northern boundary of the New Amsterdam settlement and a stockade wall was constructed there to protect against Indian attacks and English colonial encroachment.
- By the late eighteenth century, a buttonwood tree at the foot of Wall Street had become the daily gathering place for traders and speculators; in 1792, the traders formalized their association through the Buttonwood Agreement, which led directly to the foundation of the New York Stock Exchange.
- In 1817 the signers of the Buttonwood Agreement adopted a constitution and named themselves the New York Stock and Exchange Board, moving into rented quarters at 40 Wall Street.
- The name was officially shortened to the New York Stock Exchange in 1863.
- Two years later, in 1865, the NYSE moved to 10–12 Broad Street, just south of Wall Street, where it remained until its move to 18 Broad Street in 1903.
- Wall Street's architecture was generally rooted in the Gilded Age, the era of the robber barons, extending approximately from the end of Reconstruction in 1878 until the turn of the century.
- "Wall Street" swiftly came to symbolize financial and economic power and elitism.
- The business of business was highly pleasurable for many Americans in the second half of the 1920s.
- America was producing five million automobiles a year; overall corporate earnings were rising rapidly, and it was a good time to be in business.
- Wall Street was attracting an army of investors, eager to live the American dream; everyone knew someone who had done well in the market.
- A broad market rise began in the last six months of 1924.
- In May 1924 the *New York Times* put the average price for 25 industrial stocks at 106; in December 1926, the *Times* industrial average had more than doubled, to 245, a gain of 69 points for that year alone.
- In June 1928 five million shares changed hands.
- The year ended with the *Times* industrial average up 86 points for the year, at 331, with a dramatic increase in brokers' loans, or stocks purchased on margin with little or no money down.
- In 1928 brokered loans increased from $1.5 billion to $6 billion.
- Speculative fever had been intensified by the decision of the Federal Reserve System to lower the rediscount rate from 4 percent to 3.5 percent in August 1927, and to allow the purchase of government securities in the open market.
- In January 1928 President Coolidge publicly stated that he did not consider the volume of brokers' loans too high, giving White House approbation to the inflation that was already worrying the more sober minds of the financial community.
- These analysts had already recognized that while stock prices had been climbing, business activity was subsiding.
- By February 1928 the director of the Charity Organization Society in New York reported that unemployment was more serious than at any time since immediately after the Great War.

- Moody's Investors Service said that stock prices had "over-discounted anticipated progress" and wondered "how much of a readjustment may be required to place the stock market in a sound position."
- The financial editor of the *New York Times* described the picture of current conditions presented by the mercantile agencies as one of "hesitation."
- The newspaper advertisements of investment services asked, "Will You 'Overstay' This Bull Market?" and "Is the Process of Deflation Under Way?"
- The air was fogged with uncertainty; despite the qualms of the experts, however, delirium reigned in the market.

Unemployment line

William Allen Rogers, "The Makers of Wall Street," from the New York Herald, *October 16, 1916 (Cabinet of American Illustration, Library of Congress)*

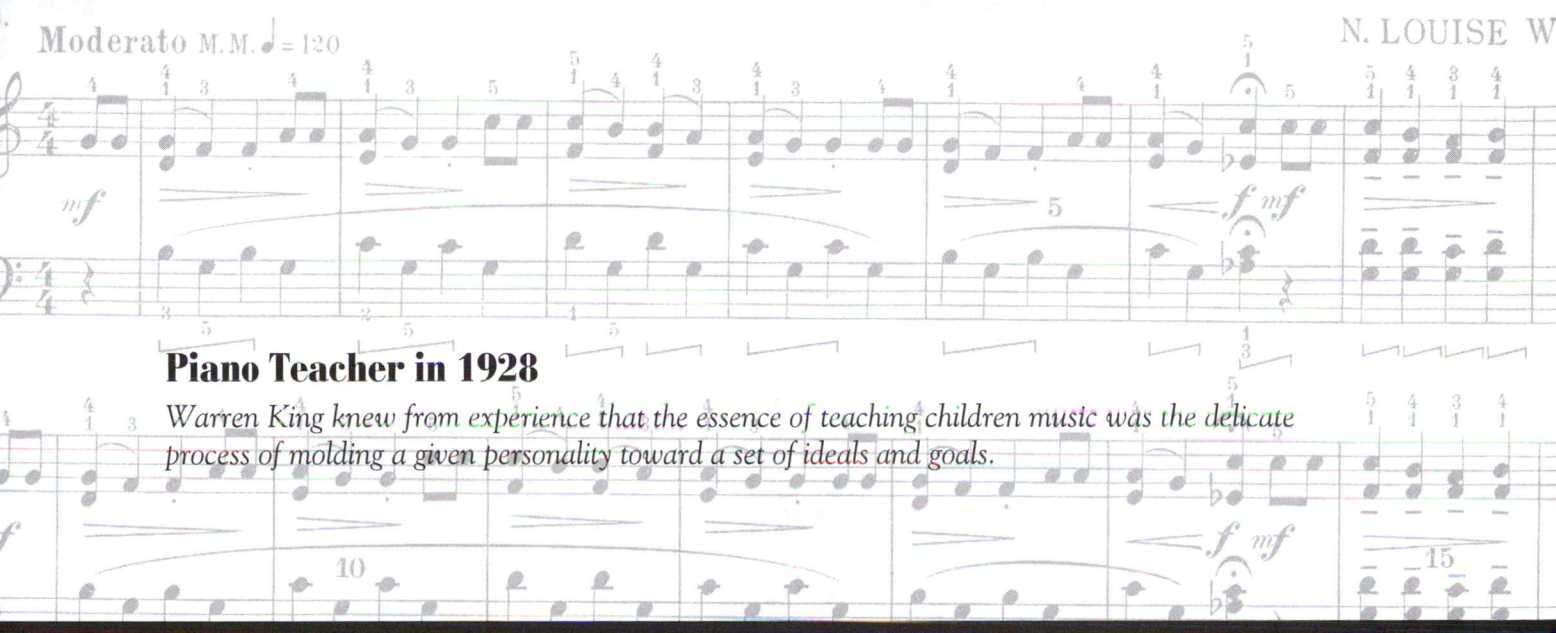

Piano Teacher in 1928

Warren King knew from experience that the essence of teaching children music was the delicate process of molding a given personality toward a set of ideals and goals.

Life at Home

- The third of five children, Warren King had no desire to compete with his athletic older brothers or his artistic younger sisters, both of whom, encouraged by their mother, were showing promise as painters.
- Warren first played the piano while sitting on his father's lap; at age three he would sneak into the music room and attempt to pick out notes he had heard his eldest brother play during his weekly lesson.
- One day, he was found perched on the piano bench composing a little song; lessons were started the next day.
- Warren's father was a successful contractor who had substantially increased his fortune by prudently riding the economic wave of the 1920s; Baltimore, Maryland, was prospering, and that meant that the King family was doing well.
- Two major office buildings in the center of town and a 3,000-acre subdivision on the edge of town were all the work of King Construction.
- In their social circle, the Kings were considered trendsetters; they were among the first to get a radio, install a telephone in their home, and purchase an electric toaster.
- The latest-model car was always parked in the family garage, protected from the weather; it shared the space with a child's motorbike and the most inventive toys available.
- Warren's mother led a ladies' group discussion on the first Tuesday of the month, intellectually wrestling with some of the major issues of the day.
- The group, to which a number of the leading women of the city belonged, was currently debating the right of professional women to receive pay equal to that of men's for the same work.
- Warren was educated in private schools and was tutored each afternoon in music, Greek, Latin, and fine art.

Warren King

Warren started playing at a young age (Library of Congress)

- Pampered for most of his childhood because of severe asthma and an early childhood episode with whooping cough, Warren learned early that playing the piano not only delighted him but brought him welcome attention.
- Although he was accepted at half a dozen elite colleges, Warren elected to attend the University of Maryland.
- There he came to understand—through good examples and bad—that the characteristic that most distinguished an effective teacher was an incessant desire for learning.
- This trait, he thought, should follow from the natural curiosity of children, who were forever bubbling over with wonder and curiosity about all the things around them.
- But this sense of curiosity was often blocked through faulty teaching, unsympathetic parents, the child's environment, and other factors, causing children to grow into maturity with a dull and stunted interest in the world around them.
- Therefore they tended to grow up concerned about only their own personal advancement.
- Following college, Warren went to work in the family construction business.
- It was his job to attend civic functions to meet the city's most influential people, to prospect for new business, and to create a marketing department.
- His father and two older brothers would focus on the actual construction projects, estimating costs, negotiating the final contract prices, and overseeing every detail of the projects.
- Warren tried hard to fit into the rough, hypermasculine world of heavy construction, but after three years, it had become clear that four Kings at King Construction was one King too many.
- At the insistence of his highly talented and super-competitive brothers, King Construction bought out Warren's financial interest in the company.
- Bored, Warren couldn't have been more pleased: no more civic functions, no more construction; no more brotherly competition, or irritation; plenty of money to live on; and a chance to test his teaching theories on dozens of developing talents.
- Baltimore possessed a long and rich artistic tradition; Warren set his sights on lifting the city's talent to the next level by properly training the fingers, minds, and hearts of his piano students.

Life at Work

- As a teacher Warren worked at something of a disadvantage; he himself had been a child prodigy who never seriously desired to do anything except play and teach piano.
- For him practice was play and performance a reward; as a child he had enjoyed bicycle riding and games of cowboys and Indians with his friends, but such activities paled in comparison with creating sublime music at the piano.
- It was difficult for him to understand how it was that everyone did not regard playing the piano as a privilege.
- His devotion to music did not, however, take the form of a desire for a solo performing career.

Billboard for Jordan Piano Company (National Photo Collection, Library of Congress)

- Warren had relished attending Baltimore Symphony Orchestra concerts at the Lyric Theatre since the orchestra's first concert in 1916; the Lyric was modeled after Amsterdam's Concertgebouw, a hall Warren had visited and admired.
- Much as he enjoyed hearing and learning from the piano soloists who appeared at the Lyric—their interpretations sometimes revealed new emotional depths in music Warren himself knew and had played—he thought his own talents were best employed elsewhere.
- In early 1923 Warren opened a ground-floor studio for piano lessons; the studio featured a sweeping view of the harbor and landscaping that pleased the eye and encouraged birds to linger.

Warren looked forward to working with young talent

- After five years of intense work, he well understood that teaching was indirect and subtle.
- Any direct effort to mold another's musical personality, even a young student's, was likely to meet with resistance.
- In fact, the more he taught, the more Warren came to believe that the word "teach" was inadequate for what he and his best pupils were trying to accomplish.
- At age 28, Warren King got up each morning with optimism; he looked forward to working with young talent and influencing his students' musical development.
- Warren's teaching style emphasized the need to nurture both the personality and the musical ability of his piano students.
- Success could not be achieved unless both areas were addressed.

Warren nurtured individual personalities and abilities (G. G. Bain Collection, Library of Congress)

- "The type of person that the teacher is will gradually be communicated to the pupil according to his sensitivity, and the pupil comes to strive to be likewise in some manner," Warren wrote, in an attempt to explain his approach to a college friend.
- It was a form of education by which results could be achieved simply by being in the presence of someone who was interested in the student's welfare.
- Parents, for example, had a very strong influence on their children over and above the education they attempted to impart, simply by their presence.
- Warren had observed that parents' attitudes and habits often affected the lives of their children more than anything the parents attempted to impart by way of instruction.
- The same principle applied to the piano teacher and to teaching the piano.
- Warren believed that over time, his own ideals and goals, seriousness of purpose, love of music, and sincerity would all have important effects on his pupils.
- Warren fully understood that few piano teachers approached their job in this way, but considering the

number of children who started playing the piano but stopped before achieving anything of lasting value, he thought he was justified in trying to find a better way.

- Alongside his earnestness about his vocation, Warren had a sense of humor and abundant dry wit, which often made his lessons delightful as well as absorbing.
- The majority of Warren's students were children, of varying degrees of natural ability and training, but he also had a substantial number of adult pupils.
- Warren was fascinated by the distinct challenges posed by teaching each group and experimented with different methods accordingly.
- Writing to another college friend who had taken a job at a music school in Philadelphia, Warren commented, "Treating all pupils alike connotes a lack of ability to distinguish essential differences in personalities; the greater the lack, the less talent one may be said to have for teaching."
- The best teachers, Warren believed, worked for the day when their pupils could take flight on their own as fully mature artists.
- For the very best, this might mean further training in Europe with one of a handful of almost legendary piano teachers who could trace their musical lineage back to a Liszt or a Czerny.

Life in the Community: Baltimore, Maryland

- Founded in 1729, Baltimore was the largest seaport in the Mid-Atlantic United States, situated closer to Midwestern markets than any other major seaport on the East Coast.
- Baltimore's Inner Harbor was the third leading port of entry for immigrants to the United States, behind only New York City and Boston, as well as a major manufacturing center.
- Named after Lord Baltimore, a member of the Irish House of Lords and the founding proprietor of the Maryland Colony, Baltimore was an Anglicization of the Irish Gaelic name *Baile an Tí Mhóir*, meaning "town of the big house."
- Baltimore played a key role in events leading to and including the American Revolution.
- The Second Continental Congress met in the Henry Fite House from December 1776 to February 1777, effectively making the city the capital of the United States during this period.
- The port city was the site of the Battle of Baltimore during the War of 1812.
- After burning Washington, D.C., the British attacked Baltimore on the night of September 13, 1814.
- Francis Scott Key, a Maryland lawyer, was aboard a British ship where he had been negotiating for the release of an American prisoner, Dr. William Beanes.
- Key witnessed the bombardment from his ship and later wrote "The Star-Spangled Banner," a poem recounting the attack.

Lexington Market, Baltimore (Library of Congress)

- Following the Battle of Baltimore, the city's population grew rapidly.
- The construction of the federally funded National Road and the private Baltimore and Ohio Railroad (B&O) made Baltimore a major shipping and manufacturing center by linking the city with prominent markets in the Midwest.
- Maryland did not secede from the Union during the Civil War; however, when Union soldiers marched through the city at the start of the war, Confederate sympathizers attacked the troops, which led to the Baltimore Riot of 1861.
- In 1904 the Great Baltimore Fire destroyed more than 1,500 buildings in 30 hours,

leaving more than 70 blocks of the downtown area burned to the ground; damages were estimated at $150 million.

- The fire began on February 7 in the five-story Hurst Building at Hopkins Place in the western part of downtown Baltimore, and it quickly went out of control.
- Fire officials tried to establish a firebreak; the Mayor Robert McLane ordered the dynamiting of buildings around the area already alight, but this tactic failed to stop the blaze.
- Firefighters and equipment arrived from Philadelphia and Washington, D.C.; equipment was also sent from New York City, but owing to a derailment, it failed to arrive until the next day,.
- The firefighting equipment rushed to Baltimore proved to be of limited use, chiefly because the hose couplings did not fit Baltimore's hydrants.
- High winds and freezing temperatures further complicated the firefighters' task.
- Horse-drawn pumpers were used by firemen trying to combat the blaze.

Ruins in the heart of the city after the Great Baltimore Fire, February 1904; Hurst Building at left (stereograph, Library of Congress)

- The Maryland National Guard and city police were deployed to maintain order, prevent looting, and keep citizens out of the fire zone; meanwhile, the Naval Brigade blockaded the harbor.
- In the harbor district the fire swept down to the water's edge.
- The offices of all of the city's major newspapers—the *Baltimore Herald, Baltimore Sun, Baltimore News,* and *Baltimore American*—were variously destroyed or heavily damaged.
- In exchange for photographs, the *Baltimore Herald* was able to publish an edition on the evening of February 7 from the presses of the *Washington Post;* it published in subsequent days from the presses of the *Philadelphia Evening Telegraph,* with the papers transported the 100 miles to Baltimore by a train provided free of charge by the B&O Railroad.
- Remarkably, it seemed at first that no lives had been lost directly to the blaze; two weeks afterward a body was recovered from the harbor, and four deaths among firefighters who had been on the scene were later ascribed to the fire.
- Just two years after "one of the greatest disasters of modern times," the *Baltimore Sun* declared that Baltimore was a "boom city," citing "marvelous progress in building, manufactures, municipal improvements and general business."
- The Baltimore Equitable Society had insured many of the buildings destroyed by the fire, and it paid off every claim.
- Only one church was destroyed by the fire, the Church of the Messiah at Fayette and Gay streets; the congregation retrieved the church's enormous bell and raised money for a new church by recasting the large bell as 2,800 smaller bells and selling them.
- Led by Mayor Robert McLane (until his untimely death, by suicide or murder, just four months after the fire) and Sherlock Swann, chairman of the four-member Burnt District Commission, Baltimore modernized as it rebuilt, adopting its first building code and making municipal improvements such as widening streets, creating parks, digging sewers, and piping running water to residential areas.
- Nationwide the fire inspired an effort to standardize firefighting equipment, particularly hose couplings.
- The city grew in area by annexing new suburbs from the surrounding counties, the last being in 1918, when the city acquired portions of Baltimore County and Anne Arundel County.

Grace Coolidge presents piano to Friendship House (National Photo Company Collection, Library of Congress)

Female Auto Engineer in 1929

Susan Burdick, a native of New York City, worked in the engineering department of Mack Trucks in Plainfield, New Jersey; in 1929 she had been with the company for more than ten years.

Life at Home

- Susan was born and raised on Sixtieth Street in New York City; her grandfather was a successful florist.
- After graduation from high school, she studied interior decorating at the School of Applied Design in New York City.
- A class in architecture captured her attention, and she migrated away from interior decorating.
- After the death of her father, she was able to travel to France, Switzerland, and Germany.
- When the First World War erupted, she returned to the United States and began doing animated cartooning for the International Film Company.
- There she was made a supervisor of other women.
- Woman suffrage and Prohibition have been features of her entire adult life.
- Mack Trucks was looking for women to replace the men going to war; she answered an advertisement and was hired.
- She did well with the company, working at the Plainfield facility; Mack Trucks had expanded in Plainfield after its 1911 merger with Saurer Motor Company.
- After moving to Plainfield, Susan still did much of her shopping in New York City, which was easily accessible by train; a year or so after her arrival in Plainfield, she was delighted when Tepper's, a grand new department store, opened on West Front Street.
- Tepper's offered stylish women's clothing reflecting the newest trends, and Susan loved to shop there.
- Both at home and at work, Susan prided herself on being patient and skillful with details.
- At work she took care to avoid any work habits she thought might lead co-workers to view her as a stereotypical female rather than as a colleague and an equal; she was not considered talkative.
- This year, in keeping with the current airplane craze, her boyfriend Carl, a co-worker, gave her a delightful valentine card showing a passenger airplane circling the Capitol, surrounded by a heart.

Susan Burdick

- Better still, he brought her chocolates from the confectioner's on East Front Street; Susan considered this shop to be the best confectioner's in town.
- Susan and Carl liked to go out to Plainfield's theaters, especially to see movies at the Paramount, and they often stopped at the new Clara Louise Tearoom on East Front Street, which was conveniently located just two blocks from the theater—and two blocks from Tepper's as well.
- Susan never failed to feel inspired by the Plainfield Public Library's sweeping entry staircase and its light-filled reading room; it was wonderful to have access to the materials acquired for the Babcock Scientific Library.
- She loved to cook and enjoyed all the new gadgets; she owned an electric mixer and an electric vacuum cleaner. She had looked at the new electric ranges but had not yet decided whether to purchase one.

- She rented her apartment in Plainfield but knew that one day she would have a house of her own, whether she married or not.
- Most of her clothes were cleaned at the commercial laundry; if she had the time, she liked to use the wet wash, picking up her clothes wet and taking them home to dry and iron. She did not like the way the laundry folded her clothes.
- Susan preferred to do her own ironing; her electric iron was so much easier to operate than the cast-iron, stovetop instrument her mother continued to use.

Life at Work

- Susan got her job by answering a newspaper advertisement from Mack Trucks seeking women with training in technical drawing.
- The flood of men going to Europe to fight in the First World War had reduced the number of available draftsmen, and Mack purposely sought out women.
- Encouraged by her success at Mack, she began studying engineering at night.
- While still working at Mack, she went to Cooper Union in Manhattan, becoming the first woman admitted to engineering classes; her course work took three years.
- Her artistic skills and love of mathematics helped her in her studies.
- Susan regularly read technical papers with titles like "Springs and Shock Insulators" in preparation for her degree.

Susan at work

- She graduated with honors and was admitted into the Society of Automotive Engineers, becoming the first woman to earn that honor.
- At first Susan was asked to work on the interior design of the Mack Truck, a more traditionally female job; this was a disappointment, but she said little and did her work.
- Then help was needed to design the drive train of an engine.

- Having done well with that project, Susan was assigned to design brake piping for air brakes; she was proud that she was no longer confined to work traditionally allocated to women.
- Nevertheless, the company's internal publication, the *Mack Bulldog*, had recently done a story about the company's "girl designer."
- Few middle-class women worked outside the home; almost all of the professional jobs open to women were in teaching, social work, and nursing.
- Even now colleges and universities offered few women the opportunity to become professors.
- The only woman in her 20-person design department, Susan was careful of how she dressed; most days she wore a silk dress and light smock.
- The men dressed in dark business suits and ties every day; currently, most wore a double-breasted suit with wide lapels and padded shoulders.
- The style allowed businessmen to appear more athletic and aggressive, both qualities associated with success.
- The men were all clean-shaven, and all wore hats to work—taking care to remove them on entering a building and in the presence of a woman.
- Everyone understood how important it was to "fit in" if you wished to be successful in the "modern world."
- Susan's office fully adopted the scientific management methods of specialization; consultant Frederick Taylor believed that efficiency was enhanced if employees did only one job, such as opening mail, bookkeeping, or designing truck parts.
- Roll-top desks were replaced by more efficient, three-draw desks backed by file cabinets.
- Desktop neatness was paramount: too many papers would only distract workers.
- At Mack all of the clerks used identical nibs on dipping pens; executives and middle-level employees such as Susan were allowed to use fountain pens instead.
- As a designer, Susan believed that appearances should matter down to the tiniest detail, and she liked scientific management.

Susan with colleague

Mack buses

Life in the Community: Plainfield, New Jersey

- Plainfield's growth resulted from the opening of railroad service in 1838 between Plainfield and Elizabethtown, where passengers could board a ferry and cross Newark Bay to New York.
- As railroad service improved, it became feasible for residents to commute to New York City.
- With the Watchung Mountains—actually three long volcanic ridges stretching some 40 miles and offering fine views, including of the New York City skyline—close by, Plainfield had established itself as a country resort town.

- From 1879 the Netherwood Hotel was a popular destination, and tourist attractions included Tier's Pond and the Plainfield Amusement Academy, which offered a variety of attractions, including circuses.
- Many city dwellers from New York and Philadelphia who came to Plainfield for vacations and recreation eventually decided to move there and commute to their city jobs.
- By the mid-1880s, the area's once predominately agricultural economy had been transformed, chiefly owing to the railroad; hats, clothing, carriages, and other manufactured goods were produced in the city.
- There were two train depots, the Clinton Avenue station, a three-story building housing the stationmaster's family on the second floor, and the newer Grant Avenue station; both were in the southwestern part of Plainfield.
- The main business section coalesced on Front Street between Cherry Street and Peace Street.
- Plainfield drew vacationers but also residents of the surrounding areas, who came to shop, do business, and enjoy movies and other entertainment on offer.

- The city had advanced public health institutions; Muhlenberg Hospital was incorporated in 1877 and moved to a new location at Park Avenue and Randolph Road in 1903; the Visiting Nurse Association (VNA) in the Babcock Building was first organized in 1911 and was incorporated in 1915.
- By 1927 the VNA offered services not only to Plainfield proper but to five surrounding towns; the VNA staffed ten well-baby stations as well as dental and hygiene clinics, and it conducted school health screenings for 35 schools.
- Andrew Carnegie underwrote Plainfield's new public library on Library Park; the library was dedicated in February 1913.
- In 1919 the Plainfield Symphony Orchestra was established.
- For most of the 1920s, the economy in New Jersey was booming, as was true of much of the rest of the country.
- Nationwide the number of gainfully employed persons increased from 41.6 million in 1920 to 48.8 million in 1930.
- The number of manufacturing jobs remained steady, at approximately 11 million, during most of the decade; the number of middle-class occupations increased from 11.5 million to 16.7 million.
- Office machines such as typewriters, addressing machines, mechanical accounting machines, and dictating machines were in widespread use.

Mack commercial trucks (above and above right)

- Although the telephone was accepted as standard for business, more Americans owned cars than rented telephones.
- Mack began its operations in Allentown, Pennsylvania, and through a merger with Saurer Motor Company in 1911 expanded its operations in Plainfield.
- Trucks were part of America's love affair with the automobile; in 1920, Secretary of the Interior Franklin K. Lane had reported that the United States had more automobiles than did all of the nations of the world combined.
- By 1929 the number of automobiles in the nation had increased fourfold over the number in 1920.
- Trucks had begun to appear in 1904 but became numerous only in the 1920s.

- Jack Mack was inspired to build a large commercial motor vehicle in 1901 after riding in a neighbor's new two-cylinder Winton automobile.
- The first Mack Brothers' sightseeing bus used a four-cylinder, 24-horsepower engine capable of speeds up to 20 miles per hour.
- Solid tires were standard on all trucks weighing a ton or more, which allowed a top speed of 20 miles per hour on good roads and 15 miles per hour on country roads; pneumatic tires were introduced in 1919, permitting higher speeds.
- In 1916 Mack introduced the model AC, with its highly distinctive hood and the nickname "Bulldog": the 74-horsepower vehicle helped the company launch the slogan "Built Like a Mack Truck."
- More than 4,000 Mack AC trucks were ordered for the American armed forces during World War I; the trucks were so successful that the American Expeditionary Forces declared the Bulldog to be their only standard truck in capacities of five tons or more.
- The name of the company was changed from the International Motor Truck Company to Mack Trucks, Incorporated, in 1922 in order to avoid confusion with a competitor, International Harvester Company.

Mack logo and company mascot

- Over 1926-1927, Mack introduced a complete line of high-speed, six-cylinder Mack trucks featuring four-speed transmission, dual-reduction rear axle, and four-wheel brakes.
- Mack products now included a line of truck equipment, such as winches, dump bodies, full trailers, and an aluminum container unit used for less-than-railcar-load-sized railroad freight.
- By 1910 only 10,000 trucks had been produced; in 1915 the annual output was 75,000 trucks, and by 1925 a half-million trucks were being built per year.
- At first most trucks were local carriers; few were used for interstate commerce. By 1929 trucks clearly were beginning to challenge the railroads for freight business.

- The "Good Roads" movement was gaining momentum nationwide; heavy-duty Mack Trucks were needed to haul crushed rock and asphalt for highway construction.
- Many of America's first modern highways were built by Mack equipment, which was used to spray a hot, bituminous binder on crushed rock to form a solid road surface.

*F*RIGIDAIRE supplies an *abundance* of protected drinking water at the proper temperature

Adam Checler, a Belgian immigrant and a successful lawyer, divided his time between his family's home in Houston, Texas, and offices in Washington, D.C., where he lobbied against the prevailing anti-immigration mood sweeping the government.

Life at Home

- In 1924 Adam Checler was a 51-year-old successful lawyer, already a grandfather nine times over and generally happy with his life.
- A Belgian immigrant and himself a proud naturalized citizen, Checler was grateful to the United States for all it had offered him and was fervently devoted to its founding principles of equality and justice under the law.
- As a lawyer and an informed citizen, he knew full well that the American reality frequently did not live up to those high ideals, but he thought it was the highest duty of every American to strive to uphold them.
- He had grown increasingly disturbed, he told friends, by the insidious nature of racist laws dressed up as economic protectionism.
- By 1929 Adam was living part-time in Washington, D.C., away from his precious children and grandchildren back in his beloved Houston, Texas, to work to defeat the anti-immigrant mood that was sweeping the nation.
- Americans, he observed, loved to describe their country as a "nation of immigrants" and to rhapsodize about how their own ancestors had arrived in America decades or even centuries before; yet they would go on to insist that "immigration today" was different, more dangerous, even a threat to the cause of democracy.

Adam Checler

- Adam had his own passionate opinions on that subject.
- Adam's parents had immigrated to New York City in 1881 when his father, Jean Checler, was named head of the American branch of a Belgian bank heavily invested in the import and export business with the United States.
- The bank needed a representative in the United States who could get along with Americans, who understood the shipping business, and—most of all—who could be trusted with complicated financial transactions.
- At the urging of his wife, the elder Checler accepted the short-term assignment, quickly

booked first-class passage to the United States for his family, and told friends to keep his seat warm at his downtown Brussels men's club; he would be back.

- Belgium was a growing, prosperous country in 1881; it was in the midst of an explosion of innovation in technical fields and in the arts.
- With so much going on in Europe, Jean Checler was eager for the experience offered by an American assignment, yet he had no desire to be abandoned in an American backwater for too long.
- Adam was a precocious eight-year-old at the time of the move.

Adam as a child

- He immediately fell in love with ice skating in Central Park, speaking English to his nanny, and playing in the park with his dog.
- He named the Irish wolfhound Hermina, after his Dutch grandmother, who had died the year he moved to America.
- Adam made friends easily; pupils at his private school were mostly middle or upper-middle class, but perhaps because he was not a native New Yorker, he was more or less indifferent to matters of class and wealth.
- In the United States, Adam's father prospered, away from the encumbrances of too many rules, too much supervision, too much fear of violating the old ways of doing business.
- In the business atmosphere of New York, his father worked meticulously and built a reputation for making solid deals that produced substantial income on both sides of the Atlantic.
- He also acquired a reputation as a knower of men, capable of remembering clients' names and the gist of their previous transactions without extensive notes or cumbersome bundles of legal documents.
- Although an alien who spoke with a pronounced accent, Jean Checler found in the United States the freedom to be successful, to experiment, and to be his own man.

Checker family photo

- The joy in resolving complex problems and the knack for remembering names were both qualities passed along to his son.
- Adam saw his father becoming somehow lighter and less burdened, yet he did not fully understand his father's attachment to America until the family was ordered by the bank to return to Belgium.
- The return trip included a month-long holiday, lots of visiting, and then a series of mysterious meetings.
- Within six months the family was back in New York City, his father now president of a newly created import/export financing business; permanently returning to Belgium was never discussed again.

Life at Work

- Adam Checler moved to Houston, Texas, after completing law school; he loved Houston's energy and considered it a wide-open canvas for a man seeking to make his fortune.
- Since 1924, Adam had been working on ways to ameliorate the harsh impact of immigration quotas set out in the Immigration Act of that year.
- The law was rooted in the viewpoint that the racial composition of the United States should not be altered by immigration.
- Political minds had decided that the best way to ensure that goal in the 1920s was to permit immigrants only in the same ratio as they had arrived in 1890.

Immigration officers boarding a tug (Library and Archives Canada)

- That way, the lawmakers said, the United States would maintain the "proper" mix of people and forestall the immigration of persons of nationalities that had shown themselves, so it was asserted, to be uninterested in learning English and unwilling to practice democracy or work hard.
- During the very public debate of the immigration bill, American "nativists" commonly referred to Southern and Eastern European immigrants as "undesirable races" and fought hard to continue the exclusion of Chinese and Japanese immigrants from eligibility for citizenship.
- Harvard-educated, Adam Checler was drawn into the debate by his legal work; from parsing legal nuances, he soon transitioned to making a full-throated defense of the downtrodden newcomers in Texas.
- "To those to whom much is given, much is expected," he repeatedly told his wife, Marie, as he planned yet another trip to Washington to lobby Congress.
- Between 1887 and 1923, the federal courts had handled 25 challenges to racial assumptions affecting citizenship rights, culminating in two landmark race rulings by the U.S. Supreme Court.
- In each case the Supreme Court's decision turned on whether the petitioner could be considered a "white person" within the meaning of the statute.
- Adam had become involved in his first legal case in 1921, following the First World War.
- In that case he confronted race-based restrictions that handicapped nonwhites in their effort to become citizens.
- Simply using a person's presumed "color" to determine nationality and eligibility for citizenship was insufficient, given the "overlapping of races and gradual merging of one into another without any practical line of separation," he had argued.
- That was legal reasoning and the argument from pragmatism, but in truth Adam was simply outraged by the notion of judging a person's worth not as an individual but as a member of a race or nationality, as though everyone of a given race or nationality were the same.

- Adam was repelled by what he saw as the hypocrisy of those who proclaimed their deep devotion to the ideals of the Declaration of Independence yet sought to deny others the rights they claimed for themselves.

- Adam was also unsettled by the evidence that all too many Americans welcomed immigrants when cheap labor was needed but considered them disposable afterward.

- Particularly offensive, he believed, were laws passed the decade before that were designed to drive Japanese and other Asians out of farming.

Naturalization class (National Photo Company, Library of Congress)

- He was aghast that the courts had ruled that the alien land laws were nondiscriminatory against Japanese because the law made all aliens ineligible to be citizens, making them all equally unequal.

- This, Adam proclaimed, was utter nonsense.

- To Marie's dismay and the wonderment of his friends, Adam poured his energy into filing lawsuits and conducting long-distance lobbying efforts against lawmakers who treated immigrants from different countries unequally.

- He was appalled that elected officials believed that white America needed to be protected from Spanish, Japanese, and Mexican immigrants "bent on taking over the land."

- Experience had taught him that the children and grandchildren of immigrants learned English, wanted to be Americans, and uniformly were assimilated into American culture, no matter their skin color.

- The battle to control immigration had become more intense in the last few years.

- Many Americans were unsettled by the shifts in immigration patterns that brought more workers from Southern and Eastern Europe and from parts of Asia and Mexico.

- Italians, for example, who made up 12 percent of immigrants in the early 1920s, attracted negative attention because of their darker skin.

- Groups formed around slogans such as "America for Americans."

Ku Klux Klan march, Washington D.C., 1926 (Library of Congress)

- The rapid growth and acceptance of the revived Ku Klux Klan was linked to halting the "encroachment of foreigners," especially those who did not speak English or who answered to a "foreign Pope as their religious authority."

- Protestant fundamentalist groups, in particular, championed anti-Catholic immigration campaigns.

- Immigrants were linked to excessive drinking by the supporters of Prohibition, and especially after the Bolshevik Revolution, anti-Communist groups preached about the immigrants' supposed secret agenda of spreading anarchism and Communism.

- Industrialists blamed the newcomers for the rising demands of labor unions, whose strikes were often branded as radical uprisings fomented by outside agitators.
- But despite the popularity of the immigration legislation passed in 1924, which limited immigration into the United States to 150,000 people a year and according to nation-based quotas, its implementation had been postponed several times.
- The first two reports submitted to Congress criticized Irish, German, and Scandinavian Americans for failing to take their populations in 1890 fully into account.
- Many Japanese, Chinese, and other Asians were angered that they were largely excluded altogether—a continuation of American policy dating back 50 years.
- Since the mid-nineteenth century, "scientific" race theorists had been working to develop systems of racial classification and typology.
- Toward this end, new questions were added to the 1910 and 1920 censuses in the hope of quantifying levels of assimilation by immigrant groups.
- These questions concerned literacy, ability to speak English, mother tongue, number of children born and living, and length of time in the United States.
- By 1928 the restrictive quotas had united in opposition the Young Men's Christian Association, church congregations, and the League of Women Voters, among other groups; favoring the quotas were the American Legion, the Grange, and the Daughters of the American Revolution.
- The issues universally concerned the quota system allotting immigration permits to countries in the same proportion that the American people traced their origins, using the 1890 census as a base.
- The Daughters of the American Revolution and the American Legion called on Congress to stand firm against the efforts of "hyphates" who would "play politics with the nation's bloodstream."
- The law rewarded whiteness while limiting ethnic Japanese, Chinese, Mexicans, and even Filipinos, despite the fact that the Philippines was a territory of the United States.

Immigrant family at Ellis Island (Lewis W. Hine)

- The act was not the first to limit or bar "undesirables" from American shores.
- The 1917 Immigration Act, which increased the entry head tax to $8.00, also excluded "all idiots, imbeciles, feeble-minded persons, epileptics, insane persons; persons who have had one or more attacks of insanity in any time previously; persons of constitutional psychopathic inferiority; persons with chronic alcoholism, paupers, professional beggars, vagrants, persons afflicted with tuberculosis in any form or with a loathsome or dangerous contagious disease; persons not comprehended within any of the foregoing excluded classes found to be certified by the examining surgeon as being mentally or physically defective, such physical defect being of a nature which may affect the ability of such alien to earn a living; persons who have been convicted of or admit having committed a felony or any other crime or misdemeanor involving moral turpitude; polygamists, or persons who practice polygamy or believe in the practice of polygamy; anarchists, or

persons who believe in or advocate the overthrow by force or violence of the government of the United States."

- The most controversial aspect of the 1917 act was the plan to exclude all aliens over 16 years of age who could not read "the English language, or some other language or dialect, including Hebrew or Yiddish."

- Attempts at introducing literacy tests into the immigration process had been vetoed by presidents Grover Cleveland (in 1891) and William Howard Taft (in 1913; Taft had been the first civilian governor-general of the Philippines).

- President Woodrow Wilson also objected to the literacy clause in the 1917 Immigration Act, but it was approved by Congress nevertheless.

- Now Adam was faced with new controversies over the Mexican "race problem" emerging in the Southwest, where he was from, sparked by all-time-high Mexican immigration; the immigrants were attracted by agricultural jobs.

Mexican American workmen (California Historical Society Collection)

- Immigration was threatening the region's current political and economic structure, and the pressure was on Mexico to refuse visas to all Mexican workers except those with prior residency in the United States.

- To halt illegal immigration from Mexico, Congress was even discussing making unlawful entry into the United States a felony offense.

- Adam argued that the new wave of immigration coincided with the emergence of a form of commercial agriculture that actually required the creation of a large migratory workforce.

- It was extremely unfortunate, he said, that the term "illegals" had become a synonym for "Mexican immigrant workers."

- Adam was in Texas on the day the new regulations were finally approved in 1929.

- His nine young grandchildren were more interested in learning to ride horses than in their grandfather's apprehensions about how the struggle over immigration was going to change the country.

Life in the Community: Houston, Texas

- Civil War General Sheridan was quoted as saying, "If I owned Texas and Hades, I'd rent Texas and move to the other place."

- But modern Texas was praised by *National Geographic* magazine in 1928: "Power and political experience have taught her tolerance. In her easy-going, slightly Mexican manner, she is too busy working out her own social problems and her huge economic destiny to worry over her past, sensational though it may have been."

- The rapid expansion of Texas agriculture was primarily responsible for the migration of Mexicans into the state after 1900.

- Texas had become so prosperous that employers found it difficult to get enough Mexican workers to pick its cotton, work its oil fields, or handle trainloads of fresh vegetables shipped annually from the lower Rio Grande.

- Mexicans were essential to the operations of the newly developed cotton fields of West Texas, and the development of large fruit and truck farming areas in Texas from about 1910 was the result of new irrigation projects and the availability of cheap Mexican labor.
- A million and a half cars of freight, mostly carrying farm products, originated in Texas every year; all told, approximately 3.5 billion cars of freight crossed the state annually.
- To meet this huge economic demand, workers came both lawfully, through immigration offices at the border, and illegally, across the Rio Grande—10,000 every year.

Burkburnett, Texas, oil field (Texas State Library and Archives Commission)

- Texas required a veritable army of Mexican and American labor to do its work.
- In addition to its enormous agricultural potential, Texas had produced more than $1 billion worth of oil over the second half of the decade.
- Texas surpassed Oklahoma in 1928 as the top oil producer among the states.
- In 1929 the four southwestern states of Texas, Oklahoma, Arkansas, and Louisiana accounted for some 60 percent of the crude oil production in the United States.
- The massive oil strike at Spindletop to the east of Houston in 1901 had marked the beginning of the oil industry in Houston, which soon was viewed as the energy capital of the nation, if not the world.
- By 1913, twelve oil companies were headquartered in Houston.
- Houston nearly doubled in size between 1910 and 1920, growing from 16 to 38 square miles, and, at 72 square miles, had nearly doubled again by 1929; the population was some 300,000.
- In the 1910s, like so many other American cities, Houston embarked on an era of civic improvements; the city began the creation of a chain of parkway corridors along the banks of its bayous.
- The main commercial artery and elite residential district were both on Main Street, a grand avenue that ran from the Buffalo Bayou through downtown and south to Rice Institute and Hermann Park.
- The financial district was on Main Street at Franklin Avenue; the residential area was to its south.
- North of Buffalo Bayou were numerous railroad lines that ran through Houston and the residential districts of much of the city's working class.
- Railroads were the underpinning of Houston's economy.

Main Street, Houston (stereograph, Library of Congress)

- By the 1890s, in Houston as in other American cities, people were ready to leave the city center for more serene and secure surroundings, and suburbs sprang up in every direction beyond what was then the edge of town.
- The electrification of the streetcar system made the suburbs accessible, especially for working families; the developers of Houston's Houston Heights suburb

actually bought Houston's streetcar system so that they could electrify it and extend it out to the Heights.

- The connection between real estate development and urban infrastructure improvements in Houston was unmistakable.
- Cotton and timber flowed through the Houston port, which was finally opened in 1914, nearly 75 years work on the port began.
- The opening of the Houston Ship Channel in 1917 led to the construction of two military installations in Harris County: Camp Logan and Ellington Field.
- Houston was a rigidly segregated city, and when the Army deployed a battalion of the all-black 24th Infantry Regiment to guard the Camp Logan construction site, racial tensions simmered and then flared.
- After an incident on August 17 in which a white policemen bludgeoned a black soldier, panic and confusion swelled into a riot as the soldiers poured into the city; the Camp Logan Riot resulted in the deaths of 15 whites and 4 black soldiers.
- In subsequent courts-martial, 110 soldiers (out of 118 indicted) were found guilty of mutiny and riot; 19 were hanged and 63 received life sentences. No white policemen or civilians were punished.
- During the early 1920s the reorganized Ku Klux Klan, first revived in Georgia in 1915, was the primary force in the politics of the Southwest.
- Wartime propaganda, xenophobia, and the hysteria of the Red Summer of 1919, when race riots flared across the country, fed the popularity of the Klan.
- The rise of the Klan was also a reaction to unprecedented technological progress, prosperity, and social changes felt by many as deeply threatening.
- White supremacy, hatred of Jews and Catholics, antiradicalism, and opposition to immigration were all Klan tenets that appealed to people who thought their livelihoods were precarious and their way of life was under siege.
- Urbanization was an obvious symptom of modernization; the Klan in fact took firm root in Texas cities, particularly in Dallas.
- Houston's first skyscraper was the six-story Binz Building, constructed in 1894. By the 1920s skyscrapers were setting new height records in the city.
- Newly available, air-conditioning countered the stifling heat and humidity for which Houston was known.
- The National Democratic Convention of 1928 was held in Houston, dramatizing Houston as a modern metropolis; state delegates' flags were hung from all of the lamp posts on Main Street.

Panorama of Houston's business district, 1921 (F. J. Schlueter, Library of Congress)

Dock Boggs, Banjo Player and Singer, in 1929

The career of banjo picker-singer Dock Boggs was shaped by the rough landscape of Virginia's coal country and the newly emerging entertainment medium known as radio.

Life at Home

- When Moran Lee Boggs was born in West Norton, Virginia, in February 1898, radio was in its infancy; by 1927, when he recorded his first record, no home was complete without one.
- Named for a local physician but always called Dock, he grew up in the same region of Virginia as the Stanley Brothers and the Carter family—all musicians with deep country roots.
- His father was a mountain farmer, blacksmith and singer who encouraged his children's musical talents.
- The youngest of ten children, Dock was one of many siblings who could sing and play the banjo.
- Some of his earliest music lessons came from an African American guitarist called Go Lightning, whom Dock would follow up and down the railroad tracks between Norton and Dorchester.
- Dock would also sneak over at night to the African American camps in Dorchester, where he watched string bands playing at dances and parties.
- Dock started working in the coal mines in 1910, when he was 12 years old.
- He continued his musical education by playing the banjo with the black miners.
- Although he initially learned the claw-hammer style of playing the banjo, Dock began picking the banjo with a three-finger style, rather like the way a guitarist picks a guitar.
- During this time an itinerant musician named Homer Crawford taught him to play "Hustlin' Gambler," and he added "Turkey in the Straw" to his repertoire thanks to musician Jim White.
- By 1918 coal miner Dock Boggs had begun building a reputation playing and singing at parties in the region.
- He was widely influenced by a blend of "old-time" and blues music played in the isolated backwoods of Virginia.
- At the same time, much of the nation was falling in love with a new phenomenon called radio.
- Radio's increasing popularity during the 1920s was extremely important to the growth of country music; many stations gave airtime to live and recorded music that appealed to rural white people.

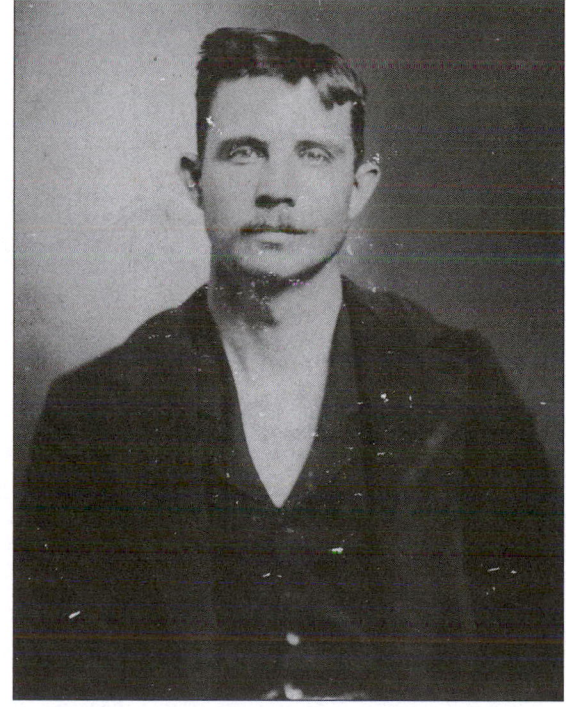

Dock Boggs

- Big-city record labels flocked to the South to record old-time songs and to the West to find singing cowboys; in the process, they sought out musicians like Dock.
- Encouraged by the radio response, in 1923, a 55-year-old Georgia fiddler, Fiddlin' John Carson, recorded two Southern rural songs, starting the march of "hillbilly" or "country" music.
- The term "hillbilly" was introduced in 1924 by "Uncle" Dave Macon's *Hill Billie Blues*.
- In 1924 Chicago's radio station WLS, which stood for "World's Largest Store," began broadcasting a barn dance that could be heard throughout the Midwest.

Child coal miners (Lewis W. Hine, Library of Congress)

- This was followed the next year by Nashville's first radio station, WSM, which started a barn dance of its own that would eventually be called the Grand Ole Opry.
- Old-time "hillbilly" music was an amalgamation of styles, rather than a monolithic style.
- Its origins incorporated Scottish reels, Irish jigs, square dances, British ballads, and religious hymns sung at church and at camp meetings.
- It was a mongrel mix as unique as America itself.
- Across America, families by the millions gathered around their radios for night-time entertainment—mesmerized by the sounds magically coming from the box.
- That meant money was to be made, setting off a mad scramble for listeners; chaos reigned.
- Without radio wave regulations, programs overlapped as stations arbitrarily changed their broadcasting ban to gain an advantage.
- Listeners of one program were frequently interrupted by a competing program.
- Initially, the government viewed radio as a public service, not a commercial enterprise, setting off additional battles with advertisers.
- Eventually, government intervention was demanded to end the free-for-all, resulting in the Federal Radio Commission in 1926 and the Radio Act of 1927.

Life at Work

- Dock Boggs's big moment came when the Brunswick Label held a mass audition in western Virginia, searching for unknown talent.

Boggs's fellow coal miners (Library of Congress)

- Old-time music was hot, and the record companies were willing to go into the isolated corners of Appalachia to find unique voices and sounds.
- Auditions were held at the Norton Hotel, where Dock used a borrowed banjo and a bracer of whiskey to display his talents.
- Dock's style personified the authentic folk strain of country music; strong, personal, cruel, and tinged with the blues.
- A hard life working in the coal mines of western Virginia was reflected in his tone.
- Out of the dozens who tried out—some 75 musicians performed—two were selected: Dock Boggs and the Dykes Magic City Trio.

- Dock played "Country Blues," which was an arrangement of "Hustlin' Gamblers," and "Down South Blues." Dock was one of the few banjo players at the audition.
- The Carter family participated in the audition but was not selected.
- The reward for winning the audition was a recording session in New York City.
- Boggs made his first trip out of the mountains, accompanied by his banjo.
- Dressed in his trademark dark suit, necktie and polished shoes, Dock cut eight sides, featuring a raw, bluesy mountain voice and five-string banjo.
- Brunswick wanted more, but Dock decided that his remuneration was worth eight sides—no more.

White boy watching African American musicians (National Photo Collection, Library of Congress)

- The path for mountain-style music had been smoothed by banjoist Charlie Poole of the North Carolina Ramblers, who recorded "Don't Let Your Deal Go Down" in 1925 and the "White House Blues" in 1926.
- "Uncle" Dave Macon, one of the bestselling artists of the twenties, had recorded "Keep My Skillet Good and Greasy," "Chewing Gum," and "Sail Away Ladies."
- They used the banjo as more than a mere rhythmic device, but Dock Boggs was perhaps the first white banjoist to play the instrument like a blues guitar.
- During his sessions in 1927, he recorded six plantation blues numbers and "Sugar Baby," a rockabilly tune.
- His records sold moderately well, and he returned to southwestern Virginia, where he played at parties and mining camps.
- By 1928 he had added numerous gospel and religious songs to his repertoire, thanks to his brother-in-law, Lee Hunsucker, a Holiness preacher and singer.
- Dock also began making enough money singing and playing the banjo so that he could quit working in the mine and focus exclusively on music.

- He bought a new banjo and formed a band called Dock Boggs and His Cumberland Entertainers.
- At times he was making $300 to $400 dollars a week.
- Until the late 1920s, hillbilly artists were comedians as much as musicians, with a mixed repertoire of songs and skits.
- The Skillet Lickers were probably instrumental in creating the charisma of the country musician, as opposed to the image of the hillbilly clown.
- But Dock's success was tempered by problems at home.
- His religious neighbors equated the life of a traveling musician with a life of sin; his wife, Sara, despised secular music and objected to her husband earning a living by playing music.

Musicians gathered for a Klan-sponsored Fiddler's Convention in Mountain City, Tennessee, in 1925; Fiddlin' John Carson, far right (John Edwards Memorial Foundation Records #20001, Southern Folklife Collection, The Wilson Library, University of North Carolina at Chapel Hill)

- The mining camps where Dock and his band played were often violent, and Dock did not always escape the drunken brawls unscathed.
- Finally, he returned to the studio in 1929, this time for Lonesome Ace Records in Chicago.
- He recorded just four songs for Lonesome Ace.
- But the stock market crash of October 1929 ushered the tiny recording company into bankruptcy almost immediately afterward. It also dried up the party income and put Dock back into the coal mines.
- Automaker Henry Ford invested heavily in promoting country music in the 1920s, terrified by what he saw as the urban decadence of couples jazz dancing.
- In response, he organized fiddling contests and promoted square dances across the country to encourage what he saw as the older, more wholesome forms of entertainment.
- Fiddling contests were sponsored by others as well, including the Ku Klux Klan.
- Yet much of country music of the 1920s could be rowdy and bawdy, too.
- The B side of one of the first country music records, by Fiddlin' John Carson, had the barnyard double-entendre lyric, "The old hen cackled, and the rooster's going to crow."
- Country music was cleaned up as radio became the major medium for promoting country music performers; advertisers, such as Crazy Water Crystals, insisted on sanitized lyrics.

Life in the Community: Norton, Virginia

- Norton, Virginia, tucked in the Appalachian Mountains, was one of the Commonwealth of Virginia's smallest towns in one of its poorest regions.
- Located in far southwestern Virginia, in one of the last parts of the state to be settled by Europeans, Norton had a population largely of English, German, and Scots-Irish ancestry; most people in the region engaged in subsistence farming on the rocky hillsides.
- During the American Revolution, men from southwestern Virginia were among those who participated in the Battle of King's Mountain; during the Civil War, the area's allegiance was deeply divided between supporters of the Union and supporters of the Confederacy.
- Often blamed for isolating residents from the rest of Virginia, the Appalachian Mountains defined the people and fostered the region's unique language and musical styles.
- Researchers could still find remnants of seventeenth-century Elizabethan speech in the 1920s, despite the intrusion of Big Coal into the region.
- Prior to the Civil War, the coal counties in southwestern Virginia were unable to ship their product to market.

Clayton McMichen (fiddle) and the Whitten brothers, Charlie (tenor banjo) and Mike (guitar), billed as the Home Town Boys, 1922

- After 1865 Northern financiers supported the extension of Virginia railroads into the timber-rich and coal-rich mountains.
- By World War I, the Norfolk and Western Railroad had built a rail line capable of moving the coal to the East; the Pocahontas Mine became a major supplier of coal for the U.S. Navy.
- The musical traditions of Appalachia were well established by that time, including those of the banjo and the fiddle.
- Originally, the American banjo was developed from an instrument the Africans played, variously called banjars, banzas, banias, and bangoes.
- Africans, brought to the New World in bondage and not allowed to play drums, started making their banjars from calabash gourds.
- To Americans the banjo was an oddity; denied respectability, it was considered a musical outcast—lowlier than the fiddle, which many "righteous people" knew was the gift of the devil.
- By the 1840s a fifth string had been added, called the short thumb string or bass string.
- Among mountain people the fiddle and the banjo were commonly paired in performances.
- The instrument found its greatest growth in popularity during the Civil War years; in the long days of boredom between battles, both Union and Confederate soldiers who played the banjo taught other soldiers, many belonging to units from distant places, how to play.
- Banjos and fiddles also moved West after the war, in the largest migration ever.
- Most of the men who became cowboys were from the South, due to Reconstruction and economic disruption in the South after the devastation of the region's economy.
- At the same time, touring minstrel shows—with white musicians in blackface, and sometimes even black musicians in blackface—popularized the banjo.
- The most popular minstrel troupes—Christy's Minstrels, Buckley's Serenaders, The Congo Melodists, and the Virginia Minstrels—remained on Broadway in New York and other big Eastern cities, where they reigned for 50 years.
- Lesser-known minstrel troupes traveled to small towns and territories to make a living.
- As early as the 1850s, some players stepped away from the banjo-stroke style of playing, which employed the back of the fingernails, and adopted the thumb-and-fingers technique, playing the banjo just as the guitar was played.
- Noted musician Frank Converse perfected this style and introduced it in his 1865 banjo instruction book.
- Together with another instruction book published in 1868 by minstrel banjoist James Buckley, the finger-picking style was developed and taught.
- Around 1880 Henry Dobson became the first person to manufacture banjos with frets, which increased the accuracy of the notes when playing up the neck.
- As the banjo started to become more sophisticated, it moved into high society, and more ladies started to play.
- In the 1880s and 1890s, people often created their own entertainment in social clubs organized around a common interest, whether poetry, railroads, rowing, bicycling, theater, science, or music.

Virginia Minstrels handbill (Minstrels Poster Collection, Library of Congress)

- Countless banjo clubs were formed all over the country and in the leading universities and colleges, all of which had their own banjo orchestras.
- The social elite thought it fashionable to play banjo in these orchestras, with the music ranging from classical to marches to waltzes to rags.
- Radio broadcasting began in 1920, with a broadcast by station KDKA of Pittsburgh, Pennsylvania; listeners were limited to the few who had built their own radio receivers.
- Nevertheless, public response was immediate: manufacturers were overwhelmed by the demand for receivers, as customers stood in line to complete order forms for radios after dealers had sold out.

Farmer listening to crystal radio, around 1922 (National Archives)

- In 1922 radio station WSM, based in Georgia, became the first to broadcast folk songs to its audience.
- "Crystal" radios were among the first radios to be used and manufactured.
- These sets used a piece of lead galena crystal and a cat whisker to find the radio signal.
- Magazines encouraged young boys to make their own radios, providing step-by-step instructions for the crystal radio.
- Supplies could be purchased for as little as $6.00.
- Prior to 1920, most Americans couldn't fathom the idea of voices and music coming over the air into their homes.

Sharps Station, Tennessee, M.E. church congregation (Lewis W. Hine)

Known as the Roaring Twenties, the 1920s was marked by social, artistic, cultural, and economic peaks. Affluence roared. Income roared. GNP roared. Music, movies, even baseball roared to new heights of popularity with the general public. Also known as the Jazz Age, the decade was associated with new technology—automobiles and moving pictures—and a loosening of traditional values. Prosperity was so widespread that the second half of the decade was known as the Golden Twenties, before the Great Depression in 1929 brought everything to a screeching halt. This section highlights significant firsts and milestones of the 1920s, including the founding of the Walt Disney Company and Babe Ruth's rise to fame.

Early 1920s

- Congress overrode President Wilson's veto, reactivating the War Finance Corps to aid struggling farmers
- The U.S. Navy ordered the sale of 125 flying boats to encourage commercial aviation
- Milk drivers on strike dumped thousands of gallons of milk onto New York City streets
- The movie *The Sheik*, starring Rudolph Valentino, was released
- The Cherokee Indians asked the U.S. Supreme Court to review their claim to one million acres of land in Texas
- New York City discussed ways to vary work hours to avoid long traffic jams
- The first successful helium dirigible made a test flight in Portsmouth, Virginia
- President Harding freed socialist Eugene Debs and 23 other political prisoners
- Sears, Roebuck President Julius Rosenwald pledged $20 million of his personal fortune to help Sears through hard times
- J. D. Rockefeller pledged $1 million for the relief of Europe's destitute
- Albert Einstein proposed the possibility of measuring the universe
- Airmail service opened between New York and San Francisco
- The U.S. Red Cross reported that 20,000 children died annually in auto accidents
- The National Association of the Moving Picture Industry announced its intention to censor U.S. movies
- Junior Achievement, created to encourage business skills in young people, was incorporated
- West Virginia imposed the first state sales tax
- Congress passed the Emergency Quota Act, which established national quotas for immigrants entering the United States

THE WORLD'S WORK

DEC. 1923   35 CENTS

The Immigration Peril
What The Aliens Are Doing to Us
The March of Events

- Race riots erupted in Tulsa, Oklahoma, killing 85 people
- U.S. Army Air Service pilots bombed the captured German battleship *Ostfriesland* to demonstrate the effectiveness of aerial bombing on warships
- Italian anarchists Nicola Sacco and Bartolomeo Vanzetti were convicted for the killing of a paymaster and guard at a shoe factory in South Braintree, Massachusetts
- The United States, which had never ratified the Versailles Treaty ending World War I, finally signed a peace treaty with Germany
- The baseball World Series was broadcast on radio for the first time
- The first religious radio broadcast was heard over station KDKA AM in Pittsburgh, Pennsylvania
- Popular books included John Dos Passos' *Three Soldiers*; *Symptoms of Being Thirty-Five* by Ring Lardner; *The Outline of History* by H.G. Wells, and *Dream Psychology* by Sigmund Freud
- The DeYoung Museum opened in Golden Gate Park, San Francisco
- The Mounds candy bar, Eskimo Pie, Betty Crocker, Wise potato chips, Band-Aids, table tennis, and Drano all made their first appearance
- The Allies of World War I Reparations Commission decided that Germany was obligated to pay 132 billion gold marks ($33 trillion) in annual installments of 2.5 billion
- Cigarette consumption rose to 43 billion annually despite its illegality in 14 states
- The first vaccination against tuberculosis was administered
- Researchers at the University of Toronto led by biochemist Frederick Banting announced the discovery of the hormone insulin
- Adolf Hitler became Führer of the Nazi Party
- Sixteen-year-old Margaret Gorman won the Atlantic City Pageant's Golden Mermaid trophy to become the first Miss America
- Literature dealing with contraception was banned
- Centre College's football team, led by quarterback Bo McMillin, defeated Harvard University 6-0 to break Harvard's five-year winning streak
- Albert Einstein was awarded the Nobel Prize in Physics for his work with the photoelectric effect
- During an Armistice Day ceremony at Arlington National Cemetery, the Tomb of the Unknowns was dedicated by President Warren G. Harding
- Hyperinflation was rampant in Germany after the Great War, where 263 German marks were needed to buy a single American dollar
- Seventeen-year-old Clara Bow won a fan magazine contest for "The Most Beautiful Girl in the World," while Charles Atlas won the "World's Most Perfectly Developed Man" contest
- During his third trial, movie star Roscoe "Fatty" Arbuckle was exonerated of starlet Virginia Rappe's murder, but not before his name was sullied in a highly publicized sex trial
- The self-winding wristwatch, Checker Cab, Canada Dry ginger ale, and State Farm Mutual auto insurance all made their first appearance
- Automobile magnate Henry Ford was declared a billionaire by the Associated Press
- Radio station WEAF objected to airing a toothpaste commercial, deciding that care of the teeth was too delicate a subject for broadcast
- The first commercially prepared baby food was marketed
- The U.S. Post Office burned 500 copies of James Joyce's *Ulysses*, after it was declared to be too sexually explicit.
- The mah-jongg craze swept the nation
- Protestant Episcopal bishops voted to erase the word obey from the marriage ceremony
- Movie idol Wallace Reid died in a sanitarium of alcohol and morphine addiction

- Thom McAn shoe store introduced mass-produced shoes sold through chain stores for $3.99 a pair
- Hollywood's black list of "unsafe" persons stood at 117
- Radio became a national obsession, airing concerts, sermons and sports
- Syracuse University banned dancing
- A cargo ship was converted into the first U.S. aircraft carrier
- Willa Cather won the Pulitzer Prize for *One of Ours*
- The tomb of King Tutankhamun, in the Valley of the Kings, Egypt, was discovered, setting off a rage in women's fashion for fringed scarves, slave bangles, and long earrings
- The first mechanical telephone switchboard was installed in New York
- Broadway producer Florenz Ziegfeld forbade his stars to perform on radio because it "cheapens them"
- In describing the new "flapper," *Vanity Fair* reported, "She will never . . . knit you a necktie, but she'll go skiing with you. . . . "
- Even though Prohibition was the law of the land, prescription liquor for those in need remained unrestricted
- Clarence Darrow and William Jennings Bryan debated the issue of evolution versus fundamentalism in the *Chicago Tribune*
- Girls who dressed in the style of flappers in Tennessee were banned from public schools until they rolled their stockings back up over their knees
- The German shepherd Rin Tin Tin captured stardom as a top silent movie star
- Montana and Nevada became the first states to introduce old-age pensions

Harry Landgon and Joan Crawford in silent film Tramp, Tramp, Tramp

- The Dow-Jones Average hit a high of 105, a low of 86
- A sign reading HOLLYWOODLAND was erected in Los Angeles; each letter measured 30 by 50 feet
- The rubber diaphragm, Pan American World Airlines, the Milky Way candy bar, Welch's grape jelly, the name Popsicle and the Hertz Drive-Ur-Self all made their first appearance
- Evangelist Aimee Semple McPherson opened a $1.5 million temple in Los Angeles, which included a "miracle room" where the healed could discard their crutches and wheelchairs
- Music hits included "Yes! We Have No Bananas," "Who's Sorry Now?" and "That Old Gang of Mine"
- Blues singer Bessie Smith's "Downhearted Blues" sold a record two million copies
- President Warren G. Harding became the first chief executive to file an income tax report
- In a Ku Klux Klan surprise attack on a black residential area of Rosewood, Florida, at least six blacks and two whites died and almost every building in the town was burned
- The U.S. Senate debated the benefits of peyote, a catus with psychoactive properties, for the American Indian
- The United States withdrew its last troops from Germany
- The Clean Book League of Boston was formed to judge the appropriateness of modern literature, including D. H. Lawrence's *Women in Love*
- The first U.S. dance marathon was held in New York City
- Films featuring sound were shown to a paying audience at the Rialto Theater in New York City
- Insulin became generally available for diabetics
- A self-winding watch was patented in Switzerland

- The Teapot Dome scandal resulted in the bribery conviction of Harry F. Sinclair of Mammoth Oil, and Secretary of the Interior Albert B. Fall, the first cabinet member in American history to go to prison
- The play *Runnin' Wild,* which featured a dance known as the Charleston, opened on Broadway
- Goodyear Tire and Rubber Company bought the rights to manufacture Zeppelin dirigibles
- Col. Jacob Schick patented the first electric shaver
- Adolf Hitler launched his first attempt to seize power with a failed coup in Munich, Germany; while in prison he wrote *Mein Kampf,* subtitled *Four-and-a-Half Years of Struggle against Lies, Stupidity, and Cowardice*
- Nationwide, $250 million was invested in the construction of 300 hotels to accommodate a population in love with the automobile
- Oklahoma Governor Jack Walton was ousted by the state senate for advocating anti-Ku Klux Klan measures
- *Time* magazine hit newsstands for the first time
- Popular movies included *The Ten Commandments, The Hunchback of Notre Dame, The White Sister,* and *A Woman of Paris*
- Lee De Forest devised a method of recording sound on film, called fonofilm
- Roy and Walt Disney founded The Walt Disney Company
- Ida Rosenthal popularized the Maidenform bra by giving one away to each woman who visited her dress store
- "The House That Ruth Built"—Yankee Stadium—opened
- Harry Steenbock discovered that radiating food with ultraviolet light added vitamin D
- Golfer Bobby Jones won his first USGA Open
- The Moderation League of New York became part of the movement for the repeal of Prohibition in the United States

Mid 1920s

- The Popsicle was patented under the name Epsicle
- The Butterfinger candy bar was created and marketed by dropping parachuted bars from an airplane
- Commercially canned tomato juice was marketed by Libby McNeill & Libby
- A.C. Nielson Company was founded
- Zenith Radio Corporation was founded
- Ten automakers accounted for 90 percent of auto sales; a total of 108 different companies were producing cars
- Thirty percent of all bread was now baked in the home, down from 70 percent in 1910
- The first effective chemical pesticides were introduced
- *American Mercury* magazine began publication
- Radio set ownership reached three million
- Ford produced two million Model T motorcars
- Microbiologists isolated the cause of scarlet fever
- Emily Post published *Etiquette,* which made her the arbiter of American manners
- Concerns arose that the increasing number of telephones would lead to the elimination of regional dialects and of written records for historians to study
- College football, thanks to stars such as Galloping Ghost Red Grange, surpassed boxing as a national pastime

- Ernest Hemingway gained national recognition when he joined in the running of the bulls at Pamplona, Spain
- African-American actor Paul Robeson was threatened by the KKK when he was featured in the play *All God's Chillun Got Wings* as the black husband of a white woman
- News programs became more prominent on radio, challenging the popular all-dance music programs
- A popular GOP convention drink was the "Keep Cool with Coolidge" highball, consisting of raw eggs and fruit juice
- Dime magazines such as *Detective Story* and *Western Story* increased in circulation to half a million
- Walt Disney created a cartoon named "Alice's Wonderland"
- The permanent wave, contact lenses, Beech-Nut Coffee, and Wheaties all made their first appearance
- The U.S. Supreme Court declared unconstitutional an Oregon law requiring all grammar school-aged children to attend school
- Gangland king Diom O'Banion was buried in a $10,000 bronze casket; 20,000 attended the funeral
- The Methodist Episcopal General Conference lifted its ban on theatergoing and dancing
- Commercial laundry use increased 57 percent in 10 years
- Hiding places for liquor included shoe heels, flasks form-fitted to a woman's thigh, folds of coats and perfume bottles
- The first Macy's Thanksgiving Day Parade made its way down Central Park West in New York City
- James Buchanan "Buck" Duke donated $47 million to Trinity College at Durham, North Carolina; the college changed its name to Duke
- The dance, the Charleston, which originated in Charleston, South Carolina, was carried north and incorporated into the all-black show *Shuffle Along*
- When Henry Ford paid $2.4 million in income tax, 500,000 people wrote to him begging for money
- More than 50 companies sold home refrigerators, with an average price of $450
- President Calvin Coolidge declared, "The business of America is business"
- The Model-T Ford sold for its lowest price ever, $260, reduced from $950 in 1909
- Charles David Jenkins produced a working television set
- Alfred Sturtevant of Columbia University demonstrated that developmental effects of genes are influenced by neighboring genes
- Cinema-goers watched *The Phantom of the Opera*, *The Freshman*, *The Gold Rush* and *Ben-Hur*
- Americans spent more than $6 billion on building and construction
- Bootleg liquor prices appeared regularly at the end of the "Talk of the Town" section of *The New Yorker*
- The last fire engine drawn by a span of three horses in Washington, DC, was retired
- Red Grange brought his college fame to pro football, drawing unprecedented crowds as he played 10 games in 17 days
- Philip Randolph organized the Brotherhood of Sleeping Car Porters, one of the first black labor unions
- Refrigerator sales reached 75,000 annually, up from 10,000 in 1920
- The National Spelling Bee, dry ice, automatic potato peeling machine, Wesson Oil and Caterpillar tractors all made their first appearance
- *The New Yorker* and *Cosmopolitan* were first published
- Popular songs included, "Swannee," "Tea for Two," "Has Anybody Seen My Gal?", and "Sweet Georgia Brown"
- One in six Americans owned an automobile
- Cosmetics became a $141 million industry
- Nellie Taylor of Wyoming became the first female governor, finishing the term of her late husband; 15 days later, Ma Ferguson became the first female governor of Texas

- Greyhound Corporation began with General Motors as its major stockholder
- Having handed over his crime empire to Al Capone, gangster Johnny Torrino retired to Italy with between $10 and $30 million
- Benito Mussolini announced he was taking dictatorial power over Italy
- Calvin Coolidge was the first U.S. president to have his inauguration broadcast on radio
- Tennessee Governor Austin Peay signed the Butler Act, prohibiting the teaching of evolution in the state's public schools; subsequently, teacher John Scopes was convicted of teaching Charles Darwin's Theory of Evolution and fined $100
- Radio station WOWO in Ft. Wayne, Indiana, began broadcasting
- F. Scott Fitzgerald published *The Great Gatsby*
- The Chrysler Corporation was founded by Walter Percy Chrysler
- Charles Francis Jenkins achieved the first synchronized transmission of pictures and sound, which he called radiovision
- The Ku Klux Klan demonstrated its popularity by holding a parade in Washington, DC; 40,000 male and female members of the Klan marched down Pennsylvania Avenue
- The country variety show *WSM Barn Dance*, later renamed *The Grand Ole Opry*, made its radio debut
- The Great Sphinx of Giza was unearthed
- The Thompson submachine gun sold for $175 in the 1925 Sears, Roebuck and Company mail order catalog
- Florida land prices collapsed as investors discovered that many lots they had purchased were under water
- The $10 million Boca Raton Hotel in Florida was completed
- Al Capone took control of Chicago bootlegging
- Chesterfield cigarettes were marketed to women for the first time
- The Book-of-the-Month Club was founded
- Aunt Jemima Mills was acquired by Quaker Oats Company for $4 million
- Machine-made ice production topped 56 million pounds; up 1.5 million from 1894
- The first ham in a can was introduced by Hormel
- The first blue jeans with slide fasteners were introduced by J.D. Lee Company
- Synthetic rubber was pioneered by B.F. Goodrich Rubber Company chemist Waldo Lonsburg Serman
- Cars appeared for the first time in such colors as "Florentine Cream" and "Versailles Violet"
- "Yellow-Drive-It-Yourself-Systems" car rentals became popular; $0.12 a mile for a Ford and $0.22 a mile for a 6-cylinder car
- Earl Wise's potato chips were so successful he moved his business from a remodeled garage to a concrete plant
- Wesson Oil, National Spelling Bees, and the *New Yorker* magazine all made their first appearances
- Congress reduced the taxes on incomes of more than $1 million, from 66 percent to 20 percent
- To fight the depression in the automobile industry, Henry Ford introduced the eight-hour day and five-day work week
- With prohibition under way, the Supreme Court upheld a law limiting the medical prescription of whiskey to one pint every 10 days
- 2,000 people died of poisoned liquor; the illegal liquor trade netted $3.5 billion a year, with the price for bootleg Scotch at $48 a case
- The movies became America's favorite entertainment, with more than 14,500 movie houses showing 400 movies a year

- *True Story Magazine* reached a circulation of two million with stories such as "The Diamond Bracelet She Thought Her Husband Didn't Know About"
- Philadelphia's Warwick Hotel and the Hotel Carlyle in New York were opened
- Forty percent of all first-generation immigrants owned their own homes
- Kodak introduced 16 mm film
- Sinclair Lewis refused to accept the Pulitzer Prize because it "makes the writer safe, polite, obedient, and sterile"
- Martha Graham debuted in New York as a choreographer and dancer in *Three Gopi Maidens*
- Women's skirts, the shortest of the decade, now stopped just below the knee with flounces, pleats, and circular gores that extended from the hip
- Ethel Lackie of the Illinois Athletic Club broke the world's record for the 40-yard freestyle swim with a time of 21.4 seconds
- Walt Disney arrived in Hollywood and produced 10 short features composed of animation and live action
- Oscar Barnack developed the 35mm camera
- Pop-up electric toasters, the Chrysler Imperial, Safeway stores and flavored yogurt all made their first appearance
- The St. Louis Cardinals defeated the New York Yankees four games to three in the World Series; Babe Ruth hit three home runs during one game
- *The Sun Also Rises* by Ernest Hemingway, *The Love Nest* by Ring Lardner, *Abraham Lincoln: The Prairie Years* by Carl Sandburg and *Gentlemen Prefer Blondes* by Anita Loos were all published
- Harry Houdini died from a stomach punch that lead to peritonitis
- Popular songs included "Bye Bye Blackbird," "When the Red, Red Robin Comes Bob, Bob, Bobbin' Along," and Louis Armstrong's "You Made Me Love You"
- The New York Public Library began its Ten Worst Books Contest
- Freeman Gosden and Charles Correll premiered their radio program *Sam 'n' Henry*, in which the two white performers portrayed two black characters from Harlem looking to strike it rich in the big city
- Eugene O'Neill's *The Great God Brown* opened at the Greenwich Theatre
- Land on Broadway and Wall Street in New York City was sold at a record $7 per square inch
- In the Treaty of Berlin, Germany and the Soviet Union each pledged neutrality in the event of an attack on the other by a third party for the next five years
- Admiral Richard E. Byrd and Floyd Bennett claimed to have flown over the North Pole
- Congress passed the Air Commerce Act, licensing pilots and planes
- Fox Film bought the patents of the Movietone sound system for recording sound onto film
- The National Bar Association incorporated in the United States
- The Warner Brothers' Vitaphone system premiered with the movie *Don Juan* starring John Barrymore
- The League of Nations Slavery Convention abolished all types of slavery
- Gene Tunney defeated Jack Dempsey and became Heavyweight Champion of the World, a battle broadcast nationwide by radio
- Alan Alexander Milne's book *Winnie-the-Pooh* was published
- The NBC Radio Network (formed by Westinghouse, General Electric and RCA) opened with 24 stations
- In Williamsburg, Virginia, the restoration of Colonial Williamsburg began
- Phencyclidine (PCP, angel dust) was first synthesized
- U.S. Marines intervened in Nicaragua to bolster the conservative government

Late 1920s

- More than 40 percent of all American households had a telephone
- The per capita consumption of crude oil reached 7.62 barrels
- Peanut butter cracker sandwich packets were sold under the name NAB by the National Biscuit Company for $0.05 each
- Massachusetts passed the nation's first compulsory automobile insurance legislation
- Transatlantic telephone service between London and New York began at a cost of $75 for three minutes
- Film producers added sound sequences to silent movies and called them "part talkies"
- The Al Capone gang netted $100 million in the liquor trade, $30 million in protection money, $25 million in gambling, $10 million in vice and $10 million in the rackets
- The original manuscript for Lewis Carroll's *Alice's Adventures Underground* was sold for $75,000
- A record 268 plays were performed on Broadway
- Black leader Marcus Garvey, who was convicted of mail fraud in 1923, had his sentence commuted and was deported to the West Indies
- Sears and Roebuck distributed 15 million catalogues to American homes
- The car radio, Hostess Cakes, Borden's homogenized milk, Volvo, the Literary Guild of America, Lender Bagels, Gerber baby food, A&W Root Beer and the all-electric jukebox made their first appearance
- A national survey reported a "loosening" in manner and morals
- To abide by prohibition laws, restaurants hired detectives to search customers for hip flasks and bottles before serving ice and ginger ale
- The average salary reached $1,312 a year; teachers made $1,277, lawyers took home $5,205 and factory workers made $1,502
- The Ford Model A automobile, the successor to the all-black Model T, was manufactured in four colors with a self-starter, rumble seat and shatterproof windshield
- The National Football League was reduced from 32 teams to 12
- Charles Lindbergh flew solo, nonstop, from New York to Paris, traveling 3,610 miles in 33.3 hours in his plane *The Spirit of St. Louis,* for which President Coolidge awarded him the Congressional Medal of Honor; his New York ticker tape parade used 1,800 tons of paper, and $16,000 was spent to sweep it up
- The *New York Daily News* initiated the Golden Gloves program to encourage young boxers
- Coney Island introduced the world to the cyclone roller coaster
- Harvard's Philip Drinker devised the iron lung, a respirator for patients who could not breathe on their own
- "I'm Looking Over a Four-Leaf Clover," "Let a Smile Be Your Umbrella," and "Me and My Shadow" were all popular songs
- *The Jazz Singer,* the first successful talkie, opened, starring Al Jolson
- Duke Ellington's radio program premiered from the Cotton Club in New York
- All-black basketball team Harlem Globetrotters was organized by Abe Saperstein
- Fashion dictated that women's skirts rise again and stop just below the knee, the shortest length of the decade
- The U.S. Federal Radio Commission began to regulate the use of radio frequencies
- The Great Mississippi Flood of 1927 affected 700,000 people in the greatest national disaster in U.S. history to date

- The Boeing Airplane Company signed a contract with the U.S. Postal Department to fly airmail on the 1,918-mile route between Chicago, Illinois, and San Francisco, California, using the Model 40A mail plane with an air-cooled engine
- The Roxy Theater was opened by Samuel Roxy Rothafel in New York City
- The Academy of Motion Picture Arts and Sciences was founded
- FOX Films acquired the rights to the Tri-Ergon sound-on-film technology, which was developed in 1919 by German inventors, Josef Engl, Hans Vogt, and Joseph Massole
- Nearly 600 members of the American Institute of Electrical Engineers and the Institute of Radio Engineers viewed the first live demonstration of television at the Bell Telephone Building in New York
- Golfer Bobby Jones won both the British Open and the U.S. Amateur Championship

Roxy Theater, New York City

- Paul R. Redfern crashed his plane while attempting to fly from Brunswick, Georgia, non-stop to Rio de Janeiro, Brazil
- For the second straight year, the Chicago American Giants defeated the Bacharach Giants of Atlantic City, New Jersey, in the Negro League World Series
- Frank Heath and his horse Gypsy Queen completed a two-year journey of 11,356 miles to all 48 states
- The musical play *Show Boat,* based on Edna Ferber's novel, opened on Broadway
- The world population reached two billion
- The first armored car robbery was committed by the Flatheads Gang near Pittsburgh, Pennsylvania
- *To The Lighthouse* was completed by Virginia Woolf
- Saudi Arabia became independent of the United Kingdom under the Treaty of Jedda
- Mount Rushmore was dedicated with promises of national funding from President Hoover for the carvings of the heads of four presidents
- Leon Trotsky was expelled from the Soviet Communist Party, leaving Joseph Stalin with undisputed control of the Soviet Union
- The Holland Tunnel opened to traffic as the first Hudson River vehicular tunnel linking New Jersey to New York City
- Harold Stephen Black invented the feedback amplifier
- Arthur H. Compton won the Nobel prize in physics for his discovery of wavelength change in diffused x-rays
- The Voluntary Committee of Lawyers was founded to repeal Prohibition in the U.S.
- Bell Telephone Company transmitted an image of Herbert Hoover, the Secretary of Commerce — the first successful long-distance demonstration of television
- American Philo Farnsworth transmitted his first experimental electronic television pictures, as opposed to mechanical TV systems that others had tried before
- The Columbia Phonographic Broadcasting System (later CBS) was formed and went on the air with 47 radio stations
- 20 million cars were on the road, up from 13,824 in 1900
- J.C. Penney opened its 500th store, and sold stock to the public

- Wonder Bread was introduced
- Broccoli became more widely marketed in the United States
- Rice Krispies were introduced by W.K. Kellogg
- Presidential candidate Herbert Hoover called for "a chicken in every pot and two cars in every garage" and promoted the concept of the "American system of rugged individualism" in a speech at Madison Square Garden
- The Hayes list of don'ts for Hollywood films included licentious or suggestive nudity, ridicule of clergy, and inference of sexual perversion
- President Calvin Coolidge urged the nation to pray more
- A phonograph with an automatic record changer was introduced
- The German dirigible *Graf Zeppelin* landed in Lakehurst, New Jersey, on its first commercial flight across the Atlantic
- The Boston Garden officially opened
- The first successful sound-synchronized animated cartoon, Walt Disney's *Steamboat Willie* starring Mickey Mouse, premiered
- The first issue of *Time* magazine was published, featuring Japanese Emperor Hirohito on its cover
- North Carolina Governor O. Max Gardner blamed women's diet fads for the drop in farm prices
- *Bolero* by Maurice Ravel made its debut in Paris
- George Gershwin's *An American in Paris* premiered at Carnegie Hall in New York
- The clip-on tie was created
- Nationalist Chiang Kai-shek captured Peking, China, from the communists and gained United States recognition
- Aviator Amelia Earhart became the first woman to fly across the Atlantic Ocean from Newfoundland to Wales in about 21 hours
- The first all-talking movie feature, *The Lights of New York,* was released
- Fifteen nations signed the Kellogg-Briand Peace Pact, developed by French Foreign Minister Aristide Briand and U.S. Secretary of State Frank Kellogg; also known as the Pact of Paris, it outlawed war and called for the settlement of disputes through arbitration
- Actress Katharine Hepburn made her stage debut in *The Czarina*
- *My Weekly Reader* magazine made its debut
- Ruth Snyder became the first woman to die in the electric chair
- In its first show to feature a black artist, the New Gallery of New York exhibited works by Archibald Motley
- Bell Labs created a way to end the fluttering of the television image
- Paul Galvin and his brother Joseph incorporated the Galvin Manufacturing Corporation, later known as Motorola
- Radio premieres included *Real Folks, Main Street*; *The Chase and Sanborn Hour* with Maurice Chevalier; and *The Voice of Firestone* and *Shell Château* with Al Jolson
- Box office movie stars included Clara Bow, Lon Chaney Sr., and Greta Garbo
- The International Red Cross and Red Crescent Movement (ICRM) was formally established with the adoption of "Statutes of the International Red Cross"
- On Broadway, Eugene O'Neill captured the Pulitzer Prize for *Strange Interlude*
- Johnny Weissmuller retired from swimming, having set 67 world records and won three Olympic gold medals
- Personal loans were initiated by the National City Bank of New York
- The U.S. Congress approved the construction of Boulder (later Hoover) Dam

- Coca Cola entered the European market through the Amsterdam Olympics
- Frederick Griffith indirectly proved the existence of DNA
- The Episcopal Church in the United States of America ratified a new revision of the *Book of Common Prayer*
- The first patent for the transistor principle was registered in Germany to Julius Edgar Lilienfeld
- Charles Jenkins Laboratories of Washington, DC, became the first holder of a television license from the Federal Radio Commission
- The first regular schedule of television programming began in Schenectady, New York, by General Electric's television station W2XB
- The animated short *Plane Crazy* was released by Disney Studios in Los Angeles, featuring the first appearances of Mickey and Minnie Mouse
- At the Democratic National Convention in Houston, Texas, New York Governor Alfred E. Smith became the first Catholic to be nominated for president by a major political party
- The U.S. recalled its troops from China
- The moat at the Tower of London, previously drained in 1843 (and planted with grass), was completely refilled by a tidal wave
- Eliot Ness was placed in charge of enforcing Prohibition in Chicago
- Margaret Mead's influential cultural anthropology text *Coming of Age in Samoa* was published
- Russian leader Joseph Stalin launched the First Five-Year Plan
- A Baltimore survey discovered rickets in 30 percent of the city's children
- German Kurt Barthel set up the first American nudist colony in New Jersey, which began with three married couples
- Of the 20,500 movie theaters nationwide, 9,000 installed sound during the year to adapt to "talkies"
- Calvin Coolidge was elected director of the New York Life Insurance Company
- The "Age of the Car" was apparent everywhere, as one-way streets, traffic lights, stop signs, and parking regulations were hot topics
- At least 32,000 speakeasies thrived in New York City; the Midwest had similar institutions named "beer flats," "Blind Pigs," and "shock houses"
- On November 13, 1929, the Stock Market hit bottom, with U.S. securities losing $26 billion in value; within a few weeks of "Black Tuesday," unemployment rose from 700,000 to 3.1 million nationwide
- Following the stock market crash, New York Mayor Jimmy Walker urged movie houses to show cheerful movies
- Coast-to-coast commercial travel took 48 hours, via a combination of airplanes and overnight trains, at an average cost of $310
- Lt. James Doolight piloted an airplane solely using instruments
- Commander Richard E. Byrd planted a U.S. flag on the South Pole
- W.A. Morrison introduced quartz-crystal clocks for precise timekeeping
- Ford introduced a station wagon with boxed wood panels
- Admission to New York theaters ranged from $0.35 to $2.50
- On St. Valentine's Day, six notorious Chicago gangsters were machine-gunned to death by a rival gang, known as the St. Valentines Day Massacre
- American manufacturers began to make aluminum furniture, especially chairs
- The Oscar Meyer wiener trademark, 7-Up, front-wheel-drive cars, and *Business Week* magazine all made their first appearances
- The United States and Canada reached an agreement on joint action to preserve Niagara Falls

- The adventure comic strip *Tarzan,* first appeared; the Popeye character was introduced in the *Thimble Theater* cartoon strip by Elzie Segar
- Frontiersman Wyatt Earp died in Los Angeles, California, after an illustrious life in the West; cowboy stars William S. Hart and Tom Mix served as pallbearers
- Acadia National Park was established in Maine; the Grand Teton National Park opened in Wyoming
- San Francisco police took 19-year-old Frances Orlando to the police station because she was dressed in men's clothing
- The first telephone was installed in the White House
- Louie Marx introduced the yo-yo in the United States
- Harold E. Jones of the University of California Institute of Child Welfare reported that children who attended motion picture shows frequently did poorly in school and exhibited objectionable traits
- The first all-color talking picture, *On with the Show,* opened in New York
- Scientists at Bell Laboratories revealed a system for transmitting television picturest
- The comedy program *Amos 'n' Andy,* starring Freeman Gosden and Charles Correll, made its network radio debut on NBC, and became so popular that Atlantic City resorts broadcast the show over loudspeakers
- William Faulkner published *The Sound and the Fury,* Ernest Hemingway published A *Farewell to Arms* and John Steinbeck wrote *Cup of Gold*
- Edward Doisy isolated the female sex hormone estrogen in pure form
- Alexander Fleming successfully treated a skin infection with penicillin
- Radio premieres included *The Hour of Charm, Blackstone Plantation,* and *The Rise of the Goldbergs*
- New York Yankees baseball star Babe Ruth hit his 500th home run
- RCA Victor recorded the first $33\frac{1}{3}$ rpm LP—Victor Salon Suite No. 1, arranged and directed by Nathaniel Shilkret
- Dunlop Rubber Company produced foam rubber
- Broadway openings included *The Showgirl, Hot Chocolates, Street Singer* and *Death Takes a Holiday*
- The Museum of Modern of Art was founded in New York City
- Plans for the Empire State Building included mooring masts for giant zeppelins
- Louis Armstrong recorded his hit song "When You're Smiling"
- Federated Department Stores, Conoco, and auto sunroofs made their first appearance

SECTION THREE: ECONOMY OF THE TIMES

This section defines the 1920s by three economic elements: Consumer Expenditures; Annual Income of Standard Jobs; and Selected Prices. We highlighted three specific years for each category—1923, 1925, and 1929—for easy comparison. You'll find, for example, that there was a relatively large jump in how much people spent annually on utilities (from $8.97 in 1923 to $24.64 in 1929) but money spent on clothing stayed stable during the years featured. Farm laborers made less money (from $572 in 1923 to $378 in 1929) but the salaries of gas and electricity workers jumped from $1,339 in 1923 to $1,589 in 1929. Consumer electronics also skyrocketed, as the cost of a radio went from $14.50 in 1923 to $65.00 in 1929.

Consumer Expenditures

The numbers below are per capita expenditures in the years 1923, 1925, and 1929 for all workers nationwide.

Category	1923	1925	1929
Auto Parts	$4.97	$6.96	$4.92
Auto Purchases	$20.45	$20.82	$21.35
Clothing	$64.52	$62.04	$63.24
Dentists	$2.72	$3.26	$3.26
Food	$128.14	$160.59	$160.14
Furniture	$8.78	$9.49	$9.49
Gas and Oil	$12.38	$15.70	$14.78
Health Insurance	N/A	N/A	$0.82
Housing	$94.80	$98.89	$96.08
Intercity Transport	N/A	$4.95	$4.11
Local Transport	N/A	$9.13	$9.03
New Auto Purchase	N/A	N/A	N/A
Per Capita Consumption	$594.87	$619.45	N/A
Personal Business	$22.17	$27.33	$32.85
Personal Care	$7.79	$7.79	$9.03
Physicians	$7.15	$7.68	$8.21
Private Education and Research	$7.26	$7.72	$5.75
Recreation	$23.44	$24.52	$35.31
Religion/Welfare Activities	$11.57	$11.31	$9.85
Telephone and Telegraph	$2.71	$5.88	$4.93
Tobacco	$11.46	$13.13	$13.96
Utilities	$8.97	$9.82	$24.64

Annual Income, Standard Jobs

The numbers below are annual incomes for standard jobs across America in the years 1923, 1925, and 1929.

Category	1923	1925	1929
Average of all Industries, Excluding Farm Labor	N/A	N/A	$1,534
Average of all Industries, Including Farm Labor	$1,299	$1,434	$1,425
Bituminous Coal Mining	N/A	N/A	$1,816
Building Trades	N/A	N/A	$2,808
Clerical Workers in Manufacturing	$2,126	$2,239	N/A
Domestics	$711	$741	$731
Farm Labor	$572	$382	$378
Federal Civilian	N/A	N/A	$1,916
Finance, Insurance and Real Estate	N/A	N/A	$2,062
Gas and Electricity Employees	$1,339	$1,552	$1,589
Manufacturing Payroll	N/A	N/A	$1,330
Medical/Health Services Employees	$845	$916	$925
Nonprofit Organization Employees	N/A	N/A	$1,712
Public School Educators	$1,239	$1,299	$1,445
Railroad Employees	N/A	N/A	$1,749
State and Local Government Employees	$1,336	$1,377	$1,549
Telephone and Telegraph Employees	$1,069	$1,108	N/A
Wholesale and Retail Trade Employees	$1,272	$1,416	$1,359

Selected Prices

1923

Airmail Package	$0.08
All-Wool Blankets, 60"x 84" Pair	$14.50
American Kampkook Gas Grill	$15.00
Armstrong Waffle Iron	$4.00
Automobile, Buick Standard Six	$1,175.00
Baby's Portable Bathtub, Rubber	$5.75
Bath Salts, Jar	$1.50
Bathtub	$29.95
Bloomers, Mercerized Cotton	$1.10
Brassiere, in Camisole Style	$0.79
Cigarette Case, Sterling Silver	$11.72
Coat, Woman's Wool	$12.75
Cream Separator	$69.95
Crosley Radio	$14.50
Dress, Crepe	$49.50
Electric Percolator	$7.15
Floor Paint, per Gallon	$1.95
Four-month Around-the-World Cruise	$1,000.00
Frock, Cotton Voile	$13.25
Gas Grill	$15.00
Grand Piano, Steinway	$1,425.00
Hamilton Wristwatch, Man's	$38.00
Hat Box	$5.00
House Paint, Gallon	$2.15
Incense and Burner	$1.00
Instant Coffee	$0.10
Iron	$4.45
Kodak No. 1 Camera	$50.00
Lablashe Face Powder	$0.50
Licecil Insecticide, per Bottle	$1.00
Life Magazine, One Year	$5.00
Listerine Mouthwash	$0.79
Man's Bathing Suit	$5.00
Metal Bed with Mattress/Box Spring	$26.95
Milk of Magnesia Laxative	$0.39
Montague Montamower, Lawn Mower	$18.00
Oil Heater	$4.95
Pocket Watch	$63.50
Post Card	$0.01
Radio	$14.50
Refrigerator, Ice Capacity 100 Pounds	$56.95
S.C. Red Pullet, Sired by a 296-Egg Cock	$5.00
Shaving Brush	$1.25
Shirt, Man's	$2.75
Stationery, 24 Sheets and Envelopes	$1.50
Tennis Racket	$10.50

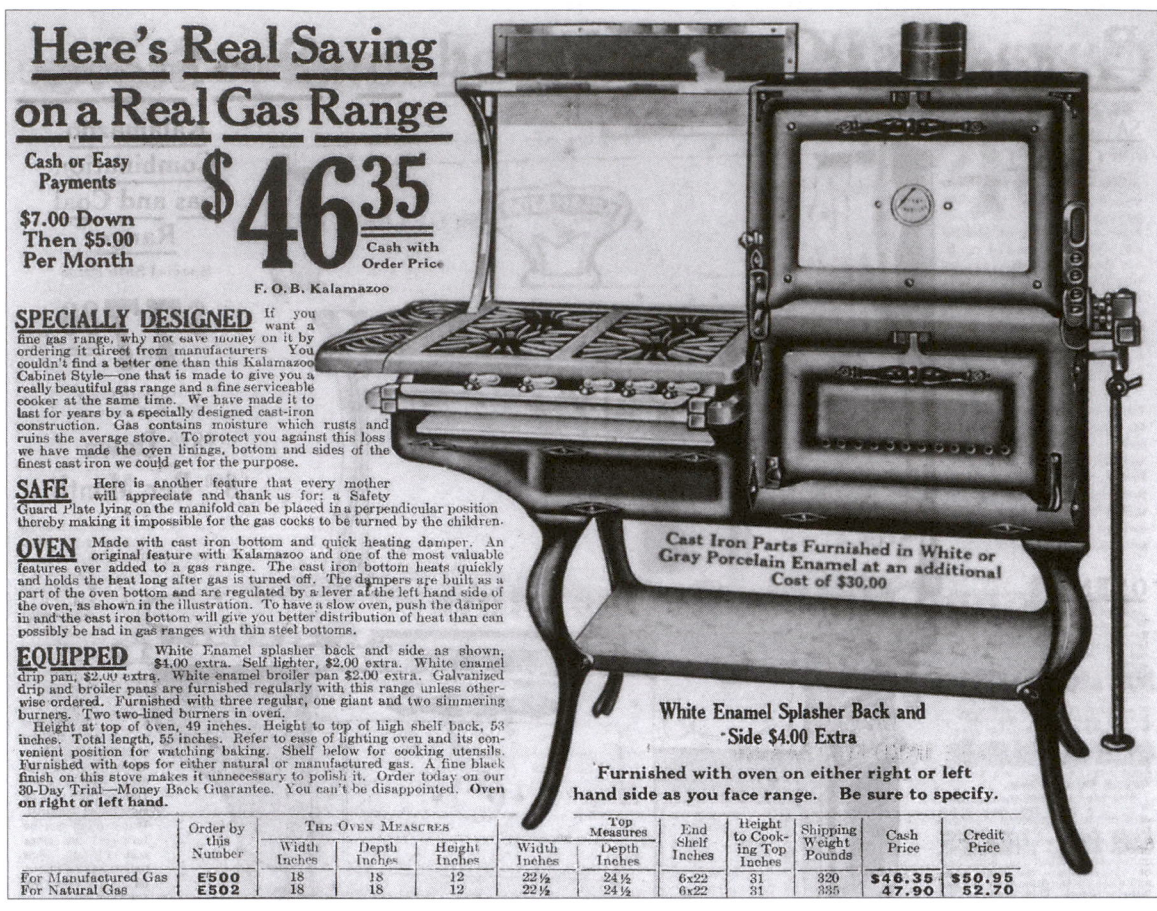

Here's Real Saving on a Real Gas Range

Cash or Easy Payments

$7.00 Down Then $5.00 Per Month

$46 35

Cash with Order Price

F. O. B. Kalamazoo

SPECIALLY DESIGNED If you want a fine gas range, why not save money on it by ordering it direct from manufacturers. You couldn't find a better one than this Kalamazoo Cabinet Style—one that is made to give you a really beautiful gas range and a fine serviceable cooker at the same time. We have made it to last for years by a specially designed cast-iron construction. Gas contains moisture which rusts and ruins the average stove. To protect you against this loss we have made the oven linings, bottom and sides of the finest cast iron we could get for the purpose.

SAFE Here is another feature that every mother will appreciate and thank us for: a Safety Guard Plate lying on the manifold can be placed in a perpendicular position thereby making it impossible for the gas cocks to be turned by the children.

OVEN Made with cast iron bottom and quick heating damper. An original feature with Kalamazoo and one of the most valuable features ever added to a gas range. The cast iron bottom heats quickly and holds the heat long after gas is turned off. The dampers are built as a part of the oven bottom and are regulated by a lever at the left hand side of the oven, as shown in the illustration. To have a slow oven, push the damper in and the cast iron bottom will give you better distribution of heat than can possibly be had in gas ranges with thin steel bottoms.

EQUIPPED White Enamel splasher back and side as shown, $4.00 extra. Self lighter, $2.00 extra. White enamel drip pan, $2.00 extra. White enamel broiler pan $2.00 extra. Galvanized drip and broiler pans are furnished regularly with this range unless otherwise ordered. Furnished with three regular, one giant and two simmering burners. Two two-lined burners in oven. Height at top of oven, 49 inches. Height to top of high shelf back, 53 inches. Total length, 55 inches. Refer to ease of lighting oven and its convenient position for watching baking. Shelf below for cooking utensils. Furnished with tops for either natural or manufactured gas. A fine black finish on this stove makes it unnecessary to polish it. Order today on our 30-Day Trial—Money Back Guarantee. You can't be disappointed. Oven on right or left hand.

Cast Iron Parts Furnished in White or Gray Porcelain Enamel at an additional Cost of $30.00

White Enamel Splasher Back and Side $4.00 Extra

Furnished with oven on either right or left hand side as you face range. Be sure to specify.

For	Order by this Number	The Oven Measures			Top Measures		End Shelf Inches	Height to Cooking Top Inches	Shipping Weight Pounds	Cash Price	Credit Price
		Width Inches	Depth Inches	Height Inches	Width Inches	Depth Inches					
For Manufactured Gas	E500	18	18	12	22½	24½	6x22	31	320	$46.35	$50.95
For Natural Gas	E502	18	18	12	22½	24½	6x22	31	335	47.90	52.70

You can't eat glass balls and tinsel but Tootsie Rolls—oh my!

Good clean pure candy wrapped in attractive rolls that look pretty on the tree and taste good afterwards.

1c Rolls
Chocolate and Butterscotch

5c Rolls
Lunch Rolls
Butterscotch Rolls
Nut Rolls
Molasses Rolls

If you do not find them at the store mail the coupon with a quarter and we will send you a Family Package. Enough to trim a tree.

The Sweets Company of America, Inc.
414 West 45th Street, New York

Enclosed is 25 cents in stamps. Please send me a Family Package of Tootsie Rolls (Mark the flavor you want with an X).
Chocolate (　)　　　　　Butterscotch (　)

Name ....

Address ....

Dealer's Name ....

Trim the Tree with Tootsie Rolls

Toilet $6.95
Underwood Typewriter $50.00
Vacuum Bottle $2.25
Walnut Dresser, Louis XVI Style $98.00
Wilbur Buds' Chocolate, per pound $1.00
Women's Kitchen Apron $0.98
Women's Wristwatch $20.00

1925

Apartment, Chicago, Five Rooms $70.00
Armstrong Waffle Iron $4.00
Arts and Crafts Misson Oak Set, Seven Pieces $28.50
Automobile, Chrysler Roadster $1,525.00
B. Altonman & Co. Handkerchiefs, Hemstitched $1.80/Dozen
Barn Paint $1.54/Gallon
Bathing Suit, Men's $5.00
Blanket, Wool $4.95
Carpet Sweeper $5.00
Colgate Ribbon Dental Cream $0.25/Tube
Condo Typrocraft Typewriter Ribbon $3.00/Dozen
Crib $17.50
Durant Four Automobile, Five Passenger $890.00
Fishing Reel $4.37
Football, Helmet $5.50
Football Pants, Red Grange $3.89
Football, Rawlings $12.00
Forham's for the Gums $0.60
Golf Tee $0.25
Hamilton Strap Watch $38.00
Handerchiefs, Dozen $1.80
Hotel Room, New York, per day $3.00
Kalamazoo Stove Company Oil Heater $4.95
Licecil Insecticide Lice Poison for Chickens $1.00/Bottle
Life Magazine, Weekly $5.00/Year
Lily White Columbia River Salmon . . . .$0.44/per Can
Marvex Women's Gloves, Suede and Kidskin $5.50
Motorcycle, Harley-Davidson $235.00
Pall Mall Cigarettes, per 20 . . . .$0.30
Pocketknife $3.50
Poker Set, 100 Chips $6.25
Radio $39.95
Shinola Shoe Polish $0.08
Starr Best Boy's Suit, Blue Denim $2.95
Steinway & Sons Piano, Upright $875.00
Typewriter, Remington $60.00
Victrola, Talking Machine, Mahogany Cabinet $125.00
Victrola 405, Talking Machine, Walnut Case, Electric $290.00
Wheelbarrow $6.25
Wrigley Juicy Fruit Gum . . . .$0.39/10 Packs

1929

Airplane, Single Engine	$2,000.00
Automobile, Willys-Knight	$1,450.00
Bathing Suit	$8.50
Brill Brothers Chauffeur's Outfit	$78.00
Cahill Fireplace Grate	$10.00
Camera	$80.00
Campbell Automatic Electric Fireless Cooking Range	$25.50
Confederate Grave Marker	$1.50
Cushion Truck Tire	$16.45
Daisy Ironing Table	$2.35
Gillette Razor Blade	$0.50
Handbag, Leather	$2.98
Hunter Ceiling Fan	$52.00
Juice Extractor	$14.95
Louisville Slugger Baseball Bat	$2.00
Luxeberry Interior Wood Varnish	$1.45
Men's Hunting Coat	$3.50
Official Boy Scout Ax	$1.65
Oliver One-Horse Plow	$8.25
Phonograph	$290.00
Pocket Watch	$63.50
Polar Cub Electric Hair Dryer	$4.95
Radio, Crosley 50	$14.50
Radio, Six Tubes	$65.00
Read Head Hunting Coat	$3.50
Remington Pocket Knife	$3.50
Shaving Soap, Pound	$0.49
Stationery, 24 Sheets and Envelopes	$0.50
Suntan Lotion	$2.50
Tennis Racket	$15.00
Train, Chicago to Yellowstone, Round Trip	$56.50
Traveling Bag	$10.50
Universal Fuse Plug	$1.20
Universal Waffle Iron	$9.75
Wall Street Journal Annual Subscription	$15.00
Westclox Big Ben Alarm Clock	$3.25
White Delivery Truck	$1,545.00

The Value of a Dollar, 1860-2013

Composite Consumer Price Index; 1860=1

Year	Amount	Year	Amount	Year	Amount	Year	Amount
1860	$1.00	1899	$1.00	1938	$1.70	1977	$7.30
1861	$1.06	1900	$1.01	1939	$1.67	1978	$7.85
1862	$1.22	1901	$1.02	1940	$1.69	1979	$8.74
1863	$1.52	1902	$1.04	1941	$1.77	1980	$9.97
1864	$1.89	1903	$1.06	1942	$1.96	1981	$10.94
1865	$1.96	1904	$1.07	1943	$2.08	1982	$11.62
1866	$1.92	1905	$1.06	1944	$2.12	1983	$11.99
1867	$1.78	1906	$1.08	1945	$2.17	1984	$12.50
1868	$1.71	1907	$1.13	1946	$2.35	1985	$12.95
1869	$1.64	1908	$1.11	1947	$2.68	1986	$13.20
1870	$1.58	1909	$1.10	1948	$2.90	1987	$13.67
1871	$1.47	1910	$1.14	1949	$2.87	1988	$14.24
1872	$1.47	1911	$1.14	1950	$2.90	1989	$14.92
1873	$1.45	1912	$1.17	1951	$3.13	1990	$15.72
1874	$1.37	1913	$1.19	1952	$3.19	1991	$16.38
1875	$1.32	1914	$1.20	1953	$3.22	1992	$16.88
1876	$1.29	1915	$1.22	1954	$3.24	1993	$17.38
1877	$1.26	1916	$1.31	1955	$3.23	1994	$17.83
1878	$1.20	1917	$1.56	1956	$3.28	1995	$18.33
1879	$1.20	1918	$1.82	1957	$3.39	1996	$18.88
1880	$1.23	1919	$2.08	1958	$3.48	1997	$19.32
1881	$1.23	1920	$2.41	1959	$3.50	1998	$19.63
1882	$1.23	1921	$2.16	1960	$3.56	1999	$20.06
1883	$1.22	1922	$2.02	1961	$3.60	2000	$20.74
1884	$1.18	1923	$2.06	1962	$3.64	2001	$21.32
1885	$1.17	1924	$2.06	1963	$3.68	2002	$21.66
1886	$1.13	1925	$2.11	1964	$3.73	2003	$22.16
1887	$1.14	1926	$2.13	1965	$3.79	2004	$22.76
1888	$1.14	1927	$2.09	1966	$3.90	2005	$23.53
1889	$1.11	1928	$2.06	1967	$4.02	2006	$24.29
1890	$1.09	1929	$2.06	1968	$4.19	2007	$24.97
1891	$1.09	1930	$2.01	1969	$4.42	2008	$25.91
1892	$1.09	1931	$1.83	1970	$4.67	2009	$25.81
1893	$1.08	1932	$1.65	1971	$4.88	2010	$26.22
1894	$1.04	1933	$1.57	1972	$5.03	2011	$27.06
1895	$1.01	1934	$1.61	1973	$5.35	2012	$27.63
1896	$1.01	1935	$1.65	1974	$5.93	2013	$28.05
1897	$1.00	1936	$1.67	1975	$6.47		
1898	$1.00	1937	$1.73	1976	$6.85		

SECTION FOUR: ALL AROUND US

This section offers a ringside seat to the issues and attitudes that defined America in the 1920s. The 60 documents in this section are reprints of magazine articles, newspaper editorials, and political speeches, designed to give readers an idea of what it was like to live in the 1920s. From "Married Women in Industry" and "Code of Conduct for Teachers" to "Comprehensive Immigration Law" and "Church and Politics" these documents deal with important social change that are still up front and center today. Also fascinating to read are "Inventions New and Interesting," (a telephone which fits in the ear!) "Sports Briefs" and "Movie Review: The Best Bad Man."

"Speech by Meyer London, Socialist Party"
Congressional Record, 67th Congress, 1st Session, 1921

"At whom are you striking in this bill? Why, at the very people whom a short while ago you announced you were going to emancipate. We sent two million men abroad to make the world 'safe for democracy' to liberate these very people. Now you shut the door to them. So far, we have made the world safe for hypocrisy and the United States incidentally unsafe for the Democratic Party, temporarily at least (laughter). The supporters of the bill claim that the law will keep out radicals. The idea that by restricting immigration you will prevent the influx of radical thought is altogether untenable. You cannot confine an idea behind prison bars. You cannot exclude it by the most drastic legislation. The field of thought recognizes no barriers. The fact that there was almost no immigration during the war did not prevent us from importing every abominable idea from Europe. We brought over the idea of deportation of radicals from France, not from the France of Rousseau, Jaurès, and Victor Hugo but from the France of the Bourbons. We imported the idea of censorship of the press and the passport system from the Russia of Nicholas II. We imported the idea of universal military service from Germany, not from the Germany of Heine, Boerne, and Freiligrath but from the Germany of the Kaiser."

శ~శ~శ~శ~శ~శ

"Inventions New and Interesting"
Scientific American, **March 26, 1921**

"A Telephone Which Fits in the Ear"

That much-abused term, "the smallest in the world," is again being used, this time in connection with the tiny telephone receiver shown in the accompanying photograph. A German concern has developed this small telephone as part of a set for deaf persons, and the idea is to have the small telephones fit inside the ears of the users so as to be as inconspicuous and out-of-the-way as possible. The telephone is a perfect bi-polar receiver, and has a diameter considerably smaller that the 5-pfennig coin shown beside it.

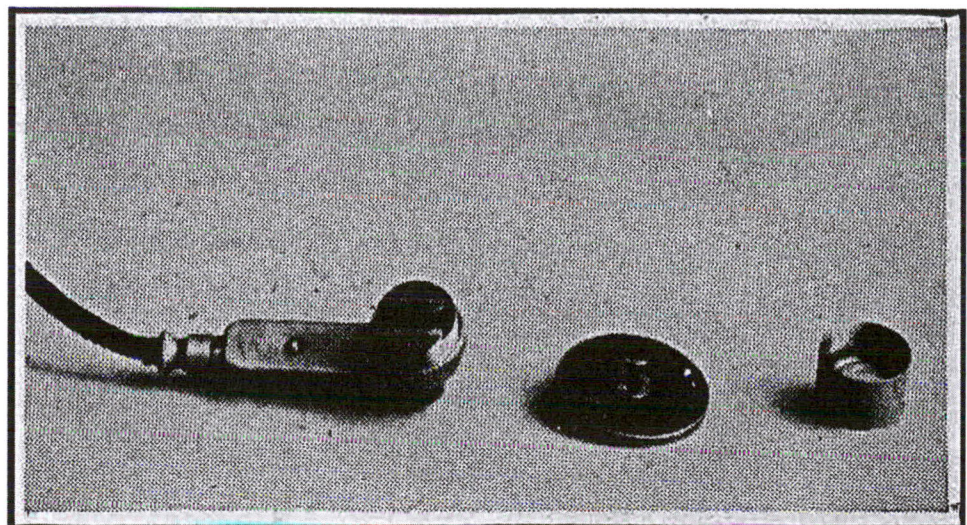

Tiny telephone receiver which is worn

Whether it is the smallest telephone receiver or not, is a question. It seems that the thermal telephone, which was described in these columns several years ago, is still smaller and also fits in the ear of the user. However, the thermal receiver works on the principle of air expansion due to the heating of a small platinum wire. The purity of sound obtained with the thermal telephone receiver is remarkable, and far superior to the general run of telephone apparatus, due to the absence of a diaphragm. In this connection it is very doubtful if the present telephone receiver with its tiny diaphragm can reproduce speech as clearly as the usual telephone receiver of far greater size.

ಹೊಹೊಹೊಹೊಹೊಹೊ

"The First Oyster-Purification Plant"
The Literary Digest, February 16, 1922

"Certified oysters will soon be in as much demand as certified milk. Processes for the sterilization of the oyster, already noted in these pages, have already passed the experimental stage, and a commercial plant, endorsed by city, state and federal health authorities, is now in successful operation near New York. Apparently no one need contract typhoid from eating oysters in the future, no matter what may be the character of the location of the beds where they have been grown. The purifying plant alluded to above is described in *The Nation's Health* (Chicago) by William Firth Wells of the New York State Conservation Commission, who had charge of the earliest experimental work on the process. 'It is unfortunate for oyster culture that these estuaries are also valuable harbors, about which population concentrates and pollutes the tidal waters.'

He goes on: 'Thus many of the finest grounds are restricted by public health regulations, and so any efficient and reliable method of purification should concern sanitarians as well as the shellfish industries. During the past year the first practical plant has been certified by the New York State Conservation Commission, thus, it is believed, marking the establishment of this process as a part of the oyster industry. Fifteen thousand bushels of oysters have been purified commercially, marketed with the approval of the authorities, and consumed by an appreciative public.

'The operation of this plant represents the consummation of successful scientific, commercial, and administrative studies. The underlying principles were carefully worked out during 1914-15 at the Fisherman's Island, Virginia, experiment station in charge of the writer. It was discovered that shellfish closed tightly in the presence of considerable excess of free chlorine, thus protecting the interior tissues from its effects, but permitting the sterilization of everything exterior to the shells; and secondly, that shellfish kept in pure salt water rapidly eliminate by their natural functions all interior contaminating materials accumulated on the tissue surfaces.' "

ಹೊಹೊಹೊಹೊಹೊಹೊ

The death toll of our country and accidents of all kinds industrial and public last year was between 75,000 and 80,000 human lives. The total death toll as a result of our engagement in the late war, covering a period of 19 months, including deaths on the front and those resulting from wounds, everything but deaths from disease, was 56,000. In our own city last year 3,800 persons were killed by accident. Of this number 1,054 were children. The weekly average was 73 resulting in death, of which approximately 20 were children.
—*Arthur Williams, President of the Safety Institute of America, 1922*

"Advertisement of the Association of Railway Executives"
Leslie's Weekly, 1923

"The old-time pack-bearer could carry 100 pounds 10 miles a day. The railroad is the modern pack-bearer. For every employee, it carries 2,000 times as much. Back of each railroad worker there is a $10,000 investment in tracks and trains and terminals, with steam and electricity harnessed like a great beast of burden.

Without this mighty transportation machine, the railroad worker could do no more than the old-time packer could. But with it he is enabled to earn the highest railroad wages paid in the world, while the country gains the lowest-cost transportation in the world. The modern railroad does as much work for half a cent as the pack-bearer could do for a full day's pay. The investment of capital in transportation and other industries increases production, spreads prosperity, and advances civilization.

To enlarge our railroads so that they may keep pace with the nation's increasing production-to improve them so that freight may be hauled with less and less human effort-a constant stream of new capital needs to be attracted. Under wise public regulation, the growth of railroads will be stimulated, the country will be adequately and economically served, labor will receive its full share of the fruits of good management, and investors will be fairly rewarded."

⟋❦⟋❦⟋❦⟋❦⟋❦

"Married Women in Industry, Radio Talks on Women in Industry"
United States Women's Bureau, 1923

"Most persons think of wage-earning women as youngsters from 18 to 25 years old, who are working for a few brief years in industry until they are fortunate enough to meet some young men who marry them and they live happily ever after.

That is just what does happen to a good many young women, as we all know. But it does not happen, by any means, to all women wage earners. There are many thousands of women in industry who never marry but keep on working through all their lives. A woman in a factory in Indiana stated that she had been making gingham aprons in that factory for more than 40 years. Besides such women who have worked steadily in industry, there are many thousands more who get married, stop work for a while, and then go back to the factory to help out with family expenses, or, in some cases, to take the places of husbands whom sickness or death has removed from the ranks of the breadwinners.

These are the women the bureau wants to tell you about, so that you may get a better idea of who goes to make up the great group of women wage earners, and so that you will know more of the human problems which must often be dealt with by these women who wait on you in stores, who make your clothes, prepare your food, and help to make almost every article you use, from a toothbrush to a railroad train.

It is an easy matter to find out how many married women are wage earners. In 1920 there were 1,920,281 married women who were gainfully employed. The census, which is taken every 10 years, tells us that. But the census does not tell us very much about them. The Women's Bureau wanted to find out more details of those women, so the records which the census had taken in 1920 for all the women in one industrial town were studied, and it was found that about half the women who were breadwinners were married women. There were about 4,000 married women earning money in this one community. When examined closely the records disclosed something that seems very important. Nearly two thirds of them were mothers who had children less than five years old. The bureau wanted to find out how these mothers managed to take care of the children and do other work at the same time, so the census records were looked at again to see whether any light on the subject could be discovered. It was found that about half of these mothers of young children earned money at home by taking in boarders or doing laundry or some other form of work which did not oblige them to leave home, so they could look out for children and work at the same time. But the other half went out to work and spent their days in mills making woolen and worsted cloth, and in factories making handkerchiefs and other manufactured articles. Wonder arose as to what became of those little children while their mothers were away from home all day; and because there was no other way to find out, agents were sent to visit as many of these families as they could.

During these visits, among every five women one was found who was working at night and looking out for her children during the daytime, and one who just left the children alone at home to look out for each other. Sometimes the father worked at night and cared for the children in the daytime while their mother was away, and sometimes the neighbors or the landlady or relatives kept an eye on the children. Only one woman in 20 had someone who was paid especially to care for her young children while she was away at work.

Does this give you a picture of the pressure under which women are working in industry? Can you see all these mothers leaving home at 6:30 or 7:00 in the morning after they have washed and dressed the children and fixed their breakfast and lunches? Can you see these mothers working all day, and can you imagine their thoughts as they wonder whether the children are all right and whether someone has seen to all the many things little children need? And at the end of the day's work in factory or mill, can you picture the homecoming of these mothers, and the tasks which await them?"

"Code of Conduct for Teachers"
W. W. Fuller, Southern Ohio District Superintendent, 1923

Some teachers, 1922-3, have failed for the following reasons: (a) lack of knowledge of subject matter and inability to manage children; (b) attention to card playing, dancing, and other social interests to the neglect of their schoolwork; (c) on account of falling in love with high school pupils; (d) on account of keeping company with sorry men; (e) on account of night riding without a chaperon; (f) on account of attendance at rotten vaudeville and sorry moving picture shows; (g) on account of entertaining company until late hours at night, making good schoolwork the next day impossible; (h) on account of failure to take any vital interest in church and Sunday school work and other community activities.

If you think this applicant will and can avoid all the above sources of failure, I shall appreciate your saying so. If you think there is doubt about her having enough sense to avoid these sources of failure, I shall appreciate your frankness. We are after teachers who are in earnest about doing what they are paid to do. We prefer that other kinds go elsewhere.

"A Vagrant Reader's Evening with the Mail"
Frater Ignotus, *The Epworth Herald*, February 24, 1923

I have spent an evening looking through some of my favorite printed matter-the stuff, good, bad and worse, which gets into many preachers' letter boxes these days.

Much of it is good. More is bad; not vicious, but plain useless. It is a sheer waste of paper, ink and postage… But what I have been reading to-night is not so far astray as some of the third-class mail that comes my way. And I want you to share some of it with me.

Here is my friend Bromley Oxman of Los Angeles, writing in his own brave broadsheet, *In Days to Come*, on Jesus's doctrine of equal rights for all. This is what he says about the right of children to play:

"I have seen little children whose ages ran from six to 10 standing in front of the machine throughout a twelve-and-one-half hour shift, and I have seen little tots dancing around the Maypole in our Los Angeles playgrounds.

Jesus says, 'Equal rights.' The relation of play to growth, to juvenile delinquency, to democracy should be studied by twentieth-century followers of Christ.

A delinquent youngster came to me one day. His nickname was 'Shrimp.' He said: 'Gee, I got pinched again. They took me in just for hooking a lawnmower. Now, what d'ye think of that?'

It was a social attitude born upon the streets. Supervised play was his right. Through it he would have developed a different social attitude, but his right had been denied him."

ᚥᚥᚥᚥᚥᚥᚥᚥᚥ

<h3 style="text-align:center">"The Currents of History in the Making"
The Epworth Herald, February 24, 1923</h3>

The world's supply of automobiles seems to be quite unequally distributed. While there are so few cars in the desert that many of the nomads live to a ripe old age and die without seeing one, there are so many in Chicago that they caused 517 deaths during the first 11 months of 1922. The significance of these figures is seen when it is remembered that typhoid, smallpox, measles and scarlet fever took only 198 lives during this period. The health department quarantines cases of contagious diseases, but it cannot quarantine reckless drivers.

"$7,000,000 for Ford Ads"
The New York Times, August 17, 1923

The Ford Motor Company has decided to spend $7,000,000 in advertising on newspapers throughout the country, and has reorganized its advertising department, after five years of inactivity, with Newton P. Brotherton at its head.

The new plan apparently contemplates display advertising to be charged directly to the Ford Company itself, presumably in addition to the dealer system of publicity.

❧❧❧❧❧❧❧❧❧

"Mob Charges Ring After Arbiter Calls Bout Draw"
Davenport Democrat and Leader (IA), October 5, 1923

Although McTigue of Ireland still retains his light heavyweight crown under the third decision rendered by referee Harry Ertie after the Irishman's 10-rounder bout yesterday, his opponent Young Stribling today is the rightful owner, in the opinion of Columbus, Georgia, fight fans. Promoter J. P. Jones of the local American Legion Post so informed Chairman Muldoon of the New York State boxing commission in a telegram sent to him last night demanding a thorough investigation by the commission of yesterday's tumultuous events.

Jones' telegram was sent after referee Ertie, who at first declared the fight a draw and then when the crowd of 8,000 displeased fans charged the ring, changed his decision giving the victory to the 18-year-old Georgia schoolboy, had issued a written statement officially declaring the fight a draw. The statement, issued from the obscurity of a private residence here, contained the assertion that the referee had been threatened with death if he did not give the decision to Stribling and a charge that Major Jones had forcibly held his arm and that of Stribling aloft.

Three hours after the fight Ertie issued a statement that his decision is a draw. Last night, on the eve of the fight, McTigue suddenly claimed that he had a broken thumb. He had doctors to back his claim. He therefore called off the match Wednesday night stating his thumb was broken Monday of this week while training here. This morning 10 of the best surgeons in this state declared after x-ray examination that the injury was an old one and that same injury to the thumb occurred prior to his signing the contract on Labor Day for the bout held today. After much wrangling McTigue agreed to defend the championship. He lost six rounds, carried two, and two were draws. This is the average opinion.

> Ford's success has startled the country, almost the world, financially, industrially, mechanically. It exhibits in higher degree than most persons would have thought possible the seemingly contradictory requirements of true efficiency, which are: constant increase of quality, great increase of pay to the workers, repeated reduction in cost to the consumer. And with these appears, as at once cause and effect, an absolutely incredible enlargement of output reaching something like one hundredfold in less than 10 years, and an enormous profit to the manufacturer.
>
> —*Charles Buxton Going, concerning Henry Ford's use of scientific management, 1915*

"Brooklyn Students Win Economic Essay Prizes"
Brooklyn Daily Standard Union, September 10, 1923

It was announced today that the first and second prizes, $1,000 and $500, respectively, offered by Alvan T. SIMONDS for the best essay on "The Lack of Economic Intelligence" which was open to high school and normal school pupils in the United States and Canada, were won by Brooklynites.

The first prize was awarded to John J. BORCHARDT, 18 years old, a graduate of Commercial High School. He is a first-generation American. His father was born in West Prussia and his mother in Gallicia. They came to the United States in 1901 and his father became a citizen. His father is employed by a furniture factory in Brooklyn and has been there ever since his arrival in this country.

The second prize was given to Morris SALTZMAN, 17, also a graduate of Commercial High. He was born in Russia. His family came to this country in 1909.

"Colored Singing"
Variety, 1923

Colored singing and playing artists are riding to fame and fortune with the current popular demand for "blues" disc recordings, and because of the recognized fact that only a Negro can do justice to the native indigo ditties, such artists are in great demand.

Mamie Smith is generally credited with having started the demand on the Okeh Records. Not only do these discs enjoy wide sales among the colored race, but they caught on with the Caucasians. As a result, practically every record-making firm, from the Victor down, has augmented its catalog with special "blues" recordings by colored artists.

As a result of this "blues" boom and demand, various colored publishers are prospering. Perry Bradford and the Clarence Williams Music Company are among the representative Negro music men cleaning up from the mechanical royalties with the sheet music angle negligible and almost incidental. No attention to professional plug-in is made; these publishers are concentrating on the disc artists.

ᔕᘏᔕᘏᔕᘏᔕᘏᔕᘏᔕᘏᔕᘏ

"Married Women in Industry"
United States Women's Bureau, 1924

"In 1920 there were 1,920,281 married women who were gainfully employed. The bureau wanted to find how these mothers managed to take care of the children and do other work at the same time, so the census records were looked at again to see whether any light on the subject could be discovered. It was found that half of these mothers of young children earned money at home by taking in boarders or doing laundry or some other form of work which did not obligate them to leave home, so they could look out for the children and work at the same time. But the other half went out to work and spent their days in mills making woolen and worsted cloth, and in factories making handkerchiefs and other manufactured articles. Wonder arose as to what became of these little children while their mothers were away from home all day, and, because there was no other way to find out, agents were sent to visit as many of these families as they could.

During these visits, among every five women one was found who was working at night and looking out for her children during the daytime, and one who just left the children alone at home to look out for each other. Sometimes, the father worked at night and cared for the children in the daytime while their mothers were away, and sometimes the neighbors or the landlady or the relatives kept an eye on the children. Only one woman in twenty had someone who was paid especially to care for her young children while she was away at work.

Does this give you a picture of the pressure under which women are working in industry? Can you see all these mothers leaving home at 6:30 or 7 in the morning after they have washed and dressed the children and fixed their breakfast and lunches? Can you see these mothers working all day, and can you imagine their thoughts as they wonder whether the children are all right and whether some one has seen to all the many little things little children need? And at the end of the day's work in factory or mill can you picture the homecoming of these mothers and the tasks which await them?"

ᔕᘏᔕᘏᔕᘏᔕᘏᔕᘏᔕᘏᔕᘏ

"Legislative Outlook"
Members of the General Federation of Women's Clubs, February 1924

"Department of Education: The President's recommendation along this line was: 'I consider it a fundamental requirement of national activity which, accompanied by allied subjects of welfare, is worthy of a separate department and a place in the Cabinet.' This does not go quite far enough to suit the National Education Association, nor the General

Federation, who think the Department of Education in the Cabinet should not be coupled with 'allied subjects of welfare.' Federal Industrial Institutions for Women: This bill, providing for the segregation of women who are committed for federal offenses, has already passed the Senate. It really opens negotiations by the appointment of a committee to select a site for such farm or institution. No definite plans could be made until it was known whether the site selected would make use of existing buildings, or require new equipment."

"The Oil Exposition Is an Immense Exhibit"
The Oil and Gas Journal, October 2, 1924

"Developing in 18 months from an idea into the largest exposition ever held by a single industry, the International Petroleum Exposition stands as a monument to the tremendous scope and power of the business of oil exploration, the production of crude petroleum, the refining of the crude into hundreds of distinctly useful products and the transportation and marketing of oil in every part of the world.

The Exposition, which opens in Tulsa on Thursday, occupies 7.5 acres of space; the size of it can better be imagined by mentally envisioning the great display as in one building. To house the show under one roof, with one big aisle, and the exhibits grouped along both sides of the aisle, would require a building that would occupy more than 20 city blocks. With the outside exhibits it would string even farther.

It occupies more space and will have a greater number of exhibits than was contained in the great machinery hall at the World's Columbian Exposition in Chicago, which was housed in the largest building ever built up to that time…Many entirely new tools, devices and instruments which manufacturers have held back for this occasion will be shown for the first time, and improvements on well-known articles of oil industrial equipment will be first noted by the crowds who attend the big oil and gas show."

"Canned Childhood"
Sarah N. Cleghon, *Poems of Child Labor*, 1924

Beneath the label "Oysters," "Shrimp,"
Is canned a pound of frolic missed
Upon a summer morn-
Lost fun and frolic, soldered tight
Where no child finds them, morn or night.
A pound of health, a pound of strength
From candles snatched, we find:
A pound of young intelligence
Robbed from a childish mind.
Packed here together, snugly fit
Teresa's eyesight, Tony's wit.
And wasted sunshine here is canned,
With wasted smells of flowers;
The wasted sparkle of green fields
Washed bright by early showers.
And pleasant scampers never run,
And shouts unheard in breeze and sun.
Yea, in the cans are voices hid
Of little sons and daughters,
That should be singing, "London Bridge,"
"I Spy," and "Sally Waters,"
"Where oats, peas, beans and barley grows
'Tis you nor I nor nobody knows."
Come buy, my fellow countrymen!
Canned childhood's selling cheap,
And what though little Jack should tire
And fall too fast asleep?
There's work for little Marianne-
Come buy sweet childhood by the can.

"Interview with German Immigrant Hans Bergner"
Island of Home, Island of Tears, 1924

Third-class passengers had to come to Ellis Island, and none of us knew exactly what this would mean. What it meant was that, first of all, the immigration officials would make sure that we knew where we were going when we arrived. We had, of course, been sponsored by someone in the United States in order to be here in the first place, but there had to be some proof shown that someone was going to pick us up or that we had some destination that we were going to go to.

The other thing they wanted to know was whether we had $25, and the third thing they wanted to know was could we read the English language (although literacy in German would have been acceptable) so each of us was asked to read a small paragraph from a book that the official would show us.

And then came the last step and, of course, the most familiar to people who have served in the armed forces, namely that there was a physical inspection awaiting us, the women on one side and the men on the other. Then came the great moment when we stood in front of the immigration official, who was a doctor, who examined us for venereal diseases. And if there was one who had a venereal disease, that particular person would not be allowed to land. There again, I had my peculiar feeling of the strange separation-that venereal diseases among first and second-class passengers were apparently acceptable, and for third class passengers, venereal diseases were not. Well, this was one of those introductions one never forgets

❧❧❧❧❧❧❧❧

"A Chance for the Rich Man's Son"
William G. Shephard, *Collier's*, June 14, 1924

The son of Frederick H. Goff, millionaire banker of Cleveland, Ohio, did not sit around twitching nervously when his father's will was read some months ago. Neither did his two sisters.

These heirs had always known they wouldn't get their father's millions. They received by the will incomes less than the salaries of a good many men in the United States. They may build homes for themselves, such as they can maintain on their incomes, but these homes will belong to the estate, cannot be mortgaged and revert to the estate when they die, unless they have children living. When the grandchildren reach the age of 25 years, the estate ceases to pay them any income.

The entire estate then goes into the philanthropic Cleveland Trust Fund. Frederick Goff was against great dynastic family fortunes.

And what do Frederick Goff's children think of this plan? I talked to William Goff, the son, about it. I found him at a clerk's desk in a bank in Cleveland.

He was in his shirtsleeves. The man at the wicket window called him to the front to meet me. I asked him whether he would be willing to tell me how much a son should expect from a rich father.

"Just wait a minute," he said, smiling. He went to the rear of the room, took his coat from a locker and put it on. Then he came out through the gateway in the railing, a brown-eyed, husky six-footer, shook hands, and led me over to a seat in the public gangway.

"Of course I'm willing to talk about what my father did in his will. I'm not married yet, and I haven't many thousands of dollars, but I made a will just like my father's the other day. It's the right kind of will to make. I call it an American will."

He laughed or smiled through all our talk; straight white teeth emphasized the clear brownness of his eyes; behind his evident content with life there was football health. What a smash he, with one of his father's millions, could make-for a while-on Broadway! But he won't-not his kind.

What he says, this boy of less than 25, who might have inherited millions but didn't-and isn't sorry-runs like this:

"I don't think any son these days has a right to be a millionaire just because his father was. If I ever become one, I'll have to make the money myself, if I can, as my father did.

"Here's what my father did with me; he fixed it so that I will never have to go hungry or cold and so that I will be taken care of if I am taken ill. If I get married and have children, I can build a home for them and I will have enough money to care for them and educate them. But when they reach the age that I am now, they must begin to shift for themselves. The same arrangement is made for my sisters…"

"What's the harm of inheriting a million dollars?" I asked.

"Why, it's like wrapping cloths around a fellow's ambition and making a mummy out of it. I know some young fellows who have inherited millions of dollars. They're the unhappiest people I know. They don't know what to do in life. There's no use of doing anything.

"And," he added with a big laugh, "they're the tightest tightwads I know. They're always trying to find out what they can get without using their money-and it's mighty little, let me tell you. They didn't get a square sort of start.

"People don't seem to understand that it's a chance that any boy wants. The son of a rich man needs it just as much as the son of a poor man.

"And that's true about the daughters of rich men, too. It isn't good for a girl to expect a lot of money all her life and then get it. If a girl has an income that keeps her safe from what I call jungle living, or the fight to keep alive, she has as good a chance in life as any other girl. And that's what girls want these days."

જ~√જ~√જ~√જ~√

"Comprehensive Immigration Law"
The President of the United States of America, 1924

Whereas it is provided in the act of Congress approved May 26, 1924, entitled "An act to limit the immigration of aliens into the United States, and for other purposes" that "The annual quota of any nationality shall be two per centum of the number of foreign-born individuals of such nationality resident in continental United States as determined by the United States Census of 1890, but the minimum quota of any nationality shall be 100 (Sec. 11 a)…

"The Secretary of State, the Secretary of Commerce, and the Secretary of Labor, jointly, shall, as soon as feasible after the enactment of this act, prepare a statement showing the number of individuals of the various nationalities resident in continental United States as determined by the United States Census of 1890, which statement shall be the population basis for the purposes of subdivision (a) of section 11 (Sec. 12 b).

"Such officials shall, jointly, report annually to the President the quota of each nationality under subdivision (a) of section 11, together with the statements, estimates, and revisions provided for in this section.

The President shall proclaim and make known the quotas so reported. (Sec. 12 e) "Now, therefore I, Calvin Coolidge, President of the United States of America acting under and by virtue of the power in me vested by the aforesaid act of Congress, do hereby proclaim and make known that on and after July 1, 1924, and throughout the fiscal year 1924-1925, the quota of each nationality provided in said act shall be as follows:

Country or Area of Birth: Quota 1924-1925

Afghanistan: 100
Albania: 100
Andorra: 100
Arabian peninsula: 100
Armenia: 124
Australia, including Papua, Tasmania, and all islands appertaining to Australia: 121
Austria: 785
Belgium: 512
Bhutan: 100
Bulgaria: 100
Cameroon (proposed British mandate): 100
Cameroon (French mandate): 100
China: 100
Czechoslovakia: 3,073
Danzig, Free City of: 228
Denmark: 2,789
Egypt: 100
Estonia: 124
Ethiopia (Abyssinia): 100
Finland: 170
France: 3,954
Germany: 51,227
Great Britain and Northern Ireland: 34,007
Greece: 100
Hungary: 473
Iceland: 100
India: 100
Iraq (Mesopotamia): 100
Irish Free State: 28,567
Italy, including Rhodes, Dodecanesia, and Castellorizzo: 3,845
Japan: 100
Latvia: 142
Liberia: 100
Liechtenstein: 100
Lithuania: 344
Luxemburg: 100
Monaco: 100
Morocco (French and Spanish Zones and Tangier): 100
Muscat (Oman): 100
Nauru (proposed British mandate): 100
Nepal: 100
Netherlands: 1648
New Zealand (including appertaining islands: 100
Norway: 6,453
New Guinea, and other Pacific Islands under proposed Australian mandate: 100
Palestine (with Trans Jordan, proposed British mandate): 100
Persia: 100
Poland: 5,982

Portugal: 503
Ruanda and Urundi (Belgium mandate): 100
Rumania: 603
Russia, European and Asiatic: 2,248
Samoa, Western (proposed mandate of New Zealand): 100
San Marino: 100
Siam: 100
South Africa, Union of: 100
South West Africa (proposed mandate of Union of South Africa): 100
Spain: 131
Sweden: 9,561
Switzerland: 2,081
Syria and The Lebanon (French mandate): 100
Tanganyika (proposed British mandate): 100
Togoland (proposed British mandate): 100
Togoland (French mandate): 100
Turkey: 100
Yap and other Pacific islands (under Japanese mandate) (4): 100
Yugoslavia: 671

"Athletics"
The Etonian (Elizabethtown, PA), 1924

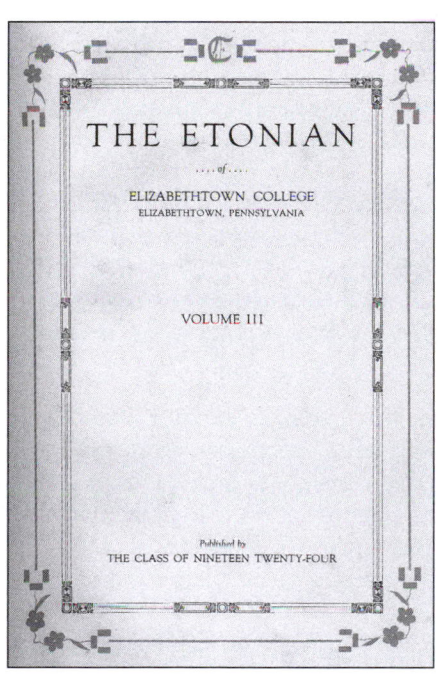

Throughout the school year we have had among the entire student body the feeling that physical exercise is one of the essential, if not the most essential, phase in an educational career. Consequently there was a need for the development of a proper attitude for this division of school activity. However, great care has been shown in determining how much exercise is needed in order to maintain sufficient body vigor and at the same time to hold the scholastic attainment of the individual in the foreground.

The true sportsman will enter into any kind of athletics wholeheartedly. By playing the game hard he will obtain the greatest amount of value in any game, both from a physical and mental standpoint. This is very evident when we consider any form of group game which requires considerable cooperation among individual players to ensure victory. In this very idea there is something that readily can be applied to everyday life.

We believe that every member of the student body needs some form of physical exercise. Bodily decay and reconstruction are taking place continually. Therefore, if we wish to establish a foursquare educational platform we must not fail to take into the structure a well-founded conception of physical education.

We Americans need to stop and step aside from our daily routine of everyday life and engage in something that will tend to give voice to our bodily systems.

"Democratic Tendencies in Education, Two Outstanding Advances in the United States"
James R. Angell, *These Eventful Years*, 1924

In the United States, undoubtedly the two outstanding features of educational development in this century have been the unprecedented growth of the public high schools and, especially since the World War, the extraordinary increase in attendance of colleges and universities. In 1900, there were 696,000 high school students. In 1922, there were 2,371,000. Nor does this mere increase in numbers at all convey the real situation, for partly as cause and partly as effect there has occurred in parallel with this growth in attendance, an amazing growth in physical appointments of many of the schools and the educational opportunities offered. Millions of dollars have been expended upon school buildings, certain of which challenge in beauty and convenience any educational buildings ever erected. In many cases, they have become centers for civic interest related to the schools: for example, the development of music, art and general public education. The pride felt by towns and cities in these buildings and their equipment reflects a radical change in the community attitude toward education....

The change in the curriculum which had begun long before the opening of the twentieth century, but which has gone on rapidly since then, is attributable chiefly to two circumstances, the first of which has affected higher education as well as secondary, and Europeans as well as American.

1) A few generations ago, the scope of American education beyond the elementary school was fundamentally comprised of Latin, Greek and mathematics. Presently, the natural sciences (astronomy, chemistry, geology, physics and biology), modern languages, including English itself, history, both modern and ancient, and the social and economic sciences, all came knocking at the door and all were admitted, with the result that, where half a dozen subjects formerly covered the entire educational offering, there are now four or five times as many, each of which can present some cogent claim to replace certain of the older subjects, hard pressed to stand upon a par with them. Some of these subjects, especially those of laboratory character, require much more elaborate and costly equipment for their proper presentation than the older and more bookish subjects. Moreover, instruction in them requires a large number of teachers who are more or less specialists and who will be difficult to secure in requisite numbers until the demand has induced a sufficient number of candidates to get the necessary preparation.

2) Again, the high school movement has been fundamentally affected by the natural desire to give students who complete their former education at this level, opportunity to acquire training which it is hoped and believed they can make immediately available in earning a livelihood and taking up the practical duties of citizenship. Considerations of this character have resulted in the establishment of new commercial and technical high schools and the introduction of many essentially vocational studies into the programme of the ostensibly non-technical schools. High schools, state colleges and state universities have all been affected by federal legislation such as the Smith-Hughes Bill of 1917, which appropriates large sums for vocational training on the condition that the state contribute dollar for dollar with the Central Government. The invasion of this material has called for the construction of costly shop laboratories of various kinds. The same motive has in part controlled the criteria offered in the continuation schools, whose pupils pursue there some fraction of the time, when they are not engaged in business or industrial employments, the school training which they interrupted to seek such remunerative occupation.

One notable circumstance deserves special emphasis. Never before has any country entered seriously a program of free education of high school grade for literally every child who may apply his intelligence and permits the pursuing of the course of study, and with the expectation that a large proportion of the eligible children will take advantage of the opportunity. This programme carries with it the necessity of providing trained teachers and physical facilities on a scale never before undertaken. The cost of the enterprise is staggering, and many communities are at present proceeding under the greatest financial embarrassment in the maintenance of their schools.

Side-by-side with the increase of the number of high schools and the number of pupils has naturally been a great increase in the number of children in the primary schools, of whom there were 20,383,222 in 1920. This increase which has been in general most marked in urban centers, has reflected in part the tremendous growth in population, and in part a better enforcement of compulsory educational laws, to say nothing of some growth in the ambition of parents to have their children educated to meet the more exacting demands of modern life.

ھ‌ہ‌ہ‌ہ‌ہ‌ہ‌ہ‌ہ

"The Library and Adult Education"
Alexander Meiklejohn, 1924

Democracy is education…. Insofar as we can educate the people, insofar as we can bring people to understanding of themselves and of their world, we can have a democracy. Insofar as we cannot do that, we have got to have control by the few.

"Annual Report of Commission of Agriculture, Commerce, and Industry of State of South Carolina" Labor Division, 1925

"The magnitude of the economic importance of the textile industry in the South is illustrated by the figures for South Carolina, where, in 1925, the produce of the cotton mills was 74 percent of the value of all the industrial products of the State, 70 percent of the wages paid were to textiles employees, 70 percent of all wage earners in the State were textile operatives, 65 percent of the total number were localized in the mills of the Piedmont with 27 percent of these centers in Spartanburg County, which since 1920 has been the premier manufacturing district of the State."

ھ‌ہ‌ہ‌ہ‌ہ‌ہ‌ہ‌ہ

"My Neighborhood" Edward Corsi
The Outlook, September 16, 1925

Edward Corsi finds in the polyglot boardinghouse of New York the makings of the America of tomorrow.

There are 27 nationalities in the neighborhood, including, of course, the Chinese laundrymen, the gypsy phrenologists, and the Greek and Syrian storekeepers. Along the banks of the East River, surrounding Thomas Jefferson Park, are the Italians; on Pleasant Avenue are the Poles, Austrians and Hungarians. West, where Fifth Avenue loses its dignity but not its charm, are the Jews, sons of many lands; near them are the Turks and Spaniards. North, where "Little Italy" makes room for "Little Africa," are the Negroes, gradually moving down, much to the discomfort of the whites. South, resisting the merciless invasion of the Jews and Italians, are the Germans and Irish, remnant of a stock that once ruled this part of town. Scattered throughout the neighborhood, with limits well-defined, are lesser groups-Finns, Russians, French, Swedes, Danes, Rumanians and Jogoslavs. Here and there, like refugees in exile, are a few Americans of old stock, heroically holding their ground.

The cosmopolitan character of the neighborhood is evidenced not only in the signs of the many languages, the chop suey, the rotisseries, and spaghetti houses, the synagogues and Catholic temples, the flags of many colors, the foreign papers on every newsstand, but in the types one meets on the streets-tall, blond Nordics, olive-skinned, dark-haired Mediterraneans, long-bearded Semites and Slavs, massive Africans, East Indians, gypsies, Japs and Chinese.

The Italians and Jews predominate, giving the neighborhood the color of the Roman Ghetto. Few people have less in common than these. They differ in language, religion, custom and temperament. But they get along, even if now and then there is an unpleasant interchange of "kike" and "wop." Under the protecting aegis of the Irish policeman's club or the American flag, even the brotherhood of man is possible…

The Great War itself, with its passions and hatreds, could not disturb the peaceful equilibrium of the neighborhood. Life in that trying hour went on as usual. All fighting was done for America. In the last political campaign the Jews and the Italians joined forces. The result was the election of "the long Progressive Congressman from the East," an American of Italian extraction, and a large vote for LaFollette.

"Sports Briefs"
Alton Evening Telegraph (IL), December 15, 1925

Because they taught physical exercises in school for salaries, three London young women tennis players have been declared by the Lawn Tennis Association to be professionals and disqualified from competition in amateur matches.

Professional hockey will make its bow in New York tonight with the New York Americans meeting the Canadians of Montréal in the National Hockey League contest. The Governor General's footguard band from Canada and the cadet banned from West Point are the advertised attractions.

The Huddle System of calling basketball signals will replace the method in which the center designates the play when Northwestern opens its floor season tonight against Notre Dame. The Purple will continue the style unless it takes too much time.

Hockey has joined baseball and football in attracting noted players from the ranks of the amateurs.

ᚦᚦᚦᚦᚦᚦᚦᚦ

"Many Miners Are Entombed by Blast"
The Morning Herald, (Uniontown, PA), May 28, 1925

Coal Glenn, N.C., May 27-The fate of threescore or more miners entombed this morning by an explosion below the 1,000-foot lateral of the Carolina Coal Company mine, near here, was undetermined tonight, although rescuers had succeeded in bringing to the surface six bodies and it was feared most of the others had perished.

Records of the mine showed that 59 men, 39 white and 20 negroes, had comprised the crew which went into the mine, while mine officials reported that 71 miners' lamps were missing and it was believed that figure might represent the number entombed.

Hope was expressed, however, by Bion H. Butler, vice president of the mining company, that some of the entombed men might still be alive.

Rescue workers said that the air was clear in the mine below the point where the bodies were found. The fans were kept going all day in an effort to purify the air so that rescuers might be able to penetrate further into the dark recesses that are believed to hold the victims.

Mr. Butler said the best information he had been able to obtain was that the first explosion occurred in the second right lateral of the mine approximately 1,000 feet from the entrance. The two explosions which followed at half-hour intervals were believed by officials to have occurred between the second right shaft and the opening. Mine authorities said the six men whose bodies were found apparently had died only a short time before they were reached.

"Henry Ford Comments: Aeronautics"
Time, July 27, 1925

I experimented twelve years with my motor car before I was convinced that it represented a lasting and stable product for the public. I have now only started to experiment with the airplane. And let me tell you that the commercial airplane is as yet a considerable distance of being a success...

The airplane motor is still unreliable-a delicate, quivering mechanism. Its vibration is so intense that there is little guaranty under such strain that it will remain intact over considerable distances. The airplane game depends greatly at present upon the flying ability of the man in the pilot's seat. Our daily trips to Chicago and Cleveland are about 90 percent skill of the men at the throttle. Stunt flying, as I see it, is about 98 percent of the same element...

Countries we have long characterized as 'heathen' have taken active steps against American movies. Even Turkey has forbidden children under 15 years of age to attend movies 'to protect young Turks from the demoralizing effects of American-made films.' The infidel nation is aroused to save its children from the Christian nation... Will Hays said in a recent speech in Berlin 'the worldwide distribution of films fills an important part in making people in different lands understand each other,' but Sir Hesketh Bell (former Governor of Uganda) says, "Nothing has done more to destroy the prestige of the white man among the colored races than these deplorable pictures."

—*Helen A. Miller, New York State Director of Motion Pictures, 1926*

"Child Labor vs. Children's Work"
Julia E. Johnsen, *Child Labor*, New York, 1925

Nothing could be further from the truth than the rather widespread notion that child labor reform is predicated on the assumption that children should have no work whatever to do. It must be said, however, that the belief that children should have work is responsible for a good deal of child labor. Though much has been done by society to abolish child labor, little has been done to establish children's work on a proper basis. Society has made no serious constructive attack on the children's work problem, but sooner or later we must come to grips with this problem. The school has not done its part toward answering the true work needs of children; neither has the home, and the urban home is under heavy handicap in this regard. Instead of enough children's work, we have had too much child labor. As part of the solution of the child labor problem, as a means to the abolition of child labor and the breaking down of opposition to reform, we must give attention to the work that children should have and see that they have it. To establish children's work is quite as important as to establish children's play or to abolish child labor. These are all aspects of a single problem.

Let us consider for a moment some of the supposed values of child labor. In defense of it, we have heard the assertion that it furnishes training in the sense of responsibility and in the habit of thrift, and that it affords the discipline of self-subordination to unpleasant tasks. However, there is abundant opportunity for developing the sense of responsibility in the home and the school through household duties, home projects under school auspices, schemes of self-government and so on. The same is true of thriftiness. Moreover, thrift is not merely a matter of money, and the virtues connected with it may be developed in relation to school supplies, home possessions, food and clothes. Child laborers have not yet been shown to be especially thrifty with their earnings. As to the disciplinary value of child labor, modern psychology teaches that the only discipline that is worthwhile is that which accords with the child's own nature, his instincts and desires-not all of them, of course, but a selected few. It is not the discipline that runs counter to his nature, resulting in nothing more than sullen obedience or strained submission. This latter kind weakens or breaks what we sometimes, rather inaccurately, call the will. The activity that develops the will is willing activity. The work performed in accordance with the child's own purposes and desires has far more disciplinary value than drudgery, which stifles initiative, individuality and expressiveness, all of which may be enlisted in the service of character building, and without which there is no character.

ఈళ-ఈళ-ఈళ-ఈళ-ఈళ

"Hints to World Cruisers Ship"
Lt. Commander J. G. P. Bisset, R.D., R.N.R., 1926

Round-the-world cruising has become almost a habit, and in the great 20,000-ton liners that make the cruises today, it is also a luxury and a very interesting one, too....

Some cruises go round the world east about, that is, through the Mediterranean and the Suez Canal, and return via the Panama Canal. Others go west about, starting out through the

Panama Canal and returning via the Mediterranean, or in some cases round South Africa. The only difference is that going east about, the clock is being put up half an hour or so each night as you steam eastward, and going west it is put back correspondingly. To make up for this, when crossing the 180 meridian east about, you will experience an eight-day week, and west about a six-day week....

The cruise ships are well-known vessels belonging to the various transatlantic lines, and they are chartered lock, stock and funnel by the travel companies, and manned by the same captain, officers and crew as they carry on their ordinary runs. This is a great factor towards smooth and efficient running. The best ships provide an experienced physician, a tip-top orchestra, gymnastic, swimming and squash instructors, barbers, ladies' hairdressers and manicurists, a well-equipped laundry and valet service, a well-stocked library, indoor and outdoor swimming tanks, garden lounges, deck games, etc., etc. The charters put a staff on board, in the charge of a cruise director, and this usually includes lecturers, clergymen, surgeons, dentists, bankers, host and hostess, photographers and travel experts, and a librarian with an ample stock of travel books, guides, etc., etc. A good supply of clothing, as ordinarily worn in temperate climates, should be taken, and also several Palm Beach suits. There is an impression that these can be best obtained abroad, in places like India or China, but my experience is that they are rarely satisfactory, and you will do well to get them at home. Bring flannels, sweaters and sneakers for deck games, also a gymnastic costume. A swimming costume suitable for the outdoor pool should be brought, as this pool is well in the public eye as it were, and always a great source of attraction. A heavy coat or wrap is required for cool evenings, and a light raincoat or dust-coat is useful for motoring. Many of the motor drives are very dusty trips, and on occasion, passengers are advised by the "staff" to wear old clothes, so bring along that old suit, and you can get it cleaned up occasionally on board.

Do not bother about a sun helmet; they are a nuisance to pack, and can be obtained better and cheaper in tropical countries.

For gentlemen, a dinner jacket is the usual dress for evenings and should be sufficient, unless you expect to attend any formal functions abroad. For hot weather, a couple of loose dinner jackets made of white alpaca or duck, look and feel cool, and can be laundered on board as required.

For ladies, I am advised by several very charming authorities that amongst other things they should bring dresses of materials that do not crush or wrinkle, and which, upon opening the trunk and being shaken out, will look "perfect." I had no idea such material existed. The same authorities also advised Kayser silk for certain items, but I'm getting into deep water now and guess I'll drop that subject…

By the way, bring a couple of fancy costumes. The masquerade ball is always a fun event, and the first one usually takes place early in the cruise, as it gets folk together.

"The Klan's Fight for Americanism"
Hiram Wesley Evans, *The North American Review*, 1926

"The greatest achievement so far has been to formulate, focus, and gain recognition for an idea, the idea of preserving and developing America first and chiefly for the benefit of the children of the pioneers who made America, and only and definitely along the lines and purpose and spirit of those pioneers. The Klan cannot claim to have created this idea: it has long been a vague stirring in the souls of the plain people. But the Klan can fairly claim to have given it purpose, method and direction and a vehicle. When the Klan first appeared the nation was in the confusion of sudden awakening, from the lovely dream of the melting pot, disorganized and helpless before the invasion of aliens and alien ideas. After ten years of the Klan it is in arms for defense. This is our greatest achievement. The second is more selfish; we have won the leadership in the movement for Americanism. Except for a few lonesome voices, almost drowned by the clamor of the alien and the alien-minded 'liberal,' the Klan has alone faced the invader. This is not to say that the Klan has gathered into its membership all who are ready to fight for America. It is an idea, a faith, a purpose, an organized crusade."

"The Honest-to-Goodness Woman"
John Martin Magazine for Boys and Girls, December 1926

"The Honest-to-Goodness Woman: Very early in the morning the Honest-to-Goodness-Woman did arise. She said to herself: 'I will not waste a minute.' She did not forget to take her bath, to clean her teeth, and to brush her hair; she did all these things in order, and neatly dressed herself besides helping the children. Then she went downstairs. She did not waste a minute. As usual she put on the steam for the porridge, and let the oatmeal cook while she busied herself at other things. There were the draughts of the stove to open; the ashes to shake down, to take out and empty; there was the bread to set for rising; the dishes to place on the table; the toast to make; the apple sauce to serve, and the cocoa to prepare."

"31 Countries Inquire for U.S. Goods"
San Francisco Examiner, March 1, 1926

"An expanding stream of American factory and farm products is entering the arteries of world commerce and finding ready reception in the marts and bazaars throughout the world.

Corned beef, fat back, lemon squeezers, broom handles, shoe polish, playground equipment, bathroom fixtures, and radio sets are among the articles being sought by foreign merchants, according to a list of foreign sales opportunities made public by the Department of Commerce. Machinery for the establishment of new industries and the reorganization of old ones, together with the everyday requirements of foreign peoples, are included in the list of opportunities."

"Bug-a-Boos" Bugs Baer
San Francisco Examiner, March 2, 1926

"A girl used to be very careful about her feet. In fact, a small foot and a trim ankle were considered the hallmarks of society. Not that society got its marks in halls, although some struggles have occurred there. The old-time flapperette used to wear dancing shoes two sizes too small so that her feet would look normal. But the girl of today, and last night, doesn't care what she puts on her feet. It is O.K. provided it doesn't fit. She wears oversized slippers, twin galoshes, and Russian boots. Those Russian boots are the last word in small bungalows. A flapper rattles around in them like a doughnut on a cane.

Of course, if it is fashionable to be silly, then 'tis folly to be on a diet. Take any girl with bobbed hair, hoot-owl glasses, a paper hat, short skirts, bowlegs, and Russian boots. Add them all together. And you will find that so far as her future is concerned, she might as well have been with Custer. She might win a beauty prize from Punch and Judy. But otherwise, she looks like a Christmas tree in an alley. They must be getting their fashions out of the retail hardware catalogue. But a young man, who is anxious to meet a nice girl and get married, can't be annoyed by carrying a mouse around in his watch pocket.

It's about time to go back to the fashions of our ancestors. Not too far back, or we will once again be in the year when leaves were full dress and pie plates were hats."

"Passages"
Town and Country Magazine, April 1, 1926

"DePolignac, Princess Edmond (Winnaretta Singer), that famous and formidable daughter of the Singer who so fortuitously sold us sewing machines, passed through New York from her visit to Florida, where she has been surveying the fantastic and magic real estate activities of her brother, Paris Singer. She is one of the few Americans to have accomplished the rare feat of establishing a salon. Much of the new music we have heard in the public concert halls of New York has had its premiere in the private music room of her Paris home. Many artists are grateful for the eager impulse her patronage has afforded them."

ॐॐॐॐॐॐॐॐ

"Prohibition and New York's Poor"
The Literary Digest, October 23, 1926

"The general feeling of our workers," says Miss Stella A. Miner of the Girls' Service League of America, "is that the families with whom we deal in our protective work with girls are in better condition since the Volstead Law has been in effect. Drink and resultant poverty enter less into the home problems…"

As far as she is able to judge, Miss Clara Bassett of the Vanderbilt Clinic believes that "the number of working days among workingmen, the number of families having bank accounts and longer periods of education for their children have greatly increased during the past few years, and that change is due to Prohibition…"

Equally strong statements are made against present conditions under Prohibition… Workers in the East Harlem Health Center, representing every type of social work in a specific district, afford, it is said, a definite cross-section of opinion. Workers who have been active in the district for a long time saw little change that could be unqualifiedly attributed to the operation of Prohibition enforcement. Where the pressure has eased at one point, it had increased at another. There might be more money in the homes, but the loosening of parental control over young people and the example to children of law-breaking by the prevalence of the home-brewing, raised new and serious issues. It is a gain that children can no longer be sent to a saloon for a pail of beer, but the most innocent-looking shop in the block may be selling liquor to disreputable customers, with the children observing and commenting cynically on the whole transaction.

ॐॐॐॐॐॐॐॐ

"Jones Termed Popular Star, Atlantan Considered
One of Greatest Golf Players"
Ogden Standard-Examiner (UT), July 11, 1926

Without a doubt the most discussed golfer in all the world today is Bobby Jones. His qualifying rounds in the British Open of 36-38-134, followed by the winning of the championship stamped him as one of the greatest golfers of all time.

Recently I received a query from a golf fan asking for some data on Jones; when he started to play in the big tournaments and a brief record of his successes. Here goes:

Jones made his debut in championship golf in Merion in 1916 playing in the amateur championship at the age of 14. At 18 he played in his first open championship at Inverness and finished tied for eighth place. Eight years after his debut at Merion he won the amateur championship over the same course.

Jones has made a most remarkable showing in the United States open championships. He finished eighth in his first attempt in 1920. A year later at Columbia, he tied for fifth; at Skokie, in 1922, he had his first big thrill, finishing in a tie for second.

Success finally crowned his efforts at Inwood in 1923 when he tied with Bobby Cruickshanx for first place and won the 18-hole playoff. The following year he was the runner-up to Cyril Walker at Detroit. Last year at Worcester he tied with Willie MacFarlane. Playing off the tie in an18-hole match the finish found them all even. MacFarlane won out on the second clash over the 18-hole route.

In the last four Open championships Jones has never been farther away than second. His remarkable showing in the British Open makes him the favorite to win at Scioto.

⇛⇛⇛⇛⇛⇛⇛⇛

"Movie Review: The Best Bad Man"
The Nevada State Journal, February 1, 1926

Beginning tonight under new management and with an enlarged orchestra, the Wigwam started the week right with the best picture Tom Mix has ever made. Leaving out much of the wild west hokum that he generally uses, *The Best Bad Man* affords thrills galore and a newcomer to filmdom, Clara Bow. This is not Miss Bow's first appearance in pictures, but it is her best. Just lately she caused considerable comment with an insignificant part in *The American Venus*. Great strides are predicted for her.

The story deals with a crooked land and company manager who steals $100,000 sent by his boss to complete a dam for irrigating several thousand acres of farmland, and tells the ranchers that the big chief is a thief. Water for even domestic purposes is running low and a delegate is sent to tell the wealthy New Orleans idler just what kind of man he is. Mix, playing the big boss, and the idler go to investigate and things begin to happen immediately. In the course of events the supply dam is blown up and a torrent of water rushes down upon the hero, heroine and Sheriff's posse. The villain and his aide also tumble in the angry water. Right here is one of the best water thrills yet. Mix is fast turning into a favorite with the children for they crowded the house during the early performances. If someone isn't careful Tom Mix will turn into an actor yet.

⇛⇛⇛⇛⇛⇛⇛⇛

"Games and Equipment; Small Rural Schools"
Department of the Interior, Bureau of Education, 1927

"Time was, and not long ago, when the activities of the school playground developed spontaneously. Their significance in life was necessary. We live, however, in a day when the instinct for play and the knowledge of games, both in rural and urban communities, have strangely diminished; and this change has not only made this importance evident, but has likewise made it needful for the educator to stimulate and instruct in these activities."

"This Smoking World"
A.E. Hamilton, The Century Company, New York, 1927

"As to why women have taken up the practice of smoking, opinion is diverse, of course. Some lay the cause to the war, when women smoked to keep doughboys company. Others attribute it to the inferred slump of moral standards following the war. One theory has it that knitting, crocheting, tatting, and their like having gone the way of spinning and weaving; women's hands are again idle and have welcomed the cigarette as a relief for nervous tension in their fingers."

"Undercover, an Interview with Bruce Bielaski"
John B. Kennedy, *Collier's*, August 13, 1927

"'In the fight against booze smugglers there have been flagrant cases of local authorities cooperating not with us but with the bootleggers,' declares A. Bruce Bielaski, recently chief of the federal forces in the Atlantic seaboard war of wits between the government and the rum barons.

Bruce Bielaski

Then this ex-official of a Republican administration adds: 'I believe that a shrewd politician like Governor Smith could, if he wanted to, enforce prohibition.'

When Hippy Werner, henchman for the Providence rum syndicate, stepped scowling into Coast Guard regional headquarters he was eagerly received. Hippy was sore on the syndicate. They had done him dirt. Revenge!

'They're bringin' a load tomorrow night,' whispered Hippy, 'on the British trawler *Minerva*, from Barbados. Four thousand cases of Scotch. The boat's due at Warwick Beach at two in the mornin'. They're protected by Coast Guard X-3. Now you guys go get 'em. I'm through.' Hippy's scowl was realistic; it seemed permanent. He withstood the cold gleams of doubt.

The government men thanked him. The next morning when the *Minerva* snorted up the channel, the mid-New England Coast Guard was concentrated to intercept her, and yowling cockney seamen found themselves betrayed after assurance that they'd go unmolested. The *Minerva* was found to have 1,000 cases in her hold-all dolled up in the authentic Scotch bottles with straw overcoats. Disappointing, but substantial. Hippy had told part of the truth.

When the bottles revealed no Scotch, but an inferior concoction of fuel oil and watered alcohol, the government sniffed suspiciously. Later they discovered that while all available Coast Guard forces were out watching for the *Minerva*, an armada of schooners had landed elsewhere on the Rhode Island coast with the biggest importation of rum in months! So much for the sincerity of Hippy Werner's scowl. The incident was humiliating. But -To Hippy Werner's superiors in Providence there went one day a captain in the Coast Guard, disgruntled and gloomy. He complained that he had been put under suspicion by the government men and that if he got the blame he might as well get the game. The syndicate paid the captain something in advance, with rosy promises of reward if the adventure succeeded. Their trawlers, loaded to the limit with authentic Scotch and Canadian ale, had no sooner got within view of shore than the captain, ostensibly protecting them, showed his guns, the government swarmed from his hold, and the biggest capture in months was made.

There are typical high spots in the continuous crossplay of strategy between the rum importers and the federal undercover forces. It's up to the government to match the ingenuity of the crafty gentlemen who play every card in the pack of human cupidity and guile to land their shipments.

A. Bruce Bielaski, who operated the New York undercover headquarters for two years, speaks frankly for the first time on the war of wits between government and bootleggers.

'The spectacular cases are few. The job of catching the rum gangs is mainly routine,' he says, 'and exasperating. Enforcement is on the defensive, resisting invasion most of the time...' Bielaski initiated and supervised scores of successful raids, uncovered seagoing corruption in the U.S. Coast Guard, and received scores of letters threatening limb, life and reputation-and forming an impressive array of unsolicited testimonials to his efficiency.

A medium-size, plump, affable, youngish man, with a clean-shaven face that has never known in 15 years of federal detective work the melodramatic adjunct of false whiskers, this son of a Methodist minister of Polish ancestry was drafted into the prohibition service to be Eastern field marshal of the cleanup campaign planned by General Lincoln C. Andrews early in 1925. He returned last spring to the quiet, downtown law practice which he had deserted to serve the government...returned with a sense of relief which an intelligent man experiences who has tackled a thankless, hopeless job.

This he brands it, not with the dulled enthusiasm of one who went brightly into his first crusade to find the disillusionment that is part of all crusading. He had turned three successful jobs for the government, one in his youth, as chief of the Bureau of Investigation on Mann Act cases; another as special assistant to the attorney general in the federal bucket-shop roundup in 1909; and the third as head of espionage during the height of the enemy propaganda wave in the war.

'Those jobs,' he says, 'were conclusively successful. Public opinion was solidly behind the Mann Act and the bucket-shop prosecutions, and approved the drive against enemy

U.S. Coast Guard, right, and rum-runner

propaganda. These campaigns were well-conceived and energetically executed. We got results because everywhere we received assistance from the local authorities, who supported us in a common cause.

'But in the fight against booze smugglers, my experience has been the opposite. Save in one instance, that of Police Commissioner George V. McLaughlin in New York City, local authorities have not regarded prohibition enforcement as of any concern to themselves. Indeed, there have been flagrant cases of their cooperating not with us but with the bootleggers…

'When I was told in the spring of 1925 that I was wanted at an important conference with General Andrews, I went to that meeting in the right mood. The picture painted to me was one of a serious and unflagging effort to check liquor smuggling and the illicit diversion of grain alcohol, to fight bootlegging by reaching for the higher-ups. It seemed an attractive picture. Although I had been out of the federal service for some years, it was apparent to me that prohibition enforcement could have progressed under resolute administration. So, knowing something of General Andrews, I accepted the appointment.

'In everything I did I had the help and encouragement of General Andrews. No bureau chief could be more inspiring to his aides. But after nearly two years of it I learned that A LARGE PERCENTAGE OF OUR POPULATION DOES NOT CONSIDER TRAFFIC IN LIQUOR AS HEINOUS AS A VIOLATION OF ALMOST ANY OTHER FEDERAL STATUTE.

'We discovered that the extension of the rum line from a three-mile limit to a 12-mile limit, or one hour's steaming from shore, had little perceptible effect. The legal boundary was meaningless if the Coast Guard supposed to patrol it was venal—AND IT WAS…'

Spying activities among the personnel of the Coast Guard, riddled with graft, covered so much flagrant crookedness that Bielaski himself wryly admits conditions were farcical. 'I have read a dozen or more cases in the official records. They are all alike, differing only in detail of quantity in bribes and identity of the bribe taker. Captain Nicholas Brown, skipper of the patrol boat No. 126, confessed that he received bribe money regularly and "slipped some of the money to higher-ups in the Coast Guard service…" Captain Frank J. Stuart of No. 129 confessed his "career of crime lasted two months. In that time I pocketed thousands of dollars in bribes. I got $2,000, a year's pay, just to let several fishing boats land liquor on Fort Pond Bay, near Montauk, Long Island." '"

❦❦❦❦❦❦❦❦

"Immigration Problems Show New Intricacies"
Arthur Cook, *The New York Times*, February 6, 1927

At no time, perhaps, in the history of the country has the United States had less of immigration problems than at the present time. The problem of populating the country by immigration has disappeared. It gave place, following the war, to one of restricting the number of alien arrivals for residents. In the meantime restrictions upon the quality of immigrants determined by measures of health, mentality and moral fitness gradually became more drastic and enforcement more efficient. The exclusion of Orientals forestalled the arising of some of the problems which have arisen in other immigration countries…

Yet the exclusion from the United States of afflicted aliens has brought criticism at times because of peculiar circumstances surrounding individual cases which have arisen. A family abroad having one or two inadmissible members is sometimes first broken by the husband and father coming to the United States and sending back from time to time for additional members; the inadmissible one remains with relatives until last and then calms over when the balance of the family is well established. If the inadmissible one is rejected, immigration officers are accused of breaking home and family ties. At such times it is not, of course, recalled that the separation took place when the admissible alien member was abandoned on the other side.

Numerical limitation, which was expressed in legislation as a permanent policy in 1924, has its special problems of administration, particularly with reference to families of residents in the United States, citizen and alien. When the head of a family leaves from abroad, and no provision is made for the issuance of quota visas for the family, it can be readily understood that when, later, the applications are filed, there may be a considerable period of waiting necessary for quota numbers before the family can be secured. The present law provides for non-quota status for wife and children under 18 years of age of American citizens, and for preference for his father and mother. The alien resident, however, no matter of how long a domicile here, must wait for the admission of his dependents until they can be reached in regular non-reference number.

The problem of keeping families together, or of uniting them at the residence of the breadwinner, is one of the major issues at this time. A remedy is suggested by the Secretary of Labor, James A. Davis, in its annual report for 1926, to solve the problem as it relates to immigrants now coming. He recommends to Congress that a provision be added to the immigration laws requiring an alien head of family seeking visa for residence in the United States to express intention regarding the future residents of the family, and in the event he expects later to have the family join him in the United States, each member of the family would be required to submit to preliminary examination to determine admissibility.

వాంళ్ళ-ళ్ళ-ళ్ళ-ళ్ళ

"The Ace of Clubs"
Grantland Rice, *Collier's*, August 13, 1927

Anyone desiring to add to the hubbub of modern sport can do so by coming out boldly and picking some one ball club as "the greatest of all time."

I found this out recently when I quoted the opinions of several rival ballplayers from the American League to the effect that the present New York Yankees could be classed as one of the greatest teams in baseball history.

The rebuttal was somewhat terrific, especially from the old-time fans, but there was a wide difference of opinion.

Ballplayers who have opposed the Yankees point to the offensive power of the team that has Ruth, Gehrig, Meusel, Lazzeri, Combs and others and at the same time backs up this tremendous attack with the best fielding record in the league. And even Wilbert Robinson, who starred with the old Orioles, picks the Yankees as the game's greatest.

But before coming to the ranking of the Yankees there are five great ball clubs to be considered from the story of the past 35 years. These five clubs come in this temporal order: Baltimore Orioles 1894-96; Boston Nationals, 1897-98; Pittsburgh Pirates, 1901-03; Chicago Cubs, 1906-1910; Philadelphia Athletics, 1910-14…

All the clubs mentioned had smart ballplayers, but the ancient and honorable Orioles had more smart ballplayers. They were nearly all smart and if there were any lapses McGraw, Jennings, Robinson, Gleason and Keller made up the difference. They turned out more managers than any lineup in baseball history (McGraw and Robinson are still at the helm), and you might be surprised to know how many letter writing fans prefer headwork to home runs.

Here was one of the smartest and wisest ball clubs of all time. Its members lived baseball, ate baseball, dreamed baseball. The salary matter was unimportant in those days. They were figuring out plays and methods on and off the field, morning, afternoon and evening. The game was everything in their lives. They won three pennants and several of them went to Brooklyn and won two more.

Then came the Boston Nationals with the great catcher in Bergen, a fine outfield in Hamilton, Duffy and Stahl, and one of the greatest infields in Tenney, Lowe, Long and Collins.

Here were four smart, brilliant infielders who all batted well over .300. Many experts still rate this is as the greatest infield of all time…

Pittsburgh from 1901 to 1903 had two good catchers, a star infield and a star outfield. But the strength of this club was a phenomenal pitching staff that carried Jess Tanneyhill, Jack Chesbro, Sam Leever and Deacon Philippe, four pitchers who could make any team look great…

It is still a question as to whether or not the Chicago Cubs from 1906 through 1910 should not be rated as the greatest all-around machine.

This club had a great catcher in Johnny Kling, smart, keen, and a great thrower and a .300 hitter. It had a great pitching staff in "Three-Finger" Brown, Overall, Reulbach, Pfeister and Lundgren.

No one can ever forget the infield (comprised of Chance, Evans, Tinker and Steinfeldt) or the outfield that held Sheckard, Schultz, Hofman and Slagle.

There wasn't a weakness in this Cub organization. In 1906 it cracked a double league record by winning 116 games, a mark that has never been approached. In 1907 it won 107 games and in 1910 it won 104 games.

This Cub team won more games over a stretch of five years than any other team ever listed. They won well over 500 games from 1906 to 1910, and no other club has approached this. It won four pennants in five years. The Athletics did the same, but they never won as many games as the Cubs…

The Yankees of 1927 have shown themselves to be a ball club carrying a cargo of dynamite. No other club ever took more high-power ammunition to the battle field. They have a great outfield in Ruth, Meusel and Combs. They have a slashing, able infield in Gehrig, Lazzeri, Koenig, Morehart and Dugan.

The Yankees have annihilating power at bat (Ruth and Gehrig are the two greatest sluggers any team ever carried). They have the greatest defensive record in their league. But the greatness of no club can be measured by one campaign. It will take at least another year to prove their place-now based on sheer power. No team of recent years has shown anything like the all-around consistency of these mentioned, and this applies in full measure to the old Cubs. But for sheer power the 1927 Yankees must take their place with the elect.

"No Thanks, Mr. Bell"
L. White Busbey, *Uncle Joe Cannon*, 1927

I met a learned Justice Supreme Court who had looked into (an invention for converting base metal into gold)…he assured me that a man who had $1,000 to invest would become a millionaire in a few years…I had been a man of frugal ways and had saved $1,000. I had the money in the bank and I took the advice of the jurist and the scientist and got in on the ground floor. The scientist and other less scientific dreamers, including myself, are no longer looking for millions but would be quite happy to get back our thousands.

A few years later I was on Newspaper Row, on 14th St., where the newspaper men had their offices, and I met Uriah Painter, one of the veteran Washington correspondents. He was also a good businessman. Painter asked me if I had ever seen a telephone and I confessed that I had not. We went into his office and he walked over to a little box on the wall. He put a little instrument to his ear, rang a bell and spoke to the box. He said, "Hey, Puss, how are you? I want you to speak to Mr. Cannon, who is here in my office." He handed me the receiver and putting it to my ear, as I had seen him do, I heard Mrs. Painter's voice distinctly. It was amazing. Then he told her to play on the piano and I heard the music. It was magic. I was very much impressed, and Mr. Painter told me about the young Scotchman Bell, how they were organizing a company and insisted the men who invested their money could not lose. He said if I had a thousand to invest, I would be sure to double, perhaps quadruple my money in a few years; and might even make ten thousand by getting in on the ground floor. I had been much impressed by hearing a human voice that I recognized come out of that little piece of metal…but I was even more impressed by the proposition to get in on the ground floor. I remembered my experience with a wonderful discovery to make gold out of an old thing, and I said, "Nay, nay, Brother Painter, I've tried these get-rich-quick inventions and I am done."

Not long afterwards I went down to the office of the Superintendent of Railway Mails to get a young man approved to that service. The superintendent, Theodore Vail, was a bright young fellow, accommodating and always ready to help me when he could. That morning Mr. Vail was not there. His assistant told me that Vail had suddenly become moonstruck and resigned to be the manager of the telephone company that had been foisted on the market. Vail had saved up about four thousand dollars, and in a crazy moment had blown it all on telephone stock and resigned from the government service.

Worse than that, he had persuaded every friend in the office who had a dollar to let him have it for investment. We all liked Vail and were much concerned about his sudden madness, for he was a good Superintendent of Railway Mails and we thought he had a future in the service. We condemned him for the reckless use of his influence over young men in the service who had saved a little money, and he we did not know what would become of them when the magic bubble burst and the telephone stock went like that of a company that was to make gold out of junk.

Some years later, I was in Boston and I met Theodore Vail. He was round and jolly and looked prosperous. He was the president of the American Telephone Company and the Western Union Telegraph Company. I asked a mutual friend how much Vail was worth, and he said at least twenty-five million. All those fool friends who had let Vail have their savings 30 years ago had made money. They accepted the offer to get in on the ground floor on telephone stock and I refused. I had been a member of Congress and Vail and his friends had been poor devils working in the treadmill. I had the same opportunity as Vail but guessed on the wrong card.

⚜⚜⚜⚜⚜⚜⚜

"Movies Foster Crime, Canon Chase Charges"
The New York Times, January 2, 1928

The motion picture screen for the past 25 years has been a school of crime, according to Canon William S. Chase, who took the affirmative in a debate at the Ingersoll Forum, 113 West Fifty-seventh Street, last night on "Should There Be Federal Supervision of Motion Pictures?" Dr. Wolf Adler upheld the negative.

"Did you notice that in his account of his dreadful crime, Hickman said it was his habit to see motion pictures daily?" Canon Chase asked.

He said the movies were a menace to the children of the world, and to the furtherance of world peace. By representing American life in a false light, he charged that motion pictures aroused the antagonism of other countries and created much ill feeling by portraying foreigners as villains and Americans as heroes.

Because moving pictures are run by interests with the sole purpose of making money, he urged that the government supervise the movies so as to further the best moral and political interests of the public.

Dr. Adler said he had no admiration at all for movies, but he did not believe there should be censorship or supervision, because all censorship was bad.

"If you start censoring motion pictures, you will soon begin regulating literature, the stage and every other activity of life," he said. "The movies do not influence morals for the worst. They merely reflect morals as they are by showing the realities of life. If they are immoral, they are an effect of immorality, not a cause. Federal control will not be of any use because it cannot abolish things as they are."

If the movies have tended to foster warlike tendencies, he continued, it is because they are used by every nation as propaganda against other nations.

❦❦❦❦❦❦❦❦

Popular Movies

1927		1928	
The Jazz Singer	Camille	The Last Command	Street Angel
Wings	The Way of All Flesh	The Racket	The Singing Fool
Napoleon	Love	The Crowd	The Mysterious Lady
The King of Kings	The Unknown	Sadie Thompson	The Circus
Flesh and the Devil	The General	Steamboat Willie	The Docks of New York
The Night of Love			

❦❦❦❦❦❦❦❦

The movies constitute much of the education of many.... Shall this (movie industry) education produce graduates of the type of the 14-year-old murderers, of the Leopold-Loeb super-intellectuals criminal breed, of the flapper who is a potential mother and may reproduce more of the same, of the foreigner, the fool and the traitor who consider the Eighteenth Amendment a joke and laugh at the Stars and Stripes?
—*Harriett Pritchard, director of the WCTU Department of Purity in Literature and Art, 1925*

❦❦❦❦❦❦❦❦

"Financial Questions That Women Ask Me"
Mrs. William Laimbeer, *The Delineator*, June 1928

"The term speculative investment has lured many a person to ruin. Perhaps if they had good judgment they might have pulled out with profit. The woman today who feels the urge to buy common stocks with a view to appreciation must do it at her own risk.

It is a recognized fact that some common stocks offer large opportunities for profit over a period of years, but it is also true they possess great possibilities of loss. In order to minimize the risk when one reaches a stage in the investment program where common stocks can be considered, diversification of commitments as to industry, company and location is the proper procedure. The general order of common stocks is-railroads, public utilities and industrials, respectively. This is because railroads and public utilities are least affected in the way of earnings from operation by changing conditions in economics and finance.

In purchasing common stock it is well to be sure on one point: That the company has a large earning power over and above dividend requirements and that it has an excellent dividend record over a long number of years. During periods of inflation or rising commodity prices, greater earnings result, particularly for industrial companies, and these earnings are usually passed on to the stockholder in the form of increased dividends. During periods of depression, dividends in common stocks are sometimes passed over altogether."

> We believe mechanically perfect, artistically beautiful, morally clean motion pictures are one of the best-known means of preserving and transmitting to future generations the best ideals and institutions of our generation. We believe the best in the life of any people presented by the silver screen to the whole people will popularize that best…The motion picture industry through constant production of the worst has failed to transmit the best. We believe federal regulation is required to change the situation.
> —*Maude M. Aldrich of Oregon, chairperson of the National Woman's Christian Temperance Union's Department of Motion Pictures, November 21, 1928*

"Innocence Abroad" Frances Warfield
Scribner's Magazine, October 1928

Tell me honestly now-do you know a college woman under 30 whose bookshelf does not display the familiar red back of *A Guide to the Louvre*? Do you know a recent sweet-girl graduate who does not, through first-hand knowledge, itch to correct your faltering pronunciation of Magdalen College, threepenny, pain au beurre, St. John Ervine, Exposition Internationale des Arts Decoratifs? Or one who does not look arch at the mention of the Follies Bergères, and who cannot quote the price of her fringed shawl in lire?

To the true college girl the European venture, as soon as possible after commencement, is wellnigh indispensable. It is the accepted thing, the cultured thing. Years ago, on the first day of her freshman year, when she faced the registrar with her health certificate and her father's check for the semester's tuition, the college girl forswore crudity for all time. At that moment she dedicated the future to the conventional, the cultured, and the cultural. During four years of expensive mental hardship, she has learned what every astute bachelor of arts must know-namely, how to separate those cultural things she must do from those she can pretend to have done. The trip abroad falls into the first class. It cannot be faked. The traveled manner gives final shine to that conversational front which is, after all, the beginning and end of culture. And, even for tea-table purposes, the traveled manner must be genuine.

"Something New in Delivery of Daily Newspaper"
Daily Citizen (Beaver Dam, WI), April 20, 1928

A new era in newspaper service was begun recently by the *Los Angeles Times,* the delivery of the morning paper by airplane on a route north to San Francisco.

The first airplane newspaper delivery was made on Sunday, April 15, according to a letter received by Mr. E. E. Parker, former Beaver Dam resident, who now resides at Altadena, California.

The plane leaves from Los Angeles shortly after the papers are off the press and makes a northerly journey to San Francisco. The plane edition is the same edition that is delivered in Los Angeles, according to Mr. Parker.

ক্ষ-ক্ষ-ক্ষ-ক্ষ-ক্ষ-ক্ষ-ক্ষ

"Church and Politics: Political Discussions in the Pulpit Grossly Unfair"
Dr. Gus W. Dyer, *Southern Agriculturist,* August 15, 1928

Most people go to church for devotional and religious purposes. It is grossly unfair to these people for the preacher to arbitrarily convert a religious service into a political powwow. Again the law gives special protection to all church services-a protection that is not given to any other service. This special protection is given on the basis that the services are religious. Members of a church congregation are not permitted under the law to take issue with the speaker. Any sort of disturbance here is against the law. Men are fined and put in prison for disturbing church meetings. When the preacher from the pulpit advocates one side of a political question, he uses the special protection given by the law in the interest of religion to take unwarranted and unfair advantage of his political opponents who are not permitted to answer or make any sort of protest, although they are in the pews of their own church. When a preacher uses the pulpit to antagonize a position taken in politics by a portion of the church membership, he hits men whose mouths are locked and whose hands are tied.

ক্ষ-ক্ষ-ক্ষ-ক্ষ-ক্ষ-ক্ষ-ক্ষ

"Harvesting and Storing Ice on the Farm"
Farmer's Bulletin, 1928

Water for the ice supply should be free from contamination or pollution. Ponds and sluggish streams usually have grass and decayed vegetable matter, which is always an objectionable condition and may be injurious to health. These should, therefore, be thoroughly cleared of such growth before cold weather. Green spawn and algae must be destroyed by the use of copper sulfate (blue vitriol). The crystals can be placed in a cloth bag which is hung on the end of a pole and trailed through the water until all the crystals are dissolved. One or two treatments during the summer season at the rate of one pound copper sulfate to 13,000 cubic feet of water will be sufficient to keep down such growths.

Careful investigation should be made to determine whether the source of ice supply is pure and free from contamination or pollution. Streams and lakes are often polluted by sewage or other impurities which it is impossible to eliminate. A pure ice supply is especially important when the ice is to be used directly in beverages or other foods.

$\approx\approx\approx\approx\approx\approx\approx\approx$

"The Spirit of the Freeholder"
G. W. Westmoreland, *Southern Agriculturist*, August 15, 1928

The best citizenry has been, in ages past, on the farm. There has always been developed a nobility of spirit in owning and enjoying a piece of land. By the possession of land there has been produced not only a desire to own the land, but a freer spirit in the owner, who has become a freeholder and an independent citizen. In such an environment, future citizens can be reared.

The right to own and enjoy a piece of property will instill into any man that love for country and home without which no country could exist. It's like the birds protecting their nests, and the animals their holes; because man loves that which is his own and is willing, if need be, to die for it. Cincinnatus left his oxen in the field that he might hasten to defend the field against the enemy. Israeli did the same thing in the Revolutionary War. As long as man can own his home he will continue to die for it and no order of conscripting will be necessary. To suffer, he must have something to suffer for.

$\approx\approx\approx\approx\approx\approx\approx\approx$

"Flatbush Man Is Named Winner in Martinson Coffee Slogan Contest"
Brooklyn Standard Union, June 16, 1928

Hyman C. Ferber, of 2177 East Twenty-first Street, Flatbush, is the winner of the Martinson coffee slogan contest, according to an announcement to-day.

"You put in less—and it tastes like more," the slogan submitted by Ferber, was the one the judges deemed best. Ferber gets the $500 first prize.

The $300 second prize goes to P.E. Moreton, of 100 Columbia Heights, for the slogan, "Measures up great!-from the ground to the sealing."

"Commended by those qualified to judge," won the $100 third prize for E. Simonson, of 3373 Twelfth Avenue. Ten other slogans drew $10 each for those submitting them. They follow:

"The blend all chefs recommend," Bertram Ellis, 185 Ralph avenue; "One swallow calls for its mate," by David M. Londoner, 784 Eastern Parkway; "Why debate? Percolate," by Robert G. Smith, 377 Fifth Avenue, Manhattan; "The blend's the thing," by Charles A. Delapierre, 345 Stratford Road; "The aroma won its diploma," by Mrs. Claude Outlaw, 240 Fifty-first Street; "The blend of millions," by Jessie H. DeLong, 255 Prospect Street; "A rhapsody in coffee harmony," by Archie Tarr, 567 West 149th Street, Manhattan; "Once tested, always requested," by Mrs. John W. Bonnett, 3601 Avenue J; "A surprise at first, a pleasure ever after," by Pauline Von Moser, 1201 Bushwick Avenue; "Worth a taste, to taste its worth," by Mae T. Keenan, 2085 Lexington Avenue, Manhattan.

The prizes were offered by Joseph Martinson, head of the coffee importing house, at 85 Water Street, Manhattan. Four judges made the winning selections.

No Congress of the United States ever assembled, on surveying the State of the Union, has met with a more pleasing prospect than that which appears at the present time. In the domestic field there is tranquility and contentment…and the highest record of years of prosperity.

—President Calvin Coolidge, December 4, 1928

ன்ன்ன்ன்ன்ன்ன்

"Huge Appreciation in General Motors, $10,000 Invested 10 Years Ago Worth $1,600,000 Now Through Extra Stock"
The New York Times, March 11, 1928

Wall Street was busy with pad and pencil yesterday figuring the profits that have been made in General Motors and the current advance and by those few fortunate investors in the stock who have held the stock since the original purchase nearly 20 years ago.

It is easy to calculate what profits have been made in any particular move, but much harder to determine what the appreciation has been in an "original investment" because of the many changes that have been made in the capital structure of the company, the extra cash disbursements that have been made, and the generous regular dividends that have been added enormously to holders' profits.

It was figured yesterday that the purchase of 100 shares at $100 a share at the origination of the company in 1908 would, if the stock had been held until the present time, represent for the holder today 10,033 shares. In other words, the purchaser would have seen an investment of $10,000 mount within 10 years to a market value of $1,600,000. Few instances of such an appreciation have taken place in American financial history.

ன்ன்ன்ன்ன்ன்ன்

"Rules Are Suggested to Make Radio Installment Sales Safe"
The New York Times, June 17, 1928

Radio installment sales were discussed last week by H. P. Lewis, Vice President of Commercial Credit Company, who spoke at the meeting of the National Electrical Manufacturer's Association. Factors that make installment selling safe, according to Mr. Lewis, are: (1) A sufficient down payment to give the buyer a sense of ownership and to penalize him heavily in case of default. (2) A sufficiently rapid rate of payment for the balance to build up his equity to complete ownership and decrease the seller's equity to nothing faster than the resale value the merchandise depreciates. (3) The title retaining instrument on which the goods are sold, which makes complete forfeiture the penalty of delinquency at any stage of the contract. (4) Careful credit work of the well-established finance companies. (5) Alert but discriminating collection work. (6) The spread of risk between thousands or millions of buyers, depending on the industry under consideration. There is no concentrated hazard or any condition approaching the frozen inventory in the installment sales picture.

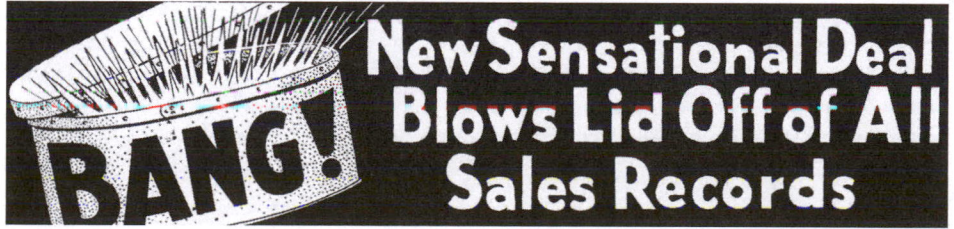

"Lowell Attacks Secondary Schools, Harvard Head Tells Teachers That They Waste Time, Effort and Money"
The New York Times, February 28, 1928

President A. Lawrence Lowell of Harvard, in an address today at the opening session of the convention of the National Education Association, declared that American public schools cost too much and are ineffective, that their courses are superficial, that they waste years of pupils' time and that at the end they leave to the college the job of giving high school work. They scatter their power in trying to teach too many things and end by teaching nothing well, he said, and in trying to make studies pleasant, has made them easy and they need to be hard. Dr. Lowell's speech anticipated the express purpose of many of the educators who came here to open fire upon the traditional interest requirements of Harvard, and during its convention counted on persuading New England colleges to their point of view. The leading candidate for the presidency of this organization is making his campaign on the issue of "domination of the high school by the college."

Dr. Lowell began by figuring out how much faster public school salaries, figured on a per pupil basis, have increased in the past 15 years more than have Harvard salaries on the same basis. He insisted that Harvard got more for its money. The difference in increased cost was between 67 percent for Harvard salaries and 167 percent for public school teacher salaries. He thought the problem of the next generation will be to make universal education "equally good and less expensive."

Then he stepped to "the more immediate question of effectiveness," and wanted to know why American schools could not finish the job of secondary education at the age of 19, as European schools do, without putting a couple of years of work preparation upon the colleges. If they could not do the job right, they ought to knock off those two years of time, he declared.

"To some aspects of education we seem to have paid insufficient attention," Dr. Lowell continued. "One of these is selective function. We hear much in the present day of vocational guidance, the determination of the pursuits for which students and schoolchildren are best adapted by somewhat artificial devices for discovering their natural abilities. But all true education is a sifting process.

"What we need is good mental training, an accurate and thorough habit of mind, not a frittering away in the attention by a multitude of small matters, of which the pupil does not get enough to develop consecutive thought."

"President Lowell seems to think the main function of the American high school is to send its pupils to college," said Dr. Boynton to newspapermen during the general meeting of the Department of Superintendents tonight. "In fact, the preparation of boys and girls for college is a mere detail in the broad program of the great high school.

"President Lowell compares American schools with European schools. That comparison is just as unfair as it would be to compare the American Constitution to the aims of government in Europe. Our objective is not to train a chosen few for higher education, but to prepare all our students for the American conditions of life."

Turning to the charge of excessive costs, he said: "The expenses per pupil of the public schools are negligible compared to those of the institutions of higher learning. You will observe that there are no empty buildings and costly monuments on the campus of the American high school." Dr. Frank D. Boynton, Superintendent of Schools in Ithaca, replied later to Pres. Lowell's charges of high school inefficiency.

"Americans are crazy people. They drink too much, do everything too much. They like something for 15 minutes, then turn about and like something else. They are faddists. They idolize some hero of the hour beyond all sensibility, then leave him flat for someone else."

—*Newspaper Cartoonist Ralph Barton, 1929*

"The Economic Condition of the World Seems on the Verge of a Great Forward Movement"
American Magazine, 1929

"For the first time in history, we have sound reason for hope for a long period of peace. For the first time, the businessmen of all nations are supplied with statistical information, together with some understanding of the laws of economics. For the first time, we have sound, centralized banking systems in the countries and close cooperation between those systems internationally. Because all these factors are favorable, and because of the universal stirring of desire and ambition…I believe in the 'industrial renaissance.' We are already seeing something of it in the United States."

"Silent Cinema, 1895–1929"
The Oxford History of World Cinema

"The Hollywood production system was not invented, but evolved in response to a number of felt imperatives, of which the most important was the need for a regular and consistent profit. A pioneering role, however, can be ascribed to producer Thomas Ince, working at Mutual in 1913. The standard studio working procedure, as devised by Ince, involved a studio boss, the film's director, and a continuity script. Once Ince, as head producer, had approved a project, he assigned available building for filming, and commissioned writers and production artists to create the necessary script, sets, and costumes. Backup systems, such as an internal police force to keep out crowds, or firefighters to assist when sets burned, meant that by the early 1920s studio lots, covering many acres, operated as veritable subcities within the urban environs of Los Angeles.

Studio bosses planned a programme of films a year in advance. Sets were efficiently used over and over again, and adapted for different stories. Art directors designed and constructed sets; casting directors found talent; makeup artists perfected the glamorous movie look; and cinematographers were picked to shoot scripts as written. Time was of the essence, so actors were shuttled from film to film. Often multiple cameras were used for complicated shots (for example, a battlefield sequence) to avoid having to stage them twice. And always present was the continuity clerk, who checked that, when shooting was completed, the film could be easily reassembled."

"Amusing Incidents"
Frank G. Young, *A Town in the Makin', History of Seaman*, Ohio, 1929

At the close of the school year in 1920, there was a lot of excitement in "this man's town," due to the activities of the senior class. One night near the close of the term, the freshmen arranged for a party, but the boys were picked up one by one, as they were going to the party, by the seniors and kidnapped. They were taken to an old house west of the village and kept captive until a late hour, when they escaped, after three or four free for-all fights in which clothes were torn and faces disfigured. The "freshies" finally got to the party. The next morning the seniors were on the streets in full force, and the freshmen, both boys and girls, were out also looking for a chance to even up for the kidnapping of the night previous. They clashed in front of the mayor's office, and engaged in another free-for-all, the girls joining in the mêlée, but the mayor soon put a stop to the scuffle.

Word had gotten out that the freshmen boys intended to kidnap the seniors as they marched from the home of the superintendent to the Presbyterian church for their graduation exercises, so John Hannah, who was the village marshal, was called upon to escort the seniors to the church, and in the name of the law, made this impossible. After the graduation exercises were over, Mr. Hannah escorted them back to the home of Supt. Fred Lott. With the exception of a wire that was stretched across the street at one point, nothing happened. This is the first thing of its kind that ever happened at graduation time, and the last.

❧❧❧❧❧❧❧

"Football Extra Saturday"
Daily Globe (Ironwood, MI), October 8, 1929

To meet the demand of the Globe readers for local, state and national football news, the *Daily Globe* will issue its first football extra of the season next Saturday evening.

Through the changes put into effect several months ago, the *Daily Globe* this season hopes to provide the fans with a greater volume of football news than it has given in previous seasons. Automatic printers will bring the Associated Press news into the *Daily Globe* office at the rate of 60 words a minute. Between three and six o'clock each Saturday afternoon all the football news available will be made ready for the green sheet sports extra. The *Daily Globe* will make every effort to make this year's sports extras better than ever.

❧❧❧❧❧❧❧

"Bear Onslaughts Encounter Little Resistance in Market"
Salt Lake Tribune, October 20, 1929

One of the most powerful bear onslaughts of the year encountered amazingly little resistance in the stock market this week, and sent prices into one of the most precipitous declines in recent financial history. Prices were driven down in bull trading, with the average turnover for full sessions averaging less than 3,300,000 shares until today, when the selling movements reached huge proportions.

Many leading industrials and several rails broke through the low levels of October 4, utilities generally tumbled to the lowest levels on record since early July. The Standard Statistics-Associated Press price index 20 utilities dropped 53.8 points during the week to 280.9 compared to the year's high of 353.1, reached early in September. An index of 50 industrials dropped 17.1 points and better than 20 rails dropped six points. Nearly 60 issues on the New York Stock Exchange drove to new lows for the year or since listing the present shares on that market, including General Motors, Montgomery Ward, United Corporation, United Gas Improvement, Baldwin, Bendix Aviation, Curtiss-Wright, Kennecott, Howe Sound, Marmon Motor, J.I. Case and several of the recently listed investment trusts.

"Motorists, Keep to the Right!"
The Oshkosh Daily Northwestern (WI), April 24, 1929

Quoting portions of a recent editorial in the *Northwestern* to the effect that the "road hog" who sticks to the center of the pavement or drives over on the left side, endangering traffic, was loose again on the highways, the *Merrill Herald* comments:

"It is our observation that the 'highway hog' is growing more numerous as the cars multiply. The highway hog is a very dangerous animal, and something ought to be done to lessen its kind. Just what can be done, we do not know. Perhaps educating him to respect the rights of others when very young might do some good."

Probably the *Merrill* editor is correct. About the only salvation for the careful motorist is a vigorous and continuous campaign of education that will make the hoggish driver see the evil of his ways. But it is not easy to educate a pig, whether it be the farm animal or a human being. It will take a lot of campaigning.

About the best cure would be for the county motorcycle officers to be on the watch for road hogs, arresting them as fast as they can be caught and bringing them into court, to be censured and fined.

The *Eau Claire Leader* says, "Back in the old days when motor chivalry and courtesy were part of the unwritten code it would not have been necessary to call the attention of road hogs to their annoying and unlawful practices. Today it is. Every holiday and every weekend emphasizes the need for some strong arm squad to keep on the right side of the highway the thoughtless and deliberate driver who regards the entire road as his.

"There is a species of mania, akin to that of speeding, that prompts some drivers to hog the road in such fashion that the vehicle in the rear cannot possibly pass. This privilege is guaranteed the trailing car by law, and the refusal to make way for it is a violation of the motor statutes.

"Drivers with a certain grain of courtesy need only a horn toot to make way for the car behind. The other style of driver needs a traffic cop, and the sooner the latter gets into action, the more safe will driving become."

At Superior a campaign was arranged to bring careless and dangerous motoring into disrepute and to focus attention on the need of safe and sane driving now that highway traffic is getting heavy. Stickers were provided upon which was printed the slogan, "KEEP TO THE RIGHT."

If a generous supply of these could be distributed to drivers anxious to spread the word to road hogs, it might help. The strips, with the warning in bold, black letters pasted on the windshield or radiator would meet the eyes of those who usurp the center of the road and they might be ashamed of themselves and move over to the right half of the pavement. The plan is worth trying anyway. Some drivers of trucks are more dangerous road hogs than the operators of pleasure cars.

"Year's Radio Sales Put at $650,550,000"
The New York Times, January 13, 1929

Radio sales in 1928 amounted to $650,550,000, against $425,600,000 in 1927. All records for the total cost and number of sets sold and the growth of the listening public were exceeded, according to Radio Retailing, which made public yesterday the statistics of its annual survey of the radio industry in this country.

The listening public was said to have increased this year in America to about 35,000,000 persons against an estimated 26,000,000 in 1927 and 75,000 in 1922. Sets of all types in use this year were said to have reached 9,000,000 in number, as compared to 7,500,000 in 1927 and 60,000 in 1922.

An itemized account of the survey, the report said, shows that 2,550,000 factory-built sets, including consoles and built-in receivers, were sold for a total of $306,000,000 in 1928, against 1,350,000 sets sold for $168,750,000 in 1927 and 100,000 sold for $5,000,000 in 1922. Radio-phonograph combinations sold last year totaled 81,000, and the outlay for them was $38,000,000.

SECTION FIVE: CENSUS DATA

This section begins with 10 state-by-state comparative tables that rank data from the 1920, 1930, and 2010 census, designed to help define the times during which the families profiled in Section One lived. Table topics are listed below. Following the state-by-state tables are reprints directly from the 1930 Census of Population, including a United States Summary and statistics on various topics listed below. This data is portrayed by maps, tables, graphs, charts and narrative, helping to visualize the environment of the 1920s.

Total Population

Area	Population 1920	Population 1930	Population 2010
Alabama	2,348,174	2,646,248	4,779,736
Alaska	55,036	59,278	710,231
Arizona	334,162	435,573	6,392,017
Arkansas	1,752,204	1,854,482	2,915,918
California	3,426,861	5,677,251	37,253,956
Colorado	939,629	1,035,791	5,029,196
Connecticut	1,380,631	1,606,903	3,574,097
D.C.	437,571	486,869	601,723
Delaware	223,003	238,380	897,934
Florida	968,470	1,468,211	18,801,310
Georgia	2,895,832	2,908,506	9,687,653
Hawaii	255,881	368,300	1,360,301
Idaho	431,866	445,032	1,567,582
Illinois	6,485,280	7,630,654	12,830,632
Indiana	2,930,390	3,238,503	6,483,802
Iowa	2,404,021	2,470,939	3,046,355
Kansas	1,769,257	1,880,999	2,853,118
Kentucky	2,416,630	2,614,589	4,339,367
Louisiana	1,798,509	2,101,593	4,533,372
Maine	768,014	797,423	1,328,361
Maryland	1,449,661	1,631,526	5,773,552
Massachusetts	3,852,356	4,249,614	6,547,629
Michigan	3,668,412	4,842,325	9,883,640
Minnesota	2,387,125	2,563,953	5,303,925
Mississippi	1,790,618	2,009,821	2,967,297
Missouri	3,404,055	3,629,367	5,988,927
Montana	548,889	537,606	989,415
Nebraska	1,296,372	1,377,963	1,826,341
Nevada	77,407	91,058	2,700,551
New Hampshire	443,083	465,293	1,316,470
New Jersey	3,155,900	4,041,334	8,791,894
New Mexico	360,350	423,317	2,059,179
New York	10,385,227	12,588,066	19,378,102
North Carolina	2,559,123	3,170,276	9,535,483
North Dakota	646,872	680,845	672,591
Ohio	5,759,394	6,646,697	11,536,504
Oklahoma	2,028,283	2,396,040	3,751,351
Oregon	783,389	953,786	3,831,074
Pennsylvania	8,720,017	9,631,350	12,702,379
Rhode Island	604,397	687,497	1,052,567
South Carolina	1,683,724	1,738,765	4,625,364
South Dakota	636,547	692,849	814,180
Tennessee	2,337,885	2,616,556	6,346,105
Texas	4,663,228	5,824,715	25,145,561
Utah	449,396	507,847	2,763,885
Vermont	352,428	359,611	625,741
Virginia	2,309,187	2,421,851	8,001,024
Washington	1,356,621	1,563,396	6,724,540
West Virginia	1,463,701	1,729,205	1,852,994
Wisconsin	2,632,067	2,939,006	5,686,986
Wyoming	194,402	225,565	563,626
United States	106,021,537	123,202,624	308,745,538

1920 Area	Rank	1930 Area	Rank	2010 Area	Rank
New York	1	New York	1	California	1
Pennsylvania	2	Pennsylvania	2	Texas	2
Illinois	3	Illinois	3	New York	3
Ohio	4	Ohio	4	Florida	4
Texas	5	Texas	5	Illinois	5
Massachusetts	6	California	6	Pennsylvania	6
Michigan	7	Michigan	7	Ohio	7
California	8	Massachusetts	8	Michigan	8
Missouri	9	New Jersey	9	Georgia	9
New Jersey	10	Missouri	10	North Carolina	10
Indiana	11	Indiana	11	New Jersey	11
Georgia	12	North Carolina	12	Virginia	12
Wisconsin	13	Wisconsin	13	Washington	13
North Carolina	14	Georgia	14	Massachusetts	14
Kentucky	15	Alabama	15	Indiana	15
Iowa	16	Tennessee	16	Arizona	16
Minnesota	17	Kentucky	17	Tennessee	17
Alabama	18	Minnesota	18	Missouri	18
Tennessee	19	Iowa	19	Maryland	19
Virginia	20	Virginia	20	Wisconsin	20
Oklahoma	21	Oklahoma	21	Minnesota	21
Louisiana	22	Louisiana	22	Colorado	22
Mississippi	23	Mississippi	23	Alabama	23
Kansas	24	Kansas	24	South Carolina	24
Arkansas	25	Arkansas	25	Louisiana	25
South Carolina	26	South Carolina	26	Kentucky	26
West Virginia	27	West Virginia	27	Oregon	27
Maryland	28	Maryland	28	Oklahoma	28
Connecticut	29	Connecticut	29	Connecticut	29
Washington	30	Washington	30	Iowa	30
Nebraska	31	Florida	31	Mississippi	31
Florida	32	Nebraska	32	Arkansas	32
Colorado	33	Colorado	33	Kansas	33
Oregon	34	Oregon	34	Utah	34
Maine	35	Maine	35	Nevada	35
North Dakota	36	South Dakota	36	New Mexico	36
South Dakota	37	Rhode Island	37	West Virginia	37
Rhode Island	38	North Dakota	38	Nebraska	38
Montana	39	Montana	39	Idaho	39
Utah	40	Utah	40	Hawaii	40
New Hampshire	41	D.C.	41	Maine	41
D.C.	42	New Hampshire	42	New Hampshire	42
Idaho	43	Idaho	43	Rhode Island	43
New Mexico	44	Arizona	44	Montana	44
Vermont	45	New Mexico	45	Delaware	45
Arizona	46	Hawaii	46	South Dakota	46
Hawaii	47	Vermont	47	Alaska	47
Delaware	48	Delaware	48	North Dakota	48
Wyoming	49	Wyoming	49	Vermont	49
Nevada	50	Nevada	50	D.C.	50
Alaska	51	Alaska	51	Wyoming	51
United States	–	United States	–	United States	–

Source: U.S. Census Bureau, 1920 Census of Population; U.S. Census Bureau, 1930 Census of Population; U.S. Census Bureau, Census 2010

White Population

Area	Percent of Population			1920		1930		2010	
	1920	1930	2010	Area	Rank	Area	Rank	Area	Rank
Alabama	61.62	64.27	68.53	New Hampshire	1	Vermont	1	Vermont	1
Alaska	n/a	n/a	66.68	Vermont	1	New Hampshire	2	Maine	2
Arizona	87.22	86.91	73.01	Maine	3	Maine	3	West Virginia	3
Arkansas	73.04	74.16	77.00	Wisconsin	4	Iowa	4	New Hampshire	4
California	95.27	95.26	57.59	Minnesota	5	Wisconsin	5	Iowa	5
Colorado	98.35	98.36	81.31	Iowa	6	Minnesota	6	Wyoming	6
Connecticut	98.41	98.12	77.57	North Dakota	7	Nebraska	7	North Dakota	7
D.C.	74.70	72.71	38.47	Massachusetts	8	North Dakota	8	Montana	8
Delaware	86.37	86.30	68.89	Nebraska	9	Massachusetts	9	Idaho	9
Florida	65.89	70.52	75.04	Idaho	10	Idaho	10	Kentucky	10
Georgia	58.33	63.16	59.74	Connecticut	11	Rhode Island	11	Wisconsin	11
Hawaii	n/a	n/a	24.74	Colorado	12	Utah	12	Nebraska	12
Idaho	98.56	98.61	89.09	Utah	13	Oregon	13	Utah	13
Illinois	97.13	95.60	71.53	Rhode Island	14	Colorado	14	South Dakota	14
Indiana	97.22	96.52	84.33	Michigan	15	Connecticut	15	Minnesota	15
Iowa	99.17	99.26	91.31	Oregon	15	Wyoming	16	Indiana	16
Kansas	96.59	96.33	83.80	New York	17	Washington	17	Kansas	17
Kentucky	90.23	91.35	87.79	Wyoming	18	South Dakota	18	Oregon	18
Louisiana	60.97	62.94	62.56	Montana	19	Montana	19	Missouri	19
Maine	99.70	99.72	95.23	Washington	20	New York	20	Ohio	20
Maryland	83.10	83.00	58.18	South Dakota	21	Indiana	21	Pennsylvania	21
Massachusetts	98.73	98.67	80.41	Indiana	22	Kansas	22	Rhode Island	22
Michigan	98.18	96.31	78.95	Illinois	23	Michigan	23	Colorado	23
Minnesota	99.24	99.17	85.30	Ohio	24	Illinois	24	Massachusetts	24
Mississippi	47.69	49.66	59.13	Pennsylvania	25	Pennsylvania	25	Michigan	25
Missouri	94.74	93.79	82.80	Kansas	26	Ohio	26	Connecticut	26
Montana	97.33	96.71	89.44	New Jersey	27	California	27	Tennessee	27
Nebraska	98.68	98.70	86.12	California	28	New Jersey	28	Washington	28
Nevada	91.33	92.81	66.16	Missouri	29	Missouri	29	Arkansas	29
New Hampshire	99.83	99.80	93.89	West Virginia	30	West Virginia	30	Florida	30
New Jersey	96.24	94.76	68.58	New Mexico	31	Nevada	31	Arizona	31
New Mexico	92.87	92.39	68.37	Nevada	32	New Mexico	32	Oklahoma	32
New York	97.95	96.55	65.75	Kentucky	33	Kentucky	33	Illinois	33
North Carolina	69.70	70.50	68.47	Oklahoma	34	Oklahoma	34	Texas	34
North Dakota	98.93	98.68	90.02	Arizona	35	Arizona	35	Delaware	35
Ohio	96.74	95.31	82.69	Delaware	36	Delaware	36	New Jersey	36
Oklahoma	89.79	88.93	72.16	Texas	37	Texas	37	Virginia	36
Oregon	98.18	98.41	83.65	Maryland	38	Maryland	38	Alabama	38
Pennsylvania	96.71	95.48	81.92	Tennessee	39	Tennessee	39	North Carolina	39
Rhode Island	98.28	98.48	81.41	D.C.	40	Arkansas	40	New Mexico	40
South Carolina	48.61	54.29	66.16	Arkansas	41	Virginia	41	Alaska	41
South Dakota	97.27	96.74	85.90	Virginia	42	D.C.	42	Nevada	42
Tennessee	80.67	81.74	77.56	North Carolina	43	Florida	43	South Carolina	42
Texas	84.02	85.28	70.40	Florida	44	North Carolina	44	New York	44
Utah	98.33	98.45	86.09	Alabama	45	Alabama	45	Louisiana	45
Vermont	99.83	99.82	95.29	Louisiana	46	Georgia	46	Georgia	46
Virginia	70.06	73.10	68.58	Georgia	47	Louisiana	47	Mississippi	47
Washington	97.28	97.33	77.27	South Carolina	48	South Carolina	48	Maryland	48
West Virginia	94.09	93.35	93.90	Mississippi	49	Mississippi	49	California	49
Wisconsin	99.43	99.23	86.20	Hawaii	n/a	Alaska	n/a	D.C.	50
Wyoming	97.81	98.08	90.71	Alaska	n/a	Hawaii	n/a	Hawaii	51
United States	89.44	89.52	72.41	United States	–	United States	–	United States	–

Source: U.S. Census Bureau, 1920 Census of Population; U.S. Census Bureau, 1930 Census of Population; U.S. Census Bureau, Census 2010

Black Population

Area	Percent of Population			1920		1930		2010	
	1920	1930	2010	Area	Rank	Area	Rank	Area	Rank
Alabama	38.36	35.70	26.18	Mississippi	1	Mississippi	1	D.C.	1
Alaska	n/a	n/a	3.28	South Carolina	2	South Carolina	2	Mississippi	2
Arizona	2.40	2.47	4.05	Georgia	3	Louisiana	3	Louisiana	3
Arkansas	26.95	25.80	15.43	Louisiana	4	Georgia	4	Georgia	4
California	1.13	1.43	6.17	Alabama	5	Alabama	5	Maryland	5
Colorado	1.20	1.14	4.01	Florida	6	Florida	6	South Carolina	6
Connecticut	1.52	1.83	10.14	Virginia	7	North Carolina	7	Alabama	7
D.C.	25.13	27.13	50.71	North Carolina	8	D.C.	8	North Carolina	8
Delaware	13.60	13.68	21.36	Arkansas	9	Virginia	9	Delaware	9
Florida	34.02	29.41	15.96	D.C.	10	Arkansas	10	Virginia	10
Georgia	41.66	36.83	30.46	Tennessee	11	Tennessee	11	Tennessee	11
Hawaii	n/a	n/a	1.57	Maryland	12	Maryland	12	Florida	12
Idaho	0.21	0.15	0.63	Texas	13	Texas	13	New York	13
Illinois	2.81	4.31	14.55	Delaware	14	Delaware	14	Arkansas	14
Indiana	2.76	3.46	9.12	Kentucky	15	Kentucky	15	Illinois	15
Iowa	0.79	0.70	2.93	Oklahoma	16	Oklahoma	16	Michigan	16
Kansas	3.27	3.53	5.88	West Virginia	17	West Virginia	17	New Jersey	17
Kentucky	9.76	8.65	7.78	Missouri	18	Missouri	18	Ohio	18
Louisiana	38.94	36.94	32.04	New Jersey	19	New Jersey	19	Texas	19
Maine	0.17	0.14	1.18	Kansas	20	Ohio	20	Missouri	20
Maryland	16.86	16.94	29.45	Pennsylvania	21	Pennsylvania	21	Pennsylvania	21
Massachusetts	1.18	1.23	6.63	Ohio	22	Illinois	22	Connecticut	22
Michigan	1.64	3.50	14.17	Illinois	23	Kansas	23	Indiana	23
Minnesota	0.37	0.37	5.17	Indiana	24	Michigan	24	Nevada	24
Mississippi	52.23	50.24	37.02	Arizona	25	Indiana	25	Kentucky	25
Missouri	5.24	6.17	11.58	New York	26	New York	26	Oklahoma	26
Montana	0.30	0.23	0.41	Rhode Island	27	Arizona	27	Massachusetts	27
Nebraska	1.02	1.00	4.54	Michigan	28	Connecticut	28	Wisconsin	28
Nevada	0.45	0.57	8.10	New Mexico	29	Rhode Island	29	California	29
New Hampshire	0.14	0.17	1.14	Connecticut	30	California	30	Kansas	30
New Jersey	3.71	5.17	13.70	Colorado	31	Massachusetts	31	Rhode Island	31
New Mexico	1.59	0.67	2.07	Massachusetts	32	Colorado	32	Minnesota	32
New York	1.91	3.28	15.86	California	33	Nebraska	33	Nebraska	33
North Carolina	29.83	28.98	21.48	Nebraska	34	Iowa	34	Arizona	34
North Dakota	0.07	0.06	1.18	Iowa	35	New Mexico	35	Colorado	35
Ohio	3.23	4.65	12.20	Wyoming	36	Nevada	36	Washington	36
Oklahoma	7.37	7.19	7.40	Washington	37	Wyoming	37	West Virginia	37
Oregon	0.27	0.23	1.81	Nevada	38	Washington	38	Alaska	38
Pennsylvania	3.26	4.48	10.85	Minnesota	39	Minnesota	39	Iowa	39
Rhode Island	1.66	1.44	5.72	Utah	40	Wisconsin	39	New Mexico	40
South Carolina	51.36	45.65	27.90	Montana	41	Montana	41	Oregon	41
South Dakota	0.13	0.09	1.25	Oregon	42	Oregon	41	Hawaii	42
Tennessee	19.32	18.25	16.66	Idaho	43	Utah	43	South Dakota	43
Texas	15.91	14.68	11.85	Wisconsin	44	New Hampshire	44	Maine	44
Utah	0.32	0.22	1.06	Maine	45	Vermont	45	North Dakota	44
Vermont	0.16	0.16	1.00	Vermont	46	Idaho	46	New Hampshire	46
Virginia	29.88	26.85	19.39	New Hampshire	47	Maine	47	Utah	47
Washington	0.51	0.44	3.57	South Dakota	48	South Dakota	48	Vermont	48
West Virginia	5.90	6.64	3.41	North Dakota	49	North Dakota	49	Wyoming	49
Wisconsin	0.20	0.37	6.32	Hawaii	n/a	Alaska	n/a	Idaho	50
Wyoming	0.71	0.55	0.84	Alaska	n/a	Hawaii	n/a	Montana	51
United States	9.87	9.65	12.61	United States	–	United States	–	United States	–

Source: U.S. Census Bureau, 1920 Census of Population; U.S. Census Bureau, 1930 Census of Population; U.S. Census Bureau, Census 2010

American Indian/Alaska Native Population

Area	Percent of Population			1920		1930		2010	
	1920	1930	2010	Area	Rank	Area	Rank	Area	Rank
Alabama	0.02	0.02	0.59	Arizona	1	Arizona	1	Alaska	1
Alaska	n/a	n/a	14.77	Nevada	2	New Mexico	2	New Mexico	2
Arizona	9.87	10.04	4.64	New Mexico	3	Nevada	3	South Dakota	3
Arkansas	0.01	0.02	0.76	Oklahoma	4	Oklahoma	4	Oklahoma	4
California	0.51	0.34	0.97	South Dakota	5	South Dakota	5	Montana	5
Colorado	0.15	0.13	1.11	Montana	6	Montana	6	North Dakota	6
Connecticut	0.01	0.01	0.31	North Dakota	7	North Dakota	7	Arizona	7
D.C.	0.01	0.01	0.35	Idaho	8	Wyoming	8	Wyoming	8
Delaware	0.00	0.00	0.47	Wyoming	9	Idaho	8	Washington	9
Florida	0.05	0.04	0.38	Washington	10	Washington	10	Oregon	10
Georgia	0.00	0.00	0.33	Utah	11	Utah	11	Idaho	11
Hawaii	n/a	n/a	0.31	Oregon	12	North Carolina	12	North Carolina	12
Idaho	0.72	0.82	1.37	California	13	Oregon	13	Nevada	13
Illinois	0.00	0.01	0.34	North Carolina	14	Minnesota	14	Utah	13
Indiana	0.00	0.01	0.28	Minnesota	15	Wisconsin	15	Minnesota	15
Iowa	0.02	0.03	0.36	Wisconsin	15	California	16	Colorado	16
Kansas	0.13	0.13	0.99	Nebraska	17	Nebraska	17	Nebraska	17
Kentucky	0.00	0.00	0.23	Michigan	18	Michigan	18	Kansas	18
Louisiana	0.06	0.07	0.67	Colorado	18	Maine	19	California	19
Maine	0.11	0.13	0.65	Kansas	20	Colorado	19	Wisconsin	20
Maryland	0.00	0.00	0.35	Maine	21	Kansas	19	Arkansas	21
Massachusetts	0.01	0.02	0.29	Louisiana	22	Louisiana	22	Texas	22
Michigan	0.15	0.15	0.63	Mississippi	22	Mississippi	22	Louisiana	23
Minnesota	0.37	0.43	1.15	New York	24	New York	24	Maine	24
Mississippi	0.06	0.07	0.51	Texas	24	South Carolina	24	Michigan	25
Missouri	0.01	0.02	0.46	Florida	24	Rhode Island	26	Alabama	26
Montana	2.00	2.75	6.32	Virginia	27	Florida	27	Rhode Island	27
Nebraska	0.22	0.24	1.01	Rhode Island	28	Iowa	28	New York	28
Nevada	6.34	5.35	1.19	Iowa	28	Virginia	28	Mississippi	29
New Hampshire	0.01	0.01	0.24	Alabama	28	Massachusetts	30	Delaware	30
New Jersey	0.00	0.01	0.33	South Carolina	28	Texas	30	Missouri	31
New Mexico	5.41	6.84	9.38	Massachusetts	32	Missouri	30	South Carolina	32
New York	0.05	0.06	0.55	Connecticut	32	Alabama	30	Florida	33
North Carolina	0.46	0.52	1.28	New Hampshire	32	Arkansas	30	Virginia	34
North Dakota	0.97	1.23	5.44	Vermont	32	Connecticut	35	Iowa	35
Ohio	0.00	0.01	0.22	D.C.	32	New Jersey	35	Maryland	36
Oklahoma	2.83	3.87	8.58	Missouri	32	New Hampshire	35	D.C.	36
Oregon	0.59	0.50	1.39	Arkansas	32	Illinois	35	Vermont	36
Pennsylvania	0.00	0.01	0.21	New Jersey	39	Pennsylvania	35	Illinois	39
Rhode Island	0.02	0.05	0.58	Illinois	39	Vermont	35	New Jersey	40
South Carolina	0.02	0.06	0.42	Pennsylvania	39	Ohio	35	Georgia	40
South Dakota	2.57	3.15	8.82	Ohio	39	D.C.	35	Tennessee	42
Tennessee	0.00	0.01	0.32	Delaware	39	Indiana	35	Hawaii	43
Texas	0.05	0.02	0.68	Maryland	39	Tennessee	35	Connecticut	43
Utah	0.60	0.56	1.19	Indiana	39	Delaware	45	Massachusetts	45
Vermont	0.01	0.01	0.35	West Virginia	39	Maryland	45	Indiana	46
Virginia	0.04	0.03	0.37	Kentucky	39	West Virginia	45	New Hampshire	47
Washington	0.67	0.72	1.54	Tennessee	39	Kentucky	45	Kentucky	48
West Virginia	0.00	0.00	0.20	Georgia	39	Georgia	45	Ohio	49
Wisconsin	0.37	0.39	0.96	Hawaii	n/a	Alaska	n/a	Pennsylvania	50
Wyoming	0.69	0.82	2.37	Alaska	n/a	Hawaii	n/a	West Virginia	51
United States	0.23	0.27	0.95	United States	–	United States	–	United States	–

Source: U.S. Census Bureau, 1920 Census of Population; U.S. Census Bureau, 1930 Census of Population; U.S. Census Bureau, Census 2010

Asian Population

Area	Percent of Population			1920		1930		2010	
	1920	1930	2010	Area	Rank	Area	Rank	Area	Rank
Alabama	0.00	0.00	1.12	California	1	California	1	Hawaii	1
Alaska	n/a	n/a	5.37	Nevada	2	Washington	2	California	2
Arizona	0.51	0.58	2.76	Washington	3	Nevada	3	New Jersey	3
Arkansas	0.01	0.02	1.24	Oregon	4	Oregon	4	New York	4
California	3.09	2.97	13.05	Wyoming	5	Utah	5	Nevada	5
Colorado	0.30	0.36	2.76	Utah	6	Arizona	6	Washington	6
Connecticut	0.05	0.04	3.79	Arizona	7	Wyoming	7	Maryland	7
D.C.	0.16	0.16	3.50	Idaho	8	Idaho	8	Virginia	8
Delaware	0.02	0.02	3.18	Montana	9	Colorado	9	Alaska	9
Florida	0.03	0.03	2.42	Colorado	10	Montana	10	Massachusetts	10
Georgia	0.01	0.01	3.25	D.C.	11	D.C.	11	Illinois	11
Hawaii	n/a	n/a	38.60	New Mexico	12	New York	12	Minnesota	12
Idaho	0.50	0.42	1.22	New York	13	New Mexico	13	Texas	13
Illinois	0.05	0.08	4.57	Nebraska	14	Massachusetts	14	Connecticut	14
Indiana	0.01	0.01	1.58	Massachusetts	15	Illinois	14	Oregon	15
Iowa	0.01	0.01	1.74	Connecticut	16	New Jersey	16	D.C.	16
Kansas	0.01	0.01	2.38	New Jersey	16	Nebraska	16	Georgia	17
Kentucky	0.00	0.00	1.13	Illinois	16	Michigan	18	Delaware	18
Louisiana	0.03	0.05	1.55	Rhode Island	19	Maryland	18	Rhode Island	19
Maine	0.02	0.02	1.02	Minnesota	20	Louisiana	18	Arizona	20
Maryland	0.03	0.05	5.52	North Dakota	20	Connecticut	21	Colorado	20
Massachusetts	0.07	0.08	5.34	Michigan	20	Pennsylvania	21	Pennsylvania	22
Michigan	0.03	0.05	2.41	Pennsylvania	20	Rhode Island	23	Florida	23
Minnesota	0.03	0.03	4.04	South Dakota	20	North Dakota	23	Michigan	24
Mississippi	0.02	0.03	0.87	Texas	20	Minnesota	23	Kansas	25
Missouri	0.02	0.03	1.64	Maryland	20	Ohio	23	Wisconsin	26
Montana	0.37	0.31	0.63	Florida	20	Texas	23	North Carolina	27
Nebraska	0.08	0.07	1.77	Louisiana	20	Florida	23	New Hampshire	28
Nevada	1.88	1.27	7.24	New Hampshire	29	Missouri	23	Utah	29
New Hampshire	0.02	0.02	2.16	Maine	29	Mississippi	23	Nebraska	30
New Jersey	0.05	0.07	8.25	Ohio	29	New Hampshire	31	Iowa	31
New Mexico	0.12	0.10	1.37	Delaware	29	Wisconsin	31	Oklahoma	32
New York	0.09	0.12	7.33	Missouri	29	Maine	31	Ohio	33
North Carolina	0.00	0.00	2.19	Oklahoma	29	Delaware	31	Missouri	34
North Dakota	0.03	0.03	1.03	Virginia	29	Virginia	31	Indiana	35
Ohio	0.02	0.03	1.67	Mississippi	29	Arkansas	31	Louisiana	36
Oklahoma	0.02	0.01	1.73	Wisconsin	37	Vermont	37	Tennessee	37
Oregon	0.96	0.86	3.69	Iowa	37	South Dakota	37	New Mexico	38
Pennsylvania	0.03	0.04	2.75	Kansas	37	Iowa	37	South Carolina	39
Rhode Island	0.04	0.03	2.89	Indiana	37	Indiana	37	Vermont	40
South Carolina	0.01	0.00	1.28	West Virginia	37	Kansas	37	Arkansas	41
South Dakota	0.03	0.01	0.93	Arkansas	37	West Virginia	37	Idaho	42
Tennessee	0.00	0.00	1.44	Georgia	37	Oklahoma	37	Kentucky	43
Texas	0.03	0.03	3.84	South Carolina	37	Georgia	37	Alabama	44
Utah	0.74	0.77	2.00	Vermont	45	Kentucky	45	North Dakota	45
Vermont	0.00	0.01	1.27	Kentucky	45	Alabama	45	Maine	46
Virginia	0.02	0.02	5.50	Alabama	45	Tennessee	45	South Dakota	47
Washington	1.54	1.51	7.15	Tennessee	45	North Carolina	45	Mississippi	48
West Virginia	0.01	0.01	0.67	North Carolina	45	South Carolina	45	Wyoming	49
Wisconsin	0.01	0.02	2.27	Hawaii	n/a	Alaska	n/a	West Virginia	50
Wyoming	0.79	0.54	0.79	Alaska	n/a	Hawaii	n/a	Montana	51
United States	0.17	0.21	4.75	United States	–	United States	–	United States	–

Source: U.S. Census Bureau, 1920 Census of Population; U.S. Census Bureau, 1930 Census of Population; U.S. Census Bureau, Census 2010

Foreign-Born Population

Area	Percent of Population			1920		1930		2010	
	1920	1930	2010	Area	Rank	Area	Rank	Area	Rank
Alabama	0.8	0.6	3.4	Rhode Island	1	New York	1	California	1
Alaska	n/a	n/a	7.2	Massachusetts	2	Massachusetts	2	New York	2
Arizona	24.1	15.1	14.2	Connecticut	3	Rhode Island	3	New Jersey	3
Arkansas	0.8	0.6	4.3	New York	4	Connecticut	4	Nevada	4
California	22.1	18.9	27.2	Arizona	5	New Jersey	5	Florida	5
Colorado	12.7	9.6	9.8	New Jersey	6	California	6	Hawaii	6
Connecticut	27.4	23.9	13.2	California	7	New Hampshire	7	Texas	7
D.C.	6.7	6.3	13.0	Nevada	8	Michigan	8	Massachusetts	8
Delaware	8.9	7.1	8.2	New Hampshire	9	Nevada	9	Arizona	9
Florida	5.6	4.8	19.2	Minnesota	10	Washington	10	Illinois	10
Georgia	0.6	0.5	9.6	North Dakota	10	Illinois	10	Maryland	11
Hawaii	n/a	n/a	17.7	Michigan	12	North Dakota	12	Connecticut	11
Idaho	9.4	7.3	5.9	Washington	13	Minnesota	13	D.C.	13
Illinois	18.7	16.3	13.6	Illinois	14	Arizona	14	Washington	14
Indiana	5.2	4.4	4.4	Wisconsin	15	Montana	15	Rhode Island	15
Iowa	9.4	6.8	4.1	Montana	16	Wisconsin	16	Virginia	16
Kansas	6.3	4.3	6.3	Pennsylvania	17	Pennsylvania	17	Colorado	17
Kentucky	1.3	0.8	3.1	Maine	18	Maine	18	New Mexico	18
Louisiana	2.6	1.8	3.6	Oregon	19	Vermont	19	Oregon	18
Maine	14.0	12.6	3.3	Wyoming	19	Oregon	20	Georgia	20
Maryland	7.1	5.9	13.2	Utah	21	Wyoming	21	Utah	21
Massachusetts	28.3	25.1	14.5	South Dakota	22	Ohio	22	Delaware	21
Michigan	19.9	17.6	5.9	Colorado	23	Colorado	23	North Carolina	23
Minnesota	20.4	15.2	7.0	Vermont	24	South Dakota	24	Alaska	24
Mississippi	0.5	0.4	2.2	Ohio	25	Utah	24	Minnesota	25
Missouri	5.5	4.2	3.7	Nebraska	26	Nebraska	26	Kansas	26
Montana	17.4	14.1	2.0	Idaho	27	Idaho	27	Michigan	27
Nebraska	11.6	8.7	5.9	Iowa	27	Delaware	28	Idaho	27
Nevada	20.7	16.6	19.3	Delaware	29	Iowa	29	Nebraska	27
New Hampshire	20.6	17.8	5.3	New Mexico	30	D.C.	30	Pennsylvania	30
New Jersey	23.5	21.0	20.3	Texas	31	Texas	31	New Hampshire	31
New Mexico	8.3	5.7	9.7	Maryland	32	Maryland	32	Oklahoma	32
New York	27.2	25.9	21.7	D.C.	33	New Mexico	33	South Carolina	33
North Carolina	0.3	0.3	7.4	Kansas	34	Florida	34	Wisconsin	34
North Dakota	20.4	15.5	2.4	Florida	35	Indiana	35	Tennessee	35
Ohio	11.8	9.8	3.8	Missouri	36	Kansas	36	Indiana	35
Oklahoma	2.0	1.3	5.2	Indiana	37	Missouri	37	Arkansas	37
Oregon	13.7	11.6	9.7	West Virginia	38	West Virginia	38	Iowa	38
Pennsylvania	16.0	12.9	5.6	Louisiana	39	Louisiana	39	Vermont	39
Rhode Island	29.0	25.0	12.6	Oklahoma	40	Oklahoma	40	Ohio	40
South Carolina	0.4	0.3	4.7	Virginia	41	Virginia	41	Missouri	41
South Dakota	13.0	9.5	2.3	Kentucky	42	Kentucky	42	Louisiana	42
Tennessee	0.7	0.5	4.4	Arkansas	43	Alabama	43	Alabama	43
Texas	7.8	6.2	16.1	Alabama	43	Arkansas	43	Maine	44
Utah	13.2	9.5	8.2	Tennessee	45	Georgia	45	Wyoming	45
Vermont	12.6	12.0	4.0	Georgia	46	Tennessee	45	Kentucky	45
Virginia	1.4	1.0	10.8	Mississippi	47	Mississippi	47	North Dakota	47
Washington	19.6	16.3	12.7	South Carolina	48	North Carolina	48	South Dakota	48
West Virginia	4.2	3.0	1.3	North Carolina	49	South Carolina	48	Mississippi	49
Wisconsin	17.5	13.2	4.6	Hawaii	n/a	Alaska	n/a	Montana	50
Wyoming	13.7	10.3	3.1	Alaska	n/a	Hawaii	n/a	West Virginia	51
United States	13.2	11.6	12.7	United States	–	United States	–	United States	–

Source: U.S. Census Bureau, 1920 Census of Population; U.S. Census Bureau, 1930 Census of Population; U.S. Census Bureau, Census 2010

Urban Population

Area	Percent of Population			1920		1930		2010	
	1920	1930	2010	Area	Rank	Area	Rank	Area	Rank
Alabama	21.7	28.1	55.0	D.C.	1	D.C.	1	D.C.	1
Alaska	5.6	13.2	60.5	Rhode Island	2	Rhode Island	2	New Jersey	2
Arizona	36.1	34.4	86.7	Massachusetts	3	Massachusetts	3	California	3
Arkansas	16.6	20.6	52.0	New York	4	New York	4	Massachusetts	4
California	67.9	73.3	93.2	New Jersey	5	New Jersey	5	Rhode Island	5
Colorado	48.2	50.2	82.0	California	6	Illinois	6	Nevada	6
Connecticut	67.8	70.4	87.9	Illinois	6	California	7	Hawaii	7
D.C.	100.0	100.0	100.0	Connecticut	8	Connecticut	8	Florida	8
Delaware	54.2	51.7	80.1	Pennsylvania	9	Michigan	9	Connecticut	9
Florida	36.5	51.7	89.3	Ohio	10	Pennsylvania	10	Illinois	10
Georgia	25.1	30.8	70.7	Michigan	11	Ohio	10	Arizona	11
Hawaii	36.1	53.7	90.0	Maryland	12	Maryland	12	Maryland	12
Idaho	27.6	29.1	63.8	New Hampshire	13	New Hampshire	13	New York	13
Illinois	67.9	73.9	87.3	Washington	14	Washington	14	Utah	14
Indiana	50.6	55.5	72.1	Delaware	15	Indiana	15	Colorado	15
Iowa	36.4	39.6	61.4	Indiana	16	Hawaii	16	Washington	16
Kansas	34.8	38.8	71.1	Oregon	17	Wisconsin	17	Texas	17
Kentucky	26.2	30.6	55.9	Colorado	18	Utah	18	Delaware	18
Louisiana	34.9	39.7	72.1	Utah	19	Delaware	19	Ohio	19
Maine	39.0	40.3	36.6	Wisconsin	20	Florida	19	Oregon	20
Maryland	60.0	59.8	86.4	Missouri	21	Oregon	21	Pennsylvania	21
Massachusetts	90.0	90.2	91.1	Minnesota	22	Missouri	22	New Mexico	22
Michigan	61.1	68.2	72.2	Maine	23	Colorado	23	Michigan	23
Minnesota	44.1	49.0	68.3	Florida	24	Minnesota	24	Indiana	24
Mississippi	13.4	16.9	48.7	Iowa	25	Texas	25	Louisiana	24
Missouri	46.6	51.2	68.3	Arizona	26	Maine	26	Virginia	26
Montana	31.3	33.7	52.0	Hawaii	26	Louisiana	27	Kansas	27
Nebraska	31.3	35.3	68.4	Louisiana	28	Iowa	28	Georgia	28
Nevada	19.7	37.8	90.6	Kansas	29	Kansas	29	Nebraska	29
New Hampshire	56.5	58.7	55.6	Texas	30	Nevada	30	Minnesota	30
New Jersey	79.9	82.6	94.7	Montana	31	Nebraska	31	Missouri	30
New Mexico	18.0	25.2	73.7	Nebraska	31	Arizona	32	Wisconsin	32
New York	82.7	83.6	85.6	Vermont	33	Oklahoma	33	Oklahoma	33
North Carolina	19.2	25.5	59.1	Wyoming	34	Tennessee	33	Idaho	34
North Dakota	13.6	16.6	54.0	Virginia	35	Montana	35	Tennessee	35
Ohio	63.8	67.8	78.9	Idaho	36	Vermont	36	Wyoming	36
Oklahoma	26.5	34.3	65.1	Oklahoma	37	Virginia	37	Iowa	37
Oregon	49.8	51.3	77.9	Kentucky	38	Wyoming	38	South Carolina	38
Pennsylvania	65.1	67.8	76.4	Tennessee	39	Georgia	39	Alaska	39
Rhode Island	91.9	92.4	90.9	West Virginia	40	Kentucky	40	North Carolina	40
South Carolina	17.5	21.3	61.2	Georgia	41	Idaho	41	Kentucky	41
South Dakota	16.0	18.9	51.6	Alabama	42	West Virginia	42	New Hampshire	42
Tennessee	26.1	34.3	63.6	Nevada	43	Alabama	43	Alabama	43
Texas	32.4	41.0	80.7	North Carolina	44	North Carolina	44	North Dakota	44
Utah	48.0	52.4	85.4	New Mexico	45	New Mexico	45	Arkansas	45
Vermont	31.2	33.0	33.6	South Carolina	46	South Carolina	46	Montana	45
Virginia	29.2	32.4	71.4	Arkansas	47	Arkansas	47	South Dakota	47
Washington	54.8	56.6	81.3	South Dakota	48	South Dakota	48	Mississippi	48
West Virginia	25.2	28.4	46.4	North Dakota	49	Mississippi	49	West Virginia	49
Wisconsin	47.3	52.9	65.8	Mississippi	50	North Dakota	50	Maine	50
Wyoming	29.4	31.1	62.4	Alaska	51	Alaska	51	Vermont	51
United States	51.2	56.1	77.6	United States	–	United States	–	United States	–

Source: U.S. Census Bureau, 1920 Census of Housing; U.S. Census Bureau, 1930 Census of Housing; U.S. Census Bureau, Census 2010

255

Rural Population

Area	Percent of Population			1920		1930		2010	
	1920	1930	2010	Area	Rank	Area	Rank	Area	Rank
Alabama	78.3	71.9	45.0	Alaska	1	Alaska	1	Vermont	1
Alaska	94.4	86.8	39.5	Mississippi	2	North Dakota	2	Maine	2
Arizona	63.9	65.6	13.3	North Dakota	3	Mississippi	3	West Virginia	3
Arkansas	83.4	79.4	48.0	South Dakota	4	South Dakota	4	Mississippi	4
California	32.1	26.7	6.8	Arkansas	5	Arkansas	5	South Dakota	5
Colorado	51.8	49.8	18.0	South Carolina	6	South Carolina	6	Arkansas	6
Connecticut	32.2	29.6	12.1	New Mexico	7	New Mexico	7	Montana	6
D.C.	0.0	0.0	0.0	North Carolina	8	North Carolina	8	North Dakota	8
Delaware	45.8	48.3	19.9	Nevada	9	Alabama	9	Alabama	9
Florida	63.5	48.3	10.7	Alabama	10	West Virginia	10	New Hampshire	10
Georgia	74.9	69.2	29.3	Georgia	11	Idaho	11	Kentucky	11
Hawaii	63.9	46.3	10.0	West Virginia	12	Kentucky	12	North Carolina	12
Idaho	72.4	70.9	36.2	Tennessee	13	Georgia	13	Alaska	13
Illinois	32.1	26.1	12.7	Kentucky	14	Wyoming	14	South Carolina	14
Indiana	49.4	44.5	27.9	Oklahoma	15	Virginia	15	Iowa	15
Iowa	63.6	60.4	38.6	Idaho	16	Vermont	16	Wyoming	16
Kansas	65.2	61.2	28.9	Virginia	17	Montana	17	Tennessee	17
Kentucky	73.8	69.4	44.1	Wyoming	18	Oklahoma	18	Idaho	18
Louisiana	65.1	60.3	27.9	Vermont	19	Tennessee	18	Oklahoma	19
Maine	61.0	59.7	63.4	Montana	20	Arizona	20	Wisconsin	20
Maryland	40.0	40.2	13.6	Nebraska	20	Nebraska	21	Minnesota	21
Massachusetts	10.0	9.8	8.9	Texas	22	Nevada	22	Missouri	21
Michigan	38.9	31.8	27.8	Kansas	23	Kansas	23	Nebraska	23
Minnesota	55.9	51.0	31.7	Louisiana	24	Iowa	24	Georgia	24
Mississippi	86.6	83.1	51.3	Arizona	25	Louisiana	25	Kansas	25
Missouri	53.4	48.8	31.7	Hawaii	25	Maine	26	Virginia	26
Montana	68.7	66.3	48.0	Iowa	27	Texas	27	Indiana	27
Nebraska	68.7	64.7	31.6	Florida	28	Minnesota	28	Louisiana	27
Nevada	80.3	62.2	9.4	Maine	29	Colorado	29	Michigan	29
New Hampshire	43.5	41.3	44.4	Minnesota	30	Missouri	30	New Mexico	30
New Jersey	20.1	17.4	5.3	Missouri	31	Oregon	31	Pennsylvania	31
New Mexico	82.0	74.8	26.3	Wisconsin	32	Delaware	32	Oregon	32
New York	17.3	16.4	14.4	Utah	33	Florida	32	Ohio	33
North Carolina	80.8	74.5	40.9	Colorado	34	Utah	34	Delaware	34
North Dakota	86.4	83.4	46.0	Oregon	35	Wisconsin	35	Texas	35
Ohio	36.2	32.2	21.1	Indiana	36	Hawaii	36	Washington	36
Oklahoma	73.5	65.7	34.9	Delaware	37	Indiana	37	Colorado	37
Oregon	50.2	48.7	22.1	Washington	38	Washington	38	Utah	38
Pennsylvania	34.9	32.2	23.6	New Hampshire	39	New Hampshire	39	New York	39
Rhode Island	8.1	7.6	9.1	Maryland	40	Maryland	40	Maryland	40
South Carolina	82.5	78.7	38.8	Michigan	41	Pennsylvania	41	Arizona	41
South Dakota	84.0	81.1	48.4	Ohio	42	Ohio	41	Illinois	42
Tennessee	73.9	65.7	36.4	Pennsylvania	43	Michigan	43	Connecticut	43
Texas	67.6	59.0	19.3	Connecticut	44	Connecticut	44	Florida	44
Utah	52.0	47.6	14.6	California	45	California	45	Hawaii	45
Vermont	68.8	67.0	66.4	Illinois	45	Illinois	46	Nevada	46
Virginia	70.8	67.6	28.6	New Jersey	47	New Jersey	47	Rhode Island	47
Washington	45.2	43.4	18.7	New York	48	New York	48	Massachusetts	48
West Virginia	74.8	71.6	53.6	Massachusetts	49	Massachusetts	49	California	49
Wisconsin	52.7	47.1	34.2	Rhode Island	50	Rhode Island	50	New Jersey	50
Wyoming	70.6	68.9	37.6	D.C.	51	D.C.	51	D.C.	51
United States	48.8	43.9	22.4	United States	–	United States	–	United States	–

Source: U.S. Census Bureau, 1920 Census of Housing; U.S. Census Bureau, 1930 Census of Housing; U.S. Census Bureau, Census 2010

Males per 100 Females

Area	Males per 100 Females			1920		1930		2010	
	1920	1930	2010	Area	Rank	Area	Rank	Area	Rank
Alabama	99.8	98.8	94.3	Nevada	1	Nevada	1	Alaska	1
Alaska	n/a	n/a	108.5	Wyoming	2	Wyoming	2	Wyoming	2
Arizona	121.9	113.2	98.7	Arizona	3	Montana	3	North Dakota	3
Arkansas	104.5	102.8	96.5	Montana	4	Idaho	4	Nevada	4
California	112.4	107.6	98.8	Idaho	5	Arizona	5	Utah	5
Colorado	110.3	105.1	100.5	Washington	6	Washington	6	Montana	6
Connecticut	101.5	99.5	94.8	Oregon	7	North Dakota	7	Colorado	7
D.C.	87.0	90.9	89.5	South Dakota	8	South Dakota	8	Idaho	8
Delaware	104.1	103.5	93.9	California	9	Oregon	9	Hawaii	9
Florida	104.7	101.0	95.6	New Mexico	10	Michigan	10	South Dakota	10
Georgia	99.6	97.3	95.4	North Dakota	11	California	11	Washington	11
Hawaii	n/a	n/a	100.3	Michigan	12	New Mexico	12	California	12
Idaho	118.2	114.3	100.4	Colorado	13	Oklahoma	13	Arizona	13
Illinois	103.9	103.1	96.2	Minnesota	14	West Virginia	14	Minnesota	14
Indiana	103.3	102.6	96.8	Oklahoma	15	Wisconsin	15	Nebraska	14
Iowa	104.7	103.2	98.1	West Virginia	16	Minnesota	16	Wisconsin	14
Kansas	105.7	104.5	98.4	Nebraska	17	Nebraska	17	Texas	17
Kentucky	103.2	102.4	96.8	Texas	18	Colorado	18	Kansas	17
Louisiana	100.9	99.4	95.9	Utah	19	Utah	19	Iowa	19
Maine	102.5	101.3	95.8	Wisconsin	20	Kansas	20	Oregon	20
Maryland	101.3	101.3	93.6	Kansas	21	Vermont	21	Oklahoma	20
Massachusetts	96.3	95.1	93.7	Ohio	22	Texas	22	New Mexico	22
Michigan	110.8	108.4	96.3	Iowa	23	Delaware	23	New Hampshire	23
Minnesota	109.1	105.5	98.5	Florida	23	Iowa	24	West Virginia	23
Mississippi	100.4	100.0	94.4	Arkansas	25	Illinois	25	Vermont	25
Missouri	102.5	100.9	96.0	Delaware	26	Arkansas	26	Indiana	26
Montana	120.5	120.0	100.8	Illinois	27	Indiana	27	Kentucky	26
Nebraska	107.9	105.2	98.5	Indiana	28	Kentucky	28	Arkansas	28
Nevada	148.4	140.3	102.0	Pennsylvania	29	Ohio	29	Virginia	29
New Hampshire	100.5	99.2	97.3	Kentucky	29	Maine	30	Michigan	29
New Jersey	101.5	101.0	94.8	Vermont	31	Maryland	30	Illinois	31
New Mexico	112.1	107.4	97.7	Maine	32	Pennsylvania	32	Missouri	32
New York	99.8	100.6	93.8	Missouri	32	New Jersey	33	Louisiana	33
North Carolina	99.9	98.8	95.0	Virginia	34	Florida	33	Maine	34
North Dakota	112.0	111.9	102.1	Connecticut	35	Missouri	35	Florida	35
Ohio	105.4	102.3	95.4	New Jersey	35	Virginia	36	Georgia	36
Oklahoma	109.0	106.1	98.0	Maryland	37	New York	37	Ohio	36
Oregon	113.4	110.0	98.0	Louisiana	38	Mississippi	38	Pennsylvania	38
Pennsylvania	103.2	101.2	95.1	Tennessee	38	Connecticut	39	Tennessee	38
Rhode Island	97.0	95.2	93.4	New Hampshire	40	Louisiana	40	North Carolina	40
South Carolina	99.2	96.3	94.7	Mississippi	41	Tennessee	40	New Jersey	41
South Dakota	112.6	110.5	100.1	North Carolina	42	New Hampshire	42	Connecticut	41
Tennessee	100.9	99.4	95.1	New York	43	Alabama	43	South Carolina	43
Texas	106.9	103.8	98.4	Alabama	43	North Carolina	43	Mississippi	44
Utah	106.8	104.9	100.9	Georgia	45	Georgia	45	Alabama	45
Vermont	103.0	103.9	97.1	South Carolina	46	South Carolina	46	Delaware	46
Virginia	102.4	100.8	96.3	Rhode Island	47	Rhode Island	47	New York	47
Washington	118.1	112.1	99.3	Massachusetts	48	Massachusetts	48	Massachusetts	48
West Virginia	108.9	106.0	97.3	D.C.	49	D.C.	49	Maryland	49
Wisconsin	106.4	105.8	98.5	Hawaii	n/a	Alaska	n/a	Rhode Island	50
Wyoming	131.3	123.8	104.1	Alaska	n/a	Hawaii	n/a	D.C.	51
United States	104.0	102.5	96.7	United States	–	United States	–	United States	–

Source: U.S. Census Bureau, 1920 Census of Population; U.S. Census Bureau, 1930 Census of Population; U.S. Census Bureau, Census 2010

Homeownership

Area	Percent of Population 1920	1930	2010	1920 Area	Rank	1930 Area	Rank	2010 Area	Rank
Alabama	35.0	34.2	69.7	North Dakota	1	Wisconsin	1	West Virginia	1
Alaska	n/a	n/a	63.1	Wisconsin	2	Maine	2	Minnesota	2
Arizona	42.8	44.8	66.0	South Dakota	3	Utah	3	Michigan	3
Arkansas	45.1	40.1	66.9	Idaho	4	Vermont	4	Iowa	3
California	43.7	46.1	56.0	Minnesota	5	Washington	5	Delaware	5
Colorado	51.6	50.7	65.5	Montana	6	Oregon	6	Maine	6
Connecticut	37.6	44.5	67.5	Utah	7	Michigan	7	New Hampshire	7
D.C.	30.3	38.6	42.0	Maine	8	Minnesota	8	Vermont	8
Delaware	44.7	52.1	72.0	New Mexico	9	North Dakota	9	Utah	9
Florida	42.5	42.0	67.3	Michigan	10	New Mexico	10	Idaho	10
Georgia	30.9	30.6	65.7	Iowa	11	Indiana	11	Indiana	11
Hawaii	n/a	n/a	57.7	Vermont	12	Idaho	12	Alabama	12
Idaho	60.9	57.0	69.9	Nebraska	13	Kansas	13	Pennsylvania	13
Illinois	43.8	46.5	67.4	Kansas	14	Maryland	14	Mississippi	13
Indiana	54.8	57.3	69.8	Oregon	15	New Hampshire	15	South Carolina	15
Iowa	58.1	54.7	72.1	Indiana	15	Iowa	16	Wyoming	15
Kansas	56.9	56.0	67.7	Washington	17	Montana	17	Missouri	17
Kentucky	51.6	51.3	68.7	Wyoming	18	Pennsylvania	18	Kentucky	18
Louisiana	33.7	35.0	67.3	Colorado	19	Ohio	18	New Mexico	19
Maine	59.6	61.7	71.3	Ohio	19	Nebraska	20	Tennessee	20
Maryland	49.9	55.2	67.5	Kentucky	19	South Dakota	21	Wisconsin	21
Massachusetts	34.8	43.5	62.3	Virginia	22	Virginia	22	South Dakota	21
Michigan	58.9	59.0	72.1	Maryland	23	Delaware	23	Montana	23
Minnesota	60.7	58.9	73.1	New Hampshire	24	Kentucky	24	Kansas	24
Mississippi	34.0	32.5	69.6	Missouri	25	Colorado	25	Ohio	25
Missouri	49.5	49.9	68.8	Tennessee	26	Missouri	26	Maryland	26
Montana	60.5	54.5	68.0	Nevada	27	New Jersey	27	Connecticut	26
Nebraska	57.4	54.3	67.2	North Carolina	28	Wyoming	28	Illinois	28
Nevada	47.6	47.1	58.8	West Virginia	29	Nevada	29	Florida	29
New Hampshire	49.8	55.0	70.9	Oklahoma	30	Illinois	30	Oklahoma	29
New Jersey	38.3	48.4	65.4	Pennsylvania	31	Tennessee	31	Louisiana	29
New Mexico	59.4	57.4	68.5	Arkansas	32	California	32	Virginia	32
New York	30.7	37.1	53.3	Delaware	33	West Virginia	33	Nebraska	32
North Carolina	47.4	44.5	66.7	Illinois	34	Arizona	34	Arkansas	34
North Dakota	65.3	58.6	65.4	California	35	Connecticut	35	North Carolina	35
Ohio	51.6	54.4	67.6	Arizona	36	North Carolina	35	Arizona	36
Oklahoma	45.5	41.3	67.3	Texas	36	Massachusetts	37	Georgia	37
Oregon	54.8	59.1	62.1	Florida	38	Florida	38	Colorado	38
Pennsylvania	45.2	54.4	69.6	New Jersey	39	Texas	39	New Jersey	39
Rhode Island	31.1	41.2	60.7	Connecticut	40	Oklahoma	40	North Dakota	39
South Carolina	32.2	30.9	69.3	Alabama	41	Rhode Island	41	Washington	41
South Dakota	61.5	53.1	68.1	Massachusetts	42	Arkansas	42	Texas	42
Tennessee	47.7	46.2	68.2	Mississippi	43	D.C.	43	Alaska	43
Texas	42.8	41.7	63.7	Louisiana	44	New York	44	Massachusetts	44
Utah	60.0	60.9	70.5	South Carolina	45	Louisiana	45	Oregon	45
Vermont	57.5	59.8	70.7	Rhode Island	46	Alabama	46	Rhode Island	46
Virginia	51.1	52.4	67.2	Georgia	47	Mississippi	47	Nevada	47
Washington	54.7	59.4	63.9	New York	48	South Carolina	48	Hawaii	48
West Virginia	46.8	45.9	73.4	D.C.	49	Georgia	49	California	49
Wisconsin	63.6	63.2	68.1	Hawaii	n/a	Alaska	n/a	New York	50
Wyoming	51.9	48.3	69.3	Alaska	n/a	Hawaii	n/a	D.C.	51
United States	45.6	47.8	65.1	United States	–	United States	–	United States	–

Source: U.S. Census Bureau, 1920 Census of Population; U.S. Census Bureau, 1930 Census of Population; U.S. Census Bureau, Census 2010

POPULATION—UNITED STATES SUMMARY

Introduction.—This section or chapter summarizes the population of the United States as returned in the 1930 census, by States, for cities and other urban areas arranged in groups according to size, and for incorporated places having from 1,000 to 2,500 inhabitants. Comparative figures are presented for the States and the larger cities for all censuses, beginning with the first in which the area was represented. For the smaller cities, comparative figures are given for at least one earlier census. The population of the townships or corresponding minor civil divisions of the counties in the several States, and of incorporated places having less than 1,000 inhabitants, is given in the sections relating to the various States.

United States and possessions.—Table 1 shows the population of the United States and its outlying territories and possessions for 1930, 1920, and 1910. The statistics for the territories and possessions which were enumerated in 1930 are presented in detail in a series of sections or chapters at the end of this volume. Elsewhere the figures are limited to what has been termed Continental United States, that is, the 48 States and the District of Columbia.

TABLE 1.—POPULATION OF THE UNITED STATES AND ITS OUTLYING TERRITORIES AND POSSESSIONS: 1930, 1920, AND 1910

AREA	Gross area (land and water) in square miles, 1930	POPULATION		
		1930	1920	1910
United States, with outlying possessions	3,738,395	137,008,435	117,823,165	101,146,530
Continental United States	3,026,789	122,775,046	105,710,620	91,972,266
Outlying territories and possessions	711,606	14,233,389	12,112,545	9,174,264
Alaska	586,400	59,278	55,036	64,356
American Samoa	[1]76	10,055	8,056	[2]7,251
Guam	206	[3]18,509	[4]13,275	11,806
Hawaii	[5]6,407	368,336	255,912	191,909
Panama Canal Zone	549	39,467	22,858	[2]62,810
Philippine Islands	114,400	[6]12,082,366	[7]10,314,310	[8]7,635,426
Porto Rico	3,435	1,543,913	1,299,809	1,118,012
Virgin Islands of the United States	133	22,012	[9]26,051	[10]27,086
Military and naval services, etc., abroad [11]		89,453	117,238	55,608

[1] Includes Swain Island.   [2] Population in 1912.

[3] Includes population (1,118) of United States naval reservations, and persons on the United States ships stationed at Guam.

[4] Includes native men enlisted in United States Navy, but excludes United States naval station personnel, numbering 309.

[5] Includes Midway Islands.

[6] Estimated population, July 1, 1929 (Thirteenth Annual Report of the Director of Education).

[7] Population Dec. 31, 1918.   [8] Population in 1903.

[9] Population Nov. 1, 1917.   [10] Population in 1911.

[11] This item represents the following class of persons: Officers and enlisted men in the military service abroad; persons in the service of the American Red Cross abroad, or in the Consular Service of the United States abroad, together with members of their families who were actually residing with them at their post of duty; and officers and enlisted men in the naval service abroad or in American waters, but not on fixed station.

5

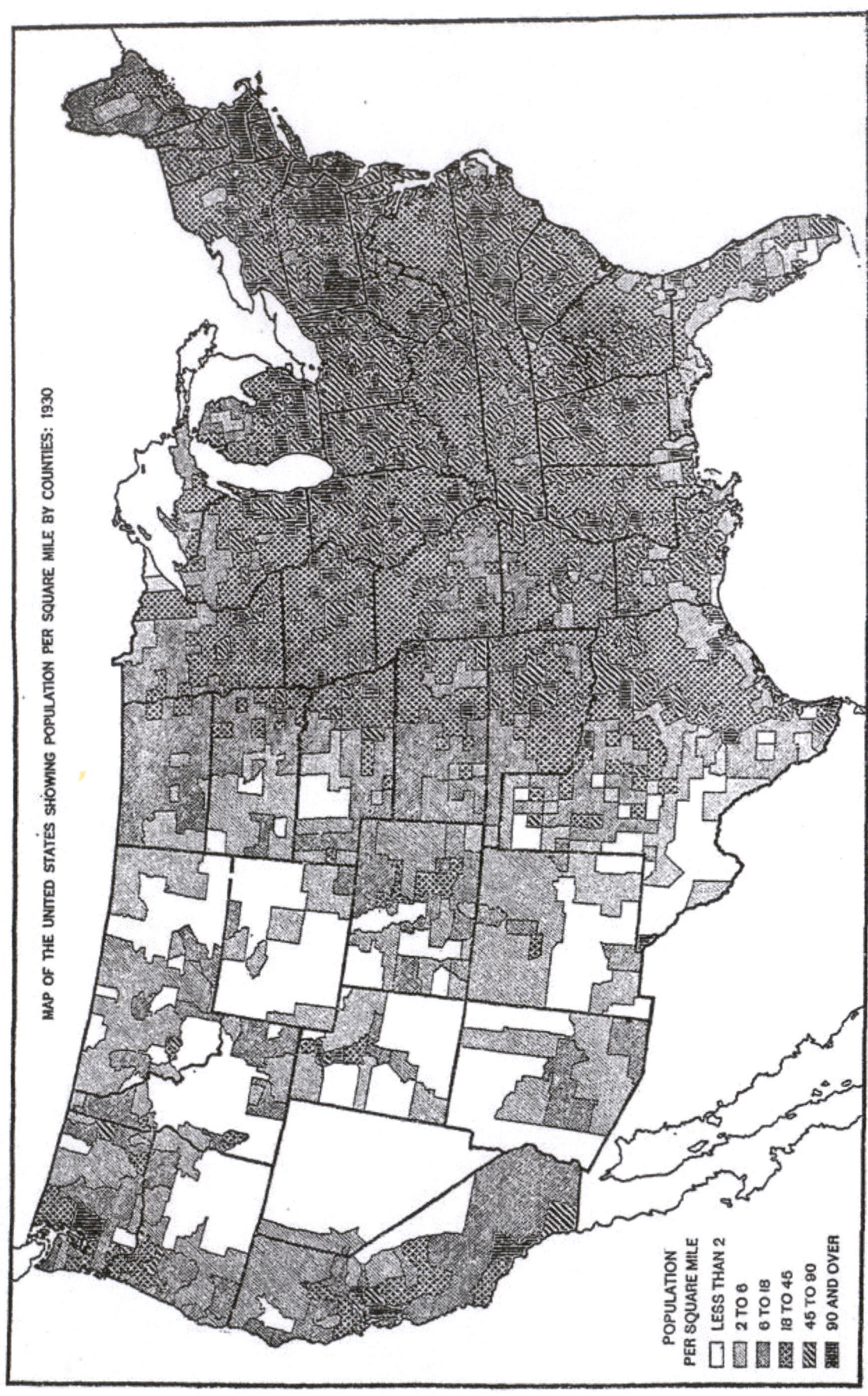

MAP OF THE UNITED STATES SHOWING POPULATION PER SQUARE MILE BY COUNTIES: 1930

POPULATION
PER SQUARE MILE

LESS THAN 2
2 TO 6
6 TO 18
18 TO 45
45 TO 90
90 AND OVER

6   POPULATION—UNITED STATES SUMMARY

Population of continental United States from 1790.—The area now forming the 48 States and the District of Columbia was first completely enumerated in 1890, though the whole area, except for what is now the State of Oklahoma, was included also in the censuses of 1860, 1870, and 1880. The gradual increase in the territory covered by the census may be indicated as follows:

The First Census, taken in 1790, covered the area now occupied by the District of Columbia and the following States: Maine, New Hampshire, Vermont, Massachusetts, Rhode Island, Connecticut, New York, New Jersey, Pennsylvania, Delaware, Maryland, Virginia, West Virginia, North Carolina, South Carolina, Georgia, Kentucky, and Tennessee.

In 1800 there was added the area now constituting the States of Ohio, Indiana, Illinois, Michigan, and Wisconsin, and the southern parts of Alabama and Mississippi.

In 1810 there were further additions comprising the territory now forming the States of Louisiana, Arkansas, and Missouri, and the northern parts of Mississippi and Alabama.

In 1820 there was no change in the census area. In 1830, Florida was added, and in 1840, Iowa territory, including the greater part of what is now Minnesota.

In 1850 still further additions were made, comprising the territory which now forms Washington, Oregon, California, Utah, Texas, and most of New Mexico.

In 1860 the area covered was brought up to its present extent, except for Oklahoma.

Table 2 shows the population and area of continental United States from 1790 to 1930, with the decennial increase, the land area, and the population per square mile.

TABLE 2.—POPULATION AND AREA OF CONTINENTAL UNITED STATES: 1790 to 1930

CENSUS YEAR	Population	INCREASE OVER PRECEDING CENSUS		Land area in square miles [1]	Population per square mile
		Number	Per cent		
1930	122,775,046	17,064,426	[2] 16.1	2,973,776	41.3
1920	105,710,620	13,738,354	14.9	2,973,776	35.5
1910	91,972,266	15,977,691	21.0	2,973,890	30.0
1900	75,994,575	13,046,861	20.7	2,974,159	25.6
1890	62,947,714	12,791,931	25.5	2,973,965	21.2
1880	50,155,783	11,597,412	30.1	2,973,965	16.9
1870	38,558,371	7,115,050	22.6	2,973,965	13.0
1860	31,443,321	8,251,445	35.6	2,973,965	10.6
1850	23,191,876	6,122,423	35.9	2,944,337	7.9
1840	17,069,453	4,203,433	32.7	1,753,588	9.7
1830	12,866,020	3,227,567	33.5	1,753,588	7.3
1820	9,638,453	2,398,572	33.1	1,753,588	5.5
1810	7,239,881	1,931,398	36.4	1,685,865	4.3
1800	5,308,483	1,379,269	35.1	867,980	6.1
1790	3,929,214	--------	--------	867,980	4.5

[1] The figures given for the various census years represent the area of all the land within the present boundaries of continental United States which was under the jurisdiction of the United States on the date in question, including in some cases considerable areas of land not then organized or settled and not covered by the census.

[2] In comparing this percentage of increase with that shown for the decade 1910-1920, allowance should be made for the fact that the period between the censuses of 1910 and 1920 was less than a full decade, and that between the 1920 and 1930 censuses was more than a full decade. An increase of 16.1 per cent for 123 months (the time between Jan. 1, 1920, and Apr. 1, 1930) is equivalent to 15.7 per cent for exactly 10 years; and the 1920 increase for 116½ months (the time between Apr. 15, 1910, and Jan. 1, 1920) is equivalent to 15.4 per cent for 120 months. Making this adjustment, the rate of increase for the decade ending in 1930 is only slightly higher than that for the preceding decade.

URBAN AND RURAL AREAS   7

Urban and rural areas.—The distinction between the urban population and the rural population of the United States is based on the classification of areas, the urban population being that living in the urban areas, and the rural population that living in the rural areas.

Urban areas, as defined by the Census Bureau in recent censuses, have included all cities and other incorporated places having 2,500 inhabitants or more. For use in connection with the 1930 census the definition has been slightly modified and extended so as to include townships and other political subdivisions (not incorporated as municipalities, nor containing any areas so incorporated) which had a total population of 10,000 or more, and a population density of 1,000 or more per square mile. This extension adds to the urban group 11 townships in New Jersey (population, 208,722), 10 townships in Pennsylvania (population, 210,505), 4 towns in Connecticut (population, 87,086), 2 townships in California (population, 48,992), and 1 town in New York (population, 18,024). The aggregate population of these 28 places, which would have been classified as rural under the rules governing the urban-rural classification in 1920, is 573,329.

In three of the New England States, New Hampshire, Massachusetts, and Rhode Island, conditions are exceptional in that the compactly built portions of the towns (townships) are not separately incorporated or politically distinct in any way from the rural territory within the same town; nor is it the practice to incorporate even the larger places as cities until they attain a population of ten or fifteen thousand. Consequently, if only the cities were counted in the urban population the classification would be quite inadequate. In 1920 and 1910 all towns in these States which had a population of 2,500 or more were classified as urban. This resulted in including a considerable number of places that were mainly rural in their general characteristics. In 1930, the special rule for these States has been modified so as to place in the urban classification, in addition to the regularly incorporated cities, only those towns in which there is a village or thickly settled area having more than 2,500 inhabitants and comprising, either by itself or when combined with other villages within the same town, more than 50 per cent of the total population of the town. The result of this modification has been to transfer from the urban to the rural classification 12 towns in New Hampshire (population, 35,389), 56 towns in Massachusetts (population, 218,231), and 8 towns in Rhode Island (population, 35,001) which would have been counted as urban if the 1920 rule had been followed in 1930. The aggregate population in 1930 of these towns which were in effect transferred from the urban to the rural classification is 288,621.

Since it has been found impracticable to go back and readjust the earlier urban and rural figures to the new basis, through the several tabulations by color, sex, age, etc., they are presented in all tables as established in 1920. The comparative figures therefore show differences, in a few cases, which must be considered or interpreted as solely or mainly the result of the change in the method of classification. This is particularly true of the nominal or apparent increase in the rural population of Massachusetts and Rhode Island, of the nominal decrease in the urban population of New Hampshire, and of the decrease in the percentage urban shown for all three of these States.

So far as concerns the urban and rural classification of the total population of the United States, it will be seen that the net result of the two changes described above is to increase the urban population by 284,708. In other words, if the classification had been made in 1930 on exactly the same basis as in 1920, the

8   POPULATION—UNITED STATES SUMMARY

urban population would have been 68,670,115, instead of 68,954,823, and the percentage urban would have been 55.9 instead of 56.2.[1]

The individual places which have been brought into the urban classification under the two special rules are marked with an asterisk (*) in the tables presenting the population of the various groups of cities (Tables 12 to 15). A complete list of the urban places in any State may therefore be obtained by taking from each of these tables the places listed under the State name.

The total urban and rural population of the United States is presented for the census years from 1880 to 1930 in Table 3, and by States for 1930 and 1920, in Table 9.

TABLE 3.—URBAN AND RURAL POPULATION OF THE UNITED STATES: 1880 TO 1930

CLASS	1930	1920	1910	1900	1890	1880
Total, number	122,775,046	105,710,620	91,972,266	75,994,575	62,947,714	50,155,783
Urban	68,954,823	54,304,603	42,166,120	30,380,433	22,298,359	14,358,167
Rural	53,820,223	51,406,017	49,806,146	45,614,142	40,649,355	35,797,616
Total, per cent	100.00	100.0	100.0	100.0	100.0	100.0
Urban	56.2	51.4	45.8	40.0	35.4	28.6
Rural	43.8	48.6	54.2	60.0	64.6	71.4

Cities grouped according to size.—For the convenience of those who are interested in cities of various sizes, statistics are presented in Tables 11 to 15 for the cities and other urban places arranged in groups according to size. In Table 11 is presented the population of cities having 100,000 inhabitants or more in 1930, with comparative figures running back to the first census in which the city appears. Table 12 shows the population of places having 25,000 inhabitants or more in 1930, with comparative figures from 1900; Table 13 shows the population for 1930 and 1920 of cities and other urban places having from 10,000 to 25,000 inhabitants; Table 14 presents similar figures for places having from 5,000 to 10,000 inhabitants; and Table 15, for places having from 2,500 to 5,000 inhabitants. All of these places are included in the urban classification in 1930.

Table 16 shows the population of the larger incorporated places which are included in the rural classification, namely, those having from 1,000 to 2,500 inhabitants.[2]

The total population in each of these various groups is summarized for the United States in Table 8, which presents figures for the several censuses from 1890 to 1930. Table 10 gives the number of places in each of the city groups, with their population, by divisions and States. for 1930 only.

---

[1] The percentage urban in the population of New Jersey, if the 11 townships having a population of more than 10,000 and a population density of more than 1,000 per square mile had been classified as rural, as they would have been under the rule followed in 1920, would have been 77.5 instead of 82.6; likewise, under the 1920 rule, the urban population of Pennsylvania would have formed only 65.7 per cent of the total, instead of 67.8 per cent; the percentage of the population urban in Connecticut would have been 65.0 instead of 70.4; in California, 72.4 instead of 73.3; and in New York, 83.4 instead of 83.6. On the other hand, if all the towns having 2,500 inhabitants or more had been included in the urban population of New Hampshire, as they would have been under the rule followed in 1920, the percentage urban would have been 66.3 instead of 58.7; likewise, under the 1920 rule, the percentage of the population urban in Massachusetts would have been 95.3 instead of 90.2; and in Rhode Island, 97.5 instead of 92.4.

[2] The population of the smaller incorporated places in any State is shown in Table 5 in the section for that State.

URBAN AND RURAL AREAS

9

Population in places of 8,000 or more, 1790 to 1930.—The present urban and rural classification, with the basic requirement of population of 2,500 in an incorporated place in order to give it urban classification, was established in 1910, and the figures were compiled for the censuses back to and including 1880. It would hardly be practicable to carry this classification back further. A table has been presented in the Census Reports for many decades, however, giving the population in places of 8,000 inhabitants or more, back to the First Census, that of 1790. These figures are given in Table 4.

TABLE 4.—POPULATION IN PLACES OF 8,000 INHABITANTS OR MORE: 1790 to 1930

CENSUS YEAR	Total population	PLACES OF 8,000 INHABITANTS OR MORE		
		Population	Number of places	Per cent of total population
1930	122,775,046	60,333,452	1,208	49.1
1920	105,710,620	46,307,640	924	43.8
1910	91,972,266	35,570,334	768	38.7
1900	75,994,575	25,018,335	547	32.9
1890	62,947,714	18,244,239	445	29.0
1880	50,155,783	11,365,698	285	22.7
1870	38,558,371	8,071,875	226	20.9
1860	31,443,321	5,072,256	141	16.1
1850	23,191,876	2,897,586	85	12.5
1840	17,069,453	1,453,994	44	8.5
1830	12,866,020	864,509	26	6.7
1820	9,638,453	475,135	13	4.9
1810	7,239,881	356,920	11	4.9
1800	5,308,483	210,873	6	4.0
1790	3,929,214	131,472	6	3.3

10   POPULATION—UNITED STATES SUMMARY

TABLE 5.—POPULATION OF THE UNITED

	DIVISION AND STATE	1930	1920	1910	1900	1890	1880
1	United States	122,775,046	105,710,620	91,972,266	75,994,575	[1] 62,947,714	50,155,783
	GEOGRAPHIC DIVISIONS:						
2	New England	8,166,341	7,400,909	6,552,681	5,592,017	4,700,749	4,010,529
3	Middle Atlantic	26,260,750	22,261,144	19,315,892	15,454,678	12,706,220	10,496,878
4	East North Central	25,297,185	21,475,543	18,250,621	15,985,581	13,478,305	11,206,668
5	West North Central	13,296,915	12,544,249	11,637,921	10,347,423	8,932,112	6,157,443
6	South Atlantic	15,793,589	13,990,272	12,194,895	10,443,480	8,857,922	7,597,197
7	East South Central	9,887,214	8,893,307	8,409,901	7,547,757	6,429,154	5,585,151
8	West South Central	12,176,830	10,242,224	8,784,534	6,532,290	4,740,983	3,334,220
9	Mountain	3,701,789	3,336,101	2,633,517	1,674,657	1,213,935	653,119
10	Pacific	8,194,433	5,566,871	4,192,304	2,416,692	1,888,334	1,114,578
	NEW ENGLAND:						
11	Maine	797,423	768,014	742,371	694,466	661,086	648,936
12	New Hampshire	465,293	443,083	430,572	411,588	376,530	346,991
13	Vermont	359,611	352,428	355,956	343,641	332,422	332,286
14	Massachusetts	4,249,614	3,852,356	3,366,416	2,805,346	2,238,947	1,783,085
15	Rhode Island	687,497	604,397	542,610	428,556	345,506	276,531
16	Connecticut	1,606,903	1,380,631	1,114,756	908,420	746,258	622,700
	MIDDLE ATLANTIC:						
17	New York	12,588,066	10,385,227	9,113,614	7,268,894	6,003,174	5,082,871
18	New Jersey	4,041,334	3,155,900	2,537,167	1,883,669	1,444,933	1,131,116
19	Pennsylvania	9,631,350	8,720,017	7,665,111	6,302,115	5,258,113	4,282,891
	EAST NORTH CENTRAL:						
20	Ohio	6,646,697	5,759,394	4,767,121	4,157,545	3,672,329	3,198,062
21	Indiana	3,238,503	2,930,390	2,700,876	2,516,462	2,192,404	1,978,301
22	Illinois	7,630,654	6,485,280	5,638,591	4,821,550	3,826,352	3,077,871
23	Michigan	4,842,325	3,668,412	2,810,173	2,420,982	2,093,890	1,636,937
24	Wisconsin	2,939,006	2,632,067	2,333,860	2,069,042	1,693,330	1,315,497
	WEST NORTH CENTRAL:						
25	Minnesota	2,563,953	2,387,125	2,075,708	1,751,394	1,310,283	780,773
26	Iowa	2,470,939	2,404,021	2,224,771	2,231,853	1,912,297	1,624,615
27	Missouri	3,629,367	3,404,055	3,293,335	3,106,665	2,679,185	2,168,380
28	North Dakota	680,845	646,872	577,056	319,146	190,983	} [4] 135,177
29	South Dakota	692,849	636,547	583,888	401,570	348,600	
30	Nebraska	1,377,963	1,296,372	1,192,214	1,066,300	1,062,656	452,402
31	Kansas	1,880,999	1,769,257	1,690,949	1,470,495	1,428,108	996,096
	SOUTH ATLANTIC:						
32	Delaware	238,380	223,003	202,322	184,735	168,493	146,608
33	Maryland	1,631,526	1,449,661	1,295,346	1,188,044	1,042,390	934,943
34	District of Columbia	486,869	437,571	331,069	278,718	230,392	177,624
35	Virginia	2,421,851	2,309,187	2,061,612	1,854,184	1,655,980	1,512,565
36	West Virginia	1,729,205	1,463,701	1,221,119	958,800	762,794	618,457
37	North Carolina	3,170,276	2,559,123	2,206,287	1,893,810	1,617,949	1,399,750
38	South Carolina	1,738,765	1,683,724	1,515,400	1,340,316	1,151,149	995,577
39	Georgia	2,908,506	2,895,832	2,609,121	2,216,331	1,837,353	1,542,180
40	Florida	1,468,211	968,470	752,619	528,542	391,422	269,493
	EAST SOUTH CENTRAL:						
41	Kentucky	2,614,589	2,416,630	2,289,905	2,147,174	1,858,635	1,648,690
42	Tennessee	2,616,556	2,337,885	2,184,789	2,020,616	1,767,518	1,542,359
43	Alabama	2,646,248	2,348,174	2,138,093	1,828,697	1,513,401	1,262,505
44	Mississippi	2,009,821	1,790,618	1,797,114	1,551,270	1,289,600	1,131,597
	WEST SOUTH CENTRAL:						
45	Arkansas	1,854,482	1,752,204	1,574,449	1,311,564	1,128,211	802,525
46	Louisiana	2,101,593	1,798,509	1,656,388	1,381,625	1,118,588	939,946
47	Oklahoma	2,396,040	2,028,283	1,657,155	[7] 790,391	[7] 258,657	--------
48	Texas	5,824,715	4,663,228	3,896,542	3,048,710	2,235,527	1,591,749
	MOUNTAIN:						
49	Montana	537,606	548,889	376,053	243,329	142,924	89,159
50	Idaho	445,032	431,866	325,594	161,772	88,548	32,610
51	Wyoming	225,565	194,402	145,965	92,531	62,555	20,789
52	Colorado	1,035,791	939,629	799,024	539,700	413,249	194,327
53	New Mexico	423,317	360,350	327,301	195,310	160,282	119,565
54	Arizona	435,573	334,162	204,354	122,931	88,243	40,440
55	Utah	507,847	449,396	373,351	276,749	210,779	143,963
56	Nevada	91,058	77,407	81,875	42,335	47,355	62,266
	PACIFIC:						
57	Washington	1,563,396	1,356,621	1,141,990	518,103	357,232	75,116
58	Oregon	953,786	783,389	672,765	413,536	317,704	174,768
59	California	5,677,251	3,426,861	2,377,549	1,485,053	1,213,398	864,694

[1] Includes population (325,464) of Indian Territory and Indian reservations, specially enumerated in 1890, but not included in the general report on population for 1890.

[2] Includes persons (6,100 in 1840 and 5,318 in 1830) on public ships in the service of the United States, not credited to any division or State.

[3] Population of area taken to form State of Missouri in 1821; part of Louisiana territory in 1810.

DIVISIONS AND STATES

STATES, BY DIVISIONS AND STATES: 1790 TO 1930

1870	1860	1850	1840	1830	1820	1810	1800	1790	
38,558,371	31,443,321	23,191,876	[2]17,069,453	[2]12,866,020	9,638,453	7,239,881	5,308,483	3,929,214	1
3,487,924	3,135,283	2,728,116	2,234,822	1,954,717	1,660,071	1,471,973	1,233,011	1,009,408	2
8,810,806	7,458,985	5,898,735	4,526,260	3,587,664	2,699,845	2,014,702	1,402,565	958,632	3
9,124,517	6,926,884	4,523,260	2,924,728	1,470,018	792,719	272,324	51,006	----	4
3,856,594	2,169,832	880,335	426,814	140,455	66,586	19,783	----	----	5
5,853,610	5,364,703	4,679,090	3,925,299	3,645,752	3,061,063	2,674,891	2,236,494	1,851,806	6
4,404,445	4,020,991	3,363,271	2,575,445	1,815,969	1,190,489	708,590	335,407	109,368	7
2,029,965	1,747,667	940,251	449,985	246,127	167,680	77,618	----	----	8
315,385	174,923	72,927	----	----	----	----	----	----	9
675,125	444,053	105,891	----	----	----	----	----	----	10
626,915	628,279	583,169	501,793	399,455	293,335	228,705	151,719	96,540	11
318,300	326,073	317,976	284,574	269,328	244,161	214,460	183,858	141,885	12
330,551	315,098	314,120	291,948	280,652	235,981	217,895	154,465	85,425	13
1,457,351	1,231,066	994,514	737,699	610,408	523,287	472,040	422,845	378,787	14
217,353	174,620	147,545	108,830	97,199	83,059	76,931	69,122	68,825	15
537,454	460,147	370,792	309,978	297,675	275,248	261,942	251,002	237,946	16
4,382,759	3,880,735	3,097,394	2,428,921	1,918,608	1,372,812	959,049	589,051	340,120	17
906,096	672,035	489,555	373,306	320,823	277,575	245,562	211,149	184,139	18
3,521,951	2,906,215	2,311,786	1,724,033	1,348,233	1,049,458	810,091	602,365	434,373	19
2,665,260	2,339,511	1,980,329	1,519,467	937,903	581,434	230,760	45,365	----	20
1,680,637	1,350,428	988,416	685,866	343,031	147,178	24,520	5,641	----	21
2,539,891	1,711,951	851,470	476,183	157,445	55,211	12,282	----	----	22
1,184,059	749,113	397,654	212,267	31,639	8,896	4,762	----	----	23
1,054,670	775,881	305,391	30,945	----	----	----	----	----	24
439,706	172,023	6,077	----	----	----	----	----	----	25
1,194,020	674,913	192,214	43,112	----	----	----	----	----	26
1,721,295	1,182,012	682,044	383,702	140,455	66,586	[3]19,783	----	----	27
[4]14,181	[5]4,837	----	----	----	----	----	----	----	{28 29
122,993	28,841	----	----	----	----	----	----	----	30
364,399	107,206	----	----	----	----	----	----	----	31
125,015	112,216	91,532	78,085	76,748	72,749	72,674	64,273	59,096	32
780,894	687,049	583,034	470,019	447,040	407,350	380,546	341,548	319,728	33
131,700	75,080	51,687	43,712	39,834	33,039	24,023	14,093	----	34
1,225,163	1,596,318	1,421,661	1,230,797	1,211,405	1,065,366	974,600	880,200	747,610	35
442,014	----	----	----	----	----	----	----	----	36
1,071,361	992,622	869,039	753,419	737,987	638,829	555,500	478,103	393,751	37
705,606	703,708	668,507	594,398	581,185	502,741	415,115	345,591	249,073	38
1,184,109	1,057,286	906,185	691,392	516,823	340,989	252,433	162,686	82,548	39
187,748	140,424	87,445	54,477	34,730	----	----	----	----	40
1,321,011	1,155,684	982,405	779,828	687,917	564,317	406,511	220,955	73,677	41
1,258,520	1,109,801	1,002,717	829,210	681,904	422,823	261,727	105,602	35,691	42
996,992	964,201	771,623	590,756	309,527	127,901	----	----	----	43
827,922	791,305	606,526	375,651	136,621	75,448	40,352	8,850	----	44
484,471	435,450	209,897	97,574	30,388	14,273	[6]1,062	----	----	45
726,915	708,002	517,762	352,411	215,739	153,407	76,556	----	----	46
----	----	----	----	----	----	----	----	----	47
818,579	604,215	212,592	----	----	----	----	----	----	48
20,595	----	----	----	----	----	----	----	----	49
14,999	----	----	----	----	----	----	----	----	50
9,118	----	----	----	----	----	----	----	----	51
39,864	34,277	----	----	----	----	----	----	----	52
91,874	93,516	61,547	----	----	----	----	----	----	53
9,658	----	----	----	----	----	----	----	----	54
86,786	40,273	11,380	----	----	----	----	----	----	55
42,491	6,857	----	----	----	----	----	----	----	56
23,955	11,594	----	----	----	----	----	----	----	57
90,923	52,465	13,294	----	----	----	----	----	----	58
560,247	379,994	92,597	----	----	----	----	----	----	59

[4] Population of that part of Dakota territory taken to form North Dakota: 1880, 36,909; 1870, 2,405. Population of part taken to form South Dakota: 1880, 98,268; 1870, 11,776.
[5] Dakota territory.
[6] Population of area taken to form Arkansas territory in 1819; part of Louisiana territory in 1810.
[7] Includes population of Indian Territory, as follows: 1900, 392,060; 1890, 180,182.

12 POPULATION—UNITED STATES SUMMARY

TABLE 6.—DECENNIAL RATES OF INCREASE IN POPULATION, BY DIVISIONS AND STATES: 1850 TO 1930

[A minus sign (−) denotes decrease]

DIVISION AND STATE	INCREASE, 1920–1930		PER CENT OF INCREASE						
	Number	Per cent	1910 to 1920	1900 to 1910	1890 to 1900	1880 to 1890	1870 to 1880	1860 to 1870	1850 to 1860
United States	17,064,426	16.1	14.9	21.0	20.7	25.5	30.1	22.6	35.6
GEOGRAPHIC DIVISIONS:									
New England	765,432	10.3	12.9	17.2	19.0	17.2	15.0	11.2	14.9
Middle Atlantic	3,999,606	18.0	15.2	25.0	21.6	21.0	19.1	18.1	26.5
East North Central	3,821,642	17.8	17.7	14.2	18.6	20.3	22.8	31.7	53.1
West North Central	752,666	6.0	7.8	12.5	15.8	45.1	59.7	77.7	146.5
South Atlantic	1,803,317	12.9	14.7	16.8	17.9	16.6	29.8	9.1	14.7
East South Central	993,907	11.2	5.7	11.4	17.4	15.1	26.8	9.5	19.6
West South Central	1,934,606	18.9	16.6	34.5	37.8	42.2	64.3	16.2	85.9
Mountain	365,688	11.0	26.7	57.3	38.0	85.9	107.1	80.3	139.9
Pacific	2,627,562	47.2	32.8	73.5	28.0	69.4	65.1	52.0	319.3
NEW ENGLAND:									
Maine	29,409	3.8	3.5	6.9	5.0	1.9	3.5	−0.2	7.7
New Hampshire	22,210	5.0	2.9	4.6	9.3	8.5	9.0	−2.4	2.5
Vermont	7,183	2.0	−1.0	3.6	3.4	(1)	0.5	4.9	0.3
Massachusetts	397,258	10.3	14.4	20.0	25.3	25.6	22.4	18.4	23.8
Rhode Island	83,100	13.7	11.4	26.6	24.0	24.9	27.2	24.5	18.4
Connecticut	226,272	16.4	23.9	22.7	21.7	19.8	15.9	16.8	24.1
MIDDLE ATLANTIC:									
New York	2,202,839	21.2	14.0	25.4	21.1	18.1	16.0	12.9	25.3
New Jersey	885,434	28.1	24.4	34.7	30.4	27.7	24.8	34.8	37.3
Pennsylvania	911,333	10.5	13.8	21.6	19.9	22.8	21.6	21.2	25.7
EAST NORTH CENTRAL:									
Ohio	887,303	15.4	20.8	14.7	13.2	14.8	20.0	13.9	18.1
Indiana	308,113	10.5	8.5	7.3	14.8	10.8	17.7	24.5	36.6
Illinois	1,145,374	17.7	15.0	16.9	26.0	24.3	21.2	48.4	101.1
Michigan	1,173,913	32.0	30.5	16.1	15.6	27.9	38.2	58.1	88.4
Wisconsin	306,939	11.7	12.8	12.8	22.2	28.7	24.7	35.9	154.1
WEST NORTH CENTRAL:									
Minnesota	176,828	7.4	15.0	18.5	33.7	67.8	77.6	155.6	2,730.7
Iowa	66,918	2.8	8.1	−0.3	16.7	17.7	36.1	76.9	251.1
Missouri	225,312	6.6	3.4	6.0	16.0	23.6	26.0	45.6	73.3
North Dakota	33,973	5.3	12.1	80.8	67.1	} [2]299.2	[2]853.2	[2]193.2	--------
South Dakota	56,302	8.8	9.0	45.4	15.2				--------
Nebraska	81,591	6.3	8.7	11.8	0.3	134.9	267.8	326.5	--------
Kansas	111,742	6.3	4.6	15.0	3.0	43.4	173.4	239.9	--------
SOUTH ATLANTIC:									
Delaware	15,377	6.9	10.2	9.5	9.6	14.9	17.3	11.4	22.6
Maryland	181,865	12.5	11.9	9.0	14.0	11.5	19.7	13.7	17.8
District of Columbia	49,298	11.3	32.2	18.8	21.0	29.7	34.9	75.4	45.3
Virginia	112,664	4.9	12.0	11.2	12.0	9.5	23.5	[3]−23.3	12.3
West Virginia	265,504	18.1	19.9	27.4	25.7	23.3	39.9		
North Carolina	611,153	23.9	16.0	16.5	17.1	15.6	30.7	7.9	14.2
South Carolina	55,041	3.3	11.1	13.1	16.4	15.6	41.1	0.3	5.3
Georgia	12,674	0.4	11.0	17.7	20.6	19.1	30.2	12.0	16.7
Florida	499,741	51.6	28.7	42.4	35.0	45.2	43.5	33.7	60.6
EAST SOUTH CENTRAL:									
Kentucky	197,959	8.2	5.5	6.6	15.5	12.7	24.8	14.3	17.6
Tennessee	278,671	11.9	7.0	8.1	14.3	14.6	22.6	13.4	10.7
Alabama	298,074	12.7	9.8	16.9	20.8	19.9	26.6	3.4	25.0
Mississippi	219,203	12.2	−0.4	15.8	20.3	14.0	36.7	4.6	30.5
WEST SOUTH CENTRAL:									
Arkansas	102,278	5.8	11.3	20.0	16.3	40.6	65.6	11.3	107.5
Louisiana	303,084	16.9	8.6	19.9	23.5	19.0	29.3	2.7	36.7
Oklahoma	367,757	18.1	22.4	109.7	205.6	--------	--------	--------	--------
Texas	1,161,487	24.9	19.7	27.8	36.4	40.4	94.5	35.5	184.2
MOUNTAIN:									
Montana	−11,283	−2.1	46.0	54.5	70.3	265.0	90.1	--------	--------
Idaho	13,166	3.0	32.6	101.3	82.7	171.5	117.4	--------	--------
Wyoming	31,163	16.0	33.2	57.7	47.9	200.9	128.0	--------	--------
Colorado	96,162	10.2	17.6	48.0	30.6	112.7	387.5	16.3	--------
New Mexico	62,967	17.5	10.1	67.6	21.9	34.1	30.1	−1.8	51.9
Arizona	101,411	30.3	63.5	66.2	39.3	118.2	313.7		
Utah	58,451	13.0	20.4	34.9	31.3	46.4	65.9	115.5	253.9
Nevada	13,651	17.6	−5.5	93.4	−10.6	−23.9	46.5	519.7	
PACIFIC:									
Washington	206,775	15.2	18.8	120.4	45.0	375.6	213.6	106.6	--------
Oregon	170,397	21.8	16.4	62.7	30.2	81.8	92.2	73.3	294.7
California	2,250,390	65.7	44.1	60.1	22.4	40.3	54.3	47.4	310.4

[1] Less than one-tenth of 1 per cent.
[2] Dakota Territory.
[3] Decrease due to loss of territory, West Virginia having been detached from Virginia and admitted as a separate State in 1863.

DIVISIONS AND STATES

TABLE 7.—POPULATION PER SQUARE MILE, BY DIVISIONS AND STATES: 1900 TO 1930

DIVISION AND STATE	Population, 1930	Land area in square miles, 1930	POPULATION PER SQUARE MILE			
			1930	1920	1910	1900
United States	122,775,046	2,973,776	41.3	35.5	30.9	25.6
GEOGRAPHIC DIVISIONS:						
New England	8,166,341	61,976	131.8	119.4	105.7	90.2
Middle Atlantic	26,260,750	100,000	262.6	222.6	193.2	154.5
East North Central	25,297,185	245,564	103.0	87.5	74.3	65.2
West North Central	13,296,915	510,804	26.0	24.6	22.8	20.3
South Atlantic	15,793,589	269,073	58.7	52.0	45.3	38.8
East South Central	9,887,214	179,509	55.1	49.5	46.8	42.0
West South Central	12,176,830	429,746	28.3	23.8	20.4	15.2
Mountain	3,701,789	859,009	4.3	3.9	3.1	1.9
Pacific	8,194,433	318,095	25.8	17.5	13.2	7.6
NEW ENGLAND:						
Maine	797,423	29,895	26.7	25.7	24.8	23.2
New Hampshire	465,293	9,031	51.5	49.1	47.7	45.6
Vermont	359,611	9,124	39.4	38.6	39.0	37.7
Massachusetts	4,249,614	8,039	528.6	479.2	418.8	349.0
Rhode Island	687,497	1,067	644.3	566.4	508.5	401.6
Connecticut	1,606,903	4,820	333.4	286.4	231.3	188.5
MIDDLE ATLANTIC:						
New York	12,588,066	47,654	264.2	217.9	191.2	152.5
New Jersey	4,041,334	7,514	537.8	420.0	337.7	250.7
Pennsylvania	9,631,350	44,832	214.8	194.5	171.0	140.6
EAST NORTH CENTRAL:						
Ohio	6,646,697	40,740	163.1	141.4	117.0	102.1
Indiana	3,238,503	36,045	89.8	81.3	74.9	70.1
Illinois	7,630,654	56,043	136.2	115.7	100.6	86.1
Michigan	4,842,325	57,480	84.2	63.8	48.9	42.1
Wisconsin	2,939,006	55,256	53.2	47.6	42.2	37.4
WEST NORTH CENTRAL:						
Minnesota	2,563,953	80,858	31.7	29.5	25.7	21.7
Iowa	2,470,939	55,586	44.5	43.2	40.0	40.2
Missouri	3,629,367	68,727	52.8	49.5	47.9	45.2
North Dakota	680,845	70,183	9.7	9.2	8.2	4.5
South Dakota	692,849	76,868	9.0	8.3	7.6	5.2
Nebraska	1,377,963	76,808	17.9	16.9	15.5	13.9
Kansas	1,880,999	81,774	23.0	21.6	20.7	18.0
SOUTH ATLANTIC:						
Delaware	238,380	1,965	121.3	113.5	103.0	94.0
Maryland	1,631,526	9,941	164.1	145.8	130.3	119.5
District of Columbia	486,869	62	7,852.7	7,292.9	5,517.8	4,645.3
Virginia	2,421,851	40,262	60.2	57.4	51.2	46.1
West Virginia	1,729,205	24,022	72.0	60.9	50.8	39.9
North Carolina	3,170,276	48,740	65.0	52.5	45.3	38.9
South Carolina	1,738,765	30,495	57.0	55.2	49.7	44.0
Georgia	2,908,506	58,725	49.5	49.3	44.4	37.7
Florida	1,468,211	54,861	26.8	17.7	13.7	9.6
EAST SOUTH CENTRAL:						
Kentucky	2,614,589	40,181	65.1	60.1	57.0	53.4
Tennessee	2,616,556	41,687	62.8	56.1	52.4	48.5
Alabama	2,646,248	51,279	51.6	45.8	41.7	35.7
Mississippi	2,009,821	46,362	43.4	38.6	38.8	33.5
WEST SOUTH CENTRAL:						
Arkansas	1,854,482	52,525	35.3	33.4	30.0	25.0
Louisiana	2,101,593	45,409	46.3	39.6	36.5	30.4
Oklahoma	2,396,040	69,414	34.5	29.2	23.9	[1] 11.4
Texas	5,824,715	262,398	22.2	17.8	14.8	11.6
MOUNTAIN:						
Montana	537,606	[2] 146,131	3.7	3.8	2.6	1.7
Idaho	445,032	[2] 83,354	5.3	5.2	3.9	1.9
Wyoming	225,565	[2] 97,548	2.3	2.0	1.5	0.9
Colorado	1,035,791	103,658	10.0	9.1	7.7	5.2
New Mexico	423,317	122,503	3.5	2.9	2.7	1.6
Arizona	435,573	113,810	3.8	2.9	1.8	1.1
Utah	507,847	82,184	6.2	5.5	4.5	3.4
Nevada	91,058	109,821	0.8	0.7	0.7	0.4
PACIFIC:						
Washington	1,563,396	66,836	23.4	20.3	17.1	7.8
Oregon	953,786	95,607	10.0	8.2	7.0	4.3
California	5,677,251	155,652	36.5	22.0	15.3	9.5

[1] Based on combined figures for Indian Territory and Oklahoma Territory for 1900.
[2] Total land area includes part of Yellowstone National Park, geographically located in Idaho (47 square miles), Montana (240 square miles), and Wyoming (2,973 square miles). Total population of park returned as in Wyoming in years prior to 1930.

67981°—31——2

14   POPULATION—UNITED STATES SUMMARY

TABLE 8.—POPULATION IN GROUPS OF CITIES CLASSIFIED ACCORDING TO SIZE, AND IN RURAL TERRITORY, FOR THE UNITED STATES: 1890 TO 1930

SUBJECT AND CLASS OF PLACES	1930	1920	1910	1900	1890
NUMBER OF PLACES [1]					
Urban territory	3,185	2,787	2,313	1,801	1,417
Places of 1,000,000 or more	5	3	3	3	3
Places of 500,000 to 1,000,000	8	9	5	3	1
Places of 250,000 to 500,000	24	13	11	9	7
Places of 100,000 to 250,000	56	43	31	23	17
Places of 50,000 to 100,000	93	76	59	40	30
Places of 25,000 to 50,000	185	143	119	82	66
Places of 10,000 to 25,000	606	459	367	280	228
Places of 5,000 to 10,000	851	721	612	468	339
Places of 2,500 to 5,000	1,332	1,320	1,106	893	726
Rural territory	13,433	12,857	11,832	8,930	6,490
Incorporated places of 1,000 to 2,500	3,087	12,857	11,832	8,930	6,490
Incorporated places under 1,000	10,346				
POPULATION					
UNITED STATES	122,775,046	105,710,620	91,972,266	75,994,575	62,947,714
Urban territory	68,954,823	54,304,603	42,166,120	30,380,433	22,298,359
Places of 1,000,000 or more	15,064,555	10,145,532	8,501,174	6,429,474	3,662,115
Places of 500,000 to 1,000,000	5,763,987	6,223,769	3,010,667	1,645,087	806,343
Places of 250,000 to 500,000	7,956,228	4,540,838	3,949,839	2,861,296	2,447,608
Places of 100,000 to 250,000	7,540,966	6,519,187	4,840,458	3,272,490	2,781,894
Places of 50,000 to 100,000	6,491,448	5,265,747	4,178,915	2,709,338	2,022,822
Places of 25,000 to 50,000	6,425,693	5,075,041	4,026,045	2,800,627	2,268,786
Places of 10,000 to 25,000	9,097,200	6,942,742	5,524,434	4,338,250	3,429,247
Places of 5,000 to 10,000	5,897,156	4,997,794	4,254,856	3,220,766	2,372,717
Places of 2,500 to 5,000	4,717,590	4,593,953	3,879,732	3,103,105	2,506,827
Rural territory	53,820,223	51,406,017	49,806,146	45,614,142	40,649,355
Incorporated places of 1,000 to 2,500	4,820,707	8,969,241	8,169,149	6,301,533	4,757,974
Incorporated places under 1,000	4,362,746				
Other rural territory	44,636,770	42,436,776	41,636,997	39,312,609	35,891,381
PER CENT OF TOTAL POPULATION					
UNITED STATES	100.0	100.0	100.0	100.0	100.0
Urban territory	56.2	51.4	45.8	40.0	35.4
Places of 1,000,000 or more	12.3	9.6	9.2	8.5	5.8
Places of 500,000 to 1,000,000	4.7	5.9	3.3	2.2	1.3
Places of 250,000 to 500,000	6.5	4.3	4.3	3.8	3.9
Places of 100,000 to 250,000	6.1	6.2	5.3	4.3	4.4
Places of 50,000 to 100,000	5.3	5.0	4.5	3.6	3.2
Places of 25,000 to 50,000	5.2	4.8	4.4	3.7	3.6
Places of 10,000 to 25,000	7.4	6.6	6.0	5.7	5.4
Places of 5,000 to 10,000	4.8	4.7	4.6	4.2	3.8
Places of 2,500 to 5,000	3.8	4.3	4.2	4.1	4.0
Rural territory	43.8	48.6	54.2	60.0	64.6
Incorporated places of 1,000 to 2,500	3.9	8.5	8.9	8.3	7.6
Incorporated places under 1,000	3.6				
Other rural territory	36.4	40.1	45.3	51.7	57.0

[1] The total number of places of certain classes for the United States as a whole is less than the sum of the numbers shown for the individual States in Table 10, for the reason that there are a few places which lie in two adjoining States and are counted in each State. In 1930, these places included Bluefield (Virginia and West Virginia), Bristol (Tennessee and Virginia), Delmar (Delaware and Maryland), Harrison and West Harrison (Ohio and Indiana), Junction City (Arkansas and Louisiana), Texarkana (Arkansas and Texas), Texhoma (Oklahoma and Texas), and Union City (Indiana and Ohio). Each of these places consists of two incorporated municipalties, but is, from the statistical standpoint, one place and is classed according to its total population. In each case that part of the population living in each State, whatever its number, is credited to the group to which, according to its total population, the place belongs. There are included in some of the groups in this table a small number of places not having a municipal incorporation, which are classified as urban in 1930 under special ruling (see p. 7).

URBAN AND RURAL BY STATES

15

TABLE 9.—URBAN AND RURAL POPULATION, BY DIVISIONS AND STATES: 1930 AND 1920

[See explanation of minor changes in basis of urban-rural classification on p. 7]

DIVISION AND STATE	POPULATION: 1930			POPULATION: 1920		PER CENT URBAN	
	Total	Urban	Rural	Urban	Rural	1930	1920
United States	122,775,046	68,954,823	53,820,223	54,304,603	51,406,017	56.2	51.4
GEOGRAPHIC DIVISIONS:							
New England	8,166,341	6,311,976	1,854,365	5,865,073	1,535,836	77.3	79.2
Middle Atlantic	26,260,750	20,394,707	5,866,043	16,672,595	5,588,549	77.7	74.9
East North Central	25,297,185	16,794,908	8,502,277	13,049,272	8,426,271	66.4	60.8
West North Central	13,296,915	5,556,181	7,740,734	4,727,372	7,816,877	41.8	37.7
South Atlantic	15,793,589	5,698,122	10,095,467	4,338,792	9,651,480	36.1	31.0
East South Central	9,887,214	2,778,687	7,108,527	1,994,207	6,899,100	28.1	22.4
West South Central	12,176,830	4,427,439	7,749,391	2,970,829	7,271,365	36.4	29.0
Mountain	3,701,789	1,457,922	2,243,867	1,214,980	2,121,121	39.4	36.4
Pacific	8,194,433	5,534,881	2,659,552	3,471,483	2,095,388	67.5	62.4
NEW ENGLAND:							
Maine	797,423	321,506	475,917	299,569	468,445	40.3	39.0
New Hampshire	465,293	273,079	192,214	279,761	163,322	[1] 58.7	63.1
Vermont	359,611	118,766	240,845	109,976	242,452	33.0	31.2
Massachusetts	4,249,614	3,831,426	418,188	3,650,248	202,108	[1] 90.2	94.8
Rhode Island	687,497	635,429	52,068	589,180	15,217	[1] 92.4	97.5
Connecticut	1,606,903	1,131,770	475,133	936,339	444,292	[1] 70.4	67.8
MIDDLE ATLANTIC:							
New York	12,588,066	10,521,952	2,066,114	8,589,844	1,795,383	[1] 83.6	82.7
New Jersey	4,041,334	3,339,244	702,090	2,474,986	680,904	[1] 82.6	78.4
Pennsylvania	9,631,350	6,533,511	3,097,839	5,607,815	3,112,202	[1] 67.8	64.3
EAST NORTH CENTRAL:							
Ohio	6,646,697	4,507,371	2,139,326	3,677,136	2,082,258	67.8	63.8
Indiana	3,238,503	1,795,892	1,442,611	1,482,855	1,447,535	55.5	50.6
Illinois	7,630,654	5,635,727	1,994,927	4,403,153	2,082,127	73.9	67.9
Michigan	4,842,325	3,302,075	1,540,250	2,241,560	1,426,852	68.2	61.1
Wisconsin	2,939,006	1,553,843	1,385,163	1,244,568	1,387,499	52.9	47.3
WEST NORTH CENTRAL:							
Minnesota	2,563,953	1,257,616	1,306,337	1,051,593	1,335,532	49.0	44.1
Iowa	2,470,939	979,292	1,491,647	875,495	1,528,526	39.6	36.4
Missouri	3,629,367	1,859,119	1,770,248	1,586,903	1,817,152	51.2	46.6
North Dakota	680,845	113,306	567,539	88,239	558,633	16.6	13.6
South Dakota	692,849	130,907	561,942	101,872	534,675	18.9	16.0
Nebraska	1,377,963	486,107	891,856	405,306	891,066	35.3	31.3
Kansas	1,880,999	729,834	1,151,165	617,964	1,151,293	38.8	34.9
SOUTH ATLANTIC:							
Delaware	238,380	123,146	115,234	120,767	102,236	51.7	54.2
Maryland	1,631,526	974,869	656,657	869,422	580,239	59.8	60.0
District of Columbia	486,869	486,869	----------	437,571	----------	100.0	100.0
Virginia	2,421,851	785,537	1,636,314	673,984	1,635,203	32.4	29.2
West Virginia	1,729,205	491,504	1,237,701	369,007	1,094,694	28.4	25.2
North Carolina	3,170,276	809,847	2,360,429	490,370	2,068,753	25.5	19.2
South Carolina	1,738,765	371,080	1,367,685	293,987	1,389,737	21.3	17.5
Georgia	2,908,506	895,492	2,013,014	727,859	2,167,973	30.8	25.1
Florida	1,468,211	759,778	708,433	355,825	612,645	51.7	36.7
EAST SOUTH CENTRAL:							
Kentucky	2,614,589	799,026	1,815,563	633,543	1,783,087	30.6	26.2
Tennessee	2,616,556	896,538	1,720,018	611,226	1,726,659	34.3	26.1
Alabama	2,646,248	744,273	1,901,975	509,317	1,838,857	28.1	21.7
Mississippi	2,009,821	338,850	1,670,971	240,121	1,550,497	16.9	13.4
WEST SOUTH CENTRAL:							
Arkansas	1,854,482	382,878	1,471,604	290,497	1,461,707	20.6	16.6
Louisiana	2,101,593	833,532	1,268,061	628,163	1,170,346	39.7	34.9
Oklahoma	2,396,040	821,681	1,574,359	539,480	1,488,803	34.3	26.6
Texas	5,824,715	2,389,348	3,435,367	1,512,689	3,150,539	41.0	32.4
MOUNTAIN:							
Montana	537,606	181,036	356,570	172,011	376,878	33.7	31.3
Idaho	445,032	129,507	315,525	119,037	312,829	29.1	27.6
Wyoming	225,565	70,097	155,468	57,348	137,054	31.1	29.5
Colorado	1,035,791	519,882	515,909	453,259	486,370	50.2	48.2
New Mexico	423,317	106,816	316,501	64,960	295,390	25.2	18.0
Arizona	435,573	149,856	285,717	117,527	216,635	34.4	35.2
Utah	507,847	266,264	241,583	215,584	233,812	52.4	48.0
Nevada	91,058	34,464	56,594	15,254	62,153	37.8	19.7
PACIFIC:							
Washington	1,563,396	884,539	678,857	748,735	607,886	56.6	55.2
Oregon	953,786	489,746	464,040	391,019	392,370	51.3	49.9
California	5,677,251	4,160,596	1,516,655	2,331,729	1,095,132	[1] 73.3	68.0

[1] See footnote on p. 8.

16   POPULATION—UNITED STATES SUMMARY

TABLE 10.—NUMBER AND POPULATION OF PLACES OF SPECIFIED SIZES, AND POPULATION OF UNINCORPORATED TERRITORY, BY DIVISIONS AND STATES: 1930

DIVISION AND STATE	URBAN PLACES							
	Cities of 100,000 or more		Places of 25,000 to 100,000		Places of 10,000 to 25,000		Places of 5,000 to 10,000	
	Number of cities	Population	Number of places	Population	Number of places	Population	Number of places	Population
United States	93	36,325,736	283	12,917,141	606	9,097,200	851	5,897,156
GEOGRAPHIC DIVISIONS:								
New England	13	2,500,799	42	1,956,666	78	1,242,450	68	491,561
Middle Atlantic	18	12,650,337	58	2,849,321	162	2,497,660	194	1,363,751
East North Central	19	9,403,178	78	3,407,680	121	1,788,908	186	1,282,329
West North Central	9	2,648,663	18	833,349	62	890,322	82	558,719
South Atlantic	0	2,322,602	32	1,503,423	51	725,071	87	589,342
East South Central	6	1,200,032	10	442,944	32	478,377	45	304,737
West South Central	8	1,835,646	18	772,340	42	626,033	89	605,546
Mountain	2	428,128	8	209,153	17	239,867	39	269,556
Pacific	9	3,336,261	19	852,265	42	608,512	61	431,615
NEW ENGLAND:								
Maine			3	134,507	6	93,503	9	64,962
New Hampshire			3	133,525	7	96,937	4	24,460
Vermont					3	53,411	7	50,278
Massachusetts	9	1,774,375	21	1,036,878	43	693,428	39	287,939
Rhode Island	1	252,981	6	252,941	7	95,671	4	30,170
Connecticut	3	473,443	9	398,815	12	209,500	5	33,752
MIDDLE ATLANTIC:								
New York	7	8,404,778	16	800,121	47	730,349	41	277,831
New Jersey	6	1,254,210	20	936,186	40	609,321	50	351,371
Pennsylvania	5	2,991,349	22	1,113,014	75	1,157,990	103	734,549
EAST NORTH CENTRAL:								
Ohio	8	2,663,801	18	734,964	33	517,498	51	359,925
Indiana	5	785,975	12	474,215	17	237,807	27	172,871
Illinois	2	3,481,407	22	1,005,034	34	482,439	56	393,926
Michigan	3	1,893,746	14	712,589	23	327,343	32	213,702
Wisconsin	1	578,249	12	480,878	14	223,821	20	141,905
WEST NORTH CENTRAL:								
Minnesota	3	837,425			11	159,580	18	123,500
Iowa	1	142,559	9	406,505	11	167,405	14	94,173
Missouri	2	1,221,706	4	197,725	10	165,060	21	151,136
North Dakota			1	28,619	3	44,301	6	34,074
South Dakota			1	33,362	5	58,971	2	11,805
Nebraska	1	214,006	1	75,933	6	78,013	9	62,216
Kansas	2	232,967	2	91,205	16	216,992	12	81,815
SOUTH ATLANTIC:								
Delaware	1	106,597						
Maryland	1	804,874	2	68,608	3	37,962	3	20,547
District of Columbia	1	486,869						
Virginia	2	312,639	5	218,552	[1]9	118,830	10	68,993
West Virginia			5	256,123	[2]5	87,952	12	85,750
North Carolina			8	420,142	13	172,672	17	113,693
South Carolina			4	171,723	5	63,279	12	73,855
Georgia	1	270,366	4	242,326	10	153,017	16	113,785
Florida	3	341,347	4	125,944	7	91,359	17	112,719
EAST SOUTH CENTRAL:								
Kentucky	1	307,745	5	203,347	7	89,511	16	112,451
Tennessee	4	632,609	1	25,080	[2]3	46,091	14	99,184
Alabama	1	259,678	2	134,281	11	185,622	11	69,654
Mississippi			2	80,236	11	157,153	4	23,448
WEST SOUTH CENTRAL:								
Arkansas			[2]3	123,872	6	97,261	9	56,416
Louisiana	1	458,762	3	133,412	4	67,480	11	72,564
Oklahoma	2	326,647	2	58,425	12	168,698	22	162,358
Texas	5	1,050,237	[2]11	456,631	20	292,594	47	314,208
MOUNTAIN:								
Montana			2	68,354	4	55,334	6	38,245
Idaho					2	38,015	5	44,122
Wyoming					2	33,980	3	25,585
Colorado	1	287,861	2	83,333	5	56,894	10	60,916
New Mexico			1	26,570	2	22,349	4	25,920
Arizona			2	80,624			6	44,224
Utah	1	140,267	1	40,272	1	14,766	4	25,379
Nevada					1	18,529	1	5,165
PACIFIC:								
Washington	3	587,914	2	61,390	10	142,702	4	27,976
Oregon	1	301,815	1	26,266	4	56,350	9	61,218
California	5	2,446,532	16	764,609	28	409,460	48	342,421

[1] Includes 2 places counted also in other States. (See footnote 1, p. 14.)
[2] Includes 1 place counted also in another State. (See footnote 1, p. 14.)

URBAN AND RURAL BY STATES 17

TABLE 10.—NUMBER AND POPULATION OF PLACES OF SPECIFIED SIZES, AND POPULATION OF UNINCORPORATED TERRITORY, BY DIVISIONS AND STATES: 1930—Continued

DIVISION AND STATE	URBAN PLACES—con. Places of 2,500 to 5,000		RURAL TERRITORY Incorporated places of 1,000 to 2,500		Incorporated places under 1,000		Population outside incorporated places
	Number of places	Population	Number of places	Population	Number of places	Population	
United States	1,332	4,717,590	3,087	4,820,707	10,346	4,362,746	44,636,770
GEOGRAPHIC DIVISIONS:							
New England	31	120,500	35	60,735	69	27,436	1,766,194
Middle Atlantic	287	1,033,638	447	727,558	765	382,897	4,755,588
East North Central	253	912,813	665	1,031,344	2,167	996,420	6,474,513
West North Central	180	625,128	560	832,209	3,241	1,212,142	5,696,383
South Atlantic	161	557,594	428	676,858	1,488	595,044	8,823,565
East South Central	100	352,597	242	376,610	776	337,891	6,394,026
West South Central	166	587,874	398	630,591	967	438,095	6,680,705
Mountain	64	221,218	164	251,571	546	227,093	1,765,203
Pacific	90	306,228	148	233,231	336	145,728	2,280,593
NEW ENGLAND:							
Maine	8	28,534	8	15,338	14	7,992	452,587
New Hampshire	4	18,157					192,214
Vermont	4	15,077	20	32,433	41	16,943	191,469
Massachusetts	10	38,806					418,188
Rhode Island	1	3,666					52,068
Connecticut	4	16,260	7	12,964	5	2,501	459,668
MIDDLE ATLANTIC:							
New York	85	308,873	146	228,791	254	135,139	1,702,184
New Jersey	53	188,156	85	144,318	86	43,580	514,192
Pennsylvania	149	536,609	216	354,449	425	204,178	2,539,212
EAST NORTH CENTRAL:							
Ohio	¹64	231,183	¹160	247,358	528	236,786	1,655,182
Indiana	¹34	125,024	¹97	148,483	331	154,570	1,139,553
Illinois	78	272,921	211	327,745	726	323,523	1,343,659
Michigan	42	154,695	111	171,380	250	122,939	1,245,931
Wisconsin	36	128,990	87	136,373	332	158,602	1,090,188
WEST NORTH CENTRAL:							
Minnesota	41	137,111	93	135,139	562	205,208	965,990
Iowa	46	168,650	123	186,409	713	278,513	1,026,725
Missouri	35	123,492	116	178,685	585	203,301	1,388,262
North Dakota	2	6,312	29	39,232	285	98,709	429,598
South Dakota	8	26,769	41	56,947	242	87,978	417,017
Nebraska	18	55,939	73	107,172	421	162,661	622,023
Kansas	30	106,855	85	128,625	433	175,772	846,768
SOUTH ATLANTIC:							
Delaware	4	16,549	¹11	17,744	36	14,050	83,440
Maryland	12	42,878	¹26	36,797	90	42,050	577,810
District of Columbia							
Virginia	19	66,523	42	69,099	128	57,653	1,509,562
West Virginia	17	61,674	62	98,609	107	53,583	1,085,509
North Carolina	30	103,340	91	141,572	339	134,346	2,084,511
South Carolina	19	62,223	54	88,114	171	62,129	1,217,442
Georgia	33	115,998	91	143,903	438	155,841	1,713,270
Florida	27	88,409	52	81,020	179	75,392	552,021
EAST SOUTH CENTRAL:							
Kentucky	24	85,972	74	117,656	242	97,497	1,600,410
Tennessee	26	93,574	49	72,008	136	63,828	1,584,182
Alabama	28	95,038	64	99,268	179	81,209	1,721,498
Mississippi	22	78,013	55	87,678	219	95,357	1,487,936
WEST SOUTH CENTRAL:							
Arkansas	31	105,329	¹58	89,513	282	106,577	1,275,514
Louisiana	29	101,314	¹53	78,415	109	55,639	1,134,007
Oklahoma	30	105,553	¹99	160,698	345	137,734	1,275,927
Texas	76	275,678	¹190	301,965	231	138,145	2,995,257
MOUNTAIN:							
Montana	6	19,103	24	36,270	74	34,109	286,191
Idaho	14	47,370	22	33,521	107	41,777	240,227
Wyoming	3	10,532	17	27,916	59	18,751	108,801
Colorado	9	30,878	42	60,826	172	60,839	394,244
New Mexico	9	31,977	11	17,458	29	15,335	283,708
Arizona	6	25,008	9	14,911	11	9,169	261,637
Utah	14	45,580	34	53,058	88	44,909	143,616
Nevada	3	10,770	5	7,611	6	2,204	46,779
PACIFIC:							
Washington	19	64,557	42	63,013	141	64,312	551,532
Oregon	13	44,097	29	46,354	147	50,996	366,690
California	58	197,574	77	123,864	48	30,420	1,362,371

¹ Includes 1 place counted also in another State. (See footnote 1, p. 14.)

18   POPULATION—UNITED STATES SUMMARY

TABLE 11.—POPULATION OF CITIES HAVING, IN

	CITY	1930	1920	1910	1900	1890	1880
1	New York, N. Y.[1]	6, 930, 446	5, 620, 048	4, 766, 883	3, 437, 202	2, 507, 414	1, 911, 698
	Bronx Borough	1, 265, 258	732, 016	430, 980	200, 507	88, 908	51, 980
	Brooklyn Borough	2, 560, 401	2, 018, 356	1, 634, 351	1, 166, 582	838, 547	599, 495
	Manhattan Borough	1, 867, 312	2, 284, 103	2, 331, 542	1, 850, 093	1, 441, 216	1, 104, 673
	Queens Borough	1, 079, 129	469, 042	284, 041	152, 999	87, 050	56, 559
	Richmond Borough	158, 346	116, 531	85, 969	67, 021	51, 693	38, 991
2	Chicago, Ill	3, 376, 438	2, 701, 705	2, 185, 283	1, 698, 575	1, 099, 850	503, 185
3	Philadelphia, Pa	1, 950, 961	1, 823, 779	1, 549, 008	1, 293, 697	1, 046, 964	847, 170
4	Detroit, Mich	1, 568, 662	993, 678	465, 766	285, 704	205, 876	116, 340
5	Los Angeles, Calif	1, 238, 048	576, 673	319, 198	102, 479	50, 395	11, 183
6	Cleveland, Ohio	900, 429	796, 841	560, 663	381, 768	261, 353	160, 146
7	St. Louis, Mo	821, 960	772, 897	687, 029	575, 238	451, 770	350, 518
8	Baltimore, Md	804, 874	733, 826	558, 485	508, 957	434, 439	332, 313
9	Boston, Mass.[2]	781, 188	748, 060	670, 585	560, 892	448, 477	362, 839
10	Pittsburgh, Pa.[3]	669, 817	588, 343	533, 905	451, 512	343, 904	235, 071
11	San Francisco, Calif	634, 394	506, 676	416, 912	342, 782	298, 997	233, 959
12	Milwaukee, Wis	578, 249	457, 147	373, 857	285, 315	204, 468	115, 587
13	Buffalo, N. Y	573, 076	506, 775	423, 715	352, 387	255, 664	155, 134
14	Washington, D. C.[5]	486, 869	437, 571	331, 069	278, 718	188, 932	147, 293
15	Minneapolis, Minn	464, 356	380, 582	301, 408	202, 718	164, 738	46, 887
16	New Orleans, La	458, 762	387, 219	339, 075	287, 104	242, 039	216, 090
17	Cincinnati, Ohio	451, 160	401, 247	363, 591	325, 902	296, 908	255, 139
18	Newark, N. J	442, 337	414, 524	347, 469	246, 070	181, 830	136, 508
19	Kansas City, Mo	399, 746	324, 410	248, 381	163, 752	132, 716	55, 785
20	Seattle, Wash	365, 583	315, 312	237, 194	80, 671	42, 837	3, 533
21	Indianapolis, Ind	364, 161	314, 194	233, 650	169, 164	105, 436	75, 056
22	Rochester, N. Y	328, 132	295, 750	218, 149	162, 608	133, 896	89, 366
23	Jersey City, N. J	316, 715	298, 103	267, 779	206, 433	163, 003	120, 722
24	Louisville, Ky	307, 745	234, 891	223, 928	204, 731	161, 129	123, 758
25	Portland, Oreg	301, 815	258, 288	207, 214	90, 426	46, 385	17, 577
26	Houston, Tex	292, 352	138, 276	78, 800	44, 633	27, 557	16, 513
27	Toledo, Ohio	290, 718	243, 164	168, 497	131, 822	81, 434	50, 137
28	Columbus, Ohio	290, 564	237, 031	181, 511	125, 560	88, 150	51, 647
29	Denver, Colo	287, 861	256, 491	213, 381	133, 859	106, 713	35, 629
30	Oakland, Calif	284, 063	216, 261	150, 174	66, 960	48, 682	34, 555
31	St. Paul, Minn	271, 606	234, 698	214, 744	163, 065	133, 156	41, 473
32	Atlanta, Ga.[6]	270, 366	200, 616	154, 839	89, 872	65, 533	37, 409
33	Dallas, Tex	260, 475	158, 976	92, 104	42, 638	38, 067	10, 358
34	Birmingham, Ala	259, 678	178, 806	132, 685	38, 415	26, 178	3, 086
35	Akron, Ohio	255, 040	208, 435	69, 067	42, 728	27, 601	16, 512
36	Memphis, Tenn	253, 143	162, 351	131, 105	102, 320	64, 495	33, 592
37	Providence, R. I	252, 981	237, 595	224, 326	175, 597	132, 146	104, 857
38	San Antonio, Tex	231, 542	161, 379	96, 614	53, 321	37, 673	20, 550
39	Omaha, Nebr.[7]	214, 006	191, 601	124, 096	102, 555	140, 452	30, 518
40	Syracuse, N. Y	209, 326	171, 717	137, 249	108, 374	88, 143	51, 792
41	Dayton, Ohio	200, 982	152, 559	116, 577	85, 333	61, 220	38, 678
42	Worcester, Mass	195, 311	179, 754	145, 986	118, 421	84, 655	58, 291
43	Oklahoma City, Okla	185, 389	91, 295	64, 205	10, 037	4, 151	------------
44	Richmond, Va	182, 929	171, 667	127, 628	85, 050	81, 388	63, 600
45	Youngstown, Ohio	170, 002	132, 358	79, 066	44, 885	33, 220	15, 435
46	Grand Rapids, Mich	168, 592	137, 634	112, 571	87, 565	60, 278	32, 016
47	Hartford, Conn	164, 072	138, 036	98, 915	79, 850	53, 230	42, 015
48	Fort Worth, Tex	163, 447	106, 482	73, 312	26, 688	23, 076	6, 663
49	New Haven, Conn	162, 655	162, 537	133, 605	108, 027	81, 298	62, 882
50	Flint, Mich	156, 492	91, 599	38, 550	13, 103	9, 803	8, 409
51	Nashville, Tenn	153, 866	118, 342	110, 364	80, 865	76, 168	43, 350
52	Springfield, Mass	149, 900	129, 614	88, 926	62, 059	44, 179	33, 340
53	San Diego, Calif	147, 995	74, 361	39, 578	17, 700	16, 159	2, 637
54	Bridgeport, Conn	146, 716	143, 555	102, 054	70, 996	48, 866	27, 643
55	Scranton, Pa	143, 433	137, 783	129, 867	102, 026	75, 215	45, 850
56	Des Moines, Iowa	142, 559	126, 468	86, 368	62, 139	50, 093	22, 408

[1] Population shown for years prior to 1900 is for New York and its boroughs as constituted under the act of consolidation in 1898.

[2] Hyde Park town annexed to Boston city between 1910 and 1920. Combined population: 1910, 686,092; 1900, 574, 136; 1890, 458,670; 1880, 369,927; 1870, 254,662. Hyde Park not returned separately at earlier censuses.

[3] Includes population of Allegheny, as follows: 1900, 129,896; 1890, 105,287; 1880, 78,682; 1870, 53,180; 1860, 28,702; 1850, 21,262; 1840, 10,089; and 1830, 2,801. Allegheny not returned separately at earlier censuses.

[4] Population as reported by State census of 1852; returns for 1850 for San Francisco were destroyed by fire.

PRINCIPAL CITIES 19

1930, 100,000 Inhabitants or More: 1790 to 1930

1870	1860	1850	1840	1830	1820	1810	1800	1790	
1,478,103	1,174,779	696,115	391,114	242,278	152,056	119,734	79,216	49,401	1
37,393	23,593	8,032	5,346	3,023	2,782	2,267	1,755	1,781	
419,921	279,122	138,882	47,613	20,535	11,187	8,303	5,740	4,495	
942,292	813,669	515,547	312,710	202,589	123,706	96,373	60,515	33,131	
45,468	32,903	18,593	14,480	9,049	8,246	7,444	6,642	6,159	
33,029	25,492	15,061	10,965	7,082	6,135	5,347	4,564	3,835	
298,977	109,260	29,963	4,470	---	---	---	---	---	2
674,022	565,529	121,376	93,665	80,462	63,802	53,722	41,220	28,522	3
79,577	45,619	21,019	9,102	2,222	1,422	---	---	---	4
5,728	4,385	1,610	---	---	---	---	---	---	5
92,829	43,417	17,034	6,071	1,076	606	---	---	---	6
310,864	160,773	77,860	16,469	---	---	---	---	---	7
267,354	212,418	169,054	102,313	80,620	62,738	46,555	26,514	13,503	8
250,526	177,840	136,881	93,383	61,392	43,298	33,787	24,937	18,320	9
139,256	77,923	67,863	31,204	15,369	7,248	4,768	1,565	---	10
149,473	56,802	34,776	---	---	---	---	---	---	11
71,440	45,246	20,061	1,712	---	---	---	---	---	12
117,714	81,129	42,261	18,213	8,668	2,095	---	---	---	13
109,199	61,122	40,001	23,364	18,826	13,247	8,208	---	---	14
13,066	2,564	---	---	---	---	---	---	---	15
191,418	168,675	116,375	102,193	46,082	27,176	17,242	---	---	16
216,239	161,044	115,435	46,338	24,831	9,642	2,540	---	---	17
105,059	71,941	38,894	17,290	---	---	---	---	---	18
32,260	4,418	---	---	---	---	---	---	---	19
1,107	---	---	---	---	---	---	---	---	20
48,244	18,611	8,091	2,692	---	---	---	---	---	21
62,386	48,204	36,403	20,191	9,207	---	---	---	---	22
82,546	29,226	6,856	3,072	---	---	---	---	---	23
100,753	68,033	43,194	21,210	10,341	4,012	1,357	359	200	24
8,293	2,874	---	---	---	---	---	---	---	25
9,382	4,845	2,396	---	---	---	---	---	---	26
31,584	13,768	3,829	1,222	---	---	---	---	---	27
31,274	18,554	17,882	6,048	2,435	---	---	---	---	28
4,759	---	---	---	---	---	---	---	---	29
10,500	1,543	---	---	---	---	---	---	---	30
20,030	10,401	1,112	---	---	---	---	---	---	31
21,789	9,554	2,572	---	---	---	---	---	---	32
---	---	---	---	---	---	---	---	---	33
---	---	---	---	---	---	---	---	---	34
10,006	3,477	3,266	---	---	---	---	---	---	35
40,226	22,623	8,841	---	---	---	---	---	---	36
68,904	50,666	41,513	23,171	16,833	11,767	10,071	7,614	6,380	37
12,256	8,235	3,488	---	---	---	---	---	---	38
16,083	1,883	---	---	---	---	---	---	---	39
43,051	28,119	22,271	---	---	---	---	---	---	40
30,473	20,081	10,977	6,067	2,950	1,000	383	---	---	41
41,105	24,960	17,049	7,497	4,173	2,962	2,577	2,411	2,095	42
---	---	---	---	---	---	---	---	---	43
51,038	37,910	27,570	20,153	16,060	12,067	9,735	5,737	3,761	44
8,075	2,759	2,802	---	---	---	---	---	---	45
16,507	8,085	2,636	---	---	---	---	---	---	46
37,180	29,152	17,966	9,468	7,074	4,726	3,955	---	---	47
---	---	---	---	---	---	---	---	---	48
50,840	39,267	20,345	12,960	10,180	7,147	5,772	4,049	---	49
5,336	2,950	---	---	---	---	---	---	---	50
25,865	16,988	10,165	6,929	5,566	---	---	---	---	51
26,703	15,199	11,766	10,985	6,784	3,914	2,767	2,312	1,574	52
2,300	731	---	---	---	---	---	---	---	53
18,969	13,299	7,560	3,294	---	---	---	---	---	54
35,092	9,223	---	---	---	---	---	---	---	55
12,035	3,965	---	---	---	---	---	---	---	56

5 City has been coextensive with the District of Columbia since 1895.

6 The population of the "Municipality of 'Atlanta,'" established by act of the Georgia State Legislature, approved Aug. 17, 1929, was 360,691. See footnote 4, p. 23.

7 Omaha and South Omaha cities consolidated between 1910 and 1920. Combined population: 1910, 150,355; 1900, 128,556; 1890, 148,514. South Omaha not returned separately at earlier censuses.

20   POPULATION——UNITED STATES SUMMARY

TABLE 11.—POPULATION OF CITIES HAVING, IN 1930,

	CITY	1930	1920	1910	1900	1890	1880
57	Long Beach, Calif	142,032	55,593	17,809	2,252	564	
58	Tulsa, Okla	141,258	72,075	18,182	1,390		
59	Salt Lake City, Utah	140,267	118,110	92,777	53,531	44,843	20,768
60	Paterson, N. J	138,513	135,875	125,600	105,171	78,347	51,031
61	Yonkers, N. Y	134,646	100,176	79,803	47,931	32,033	18,892
62	Norfolk, Va	129,710	115,777	67,452	46,624	34,871	21,966
63	Jacksonville, Fla	129,549	91,558	57,699	28,429	17,201	7,650
64	Albany, N. Y	127,412	113,344	100,253	94,151	94,923	90,758
65	Trenton, N. J	123,356	119,289	96,815	73,307	57,458	29,910
66	Kansas City, Kans	121,857	101,177	82,331	51,418	38,316	3,200
67	Chattanooga, Tenn	119,798	57,895	44,604	30,154	29,100	12,892
68	Camden, N. J	118,700	116,309	94,538	75,935	58,313	41,659
69	Erie, Pa	115,967	93,372	66,525	52,733	40,634	27,737
70	Spokane, Wash	115,514	104,437	104,402	36,848	19,922	
71	Fall River, Mass	115,274	120,485	119,295	104,863	74,398	48,961
72	Fort Wayne, Ind	114,946	86,549	63,933	45,115	35,393	26,880
73	Elizabeth, N. J	114,589	95,783	73,409	52,130	37,764	28,229
74	Cambridge, Mass	113,643	109,694	104,839	91,886	70,028	52,669
75	New Bedford, Mass	112,597	121,217	96,652	62,442	40,733	26,845
76	Reading, Pa	111,171	107,784	96,071	78,961	58,661	43,278
77	Wichita, Kans	111,110	72,217	52,450	24,671	23,853	4,911
78	Miami, Fla	110,637	29,571	5,471	1,681		
79	Tacoma, Wash	106,817	96,965	83,743	37,714	36,006	
80	Wilmington, Del	106,597	110,168	87,411	76,508	61,431	42,478
81	Knoxville, Tenn	105,802	77,818	36,346	32,637	22,535	9,693
82	Peoria, Ill	104,969	76,121	66,950	56,100	41,024	29,259
83	Canton, Ohio	104,906	87,091	50,217	30,667	26,189	12,258
84	South Bend, Ind	104,193	70,983	53,684	35,999	21,819	13,280
85	Somerville, Mass	103,908	93,091	77,236	61,643	40,152	24,933
86	El Paso, Tex	102,421	77,560	39,279	15,906	10,338	736
87	Lynn, Mass	102,320	99,148	89,336	68,513	55,727	38,274
88	Evansville, Ind	102,249	85,264	69,647	59,007	50,756	29,280
89	Utica, N. Y	101,740	94,156	74,419	56,383	44,007	33,914
90	Duluth, Minn	101,463	98,917	78,466	52,969	33,115	3,483
91	Tampa, Fla	101,161	51,608	37,782	15,839	5,532	720
92	Gary, Ind	100,426	55,378	16,802			
93	Lowell, Mass	100,234	112,759	106,294	94,969	77,696	59,475

³ Not returned separately.

PRINCIPAL CITIES

100,000 Inhabitants or More: 1790 to 1930—Continued

1870	1860	1850	1840	1830	1820	1810	1800	1790	No.
									57
									58
									59
12,854	8,236								60
33,579	19,586								61
12,733									
19,229	14,620	14,326	10,920	9,814	8,478	9,193	6,926	2,959	62
6,912	2,118	1,045							63
69,422	62,367	50,763	33,721	24,209	12,630	10,762	5,349	3,498	64
22,874	17,228	6,461	4,035	3,925	3,942	3,002			65
									66
6,093									67
20,045	14,358	9,479	3,371				81		68
19,646	9,419	5,858	3,412	1,465	635	394			69
									70
26,766	14,026	11,524	6,738	4,158	1,594	1,296			71
									72
17,718	(8)	4,282							73
20,832	11,567								74
39,634	26,060	15,215	8,409	6,072	3,295	2,323	2,453	2,115	75
21,320	22,300	16,443	12,087	7,592	3,947	5,651	4,361	3,313	76
33,930	23,162	15,743	8,410	5,856	4,332	(8)	2,386		
									77
									78
									79
									80
30,841	21,258	13,979	8,367						81
8,682	(8)	2,076							
22,849	14,045	5,095	1,467						82
8,660	4,041	2,603	(8)	1,257					83
7,206	3,832	1,652							84
14,685	8,025	3,540							85
									86
28,233	19,083	14,257	9,367	6,138	4,515	4,087	2,837	2,291	87
21,830	11,484	3,235							88
28,804	22,529	17,565	12,782	8,323	2,972				89
									90
3,131	80								91
796									92
40,928	36,827	33,383	20,796	6,474					93

22   POPULATION—UNITED STATES SUMMARY

TABLE 12.—POPULATION OF CITIES AND OTHER URBAN PLACES HAVING, IN 1930, 25,000 INHABITANTS OR MORE: 1900 TO 1930

[Besides the cities, there are included in this table a small number of places not having a regular municipal incorporation, which are classified as urban for 1930; these are listed in the table with their proper designations, as townships, towns, etc. Except as explained in footnotes, population shown for each census year does not include that of territory subsequently annexed. A minus sign (−) denotes decrease]

CITY OR OTHER URBAN PLACE	POPULATION				INCREASE			
	1930	1920	1910	1900	1920 to 1930		1910 to 1920	1900 to 1910
					Number	Per cent	Per cent	Per cent
ALABAMA								
Birmingham	259,678	178,806	132,685	38,415	80,872	45.2	34.8	245.4
Mobile	68,202	60,777	51,521	38,460	7,425	12.2	18.0	33.9
Montgomery	66,079	43,464	38,136	30,346	22,615	52.0	14.0	25.7
ARIZONA								
Phoenix	48,118	29,053	11,134	5,544	19,065	65.6	160.9	100.8
Tucson	32,506	20,292	13,193	7,531	12,214	60.2	53.8	75.2
ARKANSAS								
Fort Smith	31,429	28,870	23,975	11,587	2,559	8.9	20.4	106.9
Little Rock	81,679	65,142	45,941	38,307	16,537	25.4	41.8	19.9
Texarkana	[1] 10,764	8,257	5,655	4,914	2,507	30.4	46.0	15.1
CALIFORNIA								
Alameda	35,033	28,806	23,383	16,464	6,227	21.6	23.2	42.0
Alhambra	29,472	9,096	5,021	----------	20,376	224.0	81.2	----------
Bakersfield	26,015	18,638	12,727	4,836	7,377	39.6	46.4	163.2
Belvedere township*	33,023	6,339	2,621	----------	26,684	420.9	141.9	----------
Berkeley	82,109	56,036	40,434	13,214	26,073	46.5	38.6	206.0
Fresno	52,513	45,086	24,892	12,470	7,427	16.5	81.1	99.6
Glendale	62,736	13,536	2,746	----------	49,200	363.5	392.9	----------
Long Beach	142,032	55,593	17,809	2,252	86,439	155.5	212.2	690.8
Los Angeles	1,238,048	576,673	319,198	102,479	661,375	114.7	80.7	211.5
Oakland	234,063	216,261	150,174	66,960	67,802	31.4	44.0	124.3
Pasadena	76,086	45,354	30,291	9,117	30,732	67.8	49.7	232.2
Riverside	29,696	19,341	15,212	7,973	10,355	53.5	27.1	90.8
Sacramento	93,750	65,908	44,696	29,282	27,842	42.2	47.5	52.6
San Bernardino	37,481	18,721	12,779	6,150	18,760	100.2	46.5	107.8
San Diego	147,995	74,361	39,578	17,700	73,634	99.0	87.9	123.6
San Francisco	634,394	506,676	416,912	342,782	127,718	25.2	21.5	21.6
San Jose	57,651	39,642	28,946	21,500	18,009	45.4	37.0	34.6
Santa Ana	30,322	15,485	8,429	4,933	14,837	95.8	83.7	70.9
Santa Barbara	33,613	19,441	11,659	6,587	14,172	72.9	66.7	77.0
Santa Monica	37,146	15,252	7,847	3,057	21,894	143.5	94.4	156.7
Stockton	47,963	40,296	23,253	17,506	7,667	19.0	73.3	32.8
COLORADO								
Colorado Springs [2]	33,237	30,105	29,078	21,085	3,132	10.4	3.5	37.9
Denver	287,861	256,491	213,381	133,859	31,370	12.2	20.2	59.4
Pueblo	50,096	43,050	41,747	28,157	7,046	16.4	3.1	48.3
CONNECTICUT								
Bridgeport	146,716	143,555	102,054	70,996	3,161	2.2	40.7	43.7
Bristol	28,451	20,620	9,527	6,268	7,831	38.0	116.4	52.0
Hartford	164,072	138,036	98,915	79,850	26,036	18.9	39.6	23.9
Meriden	38,481	29,867	27,265	24,296	8,614	28.8	9.5	12.2
New Britain	68,128	59,316	43,916	25,998	8,812	14.9	35.1	68.9
New Haven	162,655	162,537	133,605	108,027	118	0.1	21.7	23.7
New London	29,640	25,688	19,659	17,548	3,952	15.4	30.7	12.0
Norwalk [3]	36,019	27,743	6,954	6,125	8,276	29.8	299.0	13.5
Stamford	46,346	35,096	25,138	15,997	11,250	32.1	39.6	57.1
Torrington	26,040	20,623	15,483	8,360	5,417	26.3	33.2	85.2
Waterbury	99,902	91,715	73,141	45,859	8,187	8.9	25.4	59.5
West Haven town*	25,808	----------	----------	----------				

* Classified as urban under special rule. See p. 7.
[1] The inclusion of Texarkana in places of 25,000 or more is based upon the combined population (27,366 in 1930) of Texarkana, Ark., and Texarkana, Tex.
[2] Colorado City and Colorado Springs city consolidated between 1910 and 1920. Combined population: 1910, 33,411; 1900, 23,999.
[3] Norwalk and South Norwalk cities consolidated and made coextensive with Norwalk town between 1910 and 1920. Population of town: 1910, 24,211; 1900, 19,932.

URBAN PLACES   23

TABLE 12.—POPULATION OF CITIES AND OTHER URBAN PLACES HAVING, IN 1930, 25,000 INHABITANTS OR MORE: 1900 TO 1930—Continued

[A minus sign (−) denotes decrease]

CITY OR OTHER URBAN PLACE	POPULATION				INCREASE			
					1920 to 1930		1910 to 1920	1900 to 1910
	1930	1920	1910	1900	Number	Per cent	Per cent	Per cent
DELAWARE								
Wilmington	106,597	110,168	87,411	76,508	−3,571	−3.2	26.0	14.3
DISTRICT OF COLUMBIA								
Washington	486,869	437,571	331,069	278,718	49,298	11.3	32.2	18.8
FLORIDA								
Jacksonville	129,549	91,558	57,699	28,429	37,991	41.5	58.7	103.0
Miami	110,637	29,571	5,471	1,681	81,066	274.1	440.5	225.5
Orlando	27,330	9,282	3,894	2,481	18,048	194.4	138.4	57.0
Pensacola	31,579	31,035	22,982	17,747	544	1.8	35.0	29.5
St. Petersburg	40,425	14,237	4,127	1,575	26,188	183.9	245.0	162.0
Tampa	101,161	51,608	37,782	15,839	49,553	96.0	36.6	138.5
West Palm Beach	26,610	8,659	1,743	564	17,951	207.3	396.8	209.0
GEORGIA								
Atlanta [4]	270,366	200,616	154,839	89,872	69,750	34.8	29.6	72.3
Augusta	60,342	52,548	41,040	39,441	7,794	14.8	28.0	4.1
Columbus	43,131	31,125	20,554	17,614	12,006	38.6	51.4	16.7
Macon [5]	53,829	52,995	40,665	23,272	834	1.6	30.3	74.7
Savannah	85,024	83,252	65,064	54,244	1,772	2.1	28.0	19.9
ILLINOIS								
Alton	30,151	24,682	17,528	14,210	5,469	22.2	40.8	23.3
Aurora	46,589	36,397	29,807	24,147	10,192	28.0	22.1	23.4
Belleville	28,425	24,823	21,122	17,484	3,602	14.5	17.5	20.8
Berwyn	47,027	14,150	5,841		32,877	232.3	142.3	
Bloomington	30,930	28,725	25,768	23,286	2,205	7.7	11.5	10.7
Chicago	3,376,438	2,701,705	2,185,283	1,698,575	674,733	25.0	23.6	28.7
Cicero	66,602	44,995	14,557	16,310	21,607	48.0	209.1	−10.7
Danville	36,765	33,776	27,871	16,354	2,989	8.8	21.2	70.4
Decatur	57,510	43,818	31,140	20,754	13,692	31.2	40.7	50.0
East St. Louis	74,347	66,767	58,547	29,655	7,580	11.4	14.0	97.4
Elgin	35,929	27,454	25,976	22,433	8,475	30.9	5.7	15.8
Evanston	63,338	37,234	24,978	19,259	26,104	70.1	49.1	29.7
Galesburg	28,830	23,834	22,089	18,607	4,996	21.0	7.9	18.7
Granite City	25,130	14,757	9,903	3,122	10,373	70.3	49.0	217.2
Joliet	42,993	38,442	34,670	29,353	4,551	11.8	10.9	18.1
Maywood	25,829	12,072	8,033	4,532	13,757	114.0	50.3	77.3
Moline	32,236	30,734	24,199	17,248	1,502	4.9	27.0	40.3
Oak Park	63,982	39,858	19,444		24,124	60.5	105.0	
Peoria	104,969	76,121	66,950	56,100	28,848	37.9	13.7	19.3
Quincy	39,241	35,978	36,587	36,252	3,263	9.1	−1.7	0.9
Rockford	85,864	65,651	45,401	31,051	20,213	30.8	44.6	46.2
Rock Island	37,953	35,177	24,335	19,493	2,776	7.9	44.6	24.8
Springfield	71,864	59,183	51,678	34,159	12,681	21.4	14.5	51.3
Waukegan	33,499	19,226	9,426	5,141	14,273	74.2	19.6	70.5

[4] An act of the Georgia State Legislature, approved Aug. 17, 1929, provides for the establishment of the "Municipality of 'Atlanta,'" including therein, in addition to the city of Atlanta, 5 other cities and 15 unincorporated communities. The act further provides that "for the purposes of this act only" these cities "shall be known as boroughs" but that it shall not be unlawful to refer to them as cities. The population of the "Municipality of 'Atlanta'" as thus defined, and of its constituent areas, is as follows:

Municipality of "Atlanta"	360,691
Atlanta city or borough	270,366
Avondale Estates city or borough	535
College Park city or borough	6,604
Decatur city or borough	13,276
East Point city or borough	9,512
Hapeville city or borough	4,224
Unincorporated communities, Nos. 1 to 15	56,174

[5] An act of the Georgia State Legislature, approved Aug. 23, 1929, provides for the establishment of the "Municipality of 'Macon,'" including therein, in addition to the city of Macon, one other city and three unincorporated communities. The act further provides that "for the purpose of this act only" these cities "shall be known as boroughs" but that it shall not be unlawful to refer to them as cities. The population of the "Municipality of 'Macon'" as thus defined, and of its constituent areas, is as follows:

Municipality of "Macon"	64,045
Macon city or borough	53,829
Payne city or borough	426
Unincorporated communities, Nos. 1 to 3	9,790

24 POPULATION—UNITED STATES SUMMARY

TABLE 12.—POPULATION OF CITIES AND OTHER URBAN PLACES HAVING, IN 1930, 25,000 INHABITANTS OR MORE: 1900 TO 1930—Continued

[A minus sign (—) denotes decrease]

| CITY OR OTHER URBAN PLACE | POPULATION | | | | INCREASE | | | |
| | | | | | 1920 to 1930 | | 1910 to 1920 | 1900 to 1910 |
	1930	1920	1910	1900	Number	Per cent	Per cent	Per cent
INDIANA								
Anderson	39,804	29,767	22,476	20,178	10,037	33.7	32.4	11.4
East Chicago	54,784	35,967	19,098	3,411	18,817	52.3	88.3	459.9
Elkhart	32,949	24,277	19,282	15,184	8,672	35.7	25.9	27.0
Evansville	102,249	85,264	69,647	59,007	16,985	19.9	22.4	18.0
Fort Wayne	114,946	86,549	63,933	45,115	28,397	32.8	35.4	41.7
Gary	100,426	55,378	16,802	---------	45,048	81.3	229.6	--------
Hammond	64,560	36,004	20,925	12,376	28,556	79.3	72.1	69.1
Indianapolis	364,161	314,194	233,650	169,164	49,967	15.9	34.5	38.1
Kokomo	32,843	30,067	17,010	10,609	2,776	9.2	76.8	60.3
Lafayette	26,240	22,486	20,081	18,116	3,754	16.7	12.0	10.8
Michigan City	26,735	19,457	19,027	14,850	7,278	37.4	2.3	28.1
Mishawaka	28,630	15,195	11,386	5,560	13,435	88.4	27.8	113.8
Muncie	46,548	36,524	24,005	20,942	10,024	27.4	52.2	14.6
New Albany	25,819	22,992	20,629	20,628	2,827	12.3	11.5	(⁶)
Richmond	32,493	26,765	22,324	18,226	5,728	21.4	19.9	22.5
South Bend	104,193	70,983	53,684	35,999	33,210	46.8	32.2	49.1
Terre Haute	62,810	66,083	58,157	36,673	—3,273	—5.0	13.6	58.6
IOWA								
Burlington	26,755	24,057	24,324	23,201	2,698	11.2	—1.1	4.8
Cedar Rapids	56,097	45,566	32,811	25,656	10,531	23.1	38.9	27.9
Clinton	25,726	24,151	25,577	22,698	1,575	6.5	—5.6	12.7
Council Bluffs	42,048	36,162	29,292	25,802	5,886	16.3	23.5	13.5
Davenport	60,751	56,727	43,028	35,254	4,024	7.1	31.8	22.1
Des Moines	142,559	126,468	86,368	62,139	16,091	12.7	46.4	39.0
Dubuque	41,679	39,141	38,494	36,297	2,538	6.5	1.7	6.1
Ottumwa	28,075	23,003	22,012	18,197	5,072	22.0	4.5	21.0
Sioux City	79,183	71,227	47,828	33,111	7,956	11.2	48.9	44.4
Waterloo	46,191	36,230	26,693	12,580	9,961	27.5	35.7	112.2
KANSAS								
Hutchinson	27,085	23,298	16,364	9,379	3,787	16.3	42.4	74.5
Kansas City	121,857	101,177	82,331	51,418	20,680	20.4	22.9	60.1
Topeka	64,120	50,022	43,684	33,608	14,098	28.2	14.5	30.0
Wichita	111,110	72,217	52,450	24,671	38,893	53.9	37.7	112.6
KENTUCKY								
Ashland	29,074	14,729	8,688	6,800	14,345	97.4	69.5	27.8
Covington	65,252	57,121	53,270	42,938	8,131	14.2	7.2	24.1
Lexington	45,736	41,534	35,099	26,369	4,202	10.1	18.3	33.1
Louisville	307,745	234,891	223,928	204,731	72,854	31.0	4.9	9.4
Newport	29,744	29,317	30,309	28,301	427	1.5	—3.3	7.1
Paducah	33,541	24,735	22,760	19,446	8,806	35.6	8.7	17.0
LOUISIANA								
Baton Rouge	30,729	21,782	14,897	11,269	8,947	41.1	46.2	32.2
Monroe	26,028	12,675	10,209	5,428	13,353	105.3	24.2	88.1
New Orleans	458,762	387,219	339,075	287,104	71,543	18.5	14.2	18.1
Shreveport	76,655	43,874	28,015	16,013	32,781	74.7	56.6	75.0
MAINE								
Bangor	28,749	25,978	24,803	21,850	2,771	10.7	4.7	13.5
Lewiston	34,948	31,791	26,247	23,761	3,157	9.9	21.1	10.5
Portland	70,810	69,272	58,571	50,145	1,538	2.2	18.3	16.8
MARYLAND								
Baltimore	804,874	733,826	558,485	508,957	71,048	9.7	31.4	9.7
Cumberland	37,747	29,837	21,839	17,128	7,910	26.5	36.6	27.5
Hagerstown	30,861	28,064	16,507	13,591	2,797	10.0	70.0	21.5

⁶ Less than one-tenth of 1 per cent.

URBAN PLACES   25

TABLE 12.—POPULATION OF CITIES AND OTHER URBAN PLACES HAVING, IN 1930, 25,000 INHABITANTS OR MORE: 1900 TO 1930—Continued

[A minus sign (−) denotes decrease]

| CITY OR OTHER URBAN PLACE | POPULATION | | | | INCREASE | | | |
| | | | | | 1920 to 1930 | | 1910 to 1920 | 1900 to 1910 |
	1930	1920	1910	1900	Number	Per cent	Per cent	Per cent
MASSACHUSETTS								
Arlington town*	36,094	18,665	11,187	8,603	17,429	93.4	66.8	30.0
Beverly	25,086	22,561	18,650	13,884	2,525	11.2	21.0	34.3
Boston [7]	781,188	748,060	670,585	560,892	33,128	4.4	11.6	19.6
Brockton	63,797	66,254	56,878	40,063	−2,457	−3.7	16.5	42.0
Brookline town*	47,490	37,748	27,792	19,935	9,742	25.8	35.8	39.4
Cambridge	113,643	109,694	104,839	91,886	3,949	3.6	4.6	14.1
Chelsea	45,816	43,184	32,452	24,072	2,632	6.1	33.1	−4.8
Chicopee	43,930	36,214	25,401	19,167	7,716	21.3	42.6	32.5
Everett	48,424	40,120	33,484	24,336	8,304	20.7	19.8	37.6
Fall River	115,274	120,485	119,295	104,863	−5,211	−4.3	1.0	13.8
Fitchburg	40,692	41,029	37,826	31,531	−337	−0.8	8.5	20.0
Haverhill	48,710	53,884	44,115	37,175	−5,174	−9.6	22.1	18.7
Holyoke	56,537	60,203	57,730	45,712	−3,666	−6.1	4.3	26.3
Lawrence	85,068	94,270	85,892	62,559	−9,202	−9.8	9.8	37.3
Lowell	100,234	112,759	106,294	94,969	−12,525	−11.1	6.1	11.9
Lynn	102,320	99,148	89,336	68,513	3,172	3.2	11.0	30.4
Malden	58,036	49,103	44,404	33,664	8,933	18.2	10.6	31.9
Medford	59,714	39,038	23,150	18,244	20,676	53.0	68.6	26.9
New Bedford	112,597	121,217	96,652	62,442	−8,620	−7.1	25.4	54.8
Newton	65,276	46,054	39,806	33,587	19,222	41.7	15.7	18.5
Pittsfield	49,677	41,763	32,121	21,766	7,914	18.9	30.0	47.6
Quincy	71,983	47,876	32,642	23,899	24,107	50.4	46.7	36.6
Revere	35,680	28,823	18,219	10,395	6,857	23.8	58.2	75.3
Salem	43,353	42,529	43,697	35,956	824	1.9	−2.7	21.5
Somerville	103,908	93,091	77,236	61,643	10,817	11.6	20.5	25.3
Springfield	149,900	129,614	88,926	62,059	20,286	15.7	45.8	43.3
Taunton	37,355	37,137	34,259	31,036	218	0.6	8.4	10.4
Waltham	39,247	30,915	27,834	23,481	8,332	27.0	11.1	18.5
Watertown town*	34,913	21,457	12,875	9,706	13,456	62.7	66.7	32.6
Worcester	195,311	179,754	145,986	118,421	15,557	8.7	23.1	23.3
MICHIGAN								
Ann Arbor	26,944	19,516	14,817	14,509	7,428	38.1	31.7	2.1
Battle Creek	43,573	36,164	25,267	18,563	7,409	20.5	43.1	36.1
Bay City	47,355	47,554	45,166	27,628	−199	−0.4	5.3	63.5
Dearborn	50,358	2,470	911	844	47,888	1,938.8	171.1	7.9
Detroit	1,568,662	993,678	465,766	285,704	574,984	57.9	113.3	63.0
Flint	156,492	91,599	38,550	13,103	64,893	70.8	137.6	194.2
Grand Rapids	168,592	137,634	112,571	87,565	30,958	22.5	22.3	28.6
Hamtramck	56,268	48,615	3,559		7,653	15.7	1,266.0	
Highland Park	52,959	46,499	4,120	427	6,460	13.9	1,028.6	864.9
Jackson	55,187	48,374	31,433	25,180	6,813	14.1	53.9	24.8
Kalamazoo	54,786	48,487	39,437	24,404	6,299	13.0	22.9	61.6
Lansing	78,397	57,327	31,229	16,485	21,070	36.8	83.6	89.4
Muskegon	41,390	36,570	24,062	20,818	4,820	13.2	52.0	15.6
Pontiac	64,928	34,273	14,532	9,769	30,655	89.4	135.8	48.8
Port Huron	31,361	25,944	18,863	19,158	5,417	20.9	37.5	−1.5
Saginaw	80,715	61,903	50,510	42,345	18,812	30.4	22.6	19.3
Wyandotte	28,368	13,851	8,287	5,183	14,517	104.8	67.1	59.9
MINNESOTA								
Duluth	101,463	98,917	78,466	52,969	2,546	2.6	26.1	48.1
Minneapolis	464,356	380,582	301,408	202,718	83,774	22.0	26.3	48.7
St. Paul	271,606	234,698	214,744	163,065	36,908	15.7	9.3	31.7
MISSISSIPPI								
Jackson	48,282	22,817	21,262	7,816	25,465	111.6	7.3	172.0
Meridian	31,954	23,399	23,285	14,050	8,555	36.6	0.5	65.7
MISSOURI								
Joplin	33,454	29,902	32,073	26,023	3,552	11.9	−6.8	23.2
Kansas City	399,746	324,410	248,381	163,752	75,336	23.2	30.6	51.7
St. Joseph	80,935	77,939	77,403	102,979	2,996	3.8	0.7	−24.8
St. Louis	821,960	772,897	687,029	575,238	49,063	6.3	12.5	19.4
Springfield	57,527	39,631	35,201	23,267	17,896	45.2	12.6	51.3
University City	25,809	6,792	2,417		19,017	280.0	181.0	

* Classified as urban under special rule. See p. 7.
[7] Hyde Park town annexed to Boston city between 1910 and 1920. Combined population: 1910, 686,092; 1900, 574,136.

26 POPULATION—UNITED STATES SUMMARY

TABLE 12.—POPULATION OF CITIES AND OTHER URBAN PLACES HAVING, IN 1930, 25,000 INHABITANTS OR MORE: 1900 TO 1930—Continued

[A minus sign (−) denotes decrease]

CITY OR OTHER URBAN PLACE	POPULATION 1930	1920	1910	1900	INCREASE 1920 to 1930 Number	Per cent	1910 to 1920 Per cent	1900 to 1910 Per cent
MONTANA								
Butte	39,532	41,611	39,165	30,470	−2,079	−5.0	6.2	28.5
Great Falls	28,822	24,121	13,948	14,930	4,701	19.5	72.9	−6.6
NEBRASKA								
Lincoln	75,933	54,948	43,973	40,169	20,985	38.2	25.0	9.5
Omaha §	214,006	191,601	124,096	102,555	22,405	11.7	54.4	21.0
NEW HAMPSHIRE								
Concord	25,228	22,167	21,497	19,632	3,061	13.8	3.1	9.5
Manchester	76,834	78,384	70,063	56,987	−1,550	−2.0	11.9	22.9
Nashua	31,463	28,379	26,005	23,898	3,084	10.9	9.1	8.8
NEW JERSEY								
Atlantic City	66,198	50,707	46,150	27,838	15,491	30.6	9.9	65.8
Bayonne	88,979	76,754	55,545	32,722	12,225	15.9	38.2	69.7
Belleville	26,974	15,660	--------	--------	11,314	72.2		
Bloomfield	38,077	22,019	15,070	9,668	16,058	72.9	46.1	55.9
Camden	118,700	116,309	94,538	75,935	2,391	2.1	23.0	24.5
Clifton	46,875	26,470	--------	--------	20,405	77.1		
East Orange	68,020	50,710	34,371	21,506	17,310	34.1	47.5	59.8
Elizabeth	114,589	95,783	73,409	52,130	18,806	19.6	30.5	40.8
Garfield	29,739	19,381	10,213	3,504	10,358	53.4	89.8	191.5
Hoboken	59,261	68,166	70,324	59,364	−8,905	−13.1	−3.1	18.5
Irvington	56,733	25,480	11,877	5,255	31,253	122.7	114.5	126.0
Jersey City	316,715	298,103	267,779	206,433	18,612	6.2	11.3	29.7
Kearny	40,716	26,724	18,659	10,896	13,992	52.4	43.2	71.2
Montclair	42,017	28,810	21,550	13,962	13,207	45.8	33.7	54.3
Newark	442,337	414,524	347,469	246,070	27,813	6.7	19.3	41.2
New Brunswick	34,555	32,779	23,388	20,006	1,776	5.4	40.2	16.9
North Bergen township *	40,714	23,344	15,662	9,213	17,370	74.4	49.0	70.0
Orange	35,399	33,268	29,630	24,141	2,131	6.4	12.3	22.7
Passaic	62,959	63,841	54,773	27,777	−882	−1.4	16.6	97.2
Paterson	138,513	135,875	125,600	105,171	2,638	1.9	8.2	19.4
Perth Amboy	43,516	41,707	32,121	17,699	1,809	4.3	29.8	81.5
Plainfield	34,422	27,700	20,550	15,369	6,722	24.3	34.8	33.7
Trenton	123,356	119,289	96,815	73,307	4,067	3.4	23.2	32.1
Union City §	58,659	20,651	21,023	15,187	38,008	184.0	−1.8	38.4
West New York	37,107	29,926	13,560	5,267	7,181	24.0	120.7	157.5
Woodbridge township *	25,266	13,423	8,948	7,631	11,843	88.2	50.0	17.3
NEW MEXICO								
Albuquerque	26,570	15,157	11,020	6,238	11,413	75.3	37.5	76.7
NEW YORK								
Albany	127,412	113,344	100,253	94,151	14,068	12.4	13.1	6.5
Amsterdam	34,817	33,524	31,267	20,929	1,293	3.9	7.2	49.4
Auburn	36,652	36,192	34,668	30,345	460	1.3	4.4	14.2
Binghamton	76,662	66,800	48,443	39,647	9,862	14.8	37.9	22.2
Buffalo	573,076	506,775	423,715	352,387	66,301	13.1	19.6	20.2
Elmira	47,397	45,393	37,176	35,672	2,004	4.4	22.1	4.2
Jamestown	45,155	38,917	31,297	22,892	6,238	16.0	24.3	36.7
Kingston	28,088	26,688	25,908	24,535	1,400	5.2	3.0	5.6
Mount Vernon	61,499	42,726	30,919	21,228	18,773	43.9	38.2	45.7
Newburgh	31,275	30,366	27,805	24,943	909	3.0	9.2	11.5
New Rochelle	54,000	36,213	28,867	14,720	17,787	49.1	25.4	96.1
New York	6,930,446	5,620,048	4,766,883	3,437,202	1,310,398	23.3	17.9	38.7
Bronx Borough	1,265,258	732,016	430,980	200,507	533,242	72.8	69.8	114.9
Brooklyn Borough	2,560,401	2,018,356	1,634,351	1,166,582	542,045	26.9	23.5	40.1
Manhattan Borough	1,867,312	2,284,103	2,331,542	1,850,093	−416,791	−18.2	−2.0	26.0
Queens Borough	1,079,129	469,042	284,041	152,999	610,087	130.1	65.1	85.6
Richmond Borough	158,346	116,531	85,969	67,021	41,815	35.9	35.6	28.3

* Classified as urban under special rule. See p. 7.

§ Omaha and South Omaha cities consolidated between 1910 and 1920. Combined population: 1910, 150,355; 1900, 128,556.

§ Union and West Hoboken towns consolidated as Union City in 1925. Combined population: 1920, 60,725; 1910, 56,426; 1900, 38,281.

URBAN PLACES

TABLE 12.—POPULATION OF CITIES AND OTHER URBAN PLACES HAVING, IN 1930, 25,000 INHABITANTS OR MORE: 1900 TO 1930—Continued

[A minus sign (—) denotes decrease]

| CITY OR OTHER URBAN PLACE | POPULATION | | | | INCREASE | | | |
| | | | | | 1920 to 1930 | | 1910 to 1920 | 1900 to 1910 |
	1930	1920	1910	1900	Number	Per cent	Per cent	Per cent
NEW YORK—continued								
Niagara Falls	75,460	50,760	30,445	19,457	24,700	48.7	66.7	56.5
Poughkeepsie	40,288	35,000	27,936	24,029	5,288	15.1	25.3	16.3
Rochester	328,132	295,750	218,149	162,608	32,382	10.9	35.6	34.2
Rome	32,338	26,341	20,497	15,343	5,997	22.8	28.5	33.6
Schenectady	95,692	88,723	72,826	31,682	6,969	7.9	21.8	129.9
Syracuse	209,326	171,717	137,249	108,374	37,609	21.9	25.1	26.6
Troy	72,763	71,996	76,813	60,651	767	1.1	—6.3	26.6
Utica	101,740	94,156	74,419	56,383	7,584	8.1	26.5	32.0
Watertown	32,205	31,285	26,730	21,696	920	2.9	17.0	23.2
White Plains	35,830	21,031	15,949	7,899	14,799	70.4	31.9	101.9
Yonkers	134,646	100,176	79,803	47,931	34,470	34.4	25.5	66.5
NORTH CAROLINA								
Asheville	50,193	28,504	18,762	14,694	21,689	76.1	51.9	27.7
Charlotte	82,675	46,338	34,014	18,091	36,337	78.4	36.2	88.0
Durham	52,037	21,719	18,241	6,679	30,318	139.6	19.1	173.1
Greensboro	53,569	19,861	15,895	10,035	33,708	169.7	25.0	58.4
High Point	36,745	14,302	9,525	4,163	22,443	156.9	50.2	128.8
Raleigh	37,379	24,418	19,218	13,643	12,961	53.1	27.1	40.9
Wilmington	32,270	33,372	25,748	20,976	—1,102	—3.3	29.6	22.7
Winston-Salem [10]	75,274	48,395	22,700	13,650	26,879	55.5	113.2	66.3
NORTH DAKOTA								
Fargo	28,619	21,961	14,331	9,589	6,658	30.3	53.2	49.5
OHIO								
Akron	255,040	208,435	69,067	42,728	46,605	22.4	201.8	61.6
Canton	104,906	87,091	50,217	30,667	17,815	20.5	73.4	63.7
Cincinnati	451,160	401,247	363,591	325,902	49,913	12.4	10.4	11.6
Cleveland	900,429	796,841	560,663	381,768	103,588	13.0	42.1	46.9
Cleveland Heights	50,945	15,236	2,955	----------	35,709	234.4	415.6	------
Columbus	290,564	237,031	181,511	125,560	53,533	22.6	30.6	44.6
Dayton	200,982	152,559	116,577	85,333	48,423	31.7	30.9	36.6
East Cleveland	39,667	27,292	9,179	2,757	12,375	45.3	197.8	232.9
Elyria	25,633	20,474	14,825	8,791	5,159	25.2	38.1	68.6
Hamilton	52,176	39,675	35,279	23,914	12,501	31.5	12.5	47.5
Lakewood	70,509	41,732	15,181	3,355	28,777	69.0	174.9	352.5
Lima	42,287	41,326	30,508	21,723	961	2.3	35.5	40.4
Lorain	44,512	37,295	28,883	16,028	7,217	19.4	29.1	80.2
Mansfield	33,525	27,824	20,768	17,640	5,701	20.5	34.0	17.7
Marion	31,084	27,891	18,232	11,862	3,193	11.4	53.0	53.7
Massillon	26,400	17,428	13,879	11,944	8,972	51.5	25.6	16.2
Middletown	29,992	23,594	13,152	9,215	6,398	27.1	79.4	42.7
Newark	30,596	26,718	25,404	18,157	3,878	14.5	5.2	39.9
Norwood	33,411	24,966	16,185	6,480	8,445	33.8	54.3	149.8
Portsmouth	42,560	33,011	23,481	17,870	9,549	28.9	40.6	31.4
Springfield	68,743	60,840	46,921	38,253	7,903	13.0	29.7	22.7
Steubenville	35,422	28,508	22,391	14,349	6,914	24.3	27.3	56.0
Toledo	290,718	243,164	168,497	131,822	47,554	19.6	44.3	27.8
Warren	41,062	27,050	11,081	8,529	14,012	51.8	144.1	29.9
Youngstown	170,002	132,358	79,066	44,885	37,644	28.4	67.4	76.2
Zanesville	36,440	29,569	28,026	23,538	6,871	23.2	5.5	19.1
OKLAHOMA								
Enid	26,399	16,576	13,799	3,444	9,823	59.3	20.1	300.7
Muskogee	32,026	30,277	25,278	4,254	1,749	5.8	19.8	494.2
Oklahoma City	185,389	91,295	64,205	10,037	94,094	103.1	42.2	539.7
Tulsa	141,258	72,075	18,182	1,390	69,183	96.0	296.4	1,208.1
OREGON								
Portland	301,815	258,288	207,214	90,426	43,527	16.9	24.6	129.2
Salem	26,266	17,679	14,094	4,258	8,587	48.6	25.4	231.0

[10] Winston city and Salem town consolidated as Winston-Salem between 1910 and 1920. Figures shown for 1910 and 1900 represent combined population of Winston and Salem.

28   POPULATION—UNITED STATES SUMMARY

TABLE 12.—POPULATION OF CITIES AND OTHER URBAN PLACES HAVING, IN 1930, 25,000 INHABITANTS OR MORE: 1900 TO 1930—Continued

[A minus sign (—) denotes decrease]

| CITY OR OTHER URBAN PLACE | POPULATION | | | | INCREASE | | | |
| | | | | | 1920 to 1930 | | 1910 to 1920 | 1900 to 1910 |
	1930	1920	1910	1900	Number	Per cent	Per cent	Per cent
PENNSYLVANIA								
Aliquippa [11]	27,116	2,931	1,743	620	24,185	825.1	68.2	181.1
Allentown	92,563	73,502	51,913	35,416	19,061	25.9	41.6	46.6
Altoona	82,054	60,331	52,127	38,973	21,723	36.0	15.7	33.8
Bethlehem [12]	57,892	50,358	12,837	7,293	7,534	15.0	292.3	76.0
Chester	59,164	58,030	38,537	33,988	1,134	2.0	50.6	13.4
Easton	34,468	33,813	28,523	25,238	655	1.9	18.5	13.0
Erie	115,967	93,372	66,525	52,733	22,595	24.2	40.4	26.2
Harrisburg	80,339	75,917	64,186	50,167	4,422	5.8	18.3	27.9
Hazleton	36,765	32,277	25,452	14,230	4,488	13.9	26.8	78.9
Johnstown	66,993	67,327	55,482	35,936	—334	—0.5	21.3	54.4
Lancaster	59,949	53,150	47,227	41,459	6,799	12.8	12.5	13.9
Lebanon	25,561	24,643	19,240	17,628	918	3.7	28.1	9.1
Lower Merion township*	35,166	23,866	17,671	13,271	11,300	47.3	35.1	33.2
McKeesport	54,632	46,781	42,694	34,227	7,851	16.8	9.6	24.7
Nanticoke	26,043	22,614	18,877	12,116	3,429	15.2	19.8	55.8
New Castle	48,674	44,938	36,280	28,339	3,736	8.3	23.9	28.0
Norristown	35,853	32,319	27,875	22,265	3,534	10.9	15.9	25.2
Philadelphia	1,950,961	1,823,779	1,549,008	1,293,697	127,182	7.0	17.7	19.7
Pittsburgh	669,817	588,343	533,905	[13] 451,512	81,474	13.8	10.2	18.2
Reading	111,171	107,784	96,071	78,961	3,387	3.1	12.2	21.7
Scranton	143,433	137,783	129,867	102,026	5,650	4.1	6.1	27.3
Sharon	25,908	21,747	15,270	8,916	4,161	19.1	42.4	71.3
Upper Darby township*	46,626	8,956	5,385	3,821	37,670	420.6	66.3	40.9
Wilkes-Barre	86,626	73,833	67,105	51,721	12,793	17.3	10.0	29.7
Wilkinsburg	29,639	24,403	18,924	11,886	5,236	21.5	29.0	59.2
Williamsport	45,729	36,198	31,860	28,757	9,531	26.3	13.6	10.8
York	55,254	47,512	44,750	33,708	7,742	16.3	6.2	32.8
RHODE ISLAND								
Central Falls	25,898	24,174	22,754	18,167	1,724	7.1	6.2	25.2
Cranston	42,911	29,407	21,107	13,343	13,504	45.9	39.3	58.2
East Providence town*	29,995	21,793	15,808	12,138	8,202	37.6	37.9	30.2
Newport	27,612	30,255	27,149	22,441	—2,643	—8.7	11.4	21.0
Pawtucket	77,149	64,248	51,622	39,231	12,901	20.1	24.5	31.6
Providence	252,981	237,595	224,326	175,597	15,386	6.5	5.9	27.8
Woonsocket	49,376	43,496	38,125	28,204	5,880	13.5	14.1	
SOUTH CAROLINA								
Charleston	62,265	67,957	58,833	55,807	—5,692	—8.4	15.5	5.4
Columbia	51,581	37,524	26,319	21,108	14,057	37.5	42.6	24.7
Greenville	29,154	23,127	15,741	11,860	6,027	26.1	46.9	32.7
Spartanburg	28,723	22,638	17,517	11,395	6,085	26.9	29.2	53.7
SOUTH DAKOTA								
Sioux Falls	33,362	25,202	14,094	10,266	8,160	32.4	78.8	37.3
TENNESSEE								
Chattanooga	119,798	57,895	44,604	30,154	61,903	106.9	29.8	47.9
Johnson City	25,080	12,442	8,502	4,645	12,638	101.6	46.3	83.0
Knoxville	105,802	77,818	36,346	32,637	27,984	36.0	114.1	11.4
Memphis	253,143	162,351	131,105	102,320	90,792	55.9	23.8	28.1
Nashville	153,866	118,342	110,364	80,865	35,524	30.0	7.2	36.5
TEXAS								
Amarillo	43,132	15,494	9,957	1,442	27,638	178.4	55.6	590.5
Austin	53,120	34,876	29,860	22,258	18,244	52.3	16.8	34.2
Beaumont	57,732	40,422	20,640	9,427	17,310	42.8	95.8	118.9
Corpus Christi	27,741	10,522	8,222	4,703	17,219	163.6	28.0	74.8

* Classified as urban under special rule. See p. 7.

[11] Aliquippa and Woodlawn boroughs consolidated as Aliquippa borough in 1928. Combined population: 1920, 15,426; 1910, 3,139.

[12] South Bethlehem borough and Bethlehem borough consolidated and incorporated as Bethlehem city between 1910 and 1920. Combined population: 1910, 32,810; 1900, 23,999.

[13] Includes population of Allegheny, 129,896.

URBAN PLACES

TABLE 12.—POPULATION OF CITIES AND OTHER URBAN PLACES HAVING, IN 1930, 25,000 INHABITANTS OR MORE: 1900 TO 1930—Continued

[A minus sign (−) denotes decrease]

CITY OR OTHER URBAN PLACE	POPULATION				INCREASE			
					1920 to 1930		1910 to 1920	1900 to 1910
	1930	1920	1910	1900	Number	Per cent	Per cent	Per cent
TEXAS—continued								
Dallas	260,475	158,976	92,104	42,638	101,499	63.8	72.6	116.0
El Paso	102,421	77,560	39,279	15,906	24,861	32.1	97.5	146.9
Fort Worth	163,447	106,482	73,312	26,688	56,965	53.5	45.2	174.7
Galveston	52,938	44,255	36,981	37,789	8,683	19.6	19.7	−2.1
Houston	292,352	138,276	78,800	44,633	154,076	111.4	75.5	70.6
Laredo	32,618	22,710	14,855	13,429	9,908	43.6	52.9	10.6
Port Arthur	50,902	22,251	7,663	900	28,651	128.8	190.4	751.4
San Angelo	25,308	10,050	10,321		15,258	151.8	−2.6	
San Antonio	231,542	161,379	96,614	53,321	70,163	43.5	67.0	81.2
Texarkana	[14] 16,602	11,480	9,790	5,256	5,122	44.6	17.3	86.3
Waco	52,848	38,500	26,425	20,686	14,348	37.3	45.7	27.7
Wichita Falls	43,690	40,079	8,200	2,480	3,611	9.0	388.8	230.6
UTAH								
Ogden	40,272	32,804	25,580	16,313	7,468	22.8	28.2	56.8
Salt Lake City	140,267	118,110	92,777	53,531	22,157	18.8	27.3	73.3
VIRGINIA								
Lynchburg	40,661	30,070	29,494	18,891	10,591	35.2	2.0	56.1
Newport News	34,417	35,596	20,205	19,635	−1,179	−3.3	76.2	2.9
Norfolk	129,710	115,777	67,452	46,624	13,933	12.0	71.6	44.7
Petersburg	28,564	31,012	24,127	21,810	−2,448	−7.9	28.5	10.6
Portsmouth	45,704	54,387	33,190	17,427	−8,683	−16.0	63.9	90.5
Richmond	182,929	171,667	127,628	85,050	11,262	6.6	34.5	50.1
Roanoke	69,206	50,842	34,874	21,495	18,364	36.1	45.8	62.2
WASHINGTON								
Bellingham	30,823	25,585	24,298	[15] 11,062	5,238	20.5	5.3	119.7
Everett	30,567	27,644	24,814	7,838	2,923	10.6	11.4	216.6
Seattle	365,583	315,312	237,194	80,671	50,271	15.9	32.9	194.0
Spokane	115,514	104,437	104,402	36,848	11,077	10.6	(6)	183.3
Tacoma	106,817	96,965	83,743	37,714	9,852	10.2	15.8	122.0
WEST VIRGINIA								
Charleston	60,408	39,608	22,996	11,099	20,800	52.5	72.2	107.2
Clarksburg	28,866	27,869	9,201	4,050	997	3.6	202.9	127.2
Huntington	75,572	50,177	31,161	11,923	25,395	50.6	61.0	161.4
Parkersburg	29,623	20,050	17,842	11,703	9,573	47.7	12.4	52.5
Wheeling	61,659	56,208	41,641	38,878	5,451	9.7	35.0	7.1
WISCONSIN								
Appleton	25,267	19,561	16,773	15,085	5,706	29.2	16.6	11.2
Eau Claire	26,287	20,906	18,310	17,517	5,381	25.7	14.2	4.5
Fond du Lac	26,449	23,427	18,797	15,110	3,022	12.9	24.6	24.4
Green Bay	37,415	31,017	25,236	18,684	6,398	20.6	22.9	35.1
Kenosha	50,262	40,472	21,371	11,606	9,790	24.2	89.4	84.1
La Crosse	39,614	30,421	30,417	28,895	9,193	30.2	(6)	5.3
Madison	57,899	38,378	25,531	19,164	19,521	50.9	50.3	33.2
Milwaukee	578,249	457,147	373,857	285,315	121,102	26.5	22.3	31.0
Oshkosh	40,108	33,162	33,062	28,284	6,946	20.9	0.3	16.9
Racine	67,542	58,593	38,002	29,102	8,949	15.3	54.2	30.6
Sheboygan	39,251	30,955	26,398	22,962	8,296	26.8	17.3	15.0
Superior	36,113	39,671	40,384	31,091	−3,558	−9.0	−1.8	29.9
West Allis	34,671	13,745	6,645		20,926	152.2	106.8	

[6] Less than one-tenth of 1 per cent.
[14] The inclusion of Texarkana in places of 25,000 or more is based upon the combined population (27,366 in 1930) of Texarkana, Tex., and Texarkana, Ark.
[15] Population of Fairhaven and New Whatcom cities combined.

67981°—31——3

URBAN PLACES   29

TABLE 12.—POPULATION OF CITIES AND OTHER URBAN PLACES HAVING, IN 1930, 25,000 INHABITANTS OR MORE: 1900 TO 1930—Continued

[A minus sign (—) denotes decrease]

CITY OR OTHER URBAN PLACE	POPULATION				INCREASE			
					1920 to 1930		1910 to 1920	1900 to 1910
	1930	1920	1910	1900	Number	Per cent	Per cent	Per cent
TEXAS—continued								
Dallas	260,475	158,976	92,104	42,638	101,499	63.8	72.6	116.0
El Paso	102,421	77,560	39,279	15,906	24,861	32.1	97.5	146.9
Fort Worth	163,447	106,482	73,312	26,688	56,965	53.5	45.2	174.7
Galveston	52,938	44,255	36,981	37,789	8,683	19.6	19.7	—2.1
Houston	292,352	138,276	78,800	44,633	154,076	111.4	75.5	76.6
Laredo	32,618	22,710	14,855	13,429	9,908	43.6	52.9	10.6
Port Arthur	50,902	22,251	7,663	900	28,651	128.8	190.4	751.4
San Angelo	25,308	10,050	10,321	----------	15,258	151.8	—2.6	------
San Antonio	231,542	161,379	96,614	53,321	70,163	43.5	67.0	81.2
Texarkana	[14] 16,602	11,480	9,790	5,256	5,122	44.6	17.3	86.3
Waco	52,848	38,500	26,425	20,686	14,348	37.3	45.7	27.7
Wichita Falls	43,690	40,079	8,200	2,480	3,611	9.0	388.8	230.6
UTAH								
Ogden	40,272	32,804	25,580	16,313	7,468	22.8	28.2	56.8
Salt Lake City	140,267	118,110	92,777	53,531	22,157	18.8	27.3	73.3
VIRGINIA								
Lynchburg	40,661	30,070	29,494	18,891	10,591	35.2	2.0	56.1
Newport News	34,417	35,596	20,205	19,635	—1,179	—3.3	76.2	2.9
Norfolk	129,710	115,777	67,452	46,624	13,933	12.0	71.6	44.7
Petersburg	28,564	31,012	24,127	21,810	—2,448	—7.9	28.5	10.6
Portsmouth	45,704	54,387	33,190	17,427	—8,683	—16.0	63.9	90.5
Richmond	182,929	171,667	127,628	85,050	11,262	6.6	34.5	50.1
Roanoke	69,206	50,842	34,874	21,495	18,364	36.1	45.8	62.2
WASHINGTON								
Bellingham	30,823	25,585	24,298	[15] 11,062	5,238	20.5	5.3	119.7
Everett	30,567	27,644	24,814	7,838	2,923	10.6	11.4	216.6
Seattle	365,583	315,312	237,194	80,671	50,271	15.9	32.9	194.0
Spokane	115,514	104,437	104,402	36,848	11,077	10.6	(6)	183.3
Tacoma	106,817	96,965	83,743	37,714	9,852	10.2	15.8	122.0
WEST VIRGINIA								
Charleston	60,408	39,608	22,996	11,099	20,800	52.5	72.2	107.2
Clarksburg	28,866	27,869	9,201	4,050	997	3.6	202.9	127.2
Huntington	75,572	50,177	31,161	11,923	25,395	50.6	61.0	161.4
Parkersburg	29,623	20,050	17,842	11,703	9,573	47.7	12.4	52.5
Wheeling	61,659	56,208	41,641	38,878	5,451	9.7	35.0	7.1
WISCONSIN								
Appleton	25,267	19,561	16,773	15,085	5,706	29.2	16.6	11.2
Eau Claire	26,287	20,906	18,310	17,517	5,381	25.7	14.2	4.5
Fond du Lac	26,449	23,427	18,797	15,110	3,022	12.9	24.6	24.4
Green Bay	37,415	31,017	25,236	18,684	6,398	20.6	22.9	35.1
Kenosha	50,262	40,472	21,371	11,606	9,790	24.2	89.4	84.1
La Crosse	39,614	30,421	30,417	28,895	9,193	30.2	(6)	5.3
Madison	57,899	38,378	25,531	19,164	19,521	50.9	50.3	33.2
Milwaukee	578,249	457,147	373,857	285,315	121,102	26.5	22.3	31.0
Oshkosh	40,108	33,162	33,062	28,284	6,946	20.9	0.3	16.9
Racine	67,542	58,593	38,002	29,102	8,949	15.3	54.2	30.6
Sheboygan	39,251	30,955	26,398	22,962	8,296	26.8	17.3	15.0
Superior	36,113	39,671	40,384	31,091	—3,558	—9.0	—1.8	29.9
West Allis	34,671	13,745	6,645	----------	20,926	152.2	106.8	------

[6] Less than one-tenth of 1 per cent.
[14] The inclusion of Texarkana in places of 25,000 or more is based upon the combined population (27,366 in 1930) of Texarkana, Tex., and Texarkana, Ark.
[15] Population of Fairhaven and New Whatcom cities combined.

67981°—31——3

30 POPULATION—UNITED STATES SUMMARY

TABLE 13.—POPULATION OF CITIES AND OTHER URBAN PLACES HAVING, IN 1930, FROM 10,000 TO 25,000 INHABITANTS: 1930 AND 1920

[See headnote to Table 12]

CITY OR OTHER URBAN PLACE	1930	1920	CITY OR OTHER URBAN PLACE	1930	1920
ALABAMA			**CONNECTICUT—continued**		
Anniston	22,345	17,734	Shelton	10,113	9,475
Bessemer	20,721	18,674	Stratford town *	19,212	12,347
Decatur [1]	15,593	4,752	Wallingford	11,170	9,648
Dothan	16,046	10,034	West Hartford town *	24,941	8,854
Fairfield	11,059	5,003	Willimantic	12,102	12,330
Florence	11,729	10,529			
Gadsden	24,042	14,737	**FLORIDA**		
Huntsville	11,554	8,018	Daytona Beach [3]	16,598	825
Phenix City [2]	13,862	5,432	Gainesville	10,465	6,860
Selma	18,012	15,589	Key West	12,831	18,749
Tuscaloosa	20,659	11,996	Lakeland	18,554	7,062
			St. Augustine	12,111	6,192
ARKANSAS			Sanford	10,100	5,588
Blytheville	10,098	6,447	Tallahassee	10,700	5,637
El Dorado	16,421	3,887			
Hot Springs	20,238	11,695	**GEORGIA**		
Jonesboro	10,326	9,384	Albany	14,507	11,555
North Little Rock	19,418	14,048	Athens	18,192	16,748
Pine Bluff	20,760	19,280	Brunswick	14,022	14,413
			Decatur	13,276	6,150
CALIFORNIA			Griffin	10,321	8,240
Anaheim	10,995	5,526	La Grange	20,131	17,038
Beverly Hills	17,429	674	Rome	21,843	13,252
Brawley	10,439	5,389	Thomasville	11,733	8,196
Burbank	16,662	2,913	Valdosta	13,482	10,783
Burlingame	13,270	4,107	Waycross	15,510	18,068
Compton	12,516	1,478			
Eureka	15,752	12,923	**IDAHO**		
Fullerton	10,860	4,415	Boise	21,544	21,393
Gardena township *	15,969	6,331	Pocatello	16,471	15,001
Huntington Park	24,591	4,513			
Inglewood	19,480	3,286	**ILLINOIS**		
Modesto	13,842	9,241	Blue Island	16,534	11,424
Monrovia	10,890	5,480	Brookfield	10,035	3,589
Ontario	13,583	7,280	Cairo	13,532	15,203
Palo Alto	13,652	5,900	Calumet City	12,298	7,492
Pomona	20,804	13,505	Canton	11,718	10,928
Redlands	14,177	9,571	Centralia	12,583	12,491
Richmond	20,093	16,843	Champaign	20,348	15,873
Salinas	10,263	4,308	Chicago Heights	22,321	19,653
San Buenaventura (Ventura)	11,603	4,156	East Moline	10,107	8,675
San Leandro	11,455	5,703	Elmhurst	14,055	4,594
San Mateo	13,444	5,979	Elmwood Park	11,270	1,380
Santa Cruz	14,395	10,917	Forest Park	14,555	10,768
Santa Rosa	10,636	8,758	Freeport	22,045	19,669
South Gate	19,632		Harrisburg	11,625	7,125
South Pasadena	13,730	7,652	Harvey	16,374	9,216
Vallejo	14,476	16,845	Highland Park	12,203	6,167
Whittier	14,822	7,997	Jacksonville	17,747	15,713
			Kankakee	20,620	16,753
COLORADO			Kewanee	17,093	16,026
Boulder	11,223	11,006	La Grange	10,103	6,525
Fort Collins	11,489	8,755	La Salle	13,149	13,050
Grand Junction	10,247	8,665	Lincoln	12,855	11,882
Greeley	12,203	10,958	Mattoon	14,631	13,552
Trinidad	11,732	10,906	Melrose Park	10,741	7,147
			Mount Vernon	12,375	9,815
CONNECTICUT			Ottawa	15,094	10,816
Ansonia	19,898	17,643	Park Ridge	10,417	3,383
Danbury	22,261	18,943	Pekin	16,129	12,086
Derby	10,788	11,238	Sterling	10,012	8,182
East Hartford town *	17,125	11,648	Streator	14,728	14,779
Middletown	24,554	13,638	Urbana	13,060	10,244
Naugatuck	14,315	15,051	West Frankfort	14,683	8,478
Norwich	23,021	22,304	Wilmette	15,233	7,814
			Winnetka	12,166	6,694

* Classified as urban under special rule. See p. 7.
[1] Albany and Decatur cities and Fairview town consolidated as Decatur city in 1927. Combined population in 1920, 12,772.
[2] Phenix and Girard cities consolidated as Phenix City in 1923. Combined population in 1920, 10,374.
[3] Daytona city and Daytona Beach and Seabreeze towns consolidated as Daytona Beach city in 1925. Combined population in 1920, 6,841.

URBAN PLACES   31

TABLE 13.—POPULATION OF CITIES AND OTHER URBAN PLACES HAVING, IN 1930, FROM 10,000 TO 25,000 INHABITANTS: 1930 AND 1920—Continued

CITY OR OTHER URBAN PLACE	1930	1920	CITY OR OTHER URBAN PLACE	1930	1920
INDIANA			**MARYLAND**		
Bedford	13,208	9,076	Annapolis	12,531	11,214
Bloomington	18,227	11,595	Frederick	14,434	11,066
Connersville	12,795	9,901	Salisbury	10,997	7,553
Crawfordsville	10,355	10,139	**MASSACHUSETTS**		
Elwood	10,685	10,790			
Frankfort	12,196	11,585	Adams town*	12,697	12,967
Goshen	10,397	9,525	Amesbury town*	11,899	10,036
Huntington	13,420	14,000	Athol town*	10,677	9,792
Jeffersonville	11,946	10,098	Attleboro	21,769	19,731
La Porte	15,755	15,158	Belmont town*	21,748	10,749
Logansport	18,508	21,626	Braintree town*	15,712	10,580
Marion	24,496	23,747	Clinton town*	12,817	12,979
New Castle	14,027	14,458	Danvers town*	12,957	11,108
Peru	12,730	12,410	Dedham town*	15,136	10,792
Shelbyville	10,618	9,701	Easthampton town*	11,323	11,261
Vincennes	17,564	17,160	Fairhaven town*	10,951	7,291
Whiting	10,880	10,145	Framingham town*	22,210	17,033
IOWA			Gardner	19,399	16,971
Ames	10,261	6,270	Gloucester	24,204	22,947
Boone	11,886	12,451	Greenfield town*	15,500	15,462
Fort Dodge	21,895	19,347	Leominster	21,810	19,744
Fort Madison	13,779	12,066	Marlborough	15,587	15,028
Iowa City	15,340	11,267	Melrose	23,170	18,204
Keokuk	15,106	14,423	Methuen town*	21,069	15,189
Marshalltown	17,373	15,731	Milford town*	14,741	13,471
Mason City	23,304	20,065	Milton town*	16,434	9,382
Muscatine	16,778	16,068	Natick town*	13,589	10,907
Newton	11,560	6,627	Needham town*	10,845	7,012
Oskaloosa	10,123	9,427	Newburyport	15,084	15,618
KANSAS			North Adams	21,621	22,282
			Northampton	24,381	21,951
Arkansas City	13,946	11,253	North Attleborough town*	10,197	9,238
Atchison	13,024	12,630	Norwood town*	15,049	12,627
Chanute	10,277	10,286	Peabody	21,345	19,552
Coffeyville	16,198	13,452	Plymouth town*	13,042	13,045
Dodge City	10,059	5,061	Saugus town*	14,700	10,874
El Dorado	10,311	10,995	Southbridge town*	14,264	14,245
Emporia	14,067	11,273	Stoneham town*	10,060	7,873
Fort Scott	10,763	10,693	Swampscott town*	10,346	8,101
Independence	12,782	11,920	Wakefield town*	16,318	13,025
Lawrence	13,726	12,456	Webster town*	12,992	13,258
Leavenworth	17,466	16,912	Wellesley town*	11,439	6,224
Manhattan	10,136	7,989	Westfield	19,775	18,604
Newton	11,034	9,781	West Springfield town*	16,684	13,443
Parsons	14,903	16,028	Weymouth town*	20,882	15,057
Pittsburg	18,145	18,052	Winchester town*	12,719	10,485
Salina	20,155	15,085	Winthrop town*	16,852	15,455
KENTUCKY			Woburn	19,434	16,574
Bowling Green	12,348	9,638	**MICHIGAN**		
Fort Thomas	10,008	5,028	Adrian	13,064	11,878
Frankfort	11,626	9,805	Alpena	12,166	11,101
Henderson	11,668	12,169	Benton Harbor	15,434	12,233
Hopkinsville	10,746	9,696	Ecorse	12,716	4,394
Middlesborough	10,350	8,041	Escanaba	14,524	13,103
Owensboro	22,765	17,424	Ferndale	20,855	2,640
LOUISIANA			Grosse Pointe Park	11,174	1,355
			Holland	14,346	12,183
Alexandria	23,025	17,510	Iron Mountain	11,652	8,251
Bogalusa	14,029	8,245	Ironwood	14,299	15,739
Lafayette	14,635	7,855	Lincoln Park	12,336	--------
Lake Charles	15,791	13,088	Marquette	14,789	12,718
MAINE			Menominee	10,320	8,907
			Monroe	18,110	11,573
Auburn	18,571	16,985	Mount Clemens	13,497	9,488
Augusta	17,198	14,114	Muskegon Heights	15,584	9,514
Biddeford	17,633	18,008	Niles	11,326	7,311
South Portland	13,840	9,254	Owosso	14,496	12,575
Waterville	15,454	13,351	River Rouge	17,314	9,822
Westbrook	10,807	9,453	Royal Oak	22,904	6,007
			Sault Ste. Marie	13,755	12,096
			Traverse City	12,539	10,925
			Ypsilanti	10,143	7,413

* Classified as urban under special rule. See p. 7.

32 POPULATION—UNITED STATES SUMMARY

TABLE 13.—POPULATION OF CITIES AND OTHER URBAN PLACES HAVING, IN 1930, FROM 10,000 TO 25,000 INHABITANTS: 1930 AND 1920—Continued

CITY OR OTHER URBAN PLACE	1930	1920	CITY OR OTHER URBAN PLACE	1930	1920
MINNESOTA			**NEW JERSEY—continued**		
Albert Lea	10,169	8,056	Carteret	13,339	11,047
Austin	12,276	10,118	Cliffside Park	15,267	5,709
Brainerd	10,221	9,591	Collingswood	12,723	8,714
Faribault	12,767	11,089	Cranford township*	11,126	6,001
Hibbing	15,666	15,089	Dover	10,031	9,803
Mankato	14,038	12,469	Englewood	17,805	11,627
Rochester	20,621	13,722	Gloucester	13,796	12,162
St. Cloud	21,000	15,873	Hackensack	24,568	17,667
South St. Paul	10,009	6,860	Harrison	15,601	15,721
Virginia	11,963	14,022	Hawthorne	11,868	5,135
Winona	20,850	19,143	Hillside township*	17,601	5,267
			Linden ⁴	21,206	1,756
MISSISSIPPI			Lodi	11,549	8,175
Biloxi	14,850	10,937	Long Branch	18,399	13,521
Clarksdale	10,043	7,552	Lyndhurst township*	17,362	9,515
Columbus	10,743	10,501	Maplewood township*	21,321	5,283
Greenville	14,807	11,560	Millville	14,705	14,691
Greenwood	11,123	7,793	Morristown	15,197	12,548
Gulfport	12,547	8,157	Neptune township*	10,625	6,470
Hattiesburg	18,601	13,270	Nutley	20,572	9,421
Laurel	18,017	13,037	Pensauken township*	16,915	6,474
McComb	10,057	7,775	Phillipsburg	19,255	16,923
Natchez	13,422	12,608	Pleasantville	11,580	5,887
Vicksburg	22,943	18,072	Rahway	16,011	11,042
			Red Bank	11,022	9,251
MISSOURI			Ridgefield Park	10,764	8,575
Cape Girardeau	16,227	10,252	Ridgewood	12,188	7,580
Columbia	14,967	10,392	Roselle	13,021	5,737
Hannibal	22,761	19,306	Rutherford	14,915	9,497
Independence	15,296	11,686	South Orange	13,630	7,274
Jefferson City	21,596	14,490	South River	10,759	6,596
Maplewood	12,657	7,431	Summit	14,556	10,174
Moberly	13,772	12,808	Teaneck township*	16,513	4,192
St. Charles	10,491	8,503	Union township*	16,472	3,962
Sedalia	20,806	21,144	Weehawken township*	14,807	14,485
Webster Groves	16,487	9,474	Westfield	15,801	9,063
			West Orange	24,327	15,573
MONTANA					
			NEW MEXICO		
Anaconda	12,494	11,668	Roswell	11,173	7,033
Billings	16,380	15,100	Santa Fe	11,176	7,236
Helena	11,803	12,037			
Missoula	14,657	12,668	**NEW YORK**		
			Batavia	17,375	13,541
NEBRASKA			Beacon	11,933	10,996
			Cohoes	23,226	22,987
Beatrice	10,297	9,664	Corning	15,777	15,820
Fremont	11,407	9,592	Cortland	15,043	13,294
Grand Island	18,041	13,947	Dunkirk	17,802	19,336
Hastings	15,490	11,647	Endicott ⁵	16,231	9,500
Norfolk	10,717	8,634	Floral Park	10,016	2,097
North Platte	12,061	10,466	Freeport	15,467	8,599
			Fulton	12,462	13,043
NEVADA			Geneva	16,053	14,648
Reno	18,529	12,016	Glen Cove	11,430	8,664
			Glens Falls	18,531	16,638
NEW HAMPSHIRE			Gloversville	23,099	22,075
			Hempstead	12,650	6,382
Berlin	20,018	16,104	Herkimer	10,446	10,453
Claremont town*	12,377	9,524	Hornell	16,250	15,025
Dover	13,573	13,029	Hudson	12,337	11,745
Keene	13,794	11,210	Irondequoit town*	18,024	5,123
Laconia	12,471	10,897	Ithaca	20,708	17,004
Portsmouth	14,495	13,569	Johnson City	13,567	8,587
Rochester	10,209	9,673	Johnstown	10,801	10,908
			Kenmore	16,482	3,160
NEW JERSEY			Lackawanna	23,948	17,918
			Little Falls	11,105	13,029
Asbury Park	14,981	12,400	Lockport	23,100	21,308
Bridgeton	15,699	14,323	Lynbrook	11,993	4,371
Burlington	10,844	9,049	Mamaroneck	11,766	6,571
			Massena	10,637	5,993

* Classified as urban under special rule. See p. 7.
⁴ Linden township and Linden borough consolidated as Linden city in 1925. Combined population in 1920, 8,368.
⁵ Union and Endicott villages consolidated as Endicott village in 1921. Combined population in 1920, 12,803.

URBAN PLACES   33

TABLE 13.—POPULATION OF CITIES AND OTHER URBAN PLACES HAVING, IN 1930, FROM 10,000 TO 25,000 INHABITANTS: 1930 AND 1920—Continued

CITY OR OTHER URBAN PLACE	1930	1920	CITY OR OTHER URBAN PLACE	1930	1920
NEW YORK—continued			**OHIO**—continued		
Middletown	21,276	18,420	Struthers	11,249	5,847
North Tonawanda	19,019	15,482	Tiffin	16,428	14,375
Ogdensburg	16,915	14,609	Wooster	10,742	8,204
Olean	21,790	20,506	Xenia	10,507	9,110
Oneida	10,558	10,541			
Oneonta	12,536	11,582	**OKLAHOMA**		
Ossining	15,241	10,739			
Oswego	22,652	23,626	Ada	11,261	8,012
Peekskill	17,125	15,868	Ardmore	15,741	14,181
Plattsburg	13,349	10,909	Bartlesville	14,763	14,417
Port Chester	22,662	16,573	Chickasha	14,099	10,179
Port Jervis	10,243	10,171	Lawton	12,121	8,930
Rensselaer	11,223	10,823	McAlester	11,804	10,632
Rockville Centre	13,718	6,262	Okmulgee	17,097	17,430
Saratoga Springs	13,169	13,181	Ponca City	16,136	7,051
Tonawanda	12,681	10,068	Sapulpa	10,533	11,634
Valley Stream	11,790	....	Seminole	11,459	854
Watervliet	16,083	16,073	Shawnee	23,283	15,348
			Wewoka	10,401	1,520
NORTH CAROLINA					
			OREGON		
Concord	11,820	9,903			
Elizabeth City	10,037	8,925	Astoria	10,349	14,027
Fayetteville	13,049	8,877	Eugene	18,901	10,593
Gastonia	17,093	12,871	Klamath Falls	16,093	4,801
Goldsboro	14,985	11,296	Medford	11,007	5,756
Kinston	11,362	9,771			
New Bern	11,981	12,198	**PENNSYLVANIA**		
Rocky Mount	21,412	12,742			
Salisbury	16,951	13,884	Abington township*	18,643	8,084
Shelby	10,789	3,609	Ambridge	20,227	12,730
Statesville	10,490	7,895	Arnold	10,575	6,120
Thomasville	10,090	5,676	Beaver Falls [6]	17,147	12,802
Wilson	12,613	10,612	Bellevue	10,252	8,198
			Berwick	12,660	12,181
NORTH DAKOTA			Braddock	19,329	20,879
			Bradford	19,306	15,525
Bismarck	11,090	7,122	Bristol	11,799	10,273
Grand Forks	17,112	14,010	Butler	23,568	23,778
Minot	16,099	10,476	Canonsburg	12,558	10,632
			Carbondale	20,061	18,640
OHIO			Carlisle	12,596	10,916
			Carnegie	12,497	11,516
Alliance	23,047	21,603	Chambersburg	13,788	13,171
Ashland	11,141	9,249	Charleroi	11,260	11,516
Ashtabula	23,301	22,082	Cheltenham township*	15,731	11,015
Barberton	23,934	18,811	Clairton [7]	15,291	6,264
Bellaire	13,327	15,061	Coatesville	14,582	14,515
Bucyrus	10,027	10,425	Columbia	11,349	10,836
Cambridge	16,129	13,104	Connellsville	13,290	13,804
Campbell	14,673	11,237	Conshohocken	10,815	8,481
Chillicothe	18,340	15,831	Coraopolis	10,724	6,162
Coshocton	10,908	10,847	Dickson City	12,395	11,049
Cuyahoga Falls	19,797	10,200	Donora	13,905	14,131
East Liverpool	23,329	21,411	Dormont	13,190	6,455
Euclid	12,751	3,363	Du Bois	11,595	13,681
Findlay	19,363	17,021	Dunmore	22,627	20,250
Fostoria	12,790	9,987	Duquesne	21,396	19,011
Fremont	13,422	12,468	Ellwood City	12,323	8,958
Garfield Heights	15,589	2,550	Farrell	14,359	15,586
Ironton	16,621	14,007	Franklin	10,254	9,970
Lancaster	18,716	14,706	Greensburg	16,508	15,033
Marietta	14,285	15,140	Hanover	11,805	8,664
Martins Ferry	14,524	11,634	Hanover township*	17,770	11,139
New Philadelphia	12,365	10,718	Harrison township*	12,387	9,389
Niles	16,314	13,080	Haverford township*	21,362	6,631
Painesville	10,944	7,272	Homestead	20,141	20,452
Parma	13,899	....	Jeannette	15,126	10,627
Piqua	16,009	15,044	Kingston [8]	21,600	8,952
Salem	10,622	10,305	Latrobe	10,644	9,484
Sandusky	24,622	22,897	Lewistown	13,357	9,849
Shaker Heights	17,783	1,616	McKees Rocks	18,116	16,713

* Classified as urban under special rule. See p. 7.

[6] College Hill and Beaver Falls boroughs consolidated as Beaver Falls city in 1930. Combined population in 1920, 15,445.

[7] North Clairton, Wilson, and Clairton boroughs consolidated as Clairton city in 1922. Combined population in 1920, 10,777.

[8] Dorranceton and Kingston boroughs consolidated as Kingston borough in 1922. Combined population in 1920, 15,286.

34   POPULATION—UNITED STATES SUMMARY

TABLE 13.—POPULATION OF CITIES AND OTHER URBAN PLACES HAVING, IN 1930, FROM 10,000 TO 25,000 INHABITANTS: 1930 AND 1920—Continued

CITY OR OTHER URBAN PLACE	1930	1920	CITY OR OTHER URBAN PLACE	1930	1920
PENNSYLVANIA—continued			**TEXAS—continued**		
Mahanoy City	14,784	15,599	Harlingen	12,124	1,784
Meadville	16,698	14,568	Lubbock	20,520	4,051
Monessen	20,268	18,179	Marshall	16,203	14,271
Mount Carmel	17,967	17,469	Palestine	11,445	11,039
Mount Lebanon township*	13,403	2,258	Pampa	10,470	987
Munhall	12,995	6,418	Paris	15,649	15,040
New Kensington	16,762	11,987	San Benito	10,753	5,070
North Braddock	16,782	14,928	Sherman	15,713	15,031
Oil City	22,075	21,274	Sweetwater	10,848	4,307
Old Forge	12,661	12,237	Temple	15,345	11,033
Olyphant	10,743	10,236	Tyler	17,113	12,085
Phoenixville	12,029	10,484			
Pittston	18,246	18,497	**UTAH**		
Plains township*	16,044	13,986	Provo	14,766	10,303
Plymouth	16,543	16,500			
Pottstown	19,430	17,431	**VERMONT**		
Pottsville	24,300	21,876	Barre	11,307	10,008
Shamokin	20,274	21,204	Burlington	24,789	22,779
Shenandoah	21,782	24,726	Rutland	17,315	14,954
Steelton	13,291	13,428			
Stowe township*	13,368	10,665	**VIRGINIA**		
Sunbury	15,626	15,721			
Swissvale	16,029	10,908	Alexandria	24,149	18,060
Tamaqua	12,936	12,363	Bluefield	[10] 3,906	2,752
Taylor	10,428	9,876	Bristol	[9] 8,840	6,729
Turtle Creek	10,690	8,138	Charlottesville	15,245	10,688
Uniontown	19,544	15,692	Danville	22,247	21,539
Vandergrift	11,479	9,531	Hopewell	11,327	1,397
Warren	14,863	14,272	Staunton	11,990	10,623
Washington	24,545	21,480	Suffolk	10,271	9,123
Waynesboro	10,167	9,720	Winchester	10,855	6,883
West Chester	12,325	11,717			
			WASHINGTON		
RHODE ISLAND			Aberdeen	21,723	15,337
Bristol town*	11,953	11,375	Bremerton [11]	10,170	8,918
Cumberland town*	10,304	10,077	Hoquiam	12,766	10,058
Lincoln town*	10,421	9,543	Longview	10,652	----------
North Providence town*	11,104	7,697	Olympia	11,733	7,795
Warwick town*	23,196	13,481	Port Angeles	10,188	5,351
Westerly town*	10,997	9,952	Vancouver	15,766	12,637
West Warwick town*	17,696	15,461	Walla Walla	15,976	15,503
			Wenatchee	11,627	6,324
SOUTH CAROLINA			Yakima	22,101	18,539
Anderson	14,383	10,570			
Florence	14,774	10,968	**WEST VIRGINIA**		
Greenwood	11,020	8,703	Bluefield	[10] 19,339	15,282
Rock Hill	11,322	8,809	Fairmont	23,159	17,851
Sumter	11,780	9,508	Martinsburg	14,857	12,515
			Morgantown	16,186	12,127
SOUTH DAKOTA			Moundsville	14,411	10,669
Aberdeen	16,465	14,537			
Huron	10,946	8,302	**WISCONSIN**		
Mitchell	10,942	8,478	Ashland	10,622	11,334
Rapid City	10,404	5,777	Beloit	23,611	21,284
Watertown	10,214	9,400	Cudahy	10,631	6,725
			Janesville	21,628	18,293
TENNESSEE			Manitowoc	22,963	17,563
Bristol	[9] 12,005	8,047	Marinette	13,734	13,610
Jackson	22,172	18,860	Shorewood	13,479	2,650
Kingsport	11,914	5,692	South Milwaukee	10,706	7,598
			Stevens Point	13,623	11,371
TEXAS			Two Rivers	10,083	7,305
Abilene	23,175	10,274	Watertown	10,613	9,299
Big Spring	13,735	4,273	Waukesha	17,176	12,558
Brownsville	22,021	11,791	Wausau	23,758	18,951
Brownwood	12,780	8,223	Wauwatosa	21,194	5,818
Cleburne	11,539	12,820			
Corsicana	15,202	11,356	**WYOMING**		
Del Rio	11,693	10,589	Casper	16,619	11,447
Denison	13,850	17,065	Cheyenne	17,361	13,829
Greenville	12,407	12,384			

* Classified as urban under special rule. See p. 7.
[9] The inclusion of Bristol in places of 10,000 to 25,000 is based upon the combined population (20,845 in 1930) of Bristol, Tenn., and Bristol, Va.
[10] The inclusion of Bluefield in places of 10,000 to 25,000 is based upon the combined population (23,245 in 1930) of Bluefield, Va. (formerly Graham), and Bluefield, W. Va.
[11] Bremerton and Charleston cities consolidated as Bremerton in 1923. Combined population in 1920, 12,256.

URBAN PLACES

TABLE 14.—POPULATION OF CITIES AND OTHER URBAN PLACES HAVING, IN 1930, FROM 5,000 TO 10,000 INHABITANTS: 1930 AND 1920

See headnote to Table 12]

CITY OR OTHER URBAN PLACE	1930	1920	CITY OR OTHER URBAN PLACE	1930	1920	CITY OR OTHER URBAN PLACE	1930	1920
ALABAMA			**CALIFORNIA—con.**			**ILLINOIS**		
Alabama City	8,544	5,432	Santa Paula	7,452	3,967	Batavia	5,045	4,395
Andalusia	5,154	4,023	South San Francisco	6,193	4,411	Beardstown	6,344	7,111
Eufaula	5,208	4,939	Torrance	7,271		Belvidere	8,123	7,804
Homewood	6,103		Tulare	6,207	3,539	Benton	8,219	7,201
Jasper	5,313	3,246	Visalia	7,263	5,753	Carbondale	7,528	6,267
Lanett	5,204	4,976	Watsonville	8,344	5,013	Charleston	8,012	6,615
Opelika	6,156	4,960	Woodland	5,542	4,147	Clinton	5,920	5,898
Sheffield	6,221	6,682				Collinsville	9,235	9,753
Talladega	7,596	6,546	**COLORADO**			De Kalb	8,545	7,871
Tarrant City	7,341	734				Des Plaines	8,798	3,451
Troy	6,814	5,696	Alamosa	5,107	3,171	Dixon	9,908	8,191
			Canon City	5,938	4,551	Downers Grove	8,977	3,543
ARIZONA			Durango	5,400	4,116	Duquoin	7,593	7,285
			Englewood	7,980	4,356	East Peoria	5,027	2,214
Bisbee	8,023	9,205	La Junta	7,193	4,964	Edwardsville	6,235	5,336
Douglas	9,828	9,916	Longmont	6,029	5,848	Gillespie	5,111	4,063
Globe	7,157	7,044	Loveland	5,506	5,065	Glencoe	6,295	3,381
Miami	7,693	6,689	Salida	5,055	4,689	Glen Ellyn	7,680	2,851
Nogales	6,006	8,460	Sterling	7,195	6,415	Herrin	9,708	10,986
Prescott	5,517	5,010	Walsenburg	5,503	3,565	Hinsdale	6,923	4,042
						Hoopeston	5,613	5,451
ARKANSAS			**CONNECTICUT**			Johnston City	5,955	7,137
						Lake Forest	6,554	3,657
Camden	7,273	3,238	Greenwich	5,981	5,939	Lawrenceville	6,303	5,080
Conway	5,534	4,564	Putnam	7,318	7,711	Litchfield	6,612	6,215
Fayetteville	7,394	5,362	Rockville	7,445	7,726	Lombard	6,197	1,331
Helena	8,316	9,112	Southington	5,125	5,085	Macomb	8,509	6,714
Hope	6,008	4,790	Winsted	7,883	8,248	Madison	7,661	4,996
Malvern	5,115	3,864				Marion	9,033	9,582
Paragould	5,966	6,306	**FLORIDA**			Metropolis	5,573	5,055
Russellville	5,628	4,505				Monmouth	8,666	8,116
Van Buren	5,182	5,224	Bartow	5,269	4,203	Morris	5,568	4,505
			Bradentown	5,986	3,868	Mount Carmel	7,132	7,456
CALIFORNIA			Clearwater	7,607	2,427	Murphysboro	8,182	10,703
			Coral Gables	5,697		Naperville	5,118	3,830
Albany	8,569	2,462	De Land	5,246	3,324	Niles Center	5,007	763
Arcadia	5,216	2,239	Fort Lauderdale	8,666	2,065	Normal	6,768	5,143
Bell	7,884		Fort Myers	9,082	3,678	North Chicago	8,466	5,839
Calexico	6,299	6,223	Lake Worth	5,940	1,106	Olney	6,140	4,491
Chico	7,961	9,339	Miami Beach	6,494	644	Pana	5,835	6,122
Colton	8,014	4,282	Ocala	7,281	4,914	Paris	8,781	7,985
Corona	7,018	4,129	Palatka	6,500	5,102	Peru	9,121	8,869
Coronado	5,425	3,289	Panama City	5,402	1,722	Pontiac	8,272	6,664
Culver City	5,609	503	Plant City	6,800	3,729	River Forest	8,829	4,358
Daly City	7,838	3,779	River Junction	5,624		Riverside	6,770	2,532
El Centro	8,434	5,464	Sarasota	8,398	2,149	St. Charles	5,377	4,099
Hanford	7,028	5,888	South Jacksonville	5,597	2,775	Savanna	5,086	5,237
Hawthorne	6,596		Winter Haven	7,130	1,597	Spring Valley	5,270	6,493
Hayward	5,530	3,487				Summit	6,548	4,019
Lodi	6,788	4,850	**GEORGIA**			Taylorville	7,316	5,806
Lynwood	7,323					Venice	5,362	3,895
Martinez	6,569	3,858	Americus	8,760	9,010	Villa Park	6,220	854
Marysville	5,763	5,461	Bainbridge	6,141	4,792	Wheaton	7,258	4,137
Maywood	6,794		Carrollton	5,052	4,363	Wood River	8,136	3,476
Merced	7,066	3,974	Cartersville	5,250	4,350	Woodstock	5,471	5,523
Montebello	5,498		Cedartown	8,124	4,053	Zion	5,991	5,580
Monterey	9,141	5,479	College Park	6,604	3,622			
Monterey Park	6,406	4,108	Cordele	6,880	6,538	**INDIANA**		
Napa	6,437	6,757	Dalton	8,160	5,222			
National City	7,301	3,116	Dublin	6,681	7,707	Auburn	5,088	4,650
Orange	8,066	4,884	East Point	9,512	5,241	Bicknell	5,212	7,635
Oxnard	6,285	4,417	Fitzgerald	6,412	6,870	Bluffton	5,074	5,391
Pacific Grove	5,558	2,974	Gainesville	8,624	6,272	Brazil	8,744	9,293
Petaluma	8,245	6,226	Marietta	7,638	6,190	Clinton	7,936	10,962
Piedmont	9,333	4,282	Milledgeville	5,534	4,619	Columbus	9,935	8,990
Pittsburg	9,610	4,715	Moultrie	8,027	6,789	Decatur	5,156	4,762
Porterville	5,303	4,097	Newnan	6,386	7,037	Franklin	5,682	4,969
Redondo Beach	9,347	4,913				Greensburg	5,702	5,345
Redwood City	8,962	4,020	**IDAHO**			Hartford City	6,613	6,183
Roseville	6,425	4,477				Hobart	5,787	3,450
San Fernando	7,567	3,204	Coeur d'Alene	8,297	6,447	Kendallville	5,439	5,273
San Gabriel	7,224	2,640	Idaho Falls	9,429	8,064	Lebanon	6,445	6,257
San Luis Obispo	8,276	5,895	Lewiston	9,403	6,574	Linton	5,085	5,856
San Rafael	8,022	5,512	Nampa	8,206	7,621	Madison	6,530	6,711
Santa Clara	6,302	5,220	Twin Falls	8,787	8,324	Mount Vernon	5,035	5,284
Santa Maria	7,057	3,943				Plymouth	5,290	4,338

POPULATION—UNITED STATES SUMMARY

TABLE 14.—POPULATION OF CITIES AND OTHER URBAN PLACES HAVING, IN 1930, FROM 5,000 TO 10,000 INHABITANTS: 1930 AND 1920—Continued

CITY OR OTHER URBAN PLACE	1930	1920	CITY OR OTHER URBAN PLACE	1930	1920	CITY OR OTHER URBAN PLACE	1930	1920
INDIANA—con.			**MAINE**			**MICHIGAN—con.**		
Portland	5,276	5,953	Bath	9,110	14,731	Grosse Pointe	5,173	2,084
Princeton	7,505	7,132	Brewer	6,329	6,064	Hancock	5,795	7,527
Rushville	5,709	5,498	Brunswick	6,144	5,784	Hastings	5,227	5,132
Seymour	7,508	7,348	Calais	5,470	6,084	Hillsdale	5,896	5,476
Sullivan	5,306	4,489	Gardiner	5,609	5,475	Ionia	6,562	6,935
Valparaiso	8,079	6,518	Old Town	7,266	6,956	Ishpeming	9,238	10,500
Wabash	8,840	9,872	Rockland	9,075	8,109	Kingsford	5,526	------
Warsaw	5,730	5,478	Rumford Falls	8,726	7,016	Lapeer	5,008	4,723
Washington	9,070	8,743	Saco	7,233	6,817	Ludington	8,898	8,810
West Lafayette	5,095	3,830				Manistee	8,078	9,694
			MARYLAND			Manistique	5,198	6,380
IOWA						Marshall	5,019	4,270
Atlantic	5,585	5,329	Cambridge	8,544	7,467	Midland	8,038	5,483
Cedar Falls	7,362	6,316	Frostburg	5,588	6,017	Mount Pleasant	5,211	4,819
Centerville	8,147	8,486	Takoma Park	6,415	3,163	Negaunee	6,552	7,419
Chariton	5,365	5,175				Petoskey	5,740	5,064
Charles City	8,039	7,350	**MASSACHUSETTS**			Roseville	6,836	------
Cherokee	6,443	5,824				St. Clair Shores	6,745	------
Creston	8,615	8,034	Abington town*	5,872	5,787	St. Joseph	8,349	7,251
Fairfield	6,619	5,948	Amherst town*	5,888	5,550	Sturgis	6,950	5,995
Oelwein	7,794	7,455	Andover town*	9,969	8,268	Three Rivers	6,863	5,209
Perry	5,881	5,642	Auburn town*	6,147	3,891			
Red Oak	5,778	5,578	Barnstable town*	7,271	4,836	**MINNESOTA**		
Shenandoah	6,502	5,255	Bridgewater town*	9,055	8,438			
Spencer	5,019	4,599	Canton town*	5,816	5,945	Bemidji	7,202	7,086
Webster City	7,024	5,657	Concord town*	7,477	6,461	Chisholm	8,308	9,039
			Dartmouth town*	8,778	6,493	Cloquet	6,782	5,127
KANSAS			Dracut town*	6,912	5,280	Columbia Heights	5,613	2,968
			Franklin town*	7,028	6,497	Crookston	6,321	6,825
Abilene	5,658	4,895	Great Barrington town*	5,934	6,315	Ely	6,156	4,902
Concordia	5,792	4,705	Hingham town*	6,657	5,604	Eveleth	7,484	7,205
Garden City	6,121	3,848	Hudson town*	8,469	7,607	Fairmont	5,521	4,630
Great Bend	5,548	4,460	Ipswich town*	5,599	6,201	Fergus Falls	9,389	7,581
Iola	7,160	8,513	Lexington town*	9,467	6,350	Hastings	5,086	4,571
Junction City	7,407	7,533	Ludlow town*	8,876	7,470	International Falls	5,036	3,448
Liberal	5,294	3,613	Mansfield town*	6,364	6,255	Little Falls	5,014	5,500
McPherson	6,147	4,595	Marblehead town*	8,668	7,324	Moorhead	7,651	5,720
Ottawa	9,563	9,018	Maynard town*	7,156	7,086	New Ulm	7,308	6,745
Pratt	6,322	5,183	Middleborough town*	8,608	8,453	Owatonna	7,654	7,252
Wellington	7,405	7,048	Millbury town*	6,957	5,653	Red Wing	9,629	8,637
Winfield	9,398	7,933	Montague town*	8,081	7,675	Stillwater	7,173	7,735
			North Andover town*	6,961	6,265	Willmar	6,173	5,892
KENTUCKY			Northbridge town*	9,713	10,174			
			Orange town*	5,365	5,393	**MISSISSIPPI**		
Bellevue	8,497	7,379	Palmer town*	9,577	9,896			
Catlettsburg	5,025	4,183	Randolph town*	6,553	4,756	Brookhaven	5,288	4,706
Corbin	8,036	3,406	Reading town*	9,767	7,439	Corinth	6,220	5,498
Danville	6,729	5,099	Rockland town*	7,524	7,544	Tupelo	6,361	5,055
Dayton	9,071	7,646	Somerset town*	5,398	3,520	Yazoo City	5,579	5,244
Glasgow	5,042	2,559	South Hadley town*	6,773	5,527			
Hazard	7,021	4,348	Spencer town*	6,272	5,930	**MISSOURI**		
Jenkins	8,465	4,707	Stoughton town*	8,204	6,865			
Ludlow	6,485	4,582	Uxbridge town*	6,285	5,384	Boonville	6,435	4,665
Madisonville	6,908	5,030	Walpole town*	7,273	5,446	Brookfield	6,428	6,304
Mayfield	8,177	6,583	Ware town*	7,385	8,525	Carthage	9,736	10,068
Maysville	6,557	6,107	Whitman town*	7,638	7,147	Chillicothe	8,177	6,772
Paris	6,204	6,310	Winchendon town*	6,202	5,904	Clayton	9,613	3,028
Richmond	6,495	5,622				Clinton	5,744	5,098
Somerset	5,506	4,672	**MICHIGAN**			De Soto	5,069	5,003
Winchester	8,233	8,333				Fulton	6,105	5,595
			Albion	8,324	8,354	Kirksville	8,293	7,213
LOUISIANA			Alma	6,734	7,542	Kirkwood	9,169	4,422
			Berkley	5,571	------	Marshall	8,103	5,200
Bastrop	5,121	1,216	Birmingham	9,539	3,694	Maryville	5,217	4,711
Crowley	7,656	6,108	Cadillac	9,570	9,750	Mexico	8,290	6,013
Gretna	9,584	7,197	Charlotte	5,307	5,126	Nevada	7,448	7,139
Hammond	6,072	3,855	Coldwater	6,735	6,114	Poplar Bluff	7,551	8,042
Houma	6,531	5,160	Dowagiac	5,550	5,440	Richmond Heights	9,150	2,136
Minden	5,623	6,105	East Detroit	5,955	------	Sikeston	5,676	3,613
Morgan City	5,985	5,429	Gladstone	5,170	4,953	Trenton	6,992	6,951
New Iberia	8,003	6,278	Grand Haven	8,345	7,205	Warrensburg	5,146	4,811
Opelousas	6,299	4,437				Washington	5,918	3,182
Plaquemine	5,124	4,632				Webb City	6,876	7,807
West Monroe	6,566	2,240						

* Classified as urban under special rule. See p. 7.

TABLE 14.—POPULATION OF CITIES AND OTHER URBAN PLACES HAVING, IN 1930, FROM 5,000 TO 10,000 INHABITANTS: 1930 AND 1920—Continued

CITY OR OTHER URBAN PLACE	1930	1920	CITY OR OTHER URBAN PLACE	1930	1920	CITY OR OTHER URBAN PLACE	1930	1920
MONTANA			**NEW JERSEY—con.**			**NORTH DAKOTA**		
Bozeman	6,855	6,183	Verona	7,161	3,039	Devils Lake	5,451	5,004
Havre	6,372	5,429	Vineland	7,556	6,432	Dickinson	5,025	4,122
Kalispell	6,094	5,147	Wallington	9,063	5,715	Jamestown	8,187	6,627
Lewistown	5,358	6,120	Wildwood	5,330	2,790	Mandan	5,037	4,336
Livingston	6,391	6,311	Woodbury	8,172	5,801	Valley City	5,268	4,686
Miles City	7,175	7,937	Wood Ridge	5,159	1,923	Williston	5,106	4,178
NEBRASKA			**NEW MEXICO**			**OHIO**		
Alliance	6,669	4,591	Clovis	8,027	4,904	Athens	7,252	6,418
Columbus	6,898	5,410	Gallup	5,992	3,920	Bedford	6,814	2,677
Fairbury	6,192	5,454	Las Cruces	5,811	3,909	Bellefontaine	9,543	9,336
Falls City	5,787	4,930	Raton	6,090	5,544	Bellevue	6,256	5,776
Kearney	8,575	7,702				Berea	5,697	2,959
McCook	6,688	4,308	**NEW YORK**			Bexley	7,396	1,342
Nebraska City	7,230	6,279	Bronxville	6,387	3,055	Bowling Green	6,688	5,788
Scottsbluff	8,465	6,912	Canadaigua	7,541	7,299	Cheviot	8,046	4,168
York	5,712	5,388	Catskill	5,082	4,728	Circleville	7,369	7,049
			Cedarhurst	5,065	2,838	Conneaut	9,691	9,343
NEVADA			Depew	6,536	5,850	Defiance	8,818	8,876
Las Vegas	5,165	2,304	Dobbs Ferry	5,741	4,401	Delaware	8,675	8,756
			East Rochester	6,627	3,901	Delphos	5,672	5,745
NEW HAMPSHIRE			Elmira Heights	5,061	4,188	Dover	9,716	8,101
			Fredonia	5,814	6,051	East Palestine	5,215	5,750
Derry town*	5,131	5,382	Garden City	7,180	2,420	Galion	7,674	7,374
Franklin	6,576	6,318	Hastings-on-Hudson	7,007	5,526	Gallipolis	7,106	6,070
Lebanon town*	7,073	6,162	Haverstraw	5,621	5,226	Girard	9,859	6,556
Somersworth	5,680	6,688	Hudson Falls	6,449	5,761	Grandview Heights	6,358	1,185
			Ilion	9,890	10,169	Greenville	7,036	7,104
NEW JERSEY			Lancaster	7,040	6,059	Jackson	5,922	5,842
Audubon	8,904	4,740	Larchmont	5,282	2,468	Kent	8,375	7,070
Bergenfield	8,816	3,667	Long Beach	5,817	282	Kenton	7,009	7,690
Bogota	7,341	3,906	Malone	8,657	7,556	Lockland	5,703	4,007
Boonton	6,866	5,372	Mechanicville	7,924	8,166	Logan	6,080	5,493
Bound Brook	7,372	5,906	Medina	6,071	6,011	Maple Heights	5,950	1,732
Caldwell	5,144	3,776	Mineola	8,155	3,016	Miamisburg	5,518	4,383
Carlstadt	5,425	4,472	Mount Kisco	5,127	3,944	Mingo Junction	5,030	4,616
Dumont	5,861	2,537	Newark	7,649	6,964	Mount Vernon	9,370	9,237
Dunellen	5,148	3,394	North Tarrytown	7,417	5,927	Nelsonville	5,322	6,440
East Rutherford	7,080	5,463	Norwich	8,378	8,268	New Boston	5,931	4,817
Fairlawn	5,990		Nyack	5,392	4,444	Norwalk	7,776	7,379
Fairview	9,067	4,882	Patchogue	6,860	4,031	Oakwood	6,494	1,473
Fort Lee	8,759	5,761	Penn Yan	5,329	4,517	Ravenna	8,019	7,219
Freehold	6,894	4,768	Rye	8,712	5,308	Reading	5,723	4,540
Glen Ridge	7,365	4,620	Salamanca	9,577	9,276	Rocky River	5,632	1,861
Guttenberg	6,535	6,726	Saranac Lake	8,020	5,174	St. Bernard	7,487	6,312
Haddonfield	8,857	5,646	Scarsdale	9,690	3,506	St. Marys	5,433	5,679
Haddon Heights	5,394	2,950	Scotia	7,437	4,358	Shelby	6,198	5,578
Hammonton	7,656	6,417	Seneca Falls	6,443	6,389	Sidney	9,301	8,590
Hasbrouck Heights	5,658	2,895	Solvay	7,986	7,352	Toronto	7,044	4,684
Highland Park	8,691	4,866	Tarrytown	6,841	5,807	Troy	8,675	7,260
Leonia	5,350	2,979	Tuckahoe	6,138	3,509	Uhrichsville	6,437	6,428
Madison	7,481	5,523	Tupper Lake	5,271	2,508	Urbana	7,742	7,621
Manville	5,441		Waverly	5,662	5,270	Van Wert	8,472	8,100
Metuchen	5,748	3,334	Wellsville	5,674	4,996	Wadsworth	5,930	4,742
Newton	5,401	4,125	Whitehall	5,191	5,258	Wapakoneta	5,378	5,295
North Arlington	8,263	1,767				Washington Court House	8,426	7,962
North Plainfield	9,760	6,916	**NORTH CAROLINA**			Wellston	5,319	6,687
Ocean City	5,525	2,512	Asheboro	5,021	2,559	Wellsville	7,956	8,849
Palisades Park	7,065	2,633	Burlington	9,737	5,952	Wilmington	5,332	5,037
Paulsboro	7,121	4,352	Canton	5,117	2,584			
Pennsgrove	5,895	6,060	Greenville	9,194	5,772	**OKLAHOMA**		
Pitman	5,411	3,385	Henderson	6,345	5,222			
Princeton	6,992	5,917	Hendersonville	5,070	3,720	Altus	8,439	4,522
Prospect Park	5,909	4,292	Hickory	7,363	5,076	Alva	5,121	3,913
Roselle Park	8,960	5,438	Kings Mountain	5,632	2,800	Anadarko	5,036	3,116
Salem	8,047	7,435	Lenoir	6,532	3,718	Blackwell	9,521	7,174
Sayreville	8,658	7,181	Lexington	9,652	5,254	Bristow	6,619	3,460
Secaucus	8,950	5,423	Monroe	6,100	4,084	Clinton	7,512	2,596
Somerville	8,255	6,718	Mooresville	5,619	4,315	Cushing	9,301	6,326
South Amboy	8,476	7,897	Morganton	6,001	2,867	Duncan	8,363	3,463
South Plainfield	5,047		Mount Airy	6,045	4,752	Durant	7,463	7,340
Tenafly	5,669	3,585	Reidsville	6,851	5,333	Elk City	5,666	2,814
Ventnor	6,674	2,193	Tarboro	6,379	4,568	El Reno	9,384	7,737
			Washington	7,035	6,314	Guthrie	9,582	11,757

* Classified as urban under special rule. See p. 7.

38 POPULATION—UNITED STATES SUMMARY

TABLE 14.—POPULATION OF CITIES AND OTHER URBAN PLACES HAVING, IN 1930, FROM 5,000 TO 10,000 INHABITANTS: 1930 AND 1920—Continued

CITY OR OTHER URBAN PLACE	1930	1920
OKLAHOMA—con.		
Henryetta	7,694	5,889
Holdenville	7,268	2,932
Hugo	5,272	6,368
Miami	8,064	6,802
Norman	9,603	5,004
Pawhuska	5,931	6,414
Picher	7,773	9,676
Sand Springs	6,674	4,076
Stillwater	7,016	4,701
Woodward	5,056	3,849
OREGON		
Albany	5,325	4,840
Baker	7,858	7,729
Bend	8,848	5,415
Corvallis	7,585	5,752
La Grande	8,050	6,913
Marshfield	5,287	4,034
Oregon City	5,761	5,686
Pendleton	6,621	6,837
The Dalles	5,883	5,807
PENNSYLVANIA		
Archbald	9,587	8,603
Ashland	7,164	6,666
Ashley	7,093	6,520
Avalon	5,940	5,277
Bangor	5,824	5,402
Beaver	5,665	4,135
Blairsville	5,296	4,391
Blakely	8,260	6,564
Bloomsburg	9,093	7,819
Brackenridge	6,250	4,987
Brentwood	5,381	1,695
Bridgeport	5,595	4,680
Centerville	6,467	4,793
Clearfield	9,221	8,529
Clifton Heights	5,057	3,469
Coaldale	6,921	6,336
Collingdale	7,857	3,834
Corry	7,152	7,228
Crafton	7,004	5,954
Danville	7,185	6,952
Darby	9,899	7,922
Dupont	5,161	4,576
Duryea	8,503	7,776
East Pittsburgh	6,214	6,527
East Stroudsburg	6,099	4,855
Edwardsville	8,847	9,027
Emaus	6,419	4,370
Etna	7,493	6,341
Exeter	5,724	4,176
Ford City	6,127	5,605
Forest City	5,209	6,004
Forty Fort	6,224	3,389
Frackville	8,034	5,590
Freeland	7,098	6,666
Gettysburg	5,584	4,439
Glassport	8,390	6,959
Greenville	8,028	8,101
Grove City	6,156	4,944
Hollidaysburg	5,969	4,071
Honesdale	5,490	2,756
Huntingdon	7,558	7,051
Indiana	9,569	7,043
Jersey Shore	5,781	6,103
Kane	6,232	7,283
Kittanning	7,808	7,153
Kulpmont	6,120	4,695
Lansdale	8,379	4,728
Lansdowne	9,542	4,797
Lansford	9,632	9,025
Larksville	9,322	9,438
PENNSYLVANIA—continued		
Lehighton	6,490	6,102
Lock Haven	9,608	8,557
Luzerne	6,950	5,998
McAdoo	5,239	4,674
Mechanicsburg	5,647	4,688
Media	5,372	4,109
Middletown	6,085	5,920
Midland	6,007	5,452
Millvale	8,166	8,031
Milton	8,552	8,638
Minersville	9,392	7,845
Monongahela City	8,675	8,688
Morrisville	5,368	3,639
Mount Oliver	7,071	5,575
Mount Pleasant	5,869	5,802
Nanty-Glo	5,598	5,028
Nazareth	5,505	4,288
New Brighton	9,950	9,361
Northampton	9,839	9,349
Oakmont	6,027	4,512
Palmerton	7,678	7,168
Parnassus	6,240	3,816
Pitcairn	6,317	5,738
Punxsutawney	9,266	10,311
Rankin	7,956	7,301
Ridgway	6,313	6,037
Rochester	7,726	6,957
St. Clair	7,296	6,495
St. Marys	7,433	6,967
Sayre	7,902	8,078
Schuylkill Haven	6,514	5,437
Scottdale	6,714	5,768
Sewickley	5,599	4,955
Sharpsburg	8,642	8,921
Sharpsville	5,194	4,674
South Brownsville	5,314	4,675
South Williamsport	6,058	4,341
Stroudsburg	5,961	5,278
Summit Hill	5,567	5,499
Swoyerville	9,133	6,876
Tarentum	9,551	8,925
Throop	8,027	6,672
Titusville	8,055	8,432
Tyrone	9,042	9,084
West Hazleton	7,310	5,854
West Pittston	7,940	6,968
West View	6,028	2,797
West York	5,381	3,320
Wilmerding	6,291	6,441
Wilson	8,265	------
Windber	9,205	9,462
Winton	8,508	7,583
Yeadon	5,430	1,308
RHODE ISLAND		
Barrington town*	5,162	3,897
Burrillville town*	7,677	8,606
Johnston town*	9,357	6,855
Warren town*	7,974	7,841
SOUTH CAROLINA		
Aiken	6,033	4,103
Camden	5,183	3,930
Chester	5,528	5,557
Clinton	5,643	3,767
Darlington	5,556	4,609
Gaffney	6,827	5,065
Georgetown	5,082	4,579
Hartsville	5,067	3,624
Laurens	5,443	4,629
Newberry	7,298	5,894
Orangeburg	8,776	7,290
Union	7,419	6,141
SOUTH DAKOTA		
Lead	5,733	5,013
Yankton	6,072	5,024
TENNESSEE		
Alcoa	5,255	3,358
Athens	5,385	2,580
Clarksville	9,242	8,110
Cleveland	9,136	6,522
Columbia	7,882	5,526
Dyersburg	8,733	6,444
Elizabethton	8,093	2,749
Greeneville	5,544	3,775
Morristown	7,305	5,875
Murfreesboro	7,993	5,367
Paris	8,164	4,730
Shelbyville	5,010	2,912
Springfield	5,577	3,860
Union City	5,865	4,412
TEXAS		
Bonham	5,655	6,008
Borger	6,532	---
Breckenridge	7,569	1,846
Brenham	5,974	5,066
Bryan	7,814	6,307
Childress	7,163	5,003
Cisco	6,027	7,422
Coleman	6,078	2,868
Crystal City	6,609	(1)
Denton	9,587	7,626
Eagle Pass	5,059	5,765
Electra	6,712	4,744
Ennis	7,069	7,224
Gainesville	8,915	8,648
Goose Creek	5,208	---
Highland Park	8,422	2,321
Hillsboro	7,823	6,952
Huntsville	5,028	4,689
Jacksonville	6,748	3,723
Kingsville	6,815	4,770
Longview	5,036	5,713
Lufkin	7,311	4,878
Luling	5,970	1,502
McAllen	9,074	5,331
McKinney	7,307	6,677
Marlin	5,338	4,310
Mercedes	6,608	3,414
Mexia	6,579	3,482
Midland	5,484	1,795
Mineral Wells	5,986	7,890
Mission	5,120	3,847
Nacogdoches	5,687	3,546
Navasota	5,128	5,060
New Braunfels	6,242	3,590
Orange	7,913	9,212
Plainview	8,834	3,989
Ranger	6,208	16,205
San Marcos	5,134	4,527
Seguin	5,225	3,631
Sulphur Springs	5,417	5,558
Taylor	7,463	5,965
Terrell	8,795	8,349
Uvalde	5,286	3,885
Vernon	9,137	5,142
Victoria	7,421	5,957
Waxahachie	8,042	7,958
Yoakum	5,656	6,184
UTAH		
Brigham	5,093	5,282
Logan	9,979	9,439
Murray	5,172	4,584
Tooele	5,135	3,602

* Classified as urban under special rule. See p. 7.
1 Not returned separately.

URBAN PLACES   39

TABLE 14.—POPULATION OF CITIES AND OTHER URBAN PLACES HAVING, IN 1930, FROM 5,000 TO 10,000 INHABITANTS: 1930 AND 1920—Continued

CITY OR OTHER URBAN PLACE	1930	1920	CITY OR OTHER URBAN PLACE	1930	1920	CITY OR OTHER URBAN PLACE	1930	1920
VERMONT			**WEST VIRGINIA**			**WISCONSIN—con.**		
Bennington	7,390	7,230	Beckley	9,357	4,149	Monroe	5,015	4,788
Brattleboro	8,709	7,324	Elkins	7,345	6,788	Neenah	9,151	7,171
Montpelier	7,837	7,125	Grafton	7,737	8,517	Oconto	5,030	4,920
Newport	5,094	4,976	Hinton[3]	6,654	3,912	Portage	6,308	5,582
St. Albans	8,020	7,588	Keyser	6,248	6,003	Rhinelander	8,019	6,654
St. Johnsbury	7,920	7,164	Princeton	6,955	6,224	Rice Lake	5,177	4,457
Winooski	5,308	4,932	Richwood	5,720	4,331	Waupun	5,708	4,440
			South Charleston	5,904	3,650	Whitefish Bay	5,362	882
VIRGINIA			Welch	5,376	3,232	Wisconsin Rapids	8,726	7,243
Clifton Forge	6,839	6,164	Wellsburg	6,398	4,918			
Covington	6,538	5,623	Weston	8,646	5,701	**WYOMING**		
Fredericksburg	6,819	5,882	Williamson	9,410	6,819			
Hampton	6,382	6,138				Laramie	8,609	6,301
Harrisonburg	7,232	5,875	**WISCONSIN**			Rock Springs	8,440	6,456
Martinsville	7,705	4,075				Sheridan	8,536	9,175
Pulaski	7,168	5,282	Antigo	8,610	8,451			
Radford	6,227	4,627	Baraboo	5,545	5,538			
South Norfolk	7,857	7,724	Beaver Dam	9,867	7,992			
Waynesboro[2]	6,226	1,594	Chippewa Falls	9,539	9,130			
			De Pere	5,521	5,165			
WASHINGTON			Fort Atkinson	5,793	4,915			
Anacortes	6,564	5,284	Kaukauna	6,581	5,951			
Centralia	8,058	7,549	Marshfield	8,778	7,394			
Kelso	6,260	2,228	Menasha	9,062	7,214			
Puyallup	7,094	6,323	Menomonie	5,595	5,104			
			Merrill	8,458	8,068			

[2] Basic City and Waynesboro towns consolidated as Waynesboro town in 1923. Combined population in 1920, 3,806.

[3] Avis town and Hinton city consolidated as Hinton city in 1927. Combined population in 1920, 5,547.

40 POPULATION—UNITED STATES SUMMARY

TABLE 15.—POPULATION OF CITIES AND OTHER URBAN PLACES HAVING, IN 1930, FROM 2,500 TO 5,000 INHABITANTS: 1930 AND 1920

[See headnote to Table 12]

CITY OR OTHER URBAN PLACE	1930	1920	CITY OR OTHER URBAN PLACE	1930	1920	CITY OR OTHER URBAN PLACE	1930	1920
ALABAMA			**CALIFORNIA—con.**			**DELAWARE**		
Albertville	2,716	1,666	Azusa	4,808	2,460	Dover	4,800	4,042
Alexander City	4,519	2,293	Banning	2,752	1,810	Milford	3,719	2,703
Athens	4,238	3,323	Benicia	2,913	2,693	Newark	3,899	2,183
Atmore	3,035	1,775	Chino	3,118	2,132	New Castle	4,131	3,854
Attalla	4,585	3,462	Chula Vista	3,869	1,718			
Auburn	2,800	2,143	Claremont	2,719	1,728	**FLORIDA**		
Brewton	2,818	2,682	Coalinga	2,851	2,934	Apalachicola	3,150	3,066
Carbon Hill	2,519	2,666	Covina	2,774	1,999	Arcadia	4,082	3,479
Cullman	2,786	2,467	Delano	2,632	805	Avon Park	3,355	890
Demopolis	4,037	2,779	Dinuba	2,968	3,400	De Funiak Springs	2,636	2,097
Elba	2,523	1,681	Dunsmuir	2,610	2,528	Eustis	2,835	1,193
Enterprise	3,702	3,013	El Cerrito	3,870	1,505	Fernandina	3,023	3,147
Florala	2,580	2,633	El Monte	3,479	1,253	Fort Pierce	4,803	2,115
Fort Payne	3,375	2,025	El Segundo	3,503	1,563	Haines City	3,037	651
Greenville	3,985	3,471	Escondido	3,421	1,789	Hialeah	2,600	-----
Guntersville	2,826	1,909	Exeter	2,685	1,852	Hollywood	2,869	-----
Jacksonville	2,840	2,395	Fillmore	2,893	1,597	Kissimmee	3,163	2,722
Leeds	2,529	1,600	Fort Bragg	3,022	2,616	Lake City	4,416	3,341
Opp	2,918	1,556	Gilroy	3,502	2,862	Lake Wales	3,401	796
Ozark	3,103	2,518	Glendora	2,761	2,028	Leesburg	4,113	1,835
Piedmont	3,668	2,645	Grass Valley	3,817	4,006	Live Oak	2,734	3,103
Prichard	4,580	-----	Hermosa Beach	4,796	2,327	Manatee	3,219	1,076
Roanoke	4,373	3,841	Hollister	3,757	2,781	Marianna	3,372	2,499
Russellville	3,146	2,269	Huntington Beach	3,690	1,687	Melbourne	2,677	533
Sylacauga	4,115	2,141	La Mesa	2,513	1,004	New Smyrna	4,149	2,007
Tuscumbia	4,533	3,855	La Verne	2,860	1,698	Palmetto	3,043	2,046
Tuskegee	3,314	2,475	Lindsay	3,878	2,576	Perry	2,744	1,956
Union Springs	2,875	4,125	Livermore	3,119	1,916	Pompano	2,614	636
			Lompoc	2,845	1,876	Quincy	3,788	3,118
ARIZONA			Los Gatos	3,168	2,317	Sebring	2,912	812
			Madera	4,665	3,444	Tarpon Springs	3,414	2,105
Flagstaff	3,891	3,186	Mill Valley	4,164	2,554	Wauchula	2,574	2,081
Glendale	3,665	2,737	Mountain View	3,308	1,888	Winter Park	3,686	1,078
Jerome	4,932	4,030	Needles	3,144	2,807			
Mesa	3,711	3,036	Oceanside	3,508	1,161	**GEORGIA**		
Winslow	3,917	3,730	Oroville	3,698	3,340	Barnesville	3,236	3,059
Yuma	4,892	4,237	Paso Robles	2,573	1,919	Buford	3,357	2,500
			Red Bluff	3,517	3,104	Cairo	3,169	1,908
ARKANSAS			Redding	4,188	2,962	Canton	2,892	2,679
			Reedley	2,589	2,447	Commerce	3,002	2,459
Arkadelphia	3,380	3,311	San Anselmo	4,650	2,475	Covington	3,203	3,203
Batesville	4,484	4,299	San Bruno	3,610	1,562	Cuthbert	3,235	3,022
Benton	3,445	2,933	Sanger	2,967	2,578	Dawson	3,827	3,504
Brinkley	3,046	2,714	San Marino	3,730	584	Douglas	4,206	3,401
Clarksville	3,031	2,127	Sausalito	3,667	2,790	Eastman	3,022	2,707
Crossett	2,811	2,707	Selma	3,047	3,158	East Thomaston	3,061	1,058
De Queen	2,938	2,517	Sierra Madre	3,550	2,026	Elberton	4,650	6,475
Dermott	2,942	2,330	Signal Hill	2,932	-----	Fort Valley	4,560	3,223
Fordyce	3,206	2,996	Sunnyvale	3,094	1,675	Hapeville	4,224	1,631
Forrest City	4,594	3,377	Taft	3,442	3,317	Lafayette	2,811	2,104
Harrison	3,626	3,477	Tracy	3,829	2,450	Manchester	3,745	2,776
McGehee	3,488	2,868	Turlock	4,276	3,394	Millen	2,527	2,405
Magnolia	3,008	2,158	Ukiah	3,124	2,305	Monroe	3,706	3,211
Marianna	4,314	5,074	Upland	4,713	2,912	Pelham	2,762	2,640
Mena	3,118	3,441	Willow Glen	4,167	-----	Porterdale	3,002	2,880
Monticello	2,076	2,378	Yuba City	3,605	1,708	Quitman	4,149	4,393
Morrilton	4,043	3,010				Rockmart	3,264	1,400
Newport	4,547	3,771	**COLORADO**			Rossville	3,230	1,427
Osceola	2,573	1,755				Sandersville	3,011	2,695
Paris	3,234	1,740	Brighton	3,394	2,715	Statesboro	3,996	3,807
Prescott	3,033	2,691	Delta	2,938	2,623	Thomaston	4,922	2,502
Rogers	3,554	3,318	Fort Morgan	4,423	3,818	Tifton	3,390	3,005
Searcy	3,387	2,836	Lamar	4,233	2,512	Toccoa	4,602	3,567
Smackover	2,544	-----	Las Animas	2,517	2,252	Trion	3,289	1,588
Springdale	2,763	2,263	Leadville	3,771	4,959	Vidalia	3,535	2,860
Stamps	2,705	2,564	Monte Vista	2,610	2,484	Washington	3,158	4,208
Stuttgart	4,927	4,522	Montrose	3,566	3,581	Waynesboro	3,922	3,311
Trumann	2,095	2,598	Rocky Ford	3,426	3,746	Winder	3,283	3,335
Warren	2,523	2,145						
West Helena	4,489	6,226	**CONNECTICUT**			**IDAHO**		
Wynne	3,505	2,933	Danielson	4,210	3,130	Blackfoot	3,199	3,937
			Groton	4,122	4,236	Burley	3,826	5,408
CALIFORNIA			Jewett City	4,436	3,196	Caldwell	4,974	5,106
Antioch	3,563	1,936	Stafford Springs	3,492	3,383			
Auburn	2,661	2,289						

TABLE 15.—POPULATION OF CITIES AND OTHER URBAN PLACES HAVING, IN 1930, FROM 2,500 TO 5,000 INHABITANTS: 1930 AND 1920—Continued

CITY OR OTHER URBAN PLACE	1930	1920	CITY OR OTHER URBAN PLACE	1930	1920	CITY OR OTHER URBAN PLACE	1930	1920
IDAHO—con.			**ILLINOIS—con.**			**IOWA—con.**		
Emmett	2,763	2,204	Sparta	3,385	3,340	Jefferson	3,431	3,416
Kellogg	4,124	3,017	Staunton	4,618	6,027	Knoxville	4,607	3,523
Malad	2,535	2,598	Steger	2,985	2,304	Le Mars	4,788	4,683
Moscow	4,476	3,956	Sycamore	4,021	3,602	Manchester	3,413	3,111
Payette	2,618	2,433	Tuscola	2,569	2,564	Maquoketa	3,595	3,626
Preston	3,381	3,235	Vandalia	4,342	3,316	Marion	4,348	4,133
Rexburg	3,048	3,569	Virden	3,011	4,682	Missouri Valley	4,230	3,985
St. Anthony	2,778	2,957	Washington Park	3,837	1,516	Mount Pleasant	3,743	3,987
Sandpoint	3,290	2,876	Watseka	3,144	2,817	Nevada	3,133	2,668
Wallace	3,634	2,816	West Chicago	3,477	2,594	Onawa	2,538	2,256
Weiser	2,724	3,154	Western Springs	3,894	1,258	Osage	2,964	2,878
			Westmont	2,733	-----	Osceola	2,871	2,684
ILLINOIS			Westville	3,901	4,241	Pella	3,326	3,838
			White Hall	2,928	2,954	Sac City	2,854	2,630
Abingdon	2,771	2,721	Zeigler	3,816	2,338	Sheldon	3,320	3,488
Anna	3,436	3,019				Storm Lake	4,157	3,658
Arlington Heights	4,997	2,250	**INDIANA**			Tama	2,626	2,601
Barrington	3,213	1,743				Valley Junction	4,280	3,631
Bellwood	4,991	1,881	Alexandria	4,408	4,172	Vinton	3,372	3,381
Benld	2,980	3,316	Angola	2,665	2,650	Washington	4,814	4,697
Bradley	3,048	2,128	Attica	3,700	3,392	Waukon	2,526	2,359
Bushnell	2,850	2,716	Aurora	4,386	4,299	Waverly	3,652	3,352
Carlinville	4,144	5,212	Batesville	2,838	2,361	Winterset	2,921	2,906
Carmi	2,932	2,667	Beech Grove	3,552	1,459			
Carterville	2,866	3,404	Boonville	4,208	4,451	**KANSAS**		
Chester	3,922	2,904	Columbia City	3,805	3,499			
Christopher	4,244	3,830	Crown Point	4,046	3,232	Anthony	2,947	2,740
Crystal Lake	3,732	2,249	Dunkirk	2,583	2,532	Augusta	4,033	4,219
Dolton	2,923	2,076	Garrett	4,428	4,796	Baxter Springs	4,541	3,608
Dwight	2,534	2,255	Gas City	3,087	2,870	Beloit	3,502	3,315
East Alton	4,502	1,669	Greencastle	4,613	3,780	Caney	2,794	3,427
Effingham	4,978	4,024	Greenfield	4,188	4,168	Cherryvale	4,251	4,698
Eldorado	4,482	5,004	Huntingburg	3,440	3,261	Clay Center	4,386	3,715
Fairfield	3,280	2,754	Jasonville	3,536	4,461	Columbus	3,225	3,155
Flora	4,393	3,553	Jasper	3,905	2,539	Council Grove	2,898	2,857
Fulton	2,656	2,445	Lawrenceburg	4,072	3,466	Eureka	3,698	2,606
Galena	3,878	4,742	Martinsville	4,962	4,895	Fredonia	3,446	3,954
Galva	2,875	2,974	Mitchell	3,226	3,025	Galena	4,736	4,712
Geneseo	3,406	3,375	Nappanee	2,957	2,678	Garnett	2,768	2,329
Geneva	4,607	3,327	Noblesville	4,811	4,758	Goodland	3,626	2,664
Georgetown	3,407	3,061	North Manchester	2,765	2,711	Hays	4,618	3,165
Greenville	3,233	3,091	North Vernon	2,989	3,084	Herington	4,519	4,065
Harvard	2,988	3,294	Oakland City	2,842	2,270	Hiawatha	3,302	3,222
Havana	3,451	3,614	Petersburg	2,609	2,367	Hoisington	3,001	2,395
Highland	3,319	2,902	Rensselaer	2,798	2,912	Holton	2,705	2,703
Highwood	3,500	1,446	Rochester	3,518	3,720	Horton	4,049	4,009
Hillsboro	4,435	5,074	Salem	3,194	2,836	Humboldt	2,558	2,525
Homewood	3,227	1,389	Tell City	4,873	4,086	Kingman	2,752	2,407
Jerseyville	4,309	3,839	Tipton	4,861	4,507	Larned	3,532	3,139
Kenilworth	2,501	1,188	Union City	[1]3,084	3,406	Lyons	2,939	2,516
La Grange Park	2,939	1,654	West Terre Haute	3,588	4,310	Marysville	4,013	3,048
Lansing	3,378	1,409	Winchester	4,487	4,021	Neodesha	3,381	3,943
Lemont	2,582	2,322				Norton	2,767	2,186
Libertyville	3,791	2,125	**IOWA**			Olathe	3,656	3,268
Lockport	3,383	2,684	Albia	4,425	5,067	Osawatomie	4,440	3,293
Lyons	4,787	2,564	Algona	3,985	3,724	Paola	3,762	3,238
Marseilles	4,292	3,391	Anamosa	3,579	2,881			
Mendota	4,008	3,934	Belle Plaine	3,239	3,887	**KENTUCKY**		
Morrison	3,067	3,000	Bettendorf	2,768	2,178			
Mound City	2,548	2,756	Carroll	4,691	4,254	Central City	4,321	3,108
Mount Olive	3,079	3,503	Clarinda	4,962	4,511	Clifton	3,080	2,065
Oglesby	3,910	4,135	Clarion	2,578	2,826	Cumberland	2,639	300
Paxton	2,892	3,033	Clear Lake	3,066	2,804	Cynthiana	4,386	3,857
Peoria Heights	3,279	1,111	Cresco	3,069	3,195	Earlington	3,309	3,652
Phoenix	3,033	1,933	Decorah	4,581	4,039	Elizabethtown	2,590	2,530
Pinckneyville	3,046	2,649	Denison	3,905	3,581	Elsmere	2,917	919
Princeton	4,762	4,126	Eagle Grove	4,071	4,433	Franklin	3,056	3,154
Riverdale	2,504	1,166	Eldora	3,200	3,189	Fulton	3,502	3,415
River Grove	2,741	484	Emmetsburg	2,865	2,762	Georgetown	4,229	3,903
Robinson	3,668	3,375	Estherville	4,940	4,699	Harlan	4,327	2,647
Rochelle	3,785	3,310	Glenwood	4,269	3,862	Harrodsburg	4,029	3,765
Rock Falls	3,893	2,927	Grinnell	4,949	5,362	Irvine	3,640	2,705
Roodhouse	2,621	2,928	Hampton	3,473	2,992	Lebanon	3,248	3,239
Salem	4,420	3,457	Harlan	3,145	2,831	Morganfield	2,551	2,651
Sandwich	2,611	2,409	Independence	3,691	3,672	Mount Sterling	4,350	3,995
Shelbyville	3,491	3,568	Indianola	3,488	3,628	Murray	2,891	2,415
Silvis	2,650	2,541	Iowa Falls	4,112	3,954	Nicholasville	3,128	2,786

[1] Combined population of Union City, Ind., and Union City, Ohio, 4,389 in 1930.

42   POPULATION—UNITED STATES SUMMARY

TABLE 15.—POPULATION OF CITIES AND OTHER URBAN PLACES HAVING, IN 1930, FROM 2,500 TO 5,000 INHABITANTS: 1930 AND 1920—Continued

CITY OR OTHER URBAN PLACE	1930	1920	CITY OR OTHER URBAN PLACE	1930	1920	CITY OR OTHER URBAN PLACE	1930	1920
KENTUCKY—con.			**MICHIGAN**			**MINNESOTA—con.**		
Pikeville	3,376	2,110	Allegan	3,941	3,637	Sauk Rapids	2,656	2,349
Pineville	3,567	2,908	Belding	4,140	3,911	Sleepy Eye	2,576	2,449
Princeton	4,764	3,689	Bessemer	4,035	5,482	Staples	2,667	2,570
Providence	4,742	4,151	Big Rapids	4,671	4,558	Thief River Falls	4,268	4,685
Russellville	3,297	3,124	Boyne City	2,650	4,284	Tracy	2,570	2,463
Shelbyville	4,033	3,760	Buchanan	3,922	3,187	Two Harbors	4,425	4,546
LOUISIANA			Caro	2,554	2,704	Wadena	2,512	2,186
			Centerline	2,604	------	Waseca	3,815	3,908
Abbeville	4,356	3,461	Cheboygan	4,923	5,642	West St. Paul	4,463	2,962
Amite	2,536	1,854	Clawson	3,377	------	White Bear Lake	2,600	2,022
Bossier City	4,003	1,094	Crystal Falls	2,995	3,394	Worthington	3,878	3,481
Covington	3,208	2,942	Durand	3,081	2,672			
De Quincy	3,589	1,823	East Grand Rapids	4,024	1,310	**MISSISSIPPI**		
De Ridder	3,747	3,535	East Lansing	4,389	1,889			
Donaldsonville	3,788	3,745	Eaton Rapids	2,822	2,379	Aberdeen	3,925	4,071
Eunice	3,597	3,272	Fenton	3,171	2,507	Amory	3,214	2,861
Ferriday	2,502	1,044	Grand Ledge	3,572	3,043	Bay St. Louis	3,724	3,033
Franklin	3,271	3,504	Greenville	4,730	4,304	Belzoni	2,735	2,277
Haynesville	2,541	903	Grosse Pointe Farms	3,533	1,649	Canton	4,725	3,252
Homer	2,909	3,305	Houghton	3,757	4,466	Cleveland	3,240	1,674
Jackson	3,966	2,320	Howell	3,615	2,951	Columbia	4,833	2,826
Jennings	4,036	3,824	Inkster	4,440	------	Grenada	4,349	3,402
Lake Providence	2,867	1,917	Iron River	4,665	4,295	Indianola	3,116	2,112
Leesville	3,291	2,518	Laurium	4,916	6,696	Kosciusko	3,237	2,258
Mansfield	3,837	2,564	Marine City	3,462	3,731	Lexington	2,590	1,792
Merryville	2,626	2,963	Mason	2,575	1,879	Louisville	3,013	1,777
Natchitoches	4,547	3,388	Melvindale	4,053	------	New Albany	3,187	2,531
Oakdale	3,188	4,016	Munising	3,956	5,037	Oxford	2,890	2,150
Pineville	3,612	2,188	Northville	2,566	1,738	Pascagoula	4,339	6,082
Ponchatoula	2,898	955	Norway	4,016	4,533	Pass Christian	3,004	2,357
Rayne	3,710	2,720	Otsego	3,245	3,168	Philadelphia	2,560	1,669
Ruston	4,400	3,389	Pleasant Ridge	2,885	472	Picayune	4,698	2,479
Slidell	2,807	2,958	Plymouth	4,484	2,857	Starkville	3,612	2,596
Tallulah	3,332	1,316	Rochester	3,554	2,549	Water Valley	3,738	4,315
Thibodaux	4,442	3,526	Rogers City	3,278	2,109	West Point	4,677	4,400
Westwego	3,987	(1)	St. Clair	3,389	3,204	Winona	2,607	2,572
Winnfield	3,721	2,975	St. Johns	3,929	3,925			
MAINE			South Haven	4,804	3,829	**MISSOURI**		
Belfast	4,993	5,083	Trenton	4,022	1,682			
Eastport	3,466	4,494	Wakefield	3,677	4,151	Aurora	3,875	3,575
Ellsworth	3,557	3,058	Wayne	3,423	1,899	Bonne Terre	4,021	3,815
Fairfield	3,529	2,747	Zeeland	2,850	2,275	Brentwood	2,819	------
Fort Fairfield	2,616	1,993				Butler	2,706	2,702
Hallowell	2,675	2,764	**MINNESOTA**			Cameron	3,507	3,248
Madison	3,036	2,729				Carrollton	4,058	3,218
Presque Isle	4,662	3,452	Alexandria	3,876	3,388	Caruthersville	4,781	4,750
			Anoka	4,851	4,287	Chaffee	2,902	3,035
MARYLAND			Bayport	2,590	1,936	Charleston	3,357	3,410
Brunswick	3,671	3,905	Blue Earth	2,884	2,568	Crystal City	3,057	2,243
Chestertown	2,809	2,537	Crosby	3,451	3,500	Dexter	2,714	2,635
Crisfield	3,850	4,116	Detroit Lakes	3,675	3,426	Eldon	3,171	2,636
Easton	4,092	3,442	East Grand Forks	2,922	2,490	Excelsior Springs	4,565	4,165
Elkton	3,331	2,660	Edina	3,138	1,833	Farmington	3,001	2,685
Havre de Grace	3,985	4,377	Gilbert	2,722	3,510	Fayette	2,630	2,381
Hyattsville	4,264	2,675	Grand Rapids	3,206	2,914	Ferguson	3,798	1,874
Laurel	2,532	2,239	Hopkins	3,834	3,055	Festus	4,085	3,348
Mount Rainier	3,832	2,462	Hutchinson	3,406	3,379	Fredericktown	2,954	3,124
Pocomoke City	2,609	2,444	Lake City	3,210	2,846	Higginsville	3,339	2,724
Westernport	3,440	3,977	Litchfield	2,880	2,790	Kennett	4,128	3,622
Westminster	4,463	3,521	Luverne	2,644	2,782	Lebanon	3,562	2,848
			Marshall	4,250	3,092	Lexington	4,595	4,695
MASSACHUSETTS			Montevideo	4,319	4,419	Liberty	3,516	3,097
Ayer town*	3,060	3,052	Nashwauk	2,555	2,414	Louisiana	3,549	4,060
Blackstone town*	4,674	4,299	Northfield	4,153	4,023	Macon	3,851	3,549
Dalton town*	4,220	3,752	North Mankato	2,822	1,840	Marceline	3,555	3,760
Dudley town*	4,265	3,701	North St. Paul	2,915	1,979	Monett	4,099	4,206
Hopedale town*	2,973	2,777	Pipestone	3,489	3,325	Neosho	4,485	3,968
Lee town*	4,061	4,085	Proctorknott	2,521	2,378	North Kansas City	2,574	870
Longmeadow town*	4,437	2,618	Redwood Falls	2,552	2,421	Perryville	2,964	1,763
Nantucket town*	3,678	2,797	Richfield	3,344	2,411	Richmond	4,129	4,409
Provincetown town*	3,808	4,246	Robbinsdale	4,427	1,369	Rolla	3,670	2,077
Rockport town*	3,630	3,878	St. James	2,808	2,673	Ste. Genevieve	2,662	2,046
			St. Louis Park	4,710	2,281	Slater	3,478	3,797
			St. Peter	4,811	4,335	West Plains	3,335	3,178
			Sauk Center	2,716	2,699			

* Classified as urban under special rule. See p. 7.
[1] Not returned separately.

URBAN PLACES 43

TABLE 15.—POPULATION OF CITIES AND OTHER URBAN PLACES HAVING, IN 1930, FROM 2,500 TO 5,000 INHABITANTS: 1930 AND 1920—Continued

CITY OR OTHER URBAN PLACE	1930	1920	CITY OR OTHER URBAN PLACE	1930	1920	CITY OR OTHER URBAN PLACE	1930	1920
MONTANA			**NEW JERSEY—con.**			**NEW YORK—con.**		
Deer Lodge	3,510	3,780	Midland Park	3,638	2,243	Hoosick Falls	4,755	4,896
Glendive	4,629	3,816	Milltown	2,994	2,573	Irvington	3,067	2,701
Laurel	2,558	2,239	New Milford	2,556	-----	Lake Placid	2,930	2,099
Red Lodge	3,026	4,515	Northfield	2,804	1,127	Lawrence	3,041	2,861
Roundup	2,577	2,434	Oaklyn	3,843	1,148	Le Roy	4,474	4,203
Whitefish	2,803	2,867	Palmyra	4,968	-----	Liberty	3,427	2,459
			Paramus	2,649	-----	Lindenhurst	4,040	-----
NEBRASKA			Pompton Lakes	3,104	2,008	Lowville	3,424	3,127
			Ramsey	3,258	2,090	Lyons	3,956	4,253
Auburn	3,068	2,863	Raritan	4,751	4,457	Mohawk	2,835	2,919
Aurora	2,715	2,962	Ridgefield	4,671	1,560	Monticello	3,450	2,330
Blair	2,791	2,702	Rockaway	3,132	2,655	Mount Morris	3,238	3,312
Broken Bow	2,715	2,567	Totowa	4,600	1,864	New Hyde Park	3,314	-----
Chadron	4,606	4,412	Wanaque	3,119	2,916	New York Mills	4,006	-----
Crete	2,805	2,445	Washington	4,410	3,341	North Pelham	4,890	2,385
Gering	2,531	2,508	West Caldwell	2,911	1,085	Northport	2,528	1,977
Havelock	3,659	3,602	West Paterson	3,101	1,858	Owego	4,742	4,147
Holdrege	3,263	3,108	Westville	3,462	2,380	Palmyra	2,592	2,480
Lexington	2,962	2,327	Westwood	4,861	2,597	Pelham Manor	4,908	1,754
Plattsmouth	3,793	4,190	Wharton	3,683	2,877	Perry	4,231	4,717
Schuyler	2,588	2,636	Woodlynne	2,878	1,515	Pleasantville	4,540	3,590
Seward	2,737	2,368				Potsdam	4,136	4,039
Sidney	3,306	2,852	**NEW MEXICO**			Sag Harbor	2,773	2,993
South Sioux City	3,927	2,402				Saugerties	4,000	4,013
Superior	3,044	2,719	Alamogordo	3,096	2,363	Sea Cliff	3,456	2,108
Wahoo	2,689	2,338	Carlsbad	3,708	2,205	Silver Creek	3,160	3,260
Wymore	2,680	2,592	Clayton	2,518	2,157	Sloan	3,482	1,791
			Deming	3,377	3,212	Southampton	3,737	2,891
NEVADA			Las Vegas (city)	4,719	4,304	South Glens Falls	2,689	2,158
			Las Vegas (town)	4,378	3,902	Spring Valley	3,948	3,818
Elko	3,217	2,173	Portales	2,519	1,154	Springville	2,540	2,331
Ely	3,045	2,090	Silver City	3,519	2,662	Suffern	3,757	3,154
Sparks	4,508	3,238	Tucumcari	4,143	3,117	Ticonderoga	3,680	2,102
						Walden	4,283	5,493
NEW HAMPSHIRE			**NEW YORK**			Walton	3,496	3,598
						Wappingers Falls	3,336	3,235
Exeter town*	4,872	4,604	Albion	4,878	4,683	Warsaw	3,477	3,622
Littleton town*	4,558	4,239	Amityville	4,437	3,265	Waterford	2,921	2,637
Milford town*	4,068	3,783	Babylon	4,342	2,523	Waterloo	4,047	3,809
Newport town*	4,659	4,109	Baldwinsville	3,845	3,685	Watkins Glen	2,956	2,785
			Ballston Spa	4,591	4,103	Westfield	3,466	3,413
NEW JERSEY			Bath	4,015	3,720	West Haverstraw	2,834	2,018
			Brockport	3,511	2,980	Whitesboro	3,375	3,038
Belmar	3,491	1,987	Canajoharie	2,519	2,415	Williamsville	3,119	1,667
Bernardsville	3,336	-----	Canastota	4,235	3,995	Williston Park	4,427	-----
Beverly	2,864	2,562	Canisteo	2,548	2,201	Yorkville	3,406	1,512
Bloomingdale	2,543	2,193	Canton	2,822	2,522			
Bordentown	4,405	4,371	Carthage	4,460	4,320	**NORTH CAROLINA**		
Bradley Beach	3,306	2,307	Cobleskill	2,594	2,410			
Butler	3,392	2,886	Cooperstown	2,909	2,725	Albemarle	3,493	2,691
Cape May	2,637	2,999	Corinth	2,613	2,576	Beaufort	2,957	2,968
Chatham	3,869	2,421	Dannemora	3,348	2,623	Belmont	4,121	2,941
Clementon	2,605	-----	Dansville	4,928	4,631	Bessemer City	3,739	2,176
Closter	2,502	1,840	Dolgeville	3,309	3,448	Chapel Hill	2,699	1,483
East Newark	2,686	3,057	East Aurora	4,815	3,703	Cherryville	2,756	1,884
East Paterson	4,779	2,441	East Rockaway	4,340	2,005	Clinton	2,712	2,110
Edgewater	4,089	3,530	East Syracuse	4,646	4,106	Dunn	4,558	2,805
Egg Harbor	3,478	2,622	Ellenville	3,280	3,116	Edenton	3,563	2,777
Flemington	2,729	2,590	Elmsford	2,935	1,535	Forest City	4,069	2,312
Franklin	4,176	4,075	Fairport	4,604	4,626	Graham	2,972	2,366
Garwood	3,344	2,084	Falconer	3,579	2,742	Hamlet	4,801	3,808
Glassboro	4,799	-----	Farmingdale	3,373	2,091	Laurinburg	3,312	2,643
Glen Rock	4,369	2,181	Fort Edward	3,850	3,871	Lincolnton	3,781	3,390
Hackettstown	3,038	2,936	Fort Plain	2,725	2,747	Lumberton	4,140	2,691
Haledon	4,312	3,435	Frankfort	4,203	4,198	Morehead City	3,483	2,958
Hightstown	3,012	2,674	Goshen	2,891	2,843	Mount Olive	2,685	2,297
Hillsdale	2,959	-----	Gouverneur	4,015	4,143	Newton	4,394	3,021
Keyport	4,940	4,415	Gowanda	3,042	2,673	North Wilkesboro	3,668	2,363
Lambertville	4,518	4,660	Granville	3,483	3,024	Oxford	4,101	3,606
Lindenwold	2,523	-----	Great Neck	4,010	-----	Roanoke Rapids	3,404	3,369
Little Ferry	4,155	2,715	Green Island	4,331	4,411	Rockingham	2,906	2,509
Margate City	2,913	249	Greenport	3,062	3,122	Roxboro	3,657	1,651
Maywood	3,398	1,618	Hamburg	4,731	3,185	Sanford	4,253	2,977
Merchantville	3,592	2,749	Highland Falls	2,910	2,588	Smithfield	2,543	1,895
Middlesex	3,504	1,852	Homer	3,195	2,356	Southern Pines	2,524	743

* Classified as urban under special rule. See p. 7.

44   POPULATION—UNITED STATES SUMMARY

TABLE 15.—POPULATION OF CITIES AND OTHER URBAN PLACES HAVING, IN 1930,
FROM 2,500 TO 5,000 INHABITANTS: 1930 AND 1920—Continued

CITY OR OTHER URBAN PLACE	1930	1920	CITY OR OTHER URBAN PLACE	1930	1920	CITY OR OTHER URBAN PLACE	1930	1920
NORTH CAROLINA— continued			**OHIO—continued**			**PENNSYLVANIA— continued**		
Spencer	3,128	2,510	Willard	4,514	3,889	Castle Shannon	3,810	2,353
Spindale	3,066	-----	Willoughby	4,252	2,656	Catasauqua	4,851	4,714
Wadesboro	3,124	2,648	Wyoming	3,767	2,323	Clarion	3,201	2,793
Williamston	2,731	1,800				Clarks Summit	2,604	1,404
			OKLAHOMA			Clymer	2,672	2,867
NORTH DAKOTA						Coplay	3,279	2,845
			Chandler	2,717	2,226	Coudersport	2,740	2,836
Grafton	3,136	2,512	Claremore	3,720	3,435	Curwensville	3,140	2,973
Wahpeton	3,176	3,069	Cleveland	2,959	2,717	Dale	3,364	3,115
			Commerce	2,608	2,555	Dallastown	2,849	2,124
OHIO			Cordell	2,936	1,855	Derry	3,046	2,889
			Drumright	4,972	6,460	Downingtown	4,548	4,024
Amherst	2,844	2,485	Edmond	3,576	2,452	Doylestown	4,577	3,837
Barnesville	4,602	4,865	Frederick	4,568	3,822	East Conemaugh	4,979	5,256
Bridgeport	4,655	3,977	Hartshorne	3,587	3,480	East Lansdowne	3,168	1,561
Bryan	4,689	4,252	Hobart	4,982	2,936	East McKeesport	2,922	2,430
Byersville	2,638	2,775	Hollis	2,914	1,683	East Mauch		
Cadiz	2,597	2,084	Hominy	3,485	2,875	Chunk	3,739	3,868
Carey	2,722	2,488	Idabel	2,581	3,067	Ebensburg	3,063	2,179
Celina	4,664	4,226	Kingfisher	2,726	2,447	Edgewood	4,821	3,181
Chagrin Falls	2,739	2,237	Mangum	4,806	3,405	Elizabeth	2,939	2,703
Clyde	3,159	3,099	Marlow	3,084	2,276	Elizabethtown	3,940	3,319
Crestline	4,425	4,313	Maud	4,326	637	Emporium	2,929	3,036
Crooksville	3,251	3,311	Nowata	3,531	4,435	Emsworth	2,709	2,165
Deer Park	2,642	824	Okemah	4,002	2,162	Ephrata	4,988	3,735
Dennison	4,529	5,524	Pauls Valley	4,235	3,694	Ferndale	2,742	1,450
Eaton	3,347	3,210	Pawnee	2,562	2,418	Forest Hills	4,549	-----
Elmwood Place	4,562	3,991	Perry	4,206	3,154	Fountain Hill	4,568	2,339
Fairport Harbor	4,972	4,211	Poteau	3,169	2,679	Freedom	3,227	3,452
Fairview	3,689	642	Purcell	2,817	2,938	Freeport	2,772	2,696
Franklin	4,491	3,071	Sayre	3,157	1,703	Gallitzin	3,458	3,580
Geneva	3,791	3,081	Sulphur	4,242	3,667	Gilberton	4,227	4,766
Glouster	2,903	3,140	Tonkawa	3,311	1,443	Girardville	4,891	4,482
Greenfield	3,871	4,344	Vinita	4,263	5,010	Glenolden	4,482	1,944
Hillsboro	4,040	4,356	Wagoner	2,994	3,436	Greencastle	2,557	2,271
Hubbard	4,080	3,320	Wilson	2,517	2,286	Hamburg	3,637	2,764
Lebanon	3,222	3,396				Hatboro	2,651	1,102
Lisbon	3,405	3,113	**OREGON**			Hellertown	3,851	3,008
London	4,141	4,080				Hummelstown	3,036	2,654
Louisville	3,130	2,008	Ashland	4,544	4,283	Ingram	3,866	2,900
Lowellville	2,550	2,214	Burns	2,599	1,022	Irwin	3,443	3,235
Marysville Heights	3,639	3,635	Coquille	2,732	1,642	Jenkintown	4,797	3,366
Maumee	4,588	3,195	Dallas	2,975	2,701	Jermyn	3,519	3,326
Mayfield Heights	2,612	-----	Grants Pass	4,666	3,151	Johnsonburg	4,737	5,400
Medina	4,071	3,430	Hillsboro	3,039	2,468	Kennett Square	3,091	2,398
Middleport	3,505	3,772	Hood River	2,757	3,195	Kutztown	2,841	2,684
Minerva	2,675	2,261	McMinnville	2,917	2,767	Leechburg	4,489	3,991
Montpelier	3,677	3,052	Newberg	2,951	2,566	Leetsdale	2,774	2,311
Mount Healthy	3,530	2,255	North Bend	4,012	3,268	Lemoyne	4,171	1,939
Napoleon	4,545	4,143	Roseburg	4,362	4,258	Lewisburg	3,308	3,204
Newburgh Heights	4,152	2,957	St. Helens	3,994	2,220	Lititz	4,368	3,680
Newcomerstown	4,265	3,389	Tillamook	2,549	1,964	Lykens	3,033	2,880
New Lexington	3,901	3,157				McDonald	3,281	2,751
Newton Falls	3,458	1,100	**PENNSYLVANIA**			Manheim	3,520	2,712
North Canton	2,648	1,597				Marcus Hook	4,867	5,324
North College Hill	4,139	1,104	Ambler	3,944	3,094	Masontown	3,873	1,525
North Olmsted	2,624	1,419	Apollo	3,406	3,227	Mauch Chunk	3,206	3,666
Oberlin	4,292	4,236	Aspinwall	4,263	3,170	Mayfield	3,774	3,832
Orrville	4,427	4,107	Athens	4,372	4,384	Meyersdale	3,065	3,716
Oxford	2,588	2,146	Avoca	4,943	4,950	Millersburg	2,909	2,936
Perrysburg	3,182	2,429	Barnesboro	3,506	4,183	Monaca	4,641	3,838
Pomeroy	3,563	4,294	Bedford	2,953	2,330	Montoursville	2,710	1,949
Port Clinton	4,408	3,928	Bellefonte	4,804	3,996	Moosic	4,557	4,364
Rittman	2,785	1,803	Bellwood	2,560	2,629	Mount Joy	2,716	2,192
Sebring	3,949	3,541	Bentleyville	3,609	3,679	Mount Penn	3,017	1,370
Shadyside	4,098	3,084	Birdsboro	3,542	3,299	Mount Union	4,892	4,744
South Euclid	4,399	1,605	Boyertown	3,943	3,189	Myerstown	2,593	2,385
Tippecanoe City	2,559	2,426	Bridgeville	3,939	3,092	Narberth	4,669	3,704
Union City	[3]1,305	1,534	Brockway	2,690	2,369	New Cumberland	4,283	1,577
Upper Arlington	3,059	620	Brookville	4,387	3,272	New Philadelphia	2,557	2,537
Upper Sandusky	3,889	3,708	Brownsville	2,869	2,502	North Bellevernon	3,072	2,605
Wauseon	2,889	3,035	Burnham	3,089	2,765	North Catasauqua	2,700	2,321
Westerville	2,879	2,480	Camp Hill	3,111	1,636	North Charleroi	2,879	1,931

[3] The inclusion of Union City in places of 2,500 to 5,000 is based upon the combined population (4,389 in 1930) of Union City, Ohio, and Union City, Ind.

TABLE 15.—POPULATION OF CITIES AND OTHER URBAN PLACES HAVING, IN 1930, FROM 2,500 TO 5,000 INHABITANTS: 1930 AND 1920—Continued

CITY OR OTHER URBAN PLACE	1930	1920	CITY OR OTHER URBAN PLACE	1930	1920	CITY OR OTHER URBAN PLACE	1930	1920
PENNSYLVANIA—continued			SOUTH CAROLINA—continued			TEXAS—continued		
North East	3,670	3,481	Cheraw	3,573	3,150	Colorado	4,671	1,766
Northumberland	4,483	4,061	Clover	3,111	1,608	Commerce	4,267	3,842
Norwood	3,878	2,353	Conway	3,011	1,989	Cotulla	3,175	1,058
Oxford	2,606	2,093	Dillon	2,731	2,205	Crockett	4,441	3,061
Palmyra	4,377	3,646	Easley	4,886	3,568	Cuero	4,672	3,671
Patton	2,988	3,628	Eau Claire	2,915	2,566	Dalhart	4,691	2,676
Pen Argyl	4,310	4,096	Honea Path	2,740	1,900	Donna	4,103	1,579
Penbrook	3,567	2,072	Lancaster	3,545	3,032	Eastland	4,648	9,368
Perkasie	3,463	3,150	Marion	4,921	3,892	Edinburg	4,821	1,406
Philipsburg	3,600	3,900	Mullins	3,158	2,379	Floydada	2,637	1,384
Polk	3,337	2,662	Summerville	2,579	2,550	Fort Stockton	2,695	1,297
Portage	4,432	4,804	Walterboro	2,592	1,853	Freeport	3,162	1,798
Port Carbon	3,225	2,882	Whitmire	2,763	1,955	Gatesville	2,601	2,499
Port Vue	3,510	2,538	Woodruff	3,175	2,396	Georgetown	3,583	2,871
Prospect Park	4,623	2,536	York	2,827	2,731	Gonzales	3,859	3,128
Quakertown	4,883	4,391				Graham	4,981	2,544
Red Lion	4,757	3,198	SOUTH DAKOTA			Haskell	2,632	2,800
Renovo	3,947	5,877				Hearne	2,956	2,741
Reynoldsville	3,480	4,116	Brookings	4,376	3,924	Henderson	2,932	2,273
Ridley Park	3,356	2,313	Deadwood	2,559	2,403	Jasper	3,393	------
Roaring Spring	2,724	2,379	Hot Springs	2,908	1,697	Kenedy	2,610	2,015
Royersford	3,719	3,278	Madison	4,289	4,144	Kerrville	4,546	2,353
Selinsgrove	2,797	1,937	Mobridge	3,464	3,517	Lamesa	3,528	1,188
Sharon Hill	3,825	1,780	Pierre	3,659	3,209	Lampasas	2,709	2,107
Shillington	4,401	2,175	Redfield	2,664	2,755	Littlefield	3,218	------
Shippensburg	4,345	4,372	Vermillion	2,850	2,590	Lockhart	4,367	3,731
Slatington	4,134	4,014				McCamey	3,446	------
Somerset	4,395	3,121	TENNESSEE			Marfa	3,909	3,553
Souderton	3,857	3,125				Mart	2,853	3,105
South Connellsville	2,516	2,196	Brownsville	3,204	3,062	Memphis	4,257	2,839
South Fork	3,227	4,239	Cookeville	3,738	2,395	Mineola	3,304	2,299
South Greensburg	2,520	2,188	Covington	3,397	3,410	Mount Pleasant	3,541	4,099
Southwest Greensburg	3,105	2,538	Dickson	2,902	2,263	Olney	4,138	1,164
Spangler	2,761	3,035	Erwin	3,623	2,965	Paducah	2,802	1,357
Spring City	2,963	2,944	Etowah	4,209	2,516	Pearsall	2,536	2,161
Springdale	4,781	2,929	Fayetteville	3,822	3,629	Pecos	3,304	1,445
State College	4,450	2,405	Franklin	3,377	3,123	Pelly	3,452	------
Sugar Notch	2,768	2,612	Gallatin	3,050	2,757	Perryton	2,824	------
Susquehanna Depot	3,203	3,764	Harriman	4,588	4,019	Pharr	3,225	1,565
Swarthmore	3,405	2,350	Humboldt	4,613	3,913	Pittsburg	2,640	2,540
Towanda	4,104	4,269	La Follette	2,637	3,056	Quanah	4,464	3,691
Trafford	4,187	2,859	Lawrenceburg	3,102	2,461	Robstown	4,183	948
Union City	3,788	3,850	Lebanon	4,656	4,084	Rusk	3,859	2,348
Upland	2,500	2,486	Lenoir City	4,470	4,210	Seymour	2,626	2,121
Verona	4,376	3,938	Lewisburg	3,112	2,711	Shamrock	3,780	1,227
Waynesburg [4]	4,915	3,332	Loudon	2,578	------	Slaton	3,876	1,525
Weatherly	2,531	2,356	McMinnville	3,914	2,814	Smithville	3,296	3,204
Wellsboro	3,643	3,452	Martin	3,300	2,837	Snyder	3,008	2,179
Wesleyville	2,354	1,457	Maryville	4,958	3,739	South San Antonio	2,708	------
West Conshohocken	2,579	2,331	Milan	3,155	2,057	Stamford	4,095	3,704
West Homestead	3,552	3,435	Newport	2,989	2,753	Stephenville	3,944	3,891
Westmont	3,388	1,976	Pulaski	3,367	2,780	Teague	3,509	3,306
West Newton	2,953	2,645	Rockwood	3,898	4,652	Texas City	3,534	2,509
West Reading	4,908	2,921	Trenton	2,892	2,751	University Park	4,200	------
West Wyoming	2,769	1,938	Tullahoma	4,023	3,479	Weatherford	4,912	6,203
Williamstown	2,958	2,878				Wellington	3,570	1,968
Wyoming	4,648	3,582	TEXAS			Weslaco	4,879	------
Wyomissing	3,111	2,062				Wharton	2,691	2,346
Youngwood	2,783	2,275	Alamo Heights	3,874	------	Wink	3,963	------
			Alice	4,239	1,880			
RHODE ISLAND			Alpine	3,495	931	UTAH		
			Arlington	3,661	3,031	American Fork	3,047	2,763
East Greenwich town*	3,666	3,290	Athens	4,342	3,176	Bingham Canyon	3,248	2,676
			Ballinger	4,187	2,767	Bountiful	2,571	2,063
SOUTH CAROLINA			Bay City	4,070	3,454	Cedar City	3,615	2,462
			Beeville	4,806	3,063	Eureka	3,041	3,608
Abbeville	4,414	4,570	Belton	3,779	5,098	Helper	2,707	1,606
Batesburg	2,839	2,848	Bowie	3,131	3,179	Lehi	2,826	3,078
Beaufort	2,776	2,831	Brady	3,983	2,197	Nephi	2,573	2,603
Bennettsville	3,667	3,197	Burkburnett	3,281	5,300	Park City	4,281	3,393
			Cameron	4,565	4,298	Payson	3,045	3,031
			Canyon	2,821	1,618	Price	4,084	2,364
			Center	2,510	1,838	Richfield	3,067	3,262
			Clarendon	2,756	2,456	Spanish Fork	3,727	4,036
			Clarksville	2,952	3,386	Springville	3,748	3,010

*Classified as urban under special rule. See p. 7.
[4] Waynesburg and East Waynesburg boroughs consolidated as Waynesburg borough in 1923. Combined population in 1920, 4,218.

67981°—31——4

46 POPULATION—UNITED STATES SUMMARY

TABLE 15.—POPULATION OF CITIES AND OTHER URBAN PLACES HAVING, IN 1930, FROM 2,500 TO 5,000 INHABITANTS: 1930 AND 1920—Continued

CITY OR OTHER URBAN PLACE	1930	1920	CITY OR OTHER URBAN PLACE	1930	1920	CITY OR OTHER URBAN PLACE	1930	1920
VERMONT			**WASHINGTON—con.**			**WISCONSIN—con.**		
Bellows Falls	3,930	4,860	Omak	2,547	525	Edgerton	2,906	2,688
Proctor	2,515	2,692	Pasco	3,496	3,362	Hartford	3,754	4,515
Springfield	4,943	5,283	Port Townsend	3,979	2,847	Hudson	2,725	3,014
Windsor	3,689	3,061	Pullman	3,322	2,440	Hurley	3,264	3,188
			Raymond	3,828	4,260	Jefferson	2,639	2,572
VIRGINIA			Renton	4,062	3,301	Ladysmith	3,493	3,581
			Sedro-Wooley	2,719	2,379	Lake Geneva	3,073	2,632
Abingdon	2,877	2,532	Shelton	3,091	984	Little Chute	2,833	2,017
Appalachia	3,595	2,036	Snohomish	2,638	2,985	Mayville	2,521	3,011
Bedford	3,713	3,243	Toppenish	2,774	3,120	New London	4,661	4,667
Big Stone Gap	3,908	3,009				Oconomowoc	4,190	3,301
Buena Vista	4,002	3,911	**WEST VIRGINIA**			Park Falls	3,036	2,676
Cape Charles	2,527	2,517				Platteville	4,047	4,353
Farmville	3,133	2,586	Benwood	3,950	4,773	Plymouth	3,882	3,415
Franklin	2,930	2,563	Buckhannon	4,374	3,785	Port Washington	3,693	3,340
Galax	2,544	1,250	Chester	3,701	3,283	Prairie du Chien	3,943	3,537
Lexington	3,752	2,870	Dunbar	4,189	......	Reedsburg	2,967	2,997
Marion	4,156	3,253	Follansbee	4,841	3,135	Richland Center	3,632	3,409
Norton	3,077	3,068	Hollidays Cove	4,480	1,213	Ripon	3,984	3,929
Phoebus	2,956	3,043	Kenova	3,680	2,162	Shawano	4,188	3,544
Salem	4,833	4,159	Logan	4,396	2,998	Sheboygan Falls	2,934	2,002
Saltville	2,964	2,248	McMechen	3,710	3,356	Sparta	4,949	4,466
South Boston	4,841	4,338	Mannington	3,261	3,673	Stoughton	4,497	5,101
Vinton	3,610	2,779	Montgomery	2,906	2,130	Sturgeon Bay	4,983	4,553
Williamsburg	3,778	2,462	New Martinsville	2,814	2,341	Tomah	3,354	3,257
Wytheville	3,327	2,947	Point Pleasant	3,301	3,059	Tomahawk	2,919	2,898
			St. Albans	3,254	2,825	Viroqua	2,792	2,574
WASHINGTON			Salem	2,943	2,920	Waupaca	3,131	2,839
			Shinnston	2,802	1,679	West Bend	4,760	3,378
Auburn	3,906	3,163	Sistersville	3,072	3,238	West Milwaukee	4,168	2,101
Camas	4,239	1,843				Whitewater	3,465	3,215
Chehalis	4,907	4,558	**WISCONSIN**					
Clarkston	2,870	1,859				**WYOMING**		
Cle Elum	2,508	2,661	Berlin	4,106	4,400			
Colfax	2,782	3,027	Burlington	4,114	3,626	Evanston	3,075	3,226
Dayton	2,528	2,695	Clintonville	3,572	3,275	Green River	2,589	2,140
Ellensburg	4,621	3,967	Columbus	2,514	2,460	Rawlins	4,868	3,969
Mount Vernon	3,690	3,341	Delavan	3,301	3,016			

RURAL INCORPORATED PLACES   47

TABLE 16.—POPULATION OF INCORPORATED PLACES HAVING, IN 1930, FROM 1,000 TO 2,500 INHABITANTS: 1930 AND 1920

CITY, TOWN, VILLAGE, OR BOROUGH	1930	1920	CITY, TOWN, VILLAGE, OR BOROUGH	1930	1920	CITY, TOWN, VILLAGE, OR BOROUGH	1930	1920
ALABAMA			**ARKANSAS**			**CALIFORNIA—con.**		
Abbeville	2,047	1,267	Arkansas City	1,432	1,482	Corcoran	1,768	1,101
Aliceville	1,066	944	Ashdown	1,607	2,052	Corning	1,377	1,449
Altoona	1,098	1,078	Atkins	1,364	1,529	Corte Madera	1,027	607
Ashland	1,476	1,655	Augusta	2,243	1,781	Crescent City	1,720	955
Bay Minette	1,545	1,092	Bald Knob	1,273	958	Davis	1,243	939
Bevelle	1,276	------	Bearden	1,147	687	Dixon	1,000	926
Blue Mountain	1,134	605	Beebe	1,108	995	El Cajon	1,050	469
Boaz	1,691	1,369	Bentonville	2,203	2,313	Elsinore	1,350	633
Brantley	1,053	702	Berryville	1,286	1,474	Emeryville	2,336	2,390
Bridgeport	2,124	2,018	Booneville	2,099	2,199	Fairfield	1,131	1,008
Brighton	1,708	3,065	Clarendon	2,149	2,638	Fortuna	1,239	986
Brundidge	1,434	941	Coal Hill	1,169	1,057	Fowler	1,171	1,528
Camp Hill	1,131	952	Corning	1,550	1,564	Gridley	1,941	1,636
Chapman	1,189	1,142	Cotter	1,064	884	Gustine	1,016	716
Citronelle	1,082	932	Cotton Plant	1,689	1,661	Healdsburg	2,296	2,412
Clanton	1,847	1,411	Dardanelle	1,832	1,835	Hemet	2,235	1,480
Clayton	1,717	989	De Witt	1,853	1,422	Hillsborough	1,891	931
Columbiana	1,180	1,073	Des Arc	1,348	1,307	Holtville	1,758	1,347
Cordova	1,830	1,622	Dierks	1,544	1,495	Imperial	1,943	1,885
Dadeville	1,549	1,146	Dumas	1,669	1,124	Isleton	2,090	------
Dora	1,143	1,117	Earle	2,062	2,091	Jackson	2,005	1,601
East Brewton	1,002	826	England	2,130	2,408	King City	1,483	1,048
Eutaw	1,721	1,359	Eudora	2,020	1,197	Kingsburg	1,322	1,316
Evergreen	2,007	1,813	Eureka Springs	2,276	2,429	Laguna Beach	1,981	------
Fairhope	1,549	853	Glenwood	1,310	891	La Habra	2,273	------
Fayette	2,109	1,741	Gurdon	2,172	1,469	Lakeport	1,318	1,024
Five Points	1,010	835	Hamburg	1,517	1,538	Larkspur	1,241	612
Fort Deposit	1,092	830	Harrisburg	1,111	1,315	Lemoore	1,399	1,355
Frisco City	1,021	576	Hartford	1,210	2,067	Lincoln	2,094	1,325
Geneva	1,593	1,581	Heber Springs	1,401	1,675	Los Banos	1,875	1,276
Georgiana	1,480	1,550	Horatio	1,028	1,038	Manhattan Beach	1,891	859
Greensboro	1,795	1,809	Hoxie	1,448	1,711	Manteca	1,614	1,286
Guin	1,099	596	Huttig	1,386	1,261	Maricopa	1,071	1,121
Haleyville	2,115	1,404	Judsonia	1,123	899	Menlo Park	2,254	------
Hartford	1,419	1,561	Junction City	[1] 814	653	Mount Shasta	1,009	542
Hartselle	2,204	2,009	Lake Village	1,582	1,449	Newman	1,269	1,251
Headland	1,811	1,252	Leachville	1,157	(2)	Newport Beach	2,203	894
Heflin	1,281	1,026	Lepanto	1,195	986	Nevada City	1,701	1,782
Irondale	1,517	809	Levy	1,197	673	North Sacramento	2,097	------
Jackson	1,828	1,331	Lewisville	1,061	1,067	Oakdale	2,112	1,745
Lafayette	2,119	1,911	Lonoke	1,674	1,711	Ojai	1,468	------
Lineville	1,329	1,507	Luxora	1,074	1,179	Orland	1,195	1,582
Lipscomb	1,774	1,605	Manila	1,226	971	Placentia	1,606	------
Livingston	1,072	968	Marked Tree	2,276	1,313	Placerville	2,322	1,650
Luverne	1,874	1,464	Monette	1,111	1,066	Pleasanton	1,237	991
Marion	2,141	2,035	Nashville	2,469	2,144	Rialto	1,642	961
Mignon	2,407	2,028	New Rocky Comfort	1,056	1,408	Rio Vista	1,309	1,104
Monroeville	1,355	1,017	Norphlet	1,063	------	Ross	1,355	727
Montevallo	1,245	850	Ozark	1,564	1,262	St. Helena	1,582	1,346
Northport	2,173	1,606	Parkin	1,676	1,878	San Carlos	1,132	------
Oneonta	1,387	876	Piggott	1,885	2,016	San Jacinto	1,346	945
Oxford	1,206	1,108	Pocahontas	1,896	1,806	Seal Beach	1,156	669
Prattville	2,331	2,316	Rector	1,617	1,801	Sebastopol	1,762	1,493
Red Bay	1,297	753	Sheridan	1,590	695	Sonora	2,278	1,684
Samson	1,656	1,646	Siloam Springs	2,378	2,569	Susanville	1,358	918
Scottsboro	2,304	1,417	Stephens	1,045	769	Sutter Creek	1,013	920
Sulligent	1,078	1,071	Waldron	1,077	918	Tujunga	2,311	------
Thomasville	1,504	1,002	Walnut Ridge	2,007	2,226	Vacaville	1,556	1,254
Uniontown	1,424	1,359				Vernon	1,269	1,005
Vincent	1,192	1,034	**CALIFORNIA**			Walnut Creek	1,014	538
West Blocton	1,070	1,023				Willits	1,424	1,468
Wetumpka	2,357	1,520	Alturas	2,338	979	Willows	2,024	2,190
Winfield	1,254	753	Arcata	1,709	1,486	Yreka	2,126	1,277
York	1,796	1,651	Atherton	1,324	------			
			Avalon	1,897	586	**COLORADO**		
ARIZONA			Beaumont	1,332	857			
			Bishop	1,159	1,304	Aguilar	1,383	1,236
Buckeye	1,077	------	Blythe	1,020	1,622	Akron	1,135	1,401
Casa Grande	1,351	948	Brea	2,435	1,037	Arvada	1,276	915
Chandler	1,378	------	Calipatria	1,554	785	Aurora	2,295	983
Clifton	2,305	4,163	Calistoga	1,000	850	Brush	2,312	2,103
Florence	1,318	1,161	Carmel-by-the-Sea	2,260	638	Burlington	1,280	991
Holbrook	1,115	1,296	Clovis	1,316	1,157	Center	1,011	547
Safford	1,706	1,336	Colusa	2,116	1,846	Craig	1,418	1,297
Tempe	2,495	1,963	Concord	1,125	912	Crested Butte	1,251	1,213
Williams	2,166	1,350				Cripple Creek	1,427	2,325

[1] The inclusion of Junction City in places of 1,000 to 2,500 is based upon the combined population (1,202 in 1930) of Junction City, Ark., and Junction City, La.

[2] Not returned separately.

48 POPULATION—UNITED STATES SUMMARY

TABLE 16.—POPULATION OF INCORPORATED PLACES HAVING, IN 1930, FROM 1,000 TO 2,500 INHABITANTS: 1930 AND 1920—Continued

CITY, TOWN, VILLAGE, OR BOROUGH	1930	1920
COLORADO—con.		
Delagua	1,021	1,035
Del Norte	1,410	1,007
Eaton	1,221	1,289
Edgewater	1,473	664
Florence	2,475	2,629
Fort Lupton	1,578	1,014
Fruita	1,053	1,193
Glenwood Springs	1,825	2,073
Golden	2,426	2,135
Gunnison	1,415	1,329
Haxtun	1,027	1,118
Holyoke	1,226	1,205
Idaho Springs	1,207	1,192
Julesburg	1,467	1,320
Lafayette	1,842	1,815
Limon	1,100	1,047
Littleton	2,019	1,636
Louisville	1,681	1,799
Manitou	1,205	1,129
Meeker	1,069	935
Oak Creek	1,211	967
Ordway	1,139	1,186
Rifle	1,287	865
Saguache	1,010	948
Silverton	1,301	1,150
South Canon	1,471	1,281
Springfield	1,393	295
Steamboat Springs	1,198	1,249
Victor	1,291	1,777
Windsor	1,852	1,290
Wray	1,785	1,538
Yuma	1,360	1,177
CONNECTICUT		
Branford	2,365	2,619
Farmington	1,131	1,021
Guilford	1,880	1,612
Litchfield	1,075	707
New Canaan	2,372	1,918
Stonington	2,006	2,100
Unionville	2,135	------
DELAWARE		
Delaware City	1,005	1,064
Delmar	³838	780
Elsmere	1,323	620
Georgetown	1,763	1,710
Harrington	1,812	1,617
Laurel	2,277	2,253
Lewes	1,923	2,074
Middletown	1,247	1,260
Milton	1,130	898
Seaford	2,468	2,141
Smyrna	1,958	1,953
FLORIDA		
Apopka	1,134	798
Auburndale	1,849	715
Blountstown	1,270	863
Bonifay	1,292	1,230
Bowling Green	1,025	692
Boynton Beach	1,053	------
Brooksville	1,405	1,011
Caryville	1,022	440
Cedar Keys	1,066	695
Chipley	1,878	1,806
Clermont	1,086	496
Cocoa	2,164	1,445
Cross City	1,071	------
Dade City	1,811	1,296

CITY, TOWN, VILLAGE, OR BOROUGH	1930	1920
FLORIDA—con.		
Dania	1,674	762
Deerfield	1,483	------
Delray Beach⁴	2,333	1,051
Dunedin	1,435	642
Dunnellon	1,194	1,185
Fort Meade	1,981	2,029
Frostproof	1,406	(²)
Graceville	1,012	840
Green Cove Springs	1,719	2,093
Hallandale	1,012	------
Havana	1,169	448
High Springs	1,864	1,719
Holly Hill	1,146	332
Homestead	2,319	1,307
Inverness	1,215	1,132
Jasper	1,748	1,260
Largo	1,429	599
Madison	2,189	1,952
Milton	1,466	1,594
Monticello	1,901	1,704
Mount Dora	1,613	725
Mulberry	2,029	1,499
Okeechobee	1,795	900
Ormond	1,517	1,292
Oviedo	1,042	------
Pahokee	2,256	------
Palm Beach	1,707	1,135
Port Tampa	1,242	1,030
Punta Gorda	1,833	1,295
St. Cloud	1,863	2,011
South Miami	1,160	------
Starke	1,339	1,023
Stuart	1,924	778
Tavares	1,090	359
Titusville	2,089	1,361
Vero Beach	2,268	798
Wildwood City	1,409	480
Winter Garden	2,023	1,021
GEORGIA		
Abbeville	1,018	1,119
Acworth	1,163	1,117
Adel	1,796	1,720
Alma	1,235	1,061
Arlington	1,232	1,331
Ashburn	2,073	2,116
Baxley	2,122	1,142
Bibb City	1,707	1,090
Blackshear	1,817	1,329
Blakely	2,166	1,935
Blue Ridge	1,190	904
Boston	1,243	1,640
Bowdon	1,024	1,047
Bremen	1,030	917
Buena Vista	1,097	1,230
Calhoun	2,371	1,955
Camilla	2,025	2,136
Chickamauga	1,715	965
Claxton	1,584	1,265
Cochran	2,257	2,021
Conyers	1,495	1,517
Cornelia	1,542	1,274
Dallas	1,412	1,245
Donalsonville	1,183	1,031
Douglasville	2,316	2,159
Eatonton	1,876	2,519
Edison	1,321	885
Fairburn	1,372	1,600
Forsyth	2,277	2,241
Fort Gaines	1,272	1,237
Glennville	1,503	1,069

CITY, TOWN, VILLAGE, OR BOROUGH	1930	1920
GEORGIA—con.		
Gordon	1,199	1,081
Grantville	1,346	1,200
Greensboro	2,125	2,128
Hampton	1,002	927
Hartwell	2,048	2,323
Hawkinsville	2,484	3,070
Hazelhurst	1,378	1,383
Hogansville	2,355	1,591
Homerville	1,150	627
Jackson	1,776	2,027
Jefferson	1,869	1,626
Jesup	2,303	1,941
Jonesboro	1,065	1,060
Lakeland	1,006	860
Lavonia	1,511	1,644
Lawrenceville	2,156	2,059
Lithonia	1,457	1,269
Louisville	1,650	1,040
Lumber City	1,043	978
Lumpkin	1,103	934
Lyons	1,445	873
McCaysville	1,969	2,166
McDonough	1,068	1,263
McRae	1,314	1,273
Madison	1,966	2,348
Meigs	1,000	1,111
Metter	1,424	908
Montezuma	2,284	1,827
Monticello	1,593	1,828
Nashville	1,672	2,025
Ocilla	2,034	2,180
Perry	1,398	678
Richland	1,577	1,529
Rochelle	1,053	1,046
Roswell	1,432	1,227
Royston	1,447	1,681
Shellman	1,117	1,074
Silvertown	2,171	------
Smyrna	1,178	791
Social Circle	1,766	1,781
Soperton	1,081	1,033
Sparta	1,613	1,895
Stone Mountain	1,335	1,266
Swainsboro	2,442	1,578
Sylvania	1,781	1,413
Sylvester	1,984	1,547
Talbotton	1,064	1,093
Tallapoosa	2,417	2,719
Tennille	1,666	1,768
Thomson	1,914	2,140
Unadilla	1,203	1,103
Union Point	1,627	1,126
Vienna	1,832	2,019
Villa Rica	1,304	1,047
Wadley	1,055	1,126
Warrenton	1,289	1,407
West Point	2,146	2,138
Willacoochee	1,006	1,211
Wrens	1,085	1,074
Wrightsville	1,741	1,476
IDAHO		
Alameda⁵	1,885	------
American Falls	1,280	1,547
Ashton	1,003	1,022
Bonners Ferry	1,418	1,236
Buhl	1,883	2,245
Filer	1,011	1,012
Glenns Ferry	1,414	1,243
Gooding	1,592	1,843
Grangeville	1,860	1,430
Jerome	1,976	1,759

² Not returned separately.

³ The inclusion of Delmar in places of 1,000 to 2,500 is based upon the combined population (2,018 in 1930) of Delmar, Del., and Delmar, Md.

⁴ Delray and Delray Beach towns consolidated as Delray Beach city in 1927.

⁵ Fairview and North Pocatello villages consolidated as Alameda village in 1924. Combined population in 1920, 772.

RURAL INCORPORATED PLACES   49

TABLE 16.—POPULATION OF INCORPORATED PLACES HAVING, IN 1930, FROM 1,000 TO 2,500 INHABITANTS: 1930 AND 1920—Continued

CITY, TOWN, VILLAGE, OR BOROUGH	1930	1920	CITY, TOWN, VILLAGE, OR BOROUGH	1930	1920	CITY, TOWN, VILLAGE, OR BOROUGH	1930	1920
IDAHO—con.			**ILLINOIS—con.**			**ILLINOIS—con.**		
Meridian	1,004	1,000	Evergreen Park	1,594	705	Nokomis	2,454	3,465
Montpelier	2,436	2,984	Fairbury	2,310	2,532	Norris City	1,109	1,300
Mountain Home	1,243	1,644	Fairmont City	1,827	1,056	Northbrook [8]	1,193	554
Mullan	1,891	1,320	Farmer City	1,621	1,678	North Chillicothe	1,004	1,002
Orofino	1,078	537	Farmington	2,269	2,631	North Utica	1,120	1,037
Rigby	1,531	1,629	Franklin Park	2,425	914	Oakland	1,036	1,210
Rupert	2,250	2,372	Freeburg	1,434	1,594	Oak Lawn	2,045	489
St. Marie	1,996	1,962	Genoa	1,168	1,228	Oblong	1,427	1,547
Salmon	1,371	1,311	Gibson	2,163	2,234	Odin	1,204	1,385
Shelley	1,447	1,223	Gilman	1,620	1,448	O'Fallon	2,373	2,379
Shoshone	1,211	1,165	Girard	1,760	2,387	Onarga	1,469	1,302
Spirit Lake	1,241	940	Glen Carbon	1,340	1,323	Oregon	2,376	2,227
			Glenview	1,886	760	Orient City	1,267	1,388
ILLINOIS			Golconda	1,184	1,242	Palatine	2,118	1,210
			Grafton	1,026	949	Palestine	1,670	1,803
Albion	1,666	1,584	Grays Lake	1,120	736	Panama	1,026	1,281
Aledo	2,203	2,231	Grayville	1,904	1,749	Pecatonica	1,152	1,088
Altamont	1,225	1,352	Greenfield	1,038	1,149	Peotone	1,154	1,090
Amboy	1,972	1,944	Greenup	1,062	1,230	Petersburg	2,319	2,432
Antioch	1,101	775	Griggsville	1,184	1,343	Pittsfield	2,356	2,129
Arcola	1,686	1,831	Hamilton	1,687	1,698	Plainfield	1,428	1,147
Arthur	1,361	998	Hartford	1,566	------	Plano	1,785	1,473
Ashland	1,007	1,122	Hazel Crest	1,162	488	Polo	1,871	1,867
Assumption	1,554	1,852	Henry	1,658	1,637	Posen	1,329	947
Astoria	1,189	1,340	Hillside	1,004	555	Prophetstown	1,353	1,159
Athens	1,019	1,241	Hurst	1,123	1,222	Rantoul	1,555	1,551
Atlanta	1,169	1,173	Jonesboro	1,241	1,060	Redbud	1,208	1,141
Auburn	2,242	2,600	Keithsburg	1,081	1,148	Riverton	1,582	1,916
Augusta	1,011	1,085	Kincaid	1,583	1,453	Roanoke	1,088	1,368
Barry	1,506	1,490	Knoxville	1,867	1,708	Rockdale	1,701	1,478
Bartonville	1,886	1,588	Lacon	1,548	1,464	Rockton	1,077	899
Bement	1,517	1,663	Ladd	1,318	2,040	Rosiclare	1,794	1,522
Bensenville	1,680	650	La Harpe	1,175	1,323	Rossville	1,453	1,588
Braidwood	1,161	1,297	Lake Bluff	1,452	819	Roxanna	1,139	------
Breese	1,957	2,399	Lanark	1,208	1,297	Royalton	2,108	2,043
Bridgeport	2,315	2,229	Lebanon	1,828	1,883	Rushville	2,388	2,275
Broadview	2,334	430	Lena	1,145	1,140	St. Anne	1,078	1,067
Brooklyn	2,063	1,685	Leroy	1,595	1,680	St. Elmo	1,329	1,337
Brookport	1,336	1,098	Lewistown	2,249	2,279	St. Francisville	1,202	1,164
Buckner	1,409	1,827	Lexington	1,202	1,301	Sandoval	1,264	1,768
Calumet Park [6]	1,429	1,237	Livingston	1,447	1,365	Sesser	2,315	2,841
Cambridge	1,355	1,835	Lovington	1,121	1,479	Shawneetown	1,440	1,368
Camp Point	1,000	994	McHenry	1,354	1,146	Sheldon	1,121	1,182
Carlyle	2,078	2,027	McLeansboro	2,102	1,927	South Beloit	2,361	1,436
Carpentersville	1,461	1,036	Manteno	1,149	1,182	South Chicago		
Carrier Mills	2,140	2,343	Marengo	1,948	1,758	Heights	1,691	949
Carrollton	2,075	2,020	Marissa	1,680	1,900	South Holland	1,873	1,247
Carthage	2,240	2,129	Maroa	1,154	1,193	South Pekin	1,222	944
Casey	2,200	2,189	Marshall	2,368	2,222	Stickney	2,005	550
Central City	1,148	1,248	Martinsville	1,206	1,437	Stockton	1,505	1,449
Chenoa	1,325	1,311	Mascoutah	2,311	2,343	Stonington	1,057	1,466
Chillicothe	1,978	1,986	Mason City	1,941	1,830	Sullivan	2,339	2,532
Chrisman	1,092	1,101	Midlothian	1,775	------	Swansea	1,201	1,048
Coal City	1,637	1,744	Milford	1,442	1,466	Thornton	1,012	767
Cobden	1,036	944	Millstadt	1,014	907	Tilton	1,394	909
Colchester	1,342	1,387	Minonk	1,910	2,109	Toluca	1,413	2,503
Colp	1,250	584	Momence	2,236	2,218	Toulon	1,203	1,235
Columbia	1,791	1,592	Monticello	2,378	2,280	Trenton	1,271	1,200
Coulterville	1,337	1,407	Morton	1,501	1,179	Troy	1,122	1,312
Crete	1,429	945	Morton Grove	1,974	1,079	Valier	1,176	876
Crotty	1,185	994	Mounds	2,129	2,661	Villa Grove	2,001	2,493
Cuba	1,479	1,484	Mount Carroll	1,775	1,806	Virginia	1,494	1,501
Dallas City	1,114	1,140	Mount Morris	1,902	1,250	Wamac	1,232	1,180
Deerfield	1,852	610	Mount Prospect	1,225	349	Warren	1,179	1,253
Delavan	1,084	1,191	Mount Pulaski	1,445	1,510	Warsaw	1,866	2,031
Depue	2,200	2,428	Mount Sterling	1,724	1,932	Washington	1,741	1,643
Divernon	1,170	2,382	Moweaqua	1,478	1,591	Waterloo	2,239	1,930
Dupo	2,082	1,393	Mundelein [7]	1,011	420	Waverley	1,390	1,510
Earlville	1,028	1,012	Nameoki	2,257	1,181	Wenona	1,005	1,203
East Duhuque	1,395	1,163	Nashville	2,243	2,209	West City	1,091	525
East Dundee	1,341	1,303	New Athens	1,269	1,406	West Dundee	1,697	1,587
Elkville	1,133	990	New Baden	1,243	1,550	Wilmington	1,741	1,384
Elmwood	1,166	1,242	Newman	1,054	1,225	Wilsonville	1,220	837
El Paso	1,578	1,638	Newton	2,076	2,083	Winchester	1,532	1,540
Eureka	1,534	1,559	Niles	2,135	1,258	Witt	1,516	2,443

[6] Name changed from Burr Oak in 1925.
[7] Name changed from Area in 1925.
[8] Name changed from Shermerville since 1920.

50   POPULATION—UNITED STATES SUMMARY

TABLE 16.—POPULATION OF INCORPORATED PLACES HAVING, IN 1930, FROM 1,000 TO 2,500 INHABITANTS: 1930 AND 1920—Continued

CITY, TOWN, VILLAGE, OR BOROUGH	1930	1920
ILLINOIS—con.		
Worden	1,111	1,252
Wyoming	1,408	1,376
INDIANA		
Albany	1,413	1,333
Albion	1,108	1,142
Argos	1,211	1,111
Berne	1,883	1,537
Bloomfield	2,298	1,872
Bourbon	1,193	1,259
Bremen	2,105	2,084
Brookville	2,148	2,220
Brownsburg	1,042	1,063
Brownstown	1,758	1,554
Butler	1,643	1,745
Cambridge City	2,113	1,963
Cannelton	2,265	2,008
Chesterton	2,231	1,604
Churubusco	1,095	916
Clarksville	2,243	2,322
Clay City	1,079	1,226
Corydon	2,009	1,785
Covington	2,003	1,945
Culver	1,502	1,080
Danville	1,930	1,729
Delphi	1,929	2,087
Dugger	1,383	1,679
East Gary	2,409	813
Eaton	1,273	1,214
Edinburg	2,209	2,378
Fairmount	2,056	2,155
Fairview Park	1,106	1,301
Flora	1,449	1,441
Fort Branch	1,341	1,339
Fortville	1,289	1,213
Fowler	1,564	1,442
French Lick	2,462	1,980
Greendale	1,050	763
Greentown	1,021	1,163
Greenwood	2,377	1,907
Griffith	1,176	630
Hagerstown	1,262	1,238
Highland	1,553	542
Hope	1,085	1,183
Hymera	1,152	1,599
Jonesboro	1,496	1,429
Kentland	1,355	1,288
Knightstown	2,209	1,918
Knox	1,815	1,577
Lagrange	1,640	1,610
Lapel	1,140	1,079
Liberty	1,241	1,292
Ligonier	2,064	2,037
Loogootee	2,203	2,335
Lowell	1,274	1,197
Middletown	1,348	1,273
Monon	1,374	1,357
Montezuma	1,292	1,178
Monticello	2,331	2,536
Montpelier	1,859	2,207
Mooresville	1,910	1,781
Morocco	1,006	1,064
Newburg	1,262	1,295
New Harmony	1,022	1,128
New Haven	1,702	1,237
North Judson	1,348	1,189
Oolitic	1,210	883
Orleans	1,422	1,408
Osgood	1,173	1,093
Owensville	1,056	1,239
Paoli	2,016	1,520
Pendleton	1,538	1,244
Plainfield	1,617	1,373
Redkey	1,370	1,386
Rising Sun	1,379	1,411

CITY, TOWN, VILLAGE, OR BOROUGH	1930	1920
INDIANA—con.		
Rockport	2,396	2,581
Rockville	1,832	1,968
Scottsburg	1,702	1,609
Sellersburg	1,050	915
Shelburn	1,548	1,814
Sheridan	1,763	1,761
Shoals	1,128	1,034
South Whitley	1,102	1,074
Speedway	1,420	
Spencer	2,179	2,066
Summitville	1,017	1,001
Syracuse	1,190	1,171
Thorntown	1,325	1,432
Veedersburg	1,606	1,580
Vevay	1,183	1,175
Walkerton	1,137	1,031
Warren	1,177	1,520
Waterloo	1,244	1,172
West Baden	1,174	832
West Harrison	[9] 279	258
Williamsport	1,053	1,088
Winamac	1,679	1,684
Winslow	1,175	1,140
Woodruff Place	1,216	1,158
Worthington	1,687	1,853
Zionsville	1,131	957
IOWA		
Ackley	1,524	1,529
Adel	1,669	1,455
Afton	1,013	926
Akron	1,304	1,324
Alta	1,297	1,290
Alton	1,014	1,007
Anita	1,106	1,236
Audubon	2,255	2,108
Avoca	1,673	1,482
Bedford	2,100	2,073
Bellevue	1,717	1,663
Belmond	1,738	1,797
Bloomfield	2,226	2,064
Britt	1,593	1,619
Brooklyn	1,345	1,533
Cascade	1,221	1,249
Clarksville	1,143	1,003
Colfax	2,213	2,504
Coon Rapids	1,303	1,328
Corning	2,026	1,840
Correctionville	1,058	1,016
Corydon	1,768	1,867
DeWitt	2,041	1,849
Dunlap	1,522	1,455
Dyersville	2,046	1,933
Eldon	1,788	2,091
Elkader	1,382	1,223
Farmington	1,012	1,086
Fayette	1,083	1,085
Fonda	1,027	1,136
Forest City	2,016	2,145
Garner	1,241	1,311
Gowrie	1,059	*895
Grand Junction	1,025	1,010
Greene	1,268	1,375
Greenfield	1,837	1,707
Griswold	1,139	1,264
Grundy Center	1,793	1,749
Guthrie Center	1,813	1,727
Guttenberg	1,918	1,666
Hamburg	2,103	2,017
Hartley	1,272	1,306
Hawarden	2,459	2,491
Holstein	1,300	1,248
Humboldt	2,251	2,232
Ida Grove	2,206	2,020
Kingsley	1,093	1,072

CITY, TOWN, VILLAGE, OR BOROUGH	1930	1920
IOWA—con.		
Lake City	2,012	2,110
Lake Mills	1,474	1,529
Lamoni	1,739	1,787
Lansing	1,321	1,447
La Porte City	1,470	1,443
Laurens	1,071	914
Lenox	1,171	1,197
Leon	2,006	2,193
Logan	1,654	1,637
McGregor	1,299	1,289
Madrid	2,061	1,783
Malvern	1,320	1,195
Manilla	1,032	1,142
Manly	1,447	1,476
Manning	1,817	1,863
Manson	1,382	1,409
Mapleton	1,622	1,367
Marcus	1,138	1,091
Marengo	2,112	2,048
Melcher	1,673	1,582
Milford	1,062	903
Monona	1,163	1,049
Montezuma	1,257	1,273
Monticello	2,259	2,257
Moulton	1,476	1,387
Mount Ayr	1,704	1,738
Mount Vernon	1,441	1,466
Mystic	1,953	2,796
Nashua	1,363	1,317
New Hampton	2,458	2,539
New London	1,336	1,144
New Sharon	1,052	1,084
Nora Springs	1,070	1,055
Northwood	1,554	1,597
Oakland	1,181	1,188
Odebolt	1,388	1,445
Ogden	1,429	1,451
Orange City	1,727	1,632
Panora	1,014	966
Parkersburg	1,046	1,108
Paullina	1,013	987
Pocahontas	1,308	1,302
Postville	1,060	1,039
Reinbeck	1,425	1,415
Remsen	1,181	1,144
Rock Rapids	2,221	2,172
Rock Valley	1,204	1,347
Rockwell City	2,108	2,039
Rolfe	1,012	1,081
Sanborn	1,213	1,497
Scranton	1,058	843
Seymour	1,571	1,746
Sheffield	1,057	1,106
Sibley	1,870	1,803
Sidney	1,074	1,154
Sigourney	2,262	2,210
Sioux Center	1,497	1,389
Spirit Lake	1,778	1,701
State Center	1,012	975
Story City	1,434	1,591
Strawberry Point	1,128	1,101
Stuart	1,626	1,716
Sumner	1,561	1,511
Tabor	1,017	1,186
Tipton	2,145	2,142
Toledo	1,825	1,604
Traer	1,417	1,329
Villisca	2,032	2,111
Wapello	1,502	1,480
West Burlington	1,333	1,212
West Liberty	1,679	1,834
West Union	2,056	1,777
What Cheer	1,310	1,626
Williamsburg	1,219	1,251
Wilton	1,104	1,178
Woodbine	1,348	1,463

[9] The inclusion of West Harrison in places of 1,000 to 2,500 is based upon the combined population (1,728 in 1930) of West Harrison, Ind., and Harrison, Ohio.

RURAL INCORPORATED PLACES 51

TABLE 16.—POPULATION OF INCORPORATED PLACES HAVING, IN 1930, FROM 1,000 TO 2,500 INHABITANTS: 1930 AND 1920—Continued

CITY, TOWN, VILLAGE, OR BOROUGH	1930	1920	CITY, TOWN, VILLAGE, OR BOROUGH	1930	1920	CITY, TOWN, VILLAGE, OR BOROUGH	1930	1920
KANSAS			**KANSAS—con.**			**KENTUCKY—con.**		
Arma	2,004	2,180	Stockton	1,291	1,324	South Fort Mitchell	1,617	----
Ashland	1,232	1,147	Syracuse	1,383	1,059	Southgate	1,735	699
Atwood	1,166	919	Tonganoxie	1,109	971	Springfield	1,487	1,529
Baldwin City	1,127	1,137	Troy	1,042	1,013	Stanford	1,544	1,397
Belleville	2,383	2,254	Ulysses	1,140	103	Sturgis	2,154	1,750
Blue Rapids	1,465	1,534	Valley Falls	1,238	1,218	Uniontown	1,235	1,094
Bonner Springs	1,837	1,599	Wakeeney	1,408	1,003	Vanceburg	1,388	1,353
Burlingame	1,127	1,330	Wamego	1,647	1,585	Van Lear	2,338	2,056
Burlington	2,273	2,236	Washington	1,370	1,406	Versailles	2,244	2,061
Caldwell	2,046	2,191	Weir	1,115	1,945	Wayland	2,436	1,362
Cedarvale	1,000	1,044	Wilson	1,038	1,020	Weeksbury	1,509	1,016
Cherokee	1,158	1,091	Yates Center	2,013	2,306	Wheelwright	1,822	506
Chetopa	1,344	1,519				Whitesburg	1,804	706
Cimarron	1,035	599	**KENTUCKY**			Wickliffe	1,108	969
Clyde	1,174	1,063				Williamsburg	1,826	1,767
Colby	2,153	1,114	Augusta	1,675	1,820	Wilmore	1,329	1,157
Coldwater	1,296	1,207	Barbourville	2,380	1,877			
Downs	1,383	1,508	Bardstown	1,767	1,717	**LOUISIANA**		
Elkhart	1,435	1,160	Bardwell	1,139	1,120			
Ellinwood	1,115	1,103	Beaver Dam	1,036	788	Arcadia	1,809	1,240
Ellis	1,957	1,876	Benton	1,021	897	Berwick	1,679	1,691
Ellsworth	2,072	2,065	Berea	1,827	1,640	Breaux Bridge	1,399	1,171
Erie	1,184	1,167	Bromley	1,017	736	Bunkie	2,464	1,743
Florence	1,493	1,517	Cadiz	1,114	897	Church Point	1,037	557
Frankfort	1,346	1,314	Campbellsville	1,923	1,535	Colfax	1,141	1,449
Frontenac	2,085	3,225	Carlisle	1,469	1,569	Cottonport	1,015	720
Girard	2,442	3,161	Carrollton	2,409	2,281	Cotton Valley	1,138	(2)
Greensburg	1,338	1,215	Clay	1,551	1,378	Delhi	1,043	980
Halstead	1,373	1,163	Clinton	1,204	1,455	Denham Springs	1,002	500
Harper	1,485	1,770	Cloverport	1,324	1,509	Farmerville	1,137	632
Hill City	1,027	732	Columbia	1,195	1,076	Gibsland	1,000	798
Hillsboro	1,458	1,451	Dawson Springs	2,311	1,762	Glenmora	1,875	2,298
Howard	1,069	1,060	Drakesboro	1,242	1,164	Gueydan	1,313	1,233
Hugoton	1,368	644	Eddyville	1,990	1,182	Hodge	1,367	----
Kinsley	2,270	1,986	Eminence	1,323	1,317	Independence	1,700	1,032
Kiowa	1,501	1,539	Erlanger	1,853	711	Jeanerette	2,228	2,512
La Crosse	1,355	808	Evarts	1,438	502	Jena	1,007	520
Lacygne	1,019	1,028	Falmouth	1,876	1,330	Jonesboro	1,949	837
Lincoln	1,732	1,613	Fleming	1,389	2,069	Jonesville	1,123	1,029
Lindsborg	2,016	1,897	Flemingsburg	1,265	1,562	Junction City	10 388	322
Madison	1,488	795	Fullerton	1,237	(2)	Kaplan	1,653	876
Mankato	1,404	1,326	Grayson	1,022	822	Kenner	2,440	1,582
Marion	1,959	1,928	Greenup	1,125	910	Kentwood	1,726	3,059
Meade	1,552	838	Greenville	2,451	1,917	Lake Arthur	1,602	1,582
Medicine Lodge	1,655	1,305	Guthrie	1,272	1,160	Lecompte	1,247	1,034
Minneapolis	1,741	1,842	Hartford	1,106	960	Logansport	1,040	632
Mulberry	1,596	2,697	Hellier	2,112	1,884	Lutcher	1,481	1,700
Mulvane	1,042	1,239	Hickman	2,321	2,633	Mandeville	1,069	1,180
Ness City	1,509	905	Hodgenville	1,104	1,100	Mansura	1,067	829
Nickerson	1,052	1,049	Horse Cave	1,259	864	Many	1,239	663
Oakley	1,159	768	Jackson	2,109	1,503	Marksville	1,527	1,185
Oberlin	1,629	1,247	La Grange	1,121	1,060	Melville	1,541	958
Osage City	2,402	2,376	Lancaster	1,630	2,166	Napoleonville	1,180	1,171
Osborne	1,881	1,635	Lawrenceburg	1,763	1,811	New Roads	1,473	1,294
Oswego	1,845	2,386	Lebanon Junction	1,267	882	Oak Grove	1,241	700
Oxford	1,129	748	Livermore	1,573	1,426	Patterson	2,206	2,538
Peabody	1,491	2,455	London	1,950	1,707	Plain Dealing	1,412	655
Phillipsburg	1,543	1,310	Louisa	1,961	2,011	Port Allen	1,524	920
Plainville	1,058	1,004	Loyal	1,468	----	Rayville	2,076	1,499
Pleasanton	1,214	1,291	McVeigh	1,298	802	Roseland	1,139	603
Protection	1,072	1,109	Marion	1,892	1,718	St. Martinsville	2,455	2,465
Russell	2,352	1,700	Monticello	1,503	1,514	Springhill	1,546	748
Sabetha	2,332	2,003	Mortons Gap	1,068	1,061	Sulphur	1,888	1,714
St. John	1,552	1,671	Neon	1,077	493	Vidalia	1,141	1,246
St. Marys	1,304	1,321	Olive Hill	1,484	1,395	Ville Platte	1,722	1,364
Scammon	1,093	1,694	Paintsville	2,411	1,383	Vinton	1,989	1,441
Scott City	1,544	1,112	Park Hills	1,275	----	Vivian	1,646	1,864
Sedan	1,776	1,885	Prestonsburg	2,105	1,667	Washington	1,004	1,041
Seneca	1,864	1,885	Raceland	1,088	----	Welsh	1,514	1,456
Smith Center	1,736	1,567	Ravenna	1,189	----	White Castle	1,499	1,566
Solomon	1,032	1,071	Russell	2,084	1,756	Winnsboro	1,965	1,176
Stafford	1,614	1,752	Scottsville	1,867	2,179	Zwolle	1,264	909
Sterling	1,868	2,060	Seco	1,150	535			

2 Not returned separately.
10 The inclusion of Junction City in places of 1,000 to 2,500 is based upon the combined population (1,202 in 1930) of Junction City, La., and Junction City, Ark.

52   POPULATION—UNITED STATES SUMMARY

TABLE 16.—POPULATION OF INCORPORATED PLACES HAVING, IN 1930, FROM 1,000 TO 2,500 INHABITANTS: 1930 AND 1920—Continued

CITY, TOWN, VILLAGE, OR BOROUGH	1930	1920	CITY, TOWN, VILLAGE, OR BOROUGH	1930	1920	CITY, TOWN, VILLAGE, OR BOROUGH	1930	1920
MAINE			**MICHIGAN—con.**			**MINNESOTA**		
Bridgton Center	1,625	1,545	Frankfort	1,468	1,244	Ada	1,285	1,411
Farmington	1,737	1,650	Fremont	2,157	2,180	Adrian	1,000	1,087
Fort Kent	2,245	(2)	Garden City	2,081	-----	Aitkin	1,545	1,490
Gorham	1,088	(2)	Gaylord	1,627	1,701	Appleton	1,625	1,579
Lincoln	2,161	1,586	Gladwin	1,248	1,225	Aurora	1,463	2,809
Norway	2,446	2,208	Grandville	1,346	799	Barnesville	1,279	1,564
Pittsfield	2,075	2,146	Grayling	1,973	2,450	Belle Plaine	1,236	1,251
South Paris	1,961	1,793	Harbor Beach	1,892	1,927	Benson	2,095	2,111
			Harbor Springs	1,429	1,600	Bird Island	1,004	976
MARYLAND			Hart	1,690	1,590	Biwabik	1,383	2,024
Aberdeen	1,240	1,067	Hartford	1,484	1,361	Blooming Prairie	1,046	1,012
Bel Air	1,650	1,091	Holly	2,252	1,888	Bovey	1,248	1,324
Berlin	1,480	1,366	Homer	1,108	1,076	Breckinridge	2,204	2,401
Brentwood	1,842	-----	Hudson	2,361	2,464	Brooklyn Center	1,344	788
Capitol Heights	1,611	1,194	Imlay City	1,495	1,211	Buffalo	1,409	1,438
Centreville	1,291	1,765	Ithaca	1,780	1,929	Buhl	1,634	2,007
Chesapeake City	1,016	958	Jonesville	1,316	1,274	Caledonia	1,554	1,570
Colmar Manor	1,225		Lake Linden	1,714	2,182	Cambridge	1,183	1,080
Delmar	11 1,180	1,291	Lake Odessa	1,220	1,246	Canby	1,738	1,754
Denton	1,604	1,570	Lake Orion	1,369	929	Cannon Falls	1,358	1,315
Ellicott City	1,216	1,246	L'Anse	2,421	1,013	Cass Lake	1,409	2,109
Emmitsburg	1,235	940	Lawton	1,164	1,073	Chaska	1,901	1,966
Fairmont Heights	1,218		Leslie	1,105	1,089	Chatfield	1,269	1,382
Federalsburg	1,369	1,288	Lowell	1,919	1,730	Cokato	1,125	1,014
Gaithersburg	1,068	729	Mancelona	1,143	1,214	Cold Springs	1,147	705
Indianhead	1,240		Manchester	1,037	1,024	Coleraine	1,243	1,300
Lonaconing	2,426	2,054	Manton	1,008	793	Crystal	1,865	814
Luke	1,064		Marysville	1,405	941	Dawson	1,386	1,511
North East	1,412	1,112	Milan	1,947	1,557	Elk River	1,026	983
Oakland	1,583	1,225	Milford	1,364	1,088	Excelsior	1,072	799
Riverdale	1,533		Morenci	1,773	1,697	Farmington	1,342	1,449
Rockville	1,422	1,145	Mount Morris	1,982	1,174	Frazee	1,041	1,277
St. Michaels	1,308	1,347	Nashville	1,249	1,376	Glencoe	1,925	1,747
Snow Hill	1,004	1,684	Newaygo	1,227	1,160	Glenwood	2,220	2,187
Thurmont	1,185	1,074	New Baltimore	1,148	974	Golden Valley	1,326	830
Williamsport	1,775	1,615	Newberry	2,465	2,172	Granite Falls	1,791	1,611
			New Buffalo	1,051	496	Ironton	1,033	1,165
MICHIGAN			North Muskegon	1,370	630	Jackson	2,206	2,144
Algonac	1,736	1,303	Oak Park	1,079	-----	Janesville	1,184	1,261
Bad Axe	2,332	2,140	Onaway	1,492	2,739	Jordan	1,119	1,106
Bangor	1,274	1,243	Ontonagon	1,937	1,406	Kasson	1,019	1,150
Baraga	1,045	942	Ovid	1,131	1,067	Keewatin	2,134	1,879
Bellevue	1,029	1,035	Oxford	2,052	1,668	Kenyon	1,382	1,362
Berrien Springs	1,413	918	Paw Paw	1,684	1,556	Lake Crystal	1,173	1,204
Blissfield	2,103	1,906	Plainwell	2,279	2,049	Lakefield	1,349	1,346
Bloomfield Hills	1,127		Portland	1,902	1,899	Lanesboro	1,014	1,015
Brighton	1,287	800	Quincy	1,265	1,251	Le Sueur	1,897	1,795
Bronson	1,651	1,257	Reed City	1,792	1,803	Long Prairie	1,854	1,346
Calumet	1,557	2,390	Richmond	1,493	1,303	Madelia	1,397	1,447
Caspian	1,888	1,912	Rockford	1,613	1,143	Madison	1,916	1,838
Cass City	1,261	1,228	Romeo	2,283	2,102	Melrose	1,801	2,529
Cassopolis	1,448	1,385	St. Charles	1,463	1,489	Milaca	1,318	1,347
Cedar Springs	1,104	1,020	St. Ignace	2,109	1,852	Montgomery	1,570	1,297
Charlevoix	2,247	2,218	St. Louis	2,494	3,036	Mora	1,014	1,006
Chelsea	2,268	2,079	Saline	1,009	830	Morris	2,474	2,320
Chesaning	1,594	1,387	Sandusky	1,305	1,228	Mountain Iron	1,349	1,546
Clare	1,491	1,462	Scottville	1,002	1,045	Mountain Lake	1,388	1,309
Clinton	1,028	961	Sebewaing	1,441	1,446	New Prague	1,543	1,540
Clio	1,548	1,256	Shelby	1,152	1,288	Olivia	1,475	1,488
Constantine	1,259	1,277	South Range	1,120	1,435	Ortonville	2,017	1,758
Coopersville	1,004	914	Sparta	1,939	1,502	Osakis	1,155	1,480
Corunna	1,936	1,571	Spring Lake	1,271	973	Park Rapids	2,081	1,603
Crosswell	1,470	1,678	Stambaugh	2,400	2,263	Paynesville	1,121	1,060
Davison	1,298	811	Tawas City	1,034	1,018	Pelican Rapids	1,365	1,156
Decatur	1,582	1,270	Tecumseh	2,450	2,432	Perham	1,411	1,370
Dundee	1,364	1,108	Three Oaks	1,336	1,362	Pine City	1,343	1,303
East Jordan	1,523	2,428	Union City	1,104	1,268	Plainview	1,233	1,370
East Tawas	1,455	1,398	Vassar	1,816	1,453	Preston	1,214	1,227
Essexville	1,864	1,538	Vicksburg	1,735	1,712	Princeton	1,636	1,685
Evart	1,301	1,326	Watervliet	1,207	1,073	Red Lake Falls	1,386	1,549
Farmington	1,243	853	Wayland	1,013	853	Renville	1,064	1,142
Flat Rock	1,231		West Branch	1,164	1,015	Roseau	1,028	1,012
Flushing	1,723	1,169	Whitehall	1,304	1,230	Rushford	1,125	1,142
Fowlerville	1,141	1,057	Williamston	1,458	1,060	St. Charles	1,311	1,351
			Yale City	1,345	1,223	St. Joseph	1,009	717
						Sandstone	1,083	1,200

2 Not returned separately.
11 Combined population of Delmar Md. and Delmar, Del., 2,018 in 1930.

RURAL INCORPORATED PLACES 53

TABLE 16.—POPULATION OF INCORPORATED PLACES HAVING, IN 1930, FROM 1,000 TO 2,500 INHABITANTS: 1930 AND 1920—Continued

CITY, TOWN, VILLAGE, OR BOROUGH	1930	1920	CITY, TOWN, VILLAGE, OR BOROUGH	1930	1920	CITY, TOWN, VILLAGE, OR BOROUGH	1930	1920
MINNESOTA—con.			**MISSOURI**			**MISSOURI—con.**		
Shakopee	2,023	1,988	Albany	1,858	2,016	Pattonsburg	1,009	1,068
Slayton	1,102	1,045	Appleton City	1,136	1,262	Peirce City	1,135	1,476
Springfield	2,049	1,830	Ash Grove	1,107	1,000	Plattsburg	1,672	1,719
Spring Valley	1,712	1,871	Ava	1,041	845	Pleasant Hill	2,330	1,965
Wabasha	2,212	2,249	Bernie	1,031	1,571	Portageville	1,262	1,244
Waconia	1,291	901	Bethany	2,209	2,080	Potosi	1,279	984
Waite Park	1,318	963	Bevier	1,229	1,868	Princeton	1,509	1,576
Warren	1,472	1,772	Bismarck	1,185	949	Rich Hill	2,118	2,261
Warroad	1,184	1,211	Bloomfield	1,023	1,094	Rock Hill	1,309	------
Waterville	1,419	1,211	Bolivar	2,256	1,980	Rockport	1,162	1,136
Wayzata	1,100	633	Bowling Green	1,855	1,965	St. Clair	1,135	442
Wells	1,795	1,894	Brunswick	1,715	1,411	St. Ferdinand	1,039	682
Wheaton	1,279	1,337	California	2,384	2,218	St. James	1,294	1,117
Windom	2,123	2,123	Campbell	1,592	2,025	Salem	2,250	1,771
Winnebago	1,701	1,641	Canton	2,044	1,949	Salisbury	1,768	1,757
Winthrop	1,037	1,147	Carl Junction	1,042	1,377	Sarcoxie	1,017	1,023
Zumbrota	1,350	1,265	Carterville	1,600	2,434	Savannah	1,888	1,831
			Cassville	1,016	1,002	Senath	1,086	1,054
MISSISSIPPI			Centralia	2,009	2,071	Seneca	1,063	1,104
			Clarence	1,286	1,400	Shelbina	1,826	1,809
Ackerman	1,169	1,264	Concordia	1,140	962	Shrewsbury	1,525	845
Baldwyn	1,106	922	Crane	1,030	1,151	Stanberry	2,029	1,864
Batesville	1,062	1,050	Deepwater	1,093	1,391	Steele	1,219	751
Bonneville	1,703	1,495	Doniphan	1,398	1,248	Sugar Creek	1,657	------
Bude	1,378	1,121	East Prairie	1,385	1,124	Sullivan	2,013	909
Calhoun City	1,012	502	Edina	1,532	1,438	Sweet Springs	1,641	1,177
Centerville	1,344	755	Eldorado Springs	1,917	2,212	Tarkio	2,016	1,870
Charleston	2,014	3,007	Elsberry	1,204	1,255	Thayer	1,632	1,738
Cohay	1,092	------	Elvins	2,403	2,418	Tipton	1,067	1,170
Crystal Springs	2,257	1,395	Fornfelt	1,500	1,819	Troy	1,419	1,116
Drew	1,373	721	Gallatin	1,504	1,747	Union	2,143	1,605
Durant	2,480	1,870	Gideon	1,315	1,197	Unionville	1,811	1,765
Electric Mills	1,084	600	Glasgow	1,409	1,351	Valley Park	1,772	899
Ellisville	2,127	1,681	Glendale	1,451	749	Vandalia	2,450	2,158
Eupora	1,092	943	Granby	1,445	1,736	Versailles	1,662	1,651
Forest	2,176	1,188	Grant City	1,126	1,305	Warrenton	1,250	800
Gloster	1,139	1,079	Greenfield	1,304	1,440	Warsaw	1,102	925
Hazlehurst	2,447	1,762	Hamilton	1,572	1,689	Wellsville	1,525	1,551
Hollandale	1,211	799	Harrisonville	2,306	2,073	Weston	1,028	991
Holly Springs	2,271	2,113	Hayti	1,620	1,507	Willow Springs	1,430	1,441
Houston	1,477	1,408	Hermann	2,063	1,701	Windsor	1,879	2,034
Itta Bena	1,370	1,620	Holden	1,807	2,011			
Iuka	1,441	1,306	Humansville	1,022	947	**MONTANA**		
Leland	2,426	2,003	Huntsville	1,897	2,126			
Long Beach	1,346	980	Illmo	1,129	1,275	Baker	1,212	1,067
Lumberton	2,374	2,192	Jackson	2,465	2,114	Big Timber	1,224	1,282
Macon	2,198	2,051	Kahoka	1,507	1,624	Browning	1,172	986
Magnolia	1,660	2,012	King City	1,101	1,150	Chinook	1,320	1,217
Marks	1,258	1,020	La Grange	1,160	1,114	Conrad	1,499	988
Moorhead	1,553	1,600	Lamar	2,381	2,255	Dillon	2,422	2,701
Moss Point	2,453	3,340	La Plata	1,406	1,463	East Helena	1,039	------
Newton	2,011	1,604	Lees Summit	2,035	1,467	Forsyth	1,591	1,838
Northfield	1,399	1,080	Lilbourn	1,154	986	Fort Benton	1,109	1,065
Ocean Springs	1,663	1,732	Malden	2,025	2,098	Glasgow	2,216	2,059
Okolona	2,235	3,852	Marionville	1,227	1,167	Hamilton	1,839	1,700
Pelahatchie	1,599	1,212	Marshfield	1,378	1,371	Hardin	1,169	1,312
Pontotoc	2,018	1,274	Memphis	1,728	1,941	Harlowton	1,473	1,856
Poplarville	1,498	1,290	Milan	2,002	2,395	Libby	1,752	1,522
Port Gibson	1,861	1,691	Monroe City	1,820	1,941	Malta	1,342	1,427
Quitman	1,872	1,375	Montgomery City	1,510	1,688	Philipsburg	1,300	1,724
Ripley	1,468	856	Morehouse	1,165	1,913	Plentywood	1,226	888
Rosedale	2,117	1,696	Mound City	1,525	1,472	Polson	1,455	1,132
Ruleville	1,181	1,022	Mountain Grove	2,229	2,212	Poplar	1,046	1,152
Sardis	1,298	1,352	Mount Vernon	1,342	1,254	Scobey	1,259	1,170
Senatobia	1,264	1,126	Newburg	1,036	1,235	Shelby	2,004	537
Shaw	1,612	1,375	New Franklin	1,210	848	Sidney	2,010	1,400
Shelby	1,811	1,300	New Madrid	2,309	1,908	Walkerville	2,052	2,391
Summit	1,157	1,187	Norborne	1,190	1,180	Wolf Point	1,539	2,098
Sumrall	1,364	1,444	Odessa	1,861	1,786			
Tunica	1,043	955	Osceola	1,043	1,025	**NEBRASKA**		
Tylertown	1,102	1,116	Owensville	1,424	777			
Union	1,705	1,012	Pacific	1,456	1,275	Ainsworth	1,378	1,508
Waynesboro	1,120	689	Palmyra	1,967	1,964	Albion	2,172	1,978
Wiggins	1,074	1,037	Paris	1,367	1,431	Alma	1,235	1,058
Woodville	1,113	1,012	Parma	1,051	1,241	Arapahoe	1,017	894

54   POPULATION—UNITED STATES SUMMARY

TABLE 16.—POPULATION OF INCORPORATED PLACES HAVING, IN 1930, FROM 1,000 TO 2,500 INHABITANTS: 1930 AND 1920—Continued

NEBRASKA—con.

CITY, TOWN, VILLAGE, OR BOROUGH	1930	1920
Ashland	1,786	1,725
Atkinson	1,144	1,300
Bayard	1,559	2,127
Beaver City	1,024	1,103
Bellevue	1,017	695
Benkelman	1,154	1,009
Bloomfield	1,435	1,431
Bridgeport	1,421	1,235
Burwell	1,156	1,214
Cambridge	1,203	1,042
Central City	2,474	2,410
Chappell	1,061	1,131
Cozad	1,813	1,293
Crawford	1,703	1,646
Creighton	1,388	1,446
David City	2,333	2,216
Deshler	1,177	944
Franklin	1,103	1,055
Friend	1,214	1,263
Fullerton	1,680	1,595
Geneva	1,662	1,768
Genoa	1,089	1,069
Gordon	1,958	1,581
Gothenburg	2,322	1,754
Hartington	1,568	1,467
Hebron	1,804	1,513
Hemingford	1,025	708
Humboldt	1,435	1,277
Kimball	1,711	1,620
Loup City	1,446	1,364
Madison	1,842	1,735
Minatare	1,079	660
Minden	1,716	1,527
Mitchell	2,058	1,298
Neligh	1,649	1,724
Newman Grove	1,146	1,260
North Bend	1,108	1,087
Oakland	1,433	1,356
Ogallala	1,631	1,062
O'Neill	2,019	2,107
Ord	2,226	2,143
Osceola	1,054	1,209
Oxford	1,155	739
Pawnee City	1,573	1,595
Pender	1,006	992
Pierce	1,271	1,105
Plainview	1,216	1,199
Randolph	1,145	1,338
Ravenna	1,559	1,703
Red Cloud	1,519	1,856
Rushville	1,006	955
St. Edwards	1,030	1,002
St. Paul	1,621	1,615
Scribner	1,066	1,021
Stanton	1,479	1,487
Stromsburg	1,320	1,361
Sutton	1,540	1,603
Tecumseh	1,829	1,688
Tekamah	1,804	1,811
Tilden	1,106	1,101
Valentine	1,672	1,596
Valley	1,039	764
Wakefield	1,112	1,114
Walthill	1,162	1,145
Wayne	2,381	2,115
Weeping Water	1,029	1,084
West Point	2,225	2,002
Wilber	1,352	1,255
Wisner	1,327	1,210

NEVADA

CITY, TOWN, VILLAGE, OR BOROUGH	1930	1920
Carson City	1,596	1,685
Fallon	1,758	1,753
Lovelock	1,263	1,164
Winnemucca	1,989	(2)
Yerington	1,005	1,169

NEW JERSEY

CITY, TOWN, VILLAGE, OR BOROUGH	1930	1920
Absecon	2,158	702
Allendale	1,730	1,165
Alpha	2,374	2,140
Atlantic Highlands	2,000	1,629
Avon-by-the-Sea	1,220	647
Barrington	2,252	1,333
Bellmawr	1,123	------
Belvidere	2,073	1,793
Berlin	1,955	------
Brooklawn	1,753	------
Clayton	2,351	1,905
Cresskill	1,924	942
Demarest	1,013	654
Eatontown	1,938	------
Elmer	1,219	1,115
Emerson	1,394	973
Essex Fells	1,115	598
Fair Haven	2,260	1,295
Fanwood	1,681	724
Florham Park	1,269	570
Frenchtown	1,189	1,104
Hamburg	1,160	------
Harrington Park	1,251	627
Haworth	1,042	748
High Bridge	1,860	1,795
Highlands	1,877	1,731
Hopewell	1,467	1,339
Jamesburg	2,048	2,052
Keansburg	2,190	1,321
Kenilworth	2,243	1,312
Laurel Springs	1,343	911
Lawnside	1,379	------
Lincoln Park	1,831	------
Linwood	1,514	638
Little Silver	1,109	------
Magnolia	1,522	1,245
Manasquan	2,320	1,705
Matawan	2,264	1,910
Mendham	1,278	969
Montvale	1,243	779
Moonachie	1,465	1,194
Morris Plains	1,713	------
Mountain Lakes	2,132	------
Mount Ephraim	2,319	------
National Park	1,828	1,000
Neptune City	2,258	539
Netcong	2,097	1,800
New Providence	1,918	1,203
North Caldwell	1,492	683
North Haledon	2,157	887
Northvale	1,144	827
North Wildwood	2,049	807
Norwood	1,358	820
Oceanport	1,872	------
Ogdensburg	1,138	939
Oradell	2,360	1,286
Park Ridge	2,229	1,481
Peapack-Gladstone	1,273	1,226
Pennington	1,335	965
Pine Hill	1,392	------
Point Pleasant	2,058	------
Point Pleasant Beach	1,844	1,575
Ringwood	1,038	1,025
Riverdale	1,052	------
Riverside	2,210	1,077
Riverton	2,483	2,341
Roseland	1,058	609
Rumson	2,073	1,658
Runnemede	2,436	------
Somerdale	1,151	------
Somers Point	2,073	843
South Bound Brook	1,763	1,302
Spring Lake	1,745	1,009
Spring Lake Heights	1,221	------

NEW JERSEY—con.

CITY, TOWN, VILLAGE, OR BOROUGH	1930	1920
Stanhope	1,089	1,031
Sussex	1,415	1,318
Swedesboro	2,123	1,838
Tuckerton	1,429	1,106
Union Beach	1,893	------
Waldwick	1,728	1,296
Wenonah	1,245	918
West Cape May	1,048	967
West Long Branch	1,686	966
Woodbine	2,164	1,406
Woodstown	1,832	1,589

NEW MEXICO

CITY, TOWN, VILLAGE, OR BOROUGH	1930	1920
Artesia	2,427	1,115
Belen	2,116	1,306
Carrizozo	1,171	1,301
Farmington	1,350	728
Hot Springs	1,336	455
Lordsburg	2,069	1,325
Magdalena	1,371	1,867
Mountainair	1,027	577
Santa Rosa	1,127	1,093
Socorro	2,058	1,256
Tularosa	1,406	1,096

NEW YORK

CITY, TOWN, VILLAGE, OR BOROUGH	1930	1920
Adams	1,613	1,557
Addison	1,538	1,699
Akron	2,188	1,960
Alexandria Bay	1,952	1,649
Allegany	1,411	1,350
Andover	1,241	1,132
Angola	1,543	1,367
Arcade	1,643	1,609
Ardsley	1,135	730
Athens	1,618	1,844
Attica	2,212	2,015
Avon	2,403	2,585
Bainbridge	1,324	1,259
Bayville	1,042	(2)
Bellerose	1,202	------
Belmont	1,085	1,021
Blasdell	2,015	1,401
Bolivar	1,725	1,146
Boonville	2,090	1,914
Brewster	1,664	859
Briar Cliff Manor	1,794	1,027
Brightwaters	1,061	250
Broadalbin	1,341	------
Brocton	1,301	1,383
Buchanan	1,346	------
Caledonia	1,487	1,170
Cambridge	1,762	1,559
Camden	1,912	1,941
Camillus	1,036	808
Castleton-on-Hudson	1,506	1,595
Cattaraugus	1,236	1,347
Cazenovia	1,788	1,683
Celoron	1,182	757
Champlain	1,197	1,140
Chateaugay	1,169	1,291
Chatham	2,424	2,710
Chester	1,154	1,049
Clayton	1,940	1,849
Clifton Springs	1,819	1,628
Clinton	1,475	1,270
Clyde	2,374	2,528
Cold Spring	1,784	1,433
Colonie	1,176	------
Cornwall	1,910	1,755
Coxsackie	2,195	2,121
Croton-on-Hudson	2,447	2,286
Cuba	1,422	1,611
Delhi	1,840	1,669

2 Not returned separately.

RURAL INCORPORATED PLACES   55

TABLE 16.—POPULATION OF INCORPORATED PLACES HAVING, IN 1930, FROM 1,000 TO 2,500 INHABITANTS: 1930 AND 1920—Continued

CITY, TOWN, VILLAGE, OR BOROUGH	1930	1920	CITY, TOWN, VILLAGE, OR BOROUGH	1930	1920	CITY, TOWN, VILLAGE, OR BOROUGH	1930	1920
NEW YORK—con.			**NEW YORK—con.**			**NO. CAROLINA—con.**		
Deposit	1,887	1,943	Sherburne	1,077	1,104	Maxton	1,386	1,397
Dexter	1,020	1,164	Sherrill	2,150	1,761	Mayodan	1,948	1,886
Dundee	1,086	1,143	Shortsville	1,332	1,300	Mebane	1,568	1,351
East Hampton	1,934		Sidney	2,444	2,670	Mocksville	1,503	1,146
Fayetteville	2,008	1,584	Skaneateles	1,882	1,635	Mount Gilead	1,011	975
Fonda	1,170	1,208	Sloatsburg	1,623		Mount Holly	2,254	1,160
Franklinville	2,021	2,015	Sodus	1,444	1,329	Murfreesboro	1,000	621
Friendship	1,154	1,026	South Nyack	2,212	1,799	Murphy	1,612	1,314
Geneseo	2,261	2,157	Spencerport	1,249	926	Nashville	1,137	939
Great Neck Estates	1,738	339	Stamford	1,103	947	Norwood	1,452	1,221
Greene	1,379	1,207	Stewart Manor	1,291		Pilot Mountain	1,010	707
Greenwich	2,290	2,384	Stillwater	1,051	982	Pineville	1,108	650
Groton	2,004	2,235	Trumansburg	1,077	1,011	Plymouth	2,139	1,847
Hamilton	1,700	1,505	Unadilla	1,063	1,157	Raeford	1,303	1,235
Hammondsport	1,063	1,060	Valatie	1,246	1,301	Ramseur	1,220	1,014
Hancock	1,427	1,326	Victor	1,042	945	Randleman	1,863	1,967
Hillburn	1,303	1,112	Warwick	2,443	2,420	Red Springs	1,300	1,018
Holley	1,558	1,625	Waterville	1,298	1,255	Robersonville	1,181	1,199
Honeoye Falls	1,187	1,107	Wayland	1,814	1,790	Rutherfordton	2,020	1,693
Horseheads	2,430	2,078	Webster	1,552	1,247	St. Pauls	2,080	1,147
Island Park	1,002		Weedsport	1,325	1,379	Scotland Neck	2,339	2,061
Jordan	1,145	1,012	West Carthage	1,722	1,666	Selma	1,857	1,601
Keeseville	1,794	1,524	Wolcott	1,260	1,186	Siler City	1,730	1,253
Kings Point	1,294					Southport	1,760	1,664
Lakewood	1,837	714	**NORTH CAROLINA**			Spring Hope	1,222	1,221
Lewiston	1,013	723				Spruce Pine	1,546	717
Little Valley	1,196	1,253	Aberdeen	1,382	858	Stanley	1,084	584
Liverpool	2,244	1,831	Ahoskie	1,940	1,420	Sylva	1,340	863
McGrawville	1,082	1,032	Andrews	1,748	1,634	Tabor	1,165	782
Malverne	2,256		Aulander	1,041	803	Troy	1,522	1,102
Manchester	1,429	1,418	Ayden	1,607	1,673	Tryon	1,670	1,067
Manlius	1,538	1,296	Belhaven	2,458	1,816	Valdese	1,816	
Marcellus	1,083	989	Benson	1,522	1,123	Wake Forest	1,536	1,425
Maybrook	1,159		Bethel	1,149	817	Walnut Cove	1,081	651
Mayville	1,273	1,207	Boone	1,295	374	Warrenton	1,072	927
Menands	1,522		Brevard	2,339	1,658	Warsaw	1,222	1,108
Mexico	1,297	1,336	Bryson	1,806	882	Waynesville	2,414	1,942
Middleport	1,596	1,416	Burgaw	1,209	1,040	Weldon	2,323	1,872
Millbrook	1,296	1,096	Carrboro	1,242	1,129	West Hickory	1,706	1,266
Monroe	1,621	1,527	Carthage	1,129	962	Whiteville	2,203	1,664
Montour Falls	1,489	1,560	Chadbourn	1,311	1,121	Wilkesboro	1,042	814
Moravia	1,295	1,331	China Grove	1,258	1,027	Windsor	1,425	1,210
Naples	1,070	1,148	Clayton	1,533	1,423			
New Berlin	1,076	1,070	Cornelius	1,230	1,141	**NORTH DAKOTA**		
New Hartford	1,885	1,021	Dallas	1,489	1,397			
New Paltz	1,362	1,056	Davidson	1,445	1,156	Ashley	1,003	1,009
North Collins	1,165	1,158	East Flat Rock	1,062		Beach	1,263	1,106
North Syracuse	1,766		East Lumberton	1,111	1,011	Bottineau	1,322	1,172
Northville	1,250	1,190	East Spencer	2,098	2,239	Cando	1,164	1,111
Norwood	1,880	1,808	Elkin	2,357	1,195	Carrington	1,717	1,420
Nunda	1,085	1,152	Enfield	2,234	1,048	Casselton	1,253	1,538
Oakfield	1,919	1,422	Fairmont	1,314	1,000	Cooperstown	1,053	1,112
Old Westbury	1,264		Farmville	2,056	1,780	Crosby	1,271	1,147
Orchard Park	1,144		Franklin	1,094	773	Ellendale	1,264	1,334
Oriskany	1,142	1,101	Franklinton	1,320	1,058	Enderlin	1,839	1,919
Oxford	1,601	1,590	Fremont	1,316	1,294	Garrison	1,024	714
Painted Post	2,328	2,170	Gibsonville	1,605	1,302	Hankinson	1,400	1,477
Pawling	1,204	1,032	Granite Falls	2,147	1,101	Harvey	2,157	1,590
Pelham	2,053	1,056	Hazelwood	1,168	484	Hebron	1,348	1,374
Phelps	1,397	1,200	Hertford	1,914	1,704	Hettinger	1,292	817
Philmont	1,868	1,919	Highland	1,514	1,062	Hillsboro	1,317	1,183
Phoenix	1,758	1,747	Hillsboro	1,232	1,180	Kenmare	1,494	1,446
Piermont	1,765	1,600	Jonesville	1,306	787	Langdon	1,221	1,228
Pittsford	1,460	1,328	Kernersville	1,754	1,219	Lidgerwood	1,029	1,065
Port Dickinson	1,902	883	La Grange	1,500	1,399	Linton	1,192	1,011
Port Henry	2,040	2,183	Landis	1,388	972	Lisbon	1,650	1,855
Pulaski	2,046	1,895	Leaksville	1,814	1,606	Mayville	1,199	1,218
Randolph	1,308	1,310	Littleton	1,133	1,010	Mott	1,036	723
Ravena	1,963	2,093	Longview	1,262	755	New Rockford	2,195	2,111
Rhinebeck	1,569	1,397	Louisburg	2,182	1,954	Oakes	1,709	1,637
Richfield Springs	1,333	1,388	Lowell	1,664	1,151	Park River	1,131	1,114
Rouses Point	1,920	1,700	Madison	1,497	1,247	Rugby	1,512	1,424
St. Johnsville	2,273	2,469	Maiden	1,628	1,266	Wilton	1,001	1,026
Salem	1,081	1,083	Marion	2,467	1,784	Wishek	1,146	1,003
Schuylerville	1,411	1,625	Marshall	1,132	748			

56 POPULATION—UNITED STATES SUMMARY

TABLE 16.—POPULATION OF INCORPORATED PLACES HAVING, IN 1930, FROM 1,000 TO 2,500 INHABITANTS: 1930 AND 1920—Continued

CITY, TOWN, VILLAGE, OR BOROUGH	1930	1920	CITY, TOWN, VILLAGE, OR BOROUGH	1930	1920	CITY, TOWN, VILLAGE, OR BOROUGH	1930	1920
OHIO			**OHIO—continued**			**OHIO—continued**		
Ada	2,499	2,321	Loudonville	2,068	1,887	Wellington	2,235	2,245
Addyston	1,768	1,448	Loveland	1,954	1,557	West Carrollton	2,101	1,430
Adena	1,286	724	Lyndhurst	1,922	288	West Jefferson	1,376	1,170
Amsterdam	1,171	1,271	McArthur	1,188	1,307	West Lafayette	1,106	921
Antwerp	1,024	1,096	McConnelsville	1,754	1,618	West Liberty	1,248	1,347
Arcanum	1,149	1,311	McDonald	1,714	621	West Milton	1,388	1,256
Archbold	1,185	1,125	Madeira	1,162	600	West Union	1,094	992
Arlington Heights	1,214	730	Malvern	1,100	979	Wickliffe	2,491	1,508
Ashville	1,085	1,032	Manchester	2,009	1,824	Williamsburg	1,147	969
Avon	1,826	1,460	Marblehead	1,027	1,048	Woodsfield	2,317	2,394
Avon Lake	1,610	904	Mechanicsburg	1,424	1,470	Woodville	1,151	910
Batavia	1,119	1,088	Mentor	1,589	851	Worthington	1,239	705
Bay	2,294	751	Miles Heights	2,042	------	Yellow Springs	1,427	1,264
Belpre	1,724	1,317	Milford	1,915	1,525	Yorkville	1,963	1,754
Bethel	1,312	1,340	Millersburg	2,203	2,098			
Bethesda	1,159	1,182	Minster	1,331	1,538	**OKLAHOMA**		
Blanchester	1,597	1,671	Mogadore	1,502	751			
Bluffton	2,035	1,950	Monroeville	1,080	1,185	Afton	1,219	1,518
Bradford	1,732	2,356	Mount Gilead	1,871	1,837	Allen	1,438	1,377
Bratenahl	1,308	1,000	Mount Sterling	1,090	1,113	Antlers	2,246	1,842
Brecksville	1,308	------	Murray City	1,048	1,493	Apache	1,302	919
Bremen	1,232	1,134	Navarre	1,503	1,385	Atoka	1,856	2,088
Brewster	1,464	928	New Bremen	1,485	1,502	Barnsdall	2,001	2,099
Brilliant	1,682	1,500	New Carlisle	1,089	1,019	Beaver City	1,028	920
Brookville	1,403	1,336	New Concord	1,087	889	Beggs	1,531	2,327
Caldwell	1,778	1,706	New London	1,527	1,470	Bethany	2,032	485
Canal Fulton	1,160	1,057	New Miami	1,239	------	Bixby	1,251	1,249
Canfield	1,015	806	New Richmond	1,830	1,714	Blanchard	1,040	842
Cardington	1,192	1,109	New Straitsville	1,718	2,208	Boise City	1,256	------
Carrollton	2,286	2,192	North Baltimore	2,402	2,439	Boynton	1,204	1,204
Chardon	1,818	1,566	Northfield	1,750	861	Britton	2,214	1,070
Chauncey	1,269	1,178	North Royalton	1,397	------	Broken Arrow	1,954	2,086
Chesapeake	1,094	821	Oak Harbor	1,849	1,858	Broken Bow	2,291	1,983
Cleves	1,711	1,454	Oak Hill	1,578	1,394	Carnegie	2,063	1,150
Coal Grove	2,181	1,851	Osborn	1,271	1,059	Cement	1,117	1,098
Coldwater	1,787	1,531	Ottawa	2,169	2,167	Checotah	2,110	2,390
Columbiana	2,485	2,114	Ottawa Hills	1,185	------	Chelsea	1,527	1,692
Columbus Grove	1,633	1,768	Paulding	1,904	2,106	Cherokee	2,236	2,017
Corning	1,411	1,628	Payne	1,014	984	Coalgate	2,064	3,009
Covington	1,807	1,885	Peebles	1,235	1,008	Collinsville	2,219	3,801
Creston	1,029	894	Plain City	1,288	1,330	Comanche	1,704	1,427
Delta	1,778	1,543	Plymouth	1,339	1,374	Coweta	1,274	1,318
Deshler	1,538	1,514	Powhatan Point	2,329	406	Crescent	1,190	878
Dillonvale	1,434	1,643	Prospect	1,013	949	Davenport	1,072	440
Dover	2,453	1,754	Richwood	1,573	1,601	Davis	1,705	1,609
Doyleston	1,150	1,037	Ripley	1,556	1,529	Depew	1,128	(2)
Dresden	1,362	1,434	Roseville	1,413	1,349	Dewey	2,095	2,802
East Columbus	1,958	1,328	Sabina	1,296	1,504	Earlsboro	1,950	317
Elmore	1,107	937	St. Clairsville	2,440	1,561	Eldorado	1,183	967
Fairfield	1,240	329	St. Paris	1,177	1,226	Erick	2,231	971
Flushing	1,119	1,026	Salineville	2,133	2,700	Eufaula	2,073	2,286
Forest	1,103	1,143	Sharonville	1,111	753	Fairfax	2,134	1,342
Fort Recovery	1,118	1,092	Shawnee	1,457	1,918	Fairview	1,887	1,751
Fredericktown	1,257	1,194	Sheffield Lake	1,256	------	Fort Gibson	1,159	1,353
Garrettsville	1,179	1,119	Shreve	1,103	1,094	Garber City	1,356	1,446
Genoa	1,437	971	Silverton	1,843	795	Geary	1,892	1,167
Georgetown	1,531	1,670	Smithfield	1,023	620	Grandfield	1,416	1,990
Germantown	2,029	1,827	Solon	1,027	------	Granite	1,341	912
Gibsonburg	2,129	1,737	Somerset	1,297	1,339	Guymon	2,181	1,507
Glendale	2,360	1,759	South Charleston	1,208	1,267	Haileyville	1,801	2,067
Granville	1,467	1,440	South Zanesville	1,278	1,010	Haskell	1,682	2,196
Grove City	1,546	905	Spencerville	1,612	1,543	Healdton	2,017	2,157
Harrison	[11]1,449	1,309	Strasburg	1,305	917	Heavener	2,269	1,850
Hicksville	2,445	2,378	Strongsville	1,349	------	Hennessey	1,271	1,319
Hudson	1,324	1,134	Swanton	1,505	1,248	Hinton	1,009	744
Huron	1,699	1,703	Sylvania	2,106	1,222	Hooker	1,628	946
Independence	1,525	1,074	Tiltonville [13]	2,242	1,694	Jenks	1,110	1,508
Jefferson	1,601	1,532	University Heights	2,237	131	Kaw City	1,001	627
Johnstown	1,006	906	Utica	1,394	1,658	Konawa	2,070	896
Lakemore	1,670	------	Vermilion	1,464	1,436	Krebs	1,375	2,078
Leetonia	2,332	2,688	Versailles	1,465	1,563	Lindsay	1,713	1,543
Leipsic	1,571	1,788	Waverly	1,603	1,625	Lone Wolf	1,023	657
Lodi	1,273	1,240	Waynesburg	1,186	978			

[2] Not returned separately.
[11] Combined population of Harrison, Ohio, and West Harrison, Ind., 1,728 in 1930.
[13] Name changed from Grover in 1930.

RURAL INCORPORATED PLACES   57

TABLE 16.—POPULATION OF INCORPORATED PLACES HAVING, IN 1930, FROM 1,000 TO 2,500 INHABITANTS: 1930 AND 1920—Continued

CITY, TOWN, VILLAGE, OR BOROUGH	1930	1920	CITY, TOWN, VILLAGE, OR BOROUGH	1930	1920	CITY, TOWN, VILLAGE, OR BOROUGH	1930	1920
OKLAHOMA—con.			**PENNSYLVANIA**			**PENNSYLVANIA—continued**		
Madill	2,203	2,717	Albion	1,681	1,549	Hastings	2,011	2,292
Marietta	1,505	1,977	Aldan	2,269	1,136	Hatfield	1,149	830
Medford	1,084	1,050	Auburn	1,170	977	Hawley	1,811	1,939
Morris	1,706	1,926	Austin	1,116	1,556	Heidelberg	2,130	2,004
Mountain View	1,025	917	Avis	1,268	1,002	Highspire	2,327	2,031
Newkirk	2,135	2,533	Avonmore	1,240	1,242	Homer City	2,004	1,802
Oilton	1,518	2,231	Baden	1,924	895	Hooversville	1,448	1,345
O'Keene	1,035	1,084	Bath	1,625	1,401	Houston	1,742	1,398
Prague	1,299	1,127	Beaver Meadow	1,890	1,709	Houtzdale	1,351	1,504
Pryor Creek	1,823	1,767	Bellevernon	2,489	2,342	Hughestown	2,252	2,244
Quapaw	1,340	1,394	Ben Avon	2,472	2,198	Hughesville	1,868	1,577
Quinton	1,804	1,557	Berlin	1,393	1,563	Hyndman	1,190	1,179
Ringling	1,002	1,039	Bessemer	2,001	1,417	Irvona	1,213	1,157
Rush Springs	1,340	768	Blawnox	2,186	-----	Koppel	1,057	762
Ryan	1,258	1,379	Blossburg	1,696	2,033	Langhorne	1,147	1,067
Sallisaw	1,785	2,255	Boswell	1,775	2,168	Lebanon Independent	2,252	2,136
Sentinel	1,269	723	Bridgewater	1,792	1,340	Ligonier	1,978	1,807
Shattuck	1,490	1,305	Brownstown	1,586	1,489	Lilly	2,162	2,346
Shidler	1,177	-----	Burgettstown	2,266	1,990	Littlestown	2,001	1,552
Skiatook	1,789	1,653	California	2,362	2,480	Lorain	1,360	812
Snyder	1,195	1,197	Cambridge Springs	1,665	1,663	McSherrystown	2,050	1,800
Stigler	1,517	1,797	Canton	1,904	2,154	Malvern	1,551	1,286
Stilwell	1,366	1,155	Carrolltown	1,227	1,369	Manor	1,305	1,077
Stroud	1,894	1,361	Catawissa	2,023	2,025	Mansfield	1,755	1,609
Tahlequah	2,495	2,271	Central City	2,107	1,051	Marianna	1,762	1,124
Talihina	1,032	690	Centralia	2,446	2,336	Marietta	1,969	1,735
Tecumseh	2,419	1,429	Chalfant	1,192	1,044	Marion Heights	2,001	1,874
Temple	1,182	906	Cheswick	1,053	471	Mars	1,302	1,226
Texhoma[14]	819	687	Coalport	1,222	1,079	Martinsburg	1,295	955
Thomas	1,256	1,223	Cokeburg	1,550	1,691	Marysville	1,922	1,877
Tipton	1,459	727	Colwyn	2,064	1,859	Matamoras	1,784	1,535
Tishomingo	1,281	1,871	Conway	2,014	1,858	Mercer	2,125	1,932
Walters	2,262	3,032	Coopersburg	1,057	870	Mercersburg	1,634	1,663
Watonga	2,228	1,678	Cornwall	1,837	-----	Middleburg	1,024	984
Waurika	2,368	3,204	Courtdale	1,007	600	Middleport	1,225	984
Waynoka	1,840	1,500	Cresson	2,317	2,170	Mifflinburg	1,959	1,744
Weatherford	2,417	1,929	Cressona	1,946	1,739	Mifflintown	1,027	1,083
Weleetka	2,042	1,588	Dallas	1,188	581	Millerstown	1,052	802
Wetumka	2,153	1,422	Dalton	1,072	786	Mill Hall	1,421	1,288
Wilburton	1,524	2,226	Denver	1,203	1,125	Mohnton	1,824	1,640
Wynnewood	1,820	2,200	Dravosburg	2,391	2,204	Montgomery	1,903	1,798
Wynona	1,171	2,749	Du Boistown	1,049	756	Montrose	1,909	1,661
Yale	1,734	2,601	Dunbar	1,357	1,607	Morton	1,341	1,212
Yukon	1,455	1,016	Duncannon	1,732	1,679	Mount Holly Springs	1,140	1,109
			Duncansville	1,379	1,230	Mount Jewett	1,379	1,494
OREGON			East Brady	1,563	1,531	Muncy	2,413	2,054
			East Greenville	1,749	1,620	Nescopeck	1,614	1,638
Bandon	1,516	1,440	East Vandergrift	2,441	1,969	New Bethlehem	1,590	1,662
Beaverton	1,138	580	East Washington	1,859	1,561	New Eagle	1,703	1,572
Cottage Grove	2,473	1,919	Eddystone	2,414	2,670	New Freedom	1,125	906
Enterprise	1,379	1,895	Edenburg	1,037	806	New Holland	1,725	1,453
Forest Grove	1,859	1,915	Edgeworth	1,679	1,373	New Hope	1,113	1,093
Gladstone	1,348	1,069	Eldred	1,118	1,037	New Oxford	1,138	949
Gresham	1,635	1,103	Elizabethville	1,341	1,236	Newport	1,891	1,972
Heppner	1,190	1,324	Elkland	1,978	1,703	Newtown	1,824	1,703
Independence	1,248	1,143	Ellport	1,000	-----	Newville	1,482	1,482
Lakeview	1,799	1,139	Ellsworth	2,274	2,828	North Apollo	1,485	-----
Lebanon	1,851	1,805	Emlenton	1,137	1,025	North Girard	1,077	-----
Milton	1,576	1,747	Evansburg	1,561	1,548	North Irwin	1,064	908
Milwaukie	1,767	1,172	Everett	1,874	1,687	North Wales	2,393	2,041
Myrtle Point	1,302	934	Everson	1,900	1,988	North York	2,416	2,239
Newport	1,530	980	Export	2,184	2,596	Oakdale	1,703	1,611
Ontario	1,941	2,039	Fairchance	1,804	2,124	Oakland	1,040	1,120
Oswego	1,285	1,818	Falls Creek	1,231	1,364	Orwigsburg	2,031	1,985
Prineville	1,027	1,144	Fayette City	1,594	2,048	Osceola	2,002	2,512
Rainier	1,353	1,287	Fleetwood	2,150	1,652	Paint	1,336	1,283
Reedsport	1,178	850	Flemington	1,191	1,131	Palo Alto	1,908	1,667
Seaside	1,565	1,802	Folcroft	1,432	-----	Parkesburg	2,288	2,543
Sheridan	1,008	979	Franklin	2,323	2,632	Parkside	1,497	374
Silverton	2,462	2,251	Freemansburg	1,777	1,203	Paxtang	1,594	822
Springfield	2,364	1,855	Galeton	2,200	2,969	Pennsburg	1,494	1,404
Toledo	2,137	678	Girard	1,554	1,242	Pine Grove	2,257	1,778
Union	1,107	1,319	Glen Rock	1,309	1,232	Point Marion	2,039	1,607
Vernonia	1,625	142	Gordon	1,069	1,078			
West Linn	1,956	1,628	Greentree	1,457	1,043			
Woodburn	1,675	1,656	Hallstead	1,254	1,261			

[14] The inclusion of Texhoma in places of 1,000 to 2,500 is based upon the combined population (1,119 in 1930) of Texhoma, Okla., and Texhoma, Tex.

58 POPULATION—UNITED STATES SUMMARY

TABLE 16.—POPULATION OF INCORPORATED PLACES HAVING, IN 1930, FROM 1,000 TO 2,500 INHABITANTS: 1930 AND 1920—Continued

CITY, TOWN, VILLAGE, OR BOROUGH	1930	1920
PENNSYLVANIA—continued		
Port Allegany	2,193	2,356
Pringle	2,372	1,960
Quarryville	1,028	823
Rimersburg	1,319	1,060
Robesonia	1,468	1,203
Rockledge	1,920	1,029
Rockwood	1,176	1,362
Roscoe	1,310	1,480
Roseto	1,746	1,634
Rouseville	1,059	818
Royalton	1,117	1,156
Saltsburg	1,035	1,022
Saxton	1,128	1,165
Scalp Level	1,875	1,690
Sellersville	2,063	1,739
Shickshinny	2,451	2,289
Shingle House	1,380	1,169
Sinking Spring	1,771	1,270
Slippery Rock	1,165	826
Smethport	1,733	1,568
South Coatesville	1,785	------
Southmont	1,925	281
South New Castle	1,038	920
South Renovo	1,054	1,201
South Waverly	1,336	1,251
Spring Grove	1,236	1,115
Stoneboro	1,189	1,405
Summerville	1,202	1,199
Sykesville	2,103	2,507
Temple	1,378	------
Topton	1,667	1,147
Tower City	2,482	2,324
Trainer	1,648	1,367
Tremont	2,304	2,015
Troy	1,190	1,419
Tunkhannock	1,973	1,736
Vandling	1,169	1,258
Versailles	2,473	1,936
Vintondale	1,058	2,053
Wall	2,236	2,426
Walnutport	1,151	1,051
Warrior Run	1,516	1,387
Watsontown	2,248	2,153
Wernersville	1,096	797
West Brownsville	1,717	1,900
West Easton	1,564	1,408
West Elizabeth	1,074	890
West Fairview	1,794	1,800
Westfield	1,193	1,303
West Grove	1,375	1,152
West Kittanning	1,005	861
West Lawn	2,069	------
West Leechburg	1,044	------
West Middlesex	1,181	1,349
West Telford	1,252	921
Wheatland	1,518	1,742
Whitaker	2,072	1,881
White Haven	1,537	1,402
Williamsburg	1,898	1,872
Wind Gap	1,388	1,133
Windsor	1,009	854
Womelsdorf	1,484	1,331
Wormleysburg	1,404	866
Wrightsville	2,247	1,943
Yardley	1,308	1,262
Youngsville	1,907	1,611
Zelienople	1,933	1,870
SOUTH CAROLINA		
Allendale	2,066	1,893
Andrews	1,712	1,968
Bamberg	2,450	2,210
Barnwell	1,834	1,903
Belton	1,765	1,780
Bishopville	2,249	2,090
Blacksburg	1,747	1,512
Blackville	1,284	1,421
SOUTH CAROLINA—continued		
Branchville	1,689	1,814
Brookland	1,722	1,793
Calhoun Falls	1,759	897
Cayce	1,287	746
Central	1,440	898
Chesterfield	1,030	856
Cowpens	1,115	1,284
Denmark	1,713	1,254
Edgefield	2,132	1,865
Elloree	1,098	925
Estill	1,412	1,393
Fairfax	1,376	957
Fort Mill	2,112	1,946
Fountain Inn	1,264	1,100
Greer	2,419	2,292
Iva	1,273	962
Johnston	1,072	1,101
Jonesville	1,153	1,209
Kershaw	1,120	1,022
Kingstree	2,302	2,074
Lake City	1,942	1,606
Landrum	1,212	980
Latta	1,166	1,079
Leesville	1,340	1,216
Lexington	1,152	894
Liberty	2,128	1,705
McColl	1,657	2,129
McCormick	1,304	1,284
Manning	1,884	2,022
Mount Pleasant	1,415	1,575
Ninety-Six	1,381	773
North Augusta	2,003	1,742
Pendleton	1,035	1,040
Pickens	1,130	895
St. George	1,039	1,386
St. Matthews	1,750	1,780
Saluda	1,381	1,208
Seneca	1,929	1,460
Simpsonville	1,400	566
Timmonsville	1,919	1,860
Walhalla	2,388	2,068
West Greenville	1,917	869
Westminster	1,774	1,847
Williamston	2,235	2,322
Williston	1,024	854
Winnsboro	2,344	1,822
SOUTH DAKOTA		
Arlington	1,020	1,011
Armour	1,009	1,045
Belle Fourche	2,032	1,616
Beresford	1,460	1,519
Britton	1,312	1,105
Canton	2,270	2,225
Centerville	1,169	1,104
Chamberlain	1,364	1,303
Clark	1,290	1,392
Custer	1,203	595
Dell Rapids	1,657	1,677
De Smet	1,017	1,035
Edgemont	1,103	1,254
Elk Point	1,294	1,470
Eureka	1,308	1,200
Flandreau	1,934	1,929
Gettysburg	1,400	951
Gregory	1,034	1,067
Groton	1,009	1,273
Highmore	1,034	1,022
Howard	1,224	1,325
Kimball	1,111	993
Lake Andes	1,052	867
Lemmon	1,508	1,126
Lennox	1,113	1,074
Milbank	2,389	2,215
Miller	1,447	1,478
Parker	1,229	1,288
SOUTH DAKOTA—continued		
Parkston	1,336	1,230
Platte	1,207	1,242
Salem	1,115	1,187
Scotland	1,163	1,234
Sisseton	1,569	1,431
Spearfish	1,577	1,254
Sturgis	1,747	1,250
Tyndall	1,287	1,405
Wagner	1,420	1,236
Webster	1,805	1,800
Wessington Springs	1,401	1,618
Winner	2,220	2,000
Woonsocket	1,108	1,368
TENNESSEE		
Bolivar	1,217	1,031
Bruceton	1,112	------
Carthage	1,068	920
Clinton	1,927	1,409
Coal Creek	1,116	1,204
Collierville	1,008	989
Copperhill	1,050	1,102
Cowan	1,307	------
Crossville	1,128	948
Dayton	2,006	1,701
Dresden	1,047	1,007
Dunlap	1,295	1,465
Dyer	1,214	1,250
East Ridge	2,152	------
Englewood	1,471	1,271
Greenfield	1,429	1,474
Halls	1,474	1,400
Hartsville	1,015	1,023
Henderson	1,503	1,181
Huntingdon	1,286	1,121
Jasper	1,251	728
Jefferson City	1,898	1,414
Jellico	1,530	1,878
Lexington	1,823	1,792
Livingston	1,526	1,215
Lookout Mountain	1,031	623
McKenzie	1,858	1,630
Manchester	1,227	1,114
Monterey	1,731	1,445
Mountain City	1,058	724
Mount Pleasant	2,010	2,093
Newbern	1,621	1,767
Oakdale	1,123	1,552
Obion	1,100	1,376
Oneida	1,382	943
Palmer	1,158	------
Portland	1,030	869
Ripley	2,330	2,070
Rogersville	1,590	1,402
Savannah	1,129	758
Somerville	1,333	1,106
South Fulton	1,988	1,650
South Pittsburg	2,103	2,356
Sparta	2,211	1,517
Spring City	1,090	1,001
Sweetwater	2,271	1,972
Tiptonville	1,359	1,050
Waverly	1,152	1,054
Winchester	2,210	2,203
TEXAS		
Alamo	1,018	------
Albany	2,422	1,469
Alto	1,053	1,081
Alvarado	1,210	1,284
Alvin	1,511	1,519
Angleton	1,229	1,043
Anson	2,093	1,425
Aransas Pass	2,482	1,569

RURAL INCORPORATED PLACES   59

TABLE 16.—POPULATION OF INCORPORATED PLACES HAVING, IN 1930, FROM 1,000 TO 2,500 INHABITANTS: 1930 AND 1920—Continued

CITY, TOWN, VILLAGE, OR BOROUGH	1930	1920	CITY, TOWN, VILLAGE, OR BOROUGH	1930	1920	CITY, TOWN, VILLAGE, OR BOROUGH	1930	1920
TEXAS—con.			**TEXAS—con.**			**TEXAS—con.**		
Archer City	1,512	689	Italy	1,230	1,350	Schulenburg	1,604	1,246
Asherton	1,858	-----	Itasca	1,665	1,599	Shiner	1,372	1,300
Atlanta	1,685	1,469	Jacksboro	1,837	1,373	Sinton	1,852	1,058
Baird	1,965	1,902	Jefferson	2,329	2,549	Somerville	2,287	1,879
Bartlett	1,873	1,731	Junction	1,415	-----	Sonora	1,942	1,009
Bastrop	1,895	1,828	Karnes City	1,141	787	South Groveton	1,008	614
Bellville	1,533	-----	Kaufman	2,279	2,501	Spearman	1,580	-----
Boerne	1,117	1,153	Kerens	1,435	1,343	Spur	1,899	1,100
Brackettville	1,822	-----	Killeen	1,260	1,298	Stanton	1,384	-----
Bridgeport	2,464	1,872	Kirbyville	1,184	1,165	Strawn	1,429	2,457
Brownfield	1,907	-----	Ladonia	1,199	1,713	Sudan	1,014	-----
Burnet	1,055	966	La Feria	1,594	236	Taft	1,792	-----
Caldwell	1,724	1,659	La Grange	2,354	1,669	Tahoka	1,620	786
Calvert	2,103	2,099	Lancaster	1,133	1,190	Texhoma	15 300	313
Canadian	2,068	2,187	La Porte	1,280	889	Thorndale	1,002	-----
Carrizo Springs	2,171	954	Leonard	1,131	1,383	Three Rivers	1,275	-----
Carthage	1,651	1,366	Levelland	1,661	-----	Throckmorton	1,135	686
Chillicothe	1,610	1,351	Liberty	2,187	1,117	Timpson	1,545	1,526
Claude	1,041	770	Livingston	1,165	928	Trinity	2,036	1,363
Cleveland	1,422	-----	Llano	2,124	1,645	Troupe	1,318	1,258
Clifton	1,367	1,327	Lockney	1,466	1,118	Tulia	2,202	1,189
Columbus	2,054	-----	McGregor	2,041	2,081	Van Alstyne	1,453	1,588
Comanche	2,435	3,524	McLean	1,521	741	Waelder	1,048	894
Conroe	2,457	1,858	Madisonville	1,294	1,079	Weimar	1,256	1,171
Coolidge	1,169	880	Matador	1,302	692	West	1,807	1,629
Cooper	2,023	2,503	Menard	1,969	1,164	West University Place	1,322	-----
Crosbyton	1,250	809	Merkel	1,848	1,810	White Deer	1,010	-----
Cross Plains	1,507	700	Midlothian	1,198	1,298	Whitesboro	1,535	1,810
Crowell	1,946	1,175	Moody	1,014	1,106	Whitewright	1,480	1,666
Dawson	1,131	950	Mount Vernon	1,222	1,212	Wills Point	2,023	1,811
Dayton	1,207	-----	Munday	1,318	998	Winnsboro	1,905	2,184
Decatur	2,037	2,205	New Castle	1,157	1,452	Winters	2,423	1,509
De Kalb	1,023	910	Nixon	1,037	1,124	Wolfe City	1,405	1,859
De Leon	1,766	3,302	Nocona	2,352	1,422	Woodsboro	1,286	-----
Devine	1,093	995	Odessa	2,407	-----	Wortham	1,404	1,100
Diboll	1,363	-----	O'Donnell	1,026	-----	Yorktown	1,882	1,723
Dublin	2,271	3,229	Palacios	1,318	1,335			
Eagle Lake	2,343	2,017	Panhandle	2,035	638	**UTAH**		
East Mayfield	1,179	1,100	Pasadena	1,647	-----	Beaver	1,673	1,827
Eden	1,194	593	Pilot	1,108	1,499	Delta	1,183	939
Edna	1,752	-----	Plano	1,554	1,715	Ephraim	1,966	2,287
El Campo	2,034	1,766	Pleasanton	1,154	1,036	Fairview	1,120	1,423
Eldorado	1,404	-----	Port Isabel	1,177	-----	Farmington	1,339	1,170
Elgin	1,823	1,630	Port Lavaca	1,367	1,213	Fillmore	1,374	1,490
Fabens	1,623	-----	Port Neches	2,327	-----	Grantsville	1,201	1,213
Farmersville	1,878	2,167	Post	1,668	1,436	Gunnison	1,057	1,115
Ferris	1,438	1,586	Poteet	1,231	-----	Heber	2,477	1,931
Floresville	1,581	1,518	Presidio	1,202	-----	Hurricane	1,197	1,021
Forney	1,216	1,345	Pyote	1,097	-----	Hyrum	1,869	1,858
Frankston	1,109	818	Ralls	1,365	-----	Kanab	1,195	1,102
Fredericksburg	2,416	-----	Raymondville	2,050	-----	Lewiston	1,783	1,645
Garland	1,584	1,421	Refugio	2,019	933	Manti	2,200	2,412
Giddings	1,835	1,650	Richmond	1,432	1,273	Midvale	2,451	2,209
Gilmer	1,963	2,268	Rio Grande	2,283	-----	Milford	1,517	1,308
Goldthwaite	1,324	1,214	Rising Star	1,160	906	Monroe	1,247	1,719
Goliad	1,424	-----	Rockdale	2,204	2,323	Moroni	1,218	1,355
Gorman	1,154	3,200	Rockport	1,140	1,545	Mount Pleasant	2,284	2,415
Grand Prairie	1,529	1,263	Rockwall	1,071	1,388	Orem	1,915	(²)
Grand Saline	1,799	1,528	Rogers	1,032	1,256	Panguitch	1,541	1,473
Granger	1,703	1,944	Roscoe	1,250	1,079	Parowan	1,474	1,640
Grapeland	1,027	-----	Rosebud	1,565	1,516	Pleasant Grove	1,754	1,682
Groesbeck	2,059	1,522	Rosenberg	1,941	1,279	Providence	1,088	1,132
Groveton	1,046	1,103	Rotan	1,632	1,000	Richmond	1,140	1,396
Hale Center	1,007	-----	Round Rock	1,173	900	Roosevelt	1,051	1,054
Hallettsville	1,406	1,444	Royse City	1,128	1,289	St. George	2,434	2,215
Hamilton	2,084	2,018	Rule	1,094	890	Salina	1,383	1,451
Hamlin	2,328	1,633	Runge	1,136	1,070	Sandy	1,436	1,208
Henrietta	2,020	2,563	Sabinal	1,586	1,458	Santaquin	1,115	976
Hereford	2,458	1,696	San Augustine	1,247	1,268	Smithfield	2,353	2,421
Hico	1,463	1,635	Sanger	1,119	1,204	Tremonton	1,009	937
Honey Grove	2,475	2,642	San Juan	1,615	1,203	Vernal	1,744	1,309
Hubbard	1,855	2,072	San Saba	2,240	2,011	Wellsville	1,270	1,298
Iowa Park	2,009	2,041	Santa Anna	1,883	1,407			

² Not returned separately.

15 The inclusion of Texhoma in places of 1,000 to 2,500 is based upon the combined population (1,119 in 1930) of Texhoma, Tex., and Texhoma, Okla.

60   POPULATION—UNITED STATES SUMMARY

TABLE 16.—POPULATION OF INCORPORATED PLACES HAVING, IN 1930, FROM 1,000 TO 2,500 INHABITANTS: 1930 AND 1920—Continued

CITY, TOWN, VILLAGE, OR BOROUGH	1930	1920
VERMONT		
Barton	1,363	1,187
Bristol	1,190	1,251
Enosburg Falls	1,195	1,236
Essex Junction	1,621	1,410
Fair Haven	2,289	2,182
Hardwick	1,667	1,550
Ludlow	1,642	1,732
Lyndonville	1,559	1,878
Middlebury	2,003	1,993
Morrisville	1,822	1,707
Northfield	2,075	1,916
North Troy	1,045	1,072
Orleans	1,301	1,358
Poultney	1,570	1,371
Randolph	1,957	1,819
Richford	1,783	1,995
Swanton	1,558	1,371
Vergennes	1,705	1,609
Waterbury	1,776	1,515
Woodstock	1,312	1,252
VIRGINIA		
Altavista	2,367	1,206
Ashland	1,297	1,299
Berryville	1,094	1,138
Blacksburg	1,406	1,095
Blackstone	1,772	1,497
Chase City	1,590	1,646
Chatham	1,143	1,171
Chincoteague	2,130	1,418
Christiansburg	1,970	1,641
Colonial Heights	2,331	____
Crewe	2,152	2,097
Culpeper	2,379	1,819
Damascus	1,610	1,599
Emporia	2,144	1,869
Falls Church	2,019	1,659
Fries	2,205	2,029
Front Royal	2,424	1,404
Gate City	1,216	684
Lawrenceville	1,629	1,439
Leesburg	1,640	1,545
Luray	1,450	1,381
Manassas	1,215	1,305
Narrows	1,345	1,141
Onancock	1,245	1,074
Orange	1,381	1,078
Pennington Gap	1,553	940
Pocahontas	2,293	2,591
Richlands	1,355	1,171
Rocky Mount	1,339	1,076
Shenandoah	1,980	1,895
Smithfield	1,179	1,181
South Hill	1,405	1,074
Strasburg	1,901	650
Tangier	1,120	962
Tazewell	1,211	1,261
Victoria	1,568	1,445
Virginia Beach	1,719	846
Warrenton	1,450	1,545
Waverly	1,355	1,306
West Point	1,844	1,635
Wise	1,112	1,071
Woodstock	1,552	1,580
WASHINGTON		
Arlington	1,439	1,418
Blaine	1,642	2,254
Buckley	1,052	1,119
Burlington	1,407	1,360
Cashmere	1,473	1,114
Castle Rock	1,239	829
Chelan	1,403	896
Cheney	1,335	1,252

CITY, TOWN, VILLAGE, OR BOROUGH	1930	1920
WASHINGTON—Con.		
Chewelah	1,315	1,288
Colville	1,803	1,718
Cosmopolis	1,493	1,512
Deer Park	1,009	1,103
Edmonds	1,165	936
Elma	1,545	1,252
Enumclaw	2,084	1,378
Goldendale	1,116	1,274
Grandview	1,085	1,011
Kennewick	1,519	1,684
Kent	2,320	2,282
Kirkland	1,714	1,354
Leavenworth	1,415	1,791
Lynden	1,564	1,244
Marysville	1,354	1,244
Medical Lake	1,671	1,254
Monroe	1,570	1,675
Montesano	2,460	2,158
Newport	1,080	950
Okanogan	1,519	1,015
Orting	1,109	972
Palouse	1,151	1,179
Pomeroy	1,600	1,804
Port Orchard	1,145	1,393
Prosser	1,569	1,697
Ritzville	1,777	1,900
Roslyn	2,063	2,673
South Bend	1,798	1,948
Sumner	1,967	1,499
Sunnyside	2,113	1,809
Tekoa	1,408	1,520
Wapato	1,222	1,128
Washougal	1,206	765
Woodland	1,094	521
WEST VIRGINIA		
Alderson	1,458	1,401
Ansted	1,404	1,178
Barboursville	1,508	974
Belington	1,571	1,766
Berkeley Springs	1,039	980
Bramwell	1,574	1,696
Bridgeport	1,567	1,346
Cameron	2,281	2,404
Cedar Grove	1,110	918
Ceredo	1,164	1,110
Charles Town	2,434	2,527
Clendenin	1,217	1,263
Davis	1,656	2,491
East Rainelle	1,272	____
Fayetteville	1,143	659
Gassaway	1,618	1,518
Glendale	1,493	____
Grantsville	1,018	450
Harrisville	1,192	1,036
Hurricane	1,293	666
Ineger	1,066	481
Keystone	1,897	1,839
Kimball	1,467	1,428
Kingwood	1,709	1,417
Lewisburg	1,293	1,202
Lumberport	1,289	900
Mabscott	1,260	1,114
Madison	1,156	604
Marfrance	1,066	____
Marlinton	1,586	1,177
Marmet	1,200	____
Milton	1,305	1,023
Monongah	1,909	2,031
Mount Hope	2,361	1,989
Mullens	2,356	1,425
New Cumberland	2,300	1,816
Nutter Fort	1,825	____
Oak Hill	2,076	1,037

CITY, TOWN, VILLAGE, OR BOROUGH	1930	1920
WEST VIRGINIA—continued		
Paden City	2,281	1,705
Parsons	2,012	2,001
Pennsboro	1,616	1,654
Petersburg	1,410	834
Philippi	1,767	1,543
Piedmont	2,241	2,835
Ranson	1,002	699
Ravenswood	1,189	1,284
Ridgeley	1,972	1,709
Rivesville	1,700	1,061
Romney	1,441	1,028
Ronceverte	2,254	2,319
Rowlesburg	1,573	1,225
Sabraton	1,717	1,369
St. Marys	2,182	1,643
Spencer[16]	2,493	1,765
Star City	1,121	823
Sutton	1,205	947
Terra Alta	1,474	1,261
Thomas	1,660	2,099
War	1,392	____
Westover	1,633	721
White Sulphur Springs	1,484	837
Williamstown	1,657	1,793
WISCONSIN		
Adams	1,231	1,119
Algoma	2,202	1,911
Alma	1,009	970
Altoona	1,044	960
Amery	1,354	1,203
Arcadia	1,499	1,418
Augusta	1,359	1,407
Barron	1,863	1,623
Bayfield	1,195	1,441
Black River Falls	1,950	1,796
Bloomer	1,865	1,648
Boscobel	1,762	1,670
Brillion	1,167	1,102
Brodhead	1,533	1,600
Cedarburg	2,055	1,738
Chetek	1,076	1,154
Chilton	1,945	1,833
Cornell	1,510	1,337
Crandon	1,679	1,632
Cuba City	1,157	1,175
Cumberland	1,532	1,528
Darlington	1,764	1,798
Dodgeville	1,937	1,896
Durand	1,590	1,517
Eagle River	1,386	____
Elkhorn	2,340	1,991
Ellsworth	1,124	1,043
Elroy	1,546	1,713
Evansville	2,269	2,209
Fennimore	1,341	1,383
Galesville	1,069	952
Gillett	1,076	785
Grafton	1,065	898
Hayward	1,207	1,302
Horicon	2,214	2,134
Juneau	1,154	1,150
Kewaunee	2,409	1,865
Kiel	1,803	1,599
Kilbourn	1,489	1,206
Kimberly	2,256	1,382
Kohler	1,748	403
Lake Mills	2,007	1,754
Lancaster	2,432	2,485
Lodi	1,065	1,077
Mauston	2,107	1,966
Medford	1,918	1,881
Mellen	1,629	1,981

[16] Alvord and Spencer towns consolidated as Spencer city in 1921.   Combined population in 1920, 2,050

RURAL INCORPORATED PLACES   61

TABLE 16.—POPULATION OF INCORPORATED PLACES HAVING, IN 1930, FROM 1,000 TO 2,500 INHABITANTS: 1930 AND 1920—Continued

CITY, TOWN, VILLAGE, OR BOROUGH	1930	1920	CITY, TOWN, VILLAGE, OR BOROUGH	1930	1920	CITY, TOWN, VILLAGE, OR BOROUGH	1930	1920
WISCONSIN—con.			**WISCONSIN—con.**			**WYOMING**		
Menomonee Falls	1,291	1,019	Peshtigo	1,579	1,440	Buffalo	1,749	1,772
Milton	1,128	834	Pewaukee	1,067	800	Cody	1,800	1,242
Mineral Point	2,274	2,569	Phillips	1,901	1,973	Douglas	1,917	2,294
Mondovi	1,623	1,554	Princeton	1,183	1,275	Gillette	1,340	1,157
Montello	1,245	1,112	Randolph	1,161	1,183	Greybull	1,806	2,692
Montreal	1,819	1,890	Rib Lake	1,180	1,020	Kemmerer	1,884	1,517
Mosinee	1,229	1,161	River Falls	2,363	2,273	Lander	1,826	2,133
Mount Horeb	1,425	1,350	Sauk City	1,137	1,162	Lovell	1,857	1,686
Neillsville	2,118	2,160	Schofield	1,287	1,049	Lusk	1,218	2,092
Nekoosa	2,005	1,639	Seymour	1,201	1,280	Newcastle	1,201	1,003
New Glarus	1,010	981	Shullsburg	1,041	1,158	Powell	1,156	2,463
New Holstein	1,274	1,373	Spooner	2,426	2,293	Riverton	1,608	2,023
New Lisbon	1,076	994	Stanley	1,988	2,577	Superior	1,156	1,034
New Richmond	2,112	2,248	Sun Prairie	1,337	1,236	Thermopolis	2,129	2,095
Niagara	2,033	1,946	Washburn	2,238	3,707	Torrington	1,811	1,301
North Fond du Lac	2,244	2,150	Waterloo	1,272	1,262	Wheatland	1,997	1,336
Oconto Falls	1,921	1,914	Wautoma	1,044	1,046	Worland	1,461	1,225
Omro	1,255	1,042	Westby	1,366	1,228			
Onalaska	1,408	1,066	West Salem	1,011	1,027			
Owen	1,102	1,083	Weyauwega	1,067	938			

67981°—31——5

CHAPTER 1

URBAN AND RURAL POPULATION
METROPOLITAN DISTRICTS
AND CENTER OF POPULATION

5

CHAPTER 1.—URBAN AND RURAL POPULATION, METROPOLITAN DISTRICTS, AND CENTER OF POPULATION

URBAN AND RURAL POPULATION

Among the most fundamental of the census classifications are certain groupings of the population based upon the areas in which the people live rather than upon any personal characteristics of the individuals making up the population.

The simplest of these is that which provides separate population figures for the several States and for the counties, cities, and townships within the States. This requires only the presentation of the data for these areas as they are collected, since the enumeration is of necessity made for the smallest geographic units and the results later consolidated to make up the totals for the larger areas; in fact, the results of each tabulation have been made public State by State as the work progressed, without waiting for the completion of the data for the country as a whole.

Other geographic classifications, like that distinguishing the urban and the rural population, or the farm and the nonfarm, are less obvious and more artificial in their nature. The urban-rural classification, however, has been generally accepted and widely used since it was established in its present form in 1910; and when supplemented by the subdivision of the urban population into groups of cities classified according to size, and of the rural population into farm and nonfarm, it should be of even greater service.

Throughout most of the presentations of statistics of population classified in accordance with such personal characteristics as color, nativity, sex, age, marital condition, etc., figures are given for the urban, rural-farm, and rural-nonfarm areas; and statistics are provided in such detail for individual cities that totals can readily be made up for any desired groups of urban places.

Urban and rural areas.—Urban population, as defined by the Census Bureau, is in general that residing in cities and other incorporated places having 2,500 inhabitants or more, the remainder being classified as rural. In three of the New England States, New Hampshire, Massachusetts, and Rhode Island, conditions are exceptional in that the compactly built portions of the towns (townships) are not separately incorporated or politically distinct in any way from the rural territory within the same town; nor is it the usual practice to incorporate even the larger places as cities until they attain a population in excess of 10,000. Consequently, if only the cities were counted as urban the

classification would be quite inadequate. In 1920 and 1910 all towns in these three States which had a population of 2,500 or more were classified as urban. This resulted in the inclusion of a considerable number of places that were mainly rural in their general characteristics. In 1930 the special rule for these New England States has been modified so as to place in the urban classification, in addition to the regularly incorporated cities, only those towns in which there is a village or thickly settled area having more than 2,500 inhabitants and comprising, either by itself or when combined with other villages in the same town, more than 50 per cent of the total population of the town.[1]

One other modification has been made in the definition of urban population for use in connection with the 1930 census. This modification extends the classification so as to include townships and other political subdivisions (not incorporated as municipalities, nor containing any area so incorporated) which had a total population of 10,000 or more, and a population density of 1,000 or more per square mile.[2]

Since it has been found impracticable to go back and readjust to the new basis the 1920 urban and rural figures as they were tabulated by color, sex, age, etc., they are presented in all tables as established in 1920. The comparative figures for a few States therefore show differences which must be considered or interpreted as solely or mainly the result of the change in the method of classification.

Table 1 shows the population of continental United States for each census from 1880 to 1930, inclusive, with separate figures for urban and rural areas; 1880 being the earliest census for which it was practicable to compile urban and rural population on the basis of the classification adopted in 1910.

---

[1] The result of this modification has been to transfer from the urban to the rural classification 12 towns in New Hampshire (population 35,389), 56 towns in Massachusetts (population 218,231), and 8 towns in Rhode Island (population 35,001), which would have been counted as urban if the 1920 rule had been followed in 1930. The aggregate population in 1930 of these towns which were in effect transferred from the urban to the rural classification is 288,621.

[2] This extension adds to the urban group 11 townships in New Jersey (population 208,722), 10 townships in Pennsylvania (population 210,505), 4 towns in Connecticut (population 87,086), 2 townships in California (population 48,992), and 1 town in New York (population 18,024). The aggregate population of these 28 places, which would have been classified as rural under the rules governing the urban-rural classification in 1920, is 573,329.

The net effect of the two changes in the basis of the urban-rural classification is, therefore, to increase the urban population by 284,708. In other words, if the classification had been made in 1930 on exactly the same basis as in 1920, the urban population would have been 68,670,115, instead of 68,954,823, and the percentage urban would have been 55.9 instead of 56.2.

7

8   POPULATION

TABLE 1.—POPULATION OF THE UNITED STATES, URBAN AND RURAL: 1880 TO 1930

AREA	1930 (Apr. 1)	1920 (Jan. 1)	1910 (Apr. 15)	1900 (June 1)	1890 (June 1)	1880 (June 1)
Total	122,775,046	105,710,620	91,972,266	75,994,575	62,947,714	50,155,783
Increase:						
Number	17,064,426	13,738,354	15,977,691	13,046,861	12,791,931	11,597,412
Per cent	16.1	14.9	21.0	20.7	25.5	30.1
Urban	68,954,823	54,304,603	42,166,120	30,380,433	22,298,359	14,358,167
Increase:						
Number	14,650,220	12,138,483	11,785,687	8,082,074	7,940,192	----------
Per cent	27.0	28.8	38.8	36.2	55.3	----------
Rural	53,820,223	51,406,017	49,806,146	45,614,142	40,649,355	35,797,616
Increase:						
Number	2,414,206	1,599,871	4,192,004	4,964,787	4,851,739	----------
Per cent	4.7	3.2	9.2	12.2	13.6	----------
Per cent of total:						
Urban	56.2	51.4	45.8	40.0	35.4	28.6
Rural	43.8	48.6	54.2	60.0	64.6	71.4

Farm population.—The farm population as shown for 1930 comprises all persons living on farms, without regard to occupation. The farm population figures for 1920 include, in addition, those farm laborers (and their families) who, while not living on farms, nevertheless lived in strictly rural territory outside the limits of any city or other incorporated place. Though the number of additional persons thus included is believed not to have been very great, some allowance should be made for this difference in definition when comparing the figures. Further allowance should be made for the fact that the 1920 census was taken in January, when considerable numbers of farm laborers and others usually living on farms were temporarily absent, while the 1930 census was taken in April, when by reason of the advancing season the number of persons on the farms was appreciably larger. Since these two factors operate in opposite directions, it may well be that one largely offsets the other. It seems probable, however, that the change in the date added more to the 1930 returns than were omitted through the use of the narrower definition. The classification of the population as farm and nonfarm is based on the replies to a question on the schedule, reading: "Does this family live on a farm?"

Rural-farm population.—While the urban-farm population, that is, the population living on farms within the limits of cities and other urban places, is shown in Table 2 for the United States and in Table 9 by States, it is not included in any of the detailed presentations by color, sex, age, etc. which are presented elsewhere in the Census Reports. In other words, the analysis of the farm population is limited to that part living in rural territory, which is designated in every case as "rural-farm." This is done partly to simplify the classification (dividing the total population into three groups, namely, urban, rural-farm, and rural-nonfarm); partly because the urban-farm group is so small, forming as it does less than 1 per cent of the total farm population; and partly because the few farm families resident within the corporate limits of cities or towns are living under conditions that are at least somewhat urban, rather than under typical farm conditions.

Rural-nonfarm population.—The rural-nonfarm population, sometimes termed the "village" population, includes, in general, all persons living outside cities or other incorporated places having 2,500 inhabitants or more who do not live on farms. There were included in the rural areas of the United States in 1930, 13,433 incorporated places of less than 2,500 inhabitants, with an aggregate population of 9,183,453. While there are considerable numbers of farm families living in these villages, it may be assumed that well over nine-tenths of their population was counted as rural-nonfarm. These incorporated villages therefore contribute around two-fifths of the total rural-nonfarm population (which amounted to 23,662,710); and a considerable part of the remainder live in unincorporated villages.

The rural-nonfarm or village population is much less uniform in its make-up in the different parts of the United States than either the urban population or the rural-farm population. In some sections of the country it consists mainly of the inhabitants of small manufacturing villages or of suburban areas which are not incorporated. In other sections it is made up mainly of persons living in mining settlements. In still other parts of the country, where farming is the dominant industry, it is made up largely of the inhabitants of small commercial centers, including merchants, bankers, doctors, carpenters, automobile repair men, and other persons who are mainly occupied in supplying the wants of the farm population, together with retired farmers and their families.

The classification of the urban and rural population as farm and nonfarm is shown for 1930 and 1920 in Table 2.

TABLE 2.—URBAN, RURAL-FARM, AND RURAL-NONFARM POPULATION OF THE UNITED STATES: 1930 AND 1920

[A minus sign (—) denotes decrease]

CLASS OF POPULATION	NUMBER		INCREASE		PER CENT OF TOTAL	
	1930	1920	Number	Per cent	1930	1920
Total population	122,775,046	105,710,620	17,064,426	16.1	100.0	100.0
Urban population	68,954,823	54,304,603	14,650,220	27.0	56.2	51.4
Urban-farm	*287,857*	*255,629*	*32,208*	*12.6*	*0.2*	*0.2*
Rural population	53,820,223	51,406,017	2,414,206	4.7	43.8	48.6
Rural-farm	*30,157,513*	*31,358,640*	*—1,201,127*	*—3.8*	*24.6*	*29.7*
Rural-nonfarm	*23,662,710*	*20,047,377*	*3,615,333*	*18.0*	*19.3*	*19.0*
Total farm population	30,445,350	31,614,269	—1,168,919	—3.7	24.8	29.9

Population in places of 8,000 or more.—While the present urban and rural classification, with the basic requirement of a population of 2,500 in an incorporated place in order to give it urban classification, is not available for censuses earlier than 1880, a table has been presented in the Census Reports for many decades giving the population in places of 8,000 or more back to the First Census, that of 1790. These figures are shown in Table 3.

URBAN AND RURAL

9

TABLE 3.—POPULATION IN PLACES OF 8,000 OR MORE: 1790 TO 1930

CENSUS YEAR	Total population	PLACES OF 8,000 OR MORE		
		Number of places	Population	Per cent of total population
1930	122,775,046	1,208	60,333,452	49.1
1920	105,710,620	924	46,307,640	43.8
1910	91,972,266	768	35,570,334	38.7
1900	75,994,575	547	25,018,335	32.9
1890	62,947,714	445	18,244,239	29.0
1880	50,155,783	285	11,365,698	22.7
1870	38,558,371	226	8,071,875	20.9
1860	31,443,321	141	5,072,256	16.1
1850	23,191,876	85	2,897,586	12.5
1840	17,069,453	44	1,453,994	8.5
1830	12,866,020	26	864,509	6.7
1820	9,638,453	13	475,135	4.9
1810	7,239,881	11	356,920	4.9
1800	5,308,483	6	210,873	4.0
1790	3,929,214	6	131,472	3.3

URBAN AND RURAL POPULATION OF THE UNITED STATES: 1880 TO 1930

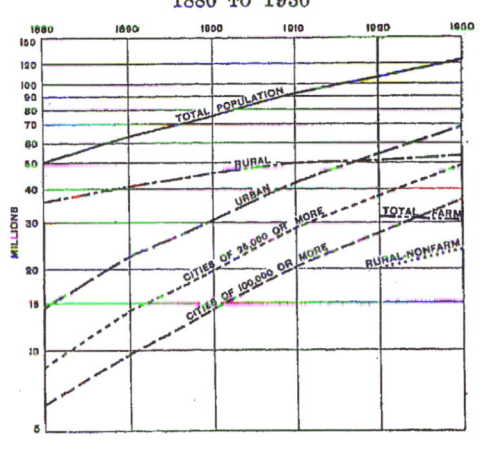

TABLE 4.—DISTRIBUTION OF POPULATION IN GROUPS OF PLACES CLASSIFIED ACCORDING TO SIZE: 1890 TO 1930

AREA	1930		1920		1910		1900		1890		PER CENT OF TOTAL POPULATION				
	Number of places	Population	Number of places	Population	Number of places	Population	Number of places	Population	Number of places	Population	1930	1920	1910	1900	1890
Total population	......	122,775,046	......	105,710,620	......	91,972,266	......	75,994,575	......	62,947,714	100.0	100.0	100.0	100.0	100.0
Urban territory	3,165	68,954,823	2,787	54,304,603	2,313	42,166,120	1,801	30,380,433	1,417	22,298,359	56.2	51.4	45.8	40.0	35.4
Places of 1,000,000 or more	5	15,064,555	3	10,145,532	3	8,501,174	3	6,429,474	3	3,662,115	12.3	9.6	9.2	8.5	5.8
Places of 500,000 to 1,000,000	8	5,763,987	9	6,223,709	5	3,010,667	3	1,645,087	1	806,343	4.7	5.9	3.3	2.2	1.3
Places of 250,000 to 500,000	24	7,956,228	13	4,540,838	11	3,949,839	9	2,861,296	7	2,447,608	6.5	4.3	4.3	3.8	3.9
Places of 100,000 to 250,000	56	7,540,966	43	6,519,187	31	4,840,458	23	3,272,490	17	2,781,894	6.1	6.2	5.3	4.3	4.4
Places of 50,000 to 100,000	98	6,491,448	76	5,205,747	59	4,178,915	40	2,709,338	30	2,022,822	5.3	5.0	4.5	3.6	3.2
Places of 25,000 to 50,000	185	6,425,693	143	5,075,041	110	4,026,045	82	2,800,627	66	2,268,786	5.2	4.8	4.4	3.7	3.6
Places of 10,000 to 25,000	606	9,007,200	459	6,942,742	367	5,524,434	280	4,338,250	228	3,429,247	7.4	6.6	6.0	5.7	5.4
Places of 5,000 to 10,000	851	5,897,156	721	4,997,704	612	4,254,856	468	3,220,766	339	2,372,717	4.8	4.7	4.6	4.2	3.8
Places of 2,500 to 5,000	1,332	4,717,590	1,320	4,593,053	1,106	3,879,732	893	3,103,105	726	2,500,827	3.8	4.3	4.2	4.1	4.0
Rural territory [1]	13,433	53,820,223	12,853	51,406,017	11,829	49,806,146	8,930	45,614,142	6,489	40,649,355	43.8	48.6	54.2	60.0	64.6
Incorporated places 1,000 to 2,500	3,087	4,820,707	12,853	8,963,125	11,829	8,164,628	8,930	6,301,533	6,489	4,745,530	8.9 / 3.6	8.5	8.9	8.3	7.5
Incorporated places under 1,000	10,346	4,362,746													
Other rural territory	......	44,636,770	......	42,442,892	......	41,641,518	......	39,312,609	......	35,903,825	30.4	40.2	45.3	51.7	57.0

[1] Minor changes have been made in the subdivision of rural territory in Table 4 for 1920, 1910, and 1890 since the publication of Volume I, Population (see p. 14 of that report), involving the transfer of several small villages in New England from rural incorporated places to "Other rural territory," as investigation has shown that these villages never have been incorporated.

TABLE 5.—POPULATION OF URBAN PLACES CLASSIFIED ACCORDING TO SIZE, IN CUMULATIVE GROUPS: 1900 TO 1930

AREA	1930			1920			1910			1900		
	Number of places	Population	Per cent of total population	Number of places	Population	Per cent of total population	Number of places	Population	Per cent of total population	Number of places	Population	Per cent of total population
Places of 2,500 or more	3,165	68,954,823	56.2	2,787	54,304,603	51.4	2,313	42,166,120	45.8	1,801	30,380,433	40.0
Places of 5,000 or more	1,833	64,237,233	52.3	1,467	49,710,650	47.0	1,207	38,286,388	41.6	908	27,277,328	35.9
Places of 10,000 or more	982	58,340,077	47.5	746	44,712,856	42.3	595	34,031,532	37.0	440	24,056,502	31.7
Places of 25,000 or more	376	49,242,877	40.1	287	37,770,114	35.7	228	28,507,098	31.0	160	19,718,312	25.9
Places of 50,000 or more	191	42,817,184	34.9	144	32,695,073	30.9	109	24,481,053	26.6	78	16,917,685	22.3
Places of 100,000 or more	93	36,325,736	29.6	68	27,429,326	25.9	50	20,302,138	22.1	38	14,208,347	18.7
Places of 250,000 or more	37	28,784,770	23.4	25	20,910,139	19.8	19	15,461,080	16.8	15	10,935,857	14.4
Places of 500,000 or more	13	20,828,542	17.0	12	16,369,301	15.5	8	11,511,841	12.5	6	8,074,561	10.6
Places of 1,000,000 or more	5	15,064,555	12.3	3	10,145,532	9.6	3	8,501,174	9.2	3	6,429,474	8.5

10

POPULATION

TABLE 6.—URBAN AND RURAL POPULATION, BY DIVISIONS AND STATES: 1930 AND 1920

[A minus sign (−) denotes decrease. Per cent not shown where less than 0.1]

DIVISION AND STATE	TOTAL POPULATION				URBAN POPULATION				RURAL POPULATION				PER CENT OF TOTAL POPULATION			
			Increase				Increase				Increase		Urban		Rural	
	1930	1920	Number	Per cent	1930	1920	Number	Per cent	1930	1920	Number	Per cent	1930	1920	1930	1920
United States	122,775,046	105,710,620	17,064,426	10.1	68,954,823	54,304,603	14,650,220	27.0	53,820,223	51,406,017	2,414,206	4.7	56.2	51.4	43.8	48.6
GEOGRAPHIC DIVS.:																
New England	8,166,341	7,400,909	765,432	10.3	6,311,976	5,865,073	446,903	7.6	1,854,365	1,535,836	318,529	20.7	77.3	79.2	22.7	20.8
Middle Atlantic	26,260,750	22,261,144	3,999,606	18.0	20,394,707	16,672,595	3,722,112	22.3	5,866,043	5,588,549	277,494	5.0	77.7	74.9	22.3	25.1
E. N. Central	25,297,185	21,475,543	3,821,642	17.8	16,794,908	13,049,272	3,745,636	28.7	8,502,277	8,426,271	76,006	0.9	66.4	60.8	33.6	39.2
W. N. Central	13,296,915	12,544,249	752,666	6.0	5,556,181	4,727,372	828,809	17.5	7,740,734	7,816,877	−76,143	−1.0	41.8	37.7	58.2	62.3
South Atlantic	15,793,589	13,990,272	1,803,317	12.9	5,698,122	4,338,792	1,359,330	31.3	10,095,467	9,651,480	443,987	4.6	36.1	31.0	63.9	69.0
E. S. Central	9,887,214	8,893,307	993,907	11.2	2,778,687	1,994,207	784,480	39.3	7,108,527	6,899,100	209,427	3.0	28.1	22.4	71.9	77.6
W. S. Central	12,176,830	10,242,224	1,934,606	18.9	4,427,439	2,970,829	1,456,610	49.0	7,749,391	7,271,395	477,996	6.6	36.4	29.0	63.6	71.0
Mountain	3,701,789	3,336,101	365,688	11.0	1,457,922	1,214,980	242,942	20.0	2,243,867	2,121,121	122,746	5.8	39.4	36.4	60.6	63.6
Pacific	8,194,433	5,566,871	2,627,562	47.2	5,534,881	3,471,483	2,063,398	59.4	2,659,552	2,095,388	564,164	26.9	67.5	62.4	32.5	37.6
NEW ENGLAND:																
Maine	797,423	768,014	29,409	3.8	321,506	299,569	21,937	7.3	475,917	468,445	7,472	1.6	40.3	39.0	59.7	61.0
N. Hampshire	465,293	443,083	22,210	5.0	273,079	279,761	−6,682	−2.4	192,214	163,322	28,892	17.7	58.7	63.1	41.3	36.9
Vermont	359,611	352,428	7,183	2.0	118,766	109,976	8,790	8.0	240,845	242,452	−1,607	−0.7	33.0	31.2	67.0	68.8
Massachusetts	4,249,614	3,852,356	397,258	10.3	3,831,426	3,650,248	181,178	5.0	418,188	202,108	216,080	106.9	90.2	94.8	9.8	5.2
Rhode Island	687,497	604,397	83,100	13.7	635,429	589,180	46,249	7.8	52,068	15,217	36,851	242.2	92.4	97.5	7.6	2.5
Connecticut	1,606,903	1,380,631	226,272	16.4	1,131,770	936,339	195,431	20.9	475,133	444,292	30,841	6.9	70.4	67.8	29.6	32.2
MIDDLE ATLANTIC:																
New York	12,588,066	10,385,227	2,202,839	21.2	10,521,952	8,589,844	1,932,108	22.5	2,066,114	1,795,383	270,731	15.1	83.6	82.7	16.4	17.3
New Jersey	4,041,334	3,155,900	885,434	28.1	3,339,244	2,474,936	864,308	34.9	702,090	680,964	21,126	3.1	82.6	78.4	17.4	21.6
Pennsylvania	9,631,350	8,720,017	911,333	10.5	6,533,511	5,607,815	925,696	16.5	3,097,839	3,112,202	−14,363	−0.5	67.8	64.3	32.2	35.7
E. N. CENTRAL:																
Ohio	6,646,697	5,759,394	887,303	15.4	4,507,371	3,677,136	830,235	22.6	2,139,326	2,082,258	57,068	2.7	67.8	63.8	32.2	36.2
Indiana	3,238,503	2,930,390	308,113	10.5	1,795,892	1,482,855	313,037	21.1	1,442,611	1,447,535	−4,924	−0.3	55.5	50.6	44.5	49.4
Illinois	7,630,654	6,485,280	1,145,374	17.7	5,635,727	4,403,153	1,232,574	28.0	1,994,927	2,082,127	−87,200	−4.2	73.9	67.9	26.1	32.1
Michigan	4,842,325	3,668,412	1,173,913	32.0	3,302,075	2,241,560	1,060,515	47.3	1,540,250	1,426,852	113,398	7.9	68.2	61.1	31.8	38.9
Wisconsin	2,939,006	2,632,067	306,939	11.7	1,553,843	1,244,568	309,275	24.8	1,385,163	1,387,499	−2,336	−0.2	52.9	47.3	47.1	52.7
W. N. CENTRAL:																
Minnesota	2,563,953	2,387,125	176,828	7.4	1,257,616	1,051,593	206,023	19.6	1,306,337	1,335,532	−29,195	−2.2	49.0	44.1	51.0	55.9
Iowa	2,470,939	2,404,021	66,918	2.8	979,292	875,495	103,797	11.9	1,491,647	1,528,526	−36,879	−2.4	39.6	36.4	60.4	63.6
Missouri	3,629,367	3,404,055	225,312	6.6	1,859,110	1,586,903	272,216	17.2	1,770,248	1,817,152	−46,904	−2.6	51.2	46.6	48.8	53.4
North Dakota	680,845	646,872	33,973	5.3	113,306	88,239	25,067	28.4	567,539	558,633	8,906	1.6	16.6	13.6	83.4	86.4
South Dakota	692,849	636,547	56,302	8.8	130,907	101,872	29,035	28.5	561,942	534,675	27,267	5.1	18.9	16.0	81.1	84.0
Nebraska	1,377,963	1,296,372	81,591	6.3	486,107	405,306	80,801	19.9	891,856	891,066	790	0.1	35.3	31.3	64.7	68.7
Kansas	1,880,999	1,769,257	111,742	6.3	729,834	617,964	111,870	18.1	1,151,165	1,151,293	−128	......	38.8	34.9	61.2	65.1
SOUTH ATLANTIC:																
Delaware	238,380	223,003	15,377	6.9	123,146	120,767	2,379	2.0	115,234	102,236	12,998	12.7	51.7	54.2	48.3	45.8
Maryland	1,631,526	1,449,661	181,865	12.5	974,869	869,422	105,447	12.1	656,657	580,239	76,418	13.2	59.8	60.0	40.2	40.0
Dist. of Columbia	486,869	437,571	49,298	11.3	486,869	437,571	49,298	11.3	(1)	(1)	......	......	100.0	100.0	......	......
Virginia	2,421,851	2,309,187	112,664	4.9	785,537	673,984	111,553	16.0	1,636,314	1,635,203	1,111	0.1	32.4	29.2	67.6	70.8
West Virginia	1,729,205	1,463,701	265,504	18.1	491,504	369,007	122,497	33.2	1,237,701	1,094,694	143,007	13.1	28.4	25.2	71.6	74.8
North Carolina	3,170,276	2,559,123	611,153	23.9	809,847	490,370	319,477	65.2	2,360,429	2,068,753	291,676	14.1	25.5	19.2	74.5	80.8
South Carolina	1,738,765	1,683,724	55,041	3.3	371,080	293,987	77,093	26.2	1,367,685	1,389,737	−22,052	−1.6	21.3	17.5	78.7	82.5
Georgia	2,908,506	2,895,832	12,674	0.4	895,492	727,859	167,633	23.0	2,013,014	2,167,973	−154,959	−7.1	30.8	25.1	69.2	74.9
Florida	1,468,211	968,470	499,741	51.6	759,778	355,825	403,953	113.5	708,433	612,645	95,788	15.6	51.7	36.7	48.3	63.3
E. S. CENTRAL:																
Kentucky	2,614,589	2,416,630	197,959	8.2	799,026	633,543	165,483	26.1	1,815,563	1,783,087	32,476	1.8	30.6	26.2	69.4	73.8
Tennessee	2,616,556	2,337,885	278,671	11.9	896,538	611,226	285,312	46.7	1,720,018	1,726,659	−6,641	−0.4	34.3	26.1	65.7	73.9
Alabama	2,646,248	2,348,174	298,074	12.7	744,273	509,317	234,956	46.1	1,901,975	1,838,857	63,118	3.4	28.1	21.7	71.9	78.3
Mississippi	2,009,821	1,790,618	219,203	12.2	338,850	240,121	98,729	41.1	1,670,971	1,550,497	120,474	7.8	16.9	13.4	83.1	86.6
W. S. CENTRAL:																
Arkansas	1,854,482	1,752,204	102,278	5.8	382,878	290,497	92,381	31.8	1,471,604	1,461,707	9,897	0.7	20.6	16.6	79.4	83.4
Louisiana	2,101,593	1,798,509	303,084	16.9	833,532	628,163	205,369	32.7	1,268,061	1,170,346	97,715	8.3	39.7	34.9	60.3	65.1
Oklahoma	2,396,040	2,028,283	367,757	18.1	821,681	539,480	282,201	52.3	1,574,359	1,488,803	85,556	5.7	34.3	26.6	65.7	73.4
Texas	5,824,715	4,663,228	1,161,487	24.9	2,389,348	1,512,689	876,659	58.0	3,435,367	3,150,539	284,828	9.0	41.0	32.4	59.0	67.6
MOUNTAIN:																
Montana	537,606	548,889	−11,283	−2.1	181,036	172,011	9,025	5.2	356,570	376,878	−20,308	−5.4	33.7	31.3	66.3	68.7
Idaho	445,032	431,866	13,166	3.0	129,507	119,037	10,470	8.8	315,525	312,829	2,696	0.9	29.1	27.6	70.9	72.4
Wyoming	225,565	194,402	31,163	16.0	70,007	57,348	12,749	22.2	155,468	137,054	18,414	13.4	31.1	29.5	68.9	70.5
Colorado	1,035,791	939,629	96,162	10.2	519,882	453,259	66,623	14.7	515,909	486,370	29,539	6.1	50.2	48.2	49.8	51.8
New Mexico	423,317	360,350	62,967	17.5	106,816	64,960	41,856	64.4	316,501	295,390	21,111	7.1	25.2	18.0	74.8	82.0
Arizona	435,573	334,162	101,411	30.3	149,856	117,527	32,329	27.5	285,717	216,635	69,082	31.9	34.4	35.2	65.6	64.8
Utah	507,847	449,396	58,451	13.0	266,264	215,584	50,680	23.5	241,583	233,812	7,771	3.3	52.4	48.0	47.6	52.0
Nevada	91,058	77,407	13,651	17.6	34,464	15,254	19,210	125.9	56,594	62,153	−5,559	−8.9	37.8	19.7	62.2	80.3
PACIFIC:																
Washington	1,563,396	1,356,621	206,775	15.2	884,539	748,735	135,804	18.1	678,857	607,886	70,971	11.7	56.6	55.2	43.4	44.8
Oregon	953,786	783,389	170,397	21.8	489,746	391,019	98,727	25.2	464,040	392,370	71,670	18.3	51.3	49.9	48.7	50.1
California	5,677,251	3,426,861	2,250,390	65.7	4,160,596	2,331,729	1,828,867	78.4	1,516,655	1,095,132	421,523	38.5	73.3	68.0	26.7	32.0

[1] The entire population of the District of Columbia is classified as urban.

URBAN AND RURAL

11

TABLE 7.—RURAL POPULATION IN SMALL INCORPORATED PLACES AND IN UNINCORPORATED TERRITORY, BY DIVISIONS AND STATES: 1930, 1920, AND 1910

DIVISION AND STATE	1930 Total rural population	1930 In incorporated places of less than 2,500 — Total	1930 Places of 1,000 to 2,500	1930 Places under 1,000	1930 Outside incorporated places	1920 Total rural population	1920 In incorporated places of less than 2,500	1920 Outside incorporated places	1910 Total rural population	1910 In incorporated places of less than 2,500	1910 Outside incorporated places	PER CENT OF RURAL POPULATION OUTSIDE INCORPORATED PLACES 1930	1920	1910	PER CENT OF TOTAL POPULATION OUTSIDE INCORPORATED PLACES 1930	1920	1910
United States	53,820,223	9,183,453	4,820,707	4,362,746	44,636,770	51,406,017	8,963,125	42,442,892	49,806,146	8,164,628	41,641,518	82.9	82.6	83.6	36.4	40.9	45.3
GEOGRAPHIC DIVISIONS:																	
New England	1,854,365	88,171	60,735	27,436	1,766,194	1,535,836	77,239	1,458,597	1,554,599	73,115	1,481,484	95.2	95.0	95.3	21.6	19.7	22.6
Mid. Atlantic	5,866,043	1,110,455	727,558	382,897	4,755,588	5,588,549	1,075,503	4,513,046	5,592,519	1,084,043	4,508,476	81.1	80.8	80.6	18.1	20.3	23.3
E. N. Central	8,502,277	2,027,764	1,031,344	996,420	6,474,513	8,426,271	2,007,078	6,419,193	8,633,350	1,952,985	6,680,365	76.2	76.2	77.4	25.0	29.9	36.6
W. N. Central	7,740,734	2,044,351	832,209	1,212,142	5,696,383	7,616,877	2,044,005	5,742,872	7,764,205	1,862,331	5,901,874	73.0	73.5	76.0	42.8	45.8	50.7
South Atlantic	10,095,467	1,271,902	676,858	595,044	8,823,565	9,651,480	1,175,440	8,476,031	9,102,742	1,064,383	8,038,359	87.4	87.8	88.3	55.9	60.6	65.0
E. S. Central	7,108,527	714,501	376,610	337,891	6,394,026	6,809,100	603,195	6,205,905	6,835,672	657,692	6,177,980	89.9	90.0	90.4	64.7	69.8	73.5
W. S. Central	7,749,391	1,068,680	630,591	438,095	6,680,705	7,271,395	980,585	6,290,810	6,827,078	771,238	6,055,840	86.2	86.5	88.7	54.9	61.4	68.9
Mountain	2,243,867	478,664	251,571	227,093	1,765,203	2,121,121	477,245	1,643,876	1,686,006	335,515	1,350,491	78.7	77.5	80.1	47.7	49.3	51.3
Pacific	2,659,552	378,959	233,231	145,728	2,280,593	2,005,388	402,826	1,602,562	1,809,975	363,326	1,446,649	85.8	80.8	79.9	27.8	30.4	34.5
NEW ENGLAND:																	
Maine	475,917	23,330	15,338	7,992	452,587	468,445	19,049	449,396	480,123	18,929	461,194	95.1	95.9	96.1	56.8	58.5	62.1
N. Hampshire	192,214	--------	--------	--------	192,214	163,322	--------	163,322	175,473	--------	175,473	100.0	100.0	100.0	41.3	36.9	40.8
Vermont	240,845	49,376	32,433	16,943	191,469	242,452	47,622	194,830	257,039	42,374	214,665	79.5	80.4	83.5	53.2	55.3	60.3
Massachusetts	418,188	--------	--------	--------	418,188	202,108	--------	202,108	241,049	--------	241,049	100.0	100.0	100.0	9.8	5.2	7.2
Rhode Island	52,068	--------	--------	--------	52,068	15,217	--------	15,217	17,956	--------	17,956	100.0	100.0	100.0	7.6	2.5	3.3
Connecticut	475,133	15,465	12,964	2,501	459,668	444,292	10,568	433,724	382,950	11,812	371,147	96.7	97.6	96.9	28.6	31.4	33.3
MID. ATLANTIC:																	
New York	2,066,114	363,930	228,701	135,139	1,702,184	1,795,383	346,877	1,448,506	1,928,120	352,294	1,575,826	82.0	80.7	81.7	13.5	13.9	17.3
New Jersey	702,090	187,898	144,318	43,580	514,192	680,964	148,702	532,262	629,957	149,790	480,167	73.2	78.2	76.2	12.7	10.9	18.9
Pennsylvania	3,097,839	558,627	354,449	204,178	2,539,212	3,112,202	579,924	2,532,278	3,034,442	581,959	2,452,483	82.0	81.4	80.8	26.4	29.0	32.0
E. N. CENTRAL:																	
Ohio	2,139,326	484,144	247,358	236,786	1,655,182	2,082,258	472,754	1,609,504	2,101,978	452,030	1,649,948	77.4	77.3	78.5	24.9	27.9	34.6
Indiana	1,442,611	303,058	148,488	154,570	1,139,553	1,447,535	295,040	1,152,495	1,557,041	300,647	1,256,394	79.0	79.6	80.7	35.2	39.3	46.5
Illinois	1,994,927	651,268	327,745	323,523	1,343,659	2,082,127	680,740	1,401,387	2,161,662	675,502	1,486,160	67.4	67.3	68.8	17.6	21.6	26.4
Michigan	1,540,250	294,319	171,380	122,939	1,245,931	1,426,852	286,644	1,140,208	1,483,129	285,955	1,197,174	80.9	79.9	80.7	25.7	31.1	42.6
Wisconsin	1,385,163	294,975	136,373	158,602	1,090,188	1,387,409	271,900	1,115,509	1,329,540	238,851	1,090,689	78.7	80.4	82.0	37.1	42.4	46.7
W. N. CENTRAL:																	
Minnesota	1,306,337	340,347	135,139	205,208	965,990	1,335,532	368,329	967,203	1,225,414	326,166	899,248	73.9	72.4	73.4	37.7	40.5	43.3
Iowa	1,491,647	464,922	186,409	278,513	1,026,725	1,528,526	477,801	1,050,725	1,544,717	438,715	1,106,002	68.8	68.7	71.6	41.6	43.7	49.7
Missouri	1,770,248	381,986	178,685	203,301	1,388,262	1,817,152	389,711	1,427,441	1,894,518	359,432	1,535,086	78.4	78.6	81.0	38.3	41.9	46.6
North Dakota	567,539	137,941	39,232	98,709	429,598	558,633	126,708	431,925	513,820	98,261	415,559	75.7	77.3	80.9	63.1	66.8	72.0
South Dakota	561,942	144,925	56,947	87,978	417,017	534,675	145,745	388,930	507,215	117,871	389,344	74.2	72.7	76.8	60.2	61.1	66.7
Nebraska	891,856	269,833	107,172	162,661	622,023	891,066	275,568	615,498	881,362	243,292	638,070	69.7	69.1	72.4	45.1	47.5	53.5
Kansas	1,151,165	304,397	128,625	175,772	846,768	1,151,293	290,203	861,090	1,197,159	278,574	918,585	73.6	74.8	76.7	45.0	48.7	54.3
S. ATLANTIC:																	
Delaware	115,234	31,794	17,744	14,050	83,440	102,236	31,679	70,557	105,237	29,027	76,210	72.4	69.0	72.4	35.0	31.6	37.7
Maryland	656,657	78,847	36,797	42,050	577,810	580,239	70,145	510,094	637,154	68,788	568,366	88.0	87.9	89.2	35.4	35.2	43.9
Dist. Columbia[1]	--------	--------	--------	--------	--------	--------	--------	--------	--------	--------	--------	--------	--------	--------	--------	--------	--------
Virginia	1,636,314	126,752	69,099	57,653	1,509,562	1,635,203	120,783	1,514,420	1,585,083	113,016	1,472,067	92.3	92.6	92.9	62.3	65.6	71.4
West Virginia	1,237,701	152,192	98,609	53,583	1,085,509	1,094,694	134,128	960,566	992,877	132,398	860,479	87.7	87.7	86.7	62.8	65.6	70.5
North Carolina	2,360,429	275,918	141,572	134,346	2,084,511	2,068,753	240,753	1,828,000	1,887,813	218,482	1,669,331	88.3	88.4	88.4	65.8	71.4	75.7
South Carolina	1,367,685	150,243	88,114	62,129	1,217,442	1,389,737	148,303	1,241,434	1,290,508	129,300	1,161,208	89.0	89.3	90.0	70.0	73.7	76.6
Georgia	2,013,014	299,744	143,903	155,841	1,713,270	2,167,973	296,795	1,871,178	2,070,471	286,803	1,784,668	85.1	86.3	86.2	58.9	64.6	68.4
Florida	708,433	156,412	81,020	75,392	552,021	612,645	132,863	479,782	533,539	87,509	446,030	77.9	78.3	83.6	37.6	49.5	59.3
E. S. CENTRAL:																	
Kentucky	1,815,563	215,153	117,656	97,497	1,600,410	1,783,087	107,551	1,585,536	1,734,463	188,872	1,545,591	88.1	88.9	89.1	61.2	65.6	67.5
Tennessee	1,720,018	135,836	72,008	63,828	1,584,182	1,726,659	131,174	1,595,485	1,743,744	133,940	1,609,804	92.1	92.4	92.3	60.5	68.2	73.7
Alabama	1,901,975	180,477	99,268	81,209	1,721,498	1,838,857	188,595	1,650,262	1,767,662	164,511	1,603,151	90.5	89.7	90.7	65.1	70.3	75.0
Mississippi	1,670,971	183,035	87,678	95,357	1,487,936	1,550,497	175,875	1,374,622	1,589,803	170,369	1,419,434	89.0	88.7	89.3	74.0	76.8	79.0
W. S. CENTRAL:																	
Arkansas	1,471,604	196,090	89,513	106,577	1,275,514	1,461,707	196,550	1,265,157	1,371,768	174,764	1,197,004	86.7	86.6	87.3	68.8	72.2	76.6
Louisiana	1,268,061	134,054	78,415	55,639	1,134,007	1,170,346	129,055	1,041,291	1,159,872	109,802	1,050,070	89.4	89.0	90.5	54.0	57.9	63.4
Oklahoma	1,574,359	298,432	160,698	137,734	1,275,927	1,488,803	291,972	1,196,831	1,337,000	230,367	1,106,633	81.0	80.4	82.8	53.3	59.0	66.8
Texas	3,435,367	440,110	301,965	138,145	2,995,257	3,150,539	363,008	2,787,531	2,958,438	256,305	2,702,133	87.2	88.5	91.3	51.4	59.8	69.3
MOUNTAIN:																	
Montana	356,570	70,379	36,270	34,109	286,191	376,878	69,699	307,179	242,633	35,186	207,447	80.3	81.5	85.5	53.2	56.0	55.2
Idaho	315,525	75,298	33,521	41,777	240,227	312,829	77,442	235,387	255,696	59,375	196,321	76.1	75.2	76.8	54.0	54.5	60.3
Wyoming	155,468	46,667	27,916	18,751	108,801	137,054	46,267	90,787	102,744	22,866	79,878	70.0	66.2	77.7	48.2	46.7	54.7
Colorado	515,909	121,665	60,826	60,839	394,244	486,370	115,103	371,267	394,184	96,757	297,427	76.4	76.3	75.5	33.1	39.5	37.2
New Mexico	316,501	32,793	17,458	15,335	283,708	295,390	30,119	265,271	280,730	17,613	263,117	89.6	89.8	93.7	67.0	73.6	80.4
Arizona	285,717	24,080	14,911	9,169	261,637	216,635	15,122	201,513	141,094	16,406	124,688	91.6	93.0	88.4	60.1	60.3	61.0
Utah	241,583	97,967	53,058	44,909	143,616	233,812	108,437	125,375	200,417	80,644	119,773	59.4	53.6	59.8	28.3	27.0	32.1
Nevada	56,594	9,815	7,611	2,204	46,779	62,153	15,056	47,097	68,508	6,668	61,840	82.7	75.8	90.3	51.4	60.8	75.5
PACIFIC:																	
Washington	678,857	127,325	63,013	64,312	551,532	607,886	130,211	477,675	536,460	120,532	415,928	81.2	78.6	77.5	35.3	35.2	36.4
Oregon	464,040	97,350	46,354	50,996	366,690	392,370	98,938	293,432	365,705	89,742	275,963	79.0	74.8	75.5	38.4	34.1	41.0
California	1,516,655	154,284	123,864	30,420	1,362,371	1,095,132	173,677	921,455	907,810	153,052	754,758	89.8	84.1	83.1	24.0	26.9	31.7

[1] See footnote 1, Table 6.

12

POPULATION

TABLE 8.—RURAL-FARM AND RURAL-NONFARM (VILLAGE) POPULATION, BY DIVISIONS AND STATES: 1930 AND 1920

[A minus sign (—) denotes decrease. Per cent not shown where less than 0.1]

DIVISION AND STATE	TOTAL RURAL POPULATION		RURAL-FARM POPULATION								RURAL-NONFARM (VILLAGE) POPULATION					
					Increase		Per cent of rural population		Per cent of total popuation				Increase		Per cent of total population	
	1930	1920	1930	1920	Number	Per cent	1930	1920	1930	1920	1930	1920	Number	Per cent	1930	1920
United States	53,820,223	51,406,017	30,157,513	31,358,640	-1,201,127	-3.8	56.0	61.0	24.6	29.7	23,662,710	20,047,377	3,615,333	18.0	19.3	19.0
GEOGRAPHIC DIVISIONS:																
New England	1,854,365	1,535,836	499,083	535,422	-36,339	-6.8	26.9	34.9	6.1	7.2	1,355,282	1,000,414	354,868	35.5	16.6	13.5
Middle Atlantic	5,866,043	5,588,549	1,673,694	1,861,161	-187,467	-10.1	28.5	33.3	6.4	8.4	4,192,349	3,727,388	464,961	12.5	16.0	16.7
East North Central	8,502,277	8,426,271	4,453,114	4,887,204	-434,090	-8.9	52.4	58.0	17.6	22.8	4,049,163	3,539,067	510,096	14.4	16.0	16.5
West North Central	7,740,734	7,816,877	5,035,561	5,153,183	-117,622	-2.3	65.1	65.9	37.9	41.1	2,705,173	2,663,694	41,479	1.6	20.3	21.2
South Atlantic	10,095,467	9,651,480	5,878,956	6,397,757	-518,801	-8.1	58.2	66.3	37.2	45.7	4,216,511	3,253,723	962,788	29.6	26.7	23.3
East South Central	7,108,527	6,899,100	5,084,435	5,174,806	-90,371	-1.7	71.5	75.0	51.4	58.2	2,024,092	1,724,294	299,798	17.4	20.5	19.4
West South Central	7,749,391	7,271,395	5,307,939	5,210,570	97,369	1.9	68.5	71.7	43.6	50.9	2,441,452	2,060,825	380,627	18.5	20.0	20.1
Mountain	2,243,867	2,121,121	1,123,693	1,152,993	-29,300	-2.5	50.1	54.4	30.4	34.6	1,120,174	968,128	152,046	15.7	30.3	29.0
Pacific	2,659,552	2,095,388	1,101,038	985,544	115,494	11.7	41.4	47.0	13.4	17.7	1,558,514	1,109,844	448,670	40.4	19.0	19.9
NEW ENGLAND:																
Maine	475,917	468,445	161,429	189,026	-27,597	-14.6	33.9	40.4	20.2	24.6	314,488	279,419	35,069	12.6	39.4	36.4
New Hampshire	192,214	163,322	54,911	64,607	-9,696	-15.0	28.6	39.6	11.8	14.6	137,303	98,715	38,588	39.1	29.5	22.3
Vermont	240,845	242,452	111,898	124,445	-12,547	-10.1	46.5	51.3	31.1	35.3	128,947	118,007	10,940	9.3	35.9	33.5
Massachusetts	418,188	202,108	80,309	61,732	18,577	30.1	19.2	30.5	1.9	1.6	337,879	140,376	197,503	140.7	8.0	3.6
Rhode Island	52,068	15,217	10,289	5,315	4,974	93.6	19.8	34.9	1.5	0.9	41,779	9,902	31,877	321.9	6.1	1.6
Connecticut	475,133	444,292	80,247	90,297	-10,050	-11.1	16.0	20.3	5.0	6.5	394,886	353,995	40,891	11.6	24.6	25.6
MIDDLE ATLANTIC:																
New York	2,066,114	1,795,383	706,446	782,954	-76,508	-9.8	34.2	43.6	5.6	7.5	1,359,668	1,012,429	347,239	34.3	10.8	9.7
New Jersey	702,090	680,964	121,008	136,847	-15,839	-11.6	17.2	20.1	3.0	4.3	581,082	544,117	36,965	6.8	14.4	17.2
Pennsylvania	3,097,839	3,112,202	846,240	941,360	-95,120	-10.1	27.3	30.2	8.8	10.8	2,251,599	2,170,842	80,757	3.7	23.4	24.9
EAST NORTH CENTRAL:																
Ohio	2,139,326	2,082,258	1,004,288	1,133,912	-129,624	-11.4	46.9	54.5	15.1	19.7	1,135,038	948,346	186,692	19.7	17.1	16.5
Indiana	1,442,611	1,447,535	808,981	902,820	-93,839	-10.4	56.1	62.4	25.0	30.8	633,630	544,715	88,915	16.3	19.6	18.0
Illinois	1,994,927	2,082,127	991,401	1,090,736	-99,335	-9.1	49.7	52.4	13.0	16.8	1,003,526	991,391	12,135	1.2	13.2	15.3
Michigan	1,540,250	1,426,852	775,436	844,499	-69,063	-8.2	50.3	59.2	16.0	23.0	764,814	582,353	182,461	31.3	15.8	15.9
Wisconsin	1,385,163	1,387,499	873,008	915,237	-42,229	-4.6	63.0	66.0	29.7	34.8	512,155	472,262	39,893	8.4	17.4	17.9
WEST NORTH CENTRAL:																
Minnesota	1,306,337	1,335,532	888,049	893,460	-5,411	-0.6	68.0	66.9	34.6	37.4	418,288	442,072	-23,784	-5.4	16.3	18.5
Iowa	1,491,647	1,528,526	964,659	977,694	-13,035	-1.3	64.7	64.0	39.0	40.7	526,988	550,832	-23,844	-4.3	21.3	22.9
Missouri	1,770,248	1,817,152	1,108,989	1,207,899	-98,980	-8.2	62.6	66.5	30.6	35.5	661,270	609,253	52,026	8.5	18.2	17.9
North Dakota	507,539	558,033	390,871	393,622	3,249	0.8	69.0	70.5	58.3	60.9	170,668	165,011	5,657	3.4	25.1	25.5
South Dakota	561,942	534,075	389,431	361,886	27,545	7.6	69.3	67.7	56.2	56.9	172,511	172,780	-278	-0.2	24.9	27.1
Nebraska	891,856	891,066	582,981	582,738	243		65.4	65.4	42.3	45.0	308,875	308,328	547	0.2	22.4	23.8
Kansas	1,151,165	1,151,293	704,601	735,884	-31,283	-4.3	61.2	63.9	37.5	41.6	446,564	415,409	31,155	7.5	23.7	23.5
SOUTH ATLANTIC:																
Delaware	115,234	102,236	46,302	51,151	-4,849	-9.5	40.2	50.0	19.4	22.9	68,932	51,085	17,847	34.9	28.9	22.0
Maryland	656,657	580,239	236,172	277,656	-41,484	-14.9	36.0	47.9	14.5	19.2	420,485	302,583	117,902	39.0	25.8	20.9
Dist. of Columbia[1]																
Virginia	1,636,314	1,635,203	948,746	1,059,913	-111,167	-10.5	58.0	64.8	39.2	45.9	687,568	575,290	112,278	19.5	28.4	24.9
West Virginia	1,237,701	1,094,694	447,750	476,631	-28,881	-6.1	36.2	43.5	25.9	32.6	789,951	618,063	171,888	27.8	45.7	42.2
North Carolina	2,360,429	2,063,753	1,597,220	1,499,946	97,274	6.5	67.7	72.5	50.4	58.6	763,209	508,807	194,402	34.2	24.1	22.2
South Carolina	1,367,685	1,380,737	914,098	1,072,479	-158,381	-14.8	66.8	77.2	52.6	63.7	453,587	317,258	136,329	43.0	26.1	18.8
Georgia	2,013,014	2,167,973	1,413,719	1,680,611	-266,892	-15.9	70.2	77.5	48.6	58.0	599,295	487,362	111,933	23.0	20.6	16.8
Florida	708,433	612,645	274,949	279,370	-4,421	-1.6	38.8	45.6	18.7	28.8	433,484	333,275	100,209	30.1	29.5	34.4
EAST SOUTH CENTRAL:																
Kentucky	1,815,563	1,783,087	1,174,232	1,302,342	-128,110	-9.8	64.7	73.0	44.9	53.9	641,331	480,745	160,586	33.4	24.5	19.9
Tennessee	1,720,018	1,726,659	1,213,065	1,269,179	-56,114	-4.4	70.5	73.5	46.4	54.3	506,953	457,480	49,473	10.8	19.4	19.6
Alabama	1,901,975	1,835,857	1,336,409	1,334,513	1,896	0.1	70.3	72.6	50.5	56.8	565,566	504,344	61,222	12.1	21.4	21.5
Mississippi	1,670,971	1,550,497	1,360,729	1,268,772	91,957	7.2	81.4	81.8	67.7	70.9	310,242	281,725	28,517	10.1	15.4	15.7
WEST SOUTH CENTRAL:																
Arkansas	1,471,604	1,461,707	1,117,330	1,144,482	-27,152	-2.4	75.9	78.3	60.3	65.3	354,274	317,225	37,049	11.7	19.1	18.1
Louisiana	1,268,061	1,170,346	826,882	784,455	42,427	5.4	65.2	67.0	39.3	43.6	441,179	385,891	55,288	14.3	21.0	21.5
Oklahoma	1,574,359	1,488,803	1,021,174	1,015,899	5,275	0.5	64.9	68.2	42.6	50.1	553,185	472,904	80,281	17.0	23.1	23.3
Texas	3,435,367	3,150,539	2,342,553	2,265,734	76,819	3.4	68.2	71.9	40.2	48.6	1,092,814	884,805	208,009	23.5	18.8	19.0
MOUNTAIN:																
Montana	356,570	376,878	203,962	225,389	-21,427	-9.5	57.2	59.8	37.9	41.1	152,608	151,489	1,119	0.7	28.4	27.6
Idaho	315,525	312,829	186,100	196,563	-10,463	-5.3	59.0	62.8	41.8	45.5	129,425	116,266	13,159	11.3	29.1	26.9
Wyoming	155,468	137,054	72,905	67,076	5,829	8.7	46.9	48.9	32.3	34.5	82,563	69,978	12,585	18.0	36.6	36.0
Colorado	515,909	486,370	281,038	265,281	15,757	5.9	54.5	54.5	27.1	28.2	234,871	221,089	13,782	6.2	22.7	23.5
New Mexico	316,501	295,390	157,906	160,542	-2,636	-1.6	49.9	54.3	37.3	44.6	158,595	134,848	23,747	17.6	37.5	37.4
Arizona	285,717	216,635	98,819	90,167	8,652	9.6	34.6	41.6	22.7	27.0	186,898	126,468	60,430	47.8	42.9	37.8
Utah	241,583	233,812	106,667	131,872	-25,205	-19.1	44.2	56.4	21.0	29.3	134,916	101,940	32,976	32.3	26.6	22.7
Nevada	56,594	62,153	16,296	16,103	193	1.2	28.8	25.9	17.9	20.8	40,298	46,050	-5,752	-12.5	44.3	59.5
PACIFIC:																
Washington	678,857	607,886	300,143	280,022	20,121	7.2	44.2	46.1	19.2	20.6	378,714	327,864	50,850	15.5	24.2	24.2
Oregon	464,040	392,370	221,545	212,009	9,536	4.5	47.7	54.0	23.2	27.1	242,495	180,361	62,134	34.4	25.4	23.0
California	1,516,655	1,095,132	579,350	493,513	85,837	17.4	38.2	45.1	10.2	14.4	937,305	601,619	335,686	55.8	16.5	17.6

[1] See footnote 1, Table 6.

URBAN AND RURAL   13

TABLE 9.—FARM POPULATION, URBAN AND RURAL, AND NUMBER OF FARMS, BY DIVISIONS AND STATES: 1930 AND 1920

[A minus sign (−) denotes decrease]

DIVISION AND STATE	TOTAL FARM POPULATION						URBAN-FARM POPULATION		RURAL-FARM POPULATION		NUMBER OF FARMS		FARM POPULATION PER FARM	
	1930	1920	Increase		Per cent of total population		1930	1920	1930	1920	1930	1920	1930	1920
			Number	Per cent	1930	1920								
United States	30,445,350	31,614,269	−1,168,919	−3.7	24.8	29.9	287,837	255,629	30,157,513	31,358,640	6,288,648	6,448,343	4.84	4.90
GEOGRAPHIC DIVISIONS:														
New England	573,251	625,877	−52,626	−8.4	7.0	8.5	74,168	90,455	499,083	535,422	124,925	156,564	4.59	4.00
Middle Atlantic	1,707,710	1,892,780	−185,070	−9.8	6.5	8.5	34,025	31,628	1,673,694	1,861,161	357,603	425,147	4.78	4.45
East North Central	4,488,933	4,913,633	−424,700	−8.6	17.7	22.9	35,819	26,429	4,453,114	4,887,204	966,502	1,084,744	4.64	4.53
West North Central	5,068,135	5,171,596	−103,461	−2.0	38.1	41.2	32,574	18,413	5,035,561	5,153,183	1,112,755	1,096,951	4.55	4.71
South Atlantic	5,898,176	6,416,698	−518,522	−8.1	37.3	45.9	19,220	18,941	5,878,956	6,397,757	1,058,468	1,158,976	5.57	5.54
East South Central	5,095,096	5,182,937	−87,841	−1.7	51.5	58.3	10,661	8,131	5,084,435	5,174,806	1,062,214	1,051,600	4.80	4.93
West South Central	5,326,412	5,228,199	98,213	1.9	43.7	51.0	18,473	17,629	5,307,939	5,210,570	1,103,134	996,088	4.83	5.25
Mountain	1,138,718	1,168,367	−29,649	−2.5	30.8	35.0	15,025	15,374	1,123,693	1,152,993	241,314	244,109	4.72	4.79
Pacific	1,148,910	1,014,173	134,737	13.3	14.0	18.2	47,872	28,629	1,101,038	985,544	261,733	234,164	4.39	4.33
NEW ENGLAND:														
Maine	170,995	197,601	−26,606	−13.5	21.4	25.7	9,566	8,575	161,429	189,026	39,006	48,227	4.38	4.10
New Hampshire	62,850	76,021	−13,171	−17.3	13.5	17.2	7,939	11,414	54,911	64,607	14,906	20,523	4.22	3.70
Vermont	112,904	125,263	−12,359	−9.9	31.4	35.5	1,006	818	111,898	124,445	24,898	29,075	4.53	4.31
Massachusetts	123,255	118,554	4,701	4.0	2.9	3.1	42,946	56,822	80,309	61,732	25,598	32,001	4.82	3.70
Rhode Island	16,477	15,136	1,341	8.0	2.4	2.5	6,188	9,821	10,289	5,315	3,322	4,083	4.96	3.71
Connecticut	86,770	93,302	−6,532	−7.0	5.4	6.8	6,523	3,005	80,247	90,297	17,195	22,655	5.05	4.12
MIDDLE ATLANTIC:														
New York	719,920	800,747	−80,818	−10.1	5.7	7.7	13,483	17,793	706,446	782,954	159,806	193,195	4.51	4.14
New Jersey	131,096	143,708	−12,612	−8.8	3.2	4.6	10,088	6,861	121,008	136,847	25,378	29,702	5.17	4.84
Pennsylvania	856,694	948,334	−91,640	−9.7	8.9	10.9	10,454	6,974	846,240	941,360	172,419	202,250	4.97	4.69
EAST NORTH CENTRAL:														
Ohio	1,013,220	1,139,320	−126,100	−11.1	15.2	19.8	8,941	5,417	1,004,288	1,133,912	219,296	256,695	4.62	4.44
Indiana	813,007	907,295	−94,288	−10.4	25.1	31.0	4,026	4,475	808,981	902,820	181,570	205,126	4.48	4.42
Illinois	999,249	1,098,262	−99,013	−9.0	13.1	16.9	7,848	7,526	991,401	1,090,736	214,497	237,181	4.66	4.63
Michigan	782,394	848,710	−66,316	−7.8	16.2	23.1	6,958	4,211	775,436	844,409	169,872	196,447	4.62	4.32
Wisconsin	881,054	920,037	−38,983	−4.2	30.0	35.0	8,046	4,800	873,008	915,237	181,267	189,295	4.85	4.86
WEST NORTH CENTRAL:														
Minnesota	895,349	897,181	−1,832	−0.2	34.9	37.6	7,300	3,721	888,049	893,460	185,255	178,478	4.83	5.03
Iowa	977,906	984,700	−6,893	−0.7	39.6	41.0	13,247	7,105	964,659	977,604	214,928	213,439	4.55	4.61
Missouri	1,114,484	1,211,346	−96,862	−8.0	30.7	35.6	5,515	3,447	1,108,969	1,207,899	255,940	263,004	4.35	4.61
North Dakota	307,294	304,500	2,794	0.7	58.4	61.0	423	878	306,871	303,622	77,975	77,090	5.10	5.08
South Dakota	390,205	362,221	27,984	7.7	56.3	56.9	774	335	389,431	361,886	83,157	74,637	4.69	4.85
Nebraska	585,701	584,172	1,529	0.3	42.5	45.1	2,720	1,434	582,981	582,738	129,458	124,417	4.52	4.70
Kansas	707,196	737,377	−30,181	−4.1	37.6	41.7	2,595	1,493	704,601	735,884	166,042	165,286	4.26	4.46
SOUTH ATLANTIC:														
Delaware	46,530	51,212	−4,682	−9.1	19.5	23.0	228	61	46,302	51,151	9,707	10,140	4.79	5.05
Maryland	237,456	279,225	−41,769	−15.0	14.6	19.3	1,284	1,569	236,172	277,656	43,203	47,908	5.50	5.83
District of Columbia	435	894	−459	−51.3	0.1	0.2	435	894			104	204	4.18	4.38
Virginia	950,757	1,064,417	−113,660	−10.7	30.3	46.1	2,011	4,504	948,746	1,059,913	170,610	186,242	5.57	5.72
West Virginia	449,114	477,924	−28,810	−6.0	26.0	32.7	1,364	1,293	447,750	476,631	82,641	87,289	5.43	5.48
North Carolina	1,599,918	1,501,227	98,691	6.6	50.5	58.7	2,698	1,281	1,597,220	1,499,946	279,708	269,763	5.72	5.56
South Carolina	916,471	1,074,693	−158,222	−14.7	52.7	63.8	2,373	2,214	914,098	1,072,479	157,931	192,693	5.80	5.53
Georgia	1,418,514	1,685,213	−266,699	−15.8	48.8	58.2	4,795	4,602	1,413,719	1,680,611	255,598	310,732	5.55	5.42
Florida	278,081	281,893	−2,912	−1.0	19.0	29.1	4,082	2,523	274,949	279,370	58,966	54,005	4.73	5.22
EAST SOUTH CENTRAL:														
Kentucky	1,176,524	1,304,862	−128,338	−9.8	45.0	54.0	2,292	2,520	1,174,232	1,302,342	246,499	270,626	4.77	4.82
Tennessee	1,215,452	1,271,708	−56,256	−4.4	46.5	54.4	2,387	2,529	1,213,065	1,269,179	245,657	252,774	4.95	5.03
Alabama	1,340,277	1,335,885	4,392	0.3	50.6	58.0	3,803	1,372	1,336,400	1,334,513	257,395	256,099	5.21	5.22
Mississippi	1,362,843	1,270,482	92,361	7.3	67.8	71.0	2,114	1,710	1,360,729	1,268,772	312,663	272,101	4.36	4.67
WEST SOUTH CENTRAL:														
Arkansas	1,119,404	1,147,049	−27,585	−2.4	60.4	65.5	2,134	2,567	1,117,330	1,144,482	242,334	232,604	4.62	4.93
Louisiana	830,006	786,050	44,556	5.7	39.5	43.7	3,724	1,595	826,882	784,455	161,445	135,463	5.14	5.80
Oklahoma	1,024,070	1,017,327	6,743	0.7	42.7	50.2	2,896	1,428	1,021,174	1,015,899	203,866	191,988	5.02	5.30
Texas	2,352,272	2,277,773	74,499	3.3	40.4	48.8	9,719	12,039	2,342,553	2,265,734	495,489	436,033	4.75	5.22
MOUNTAIN:														
Montana	204,594	225,667	−21,073	−9.3	38.1	41.1	632	278	203,962	225,389	47,495	57,677	4.31	3.91
Idaho	188,365	200,902	−12,537	−6.2	42.3	46.5	2,265	4,339	186,100	196,563	41,674	42,106	4.52	4.77
Wyoming	73,152	67,306	5,846	8.7	32.4	34.6	247	230	72,905	67,076	16,011	15,748	4.57	4.27
Colorado	282,827	266,073	16,754	6.3	27.3	28.3	1,789	792	281,038	265,281	59,956	59,934	4.72	4.44
New Mexico	158,631	161,446	−2,815	−1.7	37.5	44.8	725	904	157,906	160,542	31,404	29,844	5.05	5.41
Arizona	98,995	90,560	8,435	9.3	22.7	27.1	176	393	98,819	90,167	14,173	9,975	6.98	9.08
Utah	115,713	140,249	−24,536	−17.5	22.8	31.2	9,046	8,377	106,667	131,872	27,159	25,662	4.26	5.47
Nevada	16,441	16,164	277	1.7	18.1	20.9	145	61	16,296	16,103	3,442	3,163	4.78	5.11
PACIFIC:														
Washington	304,737	283,382	21,355	7.5	19.5	20.9	4,594	3,360	300,143	280,022	70,904	66,288	4.30	4.28
Oregon	223,667	214,021	9,646	4.5	23.5	27.3	2,122	2,012	221,545	212,009	55,153	50,206	4.06	4.26
California	620,506	516,770	103,736	20.1	10.9	15.1	41,156	23,257	579,350	493,513	135,676	117,670	4.57	4.39

POPULATION

TABLE 10.—URBAN AND RURAL POPULATION, BY DIVISIONS AND STATES: 1880 TO 1930

DIVISION OR STATE AND AREA	1930	1920	1910	1900	1890	1880
United States	122,775,046	105,710,620	91,972,266	75,994,575	62,947,714	50,155,783
Urban	68,954,823	54,304,603	42,166,120	30,380,433	22,298,359	14,358,167
Per cent	56.2	51.4	45.8	40.0	35.4	28.6
Rural	53,820,223	51,406,017	49,806,146	45,614,142	40,649,355	35,797,616
Per cent	43.8	48.6	54.2	60.0	64.6	71.4
New England	8,166,341	7,400,909	6,552,681	5,592,017	4,700,749	4,010,529
Urban	6,311,976	5,865,073	4,998,082	4,053,427	3,139,899	2,339,579
Per cent	77.3	79.2	76.3	72.5	66.8	58.3
Rural	1,854,365	1,535,836	1,554,599	1,538,590	1,560,850	1,670,950
Per cent	22.7	20.8	23.7	27.5	33.2	41.7
Middle Atlantic	26,260,750	22,261,144	19,315,892	15,454,678	12,706,220	10,496,878
Urban	20,394,707	16,672,595	13,723,373	10,075,883	7,333,772	5,242,574
Per cent	77.7	74.9	71.0	65.2	57.7	49.9
Rural	5,866,043	5,588,549	5,592,519	5,378,795	5,372,448	5,254,304
Per cent	22.3	25.1	29.0	34.8	42.3	50.1
E. North Central	25,297,185	21,475,543	18,250,621	15,985,581	13,478,305	11,206,668
Urban	16,794,908	13,049,272	9,617,271	7,219,975	5,097,181	3,077,131
Per cent	66.4	60.8	52.7	45.2	37.8	27.5
Rural	8,502,277	8,426,271	8,633,350	8,765,606	8,381,124	8,129,537
Per cent	33.6	39.2	47.3	54.8	62.2	72.5
W. North Central	13,296,915	12,544,249	11,637,921	10,347,423	8,932,112	6,157,443
Urban	5,556,181	4,727,372	3,873,716	2,946,544	2,308,819	1,116,869
Per cent	41.8	37.7	33.3	28.5	25.8	18.1
Rural	7,740,734	7,816,877	7,764,205	7,400,879	6,623,293	5,040,574
Per cent	58.2	62.3	66.7	71.5	74.2	81.9
South Atlantic	15,793,589	13,990,272	12,194,895	10,443,480	8,857,922	7,597,197
Urban	5,698,122	4,338,792	3,092,153	2,232,032	1,728,019	1,146,155
Per cent	36.1	31.0	25.4	21.4	19.5	15.1
Rural	10,095,467	9,651,480	9,102,742	8,210,848	7,129,903	6,451,042
Per cent	63.9	69.0	74.6	78.6	80.5	84.9
E. South Central	9,887,214	8,893,307	8,409,901	7,547,757	6,429,154	5,585,151
Urban	2,778,687	1,994,207	1,574,229	1,131,056	817,308	470,653
Per cent	28.1	22.4	18.7	15.0	12.7	8.4
Rural	7,108,527	6,890,100	6,835,672	6,416,701	5,611,846	5,114,498
Per cent	71.9	77.6	81.3	85.0	87.3	91.6
W. South Central	12,176,830	10,242,224	8,784,534	6,532,290	4,740,983	3,334,220
Urban	4,427,439	2,970,829	1,957,450	1,057,197	715,999	407,192
Per cent	36.4	29.0	22.3	16.2	15.1	12.2
Rural	7,749,391	7,271,395	6,827,078	5,475,093	4,024,984	2,927,028
Per cent	63.6	71.0	77.7	83.8	84.9	87.8
Mountain	3,701,789	3,336,101	2,633,517	1,674,657	1,213,935	653,119
Urban	1,457,922	1,214,980	947,511	541,363	355,627	164,450
Per cent	39.4	36.4	36.0	32.3	29.3	23.6
Rural	2,243,867	2,121,121	1,686,006	1,133,294	858,308	498,669
Per cent	60.6	63.6	64.0	67.7	70.7	76.4
Pacific	8,194,433	5,566,871	4,192,304	2,416,692	1,888,334	1,114,578
Urban	5,534,881	3,471,483	2,382,329	1,122,356	801,735	403,564
Per cent	67.5	62.4	56.8	46.4	42.5	36.2
Rural	2,659,552	2,095,388	1,809,975	1,294,336	1,086,599	711,014
Per cent	32.5	37.6	43.2	53.6	57.5	63.8
NEW ENGLAND						
Maine	797,423	768,014	742,371	694,466	661,086	648,936
Urban	321,506	299,569	262,248	232,827	173,781	146,608
Per cent	40.3	39.0	35.3	33.5	26.3	22.6
Rural	475,917	468,445	480,123	461,639	487,305	502,328
Per cent	59.7	61.0	64.7	66.5	73.7	77.4
New Hampshire	465,293	443,083	430,572	411,588	376,530	346,991
Urban	273,079	279,761	255,099	226,269	192,479	135,014
Per cent	58.7	63.1	59.2	55.0	51.1	38.9
Rural	192,214	163,322	175,473	185,319	184,051	211,977
Per cent	41.3	36.9	40.8	45.0	48.9	61.1
Vermont	359,611	352,428	355,956	343,641	332,422	332,286
Urban	118,760	109,976	98,917	75,831	50,638	29,531
Per cent	33.0	31.2	27.8	22.1	15.2	8.9
Rural	240,845	242,452	257,039	267,810	281,784	302,755
Per cent	67.0	68.8	72.2	77.9	84.8	91.1
Massachusetts	4,249,614	3,852,356	3,366,416	2,805,346	2,238,947	1,783,085
Urban	3,831,420	3,650,248	3,125,367	2,567,098	2,003,854	1,513,312
Per cent	90.2	94.8	92.8	91.5	89.5	84.9
Rural	418,188	202,108	241,049	238,248	235,093	269,773
Per cent	9.8	5.2	7.2	8.5	10.5	15.1
Rhode Island	687,497	604,397	542,610	428,556	345,506	276,531
Urban	635,429	589,180	524,654	407,647	326,602	258,527
Per cent	92.4	97.5	96.7	95.1	94.5	93.5
Rural	52,068	15,217	17,956	20,909	18,904	18,004
Per cent	7.6	2.5	3.3	4.9	5.5	6.5
Connecticut	1,606,903	1,380,631	1,114,756	908,420	746,258	622,700
Urban	1,131,770	936,339	731,797	543,755	392,545	256,587
Per cent	70.4	67.8	65.6	59.9	52.6	41.2
Rural	475,133	444,292	382,959	364,665	353,713	366,113
Per cent	29.6	32.2	34.4	40.1	47.4	58.8

DIVISION OR STATE AND AREA	1930	1920	1910	1900	1890	1880
MIDDLE ATLANTIC						
New York	12,588,066	10,385,227	9,113,614	7,268,894	6,003,174	5,082,871
Urban	10,521,952	8,589,844	7,185,494	5,298,111	3,899,737	2,852,010
Per cent	83.6	82.7	78.8	72.9	65.0	56.1
Rural	2,066,114	1,795,383	1,928,120	1,970,783	2,103,437	2,230,861
Per cent	16.4	17.3	21.2	27.1	35.0	43.9
New Jersey	4,041,334	3,155,900	2,537,167	1,883,669	1,444,933	1,131,116
Urban	3,339,244	2,474,930	1,907,210	1,329,162	876,638	607,186
Per cent	82.6	78.4	75.2	70.6	60.7	53.7
Rural	702,090	680,964	629,957	554,507	568,295	523,930
Per cent	17.4	21.6	24.8	29.4	39.3	46.3
Pennsylvania	9,631,350	8,720,017	7,665,111	6,302,115	5,258,113	4,282,891
Urban	6,533,511	5,607,815	4,630,606	3,448,610	2,557,307	1,783,378
Per cent	67.8	64.3	60.4	54.7	48.6	41.6
Rural	3,097,839	3,112,202	3,034,442	2,853,505	2,700,716	2,499,513
Per cent	32.2	35.7	39.6	45.3	51.4	58.4
EAST NORTH CENTRAL						
Ohio	6,646,697	5,759,394	4,767,121	4,157,545	3,672,329	3,198,062
Urban	4,507,371	3,677,136	2,665,143	1,998,382	1,504,300	1,030,769
Per cent	67.8	63.8	55.9	48.1	41.0	32.2
Rural	2,139,326	2,082,258	2,101,978	2,159,163	2,167,939	2,167,293
Per cent	32.2	36.2	44.1	51.9	59.0	67.8
Indiana	3,238,503	2,930,390	2,700,876	2,516,462	2,192,404	1,978,301
Urban	1,795,892	1,482,855	1,143,835	862,689	590,039	386,211
Per cent	55.5	50.6	42.4	34.3	26.9	19.5
Rural	1,442,611	1,447,535	1,557,041	1,653,773	1,602,365	1,592,090
Per cent	44.5	49.4	57.6	65.7	73.1	80.5
Illinois	7,630,654	6,485,280	5,638,591	4,821,550	3,826,352	3,077,871
Urban	5,635,727	4,403,153	3,476,929	2,616,368	1,710,172	940,504
Per cent	73.9	67.9	61.7	54.3	44.7	30.6
Rural	1,994,927	2,082,127	2,161,662	2,205,182	2,116,180	2,137,367
Per cent	26.1	32.1	38.3	45.7	55.3	69.4
Michigan	4,842,325	3,668,412	2,810,173	2,420,982	2,093,890	1,636,937
Urban	3,302,075	2,241,560	1,327,044	952,323	730,294	405,412
Per cent	68.2	61.1	47.2	39.3	34.9	24.8
Rural	1,540,250	1,426,852	1,483,129	1,468,650	1,363,596	1,231,525
Per cent	31.8	38.9	52.8	60.7	65.1	75.2
Wisconsin	2,939,006	2,632,067	2,333,860	2,069,042	1,693,330	1,315,497
Urban	1,553,843	1,244,568	1,004,320	700,213	562,286	314,285
Per cent	52.9	47.3	43.0	38.2	33.2	23.9
Rural	1,385,163	1,387,499	1,329,540	1,278,829	1,131,044	1,001,262
Per cent	47.1	52.7	57.0	61.8	66.8	76.1
WEST NORTH CENTRAL						
Minnesota	2,563,953	2,387,125	2,075,708	1,751,394	1,310,283	780,773
Urban	1,257,616	1,051,593	850,294	598,100	443,049	147,920
Per cent	49.0	44.1	41.0	34.1	33.8	18.9
Rural	1,306,337	1,335,532	1,225,414	1,153,294	867,234	632,853
Per cent	51.0	55.9	59.0	65.9	66.2	81.1
Iowa	2,470,939	2,404,021	2,224,771	2,231,853	1,912,297	1,624,615
Urban	979,292	875,495	680,054	572,386	405,764	247,427
Per cent	39.6	36.4	30.6	25.6	21.2	15.2
Rural	1,491,647	1,528,526	1,544,717	1,659,467	1,506,533	1,377,188
Per cent	60.4	63.6	69.4	74.4	78.8	84.8
Missouri	3,629,367	3,404,055	3,293,335	3,106,665	2,679,185	2,168,380
Urban	1,859,119	1,586,903	1,398,817	1,128,104	856,966	545,903
Per cent	51.2	46.6	42.5	36.3	32.0	25.2
Rural	1,770,248	1,817,152	1,894,518	1,978,561	1,822,219	1,622,387
Per cent	48.8	53.4	57.5	63.7	68.0	74.8
North Dakota	680,845	646,872	577,056	319,146	190,983	36,909
Urban	113,306	88,239	63,236	23,413	10,643	2,693
Per cent	16.6	13.6	11.0	7.3	5.6	7.3
Rural	567,539	558,633	513,820	295,733	180,340	34,216
Per cent	83.4	86.4	89.0	92.7	94.4	92.7
South Dakota	692,849	636,547	583,888	401,570	348,600	98,268
Urban	130,907	101,872	76,673	40,936	28,555	7,208
Per cent	18.9	16.0	13.1	10.2	8.2	7.3
Rural	561,942	534,675	507,215	360,634	320,045	91,060
Per cent	81.1	84.0	86.9	89.8	91.8	92.7
Nebraska	1,377,963	1,296,372	1,192,214	1,066,300	1,062,656	452,402
Urban	486,107	405,306	310,852	252,702	291,641	60,672
Per cent	35.3	31.3	26.1	23.7	27.4	13.4
Rural	891,856	891,066	881,362	813,598	771,015	391,730
Per cent	64.7	68.7	73.9	76.3	72.6	86.6
Kansas	1,880,999	1,769,257	1,690,949	1,470,495	1,428,108	996,096
Urban	729,834	617,964	493,790	330,903	272,201	104,956
Per cent	38.8	34.9	29.2	22.5	19.1	10.5
Rural	1,151,165	1,151,293	1,197,159	1,139,592	1,155,907	891,140
Per cent	61.2	65.1	70.8	77.5	80.9	89.5

URBAN AND RURAL

15

TABLE **10.**—URBAN AND RURAL POPULATION, BY DIVISIONS AND STATES: 1880 TO 1930—Continued

DIVISION OR STATE AND AREA	1930	1920	1910	1900	1890	1880
SOUTH ATLANTIC						
Delaware	238,380	223,003	202,322	184,735	168,493	146,608
Urban	123,146	120,707	97,085	85,717	71,067	48,089
Per cent	51.7	54.2	48.0	46.4	42.2	33.4
Rural	115,234	102,236	105,237	99,018	97,426	97,619
Per cent	48.3	45.8	52.0	53.6	57.8	66.6
Maryland	1,631,526	1,449,661	1,295,346	1,188,044	1,042,390	934,943
Urban	974,869	869,422	658,192	591,206	495,702	375,843
Per cent	59.8	60.0	50.8	49.8	47.6	40.2
Rural	656,657	580,239	637,154	596,838	546,688	559,100
Per cent	40.2	40.0	49.2	50.2	52.4	59.8
District of Columbia	486,869	437,571	331,069	278,718	230,392	177,624
Urban	486,869	437,571	331,069	278,718	230,392	177,624
Per cent	100.0	100.0	100.0	100.0	100.0	100.0
Rural	---	---	---	---	---	---
Per cent	---	---	---	---	---	---
Virginia	2,421,851	2,309,187	2,061,612	1,854,184	1,655,980	1,512,565
Urban	785,537	673,984	476,529	340,067	282,721	187,957
Per cent	32.4	29.2	23.1	18.3	17.1	12.4
Rural	1,636,314	1,635,203	1,585,083	1,514,117	1,373,259	1,324,608
Per cent	67.6	70.8	76.9	81.7	82.9	87.6
West Virginia	1,729,205	1,463,701	1,221,119	958,800	762,794	618,457
Urban	491,504	369,007	228,242	125,465	81,365	54,050
Per cent	28.4	25.2	18.7	13.1	10.7	8.7
Rural	1,237,701	1,094,694	992,877	833,335	681,429	564,407
Per cent	71.6	74.8	81.3	86.9	89.3	91.3
North Carolina	3,170,276	2,559,123	2,206,287	1,893,810	1,617,949	1,399,750
Urban	809,847	490,370	318,474	186,790	115,759	55,116
Per cent	25.5	19.2	14.4	9.9	7.2	3.9
Rural	2,360,429	2,068,753	1,887,813	1,707,020	1,502,190	1,344,634
Per cent	74.5	80.8	85.6	90.1	92.8	96.1
South Carolina	1,738,765	1,683,724	1,515,400	1,340,316	1,151,149	995,577
Urban	371,080	293,987	224,832	171,256	116,183	74,539
Per cent	21.3	17.5	14.8	12.8	10.1	7.5
Rural	1,367,685	1,389,737	1,290,568	1,169,060	1,034,966	921,038
Per cent	78.7	82.5	85.2	87.2	89.9	92.5
Georgia	2,908,506	2,895,832	2,609,121	2,216,331	1,837,353	1,542,180
Urban	895,492	727,859	538,650	346,382	257,472	145,090
Per cent	30.8	25.1	20.6	15.6	14.0	9.4
Rural	2,013,014	2,167,973	2,070,471	1,869,949	1,579,881	1,397,090
Per cent	69.2	74.9	79.4	84.4	86.0	90.6
Florida	1,468,211	968,470	752,619	528,542	391,422	269,493
Urban	759,778	355,825	219,080	107,031	77,358	26,947
Per cent	51.7	36.7	29.1	20.3	19.8	10.0
Rural	708,433	612,645	533,539	421,511	314,064	242,546
Per cent	48.3	63.3	70.9	79.7	80.2	90.0
EAST SOUTH CENTRAL						
Kentucky	2,614,589	2,416,630	2,289,905	2,147,174	1,858,635	1,648,690
Urban	799,020	633,543	555,442	467,668	356,713	249,023
Per cent	30.6	26.2	24.3	21.8	19.2	15.2
Rural	1,815,683	1,783,087	1,734,463	1,679,506	1,501,922	1,398,767
Per cent	69.4	73.8	75.7	78.2	80.8	84.8
Tennessee	2,616,556	2,337,885	2,184,789	2,020,616	1,767,518	1,542,359
Urban	896,538	611,226	441,045	326,639	238,394	117,631
Per cent	34.3	26.1	20.2	16.2	13.5	7.6
Rural	1,720,018	1,726,659	1,743,744	1,693,977	1,529,124	1,424,728
Per cent	65.7	73.9	79.8	83.8	86.5	92.4
Alabama	2,646,248	2,348,174	2,138,093	1,828,697	1,513,401	1,262,505
Urban	744,273	509,317	370,431	216,714	152,235	68,518
Per cent	28.1	21.7	17.3	11.9	10.1	5.4
Rural	1,901,975	1,838,857	1,767,662	1,611,983	1,361,166	1,193,987
Per cent	71.9	78.3	82.7	88.1	89.9	94.6
Mississippi	2,009,821	1,790,618	1,797,114	1,551,270	1,289,600	1,131,597
Urban	338,850	240,121	207,311	120,035	69,060	34,581
Per cent	16.9	13.4	11.5	7.7	5.4	3.1
Rural	1,670,971	1,550,497	1,589,803	1,431,235	1,210,034	1,097,016
Per cent	83.1	86.6	88.5	92.3	94.6	96.9
WEST SOUTH CENTRAL						
Arkansas	1,854,482	1,752,204	1,574,449	1,311,564	1,128,211	802,525
Urban	382,878	290,497	202,681	111,733	73,159	32,020
Per cent	20.6	16.6	12.9	8.5	6.5	4.0
Rural	1,471,604	1,461,707	1,371,768	1,199,831	1,055,052	770,505
Per cent	79.4	83.4	87.1	91.5	93.5	96.0

DIVISION OR STATE AND AREA	1930	1920	1910	1900	1890	1880
WEST SOUTH CENTRAL—Contd.						
Louisiana	2,101,593	1,798,509	1,656,388	1,381,625	1,118,588	939,946
Urban	833,532	628,163	496,516	366,288	283,845	239,300
Per cent	39.7	34.9	30.0	26.5	25.4	25.5
Rural	1,268,061	1,170,346	1,159,872	1,015,337	834,743	700,556
Per cent	60.3	65.1	70.0	73.5	74.6	74.5
Oklahoma	2,396,040	2,028,283	1,657,155	¹790,391	¹258,657	---
Urban	821,081	539,480	320,155	58,417	9,484	---
Per cent	34.3	26.6	19.3	7.4	3.7	---
Rural	1,574,959	1,488,803	1,337,000	731,974	249,173	---
Per cent	65.7	73.4	80.7	92.6	96.3	---
Texas	5,824,715	4,663,228	3,896,542	3,048,710	2,235,527	1,591,749
Urban	2,389,348	1,512,689	938,104	520,759	349,511	135,782
Per cent	41.0	32.4	24.1	17.1	15.6	8.5
Rural	3,435,367	3,150,539	2,958,438	2,527,951	1,886,016	1,455,967
Per cent	59.0	67.6	75.9	82.9	84.4	91.5
MOUNTAIN						
Montana	537,606	548,889	376,053	243,329	142,924	39,159
Urban	181,036	172,011	133,420	84,554	38,787	6,987
Per cent	33.7	31.3	35.5	34.7	27.1	17.8
Rural	356,570	376,878	242,633	158,775	104,137	32,172
Per cent	66.3	68.7	64.5	65.3	72.9	82.2
Idaho	445,032	431,866	325,594	161,772	88,548	32,610
Urban	129,507	119,037	69,898	10,003	---	---
Per cent	29.1	27.6	21.5	6.2	---	---
Rural	315,525	312,829	255,696	151,769	88,548	32,610
Per cent	70.9	72.4	78.5	93.8	100.0	100.0
Wyoming	225,565	194,402	145,965	92,531	62,555	20,789
Urban	70,097	57,348	43,221	26,657	21,484	6,152
Per cent	31.1	29.5	29.6	28.8	34.3	29.6
Rural	155,468	137,054	102,744	65,874	41,071	14,637
Per cent	68.9	70.5	70.4	71.2	65.7	70.4
Colorado	1,035,791	939,629	799,024	539,700	413,249	194,327
Urban	519,882	453,259	404,840	260,051	185,905	74,651
Per cent	50.2	48.2	50.7	48.3	45.0	38.4
Rural	515,909	486,370	394,184	279,049	227,344	119,676
Per cent	49.8	51.8	49.3	51.7	55.0	61.6
New Mexico	423,317	360,350	327,301	195,310	160,282	119,565
Urban	106,816	64,960	46,571	27,881	9,970	6,635
Per cent	25.2	18.0	14.2	14.0	6.2	5.5
Rural	316,501	295,390	280,730	167,929	150,312	112,930
Per cent	74.8	82.0	85.8	86.0	93.8	94.5
Arizona	435,573	334,162	204,354	122,931	88,243	40,440
Urban	149,856	117,527	63,260	19,495	8,302	7,007
Per cent	34.4	35.2	31.0	15.9	9.4	17.3
Rural	285,717	216,635	141,094	103,436	79,941	33,433
Per cent	65.6	64.8	69.0	84.1	90.6	82.7
Utah	507,847	449,396	373,351	276,749	210,779	143,963
Urban	266,264	215,584	172,934	105,427	75,155	33,665
Per cent	52.4	48.0	46.3	38.1	35.7	23.4
Rural	241,583	233,812	200,417	171,322	135,624	110,298
Per cent	47.6	52.0	53.7	61.9	64.3	76.6
Nevada	91,058	77,407	81,875	42,335	47,355	62,266
Urban	34,464	15,254	13,367	7,195	16,024	19,353
Per cent	37.8	19.7	16.3	17.0	33.8	31.1
Rural	56,594	62,153	68,508	35,140	31,331	42,913
Per cent	62.2	80.3	83.7	83.0	66.2	68.9
PACIFIC						
Washington	1,563,396	1,356,621	1,141,990	518,103	357,232	75,116
Urban	884,539	748,735	605,530	211,477	127,178	7,121
Per cent	56.6	55.2	53.0	40.8	35.6	9.5
Rural	678,857	607,886	536,460	306,626	230,054	67,995
Per cent	43.4	44.8	47.0	59.2	64.4	90.5
Oregon	953,786	783,389	672,765	413,536	317,704	174,768
Urban	489,746	391,019	307,060	133,180	85,093	25,832
Per cent	51.3	49.9	45.6	32.2	26.8	14.8
Rural	464,040	392,370	365,705	280,356	232,611	148,936
Per cent	48.7	50.1	54.4	67.8	73.2	85.2
California	5,677,251	3,426,861	2,377,549	1,485,053	1,213,398	864,694
Urban	4,160,596	2,331,720	1,469,739	777,000	589,464	370,011
Per cent	73.3	68.0	61.8	52.4	48.0	42.9
Rural	1,516,655	1,095,132	907,810	707,354	623,934	494,683
Per cent	26.7	32.0	38.2	47.6	51.4	57.1

¹ Includes population of Indian Territory.

METROPOLITAN DISTRICTS

In giving the population of cities and incorporated towns and villages the Census must necessarily deal with political units, or with the population contained within the legally established limits of the city or town. In other words, the population of the city as a political unit with a definite corporate name can not properly or legitimately be anything more or less than the population within the corporate limits of the city. Any departure from this principle would lead to endless confusion.

Cities and their suburbs.—It is a familiar fact, however, that the population of the corporate city frequently gives a very inadequate idea of the population massed in and around that city, constituting the "greater" city, as it is sometimes called; and that as regards large cities in few cases do the boundaries of the city limit the urban population which that city represents or of which it is the center. The suburbs are from many standpoints as much a part of the city as the area which is under the municipal government. The suburban residents share in the economic and social activities of the city; many of them have their business or employment in the city; and to a less extent persons residing in the city are employed in the suburbs. If we are to have a correct picture of the massing or concentration of population in extensive urban areas, and of the size and relative importance of the aggregations of urban population in different parts of the country, it is necessary to establish metropolitan districts which will show the magnitude of each of the principal population centers taken as a whole, by including in a single total both the population of the central city itself and that of the suburbs or urbanized areas surrounding it—or, in some cases, the population of two or more cities which are located in close proximity and that of their suburbs.

Method of defining metropolitan districts.—The metropolitan districts for the census of 1930, as here presented, include, in addition to the central city or cities, all adjacent and contiguous civil divisions having a density of 150 inhabitants or more per square mile, and also, as a rule, those civil divisions of less density that are directly contiguous to the central cities, or are entirely or nearly surrounded by minor civil divisions

16

that have the required density. This is essentially the same procedure as that followed in determining the metropolitan districts for cities of over 200,000 inhabitants at the censuses of 1910 and 1920, except that the area which might be included within the metropolitan district was then limited to the territory within 10 miles of the city boundary, while no such limit is now applied.

Ninety-six metropolitan districts have been established, each having an aggregate population of 100,000 or more and containing one or more central cities of 50,000 or more inhabitants. No metropolitan district was established for those cities which did not have in the central city and surrounding area a population of at least 100,000. The metropolitan districts are designated by the name of the central city, or in those cases where the area includes two or more important cities no one of which can properly be regarded as the central or dominant city, by the combined names of such cities. The total population and area and the population density of these 96 metropolitan districts are shown in Table 11. The location of the various districts is indicated on the accompanying map by a series of circles so drawn that their areas are in proportion to the size (population) of the districts which they represent.

While the aggregate area of the metropolitan districts is only 1.2 per cent of the total land area of the United States, the population of these districts is nearly 45 per cent of the total population of the United States. It may be noted that the suburban area outside of the central cities represents almost nine-tenths of the entire area of the metropolitan districts and that the population of the outside area comprises over three-tenths of the entire population of the districts.

Additional statistics for these metropolitan districts, including figures for the individual places making up the "outside area" in each case, and classifications of the population by color and nativity, by sex, and by age, are presented in a 253-page publication entitled "Metropolitan Districts." [3]

---

[3] This publication may be secured from the Superintendent of Documents, Washington, D. C.; price, in paper, 85 cents; in cloth, $1.35.

METROPOLITAN DISTRICTS

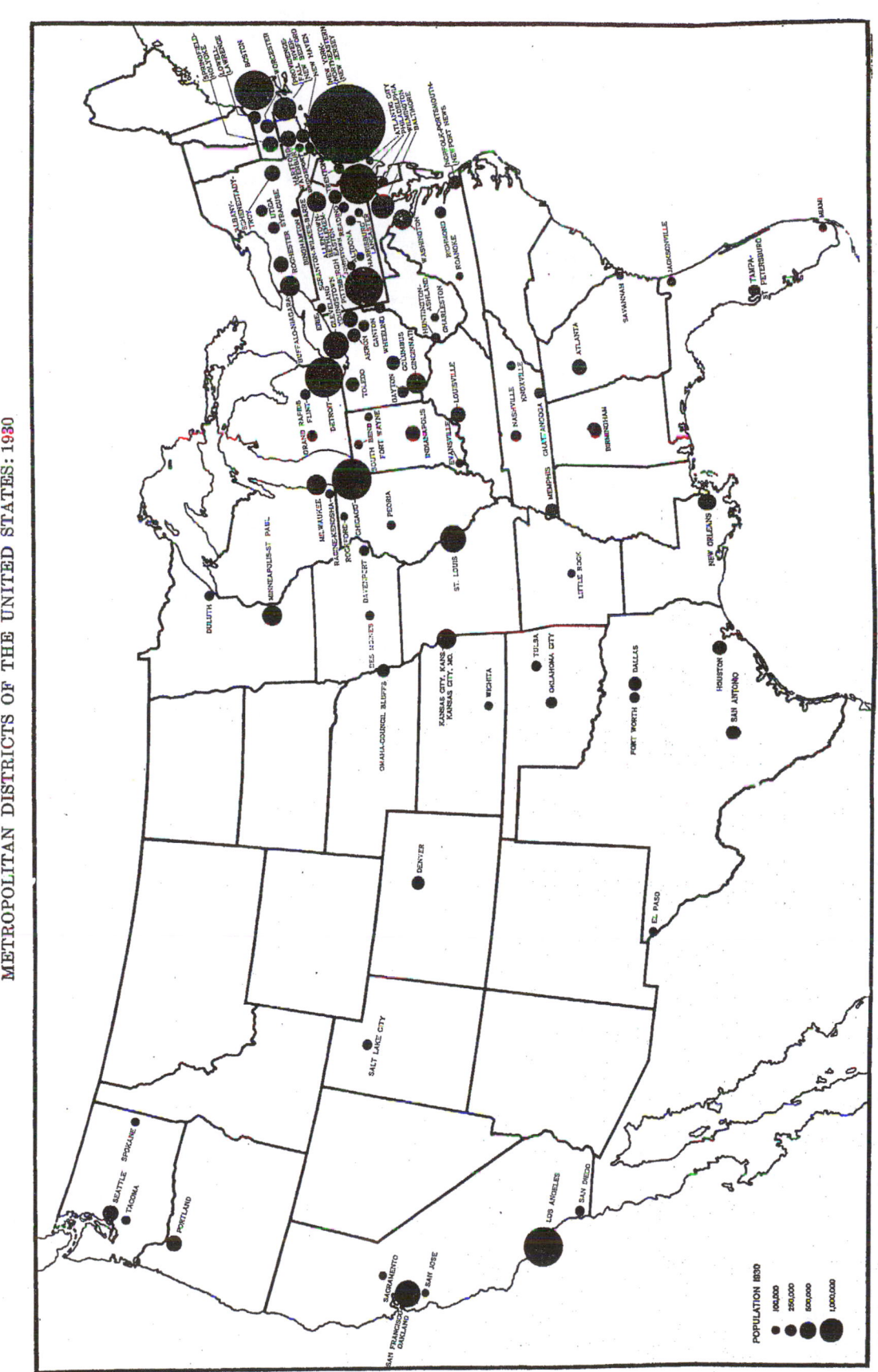

METROPOLITAN DISTRICTS OF THE UNITED STATES: 1930

18

POPULATION

TABLE 11.—POPULATION, LAND AREA, AND DENSITY, FOR METROPOLITAN DISTRICTS: 1930

AREA	Population	Land area in square miles	Population per square mile
Total (96 districts)	54,753,645	36,577.87	1,496.9
In central cities	37,814,010	4,596.05	8,227.6
Outside central cities	16,939,635	31,981.82	529.6
AKRON, OHIO			
Metropolitan District	346,681	242.76	1,428.0
Akron city	255,040	37.60	6,783.0
Outside city	91,641	205.16	446.6
ALBANY-SCHENECTADY-TROY, N.Y.			
Metropolitan District	425,259	472.45	900.1
In central cities	295,867	38.54	7,676.9
Albany city	127,412	18.87	6,752.1
Schenectady city	95,692	10.35	9,245.6
Troy city	72,763	9.32	7,807.2
Outside central cities	129,392	433.91	298.2
ALLENTOWN-BETHLEHEM-EASTON, PA.			
Metropolitan District	322,172	334.53	962.8
In central cities	184,923	32.13	5,755.5
Allentown city	92,503	11.41	8,112.4
Bethlehem city	57,892	17.46	3,315.7
Easton city	34,468	3.26	10,573.0
Outside central cities	137,249	302.40	453.9
ALTOONA, PA.			
Metropolitan District	114,232	133.06	858.5
Altoona city	82,054	8.64	9,497.0
Outside city	32,178	124.42	258.6
ATLANTA, GA.			
Metropolitan District	370,920	221.31	1,676.0
Atlanta city	270,366	34.79	7,771.4
Outside city	100,554	186.52	539.1
ATLANTIC CITY, N.J.			
Metropolitan District	102,024	52.77	1,933.4
Atlantic City	66,108	11.50	5,756.4
Outside city	35,826	41.27	868.1
BALTIMORE, MD.			
Metropolitan District	949,247	558.51	1,699.6
Baltimore city	804,874	78.72	10,224.5
Outside city	144,373	479.79	300.9
BINGHAMTON, N.Y.			
Metropolitan District	130,005	183.19	709.7
Binghamton city	76,662	9.29	8,252.1
Outside city	53,343	173.90	306.7
BIRMINGHAM, ALA.			
Metropolitan District	382,792	307.86	1,243.4
Birmingham city	259,678	50.26	5,166.7
Outside city	123,114	257.60	477.9
BOSTON, MASS.			
Metropolitan District	2,307,897	1,022.60	2,256.9
Boston city	781,188	43.90	17,794.7
Outside city	1,526,709	978.70	1,560.0
BRIDGEPORT, CONN.			
Metropolitan District	203,969	169.33	1,204.6
Bridgeport city	146,716	14.64	10,021.6
Outside city	57,253	154.69	370.1
BUFFALO-NIAGARA, N.Y.			
Metropolitan District	820,573	458.85	1,778.3
In central cities	648,536	51.57	12,575.8
Buffalo city	573,076	38.90	14,732.0
Niagara Falls city	75,460	12.67	5,955.8
Outside central cities	172,037	407.28	422.4
CANTON, OHIO			
Metropolitan District	191,231	238.38	802.2
Canton city	104,906	13.62	7,702.3
Outside city	86,325	224.76	384.1
CHARLESTON, W. VA.			
Metropolitan District	108,160	276.78	390.8
Charleston city	60,408	7.69	7,855.4
Outside city	47,752	269.09	177.5
CHATTANOOGA, TENN.			
Metropolitan District	168,589	489.72	344.3
Chattanooga city	119,798	16.17	7,408.7
Outside city	48,791	473.55	103.0
CHICAGO, ILL.			
Metropolitan District	4,364,755	1,119.29	3,899.6
Chicago city	3,376,438	201.90	16,723.3
Outside city	988,317	917.39	1,077.3
CINCINNATI, OHIO			
Metropolitan District	759,464	519.56	1,461.7
Cincinnati city	451,160	71.41	6,317.9
Outside city	308,304	448.15	687.9
CLEVELAND, OHIO			
Metropolitan District	1,194,989	310.20	3,852.3
Cleveland city	900,429	70.76	12,725.1
Outside city	294,560	239.44	1,230.2
COLUMBUS, OHIO			
Metropolitan District	340,400	219.17	1,553.1
Columbus city	290,564	38.46	7,555.0
Outside city	49,836	180.71	275.8
DALLAS, TEX.			
Metropolitan District	309,658	504.42	613.9
Dallas city	260,475	41.78	6,234.4
Outside city	49,183	462.64	106.3
DAVENPORT, IOWA			
Metropolitan District	154,491	126.55	1,220.8
Davenport city	60,751	18.07	3,362.0
Outside city	93,740	108.48	864.1
DAYTON, OHIO			
Metropolitan District	251,928	180.12	1,398.7
Dayton city	200,982	18.13	11,085.6
Outside city	50,946	161.99	314.5
DENVER, COLO.			
Metropolitan District	330,761	305.09	1,084.1
Denver city	287,861	57.95	4,967.4
Outside city	42,900	247.14	173.6
DES MOINES, IOWA			
Metropolitan District	160,963	203.07	792.6
Des Moines city	142,559	54.00	2,640.0
Outside city	18,404	149.07	123.5
DETROIT, MICH.			
Metropolitan District	2,104,764	746.52	2,819.4
Detroit city	1,568,662	137.90	11,375.4
Outside city	536,102	608.62	880.8
DULUTH, MINN.			
Metropolitan District	155,390	443.65	350.3
Duluth city	101,463	62.34	1,627.6
Outside city	53,927	381.31	141.4
EL PASO, TEX.			
Metropolitan District	118,481	290.82	407.3
El Paso city	102,421	13.50	7,586.7
Outside city	16,040	277.32	57.8
ERIE, PA.			
Metropolitan District	129,817	89.00	1,458.6
Erie city	115,967	19.25	6,024.3
Outside city	13,850	69.75	198.6
EVANSVILLE, IND.			
Metropolitan District	123,130	148.60	828.6
Evansville city	102,249	8.71	11,739.5
Outside city	20,881	139.89	149.3
FLINT, MICH.			
Metropolitan District	179,939	141.44	1,272.2
Flint city	156,492	29.67	5,274.4
Outside city	23,447	111.77	209.8
FORT WAYNE, IND.			
Metropolitan District	126,558	138.58	913.2
Fort Wayne city	114,946	17.19	6,686.8
Outside city	11,612	121.39	95.7
FORT WORTH, TEX.			
Metropolitan District	174,575	170.60	1,023.3
Fort Worth city	163,447	46.40	3,522.6
Outside city	11,128	124.20	89.6
GRAND RAPIDS, MICH.			
Metropolitan District	207,154	136.35	1,519.3
Grand Rapids city	168,592	23.02	7,323.7
Outside city	38,562	113.33	340.3
HARRISBURG, PA.			
Metropolitan District	161,672	129.52	1,248.2
Harrisburg city	80,339	6.19	12,978.8
Outside city	81,333	123.33	659.5
HARTFORD, CONN.			
Metropolitan District	471,185	565.05	833.9
Hartford city	164,072	15.88	10,332.0
Outside city	307,113	549.17	559.2
HOUSTON, TEX.			
Metropolitan District	339,216	799.20	424.4
Houston city	292,352	71.79	4,072.3
Outside city	46,864	727.41	64.4
HUNTINGTON, W. VA.-ASHLAND, KY.			
Metropolitan District	163,367	264.27	618.2
In central cities	104,646	23.77	4,402.4
Huntington city	75,572	16.27	4,644.9
Ashland city	29,074	7.50	3,876.5
Outside central cities	58,721	240.50	244.1
INDIANAPOLIS, IND.			
Metropolitan District	417,685	311.75	1,339.8
Indianapolis city	364,161	54.15	6,725.0
Outside city	53,524	257.60	207.8
JACKSONVILLE, FLA.			
Metropolitan District	148,713	218.06	682.0
Jacksonville city	129,549	26.38	4,910.9
Outside city	19,164	191.68	100.0
JOHNSTOWN, PA.			
Metropolitan District	147,611	179.90	820.5
Johnstown city	66,993	5.45	12,292.3
Outside city	80,618	174.45	462.1
KANSAS CITY, KANS.-KANSAS CITY, MO.			
Metropolitan District	608,186	454.51	1,338.1
In Kansas	143,606	119.27	1,204.0
Kansas City	121,857	20.46	5,955.9
Outside city	21,749	98.81	220.1
In Missouri	464,580	335.24	1,385.8
Kansas City	399,746	58.55	6,827.4
Outside city	64,834	276.69	234.3
KNOXVILLE, TENN.			
Metropolitan District	135,714	192.63	704.5
Knoxville city	105,802	26.40	4,007.7
Outside city	29,912	166.23	179.9
LANCASTER, PA.			
Metropolitan District	123,156	231.70	531.5
Lancaster city	59,949	3.27	18,333.0
Outside city	63,207	228.43	276.7
LITTLE ROCK, ARK.			
Metropolitan District	113,137	108.99	1,038.0
Little Rock city	81,679	17.75	4,601.6
Outside city	31,458	91.24	344.8
LOS ANGELES, CALIF.			
Metropolitan District	2,318,526	1,474.34	1,572.6
Los Angeles city	1,238,048	440.32	2,811.7
Outside city	1,080,478	1,034.02	1,044.9
LOUISVILLE, KY.			
Metropolitan District	404,396	463.92	871.7
Louisville city	307,745	35.98	8,553.2
Outside city	96,651	427.94	225.9
LOWELL-LAWRENCE, MASS.			
Metropolitan District	332,028	292.18	1,136.4
In central cities	185,302	20.13	9,205.3
Lowell city	100,234	13.38	7,491.3
Lawrence city	85,068	6.75	12,602.7
Outside central cities	146,726	272.05	539.3
MEMPHIS, TENN.			
Metropolitan District	276,126	221.16	1,248.5
Memphis city	253,143	45.67	5,542.9
Outside city	22,983	175.49	131.0
MIAMI, FLA.			
Metropolitan District	132,189	111.56	1,184.9
Miami city	110,637	43.00	2,573.0
Outside city	21,552	68.56	314.4

METROPOLITAN DISTRICTS   19

TABLE 11.—POPULATION, LAND AREA, AND DENSITY, FOR METROPOLITAN DISTRICTS: 1930—Continued

AREA	Population	Land area in square miles	Population per square mile
MILWAUKEE, WIS.			
Metropolitan District	743,414	241.70	3,075.8
Milwaukee city	578,249	41.14	14,055.6
Outside city	165,165	200.56	823.5
MINNEAPOLIS-ST. PAUL, MINN.			
Metropolitan District	832,258	525.37	1,584.1
In central cities	735,962	107.55	6,843.0
Minneapolis city	464,356	55.38	8,384.9
St. Paul city	271,606	52.17	5,200.2
Outside central cities	96,296	417.82	230.5
NASHVILLE, TENN.			
Metropolitan District	209,422	323.36	647.6
Nashville city	153,866	25.97	5,924.8
Outside city	55,556	297.39	186.8
NEW HAVEN, CONN.			
Metropolitan District	293,724	249.07	1,179.3
New Haven city	162,655	17.91	9,081.8
Outside city	131,069	231.16	567.0
NEW ORLEANS, LA.			
Metropolitan District	494,877	287.02	1,724.2
New Orleans city	458,762	196.00	2,340.6
Outside city	36,115	91.02	396.8
NEW YORK-NORTHEASTERN NEW JERSEY			
Metropolitan District	10,901,424	2,514.11	4,336.1
New York Division	7,986,368	1,354.27	5,897.2
New York City	6,930,446	299.00	23,178.7
Outside city	1,055,922	1,055.27	1,000.6
New Jersey Division	2,915,056	1,159.84	2,513.3
In central cities	1,012,154	54.36	18,619.5
Elizabeth city	114,589	9.73	11,776.9
Jersey City	316,715	13.00	24,362.7
Newark city	442,337	23.57	18,767.0
Paterson city	138,513	8.06	17,185.2
Outside central cities	1,902,902	1,105.48	1,721.3
NORFOLK-PORTSMOUTH-NEWPORT NEWS, VA.			
Metropolitan District	273,233	468.59	583.1
In central cities	209,831	37.00	5,671.1
Norfolk city	129,710	28.00	4,632.5
Portsmouth city	45,704	5.00	9,140.1
Newport News city	34,417	4.00	8,604.3
Outside central cities	63,402	431.59	146.9
OKLAHOMA CITY, OKLA.			
Metropolitan District	202,163	181.78	1,112.1
Oklahoma City	185,389	30.35	6,108.4
Outside city	16,774	151.43	110.8
OMAHA, NEBR.-COUNCIL BLUFFS, IOWA			
Metropolitan District	273,851	204.98	1,336.0
In central cities	256,054	52.80	4,849.5
Omaha city	214,006	39.10	5,473.3
Council Bluffs city	42,048	13.70	3,069.2
Outside central cities	17,797	152.18	116.9
PEORIA, ILL.			
Metropolitan District	144,732	105.54	1,371.3
Peoria city	104,969	12.28	8,548.0
Outside city	39,763	93.26	426.4
PHILADELPHIA, PA.			
Metropolitan District	2,847,148	993.89	2,864.7
Philadelphia city	1,950,961	128.00	15,241.9
Outside city	896,187	865.89	1,035.0
PITTSBURGH, PA.			
Metropolitan District	1,953,668	1,626.05	1,201.5
Pittsburgh city	669,817	51.30	13,050.0
Outside city	1,283,851	1,574.75	815.3
PORTLAND, OREG.			
Metropolitan District	378,728	277.46	1,365.0
Portland city	301,815	63.45	4,756.7
Outside city	76,913	214.01	359.4
PROVIDENCE, R.I.-FALL RIVER-NEW BEDFORD, MASS.			
Metropolitan District	963,686	817.83	1,178.3
In central cities	480,852	69.72	6,896.9
Providence city	252,981	17.83	14,188.5
Fall River city	115,274	32.90	3,503.8
New Bedford city	112,597	18.99	5,929.3
Outside central cities	482,834	748.11	645.4

AREA	Population	Land area in square miles	Population per square mile
RACINE-KENOSHA, WIS.			
Metropolitan District	133,463	185.20	720.6
In central cities	117,804	15.99	7,367.4
Racine city	67,542	8.61	7,844.6
Kenosha city	50,262	7.38	6,810.6
Outside central cities	15,659	169.21	92.5
READING, PA.			
Metropolitan District	170,486	157.07	1,085.4
Reading city	111,171	9.52	11,677.6
Outside city	59,315	147.55	402.0
RICHMOND, VA.			
Metropolitan District	220,518	334.00	660.0
Richmond city	182,920	24.00	7,622.0
Outside city	37,584	310.60	121.0
ROANOKE, VA.			
Metropolitan District	103,120	231.00	446.4
Roanoke city	69,206	10.00	6,920.6
Outside city	33,014	221.00	153.5
ROCHESTER, N.Y.			
Metropolitan District	398,591	304.24	1,310.1
Rochester city	328,132	34.23	9,586.1
Outside city	70,459	270.01	260.9
ROCKFORD, ILL.			
Metropolitan District	103,204	138.77	743.7
Rockford city	85,864	11.74	7,313.8
Outside city	17,340	127.03	136.5
SACRAMENTO, CALIF.			
Metropolitan District	126,995	462.02	274.9
Sacramento city	93,750	13.71	6,838.1
Outside city	33,245	448.31	74.2
ST. LOUIS, MO.			
Metropolitan District	1,293,516	821.54	1,574.5
In Missouri	1,039,823	441.37	2,355.9
St. Louis city	821,960	61.00	13,474.8
Outside city	217,863	380.37	572.8
In Illinois	253,693	380.17	667.3
East St. Louis city	74,347	13.31	5,585.8
Outside city	179,346	366.86	488.9
SALT LAKE CITY, UTAH			
Metropolitan District	184,451	450.85	409.1
Salt Lake City	140,267	52.04	2,695.4
Outside city	44,184	398.81	110.8
SAN ANTONIO, TEX.			
Metropolitan District	279,271	467.34	597.6
San Antonio city	231,542	35.72	6,482.1
Outside city	47,729	431.62	110.6
SAN DIEGO, CALIF.			
Metropolitan District	181,020	332.37	544.6
San Diego city	147,995	93.64	1,580.5
Outside city	33,025	238.73	138.3
SAN FRANCISCO-OAKLAND, CALIF.			
Metropolitan District	1,290,094	825.60	1,562.6
In central cities	918,457	95.16	9,651.7
San Francisco city	634,394	42.00	15,104.6
Oakland city	284,063	53.16	5,343.5
Outside central cities	371,637	730.44	508.8
SAN JOSE, CALIF.			
Metropolitan District	103,428	210.39	491.6
San Jose city	57,651	7.75	7,438.8
Outside city	45,777	202.64	225.9
SAVANNAH, GA.			
Metropolitan District	105,431	370.01	284.9
Savannah city	85,024	7.60	11,187.4
Outside city	20,407	362.41	56.3
SCRANTON-WILKES-BARRE, PA.			
Metropolitan District	653,312	394.73	1,652.6
In central cities	230,059	26.27	8,757.5
Scranton city	143,433	19.32	7,424.1
Wilkes-Barre city	86,626	6.95	12,464.2
Outside central cities	422,253	368.46	1,146.0
SEATTLE, WASH.			
Metropolitan District	420,663	209.90	2,004.1
Seattle city	365,583	68.50	5,337.0
Outside city	55,080	141.40	389.5

AREA	Population	Land area in square miles	Population per square mile
SOUTH BEND, IND.			
Metropolitan District	146,569	153.60	954.2
South Bend city	104,193	16.86	6,179.9
Outside city	42,376	136.74	309.9
SPOKANE, WASH.			
Metropolitan District	128,798	270.25	476.6
Spokane city	115,514	40.37	2,861.4
Outside city	13,284	229.88	57.8
SPRINGFIELD-HOLYOKE, MASS.			
Metropolitan District	398,991	518.69	769.2
In central cities	206,437	52.86	3,905.4
Springfield city	149,900	31.70	4,728.7
Holyoke city	56,537	21.16	2,671.9
Outside central cities	192,554	465.83	413.4
SYRACUSE, N.Y.			
Metropolitan District	245,015	139.73	1,753.5
Syracuse city	209,326	25.34	8,260.7
Outside city	35,689	114.39	312.0
TACOMA, WASH.			
Metropolitan District	146,771	190.67	769.8
Tacoma city	106,817	46.35	2,304.6
Outside city	39,954	144.32	276.8
TAMPA-ST. PETERSBURG, FLA.			
Metropolitan District	169,010	266.18	634.9
In central cities	141,586	71.58	1,978.0
Tampa city	101,161	19.00	5,324.3
St. Petersburg city	40,425	52.58	768.8
Outside central cities	27,424	194.60	140.9
TOLEDO, OHIO			
Metropolitan District	346,530	204.36	1,695.7
Toledo city	290,718	32.07	8,817.7
Outside city	55,812	171.30	325.6
TRENTON, N.J.			
Metropolitan District	190,219	172.97	1,099.7
Trenton city	123,356	7.23	17,061.7
Outside city	66,863	165.74	403.4
TULSA, OKLA.			
Metropolitan District	183,207	391.40	468.1
Tulsa city	141,258	21.60	6,539.7
Outside city	41,949	369.80	113.4
UTICA, N.Y.			
Metropolitan District	190,918	358.15	533.1
Utica city	101,740	21.20	4,799.1
Outside city	89,178	336.95	264.7
WASHINGTON, D.C.			
Metropolitan District	621,059	484.99	1,280.6
Washington city	486,869	62.00	7,852.7
Outside city	134,190	422.99	317.2
WATERBURY, CONN.			
Metropolitan District	140,575	206.66	680.2
Waterbury city	99,902	28.10	3,555.2
Outside city	40,673	178.56	227.8
WHEELING, W. VA.			
Metropolitan District	190,823	399.31	477.4
Wheeling city	61,659	9.00	6,851.0
Outside city	128,964	390.31	330.4
WICHITA, KANS.			
Metropolitan District	119,174	142.97	833.6
Wichita city	111,110	20.71	5,365.0
Outside city	8,064	122.26	66.0
WILMINGTON, DEL.			
Metropolitan District	163,592	228.64	715.5
Wilmington city	106,597	7.19	14,825.7
Outside city	56,995	221.45	257.4
WORCESTER, MASS.			
Metropolitan District	305,293	399.56	764.1
Worcester city	195,311	37.20	5,250.3
Outside city	109,982	362.36	303.5
YOUNGSTOWN, OHIO			
Metropolitan District	364,560	363.47	1,003.0
Youngstown city	170,002	33.84	5,023.7
Outside city	194,558	329.63	590.2

CENTER OF POPULATION

The term "center of population" as used by the Census Bureau has a somewhat technical significance different from that frequently attached to it in popular usage. The center is often understood to be the point of intersection of a north and south line which divides the population into two equal parts, with an east and west line which likewise divides it into two equal parts. The point of intersection of two such lines is more accurately designated "median point," and this term has been used in Census reports to distinguish it from the point technically defined as the center of population.

The center of population may be said to represent the center of gravity of the population. If the surface of the United States be considered as a rigid level plane without weight and the population distributed thereon, all individuals being assumed to have equal weight, the point on which this plane would balance would be the center of population. This pivotal point would be the center of gravity of the hypothetical plane; and its location would be affected not only by the numbers of persons on the different parts of the plane, but also by the distance of each individual from the "center." [4]

The computations for the center of population are made for continental United States, omitting Alaska and the other outlying territories and possessions.

On the basis of returns for the Fifteenth Census, taken as of April 1, 1930, the center of population was found to be in latitude 39° 3' 45" north and longitude 87° 8' 6" west. This point is in southwestern Indiana, 2.9 miles northeast of Linton, Stockton township, Greene County, Ind., as shown on the first map on the opposite page.

During the decade from 1920 to 1930 the center of population moved west 24' 51", or approximately 22.3 miles. The advance towards the west is to a large extent due to the increase in the population of the Pacific Coast States, their distance from the center giving any increase of population in those States much greater weight than an equal increase in the populous States of the East which are nearer the center.

Location of center at earlier censuses.—The location of the center of population at each Federal census from 1790 to 1930 is shown in Table 12, and also represented on the second map.

TABLE 12.—POSITION OF THE CENTER OF POPULATION: 1790 TO 1930

CENSUS YEAR	North latitude	West longitude	Approximate location by important towns	MOVEMENT IN MILES DURING PRECEDING DECADE			
				From point to point in direct line	Westward	Northward	Southward
	° ' "	° ' "					
1790	39 16 30	76 11 12	23 miles east of Baltimore, Md.				
1800	39 16 6	76 56 30	18 miles west of Baltimore, Md.	40.6	40.6		0.5
1810	39 11 30	77 37 12	40 miles northwest by west of Washington, D. C. (in Virginia)	36.9	36.5		5.3
1820	39 5 42	78 33 0	16 miles east of Moorefield, W. Va.[1]	50.5	50.1		6.7
1830	38 57 54	79 16 54	19 miles west-southwest of Moorefield, W. Va.[1]	40.4	39.4		9.0
1840	39 2 0	80 18 0	16 miles south of Clarksburg, W. Va.[1]	55.0	54.8	4.7	
1850	38 59 0	81 19 0	23 miles southeast of Parkersburg, W. Va.[1]	54.8	54.7		3.5
1860	39 0 24	82 48 48	20 miles south by east of Chillicothe, Ohio.	80.6	80.6	1.6	
1870	39 12 0	83 35 42	48 miles east by north of Cincinnati, Ohio.	44.1	42.1	13.3	
1880	39 4 8	84 39 40	8 miles west by south of Cincinnati, Ohio (in Kentucky).	58.1	57.4		9.1
1890	39 11 56	85 32 53	20 miles east of Columbus, Ind.	48.6	47.7	9.0	
1900	39 9 36	85 48 54	6 miles southeast of Columbus, Ind.	14.6	14.4		2.8
1910	39 10 12	86 32 20	In the city of Bloomington, Ind.	39.0	38.9	0.7	
1920	39 10 21	86 43 15	1.9 miles west of Whitehall, Clay Township, Owen County, Ind.; 8.3 miles south-southeast of Spencer, Washington Township, Owen County, Ind.	9.8	9.8	0.2	
1930	39 3 45	87 8 6	2.9 miles northeast of Linton, Stockton Township, Greene County, Ind.	23.6	22.3		7.6

[1] West Virginia was set off from Virginia Dec. 31, 1862; admitted as a State June 19, 1863.

In the period of 140 years, from 1790 to 1930, the center of population advanced westward 591 miles from its position in 1790, 23 miles east of Baltimore. The progress westward from census to census has been uninterrupted, being greatest—80.6 miles—during the decade 1850–1860, and least—9.8 miles—during the decade 1910–1920. The net advance southward during this period of 140 years was only 15.1 miles.

[4] In making the computations for the location of the center of population it is necessary to assume that the center is at a certain point. Through this point a parallel and a meridian are drawn, crossing the entire country. In making the computations for 1930, the same point was selected as in 1920; this intersection was assumed to be where the parallel of 39° north latitude intersects the meridian of 86° west longitude, which lines were taken as the axes of moments.

The product of the population of a given area by its distance from the assumed parallel is called a north or south moment, and the product of the population of the area by its distance from the assumed meridian is called an east or west moment. In calculating north and south moments the distances are measured in minutes of arc; in calculating east and west moments it is necessary to use miles, on account of the unequal length of the degrees and minutes in different latitudes. The population of the country is grouped by square degrees—that is, by areas included between consecutive parallels and meridians—as they are convenient units with which to work. The population of the principal cities is then deducted from that of the respective square degrees in which they lie and treated separately. The center of population of each square degree is assumed to be at its geographical center except where such an assumption is manifestly incorrect; in these cases the position of the center of population of the square degree is estimated as nearly as possible. The population of each square degree north and south of the assumed parallel is multiplied by the distance of its center from that parallel; a similar calculation is made for the principal cities; and the sum of the north moments and the sum of the south moments are ascertained. The difference between these two sums, divided by the total population of the country, gives a correction to the latitude. In a similar manner the sums of the east and of the west moments are ascertained and from them the correction in longitude is made.

POPULATION

CENTER OF POPULATION 1930 AND 1920

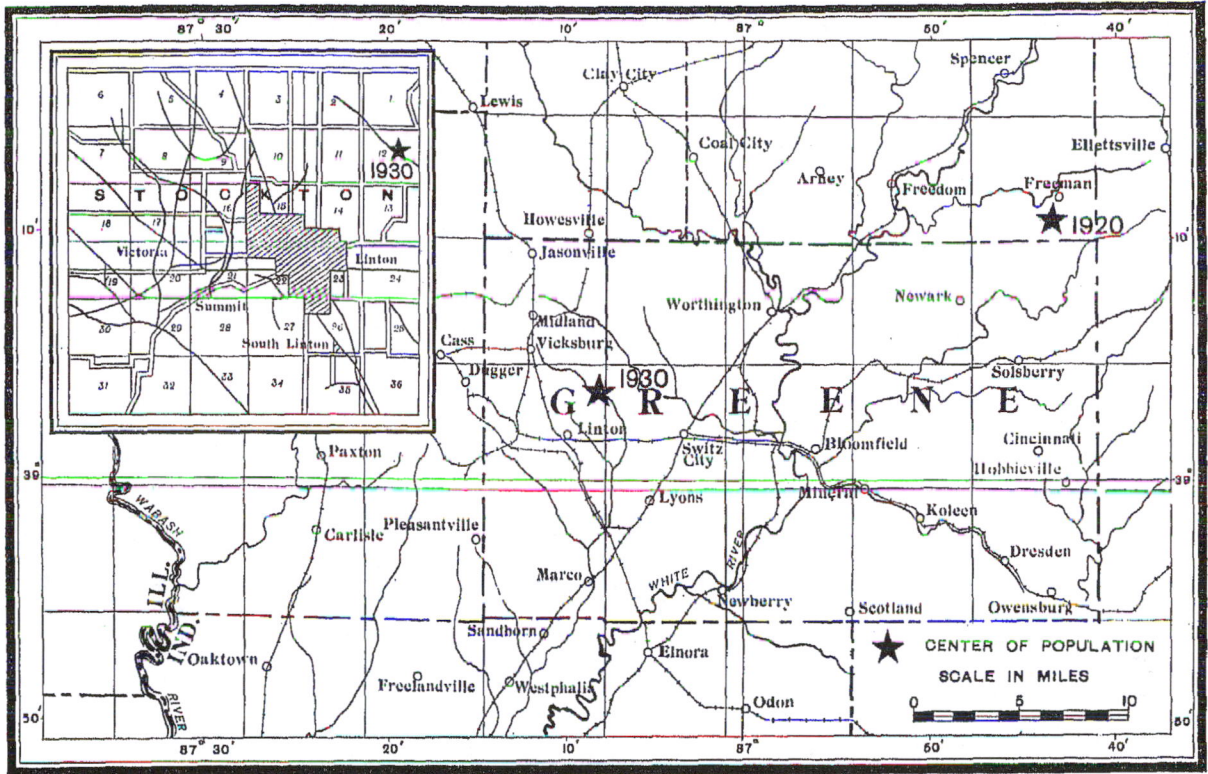

CENTERS OF POPULATION 1790-1930

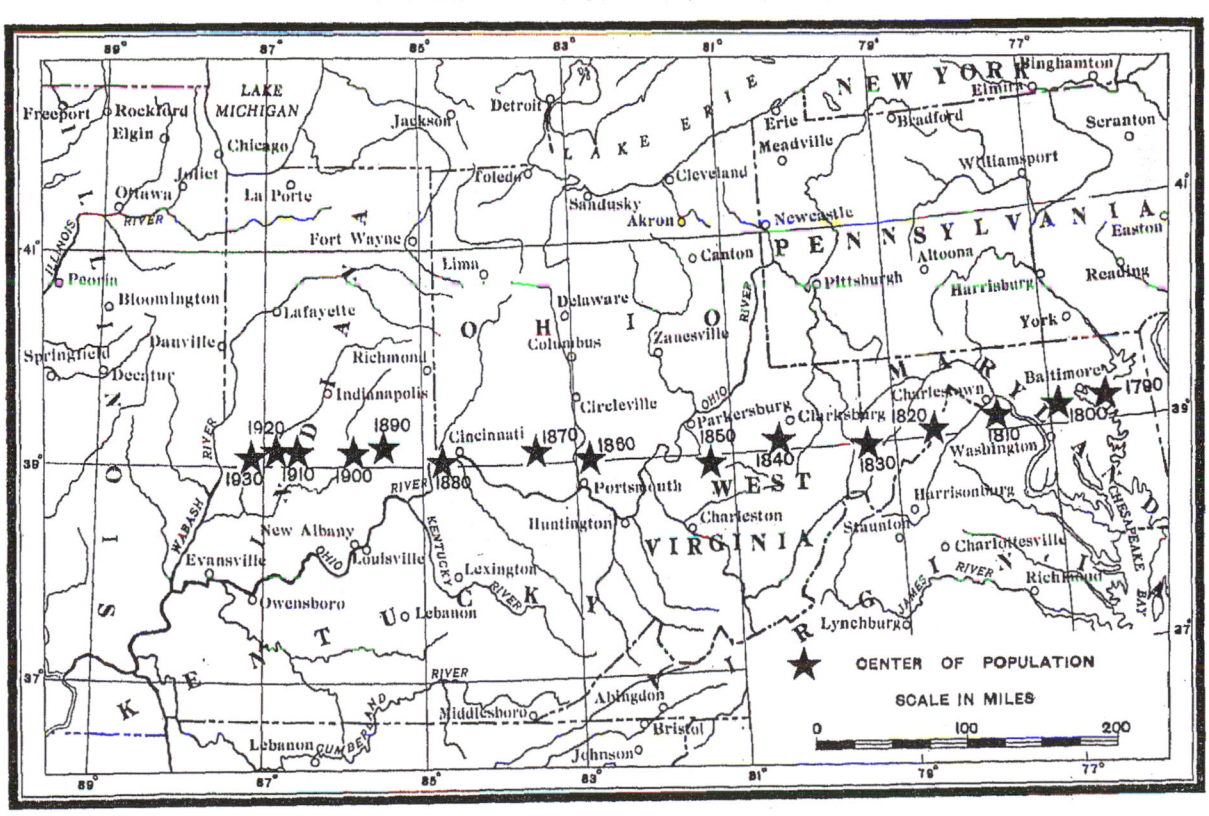

CHAPTER 2

———

COLOR OR RACE, NATIVITY
AND PARENTAGE

CHAPTER 2.—COLOR OR RACE, NATIVITY, AND PARENTAGE

INTRODUCTION

The classification of the population of the United States by color or race distinguishes in many cases only three main groups, namely, white, Negro, and "Other races." The "Other race" group includes Mexican, Indian, Chinese, Japanese, Filipino, Hindu, Korean, Hawaiian, Malay, Siamese, and Samoan, the last three represented by less than 100 persons each.

In classifying the population by nativity, all persons born in continental United States or in any of the outlying territories or possessions are regarded as native and all other persons as foreign born. In the classification by parentage there are three primary groups, as follows: (1) Native parentage, that is, having both parents born in the United States or in the outlying possessions; (2) Foreign parentage, that is, having both parents foreign born; (3) Mixed parentage, that is, having one parent native and the other foreign born. In many of the tables persons of foreign parentage and those of mixed parentage are combined into one group designated "Foreign or mixed parentage." Conversely, in a few tables the mixed parentage group is separated into two parts, designated (a) Father foreign, and (b) Mother foreign.

The distinction as to parentage is generally confined to the native white population, so that in most of the tables there are five principal classes: (1) Native white of native parentage; (2) Native white of foreign or mixed parentage; (3) Foreign-born white; (4) Negro; (5) Other races. The number of classes is expanded to six in many cases by the separate presentation of native white of foreign parentage and native white of mixed parentage. The group designated "Other races," being relatively unimportant in most areas, is frequently omitted from the tables altogether. Figures are presented, however, for this group and for its constituent races—Mexicans, Indians, Chinese, Japanese, etc.—in separate tables containing such details in each case as the number of persons in the group seems to justify.

Statistics of color or race, nativity, and parentage are presented in this chapter for continental United States, by States, and for cities of 25,000 or more. Less detailed statistics are presented for counties and townships, and for incorporated places of 1,000 or more, in Volume III of the Fifteenth Census Reports on Population; and statistics for the outlying territories and possessions enumerated at the Fifteenth Census are presented in a volume entitled "Outlying Territories and Possessions."

The 1930 figures for the various color or race groups are shown by nativity in Table 1.

TABLE 1.—POPULATION OF THE UNITED STATES BY COLOR OR RACE AND NATIVITY: 1930

[Per cent not shown where less than 0.1 or where base is less than 100]

COLOR OR RACE	Total population	NATIVE		FOREIGN BORN		PER CENT DISTRIBUTION		
		Number	Per cent of total	Number	Per cent of total	Total	Native	Foreign born
Total	122,775,046	108,570,897	88.4	14,204,149	11.6	100.0	100.0	100.0
White	108,864,207	95,497,800	87.7	13,366,407	12.3	88.7	88.0	94.1
Negro	11,891,143	11,792,523	99.2	98,620	0.8	9.7	10.9	0.7
Mexican	1,422,533	805,535	56.6	616,998	43.4	1.2	0.7	4.3
Indian	332,397	328,845	98.9	3,552	1.1	0.3	0.3	
Chinese	74,954	30,868	41.2	44,086	58.5	0.1		0.3
Japanese	138,834	68,357	49.2	70,477	50.8	0.1	0.1	0.5
Filipino	45,208	45,026	99.6	182	0.4			
Hindu	3,130	412	13.2	2,718	86.8			
Korean	1,860	816	43.9	1,044	56.1			
Hawaiian	660	654	99.1	6	0.9			
Malay	96	48		48				
Siamese	18	7		11				
Samoan	6	6						

Correction for 1870.—The corrected figures for 1870 in Table 4 and for the decades 1860 to 1870 and 1870 to 1880 in Table 5 are based on estimates of the true population in 1870, the census taken in that year having been generally deficient in the Southern States. The number of omissions in these States in 1870 is estimated to have been 1,260,000, comprising 748,000 whites and 512,000 Negroes. (See Reports of the Eleventh Census, Population, Pt. I, pp. xi, xii, and xvi.)

White population.—The proportion of whites in the total population, which was a little over 80 per cent in 1790, has increased at each succeeding census, except for a slight decline in 1810 as compared with 1800 and a decrease from 89.0 per cent (for the white population excluding Mexicans) in 1920 to 88.7 per cent in 1930 (see Table 4). This last decline is the result of a very considerable influx of Mexicans between 1920 and 1930. If Mexicans had been classed as white in 1930, the proportion would have been slightly higher than in 1920.

Accepting the estimate for 1870 as approximately correct, each decade since 1790, except the decade 1910 to 1920, has shown for the white population a numerical increase greater than for the decade immediately preceding; and the percentage of increase for the white population has exceeded that for the Negro population in every decade since 1810 (see Table 5).

In considering the growth of the white population it must be kept in mind that in the case of only one of the four nativity and parentage classes is the increase

25

335

due in any measure to the excess of births over deaths within the class itself. The number of natives of native parentage is increased in part by the children born to natives of native parentage and in part by the children of the natives of foreign or mixed parentage; the number of natives of mixed parentage is increased by the children of intermarriages between the native and the foreign born; the number of natives of foreign parentage, by the children born to immigrants after their arrival in this country; and the number of foreign born, by immigration.

Of the four classes of whites, therefore, the natives of native parentage constitute the only one whose increase is affected in any degree by its own reproductivity, since the children born in this country to each of the other classes belong to a class different from that to which their parents belong (except that in some cases one parent of a native of mixed parentage is also a native of mixed parentage). While the increase in the number of native whites of native parentage must, so long as there is any element of foreign birth or parentage in the population, necessarily exceed the natural increase by excess of births over deaths within this class, the numerical increase of any of the other classes may or may not exceed the natural increase which would result if the children were included in the same class with the parents. The numerical increases within the several nativity and parentage classes, therefore, bear no specific relationship to the natural increase.

The 1930 figures for the white population classified by nativity and parentage are summarized in Table 2. For comparative figures for earlier censuses, see Table 6.

TABLE 2.—WHITE POPULATION OF THE UNITED STATES BY NATIVITY AND PARENTAGE: 1930

NATIVITY AND PARENTAGE	Number	Per cent of total population	Per cent of white population	Per cent of native white population
Total white	108,864,207	88.7	100.0	
Native	95,497,800	77.8	87.7	100.0
Native parentage	70,136,614	57.1	64.4	73.4
Foreign or mixed parentage	25,361,186	20.7	23.3	26.6
Foreign parentage	16,999,221	13.8	15.6	17.8
Mixed parentage	8,361,965	6.8	7.7	8.8
Father foreign	5,459,530	4.4	5.0	5.7
Mother foreign	2,902,435	2.4	2.7	3.0
Foreign born	13,366,407	10.9	12.3	

Negro population.—The distinction between white and colored is the only racial classification which has been carried through all the 15 censuses. There is some doubt as to whether the small number of taxed Indians were counted with the white or with the colored population prior to 1860.

With adjustment for the undercount of Negroes in 1870, the proportion of Negroes in the total population has decreased at each census since 1810. The rate of increase in the Negro population has also shown a downward trend since 1810, but the rates, even with adjustment for 1870, show fluctuations which are difficult to explain. For example, the rate of increase dropped from 22.0 per cent (adjusted) in

the decade 1870 to 1880 to 13.5 per cent between 1880 and 1890, and then rose to 18.0 per cent in the following decade.

In the face of this fluctuation in the decennial rate of increase, the Census Bureau has admitted the possibility of an undercount of Negroes in 1890. A similar fluctuation in the rate of increase was that from 11.2 between 1900 and 1910 to 6.5 in the decade 1910 to 1920, followed by a rate of 13.6 between 1920 and 1930. This fluctuation is even greater than that of 30 years earlier, and suggests the probability of an undercount of Negroes in 1920, as well as in 1890. It would be a mistake, however, to assume that the entire fluctuation in the latter period was due to an undercount. The decade 1910 to 1920 included the years of the World War, with its consequent disorganization of the Negro population through military service and labor migrations, and also the influenza epidemic of 1918 and 1919. The disorganization of the War and migration period would tend to decrease births, and the epidemic probably increased the number of deaths of Negroes within the decade by at least 100,000. The number of deaths in the decade 1910 to 1919 of Negroes living at the census of 1910, on the assumption that the death rate of Negroes in the registration area was typical of that for Negroes in the United States as a whole, was 1,754,956, as compared with 1,522,665 Negro deaths similarly calculated for the decade 1920 to 1929 in the population living at the census of 1920. A comparison by five-year age periods of the Negro population in 1910, 1920, and 1930, arranging these periods by groups of birth years and allowing for calculated deaths in each birth-year group, would indicate a shortage of about 150,000 in the Negro enumeration of 1920, as compared with the enumerations of 1910 and 1930. This shortage in the enumeration is in addition to the usual shortage of perhaps 100,000 in the enumeration of Negro children under 5 years old. This latter shortage can be shown for every census by comparing the number of children under 5 with the number 10 to 14 in the following census, taking into account deaths within the 10-year period.

The following statement shows the rates of increase in the Negro population for the last six decades, first, as reported, and second, with the adjustments suggested above:

DECADE	As reported	Adjusted
1920–1930	13.6	12.0
1910–1920	6.5	8.0
1900–1910	11.2	11.2
1890–1900	18.0	13.8
1880–1890	13.5	17.6
1870–1880	34.9	22.0

The rapid downward trend in the decennial rate of increase in the Negro population from 1870 to 1920 can only be accounted for by the assumption of a declining birth rate, parallel with the decline which has been recorded for the white race. The Negro

COLOR OR RACE, NATIVITY, AND PARENTAGE

death rate apparently remained stationary or declined less rapidly than did the birth rate. In the decade 1920 to 1930, both birth and death registration figures for Negroes are for the first time sufficiently complete to be used as a check on the indicated decennial increase. These figures show that during the decade the Negro death rate declined more rapidly than the Negro birth rate. This offers an explanation of the apparent reversal in the trend of the rate of increase. Whether this reversal is temporary or permanent remains to be seen.

Mexican population.—The Mexican element in the population has increased very rapidly in certain parts of the United States during the past 10 years. By reason of its growing importance, it was given a separate classification in the census returns for 1930, having been included for the most part with the white population at prior censuses. The instructions given to enumerators for making this classification were to the effect that "all persons born in Mexico, or having parents born in Mexico, who are not definitely white, Negro, Indian, Chinese, or Japanese, should be returned as Mexican." Under these instructions, 1,422,533 persons were returned as Mexican in 1930, and 65,968 persons of Mexican birth or parentage were returned as white. Using as a basis the 1920 returns for persons born in Mexico and persons having one or both parents born in Mexico, it has been estimated that there were in that year 700,541 persons who would have been classified as Mexican under the 1930 instructions.[1] Similarly it was estimated that there were included in the white classification in 1910, 367,510 persons who would have been counted as Mexican in 1930.

Indian population.—The census of 1860 was the first at which Indians were distinguished from the other classes, but no enumeration was made of the Indians in Indian Territory or on Indian reservations until 1890. Prior to that time the enumeration of Indians was confined to those found living among the general population of the various States. The returns for Indians are subject to some degree of uncertainty because of the practice of treating as Indians all persons having any trace of Indian blood. Such persons in many cases can not be distinguished by their appearance from pure-blooded white persons, and as a result some of them have doubtless been reported as white at one census and as Indian at another, since the enumerators are not always able to interview directly the persons whom they enumerate but are obliged to secure information regarding them from other persons.

At the census of 1910 a special effort was made to secure a complete enumeration of all persons having any perceptible amount of Indian blood, for the purpose of preparing a special report showing tribal relation, degree of Indian blood, etc.; and it is probable that this resulted in the enumeration as Indian of a considerable number of persons who would ordinarily have been reported as white. In 1920 no special instructions were given to the enumerators on this point, and the returns showed a much smaller number of Indians than in 1910.

In 1930, however, a special effort was again made to secure a complete count of persons of Indian blood, and the enumerators were instructed specifically to return as Indian all persons of mixed white and Indian blood, except where the percentage of Indian blood was very small, or where the person was regarded as white in the community where he lived. The results of this enumeration show 87,960, or 36.0 per cent, more Indians than were returned in 1920, but for reasons already indicated, it seems likely that this figure overstates the actual increase in the number of Indians.

Urban, rural-farm, and rural-nonfarm population.—Urban population, as defined by the Census Bureau, is in general that residing in cities and other incorporated places having 2,500 inhabitants or more, the remainder being classified as rural. In three of the New England States, New Hampshire, Massachusetts, and Rhode Island, towns (townships) are classified as urban if they have a population of 2,500 or more and certain urban characteristics; and a few large and densely populated townships in other States are likewise classified, even though not formally incorporated as municipalities.

In addition to the classification of the population as urban and rural, the rural population is further subdivided into rural-farm and rural-nonfarm, on the basis of the replies to a question reading "Does this family live on a farm?" The rural-farm population includes all persons living on farms in the rural areas. The rural-nonfarm or "village" population is made up largely of persons living in small towns or villages both incorporated and unincorporated, though in many areas there are considerable numbers of families living in the open country but not on farms.

The population of the United States distributed by color or race is shown for these urban and rural areas in Table 3.

TABLE 3.—URBAN, RURAL-FARM, AND RURAL-NONFARM POPULATION OF THE UNITED STATES, BY COLOR, NATIVITY, AND PARENTAGE: 1930

COLOR, NATIVITY, AND PARENTAGE	Total population	Urban	Rural-farm	Rural nonfarm
All classes	122,775,046	68,954,823	30,157,513	23,662,710
White	108,864,207	62,836,605	24,884,834	21,142,768
Native	95,497,800	52,109,746	23,800,747	19,587,307
Native parentage	70,136,614	33,497,232	20,495,382	16,144,000
Foreign or mixed parentage	25,361,186	18,612,514	3,305,305	3,443,307
Foreign parentage	16,999,221	12,959,015	1,953,554	2,086,652
Mixed parentage	8,361,965	5,653,499	1,351,811	1,356,655
Foreign born	13,366,407	10,726,859	1,084,087	1,555,461
Negro	11,891,143	5,193,913	4,680,523	2,016,707
Mexican	1,422,533	723,428	341,411	357,694
Indian	332,397	32,816	188,946	110,635
Chinese	74,954	65,778	3,211	5,965
Japanese	138,834	74,675	46,186	17,973
Filipino	45,208	24,414	10,735	10,059
Hindu	3,130	1,297	1,273	560
Korean	1,860	1,250	330	280
All other	780	647	64	69

[1] This estimate is based on the assumption that the ratio between white persons of Mexican birth or parentage and persons who should be classified as "Mexicans" was the same in 1920 as in 1930, when the total number of persons of Mexican origin (1,488,501) comprised 1,422,533 Mexicans and 65,968 white persons of Mexican birth or parentage. The total number of white persons of Mexican birth or parentage in 1920 was 731,559.

119652—33——3

28

POPULATION

PERCENTAGE OF FOREIGN-BORN WHITE IN THE TOTAL POPULATION, BY STATES: 1930

[District of Columbia, 6.1 per cent, not shown separately on the map]

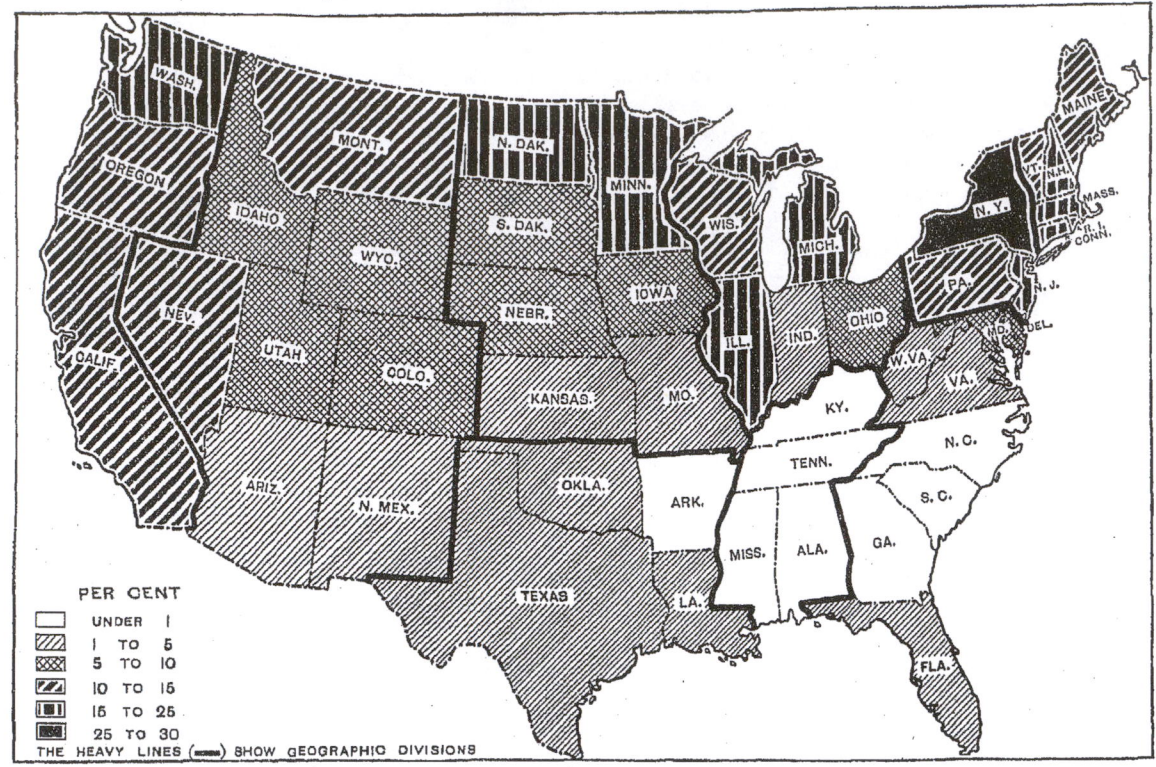

PER CENT

	UNDER 1
	1 TO 5
	5 TO 10
	10 TO 15
	15 TO 25
	25 TO 30

THE HEAVY LINES (▬) SHOW GEOGRAPHIC DIVISIONS

PERCENTAGE OF NEGROES IN THE TOTAL POPULATION, BY STATES: 1930

[District of Columbia, 27.1 per cent, not shown separately on the map]

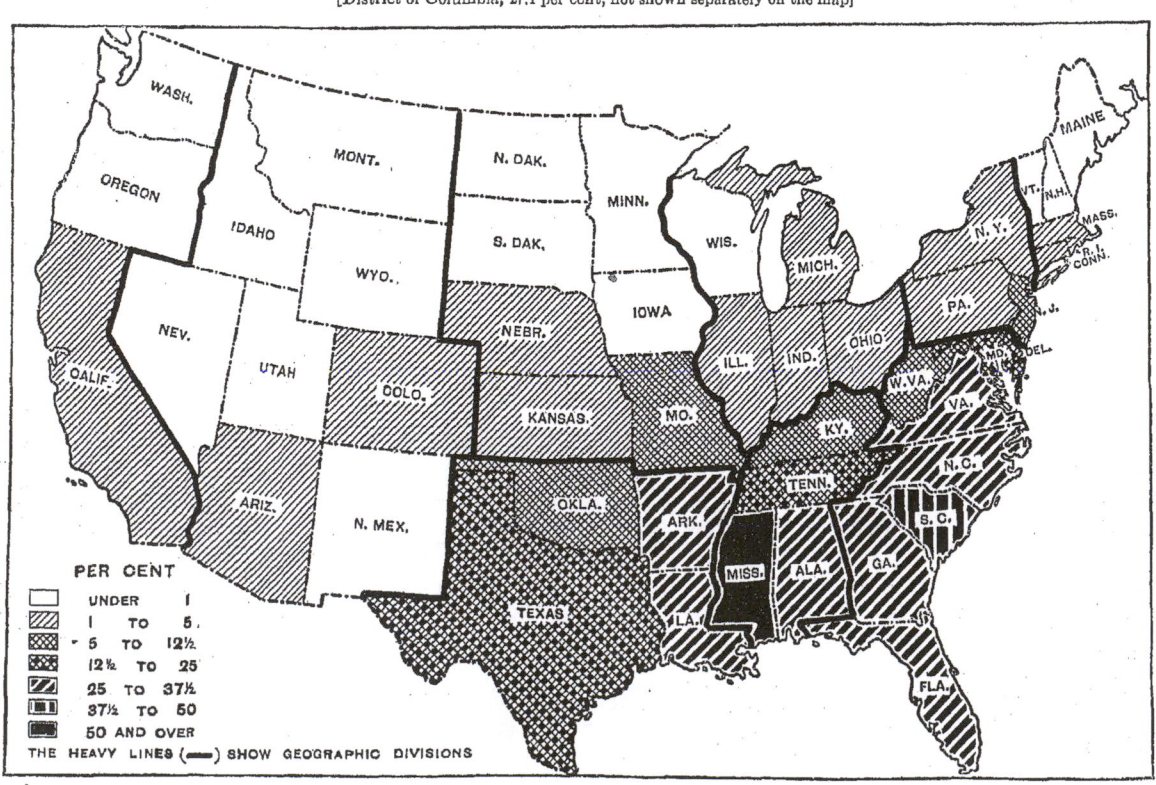

PER CENT

	UNDER 1
	1 TO 5
	5 TO 12½
	12½ TO 25
	25 TO 37½
	37½ TO 50
	50 AND OVER

THE HEAVY LINES (▬) SHOW GEOGRAPHIC DIVISIONS

COLOR OR RACE, NATIVITY, AND PARENTAGE

DISTRIBUTION OF THE TOTAL POPULATION BY COLOR AND NATIVITY: 1850 TO 1930

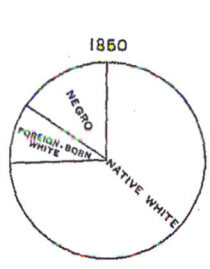

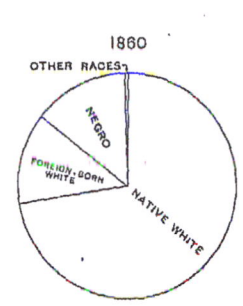

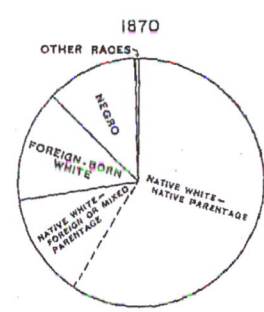

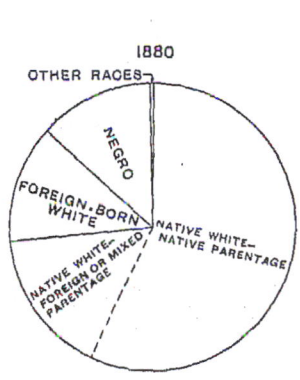

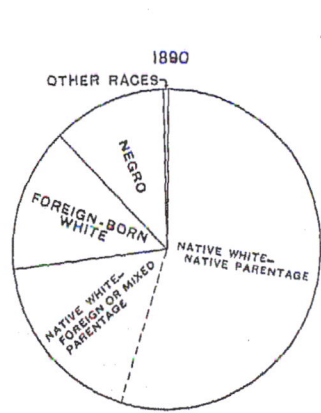

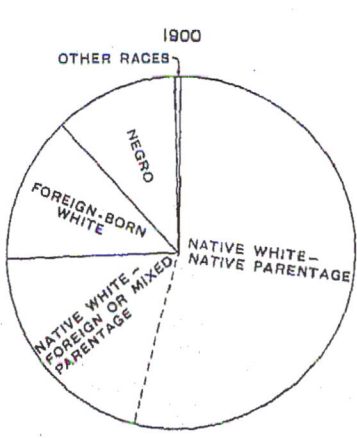

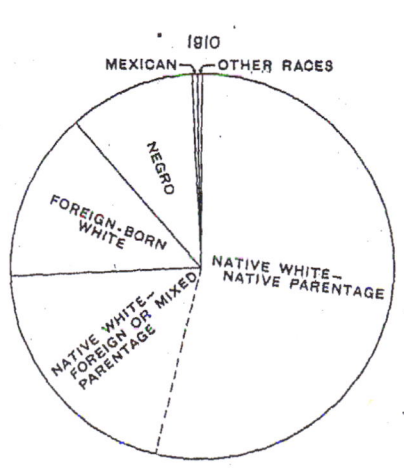

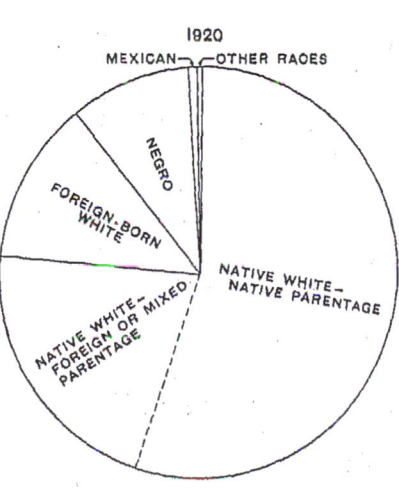

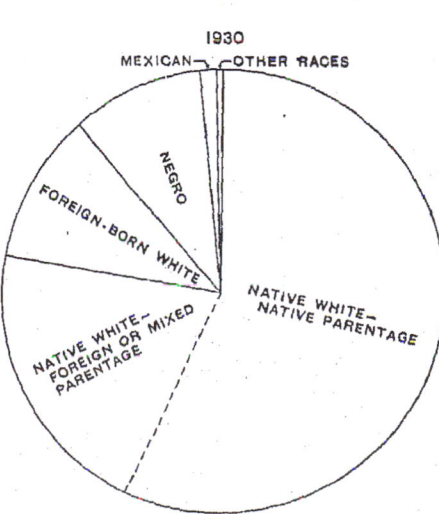

POPULATION

DISTRIBUTION OF THE URBAN, RURAL-FARM, AND RURAL-NONFARM POPULATION BY COLOR AND NATIVITY: 1930

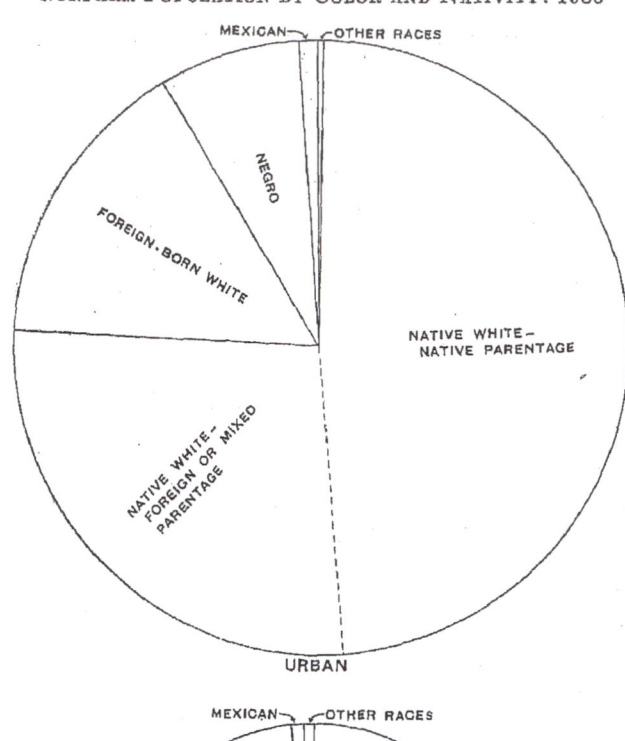

URBAN

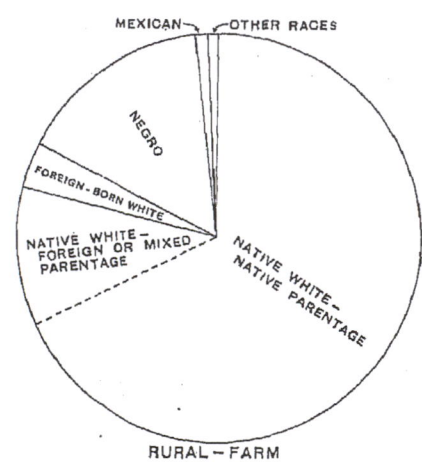

RURAL—FARM

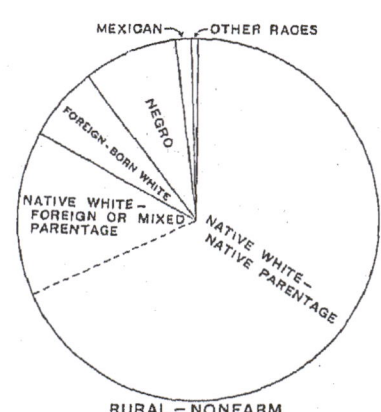

RURAL—NONFARM

COLOR, NATIVITY, AND PARENTAGE, BY STATES: 1930

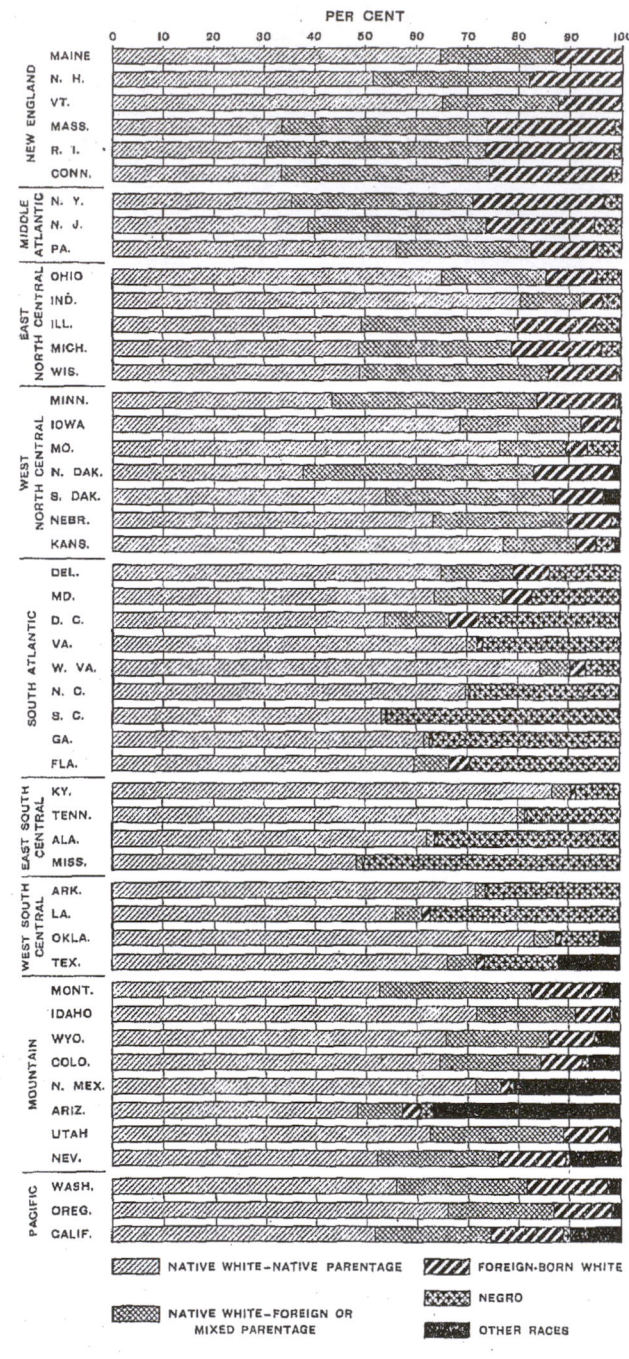

COLOR OR RACE, NATIVITY, AND PARENTAGE

31

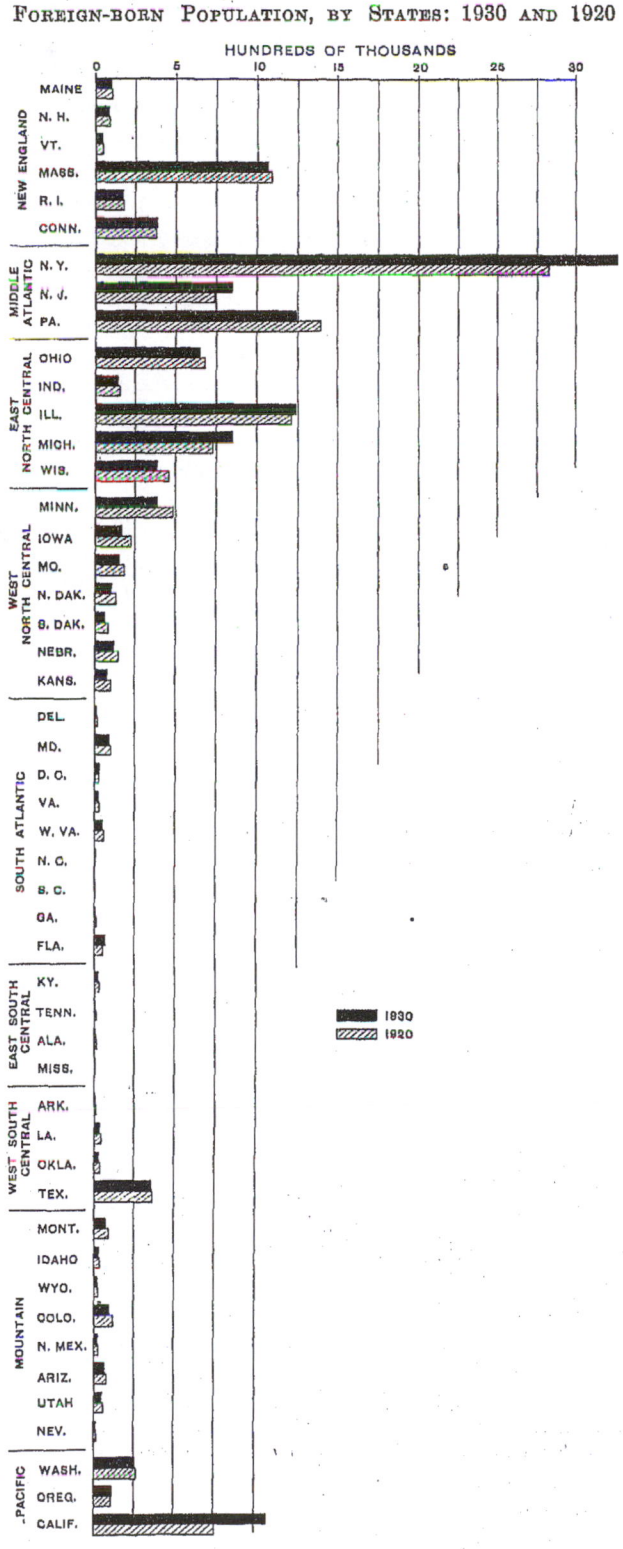

FOREIGN-BORN POPULATION, BY STATES: 1930 AND 1920

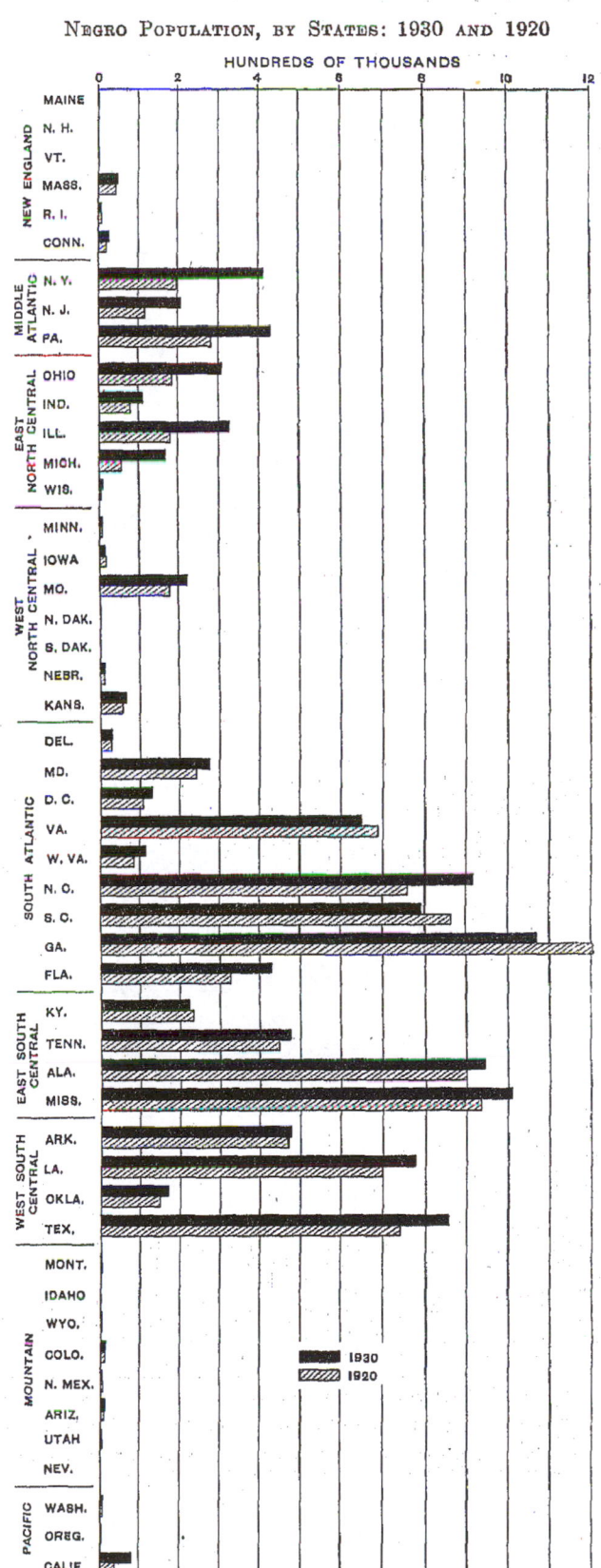

NEGRO POPULATION, BY STATES: 1930 AND 1920

32

POPULATION

Adjusted figures for white population.—The change in the classification of Mexicans introduces many complications into the process of comparing the 1930 figures for the white population and its various subdivisions with the corresponding figures for 1920 and 1910. In order to provide a basis for more satisfactory comparisons, the estimated numbers of Mexicans included in the white classification in 1920 and 1910 have been subtracted from the figures as published for these years and the difference is presented in various tables as an "adjusted"

figure for the 1920 and 1910 white population. Data are not available on which to base adjustments for census years prior to 1910, but the number of Mexicans in the United States in 1900 was relatively small. In some of the tables the adjusted figures are presented in the body of the table; in connection with other tables the effect of the adjustment is indicated in a footnote. The adjusted figures for both 1920 and 1910 for all of the classes of the white population are shown in a footnote to Table 6.

TABLE 4.—TOTAL POPULATION BY COLOR OR RACE, FOR THE UNITED STATES: 1790 TO 1930

[Figures are given under each class for all census years for which data are available. Per cent not shown where less than 0.1]

CENSUS YEAR	POPULATION									PER CENT OF TOTAL POPULATION					
	Total	White	Negro	Mexican	Indian	Chinese	Japanese	Filipino	All other	White	Negro	Mexican	Indian	Chinese	Japanese
1930	122,775,046	108,864,207	11,891,143	1,422,533	332,397	74,954	138,834	45,208	[1] 5,770	88.7	9.7	1.2	0.3	0.1	0.1
1920	105,710,620	[2] 94,820,915	10,463,131	[2] 700,541	244,437	61,639	111,010	5,603	[3] 3,885	[2] 89.7	9.9	0.7	0.2	0.1	0.1
1910	91,972,266	[2] 81,731,957	9,827,763	[2] 367,510	265,683	71,531	72,157	160	[4] 3,015	[2] 88.9	10.7	0.4	0.3	0.1	0.1
1900	75,994,575	66,809,196	8,833,994		237,196	89,863	24,326			87.9	11.6		0.3	0.1	
1890	62,947,714	55,101,258	7,488,676		248,253	107,488	2,039		[a]	87.5	11.9		0.4	0.2	
1880	50,155,783	43,402,970	6,580,793		[5] 66,407	105,465	148			86.5	13.1		0.1	0.2	
1870	38,558,371	33,589,377	4,880,000		[5] 25,731	63,199	55			87.1	12.7		0.1	0.2	
1870 [6]	*39,818,449*	*34,337,292*	*5,392,172*		*[5] 25,731*	*63,199*	*55*			*86.2*	*13.5*		*0.1*	*0.2*	
1860	31,443,321	26,922,537	4,441,830		[5] 44,021	34,933				85.6	14.1		0.1	0.1	
1850	23,191,876	19,553,068	3,638,808							84.3	15.7				
1840	17,069,453	14,195,805	2,873,648							83.2	16.8				
1830	12,866,020	10,537,378	2,328,642							81.9	18.1				
1820	9,638,453	7,866,797	1,771,656							81.6	18.4				
1810	7,239,881	5,862,073	1,377,808							81.0	19.0				
1800	5,308,483	4,306,446	1,002,037							81.1	18.9				
1790	3,929,214	3,172,006	757,208							80.7	19.3				

[1] Comprises 3,130 Hindus, 1,860 Koreans, 660 Hawaiians, 96 Malays, 18 Siamese, and 6 Samoans.
[2] The white population as classified in 1920 and 1910 included 700,541 and 367,510 persons, respectively (estimated), who would have been classified as Mexican in 1930. If the figures are adjusted by deducting these estimates, the number of white persons in 1920 becomes 94,120,374, or 89.0 per cent of the total, and in 1910, 81,364,447, or 88.5 per cent of the total.
[3] Comprises 2,507 Hindus, 1,224 Koreans, 110 Hawaiians, 19 Malays, 17 Siamese, 6 Samoans, and 2 Maoris.
[4] Comprises 2,545 Hindus, 462 Koreans, and 8 Maoris.
[5] Exclusive of Indians in Indian Territory and on Indian reservations, not enumerated at censuses prior to 1890.
[6] Estimated corrected figures. See explanation in text.

TABLE 5.—INCREASE IN THE POPULATION, BY COLOR OR RACE, FOR THE UNITED STATES: 1790 TO 1930

[A minus sign (−) denotes decrease. Per cent not shown where base is less than 100]

DECADE	TOTAL POPULATION		WHITE		NEGRO		MEXICAN		INDIAN		CHINESE		JAPANESE		FILIPINO	
	Number	Per cent	Number	Per cent	Number	Per cent	Number	Per cent	Number	Per cent	Number	Per cent	Number	Per cent	Number	Per cent
1920–1930	17,064,426	16.1	[1] 14,743,833	[1] 15.7	1,428,012	13.6	[1] 721,992	[1] 103.1	87,960	36.0	13,315	21.6	27,824	25.1	39,605	706.9
1910–1920	13,738,354	14.9	[1] 12,755,927	[1] 15.7	635,368	6.5	[1] 333,031	[1] 90.6	−21,246	−8.0	−9,892	−13.8	38,853	53.8	5,443	3,401.9
1900–1910	15,977,691	21.0	[1] 14,555,251	[1] 21.8	993,769	11.2			28,487	12.0	−18,332	−20.4	47,831	196.6		
1890–1900	13,046,861	20.7	11,707,938	21.2	1,345,318	18.0			−11,057	−4.5	−17,625	−16.4	22,287	1,093.0		
1880–1890	[2] 12,466,467	24.9	[2] 11,580,920	26.7	[2] 889,247	13.5			[2] −7,601	−11.4	[2] 2,010	1.9	1,891	1,277.7		
1870–1880 [4]	11,597,412	30.1	9,813,593	29.2	1,700,784	34.9			[3] 40,676	158.1	42,266	66.9	93			
1870–1880 [4]	*10,387,334*	*26.0*	*9,065,678*	*26.4*	*1,188,621*	*22.0*			*[3] 40,676*	*158.1*	*42,266*	*66.9*	*93*			
1860–1870 [4]	*8,375,128*	*26.6*	*7,414,755*	*27.5*	*950,342*	*21.4*			*[3] −18,290*	*−41.5*	*28,966*	*80.9*				
1860–1870	7,115,050	22.6	6,666,840	24.8	438,179	9.9			[3] −18,290	−41.5	28,266	80.9				
1850–1860	8,251,445	35.6	7,369,469	37.7	803,022	22.1										
1840–1850	6,122,423	35.9	5,357,263	37.7	765,160	26.6										
1830–1840	4,203,433	32.7	3,658,427	34.7	545,006	23.4										
1820–1830	3,227,567	33.5	2,670,581	33.9	556,986	31.4										
1810–1820	2,398,572	33.1	2,004,724	34.2	393,848	28.6										
1800–1810	1,931,398	36.4	1,555,627	36.1	375,771	37.5										
1790–1800	1,379,269	35.1	1,134,440	35.8	244,829	32.3										

[1] Increase in white and Mexican based upon adjusted figures, excluding from the white population of 1920 and 1910 the estimated number of Mexicans. See footnote 2, Table 4.
[2] Exclusive of population specially enumerated in 1890 in Indian Territory and on Indian reservations (total, 325,464; white, 117,368; Negro, 18,636; Indian, 189,447; Chinese, 13).
[3] Exclusive of Indians in Indian Territory and on Indian reservations, not enumerated prior to 1890.
[4] Increase based upon corrected figures for 1870. See Table 4.

COLOR OR RACE, NATIVITY, AND PARENTAGE — 33

TABLE 6.—POPULATION BY COLOR OR RACE, BY NATIVITY AND PARENTAGE, FOR THE UNITED STATES: 1850 TO 1930

COLOR OR RACE AND CENSUS YEAR	Total population	NATIVE POPULATION							Foreign-born population	PER CENT OF TOTAL POPULATION		PER CENT OF NATIVE POPULATION			
		Total	Native parentage	Foreign or mixed parentage	Foreign parentage	Mixed parentage				Native	Foreign born	Native parentage	Foreign or mixed parentage	Foreign parentage	Mixed parentage
						Total	Father foreign	Mother foreign							
All classes:															
1930	122,775,046	108,570,897	82,488,768	26,082,129	17,535,071	8,547,058	5,579,987	2,967,071	14,204,149	88.4	11.6	76.0	24.0	16.2	7.9
1920	105,710,620	91,789,928	68,994,682	22,795,246	15,764,366	7,030,880	4,564,295	2,466,585	13,920,692	86.8	13.2	75.2	24.8	17.2	7.7
1910	91,972,266	78,456,380	59,401,427	18,064,953	12,949,181	6,015,772	3,946,435	2,069,337	13,515,886	85.3	14.7	75.8	24.2	16.5	7.7
1900	75,994,575	65,653,299	49,956,178	15,697,121	10,650,802	5,046,319	3,368,228	1,678,091	10,341,276	86.4	13.6	76.1	23.9	16.2	7.7
1890	62,947,714	53,698,154							9,249,560	85.3	14.7				
1880	50,155,783	43,475,840							6,679,943	86.7	13.3				
1870	38,558,371	32,991,142							5,567,229	85.6	14.4				
1860	31,443,321	27,304,624							4,138,697	86.8	13.2				
1850	23,191,876	20,947,274							2,244,602	90.3	9.7				
White:															
1930	108,864,207	95,497,800	70,136,614	25,361,186	16,999,221	8,361,965	5,459,530	2,902,435	13,366,407	87.7	12.3	73.4	26.6	17.8	8.8
1920 [1]	94,820,915	81,108,161	58,421,957	22,686,204	15,694,539	6,991,665	4,539,776	2,451,889	13,712,754	85.5	14.5	72.0	28.0	19.4	8.6
1910 [1]	81,731,957	68,386,412	49,488,575	18,897,837	12,916,311	5,981,526	3,923,845	2,057,681	13,345,545	83.7	16.3	72.4	27.6	18.9	8.7
1900	66,809,196	56,595,379	40,949,362	15,646,017	10,632,280	5,013,737	3,346,652	1,667,085	10,213,817	84.7	15.3	72.4	27.6	18.8	8.9
1890	55,101,258	45,979,391	34,475,716	11,503,675	8,085,019	3,418,656	2,378,729	1,039,927	9,121,867	83.4	16.6	75.0	25.0	17.6	7.4
1880	43,402,970	36,843,291	28,568,424	8,274,867	6,363,789	1,911,098			6,559,679	84.9	15.1	77.5	22.5	17.3	5.2
1870	33,589,377	28,095,665	22,771,397	5,324,268	4,167,098	1,157,170			5,493,712	83.6	16.4	81.0	19.0	14.8	4.1
1860	26,922,537	22,825,784							4,096,753	84.8	15.2				
1850	19,553,068	17,312,533							2,240,535	88.5	11.5				
Negro:															
1930	11,891,143	11,792,523	11,709,102	83,361	43,452	39,909	26,310	13,599	98,620	99.2	0.8	99.3	0.7	0.4	0.3
1920	10,463,131	10,389,328	10,334,151	55,177	25,843	29,334	18,193	11,141	73,803	99.3	0.7	99.5	0.5	0.2	0.3
1910	9,827,763	9,787,424	9,748,439	38,985	14,500	24,425	15,332	9,093	40,339	99.6	0.4	99.6	0.4	0.1	0.2
1900	8,833,994	8,813,658	8,779,267	34,391	9,198	25,193	15,720	9,473	20,336	99.8	0.2	99.6	0.4	0.1	0.3
Other races:															
1930	2,019,696	1,280,574	642,992	637,582	492,398	145,184	94,147	51,037	739,122	63.4	36.6	50.2	49.8	38.5	11.3
1920	426,574	292,439	238,574	53,865	43,984	9,881	6,326	3,555	134,135	68.6	31.4	81.6	18.4	15.0	3.4
1910	412,546	282,544	254,413	28,131	18,310	9,821	7,258	2,563	130,002	68.5	31.5	90.0	10.0	6.5	3.5
1900	351,385	244,262	227,549	16,713	9,324	7,389	5,856	1,533	107,123	69.5	30.5	93.2	6.8	3.8	3.0

[1] The number of Mexicans as estimated for 1920 and 1910 and the adjusted figures for the different classes in the white population with which they were included in those years are as follows:

CLASS OF POPULATION	WHITE		1920, Mexicans (est.)	WHITE		1910, Mexicans (est.)
	1920, as reported	1920, as adjusted		1910, as reported	1910, as adjusted	
Total	94,820,915	94,120,374	700,541	81,731,957	81,364,447	367,510
Native	81,108,161	80,864,980	243,181	68,386,412	68,230,135	156,277
Native parentage	58,421,957			49,488,575		
Foreign or mixed parentage	22,686,204	22,443,023	243,181	18,897,837	18,741,560	156,277
Foreign parentage	15,694,539	15,521,835	172,704	12,916,311	12,812,090	104,221
Mixed parentage	6,991,665	6,921,188	70,477	5,981,526	5,929,470	52,056
Foreign born	13,712,754	13,255,394	457,360	13,345,545	13,134,312	211,233

TABLE 7.—INCREASE IN THE TOTAL POPULATION BY NATIVITY, AND IN THE WHITE POPULATION BY PARENTAGE, FOR THE UNITED STATES: 1850 TO 1930

DECADE	TOTAL POPULATION				WHITE POPULATION													
	Native		Foreign born		Native												Foreign born	
					Total		Native parentage		Foreign or mixed parentage		Foreign parentage		Mixed parentage					
	Number	Per cent	Number	Per cent	Number	Per cent	Number	Per cent	Number	Per cent	Number	Per cent	Number	Per cent			Number	Per cent
1920–1930 [1]	16,780,969	18.3	283,457	2.0	14,632,820	18.1	11,714,657	20.1	2,918,163	13.0	1,477,386	9.5	1,440,777	20.8			111,013	0.8
1910–1920 [1]	13,333,548	17.0	404,806	3.0	12,634,845	18.5	8,933,382	18.1	3,701,463	19.8	2,700,745	21.1	991,718	16.7			121,082	0.9
1900–1910 [1]	12,803,081	19.5	3,174,610	30.7	11,634,750	20.6	8,539,213	20.9	3,095,543	19.8	2,179,810	20.5	915,733	18.3			2,920,495	28.6
1890–1900	11,955,145	22.3	1,091,710	11.8	10,615,988	23.1	6,473,646	18.8	4,142,342	36.0	2,547,261	31.5	1,595,081	46.7			1,091,950	12.0
1880–1890	[2] 9,896,863	22.8	[2] 2,569,604	38.5	[2] 9,018,732	24.5	[2] 5,789,924	20.3	3,228,808	39.0	1,721,250	27.0	1,507,558	78.9			2,562,188	39.1
1870–1880	10,484,698	31.8	1,112,714	20.0	8,747,626	20.0	5,707,027	25.5	2,950,599	55.4	2,196,671	52.7	753,928	65.2			1,065,967	19.4
1860–1870 [3]	5,686,518	20.8	1,428,532	34.5	5,269,881	23.1											1,396,959	34.1
1850–1860	6,357,350	30.3	1,894,095	84.4	5,513,251	31.8											1,856,218	82.8

[1] Increase in the white classes based upon adjusted figures for Mexicans in 1920 and 1910. See footnote 1, Table 6.
[2] Exclusive of population specially enumerated in 1890 in Indian Territory and on Indian reservations.
[3] Increase based upon 1870 figures as reported. See text, p. 25.

34 POPULATION

TABLE 8.—POPULATION OF THE MINOR RACES BY NATIVITY, FOR THE UNITED STATES: 1900 TO 1930

RACE AND CENSUS YEAR	Total	Native	Foreign born	PER CENT Native	PER CENT Foreign born	RACE AND CENSUS YEAR	Total	Native	Foreign born	PER CENT Native	PER CENT Foreign born
Mexican:						Japanese:					
1930	1,422,533	805,535	616,998	56.6	43.4	1930	138,834	68,357	70,477	49.2	50.8
1920 (estimated)[1]	700,541	243,181	457,360	34.7	65.3	1920	111,010	29,672	81,338	26.7	73.3
1910 (estimated)[1]	367,510	156,277	211,233	42.5	57.5	1910	72,157	4,502	67,655	6.2	93.8
Indian:						1900	24,326	269	24,057	1.1	98.9
1930	332,397	328,845	3,552	98.9	1.1	Filipino:					
1920	244,437	238,138	6,299	97.4	2.6	1930	45,208	45,026	182	99.6	0.4
1910	265,683	262,930	2,753	99.0	1.0	1920	5,603	5,593	10	99.8	0.2
1900	237,196	234,983	2,213	99.1	0.9	1910	160	155	5	96.9	3.1
Chinese:						All other:					
1930	74,954	30,868	44,086	41.2	58.8	1930	[2] 5,770	1,943	3,827	33.7	66.3
1920	61,639	18,532	43,107	30.1	69.9	1920	3,885	504	3,381	13.0	87.0
1910	71,531	14,935	56,596	20.9	79.1	1910	3,015	22	2,993	0.7	99.3
1900	89,863	9,010	80,853	10.0	90.0						

[1] Estimate based upon the number of white persons reported as born in Mexico or as having one or both parents born in Mexico.
[2] Comprises 3,130 Hindus (412 native, 2,718 foreign born); 1,860 Koreans (816 native, 1,044 foreign born); 660 Hawaiians (654 native, 6 foreign born); 96 Malays (48 native, 48 foreign born); 18 Siamese (7 native, 11 foreign born); and 6 Samoans (all native).

TABLE 9.—NATIVE MEXICANS, CHINESE, AND JAPANESE BY PARENTAGE, FOR THE UNITED STATES: 1900 TO 1930

RACE AND CENSUS YEAR	Total native	Native parentage	Foreign or mixed parentage	Foreign parentage	Mixed parentage	PER CENT OF TOTAL NATIVE Native parentage	PER CENT OF TOTAL NATIVE Foreign or mixed parentage	PER CENT OF TOTAL NATIVE Foreign parentage	PER CENT OF TOTAL NATIVE Mixed parentage
Mexican:									
1930	805,535	264,338	541,197	408,304	132,893	32.8	67.2	50.7	16.5
1920 (estimated)[1]	243,181	(1)	243,181	172,704	70,477	(1)	100.0	71.0	29.0
1910 (estimated)[1]	156,277	(1)	156,277	104,221	52,056	(1)	100.0	66.7	33.3
Chinese:									
1930	30,868	4,325	26,543	18,134	8,409	14.0	86.0	58.7	27.2
1920	18,532	2,391	16,141	11,952	4,189	12.9	87.1	64.5	22.6
1910	14,935	738	14,197	12,076	2,121	4.9	95.1	80.9	14.2
1900	9,010	245	8,765	7,762	1,003	2.7	97.3	86.1	11.1
Japanese:									
1930	68,357	839	67,518	65,037	2,481	1.2	98.8	95.1	3.6
1920	29,672	212	29,460	28,948	512	0.7	99.3	97.6	1.7
1910	4,502	44	4,458	4,313	145	1.0	99.0	95.8	3.2
1900	269	32	237	204	33	11.9	88.1	75.8	12.3

[1] Estimate based upon the number of native white persons reported as having one or both parents born in Mexico. No satisfactory basis was available for estimating the number of Mexicans of native parentage.

TABLE 10.—COLOR OR RACE AND NATIVITY OF THE URBAN, RURAL-FARM, AND RURAL-NONFARM POPULATION, FOR THE UNITED STATES: 1930 AND 1920

[Figures for white in 1920 are as reported, and not adjusted for Mexicans]

COLOR AND NATIVITY	TOTAL POPULATION Number 1930	Number 1920	Per cent distribution 1930	Per cent distribution 1920	URBAN POPULATION Number 1930	Number 1920	Per cent distribution 1930	Per cent distribution 1920	Per cent of total 1930	Per cent of total 1920
All classes	122,775,046	105,710,620	100.0	100.0	68,954,823	54,304,603	100.0	100.0	56.2	51.4
White	108,864,207	94,820,915	88.7	89.7	62,836,605	50,620,084	91.1	93.2	57.7	53.4
Native	95,497,800	81,108,161	77.8	76.7	52,109,746	40,263,101	75.6	74.1	54.6	49.6
Native parentage	70,136,614	58,421,957	57.1	55.3	33,497,232	24,556,729	48.6	45.2	47.8	42.0
Foreign or mixed parentage	25,361,186	22,686,204	20.7	21.5	18,612,514	15,706,372	27.0	28.9	73.4	69.2
Foreign parentage	16,999,221	15,694,539	13.8	14.8	12,959,015	11,304,886	18.8	20.8	76.2	72.0
Mixed parentage	8,361,965	6,991,665	6.8	6.6	5,653,499	4,401,486	8.2	8.1	67.6	63.0
Foreign born	13,366,407	13,712,754	10.9	13.0	10,726,859	10,356,983	15.6	19.1	80.3	75.5
Negro	11,891,143	10,463,131	9.7	9.9	5,193,913	3,559,473	7.5	6.6	43.7	34.0
Other races	2,019,696	426,574	1.6	0.4	924,305	125,046	1.3	0.2	45.8	29.3

COLOR AND NATIVITY	RURAL-FARM POPULATION Number 1930	Number 1920	Per cent distribution 1930	Per cent distribution 1920	Per cent of total 1930	Per cent of total 1920	RURAL-NONFARM POPULATION Number 1930	Number 1920	Per cent distribution 1930	Per cent distribution 1920	Per cent of total 1930	Per cent of total 1920
All classes	30,157,513	31,358,640	100.0	100.0	24.6	29.7	23,662,710	20,047,377	100.0	100.0	19.3	19.0
White	24,884,834	26,072,800	82.5	83.1	22.9	27.5	21,142,768	18,128,031	89.4	90.4	19.4	19.1
Native	23,800,747	24,639,376	78.9	78.6	24.9	30.4	19,587,307	16,205,084	82.8	80.8	20.5	20.0
Native parentage	20,495,382	20,906,521	68.0	66.7	29.2	35.8	16,144,000	12,958,707	68.2	64.6	23.0	22.2
Foreign or mixed parentage	3,305,365	3,732,855	11.0	11.9	13.0	16.5	3,443,307	3,246,977	14.6	16.2	13.6	14.3
Foreign parentage	1,953,554	2,282,447	6.5	7.3	11.5	14.5	2,086,652	2,107,206	8.8	10.5	12.3	13.4
Mixed parentage	1,351,811	1,450,408	4.5	4.6	16.2	20.7	1,356,655	1,139,771	5.7	5.7	16.2	16.3
Foreign born	1,084,087	1,433,424	3.6	4.6	8.1	10.5	1,555,461	1,922,947	6.6	9.6	11.6	14.0
Negro	4,680,523	5,099,963	15.5	16.3	39.4	48.7	2,016,707	1,803,695	8.5	9.0	17.0	17.2
Other races	592,156	185,877	2.0	0.6	29.3	43.6	503,235	115,651	2.1	0.6	24.9	27.1

COLOR OR RACE, NATIVITY, AND PARENTAGE   35

TABLE 11.—COLOR OR RACE AND NATIVITY, BY DIVISIONS AND STATES: 1930

DIVISION AND STATE	Total population	White	Negro	Mexican	Indian	Chinese	Japanese	Filipino	All other	Total native population	Total foreign-born population	PER CENT OF TOTAL POPULATION Native	PER CENT OF TOTAL POPULATION Foreign-born
United States	122,775,046	108,864,207	11,891,143	1,422,533	332,397	74,954	138,834	45,208	5,770	108,570,897	14,204,149	88.4	11.6
GEOGRAPHIC DIVISIONS:													
New England	8,166,341	8,065,113	94,086	107	2,466	3,794	352	358	65	6,317,398	1,848,943	77.4	22.6
Middle Atlantic	26,260,750	25,172,104	1,052,899	6,757	7,709	14,005	3,662	2,882	732	20,908,019	5,352,731	79.6	20.4
East North Central	25,297,185	24,277,663	930,450	58,317	19,817	6,340	1,022	3,027	549	22,021,462	3,275,723	87.1	12.9
West North Central	13,296,915	12,873,487	331,784	39,805	48,245	1,738	1,003	784	69	12,212,762	1,084,153	91.8	8.2
South Atlantic	15,793,589	11,349,284	4,421,388	691	19,060	1,899	393	861	43	15,474,892	318,697	98.0	2.0
East South Central	9,887,214	7,224,614	2,658,238	1,403	2,106	743	46	50	14	9,827,850	59,364	99.4	0.6
West South Central	12,176,830	9,099,081	2,281,951	695,996	95,670	1,582	687	830	124	11,736,277	440,553	96.4	3.6
Mountain	3,701,789	3,303,589	30,225	249,314	102,083	3,252	11,418	1,391	520	3,317,466	384,323	89.6	10.4
Pacific	8,194,433	7,498,375	90,122	370,143	35,241	41,631	120,251	35,016	3,654	6,754,771	1,439,662	82.4	17.6
NEW ENGLAND:													
Maine	797,423	795,183	1,096	2	1,012	115	3	12	----	696,695	100,728	87.4	12.6
New Hampshire	465,293	464,350	790	1	64	84	----	3	1	382,364	82,929	82.2	17.8
Vermont	359,611	358,965	568	1	36	34	1	1	5	316,510	43,101	88.0	12.0
Massachusetts	4,249,614	4,192,926	52,365	66	874	2,973	201	157	52	3,183,994	1,065,620	74.9	25.1
Rhode Island	687,497	677,016	9,913	10	318	197	17	25	1	515,568	171,929	75.0	25.0
Connecticut	1,606,903	1,576,673	29,354	27	162	391	130	160	6	1,222,267	384,636	76.1	23.9
MIDDLE ATLANTIC:													
New York	12,588,066	12,150,293	412,814	2,898	6,973	9,003	2,930	1,982	511	9,325,788	3,262,278	74.1	25.9
New Jersey	4,041,334	3,829,209	208,828	454	213	1,783	439	286	122	3,191,296	850,038	79.0	21.0
Pennsylvania	9,631,350	9,192,602	431,257	3,405	523	2,557	293	614	99	8,390,935	1,240,415	87.1	12.9
EAST NORTH CENTRAL:													
Ohio	6,646,697	6,331,136	309,304	4,037	435	1,425	187	88	85	5,997,477	649,220	90.2	9.8
Indiana	3,238,503	3,116,136	111,982	9,642	285	279	71	77	31	3,095,504	142,999	95.6	4.4
Illinois	7,630,654	7,266,361	328,972	28,906	469	3,192	564	2,011	179	6,388,207	1,242,447	83.7	16.3
Michigan	4,842,325	4,650,171	169,453	13,336	7,080	1,081	176	787	241	3,989,567	852,758	82.4	17.6
Wisconsin	2,939,006	2,913,859	10,739	2,396	11,548	363	24	64	13	2,550,707	388,299	86.8	13.2
WEST NORTH CENTRAL:													
Minnesota	2,563,953	2,538,973	9,445	3,626	11,077	524	69	236	3	2,173,163	390,790	84.8	15.2
Iowa	2,470,939	2,448,382	17,380	4,205	660	153	19	40	10	2,302,689	168,250	93.2	6.8
Missouri	3,629,367	3,398,887	223,840	4,989	578	634	94	321	24	3,476,282	153,085	95.8	4.2
North Dakota	680,845	671,243	377	608	8,387	103	91	30	6	574,974	105,871	84.5	15.5
South Dakota	692,849	669,453	646	816	21,833	70	19	7	5	626,788	66,061	90.5	9.5
Nebraska	1,377,963	1,353,702	13,752	6,321	3,256	194	674	55	9	1,258,764	119,199	91.3	8.7
Kansas	1,880,999	1,792,847	66,344	19,150	2,454	60	37	95	12	1,800,102	80,897	95.7	4.3
SOUTH ATLANTIC:													
Delaware	238,380	205,694	32,602	24	5	38	8	9	----	221,355	17,025	92.9	7.1
Maryland	1,631,526	1,354,170	276,379	56	50	492	38	327	14	1,535,196	96,330	94.1	5.9
District of Columbia	486,869	353,914	132,068	67	40	398	78	294	10	456,136	30,733	93.7	6.3
Virginia	2,421,851	1,770,405	650,165	36	779	293	43	126	4	2,397,484	24,367	99.0	1.0
West Virginia	1,729,205	1,613,934	114,893	257	18	86	9	6	2	1,677,340	51,865	97.0	3.0
North Carolina	3,170,276	2,234,948	918,647	10	16,579	68	17	6	1	3,161,307	8,969	99.7	0.3
South Carolina	1,738,765	944,040	793,681	9	959	41	15	18	2	1,733,407	5,358	99.7	0.3
Georgia	2,908,506	1,836,974	1,071,125	47	43	253	32	29	3	2,894,203	14,303	99.5	0.5
Florida	1,468,211	1,035,205	431,828	186	587	200	153	46	7	1,398,464	69,747	95.2	4.8
EAST SOUTH CENTRAL:													
Kentucky	2,614,589	2,388,364	226,040	88	22	60	9	5	1	2,592,582	22,007	99.2	0.8
Tennessee	2,616,556	2,138,619	477,646	25	161	70	11	14	10	2,603,305	13,251	99.5	0.5
Alabama	2,646,248	1,700,775	944,834	69	465	52	25	25	3	2,630,187	16,061	99.4	0.6
Mississippi	2,009,821	998,856	1,009,718	1,221	1,458	561	1	6	----	2,001,776	8,045	99.6	0.4
WEST SOUTH CENTRAL:													
Arkansas	1,854,482	1,374,906	478,463	409	408	251	12	15	18	1,843,850	10,632	99.4	0.6
Louisiana	2,101,593	1,318,160	776,326	4,552	1,536	422	52	515	30	2,064,517	37,076	98.2	1.8
Oklahoma	2,396,040	2,123,424	172,198	7,354	92,725	206	104	21	8	2,365,482	30,558	98.7	1.3
Texas	5,824,715	4,283,491	854,964	683,681	1,001	703	519	288	68	5,462,428	362,287	93.8	6.2
MOUNTAIN:													
Montana	537,606	517,327	1,256	2,571	14,798	486	753	295	120	461,703	75,903	85.9	14.1
Idaho	445,032	437,562	668	1,278	3,638	335	1,421	97	33	412,748	32,284	92.7	7.3
Wyoming	225,565	214,067	1,250	7,174	1,845	130	1,026	45	28	202,222	23,343	89.7	10.3
Colorado	1,035,791	961,117	11,828	57,676	1,395	233	3,213	250	79	935,916	99,875	90.4	9.6
New Mexico	423,317	331,755	2,850	59,340	28,941	133	249	27	22	399,265	24,052	94.3	5.7
Arizona	435,573	264,378	10,749	114,173	43,726	1,110	879	472	86	369,817	65,756	84.9	15.1
Utah	507,847	495,955	1,108	4,012	2,869	342	3,269	158	134	459,832	48,015	90.5	9.5
Nevada	91,058	81,425	516	3,090	4,871	483	608	47	18	75,963	15,095	83.4	16.6
PACIFIC:													
Washington	1,563,396	1,521,099	6,840	562	11,253	2,195	17,837	3,480	130	1,308,138	255,258	83.7	16.3
Oregon	953,786	937,029	2,234	1,568	4,776	2,075	4,958	1,066	80	843,346	110,440	88.4	11.6
California	5,677,251	5,040,247	81,048	368,013	19,212	37,361	97,456	30,470	3,444	4,603,287	1,073,964	81.1	18.9

119652—33——4

POPULATION

TABLE **12.**—WHITE POPULATION BY NATIVITY AND PARENTAGE, BY DIVISIONS AND STATES: 1930

DIVISION AND STATE	Total white population	NATIVE WHITE							Foreign-born white	PER CENT OF TOTAL POPULATION						
		Total	Native parentage	Foreign or mixed parentage	Foreign parentage	Mixed parentage				Total white	Native white				Mixed par.	Foreign born white
						Total	Father foreign	Mother foreign			Total	Native par.	For. or mixed par.	Foreign par.		
United States	108,864,207	95,497,800	70,136,614	25,361,186	16,999,221	8,361,965	5,459,530	2,902,435	13,366,407	88.7	77.8	57.1	20.7	13.8	6.8	10.9
GEOGRAPHIC DIVS.:																
New England	8,065,113	6,230,803	3,167,082	3,063,721	2,120,423	943,298	504,268	439,030	1,834,310	98.8	76.3	38.8	37.5	26.0	11.6	22.5
Middle Atlantic	25,172,104	19,903,062	11,449,898	8,453,164	6,254,301	2,198,863	1,428,629	770,234	5,269,042	95.9	75.8	43.6	32.2	23.8	8.4	20.1
E. North Central	24,277,663	21,053,739	14,500,575	6,553,164	4,370,186	2,182,978	1,460,208	722,770	3,223,924	96.0	83.2	57.3	25.9	17.3	8.6	12.7
W. North Central	12,873,487	11,814,210	8,547,483	3,266,727	1,946,472	1,320,255	913,029	407,226	1,059,277	96.8	88.8	64.3	24.6	14.6	9.9	8.0
South Atlantic	11,349,284	11,045,006	10,412,368	632,638	384,837	247,801	171,084	76,717	304,278	71.9	69.9	65.9	4.0	2.4	1.6	1.9
E. South Central	7,224,614	7,166,949	6,971,937	195,012	103,333	91,679	69,340	22,339	57,665	73.1	72.5	70.5	2.0	1.0	0.9	0.6
W. South Central	9,099,981	8,929,749	8,353,280	576,469	300,278	276,191	200,853	75,338	170,232	74.7	73.3	68.6	4.7	2.5	2.3	1.4
Mountain	3,303,586	3,015,672	2,300,255	715,417	401,071	314,346	201,261	113,085	287,914	89.2	81.5	62.1	19.3	10.8	8.5	7.8
Pacific	7,498,375	6,338,610	4,433,736	1,904,874	1,118,320	786,554	510,858	275,696	1,159,765	91.5	77.4	54.1	23.2	13.6	9.6	14.2
NEW ENGLAND:																
Maine	796,183	694,815	515,243	179,572	87,094	92,478	47,554	44,924	100,368	99.7	87.1	64.6	22.5	10.9	11.6	12.6
New Hampshire	464,350	381,690	239,438	142,252	83,791	58,461	30,094	28,367	82,660	99.8	82.0	51.5	30.6	18.0	12.6	17.8
Vermont	358,965	315,904	234,090	81,814	40,771	41,043	23,139	17,904	43,061	99.8	87.8	65.1	22.8	11.3	11.4	12.0
Massachusetts	4,192,920	3,138,290	1,429,784	1,708,506	1,202,191	506,315	262,748	243,567	1,054,636	98.7	73.8	33.6	40.2	28.3	11.9	24.8
Rhode Island	677,016	506,302	210,963	295,339	207,032	88,307	48,381	39,926	170,714	98.5	73.6	30.7	43.0	30.1	12.8	24.8
Connecticut	1,576,673	1,193,802	537,564	656,238	499,544	156,694	92,352	64,342	382,871	98.1	74.3	33.5	40.8	31.1	9.8	23.8
MID. ATLANTIC:																
New York	12,150,293	8,958,744	4,473,946	4,484,798	3,351,491	1,133,307	719,529	413,778	3,191,549	96.5	71.2	35.5	35.6	26.6	9.0	25.4
New Jersey	3,829,209	2,984,767	1,571,528	1,413,239	1,044,704	368,535	232,019	136,516	844,442	94.8	73.9	38.9	35.0	25.9	9.1	20.9
Pennsylvania	9,192,602	7,959,551	5,404,424	2,555,127	1,858,106	697,021	477,081	219,940	1,233,051	95.4	82.6	56.1	26.5	19.3	7.2	12.8
E. N. CENTRAL:																
Ohio	6,331,130	5,686,985	4,325,311	1,361,674	921,783	439,891	299,354	140,537	644,151	95.3	85.6	65.1	20.5	13.9	6.6	9.7
Indiana	3,116,136	2,981,002	2,605,744	375,258	225,153	150,105	105,704	44,401	135,134	96.2	92.0	80.5	11.6	7.0	4.6	4.2
Illinois	7,266,361	6,048,203	3,768,990	2,279,213	1,606,599	672,614	454,405	218,209	1,218,158	95.2	79.3	49.4	29.9	21.1	8.8	16.0
Michigan	4,650,171	3,809,903	2,364,038	1,445,865	917,856	528,009	332,802	195,207	840,268	96.0	78.7	48.8	29.9	19.0	10.9	17.4
Wisconsin	2,913,859	2,527,646	1,436,492	1,091,154	698,795	392,359	267,943	124,416	386,213	99.1	86.0	48.9	37.1	23.8	13.4	13.1
W. N. CENTRAL:																
Minnesota	2,538,973	2,150,679	1,114,316	1,036,363	655,750	380,613	259,767	120,846	388,294	99.0	83.9	43.5	40.4	25.6	14.8	15.1
Iowa	2,448,382	2,282,647	1,697,538	585,109	332,051	253,058	173,918	79,140	165,735	99.1	92.4	68.7	23.7	13.4	10.2	6.7
Missouri	3,398,887	3,249,497	2,776,338	473,159	272,240	200,919	147,151	53,768	149,390	93.6	89.5	76.5	13.0	7.5	5.5	4.1
North Dakota	671,243	566,095	256,622	309,473	193,107	116,366	78,394	37,972	105,148	98.6	83.1	37.7	45.5	28.4	17.1	15.4
South Dakota	669,453	603,805	375,378	228,427	132,497	95,930	64,935	30,995	65,648	96.6	87.1	54.2	33.0	19.1	13.8	9.5
Nebraska	1,353,702	1,238,356	873,849	364,507	216,227	148,280	101,592	46,688	115,346	98.2	89.9	63.4	26.5	15.7	10.8	8.4
Kansas	1,792,847	1,723,131	1,453,442	269,689	144,600	125,089	87,272	37,817	69,716	95.3	91.6	77.3	14.3	7.7	6.7	3.7
SOUTH ATLANTIC:																
Delaware	205,694	188,809	155,024	33,785	23,477	10,308	6,682	3,626	16,885	86.3	79.2	65.0	14.2	9.8	4.3	7.1
Maryland	1,354,170	1,259,077	1,039,796	219,281	144,418	74,863	49,991	24,872	95,093	83.0	77.2	63.7	13.4	8.9	4.6	5.8
Dist. Columbia	353,914	323,982	262,427	61,555	36,809	24,746	15,820	8,926	29,932	72.7	66.5	53.9	12.6	7.5	5.1	6.1
Virginia	1,770,405	1,746,585	1,692,703	53,882	28,552	25,330	17,916	7,414	23,820	73.1	72.1	69.9	2.2	1.2	1.0	1.0
West Virginia	1,613,934	1,562,414	1,461,544	100,870	66,854	34,016	25,729	8,287	51,520	93.3	90.4	84.5	5.8	3.9	2.0	3.0
North Carolina	2,234,948	2,226,160	2,208,563	17,597	7,919	9,678	6,907	2,771	8,788	70.5	70.2	69.7	0.6	0.2	0.3	0.3
South Carolina	944,040	938,774	925,439	13,335	6,477	6,858	5,174	1,684	5,266	54.3	54.0	53.2	0.8	0.4	0.4	0.3
Georgia	1,836,974	1,823,057	1,792,499	30,558	15,215	15,343	11,467	3,876	13,917	63.2	62.7	61.6	1.1	0.5	0.5	0.5
Florida	1,035,205	976,148	874,373	101,775	55,116	46,659	31,398	15,261	59,057	70.5	66.5	59.6	6.9	3.8	3.2	4.0
E. S. CENTRAL:																
Kentucky	2,388,364	2,366,524	2,269,540	96,984	54,320	42,664	31,435	11,229	21,840	91.3	90.5	86.8	3.7	2.1	1.6	0.8
Tennessee	2,138,619	2,125,553	2,087,383	38,170	19,303	18,867	14,199	4,668	13,066	81.7	81.2	79.8	1.5	0.7	0.7	0.5
Alabama	1,700,775	1,685,065	1,646,339	38,726	19,700	19,026	14,671	4,355	15,710	64.3	63.7	62.2	1.5	0.7	0.7	0.6
Mississippi	996,856	989,807	968,675	21,132	10,010	11,122	9,035	2,087	7,049	49.6	49.2	48.2	1.1	0.5	0.6	0.4
W. S. CENTRAL:																
Arkansas	1,374,906	1,364,733	1,329,205	35,528	16,130	19,398	14,660	4,738	10,173	74.1	73.6	71.7	1.9	0.9	1.0	0.5
Louisiana	1,318,160	1,283,250	1,172,572	110,678	61,797	48,881	38,847	10,034	34,910	62.7	61.1	55.8	5.3	2.9	2.3	1.7
Oklahoma	2,123,424	2,096,671	1,994,305	102,366	48,465	53,901	38,202	15,699	26,753	88.6	87.5	83.2	4.3	2.0	2.2	1.1
Texas	4,283,491	4,185,095	3,857,198	327,897	173,886	154,011	109,144	44,867	98,396	73.5	71.9	66.2	5.6	3.0	2.6	1.7
MOUNTAIN:																
Montana	517,327	444,366	283,539	160,827	94,580	66,247	43,197	23,050	72,961	96.2	82.7	52.7	29.9	17.6	12.3	13.6
Idaho	437,562	407,108	320,189	86,919	42,888	44,031	27,867	16,164	30,454	98.3	91.5	71.9	19.5	9.6	9.9	6.8
Wyoming	214,067	194,409	148,381	46,028	26,439	19,589	12,548	7,041	19,658	94.9	86.2	65.8	20.4	11.7	8.7	8.7
Colorado	961,117	875,711	669,106	206,605	125,631	80,974	55,146	25,828	85,406	92.8	84.5	64.6	19.9	12.1	7.8	8.2
New Mexico	331,755	323,958	302,753	21,205	10,741	10,464	7,281	3,183	7,797	78.4	76.5	71.5	5.0	2.5	2.5	1.8
Arizona	264,378	248,787	210,247	38,540	18,902	19,638	11,786	7,852	15,591	60.7	57.1	48.3	8.8	4.3	4.5	3.6
Utah	495,955	452,183	318,470	133,713	69,525	64,188	37,378	26,810	43,772	97.7	89.0	62.7	26.3	13.7	12.6	8.6
Nevada	81,425	69,150	47,570	21,580	12,365	9,215	6,058	3,157	12,275	89.4	75.9	52.2	23.7	13.6	10.1	13.5
PACIFIC:																
Washington	1,521,099	1,276,843	873,627	403,216	229,063	174,153	110,782	63,371	244,256	97.3	81.7	55.9	25.8	14.7	11.1	15.6
Oregon	937,029	831,554	629,974	201,580	108,797	92,783	60,841	31,942	105,475	98.2	87.2	66.0	21.1	11.4	9.7	11.1
California	5,040,247	4,230,213	2,930,135	1,300,078	780,460	519,618	339,235	180,383	810,034	88.8	74.5	51.6	22.9	13.7	9.2	14.3

COLOR OR RACE, NATIVITY, AND PARENTAGE

TABLE 13.—PER CENT DISTRIBUTION OF POPULATION BY COLOR, NATIVITY, AND PARENTAGE, BY DIVISIONS AND STATES: 1900 TO 1930

[Percentages for native whites of foreign or mixed parentage, and for foreign-born whites, are based on figures adjusted for Mexicans, as presented for 1920 and 1910 in Table 16. "Other races" for 1920 and 1910 include estimated number of Mexicans. Per cent not shown where less than 0.1]

DIVISION AND STATE	NATIVE WHITE—NATIVE PARENTAGE				NATIVE WHITE—FOREIGN OR MIXED PARENTAGE				FOREIGN-BORN WHITE				NEGRO				OTHER RACES			
	1930	1920	1910	1900	1930	1920	1910	1900	1930	1920	1910	1900	1930	1920	1910	1900	1930	1920	1910	1900
United States	57.1	55.3	53.8	53.9	20.7	21.2	20.4	20.6	10.9	12.5	14.3	13.4	9.7	9.9	10.7	11.6	1.6	1.1	0.8	0.5
GEOGRAPHIC DIVISIONS:																				
New England	38.8	37.9	39.9	44.9	37.5	35.7	31.3	28.2	22.5	25.3	27.7	25.7	1.2	1.1	1.0	1.1	0.1	0.1	0.1	0.1
Middle Atlantic	43.6	43.3	43.8	47.9	32.2	31.9	28.9	28.5	20.1	22.1	25.0	21.4	4.0	2.7	2.2	2.1	0.1	0.1	0.1	0.1
East North Central	57.3	54.9	53.4	53.1	25.9	27.6	28.0	28.8	12.7	15.0	16.8	16.4	3.7	2.4	1.6	1.6	0.4	0.1	0.1	0.1
West North Central	64.3	59.6	56.1	54.7	24.6	26.9	27.6	27.8	8.0	10.8	13.8	14.8	2.5	2.2	2.1	2.3	0.7	0.5	0.5	0.4
South Atlantic	65.9	62.8	60.2	58.5	4.0	4.0	3.6	3.7	1.9	2.3	2.4	2.0	28.0	30.9	33.7	35.7	0.1	0.1	0.1	0.1
East South Central	70.5	68.5	64.8	62.6	2.0	2.3	2.6	3.0	0.6	0.8	1.0	1.2	26.9	28.4	31.5	33.1				
West South Central	68.6	68.0	65.7	61.7	4.7	5.4	5.7	7.3	1.4	2.0	2.6	4.0	18.7	20.1	22.6	25.9	6.5	4.5	3.5	1.0
Mountain	62.1	60.0	55.7	51.1	19.3	21.2	22.2	26.1	7.8	10.8	14.9	17.2	0.8	0.9	0.8	0.9	9.9	7.0	6.3	4.7
Pacific	54.1	51.9	50.3	48.2	23.2	25.0	24.7	27.1	14.2	17.1	19.8	19.0	1.1	0.9	0.7	0.6	7.4	5.2	4.5	4.5
NEW ENGLAND:																				
Maine	64.6	64.6	66.7	71.0	22.5	21.2	18.2	15.3	12.0	14.0	14.8	13.4	0.1	0.2	0.2	0.2	0.1	0.1	0.1	0.1
New Hampshire	51.5	50.9	53.5	58.9	30.6	28.3	23.9	19.5	17.8	20.6	22.4	21.4	0.2	0.1	0.1	0.2				
Vermont	65.1	64.8	64.4	65.6	22.8	22.4	21.1	21.2	12.0	12.6	14.0	13.0	0.2	0.2	0.5	0.2				
Massachusetts	33.6	31.9	32.8	36.8	40.2	38.8	34.8	32.0	24.8	28.0	31.2	29.0	1.2	1.2	1.1	1.1	0.1	0.1	0.1	0.1
Rhode Island	30.7	28.7	29.5	33.8	43.0	40.9	35.9	32.7	24.8	28.7	32.8	31.2	1.4	1.7	1.8	2.1	0.1	0.1	0.1	0.1
Connecticut	33.5	32.5	35.5	41.0	40.8	38.6	33.6	31.1	23.8	27.3	29.5	26.1	1.8	1.5	1.4	1.7	0.1	0.1	0.1	0.1
MIDDLE ATLANTIC:																				
New York	35.5	35.3	35.4	39.2	35.6	35.8	33.0	33.2	25.4	26.8	29.0	26.0	3.3	1.9	1.5	1.4	0.2	0.2	0.1	0.2
New Jersey	38.9	38.4	39.8	43.8	35.0	34.4	30.7	29.5	20.9	23.4	25.9	22.8	5.2	3.7	3.5	3.7	0.1	0.1	0.1	0.1
Pennsylvania	56.1	54.5	55.1	59.2	26.5	26.3	23.6	22.7	12.8	15.9	18.8	15.6	4.5	3.3	2.5	2.5	0.1			0.1
EAST NORTH CENTRAL:																				
Ohio	65.1	63.7	63.6	63.8	20.5	21.3	21.5	22.9	9.7	11.8	12.5	11.0	4.7	3.2	2.3	2.3	0.1			
Indiana	80.5	79.5	78.9	77.6	11.6	12.6	13.0	14.5	4.2	5.1	5.9	5.6	3.5	2.8	2.2	2.3	0.3			
Illinois	49.4	47.3	46.1	47.1	29.9	31.2	30.6	31.1	16.0	18.6	21.3	20.0	4.3	2.8	1.9	1.8	0.5	0.1	0.1	
Michigan	48.8	45.5	43.0	42.4	29.0	32.8	34.3	34.4	17.4	19.8	21.2	22.3	3.5	1.6	0.6	0.7	0.5	0.2	0.3	0.3
Wisconsin	48.9	40.1	32.7	28.3	37.1	41.9	44.8	46.2	13.1	17.5	22.0	24.9	0.4	0.2	0.1	0.1	0.5	0.4	0.4	0.4
WEST NORTH CENTRAL:																				
Minnesota	43.5	34.7	27.7	24.3	40.4	44.2	45.3	46.0	15.1	20.4	26.2	28.8	0.4	0.4	0.3	0.3	0.6	0.4	0.5	0.5
Iowa	68.7	63.6	58.6	56.5	23.7	26.2	28.4	29.2	6.7	9.3	12.3	13.7	0.7	0.8	0.7	0.6	0.2	0.2	0.1	
Missouri	76.5	74.5	72.5	71.0	13.0	14.7	15.7	16.0	4.1	5.4	6.9	6.9	6.2	5.2	4.8	5.2	0.2	0.1	0.1	
North Dakota	37.7	32.1	28.2	20.6	45.5	46.4	43.5	41.8	15.4	20.3	27.1	35.3	0.1	0.1	0.1	0.1	1.4	1.0	1.1	2.2
South Dakota	54.2	48.5	42.1	33.9	33.0	35.8	37.2	38.9	9.5	12.9	17.2	22.0	0.1	0.1	0.1	0.1	3.3	2.6	3.8	5.1
Nebraska	63.4	58.4	53.9	51.9	20.5	28.7	30.4	30.6	8.4	11.4	14.7	16.6	1.0	1.0	0.6	0.6	0.8	0.5	0.4	0.3
Kansas	77.3	74.0	71.4	68.9	14.3	16.2	17.3	18.8	3.7	5.5	7.5	8.6	3.5	3.3	3.2	3.5	1.2	1.1	0.6	0.1
SOUTH ATLANTIC:																				
Delaware	65.0	62.7	63.2	63.9	14.2	14.8	12.8	12.0	7.1	8.0	8.6	7.4	13.7	13.6	15.4	16.6				
Maryland	63.7	61.6	59.2	57.2	13.4	14.4	14.8	15.1	5.8	7.0	8.0	7.8	16.9	16.9	17.9	19.8	0.1			
Dist. of Columbia	53.9	54.7	50.4	48.1	12.6	13.4	13.6	13.6	6.1	6.5	7.4	7.0	27.1	25.1	28.5	31.1	0.2	0.2	0.2	0.2
Virginia	69.9	66.5	64.3	61.5	2.2	2.3	1.8	1.8	1.0	1.3	1.3	1.0	26.8	29.9	32.6	35.6	0.1	0.1		
West Virginia	84.5	84.2	85.3	88.0	5.8	5.6	4.7	5.1	3.0	4.2	4.7	2.3	6.6	5.0	5.3	4.5				
North Carolina	69.7	69.0	67.3	66.0	0.6	0.4	0.4	0.4	0.3	0.3	0.3	0.2	29.0	29.8	31.6	33.0	0.5	0.5	0.4	0.3
South Carolina	53.2	47.5	43.7	40.3	0.8	0.8	0.7	0.9	0.3	0.4	0.4	0.4	45.6	51.4	55.2	58.4	0.1			
Georgia	61.6	50.7	53.3	51.6	1.1	1.0	1.0	1.1	0.5	0.6	0.6	0.5	36.8	41.7	45.1	46.7				
Florida	59.6	55.0	49.7	48.1	6.9	6.5	4.8	4.5	4.0	4.4	4.5	3.6	29.4	34.0	41.0	43.7	0.1	0.1	0.1	0.1
EAST SOUTH CENTRAL:																				
Kentucky	86.8	84.4	81.4	77.9	3.7	4.6	5.4	6.5	0.8	1.3	1.7	2.3	8.6	9.8	11.4	13.3				
Tennessee	79.8	78.4	75.7	73.3	1.5	1.6	1.8	2.0	0.5	0.7	0.8	0.9	18.3	19.3	21.7	23.8				
Alabama	62.2	59.4	55.1	52.3	1.5	1.5	1.5	1.6	0.6	0.8	0.9	0.8	35.7	38.4	42.5	45.2				
Mississippi	48.2	46.2	42.1	39.6	1.1	1.1	1.1	1.3	0.4	0.4	0.5	0.5	50.2	52.2	56.2	58.5	0.2	0.1	0.1	0.2
WEST SOUTH CENTRAL:																				
Arkansas	71.7	70.0	68.4	68.4	1.9	2.2	2.3	2.5	0.5	0.8	1.1	1.1	25.8	27.0	28.1	28.0	0.1			
Louisiana	55.8	52.4	46.9	41.3	5.3	6.1	6.8	7.8	1.7	2.4	3.1	3.8	36.9	38.9	43.1	47.1	0.3	0.2	0.2	0.1
Oklahoma	83.2	82.8	79.1	76.1	4.3	5.0	5.6	6.1	1.1	1.7	2.3	2.6	7.2	7.4	8.3	7.0	4.2	3.2	4.7	8.2
Texas	66.2	66.7	66.8	64.3	5.6	6.4	6.6	9.5	1.7	2.5	3.1	5.8	14.7	15.9	17.7	20.4	11.8	8.4	5.9	
MOUNTAIN:																				
Montana	52.7	50.2	43.1	38.2	29.9	30.0	28.4	29.2	13.6	17.0	24.4	25.6	0.2	0.3	0.5	0.6	3.5	2.4	3.7	6.4
Idaho	71.9	68.1	62.5	55.5	19.5	21.4	23.1	26.4	6.8	8.8	12.4	13.5	0.2	0.2	0.2	0.2	1.5	1.5	1.8	4.3
Wyoming	65.8	63.2	55.3	51.9	20.4	21.5	22.2	26.5	8.7	12.1	18.5	17.9	0.6	0.7	1.5	1.0	4.5	2.5	2.6	2.7
Colorado	64.6	64.2	59.5	57.7	19.9	21.3	22.6	23.6	8.2	11.3	15.6	16.8	1.1	1.2	1.4	1.6	6.1	2.0	1.0	
New Mexico	71.5	75.8	79.1	76.3	5.0	5.1	5.1	9.2	1.8	2.8	3.4	6.8	0.7	1.6	0.5	0.8	21.0	14.6	12.9	6.9
Arizona	48.3	45.2	40.4	36.5	8.8	9.5	10.5	20.9	3.6	6.0	9.1	18.2	2.5	2.4	1.0	1.5	36.8	36.9	39.1	22.9
Utah	62.7	54.7	46.0	37.6	26.3	31.0	35.2	41.8	8.6	12.4	16.9	19.1	0.2	0.3	0.3	0.2	2.1	1.6	1.5	1.3
Nevada	52.2	46.9	43.1	35.7	23.7	25.1	25.4	27.7	13.5	17.7	21.1	20.3	0.6	0.4	0.6	0.3	10.0	9.9	9.7	16.1
PACIFIC:																				
Washington	55.9	52.5	51.3	51.2	25.8	26.4	24.7	24.9	15.6	18.4	21.1	19.7	0.4	0.5	0.5	0.5	2.3	2.2	2.4	3.7
Oregon	66.0	63.5	62.0	61.9	21.1	21.6	20.1	20.5	11.1	13.0	15.3	13.0	0.2	0.3	0.2	0.8	1.5	1.6	2.4	4.3
California	51.6	49.0	46.5	43.4	22.9	25.3	26.0	20.7	14.3	17.5	20.4	21.3	1.4	1.1	0.9	0.7	9.8	7.1	6.1	4.8

POPULATION

38

TABLE 14.—WHITE AND NEGRO POPULATION, 1930 AND 1920, AND PER CENT NEGRO, 1850 TO 1930, BY DIVISIONS AND STATES

[Figures for white in 1920 are as reported, and not adjusted for Mexicans]

DIVISION AND STATE	1930 Total population	1930 White	1930 Negro	1920 Total population	1920 White	1920 Negro	1930	1920	1910	1900	1890	1880	1870	1860	1850
United States	122,775,046	108,864,207	11,891,143	105,710,620	94,820,915	10,463,131	9.7	9.9	10.7	11.6	11.9	13.1	12.7	14.1	15.7
GEOGRAPHIC DIVISIONS:															
New England	8,166,341	8,065,113	94,086	7,400,909	7,316,079	79,051	1.2	1.1	1.0	1.1	0.9	1.0	0.9	0.8	0.8
Middle Atlantic	26,260,750	25,172,104	1,052,899	22,261,144	21,641,840	600,183	4.0	2.7	2.2	2.1	1.8	1.8	1.7	1.8	2.1
East North Central	25,297,185	24,277,663	930,450	21,475,543	20,938,862	514,554	3.7	2.4	1.6	1.6	1.5	1.6	1.4	0.9	1.0
West North Central	13,296,915	12,873,487	331,784	12,544,249	12,225,387	278,521	2.5	2.2	2.1	2.3	2.5	3.3	3.7	5.6	10.3
South Atlantic	15,793,589	11,349,284	4,421,388	13,990,272	9,648,940	4,325,120	28.0	30.9	33.7	35.7	36.8	38.7	37.9	38.4	39.8
East South Central	9,887,214	7,224,614	2,658,238	8,893,307	6,367,547	2,523,532	26.9	28.4	31.5	33.1	33.0	34.5	33.2	34.7	33.4
West South Central	12,176,830	9,099,981	2,281,951	10,242,224	8,115,727	2,063,579	18.7	20.1	22.6	25.9	29.1	32.6	36.4	36.9	39.2
Mountain	3,701,789	3,303,586	30,225	3,336,101	3,212,899	30,801	0.8	0.9	0.8	0.9	1.1	0.8	0.5	0.1	0.1
Pacific	8,194,433	7,498,375	90,122	5,566,871	5,353,634	47,790	1.1	0.9	0.7	0.6	0.7	0.6	0.7	1.0	1.1
NEW ENGLAND:															
Maine	797,423	795,183	1,096	768,014	765,695	1,310	0.1	0.2	0.2	0.2	0.2	0.2	0.3	0.2	0.2
New Hampshire	465,293	464,350	790	443,083	442,331	621	0.2	0.1	0.1	0.2	0.2	0.2	0.2	0.2	0.2
Vermont	359,611	358,965	568	352,428	351,817	572	0.2	0.2	0.5	0.2	0.3	0.3	0.3	0.2	0.2
Massachusetts	4,249,614	4,192,926	52,365	3,852,356	3,803,524	45,466	1.2	1.2	1.1	1.1	1.0	1.0	1.0	0.8	0.9
Rhode Island	687,497	677,016	9,913	604,397	593,980	10,036	1.4	1.7	1.8	2.1	2.1	2.3	2.3	2.3	2.5
Connecticut	1,606,903	1,576,673	29,354	1,380,631	1,358,732	21,046	1.8	1.5	1.4	1.7	1.6	1.9	1.8	1.9	2.1
MIDDLE ATLANTIC:															
New York	12,588,066	12,150,293	412,814	10,385,227	10,172,027	198,483	3.3	1.9	1.5	1.4	1.2	1.3	1.2	1.3	1.6
New Jersey	4,041,334	3,829,209	208,828	3,155,900	3,037,087	117,132	5.2	3.7	3.5	3.7	3.3	3.4	3.4	3.8	4.9
Pennsylvania	9,631,350	9,192,602	431,257	8,720,017	8,432,726	284,568	4.5	3.3	2.5	2.5	2.0	2.0	1.9	2.0	2.3
EAST NORTH CENTRAL:															
Ohio	6,646,697	6,331,136	309,304	5,759,394	5,571,893	186,187	4.7	3.2	2.3	2.3	2.4	2.5	2.4	1.6	1.3
Indiana	3,238,503	3,116,136	111,982	2,930,390	2,849,071	80,810	3.5	2.8	2.2	2.3	2.1	2.0	1.5	0.9	1.1
Illinois	7,630,654	7,266,361	328,972	6,485,280	6,299,333	182,274	4.3	2.8	1.9	1.8	1.5	1.5	1.1	0.5	0.6
Michigan	4,842,325	4,650,171	169,453	3,668,412	3,601,627	60,082	3.5	1.6	0.6	0.7	0.7	0.9	1.0	0.7	0.7
Wisconsin	2,939,006	2,913,859	10,739	2,632,067	2,616,938	5,201	0.4	0.2	0.1	0.1	0.1	0.2	0.2	0.2	0.2
WEST NORTH CENTRAL:															
Minnesota	2,563,953	2,538,973	9,445	2,387,125	2,368,936	8,809	0.4	0.4	0.3	0.3	0.3	0.2	0.2	0.2	0.6
Iowa	2,470,939	2,448,382	17,380	2,404,021	2,384,181	19,005	0.7	0.8	0.7	0.6	0.6	0.6	0.5	0.2	0.2
Missouri	3,629,367	3,398,887	223,840	3,404,055	3,225,044	178,241	6.2	5.2	4.8	5.2	5.6	6.7	6.9	10.0	13.2
North Dakota	680,845	671,243	377	646,872	639,954	467	0.1	0.1	0.1	0.1	0.2	0.3	0.7	------	------
South Dakota	692,849	669,453	646	636,547	619,147	832	0.1	0.1	0.1	0.1	0.2	0.3		------	------
Nebraska	1,377,963	1,353,702	13,752	1,296,372	1,279,219	13,242	1.0	1.0	0.6	0.6	0.8	0.5	0.6	0.3	------
Kansas	1,880,999	1,792,847	66,344	1,769,257	1,708,906	57,925	3.5	3.3	3.2	3.5	3.5	4.3	4.7	0.6	------
SOUTH ATLANTIC:															
Delaware	238,380	205,694	32,602	223,003	192,615	30,335	13.7	13.6	15.4	16.6	16.8	18.0	18.2	19.3	22.3
Maryland	1,631,526	1,354,170	276,379	1,449,661	1,204,737	244,479	16.9	16.9	17.9	19.8	20.7	22.5	22.5	24.9	28.3
District of Columbia	486,869	353,914	132,068	437,571	326,860	109,966	27.1	25.1	28.5	31.1	32.8	33.6	33.0	19.1	26.6
Virginia	2,421,851	1,770,405	650,165	2,309,187	1,617,909	690,017	26.8	29.9	32.6	35.6	38.4	41.8	41.9	34.4	37.1
West Virginia	1,729,205	1,613,934	114,893	1,463,701	1,377,235	86,345	6.6	5.9	5.3	4.5	4.3	4.2	4.1		
North Carolina	3,170,276	2,234,948	918,647	2,559,123	1,783,779	763,407	29.0	29.8	31.6	33.0	34.7	38.0	36.6	36.4	36.4
South Carolina	1,738,765	944,040	793,681	1,683,724	818,538	864,719	45.6	51.4	55.2	58.4	59.8	60.7	58.9	58.6	58.9
Georgia	2,908,506	1,836,974	1,071,125	2,895,832	1,689,114	1,206,365	36.8	41.7	45.1	46.7	46.7	47.0	46.0	44.1	42.4
Florida	1,468,211	1,035,205	431,828	968,470	638,153	329,487	29.4	34.0	41.0	43.7	42.5	47.0	48.8	44.6	46.0
EAST SOUTH CENTRAL:															
Kentucky	2,614,589	2,388,364	226,040	2,416,630	2,180,560	235,938	8.6	9.8	11.4	13.3	14.4	16.5	16.8	20.4	22.5
Tennessee	2,616,556	2,138,619	477,646	2,337,885	1,885,993	451,758	18.3	19.3	21.7	23.8	24.4	26.1	25.6	25.5	24.5
Alabama	2,646,248	1,700,775	944,834	2,348,174	1,447,032	900,652	35.7	38.4	42.5	45.2	44.8	47.5	47.7	45.4	44.7
Mississippi	2,009,821	996,856	1,009,718	1,790,618	853,962	935,184	50.2	52.2	56.2	58.5	57.6	57.5	53.7	55.3	51.2
WEST SOUTH CENTRAL:															
Arkansas	1,854,482	1,374,900	478,463	1,752,204	1,270,757	472,220	25.8	27.0	28.1	28.0	27.4	26.3	25.2	25.6	22.7
Louisiana	2,101,593	1,318,160	776,326	1,798,509	1,096,611	700,257	36.9	38.9	43.1	47.1	50.0	51.5	50.1	49.5	50.7
Oklahoma	2,396,040	2,123,424	172,198	2,028,283	1,821,194	149,408	7.2	7.4	8.3	7.0	8.4	------	------	------	------
Texas	5,824,715	4,283,491	854,964	4,663,228	3,918,165	741,694	14.7	15.9	17.7	20.4	21.8	24.7	31.0	30.3	27.5
MOUNTAIN:															
Montana	537,606	517,327	1,256	548,889	534,260	1,658	0.2	0.3	0.5	0.6	1.0	0.9	0.9	------	------
Idaho	445,032	437,562	668	431,866	425,668	920	0.2	0.2	0.2	0.2	0.2	0.2	0.4	------	------
Wyoming	225,565	214,067	1,250	194,402	190,146	1,375	0.6	0.7	1.5	1.0	1.5	1.4	2.0	------	------
Colorado	1,035,791	961,117	11,828	939,629	924,103	11,318	1.1	1.2	1.4	1.6	1.5	1.3	1.1	0.1	------
New Mexico	423,317	331,755	2,850	360,350	334,673	5,733	0.7	1.6	0.5	0.8	1.2	0.8	0.2	0.1	------
Arizona	435,573	264,378	10,749	334,162	291,449	8,005	2.5	2.4	1.0	1.5	1.5	0.4	0.3	------	------
Utah	507,847	495,955	1,108	449,396	441,901	1,446	0.2	0.3	0.3	0.2	0.3	0.2	0.1	0.2	0.4
Nevada	91,058	81,425	516	77,407	70,699	346	0.6	0.4	0.6	0.3	0.5	0.8	0.7	------	------
PACIFIC:															
Washington	1,563,396	1,521,099	6,840	1,356,621	1,319,777	6,883	0.4	0.5	0.5	0.5	0.4	0.4	0.9	0.3	------
Oregon	953,786	937,029	2,234	783,389	769,146	2,144	0.2	0.3	0.2	0.3	0.4	0.3	0.4	0.2	1.6
California	5,677,251	5,040,247	81,048	3,426,861	3,264,711	38,763	1.4	1.1	0.9	0.7	0.9	0.7	0.8	1.1	1.0

COLOR OR RACE, NATIVITY, AND PARENTAGE

TABLE 15.—NATIVE AND FOREIGN-BORN POPULATION, 1930 AND 1920, AND PER CENT FOREIGN BORN, 1850 TO 1930, BY DIVISIONS AND STATES

DIVISION AND STATE	1930 Total population	1930 Native population	1930 Foreign-born population	1920 Total population	1920 Native population	1920 Foreign-born population	PER CENT FOREIGN BORN IN TOTAL POPULATION 1930	1920	1910	1900	1890	1880	1870	1860	1850
United States	122,775,046	108,570,897	14,204,149	105,710,620	91,789,928	13,920,692	11.6	13.2	14.7	13.6	14.7	13.3	14.4	13.2	9.7
GEOGRAPHIC DIVISIONS:															
New England	8,166,341	6,317,398	1,848,943	7,400,909	5,514,964	1,885,945	22.6	25.5	27.9	25.8	24.3	19.8	18.6	15.0	11.2
Middle Atlantic	26,260,750	20,908,019	5,352,731	22,261,144	17,300,726	4,960,418	20.4	22.3	25.1	21.5	21.6	19.3	21.3	20.8	17.3
East North Central	25,297,185	22,021,462	3,275,723	21,475,543	18,243,402	3,232,141	12.9	15.1	16.8	16.4	18.6	17.1	18.2	17.3	12.2
West North Central	13,296,915	12,212,762	1,084,153	12,544,249	11,169,596	1,375,053	8.2	11.0	13.0	14.8	17.3	16.2	17.4	16.0	11.3
South Atlantic	15,793,589	15,474,892	318,697	13,990,272	13,659,735	330,537	2.0	2.4	2.5	2.1	2.4	2.3	2.9	3.0	2.2
East South Central	9,887,214	9,827,850	59,364	8,893,307	8,820,318	72,989	0.6	0.8	1.0	1.2	1.6	1.7	2.4	2.5	1.5
West South Central	12,176,830	11,736,277	440,553	10,242,224	9,777,396	464,828	3.6	4.5	4.0	4.1	4.6	5.4	6.4	7.3	9.3
Mountain	3,701,789	3,317,466	384,323	3,336,101	2,868,481	467,620	10.4	14.0	17.2	18.0	21.2	24.6	27.6	13.8	5.8
Pacific	8,194,433	6,754,771	1,439,662	5,566,871	4,436,310	1,130,561	17.6	20.3	22.8	22.5	27.2	30.4	33.5	34.0	21.6
NEW ENGLAND:															
Maine	797,423	696,695	100,728	768,014	660,200	107,814	12.6	14.0	14.9	13.4	11.9	9.1	7.8	6.0	5.5
New Hampshire	465,293	382,364	82,929	443,083	351,686	91,397	17.8	20.6	22.5	21.4	19.2	13.3	9.8	6.4	4.5
Vermont	359,611	316,510	43,101	352,428	307,870	44,558	12.0	12.6	14.0	13.0	13.3	12.3	14.3	10.4	10.7
Massachusetts	4,249,614	3,183,994	1,065,620	3,852,356	2,763,808	1,088,548	25.1	28.3	31.5	30.2	29.4	24.9	24.2	21.1	16.5
Rhode Island	687,497	515,568	171,929	604,397	429,208	175,189	25.0	29.0	33.0	31.4	30.8	26.8	25.5	21.4	16.2
Connecticut	1,606,903	1,222,207	384,636	1,380,631	1,002,192	378,439	23.0	27.4	29.6	26.2	24.6	20.9	21.1	17.5	10.4
MIDDLE ATLANTIC:															
New York	12,588,066	9,325,788	3,262,278	10,385,227	7,559,852	2,825,375	25.9	27.2	30.2	26.1	26.2	23.8	26.0	25.8	21.2
New Jersey	4,041,334	3,191,296	850,038	3,155,900	2,413,414	742,486	21.0	23.5	26.0	22.9	22.8	19.6	20.9	18.3	12.2
Pennsylvania	9,631,350	8,390,935	1,240,415	8,720,017	7,327,460	1,392,557	12.9	16.0	18.8	15.6	16.1	13.7	15.5	14.8	13.1
EAST NORTH CENTRAL:															
Ohio	6,646,697	5,997,477	649,220	5,759,394	5,078,942	680,452	9.8	11.8	12.6	11.0	12.5	12.3	14.0	14.0	11.0
Indiana	3,238,503	3,095,504	142,999	2,930,390	2,779,062	151,328	4.4	5.2	5.9	6.7	7.3	8.4	8.8	8.6	5.6
Illinois	7,630,654	6,388,207	1,242,447	6,485,280	5,274,696	1,210,584	16.3	18.7	21.4	20.1	22.0	19.0	20.3	19.0	13.1
Michigan	4,842,325	3,989,567	852,758	3,668,412	2,939,120	729,292	17.6	19.9	21.3	22.4	26.0	23.7	22.6	19.9	13.8
Wisconsin	2,939,006	2,550,707	388,299	2,632,067	2,171,582	460,485	13.2	17.5	22.0	24.9	30.7	30.8	34.6	35.7	36.2
WEST NORTH CENTRAL:															
Minnesota	2,563,953	2,173,163	390,790	2,387,125	1,900,330	486,795	15.2	20.4	26.2	28.9	35.7	34.3	36.5	34.1	32.5
Iowa	2,470,939	2,302,689	168,250	2,404,021	2,178,027	225,994	6.8	9.4	12.3	13.7	16.9	16.1	17.1	15.7	10.9
Missouri	3,629,367	3,476,282	153,085	3,404,055	3,217,220	186,835	4.2	5.5	7.0	7.0	8.8	9.8	12.9	13.6	11.2
North Dakota	680,845	574,974	105,871	646,872	515,009	131,863	15.5	20.4	27.1	35.4	42.7	49.4	......	......	......
South Dakota	692,849	626,788	66,061	636,547	554,013	82,534	9.5	13.0	17.3	22.0	26.1	34.2	84.0	36.7	......
Nebraska	1,377,963	1,258,764	119,199	1,296,372	1,145,707	150,665	8.7	11.6	14.8	16.6	19.1	21.5	25.0	22.0	......
Kansas	1,880,999	1,800,102	80,897	1,769,257	1,658,290	110,967	4.3	6.3	8.0	8.6	10.4	11.1	13.3	11.8	......
SOUTH ATLANTIC:															
Delaware	238,380	221,355	17,025	223,003	203,102	19,901	7.1	8.9	8.6	7.5	7.8	6.5	7.3	8.2	5.7
Maryland	1,631,526	1,535,196	96,330	1,449,661	1,346,482	103,179	5.9	7.1	8.1	7.9	9.0	8.9	10.7	11.3	8.7
District of Columbia	486,869	456,136	30,733	437,571	408,206	29,365	6.3	6.7	7.5	7.2	8.1	9.6	12.3	16.6	9.5
Virginia	2,421,851	2,397,484	24,367	2,309,187	2,277,482	31,705	1.0	1.4	1.3	1.0	1.1	1.0	1.1	2.2	1.6
West Virginia	1,729,205	1,677,340	51,865	1,463,701	1,401,596	62,105	3.0	4.2	4.7	2.3	2.5	3.0	3.9	2.2	1.6
North Carolina	3,170,276	3,161,307	8,969	2,559,123	2,551,851	7,272	0.3	0.3	0.3	0.2	0.2	0.3	0.3	0.3	0.3
South Carolina	1,738,765	1,733,407	5,358	1,683,724	1,677,142	6,582	0.3	0.4	0.4	0.4	0.5	0.8	1.1	1.4	1.3
Georgia	2,908,506	2,894,203	14,303	2,895,832	2,879,268	16,564	0.5	0.6	0.6	0.6	0.7	0.7	0.9	1.1	0.7
Florida	1,468,211	1,398,464	69,747	968,470	914,606	53,864	4.8	5.6	5.4	4.5	5.9	3.7	2.6	2.4	8.2
EAST SOUTH CENTRAL:															
Kentucky	2,614,589	2,592,582	22,007	2,416,630	2,385,724	30,906	0.8	1.3	1.8	2.3	3.2	3.6	4.8	5.2	3.2
Tennessee	2,616,556	2,603,305	13,251	2,337,885	2,322,237	15,648	0.5	0.7	0.9	0.9	1.1	1.1	1.5	1.9	0.6
Alabama	2,646,248	2,630,187	16,061	2,348,174	2,330,147	18,027	0.6	0.8	0.9	0.8	1.0	0.8	1.0	1.3	1.0
Mississippi	2,009,821	2,001,776	8,045	1,790,618	1,782,210	8,408	0.4	0.5	0.5	0.5	0.6	0.8	1.4	1.1	0.8
WEST SOUTH CENTRAL:															
Arkansas	1,854,482	1,843,850	10,632	1,752,204	1,738,067	14,137	0.6	0.8	1.1	1.1	1.3	1.3	1.0	0.8	0.7
Louisiana	2,101,593	2,064,517	37,076	1,798,509	1,752,082	46,427	1.8	2.6	3.2	3.8	4.4	5.8	8.5	11.4	13.2
Oklahoma	2,396,040	2,365,482	30,558	2,028,283	1,987,851	40,432	1.3	2.0	2.4	2.6	1.1	......	......	......	......
Texas	5,824,715	5,462,428	362,287	4,663,228	4,299,396	363,832	6.2	7.8	6.2	5.9	6.8	7.2	7.6	7.2	8.3
MOUNTAIN:															
Montana	537,606	461,703	75,903	548,889	453,298	95,591	14.1	17.4	25.2	27.6	30.2	29.4	38.7	......	......
Idaho	445,032	412,748	32,284	431,866	391,119	40,747	7.3	9.4	13.1	15.2	19.7	30.6	52.6	......	......
Wyoming	225,565	202,222	23,343	194,402	167,835	26,567	10.3	13.7	19.9	18.8	23.8	28.1	38.5	......	......
Colorado	1,035,791	935,916	99,875	939,629	820,491	119,138	9.6	12.7	16.2	16.9	20.3	20.5	16.8	7.8	......
New Mexico	423,317	399,265	24,052	360,350	330,542	29,808	5.7	8.3	7.1	7.0	7.0	6.7	6.1	7.2	3.5
Arizona	435,573	369,817	65,756	334,162	253,596	80,566	15.1	24.1	23.9	19.7	21.3	39.7	60.1	......	......
Utah	507,847	459,832	48,015	449,396	390,196	59,200	9.5	13.2	17.6	19.4	25.2	30.6	35.4	31.7	18.0
Nevada	91,058	75,963	15,095	77,407	61,404	16,003	16.6	20.7	24.1	23.8	31.1	41.2	44.2	30.1	......
PACIFIC:															
Washington	1,563,396	1,308,138	255,258	1,356,621	1,091,329	265,292	16.3	19.6	22.4	21.5	25.2	21.0	21.0	27.1	......
Oregon	953,786	843,346	110,440	783,389	675,745	107,644	11.6	13.7	16.8	15.9	18.0	17.5	12.8	9.8	7.7
California	5,677,251	4,603,287	1,073,964	3,426,861	2,669,236	757,625	18.9	22.1	24.7	24.7	30.2	33.9	37.5	38.6	23.5

40

POPULATION

TABLE 16.—NATIVE WHITE POPULATION OF MIXED PARENTAGE, BY NATIVITY OF FATHER AND MOTHER, BY DIVISIONS AND STATES: 1890 TO 1930

[Figures for 1920 and 1910 are not adjusted for Mexicans]

DIVISION AND STATE	TOTAL NATIVE WHITE OF MIXED PARENTAGE					FATHER FOREIGN					MOTHER FOREIGN				
	1930	1920	1910	1900	1890	1930	1920	1910	1900	1890	1930	1920	1910	1900	1890
United States	8,361,965	6,991,665	5,981,526	5,013,737	3,418,656	5,459,530	4,539,776	3,923,845	3,346,652	2,378,729	2,902,435	2,451,889	2,057,681	1,667,085	1,039,927
GEOGRAPHIC DIVS.:															
New England	943,298	735,936	592,144	461,951	279,870	504,268	381,769	310,671	245,247	160,382	439,030	354,167	281,473	216,704	119,488
Middle Atlantic	2,198,863	1,700,302	1,478,236	1,250,146	904,598	1,428,629	1,074,872	939,065	819,768	617,957	770,234	625,430	539,171	430,378	286,641
E. North Central	2,182,978	1,881,521	1,658,419	1,490,956	1,033,987	1,460,208	1,254,710	1,116,883	1,020,403	733,175	722,770	626,811	541,536	470,553	300,812
W. North Central	1,320,255	1,251,752	1,112,000	940,692	641,635	913,029	859,007	767,346	653,667	460,904	407,226	392,745	344,654	287,025	180,731
South Atlantic	247,801	199,961	165,392	155,990	122,922	171,084	139,452	117,001	112,895	91,317	76,717	60,509	48,391	43,095	31,605
E. South Central	91,679	87,342	91,062	98,343	77,386	69,340	67,136	70,389	76,559	61,241	22,339	20,206	20,673	21,784	16,145
W. South Central	276,101	280,810	241,251	192,330	114,901	200,853	203,986	177,764	144,446	89,764	75,338	76,824	63,487	47,884	25,137
Mountain	314,346	306,034	246,912	170,138	94,638	201,261	194,176	156,557	106,432	60,009	113,085	111,858	90,355	63,706	34,539
Pacific	786,554	548,007	396,110	244,191	148,710	510,858	364,668	268,169	167,235	103,890	275,696	183,339	127,041	76,956	44,829
NEW ENGLAND:															
Maine	92,478	76,416	61,500	47,903	31,804	47,554	38,966	32,070	24,878	18,020	44,924	37,450	29,430	23,025	13,284
New Hampshire	58,461	44,547	35,516	26,934	15,315	30,094	22,284	18,106	13,596	8,488	28,367	22,263	17,410	13,338	6,827
Vermont	41,043	36,866	35,548	34,457	25,956	23,139	20,801	21,104	20,127	16,296	17,904	16,065	14,444	14,330	9,660
Massachusetts	506,315	401,959	323,627	246,692	143,947	262,748	202,890	165,577	127,475	80,536	243,567	199,069	158,050	119,217	63,411
Rhode Island	88,307	64,208	50,376	36,205	21,252	48,381	33,578	26,049	19,097	11,555	39,926	30,690	24,327	17,108	9,697
Connecticut	156,894	111,880	85,577	69,760	42,096	92,352	63,250	47,765	40,074	25,487	64,342	48,630	37,812	29,686	16,609
MIDDLE ATLANTIC:															
New York	1,133,307	873,566	765,411	653,977	471,709	719,529	542,468	479,764	417,597	315,002	413,778	331,098	285,647	236,380	156,707
New Jersey	368,535	256,741	201,786	153,401	97,814	232,019	156,351	123,247	96,743	65,433	136,516	100,390	78,539	56,658	32,381
Pennsylvania	697,021	569,995	511,039	451,768	335,075	477,081	376,053	336,054	305,428	237,522	219,940	193,942	174,985	140,340	97,553
E. NORTH CENTRAL:															
Ohio	439,891	385,823	353,118	338,346	262,187	299,354	261,637	243,787	237,993	190,917	140,537	124,186	109,331	100,353	71,270
Indiana	150,105	141,593	139,543	148,062	113,509	105,704	101,176	100,665	108,658	85,642	44,401	40,417	38,878	40,004	27,867
Illinois	672,614	558,783	491,692	428,262	277,427	454,405	375,706	333,510	295,854	199,982	218,209	183,077	158,182	132,408	77,445
Michigan	528,009	429,257	353,563	298,106	209,142	332,802	268,777	220,621	182,895	133,783	195,207	160,480	132,942	115,211	75,359
Wisconsin	392,359	366,065	320,503	277,580	171,722	267,943	247,414	218,300	195,003	122,851	124,416	118,651	102,203	82,577	48,871
W. NORTH CENTRAL:															
Minnesota	380,613	347,019	273,676	208,521	111,343	259,767	232,719	182,518	139,322	76,761	120,840	114,300	91,158	69,199	34,582
Iowa	253,058	253,271	236,640	232,694	165,407	173,918	173,228	163,211	161,451	118,165	79,140	80,043	73,429	71,243	47,242
Missouri	200,919	202,018	206,174	205,094	152,854	147,151	149,436	153,746	154,641	118,072	53,768	52,582	52,428	50,443	34,782
North Dakota	116,366	96,512	71,182	30,631	13,239	78,394	62,579	45,581	18,581	8,363	37,972	33,933	25,601	12,050	4,876
South Dakota	95,930	86,817	74,446	45,279	20,871	64,935	57,552	49,293	29,397	19,742	30,995	29,265	25,153	15,882	10,129
Nebraska	148,280	140,555	127,683	103,902	74,478	101,592	95,358	86,930	69,751	51,433	46,688	45,197	40,753	34,151	23,045
Kansas	125,089	125,560	122,199	114,581	94,443	87,272	88,135	86,067	80,524	68,368	37,817	37,425	36,132	34,057	26,075
SOUTH ATLANTIC:															
Delaware	10,308	9,641	8,307	7,452	5,552	6,682	6,038	5,108	4,789	3,700	3,626	3,603	3,199	2,663	1,852
Maryland	74,863	66,269	61,517	60,043	50,075	49,991	44,541	41,880	42,037	36,434	24,872	21,728	19,637	18,006	13,641
Dist. of Columbia	24,746	23,695	18,544	15,490	10,753	15,820	15,189	12,083	10,381	7,293	8,926	8,506	6,461	5,109	3,460
Virginia	25,330	22,116	16,330	15,475	11,931	17,916	15,891	12,139	11,863	9,467	7,414	6,225	4,191	3,612	2,464
West Virginia	34,016	25,847	22,231	22,035	17,505	25,729	18,992	16,387	16,310	13,280	8,287	6,855	5,844	5,725	4,225
North Carolina	9,678	5,740	4,965	5,077	4,701	6,907	4,327	3,696	3,923	3,547	2,771	1,413	1,269	1,154	1,154
South Carolina	6,858	5,694	5,378	5,734	5,011	5,174	4,377	4,180	4,491	3,973	1,684	1,317	1,198	1,243	1,038
Georgia	15,343	13,860	12,440	12,907	9,964	11,467	10,858	9,934	10,332	8,145	3,876	3,002	2,506	2,575	1,819
Florida	46,659	27,099	15,680	11,777	7,430	31,398	19,239	11,594	8,769	5,508	15,261	7,860	4,086	3,008	1,922
E. SOUTH CENTRAL:															
Kentucky	42,664	44,715	48,181	52,527	41,882	31,435	33,465	36,287	40,165	32,772	11,229	11,250	11,894	12,362	9,110
Tennessee	18,867	17,335	17,795	19,688	15,547	14,199	13,439	13,897	15,256	12,156	4,668	3,896	3,898	4,427	3,391
Alabama	19,026	15,650	14,750	14,970	10,580	14,671	12,183	11,500	11,862	8,420	4,355	3,467	3,250	3,108	2,151
Mississippi	11,122	9,642	10,336	11,163	9,377	9,035	8,049	8,705	9,276	7,884	2,087	1,593	1,631	1,887	1,493
W. SOUTH CENTRAL:															
Arkansas	10,398	20,060	18,221	17,527	12,848	14,660	15,344	13,763	13,556	10,375	4,738	4,716	4,458	3,971	2,473
Louisiana	48,881	43,000	44,328	44,480	36,769	38,847	33,929	34,881	35,094	29,158	10,034	9,071	9,447	9,386	7,611
Oklahoma	53,901	49,036	44,167	23,579	2,238	38,202	35,575	31,639	16,749	1,607	15,699	13,461	12,528	6,830	631
Texas	154,011	168,714	134,535	106,744	63,046	109,144	119,138	97,481	79,047	48,624	44,867	49,576	37,054	27,697	14,422
MOUNTAIN:															
Montana	66,247	62,919	38,203	24,727	10,178	43,197	40,449	24,493	15,850	7,026	23,050	22,470	13,710	8,877	3,152
Idaho	44,031	44,533	35,120	19,381	8,393	27,867	28,153	22,283	12,030	5,412	16,164	16,380	12,837	7,351	2,981
Wyoming	19,589	16,773	12,753	9,037	4,908	12,548	10,509	7,863	5,369	3,029	7,041	6,264	4,890	3,668	1,879
Colorado	80,974	74,049	66,681	47,544	27,444	55,146	49,817	44,039	31,252	18,804	25,828	24,232	22,642	16,292	8,640
New Mexico	10,464	13,414	11,921	8,240	5,485	7,281	9,128	8,210	5,619	3,857	3,183	4,286	3,711	2,621	1,628
Arizona	19,638	22,671	16,050	10,212	4,819	11,786	13,880	10,032	6,058	2,655	7,852	8,791	6,027	4,154	2,164
Utah	64,188	63,764	57,544	46,431	29,302	37,378	37,025	33,811	27,232	16,747	26,810	26,739	23,733	19,199	12,645
Nevada	9,215	7,911	8,631	4,566	4,019	6,058	5,215	5,826	3,022	2,560	3,157	2,696	2,805	1,544	1,450
PACIFIC:															
Washington	174,153	143,398	107,683	49,689	25,574	110,782	92,163	70,048	32,659	17,653	63,371	51,235	37,635	17,030	7,921
Oregon	92,783	73,442	55,902	35,538	20,734	60,841	49,643	38,486	24,825	15,119	31,942	23,799	17,416	10,713	5,615
California	519,618	331,167	232,525	158,964	102,411	339,235	222,862	159,635	109,751	71,118	180,383	108,305	72,890	49,213	31,293

COLOR OR RACE, NATIVITY, AND PARENTAGE

41

TABLE **17.**—NATIVE AND FOREIGN-BORN POPULATION BY COLOR OR RACE, BY DIVISIONS AND STATES: 1930, 1920, AND 1910

Figures for the white population in 1920 and 1910 adjusted by deducting the estimated numbers of Mexicans which are shown separately in italics. Per cent not shown where less than 0.1 or where base is less than 100]

DIVISION OR STATE AND COLOR OR RACE	TOTAL						NATIVE			FOREIGN BORN			PER CENT FOREIGN BORN		
	Number			Per cent distribution											
	1930	1920	1910	1930	1920	1910	1930	1920	1910	1930	1920	1910	1930	1920	1910
United States	122,775,046	105,710,620	91,972,266	100.0	100.0	100.0	108,570,897	91,789,928	78,456,380	14,204,149	13,920,692	13,515,886	11.6	13.2	14.7
White, as reported	108,864,207	94,820,915	81,731,957	88.7	89.7	88.9	95,497,800	81,108,161	68,386,412	13,366,407	13,712,754	13,345,545	12.3	14.5	16.3
White, as adjusted		*94,120,374*	*81,564,447*		*89.0*	*88.5*		*80,864,980*	*68,230,135*		*13,255,394*	*13,134,312*		*14.1*	*16.1*
Negro	11,891,143	10,463,131	9,827,763	9.7	9.9	10.7	11,792,523	10,389,328	9,787,424	98,620	73,803	40,339	0.8	0.7	0.4
Mexican	1,422,533	700,541	367,510	1.2	0.7	0.4	805,535	243,181	156,277	616,998	457,360	211,233	43.4	65.3	57.5
Indian, Chinese, etc	597,163	426,574	412,546	0.5	0.4	0.4	475,039	292,439	282,544	122,124	134,135	130,002	20.5	31.4	31.5
New England	8,166,341	7,400,909	6,552,681	100.0	100.0	100.0	6,317,398	5,514,964	4,727,571	1,848,943	1,885,945	1,825,110	22.6	25.5	27.9
White, as reported	8,065,113	7,316,070	6,480,514	98.8	98.9	98.9	6,230,803	5,445,425	4,666,128	1,834,310	1,870,654	1,814,386	22.7	25.6	28.0
White, as adjusted		*7,315,995*	*6,480,468*		*98.9*	*98.9*		*5,445,395*	*4,666,112*		*1,870,600*	*1,814,356*		*25.6*	*28.0*
Negro	94,086	79,051	66,306	1.2	1.1	1.0	82,300	66,795	58,596	11,786	12,256	7,710	12.5	15.5	11.6
Mexican	107	84	46				39	30	16	68	54	30	63.6		
Indian, Chinese, etc	7,035	5,779	5,861	0.1	0.1	0.1	4,256	2,744	2,847	2,779	3,035	3,014	39.5	52.5	51.4
Middle Atlantic	26,260,750	22,261,144	19,315,892	100.0	100.0	100.0	20,908,019	17,300,726	14,464,719	5,352,731	4,960,418	4,851,173	20.4	22.3	25.1
White, as reported	25,172,104	21,041,840	18,880,452	95.9	97.2	97.7	19,903,062	16,730,205	14,054,273	5,269,042	4,920,179	4,825,900	20.9	22.7	25.6
White, as adjusted		*21,693,625*	*18,879,881*		*97.2*	*97.7*		*16,788,720*	*14,054,064*		*4,900,899*	*4,825,817*		*22.7*	*25.6*
Negro	1,052,899	600,183	417,870	4.0	2.7	2.2	988,334	562,558	401,548	64,565	37,625	16,322	6.1	6.3	3.9
Mexican	6,757	5,215	671				1,528	539	209	5,229	2,676	562	77.4	83.2	65.4
Indian, Chinese, etc	28,990	19,121	17,570	0.1	0.1	0.1	15,095	8,903	8,898	13,895	10,218	8,672	47.9	53.4	49.4
East North Central	25,297,185	21,475,543	18,250,621	100.0	100.0	100.0	22,021,462	18,243,402	15,176,855	3,275,723	3,232,141	3,073,766	12.9	15.1	16.8
White, as reported	24,277,663	20,938,862	17,927,622	96.0	97.5	98.2	21,053,739	17,715,583	14,860,402	3,223,924	3,223,279	3,067,220	13.3	15.4	17.1
White, as adjusted		*20,931,279*	*17,926,513*		*97.5*	*98.2*		*17,714,274*	*14,860,123*		*3,217,005*	*3,066,390*		*15.4*	*17.1*
Negro	930,460	514,554	300,830	3.7	2.4	1.6	925,293	510,292	297,452	5,167	4,202	3,384	0.6	0.8	1.1
Mexican	58,317	7,585	1,109	0.2			17,104	1,309	270	41,213	6,274	839	70.7	82.7	74.8
Indian, Chinese, etc	30,755	22,127	22,163	0.1	0.1	0.1	25,326	17,527	10,001	5,429	4,600	3,162	17.7	20.8	14.3
West North Central	13,296,915	12,544,249	11,637,921	100.0	100.0	100.0	12,212,762	11,168,596	10,021,226	1,084,153	1,375,653	1,616,695	8.2	11.0	13.9
White, as reported	12,873,487	12,225,387	11,351,621	96.8	97.5	97.5	11,814,210	10,853,426	9,738,390	1,059,277	1,371,961	1,613,231	8.2	11.2	14.2
White, as adjusted		*12,199,713*	*11,340,736*		*97.3*	*97.4*		*10,848,881*	*9,737,825*		*1,350,832*	*1,602,911*		*11.1*	*14.2*
Negro	331,784	278,521	242,662	2.5	2.2	2.1	331,256	277,472	241,855	528	1,049	807	0.2	0.4	0.3
Mexican	39,805	25,674	10,885	0.3	0.2	0.1	17,405	4,545	565	22,400	21,129	10,320	56.3	82.3	94.8
Indian, Chinese, etc	51,839	40,341	43,638	0.4	0.3	0.4	49,891	37,608	40,981	1,948	2,643	2,657	3.8	6.6	6.1
South Atlantic	15,793,589	13,990,272	12,194,895	100.0	100.0	100.0	15,474,892	13,659,735	11,894,901	318,697	330,537	299,994	2.0	2.4	2.5
White, as reported	11,349,284	9,648,940	8,071,603	71.9	69.0	66.2	11,045,006	9,333,020	7,781,048	304,278	315,920	290,555	2.7	3.3	3.6
White, as adjusted		*9,648,550*	*8,071,473*		*69.0*	*66.2*		*9,332,880*	*7,780,997*		*315,676*	*290,476*		*3.3*	*3.6*
Negro	4,421,388	4,325,120	4,112,488	28.0	30.9	33.7	4,408,804	4,312,158	4,104,413	12,584	12,962	8,075	0.3	0.3	0.2
Mexican	691	384	130				232	140	51	459	244	79	66.4	63.5	60.8
Indian, Chinese, etc	22,226	16,212	10,804	0.1	0.1	0.1	20,850	14,557	9,440	1,376	1,655	1,364	6.2	10.2	12.6
East South Central	9,887,214	8,893,307	8,409,901	100.0	100.0	100.0	9,827,550	8,820,318	8,322,076	59,664	72,989	87,825	0.6	0.8	1.0
White, as reported	7,224,014	6,307,547	5,754,320	73.1	71.6	68.4	7,166,949	6,295,608	5,667,469	57,665	71,939	86,857	0.8	1.1	1.5
White, as adjusted		*6,307,160*	*5,754,154*		*71.6*	*68.4*		*6,295,408*	*5,667,409*		*71,698*	*86,745*		*1.1*	*1.5*
Negro	2,658,238	2,523,582	2,652,613	26.9	28.4	31.5	2,657,706	2,522,896	2,651,888	532	636	625			
Mexican	1,403	381	172				724	140	60	679	241	112	48.4	63.3	65.1
Indian, Chinese, etc	2,959	2,228	3,002				2,471	1,814	2,719	488	414	343	16.5	18.6	11.2
West South Central	12,176,830	10,242,224	8,784,534	100.0	100.0	100.0	11,736,277	9,777,396	8,432,342	440,553	464,828	352,192	3.6	4.5	4.0
White, as reported	9,600,081	8,115,727	6,721,491	74.7	79.2	76.5	8,929,749	7,656,394	6,372,732	170,232	459,333	348,759	1.9	5.7	5.2
White, as adjusted		*7,718,177*	*6,496,026*		*75.3*	*73.9*		*7,507,981*	*6,266,020*		*208,196*	*224,606*		*2.7*	*3.5*
Negro	2,281,951	2,063,570	1,984,426	18.7	20.1	22.6	2,280,539	2,000,588	1,982,557	1,412	2,991	1,869	0.1	0.1	0.1
Mexican	695,096	309,550	290,805	5.7	3.9	3.6	428,538	148,413	166,712	267,458	251,137	124,153	38.4	62.9	53.8
Indian, Chinese, etc	98,902	82,018	78,817	0.8	0.8	0.9	97,451	80,414	77,053	1,451	2,504	1,584	1.5	4.0	2.0
Mountain	3,701,789	3,336,101	2,633,517	100.0	100.0	100.0	3,317,466	2,868,481	2,180,195	384,323	467,620	453,322	10.4	14.0	17.2
White, as reported	3,303,586	3,212,899	2,520,455	89.2	96.3	95.7	3,015,672	2,759,674	2,083,545	287,914	453,225	436,910	8.7	14.1	17.3
White, as adjusted		*3,071,405*	*2,445,515*		*92.1*	*92.9*		*2,710,874*	*2,051,932*		*360,531*	*393,583*		*11.7*	*16.1*
Negro	30,225	30,801	21,467	0.8	0.9	0.8	30,038	30,220	21,094	187	581	373	0.6	1.9	1.7
Mexican	249,314	141,494	74,840	6.7	4.2	2.8	162,818	48,800	31,563	86,496	92,694	43,277	34.7	65.5	57.9
Indian, Chinese, etc	118,664	92,401	91,595	3.2	2.8	3.5	108,938	78,587	75,556	9,726	13,814	16,039	8.2	15.0	17.5
Pacific	8,194,433	5,566,871	4,192,304	100.0	100.0	100.0	6,754,771	4,436,310	3,236,495	1,439,662	1,130,561	955,809	17.6	20.3	22.8
White, as reported	7,498,375	5,353,634	4,023,873	91.5	96.2	96.0	6,338,610	4,319,766	3,162,425	1,159,765	1,033,868	861,448	15.5	19.3	21.4
White, as adjusted		*5,251,458*	*3,975,081*		*94.0*	*94.8*		*4,280,501*	*3,145,603*		*970,957*	*829,478*		*18.5*	*20.9*
Negro	90,122	47,790	29,195	1.1	0.9	0.7	88,253	46,349	28,021	1,869	1,441	1,174	2.1	3.0	4.0
Mexican	370,143	122,176	48,792	4.5	2.2	1.2	177,147	39,265	16,822	192,996	82,911	31,970	52.1	67.9	65.5
Indian, Chinese, etc	235,793	165,447	139,230	2.9	3.0	3.3	150,761	70,105	46,049	85,032	95,252	93,187	36.1	57.6	66.9
NEW ENGLAND															
Maine	797,423	768,014	742,371	100.0	100.0	100.0	696,695	660,200	631,809	100,728	107,814	110,562	12.6	14.0	14.9
White, as reported	795,183	765,695	739,995	99.7	99.7	99.7	694,815	658,346	629,862	100,368	107,340	110,133	12.6	14.0	14.9
White, as adjusted		*765,693*	*739,991*		*99.7*	*99.7*		*658,346*	*629,862*		*107,347*	*110,129*		*14.0*	*14.9*
Negro	1,096	1,310	1,363	0.1	0.2	0.2	893	1,036	1,126	203	274	237	18.5	20.9	17.4
Mexican	2	2	4				2				2	4			
Indian, Chinese, etc	1,142	1,009	1,013	0.1	0.1	0.1	985	818	821	167	191	192	13.7	18.9	19.0
New Hampshire	465,293	443,083	430,572	100.0	100.0	100.0	382,364	351,686	333,905	82,929	91,397	96,667	17.8	20.6	22.5
White, as reported	464,350	442,331	429,906	99.8	99.8	99.8	381,690	351,098	333,348	82,660	91,233	96,558	17.8	20.6	22.5
White, as adjusted		*442,330*	*429,906*		*99.8*	*99.8*		*351,098*	*333,348*		*91,232*	*96,558*		*20.6*	*22.5*
Negro	790	621	564	0.2	0.1	0.1	595	551	524	195	70	40	24.7	11.3	7.1
Mexican	1	1								1	1				
Indian, Chinese, etc	152	131	102				79	37	33	73	94	69	48.0	71.8	67.6
Vermont	359,611	352,428	355,956	100.0	100.0	100.0	316,510	307,870	306,035	43,101	44,558	49,921	12.0	12.6	14.0
White, as reported	358,965	351,817	354,298	99.8	99.8	99.5	315,904	307,291	304,437	43,061	44,526	49,861	12.0	12.7	14.1
White, as adjusted		*351,816*	*354,298*		*99.8*	*99.5*		*307,291*	*304,437*		*44,525*	*49,861*		*12.7*	*14.1*
Negro	568	572	1,621	0.2	0.2	0.5	555	556	1,581	13	16	40	2.3	2.8	2.5
Mexican	1	1	1							1	1				
Indian, Chinese, etc	77	39	37				51	23	17	26	16	20			

POPULATION

TABLE 17.—NATIVE AND FOREIGN-BORN POPULATION BY COLOR OR RACE, BY DIVISIONS AND STATES: 1930, 1920, AND 1910—Continued

DIVISION OR STATE AND COLOR OR RACE	TOTAL Number 1930	1920	1910	TOTAL Per cent distribution 1930	1920	1910	NATIVE 1930	1920	1910	FOREIGN BORN 1930	1920	1910	PER CENT FOREIGN BORN 1930	1920	1910
NEW ENGLAND—Con.															
Massachusetts	4,249,614	3,852,356	3,366,416	100.0	100.0	100.0	3,183,994	2,763,808	2,307,171	1,065,620	1,088,548	1,059,245	25.1	28.3	31.5
White, as reported	4,192,926	3,803,524	3,324,926	98.7	98.7	98.8	3,138,290	2,725,990	2,273,876	1,054,636	1,077,534	1,051,050	25.2	28.3	31.6
White, as adjusted		*3,803,467*	*3,324,897*		*98.7*	*98.8*		*2,725,968*	*2,273,866*		*1,077,499*	*1,051,031*		*28.3*	*31.6*
Negro	52,365	45,466	38,055	1.2	1.2	1.1	43,431	36,429	31,903	8,934	9,037	6,152	17.1	19.9	16.2
Mexican	66	57	29				25	22	10	41	35	19			
Indian, Chinese, etc.	4,257	3,366	3,435	0.1	0.1	0.1	2,248	1,389	1,392	2,009	1,977	2,043	47.2	58.7	59.5
Rhode Island	687,497	604,397	542,610	100.0	100.0	100.0	515,568	429,208	363,469	171,929	175,189	179,141	25.0	29.0	33.0
White, as reported	677,016	593,980	532,492	98.5	98.3	98.1	506,302	420,481	354,467	170,714	173,499	178,025	25.2	29.2	33.4
White, as adjusted		*593,976*	*532,488*		*98.3*	*98.1*		*420,481*	*354,465*		*173,495*	*178,023*		*29.2*	*33.4*
Negro	9,913	10,036	9,529	1.4	1.7	1.8	8,850	8,540	8,657	1,063	1,496	872	10.7	14.9	9.2
Mexican	10	4	4				4	2	2	6	2	2			
Indian, Chinese, etc.	558	381	589	0.1	0.1	0.1	412	187	345	146	194	244	26.2	50.9	41.4
Connecticut	1,606,903	1,380,631	1,114,756	100.0	100.0	100.0	1,222,267	1,002,192	785,182	384,636	378,439	329,574	23.9	27.4	29.6
White, as reported	1,576,673	1,358,732	1,098,897	98.1	98.4	98.6	1,193,802	982,219	770,138	382,871	376,513	328,759	24.3	27.7	29.9
White, as adjusted		*1,358,713*	*1,098,888*		*98.4*	*98.6*		*982,211*	*770,134*		*376,502*	*328,754*		*27.7*	*29.9*
Negro	29,354	21,046	15,174	1.8	1.5	1.4	27,976	19,683	14,805	1,378	1,363	369	4.7	6.5	2.4
Mexican	27	19	9				8	8	4	19	11	5			
Indian, Chinese, etc.	849	853	685	0.1	0.1	0.1	481	200	239	368	563	446	43.3	66.0	65.1
MIDDLE ATLANTIC															
New York	12,588,066	10,385,227	9,113,614	100.0	100.0	100.0	9,325,788	7,559,852	6,365,603	3,262,278	2,825,375	2,748,011	25.9	27.2	30.2
White, as reported	12,150,293	10,172,027	8,966,845	96.5	97.9	98.4	8,958,744	7,385,915	6,237,573	3,191,549	2,786,112	2,729,272	26.3	27.4	30.4
White, as adjusted		*10,170,548*	*8,966,525*		*97.9*	*98.4*		*7,385,653*	*6,237,473*		*2,784,895*	*2,729,052*		*27.4*	*30.4*
Negro	412,814	198,483	134,191	3.3	1.9	1.5	354,909	166,512	121,340	57,895	31,971	12,851	14.0	16.1	9.6
Mexican	2,898	1,479	920				505	262	100	2,393	1,217	820	82.6	82.3	68.8
Indian, Chinese, etc.	22,061	14,717	12,578	0.2	0.1	0.1	11,620	7,425	6,690	10,441	7,292	5,888	47.3	49.5	46.8
New Jersey	4,041,334	3,155,900	2,537,167	100.0	100.0	100.0	3,191,296	2,413,414	1,876,379	850,038	742,486	660,788	21.0	23.5	26.0
White, as reported	3,829,209	3,037,087	2,445,894	94.8	96.2	96.4	2,984,767	2,298,474	1,787,706	844,442	738,613	658,188	22.1	24.3	26.9
White, as adjusted		*3,036,892*	*2,445,820*		*96.2*	*96.4*		*2,298,404*	*1,787,672*		*738,428*	*658,148*		*24.3*	*26.9*
Negro	208,828	117,132	89,760	5.2	3.7	3.5	205,109	114,408	88,273	3,719	2,634	1,487	1.8	2.2	1.7
Mexican	454	255	74				112	70	34	342	185	40	75.3	72.5	
Indian, Chinese, etc.	2,843	1,681	1,513	0.1	0.1	0.1	1,308	442	400	1,535	1,239	1,113	54.0	73.7	73.6
Pennsylvania	9,631,350	8,720,017	7,665,111	100.0	100.0	100.0	8,390,935	7,327,460	6,222,737	1,240,415	1,392,557	1,442,374	12.9	16.0	18.8
White, as reported	9,192,602	8,432,720	7,467,713	95.4	96.7	97.4	7,959,551	7,044,876	6,028,994	1,233,051	1,387,850	1,438,719	13.4	16.5	19.3
White, as adjusted		*8,431,245*	*7,467,536*		*96.7*	*97.4*		*7,044,669*	*6,028,919*		*1,386,576*	*1,438,617*		*16.4*	*19.3*
Negro	431,257	284,568	193,919	4.5	3.3	2.5	428,306	281,548	191,935	2,951	3,020	1,984	0.7	1.1	1.0
Mexican	3,405	1,481	177				911	207	75	2,494	1,274	102	73.2	86.0	57.6
Indian, Chinese, etc.	4,086	2,723	3,479				2,167	1,036	1,808	1,919	1,687	1,671	47.0	62.0	48.0
EAST NORTH CENTRAL															
Ohio	6,646,697	5,759,394	4,767,121	100.0	100.0	100.0	5,997,477	5,078,942	4,168,747	649,220	680,452	598,374	9.8	11.8	12.6
White, as reported	6,331,136	5,571,893	4,654,897	95.3	96.7	97.6	5,686,985	4,893,196	4,057,652	644,151	678,697	597,245	10.2	12.2	12.8
White, as adjusted		*5,570,951*	*4,654,758*		*96.7*	*97.6*		*4,893,057*	*4,057,582*		*677,894*	*597,176*		*12.2*	*12.8*
Negro	309,304	186,187	111,452	4.7	3.2	2.3	308,227	185,236	110,797	1,077	951	655	0.3	0.5	0.6
Mexican	4,037	942	139	0.1			1,100	139	70	2,937	803	69	72.8	85.2	49.6
Indian, Chinese, etc.	2,220	1,314	772				1,165	510	298	1,355	804	474	47.5	61.2	61.4
Indiana	3,238,503	2,930,390	2,700,876	100.0	100.0	100.0	3,095,504	2,779,062	2,541,213	142,999	151,328	159,663	4.4	5.2	5.9
White, as reported	3,116,136	2,849,071	2,639,961	96.2	97.2	97.7	2,981,002	2,698,203	2,480,639	135,134	150,868	159,322	4.3	5.3	6.0
White, as adjusted		*2,848,346*	*2,639,876*		*97.2*	*97.7*		*2,698,116*	*2,480,597*		*150,230*	*159,279*		*5.3*	*6.0*
Negro	111,982	80,810	60,320	3.5	2.8	2.2	111,782	80,626	60,223	200	184	97	0.2	0.2	0.2
Mexican	9,642	725	85	0.3			2,231	87	42	7,411	638	43	76.9	88.0	
Indian, Chinese, etc.	743	509	595				489	233	351	254	276	244	34.2	54.2	41.0
Illinois	7,630,654	6,485,280	5,638,591	100.0	100.0	100.0	6,388,207	5,274,696	4,433,277	1,242,447	1,210,584	1,205,314	16.3	18.7	21.4
White, as reported	7,266,361	6,299,333	5,526,962	95.2	97.1	98.0	6,048,203	5,092,382	4,324,402	1,218,158	1,206,951	1,202,560	16.8	19.2	21.8
White, as adjusted		*6,294,999*	*5,526,241*		*97.1*	*98.0*		*5,091,603*	*4,324,292*		*1,203,396*	*1,201,949*		*19.1*	*21.7*
Negro	328,072	182,274	109,049	4.3	2.8	1.9	327,406	181,029	108,121	1,566	1,245	928	0.5	0.7	0.9
Mexican	28,906	4,354	721	0.4	0.1		8,837	779	110	20,069	3,555	611	69.4	82.0	84.7
Indian, Chinese, etc.	6,415	3,673	2,580	0.1	0.1		3,761	1,285	754	2,654	2,388	1,826	41.4	65.0	70.8
Michigan	4,842,325	3,668,412	2,810,173	100.0	100.0	100.0	3,989,567	2,939,120	2,212,623	852,758	729,292	597,550	17.6	19.9	21.3
White, as reported	4,650,171	3,601,627	2,785,247	96.0	98.2	99.1	3,809,903	2,874,992	2,189,723	840,268	726,635	595,524	18.1	20.2	21.4
White, as adjusted		*3,600,283*	*2,785,195*		*98.1*	*99.0*		*2,874,795*	*2,189,685*		*725,488*	*595,450*		*20.2*	*21.4*
Negro	169,453	60,082	17,115	3.5	1.6	0.6	167,191	58,313	15,475	2,262	1,769	1,640	1.3	2.9	9.6
Mexican	13,336	1,344	112	0.3			4,307	197	38	9,029	1,147	74	67.7	85.3	66.1
Indian, Chinese, etc.	9,365	6,703	7,811	0.2	0.2	0.3	8,166	5,815	7,425	1,199	888	386	12.8	13.2	4.0
Wisconsin	2,939,006	2,632,067	2,333,860	100.0	100.0	100.0	2,550,707	2,171,582	1,820,995	388,299	460,485	512,865	13.2	17.5	22.0
White, as reported	2,913,859	2,616,938	2,320,555	99.1	99.4	99.4	2,527,646	2,156,810	1,807,986	386,213	460,128	512,569	13.3	17.6	22.1
White, as adjusted		*2,616,700*	*2,320,503*		*99.4*	*99.4*		*2,156,703*	*1,807,967*		*459,997*	*512,536*		*17.6*	*22.0*
Negro	10,739	5,201	2,900	0.4	0.2	0.1	10,687	5,088	2,836	52	113	64	0.5	2.2	2.2
Mexican	2,396	268	52	0.1			629	107	19	1,767	161	33	73.7	55.0	
Indian, Chinese, etc.	12,012	9,928	10,405	0.4	0.4	0.4	11,745	9,684	10,173	267	244	232	2.2	2.5	2.2
WEST NORTH CENTRAL															
Minnesota	2,563,953	2,387,125	2,075,708	100.0	100.0	100.0	2,173,163	1,900,330	1,532,113	390,790	486,795	543,595	15.2	20.4	26.2
White, as reported	2,538,973	2,368,936	2,059,227	99.0	99.2	99.2	2,150,679	1,882,772	1,516,217	388,294	486,164	543,010	15.3	20.5	26.4
White, as adjusted		*2,368,586*	*2,059,143*		*99.2*	*99.2*		*1,882,645*	*1,516,180*		*485,941*	*542,963*		*20.5*	*26.4*
Negro	9,445	8,809	7,084	0.4	0.4	0.3	9,340	8,655	6,884	105	154	200	1.1	1.7	2.8
Mexican	3,626	550	84	0.1			1,640	127	37	1,986	223	47	54.8	63.7	
Indian, Chinese, etc.	11,909	9,380	9,397	0.5	0.4	0.5	11,504	8,903	9,012	405	477	385	3.4	5.1	4.1

COLOR OR RACE, NATIVITY, AND PARENTAGE

TABLE 17.—NATIVE AND FOREIGN-BORN POPULATION BY COLOR OR RACE, BY DIVISIONS AND STATES: 1930, 1920, AND 1910—Continued

DIVISION OR STATE AND COLOR OR RACE	TOTAL — Number			Per cent distribution			NATIVE			FOREIGN BORN			PER CENT FOREIGN BORN		
	1930	1920	1910	1930	1920	1910	1930	1920	1910	1930	1920	1910	1930	1920	1910
WEST NORTH CENTRAL—Continued															
Iowa	2,470,939	2,404,021	2,224,771	100.0	100.0	100.0	2,302,689	2,178,027	1,951,006	168,250	225,994	273,765	6.8	9.4	12.3
White, as reported	2,448,382	2,384,181	2,209,191	99.1	99.2	99.3	2,282,647	2,158,534	1,935,707	165,735	225,647	273,484	6.8	9.5	12.4
White, as adjusted		*2,381,295*	*2,208,682*		*99.1*	*99.3*		*2,158,001*	*1,935,667*		*223,292*	*273,015*		*9.4*	*12.4*
Negro	17,380	19,005	14,973	0.7	0.8	0.7	17,330	18,908	14,918	50	107	55	0.3	0.6	0.4
Mexican	4,295	2,888	509	0.2	0.1		1,950	533	40	2,345	2,355	469	54.6	81.5	92.1
Indian, Chinese, etc	882	835	607				762	595	381	120	240	226	13.6	28.7	37.2
Missouri	3,629,367	3,404,055	3,293,335	100.0	100.0	100.0	3,476,282	3,217,220	3,063,556	153,085	186,835	229,779	4.2	5.5	7.0
White, as reported	3,398,887	3,225,044	3,134,932	93.6	94.7	95.2	3,249,497	3,039,018	2,906,030	149,390	186,026	228,896	4.4	5.8	7.3
White, as adjusted		*3,221,661*	*3,133,570*		*94.6*	*95.1*		*3,033,428*	*2,905,897*		*187,673*	*227,673*		*5.7*	*7.3*
Negro	223,840	178,241	157,452	6.2	5.2	4.8	223,031	177,865	157,126	809	376	326	0.4	0.2	0.2
Mexican	4,989	3,383	1,362	0.1	0.1		1,970	595	139	3,019	2,788	1,223	60.5	82.4	89.8
Indian, Chinese, etc	1,651	770	951				1,184	337	394	467	433	557	28.3	56.2	58.6
North Dakota	680,845	646,872	577,056	100.0	100.0	100.0	574,974	515,009	420,402	105,871	131,863	156,654	15.5	20.4	27.1
White, as reported	671,243	639,954	569,855	98.6	98.9	98.8	566,095	508,461	413,097	105,148	131,503	156,158	15.7	20.5	27.4
White, as adjusted		*639,912*	*569,845*		*98.9*	*98.8*		*508,434*	*413,694*		*131,478*	*156,151*		*20.5*	*27.4*
Negro	377	467	617	0.1	0.1	0.1	370	446	615	7	21	2	1.0	4.5	0.3
Mexican	608	42	10	0.1			275	17	3	333	25	7	54.8		
Indian, Chinese, etc	8,617	6,451	6,584	1.3	1.0	1.1	8,234	6,112	6,090	383	339	494	4.4	5.3	7.5
South Dakota	692,849	636,547	583,888	100.0	100.0	100.0	626,788	554,013	483,098	66,061	82,534	100,790	9.5	13.0	17.3
White, as reported	669,453	619,147	563,771	96.6	97.3	96.6	603,805	536,756	463,143	65,648	82,391	100,628	9.8	13.3	17.8
White, as adjusted		*619,062*	*563,747*		*97.3*	*96.6*		*536,737*	*463,131*		*82,325*	*100,616*		*13.3*	*17.8*
Negro	646	832	817	0.1	0.1	0.1	639	818	808	7	14	9	1.1	1.7	1.1
Mexican	816	95	24	0.1			522	29	12	294	66	12	36.0		
Indian, Chinese, etc	21,934	16,568	19,300	3.2	2.6	3.3	21,822	16,439	19,147	112	129	153	0.5	0.8	0.8
Nebraska	1,377,963	1,296,372	1,192,214	100.0	100.0	100.0	1,259,784	1,145,707	1,015,552	118,190	150,665	176,662	8.7	11.6	14.8
White, as reported	1,353,702	1,270,219	1,180,293	98.2	98.7	99.0	1,238,356	1,120,567	1,004,428	115,346	149,652	175,865	8.5	11.7	14.9
White, as adjusted		*1,276,475*	*1,179,904*		*98.5*	*99.0*		*1,129,128*	*1,004,401*		*147,345*	*175,503*		*11.5*	*14.9*
Negro	13,752	13,242	7,689	1.0	1.0	0.6	13,697	13,102	7,592	55	140	97	0.4	1.1	1.3
Mexican	6,321	2,746	299	0.5	0.2		2,910	439	27	3,411	2,307	272	54.0	84.0	91.0
Indian, Chinese, etc	4,188	3,011	4,232	0.3	0.3	0.4	3,801	2,138	3,532	387	873	700	9.2	22.3	16.5
Kansas	1,880,999	1,769,257	1,690,949	100.0	100.0	100.0	1,800,102	1,658,290	1,555,499	80,897	110,967	135,450	4.3	6.3	8.0
White, as reported	1,792,847	1,708,906	1,634,352	95.3	96.6	96.7	1,723,131	1,598,328	1,499,162	69,716	110,578	135,190	3.9	6.5	8.3
White, as adjusted		*1,692,796*	*1,625,755*		*95.7*	*96.1*		*1,595,583*	*1,498,855*		*97,213*	*126,900*		*5.7*	*7.8*
Negro	66,344	57,925	54,030	3.5	3.3	3.2	66,249	57,688	53,912	95	237	118	0.1	0.4	0.2
Mexican	19,150	16,170	8,697	1.0	0.9	0.5	8,138	2,805	407	11,012	13,365	8,290	57.5	82.7	96.4
Indian, Chinese, etc	2,658	2,426	2,567	0.1	0.1	0.2	2,584	2,274	2,425	74	152	142	2.8	6.3	5.5
SOUTH ATLANTIC															
Delaware	238,380	223,003	202,322	100.0	100.0	100.0	221,355	203,102	184,830	17,025	19,901	17,492	7.1	8.9	8.6
White, as reported	205,604	192,615	171,102	86.3	86.4	84.6	188,809	172,805	153,682	16,885	19,810	17,420	8.2	10.3	10.2
White, as adjusted		*192,585*	*171,100*		*86.4*	*84.6*		*172,800*	*153,681*		*19,785*	*17,419*		*10.3*	*10.2*
Negro	32,602	30,335	31,181	13.7	13.6	15.4	32,515	30,284	31,146	87	51	35	0.3	0.2	0.1
Mexican	24	30	2				2	5	1	22	25	1			
Indian, Chinese, etc	60	53	39				29	13	2	31	40	37			
Maryland	1,631,526	1,449,661	1,295,346	100.0	100.0	100.0	1,535,196	1,346,482	1,190,402	96,330	103,179	104,944	5.9	7.1	8.1
White, as reported	1,354,170	1,204,737	1,062,639	83.0	83.1	82.0	1,259,077	1,102,560	958,465	95,093	102,177	104,174	7.0	8.5	9.8
White, as adjusted		*1,204,690*	*1,062,627*		*83.1*	*82.0*		*1,102,546*	*958,457*		*102,144*	*104,170*		*8.5*	*9.8*
Negro	276,379	244,479	232,250	16.9	16.9	17.9	275,507	243,783	231,799	872	696	451	0.3	0.3	0.2
Mexican	56	47	12				8	14	8	48	33	4			
Indian, Chinese, etc	921	445	457	0.1			604	137	147	317	308	310	34.4	68.8	69.8
District of Columbia	486,869	437,571	331,069	100.0	100.0	100.0	456,136	408,206	306,167	30,733	29,365	24,902	6.3	6.7	7.5
White, as reported	353,914	326,860	236,128	72.7	74.7	71.3	323,082	298,312	211,777	29,032	28,548	24,351	8.5	8.7	10.3
White, as adjusted		*326,825*	*236,115*		*74.7*	*71.3*		*298,303*	*211,771*		*28,522*	*24,343*		*8.7*	*10.3*
Negro	132,068	109,966	94,446	27.1	25.1	28.5	131,611	109,602	94,208	457	364	238	0.3	0.3	0.3
Mexican	67	35	15				13	9	6	54	26	9			
Indian, Chinese, etc	820	745	495	0.2	0.2	0.1	530	292	182	290	453	313	35.4	60.8	63.2
Virginia	2,421,851	2,309,187	2,061,612	100.0	100.0	100.0	2,397,484	2,277,482	2,034,555	24,367	31,705	27,057	1.0	1.4	1.3
White, as reported	1,770,405	1,617,909	1,389,809	73.1	70.1	67.4	1,746,585	1,587,124	1,363,181	23,820	30,785	26,628	1.3	1.9	1.9
White, as adjusted		*1,617,871*	*1,389,802*		*70.1*	*67.4*		*1,587,121*	*1,363,512*		*30,760*	*26,624*		*1.9*	*1.9*
Negro	650,165	690,017	671,096	26.8	29.9	32.6	649,835	689,361	670,800	330	656	296	0.1	0.1	
Mexican	36	38	7				16	13	3	20	25	4			
Indian, Chinese, etc	1,245	1,201	707	0.1	0.1		1,048	997	574	197	204	133	15.8	20.9	18.8
West Virginia	1,729,205	1,463,701	1,221,119	100.0	100.0	100.0	1,677,340	1,401,596	1,163,901	51,865	62,105	57,218	3.0	4.2	4.7
White, as reported	1,613,934	1,377,235	1,156,817	93.3	94.1	94.7	1,562,414	1,315,329	1,099,745	51,520	61,906	57,072	3.2	4.5	4.9
White, as adjusted		*1,377,180*	*1,156,811*		*94.1*	*94.7*		*1,315,316*	*1,099,744*		*61,864*	*57,067*		*4.5*	*4.9*
Negro	114,893	86,345	64,173	6.6	5.9	5.3	114,774	86,218	64,091	119	127	82	0.1	0.1	0.1
Mexican	257	55	6				98	13	1	159	42	5	61.9	59.5	
Indian, Chinese, etc	121	66	129				54	49	65	67	17	64	55.4		49.6
North Carolina	3,170,276	2,559,123	2,206,287	100.0	100.0	100.0	3,161,307	2,551,851	2,200,195	8,969	7,272	6,092	0.3	0.3	0.3
White, as reported	2,234,948	1,783,779	1,500,511	70.5	69.7	68.0	2,226,160	1,776,680	1,494,569	8,788	7,099	5,942	0.4	0.4	0.4
White, as adjusted		*1,783,769*	*1,500,508*		*69.7*	*68.0*		*1,776,677*	*1,494,568*		*7,092*	*5,940*		*0.4*	*0.4*
Negro	918,647	763,407	697,843	29.0	29.8	31.6	918,529	763,316	697,755	118	91	88			
Mexican	10	10	3				4	3	1	6	7	2			
Indian, Chinese, etc	16,671	11,937	7,933	0.5	0.5	0.4	16,614	11,855	7,871	57	82	62	0.3	0.7	0.8
South Carolina	1,738,765	1,683,724	1,515,400	100.0	100.0	100.0	1,733,407	1,677,142	1,509,221	5,358	6,582	6,179	0.3	0.4	0.4
White, as reported	944,040	818,538	679,161	54.3	48.6	44.8	938,774	812,137	673,107	5,266	6,401	6,054	0.6	0.8	0.9
White, as adjusted		*818,532*	*679,159*		*48.6*	*44.8*		*812,135*	*673,106*		*6,397*	*6,053*		*0.8*	*0.9*
Negro	793,681	864,719	835,843	45.6	51.4	55.2	793,627	864,623	835,771	54	96	72			
Mexican	9	10	4				6	8	3	3	2	1			
Indian, Chinese, etc	1,035	467	396	0.1			1,000	382	343	35	85	53	3.4	18.2	13.4

POPULATION

Table 17.—NATIVE AND FOREIGN-BORN POPULATION BY COLOR OR RACE, BY DIVISIONS AND STATES: 1930, 1920, AND 1910—Continued

DIVISION OR STATE AND COLOR OR RACE	TOTAL Number 1930	1920	1910	Per cent distribution 1930	1920	1910	NATIVE 1930	1920	1910	FOREIGN BORN 1930	1920	1910	PER CENT FOREIGN BORN 1930	1920	1910
SOUTH ATLANTIC—Con.															
Georgia	2,908,506	2,895,832	2,609,121	100.0	100.0	100.0	2,894,203	2,879,268	2,593,644	14,303	16,564	15,477	0.5	0.6	0.6
White, as reported	1,836,974	1,689,114	1,431,802	63.2	58.3	54.9	1,823,057	1,672,928	1,416,730	13,917	16,186	15,072	0.8	1.0	1.1
White, as adjusted		*1,689,070*	*1,431,786*		*58.3*	*54.9*		*1,672,907*	*1,416,723*		*16,163*	*15,063*		*1.0*	*1.1*
Negro	1,071,125	1,206,365	1,176,987	36.8	41.7	45.1	1,070,925	1,206,149	1,176,759	200	216	228			
Mexican	47	44	16				21	21	7	26	23	9			
Indian, Chinese, etc	360	353	332				200	191	155	160	162	177	44.4	45.9	53.3
Florida	1,468,211	968,470	752,619	100.0	100.0	100.0	1,398,464	914,606	711,986	69,747	53,864	40,633	4.8	5.6	5.4
White, as reported	1,035,205	638,153	443,634	70.5	65.9	58.9	976,148	595,145	409,792	59,057	43,008	33,842	5.7	6.7	7.6
White, as adjusted		*638,034*	*443,567*		*65.9*	*58.9*		*595,085*	*409,769*		*42,949*	*33,798*		*6.7*	*7.6*
Negro	431,828	329,487	308,669	29.4	34.0	41.0	421,481	318,822	302,034	10,347	10,665	6,585	2.4	3.2	2.1
Mexican	185	110	67				64	60	23	121	50	44	65.4	45.6	65.2
Indian, Chinese, etc	993	830	316	0.1	0.1		771	639	110	222	191	206	22.4	23.0	
EAST SOUTH CENTRAL															
Kentucky	2,614,589	2,416,630	2,289,905	100.0	100.0	100.0	2,592,582	2,385,724	2,249,743	22,007	30,906	40,162	0.8	1.3	1.8
White, as reported	2,388,364	2,180,560	2,027,951	91.3	90.2	88.6	2,366,524	2,149,780	1,987,898	21,840	30,780	40,053	0.9	1.4	2.0
White, as adjusted		*2,180,462*	*2,027,926*		*90.2*	*88.6*		*2,149,755*	*1,987,885*		*30,707*	*40,041*		*1.4*	*2.0*
Negro	226,040	235,938	261,656	8.6	9.8	11.4	225,972	235,862	261,590	68	76	66			
Mexican	88	98	25				30	25	13	58	73	12			
Indian, Chinese, etc	97	132	298				56	82	255	41	50	43	37.9	14.4	
Tennessee	2,616,556	2,337,885	2,184,789	100.0	100.0	100.0	2,603,305	2,322,237	2,166,182	13,251	15,648	18,607	0.5	0.7	0.9
White, as reported	2,138,619	1,885,993	1,711,432	81.7	80.7	78.3	2,125,553	1,870,515	1,692,973	13,066	15,478	18,459	0.6	0.8	1.1
White, as adjusted		*1,885,939*	*1,711,417*		*80.7*	*78.3*		*1,870,496*	*1,692,967*		*15,443*	*18,450*		*0.8*	*1.1*
Negro	477,646	451,758	473,088	18.3	19.3	21.7	477,646	451,647	472,989	100	111	99			
Mexican	25	54	15				4	19	6	21	35	9			
Indian, Chinese, etc	266	134	260				202	75	220	64	59	49	24.1	44.0	18.2
Alabama	2,646,248	2,348,174	2,138,093	100.0	100.0	100.0	2,630,187	2,330,147	2,118,807	16,061	18,027	19,286	0.6	0.8	0.9
White, as reported	1,700,775	1,447,032	1,228,832	64.3	61.6	57.5	1,685,065	1,429,370	1,209,876	15,710	17,662	18,956	0.9	1.2	1.5
White, as adjusted		*1,446,958*	*1,228,789*		*61.6*	*57.5*		*1,429,341*	*1,209,859*		*17,617*	*18,930*		*1.2*	*1.5*
Negro	944,834	900,652	908,282	35.7	38.4	42.5	944,566	900,339	908,000	268	313	282			
Mexican	69	74	48				30	29	17	39	45	26			
Indian, Chinese, etc	570	490	979				526	438	931	44	52	48	7.7	10.6	4.9
Mississippi	2,009,821	1,790,618	1,797,114	100.0	100.0	100.0	2,001,776	1,782,210	1,787,344	8,045	8,408	9,770	0.4	0.5	0.5
White, as reported	998,856	853,962	786,111	49.6	47.7	43.7	989,807	845,943	776,722	7,049	8,019	9,389	0.7	0.9	1.2
White, as adjusted		*853,807*	*786,022*		*47.7*	*43.7*		*845,876*	*776,693*		*7,931*	*9,324*		*0.9*	*1.2*
Negro	1,009,718	935,184	1,009,487	50.2	52.2	56.2	1,009,022	935,048	1,009,309	96	136	65	45.9	56.8	
Mexican	1,221	155	89	0.1			660	67	24	561	88	178	10.7	17.2	13.4
Indian, Chinese, etc	2,026	1,472	1,516	0.1	0.1	0.1	1,687	1,219	1,313	339	253	203			
WEST SOUTH CENTRAL															
Arkansas	1,854,482	1,752,204	1,574,449	100.0	100.0	100.0	1,843,850	1,738,067	1,557,403	10,632	14,137	17,046	0.6	0.8	1.1
White, as reported	1,374,906	1,279,757	1,131,026	74.1	73.0	71.8	1,364,733	1,265,782	1,114,117	10,173	13,975	16,909	0.7	1.1	1.5
White, as adjusted		*1,279,479*	*1,130,878*		*73.0*	*71.8*		*1,265,698*	*1,114,047*		*13,781*	*16,831*		*1.1*	*1.5*
Negro	478,463	472,220	442,891	25.8	27.0	28.1	478,393	472,134	442,811	70	86	80			
Mexican	409	278	148				200	84	70	209	194	78	51.1	69.8	52.7
Indian, Chinese, etc	704	227	532				524	151	475	180	76	57	25.6	33.5	10.7
Louisiana	2,101,593	1,798,509	1,656,388	100.0	100.0	100.0	2,064,517	1,752,082	1,603,622	37,076	46,427	52,766	1.8	2.6	3.2
White, as reported	1,318,160	1,096,611	941,086	62.7	61.0	56.8	1,283,250	1,051,740	889,304	34,910	44,871	51,782	2.6	4.1	5.5
White, as adjusted		*1,093,991*	*939,789*		*60.8*	*56.7*		*1,051,015*	*888,794*		*42,976*	*50,995*		*3.9*	*5.4*
Negro	776,326	700,257	713,874	36.9	38.9	43.1	775,517	699,040	713,299	809	1,217	575	0.1	0.2	0.1
Mexican	4,552	2,620	1,297	0.2	0.1	0.1	3,471	725	510	1,081	1,895	787	23.7	72.3	60.7
Indian, Chinese, etc	2,555	1,641	1,428	0.1	0.1	0.1	2,279	1,302	1,019	276	339	409	10.8	20.7	28.6
Oklahoma	2,396,040	2,028,283	1,657,155	100.0	100.0	100.0	2,365,482	1,987,851	1,616,713	30,558	40,432	40,442	1.3	2.0	2.4
White, as reported	2,123,424	1,821,194	1,444,531	88.6	89.8	87.2	2,096,671	1,781,220	1,404,447	26,753	39,908	40,084	1.3	2.2	2.8
White, as adjusted		*1,813,217*	*1,441,577*		*89.4*	*87.0*		*1,779,562*	*1,405,988*		*33,655*	*37,591*		*1.9*	*2.6*
Negro	172,198	149,408	137,612	7.2	7.4	8.3	172,131	149,252	137,489	67	156	123	0.1	0.1	0.1
Mexican	7,354	7,977	2,954	0.3	0.4	0.2	3,858	1,664	461	3,496	6,313	2,493	47.5	79.1	84.4
Indian, Chinese, etc	93,064	57,681	75,012	3.9	2.8	4.5	92,822	57,373	74,777	242	308	235	0.3	0.5	0.3
Texas	5,824,715	4,663,228	3,896,542	100.0	100.0	100.0	5,462,428	4,299,396	3,654,604	362,287	363,832	241,938	6.2	7.8	6.2
White, as reported	4,283,491	3,918,165	3,204,848	73.5	84.0	82.2	4,185,095	3,557,646	2,964,864	98,396	360,519	239,984	2.3	9.2	7.5
White, as adjusted		*3,529,490*	*2,978,382*		*75.7*	*76.4*		*3,411,706*	*2,859,193*		*117,784*	*119,189*		*3.3*	*4.0*
Negro	854,964	741,694	690,049	14.7	15.9	17.7	854,498	740,162	688,958	466	1,532	1,091	0.1	0.2	0.2
Mexican	683,681	388,675	226,466	11.7	8.3	5.8	421,009	145,940	105,671	262,672	242,735	120,795	38.4	62.5	53.3
Indian, Chinese, etc	2,579	3,309	1,645		0.1		1,826	1,588	782	753	1,781	863	29.2	52.9	52.5
MOUNTAIN															
Montana	537,606	548,889	376,053	100.0	100.0	100.0	461,703	453,298	281,340	75,903	95,591	94,713	14.1	17.4	25.2
White, as reported	517,327	534,280	360,580	96.2	97.3	95.9	444,366	440,640	268,936	72,961	93,620	91,644	14.1	17.5	25.4
White, as adjusted		*533,991*	*360,491*		*97.3*	*95.9*		*440,571*	*268,902*		*93,420*	*91,589*		*17.5*	*25.4*
Negro	1,256	1,058	1,834	0.2	0.3	0.5	1,242	1,010	1,773	14	48	61	1.1	2.9	3.3
Mexican	2,571	269	89	0.5			884	69	34	1,687	200	55	65.6	74.3	
Indian, Chinese, etc	16,452	12,971	13,639	3.1	2.4	3.6	15,211	11,048	10,631	1,241	1,923	3,008	7.5	14.8	22.1
Idaho	445,032	431,866	325,594	100.0	100.0	100.0	412,748	391,119	283,016	32,284	40,747	42,578	7.3	9.4	13.1
White, as reported	437,562	425,668	319,221	98.3	98.6	98.0	407,108	386,705	278,794	30,454	38,963	40,427	7.0	9.2	12.7
White, as adjusted		*424,540*	*319,074*		*98.3*	*98.0*		*386,551*	*278,759*		*37,989*	*40,315*		*8.9*	*12.6*
Negro	668	920	651	0.2	0.2	0.2	653	886	623	15	34	28	2.2	3.7	4.3
Mexican	1,278	1,128	147	0.3	0.3		429	154	35	849	974	112	66.4	86.3	76.2
Indian, Chinese, etc	5,524	5,278	5,722	1.2	1.2	1.8	4,558	3,528	3,599	966	1,750	2,123	17.5	33.2	37.1

COLOR OR RACE, NATIVITY, AND PARENTAGE

45

TABLE 17.—NATIVE AND FOREIGN-BORN POPULATION BY COLOR OR RACE, BY DIVISIONS AND STATES: 1930, 1920, AND 1910—Continued

| DIVISION OR STATE AND COLOR OR RACE | TOTAL | | | | | | NATIVE | | | FOREIGN BORN | | | PER CENT FOREIGN BORN | | |
| | Number | | | Per cent distribution | | | | | | | | | | | |
	1930	1920	1910	1930	1920	1910	1930	1920	1910	1930	1920	1910	1930	1920	1910
MOUNTAIN—Con.															
Wyoming	225,565	194,402	145,965	100.0	100.0	100.0	202,222	167,835	116,945	23,343	26,567	29,020	10.3	13.7	19.9
White, as reported	214,007	190,146	140,318	94.9	97.8	96.1	194,409	164,891	113,200	19,658	25,255	27,118	9.2	13.3	19.3
White, as adjusted		*188,140*	*139,990*		*96.8*	*95.9*		*164,644*	*113,055*		*23,502*	*26,935*		*12.5*	*19.2*
Negro	1,250	1,375	2,235	0.6	0.7	1.5	1,242	1,345	2,107	8	30	128	0.6	2.2	1.7
Mexican	7,174	2,000	528	3.2	1.0	0.2	4,163	247	145	3,011	1,753	383	42.0	87.7	55.3
Indian, Chinese, etc.	3,074	2,881	3,412	1.4	1.5	2.3	2,408	1,599	1,548	666	1,282	1,864	21.7	44.5	54.6
Colorado	1,035,791	939,629	799,024	100.0	100.0	100.0	935,916	820,491	669,437	99,875	119,138	129,587	9.6	12.7	16.2
White, as reported	961,117	924,103	783,415	92.8	98.3	98.0	875,711	807,149	656,564	85,406	116,954	120,851	8.9	12.7	16.2
White, as adjusted		*909,763*	*780,146*		*96.8*	*97.6*		*803,504*	*655,791*		*106,259*	*124,355*		*11.7*	*15.9*
Negro	11,828	11,318	11,453	1.1	1.2	1.4	11,767	11,186	11,323	61	132	130	0.5	1.2	1.1
Mexican	57,676	14,340	3,209	5.6	1.5	0.4	44,860	3,645	773	12,816	10,695	2,406	22.2	74.6	76.4
Indian, Chinese, etc.	5,170	4,208	4,156	0.5	0.4	0.5	3,578	2,156	1,550	1,592	2,052	2,606	30.8	48.8	62.7
New Mexico	423,317	360,350	327,301	100.0	100.0	100.0	399,265	330,542	304,155	24,052	29,808	23,146	5.7	8.3	7.1
White, as reported	331,756	334,673	304,504	78.4	92.9	93.1	323,058	305,596	281,940	7,707	29,077	22,564	2.4	8.7	7.4
White, as adjusted		*301,879*	*283,574*		*83.8*	*86.6*		*291,866*	*272,334*		*10,013*	*11,240*		*3.3*	*4.0*
Negro	2,850	5,733	1,628	0.7	1.6	0.5	2,836	5,637	1,594	14	96	34	0.5	1.7	2.1
Mexican	59,340	32,704	21,020	14.0	9.1	6.4	43,357	13,730	9,606	15,983	19,004	11,414	26.9	58.1	54.3
Indian, Chinese, etc.	29,372	19,944	21,070	6.9	5.5	6.4	29,114	19,309	20,621	258	635	458	0.9	3.2	2.2
Arizona	435,573	334,162	204,354	100.0	100.0	100.0	369,817	253,596	155,589	65,756	80,566	48,765	15.1	24.1	23.9
White, as reported	264,378	291,440	171,468	60.7	87.2	83.9	248,787	213,350	124,644	15,591	78,090	46,824	5.9	26.8	27.3
White, as adjusted		*202,985*	*122,360*		*60.7*	*59.9*		*182,857*	*103,859*		*20,128*	*18,521*		*9.9*	*15.1*
Negro	10,749	8,005	2,009	2.5	2.4	1.0	10,696	7,827	1,978	53	178	31	0.5	2.2	1.5
Mexican	114,173	88,464	29,108	26.2	26.5	24.0	66,318	30,493	20,805	47,855	57,971	28,303	41.9	65.5	57.6
Indian, Chinese, etc.	46,273	34,708	30,877	10.6	10.4	15.1	44,016	32,419	28,967	2,257	2,289	1,910	4.9	6.6	6.2
Utah	507,847	449,396	373,351	100.0	100.0	100.0	459,832	390,196	307,529	48,015	59,200	65,822	9.5	13.2	17.6
White, as reported	495,955	441,901	366,583	97.7	98.3	98.2	452,183	385,446	303,190	43,772	56,455	63,393	8.8	12.8	17.3
White, as adjusted		*440,690*	*366,425*		*98.1*	*98.1*		*385,173*	*303,157*		*55,526*	*63,268*		*12.6*	*17.3*
Negro	1,108	1,446	1,144	0.2	0.3	0.3	1,096	1,390	1,112	12	56	32	1.1	3.9	2.8
Mexican	4,012	1,203	158	0.8	0.3		1,795	273	33	2,217	929	125	55.3	77.3	79.1
Indian, Chinese, etc.	6,772	6,040	5,624	1.3	1.3	1.5	4,758	3,380	3,227	2,014	2,089	2,397	29.7	44.5	42.6
Nevada	91,058	77,407	81,875	100.0	100.0	100.0	75,963	61,404	62,184	15,095	16,003	19,891	16.6	20.7	24.1
White, as reported	81,425	70,690	74,276	89.4	91.3	90.7	69,150	55,807	56,277	12,275	14,802	17,999	15.1	20.9	24.2
White, as adjusted		*69,402*	*73,455*		*89.7*	*89.7*		*55,708*	*56,145*		*13,694*	*17,310*		*19.7*	*23.6*
Negro	516	340	513	0.6	0.4	0.6	506	330	494	10	7	19	1.9	2.0	3.7
Mexican	3,090	1,297	821	3.4	1.7	1.0	1,012	189	132	2,078	1,108	689	67.2	85.4	83.9
Indian, Chinese, etc.	6,027	5,302	7,086	6.6	8.2	8.7	5,295	5,108	5,413	732	1,104	1,673	12.1	18.8	23.0
PACIFIC															
Washington	1,563,396	1,356,621	1,141,990	100.0	100.0	100.0	1,308,138	1,091,329	885,749	255,258	265,292	256,241	16.3	19.6	22.4
White, as reported	1,521,099	1,319,777	1,109,111	97.3	97.3	97.1	1,276,843	1,069,722	867,014	244,256	250,055	241,197	16.1	18.9	21.7
White, as adjusted		*1,319,393*	*1,108,967*		*97.3*	*97.1*		*1,069,627*	*867,859*		*249,766*	*241,108*		*18.9*	*21.7*
Negro	6,840	6,883	6,058	0.4	0.5	0.5	6,673	6,612	5,820	167	271	238	2.4	3.9	3.9
Mexican	562	384	144				152	95	55	410	289	89	73.0	75.3	61.8
Indian, Chinese, etc.	34,895	29,961	26,821	2.2	2.2	2.3	24,470	14,995	12,015	10,425	14,966	14,806	29.9	50.0	55.2
Oregon	953,786	783,389	672,765	100.0	100.0	100.0	843,346	675,745	559,629	110,440	107,644	113,136	11.6	13.7	16.8
White, as reported	937,029	769,140	655,090	98.2	98.2	97.4	831,554	666,995	552,089	105,475	102,151	103,001	11.3	13.3	15.7
White, as adjusted		*768,530*	*654,838*		*98.1*	*97.3*		*666,882*	*552,003*		*101,648*	*102,890*		*13.2*	*15.7*
Negro	2,234	2,144	1,492	0.2	0.3	0.2	2,184	2,097	1,430	50	47	62	2.2	2.2	4.2
Mexican	1,568	616	257	0.2	0.1		328	113	86	1,240	503	171	79.1	81.7	66.5
Indian, Chinese, etc.	12,955	12,009	16,183	1.4	1.5	2.4	9,280	6,053	6,110	3,675	5,446	10,073	28.4	45.0	62.2
California	5,677,251	3,426,861	2,377,549	100.0	100.0	100.0	4,603,287	2,669,236	1,791,117	1,073,964	757,625	586,432	18.9	22.1	24.7
White, as reported	5,040,247	3,264,711	2,259,672	88.8	95.3	95.0	4,230,213	2,583,049	1,742,422	810,034	681,662	517,250	16.1	20.9	22.9
White, as adjusted		*3,142,556*	*2,211,281*		*91.7*	*93.0*		*2,543,992*	*1,725,741*		*599,543*	*485,540*		*19.1*	*22.0*
Negro	81,048	38,763	21,645	1.4	1.1	0.9	79,396	37,640	20,771	1,652	1,123	874	2.0	2.9	4.0
Mexican	368,013	121,176	48,391	6.5	3.5	2.0	176,667	39,057	16,681	191,346	82,119	31,710	52.0	67.8	65.5
Indian, Chinese, etc.	187,943	123,387	96,232	3.3	3.6	4.0	117,011	48,547	27,924	70,932	74,840	68,308	37.7	60.7	71.0

CHAPTER 3

SEX DISTRIBUTION

CHAPTER 3.—SEX DISTRIBUTION

INTRODUCTION

The distribution by sex of the white population of the United States has been ascertained at every Federal census, but data on this subject for the total population were collected for the first time in 1820.

The distribution of the population by sex is a fundamental classification, essential to the proper interpretation of almost every other phase of population statistics. The sex distinction is therefore extensively presented in correlation with other classifications. This chapter is devoted mainly to a consideration of the relative numerical importance of the two sexes in different sections of the country and in the principal color, nativity, and parentage classes of the population.

The question as to sex is the simplest inquiry on the population schedule. There is no ambiguity of terms, and but rarely any motive for misrepresenting the facts to the enumerator. The sex classification of the population as a whole may therefore be accepted as the most dependable of all the classifications. Imperfect returns as to color, nativity, or parentage are more likely to occur, however, in the case of males than in the case of females, since males predominate among the foreign born and among the floating population, for both of which classes accurate information is sometimes difficult to obtain. A certain number of foreign-born persons, for example, are likely to be returned as native; and of these, far more will be males than females. From such sources may arise slight errors in the sex distribution of the several classes of the white population, but these will not be large enough to affect appreciably the sex ratio—that is, the number of males per 100 females.

Total population.—The statistics relating to the sex distribution of the population of continental United States, as returned at the Fifteenth Decennial Census, are summarized in Table 1, and comparative figures are presented for prior censuses. Statistics relating to sex distribution for the population of all the outlying possessions except the Philippine Islands are given in the special report entitled "Outlying Territories and Possessions."

The following statement shows the excess of males in the total population for each census year beginning with 1820.

CENSUS YEAR	Excess of males	CENSUS YEAR	Excess of males	CENSUS YEAR	Excess of males
1930	1,499,114	1890	1,526,488	1850	483,444
1920	2,090,242	1880	881,857	1840	307,611
1910	2,692,288	1870	428,759	1830	198,958
1900	1,638,321	1860	727,087	1820	154,757

This preponderance of males is due in part to the fact that the total population includes a considerable proportion of foreign-born persons, among whom the males greatly outnumber the females; but in the most important class of the native population, namely, the native whites of native parentage, there is also a marked excess of males.

White population.—The preponderance of males over females in the white population is due in part to the abnormal sex distribution of the foreign-born whites, but among the native whites also the males outnumbered the females in 1930 by 522,490. This excess, however, occurs only among the native whites of native parentage, the foreign-parentage and mixed-parentage groups both showing an excess of females in 1930. (See Table 1.)

The preponderance of males among the native whites of native parentage has appeared at each census beginning with that for 1890, at which the distinction between native and foreign parentage was first made by sex. For all native whites combined an excess of males has also been shown at each census beginning with 1850, when the classification according to nativity was first made.

The sex ratio for the total native white population has shown a decline at each census since 1890. This reduction has been particularly rapid since 1910. Between 1910 and 1920, emigration, war losses, and increase in military and naval services stationed abroad at the time the 1920 census was taken and therefore not included in the population of continental United States, all contributed to a relative decrease in the male population. In general, however, the reduction in the sex ratio is mainly due to the rapid fall in the birth and death rates and the consequent aging of the population. In every population, there is a preponderance of male births, but the death rate of males, both in early and in late age periods, is higher than that of females. Consequently, a decreased proportion of children in the population relative to that of adults will result in a decline in the sex ratio.

The sex ratios for the native whites of native parentage, of foreign parentage, and of mixed parentage have all declined about equally since 1910.

The ratio for the foreign-born white population has declined sharply since 1910. In that year, following a decade of heavy immigration, the sex ratio of the foreign-born whites was 129.2. In 1920 it had fallen to 121.7, and in 1930 to 115.1, the lowest ratio since 1860. Under free immigration there was always a

93

94 POPULATION

large surplus of males over females in the foreign-born population, but with the outbreak of the World War many thousands of males returned to their native countries for military service. Since the World War, under selective immigration, the surplus of males has been more than balanced by the still larger surplus of males among emigrant aliens, so that in the net accession to the population from abroad there has been an actual excess of females. With restricted immigration the foreign born are rapidly aging. The median age of the foreign-born white population increased from 40 years in 1920 to 44 years in 1930. Since there are still many more males than females surviving in the older generation of immigrants, and since the death rate of males in the older age groups exceeds that of females, the excess of males is being rapidly reduced. With the continuance of present conditions, the sex ratio of the foreign-born white population will decline rapidly until there is an actual excess of females over males.

Negro population.—Differing from all other races, the Negroes have shown an excess of females over males at every census since and including that of 1840, although the returns for 1820 and 1830 showed a preponderance of males. The relative excess of females in 1930 was greater than that shown at any previous census except that of 1870.

Indian population.—At every census except that of 1870 the Indian population has shown an excess of males. No attempt was made, however, to secure a complete enumeration of this race prior to 1890, and it is doubtful whether the figures for earlier census years are of any material value as showing the true sex ratio of the total Indian population. The more recent returns also are subject to a somewhat greater margin of error than are those for the other races, by reason of the effort to count as Indian all persons having any trace of Indian blood. It is likely that some persons in whom the admixture of Indian blood was so slight as not to be readily noticeable were reported as white, and there may have been differences between the two sexes in regard to the frequency of this occurrence.

Mexican population.—Persons of Mexican birth or parentage who were not definitely returned as white or Indian were designated "Mexican" in 1930, and included in the general class of "Other races." In prior censuses most Mexicans have been classified as white. The fact that these persons were included with the white population in 1920, but were given a separate classification in 1930, affects slightly the comparison of the 1930 and 1920 data by sex as they are presented in this chapter. In the States near the Mexican border the sex ratio of the Mexicans does not differ radically from that of the total white population, but in more distant States, where the Mexican population is made

up largely of workers without families, the sex ratio of the Mexican element is more like that of the foreign-born white.

Using as a basis the 1920 returns for persons born in Mexico, and persons having one or both parents born in Mexico, it has been estimated that there were in the United States in that year 700,541 persons who would have been classified as Mexican under the 1930 instructions. These may be compared with 1,422,533 persons returned as Mexican in 1930. Similarly it has been estimated that the white classification in 1910 included 367,510 persons who would have been counted as Mexican in 1930. The estimates of the number of Mexicans in 1920 are presented in Table 1, together with adjusted figures for the white population obtained by deducting the estimated numbers of Mexicans. In the detailed tables giving statistics for States and cities, however, the presentation is limited to the Mexicans returned in 1930 and the white population as reported, without adjustment for Mexicans.[1] The effects of this change in classification on the comparability of the sex ratios is of course limited to those areas in which an appreciable number of Mexicans are shown for 1930.

Chinese, Japanese, and "All other" population.—Among the Chinese, Japanese, and other minor elements of the population, the excess of males is very great, although there has been a pronounced decrease in the sex ratio from census to census since 1890 in the case of the Chinese, and since 1900 in the case of the Japanese. The excess of males among the immigrants of these races has been much greater than that in any other immigrant group. From the passage of the Chinese exclusion law, until 1920, the number of Chinese males in the United States steadily declined, chiefly because of deaths among the older Chinese immigrants. The number of females, however, has shown a steady increase since 1890, and the sex ratio has declined rapidly. The census of 1930 shows an increase in the total Chinese population nearly equal in numbers as between the sexes, but proportionally much greater for females than for males. The Japanese population has shown an increase at each census since 1870, when it was first separately enumerated, but the increase among Japanese males since 1910 has been comparatively slow, while the increase in the number of females has been rapid. The sex ratio in 1930 had declined to 143.3. In the absence of further immigration, the natural increase in the Japanese population, together with the larger number of deaths among males than among females, will bring the proportion of the sexes nearer to equality.

[1] The estimated numbers of Mexicans in 1920 are shown in some detail in chs. 6, 7, and 8 of this volume, with sex as incidental features, having been worked out after the material in the present chapter was in type.

SEX DISTRIBUTION

Urban and rural population.—Since there are marked differences in the sex distribution of the population of urban and rural areas, statistics are presented for the urban and rural population, by sex, in Table 5.

Urban population, as defined by the Census Bureau, is in general that residing in cities and other incorporated places having 2,500 inhabitants or more, the remainder being classified as rural. In three of the New England States, New Hampshire, Massachusetts, and Rhode Island, conditions are exceptional in that the compactly built portions of towns (townships) are not separately incorporated or politically distinct in any way from the rural territory within the same town; nor is it the usual practice to incorporate even the larger places as cities until they attain a population in excess of 10,000. Consequently, if only cities were counted as urban the classification would be quite inadequate. In 1920 and 1910 all towns in these States which had a population of 2,500 or more were classified as urban. This resulted in the inclusion of a considerable number of places that were mainly rural in their general characteristics. In 1930 the special rule for these States has been modified so as to place in the urban classification, in addition to the regularly incorporated cities, only those towns in which there is a village or thickly settled area having more than 2,500 inhabitants, and comprising, either by itself or when combined with other villages in the same town, more than 50 per cent of the total population of the town.

One other modification has been made in the definition of urban population for use in connection with the 1930 census. This modification extends the definition so as to include townships and other political subdivisions (not incorporated as municipalities, nor containing any area so incorporated) which had a total population of 10,000 or more, and a population density of 1,000 or more per square mile.

Since it has been found impracticable to go back and readjust to the new basis the 1920 urban and rural figures as they are tabulated by color, sex, age, etc., they are presented in all tables as established in 1920. The comparative figures, therefore, show differences in a few cases which must be considered or interpreted as solely or mainly the result of the change in the method of classification.

The ratio of males to females is decidedly higher in rural than in urban communities, not only for the total population but for each of its elements except the numerically unimportant group designated "Other races." (See Table 7.)

This difference between urban and rural communities in regard to the sex distribution of the principal classes of the population—which exists despite the fact that the foreign born, among whom the males considerably outnumber the females, are more numerous in urban than in rural communities—is doubtless due primarily to the fact that the cities afford many more opportunities for the gainful employment of women than do the rural districts.

Rural-farm and rural-nonfarm population.—In addition to the classification of the population as urban and rural, which is based on the size (number of inhabitants) and the political status (municipal incorporation) of the geographic unit in which the persons live, the population, both urban and rural, is further classified as farm and nonfarm, on the basis of a question reading "Does this family live on a farm?"

For the farm population living in urban territory, which forms less than 1 per cent of the total farm population, no detailed tabulations were made; hence the presentation of classified data for the farm population is limited to that part living in rural territory and designated as rural-farm population. This is done partly to simplify the classification (dividing the total population into three groups, namely, urban, rural-farm, and rural-nonfarm) and partly because it is felt that in general the farm families living within the corporate limits of cities or other incorporated places are living under conditions at least somewhat urban, rather than under typical farm conditions.

The rural-nonfarm or "village" population is made up largely of persons living in small towns or villages, both incorporated and unincorporated, though in many areas there are considerable numbers of families living in the open country but not on farms.

In the matter of sex distribution, as between the two subdivisions of the rural population, the rural-farm usually shows a much higher proportion of males than the rural-nonfarm, mainly because there is more opportunity for employment on farms for men than for women.

Geographic areas.—Statistics are presented in this bulletin for continental United States as a whole; for nine groups of States designated geographic divisions; for the three main sections of the country (the North, the South, and the West), for all cities having a population of 25,000 or more in 1930; for urban and rural areas, and for the two subdivisions of the latter, designated rural-farm and rural-nonfarm. The North includes the New England, Middle Atlantic, East North Central, and West North Central divisions; the South includes the South Atlantic, East South Central, and the West South Central divisions; and the West includes the Mountain and Pacific divisions.

POPULATION

RATIO OF MALES TO FEMALES IN TOTAL POPULATION, BY STATES: 1930

[District of Columbia, females in excess, not shown separately on the map]

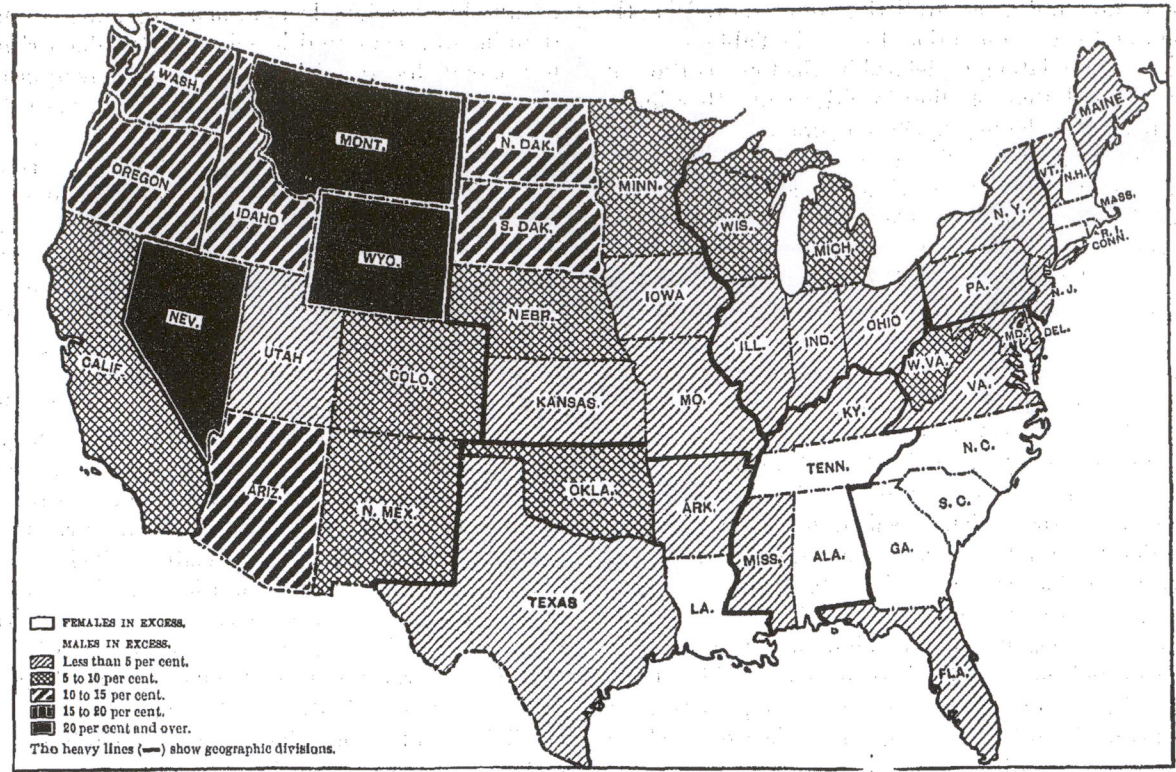

RATIO OF MALES TO FEMALES IN TOTAL POPULATION, BY STATES: 1920

[District of Columbia, females in excess, not shown separately on the map]

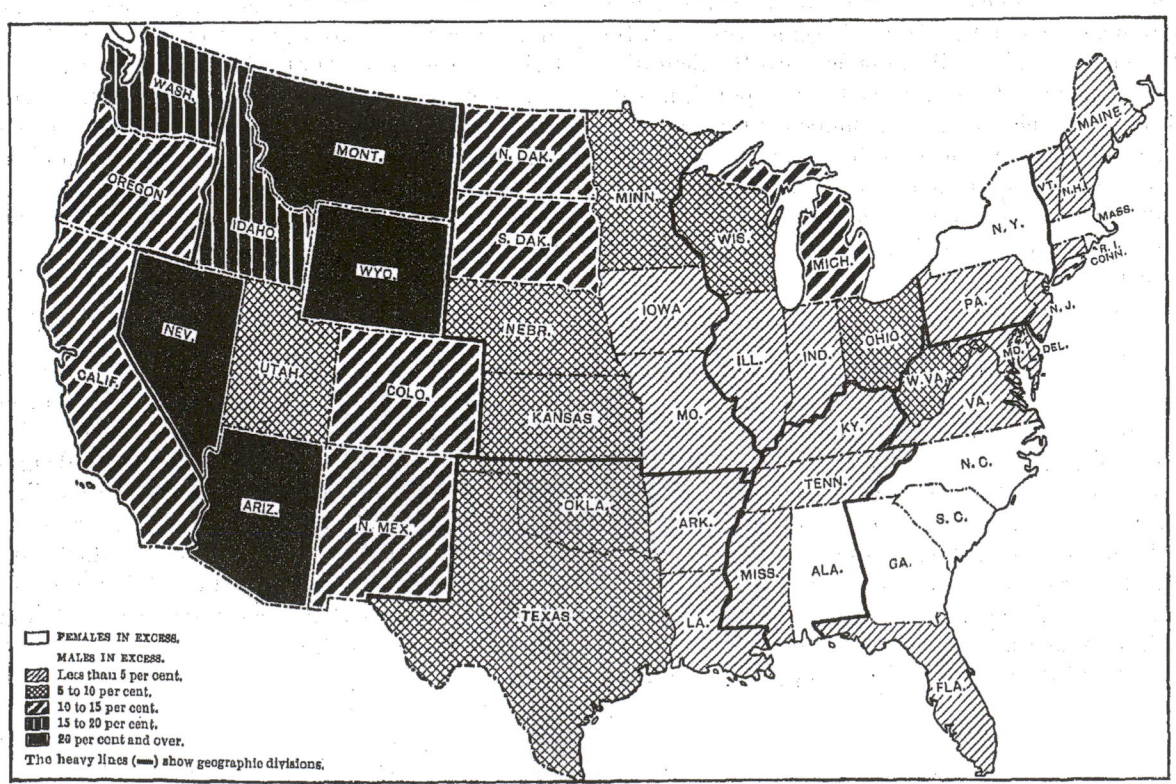

SEX DISTRIBUTION

TABLE 1.—POPULATION OF THE UNITED STATES BY SEX, COLOR, AND NATIVITY: 1790 TO 1930

[Per cent not shown where base is less than 100; sex ratio not shown where number of females is less than 100. A minus sign (—) denotes decrease]

CLASS OF POPULATION AND CENSUS YEAR	Total	Male	Female	Per cent of total — Male	Per cent of total — Female	Males per 100 females	Excess of males	Excess of females	Increase over preceding census — Males Number	Males Per cent	Increase over preceding census — Females Number	Females Per cent
All classes:												
1930	122,775,046	62,137,080	60,637,966	50.6	49.4	102.5	1,499,114		8,236,649	15.3	8,827,777	17.0
1920	105,710,620	53,900,431	51,810,189	51.0	49.0	104.0	2,090,242		6,508,154	13.9	7,170,200	16.1
1910	91,972,266	47,332,277	44,639,989	51.5	48.5	106.0	2,692,288		8,515,829	21.0	7,461,862	20.1
1900	75,994,575	38,816,448	37,178,127	51.1	48.9	104.4	1,638,321		6,579,347	20.4	6,467,514	21.1
1890	62,947,714	32,237,101	30,710,613	51.2	48.8	105.0	1,526,488		6,718,281	26.3	6,073,650	24.7
1880	50,155,783	25,518,820	24,636,963	50.9	49.1	103.6	881,857		6,025,255	30.9	5,572,157	29.2
1870	38,558,371	19,493,565	19,064,806	50.6	49.4	102.2	428,759		3,408,361	21.2	3,706,689	24.1
1860	31,443,321	16,085,204	15,358,117	51.2	48.8	104.7	727,087		4,247,544	35.8	4,003,901	35.8
1850	23,191,876	11,837,660	11,354,216	51.0	49.0	104.3	483,444		3,149,128	36.2	2,978,295	35.5
1840	17,069,453	8,688,532	8,380,921	50.9	49.1	103.7	307,611		2,155,043	33.0	2,047,390	32.3
1830	12,866,020	6,532,489	6,333,531	50.8	49.2	103.1	198,958		1,635,884	33.4	1,591,683	33.6
1820	9,638,453	4,896,605	4,741,848	50.8	49.2	103.3	154,757					
White:												
1930	108,864,207	55,163,854	53,700,353	50.7	49.3	102.7	1,463,501		6,733,199	13.9	7,310,093	15.8
1920	94,820,915	48,430,655	46,390,260	51.1	48.9	104.4	2,040,395		6,252,410	14.8	6,836,548	17.3
1920 (adjusted) [1]	94,120,374	48,049,193	46,071,181	51.1	48.9	104.3	1,978,012					
1910	81,731,957	42,178,245	39,553,712	51.6	48.4	106.6	2,624,533		8,031,356	23.3	5,776,582	21.5
1900	66,809,196	34,201,735	32,607,461	51.2	48.8	104.9	1,594,274		6,130,479	21.5	5,558,809	26.1
1890	55,101,258	28,270,379	26,830,879	51.3	48.7	105.4	1,439,500		6,139,479	27.7	5,558,809	26.1
1880	43,402,970	22,130,900	21,272,070	51.0	49.0	104.0	858,830		5,101,812	30.0	4,711,781	28.5
1870	33,589,377	17,029,088	16,560,289	50.7	49.3	102.8	468,799		3,217,701	23.3	3,449,139	26.8
1860	26,922,537	13,811,387	13,111,150	51.3	48.7	105.3	700,237		3,784,985	37.8	3,584,484	37.6
1850	19,553,068	10,026,402	9,526,666	51.3	48.7	105.2	499,736		2,770,858	38.2	2,586,405	37.3
1840	14,195,805	7,255,544	6,940,261	51.1	48.9	104.5	315,283		1,880,331	35.2	1,769,090	34.2
1830	10,537,378	5,366,213	5,171,165	50.9	49.1	103.8	195,048		1,370,404	34.3	1,300,177	33.6
1820	7,866,797	3,995,809	3,870,988	50.8	49.2	103.2	124,821		1,007,679	33.7	907,045	34.7
1810	5,862,073	2,988,130	2,873,943	51.0	49.0	104.0	114,187		792,825	36.1	762,802	36.1
1800	4,306,446	2,195,305	2,111,141	51.0	49.0	104.0	84,164		579,871	35.0	554,560	35.6
1790	3,172,006	1,615,434	1,556,572	50.9	49.1	103.8	58,862					
Native white:												
1930	95,497,800	48,010,145	47,487,655	50.3	49.7	101.1	522,490		7,107,812	17.4	7,281,827	18.1
1920	81,108,161	40,902,333	40,205,828	50.4	49.6	101.7	696,505		6,247,876	18.0	6,473,873	19.2
1920 (adjusted) [1]	80,864,980	40,780,002	40,084,978	50.4	49.6	101.7	695,024					
1910	68,386,412	34,654,457	33,731,955	50.7	49.3	102.7	922,502		5,968,007	20.8	5,823,026	20.9
1900	56,595,379	28,086,450	27,008,929	50.7	49.3	102.9	657,651		5,367,920	23.0	5,248,059	23.2
1890	45,979,391	23,318,521	22,660,870	50.7	49.3	102.9	657,651		4,709,256	25.3	4,426,844	24.3
1880	36,843,291	18,609,265	18,234,026	50.5	49.5	102.1	375,239		4,522,756	32.1	4,224,870	30.2
1870	28,095,665	14,086,509	14,009,156	50.1	49.9	100.6	77,353		2,467,352	21.2	2,802,529	25.0
1860	22,825,784	11,619,157	11,206,627	50.9	49.1	103.7	412,530		2,832,189	32.2	2,081,062	31.4
1850	17,312,533	8,786,968	8,525,565	50.8	49.2	103.1	261,403					
Native parentage:												
1930	70,136,014	35,460,001	34,676,013	50.6	49.4	102.3	783,988		5,823,220	19.6	5,891,437	20.5
1920	58,421,957	29,636,781	28,785,176	50.7	49.3	103.0	851,605		4,407,563	17.5	4,525,819	18.7
1910	49,488,575	25,229,218	24,259,357	51.0	49.0	104.0	969,861		4,379,371	21.0	4,159,842	20.7
1900	40,940,302	20,849,847	20,090,515	50.9	49.1	103.7	759,332		3,312,807	18.9	3,160,749	18.7
1800	34,475,716	17,530,950	16,938,706	50.9	49.1	103.5	598,184					
Foreign or mixed parentage:												
1930	25,361,186	12,550,144	12,811,042	49.5	50.5	98.0		260,898	1,284,592	11.4	1,390,390	12.2
1920	22,686,204	11,265,552	11,420,652	49.7	50.3	98.6		155,100	1,840,313	19.5	1,048,054	20.6
1920 (adjusted) [1]	22,443,023	11,143,221	11,299,802	49.7	50.3	98.8		156,581				
1910	18,897,837	9,425,239	9,472,598	49.9	50.1	99.5		47,359	1,588,636	20.3	1,663,184	21.3
1900	15,646,017	7,836,603	7,809,414	50.1	49.9	100.3	27,189		2,055,032	35.5	2,087,310	36.5
1890	11,503,675	5,781,571	5,722,104	50.3	49.7	101.0	59,467					
Foreign parentage:												
1930	16,999,221	8,438,676	8,560,545	49.6	50.4	98.6		121,869	628,145	8.0	676,537	8.6
1920	15,004,539	7,610,531	7,884,008	49.8	50.2	99.1		73,477	1,353,738	21.0	1,424,490	22.1
1910	12,916,311	6,456,793	6,459,518	50.0	50.0	100.0		2,725	1,115,443	20.9	1,168,588	22.1
1900	10,632,280	5,341,350	5,290,930	50.2	49.8	101.0	50,420					
Mixed parentage:												
1930	8,361,965	4,111,468	4,250,497	49.2	50.8	96.7		139,029	656,447	19.0	713,853	20.2
1920	6,991,065	3,455,021	3,536,044	49.4	50.6	97.7		81,023	486,575	16.4	523,564	17.4
1910	5,981,526	2,968,446	3,013,080	49.6	50.4	98.5		44,634	473,193	19.0	494,596	19.6
1900	5,013,737	2,495,253	2,518,484	49.8	50.2	99.1		23,231				
Foreign-born white:												
1930	13,366,407	7,153,709	6,212,698	53.5	46.5	115.1	941,011		−374,613	−5.0	28,266	0.5
1920	13,712,754	7,528,322	6,184,432	54.9	45.1	121.7	1,343,890		4,534	0.1	362,675	6.2
1920 (adjusted) [1]	13,255,394	7,269,191	5,986,203	54.8	45.2	121.4	1,282,988					
1910	13,345,545	7,523,788	5,821,757	56.4	43.6	129.2	1,702,031		2,008,503	36.4	1,123,225	23.9
1900	10,213,817	5,515,285	4,698,532	54.0	46.0	117.4	816,753		563,427	11.4	528,523	12.7
1890	9,121,867	4,951,858	4,170,009	54.3	45.7	118.7	781,849		1,430,223	40.6	1,131,965	37.3
1880	6,559,679	3,521,635	3,038,044	53.7	46.3	115.9	483,591		570,056	19.7	486,911	19.1
1870	5,493,712	2,942,579	2,551,133	53.6	46.4	115.3	391,446		750,349	34.2	646,610	34.0
1860	4,096,753	2,192,230	1,904,523	53.5	46.5	115.1	287,707		952,706	76.9	903,422	90.2
1850	2,240,535	1,239,434	1,001,101	55.3	44.7	123.8	238,333					
Negro:												
1930	11,891,143	5,855,669	6,035,474	49.2	50.8	97.0		179,805	646,233	12.4	781,779	14.9
1920	10,463,131	5,209,436	5,253,695	49.8	50.2	99.2		44,259	323,555	6.6	311,813	6.3
1910	9,827,763	4,885,881	4,941,882	49.7	50.3	98.9		56,001	490,334	11.4	404,435	11.1
1900	8,833,994	4,386,547	4,447,447	49.7	50.3	98.6		60,900	650,944	17.4	694,374	18.5
1890	7,488,676	3,735,603	3,753,073	49.9	50.1	99.5		17,470	482,488	14.8	425,395	12.8
1880	6,580,793	3,253,115	3,327,678	49.4	50.6	97.8		74,563	859,852	35.9	840,932	33.8
1870	4,880,009	2,393,263	2,486,746	49.0	51.0	96.2		93,483	176,519	8.0	261,660	11.8
1860	4,441,830	2,216,744	2,225,086	49.9	50.1	99.6		8,342	405,486	22.4	397,586	21.5
1850	3,638,808	1,811,258	1,827,550	49.8	50.2	99.1		16,292	378,270	26.4	386,890	26.9
1840	2,873,648	1,432,988	1,440,660	49.9	50.1	99.5		7,672	266,712	22.9	278,294	23.9
1830	2,328,642	1,166,276	1,162,366	50.1	49.9	100.3	3,910		265,480	29.5	291,506	33.5
1820	1,771,656	900,796	870,860	50.8	49.2	103.4	29,936					

[1] Adjusted by deducting the estimated number of Mexicans; see text, p. 94.

98

POPULATION

TABLE 1.—POPULATION OF THE UNITED STATES BY SEX, COLOR, AND NATIVITY: 1790 TO 1930—Continued

CLASS OF POPULATION AND CENSUS YEAR	Total	Male	Female	PER CENT OF TOTAL		Males per 100 females	Excess of males	Excess of females	INCREASE OVER PRECEDING CENSUS			
				Male	Female				Males		Females	
									Number	Per cent	Number	Per cent
Other races:												
1930	2,019,606	1,117,557	902,139	55.3	44.7	128.9	215,418		857,217	329.3	735,905	442.7
1920	426,574	260,340	166,234	61.0	39.0	156.6	94,106		−7,811	−2.9	21,839	15.1
1920 (adjusted) [1]	*1,127,915*	*641,802*	*486,913*	*56.9*	*43.1*	*132.2*	*156,489*					
1910	412,546	268,151	144,395	65.0	35.0	185.7	123,756		60,985	17.5	21,176	17.2
1900	351,385	228,166	123,219	64.9	35.1	185.2	104,947		−2,953	−1.3	−3,442	−2.7
1890	357,780	231,119	126,661	64.6	35.4	182.5	104,458		96,314	71.4	89,446	240.3
1880	172,020	134,805	37,215	78.4	21.6	362.2	97,590		63,591	80.3	19,444	109.4
1870	88,985	71,214	17,771	80.0	20.0	400.7	53,443		14,141	24.8	−4,110	−18.8
1860	78,954	57,073	21,881	72.3	27.7	260.8	35,192					
Mexican—												
1930	1,422,533	758,674	663,859	53.3	46.7	114.3	94,815					
1920 (estimated)	*700,541*	*381,462*	*319,079*	*54.5*	*45.5*	*119.6*	*62,383*					
Indian—												
1930	332,397	170,350	162,047	51.2	48.8	105.1	8,303		45,282	36.2	42,678	35.8
1920	244,437	125,068	119,369	51.2	48.8	104.8	5,699		−10,065	−7.4	−11,181	−8.6
1910	265,683	135,133	130,550	50.9	49.1	103.5	4,583		15,649	13.1	12,838	10.9
1900	237,196	119,484	117,712	50.4	49.6	101.5	1,772		−6,235	−5.0	−4,822	−3.9
1890	248,253	125,719	122,534	50.6	49.4	102.6	3,185		91,734	269.9	90,112	277.9
1880	66,407	33,985	32,422	51.2	48.8	104.8	1,563		21,451	171.1	19,225	145.7
1870	25,731	12,534	13,197	48.7	51.3	95.0		663	−11,390	−47.6	−6,900	−34.3
1860	44,021	23,924	20,097	54.3	45.7	119.0	3,827					
Chinese—												
1930	74,954	59,802	15,152	79.8	20.2	394.7	44,650		5,911	11.0	7,404	95.6
1920	61,639	53,891	7,748	87.4	12.6	695.5	46,143		−12,965	−19.4	3,073	65.7
1910	71,531	66,856	4,675	93.5	6.5	1,430.1	62,181		−18,485	−21.7	153	3.4
1900	89,863	85,341	4,522	95.0	5.0	1,887.2	80,819		−18,279	−17.6	654	16.9
1890	107,488	103,620	3,868	96.4	3.6	2,678.9	99,752		2,934	2.9	−911	−19.1
1880	105,465	100,686	4,779	95.5	4.5	2,106.8	95,907		42,053	71.7	213	4.7
1870	63,199	58,633	4,566	92.8	7.2	1,284.1	54,067		25,484	76.9	2,782	155.9
1860	34,933	33,149	1,784	94.9	5.1	1,858.1	31,365					
Japanese—												
1930	138,834	81,771	57,063	58.9	41.1	143.3	24,708		9,064	12.5	18,760	49.0
1920	111,010	72,707	38,303	65.5	34.5	189.8	34,404		9,637	15.3	20,216	321.5
1910	72,157	63,070	9,087	87.4	12.6	694.1	53,983		39,729	170.2	8,102	822.5
1900	24,326	23,341	985	96.0	4.0	2,369.6	22,356		21,561	1,211.3	726	280.3
1890	2,039	1,780	259	87.3	12.7	687.3	1,521		1,646	1,228.4	245	0
1880	148	134	14	90.5	9.5		120		87		6	
1870	55	47	8				39					
Filipino—												
1930	45,208	42,268	2,940	93.5	6.5	1,437.7	39,328		37,036	707.9	2,569	692.5
1920	5,603	5,232	371	93.4	6.6	1,410.2	4,861		5,088	3,533.3	355	
1910	160	144	16	90.0	10.0		128					
Hindu—												
1930	3,130	2,860	270	91.4	8.6	1,059.3	2,590		451	18.7	172	
1920	2,507	2,409	98	96.1	3.9		2,311		−117	−4.6	79	
1910	2,545	2,526	19	99.3	0.7		2,507					
Korean—												
1930	1,860	1,223	637	65.8	34.2	192.0	586		300	32.5	336	111.6
1920	1,224	923	301	75.4	24.6	306.6	622		504	120.3	258	
1910	462	419	43	90.7	9.3		376					
All other—												
1930	[2] 780	609	171	78.1	21.9	356.1	438		490	453.6	127	
1920	154	110	44	71.4	28.6		66		107		39	
1910	8	3	5					2				

[1] Adjusted by adding the estimated number of Mexicans shown in italics below.
[2] Comprises 660 Hawaiians (507 males, 153 females); 96 Malays (87 males, 9 females); 18 Siamese (12 males, 6 females); and 6 Samoans (3 males, 3 females).

SEX DISTRIBUTION 99

TABLE 2.—WHITE AND NEGRO POPULATION BY SEX, WITH NUMBER OF MALES PER 100 FEMALES, BY DIVISIONS AND STATES: 1930 AND 1920

DIVISION AND STATE OR SECTION	TOTAL POPULATION 1930 Male	1930 Female	1920 Male	1920 Female	Males per 100 females 1930	Males per 100 females 1920	WHITE 1930 Male	1930 Female	Males per 100 females 1930	Males per 100 females 1920	NEGRO 1930 Male	1930 Female	Males per 100 females 1930	Males per 100 females 1920
United States	62,137,080	60,637,966	53,900,431	51,810,189	102.5	104.0	55,163,854	53,700,353	102.7	104.4	5,855,669	6,035,474	97.0	99.2
GEOGRAPHIC DIVISIONS:														
New England	4,024,657	4,141,684	3,672,591	3,728,318	97.2	98.5	3,972,465	4,002,048	97.1	98.4	46,963	47,123	99.7	103.2
Middle Atlantic	13,188,681	13,072,069	11,200,445	11,054,690	100.9	101.4	12,640,834	12,531,270	100.9	101.3	520,826	532,073	97.9	100.7
East North Central	12,904,788	12,392,402	11,035,041	10,440,502	104.1	105.7	12,371,575	11,906,088	103.9	105.5	475,368	455,082	104.5	113.0
West North Central	6,785,442	6,511,473	6,459,067	6,085,182	104.2	106.1	6,567,265	6,306,222	104.1	106.1	167,550	164,234	102.0	106.7
South Atlantic	7,880,634	7,912,955	7,035,843	6,954,429	99.6	101.2	5,711,447	5,637,837	101.3	102.9	2,156,531	2,264,857	95.2	97.3
East South Central	4,947,502	4,939,712	4,471,690	4,421,617	100.2	101.1	3,643,406	3,581,208	101.7	102.7	1,301,552	1,356,686	95.9	97.2
West South Central	6,186,024	5,989,906	5,265,829	4,976,395	103.3	105.8	4,652,565	4,447,416	104.6	107.5	1,125,508	1,156,443	97.3	99.5
Mountain	1,949,798	1,751,991	1,789,290	1,546,802	111.3	115.7	1,736,707	1,566,879	110.8	114.9	16,312	13,913	117.2	178.1
Pacific	4,268,650	3,925,774	2,964,626	2,602,245	108.7	113.0	3,867,590	3,630,785	106.5	112.1	45,050	45,063	100.0	109.6
NEW ENGLAND:														
Maine	401,285	396,138	388,752	379,262	101.3	102.5	400,063	395,120	101.3	102.4	597	499	119.6	120.5
New Hampshire	231,759	233,534	222,112	220,971	99.2	100.5	231,127	233,223	99.1	100.5	524	266	197.0	115.6
Vermont	183,200	176,345	178,854	173,574	103.9	103.0	182,904	176,061	103.9	103.0	310	258	120.2	127.0
Massachusetts	2,071,072	2,177,942	1,890,014	1,902,342	95.1	96.3	2,042,213	2,150,713	95.0	96.1	26,097	26,268	99.3	101.6
Rhode Island	335,372	352,125	297,524	306,873	95.2	97.0	330,140	346,876	95.2	96.8	4,862	5,051	96.3	103.2
Connecticut	801,303	805,600	695,335	685,296	99.5	101.5	786,018	790,055	99.4	101.3	14,573	14,781	98.6	105.0
MIDDLE ATLANTIC:														
New York	6,312,520	6,275,546	5,187,350	5,197,877	100.6	99.8	6,004,500	6,055,793	100.6	99.8	199,485	213,320	93.5	92.6
New Jersey	2,030,644	2,010,690	1,590,075	1,565,825	101.0	101.5	1,924,094	1,904,215	101.1	101.7	102,929	105,899	97.2	96.2
Pennsylvania	4,845,517	4,785,833	4,429,020	4,290,997	101.2	103.2	4,621,840	4,571,262	101.1	103.0	218,412	212,845	102.6	108.8
EAST NORTH CENTRAL:														
Ohio	3,361,141	3,285,556	2,955,980	2,803,414	102.3	105.4	3,197,509	3,133,627	102.0	105.1	150,128	150,176	100.0	116.4
Indiana	1,640,061	1,598,442	1,489,074	1,441,310	102.6	103.3	1,575,729	1,540,407	102.3	103.2	57,068	54,914	103.9	107.2
Illinois	3,873,457	3,757,197	3,304,833	3,180,447	103.1	103.9	3,685,284	3,581,077	102.9	103.8	164,425	164,547	99.9	106.1
Michigan	2,519,309	2,323,016	1,928,436	1,730,976	108.4	110.8	2,416,039	2,234,132	108.1	110.5	88,936	80,517	110.5	132.6
Wisconsin	1,510,815	1,428,191	1,356,718	1,275,349	105.8	106.4	1,497,014	1,416,845	105.7	106.3	5,811	4,928	117.9	132.6
WEST NORTH CENTRAL:														
Minnesota	1,316,571	1,247,382	1,245,537	1,141,588	105.5	109.1	1,303,109	1,235,864	105.4	109.0	5,005	4,440	112.7	122.6
Iowa	1,255,101	1,215,838	1,229,392	1,174,620	103.2	104.7	1,243,197	1,205,185	103.2	104.6	8,987	8,393	107.1	113.9
Missouri	1,822,866	1,806,501	1,723,319	1,680,736	100.9	102.5	1,706,844	1,692,043	100.9	102.4	111,929	111,911	100.0	104.3
North Dakota	359,615	321,230	341,673	305,199	111.9	112.0	354,519	316,724	111.9	112.0	243	134	181.3	144.5
South Dakota	363,650	329,199	337,120	299,427	110.5	112.6	351,671	317,882	110.6	112.8	343	303	113.2	133.1
Nebraska	706,348	671,615	672,805	623,567	105.2	107.9	698,399	660,803	105.0	107.7	7,063	6,689	105.6	123.2
Kansas	961,291	919,708	909,221	860,036	104.5	105.7	914,626	878,221	104.1	105.7	33,980	32,364	105.0	105.5
SOUTH ATLANTIC:														
Delaware	121,257	117,123	113,755	109,248	103.5	104.1	104,200	101,494	102.7	103.7	16,983	15,619	108.7	100.6
Maryland	821,009	810,517	729,455	720,206	101.3	101.3	679,693	674,477	100.8	101.1	140,506	135,873	103.4	102.0
District of Columbia	231,883	254,086	203,543	234,028	90.9	87.0	168,982	184,932	91.4	87.0	62,225	69,843	89.1	86.0
Virginia	1,216,046	1,205,805	1,168,492	1,140,695	100.8	102.4	893,650	876,755	101.9	104.1	321,545	328,620	97.8	98.6
West Virginia	889,871	839,334	763,100	700,601	106.0	108.9	828,743	785,191	105.5	108.2	60,873	54,020	112.7	120.2
North Carolina	1,575,208	1,595,068	1,279,062	1,280,061	98.8	99.9	1,120,270	1,114,678	100.5	101.6	446,500	472,147	94.6	96.0
South Carolina	853,158	885,607	838,293	845,431	96.3	99.2	473,312	470,728	100.5	103.3	379,300	414,381	91.5	95.4
Georgia	1,434,527	1,473,979	1,444,823	1,451,009	97.3	99.6	920,781	916,193	100.5	102.3	513,451	557,674	92.1	95.9
Florida	737,675	730,536	495,320	473,150	101.0	104.7	521,816	513,389	101.6	105.5	215,148	216,680	99.3	103.0
EAST SOUTH CENTRAL:														
Kentucky	1,322,703	1,291,796	1,227,494	1,189,130	102.4	103.2	1,209,105	1,179,109	102.5	103.5	113,501	112,589	100.9	101.0
Tennessee	1,304,559	1,311,997	1,173,967	1,163,918	99.4	100.9	1,071,798	1,066,821	100.5	101.8	232,569	245,077	94.9	97.2
Alabama	1,315,009	1,331,239	1,173,105	1,175,069	98.8	99.8	857,522	843,253	101.7	102.7	457,146	487,690	93.7	95.4
Mississippi	1,005,141	1,004,680	897,124	893,494	100.0	100.4	504,921	491,935	102.6	103.1	498,838	511,380	97.4	98.0
WEST SOUTH CENTRAL:														
Arkansas	939,843	914,639	895,228	856,976	102.8	104.5	702,261	672,645	104.4	105.9	236,909	241,554	98.1	100.7
Louisiana	1,047,823	1,053,770	903,335	895,174	99.4	100.9	664,681	653,479	101.7	103.4	379,173	397,153	95.5	97.0
Oklahoma	1,233,264	1,162,776	1,058,044	970,239	106.1	109.0	1,095,000	1,028,424	106.5	109.7	86,818	85,380	101.7	104.3
Texas	2,965,094	2,858,721	2,409,222	2,254,006	103.8	106.9	2,190,623	2,092,868	104.7	108.1	422,608	432,356	97.7	100.3
MOUNTAIN:														
Montana	293,228	244,378	299,941	248,948	120.0	120.5	281,793	235,534	119.6	120.2	710	546	130.0	138.2
Idaho	237,347	207,685	233,919	197,947	114.3	118.2	232,954	204,608	113.9	117.7	395	273	144.7	174.6
Wyoming	124,785	100,780	110,359	84,043	123.8	131.3	117,703	96,364	122.1	130.1	699	551	126.9	168.6
Colorado	530,752	505,039	492,731	446,898	105.1	110.3	491,121	469,996	104.5	110.1	5,739	6,089	94.3	106.4
New Mexico	219,222	204,095	190,456	169,894	107.4	112.1	171,748	160,007	107.3	110.1	1,531	1,319	116.1	402.9
Arizona	231,304	204,269	183,602	150,560	113.2	121.9	141,537	122,841	115.2	120.6	6,352	4,397	144.5	273.0
Utah	259,999	247,848	232,051	217,345	104.9	106.8	252,556	243,399	103.8	105.9	609	499	122.0	130.3
Nevada	53,161	37,897	46,240	31,167	140.3	148.4	47,295	34,130	138.6	149.0	277	239	115.9	130.7
PACIFIC:														
Washington	826,392	737,004	734,701	621,920	112.1	118.1	800,924	720,175	111.2	117.0	3,797	3,043	124.8	135.2
Oregon	499,672	454,114	416,334	367,055	110.0	113.4	489,282	447,707	109.3	112.5	1,210	1,024	118.2	126.4
California	2,942,595	2,734,656	1,813,591	1,613,270	107.6	112.4	2,577,434	2,462,813	104.7	110.0	40,052	40,996	97.7	104.8
SECTIONS:														
The North	36,903,563	36,117,628	32,373,144	31,308,701	102.2	103.4	35,552,139	34,836,228	102.1	103.3	1,210,707	1,198,512	101.0	106.1
The South	19,015,060	18,842,573	16,773,362	16,352,441	100.9	102.6	14,007,418	13,666,461	102.5	104.4	4,583,591	4,777,986	95.9	97.8
The West	6,218,457	5,677,765	4,753,925	4,149,047	109.5	114.6	5,604,297	5,197,664	107.8	113.1	61,371	58,976	104.1	132.0

119652—33——8

100

POPULATION

TABLE 3.—WHITE POPULATION BY SEX, NATIVITY, AND PARENTAGE, WITH NUMBER OF MALES PER 100 FEMALES, BY DIVISIONS AND STATES: 1930 AND 1920

DIVISION AND STATE OR SECTION	NATIVE WHITE—NATIVE PARENTAGE				NATIVE WHITE—FOREIGN OR MIXED PARENTAGE				FOREIGN-BORN WHITE				MALES PER 100 FEMALES			
	1930		Males per 100 females		1930		Males per 100 females		1930		Males per 100 females		Native white—Foreign parentage		Native white—Mixed parentage	
	Male	Female	1930	1920	Male	Female	1930	1920	Male	Female	1930	1920	1930	1920	1930	1920
United States	35,460,001	34,676,613	102.3	103.0	12,550,144	12,811,042	98.0	98.6	7,153,709	6,212,698	115.1	121.7	98.6	99.1	96.7	97.7
GEOGRAPHIC DIVISIONS:																
New England	1,572,885	1,594,197	98.7	98.2	1,494,838	1,568,883	95.3	95.9	904,742	929,568	97.3	102.3	95.5	96.3	94.8	94.8
Middle Atlantic	5,718,981	5,730,917	99.8	98.9	4,160,113	4,293,051	96.9	96.4	2,761,740	2,507,302	110.1	114.1	97.6	97.1	94.9	94.3
East North Central	7,355,564	7,145,011	102.9	103.3	3,249,553	3,303,611	98.4	99.0	1,766,458	1,457,466	121.2	128.0	99.0	99.4	97.1	98.0
West North Central	4,336,030	4,211,453	103.0	103.9	1,640,141	1,626,586	100.8	101.9	591,094	468,183	126.3	131.4	101.8	102.5	99.4	100.9
South Atlantic	5,230,064	5,182,304	100.9	102.0	311,083	321,555	96.7	98.3	170,300	133,978	127.1	141.6	98.2	99.6	94.5	96.1
East South Central	3,516,816	3,455,121	101.8	102.7	93,231	101,781	91.6	93.0	33,359	24,306	137.2	141.0	90.8	92.1	92.5	94.3
West South Central	4,264,048	4,089,232	104.3	106.4	291,197	285,272	102.1	104.0	97,320	72,912	133.5	131.3	104.0	104.3	100.1	103.5
Mountain	1,198,649	1,101,606	108.8	111.5	368,061	347,356	106.0	106.5	169,997	117,917	144.2	149.2	108.4	108.0	102.9	104.3
Pacific	2,266,964	2,166,772	104.6	107.1	941,927	962,947	97.8	100.6	658,699	501,066	131.5	148.2	98.9	101.7	96.3	98.9
NEW ENGLAND:																
Maine	259,889	255,354	101.8	102.0	89,875	89,697	100.2	100.2	50,299	50,069	100.5	108.3	101.0	101.4	99.4	98.7
New Hampshire	119,967	119,471	100.4	100.2	70,000	72,252	96.9	97.4	41,160	41,500	99.2	105.5	96.9	97.7	96.9	97.0
Vermont	118,863	115,227	103.2	102.2	41,217	40,597	101.5	99.6	22,824	20,237	112.8	113.9	102.6	101.3	100.4	97.7
Massachusetts	702,083	726,801	96.7	95.6	829,768	878,738	94.4	95.3	509,402	545,174	93.4	98.0	94.7	95.8	93.8	93.8
Rhode Island	104,462	106,501	98.1	99.1	142,527	152,812	93.3	93.9	83,151	87,563	95.0	98.7	93.6	94.3	92.5	92.8
Connecticut	266,721	270,843	98.5	98.2	321,451	334,787	96.0	96.3	197,846	185,025	106.9	113.2	96.5	96.6	94.6	95.0
MIDDLE ATLANTIC:																
New York	2,237,230	2,236,716	100.0	98.6	2,204,100	2,280,698	96.6	95.6	1,653,170	1,538,379	107.5	107.4	97.2	96.3	95.0	93.3
New Jersey	786,421	785,107	100.2	99.6	695,641	717,798	96.9	96.9	443,132	401,310	110.4	112.9	97.6	97.4	94.9	95.3
Pennsylvania	2,695,330	2,709,094	99.5	98.9	1,260,572	1,294,555	97.4	97.5	665,438	567,613	117.2	129.6	98.4	98.2	94.7	95.4
EAST NORTH CENTRAL:																
Ohio	2,178,904	2,146,407	101.5	102.9	666,620	695,054	95.9	96.9	351,985	292,166	120.5	136.2	96.6	97.3	94.4	96.3
Indiana	1,313,539	1,292,205	101.7	101.9	185,233	190,025	97.5	98.3	76,957	58,177	132.3	140.7	98.5	98.9	96.0	97.3
Illinois	1,907,225	1,861,765	102.4	102.5	1,120,122	1,159,091	96.6	97.2	657,937	560,221	117.4	119.6	96.9	97.6	96.0	96.1
Michigan	1,222,115	1,141,923	107.0	107.9	729,022	716,843	101.7	102.5	464,902	375,366	123.9	132.3	103.0	103.4	99.5	100.8
Wisconsin	733,781	702,711	104.4	103.3	548,556	542,598	101.1	101.0	214,677	171,536	125.1	128.5	102.0	101.7	99.4	99.7
WEST NORTH CENTRAL:																
Minnesota	566,891	547,425	103.6	105.5	518,235	518,128	100.0	101.8	217,983	170,311	128.0	134.2	100.8	102.4	98.7	100.5
Iowa	859,183	838,355	102.5	103.0	291,885	293,224	99.5	100.8	92,129	73,606	125.2	128.9	100.4	101.4	98.4	99.9
Missouri	1,397,066	1,379,272	101.3	102.3	228,479	244,680	93.4	95.5	81,209	68,091	119.4	125.2	94.0	95.4	92.6	95.3
North Dakota	133,690	122,932	108.8	108.7	160,451	149,022	107.7	105.6	60,378	44,770	134.9	134.3	108.6	105.5	106.1	105.7
South Dakota	195,173	180,205	108.3	110.5	118,733	109,694	108.2	108.3	37,665	27,983	134.6	136.9	110.5	110.3	105.1	105.1
Nebraska	445,232	428,617	103.9	105.7	184,781	179,726	102.8	104.0	63,386	51,960	122.0	128.5	103.1	104.1	102.3	103.9
Kansas	738,795	714,647	103.4	104.1	137,577	132,112	104.1	104.7	38,254	31,462	121.6	130.9	106.3	106.0	101.7	102.9
SOUTH ATLANTIC:																
Delaware	78,215	76,809	101.8	101.7	16,704	17,081	97.8	96.4	9,281	7,604	122.1	134.7	97.8	97.2	97.9	94.5
Maryland	522,310	517,486	100.9	100.8	107,117	112,164	95.5	96.2	50,266	44,827	112.1	114.9	95.8	96.3	94.9	95.8
Dist. of Columbia	124,500	137,927	90.3	84.8	28,830	32,725	88.1	84.9	15,652	14,280	109.6	112.9	91.5	89.1	83.3	79.1
Virginia	851,882	840,821	101.3	102.9	28,067	25,815	108.7	113.9	13,701	10,119	135.4	162.4	114.7	118.4	102.4	108.0
West Virginia	745,459	716,085	104.1	105.3	50,420	50,450	99.9	101.5	32,884	18,656	176.2	209.6	100.8	102.0	98.3	100.3
North Carolina	1,106,490	1,102,073	100.4	101.4	8,691	8,900	97.6	99.9	5,089	3,699	137.6	157.4	100.1	104.5	95.6	95.6
South Carolina	463,533	461,906	100.4	102.7	6,659	6,676	99.7	108.1	3,120	2,146	145.4	177.6	104.6	109.9	95.4	100.0
Georgia	897,514	894,085	100.3	101.8	15,092	15,466	97.6	104.8	8,175	5,742	142.4	161.8	100.1	108.6	95.2	100.5
Florida	440,161	434,212	101.4	104.4	49,503	52,272	94.7	98.6	32,152	26,905	119.5	133.7	96.8	100.2	92.2	96.5
EAST SOUTH CENTRAL:																
Kentucky	1,151,622	1,117,918	103.0	103.9	45,251	51,733	87.5	89.4	12,292	9,548	128.7	131.4	85.6	87.8	90.0	92.0
Tennessee	1,045,939	1,041,444	100.4	101.6	18,465	19,705	93.7	97.7	7,304	5,672	130.4	139.7	95.4	99.0	92.1	96.2
Alabama	829,250	817,089	101.5	102.3	18,946	19,780	95.8	97.9	9,326	6,384	146.1	151.0	96.8	98.0	94.8	97.8
Mississippi	490,005	478,670	102.4	102.8	10,569	10,563	100.1	96.3	4,347	2,702	160.9	162.8	100.4	96.8	99.7	95.8
WEST SOUTH CENTRAL:																
Arkansas	677,734	651,471	104.0	105.2	18,521	17,007	108.9	112.8	6,006	4,167	144.1	159.6	115.4	119.7	108.8	106.7
Louisiana	591,828	580,744	101.9	103.3	52,477	58,201	90.2	90.5	20,376	14,534	140.2	148.4	90.5	91.0	89.7	89.9
Oklahoma	1,026,128	968,177	106.0	108.5	53,328	49,038	108.7	111.7	15,544	11,209	138.7	165.8	113.1	113.9	105.0	109.2
Texas	1,968,358	1,888,840	104.2	106.7	166,871	161,026	103.6	105.1	55,394	43,002	128.8	125.2	105.7	105.1	101.4	105.2
MOUNTAIN:																
Montana	152,209	131,330	115.9	115.2	84,685	76,142	111.2	108.3	44,899	28,002	160.0	164.5	113.5	110.0	108.0	105.6
Idaho	167,937	152,252	110.3	112.8	46,070	40,849	112.8	114.2	18,947	11,507	164.7	176.6	117.1	116.5	108.8	111.8
Wyoming	80,875	67,506	119.8	124.1	24,389	21,630	112.7	115.6	12,439	7,219	172.3	203.5	115.0	115.7	109.7	115.5
Colorado	340,403	328,703	103.6	108.5	102,714	103,891	98.9	100.4	48,004	37,402	128.3	140.0	101.0	101.7	95.6	98.2
New Mexico	156,224	146,529	106.6	108.0	10,769	10,436	103.2	105.5	4,755	3,042	156.3	137.7	104.8	106.2	101.6	104.5
Arizona	112,014	98,233	114.0	120.0	20,131	18,409	100.4	107.7	9,392	6,199	151.5	133.5	112.2	107.7	106.7	107.7
Utah	162,130	156,340	103.7	104.1	67,448	66,265	101.8	103.4	22,978	20,704	110.5	120.7	105.0	106.7	98.5	99.6
Nevada	26,857	20,713	129.7	133.2	11,855	9,725	121.9	123.7	8,583	3,692	232.5	264.1	125.1	126.5	117.8	110.6
PACIFIC:																
Washington	454,048	419,579	108.2	111.1	204,282	198,934	102.7	105.8	142,594	101,662	140.3	158.0	104.6	107.4	100.3	103.3
Oregon	325,532	304,442	106.9	108.2	101,622	99,958	101.7	103.8	62,078	43,397	143.0	156.4	103.4	105.3	99.7	101.8
California	1,487,384	1,442,751	103.1	105.2	636,023	664,055	95.8	98.1	454,027	356,007	127.5	143.6	96.7	99.1	94.4	96.4
SECTIONS:																
The North	18,983,460	18,681,578	101.6	101.6	10,544,645	10,792,131	97.7	98.1	6,024,034	5,362,519	112.3	117.7	98.3	98.5	96.5	97.1
The South	13,010,928	12,726,657	102.2	103.6	695,511	708,608	98.2	100.2	300,979	231,196	130.2	135.9	99.3	100.8	96.7	99.4
The West	3,465,613	3,268,378	106.0	108.9	1,309,988	1,310,303	100.0	102.6	828,696	618,983	133.9	148.5	101.3	103.8	98.1	100.8

SEX DISTRIBUTION

TABLE 4.—MEXICAN, INDIAN, CHINESE, JAPANESE, AND FILIPINO POPULATION BY SEX, WITH NUMBER OF MALES PER 100 FEMALES, BY DIVISIONS AND STATES: 1930 AND 1920

[Sex ratio not shown where base is less than 100]

DIVISION AND STATE OR SECTION	MEXICAN, 1930 Male	Female	Males per 100 females	INDIAN 1930 Male	Fe-male	Males per 100 females 1930	1920	CHINESE 1930 Male	Fe-male	Males per 100 females 1930	1920	JAPANESE 1930 Male	Fe-male	Males per 100 females 1930	1920	FILIPINO 1930 Male	Fe-male	Males per 100 females 1930	1920
United States	758,674	663,859	114.3	170,350	162,047	105.1	104.8	59,802	15,152	394.7	695.5	81,771	57,063	143.3	189.8	42,268	2,940	1,437.7	1,410.2
GEOGRAPHIC DIVISIONS:																			
New England	60	38		1,273	1,193	106.7	97.8	3,233	561	576.3	1,006.7	277	75			329	29		
Middle Atlantic	4,550	2,207	206.2	4,012	3,697	108.5	106.8	12,503	1,502	832.4	1,082.8	2,740	922	297.2	427.6	2,568	314	817.8	
East North Central	37,907	20,410	185.7	10,446	9,371	111.5	109.5	5,421	919	599.0	1,100.7	785	207	282.8	423.7	2,850	168	1,701.8	
West North Central	22,925	16,880	135.8	24,848	23,397	106.2	103.2	1,431	307	466.1	996.7	662	341	194.1	351.7	708	76		
South Atlantic	425	266	159.8	9,657	9,403	102.7	102.6	1,477	392	376.8	880.0	278	115	241.7		780	81		
East South Central	700	613	128.9	1,072	1,034	103.7	111.1	589	154	382.5		32	14			48	2		
West South Central	358,151	337,845	106.0	48,270	47,400	101.8	101.5	1,237	345	358.6	1,062.1	432	255	169.4	234.1	663	176	376.7	
Mountain	132,905	116,409	114.2	52,534	49,549	106.0	107.3	2,675	577	463.6	918.5	7,036	4,382	160.6	263.7	1,279	112	1,142.0	
Pacific	200,052	169,191	118.8	18,238	17,003	107.3	105.7	31,236	10,395	300.5	544.3	69,559	50,692	137.2	175.4	33,034	1,982	1,666.7	1,479.1
NEW ENGLAND:																			
Maine		2		518	494	104.9	100.2	93	22			2	1			12			
New Hampshire		1		33	31			71	13							8			
Vermont	1	1		20	16			20	5			1							
Massachusetts	43	23		458	416	110.1	80.4	2,530	443	571.1	973.4	151	50			140	17		
Rhode Island	6	4		154	164	93.9		170	27			15	2			24	1		
Connecticut	20	7		90	72			340	51			108	22			149	11		
MIDDLE ATLANTIC:																			
New York	1,879	1,019	184.4	3,584	3,389	105.8	104.8	8,649	1,016	851.3	947.6	2,201	729	301.9	441.5	1,770	212	834.9	
New Jersey	295	159	185.5	123	90			1,608	175	918.9		322	117	275.2		260	26		
Pennsylvania	2,376	1,029	230.9	305	218	139.9	139.0	2,246	311	722.2	1,204.0	217	76			538	76		
EAST NORTH CENTRAL:																			
Ohio	2,806	1,231	227.9	252	183	137.7		1,168	257	454.5		131	56			73	15		
Indiana	6,708	2,934	228.6	158	127	124.4		247	32			53	18			74	3		
Illinois	18,216	10,690	170.4	250	219	114.2		2,796	396	706.1	997.2	414	150	276.0		1,023	88		
Michigan	8,529	4,807	177.4	3,835	3,245	118.2	110.0	902	179	503.9		138	38			731	56		
Wisconsin	1,648	748	220.3	5,951	5,597	106.3	106.2	308	55			10	5			58	6		
WEST NORTH CENTRAL:																			
Minnesota	2,069	1,557	132.0	5,091	5,386	105.7	102.0	422	102	413.7		51	18			221	15		
Iowa	2,380	1,915	124.3	349	311	112.2	112.4	126	27			16	3			37	3		
Missouri	2,834	2,155	131.5	336	242	138.8		521	113	461.1		80	14			303	18		
North Dakota	376	232	162.1	4,293	4,094	104.9	103.6	93	10			60	31			29	1		
South Dakota	481	335	143.6	11,172	10,661	104.8	102.5	64	6			11	8			5	2		
Nebraska	3,585	2,736	131.0	1,674	1,582	105.8	102.1	152	42			414	260	159.2	316.6	54	1		
Kansas	11,200	7,950	140.9	1,333	1,121	118.9	111.1	53	7			30	7			59	36		
SOUTH ATLANTIC:																			
Delaware	24			3	2			32	6			8				7	2		
Maryland	38	18		34	16			389	103	377.7		27	11			309	18		
Dist. of Columbia	41	26		17	23			305	93			50	28			255	39		
Virginia	20	16		436	343	127.1	105.5	230	54			37	6			116	10		
West Virginia	155	102	152.0	15	3			74	12			6	3			3	3		
North Carolina	8	2		8,353	8,220	101.5	102.1	59	9			11	6			6			
South Carolina	4	5		474	485	97.7	91.2	38	8			11	4			17	1		
Georgia	38	9		26	17			181	72			23	9			24	5		
Florida	97	88		299	288	103.8	100.7	160	40			105	48			43	3		
EAST SOUTH CENTRAL:																			
Kentucky	53	35		16	6			47	13			7	2			3	2		
Tennessee	16	9		85	70			60	10			8	3			14			
Alabama	27	42		228	237	96.2	108.8	44	8			16	1			25			
Mississippi	604	527	131.7	743	715	103.9	111.7	438	123	356.1		1				6			
WEST SOUTH CENTRAL:																			
Arkansas	248	161	154.0	210	198	106.1		186	65			9	3			12	3		
Louisiana	2,392	2,160	110.7	800	736	108.7	106.6	327	95			33	19			390	125	312.0	
Oklahoma	4,434	2,920	151.8	46,744	45,981	101.7	100.6	178	28			67	37			15	6		
Texas	351,077	332,604	105.6	516	485	106.4	127.3	546	157	347.8		323	196	164.8	201.3	246	42		
MOUNTAIN:																			
Montana	1,766	805	219.4	7,664	7,134	107.4	107.6	427	59			510	243	209.9	362.9	203	2		
Idaho	907	371	244.5	1,833	1,805	101.6	103.7	295	40			847	574	147.6	207.0	93	4		
Wyoming	4,582	2,592	176.8	982	863	113.8	113.1	113	17			645	381	169.3	393.4	45			
Colorado	30,824	26,852	114.8	748	647	115.6	113.1	195	38			1,847	1,366	135.2	185.5	220	30		
New Mexico	30,775	28,565	107.7	14,864	14,077	105.6	108.4	108	25			157	92			20	7		
Arizona	59,102	55,071	107.3	22,471	21,255	105.7	106.7	845	265	318.9	553.4	532	347	153.3	220.3	408	64		
Utah	2,728	1,284	212.5	1,516	1,353	112.0	113.6	282	60			2,056	1,213	169.5	285.3	157	1		
Nevada	2,221	869	255.6	2,456	2,415	101.7	102.1	410	73			442	166	266.3	442.4	43	4		
PACIFIC:																			
Washington	477	85		5,778	5,475	105.5	101.0	1,723	472	365.0	759.3	10,200	7,637	133.6	186.7	3,374	106	3,183.0	
Oregon	1,247	321	388.5	2,442	2,334	104.6	100.5	1,525	550	277.3	570.3	2,919	2,039	143.2	207.7	1,035	31		
California	199,228	169,785	118.0	10,018	9,194	109.0	100.8	27,988	9,373	298.6	528.8	56,440	41,016	137.6	171.1	28,625	1,845	1,551.5	1,307.4
SECTIONS:																			
The North	65,451	39,535	165.6	40,570	37,658	107.8	104.7	22,588	3,289	686.8	1,081.9	4,434	1,605	276.3	410.2	6,464	587	1,101.2	
The South	359,366	338,724	106.1	58,990	57,837	102.0	101.9	3,303	891	370.7	913.0	742	384	193.2	280.1	1,491	259	575.7	
The West	333,857	285,600	116.9	70,772	66,552	106.3	106.8	33,911	10,972	309.1	572.1	76,595	55,074	139.1	182.5	34,313	2,094	1,638.6	1,459.5

102

POPULATION

TABLE 5.—URBAN AND RURAL POPULATION BY SEX, WITH NUMBER OF MALES PER 100 FEMALES, BY DIVISIONS AND STATES: 1930 AND 1920

DIVISION AND STATE OR SECTION	URBAN POPULATION				RURAL POPULATION				RURAL-FARM POPULATION				RURAL-NONFARM POPULATION			
	1930		Males per 100 females		1930		Males per 100 females		1930		Males per 100 females		1930		Males per 100 females	
	Male	Female	1930	1920	Male	Female	1930	1920	Male	Female	1930	1920	Male	Female	1930	1920
United States	34,154,760	34,800,063	98.1	100.4	27,982,320	25,837,903	108.3	108.0	15,864,375	14,293,138	111.0	109.1	12,117,945	11,544,765	105.0	106.5
GEOGRAPHIC DIVS:																
New England	3,075,299	3,236,677	95.0	96.9	949,358	905,007	104.9	104.8	267,482	231,601	115.5	111.4	681,876	673,406	101.3	101.5
Middle Atlantic	10,152,885	10,241,822	99.1	99.7	3,035,796	2,830,247	107.3	106.5	895,344	778,350	115.0	110.3	2,140,452	2,051,897	104.3	104.6
E. N. Central	8,441,351	8,353,557	101.1	103.9	4,463,432	4,038,845	110.5	108.6	2,383,400	2,069,714	115.2	111.5	2,080,032	1,969,131	105.6	104.7
W. N. Central	2,717,628	2,838,553	95.7	99.5	4,067,814	3,672,920	110.8	110.4	2,705,632	2,329,929	116.1	114.5	1,362,182	1,342,991	101.4	103.0
South Atlantic	2,739,047	2,959,075	92.6	95.4	5,141,587	4,953,880	103.8	103.9	3,007,955	2,871,001	104.8	103.5	2,133,632	2,082,879	102.4	104.5
E. S. Central	1,331,443	1,447,244	92.0	93.8	3,616,059	3,492,468	103.5	103.4	2,602,692	2,481,743	104.9	103.8	1,013,367	1,010,725	100.3	102.0
W. S. Central	2,172,629	2,254,810	96.4	101.0	4,014,295	3,735,096	107.5	107.9	2,768,247	2,539,692	109.0	107.9	1,246,048	1,195,404	104.2	107.7
Mountain	781,974	725,948	100.8	105.5	1,217,824	1,026,043	118.7	122.0	615,806	507,887	121.2	119.7	602,018	518,156	116.2	124.8
Pacific	2,792,504	2,742,877	101.8	100.1	1,476,155	1,183,397	124.7	128.4	617,817	483,221	127.9	127.0	858,338	700,176	122.6	129.6
NEW ENGLAND:																
Maine	155,187	166,319	93.3	94.9	246,098	229,819	107.1	107.7	86,159	75,270	114.5	111.5	150,939	154,549	103.5	105.2
New Hampshire	133,209	139,870	95.2	96.4	98,550	93,664	105.2	107.9	29,263	25,048	114.1	110.7	69,287	68,016	101.9	106.1
Vermont	57,539	61,227	94.0	94.5	125,727	115,118	109.2	107.2	60,514	51,384	117.8	113.8	65,213	63,734	102.3	101.1
Massachusetts	1,859,807	1,971,619	94.3	96.1	211,865	206,323	102.7	100.7	43,084	37,225	115.7	109.3	168,781	169,098	99.8	97.2
Rhode Island	300,093	326,336	94.7	96.7	26,279	25,789	101.9	107.2	5,448	4,841	112.5	116.7	20,831	20,948	99.4	102.5
Connecticut	560,464	571,306	98.1	101.5	240,839	234,294	102.8	101.4	43,014	37,233	115.5	110.4	197,825	197,061	100.4	99.2
MIDDLE ATLANTIC:																
New York	5,242,636	5,279,316	99.3	98.7	1,069,884	996,230	107.4	105.2	380,895	325,551	117.0	112.1	688,989	670,679	102.7	100.1
New Jersey	1,669,396	1,669,848	100.0	100.3	361,248	340,842	106.0	106.2	65,718	55,290	118.9	113.8	295,530	285,552	103.5	104.4
Pennsylvania	3,240,853	3,292,658	98.4	101.0	1,604,664	1,493,175	107.5	107.3	448,731	397,509	112.9	108.4	1,155,933	1,095,666	105.5	106.9
E. N. CENTRAL:																
Ohio	2,245,496	2,261,875	99.3	104.4	1,115,645	1,023,681	109.0	107.3	532,118	472,170	112.7	109.4	583,527	551,511	105.8	104.9
Indiana	893,132	902,760	98.9	101.3	746,929	695,682	107.4	105.4	425,773	383,208	111.1	108.7	321,156	312,474	102.8	100.1
Illinois	2,828,968	2,806,759	100.8	101.7	1,044,489	950,438	109.9	108.7	528,927	462,474	114.4	111.0	515,562	487,964	105.7	106.3
Michigan	1,700,248	1,601,827	106.1	111.2	819,061	721,189	113.6	110.3	420,860	354,576	118.7	113.6	398,201	366,613	108.6	105.5
Wisconsin	773,507	780,336	99.1	100.5	737,308	647,855	113.8	112.0	475,722	397,286	119.7	115.7	261,586	250,569	104.4	105.0
W. N. CENTRAL:																
Minnesota	618,799	638,817	96.9	101.8	697,772	608,565	114.7	115.2	485,316	402,733	120.5	118.2	212,456	205,832	103.2	109.5
Iowa	478,309	500,983	95.5	98.6	776,792	714,355	108.7	108.3	517,017	447,642	115.5	113.6	259,775	267,218	97.2	99.5
Missouri	905,948	953,171	95.0	98.0	916,918	853,330	107.5	106.7	585,358	523,611	111.8	110.3	331,560	329,719	100.6	99.9
North Dakota	55,172	58,134	94.9	97.8	304,443	263,096	115.7	114.4	217,616	179,255	121.4	118.4	86,827	83,841	103.6	105.2
South Dakota	64,507	66,400	97.1	102.2	299,143	262,799	113.8	114.7	211,976	177,455	119.5	119.3	87,167	85,344	102.1	105.6
Nebraska	238,490	247,617	96.3	103.0	467,858	423,998	110.3	110.2	313,302	269,679	116.2	116.0	154,556	154,319	100.2	100.1
Kansas	356,403	373,431	95.4	98.0	604,888	546,277	110.7	110.1	375,047	329,554	113.8	112.6	229,841	216,723	106.1	105.9
SOUTH ATLANTIC:																
Delaware	61,405	61,741	99.5	103.2	59,852	55,382	108.1	105.2	24,702	21,600	114.4	111.1	35,150	33,782	104.0	99.6
Maryland	479,180	495,689	96.7	97.5	341,829	314,828	108.6	107.3	124,948	111,224	112.3	109.7	216,881	203,604	106.5	105.2
Dist. Columbia	231,883	254,986	90.9	87.0												
Virginia	379,244	406,293	93.3	96.8	836,802	799,512	104.7	104.9	488,182	460,564	106.0	104.4	348,620	338,948	102.9	105.7
West Virginia	243,025	248,479	97.8	101.3	646,846	590,855	109.5	111.6	234,735	213,015	110.2	108.8	412,111	377,840	109.1	113.9
North Carolina	384,928	424,919	90.6	94.5	1,190,280	1,170,149	101.7	101.3	813,716	783,504	103.9	102.8	376,564	386,645	97.4	97.2
South Carolina	172,046	199,034	86.4	92.3	681,112	686,573	99.2	100.7	459,888	454,210	101.3	100.8	221,224	232,363	95.2	100.1
Georgia	418,516	476,976	87.7	93.5	1,016,011	997,003	101.9	101.7	718,705	695,014	103.4	102.2	297,306	301,989	98.4	99.9
Florida	368,820	390,958	94.3	98.2	368,855	339,578	108.6	108.7	143,079	131,870	108.5	106.4	225,776	207,708	108.7	110.6
E. S. CENTRAL:																
Kentucky	387,339	411,687	94.1	93.6	935,454	880,109	106.3	106.9	611,200	563,032	108.6	107.6	324,254	317,077	102.3	104.9
Tennessee	428,416	468,122	91.5	93.8	876,143	843,875	103.8	103.5	622,736	590,329	105.5	104.7	253,407	253,546	99.9	100.1
Alabama	356,121	388,152	91.7	95.4	958,888	943,087	101.7	101.1	676,620	659,789	102.6	100.9	282,268	283,298	99.6	101.8
Mississippi	159,567	179,283	89.0	90.9	845,574	825,397	102.4	102.0	692,136	668,593	103.5	102.3	153,438	156,804	97.9	100.4
W. S. CENTRAL:																
Arkansas	183,800	199,078	92.3	96.9	756,043	715,561	105.7	106.0	578,290	539,040	107.3	106.4	177,753	176,521	100.7	104.9
Louisiana	400,029	433,503	92.3	95.4	647,794	620,267	104.4	104.0	423,811	403,071	105.1	103.7	223,983	217,196	103.1	104.5
Oklahoma	408,828	412,853	99.0	105.6	824,436	749,923	109.9	110.3	540,221	480,953	112.3	111.8	284,215	268,970	105.7	107.3
Texas	1,179,972	1,209,376	97.6	102.6	1,786,022	1,649,345	108.3	109.0	1,225,925	1,116,628	109.8	108.5	560,097	532,717	105.1	110.4
MOUNTAIN:																
Montana	94,228	86,808	108.5	110.2	199,000	157,570	126.3	125.5	115,965	87,997	131.8	126.9	83,035	69,573	119.3	123.6
Idaho	65,537	63,970	102.4	106.8	171,810	143,715	119.5	122.8	101,530	84,570	120.1	120.4	70,280	59,145	118.8	126.9
Wyoming	36,700	33,397	109.9	126.9	88,085	67,383	130.7	133.6	41,664	31,241	133.4	126.7	46,421	36,142	128.4	140.6
Colorado	254,319	265,563	95.8	102.5	276,433	239,476	115.4	118.1	152,606	128,432	118.8	118.0	123,827	111,044	111.5	118.3
New Mexico	53,031	53,785	98.6	99.3	166,191	150,310	110.6	115.1	84,181	73,725	114.2	114.7	82,010	76,585	107.1	115.7
Arizona	76,600	73,256	104.6	110.9	154,704	131,013	118.5	128.5	53,088	45,731	116.1	118.6	101,616	85,282	119.2	136.0
Utah	132,649	133,615	99.3	100.7	127,350	114,233	111.5	112.7	56,823	49,844	114.0	110.9	70,527	64,389	109.5	115.1
Nevada	18,910	15,554	121.6	120.1	34,251	22,343	153.3	156.4	9,949	6,347	156.8	149.3	24,302	15,996	151.9	159.0
PACIFIC:																
Washington	451,985	432,554	104.5	111.9	374,407	304,450	123.0	126.3	165,607	134,536	123.1	121.8	208,800	169,914	122.9	130.3
Oregon	246,078	243,668	101.0	105.2	258,594	210,446	120.5	122.3	122,605	98,940	123.9	122.9	130,989	111,506	117.5	121.6
California	2,094,441	2,066,155	101.4	104.4	848,154	668,501	126.9	131.8	329,605	249,745	132.0	131.8	518,549	418,756	123.8	131.8
SECTIONS:																
The North	24,387,163	24,670,609	98.9	100.6	12,516,400	11,447,019	109.3	108.4	6,251,858	5,409,594	115.6	112.5	6,264,542	6,037,425	103.8	103.9
The South	6,243,119	6,661,129	93.7	96.8	12,771,941	12,181,444	104.8	104.9	8,378,894	7,992,436	106.2	105.0	4,393,047	4,289,008	102.4	104.8
The West	3,524,478	3,468,325	101.6	105.9	2,693,979	2,209,440	121.9	125.1	1,233,623	991,108	124.5	123.0	1,460,356	1,218,332	119.9	127.4

SEX DISTRIBUTION

TABLE 6.—POPULATION BY SEX, COLOR, AND NATIVITY, 1930, WITH NUMBER OF MALES PER 100 FEMALES, 1900 TO 1930, BY DIVISIONS AND STATES

[Mexicans were not returned as a separate class prior to 1930, but were counted with the white population; hence there are no comparative figures for the earlier censuses. See more detailed explanation in text. This situation frequently explains the lack of comparative figures for the group designated "Other races," which in 1930 included the Mexicans. Sex ratio not shown where number of females is less than 100]

DIVISION OR STATE AND CLASS OF POPULATION	Male, 1930	Female, 1930	1930	1920	1910	1900
UNITED STATES						
All classes	62,137,080	60,637,966	102.5	104.0	106.0	104.4
White	55,163,854	53,700,353	102.7	104.4	106.6	104.9
Native	48,010,145	47,487,655	101.1	101.7	102.7	102.8
Native parentage	35,400,001	34,676,613	102.3	103.0	104.0	103.7
Foreign or mixed par.	12,550,144	12,811,042	98.0	98.6	99.5	100.3
Foreign parentage	8,438,676	8,560,545	98.6	99.1	100.0	101.0
Mixed parentage	4,111,468	4,250,497	96.7	97.7	98.5	99.1
Foreign born	7,153,709	6,212,698	115.1	121.7	129.2	117.4
Negro	5,855,669	6,035,474	97.0	99.2	98.9	98.6
Other races	1,117,557	902,189	123.9	155.6	185.7	185.2
Mexican	758,674	663,859	114.3			
Indian	170,350	162,047	105.1	104.8	103.5	101.5
Chinese	59,802	15,152	394.7	695.5	1,430.1	1,887.2
Japanese	81,771	57,063	143.3	180.8	694.1	2,369.6
Filipino	42,268	2,940	1,437.7	1,410.2		
Hindu	2,800	270	1,059.3			
Korean	1,223	637	192.0	306.6		
Hawaiian	507	153	331.4			
All other	102	18				
GEOGRAPHIC DIVISIONS						
New England	4,024,657	4,141,684	97.2	98.5	99.3	97.7
White	3,972,465	4,092,048	97.1	98.4	99.2	97.6
Native	3,067,723	3,163,080	97.0	97.1	97.1	97.7
Native parentage	1,572,885	1,594,197	98.7	98.2	98.1	98.1
Foreign or mixed par.	1,494,838	1,568,883	95.3	95.9	96.0	96.9
Foreign parentage	1,035,731	1,084,692	95.5	96.3	96.3	96.9
Mixed parentage	459,107	484,191	94.8	94.8	95.2	96.9
Foreign born	904,742	929,568	97.3	102.3	104.8	97.5
Negro	46,963	47,123	99.7	103.2	97.8	93.6
Other races	5,220	1,913	273.3	360.8	415.9	640.2
Mexican	69	38				
Indian	1,273	1,193	106.7	97.8	103.5	112.2
Chinese	3,233	561	576.3	1,096.7		
Japanese	277	75				
Filipino	329	29				
All other	48	17				
Middle Atlantic	13,188,681	13,072,069	100.9	101.4	103.3	100.9
White	12,640,834	12,531,270	100.9	101.3	103.4	100.8
Native	9,879,094	10,023,968	98.6	97.8	98.0	98.5
Native parentage	5,718,981	5,730,917	99.8	98.9	98.9	99.1
Foreign or mixed par.	4,160,113	4,293,051	96.9	96.4	96.5	97.3
Foreign parentage	3,089,448	3,164,853	97.6	97.1	97.1	97.8
Mixed parentage	1,070,665	1,128,198	94.9	94.3	94.9	96.1
Foreign born	2,761,740	2,507,302	110.1	114.1	120.9	109.8
Negro	520,826	532,073	97.9	100.7	94.9	96.1
Other races	27,021	8,726	309.7	343.5	326.7	413.0
Mexican	4,550	2,207	206.2			
Indian	4,012	3,697	108.5	106.8	113.5	113.0
Chinese	12,503	1,502	832.4	1,082.8	2,763.3	6,219.3
Japanese	2,740	922	297.2	427.6	664.2	
Filipino	2,568	314	817.8			
Hindu	437	56				
Korean	102	24				
All other	109	4				
East North Central	12,904,783	12,392,402	104.1	105.7	106.0	104.7
White	12,371,575	11,900,088	103.9	105.5	106.0	104.6
Native	10,605,117	10,448,622	101.5	101.8	101.4	102.1
Native parentage	7,355,564	7,145,011	102.9	103.3	102.9	103.3
Foreign or mixed par.	3,249,553	3,303,611	98.4	99.0	98.6	99.0
Foreign parentage	2,174,040	2,196,146	99.0	99.4	99.1	101.1
Mixed parentage	1,075,513	1,107,465	97.1	98.0	97.7	97.5
Foreign born	1,766,458	1,457,466	121.2	128.0	131.3	118.4
Negro	475,368	455,082	104.5	113.0	108.3	109.0
Other races	57,840	31,232	185.2	171.1	146.8	143.3
Mexican	37,907	20,410	185.7			
Indian	10,446	9,371	111.5	108.5	108.8	108.6
Chinese	5,421	919	589.9	1,100.7	3,121.7	
Japanese	755	267	282.8	423.7		
Filipino	2,859	168	1,701.8			
Hindu	304	35				
Korean	127	49				
All other	21	13				
West North Central	6,785,442	6,511,473	104.2	106.1	109.9	109.7
White	6,567,265	6,306,222	104.1	106.1	109.9	109.8
Native	5,976,171	5,838,039	102.4	103.3	105.5	106.5
Native parentage	4,336,030	4,211,453	103.0	103.9	106.5	107.6
Foreign or mixed par.	1,640,141	1,626,586	100.8	101.9	103.3	104.4
Foreign parentage	981,837	964,635	101.8	102.5	104.3	105.0
Mixed parentage	658,304	661,951	99.4	100.0	101.6	103.1
Foreign born	591,094	468,183	126.3	131.4	141.3	130.5
Negro	167,550	164,234	102.0	106.7	107.8	104.0
Other races	50,627	41,017	123.4	114.8	112.5	104.9
Mexican	22,925	16,880	135.8			
Indian	24,848	23,397	106.2	103.2	102.6	98.8
Chinese	1,431	307	466.1	996.7		
Japanese	662	341	194.1	351.7		
Filipino	708	76				
All other	53	16				
GEOGRAPHIC DIVISIONS—Continued						
South Atlantic	7,880,634	7,912,955	99.6	101.2	101.2	100.0
White	5,711,447	5,637,837	101.3	102.9	103.2	101.7
Native	5,541,147	5,503,859	100.7	101.8	101.8	101.1
Native parentage	5,230,064	5,182,304	100.9	102.0	102.1	101.3
Foreign or mixed par.	311,083	321,555	96.7	98.3	97.6	97.7
Foreign parentage	190,672	194,165	98.2	99.6	98.1	98.0
Mixed parentage	120,411	127,390	94.5	96.1	96.9	97.2
Foreign born	170,300	133,978	127.1	141.6	146.9	123.3
Negro	2,155,531	2,264,857	95.2	97.3	97.5	96.9
Other races	12,656	10,261	123.3	130.4	135.6	154.4
Mexican	425	266	159.8			
Indian	9,667	9,403	102.7	102.6	102.5	102.6
Chinese	1,477	392	376.8	880.6		
Japanese	278	115	241.7			
Filipino	780	81				
All other	29	4				
East South Central	4,047,502	4,039,712	100.2	101.1	101.9	101.9
White	3,643,406	3,581,208	101.7	102.7	103.6	103.4
Native	3,610,047	3,556,902	101.5	102.4	103.1	103.0
Native parentage	3,516,816	3,455,121	101.8	102.7	103.5	103.3
Foreign or mixed par.	93,231	101,781	91.6	93.0	94.5	97.8
Foreign parentage	49,172	54,101	90.8	92.1	93.8	97.5
Mixed parentage	44,059	47,620	92.5	94.3	95.6	98.0
Foreign born	33,359	24,306	137.2	141.0	139.2	130.1
Negro	1,301,552	1,356,686	95.0	97.2	98.4	98.9
Other races	2,544	1,818	139.9	153.7	137.9	136.6
Mexican	700	613	128.0			
Indian	1,072	1,034	103.7	111.1	107.8	105.6
Chinese	589	154	382.5			
Japanese	32	14				
Filipino	48	2				
All other	13	1				
West South Central	6,186,924	5,989,906	103.3	105.8	107.2	106.7
White	4,652,565	4,447,416	104.6	107.5	109.3	100.3
Native	4,555,245	4,374,504	104.1	106.2	107.9	108.0
Native parentage	4,264,048	4,089,232	104.3	106.4	108.2	108.4
Foreign or mixed par.	291,197	285,272	102.1	104.0	105.1	104.2
Foreign parentage	153,051	147,227	104.0	104.3	106.8	104.5
Mixed parentage	138,146	138,045	100.1	103.5	104.2	103.8
Foreign born	97,320	72,912	133.5	131.3	138.8	134.3
Negro	1,125,508	1,150,443	97.3	99.5	100.4	99.0
Other races	408,851	380,047	105.9	106.8	105.7	103.5
Mexican	358,151	337,845	106.0			
Indian	48,270	47,400	101.8	101.5	101.5	99.0
Chinese	1,237	345	358.6	1,002.1		
Japanese	432	255	169.4	234.1		
Filipino	663	176	376.7			
All other	98	26				
Mountain	1,949,798	1,751,991	111.3	115.7	127.9	128.0
White	1,736,707	1,566,879	110.8	114.9	127.4	127.2
Native	1,566,710	1,448,962	108.1	110.1	117.6	120.0
Native parentage	1,198,649	1,101,606	108.8	111.5	119.8	122.8
Foreign or mixed par.	368,061	347,356	106.0	106.5	112.6	114.8
Foreign parentage	208,647	192,424	108.4	108.0	115.2	118.2
Mixed parentage	159,414	154,932	102.9	104.3	100.0	109.6
Foreign born	160,997	117,017	144.2	149.2	180.6	166.1
Negro	16,312	13,913	117.2	178.1	121.3	140.4
Other races	196,779	171,199	114.9	127.9	144.8	142.1
Mexican	132,905	116,400	114.2			
Indian	52,534	49,549	106.0	107.3	104.5	
Chinese	2,675	577	463.6	918.5	2,154.6	3,171.6
Japanese	7,036	4,382	160.6	263.7	2,505.2	
Filipino	1,279	112	1,142.0			
Hindu	118	30				
Korean	205	119	172.3			
All other	27	21				
Pacific	4,268,659	3,925,774	108.7	113.9	120.5	125.3
White	3,867,590	3,680,785	105.1	112.1	125.4	122.2
Native	3,208,891	3,129,719	102.5	104.9	113.8	113.6
Native parentage	2,266,964	2,166,772	104.6	107.1	117.4	118.1
Foreign or mixed par.	941,927	962,947	97.8	100.6	106.8	106.0
Foreign parentage	556,078	562,242	98.9	101.7	108.4	107.0
Mixed parentage	385,849	400,705	96.3	98.0	104.2	104.4
Foreign born	658,699	551,066	131.5	148.2	181.9	162.9
Negro	45,063	45,063	100.0	109.6	120.4	121.1
Other races	356,010	249,926	142.4	201.4	395.4	441.3
Mexican	200,952	169,191	118.8			
Indian	18,238	17,003	107.3	105.7	101.8	98.5
Chinese	31,236	10,395	300.5	544.3	1,133.6	1,432.8
Japanese	69,559	50,692	137.2	175.4	601.8	2,090.5
Filipino	33,034	1,982	1,666.7	1,479.1		
Hindu	1,841	120	1,534.2			
Korean	727	421	172.7	273.9		
Hawaiian	413	112	368.8			
All other	10	10				

POPULATION

TABLE 6.—POPULATION BY SEX, COLOR, AND NATIVITY, 1930, WITH NUMBER OF MALES PER 100 FEMALES, 1900 TO 1930, BY DIVISIONS AND STATES—Continued

DIVISION OR STATE AND CLASS OF POPULATION	Male, 1930	Female, 1930	MALES PER 100 FEMALES			
			1930	1920	1910	1900
NEW ENGLAND						
Maine	401,285	396,198	101.3	102.5	103.2	102.2
White	400,063	395,120	101.3	102.4	103.2	102.1
Native	349,764	345,051	101.4	101.5	101.8	101.5
Native parentage	259,889	255,354	101.8	102.0	101.9	101.2
Foreign or mixed par	89,875	89,697	100.2	100.2	101.7	102.5
Foreign parentage	43,764	43,330	101.0	101.4	101.8	102.4
Mixed parentage	46,111	46,367	99.4	98.7	101.6	102.6
Foreign born	50,299	50,069	100.5	108.3	111.1	106.7
Negro	597	499	119.6	120.5	105.6	103.2
Other races	625	519	120.4	135.7	137.2	141.1
Indian	518	494	104.9	100.2	108.9	111.7
Chinese	93	22				
All other	14	3				
New Hampshire	231,759	233,534	99.2	100.5	100.9	99.6
White	231,127	233,223	99.1	100.5	100.9	99.5
Native	189,967	191,723	99.1	99.2	98.3	98.9
Native parentage	119,967	119,471	100.4	100.2	99.2	99.3
Foreign or mixed par	70,000	72,252	96.9	97.4	96.4	97.8
Foreign parentage	41,235	42,556	96.9	97.7	96.3	98.4
Mixed parentage	28,765	29,696	96.9	97.0	96.6	96.6
Foreign born	41,160	41,500	99.2	105.5	110.4	101.9
Negro	524	266	197.0	115.6	104.3	97.6
Other races	108	45				
Vermont	183,266	176,345	103.9	103.0	105.3	103.9
White	182,904	176,061	103.9	103.0	104.9	103.9
Native	160,080	155,824	102.7	101.5	101.6	101.5
Native parentage	118,863	115,227	103.2	102.2	102.7	101.9
Foreign or mixed par	41,217	40,597	101.5	99.6	98.4	100.2
Foreign parentage	20,650	20,121	102.6	101.3	100.2	101.1
Mixed parentage	20,567	20,476	100.4	97.7	96.5	99.2
Foreign born	22,824	20,237	112.8	113.9	127.3	121.4
Negro	310	258	120.2	127.0	261.8	122.0
Other races	52	26				
Massachusetts	2,071,672	2,177,942	95.1	96.3	96.7	95.1
White	2,042,213	2,150,713	95.0	96.1	96.6	94.9
Native	1,532,751	1,605,539	95.5	95.4	95.3	95.0
Native parentage	702,983	726,801	96.7	95.6	95.2	95.7
Foreign or mixed par	829,768	878,738	94.4	95.3	95.3	96.1
Foreign parentage	584,705	617,486	94.7	95.6	95.9	96.2
Mixed parentage	245,063	261,252	93.8	93.8	94.0	95.8
Foreign born	509,462	545,174	93.4	98.0	99.5	92.6
Negro	26,097	26,268	99.3	101.6	97.1	95.2
Other races	3,362	961	349.8	479.3	714.0	1,090.8
Indian	458	416	110.1	89.4	104.8	115.0
Chinese	2,530	443	571.1	973.4		
Japanese	151	50				
Filipino	140	17				
All other	83	35				
Rhode Island	335,372	352,125	95.2	97.0	98.3	96.5
White	330,140	346,876	95.2	96.8	99.2	96.5
Native	246,989	259,313	95.2	96.0	97.1	96.7
Native parentage	104,462	106,501	98.1	99.1	99.6	98.0
Foreign or mixed par	142,527	152,812	93.3	93.9	95.2	96.4
Foreign parentage	100,085	106,947	93.6	94.3	95.6	95.3
Mixed parentage	42,442	45,865	92.5	92.8	94.1	95.6
Foreign born	83,151	87,563	95.0	95.7	103.6	96.1
Negro	4,862	5,051	96.3	103.2	95.1	89.3
Other races	370	198	186.9		263.6	
Indian	154	164	93.9		89.3	
Chinese	170	27				
All other	46	7				
Connecticut	801,303	805,600	99.5	101.5	102.3	100.0
White	786,018	790,655	99.4	101.3	102.3	100.1
Native	588,172	605,630	97.1	97.1	96.9	97.6
Native parentage	266,721	270,843	98.5	98.2	97.6	97.9
Foreign or mixed par	321,451	334,787	96.0	96.3	95.9	97.2
Foreign parentage	245,292	254,252	96.6	96.6	96.1	97.3
Mixed parentage	76,159	80,535	94.6	95.0	95.1	96.9
Foreign born	197,846	185,025	106.9	113.2	116.7	107.2
Negro	14,573	14,781	98.6	105.0	91.0	90.8
Other races	712	164	434.1	541.4		
Indian	90	72				
Chinese	340	51				
Japanese	108	22				
Filipino	149	11				
All other	25	8				
MIDDLE ATLANTIC						
New York	6,312,520	6,275,546	100.6	99.8	101.2	98.9
White	6,094,500	6,055,793	100.6	99.9	101.3	98.9
Native	4,441,330	4,517,414	98.3	97.1	97.5	97.8
Native parentage	2,237,230	2,236,716	100.0	98.9	98.9	98.9
Foreign or mixed par	2,204,100	2,280,698	96.6	95.6	95.9	96.5
Foreign parentage	1,651,841	1,699,650	97.2	96.3	96.4	96.9
Mixed parentage	552,259	581,048	95.0	93.3	94.5	95.5
Foreign born	1,653,170	1,538,379	107.5	107.4	110.5	101.9
Negro	109,485	213,329	93.5	92.6	91.3	88.6
MIDDLE ATLANTIC—Con.						
New York—Con.						
Other races	18,535	6,424	288.5	287.8	276.4	367.3
Mexican	1,879	1,019	184.4			
Indian	3,584	3,389	105.8	104.8	103.5	105.8
Chinese	8,649	1,016	851.3	947.6	2,519.9	4,049.3
Japanese	2,201	729	301.9	441.5	646.7	
Filipino	1,770	212	834.0			
Hindu	282	38				
Korean	84	21				
All other	86					
New Jersey	2,030,644	2,010,690	101.0	101.5	102.9	100.0
White	1,924,994	1,904,215	101.1	101.7	103.1	100.1
Native	1,481,862	1,502,905	98.6	98.3	98.0	97.8
Native parentage	786,107	785,107	100.2	99.6	98.9	98.3
Foreign or mixed par	695,441	717,798	96.9	96.9	96.9	97.1
Foreign parentage	516,000	528,704	97.6	97.4	97.4	97.7
Mixed parentage	179,441	189,094	94.9	95.3	95.4	95.4
Foreign born	443,132	401,310	110.4	112.9	118.2	107.8
Negro	102,029	105,899	97.2	96.2	94.5	93.5
Other races	2,721	576	472.4	813.6	1,020.1	
Mexican	295	159	185.5			
Indian	123	90				
Chinese	1,608	175	918.0			
Japanese	322	117	275.2			
Filipino	260	26				
Hindu	104	6				
All other	9	3				
Pennsylvania	4,845,517	4,785,833	101.2	103.2	105.9	103.5
White	4,621,340	4,571,262	101.1	103.0	106.1	103.4
Native	3,955,902	4,003,649	98.8	98.5	98.4	99.3
Native parentage	2,695,330	2,709,094	99.5	98.9	98.9	99.5
Foreign or mixed par	1,260,572	1,294,555	97.4	97.5	97.5	98.8
Foreign parentage	921,607	936,499	98.4	98.2	98.3	99.5
Mixed parentage	338,965	358,056	94.7	95.4	95.4	97.2
Foreign born	665,438	567,613	117.2	120.6	145.5	128.0
Negro	218,412	212,845	102.6	108.8	97.7	102.4
Other races	5,765	1,726	334.0	720.2	441.9	402.9
Mexican	2,376	1,029	230.9			
Indian	305	218	139.9	139.0	154.7	138.2
Chinese	2,246	311	722.2	1,264.0		
Japanese	217	76				
Filipino	538	70				
All other	83	16				
EAST NORTH CENTRAL						
Ohio	3,361,141	3,285,556	102.3	105.4	104.4	102.3
White	3,197,509	3,133,627	102.0	105.1	104.3	102.2
Native	2,845,524	2,841,461	100.1	101.4	100.1	100.5
Native parentage	2,178,904	2,146,407	101.5	102.9	101.5	101.6
Foreign or mixed par	666,620	695,054	95.9	96.9	96.9	97.7
Foreign parentage	453,039	468,744	96.6	97.3	96.2	97.7
Mixed parentage	213,581	226,310	94.4	96.3	95.8	97.1
Foreign born	351,985	292,166	120.5	136.2	137.8	116.8
Negro	150,128	150,176	106.0	110.4	108.5	106.6
Other races	4,504	1,753	256.9	731.6		
Mexican	2,806	1,231	227.9			
Indian	252	183	137.7			
Chinese	1,168	257	454.5			
Japanese	131	56				
All other	147	26				
Indiana	1,640,061	1,598,442	102.6	103.3	105.0	104.4
White	1,575,729	1,540,407	102.3	103.2	104.9	104.3
Native	1,498,772	1,482,230	101.1	101.4	102.3	103.3
Native parentage	1,313,539	1,292,205	101.7	101.9	102.8	103.6
Foreign or mixed par	185,233	190,025	97.5	98.3	99.3	101.4
Foreign parentage	111,719	113,434	98.5	98.9	100.4	103.0
Mixed parentage	73,514	76,591	96.0	97.3	97.7	99.3
Foreign born	76,957	58,177	132.3	140.7	156.4	123.8
Negro	57,008	54,914	103.9	107.2	106.0	106.8
Other races	7,264	3,121	232.7		337.5	250.0
Mexican	6,708	2,934	228.6			
Indian	158	127	124.4		121.4	91.3
Chinese	247	32				
All other	151	28				
Illinois	3,873,457	3,757,197	103.1	103.9	106.8	105.3
White	3,685,284	3,581,077	102.9	103.8	106.6	105.1
Native	3,027,347	3,020,856	100.2	100.3	101.5	102.5
Native parentage	1,907,225	1,861,765	102.4	102.5	103.9	104.6
Foreign or mixed par	1,120,122	1,159,091	96.6	97.2	98.1	99.6
Foreign parentage	790,607	815,992	96.9	97.6	98.5	100.0
Mixed parentage	329,515	343,099	96.0	96.1	97.4	98.5
Foreign born	657,937	560,221	117.4	119.6	127.3	115.8
Negro	164,425	164,547	99.9	106.1	109.1	112.9
Other races	23,748	11,573	205.2	719.9	1,183.6	
Mexican	18,216	10,690	170.4			
Indian	250	219	114.2			
Chinese	2,796	396	706.1	997.2		
Japanese	414	150	276.0			
Filipino	1,923	88				
All other	149	30				

SEX DISTRIBUTION

TABLE 6.—POPULATION BY SEX, COLOR, AND NATIVITY, 1930, WITH NUMBER OF MALES PER 100 FEMALES, 1900 TO 1930, BY DIVISIONS AND STATES—Continued

DIVISION OR STATE AND CLASS OF POPULATION	Male, 1930	Female, 1930	MALES PER 100 FEMALES			
			1930	1920	1910	1900
EAST NORTH CENTRAL—Con.						
Michigan	2,519,300	2,323,016	109.4	110.8	107.3	106.6
White	2,416,039	2,284,132	108.1	110.5	107.2	106.5
Native	1,951,137	1,858,706	105.0	105.6	102.4	102.8
Native parentage	1,222,115	1,141,923	107.0	107.9	104.2	103.8
Foreign or mixed par	729,022	716,843	101.7	102.5	100.1	101.6
Foreign parentage	465,738	452,118	103.0	103.4	100.6	102.4
Mixed parentage	263,284	264,725	99.5	100.8	99.1	100.1
Foreign born	464,902	375,366	123.9	132.3	127.4	120.5
Negro	89,930	80,517	110.5	132.6	111.1	108.2
Other races	14,334	8,367	171.3	141.0	119.1	118.0
Mexican	8,529	4,807	177.4			
Indian	3,835	3,245	118.2	110.0	111.7	110.0
Chinese	902	179	503.9			
Japanese	138	38				
Filipino	731	56				
Hindu	108	13				
All other	31	29				
Wisconsin	1,510,815	1,428,191	105.8	106.4	107.4	106.6
White	1,497,014	1,416,845	105.7	106.3	107.4	106.6
Native	1,282,337	1,245,309	103.0	102.1	101.0	102.1
Native parentage	733,781	702,711	104.4	103.3	103.2	103.9
Foreign or mixed par	548,556	542,598	101.1	101.0	100.4	101.1
Foreign parentage	352,937	345,858	102.0	101.7	101.3	104.6
Mixed parentage	195,619	196,740	99.4	99.7	98.6	93.0
Foreign born	214,677	171,536	125.1	128.5	130.8	121.0
Negro	5,811	4,928	117.9	132.6	103.7	126.2
Other races	7,990	6,418	124.5	111.4	111.4	112.0
Mexican	1,648	748	220.3			
Indian	5,951	5,597	106.3	100.2	106.5	100.7
Chinese	308	55	413.7			
All other	33	18				
WEST NORTH CENTRAL						
Minnesota	1,316,571	1,247,382	105.5	109.1	114.6	113.9
White	1,303,100	1,235,804	105.4	100.0	114.5	113.9
Native	1,085,120	1,065,553	101.8	103.4	105.7	107.2
Native parentage	566,891	547,425	103.6	105.5	110.2	112.2
Foreign or mixed par	518,235	518,128	100.0	101.8	102.9	104.6
Foreign parentage	329,182	326,568	100.8	102.4	103.8	105.1
Mixed parentage	180,053	191,560	98.7	100.5	100.9	103.2
Foreign born	217,983	170,311	128.0	134.2	144.0	132.2
Negro	5,005	4,440	112.7	122.6	144.2	133.6
Other races	8,457	7,078	119.5	112.1	109.1	104.5
Mexican	2,009	1,557	132.9			
Indian	5,691	5,386	105.7	102.0	102.3	100.0
Chinese	422	102	413.7			
Filipino	221	15				
All other	54	18				
Iowa	1,255,101	1,215,838	103.2	104.7	106.6	107.6
White	1,243,197	1,205,185	103.2	104.6	106.5	107.5
Native	1,151,068	1,131,570	101.7	102.3	103.0	104.8
Native parentage	859,183	838,355	102.5	103.0	103.8	105.0
Foreign or mixed par	291,885	293,224	99.5	100.8	101.4	103.2
Foreign parentage	166,377	166,674	100.4	101.4	102.7	103.8
Mixed parentage	125,508	127,550	98.4	99.0	99.2	100.2
Foreign born	92,129	73,606	125.2	128.9	135.7	126.7
Negro	8,987	8,393	107.1	113.9	118.5	118.2
Other races	2,917	2,260	129.1	203.0	242.9	165.1
Mexican	2,380	1,915	124.3			
Indian	349	311	112.2	112.4	182.0	107.6
Chinese	126	27				
All other	62	7				
Missouri	1,822,868	1,806,501	100.9	102.5	105.1	105.6
White	1,706,844	1,692,043	100.9	102.4	105.1	105.8
Native	1,625,545	1,623,952	100.1	101.2	103.0	104.5
Native parentage	1,397,066	1,379,272	101.3	102.3	104.2	105.5
Foreign or mixed par	228,479	244,680	93.4	95.5	97.7	100.3
Foreign parentage	131,876	140,364	94.0	95.4	97.9	100.5
Mixed parentage	96,603	104,310	92.6	95.5	97.5	100.0
Foreign born	81,299	68,091	119.4	125.2	135.9	124.3
Negro	111,929	111,911	100.0	104.3	104.6	101.5
Other races	4,093	2,547	160.7	454.0	419.7	
Mexican	2,834	2,155	131.5			
Indian	336	242	138.8		99.4	
Chinese	521	113	461.1			
Filipino	303	18				
All other	99	19				
North Dakota	359,615	321,230	111.9	112.0	122.4	125.3
White	354,519	316,724	111.9	112.0	122.6	125.8
Native	294,141	271,054	108.2	100.9	114.9	117.4
Native parentage	133,690	122,932	108.8	108.7	121.6	130.9
Foreign or mixed par	160,451	148,122	107.7	105.6	110.8	111.1
Foreign parentage	100,549	92,558	108.6	105.5	111.5	111.4
Mixed parentage	59,902	56,464	106.1	105.7	109.1	111.9
Foreign born	60,378	44,770	134.9	134.3	145.8	142.4
Negro	243	134	181.3	144.5	161.4	153.1
Other races	4,853	4,372	111.0	109.1	101.8	104.0
Mexican	376	232	162.1			
Indian	4,293	4,094	104.9	103.6	98.8	98.9
Chinese	93	10				
All other	91	36				

DIVISION OR STATE AND CLASS OF POPULATION	Male, 1930	Female, 1930	MALES PER 100 FEMALES			
			1930	1920	1910	1900
WEST NORTH CENTRAL—Con.						
South Dakota	363,650	329,190	110.5	112.6	118.9	118.6
White	351,571	317,882	110.6	112.8	119.5	117.8
Native	313,906	289,890	108.3	109.5	114.5	112.8
Native parentage	195,173	180,205	108.3	110.5	118.2	117.0
Foreign or mixed par	118,733	109,694	108.2	108.3	110.5	109.2
Foreign parentage	69,566	62,931	110.5	110.3	111.0	110.1
Mixed parentage	49,167	46,763	105.1	105.1	108.5	107.3
Foreign born	37,665	27,983	134.6	136.9	145.8	130.4
Negro	343	303	113.2	133.1	134.1	140.9
Other races	11,736	11,014	106.6	104.0	100.9	95.4
Mexican	481	335	143.6			
Indian	11,172	10,661	104.8	102.5	99.4	94.1
All other	83	18				
Nebraska	706,348	671,615	105.2	107.9	111.2	112.5
White	693,399	660,303	105.0	107.7	111.0	112.5
Native	630,013	608,343	103.6	105.1	107.1	109.5
Native parentage	445,232	428,617	103.9	105.7	108.5	111.5
Foreign or mixed par	184,781	179,726	102.8	104.0	104.7	106.1
Foreign parentage	109,782	106,445	103.1	114.1	105.2	106.4
Mixed parentage	74,999	73,281	102.3	103.9	103.8	105.6
Foreign born	63,386	51,960	122.0	128.9	136.7	128.8
Negro	7,063	6,689	105.6	123.2	124.2	116.1
Other races	5,886	4,623	127.3	137.8	141.7	116.4
Mexican	3,585	2,736	131.0			
Indian	1,674	1,582	105.8	102.1	103.0	105.1
Chinese	152	42				
Japanese	414	260	159.2	316.6		
All other	61	3				
Kansas	961,291	919,708	104.5	105.7	110.0	109.5
White	914,626	878,221	104.1	105.7	110.1	109.7
Native	876,372	846,759	103.5	104.2	107.1	107.7
Native parentage	738,795	714,647	103.4	104.1	107.4	108.0
Foreign or mixed par	137,577	132,112	104.1	104.7	106.1	106.3
Foreign parentage	74,505	70,005	106.3	106.0	107.5	107.7
Mixed parentage	63,072	62,017	101.7	102.9	104.2	104.2
Foreign born	38,254	31,462	121.6	130.0	149.9	132.9
Negro	33,980	32,361	105.0	105.5	107.3	104.2
Other races	12,685	9,123	139.0	121.8	143.1	135.9
Mexican	11,200	7,950	140.9			
Indian	1,333	1,121	118.9	111.1	132.8	131.5
All other	152	52				
SOUTH ATLANTIC						
Delaware	121,257	117,123	103.5	104.1	104.6	104.0
White	104,200	101,494	102.7	103.7	104.4	104.0
Native	94,919	93,890	101.1	100.6	101.6	102.4
Native parentage	78,215	76,809	101.8	101.7	102.5	102.9
Foreign or mixed par	16,704	17,081	97.8	96.4	97.7	100.0
Foreign parentage	11,605	11,872	97.8	97.2	98.0	100.0
Mixed parentage	5,099	5,209	97.9	94.5	96.9	100.0
Foreign born	9,281	7,604	122.1	134.7	132.4	121.5
Negro	16,988	15,619	108.7	106.0	105.5	103.5
Other races	74	10				
Maryland	821,009	810,517	101.3	101.3	98.9	98.4
White	670,603	674,477	100.8	101.1	99.2	98.7
Native	620,427	620,650	100.0	99.9	98.1	98.4
Native parentage	522,310	517,486	100.9	100.8	99.0	99.1
Foreign or mixed par	107,117	112,164	95.5	96.2	94.8	95.8
Foreign parentage	70,671	73,747	95.8	96.3	94.9	95.8
Mixed parentage	36,446	38,417	94.9	95.8	94.7	95.8
Foreign born	50,206	44,827	112.1	114.0	108.9	101.9
Negro	140,506	135,873	103.4	102.0	97.7	96.8
Other races	810	187	485.0			
Chinese	389	103	377.7			
Filipino	309	18				
All other	112	46				
District of Columbia	231,883	254,986	90.9	87.0	91.3	90.0
White	168,982	184,932	91.4	87.0	90.4	94.8
Native	153,330	170,652	89.8	84.8	93.1	93.2
Native parentage	124,500	137,927	90.3	84.8	93.4	94.0
Foreign or mixed par	28,830	32,725	88.1	84.9	91.9	90.6
Foreign parentage	17,597	19,222	91.5	89.1	93.4	92.0
Mixed parentage	11,243	13,503	83.3	79.1	89.7	88.8
Foreign born	15,652	14,280	109.6	112.0	113.0	109.7
Negro	62,225	69,843	89.1	86.0	82.2	79.3
Other races	676	211	320.4			
Chinese	305	93				
Filipino	255	39				
All other	116	79				
Virginia	1,216,046	1,205,805	100.8	102.4	100.9	99.7
White	893,650	876,755	101.9	104.1	102.8	101.9
Native	879,949	866,636	101.5	103.2	101.8	101.1
Native parentage	851,882	840,821	101.3	102.9	101.6	100.9
Foreign or mixed par	28,067	25,815	108.7	113.9	107.9	106.7
Foreign parentage	15,251	13,301	114.7	118.4	111.6	113.4
Mixed parentage	12,816	12,514	102.4	108.0	104.4	103.1
Foreign born	13,701	10,119	135.4	162.4	169.0	171.1

POPULATION

TABLE 6.—POPULATION BY SEX, COLOR, AND NATIVITY, 1930, WITH NUMBER OF MALES PER 100 FEMALES, 1900 TO 1930, BY DIVISIONS AND STATES—Continued

DIVISION OR STATE AND CLASS OF POPULATION	Male, 1930	Female, 1930	MALES PER 100 FEMALES 1930	1920	1910	1900
SOUTH ATLANTIC—Con.						
Virginia—Con.						
Negro	321,545	328,620	97.8	98.6	97.1	95.9
Other races	851	430	197.9	187.9	167.8	267.9
Indian	436	343	127.1	105.5	112.2	119.9
Chinese	239	54				
Filipino	116	10				
All other	60	23				
West Virginia	889,871	838,384	106.0	108.9	111.6	108.6
White	828,743	785,191	105.5	108.2	110.5	107.4
Native	795,879	766,535	103.8	105.1	106.1	106.2
Native parentage	745,459	716,085	104.1	105.3	106.3	106.4
Foreign or mixed par	50,420	50,450	99.9	101.5	101.6	102.5
Foreign parentage	33,502	33,292	100.6	102.0	102.2	103.0
Mixed parentage	16,858	17,158	98.3	100.3	100.5	101.9
Foreign born	32,864	18,656	176.2	209.6	261.8	172.4
Negro	60,873	54,020	112.7	120.2	132.8	137.3
Other races	255	123	207.3			
Mexican	155	102	152.0			
All other	100	21				
North Carolina	1,575,208	1,595,068	98.8	99.9	99.2	98.3
White	1,120,270	1,114,678	100.5	101.6	101.2	100.1
Native	1,115,181	1,110,979	100.4	101.4	101.0	99.9
Native parentage	1,106,490	1,102,073	100.4	101.4	101.0	99.9
Foreign or mixed par	8,691	8,906	97.6	99.9	99.9	98.5
Foreign parentage	3,961	3,958	100.1	104.5	100.4	99.5
Mixed parentage	4,730	4,948	95.6	95.6	97.0	100.0
Foreign born	5,089	3,699	137.6	157.4	170.5	161.2
Negro	446,500	472,147	94.6	96.0	94.8	94.6
Other races	8,438	8,243	102.4	103.3	103.9	102.0
Indian	8,353	8,226	101.5	102.1	102.0	100.4
All other	85	17				
South Carolina	853,158	885,607	96.3	99.2	98.5	98.4
White	473,312	470,728	100.5	103.3	102.4	101.6
Native	470,192	468,582	100.3	102.8	102.0	101.3
Native parentage	463,533	461,906	100.4	102.7	102.0	101.4
Foreign or mixed par	6,659	6,676	99.7	108.1	97.1	94.7
Foreign parentage	3,311	3,166	104.6	109.9	95.2	92.4
Mixed parentage	3,348	3,510	95.4	106.0	99.2	97.2
Foreign born	3,120	2,146	145.4	177.6	159.3	142.8
Negro	379,300	414,381	91.5	95.4	95.4	96.2
Other races	546	498	100.6	156.6	125.0	
Indian	474	485	97.7	91.2	99.4	
All other	72	13				
Georgia	1,434,527	1,473,979	97.3	99.6	100.1	99.1
White	920,781	916,193	100.5	102.3	102.4	100.8
Native	912,606	910,451	100.2	101.8	101.9	100.4
Native parentage	897,514	894,985	100.3	101.8	101.9	100.5
Foreign or mixed par	15,092	15,466	97.6	104.8	101.3	97.7
Foreign parentage	7,610	7,605	100.1	108.0	103.6	98.0
Mixed parentage	7,482	7,861	95.2	100.5	98.9	96.5
Foreign born	8,175	5,742	142.4	161.8	171.4	153.7
Negro	513,451	557,674	92.1	95.9	97.2	97.1
Other races	295	112	263.4			
Chinese	181	72				
All other	114	40				
Florida	737,675	730,536	101.0	104.7	110.0	108.7
White	521,816	513,389	101.6	105.5	110.2	108.5
Native	489,664	486,484	100.7	103.7	107.0	106.6
Native parentage	440,161	434,212	101.4	104.4	107.0	107.1
Foreign or mixed par	49,503	52,272	94.7	98.6	101.4	101.1
Foreign parentage	27,114	28,002	96.8	100.2	102.7	101.7
Mixed parentage	22,389	24,270	92.2	96.5	99.7	100.5
Foreign born	32,152	26,905	119.5	133.7	157.6	140.8
Negro	215,148	216,680	99.3	103.0	109.5	108.7
Other races	711	407	152.2	167.7		199.4
Mexican	97	88				
Indian	299	288	103.8	109.7		126.6
Chinese	160	40				
Japanese	105	48				
All other	50	3				
EAST SOUTH CENTRAL						
Kentucky	1,322,793	1,291,796	102.4	103.2	103.0	103.1
White	1,209,165	1,179,199	102.5	103.5	103.2	103.7
Native	1,196,873	1,169,651	102.3	103.1	103.0	103.5
Native parentage	1,151,622	1,117,918	103.0	103.9	103.8	104.2
Foreign or mixed par	45,251	51,733	87.5	89.4	91.4	95.0
Foreign parentage	25,046	29,274	85.6	87.8	90.3	94.4
Mixed parentage	20,205	22,459	90.0	92.0	93.2	96.1
Foreign born	12,292	9,548	128.7	131.4	117.2	111.6
Negro	113,501	112,539	100.9	101.0	101.0	99.6
Other races	127	58			161.4	
Tennessee	1,304,559	1,311,997	99.4	100.9	102.1	102.2
White	1,071,798	1,066,821	100.5	101.8	103.3	103.3
Native	1,064,404	1,061,149	100.3	101.5	102.9	103.0
Native parentage	1,045,939	1,041,444	100.4	101.6	103.0	103.0
Foreign or mixed par	18,465	19,705	93.7	97.7	97.9	102.1
Foreign parentage	9,422	9,881	95.4	99.0	98.5	103.1
Mixed parentage	9,043	9,824	92.1	96.2	97.2	101.0
Foreign born	7,394	5,672	130.4	139.7	152.4	141.1

DIVISION OR STATE AND CLASS OF POPULATION	Male, 1930	Female, 1930	MALES PER 100 FEMALES 1930	1920	1910	1900
EAST SOUTH CENTRAL—Con.						
Tennessee—Continued.						
Negro	232,569	245,077	94.9	97.2	97.6	98.6
Other races	192	99			144.5	
Indian	85	76			98.2	
All other	107	23				
Alabama	1,315,009	1,331,239	98.8	99.8	101.0	100.5
White	857,522	843,253	101.7	102.7	103.8	102.8
Native	848,196	836,869	101.4	102.2	103.1	102.1
Native parentage	829,250	817,089	101.5	102.3	103.2	102.0
Foreign or mixed par	18,946	19,780	95.8	97.9	99.5	102.5
Foreign parentage	9,688	10,012	96.8	98.0	100.4	105.5
Mixed parentage	9,258	9,768	94.8	97.8	98.5	99.5
Foreign born	9,326	6,384	146.1	151.0	165.9	166.1
Negro	457,144	487,000	93.7	95.4	97.2	97.0
Other races	343	296	115.9	141.4	115.2	
Indian	228	237	96.2	108.8	99.8	
All other	115	59				
Mississippi	1,005,141	1,004,680	100.0	100.4	101.6	101.5
White	504,921	491,935	102.6	103.1	104.7	103.9
Native	500,574	489,233	102.3	102.6	104.1	103.1
Native parentage	490,005	478,670	102.4	102.8	104.2	103.2
Foreign or mixed par	10,569	10,563	100.1	96.3	100.3	102.0
Foreign parentage	5,016	4,994	100.4	96.8	100.8	104.4
Mixed parentage	5,553	5,569	99.7	95.8	99.0	100.2
Foreign born	4,347	2,702	160.9	162.8	173.7	193.4
Negro	408,338	511,380	97.4	98.0	99.2	99.8
Other races	1,882	1,365	137.9	156.9	149.3	125.3
Mexican	694	527	131.7			
Indian	743	715	103.9	111.7	114.0	105.9
Chinese	438	123	356.1			
All other	7					
WEST SOUTH CENTRAL						
Arkansas	939,843	914,639	102.8	104.5	106.0	106.1
White	702,261	672,645	104.4	105.9	107.7	107.7
Native	696,255	668,478	104.2	105.4	107.0	107.0
Native parentage	677,734	651,471	104.0	105.2	106.8	106.7
Foreign or mixed par	18,521	17,007	108.9	112.8	112.8	116.7
Foreign parentage	8,640	7,490	115.4	119.7	118.8	122.1
Mixed parentage	9,881	9,517	103.8	106.7	107.0	112.3
Foreign born	6,006	4,167	144.1	159.6	168.3	108.9
Negro	236,554	241,554	98.1	100.7	101.7	102.1
Other races	673	440	153.0		113.7	
Mexican	248	161	154.0			
Indian	210	198	106.1		88.5	
Chinese	186	65				
All other	29	16				
Louisiana	1,047,823	1,053,770	99.4	100.9	101.7	101.1
White	664,681	653,479	101.7	103.4	104.8	103.5
Native	644,305	638,945	100.8	101.9	102.8	102.0
Native parentage	591,828	580,744	101.9	103.8	104.2	103.7
Foreign or mixed par	52,477	58,201	90.2	90.5	93.5	93.9
Foreign parentage	29,359	32,438	90.5	91.0	94.2	94.2
Mixed parentage	23,118	25,763	89.7	89.9	92.3	93.4
Foreign born	20,376	14,534	140.2	148.4	133.9	125.3
Negro	379,173	397,153	95.5	97.0	98.3	98.3
Other races	3,969	3,138	126.5	174.4	226.8	328.7
Mexican	2,392	2,160	110.7			
Indian	800	736	108.7	106.6	97.5	132.5
Chinese	327	95				
Filipino	390	125	312.0			
All other	60	22				
Oklahoma	1,233,264	1,162,776	106.1	109.0	113.7	115.3
White	1,095,000	1,028,424	106.5	109.7	114.7	117.9
Native	1,079,456	1,017,215	106.1	108.7	113.3	116.7
Native parentage	1,026,128	968,177	106.0	108.5	113.1	116.4
Foreign or mixed par	53,328	49,088	108.7	111.7	116.2	119.0
Foreign parentage	25,718	22,747	113.1	113.9	118.7	121.8
Mixed parentage	27,610	26,291	105.0	109.2	113.4	118.0
Foreign born	15,544	11,200	138.7	165.8	178.1	164.4
Negro	86,818	85,380	101.7	104.3	109.5	100.0
Other races	51,446	48,972	105.1	101.5	102.0	98.6
Mexican	4,434	2,920	151.8			
Indian	46,744	45,981	101.7	100.6	101.5	98.5
Chinese	178	28				
Japanese	67	37				
All other	23	6				
Texas	2,965,994	2,858,721	103.8	106.9	107.4	107.4
White	2,190,623	2,092,808	104.7	108.1	109.0	100.4
Native	2,135,229	2,049,866	104.2	106.5	107.3	107.8
Native parentage	1,968,358	1,888,840	104.2	106.7	107.5	108.3
Foreign or mixed par	166,871	161,026	103.6	105.1	105.5	104.5
Foreign parentage	89,334	84,552	105.7	105.1	105.8	104.7
Mixed parentage	77,537	76,474	101.4	105.2	105.0	104.1
Foreign born	55,394	43,002	128.8	125.2	132.6	131.6
Negro	422,008	432,356	97.7	100.3	100.0	99.9
Other races	352,763	333,497	105.8	195.5	314.4	488.8
Mexican	351,077	332,604	105.6			
Indian	510	485	106.4	127.3	117.3	127.1
Chinese	546	157	347.8			
Japanese	323	106	164.8	201.3		
Filipino	246	42				
All other	55	13				

SEX DISTRIBUTION 107

TABLE 6.—POPULATION BY SEX, COLOR, AND NATIVITY, 1930, WITH NUMBER OF MALES PER 100 FEMALES, 1900 TO 1930, BY DIVISIONS AND STATES—Continued

DIVISION OR STATE AND CLASS OF POPULATION	Male, 1930	Female, 1930	1930	1920	1910	1900
MOUNTAIN						
Montana	293,228	244,378	120.0	120.5	152.1	160.3
White	281,703	235,534	119.6	120.2	152.2	159.7
Native	236,894	207,472	114.2	112.6	132.1	141.1
Native parentage	152,209	131,330	115.9	115.2	130.6	149.7
Foreign or mixed par	84,685	76,142	111.2	108.3	121.5	130.8
Foreign parentage	50,282	44,298	113.5	110.0	124.4	137.0
Mixed parentage	34,403	31,844	108.0	105.6	116.5	120.0
Foreign born	44,899	28,062	160.0	164.5	238.4	225.5
Negro	710	546	130.0	138.2	136.3	149.3
Other races	10,725	8,298	120.2	132.3	150.5	170.8
Mexican	1,766	805	219.4			
Indian	7,664	7,134	107.4	107.6	100.4	99.5
Chinese	427	59				
Japanese	510	243	209.9	362.0		
Filipino	293	2				
Korean	60	55				
All other	5					
Idaho	237,947	207,685	114.3	118.2	132.5	136.5
White	232,054	204,608	113.9	117.7	131.3	134.0
Native	214,007	193,101	110.8	113.1	121.9	126.0
Native parentage	167,937	152,252	110.3	112.8	123.0	127.9
Foreign or mixed par	46,070	40,849	112.8	114.2	118.9	122.2
Foreign parentage	23,130	19,758	117.1	116.5	123.4	128.7
Mixed parentage	22,940	21,091	108.8	111.8	114.0	114.9
Foreign born	18,047	11,507	164.7	176.6	227.5	197.2
Negro	395	273	144.7	174.6	157.3	130.7
Other races	3,998	2,804	142.6	153.8	216.0	211.0
Mexican	907	371	244.5			
Indian	1,833	1,805	101.6	103.7	102.7	93.0
Chinese	295	40				
Japanese	847	574	147.6	207.0		
All other	116	14				
Wyoming	124,785	100,780	123.8	131.3	168.8	169.4
White	117,703	96,364	122.1	130.1	165.6	168.2
Native	105,264	89,145	118.1	121.9	147.1	156.9
Native parentage	80,875	67,506	119.8	124.1	151.8	163.0
Foreign or mixed par	24,389	21,639	112.7	115.6	136.0	145.7
Foreign parentage	14,140	12,299	115.0	115.7	139.3	148.5
Mixed parentage	10,249	9,340	109.7	115.5	130.9	141.1
Foreign born	12,439	7,219	172.3	203.5	287.2	231.9
Negro	699	551	126.9	168.6	223.4	204.2
Other races	6,383	3,865	165.1	225.2	335.8	206.0
Mexican	4,582	2,592	176.8			
Indian	982	863	113.8	113.0	104.7	103.9
Chinese	113	17				
Japanese	645	381	169.3	393.4		
All other	61	12				
Colorado	530,752	505,039	105.1	110.3	116.9	120.9
White	491,121	469,996	104.5	110.1	116.4	120.8
Native	443,117	432,594	102.4	106.4	109.7	114.5
Native parentage	340,403	328,703	103.6	108.5	112.0	117.4
Foreign or mixed par	102,714	103,891	98.9	100.4	103.8	107.5
Foreign parentage	63,131	62,500	101.0	101.7	105.4	110.2
Mixed parentage	39,583	41,391	95.6	98.2	101.1	103.0
Foreign born	48,004	37,402	128.3	140.0	160.1	158.1
Negro	5,730	6,089	94.3	106.4	105.0	109.2
Other races	33,892	28,954	117.1	170.4	421.5	191.5
Mexican	30,824	26,852	114.8			
Indian	748	647	115.6	113.1	120.5	110.7
Chinese	195	38				
Japanese	1,847	1,366	135.2	185.5	2,029.6	
Filipino	220	30				
All other	58	21				
New Mexico	219,222	204,095	107.4	112.1	115.3	114.4
White	171,748	160,007	107.3	110.1	115.8	114.1
Native	166,993	156,965	106.4	107.8	111.5	110.8
Native parentage	156,224	146,529	106.6	108.0	111.1	110.5
Foreign or mixed par	10,769	10,436	103.2	105.5	115.0	113.4
Foreign parentage	5,496	5,245	104.8	106.2	116.1	118.6
Mixed parentage	5,273	5,191	101.6	104.5	113.6	107.6
Foreign born	4,755	3,042	156.3	137.7	189.6	165.7
Negro	1,531	1,319	116.1	402.9	120.9	174.8
Other races	45,943	42,769	107.4	111.5	107.3	113.4
Mexican	30,775	28,565	107.7			
Indian	14,864	14,077	105.6	108.4	102.6	108.1
Chinese	108	25				
Japanese	157	92				
All other	39	10				
Arizona	231,304	204,268	113.2	121.9	188.2	140.4
White	141,537	122,841	115.2	120.6	142.9	146.6
Native	132,145	116,642	113.3	116.2	129.3	139.3
Native parentage	112,014	98,233	114.0	120.0	135.0	146.3
Foreign or mixed par	20,131	18,409	109.4	107.7	119.0	127.9
Foreign parentage	9,993	8,909	112.2	107.7	122.3	131.4
Mixed parentage	10,138	9,500	106.7	107.7	118.7	122.7
Foreign born	9,392	6,199	151.5	133.5	188.4	172.9
Negro	6,352	4,397	144.5	273.0	110.4	281.0
Other races	83,415	77,031	108.3	112.8	117.0	117.1
Mexican	59,102	55,071	107.3			
Indian	22,471	21,255	105.7	106.7	106.4	104.8
MOUNTAIN—Continued						
Arizona—Continued.						
Other races—Continued.						
Chinese	845	265	318.9	553.4		
Japanese	532	347	153.3	229.3		
Filipino	408	64				
All other	57	29				
Utah	259,999	247,848	104.9	106.8	111.5	104.9
White	252,556	243,399	103.8	105.9	110.1	104.0
Native	229,578	222,605	103.1	103.8	108.2	104.4
Native parentage	162,130	156,340	103.7	104.1	108.2	105.6
Foreign or mixed par	67,448	66,265	101.8	103.4	103.7	103.3
Foreign parentage	35,604	33,921	105.0	106.7	105.8	104.6
Mixed parentage	31,844	32,344	98.5	99.6	101.1	101.4
Foreign born	22,978	20,794	110.5	120.7	131.0	102.5
Negro	609	499	122.0	136.3	152.5	208.3
Other races	6,834	3,950	173.0	193.1	258.2	177.4
Mexican	2,728	1,284	212.5			
Indian	1,510	1,353	112.0	113.6	115.4	106.5
Chinese	282	60				
Japanese	2,056	1,213	169.5	285.3		
Filipino	167	1				
All other	95	39				
Nevada	53,161	37,897	140.3	148.4	179.2	153.0
White	47,295	34,180	138.6	149.0	181.5	151.3
Native	38,712	30,438	127.2	129.8	153.4	131.9
Native parentage	26,857	20,713	129.7	133.2	161.3	142.5
Foreign or mixed par	11,855	9,725	121.9	123.7	141.0	119.6
Foreign parentage	6,871	5,494	125.1	126.5	147.2	122.9
Mixed parentage	4,984	4,231	117.8	119.6	132.6	114.5
Foreign born	8,583	3,692	232.5	264.1	331.4	240.5
Negro	277	239	115.9	130.7	105.2	
Other races	5,589	3,528	158.4	142.3	163.4	162.1
Mexican	2,221	869	255.6			
Indian	2,456	2,415	101.7	102.1	101.0	106.7
Chinese	410	73				
Japanese	442	166	266.3	442.4		
All other	60	5				
PACIFIC						
Washington	826,392	737,004	112.1	118.1	136.3	142.2
White	800,024	720,175	111.2	117.0	135.4	139.0
Native	658,330	618,513	106.4	109.3	120.8	128.4
Native parentage	454,048	419,579	108.2	111.1	124.2	133.9
Foreign or mixed par	204,282	198,934	102.7	105.8	113.9	117.8
Foreign parentage	117,089	111,974	104.6	107.4	116.4	120.9
Mixed parentage	87,193	86,960	100.3	103.3	110.0	113.0
Foreign born	142,694	101,662	140.3	158.0	199.7	191.4
Negro	3,797	3,043	124.8	135.2	160.0	171.8
Other races	21,671	13,786	157.2	174.6	262.9	260.9
Mexican	477	85				
Indian	5,778	5,475	105.5	101.0	99.6	97.7
Chinese	1,723	472	365.0	759.3	1,325.8	
Japanese	10,200	7,637	133.6	186.7	665.9	2,933.2
Filipino	3,374	106	3,183.0			
All other	119	11				
Oregon	499,672	454,114	110.0	113.4	133.2	129.0
White	489,232	447,797	109.3	112.5	130.1	122.8
Native	427,154	404,400	105.6	107.0	119.5	116.8
Native parentage	325,532	304,442	106.9	108.2	121.6	118.3
Foreign or mixed par	101,622	99,958	101.7	103.8	113.2	112.7
Foreign parentage	55,308	53,494	103.4	105.3	116.5	115.8
Mixed parentage	46,319	46,464	99.7	101.8	108.7	108.4
Foreign born	62,078	43,397	143.0	156.4	209.9	169.6
Negro	1,210	1,024	118.2	126.4	155.0	158.2
Other races	9,230	5,293	174.4	193.6	410.5	490.2
Mexican	1,247	321	388.5			
Indian	2,442	2,334	104.6	100.5	99.1	93.2
Chinese	1,526	550	277.3	570.5	2,200.9	2,748.5
Japanese	2,919	2,039	143.2	207.7	1,062.0	
Filipino	1,035	31				
All other	62	18				
California	2,942,595	2,734,656	107.6	112.4	125.5	123.5
White	2,577,434	2,462,813	104.7	110.0	120.1	116.6
Native	2,123,407	2,106,806	100.8	102.6	108.7	107.7
Native parentage	1,487,384	1,442,751	103.1	105.2	112.4	112.1
Foreign or mixed par	636,023	664,055	95.8	98.1	102.5	101.7
Foreign parentage	383,686	396,774	96.7	99.1	103.6	102.0
Mixed parentage	252,337	267,281	94.4	96.4	100.7	101.0
Foreign born	454,027	356,007	127.5	143.6	169.6	153.8
Negro	40,052	40,906	97.7	104.8	100.3	100.2
Other races	325,109	230,847	140.8	209.6	448.4	511.2
Mexican	199,228	168,785	118.0			
Indian	10,018	9,194	109.0	109.8	104.3	100.9
Chinese	27,988	9,373	298.6	528.8	1,017.0	1,223.9
Japanese	56,440	41,016	137.6	171.1	562.8	1,735.6
Filipino	28,625	1,845	1,551.5	1,307.4		
Hindu	1,761	112	1,572.3			
Korean	687	410	167.6	260.7		
Hawaiian	352	104	338.5			
All other	10	8				

CHAPTER 4

STATE OF BIRTH OF THE NATIVE POPULATION

CHAPTER 4.—STATE OF BIRTH OF THE NATIVE POPULATION

INTRODUCTION

The inquiry as to State of birth has been carried on the Population Schedule at each census beginning with that of 1850. In 1850 and 1860, however, State of birth was returned for the free population only. The statistics here presented relate to the population living in continental United States at the time of the census of 1930, with comparable statistics, so far as available, back to 1850. Corresponding statistics for Alaska, Hawaii, Puerto Rico, the Panama Canal Zone, and the Virgin Islands are presented in condensed form in a volume entitled "Outlying Territories and Possessions."

The returns as to State of birth are valuable mainly for the light they throw upon the movement of the native population from one place to another within the United States. "Native population," as the term is ordinarily used by the Bureau of the Census, comprises all persons born in continental United States or any of the outlying possessions, and persons of native parentage born abroad or at sea and designated, respectively, as "American citizens born abroad," and "American citizens born at sea." Thus the term "native population," when used in the headings of tables presenting statistics by States, does not indicate that the persons are native to (that is, born in) the several States, but merely that they are born in the United States. The natives of individual States are designated in the table headings as "Population born in" the specified States.

For a certain number of persons the enumerators returned the place of birth as "United States," without specifying the State. Persons for whom the place of birth was not returned at all, and for whom the returns give no indication of foreign origin, have also been assumed to be natives of the United States and included in the group designated "United States, State not reported."

In some of the tables the statistics have been limited to persons born in continental United States, with State of birth reported, excluding both those born in the outlying possessions and those for whom the State of birth was not reported.

The fact that each census from 1850 to 1930 has shown that more than one-fifth of the native Americans had migrated from the States of their birth and were living in other States indicates a rather high degree of mobility on the part of the population. In this connection it should be noted that the census figures take account only of those persons who have removed from one State to another and are, on the census date,

living in States other than those in which they were born. The statistics therefore afford no indication of the amount of migration within a given State from rural to urban communities or from one locality to another. Much of the movement from country to city takes place within the boundaries of some one State, while some of the migration from one State to another is merely from one border county or city to another just across the State line. In fact, nearly one-half of the natives of the United States who were enumerated in 1930 outside the States in which they were born were found living in adjoining States.

Furthermore, the census figures do not give any indication of the movement of population from one State to another outside the State of birth. A person who at one or more times has removed from one State to another and has later returned to the State in which he was born is counted in the census tables as a person born in and living in that particular State, just as if he had remained there continuously; and if he has not returned to the State of his birth he is counted in the tables as born in one State and living in another, just as if he had gone directly from the State of birth to the State of present residence.

While the census figures for State of birth form practically the only source of extensive information with regard to interstate movements of population, extreme care should be exercised in the use of these figures as representing or measuring migration. Obviously, the census statistics do not indicate the whole number of persons who have migrated (removed) from the States in which they were born to other States, or to any other specific State, during any given period of time. Some of those who have gone from one State to another, from Vermont to Iowa, for example, have since died; others have returned to the States in which they were born; and still others have gone to other States, or to places outside the boundaries of continental United States. The census figure for the number of persons living in Iowa who were born in Vermont does not, therefore, represent the number of persons who have migrated from Vermont to Iowa, but that number minus those who have died or removed from the State. Again, if 50,000 Negroes had gone from Georgia to Illinois in 1922 and returned to Georgia in 1929, their double migration would have left no record in the census statistics. It is therefore with some hesitancy that the term "migration" is used at all in the headings of the tables presented herewith; for what the census figures show is not the extent of interstate

135

373

POPULATION

migration (that is, the number of persons who go from one State to another) but the net, cumulative results of such migration in combination with mortality.

Migration east and west of the Mississippi River, and between the North and the South.—Statistics indicating some of the results of the migration of the native population between the sections of the country lying east and west, respectively, of the Mississippi River are presented in Tables 2 and 4. The "Net gain of the West," which is shown in Table 4, is obtained by subtracting from the number of native persons reported as born east of the Mississippi River and living west of it (5,145,922) the number born west of the river and living east of it (1,648,832).

The results of the exchange of population between the North and South are likewise presented in Tables 3 and 4. There has been, of course, a considerable amount of migration from both the North and the South to the West; that is, to the States comprising the Mountain and Pacific divisions. It is believed, however, that the main currents of the movement of the population northward and southward are best indicated by the figures as presented in Tables 3 and 4.

Gain or loss through interdivisional or interstate migration.—The net gain or loss through interdivisional migration (Tables 7 to 12) and through interstate migration (Tables 17 to 19) represents the difference on the census date between the total number of surviving native migrants out of the specified division or State and the total number of surviving native migrants into the specified division or State. Some of these migrants are the survivors of groups who departed from, or arrived in, the division or State half a century or more before the census was taken. The figures do not, therefore, represent the migration in the sense of the number of persons coming or going during the preceding census decade or during any other specific period of time. The "change in net gain or loss as compared with preceding census," as shown in column I, Table 7, represents the algebraic difference between the net gains or the net losses at the beginning and the end of the decade. Even this figure, however, does not represent exactly the difference between the number of native migrants out of the division and the number of native migrants into the division, since it is affected also by differences in mortality and by the movement of native population between the division in question and foreign countries.

Urban and rural population.—Because of the differences between urban and rural population in respect to the proportions of persons born in other States, separate statistics are given in Tables 28 to 34 for the urban population, the rural-farm population, and the rural-nonfarm population. The extent of migration between one and another of these classes of population within the same State can not be shown, of course, as the census returns relate only to movements of population across State lines.

Urban population, as defined by the Census Bureau, is in general that residing in cities and other incorporated places having 2,500 inhabitants or more, the remainder being classified as rural. In three of the New England States, New Hampshire, Massachusetts, and Rhode Island, conditions are exceptional in that the compactly built portions of towns (townships) are not separately incorporated or politically distinct in any way from the rural territory within the same town; nor is it the usual practice to incorporate even the larger places as cities until they attain a population in excess of 10,000. Consequently, if only cities were counted as urban the classification would be quite inadequate. In 1920 and 1910 all towns in these States which had a population of 2,500 or more were classified as urban. This resulted in the inclusion of a considerable number of places that were mainly rural in their general characteristics. In 1930 the special rule for these States has been modified so as to place in the urban classification, in addition to the regularly incorporated cities, only those towns in which there is a village or thickly settled area having more than 2,500 inhabitants, and comprising, either by itself or when combined with other villages in the same town, more than 50 per cent of the total population of the town.

One other modification has been made in the definition of urban population for use in connection with the 1930 census. This modification extends the definition so as to include townships and other political subdivisions (not incorporated as municipalities, nor containing any area so incorporated) which had a total population of 10,000 or more, and a population density of 1,000 or more per square mile.

Rural-farm and rural-nonfarm population.—In addition to the classification of the population as urban and rural, which is based on the size (number of inhabitants) and the political status (municipal incorporation) of the geographic unit in which the persons live, the population, both urban and rural, is further classified as farm and nonfarm, on the basis of a question reading "Does this family live on a farm?"

For the farm population living in urban territory, which forms less than 1 per cent of the total farm population, no detailed tabulations were made; hence the presentation of classified data for the farm population is limited to that part living in rural territory and designated as rural-farm population. This is done partly to simplify the classification (dividing the total population into three groups, namely, urban, rural-farm, and rural-nonfarm) and partly because it is felt that in general the farm families living within the corporate limits of cities or other incorporated places are living under conditions at least somewhat urban, rather than under typical farm conditions.

The rural-nonfarm or "village" population is made up largely of persons living in small towns or villages, both incorporated and unincorporated, though in many areas there are considerable numbers of families living in the open country but not on farms.

STATE OF BIRTH

PER CENT WHICH POPULATION BORN IN EACH STATE AND LIVING IN OTHER STATES FORMED
OF TOTAL BORN IN EACH STATE: 1930

[District of Columbia, 34 per cent, not shown separately on the map]

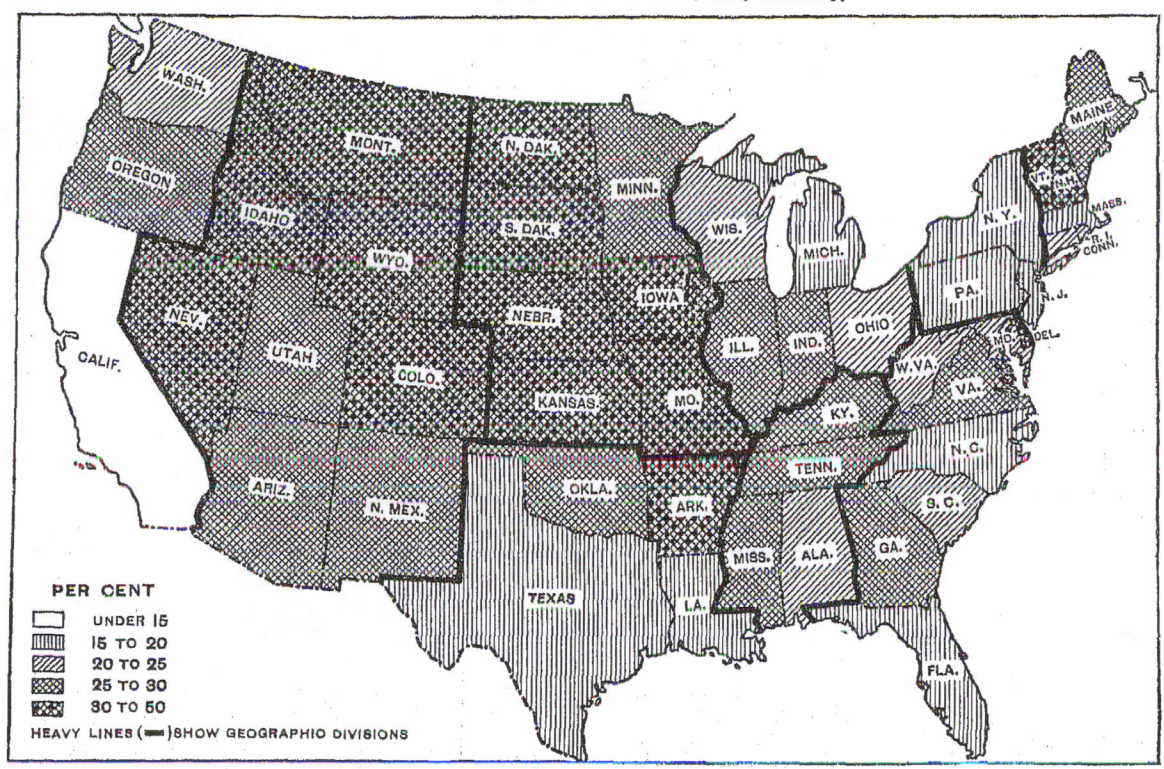

PER CENT WHICH POPULATION BORN IN OTHER STATES FORMED OF TOTAL NATIVE POPULATION
LIVING IN EACH STATE: 1930

[District of Columbia, 60 per cent, not shown separately on the map]

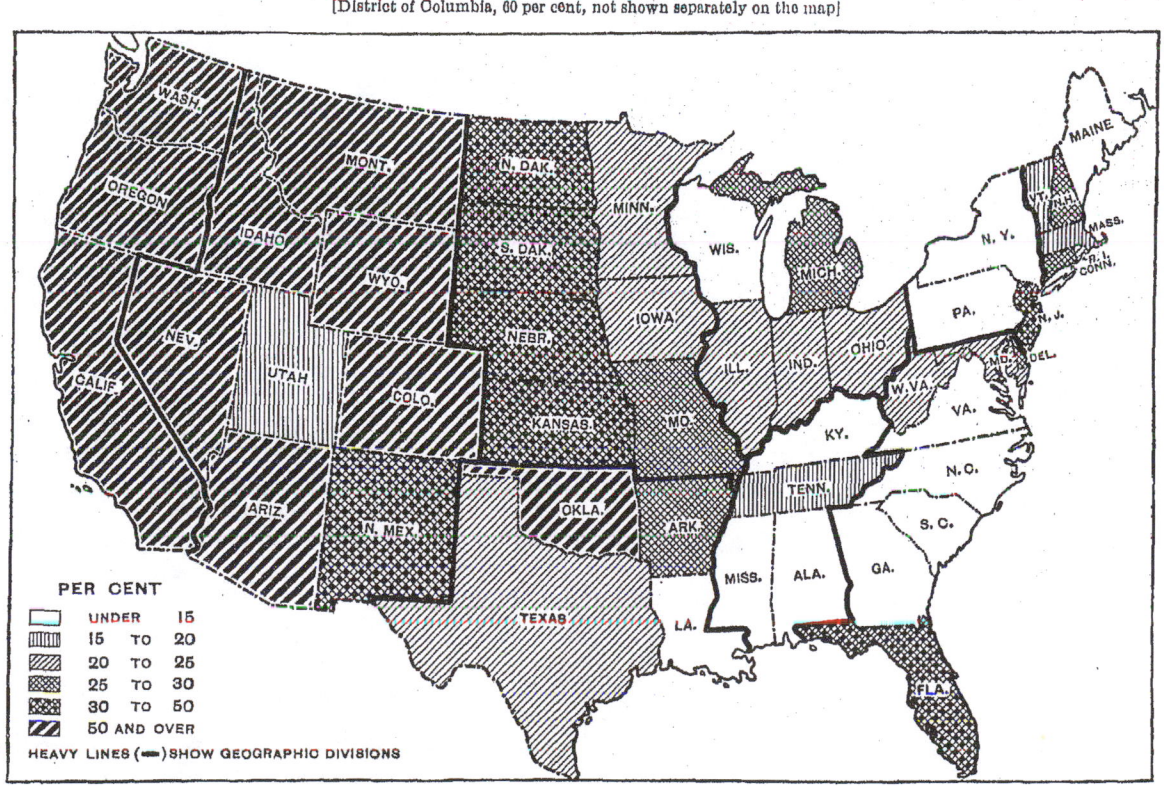

138

POPULATION

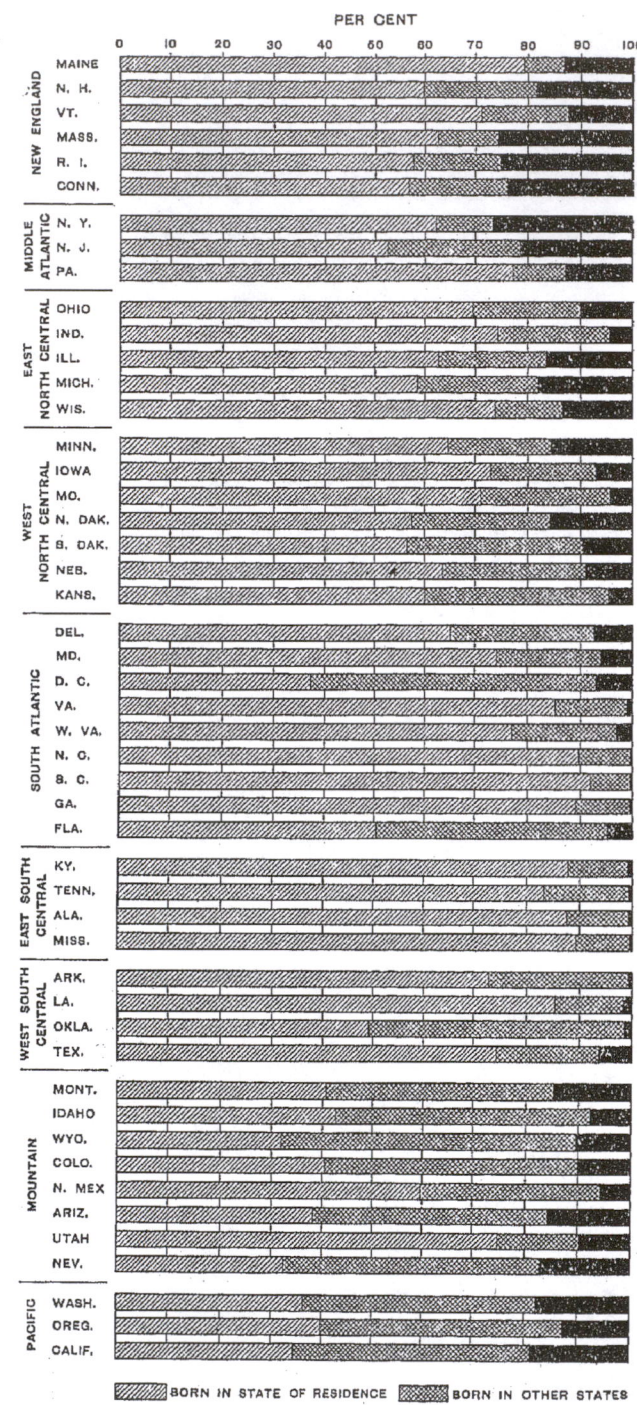

Distribution of total population of each State as born in State of residence, in other States, or in foreign countries: 1930

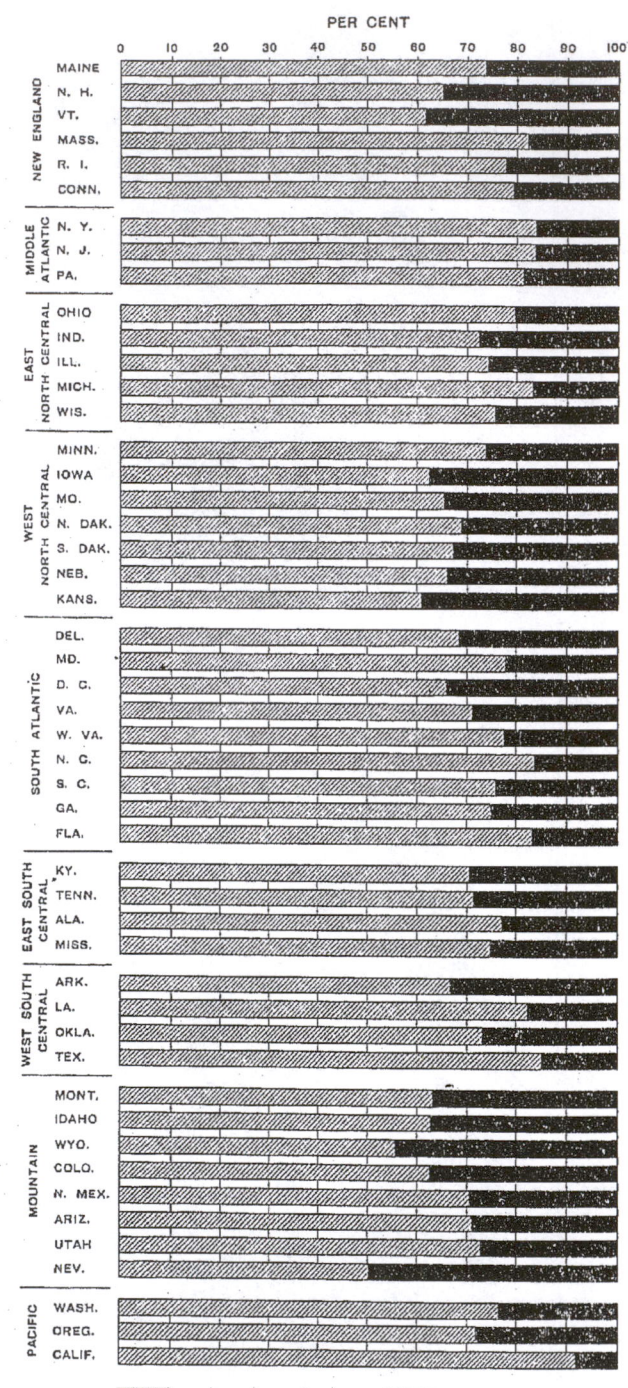

Distribution of population born in each State as living in State of birth or in other States: 1930

STATE OF BIRTH

TABLE 1.—NUMBER AND PER CENT NATIVE AND FOREIGN BORN IN THE TOTAL POPULATION, WITH CLASSIFICATION OF NATIVE ACCORDING TO WHETHER BORN IN STATE OF RESIDENCE OR ELSEWHERE, FOR THE UNITED STATES: 1850 TO 1930

CENSUS YEAR	Total population	NATIVE POPULATION								State of birth not reported	Born in outlying posses-sions	Ameri-can citizens born at sea	Ameri-can citizens born abroad	FOREIGN-BORN POPULATION	
		Total		With State of birth reported											
				Born in State of residence		Born in other States									
		Number	Per cent of total popu-lation	Number	Per cent of total popu-lation	Number	Per cent of total popu-lation	Per cent of native popu-lation					Number	Per cent of total popu-lation
1930	122,775,046	108,570,897	88.4	82,677,619	67.3	25,388,100	20.7	23.4	238,469	136,032	819	129,853	14,204,149	11.6
1920	105,710,620	91,789,928	86.8	71,071,013	67.2	20,274,450	19.2	22.1	313,582	38,020	853	92,010	13,920,692	13.2
1910	91,972,266	78,456,380	85.3	61,185,305	66.5	16,910,114	18.4	21.6	285,085	7,365	1,560	66,351	13,515,886	14.7
1900	75,994,575	65,653,299	86.4	51,901,722	68.3	13,501,045	17.8	20.6	180,458	2,923	2,252	64,899	10,341,276	13.6
1890	[1] 62,622,250	53,372,703	85.2	41,871,611	66.9	11,094,108	17.7	20.8	396,652	322	1,463	8,547	9,249,547	14.8
1880	50,155,783	43,475,840	86.7	33,882,734	67.6	9,592,764	19.1	22.1		51	291		6,679,943	13.3
1870	38,558,371	32,991,142	85.6	25,321,340	65.7	7,057,320	18.3	23.2	12,262	51	109		5,567,229	14.4
1860	27,489,561	23,353,386	85.0	17,527,069	63.8	5,774,434	21.0	24.7	49,265		2,618		[2] 4,136,175	15.0
1850	[2] 19,987,563	[2] 17,742,961	88.8	13,457,040	67.3	4,251,250	21.3	24.0	34,662				[2] 2,244,602	11.2

[1] Exclusive of population of Indian Territory and Indian reservations, specially enumerated in 1890, with a native population of 325,451 not distributed by State of birth and a foreign-born population of 13. These areas were not enumerated prior to 1890.
[2] White and free colored population only.

TABLE 2.—NATIVE POPULATION BORN EAST AND LIVING WEST OF THE MISSISSIPPI RIVER, OR VICE VERSA: 1870 TO 1930

[The small number of persons for whom State of birth was not reported are omitted from this table]

SECTION	1930	1920	1910	1900	1890	1880	1870
Total native population born in United States and with State of birth reported	108,065,719	91,345,463	78,095,419	65,402,767	52,965,719	43,475,498	32,978,660
Born east of the Mississippi River [1]	77,755,710	67,487,718	58,981,669	51,163,588	43,267,325	37,196,027	29,518,843
Living east of the Mississippi River	72,609,788	62,259,868	53,704,790	46,651,491	38,906,809	33,685,290	27,084,122
Living west of the Mississippi River	5,145,922	5,227,850	5,276,879	4,512,097	4,360,516	3,510,737	2,434,721
Per cent of total born east of the Mississippi	6.6	7.7	8.9	8.8	10.1	9.4	8.2
Born west of the Mississippi River [1]	30,310,009	23,857,745	19,113,750	14,239,179	9,698,394	6,279,471	3,459,817
Living west of the Mississippi River	28,661,177	22,818,840	18,428,977	13,720,636	9,416,035	6,069,112	3,324,048
Living east of the Mississippi River	1,648,832	1,038,905	684,773	518,543	282,359	210,359	135,769
Per cent of total born west of the Mississippi	5.4	4.4	3.6	3.6	2.9	3.3	3.9
Net gain of West (excess of persons born east and living west of the Mississippi over persons born west and living east)	3,497,090	4,188,945	4,592,106	3,993,554	4,078,157	3,300,378	2,298,952

[1] In the preparation of this table the entire States of Minnesota and Louisiana have been treated as lying west of the Mississippi River.

TABLE 3.—NATIVE POPULATION BORN IN THE NORTH AND LIVING IN THE SOUTH, OR VICE VERSA: 1870 TO 1930

[Persons born and living in the West and the small number of persons for whom State of birth was not reported are omitted from this table]

SECTION	1930	1920	1910	1900	1890	1880	1870
Population born and living in the North or in the South and with State of birth reported	97,746,825	83,852,590	72,581,780	62,098,675	50,706,023	42,183,329	32,291,720
Born in the North [1]	59,468,321	51,341,156	43,975,391	37,941,559	31,616,121	25,480,443	19,655,131
Living in the North	57,590,129	49,619,807	42,526,162	36,920,109	30,980,527	25,006,653	19,356,833
Living in the South	1,878,192	1,721,349	1,449,229	1,021,450	635,594	473,790	298,298
Per cent of total born in the North	3.2	3.4	3.3	2.7	2.0	1.9	1.5
Born in the South [1]	38,278,504	32,511,434	28,606,389	24,157,116	19,089,902	16,702,886	12,636,589
Living in the South	34,981,175	30,359,885	27,079,282	22,861,263	18,554,282	15,590,078	11,585,836
Living in the North	3,297,329	2,151,540	1,527,107	1,295,853	1,135,620	1,112,808	1,050,753
Per cent of total born in the South	8.6	6.6	5.3	5.4	5.8	6.7	8.3
Net gain of the North (excess of persons born in the South and living in the North over persons born in the North and living in the South)	1,419,137	430,200	77,878	274,403	500,026	639,018	752,455

[1] The North: New England, Middle Atlantic, East North Central, and West North Central divisions. The South: South Atlantic, East South Central, and West South Central divisions.

140

POPULATION

TABLE 4.—SUMMARY OF DATA INDICATING RESULTS OF MIGRATION OF THE NATIVE POPULATION EAST AND WEST, AND NORTH AND SOUTH, BY COLOR AND NATIVITY: 1930 AND 1920

[The small number of persons for whom State of birth was not reported are omitted from this table]

SECTION [1]	TOTAL		WHITE								NEGRO		OTHER RACES	
			Total		Of native parentage		Of foreign or mixed parentage							
	1930	1920	1930	1920	1930	1920	1930	1920			1930	1920	1930	1920
Born east and living west of the Mississippi River	5,145,922	5,227,850	4,820,182	4,882,520	3,658,859	3,745,681	1,161,323	1,136,839			320,589	342,931	5,151	2,399
Born west and living east of the Mississippi River	1,648,832	1,038,905	1,458,154	939,017	1,064,938	669,010	393,216	270,007			177,158	96,110	13,520	3,778
Net gain of the West	3,497,090	4,188,945	3,362,028	3,943,503	2,593,921	3,076,671	768,107	866,832			143,431	246,821		
Net gain of the East													8,369	1,379
Born in the North and living in the South	1,878,192	1,721,349	1,821,678	1,675,085	1,475,545	1,363,190	346,133	311,895			52,338	44,536	4,176	1,728
Born in the South and living in the North	3,297,329	2,151,549	1,931,799	1,412,779	1,718,517	1,230,611	213,282	182,168			1,355,789	737,423	9,741	1,347
Net gain of the South				262,306		132,579	132,851	129,727						381
Net gain of the North	1,419,137	430,200	110,121		242,972						1,303,451	692,887	5,565	

[1] See footnotes to Tables 2 and 3.

TABLE 5.—PER CENT DISTRIBUTION BY DIVISION OF BIRTH, FOR THE NATIVE POPULATION LIVING IN EACH DIVISION: 1930 AND 1920

[Percentages based on population with State of birth reported; not shown where less than 0.1]

DIVISION OF BIRTH	NEW ENGLAND		MIDDLE ATLANTIC		EAST NORTH CENTRAL		WEST NORTH CENTRAL		SOUTH ATLANTIC		EAST SOUTH CENTRAL		WEST SOUTH CENTRAL		MOUNTAIN		PACIFIC	
	1930	1920	1930	1920	1930	1920	1930	1920	1930	1920	1930	1920	1930	1920	1930	1920	1930	1920
Total	100.0	100.0	100.0	100.0	100.0	100.0	100.0	100.0	100.0	100.0	100.0	100.0	100.0	100.0	100.0	100.0	100.0	100.0
New England	92.2	91.8	1.9	1.5	0.5	0.6	0.3	0.5	0.4	0.4	0.1	0.1	0.1	0.1	0.6	0.9	2.1	2.5
Middle Atlantic	5.2	5.6	90.5	92.7	3.9	4.2	1.5	2.3	2.2	2.0	0.3	0.3	0.6	0.8	2.4	3.5	5.4	6.2
East North Central	0.9	0.9	1.8	1.6	84.2	87.0	9.1	11.7	1.5	1.3	1.6	1.6	2.4	3.2	8.4	11.3	13.7	15.5
West North Central	0.3	0.3	0.5	0.4	3.6	2.7	83.4	80.1	0.5	0.4	0.4	0.4	4.9	5.6	17.2	18.8	16.4	15.0
South Atlantic	0.9	0.9	4.3	3.1	2.4	1.8	0.7	0.9	92.4	93.3	3.6	3.4	1.7	2.3	1.4	1.8	1.8	1.9
East South Central	0.1	0.1	0.5	0.4	4.2	3.1	1.9	2.1	2.6	2.1	92.5	93.0	6.7	8.7	2.0	2.4	2.2	2.3
West South Central	0.1	0.1	0.2	0.2	0.8	0.4	2.2	1.6	0.3	0.3	1.3	1.1	82.9	78.8	6.1	5.0	4.7	2.0
Mountain	0.1	0.1	0.1	0.1	0.3	0.2	0.7	0.6	0.1	0.1			0.5	0.4	59.4	53.6	6.4	4.2
Pacific	0.1	0.1	0.2	0.1	0.2	0.2	0.3	0.3	0.1	0.1			0.2	0.2	2.6	2.6	47.5	48.6

TABLE 6.—PER CENT DISTRIBUTION BY DIVISION OF RESIDENCE, FOR THE POPULATION BORN IN EACH DIVISION: 1930 AND 1920

[Percentages based on population with State of birth reported]

DIVISION OF RESIDENCE	NEW ENGLAND		MIDDLE ATLANTIC		EAST NORTH CENTRAL		WEST NORTH CENTRAL		SOUTH ATLANTIC		EAST SOUTH CENTRAL		WEST SOUTH CENTRAL		MOUNTAIN		PACIFIC	
	1930	1920	1930	1920	1930	1920	1930	1920	1930	1920	1930	1920	1930	1920	1930	1920	1930	1920
Total	100.0	100.0	100.0	100.0	100.0	100.0	100.0	100.0	100.0	100.0	100.0	100.0	100.0	100.0	100.0	100.0	100.0	100.0
New England	87.9	89.0	1.6	1.7	0.2	0.3	0.2	0.2	0.4	0.3	0.1	0.1	0.1	0.1	0.2	0.3	0.3	0.3
Middle Atlantic	6.1	4.5	89.4	88.5	1.7	1.5	0.8	0.7	5.4	3.7	0.8	0.6	0.4	0.3	0.9	0.8	0.9	1.0
East North Central	1.8	1.8	4.0	4.2	82.9	82.9	5.9	4.3	3.1	2.2	7.8	5.5	1.7	0.9	2.1	1.8	1.2	1.2
West North Central	0.6	0.9	0.9	1.4	5.1	6.8	75.7	78.6	0.5	0.7	2.0	2.3	2.4	2.1	3.3	3.5	0.9	1.2
South Atlantic	1.0	0.9	1.6	1.5	1.1	1.0	0.5	0.5	86.3	88.5	3.4	2.8	0.5	0.4	0.4	0.4	0.3	0.4
East South Central	0.1	0.1	0.1	0.2	0.7	0.7	0.3	0.3	2.2	2.1	77.4	79.0	1.2	1.2	0.2	0.2	0.1	0.1
West South Central	0.2	0.2	0.3	0.4	1.3	1.6	4.3	4.8	1.2	1.0	6.7	8.1	89.1	91.8	2.0	1.9	0.6	0.7
Mountain	0.3	0.5	0.4	0.6	1.3	1.7	4.2	4.7	0.3	0.3	0.6	0.7	1.8	1.7	74.7	81.3	2.5	3.2
Pacific	2.1	1.9	1.7	1.5	4.1	3.6	8.1	6.0	0.7	0.6	1.2	1.0	2.8	1.5	16.1	9.8	93.1	91.9

STATE OF BIRTH

141

TABLE 7.—NATIVE POPULATION BY DIVISION OF BIRTH AND DIVISION OF RESIDENCE, WITH NET GAIN OR LOSS THROUGH INTERDIVISIONAL MIGRATION: 1870 TO 1930

[The small number of persons for whom State of birth was not reported are omitted from this table]

GEOGRAPHIC DIVISION AND CENSUS YEAR	BORN IN THE SPECIFIED DIVISION			Born in and living in the specified division	LIVING IN THE SPECIFIED DIVISION			Net gain (+) or loss (−) through interdivisional migration (col. E − col. A, or col. F − col. B)	Change in "net gain or loss," as compared with preceding census
	Total	Living in other divisions			Total	Born in other divisions			
		Number	Per cent			Number	Per cent		
	A	B	C	D	E	F	G	H	I
NEW ENGLAND:									
1930	6,596,477	795,680	12.1	5,800,797	6,289,484	488,687	7.8	−306,993	−136,138
1920	5,660,113	619,870	11.0	5,040,243	5,489,258	449,015	8.2	−170,855	−34,272
1910	4,907,215	568,763	11.6	4,338,452	4,702,088	363,636	7.7	−205,127	+13,638
1900	4,338,274	526,979	12.1	3,811,295	4,119,509	308,214	7.5	−218,765	+138,323
1890	3,898,003	564,572	14.5	3,333,431	3,540,915	207,484	5.9	−357,088	+69,446
1880	3,643,424	587,039	16.1	3,056,385	3,216,890	160,505	5.0	−426,534	+27,777
1870	3,293,103	568,707	17.3	2,724,396	2,838,703	114,396	4.0	−454,311	
MIDDLE ATLANTIC:									
1930	21,016,097	2,223,424	10.6	18,792,673	20,760,477	1,967,804	9.5	−255,620	+549,684
1920	18,019,528	2,060,953	11.5	15,949,575	17,214,224	1,264,649	7.3	−805,304	+127,163
1910	15,342,852	1,881,406	12.3	13,461,446	14,410,385	948,939	6.6	−932,467	+155,683
1900	13,178,117	1,808,060	13.7	11,370,057	12,089,967	719,910	6.0	−1,088,150	+248,899
1890	11,177,406	1,818,364	16.3	9,359,042	9,840,357	481,315	4.9	−1,337,049	+30,779
1880	9,843,732	1,785,831	18.1	8,057,901	8,475,904	418,003	4.9	−1,367,828	−116,551
1870	8,186,679	1,596,101	19.5	6,590,578	6,935,402	344,824	5.0	−1,251,277	
EAST NORTH CENTRAL:									
1930	21,878,346	3,402,696	15.6	18,475,650	21,948,072	3,472,416	15.8	+69,720	+967,901
1920	19,002,140	3,205,913	17.1	15,796,227	18,103,965	2,307,738	13.0	−898,175	−478,250
1910	16,479,755	3,077,070	18.7	13,402,685	15,103,330	1,700,645	11.3	−1,376,425	−520,976
1900	14,160,456	2,473,049	17.5	11,687,407	13,305,007	1,617,600	12.2	−855,449	−149,210
1890	11,596,441	2,194,918	18.9	9,401,523	10,890,202	1,488,679	13.7	−706,239	−817,075
1880	9,179,161	1,552,367	16.9	7,626,794	9,289,997	1,063,203	17.9	+110,836	−731,146
1870	6,618,328	930,119	14.1	5,688,209	7,460,310	1,772,101	23.8	+841,982	
WEST NORTH CENTRAL:									
1930	13,409,581	3,261,876	24.3	10,147,705	12,173,222	2,025,517	16.6	−1,236,359	−1,025,588
1920	11,320,725	2,426,788	21.4	8,893,937	11,109,954	2,216,017	19.9	−210,771	−723,058
1910	9,449,180	1,840,185	19.5	7,608,995	9,961,467	2,352,472	23.6	+512,287	−810,320
1900	7,448,659	1,101,856	14.8	6,346,803	8,777,275	2,430,472	27.7	+1,328,616	−687,759
1890	5,262,124	592,940	11.3	4,669,184	7,278,499	2,600,315	35.8	+2,016,375	+136,160
1880	3,276,998	333,539	10.2	2,943,459	5,167,213	2,213,754	42.9	+1,880,215	+498,626
1870	1,801,712	176,627	9.8	1,625,085	3,183,301	1,557,616	48.9	+1,381,589	
SOUTH ATLANTIC:									
1930	16,535,486	2,263,290	13.7	14,272,196	15,446,709	1,174,513	7.6	−1,088,777	−339,583
1920	14,377,095	1,658,241	11.5	12,718,854	13,627,901	909,047	6.7	−749,194	+161,972
1910	12,770,824	1,478,110	11.6	11,292,714	11,869,658	576,944	4.9	−901,166	+49,392
1900	11,161,575	1,372,186	12.3	9,789,389	10,211,017	421,628	4.1	−950,558	−40,633
1890	9,616,872	1,291,048	13.4	8,325,824	8,625,681	299,857	3.5	−991,191	−95,617
1880	8,509,714	1,335,735	15.7	7,173,979	7,422,906	248,927	3.4	−1,086,808	+55,849
1870	6,828,793	1,318,504	19.3	5,510,289	5,686,136	175,847	3.1	−1,142,657	
EAST SOUTH CENTRAL:									
1930	11,729,304	2,649,619	22.6	9,079,685	9,813,878	734,193	7.5	−1,915,426	−350,009
1920	10,368,842	2,178,394	21.0	8,190,448	8,803,425	612,977	7.0	−1,565,417	−388,496
1910	9,481,023	1,788,681	18.9	7,692,342	8,304,102	611,760	7.4	−1,176,921	−296,289
1900	8,325,166	1,482,208	17.8	6,842,958	7,444,534	601,576	8.1	−880,632	−194,042
1890	6,978,603	1,255,789	18.0	5,722,814	6,292,013	569,199	9.0	−686,590	−156,546
1880	6,019,996	1,146,840	19.1	4,873,156	5,489,952	616,796	11.2	−530,044	−237,355
1870	4,591,940	932,776	20.8	3,659,164	4,299,251	640,087	14.9	−292,689	
WEST SOUTH CENTRAL:									
1930	10,895,498	1,189,280	10.9	9,706,218	11,704,384	1,998,166	17.1	+808,886	−577,037
1920	8,339,585	680,706	8.2	7,658,879	9,725,508	2,066,629	21.2	+1,385,923	−248,650
1910	6,758,408	410,956	6.1	6,347,452	8,392,981	2,045,529	24.4	+1,634,573	+245,139
1900	4,855,385	231,088	4.8	4,624,297	6,244,819	1,620,522	25.9	+1,389,434	−351,731
1890	3,242,235	149,286	4.6	3,092,949	4,279,938	1,186,980	27.7	+1,037,703	+140,275
1880	2,257,662	108,456	4.8	2,149,206	3,155,090	1,005,884	31.9	+897,428	+266,693
1870	1,269,192	74,374	5.9	1,194,818	1,899,927	705,109	37.1	+630,735	
MOUNTAIN:									
1930	2,620,755	662,640	25.3	1,958,115	3,298,382	1,340,267	40.6	+677,627	−288,287
1920	1,870,479	349,873	18.7	1,520,606	2,836,393	1,315,787	46.4	+965,914	+96,594
1910	1,289,296	188,290	14.6	1,101,006	2,158,616	1,057,610	49.0	+869,320	+343,709
1900	835,858	84,466	10.1	751,392	1,361,469	610,077	44.8	+525,611	+112,210
1890	469,834	36,314	7.7	433,520	883,235	449,715	50.9	+413,401	+206,796
1880	285,621	17,969	6.3	267,652	492,226	224,574	45.6	+206,605	+134,039
1870	155,724	6,140	3.9	149,584	228,290	78,706	34.5	+72,566	
PACIFIC:									
1930	3,384,175	234,818	6.9	3,149,357	6,631,111	3,481,754	52.5	+3,246,936	+1,199,057
1920	2,326,956	189,210	8.1	2,137,746	4,374,835	2,237,089	51.1	+2,047,879	+471,953
1910	1,616,866	115,579	7.1	1,501,287	3,192,792	1,691,505	53.0	+1,575,926	+826,033
1900	1,099,277	74,379	6.8	1,024,898	1,849,170	824,272	44.6	+749,893	+139,215
1890	724,201	39,888	5.5	684,313	1,334,879	650,566	48.7	+610,678	+294,548
1880	459,190	25,332	5.5	433,858	775,320	341,462	44.0	+316,130	+102,058
1870	233,189	12,109	5.2	221,080	447,251	226,171	50.6	+214,062	

142   POPULATION

TABLE 8.—TOTAL POPULATION DISTRIBUTED AS BORN IN DIVISION OF RESIDENCE, IN OTHER DIVISIONS, OR IN FOREIGN COUNTRIES, BY DIVISIONS, 1930, WITH PERCENTAGES, 1900 TO 1930

GEOGRAPHIC DIVISION	Total population, 1930 [1]	POPULATION BORN IN THE UNITED STATES AND WITH STATE OF BIRTH REPORTED										FOREIGN BORN				
		Born in division of residence					Born in other divisions					Number, 1930	Per cent of total			
		Number, 1930	Per cent of total				Number, 1930	Per cent of total					1930	1920	1910	1900
			1930	1920	1910	1900		1930	1920	1910	1900					
United States	122,775,046	91,382,402	74.4	73.7	72.6	74.0	16,683,317	13.6	12.7	12.3	12.0	14,204,149	11.6	13.2	14.7	13.6
New England	8,166,341	5,800,797	71.0	68.1	66.2	68.2	488,087	6.0	6.1	5.5	5.5	1,848,943	22.6	25.5	27.9	25.8
Middle Atlantic	26,260,750	18,792,673	71.6	71.6	69.7	73.6	1,967,804	7.5	5.7	4.9	4.7	5,352,781	20.4	22.3	25.1	21.5
East North Central	25,297,185	18,475,656	73.0	70.8	73.4	73.1	3,472,416	13.7	11.0	9.3	10.1	3,275,723	12.9	15.1	16.8	16.4
West North Central	13,296,915	10,147,705	76.3	70.9	65.4	61.3	2,025,517	15.2	17.7	20.2	23.5	1,084,153	8.2	11.0	13.9	14.8
South Atlantic	15,793,589	14,272,196	90.4	90.9	92.6	93.7	1,174,513	7.4	6.5	4.7	4.0	318,697	2.0	2.4	2.5	2.1
East South Central	9,887,214	9,079,685	91.8	92.1	91.5	90.7	734,193	7.4	6.9	7.3	8.0	59,364	0.6	0.8	1.0	1.2
West South Central	12,176,830	9,706,218	79.7	74.8	72.3	70.8	1,908,166	16.4	20.2	23.3	24.8	440,553	3.6	4.5	4.0	4.1
Mountain	3,701,789	1,958,115	52.9	45.6	41.8	44.9	1,340,267	36.2	39.4	40.2	36.4	384,323	10.4	14.0	17.2	18.0
Pacific	8,194,433	3,149,357	38.4	38.4	35.8	42.4	3,481,754	42.5	40.2	40.3	34.1	1,439,662	17.6	20.3	22.8	22.5

[1] Includes persons born in the United States, State of birth not reported; persons born in outlying possessions, and American citizens born abroad or at sea. The combined number of these classes in the United States in 1930 was 505,178, or four-tenths of 1 per cent of the total population.

TABLE 9.—WHITE AND NEGRO POPULATION DISTRIBUTED AS BORN IN DIVISION OF RESIDENCE, IN OTHER DIVISIONS, OR IN FOREIGN COUNTRIES, BY DIVISIONS: 1930

GEOGRAPHIC DIVISION	WHITE POPULATION							NEGRO POPULATION						
	Total [1]	Born in the United States, and with State of birth reported				Foreign born		Total [1]	Born in the United States, and with State of birth reported				Foreign born	
		Born in division of residence		Born in other divisions					Born in division of residence		Born in other divisions			
		Number	Per cent	Number	Per cent	Number	Per cent		Number	Per cent	Number	Per cent	Number	Per cent
United States	108,864,207	80,492,581	73.9	14,606,654	13.4	13,366,407	12.3	11,891,143	9,762,855	82.1	1,976,624	16.6	98,620	0.8
New England	8,065,113	5,752,888	71.3	451,123	5.6	1,834,810	22.7	94,086	44,991	47.8	36,579	38.9	11,780	12.5
Middle Atlantic	25,172,104	18,427,461	73.2	1,352,960	5.4	5,260,042	20.9	1,052,899	354,010	33.7	611,497	58.1	64,565	6.1
East North Central	24,277,663	18,167,867	74.8	2,822,595	11.6	3,223,924	13.3	930,450	278,327	29.9	640,218	68.8	5,157	0.6
West North Central	12,873,487	9,918,618	77.0	1,860,070	14.4	1,050,277	8.2	331,784	171,547	51.7	157,008	47.3	528	0.2
South Atlantic	11,349,284	9,955,907	87.7	1,069,614	9.4	304,278	2.7	4,421,388	4,296,766	97.2	104,217	2.4	12,684	0.3
East South Central	7,224,614	6,563,867	90.9	594,613	8.2	57,065	0.8	2,658,238	2,513,498	94.6	138,805	5.2	532	--------
West South Central	9,099,981	7,117,591	78.2	1,788,887	19.7	170,232	1.9	2,281,951	2,077,617	91.0	197,058	8.6	1,412	0.1
Mountain	3,303,586	1,699,814	51.5	1,299,917	39.3	287,014	8.7	30,225	6,122	20.3	23,591	78.1	187	0.6
Pacific	7,498,375	2,888,568	38.5	3,366,875	44.9	1,159,765	15.5	90,122	19,077	21.2	67,561	75.0	1,869	2.1

[1] Includes persons born in the United States, State of birth not reported; persons born in outlying possessions, and American citizens born abroad or at sea. The combined numbers of these classes are 398,565 whites or four-tenths of 1 per cent of the white population and 53,044 Negroes, or four-tenths of 1 per cent of the Negro population.

TABLE 10.—NATIVE POPULATION, WHITE AND NEGRO, BY DIVISION OF BIRTH AND DIVISION OF RESIDENCE, 1930, WITH GAIN OR LOSS THROUGH INTERDIVISIONAL MIGRATION, 1930, 1920, AND 1910

[The small number of persons for whom State of birth was not reported are omitted from this table]

GEOGRAPHIC DIVISION	TOTAL NATIVE POPULATION, 1930							NATIVE WHITE, 1930						
	Born in the specified division			Born in and living in the specified division	Living in the specified division			Born in the specified division			Born in and living in the specified division	Living in the specified division		
	Total	Living in other divisions			Total	Born in other divisions		Total	Living in other divisions			Total	Born in other divisions	
		Number	Per cent			Number	Per cent		Number	Per cent			Number	Per cent
United States	108,065,719	16,683,317	15.4	91,382,402	108,065,719	16,683,317	15.4	95,099,235	14,606,654	15.4	80,492,581	95,099,235	14,606,654	15.4
New England	6,596,477	795,680	12.1	5,800,797	6,289,484	488,087	7.8	6,535,693	782,805	12.0	5,752,888	6,204,011	451,123	7.3
Middle Atlantic	21,016,097	2,223,424	10.6	18,792,673	20,760,477	1,967,804	9.5	20,610,693	2,183,232	10.6	18,427,461	19,780,421	1,352,960	6.8
E. North Central	21,878,346	3,402,690	15.6	18,475,656	21,948,072	3,472,416	15.8	21,523,034	3,355,167	15.6	18,167,867	20,990,462	2,822,595	13.4
W. North Central	13,409,581	3,261,876	24.3	10,147,705	12,173,222	2,025,517	16.6	13,113,764	3,195,136	24.4	9,918,618	11,778,688	1,860,070	15.8
South Atlantic	16,535,486	2,263,290	13.7	14,272,196	15,446,709	1,174,513	7.6	11,319,720	1,363,813	12.0	9,955,907	11,025,521	1,069,614	9.7
E. South Central	11,729,304	2,649,619	22.6	9,079,685	9,813,878	734,193	7.5	8,531,783	1,967,916	23.1	6,563,867	7,158,480	594,613	8.3
W. South Central	10,895,498	1,189,280	10.9	9,706,218	11,704,384	1,998,166	17.1	8,039,544	921,953	11.5	7,117,591	8,906,478	1,788,887	20.1
Mountain	2,620,755	662,640	25.3	1,958,115	3,208,382	1,340,267	40.6	2,317,079	617,265	26.6	1,699,814	2,990,731	1,290,917	43.3
Pacific	3,384,175	234,818	6.9	3,149,357	6,631,111	3,481,754	52.5	3,107,935	219,367	7.1	2,888,568	6,255,443	3,366,875	53.8

GEOGRAPHIC DIVISION	NATIVE NEGRO, 1930							GAIN (+) OR LOSS (−) THROUGH INTERDIVISIONAL MIGRATION								
	Born in the specified division			Born in and living in the specified division	Living in the specified division			Total native population			Native white			Native Negro		
	Total	Living in other divisions			Total	Born in other divisions		1930	1920	1910	1930	1920	1910	1930	1920	1910
		Number	Per cent			Number	Per cent									
United States	11,739,479	1,976,624	16.8	9,762,855	11,739,479	1,976,624	16.8	--------	--------	--------	--------	--------	--------	--------	--------	--------
New Eng.	57,580	12,539	21.8	44,991	81,570	36,579	44.8	−306,993	−170,855	−205,127	−331,682	−192,833	−226,219	+24,040	+21,325	+20,310
Mid. Atl.	394,022	39,112	9.9	354,910	966,407	611,497	63.3	−255,620	−805,304	−932,467	−830,272	−1,102,900	−1,120,078	+572,385	+296,664	+186,384
E. N. Cen.	323,198	44,871	13.9	278,327	918,545	640,218	69.7	+69,726	−808,175	−1,376,425	−532,572	−1,194,908	−1,496,074	+595,347	+296,111	+119,649
W. N. Cen.	229,719	58,172	25.3	171,547	328,645	157,098	47.8	−1,236,359	−210,771	−512,287	−1,335,066	−279,218	+472,566	+98,926	+68,222	+40,497
S. Atlantic	5,195,040	898,274	17.3	4,296,766	4,400,983	104,217	2.4	−1,088,777	−749,194	−901,166	−294,199	−293,667	−507,454	−794,057	−455,410	−392,827
E. S. Cen.	3,193,426	679,551	21.3	2,513,498	2,652,303	138,805	5.2	−1,915,426	−1,565,417	−1,176,921	−1,373,303	−1,159,135	−974,165	−541,146	−405,511	−200,876
W. S. Cen.	2,310,969	233,352	10.1	2,077,617	2,274,675	197,058	8.7	+808,886	+1,385,928	+1,634,573	+866,934	+1,257,042	+1,434,780	−36,294	+127,350	+194,658
Mountain	12,327	6,205	50.3	6,122	29,713	23,591	79.4	+677,627	+965,914	+869,320	+682,652	+945,727	+856,683	+17,386	+20,085	+13,229
Pacific	23,225	4,148	17.9	19,077	86,638	67,561	78.0	+3,246,936	+2,047,879	+1,575,926	+3,147,508	+2,019,052	+1,560,561	+63,413	+31,164	+18,976

STATE OF BIRTH

TABLE 11.—NATIVE WHITE POPULATION OF NATIVE PARENTAGE AND OF FOREIGN OR MIXED PARENTAGE, BY DIVISION OF BIRTH AND DIVISION OF RESIDENCE, 1930, WITH GAIN OR LOSS THROUGH INTERDIVISIONAL MIGRATION, 1930, 1920, AND 1910

[The small number of persons for whom State of birth was not reported are omitted from this table]

GEOGRAPHIC DIVISION AND CLASS OF POPULATION	BORN IN THE SPECIFIED DIVISION			Born in and living in the specified division	LIVING IN THE SPECIFIED DIVISION			GAIN (+) OR LOSS (−) THROUGH INTERDIVISIONAL MIGRATION		
	Total	Living in other divisions			Total	Born in other divisions		1930	1920	1910
		Number	Per cent			Number	Per cent			
NATIVE WHITE OF NATIVE PARENTAGE										
United States	69,842,445	11,113,438	15.9	58,729,007	69,842,445	11,113,438	15.9	--------	--------	--------
New England	3,335,196	443,165	13.3	2,892,031	3,152,115	260,084	8.3	−183,081	−142,364	−180,137
Middle Atlantic	11,777,098	1,318,747	11.2	10,458,351	11,364,949	906,598	8.0	−412,149	−647,973	−741,207
East North Central	14,772,813	2,366,924	16.0	12,406,889	14,453,392	2,046,503	14.2	−319,421	−290,502	−1,067,279
West North Central	9,586,522	2,435,710	25.4	7,150,812	8,517,614	1,366,802	16.0	−1,068,908	−290,502	+281,575
South Atlantic	10,729,575	1,219,662	11.4	9,509,913	10,395,375	885,462	8.5	−334,200	−321,087	−480,724
East South Central	8,300,118	1,879,440	22.6	6,420,678	6,954,048	534,370	7.7	−1,345,070	−1,130,460	−955,052
West South Central	7,536,404	834,224	11.1	6,702,180	8,332,048	1,629,868	19.6	+795,644	+1,169,159	+1,344,362
Mountain	1,712,481	451,411	26.4	1,261,070	2,287,212	1,026,142	44.9	+574,731	+754,695	+670,836
Pacific	2,083,238	165,155	7.9	1,918,083	4,375,692	2,457,609	56.2	+2,292,454	+1,451,519	+1,132,620
NATIVE WHITE OF FOREIGN OR MIXED PARENTAGE										
United States	25,256,790	3,493,216	13.8	21,763,574	25,256,790	3,493,216	13.8	--------	--------	--------
New England	3,200,497	330,640	10.6	2,860,857	3,051,896	191,039	6.3	−148,601	−50,409	−46,082
Middle Atlantic	8,833,595	864,485	9.8	7,969,110	8,415,472	446,362	5.3	−418,123	−454,987	−379,471
East North Central	6,750,221	989,243	14.7	5,760,978	6,537,070	776,092	11.9	−213,151	−300,121	−428,795
West North Central	3,527,232	750,426	21.5	2,767,806	3,261,074	493,268	15.1	−266,158	+20,284	+190,991
South Atlantic	590,145	144,151	24.4	445,994	630,146	184,152	29.2	+40,001	+27,420	−21,730
East South Central	222,665	88,476	39.7	134,189	194,432	60,243	31.0	−28,233	−28,675	−19,113
West South Central	503,140	87,729	17.4	415,411	574,430	159,019	27.7	+71,290	+87,083	+90,418
Mountain	604,598	165,854	27.4	438,744	712,519	273,775	38.4	+107,921	+191,032	+185,847
Pacific	1,024,697	54,212	5.3	970,485	1,879,751	909,266	48.4	+855,054	+568,433	+427,935

TABLE 12.—NATIVE POPULATION, BY SEX, BY DIVISION OF BIRTH AND DIVISION OF RESIDENCE, WITH GAIN OR LOSS THROUGH INTERDIVISIONAL MIGRATION: 1930

[The small number of persons for whom State of birth was not reported are omitted from this table]

GEOGRAPHIC DIVISION AND SEX	BORN IN THE SPECIFIED DIVISION			Born in and living in the specified division	LIVING IN THE SPECIFIED DIVISION			Gain (+) or loss (−) through interdivisional migration
	Total	Living in other divisions			Total	Born in other divisions		
		Number	Per cent			Number	Per cent	
NATIVE MALES								
United States	54,188,892	8,606,273	15.9	45,582,619	54,188,892	8,606,273	15.9	--------
New England	3,281,536	423,171	12.9	2,858,365	3,095,870	237,505	7.7	−185,666
Middle Atlantic	10,462,558	1,162,431	11.1	9,300,127	10,297,811	997,684	9.7	−164,747
East North Central	11,010,070	1,746,115	15.9	9,263,955	11,057,396	1,793,441	16.2	+47,326
West North Central	6,748,367	1,641,126	24.3	5,107,241	6,154,450	1,047,209	17.0	−593,917
South Atlantic	8,267,562	1,179,819	14.3	7,087,743	7,685,232	597,489	7.8	−582,330
East South Central	5,917,885	1,386,519	23.4	4,531,366	4,904,487	373,121	7.6	−1,013,398
West South Central	5,467,009	610,622	11.2	4,856,387	5,926,712	1,070,325	18.1	+459,703
Mountain	1,325,988	330,082	24.9	995,806	1,711,891	716,085	41.9	+385,903
Pacific	1,707,917	125,788	7.4	1,582,129	3,355,043	1,772,914	52.8	+1,647,126
NATIVE FEMALES								
United States	53,876,827	8,077,044	15.0	45,799,783	53,876,827	8,077,044	15.0	--------
New England	3,314,941	372,509	11.2	2,942,432	3,193,614	251,182	7.9	−121,327
Middle Atlantic	10,553,539	1,060,993	10.1	9,492,546	10,462,666	970,120	9.3	−90,873
East North Central	10,868,276	1,656,575	15.2	9,211,701	10,890,676	1,678,975	15.4	+22,400
West North Central	6,661,214	1,620,750	24.3	5,040,464	6,018,772	978,308	16.3	−642,442
South Atlantic	8,267,924	1,083,471	13.1	7,184,453	7,761,477	577,024	7.4	−506,447
East South Central	5,811,419	1,263,100	21.7	4,548,319	4,909,391	361,072	7.4	−902,028
West South Central	5,428,489	578,658	10.7	4,849,831	5,777,672	927,841	16.1	+349,183
Mountain	1,294,767	331,958	25.6	962,809	1,586,491	623,682	39.3	+291,724
Pacific	1,676,258	109,030	6.5	1,567,228	3,276,068	1,708,840	52.2	+1,599,810

144 POPULATION

TABLE 13.—PER CENT DISTRIBUTION BY DIVISION OF BIRTH, FOR THE NATIVE POPULATION LIVING IN EACH STATE: 1930 AND 1920

[Percentages based on population with State of birth reported; not shown where less than 0.1]

DIVISION OF BIRTH	MAINE 1930	MAINE 1920	NEW HAMPSHIRE 1930	NEW HAMPSHIRE 1920	VERMONT 1930	VERMONT 1920	MASSACHUSETTS 1930	MASSACHUSETTS 1920	RHODE ISLAND 1930	RHODE ISLAND 1920	CONNECTICUT 1930	CONNECTICUT 1920	NEW YORK 1930	NEW YORK 1920	NEW JERSEY 1930	NEW JERSEY 1920
Total	100.0	100.0	100.0	100.0	100.0	100.0	100.0	100.0	100.0	100.0	100.0	100.0	100.0	100.0	100.0	100.0
New England	97.8	97.6	95.9	95.6	91.6	90.8	93.4	92.9	94.0	92.9	84.2	83.7	3.0	2.3	2.5	2.0
Middle Atlantic	1.1	1.1	2.6	2.8	6.6	7.3	3.9	4.4	3.8	4.6	11.8	12.9	90.3	92.9	89.1	91.7
East North Central	0.4	0.4	0.6	0.7	0.8	0.8	0.9	1.0	0.7	0.7	1.1	1.0	1.9	1.7	1.5	1.3
West North Central	0.2	0.3	0.3	0.3	0.4	0.4	0.4	0.3	0.3	0.3	0.4	0.3	0.7	0.5	0.5	0.4
South Atlantic	0.2	0.3	0.3	0.3	0.3	0.3	0.9	0.9	0.9	1.1	1.8	1.5	3.0	1.8	5.4	3.9
East South Central	0.1	0.1	0.1	0.1	0.1	0.1	0.1	0.1	0.1	0.1	0.2	0.2	0.4	0.3	0.5	0.4
West South Central	0.1	--	0.1	--	0.1	0.1	0.1	0.1	0.1	0.1	0.1	0.1	0.3	0.2	0.2	0.2
Mountain	0.1	0.1	0.1	0.1	0.1	0.1	0.1	0.1	0.1	0.1	0.1	0.1	0.1	0.1	0.1	0.1
Pacific	0.1	0.1	0.1	--	0.1	0.1	0.2	0.1	0.1	0.1	0.1	0.1	0.2	0.2	0.2	0.1

DIVISION OF BIRTH	PENNSYLVANIA 1930	PENNSYLVANIA 1920	OHIO 1930	OHIO 1920	INDIANA 1930	INDIANA 1920	ILLINOIS 1930	ILLINOIS 1920	MICHIGAN 1930	MICHIGAN 1920	WISCONSIN 1930	WISCONSIN 1920	MINNESOTA 1930	MINNESOTA 1920	IOWA 1930	IOWA 1920
Total	100.0	100.0	100.0	100.0	100.0	100.0	100.0	100.0	100.0	100.0	100.0	100.0	100.0	100.0	100.0	100.0
New England	0.5	0.5	0.4	0.5	0.2	0.2	0.5	0.6	1.0	1.0	0.4	0.6	0.5	0.9	0.3	0.5
Middle Atlantic	91.2	92.7	6.3	6.1	1.5	1.7	2.7	3.2	5.5	6.3	1.4	2.2	1.5	2.3	1.6	2.6
East North Central	1.8	1.7	81.4	84.6	87.8	89.8	82.9	85.6	83.0	87.3	91.2	91.8	10.0	12.2	9.5	12.4
West North Central	0.4	0.3	1.1	0.9	1.9	1.4	6.3	4.7	3.1	1.8	5.7	4.4	86.5	83.0	86.4	81.8
South Atlantic	5.2	4.1	4.9	3.7	1.2	1.1	1.4	1.2	2.5	1.3	0.3	0.2	0.3	0.3	0.5	0.7
East South Central	0.5	0.4	5.3	3.8	6.5	5.2	4.1	3.5	3.3	1.5	0.4	0.3	0.3	0.3	0.6	0.8
West South Central	0.2	0.1	0.4	0.3	0.6	0.6	1.5	0.8	1.0	0.3	0.2	0.1	0.3	0.2	0.5	0.5
Mountain	0.1	0.1	0.1	0.1	0.2	0.1	0.4	0.3	0.3	0.2	0.3	0.2	0.4	0.4	0.4	0.4
Pacific	0.1	0.1	0.1	0.1	0.1	0.1	0.2	0.2	0.3	0.2	0.2	0.2	0.3	0.3	0.2	0.2

DIVISION OF BIRTH	MISSOURI 1930	MISSOURI 1920	NORTH DAKOTA 1930	NORTH DAKOTA 1920	SOUTH DAKOTA 1930	SOUTH DAKOTA 1920	NEBRASKA 1930	NEBRASKA 1920	KANSAS 1930	KANSAS 1920	DELAWARE 1930	DELAWARE 1920	MARYLAND 1930	MARYLAND 1920	DISTRICT OF COLUMBIA 1930	DISTRICT OF COLUMBIA 1920
Total	100.0	100.0	100.0	100.0	100.0	100.0	100.0	100.0	100.0	100.0	100.0	100.0	100.0	100.0	100.0	100.0
New England	0.2	0.3	0.3	0.4	0.3	0.5	0.3	0.5	0.2	0.4	0.8	0.8	0.7	0.6	2.8	3.2
Middle Atlantic	1.2	1.5	1.0	1.7	1.3	2.3	1.9	3.0	1.9	3.0	12.1	12.7	5.6	5.3	9.3	10.7
East North Central	8.5	9.6	7.6	11.5	9.4	18.5	8.4	11.8	9.9	13.8	1.1	0.9	1.3	1.1	4.6	5.8
West North Central	80.0	79.5	89.2	84.3	86.5	81.0	85.1	80.3	78.0	73.6	0.5	0.3	0.5	0.4	2.4	2.8
South Atlantic	1.0	1.3	0.3	0.5	0.3	0.6	0.7	0.9	1.1	1.4	84.8	84.7	91.0	91.7	76.4	72.9
East South Central	4.6	4.7	0.2	0.3	0.3	0.5	0.7	1.0	2.1	2.8	0.4	0.3	0.5	0.4	2.4	2.6
West South Central	3.9	2.5	0.2	0.2	0.4	0.4	1.0	0.9	5.4	3.9	0.2	0.1	0.2	0.2	1.1	1.1
Mountain	0.5	0.4	0.8	0.7	1.1	0.9	1.5	1.2	1.1	0.9	0.1	0.1	0.1	0.1	0.5	0.4
Pacific	0.2	0.2	0.3	0.3	0.3	0.3	0.3	0.3	0.3	0.3	0.1	0.1	0.1	0.1	0.4	0.5

DIVISION OF BIRTH	VIRGINIA 1930	VIRGINIA 1920	WEST VIRGINIA 1930	WEST VIRGINIA 1920	NORTH CAROLINA 1930	NORTH CAROLINA 1920	SOUTH CAROLINA 1930	SOUTH CAROLINA 1920	GEORGIA 1930	GEORGIA 1920	FLORIDA 1930	FLORIDA 1920	KENTUCKY 1930	KENTUCKY 1920	TENNESSEE 1930	TENNESSEE 1920
Total	100.0	100.0	100.0	100.0	100.0	100.0	100.0	100.0	100.0	100.0	100.0	100.0	100.0	100.0	100.0	100.0
New England	0.3	0.3	0.1	0.1	0.1	0.1	0.1	0.1	0.1	0.1	1.7	1.3	0.1	0.1	0.1	0.1
Middle Atlantic	1.5	1.6	3.1	3.3	0.4	0.3	0.3	0.3	0.4	0.4	4.4	3.3	0.4	0.4	0.3	0.4
East North Central	0.8	0.9	4.1	4.3	0.3	0.2	0.2	0.2	0.5	0.4	5.8	4.7	3.8	3.6	1.2	1.2
West North Central	0.3	0.3	0.3	0.3	0.1	0.1	0.1	0.1	0.2	0.2	1.9	1.5	0.5	0.5	0.6	0.5
South Atlantic	95.1	95.0	88.5	88.9	97.9	98.4	98.5	98.5	94.3	95.1	76.1	79.9	2.2	1.9	5.1	4.2
East South Central	1.6	1.5	3.7	2.9	0.9	0.7	0.7	0.6	4.0	3.4	8.5	7.9	92.5	93.1	91.0	92.3
West South Central	0.2	0.2	0.2	0.1	0.1	0.1	0.1	0.1	0.4	0.3	1.2	0.9	0.3	0.3	1.5	1.2
Mountain	0.1	0.1	0.1	0.1	--	--	--	--	--	--	0.2	0.2	0.1	--	0.1	0.1
Pacific	0.1	0.1	0.1	--	--	--	--	--	--	--	0.2	0.1	--	--	0.1	--

DIVISION OF BIRTH	ALABAMA 1930	ALABAMA 1920	MISSISSIPPI 1930	MISSISSIPPI 1920	ARKANSAS 1930	ARKANSAS 1920	LOUISIANA 1930	LOUISIANA 1920	OKLAHOMA 1930	OKLAHOMA 1920	TEXAS 1930	TEXAS 1920	MONTANA 1930	MONTANA 1920	IDAHO 1930	IDAHO 1920
Total	100.0	100.0	100.0	100.0	100.0	100.0	100.0	100.0	100.0	100.0	100.0	100.0	100.0	100.0	100.0	100.0
New England	0.1	0.1	--	--	0.1	0.1	0.1	0.1	0.1	0.2	0.1	0.2	0.8	1.2	0.4	0.7
Middle Atlantic	0.3	0.3	--	0.1	0.3	0.4	0.4	0.4	1.0	1.4	0.6	0.8	2.6	3.9	1.7	2.6
East North Central	0.7	0.7	0.5	0.6	2.7	3.7	0.8	0.9	5.0	7.0	1.8	2.2	12.6	17.4	8.3	11.2
West North Central	0.3	0.2	0.3	0.3	4.3	4.8	0.7	0.7	14.4	17.0	2.5	2.7	26.0	28.7	17.2	19.4
South Atlantic	5.5	5.6	1.1	1.5	1.9	2.8	1.0	1.2	1.8	2.4	1.8	2.6	1.1	1.5	1.4	1.8
East South Central	92.3	92.3	94.7	94.8	11.2	13.4	5.5	5.9	6.1	8.2	5.8	8.1	1.1	1.6	1.4	1.8
West South Central	0.8	0.7	3.1	2.5	79.4	74.6	90.9	90.5	70.5	62.9	80.5	83.0	1.3	1.5	2.3	2.4
Mountain	--	--	--	--	0.2	0.1	0.1	0.1	0.7	0.6	0.6	0.5	51.8	41.8	60.1	53.2
Pacific	0.1	--	--	--	0.1	0.1	0.1	0.1	0.3	0.3	0.2	0.2	2.6	2.6	7.1	6.9

DIVISION OF BIRTH	WYOMING 1930	WYOMING 1920	COLORADO 1930	COLORADO 1920	NEW MEXICO 1930	NEW MEXICO 1920	ARIZONA 1930	ARIZONA 1920	UTAH 1930	UTAH 1920	NEVADA 1930	NEVADA 1920	WASHINGTON 1930	WASHINGTON 1920	OREGON 1930	OREGON 1920	CALIFORNIA 1930	CALIFORNIA 1920
Total	100.0	100.0	100.0	100.0	100.0	100.0	100.0	100.0	100.0	100.0	100.0	100.0	100.0	100.0	100.0	100.0	100.0	100.0
New England	0.6	1.0	0.8	1.2	0.2	0.3	0.8	1.0	0.3	0.4	1.3	2.0	1.4	1.9	1.0	1.3	2.5	3.0
Middle Atlantic	2.9	4.2	3.5	5.2	1.0	1.5	2.8	3.5	1.0	1.6	4.1	5.3	3.6	5.1	2.9	4.0	6.4	7.2
East North Central	9.8	13.8	11.2	14.8	3.7	4.7	8.1	8.9	2.3	3.4	7.6	9.7	14.2	18.0	12.1	14.8	13.8	14.6
West North Central	31.3	32.9	25.2	25.9	5.9	6.7	9.6	9.2	3.2	4.1	9.6	9.8	19.5	20.4	18.4	18.4	15.1	13.0
South Atlantic	1.5	1.9	1.5	2.0	1.1	1.8	2.2	2.8	0.6	0.8	1.7	1.7	2.2	1.2	1.5	1.9	1.9	1.9
East South Central	1.5	1.8	2.4	3.0	3.0	3.7	3.8	4.7	0.6	0.9	1.7	1.5	2.0	1.5	1.9	2.5	2.5	2.5
West South Central	3.3	2.9	4.8	4.4	17.7	14.6	15.6	13.2	0.7	0.7	3.1	2.2	1.9	1.8	2.5	2.1	5.9	3.6
Mountain	48.0	40.3	49.7	42.6	66.7	66.2	52.8	51.6	90.2	86.9	57.4	53.9	6.2	4.7	6.1	4.2	6.5	4.0
Pacific	1.2	1.3	0.8	0.8	0.7	0.5	4.4	5.1	1.1	1.1	13.4	14.0	49.9	43.9	54.2	51.7	45.6	50.2

STATE OF BIRTH

TABLE 14.—PER CENT DISTRIBUTION BY DIVISION OF RESIDENCE, FOR THE POPULATION BORN IN EACH STATE: 1930 AND 1920

[Percentages based on population with State of birth reported; not shown where less than 0.1]

DIVISION OF RESIDENCE	MAINE 1930	MAINE 1920	NEW HAMPSHIRE 1930	NEW HAMPSHIRE 1920	VERMONT 1930	VERMONT 1920	MASSACHUSETTS 1930	MASSACHUSETTS 1920	RHODE ISLAND 1930	RHODE ISLAND 1920	CONNECTICUT 1930	CONNECTICUT 1920	NEW YORK 1930	NEW YORK 1920	NEW JERSEY 1930	NEW JERSEY 1920
Total	100.0	100.0	100.0	100.0	100.0	100.0	100.0	100.0	100.0	100.0	100.0	100.0	100.0	100.0	100.0	100.0
New England	89.5	89.6	90.4	91.1	81.8	81.5	88.7	90.2	89.8	90.7	85.2	86.8	2.5	2.9	1.4	1.6
Middle Atlantic	3.5	2.4	3.8	2.7	8.9	7.0	5.6	4.0	5.5	4.2	9.4	7.6	89.8	87.8	93.7	93.3
East North Central	1.4	1.5	1.6	1.6	2.7	3.5	1.8	1.8	1.4	1.4	1.8	1.9	3.1	3.9	1.5	1.7
West North Central	0.8	1.4	0.6	1.0	1.5	2.6	0.4	0.7	0.3	0.6	0.4	0.7	0.9	1.4	0.4	0.0
South Atlantic	1.0	0.9	1.1	0.9	1.2	1.1	1.0	0.9	1.0	1.0	1.1	1.0	1.0	1.0	1.3	1.3
East South Central	0.1	0.1	0.1	0.1	0.1	0.1	0.1	0.1	0.1	0.2	0.1	0.1	0.1	0.1	0.1	0.1
West South Central	0.2	0.3	0.2	0.2	0.3	0.4	0.2	0.2	0.2	0.3	0.2	0.2	0.3	0.4	0.2	0.2
Mountain	0.5	0.7	0.3	0.5	0.6	0.9	0.3	0.4	0.2	0.3	0.2	0.4	0.4	0.6	0.2	0.3
Pacific	3.0	3.1	2.0	1.9	2.9	2.9	2.0	1.7	1.6	1.3	1.5	1.3	1.9	1.8	1.2	1.0

DIVISION OF RESIDENCE	PENNSYLVANIA 1930	PENNSYLVANIA 1920	OHIO 1930	OHIO 1920	INDIANA 1930	INDIANA 1920	ILLINOIS 1930	ILLINOIS 1920	MICHIGAN 1930	MICHIGAN 1920	WISCONSIN 1930	WISCONSIN 1920	MINNESOTA 1930	MINNESOTA 1920	IOWA 1930	IOWA 1920
Total	100.0	100.0	100.0	100.0	100.0	100.0	100.0	100.0	100.0	100.0	100.0	100.0	100.0	100.0	100.0	100.0
New England	0.6	0.5	0.3	0.2	0.2	0.1	0.2	0.2	0.3	0.5	0.2	0.2	0.2	0.2	0.2	0.2
Middle Atlantic	87.9	88.0	2.9	2.5	1.1	0.9	1.3	1.1	1.6	1.5	0.0	0.8	0.9	0.6	0.8	0.7
East North Central	5.7	5.1	86.7	85.7	84.6	83.1	80.3	78.2	89.6	88.4	82.9	81.0	7.0	4.5	7.4	5.1
West North Central	1.0	1.6	2.3	3.7	4.3	6.1	8.4	10.8	1.9	2.8	7.9	9.9	80.5	84.4	76.6	79.9
South Atlantic	2.2	2.1	2.0	1.8	1.1	0.9	0.7	0.6	0.7	0.7	0.4	0.4	0.4	0.4	0.5	0.5
East South Central	0.2	0.2	1.1	1.1	1.4	1.5	0.5	0.5	0.3	0.3	0.2	0.2	0.1	0.1	0.2	0.2
West South Central	0.4	0.5	0.9	1.2	2.0	2.4	2.0	2.5	0.5	0.6	0.5	0.6	0.5	0.6	2.0	2.3
Mountain	0.4	0.6	0.8	1.1	1.3	1.7	1.7	2.2	1.0	1.4	1.6	2.2	2.4	3.0	3.8	4.6
Pacific	1.6	1.4	2.9	2.6	3.9	3.2	4.8	3.9	4.1	3.9	5.4	4.8	7.9	6.3	8.5	6.5

DIVISION OF RESIDENCE	MISSOURI 1930	MISSOURI 1920	NORTH DAKOTA 1930	NORTH DAKOTA 1920	SOUTH DAKOTA 1930	SOUTH DAKOTA 1920	NEBRASKA 1930	NEBRASKA 1920	KANSAS 1930	KANSAS 1920	DELAWARE 1930	DELAWARE 1920	MARYLAND 1930	MARYLAND 1920	DISTRICT OF COLUMBIA 1930	DISTRICT OF COLUMBIA 1920
Total	100.0	100.0	100.0	100.0	100.0	100.0	100.0	100.0	100.0	100.0	100.0	100.0	100.0	100.0	100.0	100.0
New England	0.1	0.1	0.1	0.2	0.1	0.2	0.2	0.2	0.1	0.1	0.8	0.9	0.5	0.6	1.4	1.4
Middle Atlantic	0.8	0.7	0.7	0.5	0.7	0.5	0.8	0.6	0.8	0.7	20.9	20.3	9.7	8.7	9.2	8.4
East North Central	6.2	4.7	4.8	3.0	4.6	3.1	3.7	2.9	4.0	3.3	1.5	1.6	2.3	2.4	2.7	2.7
West North Central	78.2	75.6	79.9	84.7	81.2	84.3	76.2	79.4	70.2	72.5	0.4	0.6	0.6	0.8	0.8	1.1
South Atlantic	0.6	0.5	0.3	0.4	0.4	0.4	0.4	0.5	0.6	0.6	74.9	75.1	85.3	85.9	82.6	82.9
East South Central	0.7	0.6	0.1	0.1	0.1	0.2	0.2	0.1	0.3	0.3	0.2	0.1	0.2	0.2	0.4	0.4
West South Central	8.0	8.9	0.4	0.4	0.9	0.9	2.0	2.2	8.3	8.0	0.2	0.2	0.3	0.3	0.6	0.6
Mountain	3.6	4.0	4.7	4.8	3.8	4.5	7.4	7.6	6.0	6.6	0.2	0.4	0.2	0.3	0.4	0.6
Pacific	6.7	4.9	8.8	5.9	8.2	5.9	9.1	6.6	9.6	7.1	1.0	0.8	0.9	0.7	2.0	1.9

DIVISION OF RESIDENCE	VIRGINIA 1930	VIRGINIA 1920	WEST VIRGINIA 1930	WEST VIRGINIA 1920	NORTH CAROLINA 1930	NORTH CAROLINA 1920	SOUTH CAROLINA 1930	SOUTH CAROLINA 1920	GEORGIA 1930	GEORGIA 1920	FLORIDA 1930	FLORIDA 1920	KENTUCKY 1930	KENTUCKY 1920	TENNESSEE 1930	TENNESSEE 1920
Total	100.0	100.0	100.0	100.0	100.0	100.0	100.0	100.0	100.0	100.0	100.0	100.0	100.0	100.0	100.0	100.0
New England	0.5	0.6	0.1	0.1	0.3	0.2	0.3	0.2	0.3	0.2	0.4	0.4	0.1	0.1	0.1	0.1
Middle Atlantic	8.1	5.9	4.0	2.9	3.2	1.7	5.8	1.9	3.0	1.4	3.9	2.6	0.9	0.8	0.8	0.5
East North Central	2.9	2.8	9.5	7.8	1.2	1.0	1.6	0.8	3.9	1.4	2.3	1.3	15.8	12.4	6.5	4.1
West North Central	0.9	1.5	0.9	1.8	0.3	0.5	0.2	0.2	0.3	0.3	0.4	0.4	2.7	3.7	2.6	3.0
South Atlantic	83.4	84.9	81.7	84.3	92.0	92.9	90.4	94.0	84.0	87.9	88.0	91.0	2.5	2.0	3.5	2.8
East South Central	2.1	1.9	1.1	0.9	1.4	1.6	1.0	1.1	5.2	4.7	2.7	2.4	72.3	74.8	76.6	78.0
West South Central	0.8	1.1	0.9	1.0	0.9	1.3	1.0	1.4	2.6	3.4	1.4	1.3	3.1	3.9	7.5	9.4
Mountain	0.4	0.5	0.5	0.6	0.2	0.3	0.1	0.1	0.2	0.3	0.2	0.3	0.8	1.0	0.7	0.4
Pacific	0.9	0.8	1.1	1.0	0.5	0.5	0.3	0.2	0.6	0.4	0.7	0.5	1.8	1.5	1.7	1.3

DIVISION OF RESIDENCE	ALABAMA 1930	ALABAMA 1920	MISSISSIPPI 1930	MISSISSIPPI 1920	ARKANSAS 1930	ARKANSAS 1920	LOUISIANA 1930	LOUISIANA 1920	OKLAHOMA 1930	OKLAHOMA 1920	TEXAS 1930	TEXAS 1920	MONTANA 1930	MONTANA 1920	IDAHO 1930	IDAHO 1920
Total	100.0	100.0	100.0	100.0	100.0	100.0	100.0	100.0	100.0	100.0	100.0	100.0	100.0	100.0	100.0	100.0
New England	0.1	0.1	—	—	0.3	—	0.1	0.1	—	—	0.1	0.1	0.3	0.3	0.1	0.1
Middle Atlantic	1.2	0.8	0.4	0.3	0.3	0.2	0.6	0.5	0.4	0.2	0.4	0.3	1.2	0.9	0.5	0.4
East North Central	3.8	2.2	3.7	1.8	3.1	1.2	2.0	1.2	1.7	1.3	0.9	0.6	3.8	2.6	1.2	1.7
West North Central	0.6	0.6	1.8	1.5	4.9	3.6	0.7	0.6	6.0	6.1	1.0	1.0	5.4	5.3	1.6	2.7
South Atlantic	6.2	5.3	0.9	0.8	0.5	0.4	0.6	0.5	0.4	0.4	0.4	0.4	0.5	0.5	0.3	0.3
East South Central	81.4	83.0	80.3	81.3	2.3	1.6	2.4	2.4	2.2	2.4	0.5	0.6	0.2	0.2	0.1	0.1
West South Central	5.8	7.4	11.8	13.4	84.5	90.1	92.0	93.6	82.7	85.6	91.7	93.4	0.8	0.8	0.6	0.8
Mountain	0.3	0.3	0.3	0.4	1.5	1.3	0.3	0.3	3.5	3.3	2.1	2.1	68.2	76.7	72.0	78.4
Pacific	0.6	0.4	0.3	0.5	2.8	1.6	1.3	0.8	4.9	2.6	2.9	1.6	19.6	12.7	23.6	15.4

DIVISION OF RESIDENCE	WYOMING 1930	WYOMING 1920	COLORADO 1930	COLORADO 1920	NEW MEXICO 1930	NEW MEXICO 1920	ARIZONA 1930	ARIZONA 1920	UTAH 1930	UTAH 1920	NEVADA 1930	NEVADA 1920	WASHINGTON 1930	WASHINGTON 1920	OREGON 1930	OREGON 1920	CALIFORNIA 1930	CALIFORNIA 1920
Total	100.0	100.0	100.0	100.0	100.0	100.0	100.0	100.0	100.0	100.0	100.0	100.0	100.0	100.0	100.0	100.0	100.0	100.0
New England	0.3	0.3	0.3	0.5	0.1	0.2	0.1	0.2	0.1	0.1	0.7	0.2	0.2	0.2	0.2	0.2	0.3	0.4
Middle Atlantic	1.3	1.8	1.5	1.4	0.4	0.6	0.6	0.6	0.4	0.5	0.4	1.1	1.0	0.9	0.6	0.6	1.1	1.1
East North Central	3.3	2.6	3.6	3.0	1.0	1.1	1.0	1.0	0.8	0.6	0.6	1.4	1.2	1.6	1.1	1.1	1.1	1.1
West North Central	7.6	7.8	6.2	6.5	1.5	1.5	0.8	1.0	0.7	0.7	1.7	1.2	1.4	1.8	1.2	1.5	0.7	0.9
South Atlantic	0.7	0.7	0.6	0.6	0.2	0.3	0.4	0.5	0.8	0.4	0.5	0.4	0.6	0.6	0.3	0.3	0.3	0.4
East South Central	0.2	0.2	0.3	0.3	0.2	0.2	0.2	0.2	0.1	0.1	0.1	0.1	0.1	0.1	0.1	0.1	0.1	0.1
West South Central	1.6	1.4	2.5	2.3	6.1	5.0	2.4	2.6	0.5	0.3	1.0	0.5	0.6	0.6	0.6	0.6	0.7	0.7
Mountain	71.5	76.5	69.2	74.6	83.3	87.9	74.2	82.5	91.9	84.8	58.4	61.3	3.9	4.7	3.6	4.4	1.8	2.3
Pacific	13.5	8.7	15.7	10.8	7.3	3.2	20.5	11.3	5.4	12.5	36.2	32.3	91.0	89.4	92.4	91.3	94.0	92.9

POPULATION

TABLE 15.—TOTAL POPULATION DISTRIBUTED AS BORN IN STATE OF RESIDENCE, IN OTHER STATES, OR IN FOREIGN COUNTRIES, BY STATES, 1930, WITH PERCENTAGES, 1900 TO 1930

STATE	Total population, 1930 [1]	POPULATION BORN IN THE UNITED STATES AND WITH STATE OF BIRTH REPORTED										FOREIGN BORN				
		Born in State of residence					Born in other States									
		Number, 1930	Per cent of total				Number, 1930	Per cent of total				Number, 1930	Per cent of total			
			1930	1920	1910	1900		1930	1920	1910	1900		1930	1920	1910	1900
United States	122,775,046	82,677,619	67.3	67.2	66.5	68.3	25,388,100	20.7	19.2	18.4	17.8	14,204,149	11.6	13.2	14.7	13.6
NEW ENGLAND:																
Maine	797,423	630,193	79.0	77.9	78.0	80.7	62,553	7.8	7.6	6.7	5.3	100,728	12.6	14.0	14.9	13.4
New Hampshire	465,293	278,028	59.8	58.0	57.7	59.1	102,041	21.9	20.8	19.2	18.9	82,929	17.8	20.6	22.5	21.4
Vermont	359,611	255,262	71.0	71.1	70.4	72.2	59,259	16.5	15.5	14.7	13.9	43,101	12.0	12.6	14.0	13.0
Massachusetts	4,249,614	2,661,016	62.6	58.8	55.3	55.0	509,214	12.0	12.6	12.9	14.3	1,065,620	25.1	28.3	31.5	30.2
Rhode Island	687,497	396,181	57.6	53.7	49.2	49.9	117,449	17.1	17.0	17.5	18.4	171,929	25.0	29.0	33.0	31.4
Connecticut	1,606,903	911,836	56.7	54.8	54.5	57.0	306,452	19.1	17.5	15.7	16.6	384,636	23.9	27.4	29.6	26.2
MIDDLE ATLANTIC:																
New York	12,588,066	7,833,595	62.2	63.9	62.0	66.5	1,374,400	10.9	8.3	7.5	6.9	3,262,278	25.9	27.2	30.2	26.1
New Jersey	4,041,334	2,126,794	52.6	53.7	53.0	56.5	1,049,365	26.0	22.5	20.7	20.3	850,038	21.0	23.5	26.0	22.9
Pennsylvania	9,631,350	7,412,375	77.0	75.3	73.6	76.5	963,948	10.0	8.5	7.4	7.7	1,240,415	12.9	16.0	18.8	15.6
EAST NORTH CENTRAL:																
Ohio	6,646,697	4,619,774	69.5	70.8	74.4	76.7	1,362,839	20.5	17.1	12.7	12.0	649,220	9.8	11.8	12.6	11.0
Indiana	3,238,503	2,399,608	74.1	75.4	75.2	74.6	688,506	21.3	19.1	18.6	19.6	142,999	4.4	5.2	5.9	5.6
Illinois	7,630,654	4,801,308	62.9	63.1	60.4	60.0	1,564,121	20.5	17.8	17.7	19.6	1,242,447	16.3	18.7	21.4	20.1
Michigan	4,842,325	2,830,978	58.5	60.6	62.7	60.1	1,136,886	23.5	19.0	15.5	16.8	852,758	17.6	19.9	21.3	22.4
Wisconsin	2,939,006	2,166,114	73.7	70.4	66.8	63.1	378,438	12.9	11.8	11.0	11.7	388,299	13.2	17.5	22.0	24.9
WEST NORTH CENTRAL:																
Minnesota	2,563,953	1,660,020	64.7	58.3	54.0	51.0	506,050	19.7	20.9	19.4	19.7	390,790	15.2	20.4	26.2	28.9
Iowa	2,470,939	1,799,730	72.8	67.6	63.7	59.1	496,579	20.1	22.6	23.6	26.9	168,250	6.8	9.4	12.3	13.7
Missouri	3,629,367	2,569,904	70.8	70.0	67.5	65.5	894,686	24.7	24.1	25.0	27.2	153,085	4.2	5.5	7.0	7.6
North Dakota	680,845	391,665	57.5	47.1	34.3	34.1	181,009	26.6	31.6	37.6	30.0	105,871	15.5	20.4	27.1	35.4
South Dakota	692,849	391,393	56.5	47.6	38.6	39.9	233,454	33.7	38.8	43.6	37.6	66,061	9.5	13.0	17.3	22.0
Nebraska	1,377,963	879,132	63.8	56.7	50.0	43.2	375,937	27.3	31.1	34.7	39.8	119,199	8.7	11.6	14.8	16.6
Kansas	1,880,999	1,129,305	60.0	54.7	48.7	42.9	664,352	35.3	38.5	42.8	48.2	80,897	4.3	6.3	8.0	8.6
SOUTH ATLANTIC:																
Delaware	238,380	155,585	65.3	64.1	67.8	70.1	65,472	27.5	26.5	23.4	22.2	17,025	7.1	8.9	8.6	7.5
Maryland	1,631,526	1,206,654	74.0	76.4	79.2	80.5	322,282	19.8	16.3	12.5	11.4	96,330	5.9	7.1	8.1	7.9
District of Columbia	486,869	180,864	37.1	36.6	42.1	43.0	270,797	55.6	55.8	49.7	49.6	30,733	6.3	6.7	7.5	7.2
Virginia	2,421,851	2,063,590	85.2	85.7	89.4	91.7	330,911	13.7	12.7	9.2	7.1	24,367	1.0	1.4	1.3	1.0
West Virginia	1,729,205	1,329,981	76.9	76.1	76.2	79.8	345,676	20.0	19.4	18.8	17.5	51,865	3.0	4.2	4.7	2.3
North Carolina	3,170,276	2,843,452	89.7	93.4	94.7	95.3	315,278	9.9	6.2	4.9	4.4	8,969	0.3	0.3	0.3	0.2
South Carolina	1,738,765	1,596,032	91.8	93.0	94.4	95.5	136,243	7.8	6.5	5.1	4.1	5,358	0.3	0.4	0.4	0.4
Georgia	2,908,506	2,590,975	89.1	89.6	90.6	90.7	300,071	10.3	9.6	8.5	8.6	14,303	0.5	0.6	0.6	0.6
Florida	1,468,211	740,706	50.4	57.8	61.5	64.9	652,040	44.4	36.1	32.5	30.2	69,747	4.8	5.6	5.4	4.5
EAST SOUTH CENTRAL:																
Kentucky	2,614,589	2,295,545	87.8	88.3	88.7	87.8	294,362	11.3	10.3	9.4	9.7	22,007	0.8	1.3	1.8	2.3
Tennessee	2,616,556	2,176,591	83.2	85.3	85.7	85.8	420,943	16.1	13.8	13.1	13.1	13,251	0.5	0.7	0.9	0.9
Alabama	2,646,248	2,318,600	87.6	87.5	86.9	86.3	308,835	11.7	11.5	12.0	12.8	16,061	0.6	0.8	0.9	0.8
Mississippi	2,009,821	1,791,615	89.1	89.1	87.0	85.5	207,387	10.3	10.2	12.2	13.9	8,045	0.4	0.5	0.5	0.5
WEST SOUTH CENTRAL:																
Arkansas	1,854,482	1,346,707	72.6	68.3	67.1	64.8	492,426	26.6	30.4	31.4	33.8	10,632	0.6	0.8	1.1	1.1
Louisiana	2,101,593	1,792,065	85.3	84.7	84.9	84.6	269,260	12.8	12.4	11.5	11.4	37,076	1.8	2.6	3.2	3.8
Oklahoma	2,396,040	1,177,814	49.2	40.4	31.1	26.5	1,179,178	49.2	57.0	65.9	70.4	30,558	1.3	2.0	2.4	2.6
Texas	5,824,715	4,317,577	74.1	70.9	70.1	66.6	1,129,348	19.4	20.8	23.3	27.2	362,287	6.2	7.8	6.2	5.9
MOUNTAIN:																
Montana	537,606	218,483	40.6	31.5	26.4	25.8	239,482	44.5	50.1	47.3	45.9	75,903	14.1	17.4	25.2	27.6
Idaho	445,032	190,940	42.9	34.3	27.7	29.9	218,952	49.2	55.6	58.4	54.5	32,284	7.3	9.4	13.1	15.2
Wyoming	225,565	71,622	31.8	25.2	21.8	21.1	129,778	57.5	60.1	57.7	59.7	23,343	10.3	13.7	19.9	18.8
Colorado	1,035,791	419,563	40.5	33.8	29.2	28.1	512,764	49.5	52.4	53.8	54.0	99,875	9.6	12.7	16.2	16.9
New Mexico	423,317	252,962	59.8	58.1	56.4	73.3	145,076	34.3	33.3	36.0	19.4	24,052	5.7	8.3	7.1	7.0
Arizona	435,573	165,303	38.0	32.9	38.6	42.9	200,597	46.1	41.2	36.6	36.7	65,756	15.1	24.1	23.9	19.7
Utah	507,847	378,778	74.6	69.9	65.1	65.7	78,713	15.5	16.5	16.2	14.5	48,015	9.5	13.2	17.6	19.4
Nevada	91,058	29,276	32.2	32.0	26.4	42.4	46,093	50.6	46.2	48.5	33.2	15,095	16.6	20.7	24.1	23.8
PACIFIC:																
Washington	1,563,396	566,360	36.2	30.2	23.0	25.7	718,109	45.9	48.8	53.3	51.3	255,258	16.3	19.6	22.4	21.5
Oregon	953,786	379,795	39.8	37.7	33.5	39.8	453,980	47.6	47.8	49.0	43.8	110,440	11.6	13.7	16.8	15.9
California	5,677,251	1,935,867	34.1	37.0	38.0	44.5	2,577,000	45.4	39.8	36.3	29.9	1,073,964	18.9	22.1	24.7	24.7

[1] Includes persons born in the United States, State of birth not reported; persons born in outlying possessions, and American citizens born abroad or at sea. The combined number of these classes in the United States in 1930 was 505,178, or four-tenths of 1 per cent of the total population.

STATE OF BIRTH

147

TABLE 16.—WHITE AND NEGRO POPULATION DISTRIBUTED AS BORN IN STATE OF RESIDENCE, IN OTHER STATES, OR IN FOREIGN COUNTRIES, BY STATES: 1930

[Per cent not shown where less than 0.1]

STATE	WHITE POPULATION							NEGRO POPULATION						
	Total [1]	Born in State of residence		Born in other States		Foreign born		Total [1]	Born in State of residence		Born in other States		Foreign born	
		Number	Per cent	Number	Per cent	Number	Per cent		Number	Per cent	Number	Per cent	Number	Per cent
United States	108,864,207	72,821,481	66.9	22,277,754	20.5	13,366,407	12.3	11,891,143	8,774,754	73.8	2,964,725	24.9	98,620	0.8
NEW ENGLAND:														
Maine	795,183	628,614	79.1	62,285	7.8	100,368	12.6	1,096	659	60.1	212	19.3	203	18.5
New Hampshire	464,350	277,763	59.8	101,647	21.9	82,660	17.8	790	223	28.2	360	45.6	195	24.7
Vermont	358,965	254,898	71.0	59,031	16.4	43,061	12.0	568	347	61.1	197	34.7	13	2.3
Massachusetts	4,192,926	2,035,316	62.9	480,784	11.7	1,054,636	25.2	52,365	24,358	46.5	18,663	35.6	8,934	17.1
Rhode Island	677,016	390,680	57.7	113,780	16.8	170,714	25.2	9,913	5,242	52.9	3,556	35.9	1,003	10.7
Connecticut	1,576,073	901,184	57.2	289,020	18.3	382,871	24.3	29,354	10,503	35.8	17,250	58.8	1,378	4.7
MIDDLE ATLANTIC:														
New York	12,150,293	7,717,141	63.5	1,144,622	9.4	3,191,549	26.3	412,814	108,351	26.2	227,880	55.2	57,895	14.0
New Jersey	3,829,209	2,062,040	53.9	900,442	23.8	844,442	22.1	208,828	64,352	30.8	139,184	66.7	3,719	1.8
Pennsylvania	9,192,602	7,264,716	70.0	682,460	7.4	1,233,051	13.4	431,257	146,374	33.0	280,257	65.0	2,951	0.7
EAST NORTH CENTRAL:														
Ohio	6,331,136	4,519,317	71.4	1,154,475	18.2	644,151	10.2	309,304	99,470	32.2	206,717	66.8	1,077	0.3
Indiana	3,116,136	2,362,470	75.8	612,185	19.6	135,134	4.3	111,082	35,727	31.9	75,110	67.1	200	0.2
Illinois	7,266,361	4,719,049	64.9	1,310,377	18.0	1,218,158	16.8	328,972	76,069	23.1	249,401	75.8	1,566	0.5
Michigan	4,650,171	2,793,520	60.1	997,352	21.4	840,208	18.1	169,453	29,121	17.2	136,315	80.4	2,262	1.3
Wisconsin	2,913,859	2,153,245	73.9	368,463	12.6	386,213	13.3	10,739	1,732	16.1	8,874	82.6	52	0.5
WEST NORTH CENTRAL:														
Minnesota	2,538,973	1,646,808	64.9	497,312	19.6	388,294	15.3	9,445	2,384	25.2	6,834	72.4	105	1.1
Iowa	2,448,382	1,701,435	73.2	485,032	19.8	105,735	6.8	17,380	6,599	38.0	10,585	60.9	50	0.3
Missouri	3,398,887	2,461,546	72.4	778,050	22.9	149,390	4.4	223,840	106,728	47.7	115,406	51.6	209	0.1
North Dakota	671,243	384,016	57.2	179,870	26.8	105,148	15.7	377	94	24.9	267	70.8	7	1.9
South Dakota	669,453	371,588	55.5	230,453	34.4	65,648	9.8	646	175	27.1	458	70.9	7	1.1
Nebraska	1,353,702	871,572	64.4	363,455	26.8	115,346	8.5	13,752	3,123	22.7	10,351	75.3	55	0.4
Kansas	1,792,847	1,093,800	61.0	623,751	34.8	69,716	3.9	66,344	27,665	41.7	37,916	57.2	95	0.1
SOUTH ATLANTIC:														
Delaware	205,694	134,264	65.3	54,289	26.4	16,885	8.2	32,602	21,311	65.4	11,171	34.3	87	0.3
Maryland	1,354,170	1,005,259	74.2	249,507	18.4	95,093	7.0	276,379	201,244	72.8	72,626	26.3	872	0.3
District of Columbia	353,914	128,226	36.2	192,714	54.5	29,932	8.5	132,068	52,513	39.8	77,937	59.0	457	0.3
Virginia	1,770,405	1,486,280	84.0	258,137	14.6	23,820	1.3	650,165	576,588	88.7	72,646	11.2	330	0.1
West Virginia	1,613,934	1,283,079	79.5	277,876	17.2	51,520	3.2	114,893	46,834	40.8	67,724	58.9	119	0.1
North Carolina	2,234,948	2,019,223	90.3	205,201	9.2	8,788	0.4	918,647	808,298	88.0	109,441	11.9	118	------
South Carolina	944,040	819,156	86.8	118,822	12.6	5,266	0.6	793,681	776,058	97.8	17,250	2.2	54	------
Georgia	1,836,974	1,594,480	86.8	226,583	12.3	13,017	0.8	1,071,125	996,411	93.0	73,373	6.0	200	------
Florida	1,035,205	480,405	46.4	492,011	47.5	59,057	5.7	431,828	259,635	60.1	159,923	37.0	10,347	2.4
EAST SOUTH CENTRAL:														
Kentucky	2,388,364	2,110,461	88.4	253,990	10.6	21,840	0.9	226,040	185,051	81.9	40,325	17.8	68	------
Tennessee	2,138,619	1,812,763	84.8	309,108	14.5	13,066	0.6	477,646	363,704	76.1	111,769	23.4	100	------
Alabama	1,700,775	1,434,802	84.4	248,639	14.6	15,710	0.9	944,834	883,289	93.5	60,117	6.4	268	------
Mississippi	996,856	851,013	85.4	137,644	13.8	7,049	0.7	1,000,718	938,911	93.0	69,137	6.8	96	------
WEST SOUTH CENTRAL:														
Arkansas	1,374,906	1,006,271	73.2	355,651	25.9	10,173	0.7	478,463	340,182	71.1	136,314	28.5	70	------
Louisiana	1,318,160	1,076,094	81.6	205,186	15.6	34,910	2.6	776,326	710,894	91.6	63,702	8.2	309	0.1
Oklahoma	2,123,424	1,005,882	47.4	1,083,967	51.0	26,753	1.3	172,198	85,760	49.8	85,490	49.6	67	------
Texas	4,283,491	3,149,781	73.5	1,023,646	23.9	98,396	2.3	854,964	755,017	88.3	97,316	11.4	466	0.1
MOUNTAIN:														
Montana	517,327	204,507	39.5	236,679	45.8	72,961	14.1	1,256	299	23.8	919	73.2	14	1.1
Idaho	437,562	186,904	42.7	217,485	49.7	30,454	7.0	668	110	16.5	533	79.8	15	2.2
Wyoming	214,067	68,422	32.0	125,246	58.5	19,658	9.2	1,250	178	14.2	1,054	84.3	8	0.6
Colorado	961,117	386,451	40.2	486,106	50.6	85,406	8.9	11,828	2,892	24.5	8,781	74.2	61	0.5
New Mexico	331,755	186,445	56.2	136,544	41.2	7,797	2.4	2,850	515	18.1	2,277	79.9	14	0.5
Arizona	264,378	67,083	25.4	179,058	67.7	15,591	5.9	10,749	1,113	10.4	9,489	88.1	53	0.5
Utah	495,955	374,196	75.4	75,962	15.3	43,772	8.8	1,108	250	22.6	828	74.7	12	1.1
Nevada	81,425	24,262	29.8	44,381	54.5	12,275	15.1	516	47	0.1	448	86.8	10	1.9
PACIFIC:														
Washington	1,521,090	545,609	35.9	711,669	46.8	244,256	16.1	6,840	1,480	21.6	4,977	72.8	167	2.4
Oregon	937,029	372,797	39.8	459,667	48.1	105,475	11.3	2,234	351	15.7	1,779	79.6	50	2.2
California	5,040,247	1,706,570	33.9	2,468,131	49.0	810,034	16.1	81,048	16,514	20.4	61,537	75.9	1,652	2.0

[1] Includes persons born in the United States, State of birth not reported; persons born in outlying possessions; and American citizens born abroad or at sea. The combined numbers of these classes are 398,565 whites, or four-tenths of 1 per cent of the white population, and 53,044 Negroes, or four-tenths of 1 per cent of the Negro population.

148

POPULATION

TABLE 17.—NATIVE POPULATION, WHITE AND NEGRO, BY STATE OF BIRTH AND STATE

[The small number of persons for whom State of birth

	STATE	TOTAL NATIVE POPULATION, 1930							NATIVE WHITE, 1930						
		Born in the specified State			Born in and living in the specified State	Living in the specified State			Born in the specified State			Born in and living in the specified State	Living in the specified State		
		Total	Living in other States			Total	Born in other States		Total	Living in other States			Total	Born in other States	
			Number	Per cent			Number	Per cent		Number	Per cent			Number	Per cent
1	United States____	108,065,719	25,388,100	23.5	82,677,619	108,065,719	25,388,100	23.5	95,099,235	22,277,754	23.4	72,821,481	95,099,235	22,277,754	23.4
	NEW ENGLAND:														
2	Maine____	854,883	224,690	26.3	630,193	692,746	62,553	9.0	852,559	223,945	26.3	628,614	690,899	62,285	9.0
3	New Hampshire__	427,271	149,243	34.9	278,028	380,069	102,041	26.8	426,705	148,942	34.9	277,763	379,410	101,647	26.8
4	Vermont____	415,337	160,075	38.5	255,262	314,521	59,259	18.8	414,444	159,546	38.5	254,898	313,929	59,031	18.8
5	Massachusetts____	3,237,815	576,799	17.8	2,661,016	3,170,230	509,214	16.1	3,204,213	568,897	17.8	2,635,316	3,125,100	480,784	15.7
6	Rhode Island____	510,453	114,272	22.4	396,181	513,630	117,449	22.9	502,665	111,985	22.3	390,680	504,460	113,780	22.6
7	Connecticut____	1,150,718	238,882	20.8	911,836	1,218,288	306,452	25.2	1,135,107	233,923	20.6	901,184	1,190,213	289,029	24.3
	MIDDLE ATLANTIC:														
8	New York____	9,346,737	1,513,142	16.2	7,833,595	9,207,995	1,374,400	14.9	9,211,743	1,494,602	16.2	7,717,141	8,861,763	1,144,622	12.9
9	New Jersey____	2,542,468	415,674	16.3	2,126,794	3,176,159	1,049,365	33.0	2,460,998	398,958	16.2	2,062,040	2,971,482	909,442	30.6
10	Pennsylvania____	9,126,892	1,714,517	18.8	7,412,375	8,376,323	963,948	11.5	8,937,952	1,673,236	18.7	7,264,716	7,947,176	682,460	8.6
	E. NORTH CENTRAL:														
11	Ohio____	5,804,095	1,184,321	20.4	4,619,774	5,982,113	1,362,339	22.8	5,673,578	1,154,261	20.3	4,519,317	5,673,792	1,154,475	20.3
12	Indiana____	3,322,930	923,322	27.8	2,399,608	3,088,114	688,506	22.3	3,268,074	905,595	27.7	2,362,479	2,974,664	612,185	20.6
13	Illinois____	6,481,000	1,679,692	25.9	4,801,308	6,365,429	1,564,121	24.6	6,371,387	1,652,338	25.9	4,719,049	6,029,426	1,310,377	21.7
14	Michigan____	3,406,702	575,724	16.9	2,830,978	3,967,864	1,136,886	28.7	3,361,626	568,106	16.9	2,793,520	3,790,872	997,352	26.3
15	Wisconsin____	2,863,619	697,505	24.4	2,166,114	2,544,552	378,438	14.9	2,848,369	695,124	24.4	2,153,245	2,521,708	368,463	14.6
	W. NORTH CENTRAL:														
16	Minnesota____	2,255,454	595,428	26.4	1,660,026	2,166,076	506,050	23.4	2,239,469	592,661	26.5	1,646,808	2,144,120	497,312	23.2
17	Iowa____	2,883,890	1,084,160	37.6	1,799,730	2,296,309	496,579	21.6	2,868,966	1,077,531	37.6	1,791,435	2,276,467	485,032	21.3
18	Missouri____	3,929,733	1,359,829	34.6	2,569,904	3,464,590	894,686	25.8	3,766,940	1,305,394	34.7	2,461,546	3,239,596	778,050	24.0
19	North Dakota____	567,488	175,823	31.0	391,665	572,674	181,009	31.6	558,477	174,461	31.2	384,016	563,886	179,870	31.9
20	South Dakota____	583,112	191,719	32.9	391,393	624,847	233,454	37.4	561,836	190,248	33.9	371,588	602,041	230,453	38.3
21	Nebraska____	1,332,288	453,156	34.0	879,132	1,255,069	375,937	30.0	1,319,947	448,375	34.0	871,572	1,235,027	363,455	29.4
22	Kansas____	1,857,616	728,311	39.2	1,129,305	1,793,657	664,352	37.0	1,798,119	704,319	39.2	1,093,800	1,717,551	623,751	36.3
	SOUTH ATLANTIC:														
23	Delaware____	227,157	71,572	31.5	155,585	221,057	65,472	29.6	194,933	60,669	31.1	134,264	188,553	54,289	28.8
24	Maryland____	1,551,593	344,939	22.2	1,206,654	1,528,936	322,282	21.1	1,276,300	271,041	21.2	1,005,259	1,254,766	249,507	19.9
25	Dist. of Columbia_	274,116	93,252	34.0	180,864	451,661	270,797	60.0	201,887	73,661	36.5	128,226	320,940	192,714	60.0
26	Virginia____	2,808,132	834,442	28.8	2,063,690	2,394,601	330,911	13.8	1,988,505	502,225	25.3	1,486,280	1,744,417	258,137	14.8
27	West Virginia____	1,716,721	386,740	22.5	1,329,981	1,675,657	345,676	20.6	1,651,656	368,577	22.3	1,283,079	1,560,955	277,876	17.8
28	North Carolina___	3,398,364	554,912	16.3	2,843,452	3,158,730	315,278	10.0	2,353,460	334,237	14.2	2,019,223	2,224,424	205,201	9.2
29	South Carolina___	2,103,834	507,802	24.1	1,596,032	1,732,275	136,243	7.9	1,007,270	188,114	18.7	819,156	937,978	118,822	12.7
30	Georgia____	3,474,698	883,723	25.4	2,590,975	2,891,046	300,071	10.4	2,070,352	475,863	23.0	1,594,489	1,821,072	226,583	12.4
31	Florida____	890,871	150,165	16.9	740,706	1,392,746	652,040	46.8	575,357	94,952	16.5	480,405	972,416	492,011	50.6
	E. SOUTH CENTRAL:														
32	Kentucky____	3,261,020	965,475	29.6	2,295,545	2,589,907	294,362	11.4	2,968,335	857,874	28.9	2,110,461	2,364,451	253,990	10.7
33	Tennessee____	3,055,701	879,110	28.8	2,176,591	2,597,534	420,943	16.2	2,515,598	702,835	27.9	1,812,763	2,121,871	309,108	14.6
34	Alabama____	3,010,218	691,618	23.0	2,318,600	2,627,435	308,835	11.8	1,875,747	440,885	23.5	1,434,862	1,683,501	248,639	14.8
35	Mississippi____	2,402,365	610,750	25.4	1,791,615	1,999,002	207,387	10.4	1,172,103	321,090	27.4	851,013	988,657	137,644	13.9
	W. SOUTH CENTRAL:														
36	Arkansas____	2,022,417	675,710	33.4	1,346,707	1,839,133	492,426	26.8	1,570,503	564,232	35.9	1,006,271	1,361,922	355,651	26.1
37	Louisiana____	2,178,273	386,208	17.7	1,792,065	2,061,334	269,269	13.1	1,290,064	213,970	16.6	1,076,094	1,281,280	205,186	16.0
38	Oklahoma____	1,614,238	436,424	27.0	1,177,814	2,356,992	1,179,178	50.0	1,408,541	402,659	28.6	1,005,882	2,089,849	1,083,967	51.9
39	Texas____	5,080,570	762,993	15.0	4,317,577	5,446,925	1,129,348	20.7	3,770,436	620,655	16.5	3,149,781	4,173,427	1,023,646	24.5
	MOUNTAIN:														
40	Montana____	345,203	126,720	36.7	218,483	457,965	239,482	52.3	329,302	124,795	37.9	204,507	441,186	236,679	53.6
41	Idaho____	304,578	113,638	37.3	190,940	409,892	218,952	53.4	299,427	112,523	37.6	186,904	404,389	217,485	53.8
42	Wyoming____	128,256	56,634	44.2	71,622	201,400	129,778	64.4	123,471	55,049	44.6	68,422	193,668	125,246	64.7
43	Colorado____	670,879	251,316	37.5	419,563	932,327	512,764	55.0	629,572	243,121	38.6	386,451	872,557	486,106	55.7
44	New Mexico____	358,750	105,788	29.5	252,962	398,038	145,076	36.4	254,960	68,515	26.9	186,445	322,989	136,544	42.3
45	Arizona____	233,290	67,987	29.1	165,303	365,900	200,597	54.8	112,473	45,390	40.4	67,083	246,141	179,058	72.7
46	Utah____	521,360	142,582	27.3	378,778	457,491	78,713	17.2	515,439	141,243	27.4	374,196	450,158	75,962	16.9
47	Nevada____	58,439	29,163	49.9	29,276	75,369	46,093	61.2	52,435	28,173	53.7	24,262	68,643	44,381	64.7
	PACIFIC:														
48	Washington____	742,179	175,819	23.7	566,360	1,284,469	718,109	55.9	718,035	172,426	24.0	545,609	1,257,278	711,669	56.6
49	Oregon____	530,417	150,622	28.4	379,795	833,775	453,980	54.4	521,635	148,838	28.5	372,797	823,464	450,667	54.7
50	California____	2,111,579	175,712	8.3	1,935,867	4,512,867	2,577,000	57.1	1,868,265	161,695	8.7	1,706,570	4,174,701	2,468,131	59.1

STATE OF BIRTH

OF RESIDENCE, 1930, WITH GAIN OR LOSS THROUGH INTERSTATE MIGRATION, 1930, 1920, AND 1910

149

was not reported are omitted from this table]

Total (Born in specified State)	Living in other States, Number	Per cent	Born in and living in the specified State	Total (Living in specified State)	Born in other States, Number	Per cent	Total native pop. 1930	1920	1910	Native white 1930	1920	1910	Native Negro 1930	1920	1910	#
11,739,479	2,964,725	25.3	8,774,754	11,739,479	2,964,725	25.3										1
1,334	675	50.6	659	871	212	24.3	−162,137	−150,192	−163,079	−161,660	−149,751	−162,610	−463	−479	−473	2
404	271	54.9	223	583	360	61.7	−47,202	−42,838	−44,331	−47,295	−42,819	−44,348	+89	−41	+9	3
853	506	59.3	347	544	197	36.2	−100,816	−101,669	−105,295	−100,515	−100,892	−105,789	−300	−779	+501	4
32,009	7,651	23.9	24,358	43,021	18,663	43.4	−67,585	+58,792	+77,767	−79,113	+45,705	+64,576	+11,012	+12,617	+12,563	5
7,468	2,226	29.8	5,242	8,798	3,556	40.4	+3,177	+9,905	+21,728	+1,795	+8,000	+18,390	+1,330	+1,864	+3,196	6
15,372	4,869	31.7	10,503	27,753	17,250	62.2	+67,570	+55,147	+8,083	+55,106	+46,924	+3,553	+12,381	+8,143	+4,514	7
125,964	17,613	14.0	108,351	336,240	227,889	67.8	−138,742	−586,206	−630,782	−349,080	−660,959	−689,393	+210,276	+83,334	+58,449	8
80,937	16,585	20.5	64,352	203,536	139,184	68.4	+633,091	+379,594	+254,565	+510,484	+319,445	+211,843	+122,500	+59,923	+42,450	9
187,121	40,747	21.8	146,374	426,631	280,257	65.7	−750,509	−598,692	−556,250	−990,776	−752,446	−643,128	+239,510	+153,407	+85,485	10
129,116	29,637	23.0	99,479	306,196	206,717	67.5	+178,018	−160,699	−558,666	+214	−256,394	−592,306	+177,080	+95,465	+33,599	11
53,032	17,305	32.6	35,727	110,837	75,110	67.8	−234,816	−290,197	−272,751	−293,410	−329,460	−297,735	+57,805	+39,270	+25,018	12
101,878	25,809	25.3	76,069	325,470	249,401	76.6	−115,571	−358,780	−310,800	−341,961	−475,807	−368,881	−223,502	+116,476	+57,577	13
35,906	6,785	18.9	29,121	165,436	136,315	82.4	+561,162	+209,219	+28,766	−420,246	+166,781	+26,091	+129,530	+42,374	−2,940	14
3,266	1,534	47.0	1,732	10,606	8,874	83.7	−319,067	−207,718	−202,878	−326,661	−300,022	−263,243	+7,340	+2,526	+515	15
3,990	1,606	40.3	2,384	9,218	6,834	74.1	−89,378	+74,658	+77,407	−95,349	+69,703	+74,106	+5,349	+5,189	+3,950	16
12,410	5,811	46.8	6,599	17,184	10,585	61.6	−587,581	−376,036	−277,062	−592,490	−383,088	−282,910	+4,774	+7,038	+5,066	17
159,113	52,385	32.9	106,728	222,194	115,466	52.0	−465,143	−315,235	−96,220	−527,344	−344,899	−101,905	+63,081	+29,463	+6,080	18
377	283	75.1	94	361	207	74.0	+5,186	+103,302	+169,033	+5,409	+103,777	+169,127	−16	−103	+295	19
504	329	65.3	175	633	458	72.4	+41,735	+117,763	+174,283	+40,205	+116,676	+172,126	+129	−30	−287	20
5,882	2,759	46.9	3,123	13,474	10,351	76.8	−77,219	+71,204	+169,824	−84,920	+63,021	+165,980	+7,592	+8,569	+4,551	21
47,443	19,778	41.7	27,665	65,581	37,916	57.8	−63,959	+113,488	+295,022	−80,568	+95,092	+276,042	+18,188	+18,096	+19,418	22
32,184	10,873	33.8	21,311	32,482	11,171	34.4	−6,100	−5,796	−13,397	−6,380	−4,901	−11,796	+298	−892	−1,597	23
275,093	73,849	26.8	201,244	273,870	72,626	26.5	−22,657	−72,769	−109,041	−21,534	−51,926	−77,953	−1,223	−20,915	−81,177	24
72,018	19,505	27.1	52,513	130,450	77,937	59.7	+177,545	+178,265	+113,521	+119,053	+131,701	+77,230	+58,432	+46,518	+41,235	25
908,551	331,963	36.5	576,588	649,234	72,646	11.2	−503,531	−388,920	−432,807	−244,088	−193,348	−225,982	−259,317	−195,515	−206,764	26
64,808	18,064	27.8	46,834	114,558	67,724	59.1	−41,064	+18,471	+42,248	−90,701	−22,003	+14,921	+49,660	+40,456	+27,316	27
1,028,538	220,240	21.4	808,208	917,739	109,441	11.9	−239,634	−285,848	−272,162	−129,036	−172,291	−162,156	−110,799	−113,716	−109,751	28
1,095,214	319,156	29.1	776,058	793,308	17,250	2.2	−371,559	−195,649	−184,524	−69,292	−43,002	−62,915	−301,906	−152,423	−121,479	29
1,403,856	407,445	29.0	996,411	1,069,784	73,373	6.9	−583,852	−254,317	−242,415	−249,280	−132,563	−166,570	−334,072	−121,576	−75,274	30
314,688	55,053	17.5	259,635	419,558	159,923	38.1	+501,875	+257,375	+192,411	+397,059	+194,666	+107,703	+104,870	+62,653	+84,664	31
292,365	107,314	36.7	185,051	225,376	40,325	17.9	−671,113	−548,069	−457,773	−603,884	−479,584	−394,792	−66,989	−68,432	−62,878	32
539,556	175,852	32.6	363,704	475,473	111,769	23.5	−458,167	−426,312	−384,788	−393,727	−362,589	−338,239	−64,083	−63,557	−46,194	33
1,133,771	250,482	22.1	883,289	943,406	60,117	6.4	−382,783	−282,019	−201,843	−192,246	−147,514	−136,250	−190,365	−134,344	−65,365	34
1,227,757	288,846	23.5	938,911	1,008,048	69,137	6.9	−403,363	−309,017	−132,517	−183,446	−169,448	−104,884	−219,700	−139,178	−26,439	35
449,451	109,269	24.3	340,182	476,490	136,314	28.6	−183,284	+89,264	+152,358	−208,581	−16,920	+47,402	+27,045	+106,039	+105,516	36
882,024	171,130	19.4	710,894	774,596	63,702	8.2	−116,939	−37,121	−3,028	−8,784	+15,753	+12,774	−107,428	−52,784	−15,741	37
115,284	29,524	25.6	85,760	171,250	85,490	49.9	+742,754	+924,950	+981,604	+681,308	+852,486	+889,691	+55,966	+69,904	+85,062	38
864,210	109,193	12.6	755,017	852,333	97,316	11.4	+306,355	+408,830	+503,639	+402,991	+405,723	+484,913	−11,877	+8,501	+19,821	39
937	638	68.1	299	1,218	919	75.5	+112,762	+207,182	+144,933	+111,884	+206,057	+143,478	+281	+712	+1,041	40
372	262	70.4	110	643	533	82.9	+105,314	+178,235	+157,900	+104,962	+177,376	+157,542	+271	+540	+140	41
596	418	70.1	178	1,232	1,054	85.6	+73,144	+84,272	+64,972	+70,197	+83,897	+63,995	+636	+902	+1,832	42
6,062	3,170	52.3	2,892	11,673	8,781	75.2	+261,448	+336,213	+340,446	+242,985	+329,680	+333,204	+5,611	+6,332	+7,583	43
1,293	778	60.2	515	2,792	2,277	81.6	+39,288	+60,619	+84,010	+68,029	+56,494	+83,565	+1,499	+4,318	+636	44
2,265	1,152	50.9	1,113	10,582	9,469	89.5	+132,610	+107,963	+57,375	+133,668	+101,587	+56,588	+8,317	+6,454	+1,407	45
627	377	60.1	250	1,078	828	76.8	−63,860	−20,833	−1,259	−85,281	−21,516	−2,439	+451	+675	+482	46
175	128	73.1	47	495	448	90.5	+16,930	+12,263	+20,943	+16,208	+12,152	+20,750	+320	+152	+108	47
2,998	1,518	50.6	1,480	6,457	4,977	77.1	+542,290	+555,590	+552,301	+539,243	+551,995	+548,472	+3,459	+3,582	+4,045	48
746	395	52.9	351	2,130	1,779	83.5	+303,358	+269,562	+261,000	+301,829	+267,830	+259,677	+1,884	+1,440	+989	49
19,481	2,967	15.2	16,514	78,051	61,537	78.8	+2,401,288	+1,222,727	+762,625	+2,306,436	+1,200,127	+752,412	+58,570	+26,133	+13,942	50

POPULATION

TABLE 18.—NATIVE WHITE POPULATION OF NATIVE PARENTAGE AND OF FOREIGN OR MIXED PARENTAGE, BY STATE OF BIRTH AND STATE OF RESIDENCE, WITH GAIN OR LOSS THROUGH INTERSTATE MIGRATION: 1930

[The small number of persons for whom State of birth was not reported are omitted from this table]

STATE	NATIVE WHITE OF NATIVE PARENTAGE								NATIVE WHITE OF FOREIGN OR MIXED PARENTAGE							
	Born in the specified State			Born in and living in the specified State	Living in the specified State			Gain (+) or loss (−) through interstate migration	Born in the specified State			Born in and living in the specified State	Living in the specified State			Gain (+) or loss (−) through interstate migration
	Total	Living in other States			Total	Born in other States			Total	Living in other States			Total	Born in other States		
		Number	Per cent			Number	Per cent			Number	Per cent			Number	Per cent	
United States	69,842,445	16,848,840	24.1	52,993,605	69,842,445	16,848,840	24.1	--------	25,256,790	5,428,914	21.5	19,827,876	25,256,790	5,428,914	21.5	--------
NEW ENGLAND:																
Maine	639,677	166,835	26.1	472,842	513,300	40,548	7.9	−126,287	212,882	57,110	26.8	155,772	177,509	21,737	12.2	−35,373
New Hampshire	268,763	97,364	36.2	171,399	238,373	66,974	28.1	−30,390	157,942	51,578	32.7	106,364	141,037	34,673	24.6	−16,905
Vermont	305,709	113,433	37.1	192,276	232,955	40,679	17.5	−72,754	108,735	46,113	42.4	62,622	80,974	18,352	22.7	−27,761
Massachusetts	1,406,884	289,752	20.6	1,117,132	1,422,090	304,958	21.4	+15,206	1,797,329	279,145	15.5	1,518,184	1,703,010	184,826	10.9	−94,319
Rhode Island	210,057	53,034	25.2	157,023	210,067	53,044	25.3	+10	292,608	58,951	20.1	233,657	294,393	60,736	20.6	+1,785
Connecticut	504,106	120,748	24.0	383,358	535,240	151,882	28.4	+31,134	631,001	113,175	17.9	517,826	654,973	137,147	20.9	+23,972
MIDDLE ATLANTIC:																
New York	4,499,719	781,050	17.4	3,718,669	4,405,545	686,876	15.6	−94,174	4,712,024	713,552	15.1	3,998,472	4,456,218	457,746	10.3	−255,806
New Jersey	1,288,473	216,219	16.8	1,072,254	1,563,953	491,699	31.4	+275,480	1,172,525	182,739	15.6	989,786	1,407,529	417,743	29.7	+235,004
Pennsylvania	5,988,906	1,075,687	18.0	4,913,219	5,395,451	482,232	8.9	−593,455	2,949,046	597,549	20.3	2,351,497	2,551,725	200,228	7.8	−397,321
E. NORTH CENTRAL:																
Ohio	4,316,360	886,113	20.5	3,430,247	4,314,552	884,305	20.5	−1,808	1,357,218	268,148	19.8	1,089,070	1,359,240	270,170	10.9	+2,022
Indiana	2,874,465	775,594	27.0	2,098,871	2,600,207	501,336	19.3	−274,258	393,609	130,001	33.0	263,608	374,457	110,849	29.6	−19,152
Illinois	4,001,644	1,149,284	28.7	2,852,360	3,754,395	902,035	24.0	−247,249	2,369,743	503,054	21.2	1,866,689	2,275,031	408,342	17.9	−94,712
Michigan	1,999,377	333,259	16.7	1,666,118	2,352,285	686,167	29.2	+352,908	1,362,249	234,847	17.2	1,127,402	1,438,587	311,185	21.6	+76,338
Wisconsin	1,580,967	355,001	22.5	1,225,966	1,431,953	205,987	14.4	−149,014	1,267,402	340,123	26.8	927,270	1,089,755	162,476	14.9	−177,647
W. NORTH CENTRAL:																
Minnesota	1,139,429	298,548	26.2	840,881	1,109,652	268,771	24.2	−29,777	1,100,040	294,113	26.7	805,927	1,034,468	228,541	22.1	−65,572
Iowa	2,127,864	794,207	37.3	1,333,657	1,692,203	358,546	21.2	−435,661	741,102	283,324	38.2	457,778	584,204	126,486	21.6	−156,838
Missouri	3,272,626	1,151,736	35.2	2,120,890	2,767,404	646,514	23.4	−505,222	494,314	153,658	31.1	340,656	472,192	131,536	27.0	−22,122
North Dakota	258,848	91,734	35.4	167,114	255,004	87,890	34.5	−3,844	299,629	82,727	27.6	216,902	308,882	91,080	29.8	+9,253
South Dakota	351,900	119,225	33.9	232,675	373,987	141,312	37.8	+22,087	209,936	71,023	33.8	138,913	228,054	89,141	39.1	+18,118
Nebraska	928,698	327,676	35.3	601,022	871,022	270,000	31.0	−57,676	391,249	120,699	30.8	270,550	364,005	93,455	25.7	−27,244
Kansas	1,507,157	592,163	39.3	914,994	1,448,342	533,348	36.8	−58,815	290,962	112,150	38.5	178,806	269,209	90,403	33.6	−21,753
SOUTH ATLANTIC:																
Delaware	159,250	49,559	31.1	109,691	154,815	45,124	29.1	−4,435	35,683	11,110	31.1	24,573	33,738	9,165	27.2	−1,945
Maryland	1,048,957	220,513	21.0	828,444	1,035,973	207,529	20.0	−12,984	227,343	50,528	22.2	176,815	218,793	41,978	19.2	−8,550
Dist. of Columbia	159,810	59,855	37.5	99,955	259,801	159,846	61.5	+99,991	42,077	13,806	32.8	28,271	61,139	32,868	53.8	+19,062
Virginia	1,931,417	474,809	24.6	1,456,608	1,690,790	234,182	13.9	−240,627	57,088	27,416	48.0	29,672	53,627	23,955	44.7	−3,461
West Virginia	1,542,344	325,993	21.1	1,216,351	1,460,307	243,956	16.7	−82,037	109,312	42,584	39.0	66,728	100,648	33,920	33.7	−8,664
North Carolina	2,337,763	326,996	14.0	2,010,767	2,206,941	196,174	8.9	−130,822	15,697	7,241	46.1	8,456	17,483	9,027	51.6	+1,786
South Carolina	991,182	181,024	18.3	810,158	924,717	114,559	12.4	−66,465	16,088	7,090	44.1	8,998	13,261	4,263	32.1	−2,827
Georgia	2,038,310	461,476	22.6	1,576,834	1,790,652	213,818	11.9	−247,658	32,042	14,387	44.9	17,655	30,420	12,765	42.0	−1,622
Florida	520,542	84,314	16.2	436,228	871,379	435,151	49.9	+350,837	54,815	10,638	19.4	44,177	101,037	56,860	50.3	+46,222
E. SOUTH CENTRAL:																
Kentucky	2,851,195	808,427	28.4	2,042,768	2,267,639	224,871	9.9	−583,556	117,140	49,447	42.2	67,693	96,812	29,119	30.1	−20,328
Tennessee	2,473,093	682,329	27.6	1,790,764	2,083,879	293,115	14.1	−389,214	42,505	20,506	48.2	21,999	37,992	15,993	42.1	−4,513
Alabama	1,836,746	425,658	23.2	1,411,088	1,644,891	233,803	14.2	−191,855	39,001	15,227	39.0	23,774	38,010	14,836	38.4	−391
Mississippi	1,148,084	309,606	27.0	838,478	967,639	129,161	13.3	−180,445	24,019	11,484	47.8	12,535	21,018	8,483	40.4	−3,001
W. SOUTH CENTRAL:																
Arkansas	1,538,165	549,118	35.7	989,047	1,326,505	337,458	25.4	−211,660	32,338	15,114	46.7	17,224	35,417	18,193	51.4	+3,079
Louisiana	1,165,530	182,106	15.6	983,424	1,170,994	187,570	16.0	+5,464	124,534	31,864	25.6	92,670	110,286	17,616	16.0	−14,248
Oklahoma	1,355,754	382,119	28.2	973,635	1,987,850	1,014,215	51.0	+632,096	52,787	20,540	38.9	32,247	101,999	69,752	68.4	+49,212
Texas	3,476,955	576,542	16.6	2,900,413	3,846,699	946,286	24.6	+369,744	293,481	44,113	15.0	249,368	326,728	77,360	23.7	+33,247
MOUNTAIN:																
Montana	210,034	83,548	39.8	126,486	281,161	154,675	55.0	+71,127	119,268	41,247	34.6	78,021	160,025	82,004	51.2	+40,757
Idaho	242,965	90,069	37.1	152,896	317,915	165,019	51.9	+74,950	56,462	22,454	39.8	34,008	86,474	52,466	60.7	+30,012
Wyoming	89,099	39,411	44.2	49,688	147,731	98,043	66.4	+58,632	34,372	15,638	45.5	18,784	45,987	27,203	59.2	+11,565
Colorado	457,763	180,873	39.5	276,890	666,480	389,590	58.5	+208,717	171,809	62,248	36.2	109,561	206,077	96,516	46.8	+34,268
New Mexico	238,249	60,229	25.3	178,020	301,901	123,881	41.0	+63,652	16,711	8,286	49.6	8,425	21,088	12,663	60.0	+4,377
Arizona	90,249	35,219	39.0	55,030	208,088	153,058	73.6	+117,839	22,224	10,171	45.8	12,053	38,053	26,000	68.3	+15,829
Utah	352,049	90,449	25.7	261,600	316,747	55,147	17.4	−35,302	163,390	50,794	31.1	112,596	133,411	20,815	15.6	−29,979
Nevada	32,073	17,334	54.0	14,739	47,189	32,450	68.8	+15,116	20,362	10,839	53.2	9,523	21,454	11,931	55.6	+1,092
PACIFIC:																
Washington	489,919	127,126	25.9	362,793	859,851	497,058	57.8	+369,932	228,116	45,300	19.9	182,816	397,427	214,611	54.0	+169,311
Oregon	407,188	118,164	29.0	289,024	623,510	334,486	53.6	+216,322	114,447	30,674	26.8	83,773	199,954	116,181	58.1	+85,507
California	1,186,131	117,312	9.9	1,068,819	2,892,331	1,823,512	63.0	+1,706,200	682,134	44,383	6.5	637,751	1,282,370	644,619	50.3	+600,236

STATE OF BIRTH 151

TABLE 19.—NATIVE POPULATION, BY SEX, BY STATE OF BIRTH AND STATE OF RESIDENCE, WITH GAIN OR LOSS THROUGH INTERSTATE MIGRATION: 1930

[The small number of persons for whom State of birth was not reported are omitted from this table]

STATE	NATIVE MALES — Born in the specified State — Total	— Living in other States — Number	— Per cent	Born in and living in the specified State	Living in the specified State — Total	— Born in other States — Number	— Per cent	Gain (+) or loss (−) through interstate migration	NATIVE FEMALES — Born in the specified State — Total	— Living in other States — Number	— Per cent	Born in and living in the specified State	Living in the specified State — Total	— Born in other States — Number	— Per cent	Gain (+) or loss (−) through interstate migration
United States	54,188,892	12,942,634	23.9	41,246,258	54,188,892	12,942,634	23.9	----------	53,876,827	12,445,466	23.1	41,431,361	53,876,827	12,445,466	23.1	----------
NEW ENGLAND:																
Maine	431,318	114,028	26.4	317,290	348,811	31,521	9.0	−82,507	423,565	110,662	26.1	312,903	343,935	31,032	9.0	−79,630
New Hampshire	212,847	73,630	34.6	139,217	189,221	50,004	26.4	−23,626	214,424	75,613	35.3	138,811	190,848	52,037	27.3	−23,576
Vermont	200,454	79,848	38.1	120,606	159,418	29,812	18.7	−50,036	205,883	80,227	39.0	125,656	155,103	29,447	19.0	−50,780
Massachusetts	1,605,241	300,167	18.7	1,305,074	1,548,194	243,120	15.7	−57,047	1,632,574	270,632	16.9	1,365,942	1,622,036	266,094	16.4	−10,538
Rhode Island	252,253	58,102	23.0	194,151	250,296	56,145	22.4	−1,957	258,200	56,170	21.8	202,030	263,334	61,304	23.3	+5,134
Connecticut	570,423	120,192	21.1	450,231	599,930	149,699	25.0	+29,507	580,295	118,690	20.5	461,605	618,358	156,753	25.3	+38,063
Mid. Atlantic:																
New York	4,645,323	767,037	16.5	3,878,286	4,556,166	677,880	14.9	−89,157	4,701,414	746,105	15.9	3,955,309	4,651,829	696,520	15.0	−49,585
New Jersey	1,205,835	205,310	16.2	1,000,525	1,575,519	514,994	32.7	+369,684	1,276,633	210,364	16.5	1,066,269	1,600,640	534,371	33.4	+324,007
Pennsylvania	4,551,400	875,237	19.2	3,676,163	4,156,126	480,963	11.8	−385,274	4,575,492	839,280	18.3	3,736,212	4,210,197	473,985	11.3	−365,295
E. N. Central:																
Ohio	2,917,244	612,598	21.0	2,304,646	2,996,403	691,757	23.1	+79,159	2,886,851	571,723	19.8	2,315,128	2,985,710	670,582	22.5	+98,859
Indiana	1,677,805	474,441	28.3	1,203,364	1,552,346	348,982	22.5	−125,459	1,645,125	448,881	27.3	1,196,244	1,535,768	339,524	22.1	−109,357
Illinois	3,254,278	853,680	26.2	2,400,598	3,184,216	783,618	24.6	−70,062	3,220,722	826,012	25.6	2,400,710	3,181,213	780,503	24.5	−45,509
Michigan	1,722,977	292,356	17.0	1,430,621	2,033,475	602,854	29.6	+310,498	1,683,725	283,368	16.8	1,400,357	1,934,389	534,032	27.6	+250,664
Wisconsin	1,437,766	341,877	23.8	1,095,889	1,290,956	195,067	15.1	−146,810	1,425,853	355,628	24.9	1,070,225	1,253,596	183,371	14.6	−172,257
W. N. Central:																
Minnesota	1,135,665	207,616	20.2	838,049	1,093,013	254,964	23.3	−42,652	1,119,789	207,812	20.6	821,977	1,073,063	251,086	23.4	−46,726
Iowa	1,452,488	540,033	37.7	905,555	1,157,743	252,188	21.8	−294,745	1,431,402	537,227	37.5	894,175	1,138,506	244,391	21.5	−292,836
Missouri	1,973,603	690,298	35.0	1,283,305	1,731,805	448,500	25.9	−241,798	1,950,070	669,531	34.2	1,280,539	1,732,725	440,186	25.8	−223,345
North Dakota	286,384	85,969	30.0	200,415	297,464	97,049	32.6	+11,080	281,104	89,854	32.0	191,250	275,210	83,960	30.5	−5,894
South Dakota	294,086	93,850	31.9	200,236	324,567	124,331	38.3	+30,481	289,026	97,869	33.9	191,157	300,280	109,123	36.3	+11,254
Nebraska	672,352	227,107	33.8	445,245	638,267	193,022	30.2	−34,085	659,936	226,040	34.3	433,887	616,802	182,915	29.7	−43,134
Kansas	933,720	364,710	39.1	569,010	911,531	342,521	37.6	−22,198	923,887	363,592	39.4	560,295	882,126	321,831	36.5	−41,761
SOUTH ATLANTIC:																
Delaware	113,707	35,700	31.4	78,007	111,649	33,642	30.1	−2,058	113,450	35,872	31.6	77,578	109,408	31,830	29.1	−4,042
Maryland	770,394	171,375	22.2	599,019	766,119	167,100	21.8	−4,275	781,199	173,564	22.2	607,635	762,817	155,182	20.3	−18,382
Dist. Columbia	132,813	46,357	34.0	86,456	213,062	126,606	59.4	+80,249	141,303	46,895	33.2	94,408	238,599	144,191	60.4	+97,296
Virginia	1,450,075	423,369	29.2	1,026,706	1,200,171	173,465	14.5	−249,904	1,448,057	411,073	28.4	1,036,984	1,194,430	157,446	13.2	−253,627
West Virginia	871,230	196,775	22.0	674,455	855,684	181,230	21.2	−15,536	845,491	189,965	22.5	655,526	810,963	104,437	20.1	−25,528
North Carolina	1,715,072	301,037	17.6	1,414,035	1,568,566	154,531	9.9	−146,506	1,683,292	253,875	15.1	1,429,417	1,590,164	160,747	10.1	−93,128
South Carolina	1,041,444	260,763	25.0	780,681	849,353	68,672	8.1	−192,091	1,062,390	247,030	23.3	815,351	882,922	67,571	7.7	−179,468
Georgia	1,728,114	457,431	26.5	1,270,683	1,424,196	153,513	10.8	−303,918	1,746,584	426,292	24.4	1,320,292	1,466,850	146,558	10.0	−279,734
Florida	444,713	78,487	17.6	366,226	696,422	330,196	47.4	+251,709	446,158	71,678	16.1	374,480	696,324	321,844	46.2	+250,166
E. S. Central:																
Kentucky	1,658,247	499,316	30.1	1,158,931	1,308,770	149,839	11.4	−349,477	1,602,773	466,159	29.1	1,136,614	1,281,137	144,523	11.3	−321,636
Tennessee	1,553,912	466,103	30.0	1,087,809	1,293,724	205,915	15.9	−260,188	1,501,789	413,007	27.5	1,088,782	1,303,810	215,028	16.5	−197,979
Alabama	1,505,804	359,698	23.0	1,146,106	1,303,625	157,519	12.1	−202,179	1,504,414	331,920	22.1	1,172,494	1,323,810	151,316	11.4	−180,604
Mississippi	1,199,922	309,210	25.8	890,712	998,368	107,656	10.8	−201,554	1,202,443	301,540	25.1	900,903	1,000,634	99,731	10.0	−201,809
W. S. Central:																
Arkansas	1,017,004	342,505	33.7	674,499	930,413	255,914	27.5	−86,591	1,005,413	333,205	33.1	672,208	908,720	236,512	26.0	−96,693
Louisiana	1,076,106	194,552	18.1	881,554	1,023,978	142,424	13.9	−52,128	1,102,167	191,656	17.4	910,511	1,037,356	126,845	12.2	−64,811
Oklahoma	814,749	221,170	27.1	593,579	1,209,631	616,052	50.9	+394,882	799,489	215,254	26.9	584,235	1,147,361	563,126	49.1	+347,872
Texas	2,559,150	395,344	15.4	2,163,806	2,762,690	598,884	21.7	+203,540	2,521,420	367,649	14.6	2,153,771	2,684,235	530,464	19.8	+162,815
MOUNTAIN:																
Montana	175,176	63,278	36.1	111,898	243,903	132,005	54.1	+68,727	170,027	63,442	37.3	106,585	214,062	107,477	50.2	+44,035
Idaho	153,903	56,106	36.5	97,797	215,393	117,596	54.6	+61,490	150,675	57,532	38.2	93,143	194,499	101,356	52.1	+43,824
Wyoming	65,023	28,307	43.5	36,716	109,140	72,424	66.4	+44,117	63,233	28,327	44.8	34,906	92,260	57,354	62.2	+29,027
Colorado	337,305	126,624	37.5	210,681	471,774	261,093	55.3	+134,469	333,574	124,692	37.4	208,882	460,553	251,671	54.6	+120,079
New Mexico	183,431	55,240	30.1	128,191	204,757	76,566	37.4	+21,326	175,319	50,548	28.8	124,771	193,281	68,510	35.4	+17,962
Arizona	119,021	34,761	29.2	84,260	192,480	108,220	56.2	+73,459	114,269	33,226	29.1	81,043	173,420	92,377	53.3	+59,151
Utah	262,728	71,781	27.3	190,947	232,539	41,592	17.9	−30,189	258,632	70,801	27.4	187,831	224,952	37,121	16.5	−33,080
Nevada	29,401	14,230	48.4	15,171	41,905	26,734	63.8	+12,504	29,038	14,933	51.4	14,105	33,464	19,359	57.9	+4,426
PACIFIC:																
Washington	376,331	88,167	23.4	288,164	661,996	373,832	56.5	+285,665	365,848	87,652	24.0	278,196	622,473	344,277	55.3	+256,625
Oregon	267,253	74,922	28.0	192,331	427,825	235,494	55.0	+160,572	263,164	75,700	28.8	187,464	405,950	218,486	53.8	+142,786
California	1,064,333	95,031	8.9	969,302	2,265,222	1,295,920	57.2	+1,200,889	1,047,246	80,681	7.7	966,565	2,247,645	1,281,080	57.0	+1,200,399

152

POPULATION

TABLE 20.—NATIVE POPULATION, BY STATE OF BIRTH WITH RESIDENCE IN ADJACENT STATES, AND BY STATE OF RESIDENCE WITH BIRTH IN ADJACENT STATES: 1930

[The small number of persons for whom State of birth was not reported are omitted from this table]

STATE	POPULATION BORN IN EACH STATE							NATIVE POPULATION LIVING IN EACH STATE						
	Total	Living in State of birth		Living in adjacent States		Living in other States		Total	Born in State of residence		Born in adjacent States		Born in other States	
		Number	Per cent	Number	Per cent	Number	Per cent		Number	Per cent	Number	Per cent	Number	Per cent
United States	108,065,719	82,677,619	76.5	12,200,290	11.3	13,187,810	12.2	108,065,719	82,677,619	76.5	12,200,290	11.3	13,187,810	12.2
NEW ENGLAND:														
Maine	854,883	630,193	73.7	18,565	2.2	206,125	24.1	692,746	630,193	91.0	13,158	1.9	49,395	7.1
New Hampshire	427,271	278,028	65.1	96,265	22.5	52,978	12.4	380,069	278,028	73.2	82,223	21.6	19,818	5.2
Vermont	415,337	255,262	61.5	96,858	23.3	63,217	15.2	314,521	255,262	81.2	45,195	14.4	14,064	4.5
Massachusetts	3,237,815	2,661,016	82.2	305,882	9.4	270,917	8.4	3,170,230	2,661,016	83.9	296,151	9.3	213,063	6.7
Rhode Island	510,453	396,181	77.6	57,892	11.3	56,380	11.0	513,630	396,181	77.1	73,215	14.3	44,234	8.6
Connecticut	1,150,718	911,836	79.2	137,348	11.9	101,534	8.8	1,218,288	911,836	74.8	187,245	15.4	119,207	9.8
MIDDLE ATLANTIC:														
New York	9,346,737	7,833,595	83.8	768,791	8.2	744,351	8.0	9,207,995	7,833,595	85.1	713,772	7.8	660,628	7.2
New Jersey	2,542,468	2,126,794	83.7	259,758	10.2	155,916	6.1	3,176,159	2,126,794	67.0	716,229	22.6	333,136	10.5
Pennsylvania	9,126,892	7,412,375	81.2	1,022,319	11.2	692,198	7.6	8,376,323	7,412,375	88.5	502,048	6.0	461,900	5.5
E. NORTH CENTRAL:														
Ohio	5,804,095	4,619,774	79.6	497,472	8.6	686,849	11.8	5,982,113	4,619,774	77.2	804,884	13.5	557,455	9.3
Indiana	3,322,930	2,399,608	72.2	432,179	13.0	491,143	14.8	3,088,114	2,399,608	77.7	451,713	14.6	236,793	7.7
Illinois	6,481,000	4,801,308	74.1	554,362	8.6	1,125,330	17.4	6,365,429	4,801,308	75.4	681,485	10.7	882,636	13.9
Michigan	3,406,702	2,830,978	83.1	146,448	4.3	429,276	12.6	3,967,864	2,830,978	71.3	342,380	8.6	794,506	20.0
Wisconsin	2,863,619	2,166,114	75.6	332,235	11.6	365,270	12.8	2,544,552	2,166,114	85.1	231,125	9.1	147,313	5.8
W. NORTH CENTRAL:														
Minnesota	2,255,454	1,660,026	73.6	204,498	9.1	390,930	17.3	2,166,076	1,660,026	76.6	299,805	13.8	206,245	9.5
Iowa	2,883,890	1,799,730	62.4	494,662	17.2	589,498	20.4	2,296,309	1,799,730	78.4	320,617	14.0	175,962	7.7
Missouri	3,929,733	2,569,904	65.4	687,876	17.5	671,953	17.1	3,464,590	2,569,904	74.2	590,401	17.0	304,285	8.8
North Dakota	567,488	391,665	69.0	71,848	12.7	103,975	18.3	572,674	391,665	68.4	91,496	16.0	89,513	15.6
South Dakota	583,112	391,393	67.1	89,984	15.4	101,735	17.4	624,847	391,393	62.6	140,842	22.5	92,612	14.8
Nebraska	1,332,288	879,132	66.0	189,973	14.3	263,183	19.8	1,255,069	879,132	70.0	194,820	15.5	181,108	14.4
Kansas	1,857,616	1,129,305	60.8	318,104	17.1	410,207	22.1	1,793,657	1,129,305	63.0	276,240	15.4	388,112	21.6
SOUTH ATLANTIC:														
Delaware	227,157	155,585	68.5	53,142	23.4	18,430	8.1	221,057	155,585	70.4	46,469	21.0	19,003	8.6
Maryland	1,551,593	1,206,654	77.8	203,022	13.1	141,917	9.1	1,528,936	1,206,654	78.9	208,773	13.7	113,509	7.4
Dist. of Columbia	274,116	180,864	66.0	40,590	14.8	52,662	19.2	451,661	180,864	40.0	122,890	27.2	147,907	32.7
Virginia	2,898,132	2,063,690	71.2	378,037	13.0	456,405	15.7	2,394,601	2,063,690	86.2	216,798	9.1	114,113	4.8
West Virginia	1,716,721	1,329,981	77.5	256,025	14.9	130,715	7.6	1,675,657	1,329,981	79.4	267,564	16.0	78,112	4.7
North Carolina	3,398,364	2,843,452	83.7	236,896	7.0	318,016	9.4	3,158,730	2,843,452	90.0	255,718	8.1	59,560	1.9
South Carolina	2,103,834	1,596,032	75.9	213,274	10.1	294,528	14.0	1,732,275	1,596,032	92.1	100,009	5.8	36,234	2.1
Georgia	3,474,698	2,590,975	74.6	466,000	13.4	417,723	12.0	2,891,046	2,590,975	89.6	230,907	8.0	69,164	2.4
Florida	890,871	740,706	83.1	45,611	5.1	104,554	11.7	1,392,746	740,706	53.2	295,590	21.2	356,450	25.6
E. SOUTH CENTRAL:														
Kentucky	3,261,020	2,295,545	70.4	615,158	18.9	350,317	10.7	2,589,907	2,295,545	88.6	227,729	8.8	66,633	2.6
Tennessee	3,055,701	2,176,591	71.2	351,976	11.5	527,134	17.3	2,597,534	2,176,591	83.8	339,573	13.1	81,370	3.1
Alabama	3,010,218	2,318,600	77.0	274,196	9.1	417,422	13.9	2,627,435	2,318,600	88.2	222,535	8.5	86,300	3.3
Mississippi	2,402,365	1,791,615	74.6	313,592	13.1	297,158	12.4	1,999,002	1,791,615	89.6	149,973	7.5	57,414	2.9
W. SOUTH CENTRAL:														
Arkansas	2,022,417	1,346,707	66.6	472,054	23.3	203,656	10.1	1,839,133	1,346,707	73.2	330,883	18.0	161,543	8.8
Louisiana	2,178,273	1,792,065	82.3	236,065	10.8	150,143	6.9	2,061,334	1,792,065	86.9	165,589	8.0	103,680	5.0
Oklahoma	1,614,238	1,177,814	73.0	270,137	16.7	166,287	10.3	2,356,992	1,177,814	50.0	768,840	32.6	410,338	17.4
Texas	5,080,570	4,317,577	85.0	388,100	7.6	374,893	7.4	5,446,925	4,317,577	79.3	409,070	7.5	720,278	13.2
MOUNTAIN:														
Montana	345,203	218,483	63.3	17,091	5.0	109,629	31.8	457,965	218,483	47.7	38,536	8.4	200,946	43.9
Idaho	304,578	190,940	62.7	69,750	22.9	43,888	14.4	409,892	190,940	46.6	74,214	18.1	144,738	35.3
Wyoming	128,256	71,622	55.8	23,982	18.7	32,652	25.5	201,400	71,622	35.6	47,928	23.8	81,850	40.6
Colorado	670,879	419,563	62.5	62,762	9.4	188,554	28.1	932,327	419,563	45.0	169,162	18.1	343,602	36.9
New Mexico	358,750	252,962	70.5	63,227	17.6	42,561	11.9	398,038	252,962	63.6	73,387	18.4	71,689	18.0
Arizona	233,290	165,303	70.9	52,447	22.5	15,540	6.7	365,900	165,303	45.2	38,098	10.4	162,499	44.4
Utah	521,360	378,778	72.7	59,537	11.4	83,045	15.9	457,491	378,778	82.8	32,063	7.0	46,650	10.2
Nevada	58,439	29,276	50.1	23,522	40.3	5,641	9.7	75,369	29,276	38.8	19,670	26.1	26,423	35.1
PACIFIC:														
Washington	742,179	566,360	76.3	62,842	8.5	112,977	15.2	1,284,469	566,360	44.1	77,937	6.1	640,172	49.8
Oregon	530,417	379,795	71.6	121,504	22.9	29,118	5.5	833,775	379,795	45.6	91,729	11.0	362,251	43.4
California	2,111,579	1,935,867	91.7	46,432	2.2	129,280	6.1	4,512,867	1,935,867	42.9	123,003	2.7	2,453,997	54.4

STATE OF BIRTH

153

TABLE 21.—NATIVE POPULATION OF EACH DIVISION AND STATE, BY DIVISION AND STATE OF BIRTH: 1930

DIVISION AND STATE	Total native population	United States	POPULATION BORN IN—									United States, State not reported	Other native population[1]
			Geographic divisions										
			New England	Middle Atlantic	East North Central	West North Central	South Atlantic	East South Central	West South Central	Mountain	Pacific		
United States	108,570,897	108,304,188	6,596,477	21,016,097	21,878,346	18,409,581	16,535,486	11,729,304	10,895,498	2,620,755	3,384,175	238,469	266,709
GEOGRAPHIC DIVISIONS:													
New England	6,317,398	6,297,826	5,800,797	326,073	53,919	21,629	58,350	9,094	5,975	5,163	8,484	8,342	19,572
Middle Atlantic	20,908,019	20,827,430	400,645	18,792,673	374,199	100,771	884,745	97,429	45,766	23,517	31,732	66,953	80,589
East North Central	22,021,462	21,990,889	115,619	847,196	18,475,656	793,974	520,134	918,409	180,556	56,042	40,480	42,817	30,573
West North Central	12,212,762	12,199,299	37,040	180,280	1,112,953	10,147,705	69,634	228,924	264,602	86,390	31,983	19,416	13,463
South Atlantic	15,474,892	15,466,125	66,989	382,186	236,595	69,634	14,272,196	395,351	51,166	11,252	11,340	19,416	8,767
East South Central	9,827,850	9,826,010	6,236	28,641	159,464	42,136	357,507	9,079,685	131,817	4,438	3,954	12,141	1,831
West South Central	11,736,277	11,728,274	12,991	70,163	282,777	570,380	198,295	788,940	9,706,218	53,268	21,352	23,890	8,003
Mountain	3,317,466	3,305,012	19,012	79,156	276,781	568,201	44,540	66,381	199,809	1,958,115	85,487	6,630	12,454
Pacific	6,754,771	6,663,314	136,248	359,729	906,002	1,086,151	116,374	145,091	309,589	422,570	3,140,357	32,203	91,457
NEW ENGLAND:													
Maine	696,695	693,354	677,281	7,643	2,775	1,518	1,627	427	356	399	720	608	3,341
New Hampshire	382,364	380,482	364,325	9,707	2,445	1,110	1,240	303	218	290	422	413	1,882
Vermont	316,510	314,781	288,194	20,602	2,422	1,253	868	238	233	315	300	260	1,729
Massachusetts	3,183,994	3,175,127	2,962,148	125,073	28,884	11,165	27,758	4,518	3,052	2,776	4,856	4,897	8,867
Rhode Island	515,568	514,233	482,780	19,504	3,438	1,333	4,661	572	451	308	583	603	1,335
Connecticut	1,222,267	1,219,849	1,026,069	143,454	13,955	5,250	22,196	3,036	1,665	1,060	1,597	1,561	2,418
MIDDLE ATLANTIC:													
New York	9,325,788	9,256,117	270,505	8,318,000	175,778	62,853	277,170	37,570	26,307	12,756	19,037	48,122	69,671
New Jersey	3,191,296	3,186,108	78,346	2,830,720	49,107	16,132	171,465	14,835	6,642	3,640	5,272	9,040	5,188
Pennsylvania	8,390,935	8,385,205	45,784	7,642,954	149,314	30,786	436,110	45,024	12,757	7,121	6,523	8,882	5,730
EAST NORTH CENTRAL:													
Ohio	5,997,477	5,992,847	26,340	374,278	4,871,792	64,300	291,528	314,408	23,444	8,755	7,199	10,734	4,630
Indiana	3,095,504	3,093,589	6,303	46,925	2,712,410	59,110	35,813	200,771	18,024	5,244	3,454	5,475	1,915
Illinois	6,388,207	6,380,024	34,875	171,266	5,277,803	400,785	87,205	262,243	92,676	15,778	14,505	8,182	13,538
Michigan	3,989,567	3,976,029	38,995	218,630	3,203,406	124,413	98,253	130,819	40,758	12,616	9,974	8,165	2,307
Wisconsin	2,550,707	2,548,400	9,046	36,097	2,320,245	145,297	7,335	10,168	5,532	6,751	4,081	3,848	2,307
WEST NORTH CENTRAL:													
Minnesota	2,173,163	2,168,743	11,617	31,754	216,317	1,873,214	5,663	5,939	5,914	9,635	6,023	2,667	4,420
Iowa	2,302,689	2,300,802	6,083	35,855	218,032	1,984,537	11,229	14,042	11,720	9,745	4,466	4,493	1,887
Missouri	3,476,282	3,474,120	7,666	40,504	292,800	2,771,763	34,549	158,458	133,718	16,828	8,214	9,530	2,162
North Dakota	574,974	573,412	1,508	5,941	43,750	510,956	1,582	1,001	1,337	4,824	1,775	738	1,562
South Dakota	626,788	625,946	1,877	8,852	58,746	540,775	2,102	2,178	2,528	6,587	1,707	1,099	842
Nebraska	1,258,764	1,257,629	4,077	23,727	105,377	1,068,254	8,537	9,101	13,008	19,028	3,870	2,560	1,135
Kansas	1,800,102	1,798,647	4,212	34,147	177,241	1,308,206	10,083	38,115	96,382	19,743	5,928	4,090	1,455
SOUTH ATLANTIC:													
Delaware	221,355	221,174	1,857	26,646	2,360	1,030	187,411	810	451	191	301	117	181
Maryland	1,535,196	1,533,458	9,009	85,251	19,743	7,430	1,391,953	7,536	3,631	1,431	1,984	2,911	1,564
District of Columbia	456,136	454,572	12,539	42,217	20,800	10,846	345,275	10,940	4,030	2,130	1,984	1,518	1,365
Virginia	2,397,484	2,396,119	7,548	36,601	19,275	7,782	2,277,414	37,897	4,038	1,363	1,780	1,305	878
West Virginia	1,677,340	1,676,962	1,994	51,551	68,409	4,996	1,482,416	61,468	2,044	1,090	780	1,305	513
North Carolina	3,161,307	3,160,704	3,908	12,843	9,124	3,607	3,093,948	20,074	4,351	256	286	802	330
South Carolina	1,733,407	1,733,077	1,744	4,513	2,994	1,454	1,706,300	12,444	2,284	256	960	2,525	632
Georgia	2,894,203	2,893,571	3,594	11,603	13,421	5,416	2,727,550	116,702	10,820	980	2,425	3,052	2,066
Florida	1,398,464	1,396,398	23,746	60,961	80,466	26,983	1,059,929	118,480	16,817	2,039	2,425	3,052	2,066
EAST SOUTH CENTRAL:													
Kentucky	2,592,582	2,592,038	1,840	9,695	99,494	12,580	58,185	2,396,657	8,938	1,387	1,131	2,131	544
Tennessee	2,603,305	2,602,765	2,076	8,844	30,643	15,828	133,047	2,364,687	30,340	1,563	1,506	5,231	540
Alabama	2,630,187	2,629,744	1,759	7,632	18,397	7,118	144,311	2,425,733	20,801	904	780	2,309	443
Mississippi	2,001,776	2,001,472	561	2,470	10,930	6,610	21,964	1,892,608	62,738	584	537	2,470	304
WEST SOUTH CENTRAL:													
Arkansas	1,843,850	1,843,535	920	5,079	49,358	78,518	34,215	206,515	1,459,795	3,018	1,715	4,402	315
Louisiana	2,064,517	2,063,194	1,963	8,002	17,450	14,448	21,532	121,778	1,873,352	1,276	1,533	1,860	1,323
Oklahoma	2,365,482	2,364,236	2,506	23,476	117,860	340,480	42,870	143,511	1,662,611	16,740	6,839	7,244	1,246
Texas	5,462,428	5,457,309	7,512	33,606	98,109	136,934	99,669	317,136	4,710,460	32,284	11,265	10,384	5,119
MOUNTAIN:													
Montana	461,703	459,023	3,670	12,099	57,822	118,908	5,014	5,082	6,100	237,285	11,985	1,058	2,680
Idaho	412,748	410,723	1,777	6,947	34,040	70,555	5,679	5,750	9,392	246,501	29,251	831	2,025
Wyoming	202,222	201,834	1,258	5,840	19,775	62,994	2,953	3,101	6,556	96,600	2,323	434	388
Colorado	935,916	934,433	7,366	32,559	104,613	235,105	14,346	22,428	44,848	463,260	7,793	2,106	1,483
New Mexico	399,265	398,613	873	4,015	14,860	23,458	4,503	11,871	70,354	265,472	2,632	575	652
Arizona	369,817	366,798	2,745	10,087	29,512	35,039	7,905	14,085	57,104	193,200	16,223	898	3,019
Utah	459,832	457,959	1,206	4,539	10,424	14,767	2,892	2,815	3,147	412,525	5,176	468	1,873
Nevada	75,963	75,620	1,017	3,070	5,735	7,375	1,248	1,249	2,308	43,263	10,104	260	334
PACIFIC:													
Washington	1,308,138	1,289,783	17,531	46,850	183,031	250,448	21,503	19,634	24,451	79,780	641,241	5,314	18,355
Oregon	843,346	837,438	8,083	24,554	101,205	153,757	10,400	12,596	20,613	50,843	451,724	3,663	5,908
California	4,603,287	4,536,093	110,634	288,325	621,766	681,946	84,471	112,861	264,525	291,947	2,055,392	23,226	67,194

[1] Includes persons born in outlying possessions and American citizens born abroad or at sea.

154

POPULATION

TABLE 21.—NATIVE POPULATION OF EACH DIVISION AND STATE, BY DIVISION AND STATE OF BIRTH: 1930—Continued

DIVISION AND STATE	POPULATION BORN IN—													
	New England division						Middle Atlantic division			East North Central division				
	Maine	New Hampshire	Vermont	Massachusetts	Rhode Island	Connecticut	New York	New Jersey	Pennsylvania	Ohio	Indiana	Illinois	Michigan	Wisconsin
United States	854,883	427,271	415,337	3,237,815	510,453	1,150,718	9,346,737	2,542,468	9,126,892	5,804,095	3,322,930	6,481,000	3,406,702	2,869,619
GEOGRAPHIC DIVISIONS:														
New England	765,329	386,211	339,501	2,870,446	458,518	980,702	237,894	36,519	51,660	15,691	5,320	15,350	11,461	6,097
Middle Atlantic	30,163	16,204	36,787	131,125	27,961	108,405	8,389,641	2,382,685	8,020,347	163,435	37,615	87,091	54,812	20,246
East North Central	12,229	6,670	11,208	57,702	6,901	20,909	287,686	39,029	520,481	5,034,083	2,811,761	5,203,451	3,052,417	2,373,944
West North Central	6,647	2,726	6,351	14,549	1,655	5,112	80,001	9,560	90,719	135,352	143,784	544,046	64,561	225,210
South Atlantic	8,348	4,526	5,036	31,629	4,966	12,484	97,033	32,052	203,101	117,505	35,500	45,955	24,742	12,833
East South Central	759	388	481	3,054	434	1,120	11,591	2,296	14,754	63,163	48,160	34,697	8,956	4,488
West South Central	1,880	815	1,263	6,111	860	2,062	27,997	4,540	37,626	52,765	65,494	132,120	17,503	14,895
Mountain	4,185	1,342	2,554	8,267	916	2,648	34,065	5,375	39,716	47,360	44,572	107,003	32,520	45,320
Pacific	25,343	8,389	12,066	64,932	8,242	17,276	180,829	30,412	148,488	169,741	130,664	311,287	130,724	154,586
NEW ENGLAND:														
Maine	630,193	13,158	3,301	26,783	1,669	2,177	4,887	990	1,766	590	311	675	740	459
New Hampshire	18,565	278,028	21,954	41,704	1,789	2,305	7,623	788	1,296	592	206	640	650	357
Vermont	3,269	12,239	255,282	14,139	1,007	2,278	18,817	730	1,145	552	224	709	582	355
Massachusetts	93,884	70,868	45,013	2,681,016	44,036	47,331	38,903	13,393	22,777	8,307	2,902	8,573	5,996	3,105
Rhode Island	5,731	4,581	3,072	58,440	398,181	14,775	12,639	2,960	3,905	1,027	302	862	835	412
Connecticut	13,687	7,337	10,089	68,364	13,356	911,836	105,025	17,658	20,771	4,623	1,375	3,891	2,658	1,408
MIDDLE ATLANTIC:														
New York	19,345	10,867	29,891	123,235	17,935	75,242	7,833,595	163,704	321,700	59,004	17,230	48,264	34,204	16,276
New Jersey	6,346	3,324	4,129	35,757	6,224	22,566	417,654	2,126,794	286,272	17,013	5,624	15,345	7,108	3,952
Pennsylvania	4,472	2,013	2,767	22,133	3,752	10,597	138,302	92,187	7,412,375	91,753	14,711	23,482	13,350	6,018
EAST NORTH CENTRAL:														
Ohio	2,370	1,427	2,127	13,310	1,684	5,422	74,095	11,512	238,671	4,619,774	114,611	59,279	64,886	13,242
Indiana	675	404	598	3,040	396	1,250	13,411	2,679	39,835	122,388	2,399,608	143,819	35,393	11,202
Illinois	3,277	1,873	3,322	18,531	1,985	5,887	79,108	12,436	79,662	99,336	172,902	4,801,308	74,091	129,266
Michigan	4,327	2,363	3,847	19,000	2,398	6,970	100,539	10,377	107,714	178,293	100,967	120,048	2,830,978	54,120
Wisconsin	1,580	603	1,314	3,731	438	1,380	20,473	2,025	13,599	14,292	14,673	78,997	46,169	2,166,114
WEST NORTH CENTRAL:														
Minnesota	3,107	860	1,747	4,231	444	1,228	18,097	1,718	11,339	11,637	10,583	53,156	25,653	115,288
Iowa	795	534	1,412	2,149	288	905	15,081	1,698	19,076	26,738	23,654	126,956	7,723	33,561
Missouri	901	468	789	3,846	400	1,262	17,921	2,750	19,883	37,084	44,231	190,320	10,310	10,945
North Dakota	344	107	289	541	74	153	3,039	258	2,644	2,954	4,542	11,780	3,758	20,716
South Dakota	363	154	433	622	72	233	4,324	393	3,635	4,182	4,635	23,458	4,152	22,319
Nebraska	555	321	844	1,486	176	695	10,076	1,287	12,364	15,449	15,022	55,664	5,712	13,530
Kansas	582	282	837	1,674	201	636	10,863	1,456	21,828	37,308	41,117	82,712	7,253	8,851
SOUTH ATLANTIC:														
Delaware	199	97	149	870	155	337	3,527	3,867	19,252	974	305	506	306	209
Maryland	1,089	490	566	5,074	829	1,921	17,566	7,083	60,602	8,443	2,749	4,777	2,280	1,494
District of Columbia	1,525	787	916	6,142	1,113	2,056	16,699	4,371	21,147	7,213	3,597	5,662	2,435	1,893
Virginia	954	446	393	3,601	657	1,437	12,375	4,249	19,977	8,006	3,061	4,047	2,559	1,605
West Virginia	204	131	154	871	136	438	4,229	1,500	45,822	58,323	4,301	3,356	1,781	648
North Carolina	449	349	331	1,863	315	691	5,340	1,580	5,923	3,315	1,899	2,130	1,211	569
South Carolina	178	106	112	808	187	263	2,139	551	1,823	1,001	561	738	470	224
Georgia	381	203	294	1,763	262	691	5,842	1,339	4,422	4,738	2,725	3,409	1,772	777
Florida	3,309	1,917	2,121	10,487	1,312	4,600	29,316	7,512	24,133	25,492	16,362	21,380	11,868	5,414
EAST SOUTH CENTRAL:														
Kentucky	219	95	143	986	111	286	3,430	666	5,599	46,715	34,699	14,270	2,669	1,141
Tennessee	251	143	161	957	173	391	3,816	767	4,261	8,705	7,387	10,037	3,214	1,300
Alabama	202	109	128	838	120	362	3,150	665	3,817	5,729	3,659	5,633	2,102	1,274
Mississippi	87	41	49	273	30	81	1,195	198	1,077	2,014	2,415	4,757	971	773
WEST SOUTH CENTRAL:														
Arkansas	135	55	124	402	66	138	2,042	287	2,750	6,225	11,830	27,206	2,441	1,656
Louisiana	300	96	118	984	149	316	4,264	665	3,073	3,769	3,525	6,938	1,910	1,308
Oklahoma	423	164	366	1,088	155	400	6,822	982	15,672	23,207	29,570	54,946	5,059	5,078
Texas	1,022	500	655	3,637	490	1,208	14,869	2,606	16,131	19,564	20,569	43,030	8,093	6,853
MOUNTAIN:														
Montana	1,089	231	504	1,383	141	322	5,143	704	6,252	6,401	6,976	16,671	9,310	18,464
Idaho	545	133	261	596	64	178	2,847	321	3,779	4,872	4,636	11,950	4,670	7,912
Wyoming	225	101	208	519	48	157	2,159	370	3,311	3,245	3,298	8,591	1,818	2,823
Colorado	1,299	493	1,009	3,077	354	1,134	14,215	2,254	10,090	20,544	18,082	46,940	8,894	10,153
New Mexico	123	60	93	301	41	165	1,605	283	2,127	2,894	3,090	6,244	1,475	1,157
Arizona	454	183	248	1,310	139	411	4,441	902	4,744	6,304	6,012	10,474	3,962	2,760
Utah	188	82	145	557	73	161	2,049	302	2,188	2,030	1,627	4,072	1,417	1,269
Nevada	262	59	86	434	56	120	1,606	239	1,225	1,061	851	2,061	980	782
PACIFIC:														
Washington	5,317	1,205	1,775	6,883	627	1,724	22,321	2,704	21,765	24,306	20,891	49,904	36,259	51,671
Oregon	2,189	569	993	3,138	308	886	11,319	1,451	11,784	15,130	13,601	30,519	17,292	24,663
California	17,837	6,615	9,298	54,911	7,307	14,666	147,189	26,197	114,939	130,305	96,172	230,864	86,173	78,252

392

STATE OF BIRTH

155

TABLE 21.—NATIVE POPULATION OF EACH DIVISION AND STATE, BY DIVISION AND STATE OF BIRTH: 1930—Continued

DIVISION AND STATE	POPULATION BORN IN—															
	West North Central division							South Atlantic division								
	Minnesota	Iowa	Missouri	North Dakota	South Dakota	Nebraska	Kansas	Delaware	Maryland	District of Columbia	Virginia	West Virginia	North Carolina	South Carolina	Georgia	Florida
United States	2,255,454	2,883,890	3,929,733	567,488	583,112	1,332,288	1,857,616	227,157	1,551,593	274,116	2,898,132	1,716,721	3,398,364	2,103,834	3,474,698	890,871
GEOGRAPHIC DIVISIONS:																
New England	5,045	4,784	5,400	838	864	2,048	2,650	1,707	7,732	3,827	15,350	2,465	8,736	5,012	8,930	3,691
Middle Atlantic	19,479	24,330	32,719	3,008	3,947	10,436	14,862	47,445	150,845	25,138	235,618	69,101	107,263	111,807	103,218	34,312
E. North Central	157,830	213,129	244,792	27,485	26,613	48,945	75,180	3,353	35,168	7,507	83,062	103,034	40,572	33,086	134,082	20,270
W. North Central	1,816,056	2,203,245	2,876,087	453,469	473,725	1,015,266	1,304,857	922	8,813	2,101	26,997	16,210	10,539	3,265	10,944	3,554
South Atlantic	9,322	15,581	23,611	1,942	2,196	5,946	11,056	170,134	1,324,268	220,308	2,418,158	1,402,350	3,127,479	1,900,932	2,918,615	783,952
E. South Central	2,537	5,817	25,558	524	521	2,071	4,994	356	3,205	1,080	59,712	19,349	48,457	20,596	180,539	24,213
W. South Central	11,402	57,092	313,675	2,546	4,961	27,231	153,473	504	4,331	1,616	23,496	16,099	29,421	20,437	90,056	12,335
Mountain	54,595	110,939	143,137	26,519	22,324	98,623	112,064	565	3,588	1,153	10,154	8,752	8,111	2,164	7,994	2,059
Pacific	179,188	243,993	264,754	50,167	47,847	121,722	178,480	2,171	13,643	5,386	25,585	19,361	17,786	5,635	20,322	6,485
NEW ENGLAND:																
Maine	502	305	264	80	66	142	153	59	203	145	336	116	190	112	174	202
New Hampshire	269	291	199	52	63	110	126	45	101	124	324	66	150	62	117	161
Vermont	269	311	177	71	95	145	185	16	185	75	199	80	81	53	83	126
Massachusetts	2,582	2,446	2,905	386	374	1,055	1,357	829	3,703	2,135	7,609	1,051	4,400	2,656	3,561	1,724
Rhode Island	355	255	304	63	49	124	183	126	809	370	1,642	211	553	311	372	267
Connecticut	1,068	1,176	1,491	180	217	472	646	632	2,461	978	5,270	941	3,362	2,718	4,623	1,211
MIDDLE ATLANTIC:																
New York	12,094	13,649	18,480	2,485	2,452	6,111	7,582	4,701	29,886	11,526	79,411	9,587	43,284	47,976	34,230	16,569
New Jersey	2,809	3,539	5,185	551	480	1,470	2,098	12,303	25,728	4,844	48,004	4,870	23,707	18,882	25,939	7,188
Pennsylvania	4,576	7,142	9,054	962	1,015	2,855	5,182	30,441	95,231	8,768	108,203	54,644	40,272	44,949	43,047	10,555
E. NORTH CENTRAL:																
Ohio	8,221	14,481	21,821	1,883	1,780	5,854	10,820	1,016	16,255	2,381	44,350	130,363	18,012	13,831	58,045	9,675
Indiana	5,751	13,910	21,268	2,230	1,546	4,212	10,184	336	2,474	560	9,828	7,456	5,456	1,292	6,730	1,681
Illinois	48,257	122,759	150,307	7,051	9,012	25,117	36,392	918	9,333	2,707	15,417	9,743	6,805	7,078	30,318	4,826
Michigan	27,517	24,104	41,841	6,089	4,753	7,360	12,749	918	6,048	1,553	12,110	14,306	9,089	10,500	37,184	6,545
Wisconsin	68,084	37,875	9,465	9,323	8,622	6,902	5,026	165	1,058	306	1,357	1,166	550	385	1,805	543
W. NORTH CENTRAL:																
Minnesota	1,660,026	114,051	10,446	41,736	28,730	12,095	6,130	116	1,033	323	1,428	922	524	270	669	378
Iowa	33,643	1,799,730	69,051	4,980	19,867	37,539	19,727	176	1,655	201	3,759	2,305	1,611	275	716	411
Missouri	7,413	60,706	2,569,904	1,733	3,100	21,410	107,488	263	2,764	785	11,771	4,921	4,540	1,658	6,395	1,473
North Dakota	70,848	23,102	3,496	391,685	7,051	3,546	1,492	27	194	41	527	428	193	32	71	69
South Dakota	31,928	67,514	7,079	10,647	391,393	26,874	4,445	38	278	62	697	470	241	54	156	106
Nebraska	7,572	91,757	40,832	1,704	10,987	879,132	36,270	126	1,037	174	3,309	1,656	976	212	583	464
Kansas	4,631	51,385	174,379	1,004	2,841	34,661	1,129,305	176	1,852	455	5,506	5,448	2,445	764	2,384	653
SOUTH ATLANTIC:																
Delaware	180	224	284	40	37	83	182	155,585	23,350	401	4,673	492	1,398	489	654	369
Maryland	1,183	1,567	2,224	295	267	756	1,138	10,398	1,206,654	26,614	85,102	25,997	21,015	9,703	4,713	1,697
Dist. of Columbia	1,676	2,700	3,227	206	383	934	1,630	1,075	50,796	180,864	72,004	5,869	14,202	12,367	6,274	1,674
Virginia	1,073	1,602	2,614	302	308	796	1,087	1,357	19,199	13,976	2,063,690	29,767	121,873	15,968	8,933	2,661
West Virginia	520	910	1,891	117	107	435	1,007	251	14,446	834	110,758	1,329,981	17,710	3,051	4,483	902
North Carolina	379	791	1,444	85	103	308	587	423	3,132	957	56,651	3,244	2,843,452	143,570	38,020	4,490
South Carolina	159	228	728	35	26	104	176	102	930	268	5,385	507	55,849	1,596,082	44,100	3,067
Georgia	561	1,027	2,299	93	148	429	859	207	1,635	1,012	7,651	1,344	26,645	69,695	2,590,975	28,386
Florida	3,582	6,512	8,902	670	817	2,101	4,390	736	4,126	1,382	12,094	5,149	25,275	50,058	220,403	740,706
E. SOUTH CENTRAL:																
Kentucky	709	1,500	7,922	158	175	546	1,570	94	989	340	25,092	15,254	5,613	1,816	7,678	1,309
Tennessee	792	1,967	10,316	148	222	649	1,734	143	1,043	389	28,280	2,807	32,529	7,482	57,498	2,876
Alabama	692	1,269	3,337	141	163	527	989	93	824	240	4,310	977	6,335	8,388	105,919	17,225
Mississippi	344	1,081	3,983	77	75	349	701	26	349	111	2,030	311	3,980	2,910	9,444	2,803
W. SOUTH CENTRAL:																
Arkansas	969	5,378	59,459	228	417	2,188	9,879	37	417	133	3,026	1,559	7,307	6,189	14,549	908
Louisiana	793	2,161	8,097	125	198	849	2,225	68	786	240	2,304	834	2,727	2,314	8,640	3,619
Oklahoma	4,135	31,838	175,520	986	1,987	15,517	110,497	160	951	353	6,465	7,650	6,338	2,861	16,702	1,399
Texas	5,505	17,715	70,599	1,207	2,359	8,677	30,872	239	2,177	890	11,701	6,056	12,959	9,073	50,165	6,409
MOUNTAIN:																
Montana	31,610	22,548	17,574	19,465	9,620	10,060	8,002	67	490	104	1,530	950	1,108	204	451	110
Idaho	8,505	14,972	17,937	3,159	2,786	10,704	12,492	53	284	65	1,575	1,163	1,781	162	511	85
Wyoming	2,628	13,580	12,094	1,077	3,964	21,778	7,873	35	288	73	711	707	560	119	327	133
Colorado	6,907	45,556	65,769	1,547	3,775	47,702	63,849	226	1,306	419	3,310	3,203	2,181	576	2,393	642
New Mexico	695	3,383	9,984	201	395	1,729	7,071	30	191	96	811	719	748	255	1,398	255
Arizona	2,308	5,689	13,939	545	1,057	3,024	8,477	84	531	223	1,382	1,327	972	541	2,244	651
Utah	1,162	3,596	3,750	327	413	2,620	2,899	43	247	109	608	477	548	245	472	143
Nevada	780	1,615	2,090	198	305	986	1,401	27	161	64	277	206	213	62	198	40
PACIFIC:																
Washington	67,116	51,856	43,430	20,334	13,879	23,766	30,067	264	1,806	586	5,515	4,297	5,736	693	1,879	727
Oregon	28,589	34,762	29,773	9,293	8,001	19,882	23,457	127	885	273	2,750	2,187	2,429	352	986	411
California	83,483	157,375	191,551	20,540	25,967	78,074	124,956	1,780	10,952	4,527	17,320	12,877	9,621	4,590	17,457	5,347

156

POPULATION

TABLE 21.—NATIVE POPULATION OF EACH DIVISION AND STATE, BY DIVISION AND STATE OF BIRTH: 1930—Continued

DIVISION AND STATE	POPULATION BORN IN—															
	East South Central division				West South Central division				Mountain division							
	Kentucky	Tennessee	Alabama	Mississippi	Arkansas	Louisiana	Oklahoma	Texas	Montana	Idaho	Wyoming	Colorado	New Mexico	Arizona	Utah	Nevada
United States....	3,281,020	3,055,701	3,010,218	2,402,365	2,022,417	2,178,273	1,614,238	5,080,570	345,203	304,578	128,256	670,879	358,750	233,290	521,360	58,439
GEOGRAPHIC DIVS.:																
New England...	3,557	2,339	2,322	876	820	1,495	793	2,867	1,002	316	395	2,273	213	284	461	219
Middle Atlantic.	28,244	23,002	37,075	9,108	6,046	13,705	5,749	20,266	4,307	1,473	1,628	10,087	1,309	1,290	2,791	632
E. N. Central..	516,294	199,202	113,292	89,621	62,943	42,787	27,939	46,887	13,007	3,584	4,290	24,379	3,534	2,326	4,078	844
W. N. Central..	87,625	79,831	17,584	43,884	99,894	15,422	96,537	52,749	18,808	4,856	9,776	41,620	5,404	1,769	3,465	692
South Atlantic..	81,610	106,035	185,484	22,222	10,280	13,987	6,328	20,571	1,859	954	855	4,286	838	821	1,377	262
E. S. Central....	2,358,331	2,341,793	2,450,966	1,928,505	46,246	51,745	7,386	26,440	600	361	265	1,749	656	434	302	71
W. S. Central....	99,751	228,898	175,776	284,515	1,709,425	2,004,223	1,334,915	4,657,655	2,674	1,976	2,088	17,030	21,912	5,487	1,646	455
Mountain......	27,110	22,180	9,520	7,571	30,138	6,855	55,943	106,873	235,354	219,145	91,680	463,930	298,838	173,097	441,930	34,132
Pacific.........	58,408	52,421	18,199	15,973	56,625	28,054	78,648	146,262	67,592	71,913	17,279	105,516	26,046	47,782	65,310	21,132
NEW ENGLAND:																
Maine.........	171	131	89	36	35	60	60	201	102	34	39	152	6	23	19	24
New Hampshire.	119	88	59	37	41	41	25	111	77	29	26	106	14	13	24	10
Vermont........	99	73	44	22	23	20	47	143	83	22	43	114	10	6	27	10
Massachusetts...	1,728	1,180	1,088	522	398	797	405	1,452	511	157	173	1,241	126	171	262	135
Rhode Island....	202	189	137	44	76	101	60	214	57	20	23	152	9	7	28	12
Connecticut.....	1,238	678	905	215	247	476	196	746	172	54	91	508	48	64	101	28
MIDDLE ATLANTIC:																
New York	12,333	10,268	10,580	4,389	3,017	8,976	2,664	11,710	2,246	852	821	5,481	657	688	1,643	368
New Jersey.....	3,780	3,040	6,761	1,254	912	1,913	811	3,006	650	206	208	1,610	183	231	432	120
Pennsylvania....	12,131	9,694	19,734	3,465	2,117	2,816	2,274	5,550	1,411	415	599	2,996	469	371	716	144
E. N. CENTRAL:																
Ohio..........	206,353	54,043	43,836	10,176	7,037	4,536	4,542	7,320	1,485	587	699	4,076	620	472	652	164
Indiana........	160,113	33,216	8,706	8,736	6,822	2,654	3,725	4,823	1,092	341	427	2,321	409	261	322	71
Illinois........	106,161	66,308	33,573	50,201	30,334	28,441	12,055	21,968	4,369	1,203	1,720	10,728	1,492	774	1,986	344
Michigan.......	48,586	43,336	26,045	12,852	17,396	6,226	6,399	10,737	3,273	872	968	5,076	785	626	811	205
Wisconsin......	5,081	2,299	1,132	1,656	1,354	930	1,218	2,030	2,788	521	476	2,178	228	193	307	60
W. N. CENTRAL:																
Minnesota......	3,136	1,477	693	633	1,081	623	1,412	2,798	5,575	625	581	1,983	191	154	445	81
Iowa..........	7,096	4,560	1,094	1,292	2,986	820	4,671	3,243	2,146	693	1,147	4,500	392	179	556	126
Missouri.......	52,405	57,703	11,383	36,907	70,492	9,999	29,868	23,350	1,094	1,008	1,284	9,260	1,480	603	1,006	175
North Dakota...	600	269	79	53	225	83	344	685	3,841	284	173	375	33	32	64	22
South Dakota...	1,157	723	155	143	583	106	948	886	2,281	305	1,603	1,722	361	70	195	50
Nebraska.......	4,278	2,669	1,267	977	2,967	886	4,768	4,387	1,667	883	3,892	11,091	570	164	672	89
Kansas........	18,953	12,430	2,913	3,819	21,560	2,905	54,526	17,391	1,304	1,058	1,096	12,674	2,368	507	527	149
SOUTH ATLANTIC:																
Delaware.......	220	217	272	101	44	141	65	201	35	19	17	74	13	13	17	3
Maryland.......	2,440	2,588	1,633	880	584	1,026	472	1,549	244	108	82	589	108	85	184	36
Dist. Columbia..	3,342	3,391	2,496	1,711	799	1,184	562	2,385	334	195	156	595	124	132	530	64
Virginia.......	12,015	19,968	4,502	1,412	989	1,112	630	2,207	255	131	100	531	92	102	125	27
West Virginia...	38,215	10,030	12,076	1,147	680	464	830	970	179	71	109	436	98	83	99	24
North Carolina..	3,526	17,408	5,966	2,114	1,092	858	548	1,853	145	120	69	326	74	60	63	6
South Carolina..	1,121	6,519	3,722	1,082	561	552	219	952	51	28	15	102	17	20	18	5
Georgia........	5,428	26,551	79,630	5,093	1,971	3,091	1,000	4,758	113	55	70	423	75	113	104	27
Florida........	15,303	19,308	75,187	8,082	3,560	5,559	2,002	5,696	503	227	237	1,210	242	213	237	70
E. S. CENTRAL:																
Kentucky.......	2,295,545	83,777	12,987	4,348	2,926	1,525	1,466	3,021	209	108	106	536	177	129	102	20
Tennessee......	49,896	2,176,591	49,875	88,325	22,854	5,645	2,603	8,238	236	157	66	636	234	110	89	35
Alabama........	7,742	55,084	2,318,600	44,307	4,476	6,437	1,788	8,100	108	48	47	379	135	109	69	9
Mississippi.....	5,148	26,341	69,504	1,791,615	15,990	38,138	1,529	7,081	47	48	46	198	110	86	42	7
W. S. CENTRAL:																
Arkansas.......	18,787	65,084	29,392	93,252	1,346,707	47,083	28,048	37,957	231	222	192	1,315	666	273	81	38
Louisiana......	4,801	8,289	20,980	87,708	34,219	1,792,065	3,400	43,662	147	66	62	513	232	158	77	21
Oklahoma......	34,700	53,036	30,898	24,877	212,107	14,231	1,177,814	258,459	1,110	904	795	7,430	4,827	1,001	528	145
Texas.........	41,463	102,489	94,506	78,678	116,392	150,844	125,647	4,317,577	1,186	784	1,039	7,772	16,187	4,055	960	251
MOUNTAIN:																
Montana.......	2,865	1,677	297	243	1,205	194	2,377	2,264	218,483	5,803	3,639	4,316	451	307	3,615	671
Idaho.........	2,270	2,863	349	208	3,112	235	3,812	2,233	7,407	190,940	3,832	6,319	462	505	36,013	1,023
Wyoming.......	1,494	948	402	257	1,152	266	2,387	2,751	3,562	2,390	71,622	10,258	2,373	258	5,976	161
Colorado.......	10,681	7,068	2,607	2,072	8,330	1,792	18,201	16,525	2,194	1,704	6,108	419,663	27,590	1,185	4,521	398
New Mexico....	3,235	4,158	2,475	2,003	7,073	1,412	13,847	48,022	275	247	392	7,611	252,962	3,309	598	78
Arizona........	4,875	4,194	2,774	2,242	8,240	2,561	18,955	32,348	1,097	1,283	646	6,703	13,006	165,803	4,406	636
Utah..........	1,142	897	430	346	611	232	822	1,482	1,684	15,057	4,908	2,935	1,551	1,723	378,778	1,889
Nevada........	548	375	186	140	355	163	542	1,248	652	1,721	533	2,174	377	507	8,023	29,276
PACIFIC:																
Washington.....	9,108	7,603	1,632	1,291	6,726	1,674	7,867	8,184	28,706	26,313	3,863	12,619	1,002	1,013	5,106	1,158
Oregon........	5,264	5,513	949	870	5,196	1,114	7,173	7,130	10,575	18,466	2,813	10,284	928	1,046	5,447	1,334
California......	44,126	39,305	15,618	13,812	44,703	25,266	63,608	130,948	28,311	27,134	10,603	82,663	24,116	45,723	54,757	18,640

STATE OF BIRTH — 157

TABLE 21.—NATIVE POPULATION OF EACH DIVISION AND STATE, BY DIVISION AND STATE OF BIRTH: 1930—Continued

DIVISION AND STATE	Pacific division — Washington	Oregon	California	United States, State not reported	Outlying possessions — Total	Alaska	American Samoa	Guam	Hawaii	Panama Canal Zone	Philippine Islands	Puerto Rico	Virgin Islands of the U.S.	American citizens born at sea	American citizens born abroad
United States	742,179	530,417	2,111,579	238,469	136,032	6,652	237	334	19,467	2,834	47,699	52,774	6,045	819	129,858
GEOGRAPHIC DIVISIONS:															
New England	1,518	815	6,151	8,342	1,765	69	4	4	343	159	520	477	160	156	17,051
Middle Atlantic	6,382	3,178	22,172	66,953	58,048	282	6	28	805	960	3,597	47,528	5,442	154	21,787
East North Central	12,166	6,080	22,240	42,817	5,477	307	9	15	579	369	3,349	737	112	104	24,902
West North Central	10,564	6,350	15,069	26,077	1,863	192	4	9	261	155	1,082	147	13	40	11,550
South Atlantic	2,962	1,453	6,925	19,416	3,660	133	10	87	440	431	1,411	1,012	145	60	5,038
East South Central	881	566	2,507	12,141	506	29	39	1	87	91	128	116	15	16	1,309
West South Central	3,750	2,960	14,042	23,890	1,040	97	68	8	265	157	799	515	40	44	6,010
Mountain	28,691	18,956	37,840	6,630	2,651	209	19	9	394	65	1,470	380	15	56	9,747
Pacific	675,265	490,059	1,984,033	32,203	59,504	5,244	78	173	16,283	447	35,334	1,862	83	189	31,764
NEW ENGLAND:															
Maine	128	97	495	608	78	9	-----	-----	14	11	24	14	6	35	3,228
New Hampshire	95	34	293	413	30	3	-----	-----	9	3	4	11	-----	7	1,845
Vermont	71	49	186	260	50	5	-----	-----	13	5	12	11	4	2	1,677
Massachusetts	704	430	3,032	4,807	967	36	4	2	223	103	255	263	81	88	7,812
Rhode Island	123	46	414	603	99	5	-----	2	16	11	34	20	11	6	1,230
Connecticut	307	159	1,131	1,561	541	11	-----	-----	68	26	200	158	78	18	1,859
MIDDLE ATLANTIC:															
New York	3,664	1,944	14,329	48,122	55,055	167	3	10	556	684	2,505	45,973	5,148	96	14,520
New Jersey	1,070	497	3,705	9,949	1,811	38	2	6	113	144	404	947	157	24	3,853
Pennsylvania	1,648	737	4,138	8,882	1,782	77	1	3	136	132	688	608	137	34	3,914
EAST NORTH CENTRAL:															
Ohio	1,852	1,076	4,271	10,734	724	52	2	6	117	100	217	188	42	25	3,881
Indiana	910	577	1,967	5,475	306	26	2	2	58	36	124	48	10	9	1,600
Illinois	4,344	2,097	9,337	14,595	2,819	103	3	2	222	116	2,085	252	36	40	5,324
Michigan	3,316	1,607	5,051	8,165	1,430	95	2	4	149	96	832	230	22	25	12,083
Wisconsin	1,744	723	1,614	3,848	198	31	-----	1	33	21	91	19	2	5	2,104
WEST NORTH CENTRAL:															
Minnesota	2,976	1,124	1,923	2,667	401	53	1	-----	81	32	209	13	2	9	4,010
Iowa	1,431	984	2,051	4,493	172	28	-----	-----	21	32	73	17	1	6	1,709
Missouri	1,975	1,198	5,041	9,530	657	86	3	2	85	48	409	69	5	13	1,492
North Dakota	848	453	474	738	70	14	-----	-----	14	-----	36	6	-----	-----	1,492
South Dakota	662	400	645	1,099	47	12	-----	-----	11	4	18	2	-----	1	794
Nebraska	1,127	976	1,767	2,560	184	23	-----	1	46	14	91	7	2	6	945
Kansas	1,545	1,215	3,168	4,090	332	26	-----	6	53	25	180	33	3	5	1,118
SOUTH ATLANTIC:															
Delaware	76	43	182	117	89	1	-----	-----	10	6	19	50	3	1	91
Maryland	521	244	1,227	4,522	932	28	-----	6	103	81	410	250	45	11	795
District of Columbia	453	246	1,285	2,911	875	43	3	10	86	81	447	185	20	18	676
Virginia	519	217	1,044	1,518	644	19	1	9	97	95	244	143	36	7	714
West Virginia	242	120	418	1,305	73	4	2	8	6	13	14	23	3	1	304
North Carolina	304	114	414	2,064	145	12	1	20	20	24	30	32	6	2	366
South Carolina	72	38	176	802	125	-----	1	22	22	13	36	25	6	3	202
Georgia	188	92	680	2,525	269	4	2	6	57	38	109	52	3	1	362
Florida	587	339	1,499	3,652	517	22	2	6	39	80	93	252	23	21	1,528
EAST SOUTH CENTRAL:															
Kentucky	275	188	673	2,131	126	8	16	-----	25	22	25	30	-----	5	413
Tennessee	341	216	949	5,231	133	12	17	1	29	10	37	24	8	5	402
Alabama	159	118	503	2,309	170	6	5	-----	24	44	46	40	5	3	270
Mississippi	106	49	382	2,470	77	3	1	-----	9	15	20	22	7	3	224
WEST SOUTH CENTRAL:															
Arkansas	394	283	1,038	4,402	59	11	3	-----	15	7	17	6	-----	3	253
Louisiana	202	163	1,108	1,860	627	16	15	1	37	57	306	169	26	6	690
Oklahoma	1,512	1,189	4,138	7,244	198	19	13	1	62	18	68	16	1	7	1,041
Texas	1,582	1,325	8,358	10,384	1,065	51	37	6	151	75	408	324	13	28	4,026
MOUNTAIN:															
Montana	6,934	2,648	2,403	1,058	409	61	1	-----	17	7	307	15	1	5	2,266
Idaho	15,822	10,117	3,312	831	226	72	-----	3	33	5	104	9	-----	3	1,796
Wyoming	756	614	953	434	115	9	1	-----	28	5	53	19	-----	3	270
Colorado	1,847	1,511	4,435	2,106	435	44	1	1	53	23	278	27	8	20	1,028
New Mexico	311	294	2,027	575	57	3	-----	-----	15	3	24	12	-----	6	589
Arizona	1,470	1,526	13,222	808	941	54	2	5	80	15	488	292	5	10	2,068
Utah	866	1,123	3,187	468	330	16	11	-----	126	7	166	3	1	9	1,534
Nevada	685	1,123	8,296	260	138	40	3	-----	42	-----	50	3	-----	-----	196
PACIFIC:															
Washington	566,360	51,624	23,257	5,314	7,271	2,992	4	7	590	35	3,593	46	4	38	11,046
Oregon	47,020	379,795	24,909	3,663	1,918	581	-----	-----	189	23	1,101	21	3	18	3,972
California	61,885	58,640	1,935,867	23,226	50,315	1,671	74	166	15,504	389	30,640	1,795	76	133	16,746

158

POPULATION

TABLE 22.—NATIVE WHITE POPULATION OF EACH DIVISION AND STATE, BY DIVISION AND STATE OF BIRTH: 1930

DIVISION AND STATE	Total native white population	United States	WHITE POPULATION BORN IN—									United States, State not reported	Other native white population [1]
			Geographic divisions										
			New England	Middle Atlantic	East North Central	West North Central	South Atlantic	East South Central	West South Central	Mountain	Pacific		
United States	95,497,800	95,301,158	6,535,693	20,610,693	21,523,034	13,113,754	11,319,720	8,531,783	8,039,544	2,317,079	3,107,935	201,923	196,642
GEOGRAPHIC DIVISIONS:													
New England	6,230,803	6,211,982	5,752,888	321,693	53,302	21,386	29,326	7,315	5,401	5,090	7,610	7,971	18,821
Middle Atlantic	19,903,062	19,841,939	392,102	18,427,461	362,359	106,542	353,731	52,209	34,716	22,734	28,567	61,518	61,123
East North Central	21,053,730	21,027,590	114,311	834,310	18,167,867	760,889	322,548	596,959	101,431	53,880	38,267	37,137	26,140
West North Central	11,814,210	11,801,789	36,849	179,234	1,102,154	9,918,618	72,008	153,991	202,164	82,608	31,062	23,101	12,421
South Atlantic	11,045,006	11,037,713	65,025	314,394	229,045	68,103	9,955,907	326,357	44,638	10,884	10,568	12,192	7,293
East South Central	7,166,949	7,165,334	6,084	27,532	151,942	39,461	271,607	6,563,867	90,120	4,219	3,048	6,854	1,615
West South Central	8,929,749	8,923,824	12,825	69,240	278,633	558,788	166,797	635,683	7,117,591	47,331	19,584	17,346	5,925
Mountain	3,015,672	3,005,549	19,829	78,751	275,415	562,360	42,006	61,895	170,510	1,699,814	80,061	5,818	10,123
Pacific	6,338,610	6,285,429	135,780	358,072	901,717	1,077,607	105,700	133,507	263,973	390,519	2,888,568	29,986	53,181
NEW ENGLAND:													
Maine	694,815	691,494	675,616	7,620	2,770	1,514	1,524	420	347	397	691	595	3,321
New Hampshire	381,690	379,813	363,939	9,676	2,421	1,106	1,084	272	208	208	406	403	1,877
Vermont	315,904	314,188	287,764	20,644	2,414	1,249	805	214	230	313	296	259	1,716
Massachusetts	3,138,290	3,129,827	2,934,661	123,168	28,527	11,031	14,407	3,649	2,733	2,731	4,193	4,727	8,463
Rhode Island	506,302	505,010	476,457	19,088	3,405	1,331	2,408	507	427	305	532	550	1,292
Connecticut	1,193,802	1,191,650	1,014,451	141,497	13,765	5,155	9,098	2,253	1,456	1,046	1,492	1,437	2,152
MIDDLE ATLANTIC:													
New York	8,958,744	8,906,901	270,605	8,187,737	170,595	61,179	95,006	25,655	20,406	12,391	18,189	45,138	51,843
New Jersey	2,984,767	2,980,191	77,021	2,751,941	47,817	15,693	57,575	7,880	5,413	3,514	4,628	8,709	4,576
Pennsylvania	7,959,551	7,954,847	44,476	7,487,783	143,947	29,670	201,150	18,674	8,897	6,829	5,750	7,671	4,704
EAST NORTH CENTRAL:													
Ohio	5,686,985	5,682,744	25,984	308,107	4,764,252	61,352	197,649	225,994	15,237	8,442	6,715	8,952	4,241
Indiana	2,981,002	2,979,244	6,284	46,275	2,669,182	56,702	28,012	148,080	11,791	5,016	3,322	4,580	1,758
Illinois	6,048,203	6,042,289	34,374	168,225	5,183,801	380,127	46,534	134,254	45,739	21,622	14,750	12,863	5,914
Michigan	3,809,903	3,797,898	38,654	215,674	3,244,735	118,978	44,885	81,574	24,736	12,141	9,495	7,026	12,005
Wisconsin	2,527,646	2,525,424	9,015	35,969	2,305,897	143,730	5,468	7,057	3,928	6,659	3,985	3,716	2,222
WEST NORTH CENTRAL:													
Minnesota	2,150,679	2,146,541	11,575	31,604	215,016	1,857,399	4,926	4,384	3,010	9,473	5,833	2,421	4,138
Iowa	2,282,647	2,280,806	6,070	35,755	217,589	1,971,445	9,978	11,733	9,886	9,600	4,411	4,339	1,841
Missouri	3,249,497	3,247,742	7,586	40,047	286,590	2,657,074	28,496	99,308	96,230	16,356	7,909	8,146	1,755
North Dakota	566,095	564,576	1,503	5,031	43,681	502,843	1,551	952	1,066	4,618	1,741	690	1,519
South Dakota	603,805	602,974	1,877	8,343	58,627	519,351	2,057	2,097	2,400	5,627	1,662	933	831
Nebraska	1,238,356	1,237,313	4,008	23,621	104,794	1,056,630	7,736	6,918	9,346	18,160	3,754	2,286	1,043
Kansas	1,723,131	1,721,837	4,170	33,933	175,857	1,353,876	17,264	28,599	79,326	18,774	5,752	4,286	1,294
SOUTH ATLANTIC:													
Delaware	188,809	188,645	1,796	25,203	2,292	1,000	156,862	568	363	184	285	92	164
Maryland	1,259,077	1,257,804	9,634	81,280	19,167	7,245	1,124,885	6,243	3,086	1,378	1,848	3,038	1,273
Dist. of Columbia	323,982	322,798	12,048	39,295	19,910	10,488	222,992	8,426	3,886	2,048	1,847	1,858	1,184
Virginia	1,746,585	1,745,428	7,101	32,600	18,517	7,638	1,637,018	34,134	4,443	1,315	1,651	1,011	1,157
West Virginia	1,562,414	1,562,065	1,925	49,936	60,144	4,676	1,389,336	44,850	2,328	1,035	725	1,110	349
North Carolina	2,226,160	2,225,687	3,822	11,434	8,646	3,602	2,164,838	26,496	3,957	844	785	1,263	473
South Carolina	938,774	938,484	1,693	3,974	2,781	1,407	913,844	11,650	2,120	246	263	506	290
Georgia	1,823,057	1,822,500	3,446	10,754	12,520	5,258	1,681,109	96,435	9,774	939	837	1,428	557
Florida	976,148	974,302	23,560	59,918	79,668	26,780	665,023	97,555	14,681	2,895	2,327	1,886	1,846
EAST SOUTH CENTRAL:													
Kentucky	2,366,524	2,366,008	1,811	9,413	95,854	11,930	50,021	2,185,471	7,532	1,339	1,080	1,557	516
Tennessee	2,125,553	2,125,064	2,026	8,550	28,811	14,854	101,422	1,934,680	28,602	1,501	1,425	3,193	489
Alabama	1,685,065	1,684,698	1,708	7,239	17,308	6,789	107,123	1,523,741	18,049	840	704	1,197	367
Mississippi	989,807	989,564	539	2,330	9,969	5,888	13,041	919,975	35,937	539	439	907	243
WEST SOUTH CENTRAL:													
Arkansas	1,364,733	1,364,444	808	4,940	48,148	76,249	20,946	122,707	1,083,417	2,015	1,612	2,522	289
Louisiana	1,283,250	1,282,363	1,911	7,780	16,727	13,880	15,826	83,861	1,138,719	1,194	1,382	1,083	887
Oklahoma	2,096,671	2,095,537	2,571	23,323	116,837	333,992	38,331	127,173	1,425,088	16,024	6,510	5,688	1,134
Texas	4,185,095	4,181,480	7,445	33,203	96,021	134,667	91,694	301,852	3,470,367	27,198	10,080	8,053	3,615
MOUNTAIN:													
Montana	444,366	441,997	3,660	12,058	57,685	117,931	4,892	4,894	5,746	222,799	11,521	811	2,369
Idaho	407,108	405,212	1,774	6,938	33,998	70,396	5,620	5,663	9,169	241,973	28,858	823	1,896
Wyoming	194,409	194,084	1,255	5,828	19,608	62,483	2,845	2,893	5,931	90,544	2,221	416	325
Colorado	875,711	874,523	7,334	32,426	104,108	232,289	13,511	20,363	40,255	414,814	7,457	1,966	1,188
New Mexico	323,958	323,457	869	3,991	14,767	23,170	4,346	11,518	64,520	197,523	2,285	468	501
Arizona	248,787	246,850	2,720	9,923	29,145	34,244	6,907	12,716	48,976	88,109	13,401	709	1,937
Utah	452,183	450,548	1,200	4,529	10,356	14,578	2,799	2,665	2,803	406,289	4,939	390	1,635
Nevada	69,150	68,878	1,017	3,058	5,688	7,269	1,176	1,183	2,110	37,763	9,379	235	272
PACIFIC:													
Washington	1,276,843	1,262,292	17,486	46,680	182,418	249,390	20,701	18,702	23,419	79,079	619,403	5,014	14,551
Oregon	831,554	826,813	8,073	24,489	101,042	153,332	10,163	12,316	19,937	50,483	443,629	3,349	4,741
California	4,230,213	4,196,324	110,221	286,903	618,257	674,885	74,836	102,489	220,617	260,957	1,825,536	21,623	33,889

[1] Includes persons born in outlying possessions and American citizens born abroad or at sea.

STATE OF BIRTH

159

TABLE 22.—NATIVE WHITE POPULATION OF EACH DIVISION AND STATE, BY DIVISION AND STATE OF BIRTH: 1930—Continued

DIVISION AND STATE	New England division						Middle Atlantic division			East North Central division				
	Maine	New Hampshire	Vermont	Massachusetts	Rhode Island	Connecticut	New York	New Jersey	Pennsylvania	Ohio	Indiana	Illinois	Michigan	Wisconsin
United States	852,559	426,705	414,444	3,204,213	502,665	1,135,107	9,211,743	2,460,998	8,937,952	5,673,573	3,266,074	6,371,387	3,361,626	2,848,369
GEOGRAPHIC DIVISIONS:														
New England	763,475	385,775	339,027	2,843,307	452,257	969,047	235,595	35,671	50,427	15,406	5,245	15,181	11,386	6,084
Middle Atlantic	29,894	16,138	36,574	176,907	26,908	105,591	8,265,374	2,306,555	7,855,532	101,644	36,010	84,511	53,760	26,119
East North Central	12,152	6,655	11,160	56,988	6,782	20,565	285,056	38,033	511,221	4,921,258	2,763,686	5,111,520	3,011,384	2,360,019
West North Central	6,633	2,721	6,335	14,443	1,637	5,080	79,667	9,448	90,119	133,916	142,548	537,140	63,984	224,566
South Atlantic	8,280	4,408	5,006	30,622	4,726	11,884	93,020	29,071	192,303	113,242	34,847	44,822	23,995	12,739
East South Central	747	385	480	2,970	419	1,083	11,318	2,172	14,042	60,718	46,178	32,176	8,455	4,415
West South Central	1,873	811	1,258	6,012	835	2,036	27,684	4,456	37,106	51,916	64,893	130,041	17,029	14,754
Mountain	4,182	1,341	2,549	8,222	907	2,628	33,934	5,327	39,490	47,002	44,349	106,450	32,307	45,217
Pacific	25,314	8,381	12,046	64,652	8,194	17,193	180,095	30,265	147,712	168,476	130,000	309,546	139,230	154,456
NEW ENGLAND:														
Maine	628,614	13,152	3,300	26,719	1,663	2,168	4,881	987	1,752	580	311	673	740	457
New Hampshire	18,560	277,763	21,023	41,620	1,709	2,295	7,600	783	1,287	588	190	627	650	357
Vermont	3,266	12,215	254,898	14,105	1,003	2,277	18,777	724	1,143	548	224	705	582	355
Massachusetts	93,655	70,741	44,893	2,695,316	43,474	46,582	88,017	13,025	22,120	8,161	2,850	8,473	5,043	3,100
Rhode Island	5,724	4,576	3,058	57,878	390,680	14,541	12,420	2,878	3,781	1,000	301	857	829	412
Connecticut	13,656	7,328	10,955	67,600	13,608	901,184	103,885	17,274	20,338	4,514	1,360	3,846	2,642	1,403
MIDDLE ATLANTIC:														
New York	19,189	10,823	29,719	120,337	17,262	73,275	7,717,141	157,208	313,298	57,006	16,710	46,823	33,703	10,194
New Jersey	6,297	3,314	4,104	35,171	6,050	22,085	412,383	2,062,040	277,518	16,334	5,464	15,045	7,033	3,941
Pennsylvania	4,408	2,001	2,751	21,489	3,596	10,231	135,850	87,217	7,264,716	88,214	14,136	22,643	12,970	5,984
EAST NORTH CENTRAL:														
Ohio	2,345	1,421	2,115	13,118	1,655	5,330	73,272	11,179	283,710	4,519,317	111,400	56,741	63,641	13,153
Indiana	666	403	595	3,002	388	1,230	13,303	2,642	30,330	120,070	2,362,479	140,602	34,708	11,143
Illinois	3,250	1,869	3,309	18,237	1,935	5,765	78,255	12,006	77,874	94,663	167,901	4,718,049	73,581	128,657
Michigan	4,303	2,350	3,836	18,021	2,373	6,862	99,802	10,098	105,774	173,144	107,420	116,824	2,793,520	53,821
Wisconsin	1,579	603	1,314	3,710	431	1,378	20,424	2,018	13,527	14,064	14,480	78,214	45,894	2,153,245
WEST NORTH CENTRAL:														
Minnesota	3,105	857	1,742	4,212	441	1,218	18,630	1,703	11,262	11,450	10,405	52,702	25,529	114,930
Iowa	794	533	1,411	2,140	288	904	15,051	1,692	19,012	26,633	23,551	126,208	7,678	33,510
Missouri	807	407	786	3,792	393	1,251	17,781	2,704	19,562	36,390	43,594	185,614	10,101	10,891
North Dakota	343	107	288	539	74	152	3,036	256	2,639	2,940	4,541	11,754	3,751	20,695
South Dakota	363	164	433	622	72	233	4,317	393	3,633	4,168	4,631	23,426	4,130	22,272
Nebraska	554	321	844	1,483	172	694	10,047	1,280	12,204	15,345	14,955	55,376	5,664	13,454
Kansas	577	282	831	1,655	197	628	10,796	1,420	21,717	36,990	40,871	82,060	7,131	8,805
SOUTH ATLANTIC:														
Delaware	198	97	147	841	150	363	3,434	3,585	18,184	942	289	495	361	205
Maryland	1,083	480	562	4,908	773	1,819	16,931	6,398	57,951	8,130	2,669	4,653	2,223	1,492
District of Columbia	1,503	781	907	5,885	1,038	1,934	15,929	3,857	19,509	6,778	3,480	5,426	2,351	1,880
Virginia	940	433	387	3,460	504	1,207	11,307	3,551	17,742	7,546	2,989	3,926	2,466	1,590
West Virginia	263	131	150	832	133	416	4,110	1,380	44,446	56,501	4,164	3,154	1,682	643
North Carolina	442	348	320	1,771	905	627	4,865	1,317	5,252	3,026	1,845	2,077	1,135	563
South Carolina	178	100	112	865	178	254	1,923	464	1,587	886	547	699	429	220
Georgia	380	200	291	1,691	254	630	5,564	1,207	3,083	4,303	2,616	3,228	1,617	756
Florida	3,302	1,918	2,121	10,379	1,301	4,544	28,957	7,312	28,649	25,135	16,248	21,164	11,731	5,300
EAST SOUTH CENTRAL:														
Kentucky	213	95	143	975	108	277	3,368	646	5,399	45,528	33,196	13,455	2,545	1,130
Tennessee	248	141	161	931	167	378	3,749	729	4,072	8,183	7,143	9,202	3,058	1,275
Alabama	199	108	128	811	115	347	3,056	611	3,572	5,264	3,524	5,310	1,953	1,257
Mississippi	87	41	48	253	29	81	1,145	186	999	1,793	2,315	4,209	899	753
WEST SOUTH CENTRAL:														
Arkansas	135	55	124	392	57	135	2,004	275	2,661	6,023	11,668	26,476	2,354	1,627
Louisiana	298	96	117	961	140	299	4,178	646	2,956	3,581	3,449	6,569	1,835	1,293
Oklahoma	422	162	364	1,072	152	399	6,767	970	15,586	22,998	29,371	54,481	4,973	5,014
Texas	1,018	498	653	3,587	486	1,203	14,735	2,565	15,903	19,314	20,405	42,515	7,867	6,820
MOUNTAIN:														
Montana	1,088	230	504	1,370	139	320	5,120	700	6,229	6,365	6,961	16,614	9,298	18,447
Idaho	545	133	261	594	64	177	2,843	320	3,775	4,858	4,629	11,932	4,668	7,911
Wyoming	225	101	208	517	48	156	2,153	369	3,306	3,207	3,281	8,552	1,811	2,817
Colorado	1,209	493	1,008	3,058	350	1,126	14,178	2,237	16,011	20,412	18,001	46,699	8,859	10,137
New Mexico	123	60	93	388	41	164	1,595	270	2,117	2,879	3,073	6,207	1,465	1,143
Arizona	452	183	244	1,298	136	407	4,388	883	4,652	6,200	5,950	10,354	3,919	2,722
Utah	188	82	145	554	73	158	2,047	301	2,181	2,027	1,612	4,047	1,406	1,264
Nevada	262	59	86	434	56	120	1,601	238	1,219	1,054	842	2,045	971	776
PACIFIC:														
Washington	5,310	1,205	1,774	6,863	621	1,713	22,249	2,754	21,677	24,118	20,787	49,673	36,204	51,636
Oregon	2,189	569	991	3,132	307	885	11,293	1,444	11,752	15,087	13,578	30,459	17,267	24,051
California	17,815	6,607	9,281	54,657	7,266	14,595	146,553	26,067	114,283	129,271	95,644	229,414	85,759	78,169

POPULATION

TABLE 22.—NATIVE WHITE POPULATION OF EACH DIVISION AND STATE, BY DIVISION AND STATE OF BIRTH: 1930—Continued

| | WHITE POPULATION BORN IN— | | | | | | | | | | | | | | | |
| DIVISION AND STATE | West North Central division | | | | | | | South Atlantic division | | | | | | | | |
	Minnesota	Iowa	Missouri	North Dakota	South Dakota	Nebraska	Kansas	Delaware	Maryland	District of Columbia	Virginia	West Virginia	North Carolina	South Carolina	Georgia	Florida
United States	2,239,469	2,868,966	3,786,940	558,477	561,836	1,319,947	1,796,119	194,933	1,276,300	201,887	1,988,505	1,651,656	2,353,460	1,007,270	2,070,352	575,357
GEOGRAPHIC DIVISIONS:																
New England	5,022	4,767	5,266	834	847	2,034	2,616	1,574	6,278	2,932	6,114	2,310	2,849	1,639	2,944	2,686
Middle Atlantic	19,332	24,029	30,788	3,938	3,908	10,262	14,285	38,187	107,753	15,667	63,834	63,404	22,942	11,600	18,524	11,820
East North Central	156,726	210,063	222,301	27,405	26,490	47,912	60,992	3,145	32,566	5,992	60,533	156,909	22,464	5,980	23,644	11,315
West North Central	1,802,122	2,198,131	2,752,996	445,185	453,162	1,005,854	1,261,168	901	8,445	1,832	24,610	15,906	9,054	1,813	6,674	2,773
South Atlantic	9,238	15,404	22,753	1,919	2,177	5,843	10,769	147,611	1,097,549	166,869	1,725,568	1,350,874	2,209,096	953,212	1,795,734	509,394
East South Central	2,477	5,665	23,479	507	620	1,989	4,724	332	2,916	932	53,716	18,546	40,303	12,840	123,078	18,944
West South Central	11,228	56,700	307,482	2,499	4,888	26,686	149,305	491	4,027	1,498	20,602	15,891	22,378	13,803	77,423	10,684
Mountain	54,424	110,701	141,063	26,080	21,900	98,132	109,970	559	3,467	1,058	9,545	8,656	7,784	1,884	7,225	1,918
Pacific	178,900	243,506	280,812	50,110	47,754	121,235	175,290	2,133	13,299	5,107	23,983	19,160	16,590	4,499	15,106	5,823
NEW ENGLAND:																
Maine	502	304	261	86	66	142	153	56	281	142	295	116	171	99	165	199
New Hampshire	269	291	199	52	62	109	124	44	179	114	256	66	124	46	103	152
Vermont	268	311	175	71	95	144	186	15	175	71	150	77	71	43	78	125
Massachusetts	2,567	2,436	2,883	385	370	1,048	1,342	748	3,093	1,631	2,094	977	1,365	703	1,529	1,277
Rhode Island	355	255	304	63	48	124	182	119	506	258	499	107	284	135	204	206
Connecticut	1,061	1,170	1,444	177	206	467	630	592	2,044	716	1,920	877	834	523	865	727
MIDDLE ATLANTIC:																
New York	12,007	13,508	17,464	2,447	2,429	6,027	7,297	3,851	21,750	7,582	20,467	8,539	9,311	6,094	10,452	6,960
New Jersey	2,782	3,504	4,942	540	475	1,455	1,995	9,765	16,252	3,099	11,354	4,256	4,690	2,425	3,559	2,175
Pennsylvania	4,543	7,017	8,382	951	1,004	2,780	4,993	24,571	69,751	4,986	32,013	50,609	8,941	3,081	4,513	2,685
EAST NORTH CENTRAL:																
Ohio	8,120	14,265	19,832	1,867	1,746	5,248	10,274	944	15,070	1,816	30,430	125,970	8,661	1,998	9,190	3,570
Indiana	5,076	13,696	19,761	2,237	1,537	4,132	9,063	321	2,373	490	8,853	7,273	4,343	622	2,380	1,357
Illinois	47,848	120,905	135,349	7,922	9,870	24,592	33,641	863	8,638	2,181	11,689	9,175	4,097	1,544	5,414	2,933
Michigan	27,369	23,665	38,370	6,070	4,725	7,154	11,616	854	5,459	1,216	8,394	13,353	4,923	1,576	6,125	2,985
Wisconsin	67,713	37,532	8,090	9,309	8,612	6,786	4,798	163	1,026	289	1,167	1,138	440	240	535	470
WEST NORTH CENTRAL:																
Minnesota	1,646,808	113,508	9,305	41,640	28,575	11,894	5,609	115	994	293	1,227	887	459	199	413	339
Iowa	33,542	1,791,435	65,514	4,970	19,824	37,160	19,000	175	1,620	247	3,119	2,315	1,463	186	493	360
Missouri	7,326	60,152	2,481,546	1,726	3,072	21,159	102,093	254	2,609	708	10,792	4,801	3,698	866	3,635	1,133
North Dakota	70,711	23,082	3,452	384,016	16,578	3,530	1,474	27	193	38	521	425	102	25	62	68
South Dakota	31,717	67,427	7,866	10,145	371,588	26,228	4,380	37	274	62	687	467	235	54	136	105
Nebraska	7,441	91,352	30,034	1,693	10,726	871,572	34,812	123	1,014	155	3,178	1,636	899	144	380	207
Kansas	4,577	51,115	166,279	995	2,799	34,311	1,093,800	170	1,741	329	5,086	5,375	2,108	339	1,555	561
SOUTH ATLANTIC:																
Delaware	180	221	262	40	37	82	178	134,264	18,010	288	2,521	454	778	160	224	163
Maryland	1,175	1,541	2,114	204	263	746	1,112	9,492	1,005,259	23,037	48,072	25,040	8,396	2,110	2,465	1,014
Dist. of Columbia	1,647	2,672	3,042	200	378	903	1,556	982	34,444	128,226	41,849	5,117	6,235	2,201	2,800	1,048
Virginia	1,070	1,585	2,545	209	304	789	1,046	1,262	16,885	11,626	1,486,280	27,709	77,495	7,245	6,453	2,063
West Virginia	522	840	1,723	112	105	421	944	235	13,897	610	79,355	1,283,079	9,404	610	1,578	568
North Carolina	363	784	1,393	84	103	303	567	392	2,820	717	47,033	2,818	2,019,223	63,767	24,674	3,394
South Carolina	151	227	694	35	26	102	172	94	843	217	4,766	476	48,791	819,156	37,227	2,274
Georgia	550	1,021	2,196	93	146	410	836	183	1,504	860	5,969	1,204	21,436	36,999	1,594,489	18,465
Florida	3,575	6,504	9,784	672	815	2,081	4,358	707	3,887	1,288	9,723	4,977	17,388	20,964	125,734	480,405
EAST SOUTH CENTRAL:																
Kentucky	698	1,452	7,443	151	169	524	1,493	93	921	301	23,126	14,796	4,608	900	4,288	988
Tennessee	769	1,925	9,517	146	220	632	1,645	133	962	334	26,204	2,666	29,023	4,079	35,612	2,319
Alabama	631	1,246	3,125	139	160	499	939	83	729	202	3,186	811	4,890	6,128	77,540	13,554
Mississippi	329	1,042	3,394	71	71	334	647	23	304	95	1,110	273	1,782	1,733	5,638	2,083
WEST SOUTH CENTRAL:																
Arkansas	949	5,321	57,500	221	415	2,155	9,688	32	366	107	2,322	1,521	4,060	2,261	9,559	718
Louisiana	777	2,121	7,678	122	198	823	2,161	68	676	214	1,488	792	1,610	1,587	6,579	2,812
Oklahoma	4,082	31,083	172,944	965	1,921	15,135	107,282	156	912	335	6,053	7,501	5,385	2,029	14,619	1,251
Texas	5,420	17,575	69,360	1,191	2,354	8,573	30,194	235	2,073	842	10,730	5,987	11,323	7,926	46,666	5,903
MOUNTAIN:																
Montana	31,522	22,528	17,427	19,064	9,419	10,043	7,928	67	479	98	1,481	947	1,088	195	429	108
Idaho	8,496	13,984	17,885	3,152	2,765	10,694	12,440	53	281	62	1,562	1,160	1,764	157	500	81
Wyoming	2,619	13,547	11,912	1,076	3,930	21,643	7,756	35	284	68	674	699	550	113	300	122
Colorado	6,885	45,434	64,573	1,538	3,754	47,490	62,615	226	1,358	395	3,042	3,164	2,085	501	2,140	600
New Mexico	689	3,372	9,899	197	381	1,707	6,925	30	189	93	778	712	723	232	1,341	248
Arizona	2,286	5,659	13,645	529	1,032	2,978	8,115	78	486	183	1,160	1,298	838	393	1,886	585
Utah	1,158	3,587	3,665	327	408	2,605	2,828	43	240	98	589	475	532	233	453	136
Nevada	769	1,610	2,057	197	301	972	1,363	27	150	61	259	201	204	60	176	38
PACIFIC:																
Washington	67,026	51,782	42,912	20,305	13,862	23,724	29,779	257	1,758	556	5,284	4,254	5,583	614	1,707	688
Oregon	28,567	34,740	29,566	9,282	7,987	19,856	23,334	125	867	260	2,697	2,180	2,399	317	929	389
California	83,307	156,984	188,334	20,523	25,905	77,655	122,177	1,751	10,674	4,291	16,002	12,726	8,608	3,568	12,470	4,746

STATE OF BIRTH

TABLE 22.—NATIVE WHITE POPULATION OF EACH DIVISION AND STATE, BY DIVISION AND STATE OF BIRTH: 1930—Continued

| | WHITE POPULATION BORN IN— | | | | | | | | | | | | | | | |
| DIVISION AND STATE | East South Central division | | | | West South Central division | | | | Mountain division | | | | | | | |
	Kentucky	Tennessee	Alabama	Mississippi	Arkansas	Louisiana	Oklahoma	Texas	Montana	Idaho	Wyoming	Colorado	New Mexico	Arizona	Utah	Nevada
United States	2,968,335	2,515,598	1,875,747	1,172,103	1,570,503	1,290,064	1,408,541	3,770,436	329,302	299,427	123,471	829,572	254,960	112,473	515,439	52,435
GEOGRAPHIC DIVISIONS:																
New England	3,225	1,918	1,468	704	729	1,268	723	2,681	990	314	387	2,247	210	274	454	214
Middle Atlantic	22,475	14,802	10,439	4,493	4,246	9,533	4,874	10,003	4,183	1,442	1,585	9,807	1,218	1,136	2,748	615
East North Central	439,313	118,061	26,964	12,621	33,799	14,665	22,379	30,588	12,847	3,524	4,137	23,311	3,156	2,079	4,009	817
West North Central	79,118	58,217	8,533	8,123	72,208	7,005	85,517	37,434	18,252	4,794	9,307	40,221	4,417	1,520	3,411	677
South Atlantic	76,968	97,117	134,814	17,458	9,391	11,079	5,714	18,454	1,798	941	833	4,163	800	738	1,300	261
East South Central	2,167,880	1,950,649	1,520,847	924,482	30,510	29,296	6,040	23,674	580	354	254	1,657	629	401	274	70
West South Central	96,606	204,519	149,322	185,236	1,337,450	1,193,121	1,155,366	3,431,654	2,561	1,923	2,001	16,201	18,284	4,334	1,590	428
Mountain	26,170	20,903	8,295	6,527	28,894	5,083	52,840	92,693	221,009	214,724	87,926	428,619	208,787	73,129	486,768	28,857
Pacific	56,571	49,412	15,065	12,459	53,276	19,014	74,488	117,195	67,082	71,411	17,041	103,356	17,459	28,853	64,821	20,496
NEW ENGLAND:																
Maine	171	120	85	35	35	56	58	108	101	34	38	152	6	23	19	24
New Hampshire	115	78	51	28	35	40	23	110	77	29	25	106	14	13	24	10
Vermont	93	64	38	10	22	20	46	142	82	22	43	114	10	6	27	9
Massachusetts	1,544	970	710	425	344	668	375	1,346	508	156	170	1,220	124	164	257	132
Rhode Island	191	164	112	40	76	94	56	201	56	20	23	151	9	7	27	12
Connecticut	1,111	513	472	157	217	390	165	684	100	53	88	504	47	61	100	27
MIDDLE ATLANTIC:																
New York	10,319	7,213	5,554	2,569	2,250	6,204	2,277	9,585	2,181	829	803	5,348	632	621	1,615	362
New Jersey	3,226	2,169	1,718	767	678	1,519	673	2,543	629	203	200	1,564	165	208	427	118
Pennsylvania	8,930	5,420	3,167	1,157	1,318	1,720	1,924	3,935	1,373	410	582	2,895	421	307	706	135
E. N. CENTRAL:																
Ohio	179,133	34,808	9,468	2,585	3,654	2,424	3,756	5,403	1,445	578	669	3,943	581	424	642	160
Indiana	124,785	19,487	2,500	1,308	4,002	1,018	3,237	3,534	1,077	386	405	2,205	361	244	320	68
Illinois	88,866	31,447	8,605	5,336	13,899	8,523	9,529	13,788	4,305	1,236	1,667	10,108	1,290	665	1,949	333
Michigan	41,937	30,834	5,829	2,974	11,451	2,174	4,835	6,276	3,244	854	933	4,858	703	557	794	198
Wisconsin	4,592	1,485	562	418	793	526	1,022	1,587	2,776	520	463	2,137	212	189	304	58
W. N. CENTRAL:																
Minnesota	2,670	1,037	379	298	800	397	1,142	1,571	5,544	622	566	1,923	166	135	438	79
Iowa	6,702	4,037	524	470	2,551	515	4,277	2,543	2,128	689	1,136	4,400	355	155	553	124
Missouri	47,439	40,854	5,416	5,599	48,901	4,309	26,167	16,853	1,970	992	1,250	9,025	1,414	545	989	171
North Dakota	585	252	73	42	217	59	335	455	3,650	280	172	371	31	29	64	21
South Dakota	1,131	701	143	122	572	96	898	834	2,034	300	1,348	1,522	140	45	192	46
Nebraska	3,953	2,181	427	357	2,234	441	3,977	2,694	1,646	864	3,706	10,628	372	134	661	89
Kansas	16,638	9,155	1,571	1,235	16,933	1,188	48,721	12,484	1,280	1,047	1,069	12,292	1,939	486	514	147
SOUTH ATLANTIC:																
Delaware	186	183	126	73	37	120	47	159	35	19	17	73	11	9	17	3
Maryland	2,185	2,267	1,125	666	494	862	404	1,326	234	107	80	576	91	72	182	36
Dist. of Columbia	2,956	2,777	1,622	1,071	661	872	472	1,881	324	190	153	562	120	107	528	64
Virginia	11,489	18,459	3,009	1,177	923	929	570	2,021	239	131	96	518	91	90	123	27
West Virginia	35,747	7,236	1,516	351	554	253	720	801	176	70	102	404	86	76	97	24
North Carolina	3,329	16,638	4,758	1,771	1,010	733	486	1,728	143	118	68	314	73	60	62	6
South Carolina	1,081	6,320	3,286	963	532	477	205	906	50	27	14	99	15	19	18	4
Georgia	5,082	25,030	62,042	4,281	1,798	2,611	914	4,451	102	54	67	412	72	103	102	27
Florida	14,913	18,207	57,330	7,105	3,382	4,222	1,896	5,181	495	225	236	1,195	241	202	231	70
E. S. CENTRAL:																
Kentucky	2,110,461	67,025	5,398	2,587	2,839	1,083	1,353	2,757	206	108	101	516	174	121	93	20
Tennessee	45,596	1,812,763	36,321	40,000	15,441	3,251	2,352	7,558	230	151	62	610	226	102	86	34
Alabama	7,197	50,800	1,434,862	30,882	3,879	4,950	1,591	7,629	103	47	46	353	122	105	55	9
Mississippi	4,635	20,061	44,266	851,013	8,851	20,012	1,344	5,730	41	48	45	178	107	73	40	7
W. S. CENTRAL:																
Arkansas	17,907	48,646	20,247	35,997	1,006,271	18,179	26,285	32,082	225	210	188	1,257	655	265	77	38
Louisiana	4,400	7,240	15,048	57,173	25,511	1,076,094	2,950	34,164	138	59	59	486	212	150	71	19
Oklahoma	33,642	48,945	25,863	18,723	197,342	6,837	1,005,882	215,027	1,051	883	766	7,181	4,566	923	518	136
Texas	40,657	99,688	88,164	73,343	108,326	92,011	120,249	3,149,781	1,147	771	988	7,277	12,851	2,996	933	235
MOUNTAIN:																
Montana	2,804	1,608	269	213	1,229	174	2,260	2,083	204,507	5,732	3,530	4,207	315	254	3,593	661
Idaho	2,256	2,826	329	252	3,090	206	3,750	2,123	7,284	186,904	3,801	5,255	410	489	35,896	934
Wyoming	1,434	890	346	223	1,120	230	2,291	2,290	3,450	2,348	68,422	9,391	662	209	5,912	150
Colorado	10,222	6,421	2,085	1,635	7,814	1,395	17,495	13,551	2,123	1,666	5,816	366,461	13,042	926	4,401	389
New Mexico	3,172	4,088	2,353	1,905	6,920	1,234	13,370	42,996	264	242	377	7,215	186,445	2,322	589	69
Arizona	4,646	3,860	2,351	1,859	7,813	1,531	12,398	27,284	1,075	1,271	618	6,431	6,762	67,083	4,277	592
Utah	1,104	853	394	314	561	187	752	1,303	1,662	14,915	4,835	6,559	887	1,435	374,196	1,800
Nevada	532	357	168	126	347	128	524	1,113	644	1,646	527	2,110	264	411	7,899	24,262
PACIFIC:																
Washington	8,853	7,319	1,433	1,097	6,575	1,455	7,684	7,705	28,473	26,144	3,833	12,480	962	956	5,084	1,147
Oregon	5,207	5,430	872	807	5,108	971	7,027	6,831	10,499	18,357	2,794	10,188	912	1,003	5,418	1,312
California	42,511	36,663	12,760	10,555	41,593	16,588	59,777	102,659	28,110	26,910	10,414	80,688	15,585	26,894	54,319	18,037

162

POPULATION

TABLE 22.—NATIVE WHITE POPULATION OF EACH DIVISION AND STATE, BY DIVISION AND STATE OF BIRTH: 1930—Continued

DIVISION AND STATE	WHITE POPULATION BORN IN—													American citizens born at sea	American citizens born abroad
	Pacific division			United States, State not reported	Outlying possessions										
	Washington	Oregon	California		Total	Alaska	American Samoa	Guam	Hawaii	Panama Canal Zone	Philippine Islands	Puerto Rico	Virgin Islands of the U. S.		
United States	718,035	521,635	1,868,265	201,923	71,582	6,242	194	256	15,349	2,222	5,323	41,117	879	771	124,289
GEOGRAPHIC DIVISIONS:															
New England	1,474	795	5,341	7,971	1,165	69	4	3	315	134	199	367	74	153	17,503
Middle Atlantic	5,710	3,094	19,763	61,518	39,967	272	6	15	603	527	1,046	36,910	588	142	21,014
East North Central	11,842	5,970	20,455	37,137	2,254	297	6	12	402	328	572	560	77	94	23,792
West North Central	10,437	6,286	14,339	23,101	1,008	180	2	9	211	151	323	124	8	40	11,373
South Atlantic	2,834	1,433	6,301	12,192	2,460	114	10	62	308	407	626	776	67	55	4,778
East South Central	851	556	2,241	6,854	357	29	30	1	78	84	68	64	3	16	1,242
West South Central	3,666	2,898	13,020	17,346	1,149	93	53	7	226	137	266	360	7	41	4,735
Mountain	28,159	18,721	33,181	5,818	1,058	270	15	8	240	61	154	298	12	54	9,011
Pacific	653,062	481,882	1,753,624	29,986	22,164	4,918	68	139	12,876	393	2,069	1,658	43	176	30,841
NEW ENGLAND:															
Maine	125	96	470	595	62	9			14	11	13	12	3	35	3,224
New Hampshire	95	84	277	403	25	3			9	2	2	9		7	1,845
Vermont	71	49	176	259	43	5			10	5	8	11	4	2	1,671
Massachusetts	770	412	3,011	4,727	679	36	4	1	207	82	108	208	33	80	7,698
Rhode Island	115	45	372	550	71	5		2	15	11	13	16	9	5	1,216
Connecticut	298	159	1,035	1,437	285	11			60	23	55	111	25	18	1,849
MIDDLE ATLANTIC:															
New York	3,353	1,886	12,950	45,138	37,736	162	3	7	425	294	741	35,617	487	90	14,017
New Jersey	907	431	3,240	8,709	1,310	34	2	6	98	132	148	846	44	23	3,243
Pennsylvania	1,450	727	3,573	7,671	921	76	1	2	80	101	157	447	57	29	3,754
EAST NORTH CENTRAL:															
Ohio	1,786	1,068	3,861	8,952	559	48		5	95	93	129	152	37	22	3,660
Indiana	890	573	1,859	4,580	192	24	2	2	47	36	49	25	4	7	1,559
Illinois	4,189	2,044	8,517	12,863	797	101	2	1	137	102	244	183	27	36	5,061
Michigan	3,243	1,568	4,684	7,026	576	93	2	3	95	76	119	181	7	24	11,405
Wisconsin	1,734	717	1,534	3,716	130	31		1	28	21	31	16	2	5	2,087
WEST NORTH CENTRAL:															
Minnesota	2,941	1,114	1,778	2,421	170	51	1		27	32	46	11	2	9	3,059
Iowa	1,420	984	2,007	4,339	135	27			19	32	41	15	1	6	1,700
Missouri	1,937	1,180	4,792	8,146	310	34	1	2	64	47	102	57	3	13	1,432
North Dakota	838	447	456	690	34	13			10		7	4			1,485
South Dakota	652	391	619	933	40	12			11	4	11	2		1	790
Nebraska	1,115	968	1,671	2,286	107	18		1	33	13	34	6	2	6	930
Kansas	1,534	1,202	3,016	4,286	212	25		6	47	23	82	29		5	1,077
SOUTH ATLANTIC:															
Delaware	70	43	172	92	75	1			8	5	11	47	3	1	88
Maryland	491	235	1,122	3,038	496	27		5	93	73	113	177	8	9	768
District of Columbia	436	243	1,168	1,858	542	29	3	8	73	80	186	153	10	13	629
Virginia	491	213	947	1,011	464	17	1	7	93	91	131	102	22	6	687
West Virginia	228	118	379	1,110	59	4	2	8	5	12	10	15	3	1	289
North Carolina	292	114	379	1,263	115	12	1	12	18	23	24	22	3	2	356
South Carolina	67	37	159	506	91		1	15	22	12	20	18	3	3	196
Georgia	181	91	565	1,428	208	4		4	52	36	80	32		1	348
Florida	578	339	1,410	1,886	410	20	2	3	34	75	51	210	15	19	1,417
EAST SOUTH CENTRAL:															
Kentucky	265	181	634	1,557	112	8	15		22	22	20	25		5	399
Tennessee	332	212	881	3,193	104	12	11	1	28	9	22	20	1	5	380
Alabama	152	115	437	1,197	103	6	3		22	40	16	15	1	3	261
Mississippi	102	48	289	907	38	3	1		6	13	10	4	1	3	202
WEST SOUTH CENTRAL:															
Arkansas	385	275	952	2,522	44	11	2		14	6	9	2		2	243
Louisiana	248	154	980	1,083	249	16	13	1	30	38	37	108	6	6	632
Oklahoma	1,472	1,163	3,875	5,688	153	16	11	1	43	18	51	13		7	974
Texas	1,561	1,306	7,213	8,053	703	50	27	5	139	75	169	237	1	26	2,886
MOUNTAIN:															
Montana	6,755	2,592	2,174	811	110	56	1		14	7	18	14		5	2,254
Idaho	15,595	10,039	3,224	823	101	54		3	22	5	10	7		3	1,792
Wyoming	738	609	874	416	63	9	1		22	5	8	18		3	259
Colorado	1,814	1,488	4,155	1,966	186	43	1	1	35	20	52	26	8	10	983
New Mexico	307	292	1,686	468	38	2			11	3	10	12		6	457
Arizona	1,439	1,489	10,473	709	376	53	1	4	46	15	37	216	4	9	1,552
Utah	846	1,112	2,981	390	104	16	9		59	6	11	3		9	1,522
Nevada	665	1,100	7,614	235	80	37	2		31		8	2			192
PACIFIC:															
Washington	545,609	51,041	22,753	5,014	3,553	2,804	4	7	449	35	217	39	3	35	10,958
Oregon	46,531	372,797	24,301	3,349	770	483			150	23	90	21	3	17	3,954
California	60,922	58,044	1,706,570	21,623	17,836	1,631	64	132	12,277	335	1,762	1,598	37	124	15,929

STATE OF BIRTH

163

TABLE **23.**—NATIVE NEGRO POPULATION OF EACH DIVISION AND STATE, BY DIVISION AND STATE OF BIRTH: 1930

DIVISION AND STATE	Total native Negro population	NEGRO POPULATION BORN IN—											Other native Negro population [1]
		United States	Geographic divisions									United States, State not reported	
			New England	Middle Atlantic	East North Central	West North Central	South Atlantic	East South Central	West South Central	Moun-tain	Pacific		
United States	11,792,523	11,771,863	57,530	394,022	323,198	229,719	5,195,040	3,193,449	2,310,969	12,327	23,225	32,384	20,660
GEOGRAPHIC DIVISIONS:													
New England	82,300	81,880	44,991	4,273	600	234	28,085	1,779	559	53	90	319	411
Middle Atlantic	988,334	971,731	8,366	354,910	11,629	3,141	530,748	45,196	10,663	687	1,117	5,824	16,603
East North Central	925,293	923,862	1,260	12,503	278,327	30,927	197,435	321,256	74,582	1,249	1,006	5,317	1,431
West North Central	331,256	331,040	182	991	9,935	171,547	11,267	74,868	58,451	1,012	392	2,395	216
South Atlantic	4,408,804	4,408,136	1,050	17,707	6,916	1,507	4,296,766	68,944	6,404	331	458	7,153	668
East South Central	2,657,706	2,657,548	150	1,101	7,493	2,654	85,801	2,513,498	41,131	208	207	5,245	158
West South Central	2,280,539	2,280,163	148	770	3,433	8,509	31,026	151,008	2,077,617	668	506	5,488	376
Mountain	30,038	29,939	74	353	1,125	3,976	2,387	4,418	10,886	6,122	372	226	99
Pacific	88,253	87,555	409	1,414	3,734	7,224	10,565	11,492	30,676	2,047	19,077	917	698
NEW ENGLAND:													
Maine	803	884	723	20	5	3	103	7	9		1	13	9
New Hampshire	595	592	326	31	24	3	156	31	10	1	1	9	3
Vermont	555	545	404	41	5	4	62	24	3	1		1	10
Massachusetts	43,431	43,176	26,081	1,859	351	130	13,332	869	309	84	56	155	255
Rhode Island	8,850	8,828	6,020	400	31	2	2,243	65	23	3	11	30	22
Connecticut	27,976	27,864	11,437	1,922	190	92	13,089	783	205	14	21	111	112
MIDDLE ATLANTIC:													
New York	354,919	339,125	5,823	123,015	5,074	1,641	182,077	11,904	5,830	814	562	2,885	15,794
New Jersey	205,109	204,768	1,299	78,205	1,279	430	113,842	6,953	1,197	103	228	1,232	341
Pennsylvania	428,306	427,838	1,244	153,690	5,276	1,070	234,829	26,339	3,636	220	327	1,207	468
EAST NORTH CENTRAL:													
Ohio	308,227	307,958	349	6,024	106,427	2,901	93,816	88,353	7,879	241	206	1,762	269
Indiana	111,782	111,718	78	635	41,599	2,155	7,786	52,678	5,739	98	69	881	64
Illinois	327,406	327,075	484	2,004	87,486	19,061	40,653	127,933	45,276	594	479	1,605	331
Michigan	167,191	166,439	322	2,830	39,840	5,147	53,315	49,190	14,284	279	229	1,003	752
Wisconsin	10,687	10,672	27	110	2,975	1,063	1,865	3,102	1,404	37	23	66	15
WEST NORTH CENTRAL:													
Minnesota	9,340	9,288	39	146	927	4,585	730	1,549	1,107	77	58	70	52
Iowa	17,330	17,322	13	91	938	11,037	1,229	2,302	1,485	61	28	138	8
Missouri	223,631	223,559	78	433	6,227	112,821	6,043	59,122	36,910	379	172	1,305	72
North Dakota	370	366	4	7	33	194	30	49	39	4	1	5	4
South Dakota	639	636		7	40	406	39	80	41	10	1	3	3
Nebraska	13,697	13,679	7	100	481	6,395	798	2,266	3,241	140	37	205	18
Kansas	66,249	66,190	41	207	1,280	36,109	2,398	9,500	15,619	332	95	609	59
SOUTH ATLANTIC:													
Delaware	32,515	32,507	61	1,439	68	30	30,539	242	87	5	11	25	8
Maryland	275,507	275,352	332	3,947	574	181	266,800	1,291	537	45	73	1,482	155
District of Columbia	131,611	131,498	485	2,902	882	352	122,134	2,512	1,032	78	73	1,048	113
Virginia	649,835	649,738	445	3,993	756	142	639,536	3,760	481	46	75	504	97
West Virginia	114,774	114,749	69	1,605	2,262	308	93,005	16,617	595	55	42	191	25
North Carolina	918,529	918,497	176	1,406	475	95	912,597	2,563	375	15	37	758	32
South Carolina	793,627	793,603	51	538	212	47	791,482	793	162	8	15	295	24
Georgia	1,070,925	1,070,881	148	844	896	158	1,046,363	20,259	1,017	38	61	1,097	44
Florida	421,481	421,311	183	1,033	791	194	394,220	20,907	2,118	41	71	1,753	170
EAST SOUTH CENTRAL:													
Kentucky	225,972	225,950	29	281	3,625	642	8,159	211,153	1,307	45	45	574	22
Tennessee	477,546	477,508	49	294	1,826	971	31,009	429,872	10,725	61	66	2,035	38
Alabama	944,566	944,516	50	393	1,086	320	37,175	901,541	2,725	61	55	1,110	50
Mississippi	1,009,622	1,000,574	22	133	956	721	8,918	970,932	26,284	41	41	1,526	48
WEST SOUTH CENTRAL:													
Arkansas	478,393	478,374	22	139	1,200	2,235	13,263	83,680	375,788	94	75	1,878	19
Louisiana	775,517	775,369	52	219	716	561	5,790	37,888	729,304	66	90	773	148
Oklahoma	172,131	172,069	18	119	727	3,983	4,180	15,283	146,602	202	136	819	62
Texas	854,498	854,351	56	293	790	1,730	7,883	15,147	825,923	306	205	2,018	147
MOUNTAIN:													
Montana	1,242	1,233	6	31	106	265	116	184	148	339	23	15	9
Idaho	653	646	2	7	37	105	57	85	162	167	21	3	7
Wyoming	1,242	1,240	3	12	90	322	107	204	209	273	12	8	2
Colorado	11,767	11,748	31	114	446	2,232	825	2,044	2,883	3,039	59	75	19
New Mexico	2,836	2,832	3	17	55	194	147	325	1,440	590	21	40	4
Arizona	10,696	10,646	23	150	296	619	979	1,361	5,656	1,306	192	64	50
Utah	1,096	1,090	6	10	60	164	88	149	259	327	15	12	6
Nevada	506	504		12	35	75	68	66	129	81	29	9	2
PACIFIC:													
Washington	6,673	6,565	40	147	561	996	794	919	955	304	1,741	108	108
Oregon	2,184	2,165	8	49	131	351	234	266	560	77	454	35	19
California	79,396	78,825	361	1,218	3,042	5,877	9,537	10,307	29,161	1,666	16,882	774	571

[1] Includes persons born in outlying possessions and American citizens born abroad or at sea.

119652—33——12

POPULATION

TABLE 23.—NATIVE NEGRO POPULATION OF EACH DIVISION AND STATE, BY DIVISION AND STATE OF BIRTH: 1930—Continued

| DIVISION AND STATE | NEGRO POPULATION BORN IN— | | | | | | | | | | | | | |
| | New England division | | | | | | Middle Atlantic division | | | East North Central division | | | | |
	Maine	New Hampshire	Vermont	Massachusetts	Rhode Island	Connecticut	New York	New Jersey	Pennsylvania	Ohio	Indiana	Illinois	Michigan	Wisconsin
United States	1,334	494	853	32,009	7,468	15,372	125,964	80,937	187,121	129,116	53,032	101,878	35,906	3,266
GEOGRAPHIC DIVISIONS:														
New England	907	372	538	25,731	5,976	11,467	2,214	838	1,221	281	75	163	74	13
Middle Atlantic	245	64	210	4,034	1,087	2,776	115,876	75,046	163,388	6,747	1,287	2,483	998	114
East North Central	68	14	36	683	115	344	2,422	984	9,097	111,681	46,458	85,265	32,342	2,581
West North Central	12	4	16	104	16	30	301	111	570	1,401	1,198	6,638	471	227
South Atlantic	58	28	30	999	236	599	3,967	2,977	10,763	4,251	713	1,123	742	87
East South Central	12	3	1	83	15	36	208	124	709	2,438	1,980	2,510	497	68
West South Central	5	3	1	91	24	24	251	75	444	782	501	1,756	321	73
Mountain	2	------	5	38	9	20	97	44	212	338	206	471	80	30
Pacific	25	6	16	246	40	76	568	138	708	1,197	614	1,409	381	73
NEW ENGLAND:														
Maine	659	3	------	51	2	8	3	3	14	1	------	2	------	2
New Hampshire	4	223	26	64	------	9	17	5	9	4	7	13	------	------
Vermont	2	17	347	33	4	1	35	5	1	4	------	1	------	------
Massachusetts	211	116	110	24,358	545	732	851	362	646	143	52	97	53	6
Rhode Island	7	5	14	538	5,242	214	195	82	123	20	1	5	5	------
Connecticut	24	8	32	687	183	10,503	1,113	381	428	109	15	45	16	5
MIDDLE ATLANTIC:														
New York	140	42	169	2,830	710	1,932	108,351	6,354	8,310	2,545	556	1,402	498	73
New Jersey	42	10	25	569	172	481	5,149	64,352	8,704	682	160	292	134	11
Pennsylvania	63	12	16	635	155	363	2,376	4,940	146,374	3,520	571	789	366	30
EAST NORTH CENTRAL:														
Ohio	24	5	12	180	27	92	803	330	4,891	99,479	3,184	2,483	1,107	84
Indiana	9	1	2	38	8	20	95	37	503	2,296	35,727	2,962	559	55
Illinois	18	4	12	278	50	122	817	334	1,753	4,631	4,885	76,069	1,360	541
Michigan	16	4	10	161	23	108	673	276	1,881	5,050	2,473	3,027	29,121	169
Wisconsin	1	------	------	17	7	2	34	7	69	225	189	724	105	1,732
WEST NORTH CENTRAL:														
Minnesota	1	2	5	18	3	10	56	14	76	184	169	392	75	107
Iowa	1	1	1	9	------	1	24	6	61	98	99	683	32	26
Missouri	3	1	3	53	7	11	126	46	261	688	632	4,667	193	47
North Dakota	1	------	1	2	------	------	1	2	4	14	1	13	3	2
South Dakota	------	------	------	------	------	------	5	------	2	8	2	24	14	1
Nebraska	------	------	------	3	2	1	26	7	67	101	62	263	42	13
Kansas	5	------	6	19	4	7	63	36	108	308	233	596	112	31
SOUTH ATLANTIC:														
Delaware	1	------	2	29	5	24	93	282	1,064	32	16	11	5	4
Maryland	5	1	4	165	56	101	626	683	2,638	312	80	123	57	2
District of Columbia	22	6	9	254	72	122	756	513	1,633	439	117	233	83	10
Virginia	14	13	6	210	62	140	1,062	697	2,234	456	72	121	92	15
West Virginia	1	------	4	39	3	22	116	120	1,369	1,822	137	199	99	5
North Carolina	7	1	2	92	10	64	473	263	670	288	54	53	74	6
South Carolina	------	------	------	33	9	9	215	87	236	115	14	39	41	3
Georgia	1	3	3	72	8	61	274	132	438	433	109	180	154	20
Florida	7	4	------	105	11	56	352	200	481	354	114	104	137	22
EAST SOUTH CENTRAL:														
Kentucky	6	------	------	11	3	9	62	20	199	1,180	1,503	808	123	11
Tennessee	3	2	------	26	6	12	67	38	189	572	244	835	155	20
Alabama	3	1	------	26	5	15	94	54	245	465	133	322	149	17
Mississippi	------	------	1	20	1	------	45	12	76	221	100	545	70	20
WEST SOUTH CENTRAL:														
Arkansas	------	------	------	10	9	3	38	12	89	202	158	726	85	29
Louisiana	2	------	1	23	9	17	85	18	116	188	75	365	74	14
Oklahoma	------	1	------	14	3	------	33	10	76	178	125	346	70	8
Texas	3	2	------	44	3	4	95	35	163	214	143	319	92	22
MOUNTAIN:														
Montana	1	------	------	1	2	2	7	4	20	36	14	47	7	2
Idaho	------	------	------	1	------	1	2	1	4	13	7	15	2	------
Wyoming	------	------	------	2	------	1	6	1	5	35	17	31	3	4
Colorado	------	------	1	18	4	8	27	15	72	126	73	212	28	7
New Mexico	------	------	------	2	------	1	5	3	9	11	12	28	3	1
Arizona	1	------	4	11	3	4	43	18	89	98	61	100	24	13
Utah	------	------	------	3	------	3	2	1	7	12	13	25	8	2
Nevada	------	------	------	------	------	------	5	1	6	7	9	13	5	1
PACIFIC:														
Washington	7	------	1	18	4	10	55	10	82	174	100	224	45	18
Oregon	------	------	1	5	1	1	14	7	28	43	19	49	18	2
California	18	6	14	223	35	65	499	121	598	980	495	1,196	318	53

STATE OF BIRTH

165

TABLE 23.—NATIVE NEGRO POPULATION OF EACH DIVISION AND STATE, BY DIVISION AND STATE OF BIRTH: 1930—Continued

| DIVISION AND STATE | NEGRO POPULATION BORN IN— | | | | | | | | | | | | | | | |
| | West North Central division | | | | | | | South Atlantic division | | | | | | | | |
	Minnesota	Iowa	Missouri	North Dakota	South Dakota	Nebraska	Kansas	Delaware	Maryland	District of Columbia	Virginia	West Virginia	North Carolina	South Carolina	Georgia	Florida
United States	3,990	12,410	159,113	377	504	5,682	47,443	32,184	275,093	72,018	908,551	64,898	1,028,538	1,095,214	1,403,856	314,688
GEOGRAPHIC DIVISIONS:																
New England	23	16	134	3	13	11	34	133	1,452	891	9,323	152	5,881	4,269	5,982	1,002
Middle Atlantic	136	293	1,916	51	27	165	553	9,242	43,076	9,446	171,603	5,684	84,268	100,179	84,685	22,475
East North Central	677	2,751	22,222	52	77	808	4,340	205	2,596	1,506	22,490	6,104	18,073	27,090	110,423	8,039
West North Central	2,043	8,191	121,165	158	288	3,949	35,153	20	367	267	2,377	296	1,456	1,446	4,262	776
South Atlantic	80	157	857	19	17	100	277	22,607	226,557	59,291	691,711	51,309	902,275	940,447	1,122,715	273,864
East South Central	58	152	2,070	12	13	80	200	24	289	145	5,993	801	8,138	7,754	57,456	5,261
West South Central	111	263	5,061	20	5	226	2,823	10	302	110	2,877	182	6,943	6,610	12,381	1,011
Mountain	51	194	1,953	30	25	190	1,533	6	110	91	598	87	316	277	762	134
Pacific	211	393	3,735	32	39	353	2,461	37	338	271	1,580	103	1,188	1,133	5,190	626
NEW ENGLAND:																
Maine			3					3	12	3	41		10	13	9	3
New Hampshire					1		2	1	12	10	68		26	10	14	9
Vermont	1		2			1		1	10	3	19	3	10	10	5	1
Massachusetts	15	10	82	1	3	4	15	81	700	504	4,607	73	3,032	1,800	2,030	445
Rhode Island					1		1	7	301	110	1,141	14	267	176	167	60
Connecticut	7	6	47	2	9	5	16	40	417	261	3,347	62	2,527	2,194	3,757	484
MIDDLE ATLANTIC:																
New York	83	138	1,010	34	12	82	282	847	8,133	3,929	58,910	1,048	33,901	41,866	23,776	9,598
New Jersey	22	35	243	9	5	14	102	2,529	9,473	1,741	36,035	613	19,010	16,450	22,380	5,011
Pennsylvania	31	120	663	8	10	69	169	5,866	25,470	3,776	76,139	4,023	31,297	41,863	38,529	7,866
EAST NORTH CENTRAL:																
Ohio	80	193	1,073	11	22	90	523	72	1,184	565	13,892	4,384	9,039	11,831	48,847	3,102
Indiana	63	171	1,481	2	4	68	366	13	99	70	971	181	1,110	669	4,350	323
Illinois	352	1,604	14,885	22	30	432	2,246	55	695	526	3,726	568	2,760	5,533	24,902	1,888
Michigan	116	393	3,414	13	20	177	1,014	63	586	329	3,711	943	4,155	8,021	31,064	3,553
Wisconsin	57	300	409	4	1	41	191	2	32	16	190	28	109	145	1,270	73
WEST NORTH CENTRAL:																
Minnesota	2,384	432	1,105	41	36	130	457	1	39	29	200	33	64	71	255	38
Iowa	67	6,599	3,500	8	26	180	648	1	34	14	638	49	134	88	220	51
Missouri	81	527	106,728	6	22	242	5,215	9	155	77	977	120	848	791	2,729	337
North Dakota	23	17	39	94	5	5	11		1	2	6	3	1	7	9	1
South Dakota	23	47	104		175	28	29	1	4		10	2	1		20	1
Nebraska	27	342	1,762	2	11	3,123	1,128	3	23	19	131	20	76	66	203	257
Kansas	38	227	7,927	7	13	232	27,665	5	111	126	415	69	332	423	826	91
SOUTH ATLANTIC:																
Delaware		3	22			1	4	21,311	5,340	113	2,152	38	620	329	430	206
Maryland	7	26	110	1	3	8	26	906	201,244	3,562	37,090	949	12,616	7,593	2,248	682
District of Columbia	27	28	185	5	4	30	73	87	16,346	52,513	30,236	751	8,026	10,166	3,383	626
Virginia	3	17	68	3	4	7	40	95	2,311	2,347	576,588	2,058	44,354	8,711	2,479	593
West Virginia	6	61	168	2	2	14	55	16	548	222	31,401	46,834	8,304	2,441	2,905	334
North Carolina	11	7	51	1		5	20	31	311	239	9,578	426	808,298	79,368	13,272	1,074
South Carolina	8	1	32			2	4	8	87	51	617	31	6,913	776,058	6,924	793
Georgia	11	6	103		2	13	23	24	131	151	1,682	140	5,208	32,695	996,411	9,921
Florida	7	8	118	7	2	20	32	29	239	93	2,367	172	7,936	29,086	94,663	259,635
EAST SOUTH CENTRAL:																
Kentucky	9	48	479	3	5	22	76	1	68	37	1,965	456	1,005	916	3,390	321
Tennessee	23	42	798	2	2	15	89	10	81	54	1,985	141	3,402	3,403	21,886	557
Alabama	11	23	205	1	2	28	50	10	95	38	1,123	166	1,444	2,258	28,374	3,667
Mississippi	15	39	588	6	4	15	54	3	45	16	920	38	2,197	1,177	3,806	716
WEST SOUTH CENTRAL:																
Arkansas	20	56	1,934	7	1	33	184	5	51	26	704	38	3,336	3,926	4,987	190
Louisiana	16	38	417	3		24	63		110	26	815	42	1,117	725	2,060	805
Oklahoma	23	94	1,590	6	2	106	2,162	2	37	13	401	46	859	821	1,808	133
Texas	52	75	1,120	4	2	63	414	3	104	45	957	56	1,631	1,138	3,460	483
MOUNTAIN:																
Montana	21	18	137	19	5	10	55		10	6	47	3	17	9	22	2
Idaho	4	4	51			7	39		3	3	13	2	16	5	11	4
Wyoming	1	23	175	1	6	27	89		4	5	37	7	10	6	27	11
Colorado	9	103	1,146	3	4	92	875		36	24	267	37	96	74	253	38
New Mexico	4	10	74		3	6	97		2	3	32	6	22	21	56	5
Arizona	9	23	262	6	5	30	284	6	43	38	166	26	133	148	353	66
Utah	2	9	78		2	11	62		7	9	18	2	15	12	19	6
Nevada	1	4	30	1		7	32		11	3	18	4	7	2	21	2
PACIFIC:																
Washington	72	71	508	19	12	33	281	7	48	29	229	42	151	79	170	39
Oregon	8	18	193		2	19	111	2	18	13	51	7	30	34	57	22
California	131	304	3,034	13	25	301	2,069	28	272	229	1,309	144	1,007	1,020	4,963	565

POPULATION

TABLE 23.—NATIVE NEGRO POPULATION OF EACH DIVISION AND STATE, BY DIVISION AND STATE OF BIRTH: 1930—Continued

DIVISION AND STATE	East South Central division				West South Central division				Mountain division							
	Kentucky	Tennessee	Alabama	Mississippi	Arkansas	Louisiana	Oklahoma	Texas	Montana	Idaho	Wyoming	Colorado	New Mexico	Arizona	Utah	Nevada
United States	292,365	539,556	1,133,771	1,227,757	449,451	882,024	115,284	864,210	937	372	596	6,062	1,293	2,265	627	175
GEOGRAPHIC DIVISIONS:																
New England	332	421	854	172	91	226	61	181	7	2	7	23	2	7	5	
Middle Atlantic	5,764	8,193	26,626	4,613	1,797	4,148	779	3,939	108	30	34	261	39	121	33	11
East North Central	76,888	81,082	86,314	76,972	29,111	27,983	5,098	12,390	115	44	91	681	117	140	49	12
West North Central	8,493	21,590	9,044	35,741	27,622	8,375	9,863	12,591	75	27	102	580	105	79	37	7
South Atlantic	4,639	8,899	50,648	4,758	887	2,904	557	2,056	55	11	22	126	29	75	13	
East South Central	190,406	301,000	929,666	1,002,417	15,722	22,419	711	2,279	19	7	10	90	23	30	28	1
West South Central	3,017	24,124	26,292	98,565	369,785	805,262	92,488	810,082	27	34	22	349	91	107	30	8
Mountain	924	1,203	1,203	1,028	1,187	1,747	2,301	5,651	345	144	252	3,190	669	1,156	308	58
Pacific	1,902	2,975	3,124	3,491	3,249	8,960	3,426	15,041	186	73	56	762	218	550	124	78
NEW ENGLAND:																
Maine		2	4	1		4	2	3								
New Hampshire	4	10	8	9	6	1	2	1			1					
Vermont	6	9	6	3	1		1	1	1							
Massachusetts	184	210	378	97	54	128	24	103	2	1	3	19	1	5	3	
Rhode Island	11	25	25	4		7	4	12	1			1			1	
Connecticut	127	165	433	58	30	86	28	61	3	1	3	3	1	2	1	
MIDDLE ATLANTIC:																
New York	2,011	3,051	5,023	1,810	766	2,662	349	2,053	63	23	15	128	15	49	18	3
New Jersey	553	870	5,043	487	234	393	124	446	17	3	6	45	7	19	5	1
Pennsylvania	3,200	4,272	16,560	2,307	797	1,093	306	1,440	28	4	13	88	17	53	10	7
EAST NORTH CENTRAL:																
Ohio	27,177	19,222	34,366	7,588	3,377	2,096	739	1,667	29	6	28	103	23	41	8	3
Indiana	25,317	13,728	6,205	7,428	2,819	1,630	436	854	12	5	12	49	8	9	2	1
Illinois	17,280	34,844	24,958	50,851	16,425	19,867	2,315	6,669	46	22	25	355	60	54	28	4
Michigan	6,627	12,478	20,216	9,869	5,931	3,988	1,451	2,914	21	11	24	152	23	34	10	4
Wisconsin	487	810	569	1,236	559	402	157	286	7		2	22	3	2	1	
WEST NORTH CENTRAL:																
Minnesota	465	439	314	331	277	224	214	392	26	1	4	29	7	4	5	1
Iowa	392	522	568	820	433	304	335	413	4	3	3	35	5	7	2	2
Missouri	4,957	16,836	5,966	31,363	21,550	5,680	3,468	6,212	23	16	31	226	30	34	15	4
North Dakota	15	17	6	11	8	13	3	15	1			1	1	1		
South Dakota	26	21	12	21	8	10	7	16			4	6				
Nebraska	325	486	840	615	730	441	717	1,353	5	5	41	72	12	6	8	
Kansas	2,313	3,269	1,338	2,580	4,007	1,703	5,119	4,190	16	2	19	211	50	27	7	
SOUTH ATLANTIC:																
Delaware	34	34	146	28	7	21	18	41			1	1	3			
Maryland	254	316	508	213	90	164	64	219	8	1	2	13	10	10	1	
District of Columbia	386	613	874	639	136	312	86	498	8	4	3	33	4	24	2	
Virginia	526	1,507	1,493	234	66	183	51	181	16		4	13	1	11	1	
West Virginia	2,467	2,794	10,560	796	126	211	107	151	3	1	7	26	9	7	2	
North Carolina	196	821	1,206	340	82	125	50	118	1	1	1	12				
South Carolina	40	199	435	119	29	75	12	46	1	1	1	2	2	1		
Georgia	346	1,514	17,587	812	173	480	68	296	11	1	3	11	2	8	2	
Florida	390	1,101	17,839	1,577	178	1,333	101	506	7	2	1	15		11	5	
EAST SOUTH CENTRAL:																
Kentucky	185,051	16,752	7,589	1,761	587	442	110	258	3		5	18	2	8	9	
Tennessee	4,297	363,704	13,551	48,320	7,412	2,393	242	678	6	6	4	26	7	8	3	1
Alabama	545	4,282	883,289	13,425	594	1,485	183	463	5	1	1	26	11	3	14	
Mississippi	513	6,271	25,237	938,911	7,129	18,099	176	880	5			20	3	11	2	
WEST SOUTH CENTRAL:																
Arkansas	877	16,432	9,142	57,229	340,182	28,886	1,554	5,166	5	12	4	57	6	6	4	
Louisiana	401	1,047	5,925	30,515	8,706	710,894	447	9,257	9	7	3	25	8	6	6	2
Oklahoma	957	3,873	4,903	5,550	12,935	7,265	85,760	40,642	3	11	5	110	29	25	8	2
Texas	782	2,772	6,322	5,271	7,962	58,217	4,727	755,017	10	4	10	148	48	70	12	4
MOUNTAIN:																
Montana	59	68	28	29	33	17	27	71	299	6	8	17	1	4	1	3
Idaho	14	37	20	14	22	29	27	84	8	110	2	17	3	3	23	1
Wyoming	59	55	56	34	32	34	50	93	6	1	178	78	3	1	6	
Colorado	450	644	516	434	500	386	524	1,473	13	5	42	2,692	53	15	18	1
New Mexico	62	67	107	89	141	171	277	851	4	1	2	49	515	18	1	
Arizona	227	330	422	382	402	1,029	1,330	2,895	6	4	10	78	89	1,113	3	3
Utah	37	44	36	32	49	45	53	112	7	7	9	46	4	1	250	3
Nevada	16	18	18	14	8	36	13	72	2	10	1	13	1	1	6	47
PACIFIC:																
Washington	250	281	197	191	147	218	131	459	87	31	16	117	18	18	14	3
Oregon	51	76	76	63	75	143	74	208	16	9	5	28	2	6	10	1
California	1,601	2,618	2,851	3,237	3,027	8,599	3,221	14,314	83	33	35	617	198	526	100	74

STATE OF BIRTH

167

TABLE 23.—NATIVE NEGRO POPULATION OF EACH DIVISION AND STATE, BY DIVISION AND STATE OF BIRTH: 1930—Continued

DIVISION AND STATE	Pacific division — Washington	Oregon	California	United States, State not reported	Outlying possessions — Total	Alaska	American Samoa	Guam	Hawaii	Panama Canal Zone	Philippine Islands	Puerto Rico	Virgin Islands of the U.S.	American citizens born at sea	American citizens born abroad
United States	2,998	746	19,481	32,384	17,625	42	30	48	217	594	402	11,132	5,160	39	2,996
GEOGRAPHIC DIVISIONS:															
New England	31	3	56	319	271			1	8	25	26	107	104	3	137
Middle Atlantic	595	32	490	5,324	15,863	5		13	44	426	135	10,389	4,851	12	728
East North Central	248	40	718	5,317	264	2	2	2	13	41	34	135	35	10	1,167
West North Central	80	24	288	2,305	61	4	2		7	4	22	17	5		155
South Atlantic	123	15	320	7,153	421	16		25	19	24	31	228	78	5	242
East South Central	24	7	176	5,245	97		9		8	7	12	49	12		61
West South Central	53	29	424	5,488	171	1	14		4	20	12	87	33	2	203
Mountain	69	25	278	226	52	3	1	1	8	3	24	9	3		47
Pacific	1,775	571	16,731	917	425	11	2	6	106	44	106	111	39	7	260
NEW ENGLAND:															
Maine	1			13	5							2	3		4
New Hampshire			1	9	3					1		2			6
Vermont				1	4						4				6
Massachusetts	16	3	37	155	150			1	7	21	20	53	48	2	103
Rhode Island	6		5	30	7						1	4	2	1	14
Connecticut	8		13	111	102				1	3	1	46	51		10
MIDDLE ATLANTIC:															
New York	264	19	279	2,885	15,305	1		12	22	385	82	10,145	4,658	6	483
New Jersey	145	8	75	1,232	247	3			6	11	18	96	113	1	93
Pennsylvania	186	5	136	1,207	311	1		1	16	30	35	148	80	5	152
EAST NORTH CENTRAL:															
Ohio	52	3	151	1,762	57		1	1	8	7	9	31	5	3	209
Indiana	20		49	881	22	1			3		4	8	6	2	40
Illinois	124	19	336	1,605	97		1	1	3	14	14	55	9	4	230
Michigan	49	15	165	1,003	85	1			4	20	7	38	15	1	666
Wisconsin	3	3	17	66	3							3			12
WEST NORTH CENTRAL:															
Minnesota	25	2	31	70	5	1			2		1	1			47
Iowa	9		19	138	2	1			1						6
Missouri	32	8	132	1,365	22	2	2		1	1	2	12	2		50
North Dakota			1	5	1						1				3
South Dakota			1	3											8
Nebraska	5	2	30	205	6				1	1	3	1			12
Kansas	9	12	74	609	25				2	2	15	3	3		34
SOUTH ATLANTIC:															
Delaware	6		5	25	5				1	1		3			3
Maryland	30	5	38	1,482	128	1		1	1	8	10	70	37	2	25
District of Columbia	15	3	55	1,048	74	13		2	7	1	11	30	10		39
Virginia	25	4	46	504	69	2		2	2	4	6	39	14	1	27
West Virginia	14	2	26	191	11				1	1	1	8			14
North Carolina	12		25	758	23				8	1	1	10	3		9
South Carolina	5	1	9	205	18				7		1	7	3		6
Georgia	7		54	1,097	31				2	4	2	20	3		13
Florida	9		62	1,753	62				3	2	5	41	8	2	106
EAST SOUTH CENTRAL:															
Kentucky	10	2	33	574	9		1		2		2	4			13
Tennessee	8	3	55	2,035	16		6		1	1	2	4	2		22
Alabama	4	1	50	1,110	41		2		2	4	5	24	4		9
Mississippi	2	1	38	1,526	31				3	2	3	17	6		17
WEST SOUTH CENTRAL:															
Arkansas	7	7	61	1,878	8		1			1	2	4		1	10
Louisiana	13	4	73	773	98		2			19	1	56	20		50
Oklahoma	15	9	112	819	9		1		1		3	3	1		53
Texas	18	9	178	2,018	56	1	10		3		6	24	12	1	90
MOUNTAIN:															
Montana	12	3	8	15	3	2							1		6
Idaho	8	5	8	3	3	1						2			4
Wyoming	7	1	4	8	1							1			1
Colorado	12	6	41	75	5					3	1	1			14
New Mexico	3		18	40											4
Arizona	18	7	167	64	36		1	1	6		22	5	1		14
Utah	2	2	11	12	4				2		1		1		2
Nevada	7	1	21	9											2
PACIFIC:															
Washington	1,480	102	159	108	31	5			6		12	7	1	3	74
Oregon	45	351	58	35	6	1			4		1				13
California	250	118	16,514	774	388	5	2	6	96	44	93	104	38	4	179

CHAPTER 5

COUNTRY OF BIRTH OF THE
FOREIGN BORN

CHAPTER 5.—COUNTRY OF BIRTH OF THE FOREIGN BORN

INTRODUCTION

The inquiry as to country of birth of the foreign born has been made at each census beginning with 1850. The statistics here presented relate to the population of continental United States, the States, and those cities having 100,000 inhabitants or more. Statistics for Alaska, Hawaii, Puerto Rico, the Virgin Islands, and Panama Canal Zone are given in the Report of the Fifteenth Census on Outlying Territories and Possessions. The Philippine Islands were not enumerated as a part of the Fifteenth Census.

The foreign-born population comprises all persons born outside of the United States or any of the outlying possessions, except certain persons whose parents at the time of their birth were American citizens: Persons born in any of the outlying territories or possessions, and American citizens born abroad or at sea, are regarded as native.

Color or race.—The statistics here given, except as specified in Table 2, relate to the total foreign-born population of all races combined. Of the 14,204,149 persons of foreign birth who were enumerated in continental United States in 1930, 13,366,407 were white, and 837,742 of nonwhite races, consisting mainly of Mexicans, Negroes, Chinese, and Japanese. (See Table 2.) As a general rule, to which natives of China, Japan, India, Mexico, and the West Indies constitute the leading exceptions, the total number reported as born in a given country or region does not differ greatly from the number of white persons reported as born in that country or region.

At the census of 1930, the population of Mexican origin and Indian or mixed white and Indian descent has for the first time been tabulated as a separate nonwhite race. In the foreign-born nonwhite population, the Mexicans constitute by far the largest single element. In the foreign-born population of 1920 it is estimated that there were 457,360 persons who would have been classified as Mexican under the 1930 instructions. With adjustment for Mexicans on the basis of this estimate, for purposes of comparison with the statistics of 1930, the foreign-born population of 1920 was composed of 13,255,394 persons of the white, and 665,298 of the nonwhite races.

Country of birth.—The statistics of country of birth for 1930 have been tabulated in accordance with present political boundaries. The statistics of 1920 were also tabulated on the basis of postwar boundaries, so that, aside from a few minor changes in classifica-

tion, the country of birth figures for 1930 are comparable with those of 1920.

Table 1 shows the foreign-born population for the leading countries of birth for 1930 and 1920, with percentages of increase or decrease.

TABLE 1.—COUNTRY OF BIRTH OF THE FOREIGN-BORN POPULATION OF THE UNITED STATES: 1930 AND 1920

[A minus sign (−) denotes decrease.]

COUNTRY OF BIRTH	1930	1920	INCREASE Number	INCREASE Per cent
All countries	14,204,149	13,920,692	283,457	2.0
England	809,563	813,853	−4,290	−0.5
Scotland	354,323	254,570	99,753	39.2
Wales	60,205	67,066	−6,861	−10.2
Northern Ireland	178,832	} 1,037,234	−113,592	−11.0
Irish Free State	744,810			
Norway	347,852	363,863	−16,011	−4.4
Sweden	595,250	625,585	−30,335	−4.8
Denmark	179,474	} 189,154	−9,910	−3.7
Iceland	2,764			
Netherlands	133,133	131,766	1,367	1.0
Belgium	64,194	62,687	1,507	2.4
Switzerland	113,010	118,659	−5,649	−4.8
France	135,592	153,072	−17,480	−11.4
Germany	1,608,814	1,686,108	−77,294	−4.6
Poland	1,268,583	1,139,979	128,604	11.3
Czechoslovakia	491,638	362,438	129,200	35.6
Austria	370,914	575,627	−204,713	−35.6
Hungary	274,450	397,283	−122,833	−30.9
Yugoslavia	211,416	169,489	41,977	24.8
Russia	1,153,628	} 1,400,495	−222,644	−15.9
Latvia	20,673			
Estonia	3,550			
Lithuania	193,606	135,068	58,538	43.3
Finland	142,478	149,824	−7,346	−4.9
Rumania	146,393	102,823	43,570	42.4
Greece	174,526	175,976	−1,450	−0.8
Italy	1,790,429	1,610,113	180,316	11.2
Spain	59,362	49,535	9,827	19.8
Portugal	73,164	69,981	3,183	4.5
Syria	57,227	51,901	5,326	10.3
Turkey	48,911	16,303	32,608	200.0
China	46,129	43,560	2,569	5.9
Japan	70,993	81,502	−10,509	−12.9
Canada—French	370,852	307,786	63,066	20.5
Canada—Other	915,537	817,139	98,398	12.0
West Indies	106,241	78,902	27,279	34.5
Mexico	641,462	486,418	155,044	31.9
All other countries	244,171	194,923	49,248	25.3

Census figures prior to 1920 are strictly comparable with those of 1920 and 1930 only for those countries the boundaries of which have remained unchanged. Over the entire period from 1850 to 1930 accurate comparisons are possible only for England, Scotland, Wales, Ireland (Northern Ireland and Irish Free State in 1930), Norway, Sweden, Netherlands, Switzerland, Spain, Portugal, Canada (total of Canada—French, Canada—Other, and Newfoundland), and Mexico.

For several other countries, as for example, Italy, France, and Belgium, the figures are slightly affected by boundary changes, but these changes have not been so

225

226

POPULATION

great as to destroy entirely the value of comparative figures. The boundaries of other countries, as for example, Russia, Austria, Hungary, Rumania, and Greece, have been so changed that comparisons between pre-war and postwar years are subject to a large margin of error.

In the tabulation of country of birth, the greatest difficulties were encountered in the classification of persons born in the former Austro-Hungarian Empire. Many persons born within the pre-war boundaries of this Empire could not or did not give to the enumerator the information needed for the determination of their country of birth on the basis of postwar geography. It is therefore quite possible that some persons were assigned to Austria who were really born within the present areas of either Czechoslovakia or Yugoslavia, and that persons were assigned to Hungary who were born within the present areas of Rumania or Yugoslavia. Similarly, it is possible that some persons born in Latvia, Estonia, or Lithuania were assigned to Russia.

In the statistics of country of birth of the foreign born, the countries included in the tabulation have generally been restricted to those which had at the time of the census a separate political entity. From 1860 to 1900, however, an exception was made in the case of Poland. Although Poland was not restored to its original status as an independent country until the end of the World War, its historical position was such that Polish immigrants generally returned Poland as their country of birth regardless of the political sovereignty over their birthplace. From 1860 to 1890, persons returned as born in Poland were so tabulated without qualification. At the census of 1900 an attempt was made to distinguish Austrian, German, and Russian Poland, and separate statistics for each were presented. At the census of 1910, persons returned as born in Poland were assigned either to Russia, Germany, or Austria, but for purposes of comparison it may be assumed that the number of persons from these countries returned as of Polish mother tongue in 1910 is approximately equivalent to the number in the United States in 1910 who were born within the present boundaries of Poland. While in fact there were some Polish-speaking persons born in Austria, Germany, or Russia outside the present limits of Poland, there were also perhaps an equal number of non-Polish-speaking persons who were born within those limits. In Table 4, which shows the foreign-born population by country of birth from 1850 to 1930, the figures for 1910 for Poland have been adjusted by means of mother tongue, to conform as nearly as possible to the conditions of 1930.

Changes in the foreign-born population.—The composition of the foreign-born population of the United States has undergone a great change since 1850, and particularly since 1880, as will be seen by referring to the percentages in Table 4. Since the foreign-born population at any census is composed of the survivors of the foreign-born population of the preceding census, plus the survivors of the immigration in the 10 years preceding the census, the changes in the composition of the foreign-born population follow the changes in the character of immigration but take place less rapidly. In 1850 the great majority of the foreign born were immigrants of the previous 10 years, of whom more than 80 per cent came from Ireland, Germany, and England. Until about 1890, immigration was largely from these countries and from the Scandinavian countries and Canada. After 1890, until 1914, when immigration was checked by the World War, the greater part of the accessions to the foreign-born population were from eastern, central, and southern Europe. By reason of survival from the earlier immigration, persons of northern and western European stocks still formed a majority of the foreign-born population until the census of 1920.

Under the present system of quota immigration, future changes in the national character of the foreign-born population will be due primarily to the relative mortality of the national elements in the present population. Since quota immigration is not sufficient to replace the mortality in the foreign-born population as it is now constituted, the foreign-born population will decrease until it is limited to the survivors of immigrants allowed to enter under restrictive legislation. The rate of decrease will increase rapidly as the average age of the foreign born advances, as it must advance as the immigrants of the period of unrestricted immigration grow older. Even in the decade 1920 to 1930, the median age of the foreign-born white population advanced from 40 to 44 years. Since the heaviest immigration from Ireland, Germany, England, Norway, and Sweden took place several decades ago, the population born in those countries has already reached an age at which the age specific death rate is high. Those born in eastern, central, and southern Europe are still comparatively young. According to the probabilities of survival, the relative proportion of eastern, central, and southern Europeans in the foreign-born population will continue to increase for several decades in spite of the limitation on immigration from these countries in the present quota law.

Sex distribution.—In the early immigration from Germany, particularly that between 1845 and 1885, and in the immigration from eastern, central, and southern Europe, and that from Asia between 1890 and 1914, there was a strong predominance of males. As a result, the ratio of males to females among the foreign born has always been high. When the volume of immigration declines, or when immigration is restricted, this predominance of males in the foreign-

COUNTRY OF BIRTH OF THE FOREIGN BORN 227

born population tends to decline. This is due (1) to the repatriation of male immigrants; (2) to the admission of the wives and families of naturalized citizens, and (3) to the higher death rate of males, which results in the survival of relatively more of the female immigrants. Between 1920 and 1930 the sex ratio of the foreign-born population declined from 122.9 to 116.6, as shown in Table 3. In the population born in the Irish Free State, which is probably the oldest national group among the foreign born, there is a large excess of females. There is also a definite excess of females in the population born in Canada. The decline in the sex ratio toward an approximate equality in sex distribution was marked in nearly all of the important national groups of the foreign-born population between 1920 and 1930. This decline is particularly marked in the group born in China. As a result of the operation of the exclusion act, the male population born in China showed a decrease during the decade, but the number of females of Chinese birth more than doubled, probably because of marriages between Chinese men of American birth or Chinese merchants in the United States and women born in China.

Urban, rural-farm, and rural-nonfarm population.— Urban population, as defined by the Census Bureau, is in general that residing in cities and other incorporated places having 2,500 inhabitants or more, the remainder being classified as rural. In three of the New England States, New Hampshire, Massachusetts, and Rhode Island, towns (townships) are classified as urban if they have a population of 2,500 or more and certain urban characteristics; and a few large and

densely populated townships in other States are likewise classified, even though not formally incorporated as municipalities.

In addition to the classification of the population as urban and rural, the rural population is further subdivided into rural-farm and rural-nonfarm, on the basis of the replies to a question reading "Does this family live on a farm?" The rural-farm population includes all persons living on farms in the rural areas. The rural-nonfarm or "village" population is made up largely of persons living in small towns or villages, both incorporated and unincorporated, though in many areas there are considerable numbers of families living in the open country but not on farms.

In making comparisons between foreign countries in regard to the proportions of their natives who have settled in urban and in rural communities, respectively, consideration should be given to the fact that many of the immigrants from the northwestern European countries and from Germany came to the United States at a time when land was to be had free or at low cost, while most of the immigrants from central Europe, except Germany, and from eastern and southern Europe have arrived during a more recent period, when there has been comparatively little conveniently located and fertile land available for free settlement or obtainable at low prices. As a result, large numbers of the immigrants from northwestern Europe and from Germany went to rural localities, while most of the immigrants from the remainder of Europe have settled in urban communities, despite the fact that many of them were farmers in their native countries.

119652—38——16

228   POPULATION

FOREIGN-BORN POPULATION OF THE UNITED STATES BY COUNTRY OF BIRTH: 1930

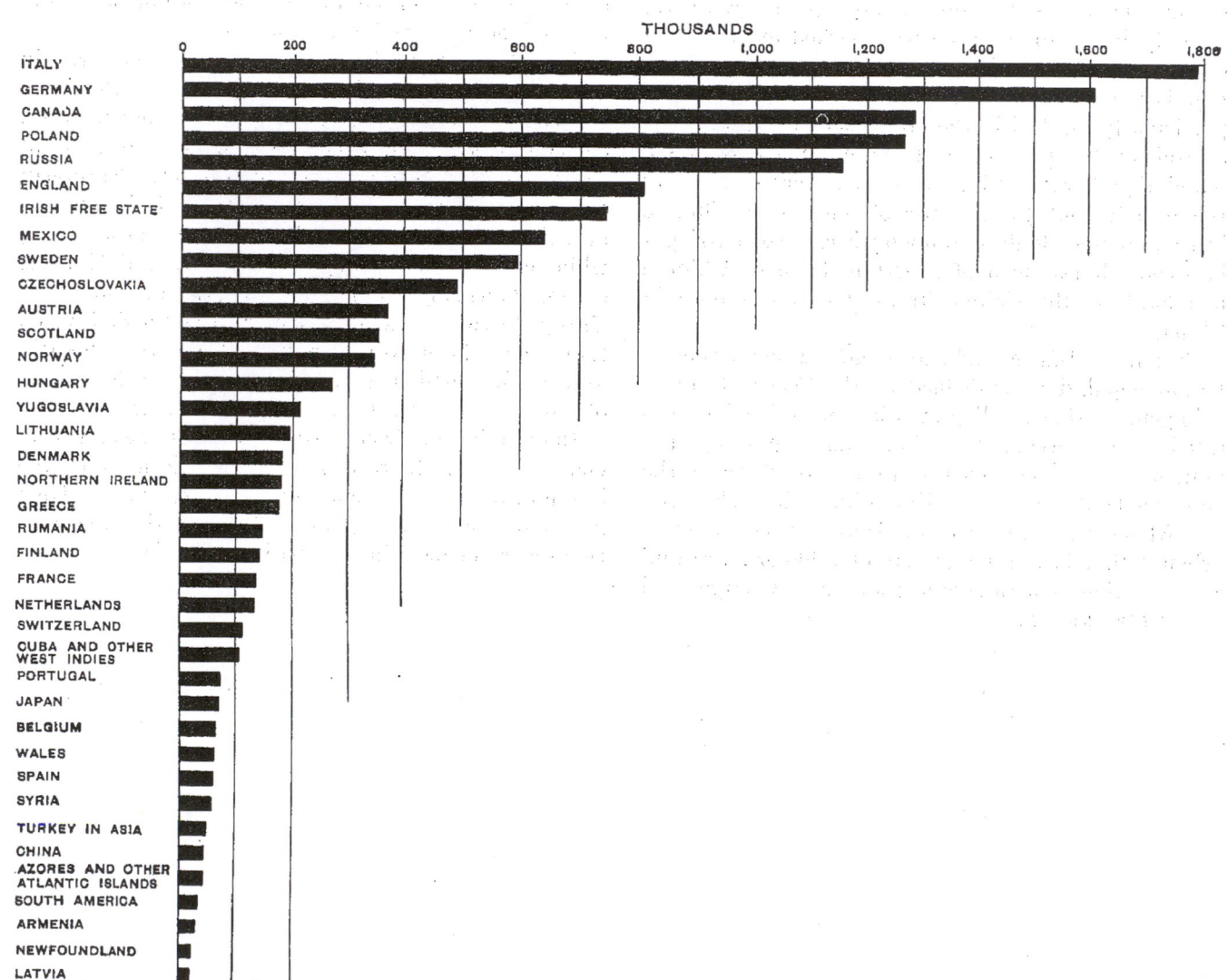

COUNTRY OF BIRTH OF THE FOREIGN BORN

FOREIGN-BORN POPULATION FROM SELECTED COUNTRIES, BY STATES: 1930

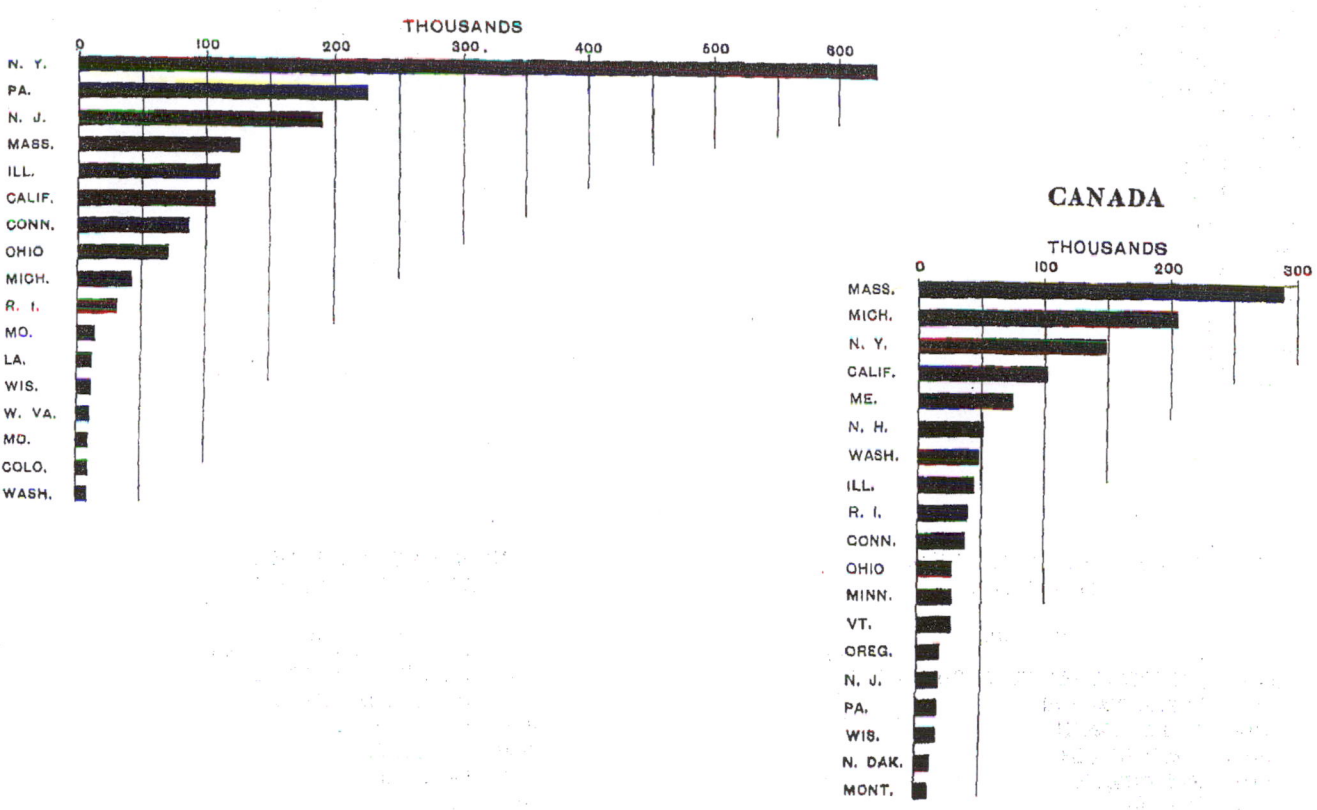

ITALY

CANADA

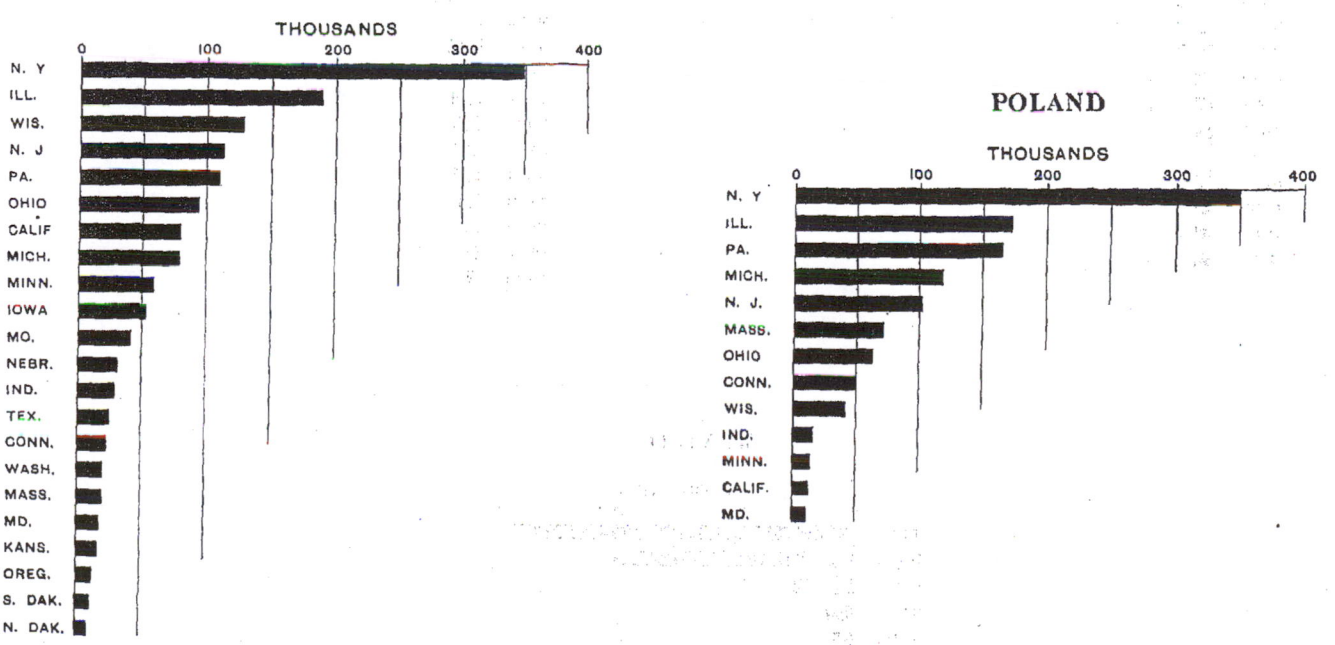

GERMANY

POLAND

230

POPULATION

FOREIGN-BORN POPULATION FROM SELECTED COUNTRIES, BY STATES: 1930—Continued

RUSSIA

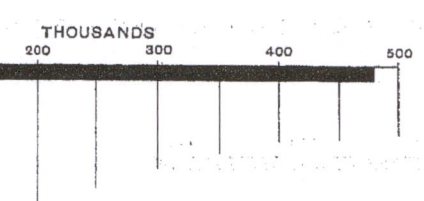

IRISH FREE STATE

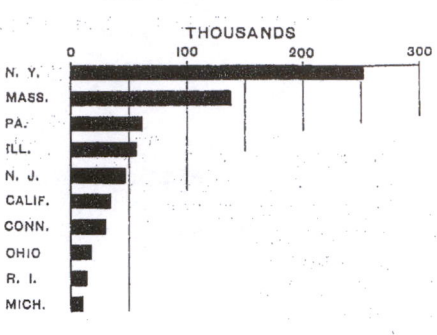

ENGLAND, SCOTLAND, AND WALES

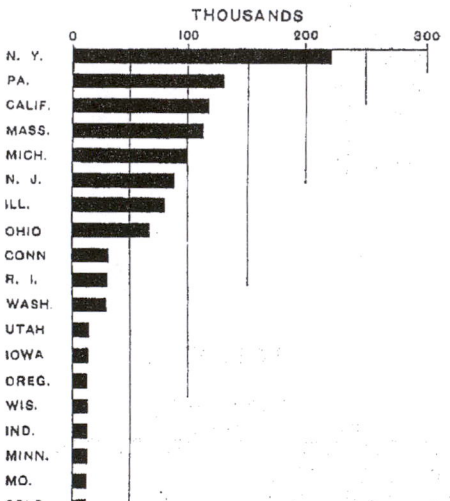

NORWAY, SWEDEN, AND DENMARK

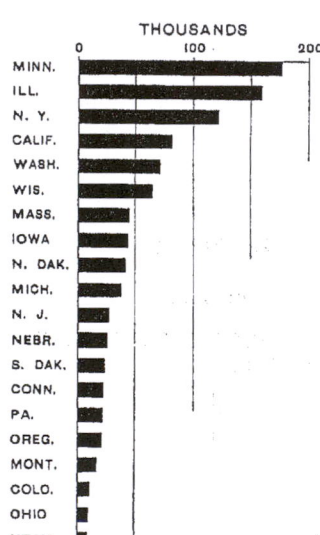

MEXICO

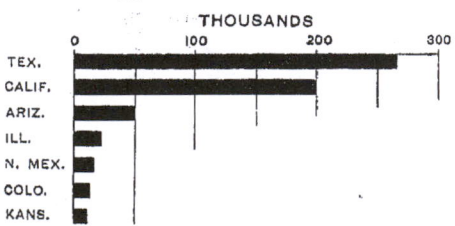

COUNTRY OF BIRTH OF THE FOREIGN BORN

231

TABLE 2.—COUNTRY OF BIRTH OF THE FOREIGN-BORN POPULATION OF THE UNITED STATES, BY COLOR OR RACE: 1930 AND 1920

PLACE OF BIRTH	ALL CLASSES		WHITE		NEGRO		MEXICAN		INDIAN		CHINESE		JAPANESE		ALL OTHER	
	1930	1920	1930	1920	1930	1920	1930	1920 (estimated)	1930	1920	1930	1920	1930	1920	1930	1920
Total population	122,775,046	105,710,620	108,864,207	[1] 04,120,374	11,891,143	10,463,131	1,422,533	700,541	332,397	244,437	74,954	61,639	138,834	111,010	50,978	9,488
Native	108,570,897	91,789,928	95,497,800	[1] 80,864,980	11,792,523	10,389,328	805,535	243,181	328,845	238,138	30,868	18,532	68,357	29,672	46,969	6,097
Foreign born	14,204,149	13,920,692	13,366,407	[1] 13,255,304	98,620	73,803	616,998	457,360	3,552	6,299	44,086	43,107	70,477	81,338	4,009	3,391
Europe	11,748,300	11,882,053	11,742,885	11,877,991	4,632	3,996	705	---	---	---	26	15	35	39	26	12
Asia	275,665	237,950	157,580	110,450	44	27	---	---	---	---	43,925	42,907	70,309	81,234	3,807	3,332
China	46,129	43,560	2,279	716	1	0	---	---	---	---	43,702	42,809	130	28	17	1
Japan	70,993	81,502	632	278	---	---	---	---	---	---	178	63	70,136	81,160	47	1
India	5,850	4,901	3,300	2,532	29	---	---	---	---	---	1	5	3	4	2,517	2,360
Other Asia	152,693	107,987	151,369	106,924	14	21	---	---	---	---	44	30	40	42	1,226	970
America	2,102,209	1,727,017	1,395,070	[1] 1,199,441	87,094	63,084	616,154	457,360	3,550	6,292	105	168	126	56	110	16
Canada	1,286,389	1,124,925	1,278,421	1,117,878	5,817	5,651	91	---	1,069	1,329	38	41	45	23	8	3
Newfoundland	23,980	13,249	23,971	13,242	9	6	---	---	---	---	---	1	---	---	---	---
Cuba	18,493	14,872	15,944	12,843	2,362	1,934	145	---	13	4	7	83	3	5	19	3
Other West Indies	87,748	64,090	15,482	13,520	72,138	50,466	29	---	60	54	10	18	1	4	22	---
Mexico	641,462	486,418	23,743	[1] 21,023	915	3,123	615,274	457,360	1,420	4,871	28	20	68	21	14	---
Central America	10,514	4,912	7,454	4,074	2,662	816	337	---	38	14	2	1	3	1	18	6
South America	33,623	18,551	30,055	16,855	3,191	1,666	278	---	50	20	14	4	6	2	29	4
All other	77,876	73,672	70,872	67,512	6,850	6,096	49	---	2	7	30	17	7	9	66	31
Africa	8,859	5,781	7,866	5,222	986	556	2	---	---	---	---	---	---	---	5	3
Australia	12,816	10,914	12,720	10,801	81	107	---	---	1	---	12	5	---	1	2	---
Azores	35,011	33,995	35,427	33,788	177	206	5	---	---	---	1	1	---	---	1	---
Other Atlantic Islands	9,467	10,345	4,052	5,196	5,411	5,143	1	---	1	2	---	3	---	1	2	---
Pacific Islands	4,527	3,712	4,364	3,643	96	40	3	---	---	---	8	1	1	3	55	25
Not specified or born at sea	6,596	8,925	6,443	8,862	99	44	38	---	---	5	9	7	6	4	1	3

[1] Adjusted figures. The white population as classified in 1920 included 700,541 persons (estimated) who would have been classified as Mexicans in 1930; 243,181 were native and 457,360 were foreign born, and these figures have been deducted from the white population as reported in 1920. (See text, p. 225.)

POPULATION

Table 3.—COUNTRY OF BIRTH OF THE FOREIGN-BORN POPULATION OF THE UNITED STATES, BY SEX, IN URBAN AND RURAL AREAS: 1930 AND 1920

[Per cent not shown where less than 0.1]

| COUNTRY OF BIRTH | TOTAL FOREIGN BORN | | | | MALE | | FEMALE | | MALES PER 100 FEMALES | | Urban, 1930 | Rural-farm, 1930 | Rural-nonfarm, 1930 |
| | Number | | Per cent | | | | | | | | | | |
	1930	1920	1930	1920	1930	1920	1930	1920	1930	1920			
All countries	14,204,149	13,920,692	100.0	100.0	7,647,090	7,675,435	6,557,059	6,245,257	116.6	122.9	11,250,815	1,224,885	1,728,449
Northwestern Europe:													
England	809,563	813,853	5.7	5.8	412,599	425,664	396,964	388,189	103.9	109.7	641,992	44,118	123,453
Scotland	354,323	254,570	2.5	1.8	181,654	133,956	172,669	120,614	105.2	111.1	295,541	13,871	44,911
Wales	60,205	67,066	0.4	0.5	32,189	36,184	28,016	30,882	114.9	117.2	45,968	4,008	10,229
Northern Ireland	178,882	} 1,037,234	{ 1.3	7.5	81,088	} 455,571	97,744	} 581,663	83.0	} 78.3	150,782	8,207	19,843
Irish Free State	744,810		5.2		324,841		419,969		77.3		671,727	17,008	56,075
Norway	347,852	363,863	2.4	2.6	196,349	202,758	151,503	161,105	129.6	125.9	194,936	91,385	61,531
Sweden	595,250	625,586	4.2	4.5	333,623	344,938	261,627	280,647	127.5	122.9	408,032	98,589	88,629
Denmark	179,474	} 189,154	{ 1.3	1.4	109,975	114,063	69,499	75,091	158.2	151.9	107,127	41,555	30,792
Iceland	2,764				1,385		1,379		100.4		1,348	772	644
Netherlands	133,133	131,766	0.9	0.9	77,574	75,510	55,559	56,256	139.6	134.2	80,466	31,408	21,259
Belgium	64,194	62,687	0.5	0.5	35,265	35,971	28,929	26,716	121.9	134.6	47,136	9,044	8,014
Luxemburg	9,048	12,585	0.1	0.1	5,456	7,671	3,592	4,914	151.9	156.1	5,693	1,955	1,400
Switzerland	113,010	118,659	0.8	0.9	64,833	67,830	48,177	50,829	134.6	133.4	67,918	25,887	19,205
France	135,592	153,072	1.0	1.1	66,388	79,475	69,204	73,597	95.9	108.0	105,178	10,358	20,056
Central Europe:													
Germany	1,608,814	1,686,108	11.3	12.1	843,136	891,293	765,678	794,815	110.1	112.1	1,176,950	215,977	215,887
Poland	1,268,583	1,139,979	8.9	8.2	681,425	646,388	587,158	493,591	116.1	131.0	1,096,114	65,166	107,303
Czechoslovakia	491,638	362,438	3.5	2.6	255,485	196,253	236,153	166,185	108.2	118.1	348,261	58,722	84,655
Austria	370,914	575,627	2.6	4.1	193,636	323,453	177,278	252,174	109.2	128.3	308,482	21,977	40,455
Hungary	274,450	397,283	1.9	2.9	139,828	216,914	134,622	180,369	103.9	120.3	228,642	14,801	31,007
Yugoslavia	211,416	169,439	1.5	1.2	131,351	114,752	80,065	54,687	164.1	209.8	154,501	12,655	44,260
Eastern Europe:													
Russia	1,153,628	} 1,400,495	{ 8.1	10.1	612,965	} 774,017	540,663	} 626,478	113.4	} 123.6	1,041,176	59,667	52,785
Latvia	20,673		0.1		11,061		9,612		115.1		18,744	672	1,257
Estonia	3,550				2,393		1,157		206.8		2,982	232	336
Lithuania	193,606	135,068	1.4	1.0	110,969	82,866	82,637	52,202	134.3	158.7	168,090	7,764	17,752
Finland	142,478	149,824	1.0	1.1	77,059	85,287	65,419	64,537	117.8	132.2	79,867	35,717	26,894
Rumania	146,393	102,823	1.0	0.7	78,685	58,135	67,708	44,688	116.2	130.1	131,465	6,469	8,459
Bulgaria	9,399	10,477	0.1	0.1	7,587	9,508	1,812	969	418.7	981.2	7,346	594	1,459
Turkey in Europe	2,257	5,284			1,269	3,658	988	1,626	128.4	225.0	2,158	31	68
Southern Europe:													
Greece	174,526	175,976	1.2	1.3	129,101	143,606	45,425	32,370	284.2	443.6	159,376	2,458	12,692
Albania	8,814	5,608	0.1		6,549	4,905	2,265	703	289.1	697.7	8,179	59	576
Italy	1,790,429	1,610,113	12.6	11.6	1,042,626	958,277	747,803	651,836	139.4	147.0	1,573,003	49,283	168,143
Spain	59,362	49,535	0.4	0.4	42,769	36,667	16,593	12,868	257.8	284.9	46,959	3,986	8,417
Portugal	73,184	69,981	0.5	0.5	44,970	41,546	28,194	28,435	159.5	146.1	54,759	9,799	8,606
Other Europe:													
Danzig	1,483	2,049			798	1,097	685	952	116.5	115.2	1,245	109	129
Europe (not specified)	14,772	3,852	0.1		8,896	2,568	5,876	1,284	151.4	200.0	12,316	877	1,579
Asia:													
Armenia	32,166	36,628	0.2	0.3	19,281	25,352	12,885	11,276	149.6	224.8	28,829	1,831	1,506
Palestine	6,137	3,203			3,636	2,062	2,501	1,141	145.4	180.7	5,875	63	199
Syria	57,227	51,901	0.4	0.4	32,510	31,241	24,717	20,660	131.5	151.2	51,482	1,081	4,664
Turkey in Asia	46,654	11,019	0.3	0.1	28,120	8,042	18,534	2,977	151.7	270.1	43,272	1,445	1,937
China	46,129	43,560	0.3	0.3	40,175	40,754	5,954	2,806	674.8	1,452.4	40,161	2,018	3,950
Japan	70,993	81,502	0.5	0.6	46,234	57,304	24,759	24,198	186.7	236.8	41,128	19,905	9,960
India	5,850	4,901			4,352	3,774	1,498	1,127	290.5	334.9	3,766	1,180	904
Other Asia	10,509	5,236	0.1		7,413	3,931	3,096	1,305	239.4	301.2	9,117	619	773
America:													
Canada—French	370,852	307,786	2.6	2.2	187,523	157,748	183,329	150,038	102.3	105.1	292,564	22,668	55,620
Canada—Other	915,537	817,139	6.4	5.9	433,239	392,931	482,298	424,208	89.8	92.6	702,236	77,729	135,572
Newfoundland	23,080	13,249	0.2	0.1	11,526	6,158	12,454	7,091	92.5	86.8	22,029	228	1,723
Cuba	18,493	14,872	0.1	0.1	11,130	8,341	7,363	6,531	151.2	127.7	17,473	165	855
Other West Indies	87,748	64,090	0.6	0.5	45,302	34,922	42,446	29,168	106.7	119.7	82,741	960	4,047
Mexico	641,462	486,418	4.5	3.5	361,787	276,526	279,675	209,892	129.4	131.7	368,453	117,553	155,456
Central America	10,514	4,912	0.1		5,596	2,849	4,918	2,063	113.8	138.1	9,882	116	516
South America	33,623	18,551	0.2	0.1	20,333	11,442	13,290	7,109	153.0	161.0	30,202	1,058	2,363
All other:													
Africa	8,859	5,781	0.1		5,241	3,433	3,618	2,348	144.9	146.2	7,745	284	830
Australia	12,816	10,914	0.1	0.1	6,730	6,019	6,086	4,895	110.6	123.0	10,286	728	1,802
Azores	35,611	33,995	0.3	0.2	19,071	18,192	16,540	15,803	115.3	115.1	23,513	8,564	3,534
Other Atlantic Islands	9,467	10,345	0.1	0.1	5,845	6,331	3,622	4,014	161.4	157.7	7,497	335	1,635
Pacific Islands	4,527	3,712			2,488	2,050	2,039	1,662	122.0	123.3	3,525	388	614
Country not specified	1,588	3,589			988	2,320	600	1,269	164.7	182.8	1,231	86	271
Born at sea	5,008	5,336			2,793	2,932	2,215	2,404	126.1	122.0	3,349	701	958

COUNTRY OF BIRTH OF THE FOREIGN BORN   233

TABLE 4.—COUNTRY OF BIRTH OF THE FOREIGN-BORN POPULATION OF THE UNITED STATES: 1850 TO 1930

[Figures are given for each country for all census years since 1850 for which data are available. Per cent not shown where less than 0.1]

COUNTRY OF BIRTH	NUMBER									PER CENT DISTRIBUTION								
	1930	1920	1910	1900	1890	1880	1870	1860	1850	1930	1920	1910	1900	1890	1880	1870	1860	1850
All countries	14,204,149	13,920,692	13,515,886	10,341,276	9,249,560	6,679,943	5,567,229	4,138,697	2,244,602	100.0	100.0	100.0	100.0	100.0	100.0	100.0	100.0	100.0
Northwestern Europe:																		
England	809,563	813,853	877,719	840,513	909,092	664,160	555,046	433,494	278,675	5.7	5.8	6.5	8.1	9.8	9.9	10.0	10.5	12.4
Scotland	354,323	254,570	261,076	233,524	242,231	170,136	140,835	108,518	70,550	2.5	1.8	1.9	2.3	2.6	2.5	2.5	2.6	3.1
Wales	60,205	67,066	82,488	93,586	100,079	83,302	74,533	45,763	29,868	0.4	0.5	0.6	0.9	1.1	1.2	1.3	1.1	1.3
Northern Ireland	178,832	} 1,037,234	1,352,251	1,615,459	1,871,509	1,854,571	1,855,827	1,611,304	961,719	1.3	} 7.5	10.0	15.6	20.2	27.8	33.3	38.9	42.8
Irish Free State	744,810									5.2								
Norway	347,852	363,863	403,877	336,388	322,665	181,729	114,246	43,995	12,678	2.4	2.6	3.0	3.3	3.5	2.7	2.1	1.1	0.6
Sweden	595,250	625,585	665,207	582,014	478,041	104,337	97,332	18,625	3,559	4.2	4.5	4.9	5.6	5.2	2.9	1.7	0.5	0.2
Denmark	179,474	} 189,154	181,649	153,690	132,543	64,196	30,107	9,962	1,838	} 1.3	} 1.4	1.3	1.5	1.4	1.0	0.5	0.2	0.1
Iceland	2,764																	
Netherlands	133,133	131,766	120,063	94,931	81,828	58,090	46,802	28,281	9,848	0.9	0.9	0.9	0.9	0.9	0.9	0.8	0.7	0.4
Belgium	64,194	62,687	49,400	29,757	22,639	15,535	12,553	9,072	1,313	0.5	0.5	0.4	0.3	0.2	0.2	0.2	0.2	0.1
Luxemburg	9,048	12,585	3,071	3,031	2,882	12,836	5,802			0.1	0.1				0.2	0.1		
Switzerland	113,010	118,659	124,848	115,593	104,069	88,621	75,153	53,327	13,358	0.8	0.9	0.9	1.1	1.1	1.3	1.3	1.3	0.6
France	135,592	153,072	117,418	104,197	113,174	106,971	116,402	109,870	54,069	1.0	1.1	0.9	1.0	1.2	1.6	2.1	2.7	2.4
Central and Eastern Europe:																		
Germany	1,608,814	1,686,108	2,311,237	2,663,418	2,784,894	1,966,742	1,690,533	1,276,075	583,774	11.3	12.1	17.1	25.8	30.1	29.4	30.4	30.8	26.0
Poland	1,268,583	1,139,070	937,884	383,407	147,440	48,557	14,436	7,298		8.9	8.2	6.9	3.7	1.6	0.7	0.3	0.2	
Czechoslovakia	491,638	362,438								3.5	2.6							
Austria	370,914	575,627	1,845,555	432,798	241,377	124,024	70,797	25,061	946	2.6	4.1	6.3	4.2	2.6	1.9	1.3	0.6	
Hungary	274,450	397,283	495,609	145,714	62,435	11,526	3,737			1.9	2.9	3.7	1.4	0.7	0.2	0.1		
Yugoslavia	211,416	169,439								1.5	1.2							
Russia	1,153,628	} 1,400,495	} 1,184,412	423,726	} 182,044	35,722	4,644	3,160	1,414	8.1	} 10.1	} 8.8	4.1	} 2.0	0.5	0.1	0.1	0.1
Latvia	20,673									0.1								
Estonia	3,550																	
Lithuania	193,606	135,068								1.4	1.0							
Finland	142,478	149,824	129,680	62,641						1.0	1.1	1.0	0.6					
Rumania	146,393	102,823	65,923	15,032						1.0	0.7	0.5	0.1					
Bulgaria	9,399	10,477	11,498							0.1	0.1	0.1						
Turkey in Europe	2,257	5,284	32,230	9,910	1,839	1,205	302	128	106			0.2	0.1					
Southern Europe:																		
Greece	174,526	175,976	101,282	8,515	1,887	776	390	328	86	1.2	1.3	0.7	0.1					
Albania	8,814	5,608	(2)							0.1								
Italy	1,790,429	1,610,113	1,343,125	484,027	182,580	44,230	17,157	11,677	3,679	12.6	11.6	9.9	4.7	2.0	0.7	0.3	0.3	0.2
Spain	59,362	49,535	22,108	7,050	6,185	5,121	3,764	4,244	3,113	0.4	0.4	0.2	0.1	0.1	0.1	0.1	0.1	0.1
Portugal	73,164	69,981	59,360	30,608	15,996	8,138	4,542	4,116	1,274	0.5	0.5	0.4	0.3	0.2	0.1	0.1	0.1	0.1
Other Europe:																		
Danzig	1,483	2,049																
Europe (not specified)	14,772	3,852	12,871	2,251	12,579	3,786	1,678	1,403		0.1		0.1		0.1	0.1			
Asia:																		
Armenia	32,166	36,628	} 59,720	(3)	(3)	(3)	(3)	(3)	(3)	0.2	0.3	} 0.4						
Palestine	6,137	8,203								0.4	0.4							
Syria	57,227	51,901								0.4	0.4							
Turkey in Asia	46,654	11,019								0.3	0.1							
China	46,129	43,560	56,756	81,534	106,701	104,468	63,042	35,565	758	0.3	0.3	0.4	0.8	1.2	1.6	1.1	0.9	
Japan	70,993	81,502	67,744	24,788	2,292	401	73			0.5	0.6	0.5	0.2					
India	5,850	4,901	4,664	2,031	2,143	1,707	586											
Other Asia	10,509	5,236	2,591	11,895	2,260	1,054	864	1,231	377	0.1		0.1						
America:																		
Canada—French	370,852	307,786	385,083	395,126	302,496					2.6	2.2	2.8	3.8	3.3				
Canada—Other	915,537	817,139	819,554	784,796	678,442	717,157	493,464	249,970	147,711	6.4	5.9	6.1	7.6	7.3	} 10.7	8.9	6.0	6.6
Newfoundland	23,980	13,249	5,080	(5)	(5)					0.2	0.1							
Cuba	18,493	14,872	15,133	11,081	} 23,256	6,917	5,319	} 7,353	} 5,772	0.1	0.1	0.1	0.1	} 0.3	0.1	0.1	} 0.2	} 0.3
Other West Indies	87,748	64,090	32,502	14,354	77,853	9,484	6,251			0.6	0.5	0.2	0.1		0.1	0.1		
Mexico	641,462	486,418	221,915	103,393	77,853	68,399	42,435	27,466	13,317	4.5	3.5	1.6	1.0	0.8	1.0	0.8	0.7	0.6
Central America	10,514	4,912	1,736	3,897	1,192	707	301	233	141	0.1								
South America	33,623	18,551	8,228	4,733	5,006	4,586	3,565	3,263	1,543	0.2	0.1	0.1		0.1	0.1	0.1	0.1	0.1
All other:																		
Africa	8,859	5,781	3,992	2,538	2,207	2,204	2,657	526	551	0.1								
Australia	12,816	10,914	9,035	6,807	5,984	4,906	3,118	1,419		0.1	0.1	0.1	0.1	0.1	0.1	0.1		
Azores	35,611	33,995	} 18,274	9,768	9,739	7,641	4,434	1,361		0.3	0.2	} 0.1	0.1	0.1	0.1	0.1		
Other Atlantic Islands	9,467	10,345								0.1	0.1							
Pacific Islands	4,527	3,712	2,415	2,013	3,369	1,953	910	721	588									
Country not specified	1,588	3,589	2,687	2,546	479		954	1,366	41,977									1.9
Born at sea	5,008	5,336	6,927	8,196	5,533	4,068	2,638	2,522			0.1	0.1	0.1	0.1		0.1		

[1] Persons reported in 1910 as of Polish mother tongue born in Germany (190,096), Austria (329,418), and Russia (418,370), have been deducted from the respective countries and combined as Poland for comparison with number reported in other years as born in Poland. (See text, p. 226.)
[2] Albania included with Turkey in Europe in 1910.
[3] Turkey in Asia included with Turkey in Europe prior to 1910.
[4] Includes 4,639 persons reported in 1910 as born in Serbia and 5,374 in Montenegro.
[5] Newfoundland included with Canada prior to 1910.

234

POPULATION

TABLE 5.—COUNTRY OF BIRTH OF THE FOREIGN-BORN POPULATION, BY DIVISIONS AND STATES: 1930

DIVISION AND STATE	All countries	England	Scotland	Wales	Northern Ireland	Irish Free State	Norway	Sweden	Denmark	Iceland	Netherlands	Belgium	Luxemburg	Switzerland	France	Germany	Poland
United States	14,204,149	809,563	354,323	60,205	178,832	744,810	347,852	595,250	179,474	2,764	133,133	64,194	9,048	113,010	135,592	1,608,814	1,268,583
GEOGRAPHIC DIVISIONS:																	
New England	1,848,943	135,586	54,226	2,834	33,527	193,113	8,860	66,023	7,625	73	2,814	3,884	76	3,541	11,741	50,005	136,774
Middle Atlantic	5,352,731	276,581	137,861	26,336	92,559	361,502	55,697	91,045	26,978	166	30,960	12,692	867	30,985	52,627	572,571	619,628
East North Central	3,275,723	170,122	84,579	14,585	23,322	93,881	74,228	165,785	42,397	227	57,443	33,053	3,976	27,066	24,144	524,437	416,569
West North Central	1,084,153	38,658	13,035	3,882	6,750	23,983	131,904	147,988	50,193	1,045	20,532	5,590	2,874	11,660	7,340	228,951	34,419
South Atlantic	318,697	25,761	8,859	1,797	3,637	12,163	2,591	4,940	2,239	33	1,624	1,397	85	2,248	3,977	38,225	26,239
East South Central	59,364	5,084	1,941	377	567	2,758	447	1,246	476	4	295	184	19	1,561	1,470	12,188	2,711
West South Central	440,553	11,228	3,241	612	1,212	4,921	2,292	5,534	2,319	13	1,044	1,009	93	2,681	5,736	38,411	6,800
Mountain	384,323	33,081	10,934	3,385	3,173	10,252	15,350	25,839	13,246	137	5,038	1,343	236	5,593	4,082	28,731	5,125
Pacific	1,439,662	113,462	39,647	6,397	14,085	42,237	56,483	86,850	33,901	1,066	18,383	5,042	822	27,675	24,475	115,295	20,318
NEW ENGLAND:																	
Maine	100,728	4,464	1,906	137	827	3,288	534	1,882	840	2	41	51	5	51	315	818	1,706
New Hampshire	82,929	3,923	1,728	72	1,010	4,807	396	1,608	166		163	528	2	82	299	1,517	4,101
Vermont	43,101	1,931	1,454	462	377	1,429	127	1,089	140	1	34	22	1	158	182	577	1,562
Massachusetts	1,065,620	78,497	32,724	1,358	20,378	138,366	5,454	36,810	3,070	61	1,890	1,956	31	1,272	6,035	20,538	71,442
Rhode Island	171,929	24,699	6,401	224	3,845	13,895	543	6,181	280	2	138	907	11	204	2,015	3,090	8,696
Connecticut	384,636	22,072	10,013	581	7,090	31,328	1,806	18,453	3,129	7	548	425	26	1,774	2,895	23,465	49,267
MIDDLE ATLANTIC:																	
New York	3,262,278	146,772	67,623	7,037	41,521	251,704	44,882	61,233	17,407	114	14,909	6,144	532	16,571	32,273	349,196	350,383
New Jersey	850,038	51,717	34,721	1,532	15,750	47,486	7,870	13,360	6,665	48	14,762	2,874	117	8,765	10,547	112,753	102,573
Pennsylvania	1,240,415	78,092	35,517	17,767	35,288	62,312	2,945	16,452	2,906	4	1,289	3,674	218	5,649	9,807	110,622	166,672
EAST NORTH CENTRAL:																	
Ohio	649,220	40,693	17,862	6,897	5,028	17,879	1,650	7,390	2,184	6	2,235	1,846	163	7,624	5,759	95,697	64,493
Indiana	142,999	7,473	3,898	934	1,045	3,931	730	4,666	964	3	1,992	3,254	56	1,624	2,160	28,152	17,482
Illinois	1,242,447	50,721	24,839	3,277	10,054	57,208	30,250	111,016	18,945	123	14,828	11,564	2,786	7,315	10,171	190,605	173,007
Michigan	852,758	62,757	35,257	2,236	6,138	11,390	7,201	23,905	7,210	32	32,128	13,931	375	2,834	4,593	81,714	119,228
Wisconsin	388,299	8,478	2,723	1,241	1,057	3,473	34,391	18,808	13,094	63	6,260	2,458	596	7,669	1,461	128,269	42,359
WEST NORTH CENTRAL:																	
Minnesota	390,790	8,448	3,241	582	1,403	5,095	71,562	90,623	13,831	266	4,832	1,701	1,032	2,041	1,248	59,993	15,015
Iowa	168,250	9,045	2,871	1,183	1,778	4,170	12,932	16,810	14,698	9	10,135	932	873	2,096	1,435	53,901	1,875
Missouri	153,085	7,924	2,419	573	1,308	8,561	575	3,895	1,497	10	706	859	54	3,578	2,360	42,276	8,324
North Dakota	105,871	1,593	891	111	329	863	31,337	8,470	2,936	724	658	238	202	360	237	10,114	2,128
South Dakota	66,061	2,159	612	265	351	862	13,061	6,540	5,298	15	3,068	239	380	618	229	12,739	717
Nebraska	119,199	4,217	1,223	383	801	2,502	1,691	14,335	10,210	19	620	523	204	1,364	558	32,544	4,445
Kansas	80,897	5,272	1,778	785	780	1,921	746	7,315	1,723	2	513	1,098	129	1,594	1,273	17,384	1,915
SOUTH ATLANTIC:																	
Delaware	17,025	1,305	562	45	900	1,364	141	294	99	1	56	29		75	147	1,459	2,954
Maryland	96,330	5,077	1,920	477	813	4,032	703	764	464	13	343	152	19	497	778	18,925	12,027
District of Columbia	30,733	2,841	884	116	493	3,026	228	435	229	6	151	92	8	360	712	3,411	1,562
Virginia	24,367	3,099	1,239	132	375	789	318	467	339	7	264	101	3	191	368	2,505	1,221
West Virginia	51,865	3,288	1,267	607	222	659	57	303	75		42	690	11	398	547	3,129	5,545
North Carolina	8,969	1,209	477	35	63	253	95	160	65	1	201	19	4	87	156	903	319
South Carolina	5,358	479	179	13	90	185	65	106	39		24	52	1	26	77	747	510
Georgia	14,303	1,334	534	83	147	546	125	266	108		67	45		114	283	1,682	1,156
Florida	69,747	7,129	1,797	289	534	1,309	859	2,145	921	5	476	217	39	500	909	5,464	945
EAST SOUTH CENTRAL:																	
Kentucky	22,007	1,482	524	114	191	1,656	46	170	72		112	59	4	915	584	7,552	899
Tennessee	13,251	1,355	433	104	160	491	68	232	123	1	56	28	3	443	220	1,788	960
Alabama	16,061	1,772	860	141	162	413	265	638	182	3	95	60	7	150	468	2,114	556
Mississippi	8,045	475	124	18	54	198	68	206	99		32	37	5	53	198	739	296
WEST SOUTH CENTRAL:																	
Arkansas	10,632	802	229	51	100	354	72	249	138		80	78	7	518	255	2,989	394
Louisiana	37,076	1,529	435	66	234	970	487	433	315	1	220	307	10	260	2,951	3,616	655
Oklahoma	30,558	2,101	866	235	262	690	243	835	516	1	166	217	31	493	720	5,893	1,162
Texas	362,287	6,796	1,711	260	616	2,907	1,490	4,017	1,350	11	578	407	45	1,410	1,810	25,913	4,589
MOUNTAIN:																	
Montana	75,903	6,021	2,721	580	1,095	3,950	8,991	5,655	2,541	16	1,253	509	108	901	653	6,155	1,144
Idaho	32,284	3,253	1,025	355	284	616	2,148	4,200	1,667	12	341	118	41	1,038	382	3,427	227
Wyoming	23,343	2,105	1,424	222	179	584	647	1,783	775	1	101	139	7	250	359	1,714	604
Colorado	99,875	6,893	2,877	1,061	900	3,184	1,261	8,328	2,374	1	810	390	51	1,202	1,074	9,988	2,488
New Mexico	24,052	650	354	99	91	218	119	263	101		64	34	5	117	259	936	97
Arizona	65,756	2,314	579	139	235	653	295	778	364	4	100	50	12	279	311	1,433	253
Utah	48,015	10,851	1,669	862	234	584	1,698	4,389	4,883	97	2,325	79	9	1,419	261	4,104	230
Nevada	15,095	994	285	67	155	463	191	443	541	6	44	24	3	387	783	974	82
PACIFIC:																	
Washington	255,258	20,311	8,024	1,694	2,154	4,942	31,429	34,084	7,175	741	3,484	1,242	263	3,578	1,988	20,542	3,942
Oregon	110,440	8,077	3,820	592	1,039	2,802	7,450	11,032	3,551	49	1,002	681	122	4,034	1,146	12,913	2,086
California	1,073,964	85,074	27,803	4,111	10,892	34,493	17,604	41,734	23,175	276	13,897	3,119	437	20,063	21,341	81,840	14,290

COUNTRY OF BIRTH OF THE FOREIGN BORN

235

TABLE 5.—COUNTRY OF BIRTH OF THE FOREIGN-BORN POPULATION, BY DIVISIONS AND STATES: 1930—Con.

DIVISION AND STATE	Czecho-slo-vakia	Austria	Hun-gary	Yugo-slavia	Russia	Latvia	Es-tonia	Lithu-ania	Fin-land	Ru-mania	Bul-garia	Tur-key in Eu-rope	Greece	Al-bania	Italy	Spain	Por-tugal	Other Eu-rope
United States	491,638	370,914	274,450	211,416	1,153,628	20,673	3,550	193,606	142,478	146,393	9,399	2,257	174,526	8,814	1,790,429	59,362	73,164	16,255
GEOGRAPHIC DIVS.:																		
New England	16,024	11,946	11,107	1,334	103,310	2,906	182	41,753	18,503	3,424	238	311	25,423	4,175	253,098	2,382	37,585	468
Middle Atlantic	199,705	216,000	136,753	54,662	659,252	9,052	1,949	69,882	22,290	72,826	1,544	1,043	51,053	2,072	1,046,150	25,787	10,949	6,532
E. North Central	190,709	82,600	100,773	102,437	175,168	4,451	401	67,872	42,946	48,871	4,914	424	49,101	1,763	244,504	4,637	600	5,737
W. North Central	46,005	22,924	7,295	17,040	83,729	684	58	3,837	26,328	9,012	692	34	8,018	334	31,653	674	35	698
S. Atlantic	8,309	7,578	6,737	3,065	35,870	1,384	119	5,681	1,191	2,743	218	106	11,449	110	39,512	6,303	495	653
E. South Central	878	1,239	1,003	550	5,023	182	12	424	154	464	43	22	2,304	52	7,288	219	41	208
W. South Central	14,885	4,590	1,241	1,141	10,850	247	53	580	297	847	220	37	3,331	20	22,185	1,625	117	587
Mountain	5,018	6,002	1,572	12,183	20,865	135	84	614	5,765	1,435	640	20	6,716	70	23,774	3,617	229	186
Pacific	10,105	18,035	7,879	19,045	59,555	1,632	692	2,963	25,004	6,771	890	260	17,131	218	122,256	14,118	23,113	1,180
NEW ENGLAND:																		
Maine	241	230	30	16	1,880	92	4	1,121	1,406	27	5	16	748	243	2,359	40	83	18
New Hampshire	132	174	47	36	1,427	46	3	1,084	1,386	35	15	7	225	193	1,938	21	251	11
Vermont	191	132	156	71	660	21	5	160	555	15	4		8	8	3,082	478	46	1
Massachusetts	2,966	4,266	905	305	67,684	2,315	89	25,219	13,077	1,680	116	217	10,780	2,938	126,103	812	25,340	178
Rhode Island	274	838	133	24	5,890	93	10	922	448	480	48	38	1,100	250	32,493	110	8,445	32
Connecticut	12,220	6,300	9,836	882	25,769	339	71	13,247	1,631	1,178	50	33	3,837	543	87,123	921	2,920	228
MIDDLE ATLANTIC:																		
New York	56,176	142,298	70,631	10,917	481,307	5,971	1,505	22,933	17,444	51,014	978	849	33,387	1,206	629,322	17,906	5,731	3,389
New Jersey	32,358	24,010	32,332	3,643	62,152	1,194	234	9,870	2,721	6,686	124	77	6,020	138	190,858	5,000	3,810	902
Pennsylvania	111,171	49,692	33,790	40,102	115,793	1,887	210	37,079	2,125	15,126	442	117	11,646	728	225,979	2,881	1,408	2,241
E. NORTH CENTRAL:																		
Ohio	68,738	20,547	47,026	38,884	32,627	721	81	7,561	5,633	19,580	1,686	96	12,050	504	71,496	1,562	232	998
Indiana	8,325	2,709	7,674	6,646	4,749	116	10	2,109	265	3,292	403	11	4,087	121	6,873	621	88	241
Illinois	76,420	33,330	20,305	28,173	87,026	2,609	127	44,733	4,302	13,172	1,037	99	20,003	365	110,449	1,050	104	1,084
Michigan	17,646	13,299	19,188	16,468	34,348	674	123	9,340	27,022	11,482	1,594	201	10,061	577	43,087	1,347	136	3,180
Wisconsin	19,580	12,709	6,490	12,266	16,418	331	60	4,109	5,724	1,345	194	17	2,900	136	12,599	57	40	234
W. NORTH CENTRAL:																		
Minnesota	11,415	7,288	1,681	8,888	11,902	255	30	1,283	24,360	2,819	238	7	1,765	23	6,401	42	6	115
Iowa	8,280	1,596	295	1,306	4,482	66	4	835	70	284	159	2	1,910	11	3,834	25	1	58
Missouri	4,495	7,928	3,484	2,753	15,689	167	9	805	100	2,321	151	19	2,405	288	15,204	465	14	250
North Dakota	1,869	1,407	808	336	22,618	33	7	121	878	2,518	39		303	2	102	8	1	25
South Dakota	2,589	678	231	223	9,023	7	3	46	825	410	46	3	270		305	10	1	25
Nebraska	14,313	1,863	372	762	11,234	145	3	589	48	336	30	3	822	7	3,642	20	4	133
Kansas	3,044	2,164	334	2,781	8,781	11	2	158	52	324	29		534		2,165	104	8	83
SOUTH ATLANTIC:																		
Delaware	159	435	157	7	1,450	20	11	90	50	91	2	4	339		3,769	121	11	33
Maryland	3,344	2,634	1,219	275	18,782	624	39	3,422	376	811	16	6	1,617	8	10,872	289	75	177
Dist. of Columbia	193	403	228	55	4,914	142	2	256	69	160	16	25	1,347	14	4,330	152	45	72
Virginia	927	492	560	67	2,989	261	9	400	68	172	9	23	1,285	19	1,853	112	70	85
West Virginia	2,831	2,254	3,683	2,440	2,209	71	6	1,009	144	667	121	12	2,479	47	12,088	1,374	51	125
North Carolina	50	146	70	9	755	31	4	121	9	33	7	6	1,006	8	438	25	13	29
South Carolina	52	74	32	13	556	49	2	60	38	21	1	6	627	3	188	19	3	27
Georgia	115	225	136	39	2,200	115	6	155	104	143	8	12	1,197	4	712	82	96	42
Florida	638	825	652	160	2,012	62	40	168	333	645	38	12	1,552	7	5,262	4,120	131	63
E. SOUTH CENTRAL:																		
Kentucky	194	484	557	201	1,629	40		186	27	202	20	14	466	16	1,580	98	26	59
Tennessee	131	223	208	25	1,803	66		106	24	98	3	3	528	35	1,946	17	3	58
Alabama	483	386	284	135	1,067	49	11	88	51	133	16	5	968	1	2,140	68	9	55
Mississippi	70	146	44	189	524	27	1	44	52	31	4		342		1,613	36	3	36
W. SOUTH CENTRAL:																		
Arkansas	404	293	67	118	401	10	2	52	10	36	33	2	312		952	7	1	31
Louisiana	332	467	361	397	1,375	23	23	31	82	127	29	12	574	4	13,526	677	59	131
Oklahoma	1,867	530	191	162	3,613	74		189	25	140	109		642		1,157	54	12	71
Texas	12,282	3,300	622	464	5,467	140	28	308	180	544	49	23	1,803	16	6,550	887	45	354
MOUNTAIN:																		
Montana	1,714	1,435	360	3,877	4,212	19	29	175	2,700	641	197	1	840	26	2,840	69	14	41
Idaho	541	399	106	489	1,153	4	9	18	858	110	29	1	414	1	1,153	1,087	18	11
Wyoming	521	457	175	1,322	1,375	6	10	35	633	55	68	2	888	5	1,653	123	24	13
Colorado	1,714	2,408	690	3,650	12,979	61	13	262	563	450	271	9	1,230	8	10,670	224	16	69
New Mexico	143	316	59	490	219	4	6	24	41	20	11		292		1,259	170	4	14
Arizona	178	341	94	784	463	18	12	58	300	75	18	2	356	10	822	558	24	14
Utah	119	410	72	989	342	15	3	36	507	64	37	5	2,197	17	2,814	277	8	10
Nevada	88	176	16	532	122	8	2	6	163	20	9		499	3	2,563	1,109	121	5
PACIFIC:																		
Washington	2,202	3,128	579	4,761	9,229	276	140	868	11,002	787	247	76	2,881	115	10,274	284	116	100
Oregon	1,691	1,664	404	1,541	6,278	167	107	319	5,507	843	174	17	1,575	10	4,728	502	103	51
California	6,212	13,243	6,896	12,743	44,048	1,189	436	1,776	8,495	5,141	469	167	12,675	93	107,254	13,332	22,894	1,029

417

236 POPULATION

TABLE 5.—COUNTRY OF BIRTH OF THE FOREIGN-BORN POPULATION, BY DIVISIONS AND STATES: 1930—Con.

DIVISION AND STATE	Armenia	Palestine	Syria	Turkey in Asia	China	Japan	India	Other Asia	Canada French	Canada Other	New-found-land	West Indies	Mexico	Central and South America	Africa	Australia	Atlantic Islands	Pacific Islands	Country not specified	Born at sea
United States	32,166	6,137	57,227	46,654	46,129	70,993	5,850	10,509	370,852	915,537	23,980	106,241	641,462	44,137	8,859	12,816	45,078	4,527	1,588	5,008
GEOGRAPHIC DIVS.:																				
New England	10,687	428	11,076	8,348	2,388	331	380	792	264,261	254,604	12,534	5,513	221	2,637	734	603	27,889	168	94	384
Middle Atlantic	8,412	3,534	17,950	21,183	10,321	2,830	1,364	3,115	33,336	149,094	8,052	71,754	8,904	24,701	3,900	2,658	2,783	704	507	1,004
E. North Central	5,927	1,037	11,561	8,593	4,304	708	839	3,553	42,308	254,688	1,726	3,432	44,191	3,654	1,251	1,697	273	371	449	1,439
W. North Central	267	167	3,127	507	1,152	511	182	203	10,531	52,899	185	464	23,506	753	293	474	42	137	85	805
South Atlantic	323	280	4,538	1,547	1,122	297	230	282	2,055	15,608	302	20,658	875	1,568	459	410	275	135	119	176
E. South Central	32	98	1,703	157	467	28	40	53	347	2,820	46	572	843	343	86	88	14	22	17	64
W. South Central	53	192	3,629	449	932	371	161	124	994	7,439	125	1,336	271,881	1,908	233	289	82	92	50	208
Mountain	193	71	1,136	298	2,037	5,723	187	287	3,678	23,835	134	258	89,870	556	277	618	177	844	34	190
Pacific	6,272	330	2,507	5,572	23,406	60,194	2,467	2,100	13,342	154,550	876	2,254	201,171	8,017	1,566	5,979	13,543	2,554	233	738
NEW ENGLAND:																				
Maine	134	11	475	131	63	4	18	6	36,947	37,048	204	89	5	34	16	20	36	8	10	43
New Hampshire	151	2	411	259	58	2	8	6	37,682	13,310	228	187	4	46	22	20	71	2	6	18
Vermont	14	7	267	17	20	4	11	1	17,320	9,874	101	18	11	30	11	14	8	3	1	13
Massachusetts	7,705	250	7,153	6,124	1,848	180	238	165	115,241	174,255	10,987	4,129	131	1,514	485	372	23,102	105	55	200
Rhode Island	1,909	31	1,218	1,084	132	19	41	42	31,501	7,824	256	228	18	359	68	56	4,321	20	7	36
Connecticut	774	127	1,552	733	267	122	64	572	25,570	12,293	758	862	52	654	132	121	351	30	15	74
MIDDLE ATLANTIC:																				
New York	4,874	2,911	10,113	16,673	7,512	2,314	920	2,293	28,955	120,193	6,378	64,466	5,218	20,145	3,003	1,676	2,027	485	317	540
New Jersey	1,947	312	2,627	2,353	1,165	297	250	360	2,470	14,195	933	4,240	628	2,644	533	436	601	122	66	190
Pennsylvania	1,591	311	5,210	2,157	1,644	219	194	462	1,911	14,706	741	3,048	3,058	1,912	424	546	155	97	124	274
E. NORTH CENTRAL:																				
Ohio	468	270	4,226	1,826	888	125	131	476	2,606	24,739	217	705	3,274	726	248	311	54	55	68	299
Indiana	127	42	741	297	210	44	45	239	682	5,585	69	144	7,612	167	45	99	10	26	17	94
Illinois	1,635	456	1,095	2,048	2,260	410	272	2,061	6,180	37,790	386	1,329	21,570	1,655	516	715	149	159	128	416
Michigan	3,322	220	4,999	3,564	705	112	343	725	28,539	175,244	975	1,175	9,778	881	374	447	53	107	195	298
Wisconsin	375	49	500	858	241	17	48	52	4,292	11,321	79	79	1,957	225	68	125	7	24	41	332
W. NORTH CENTRAL:																				
Minnesota	60	35	670	83	377	49	50	40	6,484	20,732	48	54	2,097	119	86	88	19	30	16	222
Iowa	68	10	570	67	112	15	22	38	608	5,745	42	54	2,532	88	30	82	7	29	7	154
Missouri	86	83	806	240	395	69	42	52	588	4,872	38	235	3,397	267	87	147	10	35	31	130
North Dakota	22	4	235	38	74	51	10	11	1,354	11,155	11	7	363	49	17	25	-------	3	11	71
South Dakota	3	4	229	28	40	10	8	12	492	2,922	8	8	306	16	20	18	-------	7	8	56
Nebraska	24	26	369	28	105	287	25	25	436	3,974	34	32	3,628	69	23	47	1	15	4	82
Kansas	4	5	248	23	49	30	25	25	569	3,499	4	74	11,183	145	30	67	5	18	8	90
SOUTH ATLANTIC:																				
Delaware	3	2	5	21	25	6	4	3	61	418	8	90	38	91	14	8	4	4	28	3
Maryland	30	65	68	180	292	31	32	30	291	2,016	61	814	96	330	119	86	93	42	15	49
Dist. of Columbia	68	46	259	198	226	61	39	23	223	1,506	34	415	122	286	66	44	13	12	10	15
Virginia	133	33	536	230	165	39	25	50	157	1,490	27	295	48	135	45	57	37	18	4	24
West Virginia	16	17	1,300	369	65	8	12	61	118	862	15	97	267	103	27	40	4	2	3	28
North Carolina	2	32	669	108	57	11	13	34	80	868	26	114	17	39	37	22	7	16	-------	7
South Carolina	-------	12	401	93	25	13	10	24	31	249	7	64	10	17	20	4	5	2	1	6
Georgia	23	23	388	185	145	19	16	18	109	995	20	226	49	90	46	32	14	10	5	9
Florida	48	50	912	163	122	109	79	39	985	7,204	104	18,543	228	477	85	117	98	29	53	35
E. SOUTH CENTRAL:																				
Kentucky	8	33	414	48	39	6	18	12	96	838	21	67	88	41	19	29	1	10	7	24
Tennessee	13	24	109	30	52	11	13	14	92	857	12	88	52	72	25	27	3	4	4	12
Alabama	8	21	487	62	36	9	8	15	117	802	11	342	87	137	27	20	9	5	3	20
Mississippi	3	20	693	17	340	2	1	12	42	323	2	75	616	93	15	12	1	3	3	8
W. SOUTH CENTRAL:																				
Arkansas	4	6	221	18	160	11	4	11	77	638	39	36	280	34	16	20	3	4	5	18
Louisiana	15	25	929	117	219	34	41	18	222	787	18	711	1,644	1,376	79	50	21	16	3	32
Oklahoma	10	29	809	45	124	53	16	29	243	1,903	15	53	3,737	76	29	49	5	16	7	43
Texas	24	132	1,670	269	429	273	100	66	452	4,111	53	536	266,240	422	109	170	53	56	35	115
MOUNTAIN:																				
Montana	43	11	155	79	315	438	22	74	1,966	9,227	33	27	1,776	68	36	71	10	25	5	39
Idaho	14	2	43	11	257	675	16	9	571	3,958	41	12	919	33	34	53	28	54	1	18
Wyoming	24	4	45	13	92	554	8	25	118	1,026	3	17	3,075	21	17	13	1	15	2	11
Colorado	35	27	254	78	155	1,389	48	54	572	5,273	27	87	13,144	222	48	114	11	35	9	64
New Mexico	2	1	192	8	76	108	22	8	62	556	6	16	16,406	54	15	20	2	8	4	7
Arizona	14	14	285	29	618	419	31	44	158	1,879	15	69	50,022	71	26	85	5	31	2	13
Utah	37	10	141	34	212	1,729	26	64	97	1,095	5	12	2,390	44	82	215	2	154	9	32
Nevada	24	2	21	46	312	411	14	9	134	821	4	18	2,138	43	19	47	118	22	2	6
PACIFIC:																				
Washington	113	22	272	646	1,460	8,935	139	130	4,340	43,929	250	163	520	368	175	585	52	248	60	178
Oregon	47	12	186	154	1,031	2,617	95	59	1,345	16,601	67	71	1,292	157	65	275	42	154	14	79
California	6,112	296	2,049	4,772	20,915	48,642	2,233	1,911	7,657	94,020	559	2,020	199,359	7,492	1,326	5,119	13,449	2,152	159	481

COUNTRY OF BIRTH OF THE FOREIGN BORN

237

TABLE 6.—PER CENT DISTRIBUTION OF THE FOREIGN-BORN POPULATION BY COUNTRY OF BIRTH, BY DIVISIONS AND STATES: 1930

[Per cent not shown where less than 0.1]

COUNTRY OF BIRTH	United States	GEOGRAPHIC DIVISIONS — New England	Middle Atlantic	East North Central	West North Central	South Atlantic	East South Central	West South Central	Mountain	Pacific	NEW ENGLAND — Maine	New Hampshire	Vermont	Massachusetts	Rhode Island	Connecticut	MIDDLE ATLANTIC — New York	New Jersey	Pennsylvania
All countries	100.0	100.0	100.0	100.0	100.0	100.0	100.0	100.0	100.0	100.0	100.0	100.0	100.0	100.0	100.0	100.0	100.0	100.0	100.0
Northwestern Europe:																			
England	5.7	7.3	5.2	5.2	3.6	8.1	8.6	2.5	8.6	7.9	4.4	4.7	4.5	7.4	14.4	5.7	4.5	6.1	6.3
Scotland	2.5	2.9	2.6	2.6	1.2	2.8	3.3	0.7	2.8	2.8	1.9	2.1	3.4	3.1	3.7	2.6	2.1	4.1	2.9
Wales	0.4	0.2	0.5	0.4	0.4	0.6	0.6	0.1	0.9	0.4	0.1	0.1	1.1	0.1	0.1	0.2	0.2	0.2	1.4
Northern Ireland	1.3	1.8	1.7	0.7	0.6	1.1	1.0	0.3	0.8	1.0	0.8	1.2	0.9	1.9	2.2	1.8	1.3	1.9	2.8
Irish Free State	5.2	10.4	6.8	2.0	2.2	3.8	4.6	1.1	2.7	2.9	3.3	5.8	3.3	13.0	8.1	8.1	7.7	5.6	5.0
Norway	2.4	0.5	1.0	2.3	12.2	0.8	0.8	0.5	4.0	3.9	0.5	0.5	0.3	0.5	0.3	0.5	1.4	0.9	0.2
Sweden	4.2	3.0	1.7	5.1	13.7	1.6	2.1	1.3	6.7	6.0	1.9	1.9	2.5	3.5	3.6	4.8	1.9	1.6	1.3
Denmark	1.3	0.4	0.5	1.3	4.6	0.7	0.8	0.5	3.4	2.4	0.8	0.2	0.3	0.3	0.2	0.8	0.5	0.8	0.2
Iceland					0.1					0.1									
Netherlands	0.9	0.2	0.6	1.8	1.9	0.5	0.5	0.2	1.3	0.9		0.2	0.1	0.2	0.1	0.1	0.5	1.7	0.1
Belgium	0.5	0.2	0.2	1.0	0.5	0.4	0.3	0.2	0.3	0.4	0.1	0.6	0.1	0.2	0.5	0.1	0.2	0.3	0.3
Luxemburg	0.1			0.1	0.3				0.1	0.1									
Switzerland	0.8	0.2	0.6	0.8	1.1	0.7	2.6	0.6	1.5	1.0	0.1	0.1	0.4	0.1	0.1	0.5	0.5	1.0	0.5
France	1.0	0.6	1.0	0.7	0.7	1.2	2.5	1.3	1.1	1.7	0.3	0.4	0.4	0.6	1.2	0.8	1.0	1.2	0.8
Central Europe:																			
Germany	11.3	2.7	10.7	16.0	21.1	12.0	20.5	8.7	7.5	8.0	0.8	1.8	1.3	1.0	1.8	8.1	10.7	13.3	8.9
Poland	8.0	7.4	11.6	12.7	3.2	8.2	4.6	1.5	1.3	1.4	1.7	4.9	3.6	8.7	5.1	12.8	10.7	12.1	13.4
Czechoslovakia	3.5	0.9	3.7	5.8	4.2	2.6	1.5	3.4	1.3	0.7	0.2	0.2	0.4	0.3	0.2	3.2	1.7	3.8	9.0
Austria	2.6	0.6	4.0	2.5	2.1	2.4	2.1	1.0	1.6	1.3	0.2	0.2	0.3	0.4	0.5	1.6	4.4	2.8	4.0
Hungary	1.9	0.6	2.6	3.1	0.7	2.1	1.8	0.3	0.4	0.5		0.1	0.4	0.1	0.1	2.6	2.2	3.8	2.7
Yugoslavia	1.5	0.1	1.0	3.1	1.6	1.0	0.9	0.3	3.2	1.3		0.2				0.2	0.3	0.4	3.2
Eastern Europe:																			
Russia	8.1	5.6	12.3	5.3	7.7	11.3	8.5	2.5	5.4	4.1	1.9	1.7	1.5	6.4	3.4	6.7	14.8	7.3	9.3
Latvia	0.1	0.2	0.2	0.1	0.1	0.4	0.3	0.1		0.1	0.1	0.1		0.2	0.1	0.1	0.2	0.1	0.2
Estonia																			
Lithuania	1.4	2.3	1.3	2.1	0.4	1.8	0.7	0.1	0.2	0.2	1.1	1.3	0.4	2.4	0.5	3.4	0.7	1.2	3.0
Finland	1.0	1.0	0.4	1.3	2.4	0.4	0.3	0.1	1.5	1.7	1.4	1.7	1.3	1.2	0.3	0.4	0.5	0.3	0.2
Rumania	1.0	0.2	1.4	1.5	0.8	0.9	0.8	0.2	0.4	0.5			0.2	0.3	0.3	0.3	1.6	0.8	1.2
Bulgaria	0.1		0.2	0.1	0.1	0.1	0.1			0.2									
Turkey in Europe																			
Southern Europe:																			
Greece	1.2	1.4	1.0	1.5	0.7	3.0	3.9	0.8	1.7	1.2	0.7	3.9	0.5	1.6	0.6	0.9	1.0	0.7	0.9
Albania	0.1	0.2		0.1							0.2	0.2		0.3	0.1				0.1
Italy	12.6	13.7	19.5	7.5	2.9	12.4	12.3	5.0	6.2	8.5	2.3	2.3	7.2	11.8	18.9	22.7	19.3	22.5	18.2
Spain	0.4	0.1	0.5	0.1	0.1	2.0	0.4	0.4	0.9	1.0			1.1	0.1	0.1	0.2	0.5	0.6	0.2
Portugal	0.5	2.0	0.2			0.2	0.1			1.6	0.1	0.3		2.4	4.0	0.8	0.2	0.4	0.1
Other Europe	0.1		0.1	0.2	0.1	0.2	0.4	0.1		0.1						0.1	0.1	0.1	0.2
Asia:																			
Armenia	0.2	0.6	0.2	0.2		0.1	0.1		0.1	0.4	0.1	0.2		0.7	1.1	0.2	0.1	0.2	0.1
Palestine			0.1			0.1	0.2										0.1		
Syria	0.4	0.6	0.3	0.4	0.3	1.4	2.9	0.8	0.3	0.2	0.5	0.5	0.6	0.7	0.7	0.4	0.3	0.3	0.4
Turkey in Asia	0.3	0.5	0.4	0.3		0.5	0.3	0.1	0.1	0.4	0.1	0.3		0.4	0.6	0.2	0.5	0.3	0.2
China	0.3	0.1	0.2	0.1	0.1	0.4	0.8	0.2	0.5	1.6	0.1	0.1		0.2	0.1	0.1	0.2	0.1	0.1
Japan	0.5		0.1			0.1		0.1	1.5	4.2							0.1		
India						0.1	0.1			0.2									
Other Asia	0.1		0.1	0.1		0.1	0.1		0.1	0.1						0.1	0.1		
America:																			
Canada—French	2.6	14.3	0.6	1.3	1.0	0.6	0.6	0.2	1.0	0.9	36.7	45.4	40.2	10.8	18.3	6.0	0.9	0.3	0.2
Canada—Other	6.4	13.8	2.8	7.8	4.9	4.9	4.8	1.7	6.2	10.7	36.8	16.0	22.9	16.4	4.6	3.2	3.7	1.7	1.2
Newfoundland	0.2	0.7	0.2	0.1		0.1	0.1			0.1	0.2	0.3	0.2	1.0	0.1	0.2	0.2	0.1	0.1
West Indies	0.7	0.3	1.3	0.1		6.5	1.0	0.3	0.1	0.2	0.1		0.2	0.4	0.1	0.2	2.0	0.5	0.2
Mexico	4.5		0.2	1.3	2.2	0.3	1.4	61.7	23.4	14.0							0.2	0.1	0.2
Central and South America	0.3	0.1	0.5	0.1	0.1	0.5	0.6	0.4	0.1	0.6		0.1	0.1	0.1	0.2	0.2	0.6	0.3	0.2
All other:																			
Africa	0.1		0.1			0.1	0.1	0.1	0.1	0.1							0.1	0.1	
Australia	0.1			0.1		0.1	0.1	0.1	0.2	0.4							0.1	0.1	
Atlantic Islands	0.3	1.5	0.1		0.1					0.9		0.1		2.2	2.5	0.1	0.1	0.1	
Pacific Islands									0.1	0.2									
Country not specified																			
Born at sea					0.1	0.1	0.1			0.1									

238

POPULATION

TABLE 6.—PER CENT DISTRIBUTION OF THE FOREIGN-BORN POPULATION BY COUNTRY OF BIRTH, BY DIVISIONS AND STATES: 1930—Continued

COUNTRY OF BIRTH	EAST NORTH CENTRAL					WEST NORTH CENTRAL							SOUTH ATLANTIC							
	Ohio	Indiana	Illinois	Michigan	Wisconsin	Minnesota	Iowa	Missouri	North Dakota	South Dakota	Nebraska	Kansas	Delaware	Maryland	District of Columbia	Virginia	West Virginia	North Carolina	South Carolina	Georgia
All countries	100.0	100.0	100.0	100.0	100.0	100.0	100.0	100.0	100.0	100.0	100.0	100.0	100.0	100.0	100.0	100.0	100.0	100.0	100.0	100.0
Northwestern Europe:																				
England	6.8	5.2	4.1	7.4	2.2	2.2	5.4	5.2	1.5	3.3	3.5	6.5	7.7	5.3	9.2	12.7	6.3	13.5	8.9	9.3
Scotland	2.8	2.7	2.0	4.1	0.7	0.8	1.7	1.6	0.8	0.9	1.0	2.2	3.3	2.0	2.9	5.1	2.4	5.3	3.3	3.7
Wales	1.1	0.7	0.3	0.3	0.3	0.1	0.7	0.4	0.1	0.4	0.3	1.0	0.3	0.5	0.4	0.5	1.2	0.4	0.2	0.6
Northern Ireland	0.8	0.7	0.8	0.7	0.3	0.4	1.1	0.9	0.3	0.5	0.7	1.0	5.3	0.8	1.6	1.5	0.4	0.7	1.7	1.0
Irish Free State	2.8	2.7	4.6	1.3	0.9	1.3	2.5	5.6	0.8	1.8	2.1	2.4	8.0	4.2	9.8	3.2	1.3	2.8	3.5	3.8
Norway	0.3	0.5	2.4	0.8	8.9	18.3	7.7	0.4	29.6	19.8	1.4	0.9	0.8	0.7	0.7	1.3	0.1	1.1	1.2	0.9
Sweden	1.1	3.3	8.9	2.8	4.8	23.2	10.0	2.5	8.0	9.9	12.0	9.0	1.7	0.8	1.4	1.9	0.6	1.8	2.0	1.0
Denmark	0.3	0.7	1.5	0.8	3.4	3.5	8.7	1.0	2.8	8.0	8.6	2.1	0.6	0.5	0.7	1.4	0.1	0.7	0.7	0.8
Iceland						0.1			0.7											
Netherlands	0.3	1.4	1.2	3.8	1.6	1.2	6.0	0.5	0.6	4.6	0.5	0.6	0.3	0.4	0.5	1.1	0.1	2.2	0.4	0.5
Belgium	0.8	2.3	0.9	1.6	0.6	0.4	0.6	0.6	0.2	0.4	0.4	1.4	0.2	0.2	0.3	0.4	1.3	0.2	1.0	0.3
Luxemburg			0.2		0.2	0.3	0.5		0.2	0.6	0.2	0.2								
Switzerland	1.2	1.1	0.6	0.3	2.0	0.5	1.2	2.3	0.3	0.9	1.1	2.0	0.4	0.5	1.2	0.8	0.8	1.0	0.5	0.8
France	0.9	1.5	0.8	0.5	0.4	0.3	0.9	1.5	0.2	0.3	0.5	1.6	0.9	0.8	2.3	1.5	1.1	1.7	1.4	2.0
Central Europe:																				
Germany	14.7	19.7	15.3	9.6	33.0	15.4	32.0	27.6	9.6	19.3	27.3	21.5	8.6	19.6	11.1	10.3	6.0	10.1	13.0	11.8
Poland	9.9	12.2	13.9	14.0	10.9	3.8	1.1	5.4	2.0	1.1	3.7	2.4	17.4	12.5	5.1	5.0	10.7	3.6	9.5	8.1
Czechoslovakia	10.6	5.8	6.2	2.1	5.0	2.9	4.9	2.9	1.8	3.9	12.0	3.8	0.9	3.5	0.6	3.8	5.5	0.6	1.0	0.8
Austria	3.2	1.9	2.7	1.6	3.8	1.9	0.9	5.2	1.3	1.0	1.6	2.7	2.6	2.7	1.6	2.0	4.3	1.6	1.4	1.6
Hungary	7.2	5.4	1.6	2.3	1.7	0.4	0.2	2.3	0.8	0.3	0.3	0.4	0.9	1.3	0.7	2.3	7.1	0.8	0.6	1.0
Yugoslavia	6.0	4.6	2.3	1.9	3.2	2.3	0.8	1.8	0.3	0.3	0.6	3.4		0.3	0.2	0.3	4.7	0.1	0.2	0.3
Eastern Europe:																				
Russia	5.0	3.3	7.0	4.0	4.2	3.0	2.7	10.2	21.4	13.7	9.4	10.9	8.5	19.5	16.0	12.3	4.3	8.5	10.4	15.4
Latvia	0.1	0.1	0.2	0.1	0.1	0.1		0.1			0.1		0.2	0.6	0.5	1.1	0.1	0.3	0.9	0.8
Estonia													0.1							
Lithuania	1.2	1.5	3.6	1.1	1.1	0.3	0.5	0.5	0.1	0.1	0.5	0.2	0.5	3.6	0.8	1.6	1.9	1.3	1.1	1.1
Finland	0.9	0.2	0.3	3.2	1.5	6.2		0.1	0.8	1.2		0.1	0.3	0.4	0.2	0.3	0.3	0.1	0.7	0.7
Rumania	3.0	2.3	1.1	1.3	0.3	0.7	0.2	1.5	2.4	0.6	0.3	0.4	0.5	0.8	0.5	0.7	1.3	0.4	0.4	1.0
Bulgaria	0.3	0.3	0.1	0.2		0.1	0.1	0.1		0.1					0.1		0.2	0.1		0.1
Turkey in Europe															0.1	0.1		0.1	0.1	0.1
Southern Europe:																				
Greece	1.9	2.9	1.6	1.2	0.7	0.5	1.1	1.6	0.3	0.4	0.7	0.7	2.0	1.7	4.4	5.3	4.8	11.2	11.7	8.4
Albania	0.1	0.1		0.1				0.2						0.1	0.1	0.1	0.1	0.1	0.1	
Italy	11.0	4.8	8.9	5.1	3.2	1.6	2.3	9.9	0.1	0.5	3.1	2.7	22.1	11.3	14.1	7.6	23.3	4.9	3.5	5.0
Spain	0.2	0.4	0.1	0.2				0.3				0.1	0.7	0.3	0.5	0.5	2.6	0.3	0.4	0.6
Portugal		0.1	0.1										0.1	0.1	0.1	0.3	0.1	0.1	0.1	0.7
Other Europe	0.2	0.2	0.1	0.4	0.1			0.2			0.1	0.1	0.2	0.2	0.2	0.4	0.2	0.3	0.5	0.3
Asia:																				
Armenia	0.1	0.1	0.1	0.4	0.1			0.1								0.2	0.5			0.2
Palestine								0.1						0.1	0.1	0.1		0.4	0.2	0.2
Syria	0.7	0.5	0.1	0.6	0.1		0.2	0.3	0.5	0.2	0.3	0.3		0.1	0.8	2.2	2.5	7.5	7.5	2.7
Turkey in Asia	0.3	0.2	0.2	0.4	0.2			0.2					0.1	0.2	0.6	0.9	0.7	1.2	1.7	1.3
China	0.1	0.1	0.2	0.1	0.1	0.1	0.1	0.3	0.1	0.1	0.1		0.1	0.3	0.7	0.7	0.1	0.6	0.5	1.0
Japan									0.1		0.2				0.2	0.2		0.1	0.2	0.1
India															0.1	0.1		0.1	0.2	0.1
Other Asia	0.1	0.2	0.2	0.1											0.1	0.2	0.1	0.4	0.4	0.1
America:																				
Canada—French	0.4	0.5	0.5	3.3	1.1	1.7	0.4	0.4	1.3	0.7	0.4	0.7	0.4	0.3	0.7	0.6	0.2	0.9	0.6	0.8
Canada—Other	3.8	3.9	3.0	20.6	2.9	5.3	3.4	3.2	10.5	4.4	3.3	4.3	2.5	2.1	4.9	6.1	1.7	9.7	4.6	7.0
Newfoundland			0.1												0.1	0.1		0.3	0.1	0.1
West Indies	0.1	0.1	0.1	0.1				0.2				0.1	0.5	0.8	1.4	1.2	0.2	1.3	1.2	1.6
Mexico	0.5	5.3	1.7	1.1	0.5	0.5	1.5	2.2	0.3	0.5	3.0	13.8	0.2	0.1	0.4	0.2	0.5	0.2	0.2	0.3
Central and So. America	0.1	0.1	0.1	0.1	0.1		0.1	0.2	0.1		0.1	0.2	0.5	0.3	0.9	0.6	0.2	0.4	0.3	0.6
All other:																				
Africa								0.1					0.1	0.1	0.2	0.2	0.1	0.4	0.4	0.3
Australia		0.1	0.1	0.1				0.1				0.1		0.1	0.1	0.2	0.1	0.2	0.1	0.2
Atlantic Islands															0.1	0.2		0.1	0.1	0.1
Pacific Islands																0.2		0.2		0.1
Country not specified													0.2							
Born at sea		0.1			0.1	0.1	0.1	0.1	0.1	0.1	0.1	0.1		0.1		0.1	0.1	0.1	0.1	0.1

COUNTRY OF BIRTH OF THE FOREIGN BORN

239

TABLE 6.—PER CENT DISTRIBUTION OF THE FOREIGN-BORN POPULATION BY COUNTRY OF BIRTH, BY DIVISIONS AND STATES: 1930—Continued

COUNTRY OF BIRTH	SO.ATL.-con. Florida	EAST SOUTH CENTRAL Kentucky	Tennessee	Alabama	Mississippi	WEST SOUTH CENTRAL Arkansas	Louisiana	Oklahoma	Texas	MOUNTAIN Montana	Idaho	Wyoming	Colorado	New Mexico	Arizona	Utah	Nevada	PACIFIC Washington	Oregon	California
All countries	100.0	100.0	100.0	100.0	100.0	100.0	100.0	100.0	100.0	100.0	100.0	100.0	100.0	100.0	100.0	100.0	100.0	100.0	100.0	100.0
Northwestern Europe:																				
England	10.2	6.7	10.2	11.0	5.9	7.5	4.1	6.9	1.9	7.9	10.1	9.0	6.9	2.7	3.5	22.6	6.6	8.0	7.3	7.9
Scotland	2.6	2.4	3.3	5.4	1.5	2.2	1.2	2.8	0.5	3.6	3.2	6.1	2.9	1.5	0.0	3.5	1.9	3.1	3.5	2.6
Wales	0.4	0.5	0.8	0.9	0.2	0.5	0.2	0.8	0.1	0.8	1.1	1.0	1.1	0.4	0.2	1.8	0.4	0.7	0.5	0.4
Northern Ireland	0.8	0.9	1.2	1.0	0.7	0.9	0.6	0.9	0.2	1.4	0.9	0.8	0.9	0.4	0.4	0.5	1.0	0.8	0.9	1.0
Irish Free State	1.9	7.5	3.7	2.6	2.5	3.3	2.6	2.3	0.8	5.2	1.9	2.5	3.2	0.9	1.0	1.2	3.1	1.9	2.5	3.2
Norway	1.2	0.2	0.5	1.6	0.8	0.7	1.3	0.8	0.4	11.8	6.7	2.8	1.3	0.5	0.4	3.5	1.3	12.3	10.7	1.6
Sweden	3.1	0.8	1.8	4.0	2.6	2.3	1.2	2.7	1.1	7.5	13.0	7.6	8.3	1.1	1.2	9.1	2.9	13.4	10.0	3.9
Denmark	1.3	0.3	0.9	1.1	1.2	1.3	0.8	1.7	0.4	3.3	5.2	3.3	2.4	0.4	0.6	10.2	3.6	2.8	3.2	2.2
Iceland																0.2		0.3		
Netherlands	0.7	0.5	0.4	0.6	0.4	0.8	0.6	0.5	0.2	1.7	1.1	0.4	0.8	0.3	0.2	4.8	0.3	1.4	0.9	0.8
Belgium	0.3	0.3	0.2	0.4	0.5	0.7	0.8	0.7	0.1	0.7	0.4	0.6	0.4	0.1	0.1	0.2	0.2	0.5	0.6	0.3
Luxemburg	0.1				0.1	0.1		0.1		0.1	0.1		0.1						0.1	0.1
Switzerland	0.7	4.2	3.3	0.9	0.7	4.9	0.7	1.6	0.4	1.2	3.2	1.1	1.2	0.5	0.4	3.0	2.6	1.4	3.7	1.9
France	1.3	2.7	1.7	2.0	2.5	2.4	8.0	2.4	0.5	0.9	1.2	1.5	1.1	1.1	0.5	0.5	5.2	0.8	1.0	2.0
Central Europe:																				
Germany	7.8	34.3	13.5	13.2	9.2	28.1	9.8	19.3	7.2	8.1	10.6	7.3	10.0	3.9	2.2	8.5	6.5	8.0	11.7	7.6
Poland	1.4	4.1	7.2	3.5	3.7	3.7	1.8	3.8	1.3	1.5	0.7	2.6	2.5	0.4	0.4	0.5	0.5	1.5	1.9	1.3
Czechoslovakia	0.9	0.9	1.0	3.0	0.9	3.8	0.9	6.1	3.4	2.3	1.7	2.2	1.7	0.6	0.3	0.2	0.6	0.9	1.5	0.6
Austria	1.2	2.2	1.7	2.4	1.8	2.8	1.3	1.7	0.9	1.9	1.2	2.0	2.5	1.3	0.5	0.9	1.2	1.2	1.5	1.2
Hungary	0.9	2.5	1.6	1.8	0.5	0.6	1.0	0.6	0.2	0.5	0.3	0.7	0.7	0.2	0.1	0.1	0.1	0.2	0.4	0.6
Yugoslavia	0.2	0.9	0.2	0.8	2.3	1.1	1.1	0.5	0.1	5.1	1.5	5.7	3.7	2.0	1.2	2.1	3.5	1.0	1.4	1.2
Eastern Europe:																				
Russia	2.9	7.4	13.6	6.6	6.5	3.8	3.7	11.8	1.5	5.5	3.6	5.9	13.0	0.9	0.7	0.7	0.8	3.6	5.7	4.1
Latvia	0.1	0.2	0.5	0.3	0.3	0.1	0.1	0.2				0.1					0.1	0.1	0.2	0.1
Estonia	0.1			0.1			0.1											0.1	0.1	
Lithuania	0.2	0.8	0.8	0.5	0.5	0.5	0.1	0.6	0.1	0.2	0.1	0.1	0.3	0.1	0.1	0.1		0.3	0.3	0.2
Finland	0.5	0.1	0.2	0.3	0.6	0.1	0.2	0.1		3.6	2.7	2.7	0.6	0.2	0.5	1.1	1.1	4.3	5.0	0.8
Rumania	0.9	0.9	0.7	0.8	0.4	0.3	0.3	0.5	0.2	0.8	0.3	0.2	0.5	0.1	0.1	0.1	0.1	0.3	0.8	0.5
Bulgaria	0.1			0.1		0.3	0.1	0.4		0.3	0.1	0.3	0.3			0.1	0.1	0.1	0.2	
Turkey in Europe		0.1																		
Southern Europe:																				
Greece	2.2	2.1	4.0	6.0	4.3	2.9	1.5	2.1	0.5	1.1	1.3	3.8	1.2	1.2	0.5	4.6	3.3	1.1	1.4	1.2
Albania		0.1	0.3																	
Italy	7.5	7.2	14.7	13.3	20.0	9.0	36.5	3.8	1.8	3.7	3.6	7.1	10.7	5.2	1.3	5.9	17.0	4.0	4.3	10.0
Spain	5.9	0.4	0.1	0.4	0.4	0.1	1.8	0.2	0.2	0.1	3.4	0.5	0.2	0.7	0.8	0.6	7.3	0.1	0.5	1.2
Portugal	0.2	0.1		0.1			0.2				0.1	0.1					0.8		0.1	2.1
Other Europe	0.1	0.8	0.4	0.3	0.4	0.3	0.4	0.2	0.1	0.1		0.1	0.1	0.1						0.1
Asia:																				
Armenia	0.1		0.1							0.1		0.1				0.1	0.2			0.6
Palestine	0.1	0.1	0.2		0.2	0.1	0.1	0.1												
Syria	1.3	1.9	0.8	3.0	8.6	2.1	2.5	2.6	0.5	0.2	0.1	0.2	0.3	0.8	0.4	0.3	0.1	0.1	0.2	0.2
Turkey in Asia	0.2	0.2	0.2	0.4	0.2	0.2	0.3	0.1	0.1	0.1	0.1	0.1				0.1	0.3	0.3	0.1	0.4
China	0.2	0.2	0.4	0.2	4.2	1.5	0.6	0.4	0.1	0.4	0.8	0.4	0.2	0.3	0.0	0.4	2.1	0.6	0.9	1.9
Japan	0.2		0.1	0.1		0.1	0.1	0.2	0.1	0.6	2.1		2.4	1.4	0.4	3.6	2.7	3.5	2.4	4.5
India	0.1	0.1	0.1			0.1	0.1									0.1	0.5	0.1	0.1	0.2
Other Asia	0.1	0.1		0.1	0.1	0.1				0.1		0.1				0.1	0.1	0.1	0.1	0.2
America:																				
Canada—French	1.4	0.4	0.7	0.7	0.5	0.7	0.6	0.8	0.1	2.6	1.8	0.5	0.6	0.3	0.2	0.2	0.9	1.7	1.2	0.7
Canada—Other	10.3	3.8	6.5	5.0	4.0	6.0	2.1	6.2	1.1	12.2	12.3	4.4	5.3	2.3	2.0	2.3	5.4	17.2	15.0	8.8
Newfoundland	0.1	0.1	0.1	0.1			0.4				0.1							0.1	0.1	0.1
West Indies	26.6	0.3	0.7	2.1	0.9	0.3	1.9	0.3	0.2			0.1	0.1	0.1	0.1		0.1	0.1	0.1	0.2
Mexico	0.3	0.4	0.4	0.5	7.7	2.4	4.4	12.2	73.5	2.3	2.8	13.2	13.2	68.2	76.1	5.0	14.2	0.2	1.2	18.6
Central and So. America	0.7	0.2	0.5	0.9	1.2	0.3	3.7	0.2	0.1	0.1	0.1	0.2	0.2	0.1	0.1	0.1	0.3	0.1	0.1	0.7
All other:																				
Africa	0.1	0.1	0.2	0.2	0.2	0.2	0.2	0.1			0.1	0.1		0.1		0.2	0.1	0.1	0.1	0.1
Australia	0.2	0.1	0.2	0.1	0.1	0.2		0.2		0.1	0.2	0.1	0.1		0.1	0.4	0.3	0.2	0.2	0.5
Atlantic Islands	0.1			0.1			0.1							0.1			0.8			1.3
Pacific Islands								0.1			0.1			0.2			0.3	0.1	0.1	0.2
Country not specified	0.1																			
Born at sea	0.1	0.1	0.1	0.1	0.1	0.2	0.1	0.1		0.1	0.1		0.1				0.1	0.1	0.1	

TABLE 7.—COUNTRY OF BIRTH OF THE FOREIGN-BORN POPULATION, BY SEX, BY DIVISIONS AND STATES: 1930, 1920, AND 1910

[Figures for Russia in 1920 include Latvia and Estonia. Figures for 1910 represent pre-war areas. Sex ratio (males per 100 females) not shown where number of females is less than 100]

DIVISION OR STATE OF RESIDENCE, AND COUNTRY OF BIRTH	1930					1920, total foreign born	1910, total foreign born
	Total foreign born	Per cent	Male	Female	Sex ratio		
New England	1,848,943	100.0	914,223	934,720	97.8	1,885,945	1,825,110
England	135,586	7.3	64,653	70,933	91.1	147,320	155,932
Scotland	54,226	2.9	25,682	28,544	90.0	47,501	48,421
Northern Ireland	33,527	1.8	13,941	19,586	71.2	267,429	334,486
Irish Free State	193,113	10.4	77,098	116,015	66.5		
Norway	8,860	0.5	4,603	4,257	108.1	8,564	8,448
Sweden	66,023	3.6	33,458	32,565	102.7	67,286	70,777
France	11,741	0.6	5,361	6,380	84.0	13,252	10,934
Germany	50,005	2.7	25,292	24,713	102.3	51,129	[1] 67,719
Poland	136,774	7.4	71,024	65,750	108.0	131,378	[1] 107,791
Czechoslovakia	16,024	0.9	7,982	8,042	99.3	9,653	--------
Austria	11,946	0.6	5,825	6,121	95.2	23,081	[1] 19,968
Hungary	11,107	0.6	5,394	5,713	94.4	15,187	16,907
Russia	103,310	5.6	54,832	48,478	113.1	147,371	[1] 137,071
Lithuania	41,753	2.3	22,954	18,799	122.1	35,361	
Finland	18,503	1.0	9,357	9,146	102.3	19,543	14,139
Greece	25,423	1.4	16,036	9,387	170.8	32,186	16,764
Italy	253,098	13.7	142,417	110,681	128.7	238,508	179,430
Portugal	37,585	2.0	20,693	16,892	122.5	40,302	33,916
Armenia	10,687	0.6	6,292	4,395	143.2	11,964	[2] 26,903
Syria	11,076	0.6	6,093	4,983	122.3	11,181	
Turkey	8,659	0.5	5,133	3,526	145.6	2,898	
Canada—French	264,261	14.3	130,939	133,322	98.2	240,385	278,156
Canada—Other	254,604	13.8	109,461	145,143	75.4	235,871	248,083
Newfoundland	12,534	0.7	5,921	6,613	89.5	8,201	2,252
Azores	22,429	1.2	10,977	11,452	95.9	25,140	13,665
Other Atlantic Islands	5,460	0.3	3,491	1,969	177.3	7,575	
All other countries	50,629	2.7	29,314	21,315	137.5	47,679	33,348
Middle Atlantic	5,352,731	100.0	2,811,774	2,540,957	110.7	4,960,418	4,851,173
England	276,581	5.2	137,276	139,305	98.5	273,140	306,360
Scotland	137,861	2.6	68,689	69,172	99.3	83,885	88,995
Wales	26,336	0.5	13,606	12,730	106.9	29,185	37,921
Northern Ireland	92,559	1.7	40,022	52,537	76.2	472,319	615,756
Irish Free State	361,502	6.8	154,694	206,808	74.8		
Norway	55,697	1.0	31,221	24,476	127.6	35,362	32,684
Sweden	91,045	1.7	48,528	42,517	114.1	83,547	87,719
Denmark	26,978	0.5	16,633	10,345	160.8	22,991	20,637
Netherlands	30,960	0.6	18,314	12,646	144.8	27,847	26,581
Belgium	12,692	0.2	6,552	6,140	106.7	12,478	10,601
Switzerland	30,985	0.6	16,296	14,689	110.8	30,093	31,348
France	52,627	1.0	24,277	28,350	85.6	55,250	39,715
Germany	572,571	10.7	292,577	279,994	104.5	508,227	[1] 707,384
Poland	619,628	11.6	326,659	292,969	111.5	515,708	[1] 423,636
Czechoslovakia	199,705	3.7	103,121	96,584	106.8	123,863	--------
Austria	216,000	4.0	108,604	107,396	101.1	310,844	[1] 396,424
Hungary	136,753	2.6	66,560	70,193	94.8	190,224	267,951
Yugoslavia	54,662	1.0	34,076	20,586	165.5	48,087	--------
Russia	659,252	12.3	343,979	315,273	109.1	763,894	[1] 674,614
Latvia	9,052	0.2	4,748	4,304	110.3		
Lithuania	69,882	1.3	39,383	30,499	129.1	48,504	
Finland	22,290	0.4	10,074	12,216	82.5	17,431	12,813
Rumania	72,826	1.4	37,221	35,605	104.5	55,910	44,403
Greece	51,053	1.0	35,629	15,424	231.0	44,531	15,893
Italy	1,046,159	19.5	598,791	447,368	133.8	925,222	783,769
Spain	25,787	0.5	19,702	6,085	323.8	16,921	4,615
Portugal	10,949	0.2	9,017	1,932	466.7	3,090	1,030
Syria	17,950	0.3	9,735	8,215	118.5	15,501	[3] 24,507
Turkey	22,226	0.4	12,634	9,592	131.7	6,869	
China	10,321	0.2	9,578	743	1289.1	6,909	6,882
Canada—French	33,336	0.6	16,938	16,398	103.3	17,045	27,012
Canada—Other	149,094	2.8	67,600	81,494	83.0	121,255	121,357
Newfoundland	8,052	0.2	3,868	4,184	92.4	2,775	1,619
West Indies	71,754	1.3	37,309	34,445	108.3	44,596	21,505
Mexico	8,904	0.2	6,052	2,852	212.2	5,237	805
Central and So. America	24,701	0.5	14,501	10,200	142.2	11,092	3,962
All other countries	44,001	0.8	27,310	16,691	163.6	30,496	12,675
East North Central	3,275,723	100.0	1,803,420	1,472,303	122.5	3,232,141	3,073,768
England	170,122	5.2	90,293	79,829	113.1	163,994	170,189
Scotland	84,579	2.6	44,823	39,756	112.7	51,650	48,716
Wales	14,585	0.4	7,977	6,608	120.7	15,226	18,259
Northern Ireland	23,322	0.7	11,774	11,548	102.0	135,147	179,266
Irish Free State	93,881	2.9	44,716	49,165	91.0		
Norway	74,228	2.3	40,329	33,899	119.0	82,137	99,192
Sweden	165,785	5.1	92,588	73,197	126.5	165,388	178,140
Denmark	42,397	1.3	25,592	16,805	152.3	43,018	42,875
Netherlands	57,443	1.8	32,405	25,038	129.4	59,863	59,661
Belgium	33,053	1.0	18,372	14,681	125.1	29,706	22,925
Switzerland	27,066	0.8	15,731	11,335	138.8	30,379	33,230
France	24,144	0.7	12,267	11,877	103.3	29,637	19,015
Germany	524,437	16.0	271,294	253,143	107.2	592,058	[1] 806,085
Poland	416,569	12.7	229,423	187,146	122.6	402,259	[1] 317,632
East North Central—Continued.							
Czechoslovakia	190,709	5.8	98,940	91,769	107.8	143,743	--------
Austria	82,600	2.5	44,550	38,050	117.1	145,275	[1] 221,103
Hungary	100,773	3.1	53,585	47,188	113.6	149,592	162,261
Yugoslavia	102,437	3.1	61,857	40,580	152.4	72,343	--------
Russia	175,168	5.3	97,113	78,055	124.4	236,022	[1] 169,085
Lithuania	67,872	2.1	40,177	27,695	145.1	44,307	
Finland	42,946	1.3	23,573	19,373	121.7	46,576	43,442
Rumania	48,871	1.5	27,863	21,008	132.6	29,338	9,945
Greece	49,101	1.5	37,578	11,523	326.1	45,135	17,916
Italy	244,504	7.5	148,199	96,305	153.9	203,181	146,828
Canada—French	42,308	1.3	22,694	19,614	115.7	29,267	46,614
Canada—Other	254,688	7.8	126,818	127,870	99.2	224,625	226,526
Mexico	44,191	1.3	31,241	12,950	241.2	7,181	929
All other countries	77,944	2.4	51,648	26,296	196.4	55,004	33,932
West North Central	1,084,153	100.0	607,025	477,128	127.2	1,375,653	1,616,695
England	38,658	3.6	21,134	17,524	120.6	53,551	69,052
Scotland	13,035	1.2	7,210	5,825	123.8	17,196	21,817
Wales	3,882	0.4	2,182	1,700	128.4	5,693	7,840
Northern Ireland	6,750	0.6	3,560	3,190	111.6	49,858	78,614
Irish Free State	23,983	2.2	11,886	12,097	98.3		
Norway	131,904	12.2	73,674	58,230	126.5	166,280	198,786
Sweden	147,988	13.7	85,085	62,903	135.3	187,629	213,531
Denmark	50,193	4.6	30,798	19,395	158.8	61,748	63,910
Netherlands	20,532	1.9	12,110	8,422	143.8	24,399	21,010
Belgium	5,590	0.5	3,178	2,412	131.8	7,159	6,146
Switzerland	11,660	1.1	6,706	4,954	135.4	15,838	19,171
France	7,340	0.7	3,873	3,467	111.7	11,443	9,685
Germany	228,951	21.1	124,505	104,446	119.2	293,035	[1] 411,021
Poland	34,419	3.2	19,290	15,129	127.5	38,262	[1] 40,834
Czechoslovakia	46,005	4.2	24,044	21,961	109.5	50,906	--------
Austria	22,924	2.1	12,420	10,504	118.2	37,504	[1] 103,828
Hungary	7,295	0.7	3,833	3,462	110.7	17,640	24,272
Yugoslavia	17,049	1.6	10,250	6,799	150.8	18,189	--------
Russia	83,729	7.7	44,892	38,837	115.6	110,767	[1] 105,826
Finland	26,328	2.4	15,310	11,018	139.0	31,635	20,592
Rumania	9,012	0.8	4,881	4,131	118.2	6,950	5,401
Greece	8,018	0.7	6,602	1,416	466.2	11,236	13,989
Italy	31,653	2.9	18,960	12,693	149.4	34,488	38,238
Canada—French	10,531	1.0	5,757	4,774	120.6	10,459	17,920
Canada—Other	52,899	4.9	27,306	25,593	106.7	70,246	84,929
Mexico	23,506	2.2	14,772	8,734	169.1	22,787	10,827
All other countries	20,319	1.9	12,807	7,512	170.5	20,755	20,456
South Atlantic	318,697	100.0	178,941	139,756	128.0	330,537	299,994
England	25,761	8.1	13,325	12,436	107.1	24,416	22,811
Scotland	8,859	2.8	4,690	4,169	112.5	7,456	7,145
Wales	1,797	0.6	983	814	120.8	1,773	2,007
Northern Ireland	3,637	1.1	1,640	1,997	82.1	20,145	27,485
Irish Free State	12,163	3.8	5,233	6,930	75.5		
Norway	2,591	0.8	1,694	897	188.9	2,259	1,469
Sweden	4,940	1.6	2,983	1,957	152.4	4,418	2,984
Denmark	2,339	0.7	1,625	714	227.6	2,123	1,266
Netherlands	1,624	0.5	1,061	563	188.5	1,459	630
Belgium	1,397	0.4	776	621	125.0	1,547	1,135
France	3,977	1.2	1,771	2,206	80.3	4,119	2,761
Germany	38,225	12.0	20,160	18,065	111.6	40,898	[1] 58,854
Poland	26,239	8.2	14,768	11,471	128.7	25,432	[1] 24,409
Czechoslovakia	8,309	2.6	4,431	3,878	114.3	6,620	--------
Austria	7,578	2.4	4,294	3,284	130.8	12,077	[1] 14,924
Hungary	6,737	2.1	3,992	2,745	145.4	10,696	10,600
Yugoslavia	3,065	1.0	2,175	890	244.4	3,581	--------
Russia	35,870	11.3	19,414	16,456	118.0	48,362	[1] 34,503
Lithuania	5,681	1.8	3,264	2,417	135.0	3,245	
Rumania	2,743	0.9	1,624	1,119	145.1	2,163	1,055
Greece	11,449	3.6	8,484	2,965	286.1	11,450	4,630
Italy	39,512	12.4	24,375	15,137	161.0	40,267	38,284
Spain	6,303	2.0	4,523	1,780	254.1	6,547	4,985
Syria	4,538	1.4	2,675	1,863	143.6	4,064	--------
Canada—French	2,055	0.6	1,075	980	109.7	813	763
Canada—Other	15,608	4.9	7,345	8,263	88.9	12,228	7,918
West Indies	20,658	6.5	10,973	9,685	113.3	21,256	18,387
All other countries	15,042	4.7	9,588	5,454	175.8	11,123	10,989
East South Central	59,364	100.0	34,629	24,735	140.0	72,989	87,825
England	5,084	8.6	2,807	2,277	123.3	6,085	7,806
Scotland	1,941	3.3	1,027	914	112.4	2,093	2,503
Northern Ireland	567	1.0	316	251	125.9	5,934	10,124
Irish Free State	2,758	4.6	1,269	1,489	85.2		
Sweden	1,246	2.1	776	470	165.1	1,514	1,598
Switzerland	1,561	2.6	903	658	137.2	2,176	2,748
France	1,470	2.5	757	713	106.2	2,191	1,833
Germany	12,188	20.5	6,681	5,507	121.3	16,652	[1] 28,207
Poland	2,711	4.6	1,571	1,140	137.8	2,590	[1] 1,908

See footnotes at end of table.

COUNTRY OF BIRTH OF THE FOREIGN BORN

TABLE 7.—COUNTRY OF BIRTH OF THE FOREIGN-BORN POPULATION, BY SEX, BY DIVISIONS AND STATES: 1930, 1920, AND 1910—Continued

DIVISION OR STATE OF RESIDENCE, AND COUNTRY OF BIRTH	1930 Total foreign born	Per cent	Male	Female	Sex ratio	1920 total foreign born	1910 total foreign born
East South Central—Continued.							
Czechoslovakia	878	1.5	500	378	132.3	617	
Austria	1,239	2.1	718	521	137.8	2,023	¹2,516
Hungary	1,093	1.8	655	438	149.5	1,820	1,742
Yugoslavia	550	0.9	380	170	223.5	766	
Russia	5,023	8.5	2,843	2,180	130.4	7,408	¹7,035
Greece	2,304	3.9	1,845	459	402.0	2,014	1,397
Italy	7,288	12.3	4,503	2,785	161.7	8,584	8,183
Syria	1,703	2.9	998	705	141.6	1,501	
China	467	0.8	396	71		366	313
Canada—French	347	0.6	187	160	116.9	179	331
Canada—Other	2,820	4.8	1,508	1,312	114.9	3,022	3,178
West Indies	572	1.0	397	175	226.9	686	499
Mexico	843	1.4	525	318	165.1	570	226
All other countries	4,711	7.9	3,067	1,644	186.6	4,180	5,078
West South Central	440,553	100.0	240,226	200,327	119.9	464,828	352,192
England	11,228	2.5	6,489	4,739	136.9	13,373	15,084
Scotland	3,241	0.7	1,924	1,317	146.1	3,711	4,153
Northern Ireland	1,212	0.3	665	547	121.6 }	8,330	11,994
Irish Free State	4,921	1.1	2,199	2,722	80.8 }		
Sweden	5,534	1.3	3,472	2,002	168.4	6,320	6,463
Denmark	2,319	0.5	1,627	692	235.1	2,580	2,256
Switzerland	2,681	0.6	1,539	1,142	134.8	3,433	3,768
France	5,736	1.3	3,001	2,735	109.7	8,086	8,302
Germany	38,411	8.7	21,399	17,012	125.8	47,217	¹67,221
Poland	6,800	1.5	3,815	2,985	127.8	7,206	¹7,311
Czechoslovakia	14,885	3.4	7,884	7,001	112.6	15,438	
Austria	4,590	1.0	2,639	1,951	135.3	9,195	¹25,225
Russia	10,856	2.5	6,080	4,776	127.3	14,652	¹11,438
Greece	3,331	0.8	2,671	660	404.7	3,484	1,762
Italy	22,185	5.0	12,960	9,225	140.5	27,724	31,086
Spain	1,625	0.4	1,200	425	282.4	2,522	1,623
Syria	3,629	0.8	2,144	1,485	144.4	3,436	
Canada—French	994	0.2	590	404	146.0	590	1,045
Canada—Other	7,439	1.7	4,148	3,291	126.0	8,178	7,025
West Indies	1,336	0.3	877	459	191.1	1,799	1,081
Mexico	271,881	61.7	142,713	129,168	110.5	261,478	128,917
Central and So. America	1,908	0.4	1,071	837	128.0	1,550	491
All other countries	13,811	3.1	9,119	4,692	194.4	14,526	14,747
Mountain	384,323	100.0	226,564	157,759	143.6	467,620	453,322
England	33,081	8.6	17,203	15,818	109.1	44,588	54,354
Scotland	10,934	2.8	6,312	4,622	136.6	12,986	15,143
Wales	3,385	0.9	1,913	1,472	130.0	4,907	6,157
Northern Ireland	3,173	0.8	1,828	1,345	135.9 }	19,634	26,873
Irish Free State	10,252	2.7	5,543	4,709	117.7 }		
Norway	15,350	4.0	9,500	5,850	162.4	17,400	15,129
Sweden	25,839	6.7	15,220	10,619	143.3	32,232	35,485
Denmark	13,246	3.4	7,646	5,600	136.5	17,023	17,231
Netherlands	5,038	1.3	2,792	2,246	124.3	5,252	3,667
Switzerland	5,593	1.5	3,232	2,361	136.9	6,495	6,970
France	4,082	1.1	2,468	1,614	152.9	4,968	¹4,267
Germany	28,731	7.5	16,512	12,219	135.1	33,652	42,300
Poland	5,125	1.3	3,181	1,994	159.0	4,675	¹5,633
Czechoslovakia	5,018	1.3	2,862	2,156	132.7	5,205	
Austria	6,002	1.6	3,851	2,151	179.0	13,070	¹29,271
Yugoslavia	12,133	3.2	8,067	4,066	198.4	10,771	
Russia	20,865	5.4	11,495	9,370	122.7	26,690	¹16,607
Finland	5,765	1.5	3,477	2,288	152.0	7,718	9,154
Greece	6,716	1.7	5,732	984	582.5	9,483	13,269
Italy	23,774	6.2	15,278	8,496	179.8	28,498	34,433
Spain	3,617	0.9	2,725	892	305.5	4,563	3,152
China	2,037	0.5	1,825	212	860.8	3,149	4,684
Japan	5,723	1.5	4,033	1,690	238.6	8,499	10,230
Canada—French	3,678	1.0	2,205	1,473	149.7	3,482	5,276
Canada—Other	23,835	6.2	13,161	10,674	123.3	30,615	31,336
Mexico	89,870	23.4	51,147	38,723	132.1	98,484	45,793
All other countries	11,461	3.0	7,346	4,115	178.5	13,291	16,893
Pacific	1,439,682	100.0	830,288	609,374	136.3	1,130,561	955,809
England	113,462	7.9	59,359	54,103	109.7	87,386	76,131
Scotland	39,647	2.8	21,297	18,350	116.1	28,092	24,183
Northern Ireland	14,085	1.0	7,342	6,743	108.9 }	58,438	67,653
Irish Free State	42,237	2.9	20,203	22,034	110.8 }		
Norway	56,483	3.9	33,464	23,019	145.4	48,720	45,163
Sweden	86,850	6.0	51,513	35,337	145.8	77,251	68,510
Denmark	33,901	2.4	21,290	12,611	168.8	30,682	25,228
Netherlands	18,383	0.9	13,262	5,121	161.3	8,606	5,079
Switzerland	27,675	1.9	17,417	10,258	169.8	23,934	21,821
France	24,475	1.7	12,613	11,862	106.3	24,126	20,906
Germany	115,295	8.0	64,716	50,579	128.0	103,240	¹122,437
Poland	20,318	1.4	11,744	8,574	137.0	12,469	¹8,730

DIVISION OR STATE OF RESIDENCE, AND COUNTRY OF BIRTH	1930 Total foreign born	Per cent	Male	Female	Sex ratio	1920 total foreign born	1910 total foreign born
Pacific—Continued.							
Czechoslovakia	10,105	0.7	5,721	4,384	130.5	6,303	¹82,296
Austria	18,035	1.3	10,735	7,300	147.1	22,558	5,624
Hungary	7,879	0.5	4,203	3,676	114.3	7,217	
Yugoslavia	19,045	1.3	12,963	6,082	213.1	12,030	
Russia	59,555	4.1	32,317	27,238	118.6	45,329	¹28,233
Finland	25,004	1.7	14,244	10,760	132.4	24,966	19,012
Rumania	6,771	0.5	3,651	3,120	117.0	3,177	1,589
Greece	17,131	1.2	14,524	2,607	557.1	16,457	15,602
Italy	122,256	8.5	77,143	45,113	171.0	103,641	82,274
Spain	14,118	1.0	8,868	5,250	168.9	12,105	5,076
Portugal	23,113	1.6	14,063	9,050	155.4	24,894	22,892
Armenia	6,272	0.4	3,626	2,646	137.0	6,011	
China	23,406	1.6	19,664	3,742	525.5	23,442	36,533
Japan	60,194	4.2	38,159	22,035	173.2	67,331	53,668
Canada—French	13,342	0.9	7,138	6,204	115.1	5,566	7,966
Canada—Other	154,550	10.7	75,892	78,658	96.5	111,099	88,602
Mexico	201,171	14.0	114,640	86,531	132.5	89,816	34,038
Cent. and So. America	8,017	0.6	4,573	3,444	132.8	4,417	2,382
Australia	5,979	0.4	2,929	3,050	96.0	4,848	4,121
Azores	12,755	0.9	7,809	4,946	157.9	8,572	
Other Atlantic Is.	788	0.1	521	267	105.1	479	2,943
All other countries	42,365	2.9	25,685	16,680	154.0	27,359	26,457
NEW ENGLAND							
Maine	100,728	100.0	50,507	50,221	100.6	107,814	110,562
England	4,464	4.4	2,152	2,312	93.1	5,153	5,951
Scotland	1,906	1.9	924	982	94.1	2,171	2,389
Northern Ireland	827	0.8	319	508	62.8 }	5,748	7,890
Irish Free State	3,288	3.3	1,318	1,970	66.9 }		
Sweden	1,882	1.9	1,154	728	158.5	2,026	2,203
Poland	1,706	1.7	981	725	135.3	1,717	¹1,527
Russia	1,880	1.9	1,114	766	145.4	3,763	¹3,556
Lithuania	1,121	1.1	669	452	148.0	1,032 }	
Finland	1,400	1.4	843	503	140.7	1,393	831
Italy	2,359	2.3	1,454	905	160.7	2,797	3,468
Canada—French	36,947	36.7	18,413	18,534	99.3	35,580	35,013
Canada—Other	37,048	36.8	17,703	19,345	91.5	38,840	41,210
All other countries	5,894	5.9	3,463	2,431	142.5	7,594	6,824
New Hampshire	82,929	100.0	41,400	41,529	99.7	91,397	96,667
England	3,923	4.7	1,941	1,982	97.9	4,368	4,802
Scotland	1,728	2.1	770	958	80.4	1,823	1,979
Northern Ireland	1,010	1.2	394	616	64.0 }	7,908	10,613
Irish Free State	4,807	5.8	1,920	2,887	66.5 }		
Sweden	1,608	1.9	796	812	98.0	1,886	2,008
Germany	1,517	1.8	784	733	107.0	1,714	¹1,959
Poland	4,101	4.9	2,149	1,952	110.1	3,997	¹3,728
Russia	1,427	1.7	858	569	150.8	3,467 }	
Lithuania	1,084	1.3	631	453	139.3	1,017	¹2,865
Finland	1,386	1.7	759	627	121.1	1,558	1,198
Greece	3,233	3.9	1,943	1,290	150.6	5,280	2,634
Italy	1,938	2.3	1,178	760	155.0	2,074	2,071
Canada—French	37,682	45.4	18,724	18,958	98.8	38,277	40,865
Canada—Other	13,310	16.0	6,068	7,242	83.8	14,035	17,013
All other countries	4,175	5.0	2,485	1,690	147.0	3,993	4,812
Vermont	43,101	100.0	22,856	20,245	112.9	44,558	49,921
England	1,931	4.5	1,004	927	108.3	2,197	2,464
Scotland	1,454	3.4	690	764	90.3	1,854	2,615
Northern Ireland	377	0.9	145	232	62.5 }	2,884	4,940
Irish Free State	1,429	3.3	617	812	76.0 }		
Sweden	1,089	2.5	605	484	125.0	1,128	1,331
Germany	577	1.3	304	273	111.4	630	¹773
Poland	1,562	3.6	892	670	133.1	1,726	¹2,021
Russia	660	1.5	412	248	166.1	1,333	¹1,052
Finland	555	1.3	304	251	121.1	476	293
Italy	3,082	7.2	1,778	1,300	135.4	4,067	4,594
Canada—French	17,320	40.2	9,367	7,953	117.8	14,181	14,643
Canada—Other	9,874	22.9	4,816	5,058	95.2	10,704	11,415
All other countries	3,191	7.4	1,927	1,264	152.5	3,383	3,780
Massachusetts	1,065,620	100.0	516,312	549,308	94.0	1,088,548	1,059,243
England	78,497	7.4	37,242	41,255	90.3	87,085	92,658
Scotland	32,724	3.1	15,440	17,284	89.3	28,474	28,416
Northern Ireland	20,378	1.9	8,654	11,724	73.8 }	183,172	222,867
Irish Free State	138,366	13.0	55,426	82,940	66.8 }		
Norway	5,454	0.5	2,761	2,693	102.5	5,491	5,432
Sweden	36,810	3.5	18,369	18,441	99.6	38,012	39,562
France	6,035	0.6	2,747	3,288	83.5	7,125	5,926
Germany	20,538	1.9	10,382	10,156	102.2	22,113	¹28,960
Poland	71,442	6.7	36,883	34,559	106.7	69,157	¹58,094
Russia	67,684	6.4	35,279	32,405	108.9	92,034	¹89,667
Lithuania	25,219	2.4	13,674	11,545	118.4	20,789	
Finland	13,077	1.2	6,483	6,594	98.3	14,570	10,744

See footnotes at end of table.

242

POPULATION

TABLE 7.—COUNTRY OF BIRTH OF THE FOREIGN-BORN POPULATION, BY SEX, BY DIVISIONS AND STATES: 1930, 1920, AND 1910—Continued

DIVISION OR STATE OF RESIDENCE, AND COUNTRY OF BIRTH	1930 Total foreign born	Per cent	Male	Female	Sex ratio	1920, total foreign born	1910, total foreign born
NEW ENGLAND—Continued							
Massachusetts—Con.							
Greece	16,780	1.6	10,582	6,198	170.7	20,441	11,413
Italy	126,103	11.8	71,236	54,867	129.8	117,007	85,056
Portugal	25,840	2.4	13,811	12,029	114.8	29,191	26,437
Armenia	7,705	0.7	4,514	3,191	141.5	8,640	
Syria	7,153	0.7	3,888	3,265	119.1	7,128	[1] 16,138
Turkey	6,341	0.6	3,746	2,595	144.4	2,123	
Canada—French	115,241	10.8	56,192	59,049	95.2	108,691	134,659
Canada—Other	174,255	16.4	71,957	102,298	70.3	154,787	162,710
Newfoundland	10,987	1.0	5,078	5,909	85.9	7,168	1,751
Azores	18,698	1.8	9,124	9,574	95.3	22,113	
Other Atlantic Islands	4,404	0.4	2,762	1,642	168.2	6,181	12,816
All other countries	35,889	3.4	20,082	15,807	127.0	37,056	25,939
Rhode Island	171,929	100.0	84,021	87,908	95.6	175,189	179,141
England	24,699	14.4	11,552	13,147	87.9	25,791	27,834
Scotland	6,401	3.7	2,991	3,410	87.7	5,692	6,272
Northern Ireland	3,845	2.2	1,489	2,356	63.2	22,253	20,718
Irish Free State	13,895	8.1	5,092	8,803	57.8		
Sweden	6,181	3.6	2,993	3,188	93.9	6,542	7,405
France	2,015	1.2	939	1,076	87.3	1,971	1,711
Germany	3,090	1.8	1,546	1,544	100.1	3,126	[1] 4,358
Poland	8,696	5.1	4,388	4,308	101.9	8,158	[1] 7,015
Russia	5,890	3.4	3,051	2,839	107.5	8,055	[1] 7,469
Italy	32,493	18.9	17,825	14,668	121.5	32,241	27,287
Portugal	8,445	4.9	4,559	3,886	117.3	8,999	6,501
Armenia	1,909	1.1	1,134	775	146.3	1,850	
Canada—French	31,501	18.3	15,173	16,328	92.9	28,887	34,087
Canada—Other	7,824	4.6	3,180	4,644	68.5	7,595	7,867
Azores	3,582	2.1	1,766	1,816	97.2	2,857	
Other Atlantic Islands	739	0.4	502	237	211.8	1,093	716
All other countries	10,724	6.2	5,841	4,883	119.6	10,079	10,901
Connecticut	384,636	100.0	199,127	185,509	107.3	378,439	329,574
England	22,072	5.7	10,762	11,310	95.2	22,726	22,463
Scotland	10,013	2.6	4,867	5,146	94.6	7,487	6,750
Northern Ireland	7,090	1.8	2,940	4,150	70.8	45,464	58,458
Irish Free State	31,328	8.1	12,725	18,603	68.4		
Sweden	18,453	4.8	9,541	8,912	107.1	17,697	18,208
Germany	23,465	6.1	11,837	11,628	101.8	22,614	[1] 30,408
Poland	49,267	12.8	25,731	23,536	109.3	46,623	[1] 35,406
Czechoslovakia	12,220	3.2	6,086	6,134	99.2	6,558	
Austria	6,306	1.6	2,971	3,335	89.1	12,690	[1] 10,614
Hungary	9,836	2.6	4,761	5,075	93.8	13,222	13,855
Russia	25,769	6.7	14,118	11,051	121.2	38,719	[1] 32,462
Lithuania	13,247	3.4	7,386	5,861	126.0	11,662	
Italy	87,123	22.7	48,951	38,172	128.2	80,322	56,954
Canada—French	25,570	6.6	13,070	12,500	104.6	14,769	18,889
Canada—Other	12,293	3.2	5,737	6,556	87.5	9,910	7,868
All other countries	30,584	8.0	17,644	12,940	136.4	27,967	17,239
MIDDLE ATLANTIC							
New York	3,262,278	100.0	1,693,919	1,568,359	108.0	2,825,375	2,748,011
England	146,772	4.5	73,461	73,311	100.2	135,541	146,870
Scotland	67,623	2.1	33,302	34,261	97.4	37,656	39,437
Wales	7,037	0.2	3,806	3,231	117.8	6,763	7,464
Northern Ireland	41,521	1.3	18,014	23,507	76.6	284,747	367,889
Irish Free State	251,704	7.7	109,434	142,270	76.9		
Norway	44,882	1.4	24,866	20,016	124.2	27,573	25,013
Sweden	61,233	1.9	32,293	28,940	111.6	53,025	53,705
Denmark	17,407	0.5	10,817	6,590	164.1	14,222	12,544
Netherlands	14,909	0.5	9,091	5,818	156.3	13,772	12,652
Belgium	6,144	0.2	3,190	2,954	108.0	5,300	3,484
Switzerland	16,571	0.5	8,750	7,821	111.9	15,053	16,315
France	32,273	1.0	14,529	17,744	81.9	32,252	23,472
Germany	349,196	10.7	178,139	171,057	104.1	295,651	[1] 410,876
Poland	350,388	10.7	181,174	169,209	107.1	247,519	[1] 167,379
Czechoslovakia	56,176	1.7	26,451	29,725	89.0	38,247	
Austria	142,298	4.4	70,380	71,918	97.9	151,172	[1] 189,061
Hungary	70,631	2.2	32,862	37,769	87.0	78,374	96,843
Yugoslavia	10,917	0.3	6,568	4,349	151.0	8,547	
Russia	481,307	14.8	248,909	232,398	107.1	529,243	[1] 473,555
Latvia	5,971	0.2	3,124	2,847	109.7		
Lithuania	22,933	0.7	12,722	10,211	124.6	12,121	
Finland	17,444	0.5	7,599	9,845	77.2	12,504	8,700
Rumania	51,014	1.6	25,724	25,290	101.7	40,116	34,443
Greece	33,387	1.0	23,085	10,302	224.1	26,117	10,097
Italy	629,322	19.3	356,749	272,573	130.9	545,173	472,201
Spain	17,906	0.5	13,340	4,566	292.2	12,722	3,766
Portugal	5,731	0.2	4,743	988	480.1	1,484	660

DIVISION OR STATE OF RESIDENCE, AND COUNTRY OF BIRTH	1930 Total foreign born	Per cent	Male	Female	Sex ratio	1920, total foreign born	1910, total foreign born
MIDDLE ATLANTIC—Continued							
New York—Contd.							
Syria	10,113	0.3	5,443	4,670	116.6	8,127	[1] 14,482
Turkey	17,522	0.5	9,893	7,629	129.7	5,250	
China	7,512	0.2	6,999	513	1,364.3	4,559	4,482
Canada—French	28,955	0.9	14,780	14,175	104.3	15,560	24,503
Canada—Other	120,193	3.7	54,122	66,071	81.9	97,244	98,988
Newfoundland	6,378	0.2	3,088	3,290	93.9	1,810	1,029
West Indies	64,466	2.0	33,090	31,376	105.5	38,288	17,483
Mexico	5,218	0.2	3,319	1,899	174.8	2,999	555
Cent. and So. America	20,145	0.6	11,654	8,491	137.3	8,645	2,803
All other countries	29,084	0.9	18,349	10,735	170.9	17,999	7,140
New Jersey	850,038	100.0	446,798	403,240	110.8	742,486	660,788
England	51,717	6.1	25,091	26,626	94.2	46,861	50,375
Scotland	34,721	4.1	17,422	17,299	100.7	17,781	17,512
Northern Ireland	15,750	1.9	6,806	8,944	76.1	65,971	82,758
Irish Free State	47,486	5.6	19,577	27,909	70.1		
Norway	7,870	0.9	4,566	3,304	138.2	5,343	5,351
Sweden	13,360	1.6	7,132	6,228	114.5	10,675	10,547
Denmark	6,665	0.8	4,013	2,652	151.3	5,704	5,059
Netherlands	14,762	1.7	8,381	6,381	131.3	12,737	12,698
Switzerland	8,765	1.0	4,527	4,238	106.8	8,165	7,540
France	10,547	1.2	5,115	5,432	94.2	10,108	6,240
Germany	112,753	13.3	58,594	54,159	118.2	92,382	[1] 119,598
Poland	102,573	12.1	53,471	49,102	108.9	90,419	[1] 69,244
Czechoslovakia	32,358	3.8	16,170	16,188	99.9	16,747	
Austria	24,010	2.8	11,872	12,138	97.8	36,917	[1] 30,534
Hungary	32,332	3.8	16,070	16,262	98.8	40,407	47,610
Russia	62,152	7.3	33,639	28,513	118.0	73,527	[1] 53,849
Lithuania	9,870	1.2	5,474	4,396	124.5	0,246	
Rumania	6,686	0.8	3,489	3,197	109.1	4,554	2,208
Spain	5,000	0.6	4,035	965	418.1	2,002	405
Italy	190,858	22.5	107,751	83,107	129.7	157,285	115,446
Greece	6,020	0.7	4,071	1,040	208.9	4,521	1,575
Canada—French	2,470	0.3	1,193	1,277	93.4	772	1,203
Canada—Other	14,195	1.7	6,504	7,691	84.6	9,624	7,932
All other countries	37,118	4.4	21,835	15,283	142.9	23,605	13,004
Pennsylvania	1,240,415	100.0	671,057	569,358	117.9	1,392,557	1,442,374
England	78,092	6.3	38,724	39,368	98.4	90,738	100,115
Scotland	35,517	2.9	17,905	17,612	101.7	28,448	32,046
Wales	17,767	1.4	9,008	8,759	102.8	21,107	29,255
Northern Ireland	35,288	2.8	15,202	20,086	75.7	121,001	165,109
Irish Free State	62,312	5.0	25,683	36,629	70.1		
Sweden	16,452	1.3	9,103	7,349	123.9	19,847	23,407
Switzerland	5,649	0.5	3,019	2,630	114.8	6,875	7,484
France	9,807	0.8	4,633	5,174	89.5	12,830	10,003
Germany	110,622	8.9	55,844	54,778	101.9	120,104	[1] 176,909
Poland	166,672	13.4	92,014	74,658	123.2	177,770	[1] 187,013
Czechoslovakia	111,171	9.0	60,500	50,671	119.4	68,869	
Austria	49,602	4.0	26,352	23,340	112.9	122,755	[1] 176,829
Hungary	33,790	2.7	17,628	16,162	109.1	71,380	123,498
Yugoslavia	40,102	3.2	25,448	14,654	173.7	36,227	
Russia	115,793	9.3	61,431	54,362	113.0	161,124	[1] 147,210
Lithuania	37,079	3.0	21,187	15,892	133.3	30,227	
Rumania	15,126	1.2	8,008	7,118	112.5	11,230	7,752
Greece	11,646	0.9	8,473	3,173	267.0	13,893	4,221
Italy	225,979	18.2	134,291	91,688	146.5	222,764	196,122
Syria	5,210	0.4	2,864	2,346	122.1	5,312	
Canada—French	1,911	0.2	965	946	102.0	713	1,246
Canada—Other	14,706	1.2	6,974	7,732	90.2	14,387	14,437
All other countries	40,032	3.2	25,801	14,231	181.3	34,206	30,658
E. N. CENTRAL							
Ohio	649,220	100.0	355,792	293,428	121.3	680,452	598,374
England	40,693	6.3	21,058	19,635	107.2	43,172	43,347
Scotland	17,802	2.8	9,208	8,654	106.4	12,148	10,705
Wales	6,897	1.1	3,613	3,284	110.0	7,772	9,377
Northern Ireland	5,028	0.8	2,354	2,674	88.0	29,262	40,062
Irish Free State	17,879	2.8	8,034	9,845	81.6		
Sweden	7,390	1.1	4,220	3,170	133.1	7,266	5,522
Switzerland	7,624	1.2	4,157	3,467	119.9	9,656	10,988
France	5,759	0.9	2,901	2,858	101.5	8,067	4,888
Germany	95,697	14.7	48,762	46,935	103.9	111,893	[1] 164,010
Poland	64,493	9.9	35,933	28,560	125.8	67,579	[1] 41,579
Czechoslovakia	68,738	10.6	35,682	33,056	107.9	42,121	
Austria	20,547	3.2	11,041	9,506	116.1	48,073	[1] 61,927
Hungary	47,026	7.2	24,887	22,139	112.4	73,181	85,881
Yugoslavia	38,884	6.0	22,994	15,890	144.7	30,377	
Russia	32,627	5.0	18,089	14,538	124.4	43,690	[1] 29,222
Lithuania	7,581	1.2	4,278	3,303	129.5	4,095	

See footnotes at end of table.

COUNTRY OF BIRTH OF THE FOREIGN BORN

243

TABLE 7.—COUNTRY OF BIRTH OF THE FOREIGN-BORN POPULATION, BY SEX, BY DIVISIONS AND STATES: 1930, 1920, AND 1910—Continued

DIVISION OR STATE OF RESIDENCE, AND COUNTRY OF BIRTH	1930 Total foreign born	Per cent	Male	Female	Sex ratio	1920, total foreign born	1910, total foreign born
E. N. CENTRAL—Continued							
Ohio—Continued							
Finland	5,633	0.9	2,872	2,761	104.0	6,406	3,988
Rumania	19,580	3.0	11,120	8,460	131.4	13,068	3,974
Greece	12,050	1.9	9,226	2,824	326.7	13,540	2,555
Italy	71,496	11.0	43,396	28,100	154.4	60,658	41,620
Canada—French	2,606	0.4	1,297	1,309	99.1	2,277	2,310
Canada—Other	24,739	3.8	11,891	12,848	92.6	23,393	21,382
All other countries	28,391	4.4	18,779	9,612	195.4	23,758	15,087
Indiana	142,999	100.0	82,917	60,082	138.0	151,328	159,663
England	7,473	5.2	3,962	3,511	112.8	8,528	9,783
Scotland	3,898	2.7	2,137	1,761	121.4	3,707	3,419
Northern Ireland	1,045	0.7	514	531	96.8	7,271	11,266
Irish Free State	3,931	2.7	1,871	2,060	90.8		
Sweden	4,666	3.3	2,702	1,964	137.6	4,942	5,081
Netherlands	1,992	1.4	1,180	812	145.3	2,018	2,131
Belgium	3,254	2.3	1,802	1,452	124.1	2,530	2,208
Switzerland	1,624	1.1	941	683	137.8	2,334	2,765
France	2,160	1.5	1,042	1,118	93.2	3,247	2,388
Germany	28,152	10.7	14,668	13,484	108.8	37,377	50,534
Poland	17,482	12.2	9,822	7,660	128.2	17,791	14,471
Czechoslovakia	8,325	5.8	4,674	3,651	128.0	3,041	
Austria	2,709	1.9	1,517	1,192	127.3	9,100	7,580
Hungary	7,674	5.4	4,182	3,492	119.8	9,351	14,370
Yugoslavia	6,646	4.6	4,425	2,221	199.2	4,471	
Russia	4,749	3.3	2,918	1,831	159.4	7,678	5,024
Lithuania	2,109	1.5	1,313	796	164.9	1,445	
Rumania	3,292	2.3	2,074	1,218	170.3	2,731	709
Greece	4,087	2.9	3,158	929	339.9	4,182	1,370
Italy	6,873	4.8	4,293	2,580	166.4	6,712	6,911
Canada—French	682	0.5	366	316	115.8	406	789
Canada—Other	5,585	3.9	2,949	2,636	111.9	4,741	5,049
Mexico	7,612	5.3	5,750	1,862	308.8	686	47
All other countries	6,979	4.9	4,581	2,398	191.0	6,144	7,678
Illinois	1,242,447	100.0	675,036	567,411	119.0	1,210,584	1,205,314
England	50,721	4.1	26,763	23,958	111.7	54,272	60,363
Scotland	24,839	2.0	13,271	11,568	114.7	19,598	20,755
Northern Ireland	10,054	0.8	4,992	5,062	98.6	74,274	93,455
Irish Free State	57,208	4.6	26,951	30,257	89.1		
Norway	30,256	2.4	15,665	14,591	107.4	27,785	32,013
Sweden	111,016	8.0	60,402	50,614	119.3	105,577	115,424
Denmark	18,945	1.5	11,325	7,620	148.6	17,098	17,369
Netherlands	14,828	1.2	8,466	6,362	133.1	14,344	14,402
Belgium	11,564	0.9	6,368	5,196	122.6	11,329	9,399
Switzerland	7,315	0.6	4,308	3,007	143.3	7,837	8,661
France	10,171	0.8	5,173	4,998	103.5	12,006	7,972
Germany	100,605	15.3	98,312	92,293	106.5	205,491	278,054
Poland	173,007	13.9	92,212	80,795	114.1	162,405	148,206
Czechoslovakia	76,420	6.2	38,505	37,915	101.6	66,709	
Austria	33,336	2.7	17,519	15,817	110.8	40,457	101,508
Hungary	20,395	1.6	10,519	9,876	106.5	34,437	39,859
Yugoslavia	28,173	2.3	16,939	11,234	150.8	19,285	
Russia	87,026	7.0	46,773	40,253	116.2	117,899	103,472
Lithuania	44,733	3.6	26,337	18,396	143.2	30,368	
Rumania	13,172	1.1	7,054	6,118	115.3	6,238	4,306
Greece	20,003	1.6	15,038	4,965	302.9	16,465	10,031
Italy	110,449	8.9	65,340	45,109	144.8	94,407	72,163
Canada—French	6,189	0.5	3,142	3,047	103.1	4,032	7,440
Canada—Other	37,799	3.0	18,881	18,918	99.8	34,741	38,311
Mexico	21,570	1.7	14,726	6,844	215.2	4,032	672
All other countries	32,653	2.6	20,055	12,598	159.2	23,508	20,579
Michigan	852,758	100.0	473,396	379,362	124.8	729,292	597,550
England	62,757	7.4	33,836	28,921	117.0	47,185	42,737
Scotland	35,257	4.1	18,682	16,575	112.7	13,175	9,952
Northern Ireland	6,138	0.7	3,365	2,773	121.3	16,531	20,434
Irish Free State	11,390	1.3	6,088	5,302	114.8		
Norway	7,201	0.8	4,077	3,124	130.5	6,888	7,638
Sweden	23,905	2.8	14,001	9,904	141.4	24,707	26,374
Denmark	7,210	0.8	4,424	2,786	158.8	7,178	6,315
Netherlands	32,128	3.8	17,769	14,359	123.7	33,499	33,471
Belgium	13,931	1.6	7,729	6,202	124.6	10,501	5,683
Germany	81,714	9.6	42,480	39,234	108.3	86,047	105,915
Poland	119,228	14.0	67,618	51,610	131.0	103,926	62,419
Czechoslovakia	17,646	2.1	9,600	8,046	119.3	11,161	
Austria	13,299	1.6	7,495	5,804	129.1	22,004	16,442
Hungary	19,188	2.3	10,509	8,679	121.1	22,607	11,597
Yugoslavia	16,468	1.9	10,189	6,279	162.3	9,420	
Russia	34,348	4.0	20,043	14,305	140.1	45,313	15,822
Lithuania	9,340	1.1	5,654	3,686	153.4	5,475	
Finland	27,022	3.2	15,135	11,887	127.3	30,096	31,144
Rumania	11,482	1.3	6,870	4,612	149.0	6,331	510
Greece	10,061	1.2	7,936	2,125	373.5	7,115	1,196
Italy	43,087	5.1	27,491	15,596	176.3	30,216	16,861

DIVISION OR STATE OF RESIDENCE, AND COUNTRY OF BIRTH	1930 Total foreign born	Per cent	Male	Female	Sex ratio	1920, total foreign born	1910, total foreign born
E. N. CENTRAL—Continued							
Michigan—Contd.							
Canada—French	28,539	3.3	15,434	13,105	117.8	18,635	28,083
Canada—Other	175,244	20.6	86,961	88,283	98.5	147,267	144,780
Mexico	9,778	1.1	6,809	2,969	229.3	1,333	86
All other countries	36,397	4.3	23,201	13,196	175.8	22,676	10,091
Wisconsin	388,299	100.0	216,279	172,020	125.7	460,485	512,865
England	8,478	2.2	4,674	3,804	122.9	10,837	13,959
Northern Ireland	1,057	0.3	549	508	108.1	7,809	14,049
Irish Free State	3,473	0.9	1,772	1,701	104.2		
Norway	34,391	8.9	19,171	15,220	126.0	45,433	57,000
Sweden	18,808	4.8	11,263	7,545	149.3	22,896	26,739
Denmark	13,094	3.4	7,870	5,224	150.7	15,420	16,454
Netherlands	6,260	1.6	3,645	2,615	139.4	7,473	7,379
Switzerland	7,669	2.0	4,688	2,981	157.3	7,797	8,036
Germany	128,269	33.0	67,072	61,197	109.6	151,250	201,572
Poland	42,359	10.9	23,838	18,521	128.7	50,558	50,957
Czechoslovakia	19,580	5.0	10,479	9,101	115.1	19,811	
Austria	12,709	3.3	6,978	5,731	121.8	19,641	33,046
Hungary	6,490	1.7	3,488	3,002	116.2	10,016	10,554
Yugoslavia	12,266	3.2	7,310	4,956	147.5	8,784	
Russia	16,418	4.2	9,290	7,128	130.3	21,447	15,545
Lithuania	4,109	1.1	2,595	1,514	171.4	2,934	
Finland	5,724	1.5	3,339	2,385	140.0	6,757	5,705
Italy	12,599	3.2	7,679	4,920	156.1	11,188	9,273
Canada—French	4,292	1.1	2,455	1,837	133.6	4,917	7,992
Canada—Other	11,321	2.9	6,136	5,185	118.3	14,483	17,004
All other countries	18,933	4.9	11,988	6,945	172.6	21,034	18,001
W. N. CENTRAL							
Minnesota	390,790	100.0	219,595	171,195	128.3	486,795	543,595
England	8,448	2.2	4,689	3,759	124.7	10,964	12,130
Northern Ireland	1,403	0.4	779	624	124.8	10,289	15,859
Irish Free State	5,095	1.3	2,623	2,472	106.1		
Norway	71,562	18.3	39,326	32,236	122.0	90,188	105,303
Sweden	90,623	23.2	52,324	38,299	136.6	112,117	122,428
Denmark	13,831	3.5	8,582	5,249	163.5	16,904	16,137
Netherlands	4,832	1.2	2,884	1,948	148.0	5,380	3,542
Germany	59,993	15.4	32,151	27,842	115.5	74,034	99,645
Poland	15,015	3.8	8,352	6,663	125.3	18,537	20,050
Czechoslovakia	11,415	2.9	6,016	5,399	111.4	12,626	
Austria	7,288	1.9	3,991	3,297	121.0	11,550	31,372
Yugoslavia	8,888	2.3	5,460	3,428	159.3	10,697	
Russia	11,902	3.0	6,472	5,430	119.2	16,100	13,223
Finland	24,360	6.2	14,186	10,174	139.4	29,108	26,637
Italy	6,401	1.6	3,934	2,467	159.5	7,432	9,669
Canada—French	6,484	1.7	3,591	2,893	124.1	6,798	11,062
Canada—Other	20,732	5.3	10,754	9,978	107.8	27,066	30,059
All other countries	22,518	5.8	13,481	9,037	149.2	26,407	26,470
Iowa	168,250	100.0	93,674	74,576	125.6	225,994	273,765
England	9,045	5.4	4,925	4,120	119.5	13,038	16,788
Scotland	2,871	1.7	1,524	1,347	113.1	3,967	5,162
Northern Ireland	1,778	1.1	930	848	109.7	10,686	17,756
Irish Free State	4,179	2.5	2,052	2,127	96.5		
Norway	12,932	7.7	7,033	5,899	119.2	17,344	21,924
Sweden	16,810	10.0	9,377	7,433	126.2	22,493	26,763
Denmark	14,698	8.7	8,759	5,939	147.5	18,020	17,951
Netherlands	10,135	6.0	5,844	4,291	136.2	12,471	11,337
Switzerland	2,096	1.2	1,222	874	139.8	2,871	3,675
Germany	53,901	32.0	29,343	24,558	119.5	70,642	98,291
Poland	1,875	1.1	1,076	799	134.7	2,028	2,115
Czechoslovakia	8,280	4.9	4,247	4,033	105.3	9,150	
Russia	4,482	2.7	2,455	2,027	121.1	7,319	5,494
Greece	1,910	1.1	1,599	311	514.1	2,884	3,356
Italy	3,834	2.3	2,305	1,489	166.4	4,956	5,846
Canada—French	608	0.4	304	304	100.0	401	944
Canada—Other	5,745	3.4	2,881	2,864	100.6	8,543	10,675
Mexico	2,532	1.5	1,527	1,005	151.9	2,650	620
All other countries	10,530	6.3	6,181	4,358	141.8	16,531	25,058
Missouri	153,085	100.0	83,707	69,378	120.7	186,835	229,779
England	7,924	5.2	4,235	3,689	114.8	10,407	13,760
Scotland	2,419	1.6	1,345	1,074	125.2	2,969	3,651
Northern Ireland	1,308	0.9	627	681	92.1	15,022	23,297
Irish Free State	8,561	5.6	4,034	4,527	89.1		
Sweden	3,895	2.6	2,172	1,723	126.1	4,741	5,654
Denmark	1,497	1.0	986	511	193.0	1,688	1,729
Switzerland	3,578	2.3	2,079	1,499	138.7	4,934	6,141
France	2,360	1.5	1,219	1,141	106.8	3,331	2,794
Germany	42,276	27.6	22,582	19,694	114.7	55,776	86,263
Poland	8,324	5.4	4,437	3,887	114.1	7,686	8,363

See footnotes at end of table.

244 POPULATION

TABLE 7.—COUNTRY OF BIRTH OF THE FOREIGN-BORN POPULATION, BY SEX, BY DIVISIONS AND STATES: 1930, 1920, AND 1910—Continued

DIVISION OR STATE OF RESIDENCE, AND COUNTRY OF BIRTH	1930					1920, total foreign born	1910, total foreign born
	Total foreign born	Per cent	Male	Female	Sex ratio		
W. N. CENTRAL—Continued							
Missouri—Contd.							
Czechoslovakia	4,495	2.9	2,285	2,210	103.4	4,971	----
Austria	7,928	5.2	4,178	3,750	111.4	8,676	[1]14,390
Hungary	3,484	2.3	1,772	1,712	103.5	8,080	11,532
Yugoslavia	2,753	1.8	1,633	1,120	145.8	2,327	----
Russia	15,689	10.2	8,284	7,405	111.9	18,760	[1]16,829
Rumania	2,321	1.5	1,222	1,099	111.2	1,647	1,522
Greece	2,405	1.6	1,910	495	385.9	3,022	2,790
Italy	15,204	9.9	8,887	6,317	140.7	14,609	12,984
Canada—French	588	0.4	317	271	117.0	299	779
Canada—Other	4,872	3.2	2,497	2,375	105.1	6,263	7,290
Mexico	3,397	2.2	2,090	1,307	150.9	3,411	1,413
All other countries	7,807	5.1	4,916	2,891	170.0	7,757	8,593
North Dakota	105,871	100.0	60,854	45,017	135.2	131,863	156,654
England	1,593	1.5	932	661	141.0	2,289	3,070
Northern Ireland	329	0.3	195	134	145.5	1,660	2,498
Irish Free State	863	0.8	482	381	126.5		
Norway	31,337	29.6	18,253	13,084	139.5	38,100	45,937
Sweden	8,470	8.0	5,429	3,041	178.5	10,543	12,160
Denmark	2,936	2.8	1,916	1,020	187.8	4,552	5,355
Germany	10,114	9.6	5,876	4,238	138.7	11,960	[1]15,763
Poland	2,128	2.0	1,313	815	161.1	2,236	[1]1,813
Czechoslovakia	1,869	1.8	1,065	804	132.5	2,056	----
Austria	1,407	1.3	828	579	143.0	2,059	[1]4,714
Russia	22,618	21.4	12,206	10,412	117.2	29,617	[1]31,341
Rumania	2,518	2.4	1,381	1,137	121.5	1,811	1,070
Canada—French	1,354	1.3	745	609	122.3	1,533	2,376
Canada—Other	11,155	10.5	5,835	5,320	109.7	14,210	19,131
All other countries	7,180	6.8	4,398	2,782	158.1	9,147	11,426
South Dakota	66,061	100.0	37,949	28,112	135.0	82,534	100,790
England	2,159	3.3	1,239	920	134.7	2,944	4,024
Northern Ireland	351	0.5	201	150	134.0	1,954	2,980
Irish Free State	862	1.3	466	396	117.7		
Norway	13,061	19.8	7,397	5,664	130.6	16,813	20,918
Sweden	6,540	9.9	4,006	2,534	158.1	8,573	9,998
Denmark	5,298	8.0	3,339	1,959	170.4	5,983	6,294
Netherlands	3,068	4.6	1,837	1,231	149.2	3,218	2,656
Germany	12,730	10.3	7,106	5,543	129.8	15,674	[1]21,114
Poland	717	1.1	467	250	186.8	792	[1]758
Czechoslovakia	2,589	3.9	1,396	1,193	117.0	2,819	----
Austria	678	1.0	368	310	118.7	1,151	[1]5,268
Russia	9,023	13.7	4,818	4,205	114.6	11,193	[1]12,065
Finland	825	1.2	440	385	114.3	1,085	1,381
Canada—French	492	0.7	273	219	124.7	508	998
Canada—Other	2,922	4.4	1,567	1,355	115.6	3,054	5,012
All other countries	4,787	7.2	2,939	1,798	163.5	5,873	6,424
Nebraska	119,199	100.0	65,798	53,401	123.2	150,665	176,662
England	4,217	3.5	2,257	1,960	115.2	6,000	8,009
Scotland	1,223	1.0	689	534	129.0	1,695	2,242
Northern Ireland	801	0.7	419	382	100.7	5,422	8,124
Irish Free State	2,502	2.1	1,277	1,225	104.2		
Norway	1,691	1.4	902	789	114.3	2,165	2,750
Sweden	14,335	12.0	7,843	6,492	120.8	18,825	23,219
Denmark	10,210	8.6	6,166	4,044	152.5	12,338	13,674
Switzerland	1,364	1.1	765	599	127.7	1,808	2,150
Germany	32,544	27.3	17,922	14,622	122.6	40,969	[1]55,904
Poland	4,445	3.7	2,515	1,930	130.3	4,615	[1]5,154
Czechoslovakia	14,313	12.0	7,437	6,876	108.2	15,818	----
Austria	1,863	1.6	962	901	106.8	4,551	[1]21,886
Russia	11,234	9.4	5,936	5,298	112.0	15,719	[1]11,740
Italy	3,642	3.1	2,090	1,552	134.7	3,547	3,799
Canada—French	436	0.4	228	208	109.6	351	674
Canada—Other	3,974	3.3	1,979	1,995	99.2	5,429	6,661
Mexico	3,628	3.0	2,234	1,394	160.3	2,611	290
All other countries	6,777	5.7	4,177	2,600	160.7	8,796	10,386
Kansas	80,897	100.0	45,448	35,449	128.2	110,967	135,450
England	5,272	6.5	2,857	2,415	118.3	7,903	11,262
Scotland	1,778	2.2	974	804	121.1	2,576	3,591
Wales	785	1.0	415	370	112.2	1,170	1,615
Northern Ireland	780	1.0	409	371	110.2	4,825	8,100
Irish Free State	1,921	2.4	952	969	98.2		
Sweden	7,315	9.0	3,934	3,381	116.4	10,337	13,309
Denmark	1,723	2.1	1,050	673	156.0	2,263	2,760
Belgium	1,098	1.4	581	517	112.4	1,500	1,703
Switzerland	1,594	2.0	874	720	121.4	2,238	2,853
France	1,273	1.6	690	583	118.4	2,186	2,657
Germany	17,384	21.5	9,435	7,949	118.7	23,390	[1]34,041
Poland	1,915	2.4	1,130	785	143.9	2,418	[1]2,576

DIVISION OR STATE OF RESIDENCE, AND COUNTRY OF BIRTH	1930					1920, total foreign born	1910, total foreign born
	Total foreign born	Per cent	Male	Female	Sex ratio		
W. N. CENTRAL—Continued							
Kansas—Continued.							
Czechoslovakia	3,044	3.8	1,598	1,446	110.5	3,466	----
Austria	2,164	2.7	1,173	991	118.4	5,183	[1]11,062
Yugoslavia	2,781	3.4	1,576	1,205	130.8	2,155	----
Russia	8,781	10.9	4,721	4,060	116.3	12,050	[1]14,234
Italy	2,165	2.7	1,389	776	179.0	3,355	3,520
Canada—French	569	0.7	299	270	110.7	571	1,087
Canada—Other	3,499	4.3	1,793	1,706	105.1	4,781	6,101
Mexico	11,183	13.8	7,166	4,017	178.4	13,770	8,429
All other countries	3,873	4.8	2,432	1,441	168.8	4,890	6,550
SOUTH ATLANTIC							
Delaware	17,025	100.0	9,395	7,630	123.1	19,901	17,492
England	1,305	7.7	688	617	111.5	1,497	1,558
Scotland	562	3.3	293	269	108.9	411	344
Northern Ireland	900	5.3	380	520	73.1	2,895	3,985
Irish Free State	1,364	8.0	587	777	75.5		
Germany	1,459	8.6	783	676	115.8	1,632	[1]2,045
Poland	2,954	17.4	1,581	1,373	115.1	3,847	[1]3,657
Austria	435	2.6	239	196	121.9	615	[1]467
Russia	1,450	8.5	809	641	126.2	2,244	[1]825
Greece	339	2.0	248	91	----	286	34
Italy	3,769	22.1	2,249	1,520	148.0	4,136	2,893
Canada—French	61	0.4	33	28	----	23	63
Canada—Other	418	2.5	215	203	105.9	430	441
All other countries	2,009	11.8	1,290	719	179.4	1,885	1,180
Maryland	96,330	100.0	51,294	45,036	113.9	103,179	104,944
England	5,077	5.3	2,581	2,496	103.4	5,113	5,211
Scotland	1,920	2.0	1,013	907	111.7	1,692	1,955
Northern Ireland	813	0.8	325	488	66.6	6,580	9,705
Irish Free State	4,032	4.2	1,602	2,430	65.9		
Germany	18,925	19.6	9,448	9,477	99.7	22,032	[1]33,277
Poland	12,027	12.5	6,392	5,635	113.4	12,061	[1]12,829
Czechoslovakia	3,344	3.5	1,600	1,744	91.7	3,553	----
Austria	2,634	2.7	1,358	1,276	106.4	3,620	[1]6,178
Hungary	1,219	1.3	624	595	104.9	1,947	2,080
Russia	18,782	19.5	9,660	9,122	105.9	24,791	[1]20,164
Lithuania	3,422	3.6	1,809	1,613	112.2	2,206	----
Greece	1,617	1.7	1,159	458	253.1	964	463
Italy	10,872	11.3	6,559	4,313	152.1	9,543	6,969
Canada—French	291	0.3	163	128	127.3	117	110
Canada—Other	2,016	2.1	982	1,034	95.0	1,777	1,320
All other countries	9,339	9.7	6,019	3,320	181.3	7,183	4,674
District of Columbia	30,733	100.0	16,236	14,497	112.0	29,365	24,902
England	2,841	9.2	1,355	1,486	91.2	3,001	2,638
Scotland	884	2.9	403	481	83.8	793	705
Northern Ireland	493	1.6	203	290	70.0	4,320	5,347
Irish Free State	3,026	9.8	1,261	1,765	71.4		
France	712	2.3	301	411	73.2	688	511
Germany	3,411	11.1	1,728	1,683	102.7	3,382	[1]5,082
Poland	1,562	5.1	879	683	128.7	716	[1]563
Russia	4,914	16.0	2,606	2,308	112.9	5,181	[1]2,969
Greece	1,347	4.4	918	429	214.0	1,207	342
Italy	4,330	14.1	2,626	1,704	154.1	3,784	2,761
Canada—French	223	0.7	113	110	102.7	147	109
Canada—Other	1,506	4.9	639	867	73.7	1,579	1,052
All other countries	5,484	17.8	3,204	2,280	140.5	4,587	2,823
Virginia	24,367	100.0	14,150	10,217	138.5	31,705	27,057
England	3,099	12.7	1,671	1,428	117.0	3,776	3,687
Scotland	1,239	5.1	681	558	122.0	1,327	1,246
Northern Ireland	375	1.5	205	170	120.6	1,732	2,450
Irish Free State	789	3.2	423	366	115.6		
Germany	2,505	10.3	1,465	1,040	140.9	2,802	[1]4,128
Poland	1,221	5.0	700	521	134.4	1,103	[1]1,421
Czechoslovakia	927	3.8	471	456	103.3	897	----
Austria	492	2.0	275	217	126.7	921	[1]1,137
Hungary	560	2.3	332	228	145.6	1,293	1,784
Russia	2,989	12.3	1,611	1,378	116.9	5,421	[1]3,202
Greece	1,285	5.3	961	324	296.6	1,797	721
Italy	1,853	7.6	1,214	639	190.0	2,435	2,449
Syria	536	2.2	314	222	141.4	550	----
Canada—French	157	0.6	84	73	----	106	104
Canada—Other	1,490	6.1	738	752	98.1	1,841	1,256
All other countries	4,850	19.9	3,005	1,845	162.0	5,704	3,472

See footnotes at end of table.

COUNTRY OF BIRTH OF THE FOREIGN BORN

245

TABLE 7.—COUNTRY OF BIRTH OF THE FOREIGN-BORN POPULATION, BY SEX, BY DIVISIONS AND STATES: 1930, 1920, AND 1910—Continued

DIVISION OR STATE OF RESIDENCE, AND COUNTRY OF BIRTH	1930 Total foreign born	Per cent	Male	Female	Sex ratio	1920, total foreign born	1910, total foreign born
SOUTH ATLANTIC—Continued							
West Virginia	51,865	100.0	33,126	18,739	176.8	62,105	57,218
England	3,288	6.3	1,760	1,528	115.2	3,435	3,511
Scotland	1,267	2.4	701	566	123.9	908	1,088
Wales	607	1.2	324	283	114.5	704	880
Northern Ireland	222	0.4	123	99		1,459	2,292
Irish Free State	659	1.3	344	315	100.2	938	800
Belgium	690	1.3	380	310	122.6	633	535
France	547	1.1	271	276	98.2	3,798	6,130
Germany	3,129	6.0	1,712	1,417	120.8	5,790	5,074
Poland	5,545	10.7	3,561	1,984	179.5		
Czechoslovakia	2,831	5.5	1,700	1,131	150.3	1,549	
Austria	2,254	4.3	1,425	829	171.9	5,115	5,910
Hungary	3,683	7.1	2,384	1,299	183.5	6,260	5,039
Yugoslavia	2,440	4.7	1,786	654	273.1	2,802	
Russia	2,209	4.3	1,620	589	275.0	3,911	2,707
Lithuania	1,000	1.0	730	273	260.6	717	
Rumania	667	1.3	487	180	270.0	625	259
Greece	2,479	4.8	1,855	624	297.3	3,186	787
Italy	12,088	23.3	7,860	4,228	185.9	14,147	17,202
Spain	1,374	2.6	1,029	345	298.3	1,543	464
Syria	1,300	2.5	797	503	158.4	1,235	
Canada—French	118	0.2	62	56		54	88
Canada—Other	862	1.7	450	412	109.2	927	784
All other countries	2,597	5.0	1,759	838	209.9	2,270	2,069
North Carolina	8,969	100.0	5,237	3,732	140.3	7,272	6,092
England	1,209	13.5	627	582	107.7	960	940
Scotland	477	5.3	261	216	120.8	446	435
Northern Ireland	63	0.7	29	34		301	306
Irish Free State	253	2.8	108	145	74.5	115	28
Netherlands	201	2.2	118	83		708	1,056
Germany	903	10.1	527	376	140.2	210	111
Poland	319	3.6	181	138	131.2		
Russia	758	8.5	459	299	153.5	932	637
Greece	1,006	11.2	771	235	328.1	551	174
Italy	438	4.9	278	160	173.8	453	521
Syria	669	7.5	398	271	146.9	592	
Canada—French	80	0.9	40	40		15	29
Canada—Other	868	9.7	384	484	79.3	648	514
All other countries	1,725	19.2	1,050	609	157.8	1,337	1,341
South Carolina	5,358	100.0	3,196	2,162	147.8	6,582	6,179
England	479	8.9	262	217	120.7	403	517
Scotland	179	3.3	88	91		190	239
Northern Ireland	90	1.7	38	52		442	676
Irish Free State	185	3.5	93	92		133	95
Sweden	106	2.0	83	23	123.7	1,079	1,725
Germany	747	13.9	413	334	123.7	351	231
Poland	510	9.5	282	228	123.7	1,187	612
Russia	556	10.4	316	240	131.7	578	282
Greece	627	11.7	471	156	301.9	344	316
Italy	188	3.5	132	56		306	
Syria	401	7.5	239	162	147.5	24	39
Canada—French	31	0.6	17	14		247	243
Canada—Other	249	4.6	115	134	85.8		
All other countries	1,010	18.9	647	363	178.2	1,118	1,204
Georgia	14,303	100.0	8,482	5,821	145.7	16,584	15,477
England	1,334	9.3	759	575	132.0	1,610	1,671
Scotland	534	3.7	319	215	148.4	530	527
Northern Ireland	147	1.0	73	74	80.2	1,112	1,655
Irish Free State	546	3.8	243	303	74.7	376	224
France	283	2.0	121	162	74.7	1,936	2,984
Germany	1,682	11.8	983	699	140.6	917	1,418
Poland	1,156	8.1	646	510	126.7		
Russia	2,200	15.4	1,215	985	123.4	3,462	2,914
Greece	1,197	8.4	885	312	283.7	1,478	941
Italy	712	5.0	490	222	220.7	700	545
Syria	388	2.7	230	158	145.6	473	
Canada—French	109	0.8	55	54		50	70
Canada—Other	995	7.0	509	486	104.7	915	731
All other countries	3,020	21.1	1,954	1,066	183.3	3,020	2,797
Florida	69,747	100.0	37,825	31,922	118.5	53,864	40,633
England	7,129	10.2	3,622	3,507	103.3	4,522	3,078
Scotland	1,797	2.6	931	866	107.5	1,069	806
Northern Ireland	534	0.8	264	270	97.8	1,304	1,069
Irish Free State	1,309	1.9	572	737	77.6	610	304
Norway	859	1.2	550	309	178.0	1,399	729
Sweden	2,145	3.1	1,206	939	128.4	575	295
Denmark	921	1.3	614	307	200.0	737	285
France	909	1.3	420	489	85.9	3,534	2,427
Germany	5,464	7.8	3,101	2,363	131.2	428	1,105
Poland	945	1.4	546	399	136.8		

DIVISION OR STATE OF RESIDENCE, AND COUNTRY OF BIRTH	1930 Total foreign born	Per cent	Male	Female	Sex ratio	1920, total foreign born	1910, total foreign born
SOUTH ATLANTIC—Continued							
Florida—Contd.							
Austria	825	1.2	433	392	110.5	525	216
Russia	2,012	2.9	1,118	894	125.1	1,243	1,473
Greece	1,552	2.2	1,216	336	361.9	1,408	886
Italy	5,262	7.5	2,967	2,295	129.3	4,745	4,538
Spain	4,129	5.9	2,850	1,273	224.4	4,099	4,199
Syria	912	1.3	515	397	129.7	533	
Canada—French	985	1.4	508	477	106.5	277	151
Canada—Other	7,204	10.3	3,313	3,891	85.1	3,804	1,577
West Indies	18,543	26.6	9,478	9,065	104.6	19,171	17,050
All other countries	6,311	9.0	3,595	2,716	132.4	3,821	2,645
E. S. CENTRAL							
Kentucky	22,007	100.0	12,419	9,588	129.5	30,906	40,162
England	1,482	6.7	828	654	126.6	1,865	2,619
Scotland	524	2.4	275	249	110.4	520	641
Northern Ireland	191	0.9	98	93		3,422	5,914
Irish Free State	1,056	7.5	701	955	73.4		
Switzerland	915	4.2	513	402	127.6	1,315	1,653
France	684	2.7	394	290	101.4	984	645
Germany	7,552	34.3	3,930	3,622	108.5	11,137	10,310
Poland	899	4.1	534	365	146.3	1,037	602
Austria	484	2.2	280	204	137.3	906	912
Hungary	557	2.5	348	209	166.5	1,084	725
Russia	1,629	7.4	944	685	137.8	2,736	2,872
Greece	466	2.1	399	67		401	273
Italy	1,589	7.2	1,135	454	250.0	1,032	1,316
Canada—French	96	0.4	54	42		50	98
Canada—Other	838	3.8	440	398	110.6	853	972
All other countries	2,545	11.6	1,646	899	183.1	2,664	1,701
Tennessee	13,251	100.0	7,537	5,714	131.9	15,648	18,607
England	1,355	10.2	730	625	116.8	1,070	2,045
Scotland	433	3.3	239	194	123.2	454	561
Northern Ireland	160	1.2	74	86	96.4	1,291	2,296
Irish Free State	491	3.7	241	250			
Switzerland	443	3.3	263	180	146.1	616	800
Germany	1,783	13.5	1,017	766	132.8	2,159	3,882
Poland	960	7.2	526	434	121.2	841	1,570
Russia	1,803	13.6	965	838	115.2	2,262	2,127
Greece	528	4.0	409	119	343.7	491	374
Italy	1,946	14.7	1,175	771	152.4	2,079	2,094
Canada—French	92	0.7	47	45		47	91
Canada—Other	857	6.5	438	419	104.5	941	1,065
All other countries	2,400	18.1	1,413	987	143.2	2,797	2,612
Alabama	16,061	100.0	9,589	6,472	148.2	18,027	19,286
England	1,772	11.0	960	812	118.2	1,951	2,365
Scotland	860	5.4	444	416	106.7	975	1,120
Northern Ireland	162	1.0	102	60		809	1,167
Irish Free State	413	2.6	202	211	95.7		
Sweden	638	4.0	409	229	178.6	748	753
France	468	2.9	251	217	115.7	618	592
Germany	2,114	13.2	1,271	843	150.8	2,427	3,519
Poland	556	3.5	317	239	132.6	304	513
Czechoslovakia	483	3.0	278	205	135.6	232	
Austria	386	2.4	218	168	129.8	583	724
Russia	1,067	6.6	615	452	136.1	1,582	1,282
Greece	968	6.0	756	212	356.6	915	633
Italy	2,140	13.3	1,281	859	149.1	2,732	2,696
Syria	487	3.0	271	216	125.5	482	
Canada—French	117	0.7	65	52		52	96
Canada—Other	802	5.0	438	364	120.3	852	737
West Indies	342	2.1	235	107	219.6	405	230
All other countries	2,286	14.2	1,476	810	182.2	2,272	2,859
Mississippi	8,045	100.0	5,084	2,961	171.7	8,408	9,770
England	475	5.9	289	186	155.4	599	777
Northern Ireland	54	0.7	42	12		412	747
Irish Free State	198	2.5	125	73			
Sweden	206	2.6	137	69		247	292
France	198	2.5	114	84		258	291
Germany	739	9.2	463	276	167.8	920	1,697
Poland	296	3.7	194	102	190.2	318	1,223
Yugoslavia	189	2.3	109	80		220	
Russia	524	6.5	319	205	155.6	828	754
Greece	342	4.3	281	61		207	117
Italy	1,613	20.0	912	701	130.1	1,841	2,137
Syria	603	8.6	396	297	133.3	583	
China	340	4.2	289	51		249	195
Canada—French	42	0.5	21	21		30	46
Canada—Other	323	4.0	192	131	146.6	376	404
Mexico	616	7.7	398	218	182.6	110	72
All other countries	1,197	14.9	803	394	203.8	1,201	2,078

See footnotes at end of table.

POPULATION

Table 7.—COUNTRY OF BIRTH OF THE FOREIGN-BORN POPULATION, BY SEX, BY DIVISIONS AND STATES: 1930, 1920, AND 1910—Continued

DIVISION OR STATE OF RESIDENCE, AND COUNTRY OF BIRTH	1930 Total foreign born	Per cent	Male	Female	Sex ratio	1920 total foreign born	1910 total foreign born
W. S. CENTRAL							
Arkansas	10,632	100.0	6,343	4,289	147.9	14,137	17,046
England	802	7.5	489	313	156.2	1,141	1,519
Scotland	229	2.2	140	89	----	316	442
Northern Ireland	100	0.9	67	33	---- }		
Irish Free State	354	3.3	190	164	115.9 }	676	1,079
Sweden	249	2.3	168	81	----	331	385
Switzerland	518	4.9	243	275	88.4	736	804
France	255	2.4	149	106	140.6	387	387
Germany	2,989	28.1	1,735	1,254	138.4	3,979	¹5,710
Poland	394	3.7	236	158	149.4	529	¹576
Czechoslovakia	404	3.8	208	196	106.1	492	----
Austria	293	2.8	166	127	130.7	636	¹1,071
Russia	401	3.8	243	158	153.8	662	¹486
Greece	312	2.0	255	57	----	277	179
Italy	952	9.0	563	389	144.7	1,314	1,699
Syria	221	2.1	142	79	----	213	----
Canada—French	77	0.7	37	40	----	58	119
Canada—Other	638	6.0	357	281	127.0	835	955
Mexico	260	2.4	172	88	----	280	132
All other countries	1,184	11.1	783	401	195.3	1,275	1,503
Louisiana	37,076	100.0	21,817	15,259	143.0	46,427	52,766
England	1,529	4.1	883	646	136.7	1,841	2,086
Northern Ireland	234	0.6	120	114	105.3 }		
Irish Free State	970	2.6	381	589	64.7 }	2,000	3,757
France	2,951	8.0	1,558	1,393	111.8	4,193	5,845
Germany	3,616	9.8	2,089	1,527	136.8	5,147	¹8,822
Poland	655	1.8	368	287	128.2	377	¹719
Russia	1,375	3.7	785	590	133.1	1,928	¹1,369
Greece	574	1.5	455	119	382.4	610	237
Italy	13,526	36.5	7,680	5,840	131.4	16,264	20,233
Spain	677	1.8	526	151	348.3	1,293	719
Syria	929	2.5	529	400	132.3	954	----
Canada—French	222	0.6	138	84	----	157	250
Canada—Other	787	2.1	481	306	157.2	1,029	941
Mexico	1,644	4.4	888	756	117.5	2,487	1,025
West Indies	711	1.9	458	253	181.0	1,225	630
Cent. and So. America	1,376	3.7	741	635	116.7	1,142	328
All other countries	5,300	14.3	3,737	1,563	239.1	5,780	6,305
Oklahoma	30,558	100.0	18,204	12,354	147.4	40,432	40,442
England	2,101	6.9	1,200	901	133.2	2,687	2,981
Scotland	866	2.8	477	389	122.6	1,120	1,218
Northern Ireland	262	0.9	151	111	136.0 }		
Irish Free State	690	2.3	375	315	119.0 }	1,321	1,801
Sweden	835	2.7	546	289	188.9	931	1,028
Denmark	516	1.7	337	179	188.3	561	550
France	720	2.4	392	328	119.5	962	749
Germany	5,893	19.3	3,444	2,449	140.6	7,029	¹9,934
Poland	1,162	3.8	674	488	138.1	1,253	¹1,283
Czechoslovakia	1,867	6.1	993	874	113.6	1,825	----
Austria	530	1.7	302	228	132.5	1,393	¹3,354
Russia	3,013	11.8	1,966	1,047	119.4	5,005	¹5,215
Greece	642	2.1	506	136	372.1	620	590
Italy	1,157	3.8	734	423	173.5	2,122	2,504
Syria	809	2.6	468	341	137.2	691	----
Canada—French	243	0.8	152	91	----	126	320
Canada—Other	1,903	6.2	1,053	850	123.9	2,363	2,551
Mexico	3,737	12.2	2,552	1,185	215.4	6,884	2,744
All other countries	3,012	9.9	1,882	1,130	166.5	3,530	3,560
Texas	362,287	100.0	193,862	168,425	115.1	363,832	241,938
England	6,796	1.9	3,917	2,879	136.1	7,704	8,498
Northern Ireland	616	0.2	327	289	113.1 }		
Irish Free State	2,907	0.8	1,253	1,654	75.8 }	4,333	5,357
Sweden	4,017	1.1	2,401	1,616	148.6	4,536	4,706
Germany	25,913	7.2	14,131	11,782	119.9	31,062	¹42,755
Poland	4,589	1.3	2,537	2,052	123.6	5,047	¹4,733
Czechoslovakia	12,282	3.4	6,490	5,792	112.1	12,819	----
Russia	5,467	1.5	3,086	2,381	129.6	7,057	¹4,368
Italy	6,550	1.8	3,983	2,567	155.2	8,024	7,190
Canada—French	452	0.1	263	189	139.2	249	356
Canada—Other	4,111	1.1	2,257	1,854	121.7	3,951	3,178
Mexico	266,240	73.5	139,101	127,139	109.4	251,827	125,016
All other countries	22,347	6.2	14,116	8,231	171.5	27,223	35,781
MOUNTAIN							
Montana	75,903	100.0	47,110	28,793	163.6	93,591	94,713
England	6,021	7.9	3,365	2,656	126.7	8,160	8,981
Scotland	2,721	3.6	1,679	1,042	161.1	3,279	3,373
MOUNTAIN—Contd.							
Montana—Contd.							
Northern Ireland	1,095	1.4	668	427	156.4 }		
Irish Free State	3,950	5.2	2,172	1,778	122.2 }	7,260	9,469
Norway	8,991	11.8	5,858	3,133	187.0	9,962	7,170
Sweden	5,655	7.5	3,627	2,028	178.8	7,179	6,412
Denmark	2,541	3.3	1,693	848	199.6	2,990	1,943
Netherlands	1,253	1.7	776	477	162.7	1,675	1,054
Switzerland	901	1.2	592	309	191.6	1,151	988
Germany	6,155	8.1	3,791	2,364	160.4	7,873	¹8,528
Poland	1,144	1.5	732	412	177.7	1,219	¹1,302
Czechoslovakia	1,714	2.3	990	724	136.7	1,895	----
Austria	1,435	1.9	935	500	187.0	3,298	¹7,060
Yugoslavia	3,877	5.1	2,531	1,346	188.0	3,782	----
Russia	4,212	5.5	2,382	1,830	130.2	5,203	¹1,757
Finland	2,700	3.6	1,585	1,115	142.2	3,577	4,111
Greece	840	1.1	763	77	----	1,465	1,905
Italy	2,840	3.7	1,893	947	199.9	3,842	6,592
Canada—French	1,966	2.6	1,165	801	145.4	2,211	2,874
Canada—Other	9,227	12.2	5,213	4,014	129.9	12,489	10,968
Mexico	1,776	2.3	1,369	407	336.4	236	67
All other countries	4,889	6.4	3,331	1,558	213.8	6,845	9,550
Idaho	32,284	100.0	20,333	11,951	170.1	40,747	42,578
England	3,253	10.1	1,726	1,527	113.0	4,451	4,983
Scotland	1,025	3.2	623	402	155.0	1,228	1,282
Northern Ireland	284	0.9	182	102	178.4 }		
Irish Free State	616	1.9	368	248	148.4 }	1,410	1,782
Norway	2,148	6.7	1,378	770	179.0	2,482	2,566
Sweden	4,200	13.0	2,743	1,457	188.3	5,112	4,085
Denmark	1,667	5.2	1,014	653	155.3	2,240	2,254
Switzerland	1,088	3.2	604	484	139.2	1,847	1,319
Germany	3,427	10.6	2,078	1,349	154.0	4,143	¹5,004
Czechoslovakia	541	1.7	322	219	147.0	420	----
Russia	1,153	3.6	678	475	142.7	1,458	¹574
Finland	858	2.7	554	304	182.2	989	652
Italy	1,153	3.6	789	364	216.8	1,323	2,067
Spain	1,087	3.4	802	285	281.4	1,417	1,047
Japan	675	2.1	452	223	202.7	1,180	1,330
Canada—French	571	1.8	366	205	178.5	476	796
Canada—Other	3,958	12.3	2,341	1,617	144.8	4,485	4,875
Mexico	919	2.8	712	207	344.0	1,215	133
All other countries	3,711	11.5	2,601	1,110	234.3	5,371	7,229
Wyoming	23,343	100.0	15,063	8,280	181.9	26,567	29,020
England	2,105	9.0	1,172	933	125.6	2,507	2,085
Scotland	1,424	6.1	866	558	155.2	1,439	1,812
Northern Ireland	179	0.8	112	67	---- }		
Irish Free State	584	2.5	359	225	159.6 }	956	1,359
Norway	647	2.8	427	220	194.1	651	623
Sweden	1,783	7.6	1,211	572	211.7	2,042	2,497
Denmark	775	3.3	509	266	191.4	936	962
Germany	1,714	7.3	1,066	648	164.5	2,292	¹2,477
Poland	604	2.6	395	209	189.0	544	¹903
Czechoslovakia	521	2.2	299	222	134.7	518	----
Austria	457	2.0	300	157	191.1	1,183	¹3,351
Yugoslavia	1,322	5.7	917	405	226.4	1,189	----
Russia	1,375	5.9	789	586	134.6	1,482	¹546
Finland	633	2.7	380	253	150.2	856	1,380
Greece	888	3.8	737	151	488.1	1,236	1,015
Italy	1,653	7.1	1,083	570	190.0	1,948	1,961
Japan	554	2.4	395	159	248.4	1,029	1,575
Canada—French	118	0.5	70	48	----	92	143
Canada—Other	1,026	4.4	540	486	111.1	1,348	1,288
Mexico	3,075	13.2	2,172	903	240.5	1,801	188
All other countries	1,906	8.2	1,264	642	196.9	2,518	2,965
Colorado	99,875	100.0	56,770	43,105	131.7	119,138	129,587
England	6,893	6.9	3,606	3,287	109.7	9,588	12,928
Scotland	2,877	2.9	1,593	1,284	124.1	3,357	4,269
Wales	1,061	1.1	622	439	141.7	1,482	1,989
Northern Ireland	900	0.9	448	457	96.9 }		
Irish Free State	3,184	3.2	1,511	1,673	90.3 }	6,191	8,710
Norway	1,261	1.3	659	602	109.5	1,525	1,787
Sweden	8,328	8.3	4,578	3,750	122.1	10,112	12,446
Denmark	2,374	2.4	1,444	930	155.3	2,823	2,756
Switzerland	1,202	1.2	685	517	132.5	1,510	1,767
France	1,074	1.1	564	510	110.6	1,420	1,374
Germany	9,988	10.0	5,493	4,495	122.2	11,992	¹16,908
Poland	2,488	2.5	1,422	1,066	133.4	1,807	¹2,483
Czechoslovakia	1,714	1.7	939	775	121.2	1,953	----
Austria	2,468	2.5	1,527	941	162.3	5,722	¹11,582
Yugoslavia	3,650	3.7	2,258	1,392	162.2	2,109	----
Russia	12,979	13.0	6,926	6,053	114.4	16,669	¹12,759

See footnotes at end of table.

COUNTRY OF BIRTH OF THE FOREIGN BORN

247

TABLE 7.—COUNTRY OF BIRTH OF THE FOREIGN-BORN POPULATION, BY SEX, BY DIVISIONS AND STATES: 1930, 1920, AND 1910—Continued

DIVISION OR STATE OF RESIDENCE, AND COUNTRY OF BIRTH	1930 Total foreign born	Per cent	Male	Female	Sex ratio	1920, total foreign born	1910, total foreign born
MOUNTAIN—Contd.							
Colorado—Contd.							
Greece	1,230	1.2	1,075	155	693.5	1,802	2,272
Italy	10,670	10.7	6,536	4,134	158.1	12,580	14,375
Japan	1,389	1.4	896	493	181.7	1,762	2,245
Canada—French	572	0.6	310	262	118.3	418	789
Canada—Other	5,273	5.3	2,628	2,645	99.4	7,224	8,792
Mexico	13,144	13.2	7,853	5,291	148.4	11,037	2,602
All other countries	5,156	5.2	3,202	1,954	163.9	5,995	6,754
New Mexico	24,052	100.0	13,674	10,378	131.8	29,808	23,146
England	650	2.7	370	280	132.1	889	1,101
Germany	936	3.9	521	415	125.5	1,178	[1] 1,719
Yugoslavia	490	2.0	301	189	159.3	535	
Italy	1,259	5.2	818	441	185.5	1,678	1,959
Canada—French	62	0.3	46	16		42	111
Canada—Other	556	2.3	294	262	112.2	696	912
Mexico	16,406	68.2	8,906	7,500	118.7	20,272	11,918
All other countries	3,693	15.4	2,418	1,275	189.6	4,518	5,426
Arizona	65,756	100.0	36,559	29,197	125.2	80,566	48,765
England	2,314	3.5	1,321	993	133.0	2,883	3,500
Northern Ireland	235	0.4	143	92		1,206	1,550
Irish Free State	653	1.0	351	302	116.2		
Sweden	778	1.2	492	286	172.0	859	845
Germany	1,433	2.2	890	543	163.9	1,516	[1] 1,825
Yugoslavia	784	1.2	565	219	258.0	1,167	
Italy	822	1.3	568	254	223.6	1,261	1,531
Canada—French	158	0.2	101	57		90	177
Canada—Other	1,879	2.9	1,038	841	123.4	1,874	1,650
Mexico	50,022	76.1	26,654	23,368	114.1	61,580	29,987
All other countries	6,678	10.2	4,436	2,242	197.9	8,130	7,700
Utah	48,015	100.0	26,182	21,833	119.9	59,200	65,822
England	10,851	22.6	5,125	5,726	89.5	14,839	18,053
Scotland	1,669	3.5	838	831	100.8	2,310	2,853
Wales	862	1.8	437	425	102.8	1,304	1,672
Northern Ireland	234	0.5	140	94		1,207	1,657
Irish Free State	584	1.2	369	215	171.6		
Norway	1,698	3.5	784	914	85.8	2,109	2,305
Sweden	4,389	9.1	2,081	2,308	90.2	6,073	7,227
Denmark	4,883	10.2	2,314	2,569	90.1	6,970	8,300
Netherlands	2,325	4.8	1,104	1,221	90.4	1,980	1,392
Switzerland	1,419		666	753	88.4	1,566	1,601
Germany	4,104	8.5	2,020	2,084	96.9	3,589	[1] 3,948
Yugoslavia	989	2.1	684	305	224.3	836	
Finland	507	1.1	306	201	152.2	779	1,012
Greece	2,197	4.6	1,783	414	430.7	3,029	4,039
Italy	2,814	5.9	1,802	1,012	178.1	3,225	3,117
Japan	1,729	3.6	1,242	487	255.0	2,368	2,050
Canada—French	97	0.2	63	34		45	114
Canada—Other	1,095	2.3	609	486	125.3	1,426	1,576
Mexico	2,390	5.0	1,780	610	291.8	1,166	166
All other countries	8,179	6.6	2,035	1,144	177.9	4,389	4,020
Nevada	15,095	100.0	10,873	4,222	257.5	16,003	19,691
England	994	6.6	578	416	138.9	1,271	1,793
Northern Ireland	155	1.0	101	54		970	1,702
Irish Free State	463	3.1	302	161	187.6		
Sweden	443	2.9	325	118	275.4	545	708
Denmark	541	3.6	364	177	205.6	551	616
Switzerland	387	2.6	280	107	261.7	378	468
France	783	5.2	568	215	264.2	609	653
Germany	974	6.5	653	321	203.4	1,069	[1] 1,900
Yugoslavia	532	3.5	421	111	379.3	693	
Greece	499	3.3	453	46		618	1,051
Italy	2,563	17.0	1,789	774	231.1	2,641	2,831
Spain	1,109	7.3	869	240	362.1	1,180	778
China	312	2.1	283	29		529	760
Japan	411	2.7	329	82		649	855
Canada—French	134	0.9	84	50		108	272
Canada—Other	821	5.4	498	323	154.2	1,073	1,575
Mexico	2,138	14.2	1,701	437	389.2	1,177	732
All other countries	1,836	12.2	1,275	561	227.3	1,942	2,997
PACIFIC							
Washington	255,258	100.0	149,925	105,333	142.3	265,292	256,241
England	20,311	8.0	10,937	9,374	116.7	20,821	19,430
Scotland	8,024	3.1	4,386	3,638	120.6	7,886	7,101

DIVISION OR STATE OF RESIDENCE, AND COUNTRY OF BIRTH	1930 Total foreign born	Per cent	Male	Female	Sex ratio	1920, total foreign born	1910, total foreign born
PACIFIC—Continued							
Washington—Con.							
Northern Ireland	2,154	0.8	1,218	936	130.1	8,927	10,180
Irish Free State	4,942	1.9	2,889	2,053	140.7	30,305	28,368
Norway	31,420	12.3	18,761	12,668	148.1	34,793	32,199
Sweden	34,084	13.4	21,243	12,841	165.4	34,793	32,199
Denmark	7,175	2.8	4,693	2,482	189.1	8,359	7,804
Netherlands	3,484	1.4	2,064	1,420	145.4	3,007	2,157
Switzerland	3,578	1.4	2,285	1,293	176.7	3,671	3,447
Germany	20,542	8.0	11,886	8,656	137.3	22,315	28,825
Poland	3,942	1.5	2,389	1,553	153.8	3,006	[1] 3,712
Austria	3,128	1.2	1,933	1,195	161.8	6,404	[1] 11,402
Yugoslavia	4,761	1.9	3,271	1,490	219.5	3,555	
Russia	9,229	3.6	5,185	4,044	128.2	11,125	[1] 9,155
Finland	11,002	4.3	6,459	4,543	142.2	11,863	8,719
Greece	2,881	1.1	2,579	302	854.0	4,215	4,187
Italy	10,274	4.0	6,719	3,555	189.0	10,813	13,121
Japan	8,935	3.5	5,608	3,327	168.6	12,971	12,177
Canada—French	4,340	1.7	2,363	1,977	119.5	2,581	3,711
Canada—Other	43,929	17.2	22,385	21,544	103.9	40,508	35,771
All other countries	17,114	6.7	10,672	6,442	165.7	16,987	14,775
Oregon	110,440	100.0	65,778	44,662	147.3	107,644	113,136
England	8,077	7.3	4,456	3,621	123.1	7,053	7,998
Scotland	3,820	3.5	2,197	1,623	135.4	3,600	3,387
Northern Ireland	1,039	0.9	610	429	142.2	4,203	4,995
Irish Free State	2,802	2.5	1,824	978	186.5		
Norway	7,460	6.7	4,526	2,934	154.8	6,955	6,843
Sweden	11,032	10.0	7,068	3,964	178.3	10,532	10,099
Denmark	3,551	3.2	2,244	1,307	171.7	3,602	3,215
Switzerland	4,034	3.7	2,454	1,580	155.3	4,166	3,853
France	1,146	1.0	614	532	115.4	1,273	1,159
Germany	12,913	11.7	7,419	5,494	135.0	13,740	[1] 17,778
Poland	2,086	1.9	1,228	858	143.1	1,480	[1] 1,476
Czechoslovakia	1,691	1.5	972	719	135.2	1,132	
Austria	1,664	1.5	1,026	638	160.8	2,798	[1] 4,826
Yugoslavia	1,541	1.4	1,110	431	257.5	1,186	
Russia	6,278	5.7	3,407	2,871	118.7	6,979	[1] 4,440
Finland	5,507	5.0	3,134	2,373	132.1	6,050	4,734
Greece	1,575	1.4	1,404	171	821.1	1,928	3,555
Italy	4,728	4.3	3,120	1,608	194.0	4,324	5,538
Japan	2,617	2.4	1,700	917	185.4	3,169	3,277
Canada—French	1,345	1.2	727	618	117.6	970	1,146
Canada—Other	16,601	15.0	8,480	8,121	104.4	13,121	11,263
Mexico	1,292	1.2	1,079	213	506.6	595	199
All other countries	7,651	6.9	4,979	2,672	186.3	8,170	13,355
California	1,073,964	100.0	614,585	459,379	133.8	757,625	586,432
England	85,074	7.9	43,966	41,108	107.0	58,612	48,703
Scotland	27,803	2.6	14,714	13,089	112.4	16,597	13,695
Northern Ireland	10,892	1.0	5,514	5,378	102.5	45,308	52,478
Irish Free State	34,493	3.2	17,490	17,003	102.9		
Norway	17,604	1.6	10,177	7,427	137.0	11,460	9,952
Sweden	41,744	3.9	23,202	18,532	125.2	31,026	26,212
Denmark	23,175	2.2	14,353	8,822	162.7	18,721	14,209
Netherlands	8,897	0.8	5,553	3,344	166.1	4,502	2,304
Switzerland	20,063	1.9	12,678	7,385	171.7	16,007	14,521
France	21,341	2.0	10,956	10,385	105.5	20,401	17,407
Germany	81,840	7.6	45,411	36,429	124.7	67,185	[1] 75,834
Poland	14,290	1.3	8,127	6,163	131.9	7,083	[1] 3,542
Czechoslovakia	6,212	0.6	3,452	2,760	125.1	3,379	
Austria	13,243	1.2	7,776	5,467	142.2	13,266	[1] 16,068
Hungary	6,896	0.6	3,661	3,235	113.2	5,252	3,304
Yugoslavia	12,743	1.2	8,582	4,161	206.2	7,279	
Russia	44,048	4.1	23,725	20,323	116.7	27,225	[1] 14,638
Finland	8,495	0.8	4,651	3,844	121.0	7,053	6,159
Rumania	5,141	0.5	2,746	2,395	114.7		
Greece	12,675	1.2	10,541	2,134	494.0	10,314	7,920
Italy	107,254	10.0	67,804	39,950	168.5	88,504	63,615
Spain	13,332	1.2	8,259	5,073	162.8	11,140	4,229
Portugal	22,894	2.1	13,906	8,988	154.7	24,609	22,539
Armenia	6,112	0.6	3,500	2,612	134.0	5,689	
China	20,915	1.9	17,564	3,351	524.1	19,564	27,764
Japan	48,642	4.5	30,851	17,791	173.4	51,191	38,214
Canada—French	7,657	0.7	4,048	3,609	112.2	2,306	3,109
Canada—Other	94,020	8.8	45,027	48,993	91.9	57,880	41,568
Mexico	199,359	18.6	113,117	86,242	131.2	88,771	33,694
Cent. and So. America	7,492	0.7	4,247	3,245	130.9	3,972	2,096
Australia	5,119	0.5	2,475	2,644	93.6	4,021	3,308
Azores	12,712	1.2	7,778	4,934	157.6	8,510	
Other Atlantic Islands	737	0.1	487	250	194.8	447	2,898
All other countries	31,060	2.9	18,747	12,313	152.3	19,771	16,452

1 Persons reported in 1910 as of Polish mother tongue born in Austria, Germany, or Russia have been deducted from the respective countries and combined as persons born in Poland (see text, p. 226).
2 Includes Palestine.
3 Includes Armenia and Palestine.

CHAPTER 6

COUNTRY OF ORIGIN OF
THE FOREIGN WHITE STOCK

CHAPTER 6.—COUNTRY OF ORIGIN OF THE FOREIGN WHITE STOCK

INTRODUCTION

The term "foreign white stock" is used in the Census Reports to indicate the combined total of three classes, namely, the foreign-born white, the native white of foreign parentage (both parents foreign born), and the native white of mixed parentage (one parent native and the other foreign born). In most of the tables the two native classes are combined under the term "Native white—Foreign or mixed parentage."

The inquiry as to birthplace of parents, on which is based in part the assignment of the foreign white stock to country of origin, was first made in the census of 1880, but the data then secured were not completely tabulated. The earliest published statistics pertaining to this inquiry are those for 1890. Since so large a proportion of the population of foreign birth or parentage in the United States is white, statistics as to country of origin are here presented for the white population only. The most important of the other groups is represented by the Mexican population, practically all of which is of Mexican origin. The Chinese population is likewise practically all of Chinese origin, and the Japanese population of Japanese origin. Even if the nonwhite population were relatively more important, therefore, it would not call for any detailed statistics regarding country of origin.

By reason of its growing importance the Mexican element in the population was given a separate classification in the census returns for 1930, having been included for the most part with the white population at prior censuses. The instructions given to enumerators for making this classification were to the effect that "All persons born in Mexico, or having parents born in Mexico, who are not definitely white, Negro, Indian, Chinese, or Japanese, should be returned as Mexican." Under these instructions 1,422,533 persons of Mexican birth or Mexican stock were returned as Mexican in 1930, and 65,968 persons of Mexican birth or parentage were returned as white. Using as a basis the 1920 returns for persons born in Mexico and natives having one or both parents born in Mexico, it has been estimated that there were in that year 700,541 persons who would have been classified as Mexican under the 1930 instructions. This number includes 243,181 natives of foreign or mixed parentage and 457,360 foreign born. In the tables showing comparative data the 1920 figures for the white population have been adjusted by deducting these estimates, and similar adjustments have been made for 1910.

The relative importance of the several elements in the foreign white stock is shown in Table 1.

TABLE 1.—TOTAL FOREIGN WHITE STOCK IN THE UNITED STATES, BY NATIVITY AND PARENTAGE: 1930, 1920, AND 1910

NATIVITY AND PARENTAGE	NUMBER			PER CENT DISTRIBUTION		
	1930	1920 [1]	1910 [1]	1930	1920	1910
Total foreign white stock	38,727,593	35,698,417	31,875,872	100.0	100.0	100.0
Foreign-born white	13,366,407	13,255,394	13,134,312	34.5	37.1	41.2
Native white—						
Foreign parentage	16,999,221	15,521,835	12,812,090	43.9	43.5	40.2
Mixed parentage	8,361,965	6,921,188	5,929,470	21.6	19.4	18.6
Father foreign born	5,459,530	4,496,024	3,899,302	14.1	12.6	12.2
Mother foreign born	2,902,435	2,425,164	2,030,168	7.5	6.8	6.4

[1] Adjusted figures; see text, above.

Country of origin.—The classification of the 1930 population both by country of birth and by country of birth of parents, so far as concerns European countries, has been made on the basis of postwar geography. The 1920 tabulations of country of origin were based on the pre-war boundaries of European countries, mainly by reason of the difficulty in securing correct returns on the postwar basis for the parents of the persons enumerated. The 1930 figures for those countries affected by changes resulting from the World War are therefore not comparable with those presented in the Census Reports for 1920. (For a discussion of the changes as they affect specific countries, see introduction to Chapter 5, Country of Birth of the Foreign Born.)

One other important change has been made in the classification of the native white population of foreign parentage by country of origin (country of birth of parents). In 1920 and in the earlier censuses native white persons of foreign parentage were assigned to a specific country of origin only when both parents were from that country. All cases of mixed foreign parentage (one parent born in one foreign country and the other in another) were placed in a group designated as of "Mixed foreign parentage," this group comprising about 10 per cent of the total number of natives of foreign parentage. In 1930 all persons of foreign parentage have been assigned to the country in which the father was born; and so far as possible, in the comparative tables, the figures for earlier censuses have been revised to this basis.[1]

[1] This revision is made on the basis of special tabulations showing country of birth of father by country of birth of mother which were made in 1920, 1910, and 1900. No such tabulation was made in 1930, nor could be made, because the country of birth of only one parent was punched on the population card.

263

264 POPULATION

The assignment of persons of mixed parentage to country of origin was made on the basis of the country of birth of the foreign parent. Persons having a native mother and a foreign-born father were assigned to the country of birth of the father; persons having a native father and a foreign-born mother were assigned to the country of birth of the mother. Separate figures are presented for these two classes of mixed parentage in most of the tables.

The 1930 statistics of the foreign white stock by country of origin are summarized in Table 2.

TABLE 2.—FOREIGN WHITE STOCK BY COUNTRY OF ORIGIN, BY NATIVITY AND PARENTAGE, FOR THE UNITED STATES: 1930

| COUNTRY OF ORIGIN | NUMBER | | | | PER CENT OF TOTAL | | |
	Total foreign white stock	Foreign-born white	Native white of foreign parentage	Native white of mixed parentage	Foreign born	Foreign parentage	Mixed parentage
All countries	38,727,593	13,366,407	16,999,221	8,361,965	34.5	43.9	21.6
England, Scotland, and Wales	3,658,519	1,223,200	1,104,259	1,331,060	33.4	30.2	36.4
England	2,522,261	808,672	740,066	973,523	32.1	29.3	38.6
Scotland	899,591	354,323	276,483	268,785	39.4	30.7	29.9
Wales	236,667	60,205	87,710	88,752	25.4	37.1	37.5
Northern Ireland	605,999	178,832	311,662	205,515	25.7	44.8	29.5
Irish Free State	3,086,522	744,810	1,551,760	789,952	24.1	50.3	25.6
Norway, Sweden, and Denmark	3,191,943	1,122,576	1,372,338	697,029	35.2	43.0	21.8
Norway	1,100,008	347,852	476,663	275,583	31.6	43.3	25.1
Sweden	1,562,703	595,250	676,523	290,930	38.1	43.3	18.6
Denmark	529,142	179,474	219,152	130,516	33.9	41.4	24.7
Netherlands	413,966	133,133	170,417	110,416	32.2	41.2	26.7
Switzerland	374,003	113,010	146,255	114,788	30.2	39.1	30.7
France	471,605	135,232	178,033	158,340	28.7	37.8	33.6
Germany	6,873,103	1,608,814	3,254,618	2,009,671	23.4	47.4	29.2
Poland	3,342,198	1,268,583	1,781,280	292,335	38.0	53.3	8.7
Czechoslovakia	1,382,079	491,638	707,384	183,057	35.6	51.2	13.2
Austria	954,648	370,914	458,177	125,557	38.9	48.0	13.2
Hungary	590,768	274,450	272,704	43,614	46.5	46.2	7.4
Yugoslavia	469,395	211,416	227,475	30,504	45.0	48.5	6.5
Russia	2,669,838	1,153,624	1,277,460	238,754	43.2	47.8	8.9
Lithuania	439,195	193,606	221,472	24,117	44.1	50.4	5.5
Finland	320,536	142,478	148,532	29,526	44.4	46.3	9.2
Rumania	293,453	146,393	125,479	21,581	49.9	42.8	7.4
Greece	303,751	174,526	101,608	27,557	57.5	33.5	9.1
Italy	4,546,877	1,790,424	2,306,015	450,438	39.4	50.7	9.9
Other Europe	590,997	265,226	237,147	97,624	44.2	39.5	16.3
Asia	309,927	157,580	127,695	24,652	50.8	41.2	8.0
Canada	3,337,345	1,278,421	805,801	1,253,123	38.3	24.1	37.5
Canada—French	1,106,159	370,852	389,131	346,176	33.5	35.2	31.3
Canada—Other	2,231,186	907,569	416,670	906,947	40.7	18.7	40.6
Other America	234,094	116,649	51,999	65,446	49.8	22.2	28.0
All other countries	167,832	70,872	59,601	37,359	42.2	35.5	22.3

Urban, rural-farm, and rural-nonfarm population.—Urban population, as defined by the Census Bureau, is in general that residing in cities and other incorporated places having 2,500 inhabitants or more, the remainder being classified as rural. In three of the New England

States, New Hampshire, Massachusetts, and Rhode Island, towns (townships) are classified as urban if they have a population of 2,500 or more and certain urban characteristics; and a few large and densely populated townships in other States are likewise classified, even though not formally incorporated as municipalities.

In addition to the classification of the population as urban and rural, the rural population is further subdivided into rural-farm and rural-nonfarm, on the basis of the replies to a question reading, "Does this family live on a farm?" The rural-farm population includes all persons living on farms in the rural areas. The rural-nonfarm or "village" population is made up largely of persons living in small towns or villages, both incorporated and unincorporated, though in many areas there are considerable numbers of families living in the open country but not on farms.

The relative importance of the foreign white stock and of its major elements in the urban, rural-farm, and rural-nonfarm population is indicated by the figures presented in Table 3.

TABLE 3.—TOTAL POPULATION AND FOREIGN WHITE STOCK IN THE URBAN, RURAL-FARM, AND RURAL-NONFARM POPULATION OF THE UNITED STATES: 1930

| NATIVITY AND PARENTAGE | UNITED STATES | | URBAN | |
	Number	Per cent	Number	Per cent
Total population	122,775,046	100.0	68,954,823	100.0
Native white—Native parentage	70,136,614	57.1	33,497,232	48.6
Foreign white stock	38,727,593	31.5	29,339,373	42.5
Foreign-born white	13,366,407	10.9	10,726,859	15.6
Native white—Foreign parentage	16,999,221	13.8	12,959,015	18.8
Native white—Mixed parentage	8,361,965	6.8	5,653,499	8.2
Negro	11,891,143	9.7	5,193,013	7.5
Other races	2,019,696	1.6	924,305	1.3

| NATIVITY AND PARENTAGE | RURAL-FARM | | RURAL-NONFARM | |
	Number	Per cent	Number	Per cent
Total population	30,157,513	100.0	23,662,710	100.0
Native white—Native parentage	20,495,382	68.0	16,144,000	68.2
Foreign white stock	4,389,452	14.6	4,998,768	21.1
Foreign-born white	1,084,087	3.6	1,555,461	6.6
Native white—Foreign parentage	1,953,554	6.5	2,086,652	8.8
Native white—Mixed parentage	1,351,811	4.5	1,356,655	5.7
Negro	4,680,523	15.5	2,016,707	8.5
Other races	592,156	2.0	503,235	2.1

COUNTRY OF ORIGIN OF THE FOREIGN WHITE STOCK

PER CENT DISTRIBUTION OF FOREIGN WHITE STOCK BY COUNTRY OF ORIGIN: 1930

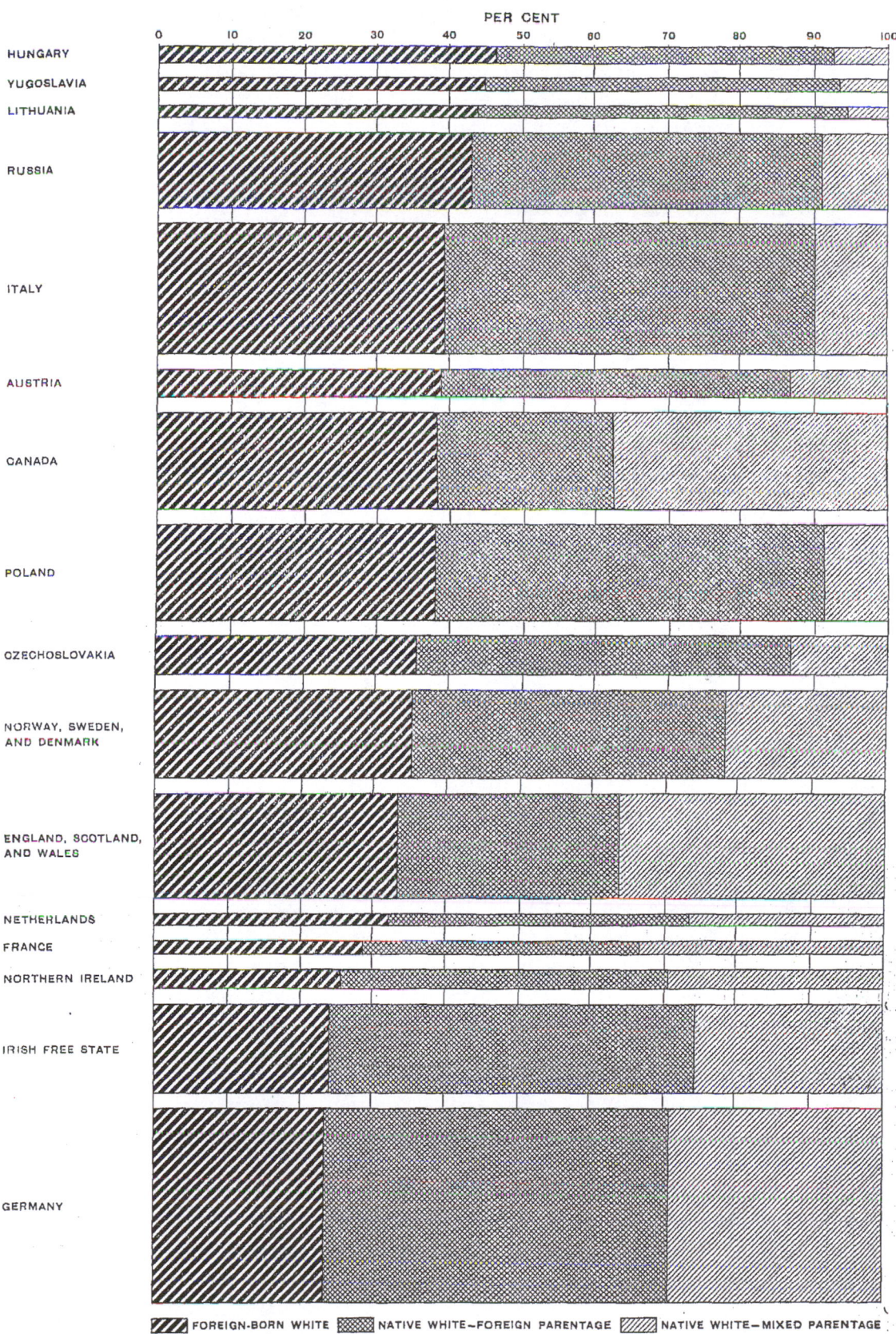

FOREIGN-BORN WHITE   NATIVE WHITE—FOREIGN PARENTAGE   NATIVE WHITE—MIXED PARENTAGE

266

POPULATION

FOREIGN WHITE STOCK BY COUNTRY OF ORIGIN: 1930

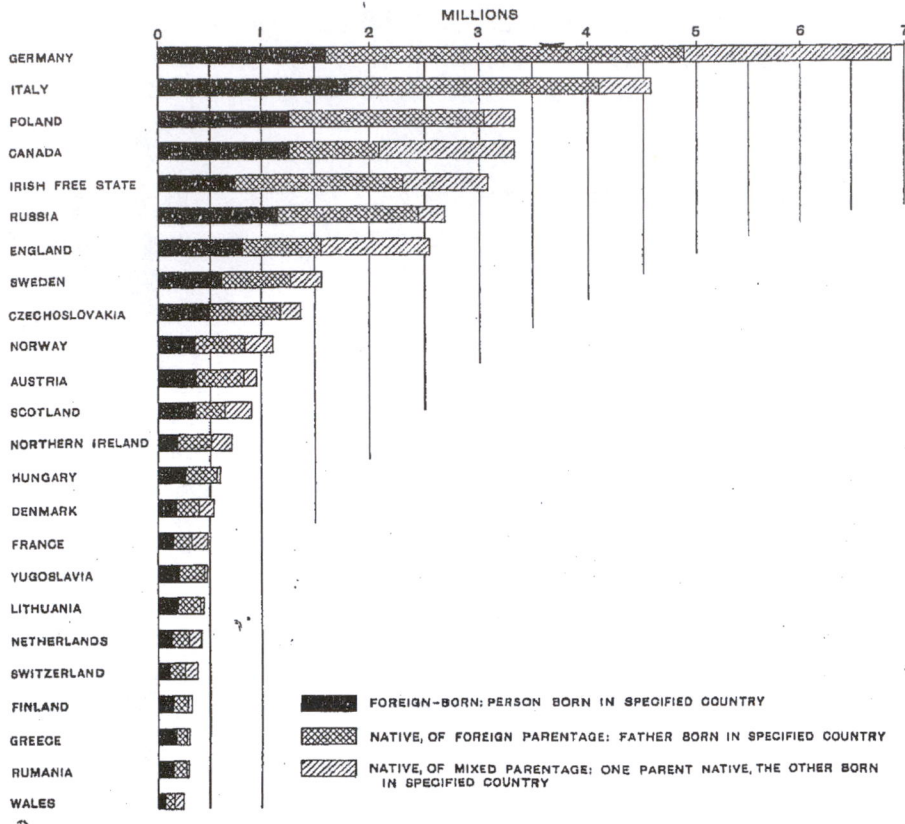

FOREIGN WHITE STOCK FROM SELECTED COUNTRIES, BY STATES: 1930

GERMANY

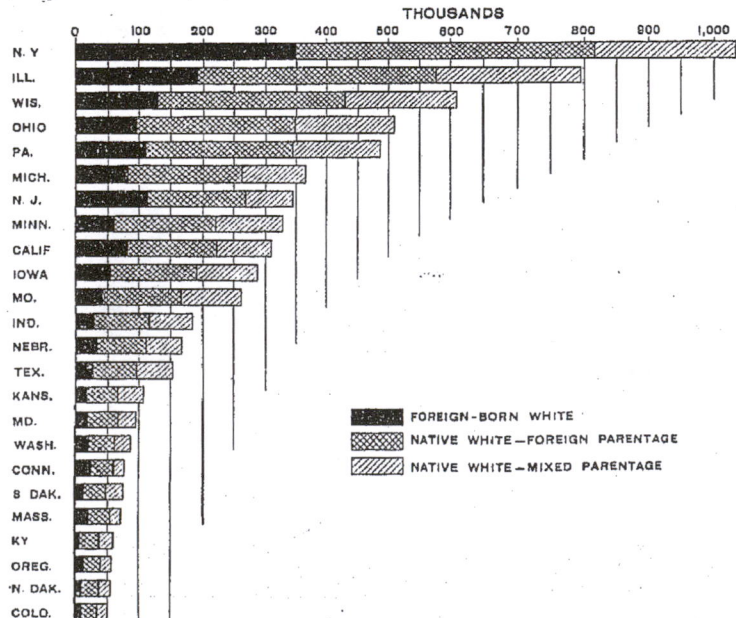

NORWAY, SWEDEN, AND DENMARK

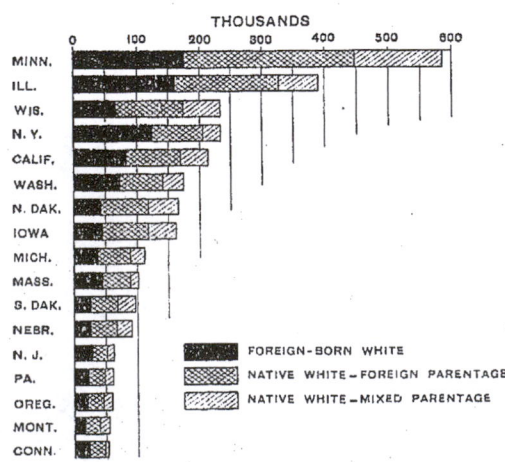

POPULATION

TABLE 4.—COUNTRY OF ORIGIN OF THE FOREIGN WHITE STOCK, BY NATIVITY AND PARENTAGE, FOR THE UNITED STATES: 1930

[The foreign-born white are classified by country of birth; the native white with both parents foreign or with father foreign and mother native are classified by country of birth of father; and the native white with mother foreign and father native, by country of birth of mother. Per cent not shown where less than 0.1]

COUNTRY OF ORIGIN	TOTAL FOREIGN WHITE STOCK		FOREIGN-BORN WHITE		NATIVE WHITE—FOREIGN OR MIXED PARENTAGE							
					Total		Both parents foreign		Father foreign		Mother foreign	
	Number	Per cent	Number	Per cent	Number	Per cent	Number	Per cent	Number	Per cent	Number	Per cent
All countries	38,727,593	100.0	13,366,407	100.0	25,361,186	100.0	16,999,221	100.0	5,459,530	100.0	2,902,435	100.0
Northwestern Europe:												
England	2,522,261	6.5	808,672	6.1	1,713,589	6.8	740,066	4.4	598,022	11.0	375,501	12.9
Scotland	899,591	2.3	354,323	2.7	545,268	2.2	276,483	1.6	164,673	3.0	104,112	3.6
Wales	236,667	0.6	60,205	0.5	176,462	0.7	87,710	0.5	56,644	1.0	32,108	1.1
Northern Ireland	695,999	1.8	178,832	1.3	517,167	2.0	311,652	1.8	117,431	2.2	88,084	3.0
Irish Free State	3,080,522	8.0	744,810	5.6	2,341,712	9.2	1,551,760	9.1	432,450	7.9	357,502	12.3
Norway	1,100,098	2.8	347,852	2.6	752,246	3.0	476,663	2.8	179,482	3.3	96,101	3.3
Sweden	1,562,703	4.0	595,250	4.5	967,453	3.8	676,523	4.0	191,037	3.5	99,893	3.4
Denmark	529,142	1.4	179,474	1.3	349,668	1.4	219,152	1.3	93,592	1.7	36,924	1.3
Iceland	7,413		2,764		4,649		3,177		799		673	
Netherlands	413,966	1.1	133,133	1.0	280,833	1.1	170,417	1.0	74,730	1.4	35,686	1.2
Belgium	147,091	0.4	64,104	0.5	82,807	0.3	52,484	0.3	20,883	0.4	9,530	0.3
Luxemburg	34,869	0.1	9,048	0.1	25,821	0.1	15,163	0.1	8,173	0.1	2,485	0.1
Switzerland	374,003	1.0	113,010	0.8	260,993	1.0	146,255	0.9	80,595	1.5	34,143	1.2
France	471,605	1.2	135,232	1.0	336,373	1.3	178,033	1.0	108,869	2.0	49,471	1.7
Central Europe:												
Germany	6,873,103	17.7	1,608,814	12.0	5,264,289	20.8	3,254,618	19.1	1,398,587	25.6	611,084	21.1
Poland	3,342,198	8.6	1,268,583	9.5	2,073,615	8.2	1,781,280	10.5	223,611	4.1	68,724	2.4
Czechoslovakia	1,382,079	3.6	491,638	3.7	890,441	3.5	707,384	4.2	123,363	2.3	59,694	2.1
Austria	954,648	2.5	370,914	2.8	583,734	2.3	458,177	2.7	84,443	1.5	41,114	1.4
Hungary	590,768	1.5	274,450	2.1	316,318	1.2	272,704	1.6	28,378	0.5	15,236	0.5
Yugoslavia	469,395	1.2	211,416	1.6	257,979	1.0	227,475	1.3	20,328	0.5	4,176	0.1
Eastern Europe:												
Russia	2,669,838	6.9	1,153,624	8.6	1,516,214	6.0	1,277,460	7.5	169,755	3.1	68,999	2.4
Latvia	38,091	0.1	20,673	0.2	17,418	0.1	14,645	0.1	2,132		641	
Estonia	5,317		3,550		1,767		1,417		265		85	
Lithuania	439,195	1.1	193,606	1.4	245,589	1.0	221,472	1.3	19,643	0.4	4,474	0.2
Finland	320,536	0.8	142,478	1.1	178,058	0.7	148,532	0.9	18,805	0.3	10,721	0.4
Rumania	293,453	0.8	146,393	1.1	147,060	0.6	125,479	0.7	15,351	0.3	6,230	0.2
Bulgaria	14,929		9,399	0.1	5,530		3,256		2,147		127	
Turkey in Europe	3,676		2,257		1,419		1,174		205		40	
Southern Europe:												
Greece	303,751	0.8	174,526	1.3	129,225	0.5	101,668	0.6	26,981	0.5	576	
Albania	13,223		8,814	0.1	4,409		3,700		678		31	
Italy	4,546,877	11.7	1,790,424	13.4	2,756,453	10.9	2,306,015	13.6	396,324	7.3	54,114	1.9
Spain	110,607	0.3	58,302	0.4	52,305	0.2	36,080	0.2	12,646	0.2	3,579	0.1
Portugal	167,891	0.4	69,974	0.5	97,917	0.4	75,202	0.4	17,920	0.3	4,795	0.2
Other Europe:												
Danzig	3,524		1,483		2,041		1,351		446		244	
Europe (not specified)	53,366	0.1	14,768	0.1	38,598	0.2	29,498	0.2	6,260	0.1	2,840	0.1
Asia:												
Armenia	58,037	0.1	32,166	0.2	25,871	0.1	23,230	0.1	2,440		201	
Palestine	10,446		6,135		4,311		3,356		680		275	
Syria	137,576	0.4	57,227	0.4	80,349	0.3	69,034	0.4	9,972	0.2	1,343	
Turkey in Asia	77,283	0.2	46,651	0.3	30,632	0.1	26,777	0.2	3,295	0.1	560	
China	3,675		2,279		1,396		278		642		476	
Japan	1,458		632		826		278		345		203	
India	7,095		3,300		3,795		1,018		1,596		1,181	
Other Asia	14,357		9,190	0.1	5,167		3,724		1,050		393	
America:												
Canada—French	1,106,159	2.9	370,852	2.8	735,307	2.9	389,131	2.3	198,512	3.6	147,664	5.1
Canada—Other	2,231,186	5.8	907,569	6.8	1,323,617	5.2	416,670	2.5	479,669	8.8	427,278	14.7
Newfoundland	45,733	0.1	23,971	0.2	21,762	0.1	12,794	0.1	4,005	0.1	4,963	0.2
Cuba	32,540	0.1	15,944	0.1	16,596	0.1	7,894		5,763	0.1	2,939	0.1
Other West Indies	31,108	0.1	15,482	0.1	15,626	0.1	6,546		5,490	0.1	3,590	0.1
Mexico	65,968	0.2	23,743	0.2	42,225	0.2	16,067	0.1	12,275	0.2	13,883	0.5
Central America	10,485		7,454	0.1	3,031		919		956		1,156	
South America	48,260	0.1	30,055	0.2	18,205	0.1	7,779		6,615	0.1	3,811	0.1
All other:												
Africa	13,469		7,866	0.1	5,603		2,001		2,228		1,374	
Australia	30,840	0.1	12,720	0.1	18,129	0.1	6,294		6,707	0.1	5,128	0.2
Azores	91,714	0.2	35,427	0.3	56,287	0.2	43,308	0.3	10,165	0.2	2,814	0.1
Other Atlantic Islands	9,711		4,052		5,659		3,362		1,527		770	
Pacific Islands	8,648		4,364		4,284		917		1,847		1,520	0.1
Country not specified	3,171		1,485		1,686		1,134		395		157	
Born at sea	10,270		4,958		5,312		2,585		1,708		1,019	

COUNTRY OF ORIGIN OF THE FOREIGN WHITE STOCK

269

TABLE 5.—COUNTRY OF ORIGIN OF THE FOREIGN WHITE STOCK, BY NATIVITY AND PARENTAGE, FOR THE UNITED STATES: 1890 TO 1930

[Persons shown as of "mixed foreign parentage" in the reports of censuses prior to 1930 have been distributed on the basis of country of birth of father. The table is limited to those countries and census years for which comparable figures are available]

COUNTRY OF ORIGIN AND CENSUS YEAR	Total foreign white stock	Foreign-born white	NATIVE WHITE OF FOREIGN OR MIXED PARENTAGE				COUNTRY OF ORIGIN AND CENSUS YEAR	Total foreign white stock	Foreign-born white	NATIVE WHITE OF FOREIGN OR MIXED PARENTAGE			
			Total	Both parents foreign	Father foreign	Mother foreign				Total	Both parents foreign	Father foreign	Mother foreign
All countries:							**Poland:**						
1930	38,727,593	13,366,407	25,361,186	16,999,221	5,459,530	2,902,435	1930	3,342,198	1,268,583	2,073,615	1,781,280	223,611	68,724
1920	36,398,958	13,712,754	22,686,204	15,694,539	4,539,776	2,451,889	1920	2,443,329	1,139,978	1,303,351	1,153,427	115,172	34,752
Adjusted [1]	*35,698,417*	*13,255,504*	*22,443,023*	*15,521,835*	*4,496,024*	*2,425,164*	1910	1,663,808	937,884	725,924	652,619	56,116	17,189
1910	32,243,382	13,345,545	18,897,837	12,916,311	3,923,845	2,057,681							
Adjusted [1]	*31,875,879*	*13,134,312*	*18,741,560*	*12,812,090*	*3,890,302*	*2,039,168*	**Austria:**						
1900	25,859,834	10,213,817	15,646,017	10,632,280	3,346,652	1,667,085	1930	954,648	370,914	583,734	458,177	84,443	41,114
1890	20,625,542	9,121,867	11,503,675	8,095,019	2,378,729	1,030,927	1920 (prewar)	1,235,097	860,004	1,034,949	134,227	65,921	
							1910	1,562,259	845,506	716,753	607,988	74,238	34,527
England:							1900	824,400	432,764	391,636	334,040	40,182	17,414
1930	2,522,261	808,672	1,713,589	740,066	598,022	375,501							
1920	2,404,871	812,828	1,592,043	773,518	571,560	336,965	**Hungary:**						
1910	2,514,112	876,455	1,637,657	783,955	546,215	307,487	1930	590,768	274,450	316,318	272,704	28,378	15,236
1900	2,358,044	839,830	1,518,214	740,764	494,929	273,521	1920 (prewar)	1,156,903	618,385	538,518	498,304	29,510	10,704
							1910	710,895	495,600	215,295	201,727	10,106	3,462
Scotland:							1900	227,006	145,709	81,897	75,872	4,895	1,130
1930	899,591	354,323	545,268	276,483	164,673	104,112							
1920	769,503	254,567	514,436	271,927	153,017	88,502	**Russia:**						
1910	745,733	261,034	484,699	261,461	145,227	78,011	1930	2,669,838	1,153,624	1,516,214	1,277,460	169,755	68,999
1900	680,907	233,473	447,524	250,691	129,735	67,098	1920	2,909,093	1,400,489	1,508,604	1,381,454	93,651	33,499
							1910	1,960,036	1,184,382	775,654	729,412	35,547	10,695
Wales:							1900	774,444	486,346	288,098	272,954	12,423	2,721
1930	236,607	60,205	176,462	87,710	56,644	32,108							
1920	249,368	67,066	182,302	96,998	54,889	30,415	**Finland:**						
1910	267,086	82,479	184,607	103,073	52,555	28,979	1930	320,536	142,478	178,058	148,532	18,805	10,721
1900	270,904	93,560	177,344	104,758	47,498	25,088	1920	301,985	149,824	152,161	136,738	9,765	5,658
							1910	215,341	129,669	85,672	80,576	3,319	1,777
Northern Ireland:													
1930	695,099	178,832	517,167	311,652	117,431	88,084	**Rumania:**						
							1930	293,453	146,393	147,060	125,479	15,351	6,230
Irish Free State:							1920	167,599	102,823	64,776	59,396	3,820	1,560
1930	3,086,522	744,810	2,341,712	1,551,760	432,450	357,502	1910	92,854	65,920	26,934	25,840	821	273
Ireland:							**Greece:**						
1920	4,159,246	1,037,238	3,122,013	2,117,293	573,021	431,699	1930	303,751	174,526	129,225	101,668	26,981	576
1910	4,656,170	1,352,155	3,304,015	2,293,387	603,013	407,615	1920	228,055	175,972	52,083	43,517	8,287	279
1900	4,990,778	1,615,232	3,375,546	2,408,115	605,987	361,444	1910	111,249	101,264	9,985	7,108	2,400	477
Norway:							**Italy:**						
1930	1,100,008	347,852	752,246	476,663	179,482	96,101	1930	4,546,877	1,790,424	2,756,453	2,306,015	396,324	54,114
1920	1,064,958	363,862	701,096	477,545	143,314	80,237	1920	3,361,200	1,610,109	1,751,091	1,585,395	146,304	19,392
1910	1,012,026	403,858	609,068	444,778	106,805	57,485	1910	2,114,715	1,343,070	771,645	711,542	52,947	7,156
1900	814,910	336,370	478,531	375,372	67,649	35,510	1900	788,513	483,963	254,550	229,419	22,442	2,689
Sweden:							**Spain:**						
1930	1,562,703	595,250	967,453	676,523	191,037	99,893	1930	110,607	58,302	52,305	36,080	12,646	3,579
1920	1,514,077	625,580	888,497	663,515	144,382	80,600	1920	80,317	49,247	31,070	20,782	7,972	2,316
1910	1,417,878	665,183	752,695	600,451	97,504	54,740	1910	36,575	21,977	14,598	7,828	5,364	1,406
1900	1,124,018	581,986	542,032	456,402	55,479	30,151							
							Portugal:						
Denmark: [2]							1930	167,891	69,974	97,917	75,202	17,920	4,795
1930	529,142	179,474	349,668	219,152	93,592	36,924	1920	136,904	67,453	69,451	55,399	11,673	2,379
1920	509,564	189,154	320,410	215,083	73,915	31,412	1910	112,090	57,623	55,367	43,548	10,359	1,460
1910	437,796	181,621	256,175	185,380	49,721	21,074							
1900	341,488	153,644	187,844	146,534	29,514	11,796	**Canada—French:**						
							1930	1,106,159	370,852	735,307	389,131	198,512	147,664
Netherlands:							1920	870,146	307,786	562,360	343,161	129,203	89,996
1930	413,966	133,133	280,833	170,417	74,730	35,686	1910	947,792	385,083	562,709	346,530	133,999	82,180
1920	381,105	131,766	249,339	163,797	57,301	28,241	1900	850,491	394,461	456,030	280,103	106,833	69,094
1910	308,068	120,053	188,015	130,825	38,199	18,991							
							Canada—Other:						
Belgium:							1930	2,231,186	907,569	1,323,617	416,670	479,669	427,278
1930	147,091	64,194	82,897	52,484	20,883	9,530	1920	2,080,337	810,092	1,279,245	426,096	467,206	385,943
1920	131,647	62,686	68,961	47,034	15,420	6,507	1910	1,899,099	810,987	1,088,112	384,013	387,617	316,482
1910	95,619	49,397	46,222	32,803	9,802	3,617	1900	1,711,839	778,399	933,440	334,707	317,988	280,745
Luxemburg:							**Newfoundland:**						
1930	34,869	9,048	25,821	15,163	8,173	2,485	1930	45,733	23,971	21,762	12,794	4,005	4,963
1920	49,348	12,585	36,763	22,754	10,847	3,162	1920	28,487	13,242	15,245	9,280	2,780	3,185
1910	7,651	3,068	4,583	3,087	1,244	252	1910	9,311	5,076	4,235	2,512	853	870
Switzerland:							**West Indies:**						
1930	374,003	113,010	260,993	146,255	80,595	34,143	1930	63,648	31,426	32,222	14,440	11,253	6,529
1920	376,000	118,659	257,341	150,266	75,315	31,760	1920	52,332	26,869	25,963	12,363	9,005	4,595
1910	342,293	124,834	217,459	131,312	61,244	24,903	1910	43,595	23,169	20,426	10,434	6,743	3,249
1900	294,272	115,581	178,691	111,797	48,806	18,088							
							Mexico:						
France:							1930	65,968	23,743	42,225	16,067	12,275	13,883
1930	471,605	135,232	336,373	178,033	108,869	49,471	1920	731,559	478,383	253,176	170,440	45,720	28,016
1920	441,240	152,890	288,350	169,472	86,549	32,329	*Adjusted* [1]	*31,025*	*9,995*	*6,786*	*1,968*	*1,291*	
1910	343,295	117,236	226,059	129,843	73,085	23,131	1910	382,761	219,802	162,959	108,625	34,995	19,339
1900	318,623	104,031	214,592	121,594	72,110	20,888	*Adjusted* [1]	*15,251*	*8,869*	*6,082*	*4,404*	*1,452*	*226*
Germany:							**Central and South America:**						
1930	6,873,103	1,608,814	5,264,289	3,254,618	1,398,587	611,084	1930	58,745	37,509	21,236	8,698	7,571	4,967
1920	7,032,106	1,686,102	5,346,004	3,448,821	1,331,531	565,652	1920	30,980	20,929	10,051	3,770	3,595	2,686
1910	7,981,696	2,311,085	5,670,611	3,845,926	1,304,201	520,484	1910	14,577	9,069	5,508	1,874	2,050	1,584
1900	8,003,351	2,663,204	5,340,147	3,761,783	1,172,697	405,667							

[1] Adjusted by deducting the estimated number of persons who would have been classified as Mexicans in 1930; see text.
[2] Included Iceland prior to 1930.

TABLE 6.—COUNTRY OF ORIGIN OF THE FOREIGN WHITE STOCK IN THE URBAN, RURAL-FARM, AND RURAL-NONFARM POPULATION, BY NATIVITY AND PARENTAGE, FOR THE UNITED STATES: 1930

[Per cent not shown where less than 0.1]

URBAN

COUNTRY OF ORIGIN	FOREIGN WHITE STOCK Number	FOREIGN WHITE STOCK Per cent	FOREIGN-BORN WHITE Number	FOREIGN-BORN WHITE Per cent	NATIVE WHITE—FOREIGN OR MIXED PARENTAGE Total Number	Total Per cent	Both parents foreign	Father foreign	Mother foreign
All countries	29,339,373	100.0	10,726,859	100.0	18,612,514	100.0	12,959,015	3,643,855	2,009,644
Europe:									
England	1,855,813	6.3	641,200	6.0	1,214,613	6.5	543,619	405,512	265,482
Scotland	694,187	2.4	295,541	2.8	398,646	2.1	210,051	114,029	74,566
Wales	170,230	0.6	45,968	0.4	124,262	0.7	62,849	38,631	22,782
Northern Ireland	558,123	1.9	150,782	1.4	407,341	2.2	254,540	84,831	67,970
Irish Free State	2,644,153	9.0	671,727	6.3	1,972,426	10.6	1,338,618	336,279	297,529
Norway	526,081	1.8	194,936	1.8	331,145	1.8	210,750	70,416	49,979
Sweden	1,010,125	3.4	408,032	3.8	602,093	3.2	438,615	103,487	59,991
Denmark	290,992	1.0	107,127	1.0	183,865	1.0	118,948	45,704	19,213
Netherlands	235,664	0.8	80,466	0.8	155,198	0.8	96,220	39,622	19,356
Belgium	98,025	0.3	47,136	0.4	50,889	0.3	32,523	12,201	6,165
Luxemburg	19,264	0.1	5,693	0.1	13,571	0.1	8,422	3,866	1,283
Switzerland	214,416	0.7	67,918	0.6	146,498	0.8	83,641	43,430	19,427
France	346,928	1.2	104,865	1.0	242,063	1.3	131,210	74,919	35,934
Germany	4,612,279	15.7	1,176,950	11.0	3,435,329	18.5	2,199,197	854,135	381,997
Poland	2,820,200	9.6	1,096,114	10.2	1,724,086	9.3	1,489,959	177,914	56,213
Czechoslovakia	925,219	3.2	348,261	3.2	576,958	3.1	471,996	69,832	35,130
Austria	771,515	2.6	308,482	2.9	463,033	2.5	370,046	62,070	30,917
Hungary	482,023	1.6	228,642	2.1	253,381	1.4	218,644	22,382	12,355
Yugoslavia	327,972	1.1	154,501	1.4	173,471	0.9	153,959	16,624	2,888
Russia	2,314,788	7.9	1,041,173	9.7	1,273,615	6.8	1,094,860	127,982	50,773
Latvia	34,493	0.1	18,744	0.2	15,749	0.1	13,305	1,875	569
Lithuania	378,533	1.3	168,090	1.6	210,443	1.1	190,267	16,389	3,787
Finland	167,277	0.6	79,867	0.7	87,410	0.5	73,735	7,908	5,767
Rumania	257,858	0.9	131,465	1.2	126,393	0.7	109,036	12,241	5,116
Bulgaria	11,421	------	7,346	0.1	4,075	------	2,600	1,385	90
Turkey in Europe	3,500	------	2,158	------	1,342	------	1,132	174	36
Greece	276,915	0.9	159,376	1.5	117,539	0.6	94,512	22,528	499
Italy	3,980,595	13.6	1,573,003	14.7	2,407,592	12.9	2,022,877	337,574	47,141
Spain	86,050	0.3	46,181	0.4	39,869	0.2	27,060	9,974	2,835
Portugal	120,171	0.4	52,141	0.5	68,030	0.4	53,473	11,189	3,368
Other Europe	64,480	0.2	26,069	0.2	38,411	0.2	29,870	5,950	2,591
Asia:									
Syria	122,127	0.4	51,482	0.5	70,645	0.4	61,688	7,768	1,189
Turkey in Asia	71,089	0.2	43,272	0.4	27,817	0.1	24,626	2,733	458
Other Asia	83,460	0.3	48,135	0.4	35,325	0.2	27,803	5,377	2,145
America:									
Canada—French	847,518	2.9	292,564	2.7	554,954	3.0	304,397	141,560	108,997
Canada—Other	1,603,023	5.5	696,174	6.5	906,849	4.9	301,518	313,128	292,203
Newfoundland	41,762	0.1	22,021	0.2	19,741	0.1	11,897	3,471	4,373
West Indies	57,818	0.2	29,088	0.3	28,730	0.2	13,460	9,728	5,542
Mexico	45,090	0.2	18,596	0.2	26,494	0.1	10,037	7,237	9,220
Central and South America	51,036	0.2	33,803	0.3	17,233	0.1	7,201	6,172	3,770
All other	117,160	0.4	51,770	0.5	65,390	0.4	40,764	15,628	8,998

RURAL

COUNTRY OF ORIGIN	FOREIGN WHITE STOCK Number	FOREIGN WHITE STOCK Per cent	FOREIGN-BORN WHITE Number	FOREIGN-BORN WHITE Per cent	NATIVE WHITE—FOREIGN OR MIXED PARENTAGE Total Number	Total Per cent	Both parents foreign	Father foreign	Mother foreign
All countries	9,388,220	100.0	2,639,548	100.0	6,748,672	100.0	4,040,206	1,815,675	892,791
Europe:									
England	666,448	7.1	167,472	6.3	498,976	7.4	196,447	192,510	110,019
Scotland	205,404	2.2	58,782	2.2	146,622	2.2	66,432	50,644	29,546
Wales	66,437	0.7	14,237	0.5	52,200	0.8	24,861	18,013	9,326
Northern Ireland	137,876	1.5	28,050	1.1	109,826	1.6	57,112	32,600	20,114
Irish Free State	442,809	4.7	73,083	2.8	369,286	5.5	213,142	96,171	59,973
Norway	574,017	6.1	152,916	5.8	421,101	6.2	256,913	109,066	55,122
Sweden	552,578	5.9	187,218	7.1	365,360	5.4	237,908	87,550	39,902
Denmark	238,150	2.5	72,347	2.7	165,803	2.5	100,204	47,888	17,711
Netherlands	178,302	1.9	52,667	2.0	125,635	1.9	74,197	35,108	16,330
Belgium	49,066	0.5	17,058	0.6	32,008	0.5	19,961	8,682	3,365
Luxemburg	15,605	0.2	3,355	0.1	12,250	0.2	6,741	4,307	1,202
Switzerland	159,587	1.7	45,092	1.7	114,495	1.7	62,614	37,165	14,716
France	124,677	1.3	30,367	1.2	94,310	1.4	46,823	33,950	13,537
Germany	2,260,824	24.1	431,864	16.4	1,828,960	27.1	1,055,421	544,452	229,087
Poland	521,998	5.6	172,469	6.5	349,529	5.2	291,321	45,697	12,511
Czechoslovakia	456,860	4.9	143,377	5.4	313,483	4.6	235,388	53,531	24,564
Austria	183,133	2.0	62,432	2.4	120,701	1.8	88,131	22,373	10,197
Hungary	108,745	1.2	45,808	1.7	62,937	0.9	54,060	5,996	2,881
Yugoslavia	141,423	1.5	56,915	2.2	84,508	1.3	73,516	9,704	1,288
Russia	355,050	3.8	112,451	4.3	242,599	3.6	182,600	41,773	18,226
Latvia	3,598	------	1,929	0.1	1,669	------	1,840	257	72
Lithuania	60,662	0.6	25,516	1.0	35,146	0.5	31,205	3,254	687
Finland	153,259	1.6	62,611	2.4	90,648	1.3	74,797	10,897	4,954
Rumania	35,595	0.4	14,928	0.6	20,667	0.3	16,443	3,110	1,114
Bulgaria	3,508	------	2,053	0.1	1,455	------	656	762	37
Turkey in Europe	176	------	99	------	77	------	42	31	4
Greece	26,836	0.3	15,150	0.6	11,686	0.2	7,156	4,453	77
Italy	566,282	6.0	217,421	8.2	348,861	5.2	283,138	58,750	6,973
Spain	24,557	0.3	12,121	0.5	12,436	0.2	9,020	2,672	744
Portugal	47,720	0.5	17,833	0.7	29,887	0.4	21,729	6,731	1,427
Other Europe	18,363	0.2	5,310	0.2	13,053	0.2	9,273	2,498	1,282
Asia:									
Syria	15,449	0.2	5,745	0.2	9,704	0.1	7,346	2,204	154
Turkey in Asia	6,194	0.1	3,379	0.1	2,815	------	2,151	562	102
Other Asia	11,608	0.1	5,567	0.2	6,041	0.1	4,081	1,376	584
America:									
Canada—French	258,641	2.8	78,288	3.0	180,353	2.7	84,734	56,952	38,667
Canada—Other	628,163	6.7	211,395	8.0	416,768	6.2	115,152	166,541	135,075
Newfoundland	3,971	------	1,950	0.1	2,021	------	897	534	590
West Indies	5,830	0.1	2,338	0.1	3,492	0.1	980	1,525	987
Mexico	20,878	0.2	5,147	0.2	15,731	0.2	6,030	5,038	4,663
Central and South America	7,709	0.1	3,706	0.1	4,003	0.1	1,407	1,399	1,197
All other	50,672	0.5	19,102	0.7	31,570	0.5	18,837	8,949	3,784

RURAL-FARM

COUNTRY OF ORIGIN	FOREIGN WHITE STOCK Number	FOREIGN WHITE STOCK Per cent	FOREIGN-BORN WHITE Number	FOREIGN-BORN WHITE Per cent	NATIVE WHITE—FOREIGN OR MIXED PARENTAGE Total Number	Total Per cent	Both parents foreign	Father foreign	Mother foreign
All countries	4,389,452	100.0	1,084,087	100.0	3,305,365	100.0	1,953,554	925,508	426,303
Europe:									
England	229,237	5.2	44,106	4.1	185,131	5.6	68,692	76,306	40,133
Scotland	63,758	1.5	13,871	1.3	49,887	1.5	21,593	18,377	9,917
Wales	22,098	0.5	4,008	0.4	18,090	0.5	8,275	6,601	3,214
North. Ireland	49,072	1.1	8,207	0.8	40,865	1.2	20,544	13,675	6,646
Irish Free State	150,107	3.4	17,008	1.6	133,099	4.0	73,762	40,382	18,955
Norway	368,727	8.4	91,385	8.4	277,342	8.4	168,814	72,421	36,107
Sweden	313,810	7.1	98,589	9.1	215,221	6.5	140,227	52,953	22,041
Denmark	143,376	3.3	41,555	3.8	101,821	3.1	62,793	29,009	10,019
Netherlands	110,067	2.5	31,408	2.9	78,659	2.4	46,987	21,972	9,700
Belgium	28,276	0.6	9,044	0.8	19,232	0.6	12,483	5,127	1,622
Luxemburg	9,992	0.2	1,955	0.2	8,037	0.2	4,251	2,967	819
Switzerland	93,963	2.1	25,887	2.4	68,076	2.1	37,633	22,119	8,324
France	49,818	1.1	10,345	1.0	39,473	1.2	19,427	15,054	4,992
Germany	1,282,760	29.2	215,977	19.9	1,066,783	32.3	605,168	326,522	135,093
Poland	209,866	4.8	65,166	6.0	144,700	4.4	117,176	21,455	6,069
Czechoslovakia	208,877	4.8	58,722	5.4	150,155	4.5	105,532	29,565	15,058
Austria	71,296	1.6	21,977	2.0	49,319	1.5	33,892	10,383	5,044
Hungary	36,374	0.8	14,801	1.4	21,573	0.7	18,682	2,009	882
Yugoslavia	33,696	0.8	12,655	1.2	21,041	0.6	18,758	1,871	412
Russia	220,606	5.0	59,667	5.5	160,939	4.9	120,307	27,931	12,701
Latvia	1,232	------	672	0.1	560	------	468	72	20
Lithuania	18,004	0.4	7,764	0.7	10,240	0.3	9,276	793	171
Finland	92,271	2.1	35,717	3.3	56,554	1.7	47,375	6,490	2,689
Rumania	18,087	0.4	6,469	0.6	11,618	0.4	9,118	1,880	620
Bulgaria	1,117	------	594	0.1	523	------	283	224	16
Turkey in Europe	58	------	31	------	27	------	14	12	1
Greece	5,037	0.1	2,458	0.2	2,579	0.1	1,544	1,018	17
Italy	131,152	3.0	49,283	4.5	81,869	2.5	67,175	12,809	1,885
Spain	7,836	0.2	3,908	0.4	3,928	0.1	3,040	718	170
Portugal	26,458	0.6	9,728	0.9	16,730	0.5	12,310	3,787	633
Other Europe	7,687	0.2	2,047	0.2	5,640	0.2	3,945	1,078	617

RURAL-NONFARM

COUNTRY OF ORIGIN	FOREIGN WHITE STOCK Number	FOREIGN WHITE STOCK Per cent	FOREIGN-BORN WHITE Number	FOREIGN-BORN WHITE Per cent	NATIVE WHITE—FOREIGN OR MIXED PARENTAGE Total Number	Total Per cent	Both parents foreign	Father foreign	Mother foreign
All countries	4,998,768	100.0	1,555,461	100.0	3,443,307	100.0	2,086,652	890,167	466,488
Europe:									
England	437,211	8.7	123,366	7.9	313,845	9.1	127,755	116,204	69,886
Scotland	141,646	2.8	44,911	2.9	96,735	2.8	44,839	32,267	19,629
Wales	44,339	0.9	10,229	0.7	34,110	1.0	16,586	11,412	6,112
North. Ireland	88,804	1.8	19,843	1.3	68,961	2.0	36,568	18,925	13,468
Irish Free State	292,262	5.8	56,075	3.6	236,187	6.9	139,380	55,789	41,018
Norway	205,290	4.1	61,531	4.0	143,759	4.2	88,099	36,045	19,015
Sweden	238,768	4.8	88,629	5.7	150,139	4.4	97,681	34,597	17,861
Denmark	94,774	1.9	30,792	2.0	63,982	1.9	37,411	18,879	7,692
Netherlands	68,235	1.4	21,259	1.4	46,976	1.4	27,210	13,136	6,630
Belgium	20,790	0.4	8,014	0.5	12,776	0.4	7,478	3,555	1,743
Luxemburg	5,613	0.1	1,400	0.1	4,213	0.1	2,490	1,340	383
Switzerland	65,624	1.3	19,205	1.2	46,419	1.3	24,981	15,046	6,392
France	74,859	1.5	20,022	1.3	54,837	1.6	27,396	18,896	8,545
Germany	978,064	19.6	215,887	13.9	762,177	22.1	450,253	217,930	93,994
Poland	312,132	6.2	107,303	6.9	204,829	5.9	174,145	24,242	6,442
Czechoslovakia	247,983	5.0	84,655	5.4	163,328	4.7	129,856	23,966	9,506
Austria	111,837	2.2	40,455	2.6	71,382	2.1	54,239	11,990	5,153
Hungary	72,371	1.4	31,007	2.0	41,364	1.2	35,378	3,987	1,999
Yugoslavia	107,727	2.2	44,260	2.8	63,467	1.8	54,758	7,833	876
Russia	134,444	2.7	52,784	3.4	81,660	2.4	62,293	13,842	5,525
Latvia	2,366	------	1,257	0.1	1,109	------	872	185	52
Lithuania	42,658	0.9	17,752	1.1	24,906	0.7	21,929	2,461	516
Finland	60,988	1.2	26,894	1.7	34,094	1.0	27,422	4,407	2,265
Rumania	17,508	0.4	8,459	0.5	9,049	0.3	7,325	1,230	494
Bulgaria	2,391	------	1,459	0.1	932	------	373	538	21
Turkey in Europe	118	------	68	------	50	------	28	19	3
Greece	21,799	0.4	12,692	0.8	9,107	0.3	5,612	3,435	60
Italy	435,130	8.7	168,138	10.8	266,992	7.8	215,963	45,941	5,088
Spain	16,721	0.3	8,213	0.5	8,508	0.2	5,980	1,954	574
Portugal	21,262	0.4	8,105	0.5	13,157	0.4	9,419	2,944	794
Other Europe	10,676	0.2	3,263	0.2	7,413	0.2	5,328	1,420	665

COUNTRY OF ORIGIN OF THE FOREIGN WHITE STOCK

271

TABLE 6.—COUNTRY OF ORIGIN OF THE FOREIGN WHITE STOCK IN THE URBAN, RURAL-FARM, AND RURAL-NONFARM POPULATION, BY NATIVITY AND PARENTAGE, FOR THE UNITED STATES: 1930—Continued

COUNTRY OF ORIGIN	FOREIGN WHITE STOCK		FOREIGN-BORN WHITE		NATIVE WHITE—FOREIGN OR MIXED PARENTAGE					FOREIGN WHITE STOCK		FOREIGN-BORN WHITE		NATIVE WHITE—FOREIGN OR MIXED PARENTAGE				
					Total		Both parents foreign	Father foreign	Mother foreign					Total		Both parents foreign	Father foreign	Mother foreign
	Number	Per cent	Number	Per cent	Number	Per cent				Number	Per cent	Number	Per cent	Number	Per cent			
	RURAL-FARM—Continued									RURAL-NONFARM—Continued								
Asia:																		
Syria	3,166	0.1	1,081	0.1	2,085	0.1	1,502	552	31	12,283	0.2	4,664	0.3	7,619	0.2	5,844	1,652	123
Turkey in Asia	2,893	0.1	1,445	0.1	1,448		1,224	193	31	3,301	0.1	1,934	0.1	1,367		927	369	71
Other Asia	5,821	0.1	2,560	0.2	3,261	0.1	2,527	494	240	5,787	0.1	3,007	0.2	2,780	0.1	1,554	882	344
America:																		
Canada—French	79,733	1.8	22,668	2.1	57,065	1.7	25,272	19,575	12,218	178,908	3.0	55,620	3.6	123,288	3.6	59,462	37,377	26,449
Canada—Other	251,204	5.7	77,069	7.1	174,135	5.3	48,005	71,236	54,894	376,959	7.5	134,326	8.6	242,633	7.0	67,147	95,305	80,181
Newfoundland	554		228		326		111	88	127	3,417	0.1	1,722	0.1	1,695		786	446	463
West Indies	1,120		380		740		171	312	257	4,710	0.1	1,958	0.1	2,752	0.1	809	1,213	730
Mexico	8,550	0.2	1,648	0.2	6,902	0.2	2,921	2,131	1,850	12,328	0.2	3,499	0.2	8,829	0.3	3,100	2,007	2,813
Central and South America	2,558	0.1	1,104	0.1	1,454		544	488	422	5,151	0.1	2,602	0.2	2,549	0.1	863	911	775
All other	29,138	0.7	10,900	1.0	18,238	0.6	11,733	4,859	1,646	21,534	0.4	8,202	0.5	13,332	0.4	7,104	4,090	2,138

POPULATION

272

TABLE 7.—COUNTRY OF ORIGIN OF THE FOREIGN WHITE STOCK, BY DIVISIONS AND STATES: 1930

DIVISION AND STATE	All countries	England	Scotland	Wales	Northern Ireland	Irish Free State	Norway	Sweden	Denmark	Iceland	Netherlands	Belgium	Luxemburg	Switzerland	France	Germany	Poland
United States	38,727,593	2,522,261	899,591	236,667	695,999	3,086,522	1,100,098	1,562,703	529,142	7,413	413,966	147,091	34,869	374,003	471,605	6,873,103	3,342,198
GEOG. DIVS.:																	
New England	4,898,031	355,071	127,784	8,588	114,335	725,374	20,032	147,920	10,283	132	6,888	7,043	194	9,508	30,040	166,024	362,285
Mid. Atlantic	13,722,206	795,413	304,356	96,311	324,471	1,293,425	99,174	198,122	59,095	316	80,719	25,618	1,980	78,989	145,756	1,864,076	1,557,700
E. N. Central	9,777,088	546,585	201,640	57,152	105,233	481,256	247,160	420,553	118,855	579	192,809	75,670	14,302	108,607	109,527	2,461,523	1,157,845
W. N. Central	4,326,004	105,223	63,342	21,249	46,295	204,552	518,617	473,252	168,505	3,452	76,442	17,395	14,305	57,586	43,710	1,282,964	106,971
South Atlantic	936,916	85,159	29,559	7,252	18,691	72,684	6,723	13,309	6,120	59	4,565	2,987	257	7,607	13,942	188,327	72,443
E. S. Central	252,677	22,669	8,499	2,020	5,263	27,394	1,514	3,912	1,701	14	1,458	583	60	7,000	8,746	84,716	6,187
W. S. Central	746,701	54,444	16,108	3,250	9,605	39,780	8,195	20,414	8,503	31	3,982	3,169	358	12,342	32,022	234,912	20,952
Mountain	1,003,331	152,043	42,830	17,213	15,689	55,060	51,485	77,907	55,551	580	14,159	3,507	890	20,450	15,137	136,476	12,614
Pacific	3,064,639	315,654	105,473	23,632	56,417	186,997	147,198	207,224	91,529	2,250	33,444	11,119	2,528	71,914	71,825	454,085	45,201
NEW ENGLAND:																	
Maine	279,940	13,649	5,379	460	8,082	15,391	1,356	5,010	2,334	4	157	106	8	185	918	2,000	3,932
N. Hampshire	224,912	11,926	4,920	252	8,810	19,202	999	3,799	495	2	322	851	2	234	919	4,423	10,506
Vermont	124,875	6,563	4,157	1,352	2,316	10,131	310	2,514	355	1	110	51	6	359	.693	2,288	4,590
Massachusetts	2,763,142	202,417	75,560	4,062	67,080	496,907	12,177	81,106	7,879	107	4,547	3,451	89	3,302	15,372	70,042	187,563
Rhode Island	466,053	58,971	15,041	679	14,296	54,911	1,294	14,117	691	3	351	1,576	23	569	3,964	10,090	22,381
Connecticut	1,039,109	61,545	22,727	1,783	23,151	128,742	3,896	41,374	7,529	15	1,401	1,008	66	4,769	8,174	76,281	133,813
MID. ATLANTIC:																	
New York	7,676,347	382,933	137,797	22,131	134,319	813,223	76,522	121,503	35,379	188	38,862	10,907	1,170	39,021	81,400	1,031,775	778,951
New Jersey	2,257,681	149,774	70,285	5,613	55,707	194,804	16,070	29,849	16,045	115	37,463	5,648	292	20,673	28,623	345,060	262,708
Pennsylvania	3,788,178	262,706	96,274	68,567	134,445	285,398	6,582	46,770	7,671	13	4,394	9,063	518	19,295	35,673	487,241	516,041
E. N. CENTRAL:																	
Ohio	2,005,825	136,330	45,203	29,111	27,040	104,422	4,713	19,864	6,346	17	8,122	4,015	578	34,861	31,285	508,914	175,608
Indiana	510,392	31,549	11,852	3,562	6,617	30,821	2,647	13,823	3,227	18	7,278	6,982	244	9,895	12,234	184,520	51,616
Illinois	3,497,371	168,877	66,323	11,910	40,013	244,950	80,730	261,374	47,852	279	44,984	24,208	9,040	26,045	39,002	704,626	470,832
Michigan	2,286,133	165,848	65,990	6,024	23,065	60,637	23,117	68,577	20,507	86	106,426	26,818	1,243	11,066	18,085	365,263	320,534
Wisconsin	1,477,367	43,981	12,272	6,545	8,498	40,417	135,953	56,915	40,023	179	25,499	12,957	3,197	26,740	8,861	698,200	139,255
W. N. CENTRAL:																	
Minnesota	1,424,657	34,565	13,038	3,281	8,802	43,493	267,012	270,773	46,220	900	17,162	5,484	5,127	10,292	7,248	327,785	48,911
Iowa	750,844	40,179	15,517	6,396	12,647	47,192	57,126	57,365	47,501	30	36,319	2,983	4,460	10,899	8,613	287,603	4,593
Missouri	622,549	38,852	11,382	3,306	9,463	57,178	2,434	13,371	5,332	29	3,506	2,640	212	16,384	14,616	262,925	21,170
North Dakota	414,621	7,249	3,634	587	1,753	6,334	124,522	29,893	10,524	2,260	2,659	857	897	1,877	1,281	54,545	7,651
South Dakota	204,075	11,069	3,245	1,520	2,481	9,209	55,712	23,503	18,214	60	10,829	849	1,789	2,717	1,581	74,337	2,656
Nebraska	479,853	23,384	6,862	2,278	5,131	21,054	7,461	50,097	33,798	62	3,200	1,430	1,130	6,495	3,638	168,329	16,179
Kansas	339,405	30,925	9,664	3,881	6,018	20,092	3,450	28,200	6,916	12	2,668	3,152	690	8,922	6,733	107,380	5,811
S. ATLANTIC:																	
Delaware	50,670	4,199	1,380	214	3,473	6,175	223	718	205	1	133	52	....	213	543	5,500	8,939
Maryland	314,374	17,495	7,035	2,029	4,792	23,508	1,493	2,088	1,194	22	1,043	314	54	1,500	2,878	94,892	35,845
Dist. Columbia	91,487	9,398	2,870	536	2,479	14,805	761	1,358	610	12	464	178	28	948	1,799	15,779	3,356
Virginia	77,702	10,865	4,020	587	1,805	6,182	894	1,359	835	13	660	175	19	689	1,485	12,959	3,005
West Virginia	152,390	11,910	4,316	2,312	1,803	7,310	194	924	270	1	249	1,480	31	1,819	1,079	19,804	14,857
N. Carolina	26,385	4,185	1,652	153	401	1,496	266	515	212	1	380	78	7	293	579	4,122	788
S. Carolina	18,601	1,872	795	63	605	1,596	141	364	143	....	63	124	9	80	378	4,398	1,156
Georgia	44,475	5,015	1,987	326	926	4,417	411	835	348	....	246	113	8	409	1,204	8,265	2,403
Florida	160,832	20,220	5,504	1,032	2,407	7,195	2,340	5,238	2,303	9	1,327	478	101	1,647	3,097	22,548	2,094
E. S. CENTRAL:																	
Kentucky	118,824	7,406	2,377	668	2,134	15,835	210	631	322	4	701	237	15	3,977	4,102	58,573	2,000
Tennessee	51,236	5,843	1,799	639	1,263	5,669	297	875	431	6	280	72	13	1,988	1,346	11,008	2,087
Alabama	54,436	7,001	3,555	618	1,149	3,536	713	1,600	576	4	341	158	20	679	1,918	10,237	1,346
Mississippi	28,181	2,419	768	95	717	2,354	285	716	372	....	136	116	12	356	1,380	4,898	745
W. S. CENTRAL:																	
Arkansas	45,701	4,546	1,385	339	714	3,385	279	951	517	....	421	246	27	1,988	1,621	16,815	1,139
Louisiana	145,588	7,046	1,970	289	2,266	9,346	1,082	1,341	1,016	4	659	1,057	30	1,271	17,313	26,745	1,556
Oklahoma	129,119	13,249	4,685	1,323	2,369	8,384	1,291	3,777	2,062	4	905	633	151	2,769	3,803	37,990	3,888
Texas	426,293	29,603	8,068	1,299	4,256	18,665	5,543	14,365	4,908	23	1,997	1,233	145	6,314	10,185	153,362	14,369
MOUNTAIN:																	
Montana	233,788	19,815	8,174	2,262	4,628	17,940	29,386	16,226	8,109	82	3,752	1,211	386	3,032	2,578	30,377	3,244
Idaho	117,373	20,227	4,991	2,689	1,619	4,003	7,226	12,328	8,494	44	1,152	330	167	4,220	1,594	17,408	463
Wyoming	65,686	8,988	4,541	1,111	888	3,449	2,127	5,908	2,968	5	404	322	36	1,036	1,179	9,201	1,674
Colorado	292,011	28,538	10,443	4,187	4,937	18,148	4,415	23,730	7,412	24	2,871	1,068	202	4,306	4,682	50,355	5,711
New Mexico	29,002	2,812	1,295	300	532	1,705	431	885	372	2	273	114	21	510	924	4,953	272
Arizona	54,131	8,133	2,209	609	1,180	3,906	1,160	2,505	1,522	10	360	159	43	987	1,389	7,932	581
Utah	177,485	50,177	9,905	5,660	1,122	3,520	6,198	15,838	24,805	393	5,201	251	25	5,201	1,204	12,338	487
Nevada	33,855	4,353	1,182	395	783	2,389	542	1,238	1,779	20	146	52	10	1,068	1,587	3,852	182
PACIFIC:																	
Washington	647,472	57,989	21,811	5,991	8,812	25,433	77,450	76,843	20,004	1,513	9,562	2,792	799	10,645	7,737	87,130	9,811
Oregon	307,055	28,063	11,664	2,379	4,634	13,254	21,182	26,778	10,710	157	3,123	1,831	372	11,571	4,870	56,546	4,686
California	2,110,112	229,602	71,998	15,262	42,971	148,310	48,566	103,603	60,815	580	20,759	6,496	1,357	49,698	59,218	310,409	30,704

COUNTRY OF ORIGIN OF THE FOREIGN WHITE STOCK　　273

TABLE 7.—COUNTRY OF ORIGIN OF THE FOREIGN WHITE STOCK, BY DIVISIONS AND STATES: 1930—Con.

DIVISION AND STATE	Czecho-slovakia	Austria	Hungary	Yugo-slavia	Russia	Latvia	Es-tonia	Lithu-ania	Fin-land	Ru-mania	Bul-garia	Turkey in Europe	Greece	Al-bania	Italy	Spain	Portu-gal	Other Europe
United States	1,382,079	954,648	590,768	469,395	2,669,838	38,091	5,317	439,195	320,536	293,453	14,929	3,676	303,751	13,223	4,546,877	110,607	167,891	56,890
GEOG. DIVS.:																		
New England	42,500	31,885	26,258	2,947	232,570	5,534	331	93,633	37,753	7,385	413	514	50,782	6,016	660,819	4,944	83,995	1,854
Mid. Atlantic	540,750	544,687	291,739	124,301	1,454,508	16,642	2,749	172,304	36,750	147,262	2,527	1,720	86,213	3,105	2,072,906	40,407	14,740	20,820
E. N. Central	509,303	207,585	214,656	219,738	388,036	7,968	646	143,324	111,825	91,072	7,494	653	83,791	2,313	598,662	8,226	1,388	17,758
W. N. Central	167,493	69,564	17,599	44,850	266,155	1,370	113	8,678	67,745	22,345	1,332	54	14,271	523	82,166	1,665	153	4,649
South Atlantic	22,277	20,424	15,246	6,505	88,082	2,849	203	12,221	2,197	5,879	398	178	20,632	161	103,209	14,143	834	2,611
E. S. Central	2,235	3,922	2,715	1,335	12,242	373	20	919	388	1,052	119	28	4,176	85	21,790	915	80	993
W. S. Central	57,306	15,737	3,324	2,681	31,852	472	60	1,353	676	2,030	402	64	6,122	28	70,415	4,710	400	3,760
Mountain	14,857	16,075	3,713	30,008	60,790	254	154	1,217	12,702	3,134	903	28	11,116	101	61,987	6,939	594	934
Pacific	25,352	43,860	15,518	36,970	134,944	2,629	1,041	5,546	50,500	13,294	1,281	437	20,648	291	268,863	28,658	65,707	3,511
NEW ENGLAND:																		
Maine	628	662	77	32	4,235	169	5	2,270	2,013	54	14	23	1,480	406	6,468	125	256	53
N. Hampshire	340	418	105	61	3,289	73	8	2,338	3,011	64	22	10	6,404	343	4,810	65	443	44
Vermont	542	394	425	121	1,073	43	14	340	1,076	40	5	------	445	9	7,567	1,051	101	21
Massachusetts	7,809	11,148	2,154	662	150,173	4,337	101	55,775	20,889	3,536	204	355	33,742	4,557	322,676	1,845	58,495	599
Rhode Island	696	2,087	322	66	13,673	200	22	2,220	800	1,045	82	67	2,188	439	92,036	291	19,999	109
Connecticut	32,491	17,176	23,175	2,005	59,536	703	121	30,690	2,974	2,646	86	59	6,523	862	227,262	1,567	4,701	1,028
MID. ATLANTIC:																		
New York	124,636	328,528	138,097	19,176	1,036,819	10,571	1,995	49,235	27,247	102,062	1,493	1,384	54,575	1,748	1,552,460	28,234	7,628	7,907
New Jersey	80,906	63,060	72,235	7,117	147,754	2,376	350	23,247	4,954	13,891	224	118	11,046	257	507,180	7,301	5,099	3,661
Pennsylvania	335,208	153,099	81,407	98,008	269,935	3,695	404	99,822	4,540	31,309	810	218	20,592	1,100	613,257	4,872	2,013	9,252
E. N. CENTRAL:																		
Ohio	184,608	52,022	102,410	84,895	74,434	1,358	128	16,754	12,800	36,919	2,537	154	10,560	726	180,452	2,614	474	4,547
Indiana	21,503	7,334	17,672	14,079	10,871	268	18	4,488	568	6,221	704	19	6,840	170	16,536	929	130	1,100
Illinois	199,350	77,634	41,238	62,171	189,888	4,546	201	92,961	9,623	24,876	1,638	152	35,861	511	271,489	2,362	463	4,705
Michigan	44,602	34,792	40,434	33,492	75,656	1,210	199	20,489	74,229	20,381	2,273	305	10,175	733	98,048	2,149	239	6,240
Wisconsin	59,150	34,903	12,872	25,101	37,837	580	100	8,632	14,598	2,675	342	23	5,346	167	32,137	172	82	1,166
W. N. CENTRAL:																		
Minnesota	41,038	23,343	4,250	24,914	28,073	528	55	2,887	60,010	5,754	451	7	3,148	34	17,175	132	25	877
Iowa	31,130	5,469	769	3,714	10,361	131	10	1,816	198	580	319	2	3,272	26	9,747	79	18	515
Missouri	13,161	19,263	6,709	5,752	34,797	320	15	1,793	229	4,513	276	26	4,259	445	39,315	1,086	62	1,622
North Dakota	7,529	4,756	8,000	881	87,072	60	15	244	3,331	8,455	82	------	554	2	272	23	4	177
South Dakota	10,650	2,519	743	565	37,632	23	7	113	3,100	1,261	82	13	511	1	841	25	5	206
Nebraska	52,031	6,720	1,075	1,851	31,820	291	6	1,431	142	746	68	5	1,513	9	8,989	55	21	731
Kansas	11,945	7,404	1,045	7,173	36,400	22	5	394	135	1,036	54	1	1,014	6	5,827	265	18	521
SOUTH ATLANTIC:																		
Delaware	355	1,192	351	10	3,488	44	11	217	85	220	2	7	604	------	10,285	158	14	82
Maryland	9,455	7,210	2,743	557	45,706	1,227	60	7,443	621	1,720	34	7	2,805	10	28,337	504	82	772
Dist. Columbia	461	1,322	521	112	11,717	208	5	575	144	340	24	37	2,080	21	10,170	306	51	224
Virginia	2,641	1,456	1,394	167	7,806	600	18	878	146	437	28	39	2,254	33	5,490	203	163	383
West Virginia	7,381	5,969	8,275	5,225	5,388	150	13	2,023	271	1,311	100	24	4,197	63	32,190	2,397	59	482
N. Carolina	133	384	175	17	2,063	89	4	276	26	69	21	14	1,818	12	1,148	60	39	112
S. Carolina	132	253	87	82	1,516	127	3	144	93	59	2	10	1,137	4	611	78	18	86
Georgia	289	690	353	81	5,444	230	15	302	174	318	9	18	2,257	4	1,717	247	135	213
Florida	1,430	1,942	1,347	304	4,954	114	74	363	637	1,405	79	22	2,811	14	13,315	10,100	273	257
E. S. CENTRAL:																		
Kentucky	524	1,443	1,301	437	4,057	73	------	405	56	465	47	16	851	27	4,553	190	34	338
Tennessee	343	684	589	55	4,341	137	------	225	62	216	6	4	997	56	5,635	80	13	262
Alabama	1,186	1,186	708	310	2,607	92	19	179	119	272	53	8	1,701	1	6,586	346	23	232
Mississippi	182	609	117	533	1,237	71	1	110	151	99	13	------	567	1	5,016	299	10	161
W. S. CENTRAL:																		
Arkansas	1,230	942	148	258	1,083	26	2	103	31	85	61	8	572	------	2,890	61	5	137
Louisiana	865	1,641	969	934	3,465	48	25	75	188	291	58	19	1,066	8	48,438	2,690	198	885
Oklahoma	6,291	1,937	581	360	12,849	144	------	473	66	398	202	1	1,134	------	3,427	171	39	416
Texas	48,920	11,217	1,626	1,120	14,455	254	33	702	391	1,256	81	36	3,350	20	21,651	1,788	158	2,322
MOUNTAIN:																		
Montana	5,078	4,163	890	9,278	13,761	42	54	369	6,051	1,450	278	1	1,220	28	6,325	169	33	194
Idaho	1,575	1,033	213	913	3,730	11	14	27	1,898	285	45	2	704	1	2,737	2,128	45	76
Wyoming	1,540	1,239	424	3,024	4,146	14	33	81	1,417	114	111	2	1,454	8	3,737	230	51	80
Colorado	5,210	7,207	1,614	10,473	36,005	117	27	496	1,252	949	403	14	1,978	13	31,353	604	53	353
New Mexico	443	903	131	1,278	688	6	6	41	74	32	25	------	494	...	3,377	361	29	55
Arizona	486	913	201	1,604	1,264	26	15	120	633	137	25	3	594	17	2,107	1,043	71	91
Utah	340	1,163	200	2,448	853	24	3	70	1,130	141	60	6	3,978	31	6,980	507	26	66
Nevada	185	354	40	1,050	253	14	2	13	247	26	10	------	694	3	5,371	1,897	286	19
PACIFIC:																		
Washington	6,135	8,285	1,208	9,842	22,976	458	237	1,577	22,048	1,661	371	150	4,090	145	22,372	694	387	469
Oregon	4,392	4,201	962	2,860	14,956	280	185	573	12,026	1,729	239	20	2,194	11	9,869	994	355	283
California	14,825	31,383	13,348	24,268	97,012	1,891	619	3,396	16,426	9,904	671	258	20,364	135	236,622	26,970	64,965	2,759

274

POPULATION

TABLE 7.—COUNTRY OF ORIGIN OF THE FOREIGN WHITE STOCK, BY DIVISIONS AND STATES: 1930—Con.

DIVISION AND STATE	Arme-nia	Pales-tine	Syria	Turkey in Asia	Other Asia	CANADA French	CANADA Other	New-found-land	West Indies	Mexico	Central and South America	Africa	Aus-tralia	Atlan-tic Islands	Pacific Is-lands	Coun-try not speci-fied	Born at sea
United States	58,087	10,446	137,576	77,283	26,595	1,106,159	2,231,186	45,733	63,648	65,968	58,745	13,469	30,849	101,425	8,648	3,171	10,270
GEOGRAPHIC DIVISIONS:																	
New England	19,678	718	26,101	14,281	2,017	743,219	602,336	24,866	3,247	321	4,072	1,120	1,572	60,776	357	175	726
Middle Atlantic	14,176	5,726	41,620	34,676	7,186	96,621	328,274	13,929	28,190	5,537	28,526	5,258	6,399	2,590	1,070	885	1,892
East North Central	9,940	1,778	27,721	13,298	7,221	146,752	628,005	3,272	2,610	5,077	5,521	1,933	4,435	874	707	889	3,165
West North Central	470	300	8,516	943	1,202	51,354	188,072	494	786	2,157	1,658	587	1,688	140	321	281	1,850
South Atlantic	604	539	11,250	2,612	1,115	5,835	37,053	633	23,396	890	2,250	595	1,020	435	276	108	332
East South Central	68	227	4,534	290	229	1,261	8,547	118	644	417	507	138	301	37	45	66	125
West South Central	104	393	9,457	856	674	4,444	26,244	261	1,810	21,278	2,481	421	934	162	195	177	456
Mountain	353	141	2,835	440	605	18,963	70,573	302	411	9,679	1,046	859	1,866	486	1,120	113	422
Pacific	12,044	624	5,542	9,887	5,736	42,710	341,482	1,858	2,548	20,612	12,084	2,558	12,634	35,925	4,557	387	1,302
NEW ENGLAND:																	
Maine	266	15	1,250	250	83	99,765	101,983	445	156	12	66	28	51	79	18	29	97
New Hampshire	308	5	1,050	485	58	101,324	36,094	502	82	18	69	34	67	166	10	13	27
Vermont	22	13	651	37	47	46,956	27,067	180	34	19	60	30	40	19	5	5	27
Massachusetts	14,033	420	16,889	10,360	994	336,871	387,929	21,847	1,846	178	2,680	715	904	50,401	225	95	387
Rhode Island	3,591	47	2,748	1,842	217	91,173	19,378	611	369	23	709	108	163	9,574	39	7	61
Connecticut	1,458	218	3,512	1,307	1,218	67,130	29,885	1,281	760	71	1,088	205	347	537	60	26	127
MIDDLE ATLANTIC:																	
New York	7,982	4,594	21,381	27,267	4,778	83,057	257,587	10,354	22,687	4,003	21,575	3,916	3,326	1,733	696	495	971
New Jersey	3,469	539	5,564	3,973	1,162	7,423	32,925	1,935	3,356	541	4,027	796	1,147	601	215	109	394
Pennsylvania	2,725	593	14,675	3,436	1,246	6,141	37,762	1,640	2,147	993	2,924	546	1,926	256	159	281	527
EAST NORTH CENTRAL:																	
Ohio	777	462	10,145	2,902	1,017	9,428	60,578	449	629	568	1,144	392	852	92	90	163	618
Indiana	228	84	1,927	458	515	3,120	16,134	138	118	352	267	73	280	21	54	79	203
Illinois	2,827	752	2,613	3,178	3,906	24,250	97,527	928	1,001	2,435	2,389	776	1,846	633	273	307	857
Michigan	5,447	388	11,760	5,296	1,501	87,911	411,091	1,546	716	1,406	1,249	550	1,042	107	224	264	705
Wisconsin	661	92	1,276	1,404	282	22,043	42,675	211	152	816	472	142	415	21	66	76	781
WEST NORTH CENTRAL:																	
Minnesota	107	63	1,704	181	316	29,384	66,551	146	88	225	231	161	324	49	76	46	557
Iowa	111	25	1,507	125	178	4,233	20,389	91	140	374	183	71	319	27	43	47	334
Missouri	140	128	2,095	407	250	2,701	17,558	102	366	775	523	144	466	22	76	84	269
North Dakota	56	7	725	70	87	6,084	34,093	30	12	64	97	33	59	5	16	27	167
South Dakota	9	11	644	53	72	2,773	11,963	27	36	30	49	39	61	3	21	16	140
Nebraska	43	50	1,128	56	145	2,591	16,477	77	52	399	194	64	178	12	38	30	200
Kansas	4	16	653	51	154	3,588	15,641	21	92	290	381	75	283	22	51	31	183
SOUTH ATLANTIC:																	
Delaware	6	7	11	36	17	177	969	14	66	23	110	14	16	8	6	28	9
Maryland	63	122	172	316	150	908	5,159	149	507	78	504	146	266	81	75	27	110
Dist. of Columbia	118	66	601	310	135	745	4,119	70	250	98	335	91	84	38	26	17	21
Virginia	253	67	1,524	375	180	574	4,097	69	209	75	191	42	142	24	41	18	37
West Virginia	29	49	3,335	647	117	371	2,287	21	77	191	162	27	131	9	6	8	47
North Carolina	11	64	1,522	179	111	227	2,264	54	103	33	51	53	57	8	37	6	17
South Carolina	1	27	1,000	193	65	132	764	22	75	21	38	21	17	10	3	6	12
Georgia	40	33	1,028	312	92	343	2,558	41	218	62	120	59	74	29	32	9	16
Florida	83	104	2,057	244	248	2,358	14,836	193	21,891	309	739	142	233	222	50	79	63
EAST SOUTH CENTRAL:																	
Kentucky	17	82	1,075	91	75	373	2,589	57	81	73	61	36	87	6	18	26	50
Tennessee	24	42	281	50	62	350	2,607	31	92	93	113	35	76	5	14	20	20
Alabama	18	59	1,405	104	60	342	2,325	23	364	133	176	40	70	19	8	15	46
Mississippi	9	44	1,773	45	32	196	1,026	7	107	118	157	27	68	7	5	5	9
WEST SOUTH CENTRAL:																	
Arkansas	6	14	579	27	35	380	2,202	47	50	139	78	25	40	2	11	31	31
Louisiana	25	52	2,536	233	101	895	2,688	48	909	1,209	1,528	123	155	29	21	11	81
Oklahoma	24	54	2,004	85	165	1,372	8,385	35	106	447	200	62	158	14	38	46	83
Texas	49	273	4,278	511	373	1,797	12,969	131	655	19,483	675	211	581	117	125	89	261
MOUNTAIN:																	
Montana	51	18	399	101	102	6,788	24,797	80	44	180	121	80	232	29	78	13	89
Idaho	18	5	115	23	59	2,075	11,640	87	19	198	54	133	159	82	193	7	54
Wyoming	37	7	103	19	57	570	3,701	11	38	135	47	41	67	6	25	11	20
Colorado	61	47	630	128	144	2,568	16,688	59	146	1,073	425	81	323	35	98	54	121
New Mexico	2	3	583	17	48	282	1,835	17	24	2,620	95	31	60	12	17	2	10
Arizona	59	29	654	39	95	652	5,220	31	92	4,636	161	63	235	20	63	9	38
Utah	101	28	313	57	75	545	4,306	11	28	666	60	380	667	9	608	13	81
Nevada	24	4	38	56	25	483	2,386	6	20	171	83	50	123	293	38	4	9
PACIFIC:																	
Washington	172	49	573	1,157	650	14,137	99,069	557	186	280	626	258	1,325	120	467	106	313
Oregon	93	24	461	266	283	4,930	40,729	150	109	207	306	153	707	124	373	31	151
California	12,379	551	4,508	8,464	4,803	23,643	201,684	1,151	2,253	20,125	11,152	2,147	10,602	35,681	3,717	250	838

COUNTRY OF ORIGIN OF THE FOREIGN WHITE STOCK 275

TABLE 8.—COUNTRY OF BIRTH OF THE FOREIGN-BORN WHITE POPULATION, BY DIVISIONS AND STATES: 1930 AND 1920

DIVISION AND STATE	ALL COUNTRIES		ENGLAND		SCOTLAND		WALES		Northern Ireland, 1930	Irish Free State, 1930	Ireland, 1920	NORWAY		SWEDEN	
	1930	1920 (adjusted)[1]	1930	1920	1930	1920	1930	1920				1930	1920	1930	1920
United States	13,366,407	13,255,394	808,672	812,828	354,323	254,567	60,205	67,066	178,832	744,810	1,037,233	347,852	363,862	595,250	625,580
GEOGRAPHIC DIVISIONS:															
New England	1,834,310	1,870,600	135,490	147,098	54,226	47,501	2,834	2,999	33,527	193,113	267,428	8,860	8,564	66,028	67,286
Middle Atlantic	5,269,042	4,909,899	276,133	272,752	137,861	83,883	26,336	29,185	92,559	361,502	472,319	55,697	35,862	91,045	83,547
East North Central	3,223,924	3,217,005	170,013	163,892	84,579	51,650	14,585	15,226	23,322	93,881	135,147	74,228	82,137	165,785	165,388
West North Central	1,059,277	1,350,882	38,641	53,523	13,035	17,196	3,882	5,693	6,750	23,983	49,858	131,904	166,280	147,988	187,625
South Atlantic	304,278	315,676	25,673	24,269	8,859	7,455	1,797	1,773	3,637	12,163	20,145	2,591	2,259	4,940	4,418
East South Central	57,665	71,698	5,059	6,060	1,941	2,093	377	455	567	2,758	5,934	447	450	1,246	1,514
West South Central	170,232	208,196	11,193	13,327	3,241	3,711	612	763	1,212	4,921	8,330	2,292	2,691	5,534	6,320
Mountain	287,914	360,531	33,070	44,576	10,934	12,986	3,385	4,007	3,173	10,252	19,634	15,350	17,400	25,830	32,232
Pacific	1,159,765	950,957	113,400	87,331	39,647	28,092	6,397	6,005	14,085	42,237	58,438	56,483	48,719	86,850	77,250
NEW ENGLAND:															
Maine	100,368	107,347	4,463	5,140	1,906	2,171	137	137	827	3,288	5,748	534	581	1,882	2,026
New Hampshire	82,660	91,232	3,922	4,367	1,728	1,823	72	51	1,010	4,807	7,908	396	427	1,608	1,886
Vermont	43,001	44,525	1,929	2,197	1,454	1,854	462	549	377	1,429	2,884	127	106	1,089	1,123
Massachusetts	1,054,636	1,077,499	78,418	86,895	32,724	28,474	1,358	1,367	20,378	138,366	183,171	5,454	5,491	36,810	38,012
Rhode Island	170,714	173,495	24,696	25,782	6,401	5,692	224	245	3,845	13,895	22,253	543	545	6,181	6,542
Connecticut	382,871	376,502	22,062	22,708	10,013	7,487	581	650	7,090	31,328	45,464	1,806	1,414	18,463	17,697
MIDDLE ATLANTIC:															
New York	3,191,549	2,784,895	146,485	135,305	67,623	37,654	7,037	6,763	41,521	251,704	284,747	44,882	27,573	61,233	53,025
New Jersey	844,442	738,428	51,629	46,781	34,721	17,781	1,532	1,255	15,750	47,486	65,971	7,870	5,343	13,360	10,675
Pennsylvania	1,233,051	1,386,576	78,019	90,666	35,517	28,448	17,767	21,167	35,288	62,312	121,601	2,945	2,446	16,452	19,847
EAST NORTH CENTRAL:															
Ohio	644,151	677,894	40,605	43,140	17,862	12,148	6,807	7,772	5,028	17,870	29,262	1,650	1,487	7,390	7,266
Indiana	135,134	150,230	7,465	8,522	3,808	3,707	934	1,106	1,045	3,931	7,271	730	544	4,666	4,942
Illinois	1,218,158	1,203,396	50,685	54,247	24,839	19,508	3,277	3,444	10,054	57,208	74,274	30,256	27,785	111,016	105,577
Michigan	840,268	725,488	62,731	47,140	35,257	13,175	2,236	1,154	6,138	11,390	16,631	7,201	6,888	23,905	24,707
Wisconsin	386,213	459,997	8,477	10,834	2,723	3,022	1,241	1,750	1,057	3,473	7,809	34,391	45,433	18,808	22,896
WEST NORTH CENTRAL:															
Minnesota	388,294	485,941	8,445	10,958	3,241	3,928	582	854	1,403	5,095	10,289	71,562	90,188	90,023	112,117
Iowa	165,735	228,292	9,045	13,036	2,871	3,967	1,188	1,733	1,778	4,179	10,086	12,932	17,344	16,810	22,493
Missouri	149,390	183,238	7,919	10,400	2,419	2,969	573	903	1,308	8,561	15,022	875	610	3,895	4,741
North Dakota	105,148	131,478	1,592	2,287	891	1,229	111	120	329	863	1,660	31,337	38,190	8,470	10,543
South Dakota	65,648	82,325	2,159	2,943	612	832	265	346	351	862	1,954	13,061	16,813	6,540	8,573
Nebraska	115,346	147,345	4,213	6,000	1,223	1,695	383	547	801	2,502	5,422	1,691	2,165	14,335	18,821
Kansas	69,716	97,213	5,268	7,899	1,778	2,576	785	1,170	780	1,921	4,825	746	970	7,315	10,337
SOUTH ATLANTIC:															
Delaware	16,885	19,785	1,302	1,497	562	411	45	44	900	1,364	2,895	141	65	294	316
Maryland	95,093	102,144	5,067	5,095	1,920	1,692	477	499	813	4,032	6,580	703	536	764	630
Dist. of Columbia	20,032	28,522	2,835	2,990	884	793	110	106	493	3,026	4,320	228	219	435	481
Virginia	23,820	30,760	3,088	3,752	1,239	1,327	132	163	375	789	1,732	318	491	407	664
West Virginia	51,520	61,864	3,282	3,433	1,267	998	607	704	222	659	1,459	57	51	303	326
North Carolina	8,788	7,092	1,208	967	477	446	35	25	63	253	301	95	70	160	170
South Carolina	5,206	6,897	479	491	179	190	13	10	90	185	442	65	85	106	133
Georgia	13,917	16,163	1,328	1,503	534	530	83	86	147	546	1,112	125	132	286	299
Florida	59,057	42,049	7,084	4,451	1,797	1,068	289	136	534	1,309	1,304	859	610	2,145	1,399
EAST SOUTH CENTRAL:															
Kentucky	21,840	30,707	1,478	1,863	524	520	114	149	191	1,656	3,422	46	75	170	214
Tennessee	13,066	15,443	1,351	1,605	433	454	104	143	160	491	1,291	68	63	232	305
Alabama	15,710	17,617	1,760	1,942	860	975	141	145	162	413	809	265	215	638	748
Mississippi	7,049	7,931	470	590	174	144	18	18	54	198	412	68	97	206	247
WEST SOUTH CENTRAL:															
Arkansas	10,173	13,781	800	1,137	229	316	51	90	100	354	676	72	99	249	331
Louisiana	34,910	42,976	1,512	1,819	435	447	66	76	234	970	2,000	487	555	433	522
Oklahoma	26,753	33,655	2,099	2,686	866	1,120	235	319	262	690	1,321	243	297	835	931
Texas	98,396	117,784	6,782	7,685	1,711	1,828	260	278	616	2,907	4,333	1,490	1,740	4,017	4,536
MOUNTAIN:															
Montana	72,961	93,420	6,020	8,159	2,721	3,279	580	879	1,095	3,950	7,260	8,991	9,902	5,655	7,179
Idaho	30,454	37,989	3,252	4,451	1,025	1,228	355	575	284	616	1,410	2,148	2,482	4,200	5,112
Wyoming	19,658	23,502	2,105	2,505	1,424	1,439	222	297	179	584	955	647	651	1,783	2,042
Colorado	85,406	106,259	6,801	9,584	2,877	3,357	1,061	1,482	900	3,154	6,191	1,261	1,525	8,328	10,112
New Mexico	7,797	10,013	648	888	354	440	99	78	91	218	434	119	128	263	310
Arizona	15,591	20,128	2,309	2,882	579	595	139	192	235	653	1,206	205	337	778	859
Utah	43,772	55,526	10,851	14,836	1,660	2,310	862	1,304	234	584	1,207	1,698	2,109	4,389	6,073
Nevada	12,275	13,694	904	1,271	285	338	67	100	155	463	970	191	206	443	545
PACIFIC:															
Washington	244,256	249,766	20,304	20,806	8,024	7,886	1,694	2,040	2,154	4,942	8,927	31,429	30,304	34,084	34,793
Oregon	105,475	101,648	8,077	7,953	3,820	3,009	592	592	1,039	2,802	4,203	7,450	6,955	11,032	10,532
California	810,034	599,543	85,019	58,572	27,803	16,597	4,111	3,433	10,892	34,493	45,308	17,604	11,460	41,734	31,925

[1] The foreign-born white population in 1920 included 457,360 persons (estimated) who would have been counted as Mexican in 1930. In the adjusted figures these have been deducted from the 1920 foreign-born white population as reported and from the number of white persons reported as having been born in Mexico.

276

POPULATION

TABLE 8.—COUNTRY OF BIRTH OF THE FOREIGN-BORN WHITE POPULATION, BY DIVISIONS AND STATES: 1930 AND 1920—Continued

DIVISION AND STATE	Denmark, 1930	Iceland, 1930	Denmark and Iceland, 1920	NETHERLANDS		BELGIUM		LUXEMBURG		SWITZERLAND		FRANCE		GERMANY		POLAND	
				1930	1920	1930	1920	1930	1920	1930	1920	1930	1920	1930	1920	1930	1920
United States	179,474	2,764	189,154	133,133	131,766	64,194	62,686	9,048	12,585	113,010	118,659	135,232	152,890	1,608,814	1,686,102	1,268,583	1,139,978
GEOGRAPHIC DIVISIONS:																	
New England	7,625	78	8,458	2,814	2,912	3,884	4,411	76	114	3,541	3,763	11,723	13,246	50,005	51,129	136,774	131,378
Middle Atlantic	26,978	166	22,991	30,960	27,847	12,692	12,478	867	1,017	30,985	30,093	52,449	55,149	572,571	508,226	619,628	515,708
East North Central	42,397	227	43,018	57,443	59,863	33,053	29,706	3,976	5,093	27,066	30,379	24,101	29,612	524,437	592,058	416,569	402,259
West North Central	50,193	1,045	61,748	20,532	24,399	5,590	7,159	2,874	4,846	11,660	15,838	7,329	11,432	228,951	293,035	34,419	38,262
South Atlantic	2,339	33	2,123	1,624	1,459	1,397	1,547	85	87	2,248	2,348	3,950	4,112	38,225	40,808	26,239	25,432
East South Central	476	4	531	295	322	184	235	19	31	1,561	2,176	1,462	2,191	12,188	16,652	2,711	2,590
West South Central	2,319	13	2,580	1,044	1,106	1,009	1,180	93	127	2,681	3,433	5,698	8,071	38,411	47,217	6,800	7,206
Mountain	13,246	137	17,023	5,038	5,252	1,343	1,608	236	372	5,593	6,695	4,071	4,965	28,731	33,052	5,125	4,675
Pacific	33,901	1,066	30,682	13,383	8,606	5,042	4,362	822	898	27,675	23,934	24,449	24,112	115,295	103,235	20,318	12,468
NEW ENGLAND:																	
Maine	840	2	1,065	41	50	51	51	5	6	51	52	314	344	818	932	1,706	1,717
New Hampshire	166		204	103	177	528	478	2	5	82	72	209	288	1,517	1,714	4,101	3,997
Vermont	140	1	155	34	32	22	15	1	2	158	187	182	197	577	630	1,562	1,726
Massachusetts	3,070	61	3,629	1,890	2,071	1,956	2,497	31	33	1,272	1,368	6,026	7,120	20,538	22,113	71,442	69,157
Rhode Island	280	2	365	138	138	907	968	11	14	204	211	2,013	1,971	3,090	3,126	8,696	8,158
Connecticut	3,129	7	3,040	548	444	425	402	26	54	1,774	1,863	2,889	3,326	23,465	22,614	49,267	46,623
MIDDLE ATLANTIC:																	
New York	17,407	114	14,222	14,909	13,772	6,144	5,300	532	564	16,571	15,053	32,145	32,170	349,196	295,650	350,383	247,519
New Jersey	6,665	48	5,704	14,762	12,737	2,874	2,483	117	167	8,765	8,165	10,520	10,165	112,753	92,382	102,573	90,419
Pennsylvania	2,906	4	3,065	1,289	1,338	3,674	4,695	218	286	5,649	6,875	9,784	12,805	110,622	120,194	166,672	177,770
E. NORTH CENTRAL:																	
Ohio	2,184	6	2,353	2,235	2,529	1,846	1,902	163	273	7,624	9,656	5,746	8,056	95,697	111,893	64,493	67,579
Indiana	964	3	969	1,092	2,018	3,254	2,530	56	101	1,624	2,334	2,160	3,247	28,152	37,377	17,482	17,791
Illinois	18,945	123	17,098	14,828	14,344	11,564	11,320	2,786	3,211	7,315	7,837	10,155	11,903	190,605	205,491	173,007	162,405
Michigan	7,210	32	7,178	32,128	33,499	13,931	10,501	375	477	2,834	2,755	4,581	4,174	81,714	86,047	119,228	103,926
Wisconsin	13,094	63	15,420	6,260	7,473	2,458	3,444	596	1,031	7,669	7,797	1,459	2,142	128,269	151,250	42,359	50,558
W. NORTH CENTRAL:																	
Minnesota	13,831	266	16,904	4,832	5,380	1,701	2,056	1,032	1,782	2,041	2,720	1,246	1,803	59,903	74,634	15,015	18,537
Iowa	14,698	9	18,020	10,135	12,471	932	1,232	873	1,630	2,096	2,871	1,435	2,125	53,901	70,642	1,875	2,028
Missouri	1,497	10	1,688	706	906	859	1,113	54	140	3,578	4,934	2,353	3,825	42,276	55,776	8,324	7,636
North Dakota	2,936	724	4,552	658	903	238	456	202	229	309	506	237	350	10,114	11,960	2,128	2,236
South Dakota	5,298	15	5,983	3,068	3,218	239	251	380	480	618	761	229	335	12,739	15,674	717	792
Nebraska	10,210	19	12,338	620	846	523	551	204	301	1,384	1,808	558	858	32,544	40,969	4,445	4,615
Kansas	1,723	2	2,263	513	675	1,098	1,500	129	284	1,594	2,238	1,271	2,136	17,384	23,380	1,915	2,418
SOUTH ATLANTIC:																	
Delaware	90	1	77	56	37	29	24		5	75	76	147	198	1,459	1,632	2,954	3,847
Maryland	464	13	382	343	314	152	135	19	22	497	500	773	818	18,025	22,082	12,027	12,061
Dist. of Columbia	229	6	237	151	127	92	76	8	13	360	358	707	687	3,411	3,382	716	716
Virginia	330	7	459	264	335	101	122	3	7	191	239	365	455	2,505	2,802	1,221	1,103
West Virginia	75		121	42	66	690	938	11	6	398	545	546	633	3,129	3,798	5,545	5,799
North Carolina	65	1	69	201	115	19	16	4	2	87	72	156	136	903	703	319	210
South Carolina	39		76	24	30	52	61	1	1	26	31	76	78	747	1,079	510	351
Georgia	108		127	67	78	45	45		7	114	161	278	376	1,682	1,936	1,156	917
Florida	921	5	575	476	357	217	130	30	24	500	357	902	731	5,464	3,534	945	428
E. SOUTH CENTRAL:																	
Kentucky	72		89	112	150	59	90	4	12	915	1,315	583	984	7,552	11,137	899	1,037
Tennessee	123	1	138	56	58	28	36	3	3	443	616	217	333	1,783	2,159	960	841
Alabama	182	3	191	95	83	60	73	7	8	150	174	466	616	2,114	2,427	556	394
Mississippi	99		113	32	31	37	36	5	8	53	71	196	258	739	929	296	318
W. SOUTH CENTRAL:																	
Arkansas	138		180	80	116	78	94	7	8	518	736	254	387	2,989	3,979	394	529
Louisiana	315	1	331	220	260	307	350	10	9	260	378	2,935	4,182	3,616	5,147	655	377
Oklahoma	516	1	561	166	176	217	289	31	52	493	629	717	958	5,893	7,029	1,162	1,253
Texas	1,350	11	1,508	578	554	407	447	45	58	1,410	1,690	1,792	2,544	25,913	31,062	4,589	5,047
MOUNTAIN:																	
Montana	2,541	16	2,990	1,253	1,675	509	672	108	153	901	1,151	653	888	6,155	7,873	1,144	1,219
Idaho	1,667	12	2,240	341	439	118	123	41	60	1,038	1,347	381	482	3,427	4,143	227	287
Wyoming	775	1	936	101	130	139	130	7	18	250	302	359	361	1,714	2,292	604	544
Colorado	2,874	1	2,823	810	853	390	430	51	91	1,202	1,510	1,072	1,420	9,988	11,992	2,488	1,867
New Mexico	101		115	64	70	34	76	5	6	117	148	259	377	936	1,178	97	153
Arizona	364	4	308	100	69	50	60	12	22	279	293	308	394	1,483	1,516	253	261
Utah	4,883	97	6,970	2,325	1,980	79	90	9	18	1,419	1,566	261	434	4,104	3,589	230	240
Nevada	541	6	551	44	36	24	27	3	4	387	378	783	609	974	1,069	82	104
PACIFIC:																	
Washington	7,175	741	8,359	3,484	3,097	1,242	1,438	203	315	3,578	3,671	1,986	2,452	20,542	22,315	3,942	3,906
Oregon	3,551	49	3,602	1,002	917	681	722	122	140	4,034	4,166	1,144	1,273	12,913	13,740	2,086	1,480
California	23,175	276	18,721	8,897	4,592	3,119	2,202	437	443	20,063	16,097	21,319	20,387	81,840	67,180	14,290	7,082

COUNTRY OF ORIGIN OF THE FOREIGN WHITE STOCK 277

TABLE 8.—COUNTRY OF BIRTH OF THE FOREIGN-BORN WHITE POPULATION, BY DIVISIONS AND STATES: 1930 AND 1920—Continued

DIVISION AND STATE	CZECHOSLOVAKIA		AUSTRIA		HUNGARY		YUGOSLAVIA		Russia, 1930	Latvia, 1930	Estonia, 1930	Russia, Latvia, and Estonia, 1920	LITHUANIA		FINLAND	
	1930	1920	1930	1920	1930	1920	1930	1920					1930	1920	1930	1920
United States	491,638	362,436	370,914	575,625	274,450	397,282	211,416	169,437	1,153,624	20,673	3,550	1,400,489	193,606	135,068	142,478	149,824
GEOGRAPHIC DIVISIONS:																
New England	16,024	9,653	11,946	23,081	11,107	15,187	1,334	2,405	103,310	2,906	182	147,371	41,753	35,361	18,503	19,543
Middle Atlantic	199,705	123,863	216,000	310,844	130,753	190,224	54,062	48,087	659,250	9,052	1,949	763,891	69,882	48,594	22,290	17,431
East North Central	190,709	143,743	82,000	145,275	100,773	149,592	102,437	72,343	175,168	4,451	401	236,022	67,872	44,307	42,946	46,576
West North Central	46,005	50,906	22,924	37,504	7,295	17,640	17,049	18,189	83,728	684	58	110,766	8,837	2,098	26,328	31,635
South Atlantic	8,309	6,620	7,578	12,077	6,737	10,096	3,005	3,581	35,870	1,384	119	48,362	5,681	3,245	1,191	1,281
East South Central	878	617	1,239	2,023	1,093	1,829	550	766	5,023	182	12	7,408	424	76	154	219
West South Central	14,885	15,438	4,590	9,195	1,241	1,664	1,141	1,267	10,856	247	53	14,552	580	219	297	455
Mountain	5,018	5,295	6,002	13,070	1,572	3,233	12,133	10,771	20,865	135	84	26,690	614	280	5,765	7,718
Pacific	10,105	6,301	18,035	22,556	7,879	7,217	19,045	12,028	59,554	1,632	692	45,327	2,963	888	25,004	24,966
NEW ENGLAND:																
Maine	241	410	230	305	30	72	16	143	1,880	92	4	3,763	1,121	1,032	1,406	1,393
New Hampshire	132	75	174	359	47	66	30	120	1,427	46	3	3,467	1,084	1,017	1,386	1,558
Vermont	101	108	132	283	156	264	71	56	660	21	5	1,333	160	67	555	476
Massachusetts	2,966	2,238	4,266	8,098	905	1,387	305	950	67,084	2,315	89	92,034	25,219	20,789	13,077	14,570
Rhode Island	274	264	838	1,307	133	176	24	140	5,800	93	10	8,055	922	794	448	320
Connecticut	12,220	6,558	6,306	12,699	9,836	13,222	882	996	26,700	339	71	38,719	13,247	11,662	1,631	1,226
MIDDLE ATLANTIC:																
New York	56,176	38,247	142,298	151,172	70,631	78,874	10,917	8,547	481,306	5,971	1,505	529,240	22,933	12,121	17,444	12,504
New Jersey	32,358	16,747	24,010	36,917	32,332	40,470	3,643	3,313	62,152	1,194	234	73,527	9,870	6,240	2,721	2,109
Pennsylvania	111,171	68,860	49,692	122,755	33,790	71,380	40,102	36,227	115,792	1,887	210	161,124	37,079	30,227	2,125	2,818
EAST NORTH CENTRAL:																
Ohio	68,738	42,121	20,547	48,073	47,026	73,181	38,884	30,377	32,027	721	81	43,090	7,581	4,095	5,633	6,406
Indiana	8,325	3,941	2,700	9,100	7,674	9,351	6,646	4,471	4,749	116	10	7,673	2,109	1,445	205	237
Illinois	76,420	66,709	33,336	46,457	20,305	34,437	28,173	19,285	87,026	2,609	127	117,899	44,733	30,358	4,302	3,080
Michigan	17,640	11,161	13,209	22,004	19,188	22,007	16,468	9,426	34,348	974	123	45,313	9,340	5,475	27,022	30,096
Wisconsin	19,586	19,811	12,700	19,641	6,400	10,016	12,266	8,784	16,418	331	60	21,447	4,109	2,034	5,724	6,757
WEST NORTH CENTRAL:																
Minnesota	11,415	12,626	7,288	11,550	1,681	4,277	8,888	10,697	11,902	255	30	16,100	1,283	741	24,360	29,108
Iowa	8,280	9,150	1,596	4,334	295	747	1,800	1,603	4,482	66	4	7,319	835	687	70	107
Missouri	4,495	4,971	7,928	8,676	3,484	8,080	2,753	2,327	15,680	167	9	18,769	805	417	100	98
North Dakota	1,809	2,056	1,407	2,059	808	2,519	336	199	22,617	33	7	29,617	121	32	873	1,108
South Dakota	2,589	2,819	678	1,151	231	585	223	470	9,023	7	8	11,193	46	14	825	1,085
Nebraska	14,313	15,818	1,863	4,551	372	810	762	738	11,234	145	3	15,718	589	139	48	78
Kansas	3,044	3,466	2,164	5,183	334	622	2,781	2,155	8,781	11	2	12,050	158	68	52	56
SOUTH ATLANTIC:																
Delaware	159	122	435	615	157	226	7	27	1,450	29	11	2,244	90	90	50	52
Maryland	3,344	3,553	2,634	3,620	1,219	1,947	275	359	18,782	624	39	24,791	3,422	2,206	376	175
Dist. of Columbia	193	122	493	525	228	219	55	43	4,914	142	2	5,181	256	38	69	104
Virginia	927	897	492	921	560	1,293	67	127	2,089	201	6	5,421	400	71	68	240
West Virginia	2,831	1,549	2,254	5,115	3,683	6,290	2,440	2,802	2,209	71	6	3,911	1,009	717	144	289
North Carolina	50	20	146	149	70	66	9	20	758	31	4	932	121	29	9	15
South Carolina	52	45	74	206	32	56	13	22	556	49	2	1,187	60	9	38	53
Georgia	115	123	225	401	136	246	39	84	2,200	115	6	3,452	155	72	104	42
Florida	638	189	825	525	652	383	160	88	2,012	62	40	1,243	108	13	333	311
EAST SOUTH CENTRAL:																
Kentucky	194	240	484	906	557	1,084	201	354	1,629	40	--------	2,736	186	56	27	50
Tennessee	131	82	223	398	208	326	25	37	1,803	66	--------	2,262	106	3	24	33
Alabama	483	232	386	583	284	372	135	155	1,067	49	11	1,582	88	12	51	74
Mississippi	70	63	146	136	44	47	189	220	524	27	1	828	44	5	52	62
WEST SOUTH CENTRAL:																
Arkansas	404	492	298	636	67	108	118	117	401	10	2	602	52	27	10	18
Louisiana	332	302	467	725	361	305	397	312	1,375	23	23	1,928	31	23	82	147
Oklahoma	1,867	1,825	530	1,393	191	311	162	218	3,613	74	--------	5,005	189	132	25	101
Texas	12,282	12,819	3,300	6,441	622	940	464	620	5,467	140	28	7,057	308	37	180	189
MOUNTAIN:																
Montana	1,714	1,895	1,435	3,298	360	935	3,877	3,782	4,212	19	29	5,203	175	80	2,700	3,577
Idaho	541	420	399	781	106	233	489	460	1,153	4	9	1,458	18	9	858	689
Wyoming	521	518	457	1,183	175	349	1,322	1,189	1,375	6	10	1,482	35	33	633	856
Colorado	1,714	1,953	2,468	5,722	690	1,157	3,650	2,109	12,970	61	13	16,669	262	115	563	879
New Mexico	143	113	316	423	59	130	490	535	219	4	6	254	24	8	41	49
Arizona	178	148	341	486	94	210	784	1,167	463	18	12	816	58	16	300	407
Utah	119	163	410	987	72	179	989	836	342	15	3	684	36	12	507	779
Nevada	88	85	176	190	16	40	532	693	122	8	2	124	6	7	163	182
PACIFIC:																
Washington	2,202	1,792	3,128	6,494	579	1,056	4,761	3,565	9,229	276	149	11,124	868	527	11,002	11,863
Oregon	1,691	1,132	1,664	2,798	404	909	1,541	1,186	6,278	167	107	6,979	319	101	5,507	6,050
California	6,212	3,377	13,243	13,264	6,896	5,252	12,743	7,277	44,047	1,189	436	27,224	1,776	260	8,495	7,053

278

POPULATION

TABLE 8.—COUNTRY OF BIRTH OF THE FOREIGN-BORN WHITE POPULATION, BY DIVISIONS AND STATES: 1930 AND 1920—Continued

DIVISION AND STATE	RUMANIA		BULGARIA		TURKEY IN EUROPE		GREECE		ALBANIA		ITALY		SPAIN		PORTUGAL		OTHER EUROPE	
	1930	1920	1930	1920	1930	1920	1930	1920	1930	1920	1930	1920	1930	1920	1930	1920	1930	1920
United States___	146,393	102,823	9,399	10,477	2,257	5,284	174,526	175,972	8,814	5,608	1,790,424	1,610,109	58,302	49,247	69,974	67,453	16,251	5,901
GEOGRAPHIC DIVISIONS:																		
New England_____	3,424	3,128	238	214	311	631	25,423	32,186	4,175	2,819	253,098	238,508	2,363	2,856	35,674	38,426	468	209
Middle Atlantic____	72,826	55,910	1,544	1,336	1,043	2,534	51,053	44,531	2,072	1,156	1,046,159	925,222	25,517	16,731	10,052	2,848	6,532	1,412
East North Central__	48,871	29,338	4,914	5,806	424	1,035	49,101	45,135	1,763	1,019	244,504	203,180	4,563	3,008	546	354	5,737	2,211
West North Central__	9,013	6,950	602	1,005	34	124	8,018	11,236	334	263	31,653	34,488	659	775	32	56	698	465
South Atlantic_____	2,743	2,163	218	161	106	203	11,449	11,449	110	19	39,512	40,267	6,277	6,523	393	436	652	355
East South Central__	464	441	43	51	22	50	2,304	2,014	52	23	7,288	8,584	213	212	39	20	207	89
West South Central__	847	663	220	241	37	101	3,331	3,483	20	12	22,185	27,724	1,437	2,495	104	183	587	336
Mountain_____	1,435	1,053	640	821	20	72	6,716	9,483	70	143	23,774	28,497	3,480	4,561	224	332	186	106
Pacific_____	6,771	3,177	990	752	260	534	17,131	16,455	218	155	122,251	103,639	13,703	12,086	22,910	24,798	1,184	718
NEW ENGLAND:																		
Maine_____	27	67	5	5	16	66	748	1,228	243	403	2,359	2,797	40	33	78	143	18	10
New Hampshire_____	35	25	15	8	7	_____	3,233	5,280	193	118	1,938	2,074	20	18	247	115	11	2
Vermont_____	15	19	4	3	_____	_____	225	167	8	6	3,082	4,067	478	661	46	29	1	4
Massachusetts_____	1,689	1,445	116	120	217	451	16,780	20,441	2,938	1,947	126,108	117,007	798	824	24,840	28,315	178	100
Rhode Island_____	480	370	48	45	38	45	1,100	1,219	250	142	32,493	32,241	110	87	8,118	8,624	32	11
Connecticut_____	1,178	1,202	50	33	33	69	3,337	3,851	543	203	87,123	80,322	917	1,233	2,345	1,200	228	82
MIDDLE ATLANTIC:																		
New York_____	51,014	40,116	978	614	849	2,050	33,387	26,117	1,206	415	629,322	545,173	17,695	12,548	5,106	1,404	3,389	842
New Jersey_____	6,686	4,564	124	66	77	195	6,020	4,521	138	54	190,858	157,285	4,982	2,000	3,655	646	902	170
Pennsylvania_____	15,126	11,230	442	656	117	289	11,646	13,893	728	687	225,979	222,764	2,840	2,183	1,291	798	2,241	400
E. NORTH CENTRAL:																		
Ohio_____	19,580	13,968	1,686	2,585	98	509	12,050	13,540	564	432	71,496	60,658	1,556	1,280	185	146	998	351
Indiana_____	3,292	2,731	403	431	11	70	4,087	4,182	121	74	6,873	6,712	597	467	88	14	241	75
Illinois_____	13,172	6,238	1,037	940	99	181	20,003	16,465	365	151	110,449	94,407	1,030	746	102	110	1,084	524
Michigan_____	11,482	6,331	1,594	1,692	201	179	10,061	7,115	577	261	43,087	30,216	1,324	441	131	67	3,180	813
Wisconsin_____	1,345	970	194	208	17	36	2,900	3,833	136	101	12,599	11,187	56	74	40	17	234	448
W. NORTH CENTRAL:																		
Minnesota_____	2,819	2,385	238	456	7	30	1,765	2,391	23	41	6,401	7,432	42	36	5	7	115	149
Iowa_____	284	297	159	209	2	18	1,910	2,884	11	7	3,834	4,956	22	41	1	14	58	78
Missouri_____	2,321	1,647	151	145	19	44	2,405	3,022	288	202	15,201	14,609	460	435	14	12	259	76
North Dakota_____	2,518	1,811	39	31	_____	17	303	420	2	_____	102	176	8	6	1	2	25	25
South Dakota_____	410	154	46	97	3	5	279	375	_____	1	305	413	7	5	1	4	25	27
Nebraska_____	336	371	30	61	3	4	822	1,504	7	9	3,642	3,547	18	38	4	6	133	53
Kansas_____	324	285	29	36	_____	6	534	640	3	2	2,165	3,355	102	214	6	11	83	57
SOUTH ATLANTIC:																		
Delaware_____	91	110	2	_____	4	3	339	286	_____	_____	3,769	4,136	121	142	7	18	33	7
Maryland_____	811	537	16	18	6	19	1,617	964	8	1	10,872	9,543	281	221	33	21	177	79
Dist. of Columbia__	160	86	16	5	25	72	1,347	1,207	14	8	4,330	3,764	148	108	23	11	71	17
Virginia_____	172	165	9	17	23	32	1,285	1,796	19	4	1,853	2,435	111	263	57	95	85	82
West Virginia_____	667	625	121	98	12	23	2,479	3,186	47	2	12,088	14,147	1,372	1,540	49	14	125	71
North Carolina____	33	31	7	1	6	17	1,006	551	8	_____	438	453	21	16	9	10	29	7
South Carolina____	21	26	1	1	6	10	627	578	3	_____	188	344	19	19	3	6	27	10
Georgia_____	143	111	8	5	12	21	1,107	1,473	4	1	712	700	79	123	90	39	42	60
Florida_____	645	472	38	16	12	6	1,552	1,408	7	3	5,262	4,745	4,125	4,091	122	222	63	22
E. SOUTH CENTRAL:																		
Kentucky_____	202	192	20	28	14	22	466	401	16	1	1,589	1,932	97	68	26	6	59	30
Tennessee_____	98	93	3	5	3	5	528	491	35	22	1,946	2,079	17	14	3	6	58	16
Alabama_____	133	120	16	18	5	22	968	915	1	_____	2,140	2,732	68	70	7	4	54	33
Mississippi_____	31	36	4	_____	_____	1	342	207	_____	_____	1,613	1,841	31	60	3	4	36	10
W. SOUTH CENTRAL:																		
Arkansas_____	36	62	33	17	2	1	312	277	_____	1	952	1,314	7	22	1	4	31	10
Louisiana_____	127	93	29	49	12	14	574	610	4	2	13,526	16,264	666	1,268	52	100	131	74
Oklahoma_____	140	65	109	105	_____	11	642	619	_____	1	1,157	2,122	50	124	12	13	71	49
Texas_____	544	443	49	70	23	75	1,803	1,977	16	8	6,550	8,024	714	1,081	39	66	354	203
MOUNTAIN:																		
Montana_____	641	344	197	264	1	28	840	1,465	26	38	2,840	3,842	67	68	14	30	41	13
Idaho_____	110	104	29	39	1	5	414	716	1	42	1,153	1,323	1,086	1,416	18	39	11	6
Wyoming_____	55	71	68	72	2	2	888	1,236	5	5	1,653	1,948	119	139	23	29	13	4
Colorado_____	450	394	271	349	9	12	1,230	1,802	8	11	10,670	12,579	210	297	15	33	69	43
New Mexico_____	20	8	11	18	_____	2	292	288	_____	_____	1,259	1,678	152	198	4	18	14	8
Arizona_____	75	51	18	28	2	10	356	329	10	6	822	1,261	473	1,013	21	30	14	8
Utah_____	64	69	37	30	5	12	2,107	3,029	17	41	2,814	3,225	274	250	8	4	10	19
Nevada_____	20	12	9	21	_____	1	499	618	3	_____	2,563	2,641	1,099	1,180	121	149	5	5
PACIFIC:																		
Washington_____	787	422	247	267	76	229	2,881	4,214	115	93	10,274	10,813	280	410	114	156	104	75
Oregon_____	843	352	174	214	17	41	1,575	1,928	10	13	4,728	4,324	497	553	101	125	51	34
California_____	5,141	2,403	469	271	167	264	12,675	10,313	93	49	107,249	88,502	13,016	11,123	22,695	24,517	1,029	609

COUNTRY OF ORIGIN OF THE FOREIGN WHITE STOCK   279

TABLE 8.—COUNTRY OF BIRTH OF THE FOREIGN-BORN WHITE POPULATION, BY DIVISIONS AND STATES:
1930 AND 1920—Continued

DIVISION AND STATE	ARMENIA		PALESTINE		SYRIA		TURKEY IN ASIA		OTHER ASIA		CANADA—FRENCH		CANADA—OTHER		NEWFOUND-LAND		WEST INDIES	
	1930	1920	1930	1920	1930	1920	1930	1920	1930	1920	1930	1920	1930	1920	1930	1920	1930	1920
United States	32,166	36,626	6,135	3,202	57,227	51,900	46,651	11,014	15,401	7,708	370,852	307,786	907,569	910,092	23,971	13,242	31,426	26,369
GEOGRAPHIC DIVS.:																		
New England	10,687	11,964	428	271	11,076	11,181	8,348	2,266	1,294	916	264,261	240,385	252,760	233,971	12,533	8,198	1,387	1,446
Middle Atlantic	8,412	10,806	3,534	1,489	17,950	15,501	21,183	4,335	4,409	2,018	33,336	17,045	147,411	120,049	8,046	2,772	16,983	11,692
East North Central	5,927	6,157	1,037	662	11,561	9,726	8,593	2,098	4,362	2,083	42,308	29,267	252,217	222,213	1,725	830	1,280	1,280
West North Central	267	717	167	142	3,127	3,405	507	322	500	417	10,531	10,459	52,323	69,785	185	181	281	366
South Atlantic	323	402	280	143	4,538	4,064	1,547	456	574	237	2,055	813	15,384	12,059	301	230	9,111	9,329
East South Central	32	61	98	77	1,703	1,501	157	93	105	71	347	179	2,763	2,967	46	32	280	303
West South Central	53	148	192	156	3,629	3,436	448	206	267	226	994	590	7,326	8,105	125	100	709	824
Mountain	193	362	71	73	1,136	1,324	298	190	267	241	3,678	3,482	23,302	30,185	134	196	174	200
Pacific	6,272	6,009	328	189	2,507	1,762	5,570	1,048	3,623	1,549	13,342	5,566	154,083	110,758	876	703	1,241	911
NEW ENGLAND:																		
Maine	134	142	11	10	475	627	131	43	35	42	36,947	35,580	36,796	38,570	204	215	56	81
New Hampshire	151	276	2	7	411	523	259	60	22	9	37,682	38,277	13,277	13,997	228	182	35	33
Vermont	14	55	7	1	267	228	17	5	16	9	17,320	14,181	9,862	10,687	101	67	16	12
Massachusetts	7,705	8,640	250	180	7,153	7,128	6,124	1,671	400	333	115,241	108,691	172,810	153,330	10,986	7,165	800	871
Rhode Island	1,909	1,850	31	14	1,218	1,285	1,084	202	92	73	31,501	28,887	7,777	7,525	256	233	142	139
Connecticut	774	1,001	127	59	1,552	1,390	733	225	609	450	25,570	14,769	12,238	9,862	758	336	338	310
MIDDLE ATLANTIC:																		
New York	4,874	5,599	2,911	1,061	10,113	8,127	16,673	3,200	3,163	1,300	28,955	15,560	118,919	96,414	6,374	1,809	14,430	9,532
New Jersey	1,947	2,275	312	160	2,627	2,062	2,353	440	579	347	2,470	772	14,051	9,520	932	476	1,575	1,120
Pennsylvania	1,591	2,932	311	268	5,210	5,312	2,157	695	667	371	1,911	713	14,441	14,115	740	487	978	1,040
E. NORTH CENTRAL:																		
Ohio	468	906	270	185	4,226	3,680	1,826	637	614	276	2,606	1,277	24,241	22,800	217	147	308	533
Indiana	127	134	42	26	741	717	297	158	288	145	682	406	5,519	4,600	60	44	52	51
Illinois	1,635	1,715	456	232	1,095	1,149	2,048	502	2,411	1,028	6,189	4,032	37,400	34,343	386	311	404	389
Michigan	3,322	2,498	220	176	4,999	3,648	3,564	663	936	468	28,539	18,635	173,777	145,867	975	245	347	239
Wisconsin	375	904	49	43	500	532	858	138	113	116	4,292	4,917	11,280	14,414	78	83	59	77
W. NORTH CENTRAL:																		
Minnesota	60	174	35	25	670	818	83	100	159	105	6,484	6,796	20,618	26,936	48	56	27	56
Iowa	68	101	10	22	570	512	67	51	76	69	608	401	5,725	8,528	42	35	41	71
Missouri	86	181	83	63	806	848	240	83	96	67	588	299	4,824	6,204	38	38	144	152
North Dakota	22	75	4	5	235	289	38	21	28	29	1,354	1,533	10,887	14,017	11	20	6	4
South Dakota	3	18	4	1	229	265	28	12	24	42	492	508	2,850	3,945	8	3	8	12
Nebraska	24	138	26	14	369	414	28	28	62	51	436	351	3,942	5,407	34	20	15	38
Kansas	4	30	5	12	248	259	23	27	55	54	569	571	3,408	4,748	4	9	40	33
SOUTH ATLANTIC:																		
Delaware	3	6	2	10	5	2	21	6	8	3	61	23	399	423	8	8	43	28
Maryland	30	43	65	15	68	72	180	39	68	41	291	117	1,975	1,747	61	61	226	215
Dist. of Columbia	68	63	46	19	259	211	198	62	64	27	223	147	1,458	1,541	33	18	129	114
Virginia	133	164	33	23	536	550	230	77	90	54	157	106	1,460	1,817	27	32	91	94
West Virginia	16	41	17	20	1,300	1,235	369	157	79	11	118	54	839	903	15	6	35	26
North Carolina	2	10	32	22	669	592	108	23	61	22	80	15	850	635	26	7	38	34
South Carolina	...	6	12	2	401	396	93	5	34	15	31	24	247	244	7	1	30	29
Georgia	23	28	23	16	388	473	185	49	37	20	109	50	985	905	20	22	101	89
Florida	48	41	50	16	912	533	163	38	133	44	985	277	7,171	3,844	104	75	8,418	8,700
E. SOUTH CENTRAL:																		
Kentucky	8	20	33	16	414	309	48	22	33	24	96	50	822	835	21	13	34	36
Tennessee	13	18	24	30	109	127	30	20	26	18	92	47	847	925	12	9	37	38
Alabama	8	22	21	16	487	482	62	39	26	15	117	52	785	840	11	3	176	201
Mississippi	3	1	20	15	693	583	17	12	20	14	42	30	309	367	2	7	33	28
W. SOUTH CENTRAL:																		
Arkansas	4	7	6	16	221	213	18	10	7	7	77	58	618	822	39	20	12	15
Louisiana	15	27	25	15	929	954	117	61	48	46	222	157	759	1,008	18	16	359	495
Oklahoma	10	15	29	20	809	691	45	21	51	53	243	126	1,876	2,349	15	11	36	43
Texas	24	99	132	105	1,670	1,578	268	114	161	120	452	249	4,073	3,926	53	53	302	271
MOUNTAIN:																		
Montana	43	140	11	8	155	192	79	62	47	50	1,966	2,211	8,787	12,105	33	63	22	25
Idaho	14	13	2	1	43	49	11	15	17	30	571	476	3,931	4,478	41	59	7	10
Wyoming	24	62	4	4	45	82	13	25	22	18	118	92	1,018	1,346	3	4	15	14
Colorado	35	46	27	41	254	289	78	30	73	62	572	418	5,244	7,203	27	39	61	91
New Mexico	2	2	1	2	192	108	8	5	17	11	62	42	551	690	6	3	10	15
Arizona	14	8	14	8	285	327	29	15	53	39	158	90	1,860	1,872	15	16	40	41
Utah	37	80	10	5	141	174	34	18	22	23	97	45	1,093	1,421	5	4	7	8
Nevada	24	11	2	4	21	13	46	20	16	8	134	108	818	1,070	4	8	12	5
PACIFIC:																		
Washington	113	259	22	18	272	318	646	288	408	297	4,340	2,581	43,724	40,407	250	318	77	100
Oregon	47	63	12	5	186	185	154	56	149	90	1,345	679	16,571	13,095	67	49	43	58
California	6,112	5,687	294	166	2,049	1,259	4,770	704	3,066	1,162	7,657	2,306	93,788	57,256	559	336	1,121	753

280

POPULATION

TABLE 8.—COUNTRY OF BIRTH OF THE FOREIGN-BORN WHITE POPULATION, BY DIVISIONS AND STATES: 1930 AND 1920—Continued

DIVISION AND STATE	MEXICO		CENTRAL AND SOUTH AMERICA		AFRICA		AUSTRALIA		ATLANTIC ISLANDS		PACIFIC ISLANDS		COUNTRY NOT SPECIFIED		BORN AT SEA	
	1930	1920 (adjusted) [2]	1930	1920	1930	1920	1930	1920	1930	1920	1930	1920	1930	1920	1930	1920
United States	23,743	21,023	37,509	20,929	7,866	5,222	12,720	10,801	39,479	38,084	4,384	3,643	1,485	3,560	4,958	5,302
GEOGRAPHIC DIVISIONS:																
New England	145	149	2,460	1,681	662	437	597	531	24,229	28,484	154	171	84	304	378	380
Middle Atlantic	3,551	2,273	20,149	9,650	3,408	1,951	2,626	2,188	1,189	835	625	462	469	647	991	1,015
East North Central	2,905	572	3,310	1,875	1,145	810	1,684	1,413	218	261	354	292	442	1,517	1,434	1,628
West North Central	1,064	1,005	711	729	272	290	470	548	35	35	134	129	85	270	802	949
South Atlantic	377	356	1,304	812	340	230	400	274	143	165	127	91	109	83	171	169
East South Central	138	288	262	181	63	62	87	80	5	11	20	18	15	28	62	90
West South Central	4,455	7,870	1,443	1,225	195	202	276	308	59	55	88	70	35	224	207	252
Mountain	2,284	3,808	513	485	264	336	616	623	176	154	336	353	30	212	186	216
Pacific	8,824	4,702	7,357	4,311	1,517	904	5,964	4,836	13,425	8,084	2,526	2,058	216	275	727	603
NEW ENGLAND:																
Maine	4	7	31	17	14	15	20	23	30	10	8	4	10	12	43	40
New Hampshire	4	8	34	31	17	10	20	21	63	40	2	4	5	14	18	11
Vermont	9	4	30	42	11	8	14	5	6	3	3	5	1	3	13	10
Massachusetts	85	96	1,390	1,056	432	283	369	337	20,213	25,230	98	100	46	62	105	212
Rhode Island	12	3	352	237	65	42	56	43	3,732	2,991	18	22	7	8	35	25
Connecticut	31	31	623	298	123	79	118	102	185	210	25	36	15	205	74	82
MIDDLE ATLANTIC:																
New York	2,744	1,680	16,032	7,430	2,580	1,390	1,659	1,360	857	569	430	317	289	249	533	479
New Jersey	288	221	2,415	1,040	485	277	428	317	247	179	108	91	59	104	185	169
Pennsylvania	519	372	1,702	1,180	343	275	539	511	85	87	87	54	121	294	273	367
EAST NORTH CENTRAL:																
Ohio	309	112	683	451	218	157	307	232	34	42	46	38	66	188	298	296
Indiana	218	23	148	80	37	37	98	77	8	7	26	26	16	43	94	133
Illinois	1,430	299	1,483	743	473	349	709	598	129	195	154	114	128	285	413	492
Michigan	760	121	774	432	352	208	445	397	40	11	104	80	191	128	297	314
Wisconsin	188	17	222	169	65	59	125	109	7	6	24	24	41	873	332	393
WEST NORTH CENTRAL:																
Minnesota	115	14	114	116	86	90	86	104	17	14	30	28	16	67	221	266
Iowa	176	205	83	109	27	32	81	101	7	8	26	37	7	30	154	165
Missouri	359	434	247	208	76	82	146	137	5	5	35	23	31	41	128	180
North Dakota	32	2	46	39	17	10	25	35	--------	--------	3	2	11	23	71	75
South Dakota	14	2	16	27	20	20	18	24	--------	--------	7	9	8	12	56	72
Nebraska	212	145	68	71	22	28	47	80	1	4	15	11	4	71	82	98
Kansas	156	203	137	159	24	28	67	67	5	4	18	19	8	20	90	93
SOUTH ATLANTIC:																
Delaware	14	25	84	15	9	9	8	12	3	1	4	5	28	--------	3	7
Maryland	40	46	279	176	83	40	86	61	20	22	38	31	11	11	47	48
District of Columbia	61	30	231	154	47	40	43	25	8	7	11	6	10	12	14	16
Virginia	24	54	114	117	26	36	53	41	12	29	17	18	3	14	23	24
West Virginia	101	32	96	48	20	8	40	38	3	3	1	2	3	31	28	28
North Carolina	11	21	30	36	32	17	22	14	3	1	16	8	--------	2	7	5
South Carolina	6	10	12	15	13	4	4	5	4	6	2	1	1	1	6	3
Georgia	21	39	70	44	31	22	30	26	10	9	10	8	4	9	9	11
Florida	99	99	388	207	79	48	114	57	80	87	28	12	49	3	34	27
EAST SOUTH CENTRAL:																
Kentucky	24	60	36	36	18	9	29	36	1	2	10	9	7	13	24	54
Tennessee	27	132	56	44	19	13	27	15	--------	2	3	4	3	8	11	16
Alabama	43	87	92	65	16	23	19	21	3	7	4	5	3	4	19	11
Mississippi	44	9	78	36	10	17	12	8	1	--------	3	--------	2	3	8	9
WEST SOUTH CENTRAL:																
Arkansas	37	65	29	23	14	16	19	25	2	4	4	7	4	1	18	26
Louisiana	557	504	1,023	844	62	53	45	60	14	13	14	10	3	5	32	39
Oklahoma	169	384	71	67	25	22	46	54	5	2	16	12	6	20	43	50
Texas	3,692	6,917	320	291	94	111	166	169	38	36	54	50	22	198	114	137
MOUNTAIN:																
Montana	88	14	65	71	35	48	71	81	10	5	25	38	5	66	39	40
Idaho	68	151	30	24	33	44	53	57	28	23	54	72	1	41	18	27
Wyoming	67	33	19	29	17	14	13	17	1	7	13	14	2	12	10	10
Colorado	336	199	213	183	44	53	114	112	11	8	34	39	9	22	64	63
New Mexico	390	842	50	20	13	25	19	14	2	2	8	4	1	2	6	5
Arizona	1,086	2,354	58	72	25	22	85	81	5	1	26	26	1	65	12	21
Utah	177	154	38	30	78	115	215	221	2	4	154	137	9	2	31	40
Nevada	72	61	40	36	19	15	46	40	117	104	22	23	2	2	6	10
PACIFIC:																
Washington	115	145	350	303	170	124	583	610	51	44	246	244	57	124	176	177
Oregon	61	66	151	122	63	72	273	213	40	48	154	158	13	13	78	53
California	8,648	4,491	6,856	3,886	1,284	708	5,108	4,013	13,334	8,892	2,126	1,656	146	138	473	373

[2] Estimated number of persons of Mexican birth returned in 1920 who would have been counted as foreign-born white even under the 1930 rules for classification.

447

CHAPTER 7

MOTHER TONGUE
OF THE FOREIGN-BORN
WHITE POPULATION

CHAPTER 7.—MOTHER TONGUE OF THE FOREIGN-BORN WHITE POPULATION

INTRODUCTION

The inquiry as to the mother tongue of the foreign-born white population was first made at the census of 1910. At that census, and also at the census of 1920, the inquiry covered all of the foreign white stock, including native white persons of foreign or mixed parentage. At the census of 1930, the inquiry was restricted to the foreign-born population. Geographically, the statistics here presented relate to the population of continental United States, the divisions and States, and cities having 25,000 inhabitants or more. No tabulation of mother tongue was made for cities of less than 25,000 nor for counties. Data for Hawaii, Puerto Rico, the Virgin Islands, and the Panama Canal Zone are shown in the report entitled "Outlying Territories and Possessions."

Although information as to "mother tongue"—that is, the language of customary speech in the home prior to immigration—was secured for all persons of foreign birth, it has been tabulated only for white persons, since most persons of each of the other races speak one characteristic language—Spanish for the Mexicans, Chinese for the Chinese, Japanese for the Japanese, etc.

While the statistics of mother tongue and of country of birth of the foreign-born white relate to the same aggregate population, they deal with essentially different characteristics. The classification by country of birth is made with reference to geographic origin, while the classification by mother tongue indicates in general the racial origin. The two classifications, while closely related in most cases, are entirely distinct, since the mother tongue of an immigrant is not necessarily the language most commonly used in the country from which he came.

The total number of foreign-born white persons reported in the census of 1930 was 13,366,407. For 1920, the adjusted figure corresponding with the total foreign-born white as reported in 1930, is 13,255,394. This figure is the total number of foreign-born white persons enumerated in 1920, minus 457,360 persons (estimated) who would have been counted as Mexican under the 1930 rules for classification. Since these persons were, with very few exceptions, of Spanish mother tongue, the whole number was subtracted from the 1920 group reporting that language. Thus the change in classification does not seriously affect the comparability of the statistics of mother tongue as between 1920 and 1930.

Classification of mother tongues.—The mother tongues for which statistics are presented in this re-

port are classified according to linguistic groups as follows:

English and Celtic (includes Irish, Scotch, and Welsh).
Germanic—
   German.
   Dutch (includes Frisian).
   Flemish.
Scandinavian—
   Swedish.
   Norwegian.
   Danish.
   Icelandic.
Latin and Greek—
   Italian (includes Romansh and Friulian).
   French (includes Breton).
   Spanish (includes Basque).
   Portuguese.
   Rumanian.
   Greek.
Slavic and Lettic—
   Polish.
   Czech.
   Slovak.
   Russian.
   Ruthenian (Russniak).
   Ukrainian.
   Slovenian.
   Croatian (includes Dalmatian).
   Serbian (includes Montenegrin)
   Bulgarian.
   Wendish.
   Lithuanian.
   Lettish.
Unclassified—
   Yiddish.
   Magyar.
   Finnish (includes Lappish).
   Estonian.
   Armenian.
   Arabic.
   Turkish.
   Albanian.
   All other (includes Persian, Gypsy, Georgian, Kurdish, and Egyptian).
Unknown.

In the main, this classification is the same as that used in 1920 and 1910. There have, however, been a few changes in designation, and a few combinations and separations. Dutch, in 1920, was designated as "Dutch and Frisian," Yiddish as "Yiddish and Hebrew" and Arabic as "Syrian and Arabic." The term "Frisian" was dropped because in the census returns the number so reported was insignificant. Hebrew and Syrian were dropped in the interest of accuracy, as these terms properly apply to languages no longer used in common speech. In 1920, Croatian and Dalmatian, and Serbian and Montenegrin, were each

341

INTRODUCTION

shown separately. These languages were very generally confused and they are so similar that the distinction was not considered of sufficient importance for retention. In fact, all of the Serbo-Croatian tongues are practically dialects of the same language, and the Serbo-Croatian total is perhaps more significant than the figures for Serbian and Croatian separately.

On the other hand, Icelandic, although similar to Danish, is shown separate from its parent language in 1930. Similarly, Ukrainian has been differentiated from Ruthenian, Lettish from Lithuanian, and Estonian from Finnish. It is believed that these separations have been made with a reasonable degree of accuracy, although in the case of Ruthenian and Ukrainian the distinction is more a matter of country of birth than of language.

The 12 leading mother tongues, as returned in the census of 1930, are shown in order of numerical importance in Table 1, with comparative figures for 1920 and 1910.

TABLE 1.—PRINCIPAL MOTHER TONGUES OF THE FOREIGN-BORN WHITE POPULATION OF THE UNITED STATES: 1930, 1920, AND 1910

MOTHER TONGUE	NUMBER			PER CENT		
	1930	1920	1910	1930	1920	1910
Total	13,366,407	[1]13,255,394	[1]13,134,312	100.0	100.0	100.0
English and Celtic	3,097,021	3,007,932	3,363,792	23.2	22.7	25.6
German	2,188,006	2,267,128	2,759,032	16.4	17.1	21.0
Italian	1,808,289	1,624,998	1,365,110	13.5	12.3	10.4
Yiddish	1,222,658	1,091,820	1,051,767	9.1	8.2	8.0
Polish	965,899	1,077,392	943,781	7.2	8.1	7.2
Swedish	615,465	643,203	683,218	4.6	4.9	5.2
French	523,207	466,956	528,842	3.9	3.5	4.0
Norwegian	345,522	362,199	402,587	2.6	2.7	3.1
Russian	315,721	392,049	57,926	2.4	3.0	0.4
Magyar	250,393	[1]290,419	229,094	1.9	2.2	1.7
Slovak	240,196	274,948	166,474	1.8	2.1	1.3
Czech	201,138	234,564	228,738	1.5	1.8	1.7
Other mother tongues	1,592,802	1,521,786	1,353,951	11.9	11.5	10.3

[1] Adjusted figures; see headnote to Table 4.   [2] Corrected figures.

Mother tongue in relation to ethnic stock.—In general, the returns for mother tongue may be taken as indicative of ethnic stock, although there are many exceptions to this rule. For example, persons reported under the linguistic group "English and Celtic" belong to several distinct ethnic stocks, of which the most important are the Anglo-Saxons of England, the Kymric Celts of Wales and Cornwall, and the Gaelic Celts of Ireland and the highlands of Scotland. English is now the mother tongue of practically all of these peoples, although Welsh is still spoken by an appreciable number of persons in Wales, and Gaelic by a small number in Ireland. In many cases the mother tongue was returned as Irish, Scotch, or Welsh, but these returns were not separately tabulated, as it was evident that the two former, in particular, often represented persons speaking English with an Irish or Scotch accent or "brogue," rather than persons speaking the distinctive Irish or Scotch (Gaelic) languages. Other ethnic distinctions not indicated by the statistics

of mother tongue are those between French and Breton stocks, Spanish and Basque, Northern and Southern Italian, and North German as distinguished from South German and Austrian.

Conversely, other ethnic groups comprise more people than those who speak the mother tongue most characteristic of the group. Yiddish as a mother tongue is spoken by only a part of the immigrants of Jewish stock. Many Jews of foreign birth report German, Russian, or other languages as their mother tongue. The returns of the census of 1920, in particular, probably exaggerate the number of Russian mother tongue at the expense of Yiddish. There is no important ethnic distinction between Norwegians, Danes, and Icelanders, yet their mother tongues are separately reported. The Welsh and the Bretons are ethnically similar, yet the first are shown with English and Celtic as their mother tongue and the second with French.

Mother tongue in relation to country of birth.—Statistics as to mother tongue are of greatest significance with reference to persons born in Austria, Belgium, Canada, Czechoslovakia, Hungary, Lithuania, Poland, Rumania, Russia, Switzerland, and Yugoslavia. Immigrants from each of these countries include persons of different ethnic groups, which may to some extent be distinguished by their mother tongue. The leading mother tongues spoken by persons in the United States who were born in these countries are shown in Table 2.

TABLE 2.—PRINCIPAL MOTHER TONGUES OF THE FOREIGN-BORN WHITE POPULATION FROM SPECIFIED COUNTRIES: 1930

COUNTRY OF BIRTH AND MOTHER TONGUE	Number	Per cent	COUNTRY OF BIRTH AND MOTHER TONGUE	Number	Per cent
Austria	370,914	100.0	Poland	1,268,583	100.0
German	191,715	51.7	Polish	918,070	72.4
Yiddish	96,052	25.9	Yiddish	243,825	10.2
All other	83,147	22.4	All other	106,688	8.4
Belgium	64,194	100.0	Rumania	146,393	100.0
Flemish	40,956	63.8	Rumanian	53,452	36.5
French	18,424	28.7	Yiddish	49,508	33.8
All other	4,814	7.5	German	28,640	19.6
			Magyar	8,830	6.0
Canada	1,278,421	100.0	All other	5,963	4.1
English and Celtic	880,754	68.9			
French	370,852	29.0	Russia	1,153,824	100.0
All other	26,815	2.1	Yiddish	743,307	64.4
			Russian	262,781	22.8
Czechoslovakia	491,638	100.0	German	103,371	9.0
Slovak	219,347	44.6	All other	44,165	3.8
Czech	188,960	38.4			
German	30,900	6.3	Switzerland	113,010	100.0
All other	52,431	10.7	German	87,073	77.0
			French	13,161	11.6
Hungary	274,450	100.0	Italian	10,339	9.1
Magyar	202,875	73.9	All other	2,437	2.2
German	48,198	17.6			
All other	23,377	8.5	Yugoslavia	211,416	100.0
			Croatian	72,138	34.1
Lithuania	193,606	100.0	Slovenian	66,793	31.6
Lithuanian	156,152	80.7	Serbian	27,663	13.1
Yiddish	25,886	18.4	German	23,403	11.1
All other	11,568	6.0	All other	21,419	10.1

In Table 6, persons of each mother tongue are classified by country of birth, and in Table 7, persons born in each specified country are classified by mother tongue. The country of birth in both tables refers to the present or postwar area.

INTRODUCTION

Since, however, a great majority of the foreign born came to the United States before the War, it is often difficult to determine the country of birth on a postwar basis. Many of the changes in country of birth shown in Tables 6 and 7 between 1920 and 1930, especially those for central and eastern Europe, are due to more specific returns or to different methods of classification, rather than to actual changes in the composition of the foreign-born population. Effort was made at both censuses to ascertain the actual birthplaces of persons born in the sections of Europe whose boundaries were changed as a result of the World War, but in 1920 these boundary changes were still too recent to be fully reflected in the returns made to the census enumerators. By 1930, the revised boundaries had become more familiar, and the returns were more in accordance with postwar areas. An illustration of the improved returns is shown in Table 6 for Slovak mother tongue. In 1920 the percentage reported as born in Austria was 32.9, which was reduced to 2.4 in 1930, with a corresponding increase in the percentage born in Czechoslovakia from 48.4 to 91.3.

Urban and rural population.—Since there are marked differences in the racial distribution of the foreign-born white population of urban and rural areas, statistics of mother tongue are presented for these areas in Tables 3, 5, and 10.

Urban population, as defined by the Census Bureau, is in general that residing in cities and other incorporated places having 2,500 inhabitants or more, the remainder being classified as rural. In three of the New England States—New Hampshire, Massachusetts, and Rhode Island—conditions are exceptional in that the compactly built portions of towns (townships) are not separately incorporated or politically distinct in any way from the rural territory within the same town; nor is it the usual practice to incorporate even the larger places as cities until they attain a population in excess of 10,000. Consequently, if only cities were counted as urban the classification would be quite inadequate. In these States the urban classification has been made to include, in addition to the regularly incorporated cities, those towns in which there is a village or thickly settled area having more than 2,500 inhabitants and comprising, either by itself or when combined with other villages in the same town, more than 50 per cent of the total population of the town.

One other modification has been made in the definition of urban population for use in connection with the 1930 census. This extends the definition so as to include townships and other political subdivisions (not incorporated as municipalities, nor containing any area so incorporated) which had a total population of 10,000 or more, and a population density of 1,000 or more per square mile.

More than four-fifths of the total foreign-born white population of the United States is found in urban territory. There are wide differences, however, among the various racial groups, as indicated by mother tongue, in this respect; 98.4 per cent of the foreign-born white persons reporting Yiddish as mother tongue were in urban territory, as compared with 54.1 per cent of those reporting Finnish as mother tongue, and 55.8 per cent of those reporting Norwegian.

Rural-farm and rural-nonfarm population.—In addition to the classification of the population as urban and rural, which is based on the size (number of inhabitants) and the political status (municipal incorporation) of the geographic unit in which the persons live, the population, both urban and rural, is further classified as farm and nonfarm, on the basis of a question reading "Does this family live on a farm?"

For the farm population living in urban territory, which forms less than 1 per cent of the total farm population, no detailed tabulations were made; hence the presentation of classified data for the farm population is limited to that part living in rural territory and designated as rural-farm population. This is done partly to simplify the classification (dividing the total population into three groups, namely, urban, rural-farm, and rural-nonfarm) and partly because it is felt that in general the farm families living within the corporate limits of cities or other incorporated places are living under conditions at least somewhat urban, rather than under typical farm conditions.

The rural-nonfarm or "village" population is made up largely of persons living in small towns or villages, both incorporated and unincorporated, though in many areas there are considerable numbers of families living in the open country but not on farms.

There are few characteristics in which the foreign-born of the different racial groups differ more widely than in their tendency to settle on farms. In Table 3 are presented the United States totals for the principal mother tongues, arranged in order of the percentage found in the rural-farm population.

TABLE 3.—MOTHER TONGUE OF THE FOREIGN-BORN WHITE POPULATION IN URBAN, RURAL-FARM, AND RURAL-NONFARM AREAS: 1930

MOTHER TONGUE	Total	URBAN		RURAL-FARM		RURAL-NONFARM	
		Number	Per cent of total	Number	Per cent of total	Number	Per cent of total
Total	13,366,407	10,726,859	80.3	1,084,087	8.1	1,555,461	11.6
Finnish	124,994	67,628	54.1	33,345	26.7	24,021	19.2
Norwegian	345,522	192,959	55.8	91,258	26.4	61,305	17.7
Dutch	133,142	79,991	60.1	31,854	23.9	21,297	16.0
Danish	178,944	106,387	59.5	41,798	23.4	30,759	17.2
Czech	201,138	133,706	66.5	39,160	19.5	28,272	14.1
Portuguese	110,197	79,622	72.3	18,563	16.8	12,012	10.9
Swedish	615,465	421,792	68.5	101,728	16.5	91,945	14.9
German	2,188,006	1,576,486	72.1	317,358	14.5	294,162	13.4
Slovak	240,196	171,907	71.6	17,338	7.2	50,951	21.2
French	523,297	408,597	78.1	35,162	6.7	79,538	15.2
Polish	965,899	810,545	83.9	58,936	6.1	96,418	10.0
English and Celtic	3,097,021	2,540,843	82.0	162,360	5.2	393,818	12.7
Magyar	250,393	205,221	82.0	13,103	5.2	32,069	12.8
Lithuanian	165,053	140,428	85.1	7,530	4.6	17,086	10.4
Spanish	126,288	107,740	85.3	5,504	4.4	13,044	10.3
Russian	315,721	274,912	87.1	13,691	4.3	27,118	8.6
Italian	1,808,289	1,584,297	87.6	53,683	3.0	170,309	9.4
Greek	189,066	172,814	91.4	2,623	1.4	13,629	7.2
Yiddish	1,222,658	1,203,659	98.4	4,532	0.4	14,467	1.2

344

POPULATION

FOREIGN-BORN WHITE POPULATION OF THE UNITED STATES BY PRINCIPAL MOTHER TONGUES:
1930, 1920, AND 1910

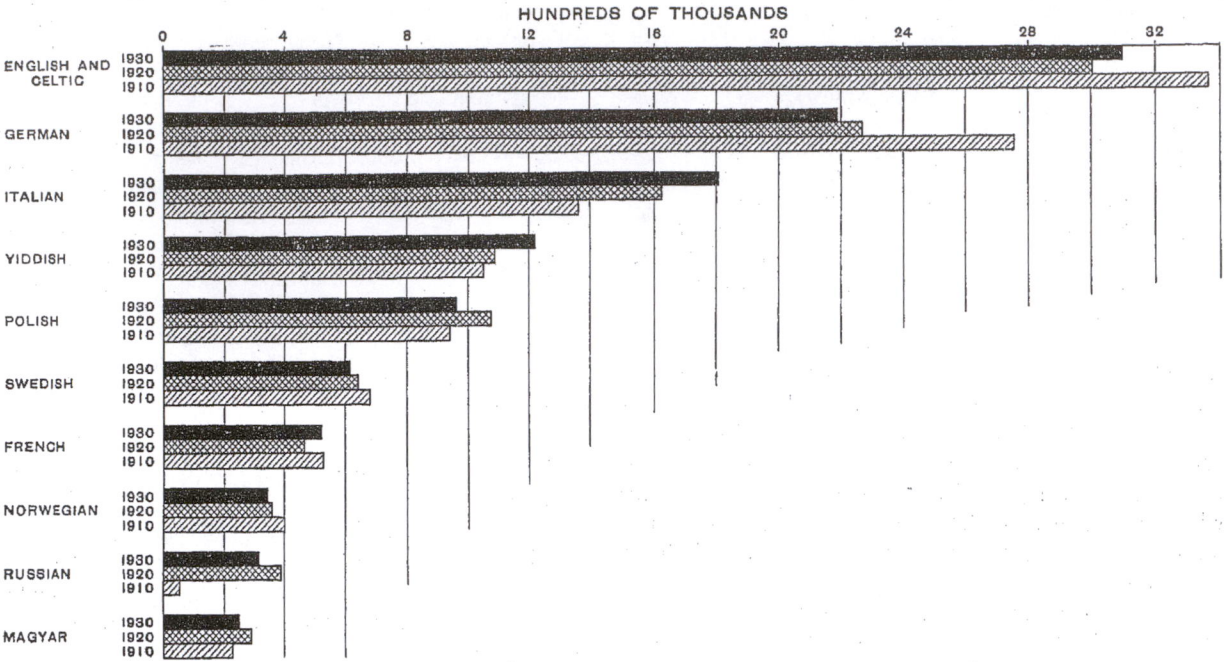

FOREIGN-BORN WHITE POPULATION OF THE UNITED STATES BY MOTHER TONGUE: 1930

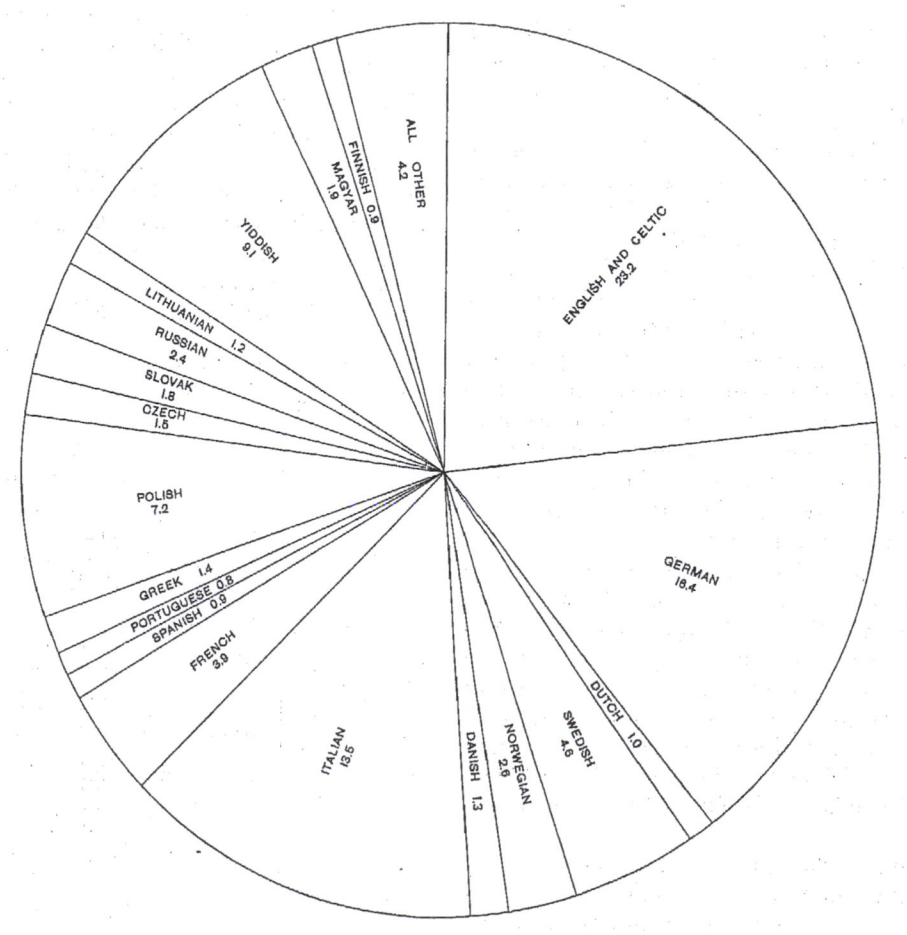

MOTHER TONGUE OF THE FOREIGN-BORN WHITE POPULATION   345

DISTRIBUTION OF FOREIGN-BORN WHITE POPULATION HAVING SPECIFIED MOTHER TONGUE, FOR
SELECTED STATES: 1930 AND 1920

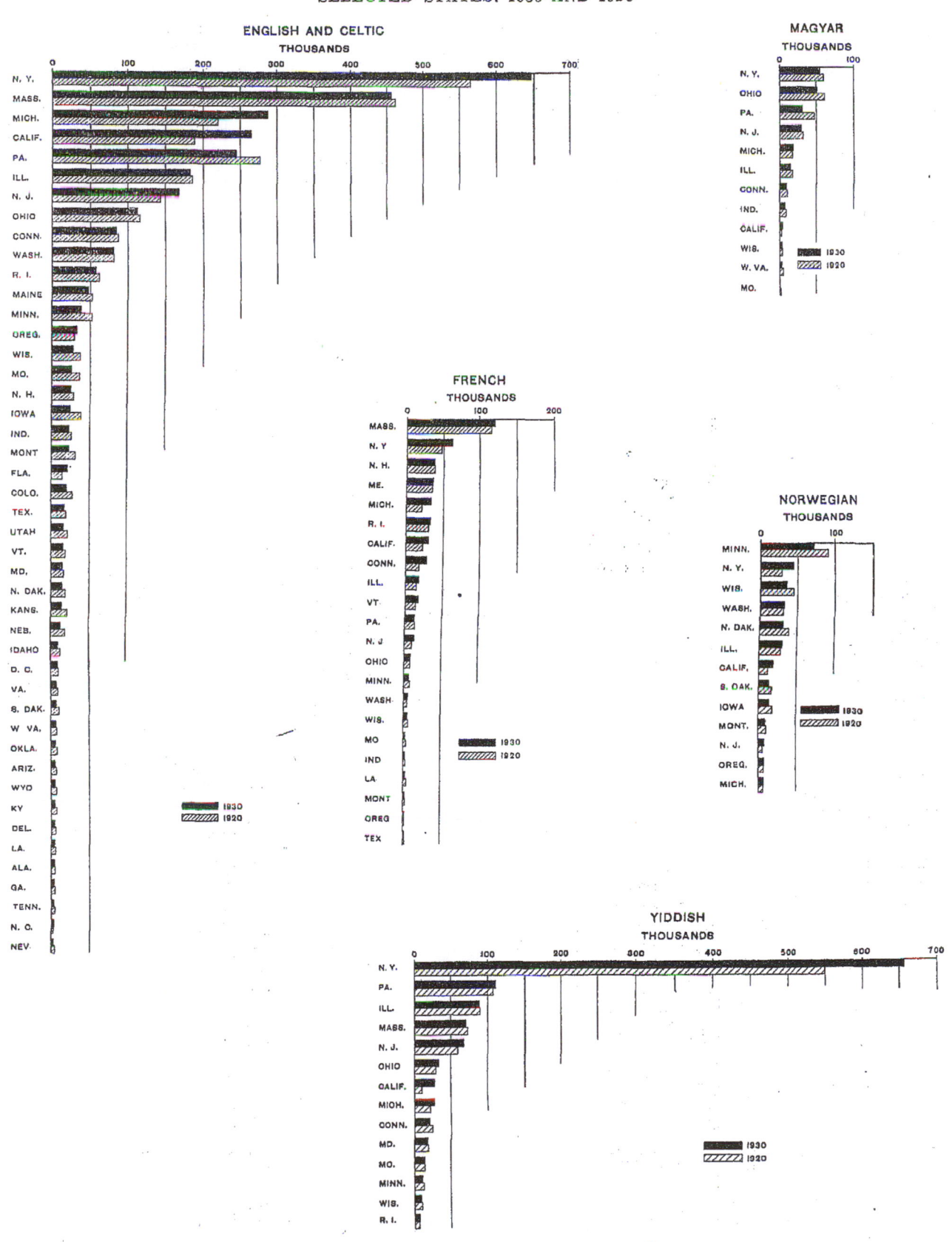

346   POPULATION

DISTRIBUTION OF FOREIGN-BORN WHITE POPULATION HAVING SPECIFIED MOTHER TONGUE, FOR
SELECTED STATES: 1930 AND 1920—Continued

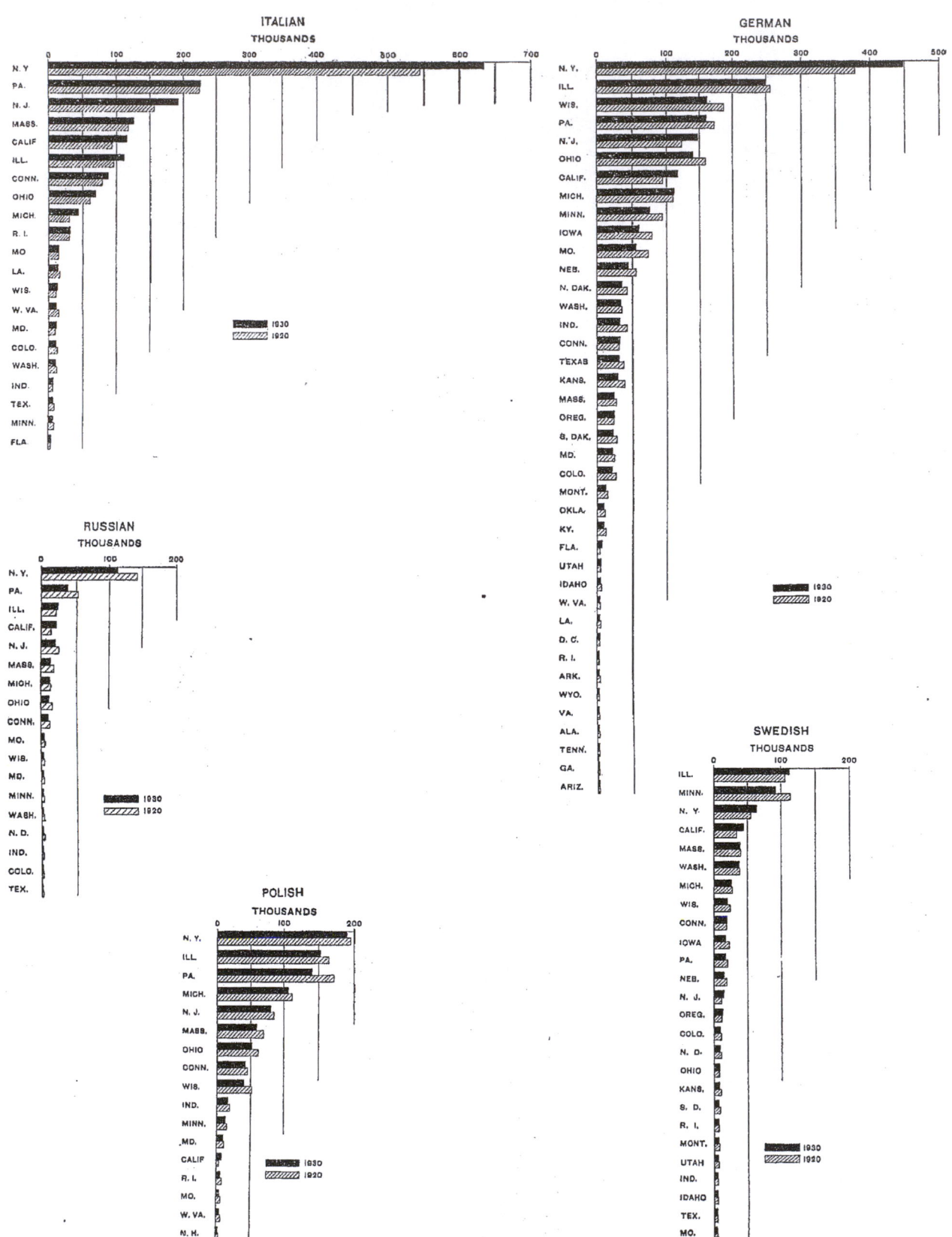

MOTHER TONGUE OF THE FOREIGN-BORN WHITE POPULATION　　347

TABLE 4.—MOTHER TONGUE OF THE FOREIGN-BORN WHITE POPULATION OF THE UNITED STATES, BY SEX: 1930, 1920, AND 1910

[Figures for 1920 and 1910 have been adjusted by deducting from the total, and from Spanish mother tongue, the estimated number of persons (457,360 in 1920; 211,233 in 1910) who would have been classified as Mexicans in 1930. Per cent not shown where less than 0.1. A minus sign (−) denotes decrease]

MOTHER TONGUE	TOTAL FOREIGN-BORN WHITE						INCREASE				MALE			FEMALE		
	Number			Per cent			1920 to 1930		1910 to 1920							
	1930	1920	1910	1930	1920	1910	Number	Per cent	Number	Per cent	1930	1920	1910	1930	1920	1910
Total	13,366,407	13,255,394	13,134,312	100.0	100.0	100.0	111,013	0.8	121,082	0.9	7,153,709	7,269,191	7,393,922	6,212,698	5,986,203	5,740,390
English and Celtic	3,097,021	3,007,932	3,363,792	23.2	22.7	25.6	89,089	3.0	−355,860	−10.6	1,483,363	1,454,967	1,669,857	1,613,658	1,552,965	1,693,935
Germanic:																
German	2,188,006	2,267,128	2,759,032	16.4	17.1	21.0	−79,122	−3.5	−491,904	−17.8	1,153,415	1,209,610	1,493,487	1,034,591	1,057,518	1,265,545
Dutch	133,142	136,540	126,045	1.0	1.0	1.0	−3,398	−2.5	10,495	8.3	77,409	78,243	71,651	55,733	58,297	54,394
Flemish	42,263	45,696	25,780	0.3	0.3	0.2	−3,433	−7.5	19,916	77.3	23,707	26,620	16,232	18,556	19,076	9,548
Scandinavian:																
Swedish	615,465	643,203	683,218	4.6	4.9	5.2	−27,738	−4.3	−40,015	−5.9	344,403	354,830	380,619	271,062	288,373	302,599
Norwegian	345,522	362,199	402,587	2.6	2.7	3.1	−16,677	−4.6	−40,388	−10.0	195,131	201,778	229,441	150,391	160,421	173,146
Danish	178,944	187,162	183,844	1.3	1.4	1.4	−8,218	−4.4	3,318	1.8	109,550	113,150	110,507	69,394	74,012	73,337
Icelandic	2,714	2,369	2,501				345	14.6	−132	−5.3	1,339	1,161	1,213	1,375	1,208	1,288
Latin and Greek:																
Italian	1,808,289	1,624,998	1,365,110	13.5	12.3	10.4	183,291	11.3	259,888	19.0	1,053,056	967,394	896,100	755,233	657,604	469,010
French	523,297	466,956	528,842	3.9	3.5	4.0	56,341	12.1	−61,886	−11.7	262,446	240,400	281,174	260,851	226,556	247,668
Spanish	126,288	98,751	46,898	0.9	0.7	0.4	27,537	27.9	51,853	110.0	80,358	65,864	31,446	45,930	32,887	15,452
Portuguese	110,197	105,895	72,649	0.8	0.8	0.6	4,302	4.1	33,246	45.8	64,306	60,279	42,630	45,891	45,616	30,019
Rumanian	56,964	62,336	42,277	0.4	0.5	0.3	−5,372	−8.6	20,059	47.4	33,111	38,841	31,661	23,853	23,495	10,616
Greek	189,066	174,658	118,379	1.4	1.3	0.9	14,408	8.2	56,279	47.5	138,780	142,477	108,922	50,286	32,181	9,457
Slavic and Lettic:																
Polish	965,899	1,077,392	943,781	7.2	8.1	7.2	−111,493	−10.3	133,611	14.2	524,243	614,876	571,255	441,656	462,516	372,526
Czech	201,138	234,564	228,738	1.5	1.8	1.7	−33,426	−14.3	5,826	2.5	101,425	121,482	120,225	99,713	113,082	108,513
Slovak	240,196	274,948	166,474	1.8	2.1	1.3	−34,752	−12.6	108,474	65.2	129,357	160,617	107,506	110,839	114,331	58,968
Russian	315,721	392,049	57,926	2.4	3.0	0.4	−76,328	−19.5	334,123	576.8	181,215	232,168	35,742	134,506	159,881	22,184
Ruthenian [1]	9,800 }	55,072	25,131	0.1 }	0.4	0.2	12,813	23.0	30,541	121.5	5,350 } 32,312	33,254	17,733	4,450 } 26,373	22,418	7,398
Ukrainian [1]	58,656 }			0.4 }												
Slovenian	77,671	[2] 80,437	123,631	0.6	0.6	0.9	−2,766	−3.4	−43,194	−34.9	46,989	50,781	83,954	30,682	29,656	39,677
Croatian	70,802	85,175	78,380	0.5	0.6	0.6	−5,373	−6.3	6,795	8.7	51,608	61,424	63,102	28,134	23,751	15,278
Serbian	30,121	40,669	27,289	0.2	0.3	0.2	−10,548	−25.9	13,380	49.0	21,076	29,086	23,592	9,045	11,583	3,697
Bulgarian	12,128	12,853	18,341	0.1	0.1	0.1	−725	−5.6	−5,488	−29.9	9,676	11,828	17,063	2,452	1,025	1,288
Wendish	1,372	[3] 2,039	1,460				−667	−32.7	579	39.7	672	1,061	884	700	978	576
Lithuanian [4]	195,053 }	182,227	140,963	1.2 } 0.1	1.4	1.1	−9,584	−5.3	41,264	29.3	96,164 } 4,383	112,557	94,277	68,889 } 3,207	69,670	46,686
Lettish [4]	7,500 }			0.1 }												
Unclassified:																
Yiddish	1,222,658	1,091,820	1,051,707	9.1	8.2	8.0	130,838	12.0	40,053	3.8	621,809	570,030	553,836	600,849	521,790	497,871
Magyar	250,393	[2] 290,419	229,094	1.9	2.2	1.7	−40,026	−13.8	61,325	26.8	129,775	161,140	140,671	120,618	129,279	88,423
Finnish	124,094	132,543	119,948	0.9	1.0	0.9	−7,549	−5.7	12,595	10.5	67,796	75,588	73,549	57,198	56,955	46,399
Estonian	2,809	1,024	138				1,785	174.3	886	642.0	1,920	742	102	889	282	36
Armenian	51,741	37,647	23,038	0.4	0.3	0.2	14,094	37.4	13,709	57.3	30,295	26,023	16,679	21,446	11,624	7,259
Arabic	67,830	57,557	32,868	0.5	0.4	0.3	10,273	17.8	24,089	75.1	39,978	35,492	20,689	27,852	22,065	12,179
Turkish	10,457	6,627	4,709	0.1			3,830	57.8	1,918	40.7	6,911	5,253	4,172	3,546	1,374	537
Albanian	7,586	5,515	2,312	0.1			2,071	37.6	3,203	138.5	6,504	4,818	2,275	1,082	697	37
All other	3,352	1,228	646				2,124	173.0	582	90.1	2,369	900	577	983	319	69
Unknown	42,233	7,166	135,824	0.3	0.1	1.0	35,067	489.4	−128,658	−94.7	22,348	4,448	81,049	19,885	2,718	54,775

[1] Ukrainian included with Ruthenian in 1920 and 1910.
[2] Corrected figures.
[3] Reported as "Slavic, not specified" in 1920, but practically all Wendish.
[4] Lettish included with Lithuanian in 1920 and 1910.

119652—33——23

POPULATION

TABLE 5.—MOTHER TONGUE OF THE FOREIGN-BORN WHITE POPULATION OF THE UNITED STATES, BY SEX, FOR URBAN, RURAL-FARM, AND RURAL-NONFARM AREAS: 1930

[Per cent not shown where less than 0.1]

MOTHER TONGUE	URBAN				RURAL-FARM				RURAL-NONFARM			
	Total		Male	Female	Total		Male	Female	Total		Male	Female
	Number	Per cent			Number	Per cent			Number	Per cent		
Total	10,726,859	100.0	5,642,087	5,084,772	1,084,087	100.0	631,169	452,918	1,555,461	100.0	880,453	675,008
English and Celtic	2,540,843	23.7	1,192,764	1,348,079	162,360	15.0	90,132	72,228	393,818	25.3	200,467	193,351
Germanic:												
German	1,576,486	14.7	810,586	765,900	317,358	29.3	183,538	133,820	294,162	18.9	159,201	134,871
Dutch	79,991	0.7	45,941	34,050	31,854	2.9	19,134	12,720	21,297	1.4	12,334	8,963
Flemish	31,689	0.3	17,398	14,291	6,743	0.6	4,058	2,685	3,831	0.2	2,251	1,580
Scandinavian:												
Swedish	421,792	3.9	228,443	193,349	101,728	9.4	61,245	40,483	91,945	5.9	54,715	37,230
Norwegian	192,959	1.8	106,176	86,783	91,258	8.4	53,446	37,812	61,305	3.9	35,509	25,796
Danish	106,387	1.0	63,990	42,397	41,798	3.9	26,729	15,069	30,750	2.0	18,831	11,928
Icelandic	1,215	------	588	627	835	0.1	425	410	664	------	326	338
Latin and Greek:												
Italian	1,584,297	14.8	913,261	671,036	53,683	5.0	33,388	20,295	170,309	10.9	106,407	63,902
French	408,597	3.8	199,203	209,394	35,162	3.2	20,726	14,436	79,538	5.1	42,517	37,021
Spanish	107,740	1.0	67,765	39,975	5,504	0.5	3,707	1,797	13,044	0.8	8,886	4,158
Portuguese	79,622	0.7	45,204	34,418	18,563	1.7	11,676	6,887	12,012	0.8	7,426	4,586
Rumanian	51,086	0.5	29,229	21,857	1,836	0.2	1,153	683	4,042	0.3	2,729	1,313
Greek	172,814	1.6	125,435	47,379	2,623	0.2	2,073	550	13,629	0.9	11,272	2,357
Slavic and Lettic:												
Polish	810,545	7.6	434,625	375,920	58,936	5.4	33,218	25,718	96,418	6.2	56,400	40,018
Czech	133,706	1.2	65,484	68,222	39,160	3.6	21,207	17,953	28,272	1.8	14,734	13,538
Slovak	171,907	1.6	91,112	80,795	17,338	1.6	9,485	7,853	50,951	3.3	28,760	22,191
Russian	274,912	2.6	155,143	119,769	13,691	1.3	8,239	5,452	27,118	1.7	17,833	9,285
Ruthenian	6,667	0.1	3,592	3,075	506	------	284	222	2,627	0.2	1,474	1,153
Ukrainian	48,132	0.4	26,463	21,669	3,494	0.3	1,880	1,614	7,059	0.5	3,969	3,090
Slovenian	52,981	0.5	31,395	21,586	5,692	0.5	3,365	2,327	18,998	1.2	12,229	6,769
Croatian	57,915	0.5	37,431	20,484	3,652	0.3	2,205	1,447	18,235	1.2	12,032	6,203
Serbian	23,014	0.2	15,880	7,134	1,124	0.1	751	373	5,983	0.4	4,445	1,538
Bulgarian	9,725	0.1	7,632	2,093	758	0.1	579	179	1,645	0.1	1,465	180
Wendish	1,198	------	584	614	71	------	37	34	103	------	51	52
Lithuanian	140,428	1.3	80,817	59,611	7,539	0.7	4,594	2,945	17,086	1.1	10,753	6,333
Lettish	6,094	0.1	3,478	2,616	679	0.1	391	288	817	0.1	514	303
Unclassified:												
Yiddish	1,203,659	11.2	611,264	592,395	4,532	0.4	2,451	2,081	14,467	0.9	8,094	6,373
Magyar	205,221	1.9	104,268	100,953	13,103	1.2	7,270	5,833	32,069	2.1	18,237	13,832
Finnish	67,628	0.6	34,834	32,794	33,345	3.1	18,482	14,863	24,021	1.5	14,480	9,541
Estonian	2,283	------	1,563	720	247	------	152	95	279	------	205	74
Armenian	46,561	0.4	27,178	19,383	2,970	0.3	1,692	1,278	2,210	0.1	1,425	785
Arabic	61,505	0.6	35,940	25,565	1,342	0.1	867	475	4,983	0.3	3,171	1,812
Turkish	9,690	0.1	6,311	3,379	151	------	103	48	616	------	497	119
Albanian	7,041	0.1	5,163	1,878	55	------	41	14	490	------	400	90
All other	2,269	------	1,568	701	587	0.1	457	130	496	------	344	152
Unknown	28,260	0.3	14,379	13,881	3,810	0.4	1,989	1,821	10,163	0.7	5,980	4,183

MOTHER TONGUE OF THE FOREIGN-BORN WHITE POPULATION 349

TABLE 6.—MOTHER TONGUE OF THE FOREIGN-BORN WHITE POPULATION BY COUNTRY OF BIRTH, FOR THE UNITED STATES: 1930 AND 1920

[Per cent not shown where less than 0.1]

MOTHER TONGUE AND COUNTRY OF BIRTH	1930 Number	1930 Per cent	1920 Number	1920 Per cent
English and Celtic	3,097,021	100.0	3,007,932	100.0
Canada	880,754	28.4	789,347	26.2
England	794,568	25.7	797,358	26.5
Irish Free State	744,280	24.0	} 1,035,944	34.4
Northern Ireland	178,660	5.8		
Scotland	352,800	11.4	252,994	8.4
Wales	60,111	1.9	66,914	2.2
Newfoundland	23,652	0.8	13,075	0.4
West Indies	13,605	0.4	11,364	0.4
Australia	11,638	0.4	9,838	0.3
Other countries	36,953	1.2	31,008	1.0
GERMANIC:				
German	2,188,006	100.0	2,267,128	100.0
Germany	1,587,052	72.5	1,641,482	72.4
Austria	191,715	8.8	201,603	8.9
Russia	103,371	4.7	116,535	5.1
Switzerland	87,073	4.0	97,087	4.3
Hungary	48,198	2.2	76,845	3.4
Poland	31,844	1.5	38,170	1.7
Czechoslovakia	30,900	1.4	16,446	0.7
Rumania	28,640	1.3	8,107	0.4
Yugoslavia	23,403	1.1	7,787	0.3
France	14,370	0.7	21,997	1.0
Canada	9,818	0.4	11,136	0.5
Luxemburg	7,927	0.4	10,844	0.5
Other countries	23,689	1.1	19,020	0.8
Dutch	133,142	100.0	136,540	100.0
Netherlands	128,774	96.7	128,905	94.4
Belgium	833	0.6	2,383	1.7
Germany	702	0.5	1,614	1.2
Canada	632	0.5	687	0.5
Russia	349	0.3	290	0.2
Africa	279	0.2	285	0.2
West Indies	270	0.2	204	0.2
Pacific islands	258	0.2	191	0.1
Other countries	1,045	0.8	1,801	1.4
Flemish	42,263	100.0	45,696	100.0
Belgium	40,950	96.9	44,776	98.0
Netherlands	490	1.2	252	0.6
France	245	0.6	249	0.5
Canada	148	0.3	104	0.2
Switzerland	107	0.3	18	
Other countries	322	0.8	297	0.6
SCANDINAVIAN:				
Swedish	615,465	100.0	643,203	100.0
Sweden	590,901	96.0	621,545	96.6
Finland	18,730	3.0	17,721	2.8
Norway	2,635	0.4	1,546	0.2
Denmark	1,018	0.2	619	0.1
Canada	986	0.2	658	0.1
Other countries	1,195	0.2	1,114	0.2
Norwegian	345,522	100.0	362,199	100.0
Norway	343,176	99.3	360,754	99.6
Canada	685	0.2	462	0.1
Sweden	639	0.2	308	0.1
Other countries	1,022	0.3	675	0.2
Danish	178,944	100.0	[1] 189,531	100.0
Denmark	175,735	98.2	185,564	97.9
Germany	1,371	0.8	2,589	1.4
Norway	480	0.3	269	0.1
Sweden	367	0.2	197	0.1
Other countries	991	0.6	912	0.5
Icelandic	2,714	100.0	(1)	--------
Iceland	2,420	89.2	--------	--------
Canada	233	8.6	--------	--------
Other countries	61	2.2	--------	--------
LATIN AND GREEK:				
Italian	1,808,289	100.0	1,624,998	100.0
Italy	1,779,698	98.4	1,604,492	98.7
Switzerland	10,339	0.6	7,527	0.5
South America	5,733	0.3	2,580	0.2
France	2,936	0.2	1,918	0.1
Austria	2,825	0.2	4,258	0.3
Other countries	6,758	0.4	4,223	0.3
French	523,297	100.0	466,956	100.0
Canada	370,852	70.9	307,790	65.9
France	113,967	21.8	125,589	26.9
Belgium	18,424	3.5	12,793	2.7
Switzerland	13,161	2.5	12,605	2.7
Luxemburg	841	0.2	1,283	0.3
Italy	826	0.2	466	0.1
Other countries	5,226	1.0	6,430	1.4

MOTHER TONGUE AND COUNTRY OF BIRTH	1930 Number	1930 Per cent	1920 Number	1920 Per cent
LATIN AND GREEK—Continued.				
Spanish	126,288	100.0	[2] 98,751	100.0
Spain	57,098	45.2	48,535	49.1
Mexico	21,227	16.8	[2] 19,258	19.5
West Indies	16,482	13.1	13,125	13.3
South America	15,263	12.1	8,263	8.4
Central America	6,217	4.9	3,228	3.3
Turkey in Asia	5,232	4.1	212	0.2
Greece	1,012	0.8	3,188	3.2
Italy	777	0.6	142	0.1
Yugoslavia	307	0.3	79	0.1
Portugal	346	0.3	165	0.2
Turkey in Europe	309	0.2	1,313	1.3
Atlantic islands	220	0.2	182	0.2
France	213	0.2	188	0.2
Other countries	1,585	1.2	878	0.9
Portuguese	110,197	100.0	105,895	100.0
Portugal	69,423	63.0	66,726	63.0
Atlantic Islands	37,549	34.1	37,314	35.2
South America	2,795	2.5	1,419	1.3
Other countries	430	0.4	436	0.4
Rumanian	56,964	100.0	62,336	100.0
Rumania	53,452	93.8	51,082	82.0
Yugoslavia	567	1.0	220	0.4
Hungary	548	1.0	4,646	7.5
Austria	482	0.8	4,399	7.1
Canada	394	0.7	188	0.3
Albania	381	0.7	98	0.2
Greece	285	0.5	383	0.6
Russia	200	0.4	164	0.3
Czechoslovakia	113	0.2	44	0.1
Turkey in Asia	112	0.2	100	0.2
Other countries	424	0.7	412	0.7
Greek	189,066	100.0	174,658	100.0
Greece	169,646	89.7	168,276	96.3
Turkey in Asia	11,409	6.1	1,451	0.8
Italy	1,493	0.8	135	0.1
Albania	1,094	0.6	187	0.1
Turkey in Europe	744	0.4	2,034	1.2
Yugoslavia	682	0.4	194	0.1
Africa	379	0.2	197	0.1
Austria	309	0.2	684	0.4
Bulgaria	288	0.2	184	0.1
Other countries	2,932	1.6	1,416	0.8
SLAVIC AND LETTIC:				
Polish	965,899	100.0	1,077,392	100.0
Poland	918,070	95.0	922,812	85.7
Russia	14,895	1.5	72,065	6.7
Austria	9,827	1.0	43,018	4.0
Germany	9,294	1.0	27,853	2.6
Lithuania	3,824	0.4	1,840	0.2
Czechoslovakia	3,437	0.4	1,537	0.1
Canada	2,141	0.2	978	0.1
Other countries	4,411	0.5	6,689	0.6
Czech	201,138	100.0	234,564	100.0
Czechoslovakia	188,960	93.9	190,868	81.4
Austria	5,478	2.7	38,820	16.5
Poland	1,971	1.0	404	0.2
Yugoslavia	1,595	0.8	637	0.3
Russia	788	0.4	908	0.4
Hungary	777	0.4	1,287	0.5
Germany	542	0.3	700	0.3
Other countries	1,027	0.5	940	0.4
Slovak	240,196	100.0	274,948	100.0
Czechoslovakia	219,347	91.3	133,179	48.4
Yugoslavia	8,309	3.5	13,815	5.0
Austria	5,710	2.4	90,370	32.9
Hungary	2,394	1.0	28,771	10.5
Poland	2,240	0.9	4,730	1.7
Russia	584	0.2	1,730	0.6
Other countries	1,612	0.7	2,353	0.9
Russian	315,721	100.0	392,049	100.0
Russia	262,781	83.2	[3] 361,843	92.3
Poland	26,797	8.5	8,781	2.2
Czechoslovakia	6,538	2.1	928	0.2
Austria	6,310	2.0	12,117	3.1
Lithuania	2,914	0.9	1,167	0.3
Latvia	1,827	0.6	(3)	--------
Rumania	1,791	0.6	936	0.2
Canada	1,245	0.4	984	0.3
England	700	0.2	1,327	0.3
Other countries	4,818	1.5	3,976	1.0

[1] Icelandic (2,369) included with Danish in 1920; can not be separated by country of birth.
[2] Adjusted figures. The foreign-born white population as classified in 1920 included 457,360 persons who would have been counted as Mexican in 1930. These have been subtracted from the white persons born in Mexico of Spanish mother tongue.
[3] Latvia included with Russia in 1920.

POPULATION

TABLE 6.—MOTHER TONGUE OF THE FOREIGN-BORN WHITE POPULATION BY COUNTRY OF BIRTH, FOR THE UNITED STATES: 1930 AND 1920—Continued

MOTHER TONGUE AND COUNTRY OF BIRTH	1930 Number	1930 Per cent	1920 Number	1920 Per cent
SLAVIC AND LETTIC—Continued.				
Ruthenian	9,800	100.0	[4]55,672	100.0
Czechoslovakia	7,218	73.7	3,228	5.8
Poland	1,580	16.1	43,534	78.2
Russia	536	5.5	545	1.0
Austria	217	2.2	7,452	13.4
Other countries	249	2.5	913	1.6
Ukrainian	58,685	100.0	([4])	
Poland	38,582	65.7		
Russia	11,689	19.9		
Austria	5,127	8.7		
Canada	1,097	1.9		
Czechoslovakia	827	1.4		
Rumania	543	0.9		
Yugoslavia	221	0.4		
Other countries	599	1.0		
Slovenian	77,671	100.0	80,437	100.0
Yugoslavia	66,793	86.0	46,388	57.7
Austria	3,969	5.1	22,304	27.7
Italy	3,301	4.2	490	0.6
Czechoslovakia	2,417	3.1	5,678	7.1
Germany	265	0.3	305	0.4
Hungary	259	0.3	3,290	4.1
Poland	127	0.2	605	0.8
Russia	121	0.2	547	0.7
Other countries	419	0.5	830	1.0
Croatian	79,802	100.0	85,175	100.0
Yugoslavia	72,138	90.4	61,969	72.8
Austria	3,902	4.9	18,201	21.4
Italy	1,348	1.7	516	0.6
Czechoslovakia	1,279	1.6	683	0.8
Hungary	430	0.5	2,790	3.3
Poland	172	0.2	224	0.3
Other countries	533	0.7	792	0.9
Serbian	30,121	100.0	40,689	100.0
Yugoslavia	27,663	91.8	32,145	79.0
Austria	747	2.5	5,827	14.3
Czechoslovakia	423	1.4	225	0.6
Rumania	378	1.3	89	0.2
Hungary	220	0.7	1,676	4.1
Other countries	690	2.3	707	1.7
Bulgarian	12,128	100.0	12,853	100.0
Bulgaria	8,112	66.9	9,462	73.6
Greece	2,215	18.3	2,651	20.6
Yugoslavia	1,086	9.0	129	1.0
Rumania	132	1.1	42	0.3
Turkey in Asia	109	0.9	35	0.3
Other countries	474	3.9	534	4.2
Wendish	1,372	100.0	2,039	100.0
Yugoslavia	717	52.3	}1,618	79.4
Hungary	431	31.4		
Austria	116	8.5	343	16.8
Other countries	108	7.9	78	3.8
Lithuanian	165,053	100.0	[5]182,227	100.0
Lithuania	156,152	94.6	126,441	69.4
Russia	5,416	3.3	[3]49,140	27.0
Poland	1,242	0.8	3,446	1.9
Scotland	507	0.3	415	0.2
Latvia	464	0.3	([3])	
England	386	0.3	404	0.2
Other countries	886	0.5	2,381	1.3
Lettish	7,590	100.0	([5])	
Latvia	5,977	78.7		
Russia	813	10.7		
Lithuania	622	8.2		
Other countries	178	2.3		
UNCLASSIFIED AND UNKNOWN:				
Yiddish	1,222,658	100.0	1,091,820	100.0
Russia	743,307	60.8	[3]791,181	72.5
Poland	243,825	19.9	114,362	10.5
Austria	96,052	7.9	99,279	9.1
Rumania	49,508	4.0	37,287	3.4
Lithuania	25,886	2.1	4,971	0.5
Hungary	16,255	1.3	16,964	1.6
England	9,480	0.8	9,845	0.9
Latvia	8,803	0.7	([3])	
Czechoslovakia	7,637	0.6	2,024	0.2
Canada	5,146	0.4	2,687	0.2
Palestine	4,150	0.3	1,588	0.1
Germany	3,494	0.3	3,100	0.3
Other countries	9,115	0.7	8,552	0.8

MOTHER TONGUE AND COUNTRY OF BIRTH	1930 Number	1930 Per cent	1920 Number	1920 Per cent
UNCLASSIFIED AND UNKNOWN—Con.				
Magyar	250,393	100.0	290,419	100.0
Hungary	202,875	81.0	253,780	87.4
Czechoslovakia	19,863	7.9	6,682	2.3
Austria	12,390	4.9	22,325	7.7
Rumania	8,830	3.5	2,606	0.9
Yugoslavia	4,506	1.8	2,678	0.9
Poland	474	0.2	817	0.3
Other countries	1,455	0.6	1,531	0.5
Finnish	124,994	100.0	[6]133,567	100.0
Finland	122,710	98.2	130,808	97.9
Sweden	855	0.7	580	0.4
Canada	565	0.5	388	0.3
Norway	304	0.3	313	0.2
Other countries	470	0.4	1,478	1.1
Estonian	2,809	100.0	([6])	
Estonia	2,422	86.2		
Russia	255	9.1		
Other countries	132	4.7		
Armenian	51,741	100.0	37,647	100.0
Armenia	30,059	58.1	35,321	93.8
Turkey in Asia	17,206	33.3	524	1.4
Syria	730	1.4	131	0.3
Russia	687	1.3	471	1.3
Turkey in Europe	576	1.1	391	1.0
Africa	232	0.4	78	0.2
Bulgaria	168	0.3	51	0.1
Greece	108	0.2	55	0.1
Other countries	1,075	2.1	625	1.7
Arabic	67,830	100.0	57,557	100.0
Syria	55,506	81.8	50,727	88.1
Palestine	1,430	2.1	1,183	2.1
Turkey in Asia	1,098	1.6	1,656	2.9
Africa	629	0.9	495	0.9
France	305	0.4	37	0.1
Canada	257	0.4	139	0.2
South America	218	0.3	96	0.2
Mexico	151	0.2	77	0.1
Yugoslavia	146	0.2	160	0.3
West Indies	125	0.2	32	0.1
Russia	115	0.2	40	0.1
Other countries	7,850	11.6	2,915	5.1
Turkish	10,457	100.0	6,627	100.0
Turkey in Asia	9,166	87.7	5,326	80.4
Armenia	290	2.8	263	4.0
Turkey in Europe	283	2.7	416	6.3
Greece	156	1.5	223	3.4
Syria	107	1.0	107	1.6
Other countries	455	4.4	292	4.4
Albanian	7,586	100.0	5,515	100.0
Albania	7,114	93.8	5,086	92.2
Italy	148	2.0	118	2.1
Greece	122	1.6	119	2.2
Other countries	202	2.7	192	3.5
All other	3,352	100.0	1,228	100.0
Spain	631	18.8		
Africa	257	7.7	173	14.1
France	233	7.0		
India	201	6.0	8	0.7
Other countries	2,030	60.6	1,047	85.3
Unknown	42,233	100.0	7,166	100.0
Austria	24,201	57.3	1,327	18.5
Russia	4,421	10.5	[7]507	7.1
Europe not specified	4,159	9.8	343	4.8
Czechoslovakia	1,672	4.0	42	0.6
Yugoslavia	1,166	2.8	203	2.8
Switzerland	990	2.3	90	1.3
Germany	887	2.1	300	4.2
Country not specified	832	2.0	1,196	16.7
At sea	533	1.3	199	2.8
Rumania	491	1.2		
Lithuania	457	1.1		
Belgium	379	0.9	72	1.0
Asia, not specified	308	0.7	78	1.1
Latvia	242	0.6	([7])	
Turkey in Asia	216	0.5	103	1.4
Africa	193	0.5	115	1.6
Estonia	193	0.5	([7])	
Hungary	168	0.4	369	5.1
South America	141	0.3	348	4.9
Poland	104	0.2	662	9.2
Other countries	480	1.1	1,212	16.9

[3] Latvia included with Russia in 1920.
[4] Ukrainian included with Ruthenian in 1920.
[5] Lettish included with Lithuanian in 1920.
[6] Estonian (1,024) included with Finnish in 1920; can not be separated by country of birth.
[7] Latvia and Estonia included with Russia in 1920.

MOTHER TONGUE OF THE FOREIGN-BORN WHITE POPULATION   351

TABLE 7.—COUNTRY OF BIRTH OF THE FOREIGN-BORN WHITE POPULATION BY MOTHER TONGUE, FOR THE UNITED STATES: 1930 AND 1920

[Per cent not shown where less than 0.1]

COUNTRY OF BIRTH AND MOTHER TONGUE	1930 Number	1930 Per cent	1920 Number	1920 Per cent
NORTHWESTERN EUROPE				
England	808,672	100.0	812,828	100.0
English and Celtic	794,568	98.3	797,358	98.1
Yiddish	9,480	1.2	9,845	1.2
German	1,230	0.2	1,488	0.2
All other	3,394	0.4	4,137	0.5
Scotland	354,323	100.0	254,567	100.0
English and Celtic	352,800	99.6	252,994	99.4
All other	1,523	0.4	1,573	0.6
Wales	60,205	100.0	67,066	100.0
English and Celtic	60,111	99.8	66,914	99.8
All other	94	0.2	152	0.2
Northern Ireland	178,832	100.0	(1)	------
English and Celtic	178,660	99.9		
All other	172	0.1		
Irish Free State	744,810	100.0	(1)	------
English and Celtic	744,280	99.9		
All other	530	0.1		
Ireland	923,642	100.0	1,037,233	100.0
English and Celtic	922,940	99.9	1,035,944	99.9
All other	702	0.1	1,289	0.1
Norway	347,852	100.0	363,862	100.0
Norwegian	343,176	98.7	360,754	99.1
Swedish	2,635	0.8	1,546	0.4
English and Celtic	838	0.2	624	0.2
All other	1,203	0.3	938	0.3
Sweden	595,250	100.0	625,580	100.0
Swedish	590,901	99.3	621,545	99.4
English and Celtic	1,469	0.2	1,221	0.2
All other	2,880	0.5	2,814	0.4
Denmark	179,474	100.0	[2] 189,154	100.0
Danish	175,735	97.9	185,564	98.1
German	1,427	0.8	1,487	0.8
Swedish	1,018	0.6	619	0.3
English and Celtic	657	0.4	551	0.3
All other	637	0.4	933	0.5
Iceland	2,764	100.0	(2)	------
Icelandic	2,420	87.6		
English and Celtic	124	4.5		
Norwegian	100	3.6		
All other	120	4.3		
Netherlands	133,133	100.0	131,766	100.0
Dutch	128,774	96.7	128,905	97.8
German	2,665	2.0	1,677	1.3
English and Celtic	720	0.5	372	0.3
Flemish	490	0.4	252	0.2
All other	484	0.4	560	0.4
Belgium	64,194	100.0	62,686	100.0
Flemish	40,956	63.8	44,776	71.4
French	18,424	28.7	12,703	20.4
German	2,509	3.9	1,910	3.0
Dutch	833	1.3	2,383	3.8
English and Celtic	511	0.8	381	0.6
Yiddish	196	0.3	131	0.2
All other	765	1.2	312	0.5
Luxemburg	9,048	100.0	12,585	100.0
German	7,927	87.6	10,844	86.2
French	841	9.3	1,283	10.2
All other	280	3.1	458	3.6
Switzerland	113,010	100.0	118,659	100.0
German	87,073	77.0	97,087	81.8
French	13,161	11.6	12,005	10.6
Italian	10,339	9.1	7,527	6.3
English and Celtic	815	0.7	693	0.6
All other	1,622	1.4	747	0.6
France	135,232	100.0	152,890	100.0
French	113,067	84.3	125,580	82.1
German	14,376	10.6	21,997	14.4
Italian	2,930	2.2	1,918	1.3
English and Celtic	1,174	0.9	1,072	0.7
Yiddish	1,057	0.8	897	0.6
Arabic	305	0.2	37	------
Flemish	245	0.2	249	0.2
Spanish	213	0.2	183	0.1
All other	959	0.7	948	0.6
CENTRAL EUROPE				
Germany	1,608,814	100.0	1,686,102	100.0
German	1,587,052	98.6	1,641,482	97.4
Polish	9,294	0.6	27,853	1.7
Yiddish	3,494	0.2	3,100	0.2
English and Celtic	2,435	0.2	3,917	0.2
All other	6,539	0.4	9,750	0.6
Poland	1,268,583	100.0	1,139,978	100.0
Polish	918,070	72.4	922,812	80.9
Yiddish	243,825	19.2	114,362	10.0
Ukrainian	38,582	3.0	} 43,534	3.8
Ruthenian	1,580	0.1	}	
German	31,844	2.5	38,170	3.3
Russian	26,797	2.1	8,781	0.8
Slovak	2,240	0.2	4,730	0.4
Czech	1,071	0.2	404	------
All other	3,674	0.3	7,176	0.6
Czechoslovakia	491,638	100.0	362,436	100.0
Slovak	219,347	44.6	133,179	30.7
Czech	188,960	38.4	190,808	52.7
German	30,900	6.3	16,446	4.5
Magyar	19,863	4.0	6,682	1.8
Yiddish	7,637	1.6	2,024	0.6
Ruthenian	7,218	1.5	} 3,228	0.9
Ukrainian	827	0.2	}	
Russian	6,538	1.3	928	0.3
Polish	3,437	0.7	1,537	0.4
Slovenian	2,417	0.5	5,678	1.6
Croatian	1,279	0.3	683	0.2
Serbian	423	0.1	225	0.1
All other	2,792	0.6	953	0.3
Austria	370,914	100.0	575,625	100.0
German	191,715	51.7	201,603	35.0
Yiddish	96,052	25.9	99,279	17.2
Magyar	12,390	3.3	22,325	3.9
Polish	9,827	2.6	43,618	7.6
Russian	6,310	1.7	12,117	2.1
Slovak	5,710	1.5	90,370	15.7
Czech	5,478	1.5	38,820	6.7
Ukrainian	5,127	1.4	} 7,452	1.3
Ruthenian	217	0.1	}	
Slovenian	3,960	1.1	22,304	3.9
Croatian	3,902	1.1	18,201	3.2
Italian	2,825	0.8	4,258	0.7
English and Celtic	834	0.2	1,039	0.2
Serbian	747	0.2	5,827	1.0
All other	25,811	7.0	8,412	1.5
Hungary	274,450	100.0	397,282	100.0
Magyar	202,875	73.9	253,780	63.9
German	48,198	17.6	76,845	19.3
Yiddish	16,255	5.9	16,964	4.3
Slovak	2,394	0.9	28,771	7.2
Polish	792	0.3	2,138	0.5
Czech	777	0.3	1,287	0.3
Rumanian	548	0.2	4,646	1.2
Wendish	431	0.2	1,615	0.4
Croatian	430	0.2	2,700	0.7
Russian	414	0.2	1,255	0.3
All other	1,336	0.5	7,101	1.8
Yugoslavia	211,416	100.0	169,437	100.0
Croatian	72,138	34.1	61,969	36.6
Slovenian	66,703	31.6	46,388	27.4
Serbian	27,663	13.1	32,145	19.0
German	23,403	11.1	7,787	4.6
Slovak	8,309	3.9	13,815	8.2
Magyar	4,508	2.1	2,678	1.6
Czech	1,595	0.8	637	0.4
Bulgarian	1,086	0.5	129	0.1
Wendish	717	0.3	3	------
Greek	682	0.3	194	0.1
Polish	577	0.3	809	0.5
Rumanian	507	0.3	220	0.1
Yiddish	433	0.2	645	0.4
Russian	405	0.2	427	0.3
Spanish	367	0.2	79	------
All other	2,175	1.0	1,512	0.9
EASTERN EUROPE				
Russia	1,153,624	100.0	[3] 1,400,489	100.0
Yiddish	743,307	64.4	791,181	56.5
Russian	262,781	22.8	361,843	25.8
German	103,371	9.0	116,535	8.3
Polish	14,805	1.3	72,065	5.1
Ukrainian	11,089	1.0	} 545	------
Ruthenian	536	------	}	
Lithuanian	5,416	0.5	} 49,140	3.5
Lettish	813	0.1	}	
English and Celtic	1,790	0.2	1,934	0.1
All other	9,026	0.8	7,246	0.5

[1] See figures for Ireland, divided since 1920 into Northern Ireland and Irish Free State.
[2] Iceland included with Denmark in 1920.
[3] Latvia and Estonia included with Russia in 1920.

352

POPULATION

TABLE 7.—COUNTRY OF BIRTH OF THE FOREIGN-BORN WHITE POPULATION BY MOTHER TONGUE, FOR THE UNITED STATES: 1930 AND 1920—Continued

COUNTRY OF BIRTH AND MOTHER TONGUE	1930		1920		COUNTRY OF BIRTH AND MOTHER TONGUE	1930		1920	
	Number	Per cent	Number	Per cent		Number	Per cent	Number	Per cent
EASTERN EUROPE—Continued					**OTHER EUROPE**				
Latvia	20,678	100.0	(²)		Other Europe	16,251	100.0	5,901	100.0
Yiddish	8,803	42.6			Arabic	3,533	21.7	809	13.7
Lettish	5,977	28.9			German	2,348	14.4	2,334	39.6
German	2,774	13.4			Yiddish	1,747	10.8	152	2.6
Russian	1,827	8.8			English and Celtic	1,160	7.1	425	7.2
Lithuanian	464	2.2			Spanish	472	2.9	108	1.8
Polish	381	1.8			Russian	409	2.5	31	0.5
All other	447	2.2			Italian	344	2.1	117	2.0
					Polish	299	1.8	443	7.5
Estonia	3,550	100.0	(²)		Magyar	278	1.7	62	1.1
Estonian	2,422	68.1			Ukrainian	228	1.4	2	
German	256	7.2			Ruthenian	18	0.1		
Russian	243	6.8			Czech	211	1.3	248	4.2
Yiddish	243	6.8			Slovak	151	0.9	200	3.4
All other	386	10.9			All other	5,053	31.1	970	16.4
Lithuania	193,606	100.0	135,068	100.0	**ASIA**				
Lithuanian	156,152	80.7	126,441	93.6	Armenia	32,166	100.0	36,626	100.0
Lettish	622	0.3			Armenian	30,959	96.2	35,321	96.4
Yiddish	25,886	13.4	-4,971	3.7	Russian	441	1.4	103	0.3
Polish	3,824	2.0	1,840	1.4	Turkish	290	0.9	263	0.7
German	3,041	1.6	417	0.3	All other	476	1.5	939	2.6
Russian	2,914	1.5	1,157	0.9					
All other	1,167	0.6	242	0.2	Palestine	6,135	100.0	3,202	100.0
					Yiddish	4,150	67.6	1,568	49.0
Finland	142,478	100.0	149,824	100.0	Arabic	1,430	23.3	1,183	36.9
Finnish	122,710	86.1	130,808	87.3	Spanish	101	1.6	58	1.8
Swedish	18,730	13.1	17,721	11.8	All other	454	7.4	393	12.3
English and Celtic	248	0.2	200	0.1					
All other	790	0.6	1,095	0.7	Syria	57,227	100.0	51,900	100.0
					Arabic	55,506	97.0	50,727	97.7
Rumania	146,393	100.0	102,823	100.0	Armenian	730	1.3	131	0.3
Rumanian	53,452	36.5	51,682	50.3	Yiddish	171	0.3	137	0.3
Yiddish	49,508	33.8	37,287	36.3	French	152	0.3	44	0.1
German	28,640	19.6	8,167	7.9	Greek	151	0.3	105	0.2
Magyar	8,830	6.0	2,606	2.5	English and Celtic	111	0.2	56	0.1
Russian	1,791	1.2	936	0.9	Turkish	107	0.2	107	0.2
Italian	588	0.4	50		All other	299	0.5	593	1.1
Polish	554	0.4	519	0.5					
Ukrainian	543	0.4			Turkey in Asia	46,651	100.0	11,014	100.0
Ruthenian	65		203	0.2	Armenian	17,206	36.9	524	4.8
Serbian	378	0.3	89	0.1	Greek	11,499	24.6	1,451	13.2
English and Celtic	285	0.2	159	0.2	Turkish	9,166	19.6	5,326	48.4
Slovak	281	0.2	343	0.3	Spanish	5,232	11.2	212	1.9
All other	1,498	1.0	782	0.8	Arabic	1,098	2.4	1,656	15.0
					Yiddish	910	2.0	796	7.2
Bulgaria	9,399	100.0	10,477	100.0	French	263	0.6	151	1.4
Bulgarian	8,112	86.3	9,462	90.3	English and Celtic	224	0.5	173	1.6
Greek	288	3.1	134	1.3	German	194	0.4	160	1.5
German	218	2.3	166	1.6	Russian	129	0.3	67	0.6
Armenian	168	1.8	51	0.5	Rumanian	112	0.2	100	0.9
Yiddish	103	1.1	83	0.8	Bulgarian	109	0.2	35	0.3
All other	510	5.4	581	5.5	All other	509	1.1	363	3.3
Turkey in Europe	2,257	100.0	5,284	100.0					
Greek	744	33.0	2,034	38.5	Other Asia	15,401	100.0	7,708	100.0
Armenian	576	25.5	391	7.4	English and Celtic	5,009	32.5	3,223	41.8
Spanish	309	13.7	1,313	24.8	Arabic	3,817	24.8	1,653	21.4
Turkish	283	12.5	416	7.9	Russian	1,397	9.1	454	5.9
All other	345	15.3	1,130	21.4	Greek	1,187	7.7	41	0.5
					Persian	1,155	7.5	801	10.4
SOUTHERN EUROPE					Armenian	588	3.8	320	4.2
Greece	174,526	100.0	175,972	100.0	Yiddish	450	2.9	285	3.7
Greek	169,646	97.2	168,276	95.6	German	407	2.6	365	4.7
Bulgarian	2,215	1.3	2,651	1.5	Turkish	134	0.9	36	0.5
Spanish	1,012	0.6	3,188	1.8	All other	1,257	8.2	530	6.9
Rumanian	285	0.2	383	0.2					
All other	1,368	0.8	1,474	0.8	**AMERICA**				
					Canada	1,278,421	100.0	1,117,878	100.0
Albania	8,814	100.0	5,608	100.0	English and Celtic	880,754	68.9	789,347	70.6
Albanian	7,114	80.7	5,086	90.7	French	370,852	29.0	307,786	27.5
Greek	1,094	12.4	187	3.3	German	9,818	0.8	11,136	1.0
Rumanian	381	4.3	98	1.7	Yiddish	5,146	0.4	2,687	0.2
All other	225	2.6	237	4.2	Polish	2,141	0.2	978	0.1
					All other	9,710	0.8	5,944	0.5
Italy	1,790,424	100.0	1,610,109	100.0					
Italian	1,779,698	99.4	1,604,492	99.7	Newfoundland	23,971	100.0	13,242	100.0
Slovenian	3,301	0.2	490		English and Celtic	23,652	98.7	13,075	98.7
All other	7,425	0.4	5,127	0.3	French	141	0.6	95	0.7
					All other	178	0.7	72	0.5
Spain	58,302	100.0	49,247	100.0					
Spanish	57,098	97.9	48,535	98.6	Cuba	15,944	100.0	12,843	100.0
English and Celtic	219	0.4	351	0.7	Spanish	14,994	94.0	12,233	95.3
All other	985	1.7	361	0.7	English and Celtic	613	3.8	328	2.6
					All other	337	2.1	282	2.2
Portugal	69,974	100.0	67,453	100.0					
Portuguese	69,423	99.2	66,726	98.9	Other West Indies	15,482	100.0	13,526	100.0
Spanish	346	0.5	165	0.2	English and Celtic	12,992	83.9	11,036	81.6
All other	205	0.3	562	0.8	Spanish	1,488	9.6	892	6.6

² Latvia and Estonia included with Russia in 1920.

MOTHER TONGUE OF THE FOREIGN-BORN WHITE POPULATION   353

TABLE 7.—COUNTRY OF BIRTH OF THE FOREIGN-BORN WHITE POPULATION BY MOTHER TONGUE, FOR THE UNITED STATES: 1930 AND 1920—Continued

COUNTRY OF BIRTH AND MOTHER TONGUE	1930 Number	1930 Per cent	1920 Number	1920 Per cent	COUNTRY OF BIRTH AND MOTHER TONGUE	1930 Number	1930 Per cent	1920 Number	1920 Percent
AMERICA—Continued					**OTHER COUNTRIES—Continued**				
Other West Indies—Continued.					Africa—Continued.				
French	370	2.4	321	2.4	Greek	379	4.8	197	3.8
Dutch	266	1.7	291	2.2	German	360	4.6	319	6.1
All other	366	2.4	986	7.3	Dutch	279	3.5	285	5.5
					Armenian	232	2.9	78	1.5
Mexico	23,743	100.0	⁷21,023	100.0	Spanish	168	2.1	156	3.0
Spanish	21,227	89.4	⁷19,258	91.6	All other	747	9.5	558	10.7
English and Celtic	1,587	6.7	941	4.5					
German	272	1.1	205	1.0	Australia	12,720	100.0	10,801	100.0
Arabic	151	0.6	77	0.4	English and Celtic	11,638	91.5	9,838	91.1
French	141	0.6	195	0.9	German	448	3.5	405	3.7
Italian	134	0.6	142	0.7	All other	634	5.0	558	5.2
All other	231	1.0	205	1.0					
					Azores	35,427	100.0	33,788	100.0
Central America	7,454	100.0	4,074	100.0	Portuguese	35,182	99.3	33,560	99.3
Spanish	6,217	83.4	3,228	79.2	English and Celtic	102	0.3	89	0.3
English and Celtic	930	12.5	550	13.5	All other	143	0.4	139	0.4
All other	307	4.1	296	7.3					
					Other Atlantic Islands	4,052	100.0	5,196	100.0
South America	30,055	100.0	16,855	100.0	Portuguese	2,367	58.4	3,754	72.2
Spanish	15,263	50.8	8,263	49.0	English and Celtic	1,358	33.5	1,156	22.2
Italian	5,733	19.1	2,580	15.3	Spanish	143	3.5	128	2.5
English and Celtic	2,869	9.5	1,734	10.3	All other	184	4.5	158	3.0
Portuguese	2,795	9.3	1,419	8.4					
German	1,181	3.9	895	5.3	Pacific Islands	4,364	100.0	3,643	100.0
Yiddish	608	2.2	320	1.9	English and Celtic	3,700	84.8	3,057	83.9
French	303	1.0	364	2.2	Dutch	258	5.9	191	5.2
Arabic	218	0.7	96	0.6	French	169	3.9	140	3.8
Polish	202	0.7	220	1.3	All other	237	5.4	255	7.0
Dutch	187	0.6	144	0.9					
Russian	106	0.4	141	0.8	All other	6,443	100.0	8,862	100.0
All other	540	1.8	679	4.0	English and Celtic	1,754	27.2	2,028	22.9
					German	1,443	22.4	2,907	32.8
OTHER COUNTRIES					Yiddish	210	3.3	303	3.4
Africa	7,866	100.0	5,222	100.0	Norwegian	210	3.3	102	2.2
English and Celtic	3,330	42.4	2,094	40.1	Polish	205	3.2	384	4.3
Italian	675	8.6	344	6.6	French	203	3.2	210	2.4
Arabic	629	8.0	495	9.5	Swedish	155	2.4	162	1.8
French	584	7.4	370	7.1	Italian	155	2.4	135	1.5
Yiddish	474	6.0	326	6.2	All other	2,108	32.7	2,541	28.7

⁷ Adjusted figures; see footnote 2, Table 6.

POPULATION

TABLE 8.—PRINCIPAL MOTHER TONGUES OF THE FOREIGN-BORN WHITE POPULATION, BY DIVISIONS AND STATES: 1930

[For mother tongues not shown in this table (representing a population of 562,404) see Tables 1 and 9]

DIVISION AND STATE	Total	English and Celtic	German	Dutch	Scandi-navian¹	Italian	French	Span-ish	Portu-guese	Greek	Polish	Czech	Slovak	Rus-sian	Lithu-anian	Yiddish	Mag-yar	Finn-ish
United States	13,366,407	3,097,021	2,188,006	133,142	1,142,645	1,808,289	523,297	126,288	110,197	189,066	965,899	201,138	240,196	315,721	165,053	1,222,658	250,393	124,994
GEOGRAPHIC DIVS.:																		
New England	1,834,310	686,850	64,980	2,820	84,682	254,886	277,458	3,442	60,244	27,663	114,674	3,599	10,551	27,585	36,869	104,573	11,286	16,176
Middle Atlantic	5,269,042	1,059,993	758,322	30,738	176,217	1,051,893	89,555	55,856	11,482	58,325	410,923	36,847	131,306	170,804	58,694	835,349	120,488	18,804
E. North Central	3,223,924	634,001	697,370	57,262	285,835	245,042	70,815	9,621	788	50,957	371,072	95,784	81,744	54,419	60,037	166,157	99,093	39,655
W. North Central	1,059,277	137,196	324,085	20,368	333,410	32,182	19,517	1,995	54	8,070	26,917	38,797	5,244	15,575	2,195	33,012	3,750	24,776
South Atlantic	304,278	71,478	47,241	1,603	9,918	39,079	7,307	14,231	515	18,132	21,509	4,491	3,862	11,169	3,726	33,682	6,425	1,031
E. South Central	57,665	14,008	15,421	295	2,164	7,337	1,887	600	53	2,398	1,353	542	269	1,840	118	5,030	900	119
W. South Central	170,232	30,143	49,616	1,159	10,167	22,315	7,301	6,816	105	3,684	4,449	13,079	1,349	3,141	244	7,421	1,040	222
Mountain	287,914	85,358	54,365	5,108	55,563	24,453	8,527	5,316	393	6,789	3,364	2,601	2,618	3,934	446	5,198	1,218	4,813
Pacific	1,159,765	377,999	176,006	13,789	184,689	130,502	40,930	28,411	36,503	18,048	11,038	5,398	3,253	27,248	1,824	32,236	6,187	19,398
NEW ENGLAND:																		
Maine	100,368	47,736	947	43	3,314	2,360	37,325	69	100	854	1,158	30	337	629	982	2,036	31	1,355
New Hampshire	82,660	25,142	1,880	155	2,167	1,957	38,024	47	309	3,317	3,679	20	50	1,120	1,105	653	35	1,378
Vermont	43,061	15,662	750	33	1,366	3,204	17,524	497	49	228	1,363	48	90	392	103	530	224	547
Massachusetts	1,054,636	456,485	25,506	1,917	46,952	126,808	121,712	1,391	45,285	18,480	59,251	1,122	1,414	14,126	21,370	72,472	725	11,352
Rhode Island	170,714	57,353	3,806	141	7,123	32,876	33,954	162	11,970	1,135	6,955	73	88	1,499	790	6,377	100	322
Connecticut	382,871	84,472	32,075	531	23,760	87,621	28,919	1,276	2,531	3,649	42,268	2,300	8,566	9,810	12,519	22,505	10,171	1,222
MIDDLE ATLANTIC:																		
New York	3,191,549	647,262	448,962	14,821	125,520	633,342	63,321	44,362	6,096	38,157	190,051	21,641	22,211	112,221	15,933	656,466	55,103	14,892
New Jersey	844,442	167,910	148,114	14,662	28,411	102,154	13,022	6,948	4,001	6,550	80,213	5,200	20,741	20,530	8,057	68,204	31,948	2,067
Pennsylvania	1,233,051	244,821	161,246	1,255	22,286	226,397	13,212	4,546	1,385	13,618	140,659	10,006	88,354	38,053	34,704	110,619	33,437	1,845
E. NORTH CENTRAL:																		
Ohio	644,151	112,786	140,175	2,144	11,102	70,819	8,016	2,291	214	13,014	52,792	21,820	39,100	11,608	5,919	34,575	51,802	5,526
Indiana	135,134	22,982	32,816	1,955	6,310	6,729	3,325	1,076	99	4,013	16,591	6,228	2,564	1,864	3,540	8,380	244
Illinois	1,218,158	182,462	250,319	14,568	161,055	111,387	18,105	3,494	254	20,639	153,038	53,797	21,205	23,641	40,955	90,419	15,537	3,576
Michigan	840,268	287,982	111,676	32,411	40,137	44,088	34,018	2,437	170	10,369	107,963	7,440	8,996	12,005	8,650	28,561	10,075	25,321
Wisconsin	386,213	27,786	162,384	6,184	67,171	12,619	6,151	323	51	2,922	40,688	11,254	6,206	4,001	3,549	9,062	4,299	4,988
W. NORTH CENTRAL:																		
Minnesota	388,294	38,551	74,140	4,742	178,232	6,506	7,908	189	9	1,744	13,265	7,814	2,339	3,443	440	11,268	919	22,867
Iowa	165,735	24,928	59,844	10,069	44,550	3,902	2,167	229	2	1,931	1,135	7,110	937	1,529	611	3,050	298	48
Missouri	149,390	25,928	56,903	644	5,883	15,429	3,372	963	21	2,435	5,740	3,445	985	4,139	505	14,993	1,750	77
North Dakota	105,148	18,964	35,374	656	43,654	113	1,662	53	1	289	1,213	1,828	168	3,003	58	468	212	873
South Dakota	65,648	7,027	23,331	3,020	24,931	322	765	23	1	201	452	2,345	137	877	19	193	110	847
Nebraska	115,346	12,889	44,760	602	26,338	3,677	1,100	247	7	840	3,053	13,839	288	1,546	427	2,598	293	32
Kansas	69,716	13,909	29,634	626	9,816	2,233	2,483	291	13	540	1,459	2,416	390	1,038	135	442	174	32
SOUTH ATLANTIC:																		
Delaware	16,885	4,639	1,717	49	541	3,778	237	214	14	362	2,744	104	110	373	49	1,286	122	44
Maryland	95,003	14,585	22,093	333	1,931	10,953	1,137	596	75	1,736	10,373	2,799	571	3,974	2,498	18,448	793	361
Dist. of Columbia	29,932	8,973	4,238	150	899	4,405	1,067	463	38	1,473	621	114	37	1,532	48	4,825	175	54
Virginia	23,820	7,316	3,126	261	1,120	1,898	596	240	75	1,466	753	555	409	993	95	3,085	516	55
West Virginia	51,520	6,947	4,855	40	426	12,069	1,246	1,534	58	2,895	5,570	551	2,353	1,786	903	770	4,088	137
North Carolina	8,788	3,026	1,137	211	315	302	400	79	11	1,121	175	16	15	330	13	679	62	5
South Carolina	5,266	1,237	879	23	222	185	135	44	6	730	176	26	9	269	9	730	25	22
Georgia	13,917	3,814	2,135	63	505	620	421	369	93	1,268	424	31	20	892	32	2,297	106	94
Florida	59,057	20,936	7,061	473	3,959	4,901	2,068	10,692	145	2,081	673	295	248	1,020	79	1,562	538	259
E. SOUTH CENTRAL:																		
Kentucky	21,840	4,916	9,231	106	280	1,636	625	142	33	490	514	56	104	573	67	1,601	499	23
Tennessee	13,066	3,473	2,460	58	417	1,971	411	87	7	546	456	86	30	597	12	1,901	152	14
Alabama	15,710	4,367	2,778	92	1,090	2,110	609	242	8	1,013	241	357	122	417	29	1,067	201	38
Mississippi	7,049	1,252	952	39	377	1,620	242	129	5	349	142	43	13	259	10	461	48	44
W. SOUTH CENTRAL:																		
Arkansas	10,173	2,252	3,788	79	455	967	467	57	5	321	322	230	154	145	30	283	39	4
Louisiana	34,910	4,394	4,467	241	1,246	13,576	3,263	2,264	68	667	277	209	86	492	10	1,207	379	57
Oklahoma	26,753	6,184	9,704	239	1,593	1,181	1,074	243	18	671	702	1,538	242	669	127	753	130	19
Texas	98,396	17,313	31,657	600	6,873	6,591	2,497	4,252	74	2,025	3,148	11,003	867	1,835	77	5,088	492	142
MOUNTAIN:																		
Montana	72,961	22,953	12,786	1,311	17,470	2,930	2,793	160	23	809	922	998	682	751	156	131	222	2,522
Idaho	30,454	9,535	5,869	336	8,182	1,217	1,059	1,007	42	414	187	408	112	315	15	55	81	723
Wyoming	19,668	5,553	3,385	114	3,213	1,467	566	187	24	888	585	216	324	342	33	104	165	619
Colorado	85,406	20,419	21,776	809	12,123	10,758	1,957	597	28	1,266	1,231	701	1,083	1,839	166	4,297	550	355
New Mexico	7,797	2,044	1,307	61	490	1,280	354	550	7	300	83	86	195	107	10	49	52	31
Arizona	15,591	6,125	2,031	99	1,487	870	501	1,441	21	388	181	97	98	337	38	222	82	245
Utah	43,772	15,840	5,897	2,330	11,353	2,890	484	378	6	2,209	119	62	49	177	23	280	52	221
Nevada	12,275	2,889	1,314	48	1,245	2,826	813	996	242	515	56	33	75	66	5	60	14	97
PACIFIC:																		
Washington	244,256	80,482	34,021	3,664	76,709	10,094	6,911	1,150	139	3,038	3,219	980	1,005	3,294	746	2,007	374	8,450
Oregon	105,475	32,534	24,852	1,052	23,080	4,758	2,770	582	137	1,602	1,080	970	411	1,637	245	1,635	253	4,586
California	810,034	264,983	117,133	9,073	84,900	115,650	31,249	26,679	36,227	13,408	7,339	3,448	1,837	22,317	833	28,594	5,560	6,362

¹ Includes Swedish, 615,465; Norwegian, 345,522; Danish, 178,944; and Icelandic, 2,714.

TABLE 9.—MOTHER TONGUE OF THE FOREIGN-BORN WHITE POPULATION, BY SEX, BY DIVISIONS AND STATES: 1930, 1920, AND 1910

[Figures for 1920 and 1910 have been adjusted by deducting from the total, and from Spanish mother tongue, the estimated number of persons who would have been classified as Mexicans in 1930. Per cent not shown where less than 0.1]

NEW ENGLAND

MOTHER TONGUE	TOTAL FOREIGN-BORN WHITE 1930 Number	1930 Per cent	1920	1910	MALE 1930	MALE 1920	FEMALE 1930	FEMALE 1920
Total	1,834,310	100.0	1,870,600	1,814,356	904,742	945,704	929,568	924,896
English and Celtic	686,850	37.4	709,298	787,710	298,557	311,950	388,293	397,348
Germanic:								
German	64,980	3.5	67,171	79,513	32,894	34,710	32,086	32,461
Dutch	2,820	0.2	3,183	2,416	1,660	1,824	1,160	1,359
Flemish	2,274	0.1	2,952	1,740	1,207	1,596	1,067	1,356
Scandinavian:								
Swedish	68,613	3.7	69,601	73,203	34,685	34,463	33,928	35,138
Norwegian	8,466	0.5	8,321	8,308	4,412	4,288	4,054	4,033
Danish	7,545	0.4	8,267	7,899	4,367	4,062	3,178	3,605
Icelandic	58	------	16	21	36	6	22	10
Latin and Greek:								
Italian	254,886	13.9	230,431	180,619	143,361	138,483	111,525	100,948
French	277,458	15.1	255,096	201,237	136,987	127,524	140,471	127,572
Spanish	3,442	0.2	3,664	1,626	2,317	2,678	1,125	986
Portuguese	60,244	3.3	66,800	44,203	31,488	35,211	28,756	31,589
Rumanian	1,372	0.1	1,527	871	756	805	616	632
Greek	27,663	1.5	32,850	21,324	17,495	22,079	10,168	9,877
Slavic and Lettic:								
Polish	114,674	6.3	132,026	108,073	59,690	72,502	54,984	59,524
Czech	3,599	0.2	3,723	3,125	1,755	1,883	1,844	1,840
Slovak	10,551	0.6	11,072	6,969	5,319	5,898	5,232	5,174
Russian	27,585	1.5	37,256	4,359	16,226	22,809	11,359	14,447
Ruthenian	247	------	3,639	1,065	118	2,000	129	1,639
Ukrainian	4,723	0.3			2,487		2,236	
Slovenian	700	------	1,112	2,862	380	610	320	493
Croatian	237	------	300	486	151	199	86	101
Serbian	159	------	1,052	165	101	564	58	488
Bulgarian	188	------	158	540	125	124	63	34
Wendish	24	------	376	1	14	204	10	172
Lithuanian	36,869	2.0	42,440	29,429	20,484	25,113	16,385	17,336
Lettish	1,523	0.1			700		733	
Unclassified:								
Yiddish	104,573	5.7	110,228	105,416	52,992	57,242	51,581	52,986
Magyar	11,286	0.6	12,803	10,491	5,539	6,640	5,747	6,163
Finnish	16,176	0.9	17,204	13,163	8,271	9,085	7,905	8,119
Estonian	137	------	79	10	89	52	48	27
Armenian	16,056	0.9	12,459	10,620	9,266	8,624	6,790	3,835
Arabic	11,710	0.6	11,730	8,154	6,497	6,976	5,213	4,754
Turkish	1,806	0.1	1,504	1,632	1,229	1,304	577	200
Albanian	3,415	0.2	2,749	1,293	2,270	2,291	1,145	458
All other	200	------	175	97	120	130	80	45
Unknown	1,201	0.1	323	5,707	607	176	594	147

MIDDLE ATLANTIC

MOTHER TONGUE	TOTAL FOREIGN-BORN WHITE 1930 Number	1930 Per cent	1920	1910	MALE 1930	MALE 1920	FEMALE 1930	FEMALE 1920
Total	5,269,042	100.0	4,909,899	4,825,817	2,761,740	2,615,613	2,507,302	2,294,286
English and Celtic	1,059,993	20.1	985,973	1,160,755	490,279	448,212	569,714	537,761
Germanic:								
German	758,322	14.4	677,547	847,088	386,913	347,786	371,409	329,761
Dutch	30,738	0.6	29,508	27,509	18,160	16,909	12,578	12,599
Flemish	6,137	0.1	6,797	3,662	3,311	3,654	2,826	3,143
Scandinavian:								
Swedish	94,667	1.8	86,037	90,435	50,341	43,451	44,326	42,586
Norwegian	54,883	1.0	34,751	32,230	30,787	18,626	24,096	16,125
Danish	26,520	0.5	22,641	20,967	16,327	13,501	10,193	9,140
Icelandic	147	------	56	23	78	31	69	25
Latin and Greek:								
Italian	1,051,893	20.0	928,944	780,639	601,843	537,322	450,050	391,622
French	89,555	1.7	72,404	74,407	42,844	34,931	46,711	37,473
Spanish	55,856	1.1	33,144	9,599	37,545	23,109	18,311	10,035
Portuguese	11,482	0.2	3,263	1,200	9,146	2,445	2,336	818
Rumanian	22,584	0.4	25,914	15,355	12,034	14,168	10,550	11,746
Greek	58,325	1.1	43,686	21,561	40,433	33,806	17,892	9,880
Slavic and Lettic:								
Polish	410,923	7.8	452,792	427,224	219,950	255,634	190,973	197,158
Czech	36,847	0.7	38,302	35,667	17,519	18,550	19,328	19,752
Slovak	131,306	2.5	165,959	108,001	70,031	95,738	61,275	70,221
Russian	170,804	3.2	220,198	38,060	95,105	124,769	75,699	95,429
Ruthenian	8,190	0.2	40,089	19,873	4,457	23,740	3,733	16,349
Ukrainian	37,873	0.7			20,507		17,366	
Slovenian	14,818	0.3	22,894	56,019	8,839	13,850	5,979	9,044
Croatian	24,443	0.5	30,654	20,500	16,109	22,164	8,334	8,490
Serbian	7,963	0.2	10,042	5,544	5,566	6,947	2,397	3,095
Bulgarian	1,641	------	1,475	2,693	1,200	1,290	441	185
Wendish	1,297	------	1,520	1,355	626	774	671	746
Lithuanian	58,694	1.1	66,238	59,357	33,653	40,084	25,041	26,154
Lettish	2,856	0.1			1,657		1,199	
Unclassified:								
Yiddish	835,349	15.9	717,974	740,636	421,379	370,959	413,970	347,015
Magyar	120,488	2.3	141,789	124,087	59,861	74,960	60,627	66,829
Finnish	18,804	0.4	14,747	10,956	8,338	6,586	10,466	8,161
Estonian	1,531	------	354	50	1,026	244	505	110
Armenian	15,156	0.3	10,908	6,086	8,611	7,165	6,545	3,743
Arabic	20,957	0.4	17,111	9,555	11,862	9,932	9,095	7,179
Turkish	4,888	0.1	2,629	999	2,905	1,789	1,983	840
Albanian	1,825	------	1,214	441	1,354	1,090	471	124
All other	685	------	380	213	460	263	225	117
Unknown	20,602	0.4	1,965	54,471	10,684	1,134	9,918	831

EAST NORTH CENTRAL

MOTHER TONGUE	TOTAL FOREIGN-BORN WHITE 1930 Number	1930 Per cent	1920	1910	MALE 1930	MALE 1920	FEMALE 1930	FEMALE 1920
Total	3,223,924	100.0	3,217,005	3,066,390	1,766,458	1,804,717	1,457,466	1,412,288
English and Celtic	634,001	19.7	583,961	628,020	323,209	298,714	310,792	285,247
Germanic:								
German	697,370	21.6	758,689	917,736	364,767	399,009	332,603	359,680
Dutch	57,262	1.8	61,105	62,718	32,242	33,988	25,020	27,117
Flemish	25,809	0.8	24,953	14,992	14,439	14,669	11,370	10,284
Scandinavian:								
Swedish	169,845	5.3	168,858	182,428	94,757	90,993	75,088	77,865
Norwegian	73,554	2.3	81,661	98,828	39,988	43,162	33,566	38,499
Danish	42,247	1.3	42,824	43,854	25,500	25,155	16,747	17,669
Icelandic	189	------	92	31	101	46	88	46
Latin and Greek:								
Italian	245,642	7.6	205,331	149,956	148,793	129,053	96,849	76,278
French	70,815	2.2	58,246	73,086	37,306	32,167	33,509	26,079
Spanish	9,621	0.3	5,042	1,069	6,886	3,799	2,735	1,243
Portuguese	788	------	638	666	552	407	236	231
Rumanian	25,101	0.8	26,309	17,560	15,483	18,230	9,618	8,079
Greek	50,957	1.6	43,945	19,896	38,750	37,574	12,207	6,371
Slavic and Lettic:								
Polish	371,072	11.5	411,825	318,863	204,961	237,967	166,111	173,858
Czech	95,784	3.0	106,075	100,949	48,091	54,427	47,693	51,648
Slovak	81,744	2.5	77,197	41,034	44,340	45,453	37,404	31,744
Russian	54,419	1.7	60,850	6,652	33,488	39,662	20,931	21,188
Ruthenian	719	------	9,017	2,427	426	5,646	293	3,371
Ukrainian	13,266	0.4			7,671		5,595	
Slovenian	36,100	1.1	32,885	35,084	20,982	20,256	15,118	12,629
Croatian	36,865	1.1	33,821	25,718	23,465	23,980	13,400	9,841
Serbian	14,728	0.5	17,365	9,227	10,070	12,276	4,658	5,089
Bulgarian	7,189	0.2	7,539	6,073	5,740	6,993	1,449	546
Wendish	34	------	91	4	20	53	14	38
Lithuanian	60,937	1.9	62,997	42,287	36,608	40,313	24,329	22,684
Lettish	1,787	0.1			1,033		754	
Unclassified:								
Yiddish	166,157	5.2	158,713	117,315	86,047	84,072	80,110	73,741
Magyar	99,093	3.1	111,139	76,126	53,226	64,445	45,867	46,694
Finnish	39,655	1.2	43,094	41,623	21,816	24,680	17,839	18,414
Estonian	276	------	135	8	191	108	85	27
Armenian	9,949	0.3	6,276	2,657	6,199	5,025	3,750	1,251
Arabic	16,640	0.5	11,660	5,183	10,493	7,802	6,147	3,858
Turkish	2,184	0.1	1,332	753	1,656	1,230	528	102
Albanian	1,618	0.1	953	218	1,383	887	235	66
All other	946	------	432	284	679	344	267	88
Unknown	9,561	0.3	1,955	23,065	5,100	1,232	4,461	723

WEST NORTH CENTRAL

MOTHER TONGUE	TOTAL FOREIGN-BORN WHITE 1930 Number	1930 Per cent	1920	1910	MALE 1930	MALE 1920	FEMALE 1930	FEMALE 1920
Total	1,059,277	100.0	1,350,832	1,602,911	591,094	765,532	468,183	585,300
English and Celtic	137,196	13.0	194,874	256,513	72,387	104,969	64,809	89,905
Germanic:								
German	324,085	30.6	412,711	517,250	176,177	226,412	147,908	186,299
Dutch	20,368	1.9	24,738	22,031	11,980	14,341	8,388	10,397
Flemish	3,536	0.3	5,430	2,994	2,032	3,212	1,504	2,218
Scandinavian:								
Swedish	150,192	14.2	189,655	215,855	86,234	108,641	63,958	81,014
Norwegian	131,859	12.4	166,146	108,717	73,677	92,674	58,182	73,472
Danish	50,292	4.7	60,852	63,974	30,823	37,087	19,469	23,765
Icelandic	1,067	0.1	1,342	1,566	512	656	555	686
Latin and Greek:								
Italian	32,182	3.0	34,930	38,968	19,278	22,216	12,904	12,714
French	19,517	1.8	22,533	30,571	10,513	12,783	9,004	9,750
Spanish	1,995	0.2	2,022	1,191	1,258	1,309	737	713
Portuguese	54	------	125	112	33	81	21	44
Rumanian	2,528	0.2	3,679	4,700	1,485	2,339	1,043	1,340
Greek	8,070	0.8	11,168	15,291	6,632	10,031	1,438	1,137
Slavic and Lettic:								
Polish	26,917	2.5	33,833	41,148	15,141	19,851	11,776	13,982
Czech	38,797	3.7	51,936	57,580	20,186	27,592	18,611	24,344
Slovak	5,244	0.5	5,845	3,827	2,857	3,593	2,387	2,252
Russian	15,575	1.5	22,994	3,549	8,982	13,718	6,593	9,276
Ruthenian	398	------	1,609	1,200	205	1,014	193	595
Ukrainian	1,515	0.1			877		638	
Slovenian	7,421	0.7	7,898	9,530	4,321	4,932	3,100	2,966
Croatian	6,805	0.6	8,829	10,395	4,160	6,254	2,645	2,575
Serbian	2,168	0.2	4,288	4,565	1,472	3,007	696	1,221
Bulgarian	887	0.1	1,380	3,374	732	1,248	155	132
Wendish	6	------	5	1	4	4	2	1
Lithuanian	2,195	0.2	2,943	3,587	1,392	2,008	803	935
Lettish	180	------			108		72	
Unclassified:								
Yiddish	33,012	3.1	37,394	34,664	17,193	20,054	15,819	17,340
Magyar	3,756	0.4	6,167	6,229	2,014	3,422	1,742	2,745
Finnish	24,776	2.3	29,971	28,589	14,500	18,309	10,276	11,662
Estonian	40	------	17	2	31	14	9	3
Armenian	431	------	658	614	309	523	122	135
Arabic	3,260	0.3	3,596	2,663	1,979	2,290	1,281	1,306
Turkish	151	------	155	522	119	130	32	19
Albanian	286	------	253	233	212	222	74	31
All other	66	------	46	7	50	24	16	22
Unknown	2,450	0.2	810	20,899	1,229	506	1,221	304

119652—33——24

POPULATION

TABLE 9.—MOTHER TONGUE OF THE FOREIGN-BORN WHITE POPULATION, BY SEX, BY DIVISIONS AND STATES: 1930, 1920, AND 1910—Continued

SOUTH ATLANTIC

MOTHER TONGUE	1930 Number	1930 Per cent	1920	1910	Male 1930	Male 1920	Female 1930	Female 1920
Total	304,278	100.0	315,676	290,476	170,300	184,979	133,978	130,697
English and Celtic	71,473	23.5	68,927	68,276	35,081	34,966	36,392	33,961
Germanic:								
German	47,241	15.5	49,214	64,141	25,297	26,747	21,944	22,467
Dutch	1,603	0.5	1,598	736	1,060	1,045	543	553
Flemish	376	0.1	882	201	227	499	149	383
Scandinavian:								
Swedish	5,048	1.7	4,508	3,005	3,063	2,770	1,985	1,738
Norwegian	2,533	0.8	2,224	1,455	1,654	1,448	879	776
Danish	2,310	0.8	2,106	1,297	1,604	1,484	706	622
Icelandic	27		10	2	18	6	9	4
Latin and Greek:								
Italian	39,079	12.8	40,484	38,334	24,044	26,372	15,035	14,112
French	7,807	2.4	5,703	4,470	3,503	2,944	3,804	2,759
Spanish	14,231	4.7	14,312	14,323	8,078	8,773	5,553	5,539
Portuguese	515	0.2	497	150	377	365	138	132
Rumanian	1,408	0.5	1,531	1,165	939	1,058	529	473
Greek	13,132	4.3	11,699	5,037	9,075	9,814	3,457	1,885
Slavic and Lettic:								
Polish	21,509	7.1	25,540	24,592	12,160	15,207	9,349	10,243
Czech	4,401	1.5	5,017	5,352	2,258	2,956	2,233	2,661
Slovak	3,862	1.3	4,724	2,873	2,200	2,084	1,602	1,740
Russian	11,169	3.7	15,289	2,000	6,652	9,528	4,517	5,761
Ruthenian	71			281	40	499	31	298
Ukrainian	760	0.2	797		429		331	
Slovenian	858	0.3	1,592	2,343	611	1,182	247	410
Croatian	1,313	0.4	1,785	1,505	935	1,357	378	428
Serbian	776	0.3	1,224	274	573	961	203	263
Bulgarian	213	0.1	190	277	184	174	29	16
Wendish			15			10		5
Lithuanian	3,726	1.2	4,403	3,637	2,236	2,752	1,490	1,651
Lettish	229	0.1			143		86	
Unclassified:								
Yiddish	33,082	11.1	34,675	26,175	17,463	18,389	16,219	16,286
Magyar	6,425	2.1	9,543	6,314	3,891	6,292	2,534	3,251
Finnish	1,031	0.3	1,116	464	608	739	423	377
Estonian	83		54		62	40	21	14
Armenian	532	0.2	897	199	332	300	200	97
Arabic	4,793	1.6	4,317	2,122	2,842	2,717	1,951	1,600
Turkish	271	0.1	224	83	209	196	62	28
Albanian	99		20	6	88	16	11	4
All other	71		25	8	53	20	18	5
Unknown	1,971	0.6	434	8,470	1,051	279	920	155

EAST SOUTH CENTRAL

MOTHER TONGUE	1930 Number	1930 Per cent	1920	1910	Male 1930	Male 1920	Female 1930	Female 1920
Total	57,665	100.0	71,698	86,745	33,359	41,949	24,306	29,749
English and Celtic	14,008	24.3	18,081	24,213	7,388	9,789	6,620	8,292
Germanic:								
German	15,421	26.7	20,771	32,575	8,605	11,322	6,816	9,449
Dutch	295	0.5	430	391	213	275	82	155
Flemish	71	0.1	106	46	43	67	28	39
Scandinavian:								
Swedish	1,260	2.2	1,526	1,617	783	973	477	553
Norwegian	435	0.8	432	492	314	292	121	140
Danish	467	0.8	518	565	339	372	128	146
Icelandic	2		1		1		1	1
Latin and Greek:								
Italian	7,337	12.7	8,624	8,277	4,535	5,338	2,802	3,286
French	1,887	3.3	2,338	2,383	904	1,278	803	1,060
Spanish	600	1.0	680	391	356	400	244	230
Portuguese	53	0.1	34	10	44	22	9	12
Rumanian	225	0.4	334	413	155	223	70	111
Greek	2,398	4.2	2,062	1,005	1,906	1,762	492	300
Slavic and Lettic:								
Polish	1,353	2.3	1,752	1,942	796	1,143	557	609
Czech	542	0.9	375	400	301	243	241	182
Slovak	269	0.5	579	331	171	412	98	167
Russian	1,846	3.2	3,123	384	1,088	1,025	758	1,198
Ruthenian	13			19	6	24	7	10
Ukrainian	12		34				3	
Slovenian	269	0.5	389	356	176	265	93	124
Croatian	143	0.2	284	95	96	248	47	36
Serbian	83	0.1	179	203	68	137	15	42
Bulgarian	56	0.1	64	107	49	64	7	
Wendish								
Lithuanian	118	0.2	137	110	79	109	39	28
Lettish	24				17		7	
Unclassified:								
Yiddish	5,030	8.7	5,353	5,025	2,766	3,017	2,264	2,336
Magyar	900	1.6	1,404	689	540	914	360	490
Finnish	119	0.2	178	156	78	130	41	48
Estonian	6		5		6	4		1
Armenian	47	0.1	60	100	37	45	10	15
Arabic	1,795	3.1	1,575	1,140	1,062	948	733	627
Turkish	53	0.1	61	65	38	40	15	21
Albanian	51	0.1	25		38	25	13	
All other	17		7	1	13	3	4	4
Unknown	460	0.8	227	2,644	249	140	211	87

WEST SOUTH CENTRAL

MOTHER TONGUE	1930 Number	1930 Per cent	1920	1910	Male 1930	Male 1920	Female 1930	Female 1920
Total	170,232	100.0	208,196	224,606	97,320	123,089	72,912	85,107
English and Celtic	30,143	17.7	35,885	39,846	16,591	21,202	13,552	14,683
Germanic:								
German	49,616	29.1	61,110	78,680	27,743	34,577	21,873	26,533
Dutch	1,159	0.7	1,378	960	812	942	347	436
Flemish	481	0.3	687	317	291	433	190	254
Scandinavian:								
Swedish	5,614	3.3	6,371	6,534	3,535	3,996	2,079	2,375
Norwegian	2,255	1.3	2,619	2,475	1,506	1,736	749	883
Danish	2,288	1.3	2,566	2,289	1,592	1,775	696	791
Icelandic	10		3	1	6	2	4	3
Latin and Greek:								
Italian	22,315	13.1	27,921	31,091	13,034	16,421	9,281	11,500
French	7,301	4.3	9,055	10,168	3,876	5,050	3,425	4,005
Spanish	6,816	4.0	11,278	5,528	3,645	6,944	3,171	4,334
Portuguese	165	0.1	227	160	132	186	33	41
Rumanian	316	0.2	394	321	194	253	122	141
Greek	3,684	2.2	3,605	2,036	2,926	3,095	758	510
Slavic and Lettic:								
Polish	4,449	2.6	5,789	7,367	2,512	3,566	1,937	2,223
Czech	13,079	7.7	17,663	17,813	6,871	9,318	6,208	8,345
Slovak	1,349	0.8	1,075	515	738	702	611	373
Russian	3,141	1.8	5,376	450	1,893	3,311	1,248	2,065
Ruthenian	17		98	34	11	65	6	33
Ukrainian	105	0.1			55		50	
Slovenian	641	0.4	740	1,143	455	550	186	190
Croatian	225	0.1	308	556	155	248	70	60
Serbian	172	0.1	447	286	125	317	47	130
Bulgarian	242	0.1	240	273	188	204	54	36
Wendish	2		30	99	1	16	1	14
Lithuanian	244	0.1	591	747	160	412	84	179
Lettish	43				34		9	
Unclassified:								
Yiddish	7,421	4.4	6,623	4,594	4,105	3,856	3,316	2,767
Magyar	1,040	0.6	1,260	837	599	780	441	480
Finnish	222	0.1	385	279	163	325	59	60
Estonian	10		5		16	4	3	1
Armenian	100	0.1	158	195	68	120	32	38
Arabic	3,909	2.3	3,697	1,939	2,324	2,265	1,585	1,432
Turkish	86	0.1	65	122	68	49	18	16
Albanian	18		9	2	16	9	2	
All other	60		17	5	44	10	16	7
Unknown	1,485	0.9	519	6,044	836	350	649	169

MOUNTAIN

MOTHER TONGUE	1930 Number	1930 Per cent	1920	1910	Male 1930	Male 1920	Female 1930	Female 1920
Total	287,914	100.0	360,531	393,533	169,997	218,945	117,917	141,586
English and Celtic	85,358	29.6	113,216	133,574	46,442	63,512	38,916	49,704
Germanic:								
German	54,365	18.9	64,628	62,662	30,909	37,778	23,456	26,850
Dutch	5,108	1.8	5,425	3,843	2,816	3,103	2,292	2,322
Flemish	791	0.3	1,136	319	514	743	277	393
Scandinavian:								
Swedish	20,929	9.4	33,594	37,000	15,872	19,677	11,057	13,917
Norwegian	15,288	5.3	17,398	15,070	9,466	10,433	5,822	6,965
Danish	13,223	4.6	16,901	17,263	7,629	9,719	5,594	7,182
Icelandic	123		154	148	58	64	65	90
Latin and Greek:								
Italian	24,453	8.5	29,303	37,910	15,706	19,792	8,747	9,511
French	8,527	3.0	9,340	10,552	5,064	5,674	3,463	3,666
Spanish	5,316	1.8	8,318	4,956	3,510	5,791	1,806	2,527
Portuguese	393	0.1	452	554	285	345	108	107
Rumanian	572	0.2	667	560	425	409	147	168
Greek	6,789	2.4	9,304	13,978	5,779	8,555	1,010	749
Slavic and Lettic:								
Polish	3,364	1.2	4,269	5,695	2,114	2,800	1,250	1,469
Czech	2,601	0.9	4,357	3,620	1,493	2,671	1,108	1,686
Slovak	2,618	0.9	4,304	1,672	1,595	2,826	1,023	1,478
Russian	3,934	1.4	6,610	692	2,417	3,996	1,517	2,614
Ruthenian	52		150	71	29	95	23	55
Ukrainian	155	0.1			98		57	
Slovenian	6,798	2.4	5,593	7,606	4,356	3,805	2,442	1,788
Croatian	3,128	1.1	4,524	5,508	2,102	3,383	1,026	1,141
Serbian	1,716	0.6	2,768	3,598	1,336	2,129	380	630
Bulgarian	725	0.3	1,002	2,986	631	970	94	32
Wendish	1						1	1
Lithuanian	446	0.2	536	477	330	412	116	124
Lettish	39				30		9	
Unclassified:								
Yiddish	5,198	1.8	5,844	5,493	2,853	3,250	2,345	2,594
Magyar	1,218	0.4	1,854	1,640	733	1,151	485	703
Finnish	4,813	1.7	6,430	8,191	2,906	4,004	1,907	2,435
Estonian	93		92	6	64	60	29	32
Armenian	231	0.1	343	288	195	304	36	39
Arabic	1,218	0.4	1,387	863	744	905	474	482
Turkish	151	0.1	159	179	135	145	16	14
Albanian	77		146	29	70	141	7	5
All other	521	0.2	36	2	400	28	121	8
Unknown	1,583	0.6	281	6,528	891	185	692	96

MOTHER TONGUE OF THE FOREIGN-BORN WHITE POPULATION   357

TABLE 9.—MOTHER TONGUE OF THE FOREIGN-BORN WHITE POPULATION, BY SEX, BY DIVISIONS AND STATES: 1930, 1920, AND 1910—Continued

PACIFIC

MOTHER TONGUE	1930 Number	1930 Per cent	1920	1910	Male 1930	Male 1920	Female 1930	Female 1920
Total	1,159,765	100.0	950,957	829,478	658,699	568,663	501,066	382,294
English and Celtic	377,999	32.6	297,717	264,885	193,429	161,653	184,570	136,064
Germanic:								
German	176,606	15.2	155,287	158,787	100,110	91,269	76,496	64,018
Dutch	13,789	1.2	9,175	5,441	8,466	5,816	5,323	3,359
Flemish	2,788	0.2	2,753	1,509	1,643	1,747	1,145	1,006
Scandinavian:								
Swedish	93,207	8.0	83,053	73,141	55,133	49,866	38,104	33,157
Norwegian	56,249	4.9	48,047	45,012	33,327	29,119	22,922	19,528
Danish	34,052	2.9	30,487	25,736	21,369	19,395	12,683	11,092
Icelandic	1,091	0.1	693	700	529	350	562	343
Latin and Greek:								
Italian	130,502	11.3	110,030	89,416	82,462	72,397	48,040	37,033
French	40,930	3.5	32,241	31,059	21,359	18,049	19,571	14,192
Spanish	28,411	2.4	20,341	8,215	16,103	13,001	12,248	7,280
Portuguese	36,503	3.1	33,859	25,504	22,249	21,217	14,254	12,642
Rumanian	2,708	0.2	1,981	1,332	1,640	1,176	1,158	805
Greek	18,048	1.6	16,333	16,751	15,184	14,861	2,864	1,472
Slavic and Lettic:								
Polish	11,036	1.0	9,566	8,877	6,919	6,116	4,710	3,450
Czech	5,308	0.5	6,516	4,232	2,951	3,842	2,447	2,674
Slovak	3,253	0.3	4,193	1,252	2,046	3,011	1,207	1,182
Russian	27,248	2.3	20,353	1,780	15,364	12,450	11,884	7,903
Ruthenian	93	...	239	161	58	171	35	68
Ukrainian	276	...			170		97	
Slovenian	10,006	0.9	7,334	8,088	6,809	5,322	3,197	2,012
Croatian	6,043	0.6	4,670	4,617	4,405	3,591	2,148	1,079
Serbian	2,356	0.2	3,304	3,427	1,765	2,688	591	616
Bulgarian	987	0.1	805	2,009	827	761	100	44
Wendish	9	...	1		7		2	1
Lithuanian	1,824	0.2	1,933	1,332	1,222	1,354	602	579
Lettish	909	0.1			571		338	
Unclassified:								
Yiddish	32,236	2.8	15,016	12,449	17,011	8,291	15,225	6,725
Magyar	6,187	0.5	4,460	2,681	3,372	2,536	2,815	1,924
Finnish	19,398	1.7	19,409	16,527	11,116	11,730	8,282	7,679
Estonian	624	0.1	283	62	435	216	189	67
Armenian	9,239	0.8	6,388	3,179	5,278	3,917	3,961	2,471
Arabic	3,548	0.3	2,484	1,249	2,175	1,657	1,373	827
Turkish	867	0.1	498	354	552	364	315	134
Albanian	197	...	146	90	173	137	24	9
All other	786	0.1	110	20	550	87	236	23
Unknown	2,920	0.3	652	7,996	1,701	446	1,219	206

MAINE

MOTHER TONGUE	1930 Number	1930 Per cent	1920	1910	Male 1930	Male 1920	Female 1930	Female 1920
Total	100,368	100.0	107,347	110,129	50,299	55,806	50,069	51,541
English and Celtic	47,736	47.6	51,976	56,913	22,557	25,137	25,179	26,839
German	947	0.9	1,067	1,417	522	633	425	434
Dutch	43	...	56	44	32	41	11	15
Flemish	13	...	20	8	8	12	5	8
Swedish	1,926	1.9	2,095	2,247	1,176	1,220	750	875
Norwegian	518	0.5	559	572	297	323	221	236
Danish	868	0.9	1,001	1,020	496	621	372	470
Icelandic	2	...	2	1	2	1	...	1
Italian	2,360	2.4	2,808	3,472	1,453	1,825	907	983
French	37,325	37.2	36,071	35,342	18,583	18,422	18,742	17,649
Spanish	69	0.1	71	147	55	55	14	16
Portuguese	100	0.1	145	84	80	107	20	38
Rumanian	11	...	10	18	7	17	4	2
Greek	854	0.9	1,281	824	558	966	296	315
Polish	1,158	1.2	1,617	1,533	688	1,051	470	566
Czech	30	...	28	27	18	17	12	11
Slovak	337	0.3	599	373	177	353	160	246
Russian	629	0.6	1,342	118	430	973	199	369
Ruthenian	2	...	27	1	2	23	...	4
Ukrainian	0	...			5		...	
Slovenian	3	...	13	113	2	8	1	5
Croatian	1	...	18	3		12	1	6
Serbian	...	...	23	22	6	14	...	9
Bulgarian	0	...	2	21		2	...	
Wendish								
Lithuanian	982	1.0	1,383	997	601	906	381	477
Lettish	44	...			27		17	
Yiddish	2,036	2.0	2,396	2,382	1,082	1,265	954	1,131
Magyar	31	...	40	24	13	25	18	15
Finnish	1,355	1.4	1,339	827	818	842	537	497
Estonian	1	...			1		...	
Armenian	199	0.2	159	219	115	122	84	37
Arabic	499	0.5	634	511	292	390	207	244
Turkish	27	...	22	52	19	18	8	4
Albanian	179	0.2	417	392	135	384	44	33
All other	2	...	1		1	1	1	
Unknown	70	0.1	25	456	42	10	28	6

NEW HAMPSHIRE

MOTHER TONGUE	1930 Number	1930 Per cent	1920	1910	Male 1930	Male 1920	Female 1930	Female 1920
Total	82,660	100.0	91,232	96,558	41,160	46,843	41,500	44,389
English and Celtic	25,142	30.4	28,282	34,321	11,258	12,840	13,884	15,442
Germanic:								
German	1,836	2.2	2,053	2,239	965	1,100	871	953
Dutch	155	0.2	189	68	96	106	59	83
Flemish	463	0.6	453	75	262	251	201	202
Scandinavian:								
Swedish	1,624	2.0	1,916	2,081	802	957	822	959
Norwegian	385	0.5	423	495	213	216	172	207
Danish	158	0.2	192	124	85	122	73	70
Icelandic	...	...		2				
Latin and Greek:								
Italian	1,957	2.4	2,077	2,083	1,157	1,307	770	770
French	38,024	46.0	38,609	41,060	18,893	19,545	19,181	19,064
Spanish	47	0.1	46	32	34	28	13	18
Portuguese	309	0.4	151	123	228	89	81	62
Rumanian	53	0.1	30	40	36	22	17	18
Greek	3,317	4.0	5,316	4,359	2,009	3,473	1,308	1,843
Slavic and Lettic:								
Polish	3,679	4.5	4,477	3,733	1,903	2,445	1,776	2,032
Czech	20	...	38	16	14	19	12	19
Slovak	50	0.1	31	3	27	23	23	8
Russian	1,129	1.4	1,716	210	703	1,188	426	528
Ruthenian	1	...	134	38	53	65	1	69
Ukrainian	105	0.1					52	
Slovenian	2	...	6	11	2	3	...	3
Croatian	...	...	8	4		6		2
Serbian	8	...	64	6	5	34	3	30
Bulgarian	11	...	9	38	8	5	3	4
Wendish	...	...		1		1		
Lithuanian	1,105	1.3	1,372	1,228	638	837	467	535
Lettish	20	...			15		11	
Unclassified:								
Yiddish	653	0.8	1,097	855	349	595	304	502
Magyar	35	...	39	31	21	25	14	14
Finnish	1,378	1.7	1,538	1,199	756	874	622	664
Estonian	1	...					1	
Armenian	288	0.3	276	330	174	211	114	65
Arabic	433	0.5	522	387	244	322	189	200
Turkish	48	0.1	41	95	42	35	6	20
Albanian	185	0.2	107	95	120	87	65	
All other								
Unknown	27	...	19	1,177	18	12	9	7

VERMONT

MOTHER TONGUE	1930 Number	1930 Per cent	1920	1910	Male 1930	Male 1920	Female 1930	Female 1920
Total	43,061	100.0	44,525	49,861	22,824	23,711	20,237	20,814
English and Celtic	15,662	36.4	18,231	22,363	7,584	8,836	8,078	9,395
German	750	1.7	840	996	416	488	334	352
Dutch	33	0.1	51	45	22	29	11	22
Flemish	11	...	7	8	6	5	5	2
Swedish	1,119	2.6	1,146	1,380	618	607	501	539
Norwegian	111	0.3	102	103	69	63	42	39
Danish	135	0.3	159	172	86	97	49	62
Icelandic	1	...		1	1			
Italian	3,204	7.4	4,201	4,950	1,843	2,562	1,361	1,689
French	17,524	40.7	14,406	14,902	9,460	7,629	8,064	6,777
Spanish	497	1.2	676	363	320	474	177	202
Portuguese	49	0.1	29	85	45	23	4	6
Rumanian	6	...	11	9	4	6	2	5
Greek	228	0.5	170	119	167	138	61	34
Polish	1,363	3.2	1,704	2,025	780	1,029	583	675
Czech	48	0.1	80	26	25	52	23	28
Slovak	96	0.2	163	118	62	97	34	66
Russian	392	0.9	733	91	274	516	118	217
Ruthenian	4	...	64	106	2	44	2	20
Ukrainian	23	0.1			15		8	
Slovenian	46	0.1	31	48	33	20	13	11
Croatian	5	...	20	6	4	11	1	9
Serbian	7	...	35	2	5	23	2	12
Bulgarian	1	...	4	32	1	2	...	
Wendish	...	...					27	
Lithuanian	103	0.2	119	107	78	84	27	35
Lettish	18	...			5		5	
Yiddish	530	1.2	607	810	283	325	247	282
Magyar	224	0.5	188	390	127	115	97	73
Finnish	547	1.3	451	262	302	255	245	196
Estonian	2	...		1			1	
Armenian	29	0.1	54	19	19	45	10	9
Arabic	270	0.6	232	205	151	132	119	100
Turkish	4	...					2	
Albanian	8	...	6	1	8	4	2	2
All other								
Unknown	16	...	5	117	5	5	11	3

358 POPULATION

TABLE 9.—MOTHER TONGUE OF THE FOREIGN-BORN WHITE POPULATION, BY SEX, BY DIVISIONS AND STATES: 1930, 1920, AND 1910—Continued

MASSACHUSETTS and RHODE ISLAND

MOTHER TONGUE	MASS. Total 1930 Number	MASS. Total 1930 Per cent	MASS. Total 1920	MASS. Total 1910	MASS. Male 1930	MASS. Male 1920	MASS. Female 1930	MASS. Female 1920	R.I. Total 1930 Number	R.I. Total 1930 Per cent	R.I. Total 1920	R.I. Total 1910	R.I. Male 1930	R.I. Male 1920	R.I. Female 1930	R.I. Female 1920
Total	1,054,636	100.0	1,077,499	1,051,031	509,462	533,297	545,174	544,202	170,714	100.0	173,495	178,023	83,151	86,162	87,563	87,333
English and Celtic	456,485	43.3	462,202	506,068	194,540	198,794	261,945	263,408	57,353	33.6	61,961	72,063	24,603	27,020	32,750	34,941
Germanic:																
German	25,506	2.4	27,401	33,282	12,938	14,173	12,568	13,228	3,866	2.3	3,988	5,121	1,964	2,000	1,902	1,988
Dutch	1,917	0.2	2,274	1,817	1,099	1,280	818	994	141	0.1	149	142	83	92	58	57
Flemish	1,264	0.1	1,747	1,255	655	941	609	806	302	0.2	457	195	146	230	156	218
Scandinavian:																
Swedish	38,684	3.7	39,613	41,261	19,258	19,363	19,426	20,250	6,343	3.7	6,680	7,508	3,069	3,199	3,274	3,481
Norwegian	5,227	0.5	5,329	5,341	2,656	2,703	2,571	2,626	498	0.3	535	568	272	277	226	258
Danish	2,992	0.3	3,451	3,406	1,768	1,979	1,224	1,472	281	0.2	334	333	153	182	128	152
Icelandic	49	---	12	18	30	4	19	8	1	---	---	---	1	---	---	---
Latin and Greek:																
Italian	126,868	12.0	117,225	85,541	71,639	68,171	55,229	49,054	32,876	19.3	32,501	27,415	18,021	18,122	14,855	14,379
French	121,712	11.5	116,304	141,266	59,110	57,259	62,602	59,105	33,954	19.9	31,270	36,549	16,339	15,424	17,615	15,846
Spanish	1,391	0.1	1,322	843	926	868	465	454	162	0.1	121	85	94	68	68	53
Portuguese	45,285	4.3	53,431	36,574	23,249	27,816	22,036	25,615	11,970	7.0	11,693	6,616	6,238	6,265	5,732	5,428
Rumanian	539	0.1	506	280	292	316	247	250	278	0.2	278	250	161	169	117	109
Greek	18,480	1.8	21,032	13,258	11,670	14,717	6,810	6,315	1,135	0.7	1,100	1,098	749	829	386	331
Slavic and Lettic:																
Polish	59,251	5.6	69,894	58,273	30,676	38,095	28,575	31,799	6,955	4.1	8,029	7,037	3,510	4,242	3,445	3,787
Czech	1,122	0.1	1,545	1,405	540	788	582	757	73	---	126	200	37	62	36	64
Slovak	1,414	0.1	1,246	845	709	693	705	553	88	0.1	126	124	41	70	47	56
Russian	14,126	1.3	18,166	1,888	8,151	10,783	5,975	7,383	1,499	0.9	2,244	124	827	1,248	672	996
Ruthenian	33	---		332	16		17		12	---		183	4		8	
Ukrainian	1,512	0.1	854		810	463	702	391	809	0.5	759		413	419	396	340
Slovenian	92	---	247	560	52	132	40	115	2	---	12	47	1	6	1	6
Croatian	43	---	80	93	30	49	13	31	1	---	12	2	1	10	---	2
Serbian	82	---	636	64	53	327	29	309	5	---	119	3	4	58	1	61
Bulgarian	80	---	82	215	59	70	21	12	37	---	35	66	18	22	19	13
Wendish	1	---			1											
Lithuanian	21,370	2.0	25,030	18,062	11,728	14,615	9,642	10,415	790	0.5	775	617	426	420	364	355
Lettish	1,318	0.1			664		654		16	---			11		5	
Unclassified:																
Yiddish	72,472	6.9	74,374	71,337	36,608	38,575	35,864	35,790	6,377	3.7	6,270	7,548	3,209	3,224	3,168	3,046
Magyar	725	0.1	878	830	369	449	356	429	100	0.1	115	101	44	55	56	60
Finnish	11,352	1.1	12,906	10,294	5,676	6,652	5,676	6,254	322	0.2	176	227	149	90	173	86
Estonian	74	---	42	2	51	27	23	15	6	---	---	---	3	---	3	---
Armenian	11,582	1.1	8,890	6,654	6,666	6,133	4,916	2,763	2,810	1.6	1,006	2,340	1,620	1,348	1,190	558
Arabic	7,269	0.7	7,444	5,482	3,977	4,411	3,292	3,033	1,308	0.8	1,325	732	717	726	591	599
Turkish	1,351	0.1	1,103	1,072	918	971	433	132	167	0.1	219	345	113	189	54	30
Albanian	2,520	0.2	1,943	757	1,639	1,584	881	359	114	0.1	107	49	72	83	42	24
All other	44	---	27	9	30	20	14	7	13	---	---	9	8	---	5	---
Unknown	404	---	137	2,638	209	76	195	61	50	---	13	320	30	4	20	9

CONNECTICUT and NEW YORK

MOTHER TONGUE	CONN. Total 1930 Number	CONN. Total 1930 Per cent	CONN. Total 1920	CONN. Total 1910	CONN. Male 1930	CONN. Male 1920	CONN. Female 1930	CONN. Female 1920	N.Y. Total 1930 Number	N.Y. Total 1930 Per cent	N.Y. Total 1920	N.Y. Total 1910	N.Y. Male 1930	N.Y. Male 1920	N.Y. Female 1930	N.Y. Female 1920
Total	382,871	100.0	376,502	328,754	197,846	199,885	185,025	176,617	3,191,549	100.0	2,784,895	2,729,052	1,653,170	1,441,808	1,538,379	1,343,087
English and Celtic	84,472	22.1	86,646	95,982	38,015	39,323	46,457	47,323	647,262	20.3	565,890	652,307	298,643	252,757	348,619	313,133
Germanic:																
German	32,075	8.4	31,822	36,458	16,089	16,316	15,986	15,506	448,962	14.1	379,919	484,310	228,362	194,036	220,600	185,883
Dutch	531	0.1	484	306	328	276	203	188	14,821	0.5	14,484	13,505	9,036	8,581	5,785	5,903
Flemish	221	0.1	268	199	130	148	91	120	3,353	0.1	2,777	1,611	1,812	1,524	1,541	1,253
Scandinavian:																
Swedish	18,917	4.9	18,151	18,726	9,762	9,117	9,155	9,034	63,928	2.0	54,790	55,739	33,617	26,780	30,311	28,010
Norwegian	1,727	0.5	1,373	1,229	905	706	822	667	44,379	1.4	27,163	24,713	24,597	14,469	19,782	12,694
Danish	3,111	0.8	3,040	2,844	1,779	1,661	1,332	1,379	17,115	0.5	13,984	12,730	10,034	8,379	6,481	5,605
Icelandic	5	---	2	---	2	1	3	1	98	---	27	10	58	14	40	13
Latin and Greek:																
Italian	87,621	22.9	80,619	57,158	49,218	46,496	38,403	34,123	633,342	19.8	546,863	474,283	359,024	307,401	274,318	239,462
French	23,919	7.6	18,376	22,118	9,602	9,245	14,317	9,131	63,321	2.0	48,238	51,366	30,231	22,813	33,090	25,425
Spanish	1,276	0.3	1,428	156	888	1,185	388	243	44,802	1.4	26,631	7,955	28,739	18,153	15,023	8,478
Portuguese	2,531	0.7	1,351	721	1,648	911	883	440	6,096	0.2	1,704	820	4,836	1,145	1,260	559
Rumanian	485	0.1	623	259	256	365	229	258	15,532	0.5	17,583	7,993	8,004	9,063	7,528	8,520
Greek	3,619	1.0	3,897	1,666	2,342	2,858	1,307	1,039	38,157	1.2	24,371	12,885	26,287	18,200	11,870	6,171
Slavic and Lettic:																
Polish	42,268	11.0	46,305	35,472	22,133	25,640	20,135	20,665	190,051	6.0	194,365	168,841	100,210	106,971	89,841	87,394
Czech	2,300	0.6	1,906	1,451	1,121	945	1,179	961	21,641	0.7	24,985	24,493	9,732	11,455	11,909	13,530
Slovak	8,566	2.2	8,907	5,506	4,303	4,662	4,263	4,245	22,211	0.7	23,081	14,319	11,024	12,008	11,187	11,073
Russian	9,810	2.6	13,055	1,928	5,841	8,101	3,969	4,954	112,221	3.5	141,865	21,127	61,104	77,783	51,117	64,082
Ruthenian	195	0.1		405	94		101		1,544	---		3,466	811		733	
Ukrainian	2,268	0.6	1,801		1,191	980	1,077	815	14,489	0.5	11,067		7,696	6,078	6,793	4,989
Slovenian	555	0.1	803	2,083	290	450	265	353	3,195	0.1	4,282	6,766	1,870	2,338	1,325	1,944
Croatian	187	---	162	378	116	111	71	51	3,324	0.1	4,246	3,757	2,277	2,917	1,047	1,329
Serbian	57	---	175	68	34	108	23	67	1,133	---	1,956	877	803	1,148	330	808
Bulgarian	53	---	26	177	33	23	20	3	857	---	579	883	612	486	245	93
Wendish	23	---	375	1	13	203	10	172	14	---	5	---	8	3	6	2
Lithuanian	12,519	3.3	13,770	8,418	7,015	8,251	5,504	5,519	15,933	0.5	15,579	12,080	9,168	9,295	6,765	6,284
Lettish	106	---			65		41		1,589	---			953		636	
Unclassified:																
Yiddish	22,505	5.9	25,484	22,534	11,461	13,258	11,044	12,226	656,466	20.6	549,879	585,543	330,308	283,574	326,158	266,305
Magyar	10,171	2.7	11,543	9,115	4,985	5,971	5,206	5,572	55,103	1.7	59,247	52,074	25,883	28,348	29,220	30,899
Finnish	1,222	0.3	794	354	570	372	652	422	14,892	0.5	10,662	7,232	6,358	4,444	8,534	6,218
Estonian	54	---	36	8	34	24	20	12	1,279	---	267	49	853	183	426	84
Armenian	1,148	0.3	1,168	1,058	672	765	476	403	9,328	0.3	5,649	3,441	5,381	3,871	3,947	1,778
Arabic	1,931	0.5	1,573	837	1,116	995	815	578	12,361	0.4	9,131	5,541	7,057	5,235	5,304	3,896
Turkish	209	0.1	119	68	135	91	74	28	3,841	0.1	2,049	827	2,274	1,321	1,567	728
Albanian	409	0.1	109	---	296	149	113	20	992	---	428	340	728	376	264	52
All other	141	---	147	78	81	109	60	38	439	---	234	146	302	155	137	79
Unknown	634	0.2	124	999	303	63	331	61	7,918	0.2	915	16,323	3,878	504	4,040	411

MOTHER TONGUE OF THE FOREIGN-BORN WHITE POPULATION   359

TABLE 9.—MOTHER TONGUE OF THE FOREIGN-BORN WHITE POPULATION, BY SEX, BY DIVISIONS AND STATES: 1930, 1920, AND 1910—Continued

NEW JERSEY / PENNSYLVANIA

MOTHER TONGUE	Total F-B White 1930 Number	Per cent	1920	1910	Male 1930	Male 1920	Female 1930	Female 1920	Total F-B White 1930 Number	Per cent	1920	1910	Male 1930	Male 1920	Female 1930	Female 1920
Total	844,442	100.0	738,428	658,148	443,132	391,536	401,310	346,892	1,233,051	100.0	1,386,576	1,438,617	665,438	782,269	567,613	604,307
English and Celtic	167,910	19.9	143,043	159,862	77,486	65,247	90,424	77,796	244,821	19.9	277,040	348,586	114,150	130,208	130,671	146,832
Germanic:																
German	148,114	17.5	123,760	140,948	76,377	63,447	71,737	60,313	161,246	13.1	173,868	222,430	82,174	90,303	79,072	83,565
Dutch	14,662	1.7	13,289	12,688	8,304	7,274	6,358	6,015	1,255	0.1	1,735	1,310	820	1,054	435	681
Flemish	2,005	0.2	1,447	951	1,064	774	941	673	779	0.1	2,573	1,300	435	1,356	344	1,217
Scandinavian:																
Swedish	14,088	1.7	11,132	10,909	7,498	5,588	6,590	5,544	16,651	1.4	20,115	23,787	9,226	11,083	7,425	9,032
Norwegian	7,682	0.9	5,262	5,304	4,466	2,843	3,216	2,419	2,822	0.2	2,326	2,213	1,724	1,314	1,098	1,012
Danish	6,598	0.8	5,699	5,202	3,959	3,324	2,639	2,375	2,807	0.2	2,958	3,035	1,734	1,798	1,073	1,160
Icelandic	43	---	28	11	17	16	26	12	6	---	1	2	3	1	3	---
Latin and Greek:																
Italian	192,154	22.8	157,820	115,084	108,445	89,833	83,709	67,996	226,307	18.4	224,252	199,372	134,374	140,088	92,023	84,164
French	13,022	1.5	10,328	8,288	6,298	5,098	6,724	5,230	13,212	1.1	13,838	14,753	6,315	7,020	6,897	6,818
Spanish	6,948	0.8	3,090	858	5,312	2,260	1,636	830	4,540	0.4	3,423	786	3,404	2,696	1,052	727
Portuguese	4,001	0.5	721	135	3,149	500	852	131	1,385	0.1	838	245	1,161	710	224	128
Rumanian	2,125	0.3	2,182	1,110	1,177	1,202	948	800	4,927	0.4	6,149	6,246	2,853	3,813	2,074	2,836
Greek	6,550	0.8	4,586	1,027	4,425	3,406	2,125	1,180	13,618	1.1	14,729	6,749	9,721	12,200	3,897	2,529
Slavic and Lettic:																
Polish	80,213	9.5	85,810	70,107	42,028	47,732	38,185	38,078	140,659	11.4	172,017	188,276	77,712	100,931	62,947	71,686
Czech	5,200	0.6	4,734	3,475	2,480	2,334	2,711	2,400	10,006	0.8	8,593	7,600	5,298	4,761	4,708	3,822
Slovak	20,741	2.5	22,053	13,668	10,530	11,977	10,211	10,076	88,354	7.2	120,825	80,014	48,477	71,753	39,877	49,072
Russian	20,530	2.4	25,190	2,355	11,810	14,969	8,720	10,221	38,053	3.1	53,143	14,578	22,191	32,017	15,862	21,126
Ruthenian	1,387	0.2	5,105	3,312	708	2,828	679	2,277	5,259	0.4	23,917	13,005	2,938	14,834	2,321	9,083
Ukrainian	7,163	0.8			3,778		3,385		16,221	1.3			9,083		7,189	
Slovenian	946	0.1	1,402	4,618	546	723	400	679	10,677	0.9	17,210	44,035	6,438	10,789	4,254	6,421
Croatian	708	0.1	669	441	499	469	269	200	20,351	1.7	25,739	25,302	13,333	18,778	7,018	6,661
Serbian	365	---	590	203	239	340	126	247	6,465	0.5	7,490	4,464	4,524	5,450	1,941	2,040
Bulgarian	85	---	57	144	56	43	29	14	699	0.1	839	1,666	532	761	107	78
Wendish	47	---	11	1	25	5	22	6	1,236	0.1	1,504	1,354	593	766	643	738
Lithuanian	8,057	1.0	8,645	5,905	4,504	5,180	3,553	3,450	34,704	2.8	42,014	41,372	19,981	25,000	14,723	16,414
Lettish	381	---			227		154		880	0.1			477		409	
Unclassified:																
Yiddish	68,204	8.1	59,919	49,128	35,036	31,345	33,228	28,574	110,619	9.0	108,176	105,965	56,035	56,040	54,584	52,136
Magyar	31,948	3.8	34,869	25,376	16,090	18,080	15,858	16,180	33,437	2.7	47,673	45,737	17,888	27,923	15,549	19,750
Finnish	2,067	0.2	1,581	1,416	939	695	1,128	880	1,845	0.1	2,504	2,308	1,041	1,447	804	1,057
Estonian	166	---	40		115	25	51	15	86	---	47	1	58	36	28	11
Armenian	3,225	0.4	2,364	1,455	1,751	1,396	1,474	968	2,003	0.2	2,895	1,190	1,470	1,898	1,124	997
Arabic	2,995	0.4	2,340	843	1,664	1,389	1,331	951	5,601	0.5	5,040	8,171	3,141	3,808	2,460	2,332
Turkish	540	0.1	194	58	305	124	235	70	507	---	386	114	326	344	181	42
Albanian	143	---	90	7	95	67	48	23	690	0.1	696	94	531	647	159	49
All other	103	---	55	26	75	38	28	17	143	---	91	41	83	70	60	21
Unknown	3,206	0.4	308	11,427	1,646	158	1,560	150	9,478	0.8	742	26,721	5,160	472	4,318	270

OHIO / INDIANA

MOTHER TONGUE	Total F-B White 1930 Number	Per cent	1920	1910	Male 1930	Male 1920	Female 1930	Female 1920	Total F-B White 1930 Number	Per cent	1920	1910	Male 1930	Male 1920	Female 1930	Female 1920
Total	644,151	100.0	677,894	597,176	351,985	390,640	292,166	287,254	135,134	100.0	150,230	159,279	76,957	87,648	58,177	62,582
English and Celtic	112,789	17.5	115,716	123,437	56,118	58,543	56,671	57,173	22,982	17.0	25,651	30,656	12,042	13,505	10,940	12,146
Germanic:																
German	140,175	21.8	159,325	198,815	72,057	83,172	68,118	76,153	32,816	24.3	43,080	60,247	17,337	22,993	15,479	20,087
Dutch	2,144	0.3	2,692	2,716	1,286	1,601	858	1,091	1,955	1.4	2,072	2,181	1,161	1,197	794	875
Flemish	651	0.1	866	305	412	517	239	349	2,614	1.9	2,106	1,438	1,457	1,184	1,157	922
Scandinavian:																
Swedish	7,442	1.2	7,313	5,564	4,236	4,266	3,206	3,047	4,679	3.5	4,924	5,128	2,708	2,785	1,971	2,139
Norwegian	1,583	0.2	1,422	1,090	935	867	648	555	701	0.5	522	519	429	295	272	227
Danish	2,131	0.3	2,275	1,908	1,346	1,412	785	863	928	0.7	934	918	576	576	352	358
Icelandic	6	---	5		4	3	2	2	2	---			2			
Latin and Greek:																
Italian	70,819	11.0	61,322	42,331	42,966	39,772	27,853	21,550	6,729	5.0	6,724	6,916	4,209	4,461	2,520	2,263
French	8,610	1.3	8,606	8,600	4,251	4,702	4,305	3,904	3,325	2.5	3,742	3,983	1,760	2,076	1,565	1,666
Spanish	2,291	0.4	1,886	215	1,667	1,512	624	374	1,076	0.8	634	84	781	446	295	188
Portuguese	214	---	199	205	153	134	61	65	99	0.1	15	4	78	9	21	6
Rumanian	9,555	1.5	12,486	10,034	5,959	9,022	3,596	3,464	2,703	2.0	2,931	318	1,763	2,094	940	837
Greek	13,014	2.0	13,216	3,220	9,848	11,844	3,166	1,372	4,013	3.0	3,654	1,996	3,086	3,259	927	395
Slavic and Lettic:																
Polish	52,792	8.2	62,508	41,828	29,608	37,282	23,184	25,226	16,591	12.3	19,434	14,530	9,351	11,343	7,240	8,091
Czech	21,820	3.4	24,127	22,701	10,874	12,247	10,946	11,880	1,473	1.1	1,630	996	811	936	662	694
Slovak	39,109	6.1	37,640	20,109	21,080	22,388	18,029	15,252	6,228	4.6	5,398	1,727	3,530	3,283	2,698	2,115
Russian	11,608	1.8	16,940	2,378	7,051	10,607	4,557	6,333	2,564	1.9	3,269	318	1,689	2,164	875	1,105
Ruthenian	308	---	4,376	1,005	183	2,733	125	1,643	74	0.1	179	161	44	109	30	70
Ukrainian	4,711	0.7			2,671		2,040		244	0.2			138		106	
Slovenian	17,487	2.7	15,325	14,911	10,095	9,506	7,392	5,819	1,026	0.8	1,104	2,063	629	672	897	432
Croatian	10,700	1.7	10,633	7,071	6,833	7,817	3,867	2,816	3,201	2.4	3,108	2,428	2,068	2,211	1,133	897
Serbian	4,741	0.7	8,437	3,082	3,165	4,502	1,576	1,935	2,095	1.6	1,819	1,225	1,526	1,403	569	416
Bulgarian	2,435	0.4	3,176	1,485	1,956	3,005	479	171	734	0.5	957	1,299	566	875	168	82
Wendish	16	---	7	3			6	2								
Lithuanian	5,919	0.9	6,048	3,326	3,445	3,885	2,474	2,163	1,864	1.4	2,150	1,383	1,177	1,393	687	757
Lettish	307	---			176		131		20	---			17			
Unclassified:																
Yiddish	34,575	5.4	30,306	24,635	17,855	16,340	16,720	13,966	3,540	2.6	3,409	3,316	1,929	1,900	1,611	1,509
Magyar	51,802	8.0	60,347	43,959	27,520	35,053	24,282	25,294	8,380	6.2	9,255	7,806	4,585	5,452	3,795	3,803
Finnish	5,526	0.9	6,254	4,069	2,818	3,405	2,708	2,849	244	0.2	216	191	151	118	93	98
Estonian	63	---	24	1	47	19	16	5	2	---	4		2	3		
Armenian	780	0.1	902	300	521	730	259	172	186	0.1	134	162	127	93	59	41
Arabic	4,810	0.7	3,984	1,762	2,878	2,489	1,932	1,495	924	0.7	801	686	561	529	363	272
Turkish	407	0.1	480	107	305	455	102	25	107	0.1	84	154	101	79	6	5
Albanian	505	0.1	414	36	440	385	65	29	135	0.1	74	44	116	70	19	4
All other	151	---	70	51	95	44	56	26	57	---	53	16	37	41	20	12
Unknown	2,149	0.3	567	5,908	1,121	376	1,028	191	806	0.6	163	2,963	410	94	396	69

TABLE 9.—MOTHER TONGUE OF THE FOREIGN-BORN WHITE POPULATION, BY SEX, BY DIVISIONS AND STATES: 1930, 1920, AND 1910—Continued

ILLINOIS

MOTHER TONGUE	TOTAL FOREIGN-BORN WHITE 1930 Number	1930 Per cent	1920	1910	MALE 1930	MALE 1920	FEMALE 1930	FEMALE 1920
Total	1,218,158	100.0	1,203,396	1,201,949	657,937	654,817	560,221	548,579
English and Celtic	182,462	15.0	185,269	214,161	92,069	93,057	90,393	92,212
Germanic:								
German	250,319	20.5	257,443	311,680	130,228	133,097	120,091	123,446
Dutch	14,568	1.2	14,664	14,767	8,282	8,231	6,286	6,433
Flemish	8,635	0.7	9,411	6,084	4,788	5,531	3,847	3,880
Scandinavian:								
Swedish	112,058	9.2	105,968	116,127	60,945	54,439	51,113	51,529
Norwegian	29,983	2.5	27,628	32,811	15,529	13,449	14,454	14,179
Danish	18,914	1.6	17,078	17,850	11,301	9,793	7,613	7,285
Icelandic	100	------	25	24	57	12	43	13
Latin and Greek:								
Italian	111,387	9.1	95,292	73,085	65,879	57,449	45,508	37,843
French	18,105	1.5	15,929	17,853	9,235	8,334	8,870	7,595
Spanish	3,494	0.3	1,558	597	2,307	1,075	1,097	483
Portuguese	254	------	322	435	153	191	101	131
Rumanian	4,255	0.3	3,388	2,573	2,468	2,057	1,787	1,331
Greek	20,639	1.7	16,313	10,487	15,480	13,237	5,159	3,076
Slavic and Lettic:								
Polish	153,038	12.6	165,594	148,809	81,620	91,544	71,418	74,050
Czech	53,797	4.4	57,036	56,448	26,639	28,772	27,158	28,264
Slovak	21,205	1.7	21,481	13,722	11,232	12,103	9,973	9,378
Russian	23,641	1.9	21,439	2,595	13,871	13,499	9,770	7,940
Ruthenian	163	------	1,710	976	91	1,026	72	684
Ukrainian	3,095	0.3			1,746		1,349	
Slovenian	9,046	0.7	8,925	10,718	5,142	5,287	3,904	3,638
Croatian	13,207	1.1	11,273	9,464	8,456	7,778	4,841	3,495
Serbian	2,599	0.2	3,505	3,596	1,779	2,412	820	1,093
Bulgarian	1,374	0.1	1,156	2,548	1,100	1,037	274	119
Wendish	10	------	66	------	5	36	5	30
Lithuanian	40,955	3.4	43,082	32,662	24,402	27,127	16,553	15,955
Lettish	1,008	0.1			564		444	
Unclassified:								
Yiddish	90,410	7.4	91,937	72,165	46,545	48,439	43,874	43,408
Magyar	15,537	1.3	18,615	14,658	8,148	10,229	7,389	8,386
Finnish	3,576	0.3	2,548	2,318	1,695	1,242	1,881	1,306
Estonian	66	------	14	------	40	12	26	2
Armenian	2,499	0.2	1,742	1,402	1,544	1,305	955	437
Arabic	2,537	0.2	1,860	1,106	1,571	1,308	966	552
Turkish	491	------	253	302	352	214	139	39
Albanian	270	------	111	75	217	101	53	10
All other	490	------	226	208	341	185	149	41
Unknown	3,872	0.3	535	8,953	2,026	309	1,846	226

MICHIGAN

MOTHER TONGUE	TOTAL FOREIGN-BORN WHITE 1930 Number	1930 Per cent	1920	1910	MALE 1930	MALE 1920	FEMALE 1930	FEMALE 1920
Total	840,268	100.0	725,488	595,450	464,902	412,963	375,366	312,525
English and Celtic	287,982	34.3	210,849	209,208	147,832	113,320	140,150	106,529
Germanic:								
German	111,676	13.3	110,758	122,497	58,834	58,557	52,842	52,201
Dutch	32,411	3.9	34,195	34,705	17,916	18,637	14,495	15,558
Flemish	12,092	1.4	9,784	4,713	6,733	5,812	5,359	3,972
Scandinavian:								
Swedish	26,059	3.1	26,895	28,667	15,178	15,396	10,881	11,499
Norwegian	6,899	0.8	6,646	7,363	3,927	3,648	2,972	2,998
Danish	7,147	0.9	7,155	6,458	4,383	4,250	2,764	2,905
Icelandic	32	------	7	2	15	4	17	3
Latin and Greek:								
Italian	44,088	5.2	30,675	18,002	28,050	20,091	16,038	10,584
French	34,618	4.1	22,798	31,246	18,596	12,812	16,022	9,986
Spanish	2,437	0.3	810	105	1,806	662	631	148
Portuguese	170	------	74	17	134	56	36	18
Rumanian	8,214	1.0	7,093	846	5,070	4,792	3,144	2,301
Greek	10,369	1.2	7,008	1,328	8,100	6,063	2,269	945
Slavic and Lettic:								
Polish	107,963	12.8	112,168	62,606	61,486	67,912	46,477	44,256
Czech	7,440	0.9	7,711	4,503	3,897	4,192	3,543	3,519
Slovak	8,996	1.1	6,477	2,068	5,104	3,933	3,892	2,544
Russian	12,605	1.5	14,524	833	8,323	10,165	4,282	4,359
Ruthenian	104	------	2,479	149	70	1,602	34	877
Ukrainian	4,984	0.6			2,977		2,007	
Slovenian	2,750	0.3	2,185	3,107	1,671	1,369	1,079	816
Croatian	5,582	0.7	5,219	4,061	3,579	3,707	2,003	1,512
Serbian	4,673	0.6	4,304	830	3,162	3,086	1,511	1,218
Bulgarian	2,383	0.3	1,940	422	1,895	1,784	488	156
Wendish	------	------	3	1	------	3	------	------
Lithuanian	8,650	1.0	7,075	2,009	5,286	4,695	3,364	2,380
Lettish	233	------			140		93	
Unclassified:								
Yiddish	28,561	3.4	23,153	8,838	14,959	12,986	13,602	10,167
Magyar	19,075	2.3	18,207	6,324	10,605	10,907	8,470	7,300
Finnish	25,321	3.0	28,148	30,321	14,207	16,351	11,114	11,797
Estonian	85	------	33	------	62	30	23	3
Armenian	5,434	0.6	2,606	472	3,360	2,000	2,074	516
Arabic	7,850	0.9	4,425	1,111	5,173	3,124	2,677	1,301
Turkish	1,026	0.1	438	58	767	412	259	26
Albanian	553	0.1	238	24	489	225	64	13
All other	231	------	72	4	193	65	38	7
Unknown	1,575	0.2	336	2,552	923	225	652	111

WISCONSIN

MOTHER TONGUE	TOTAL FOREIGN-BORN WHITE 1930 Number	1930 Per cent	1920	1910	MALE 1930	MALE 1920	FEMALE 1930	FEMALE 1920
Total	386,213	100.0	459,997	512,536	214,677	258,649	171,536	201,348
English and Celtic	27,786	7.2	37,476	50,558	15,148	20,289	12,638	17,187
Germanic:								
German	162,384	42.0	188,083	224,497	86,311	100,290	76,073	87,793
Dutch	6,184	1.6	7,482	8,349	3,597	4,322	2,587	3,160
Flemish	1,817	0.5	2,786	1,852	1,049	1,625	768	1,161
Scandinavian:								
Swedish	19,607	5.1	23,758	26,942	11,690	14,107	7,917	9,651
Norwegian	34,388	8.9	45,443	57,036	19,168	24,903	15,220	20,540
Danish	13,127	3.4	15,382	16,725	7,894	9,124	5,233	6,258
Icelandic	49	------	55	5	23	27	26	28
Latin and Greek:								
Italian	12,619	3.3	11,318	9,622	7,089	7,280	4,930	4,038
French	6,151	1.6	7,171	11,404	3,404	4,243	2,687	2,928
Spanish	323	0.1	154	68	235	104	88	50
Portuguese	51	------	28	5	34	17	17	11
Rumanian	374	0.1	411	361	223	265	151	146
Greek	2,922	0.8	3,754	2,865	2,236	3,171	686	583
Slavic and Lettic:								
Polish	40,688	10.5	52,121	51,090	22,896	29,886	17,792	22,235
Czech	11,254	2.9	15,571	16,301	5,870	8,280	5,384	7,291
Slovak	6,206	1.6	6,201	3,408	3,394	3,746	2,812	2,455
Russian	4,001	1.0	4,678	528	2,554	3,227	1,447	1,451
Ruthenian	70	------	273	136	38	176	32	97
Ukrainian	232	0.1			139		93	
Slovenian	5,791	1.5	5,346	4,285	3,445	3,422	2,346	1,924
Croatian	4,085	1.1	3,588	2,694	2,529	2,467	1,556	1,121
Serbian	620	0.2	1,300	494	438	873	182	427
Bulgarian	263	0.1	310	319	223	292	40	18
Wendish	8	------	15	------	5	9	3	6
Lithuanian	3,549	0.9	4,642	2,907	2,298	3,213	1,251	1,429
Lettish	202	0.1			133		69	
Unclassified:								
Yiddish	9,062	2.3	9,908	8,361	4,759	5,307	4,303	4,601
Magyar	4,299	1.1	4,715	3,379	2,368	2,804	1,031	1,911
Finnish	4,988	1.3	5,928	4,724	2,945	3,564	2,043	2,364
Estonian	60	------	60	7	40	44	20	16
Armenian	1,050	0.3	892	321	647	807	403	85
Arabic	519	0.1	590	518	310	352	209	238
Turkish	153	------	77	42	131	70	22	7
Albanian	155	------	116	39	121	106	34	10
All other	17	------	11	5	13	9	4	2
Unknown	1,159	0.3	354	2,689	620	228	539	126

MINNESOTA

MOTHER TONGUE	TOTAL FOREIGN-BORN WHITE 1930 Number	1930 Per cent	1920	1910	MALE 1930	MALE 1920	FEMALE 1930	FEMALE 1920
Total	388,294	100.0	485,941	542,963	217,983	278,427	170,311	207,514
English and Celtic	38,551	9.9	52,283	61,772	20,547	28,620	18,004	23,663
Germanic:								
German	74,140	19.1	94,287	111,226	40,026	51,636	34,114	42,651
Dutch	4,742	1.2	5,418	3,990	2,812	3,190	1,930	2,228
Flemish	1,280	0.3	1,670	1,039	735	1,001	545	669
Scandinavian:								
Swedish	92,633	23.9	114,076	124,443	53,366	65,725	39,267	48,351
Norwegian	71,559	18.4	90,077	105,258	39,342	49,764	32,217	40,313
Danish	13,793	3.6	16,622	16,034	8,557	10,221	5,236	6,401
Icelandic	247	0.1	330	304	110	154	137	176
Latin and Greek:								
Italian	6,506	1.7	7,533	9,882	3,986	5,028	2,520	2,505
French	7,968	2.1	8,607	12,864	4,351	4,994	3,617	3,613
Spanish	189	------	92	84	126	56	63	36
Portuguese	9	------	7	19	4	3	5	4
Rumanian	1,156	0.3	1,504	1,588	671	907	485	597
Greek	1,744	0.4	2,354	1,861	1,457	2,116	287	238
Slavic and Lettic:								
Polish	13,265	3.4	16,857	20,153	7,379	9,742	5,886	7,115
Czech	7,814	2.0	10,659	11,655	4,103	5,763	3,711	4,896
Slovak	2,339	0.6	2,744	1,427	1,290	1,712	1,049	1,032
Russian	3,443	0.9	4,232	823	2,071	2,846	1,372	1,386
Ruthenian	206	0.1	585	66	104	365	102	220
Ukrainian	647	0.2			393		254	
Slovenian	5,516	1.4	5,597	6,701	3,221	3,525	2,295	2,072
Croatian	2,267	0.6	3,793	4,281	1,473	2,912	794	881
Serbian	1,118	0.3	1,794	2,607	795	1,413	323	381
Bulgarian	280	0.1	556	1,223	247	540	33	16
Wendish	------	------	1	1	------	1	------	------
Lithuanian	440	0.1	634	420	303	458	137	176
Lettish	80	------			42		38	
Unclassified:								
Yiddish	11,268	2.9	13,344	10,995	5,818	7,173	5,450	6,171
Magyar	919	0.2	1,431	1,597	491	804	428	627
Finnish	22,867	5.9	27,571	25,553	13,412	16,931	9,455	10,640
Estonian	17	------	13	------	13	10	4	3
Armenian	92	------	177	235	57	137	35	40
Arabic	707	0.2	859	440	400	512	307	347
Turkish	24	------	41	106	20	39	4	2
Albanian	23	------	27	63	17	27	6	------
All other	26	------	8	1	20	5	6	3
Unknown	419	0.1	158	4,252	224	97	195	61

MOTHER TONGUE OF THE FOREIGN-BORN WHITE POPULATION   361

TABLE 9.—MOTHER TONGUE OF THE FOREIGN-BORN WHITE POPULATION, BY SEX, BY DIVISIONS AND STATES: 1930, 1920, AND 1910—Continued

IOWA

MOTHER TONGUE	1930 Number	1930 Per cent	1920	1910	Male 1930	Male 1920	Female 1930	Female 1920
Total	165,735	100.0	223,292	273,015	92,129	125,485	73,606	97,807
English and Celtic	24,928	15.0	38,247	52,404	13,021	20,309	11,907	17,938
Germanic:								
German	59,844	36.1	78,059	103,634	32,796	43,294	27,048	35,665
Dutch	10,069	6.1	12,542	11,436	5,806	7,126	4,263	5,416
Flemish	610	0.4	959	452	351	572	259	387
Scandinavian:								
Swedish	16,860	10.2	22,483	26,793	9,404	12,502	7,456	9,981
Norwegian	12,920	7.8	17,324	21,912	7,033	9,404	5,887	7,920
Danish	14,770	8.9	18,217	18,707	8,780	10,983	5,990	7,234
Icelandic	6	---	8	1	4	5	2	
Latin and Greek:								
Italian	3,902	2.4	5,005	5,917	2,433	3,325	1,469	1,680
French	2,107	1.3	2,529	2,966	1,156	1,419	1,011	1,110
Spanish	229	0.1	267	86	156	175	73	92
Portuguese	2	---	44	28	2	31		13
Rumanian	157	0.1	218	463	100	154	57	64
Greek	1,031	1.2	2,804	3,619	1,609	2,621	322	273
Slavic and Lettic:								
Polish	1,135	0.7	1,448	2,156	665	901	470	547
Czech	7,110	4.3	9,040	11,080	3,638	5,164	3,472	4,776
Slovak	937	0.6	783	556	491	491	446	292
Russian	1,529	0.9	2,867	342	892	1,754	637	1,103
Ruthenian	131	0.1	30	37	65	20	66	10
Ukrainian	17	---			12		5	
Slovenian	178	0.1	237	585	103	153	75	54
Croatian	878	0.5	1,152	1,200	507	743	371	409
Serbian	197	0.1	656	670	134	438	63	218
Bulgarian	167	0.1	267	408	135	232	32	35
Wendish			3			2		1
Lithuanian	611	0.4	971	678	387	667	224	304
Lettish	33	---			24		9	
Unclassified:								
Yiddish	3,050	1.8	3,893	3,671	1,612	2,112	1,438	1,781
Magyar	208	0.2	420	222	109	245	129	175
Finnish	48	---	83	162	28	44	20	80
Estonian	1	---			1			
Armenian	88	0.1	93	89	67	84	21	9
Arabic	586	0.4	540	491	350	369	236	171
Turkish	19	---	31	59	16	26	3	5
Albanian	12	---	7	2	10	7	2	
All other	5	---	26	2	5	14		12
Unknown	310	0.2	159	2,228	167	99	143	60

MISSOURI

MOTHER TONGUE	1930 Number	1930 Per cent	1920	1910	Male 1930	Male 1920	Female 1930	Female 1920
Total	149,390	100.0	183,238	227,673	81,299	101,639	68,091	81,599
English and Celtic	25,928	17.4	35,872	48,689	13,284	18,433	12,644	17,439
Germanic:								
German	56,993	38.2	72,864	102,234	30,494	39,452	26,499	33,412
Dutch	644	0.4	966	1,018	414	576	230	390
Flemish	409	0.3	796	525	247	483	162	313
Scandinavian:								
Swedish	3,881	2.6	4,738	5,706	2,177	2,647	1,704	2,091
Norwegian	542	0.4	587	650	307	336	235	251
Danish	1,454	1.0	1,635	1,738	952	1,053	502	552
Icelandic	6	---	3	1	3	1	3	2
Latin and Greek:								
Italian	15,420	10.3	14,753	13,224	9,036	9,009	6,393	5,684
French	3,372	2.3	4,184	4,451	1,775	2,335	1,597	1,849
Spanish	963	0.6	1,013	533	581	630	382	383
Portuguese	21	---	38	42	13	24	8	14
Rumanian	702	0.5	1,250	1,730	444	775	318	475
Greek	2,486	1.6	2,960	3,129	1,929	2,572	506	388
Slavic and Lettic:								
Polish	5,740	3.8	6,602	8,444	3,073	3,715	2,667	2,887
Czech	3,445	2.3	4,823	5,497	1,725	2,441	1,720	2,382
Slovak	985	0.7	1,307	1,242	526	782	459	525
Russian	4,139	2.8	5,402	728	2,267	3,030	1,872	2,372
Ruthenian	29	---	448	325	16	286	13	162
Ukrainian	287	0.2			159		128	
Slovenian	292	0.2	401	712	171	237	121	164
Croatian	1,596	1.1	1,692	2,260	997	1,193	599	499
Serbian	485	0.3	716	690	298	483	187	233
Bulgarian	221	0.1	226	681	177	207	44	19
Wendish			1			1		
Lithuanian	505	0.3	514	455	310	332	195	182
Lettish	33	---			21		12	
Unclassified:								
Yiddish	14,993	10.0	14,927	15,293	7,753	7,908	7,240	7,019
Magyar	1,750	1.2	2,921	2,861	914	1,546	836	1,375
Finnish	77	0.1	65	107	44	37	33	28
Estonian	8	---		4	6	4	2	
Armenian	180	0.1	178	156	121	148	59	30
Arabic	847	0.6	920	694	526	587	321	333
Turkish	76	0.1	46	171	52	35	24	11
Albanian	242	0.2	187	157	176	166	66	21
All other	21	---	5	2	17	1	4	4
Unknown	600	0.4	194	3,519	294	114	306	80

NORTH DAKOTA

MOTHER TONGUE	1930 Number	1930 Per cent	1920	1910	Male 1930	Male 1920	Female 1930	Female 1920
Total	105,148	100.0	131,478	156,151	60,378	75,369	44,770	56,109
English and Celtic	13,964	13.3	18,475	24,650	7,541	10,226	6,423	8,249
Germanic:								
German	35,374	33.6	43,041	46,087	19,591	23,835	15,783	19,206
Dutch	656	0.6	958	740	418	580	238	378
Flemish	165	0.2	350	60	96	188	69	162
Scandinavian:								
Swedish	8,509	8.1	10,556	12,236	5,441	6,651	3,068	3,905
Norwegian	31,430	29.9	38,253	45,972	18,314	22,080	13,116	16,173
Danish	2,939	2.8	3,045	4,289	1,917	2,331	1,022	1,314
Icelandic	776	0.7	971	1,220	383	479	393	402
Latin and Greek:								
Italian	113	0.1	181	1,267	90	152	23	29
French	1,662	1.6	1,929	2,707	908	1,067	754	862
Spanish	53	0.1	12	18	29	7	24	5
Portuguese	1	---	2	4	1	1		1
Rumanian	110	0.1	201	318	62	124	48	77
Greek	289	0.3	453	1,152	258	423	31	30
Slavic and Lettic:								
Polish	1,213	1.2	1,455	1,850	766	958	447	527
Czech	1,828	1.7	2,551	2,785	1,018	1,406	810	1,145
Slovak	168	0.2	145	65	104	89	64	56
Russian	3,003	2.9	4,680	1,151	1,720	2,619	1,283	2,061
Ruthenian	14	---	498	643	9	309	5	189
Ukrainian	544	0.5			301		243	
Slovenian	44	---	36	73	36	27	8	9
Croatian	89	---	42	77	26	29	13	13
Serbian	9	---	80	17	8	57	1	23
Bulgarian	103	0.1	116	338	69	69	34	47
Wendish								
Lithuanian	58	0.1	74	1,224	47	57	11	17
Lettish	14	---			9		5	
Unclassified:								
Yiddish	468	0.4	858	1,085	257	456	211	402
Magyar	212	0.2	343	388	116	195	96	148
Finnish	873	0.8	1,124	1,204	515	655	358	466
Estonian	11	---		2	8		3	
Armenian	34	---	30	27	32	29	2	1
Arabic	244	0.2	307	281	168	201	76	106
Turkish	10	---	10	34	10	9		1
Albanian	2	---		11	2			
All other	5	---	1		2		3	1
Unknown	211	0.2	71	4,176	106	57	105	14

SOUTH DAKOTA

MOTHER TONGUE	1930 Number	1930 Per cent	1920	1910	Male 1930	Male 1920	Female 1930	Female 1920
Total	65,648	100.0	82,325	100,616	37,665	47,561	27,983	34,764
English and Celtic	7,027	10.7	9,988	13,425	3,920	5,659	3,107	4,329
Germanic:								
German	23,331	35.5	28,109	34,906	12,869	15,783	10,462	12,376
Dutch	3,029	4.6	3,192	2,829	1,814	1,876	1,215	1,316
Flemish	180	0.3	209	136	126	139	54	70
Scandinavian:								
Swedish	6,547	10.0	8,608	10,039	4,006	5,234	2,541	3,374
Norwegian	13,022	19.8	16,821	20,929	7,375	9,432	5,647	7,389
Danish	5,350	8.1	6,019	6,375	3,374	3,727	1,976	2,292
Icelandic	12	---	17	34	7	7	5	10
Latin and Greek:								
Italian	322	0.5	430	1,214	198	280	124	150
French	23	---	26	7	19	18	4	8
Spanish	1	---	3	3	1	3	1	
Portuguese								
Rumanian	82	0.1	81	68	45	65	37	16
Greek	291	0.4	360	280	243	336	48	24
Slavic and Lettic:								
Polish	452	0.7	588	765	296	360	156	208
Czech	2,345	3.6	3,090	3,440	1,254	1,719	1,091	1,371
Slovak	137	0.2	108	96	79	73	58	35
Russian	877	1.3	1,228	118	515	732	362	496
Ruthenian	11	---	12	41	6	9	5	3
Ukrainian	43	0.1	139	233	25	94	18	45
Slovenian	123	0.2	122	358	85	87	38	35
Croatian	38	0.1	204	164	32	129	6	75
Serbian	48	0.1	116	473	44	110	4	6
Bulgarian								
Wendish	19	---			15		4	
Lithuanian	7	---	40	81	4	36	3	4
Lettish								
Unclassified:								
Yiddish	193	0.3	357	266	121	218	72	139
Magyar	110	0.2	221	296	67	135	43	86
Finnish	847	1.3	1,049	1,443	457	583	390	466
Estonian	2	---			2			2
Armenian	7	---	16	45	5	14	2	2
Arabic	242	0.4	275	203	152	194	90	81
Turkish	7	---	8	52	6		1	
Albanian			1			1		
All other			4	2		4		
Unknown	158	0.2	48	963	77	32	81	16

POPULATION

Table 9.—MOTHER TONGUE OF THE FOREIGN-BORN WHITE POPULATION, BY SEX, BY DIVISIONS AND STATES: 1930, 1920, AND 1910—Continued

NEBRASKA / KANSAS

MOTHER TONGUE	NEBRASKA — Total F.B.W. 1930 Number	Per cent	1920	1910	Male 1930	Male 1920	Female 1930	Female 1920	KANSAS — Total F.B.W. 1930 Number	Per cent	1920	1910	Male 1930	Male 1920	Female 1930	Female 1920
Total	115,346	100.0	147,345	175,593	63,386	82,557	51,960	64,788	69,716	100.0	97,213	126,900	38,254	54,494	31,462	42,719
English and Celtic	12,889	11.2	18,809	25,229	6,730	10,168	6,159	8,641	13,909	20.0	21,200	30,344	7,344	11,554	6,565	9,646
Germanic:																
German	44,769	38.8	55,925	67,603	24,385	30,746	20,384	25,179	29,634	42.5	39,526	51,560	16,016	21,716	13,618	17,810
Dutch	602	0.5	850	1,038	360	522	242	328	626	0.9	812	980	356	471	270	341
Flemish	409	0.4	455	265	211	270	198	185	483	0.7	991	517	266	559	217	432
Scandinavian:																
Swedish	14,395	12.5	18,854	23,287	7,873	10,291	6,522	8,563	7,367	10.6	10,340	13,351	3,967	5,591	3,400	4,749
Norwegian	1,660	1.4	2,140	2,723	883	1,138	777	1,002	726	1.0	944	1,273	423	520	303	424
Danish	10,266	8.9	12,453	14,018	6,203	7,398	4,063	5,055	1,720	2.5	2,261	2,813	1,040	1,374	680	887
Icelandic	17	....	11	5	5	9	12	....	3	....	2	1	1	1	2	1
Latin and Greek:																
Italian	3,677	3.2	3,534	3,842	2,112	2,151	1,565	1,383	2,233	3.2	3,494	3,622	1,423	2,211	810	1,283
French	1,100	1.0	1,259	1,532	576	702	524	557	2,483	3.6	3,169	4,719	1,319	1,752	1,164	1,417
Spanish	247	0.2	194	51	167	149	80	45	291	0.4	418	412	180	274	111	144
Portuguese	7	....	10	6	5	5	2	5	13	....	21	10	8	14	5	7
Rumanian	218	0.2	386	439	135	282	83	104	43	0.1	39	85	28	32	15	7
Greek	840	0.7	1,506	3,586	689	1,401	151	105	540	0.8	641	1,604	447	502	93	70
Slavic and Lettic:																
Polish	3,653	3.2	4,743	5,166	2,105	2,893	1,548	1,850	1,459	2.1	2,130	2,614	857	1,282	602	848
Czech	13,839	12.0	17,325	19,004	7,198	9,239	6,641	8,086	2,416	3.5	3,548	4,119	1,250	1,860	1,166	1,088
Slovak	288	0.2	146	98	157	97	131	49	390	0.6	612	343	210	349	180	263
Russian	1,546	1.3	2,260	269	876	1,286	670	974	1,038	1.5	2,335	118	641	1,451	397	884
Ruthenian	7	....	15	10	5	} 9	} 2	} 6	....	....	21	78	} 11	16	} 8	} 5
Ukrainian	1				1											
Slovenian	86	0.1	72	228	51	49	35	23	1,262	1.8	1,416	998	714	847	548	569
Croatian	378	0.3	450	430	221	309	157	141	1,524	2.2	1,578	1,789	851	981	673	597
Serbian	224	0.2	611	228	146	396	78	215	97	0.1	227	180	59	151	38	76
Bulgarian	38	....	59	137	34	55	4	4	30	....	40	114	26	35	4	5
Wendish	5				4		1		1				1			
Lithuanian	427	0.4	} 557	402	249 }	356	178 }	201	135	0.2	} 153	327	81 }	102	54 }	51
Lettish	11	....			7		4		2	....			1		1	
Unclassified:																
Yiddish	2,598	2.3	3,446	2,607	1,362	1,851	1,236	1,595	442	0.6	569	747	270	336	172	233
Magyar	293	0.3	536	615	153	318	140	218	174	0.2	295	250	104	170	70	116
Finnish	32	....	39	71	19	26	13	13	32	....	40	49	25	30	7	10
Estonian	1				1											
Armenian	24	....	138	100	21	94	3	44	6	....	26	12	6	17		9
Arabic	384	0.3	425	372	236	266	148	159	250	0.4	270	182	147	161	103	109
Turkish	4	....	7	79	4	7	....		11	....	12	21	11	12		
Albanian	6	....	29		6	19		10	1	....	2		1	2		
All other	5	....	2		3		2	2	4				3		1	
Unknown	400	0.3	99	2,153	193	55	207	44	352	0.5	81	3,608	168	52	184	20

DELAWARE / MARYLAND

MOTHER TONGUE	DELAWARE — Total F.B.W. 1930 Number	Per cent	1920	1910	Male 1930	Male 1920	Female 1930	Female 1920	MARYLAND — Total F.B.W. 1930 Number	Per cent	1920	1910	Male 1930	Male 1920	Female 1930	Female 1920
Total	18,885	100.0	19,785	17,419	9,281	11,346	7,604	8,439	95,093	100.0	102,144	104,170	50,266	54,608	44,827	47,536
English and Celtic	4,639	27.5	5,328	6,367	2,219	2,557	2,420	2,771	14,585	15.3	15,746	18,508	6,928	7,484	7,657	8,262
Germanic:																
German	1,717	10.2	1,747	2,252	933	918	784	829	22,093	23.2	25,288	36,001	11,143	12,820	10,950	12,462
Dutch	49	0.3	38	22	42	25	7	13	333	0.4	340	185	233	221	100	119
Flemish	12	0.1	12	3	8	5	4	7	53	0.1	74	12	32	46	21	28
Scandinavian:																
Swedish	299	1.8	320	332	164	152	135	168	773	0.8	639	431	549	434	224	205
Norwegian	140	0.8	66	38	91	41	49	25	697	0.7	527	360	510	327	187	200
Danish	101	0.6	79	51	69	47	32	32	447	0.5	368	241	322	265	125	103
Icelandic	6	....			1				14	....	6		12	4	2	2
Latin and Greek:																
Italian	3,778	22.4	4,145	2,901	2,256	2,765	1,522	1,380	10,953	11.5	9,571	6,977	6,599	5,961	4,354	3,610
French	237	1.4	221	250	122	108	115	113	1,137	1.2	920	720	537	477	600	443
Spanish	214	1.3	184	12	189	172	25	12	596	0.6	441	169	456	306	140	135
Portuguese	14	0.1	18	2	13	16	1	2	75	0.1	36	22	58	23	17	13
Rumanian	33	0.2	62	15	17	35	16	27	344	0.4	257	177	214	155	130	102
Greek	362	2.1	288	40	265	234	97	54	1,736	1.8	976	499	1,239	767	497	209
Slavic and Lettic:																
Polish	2,744	16.3	4,194	3,657	1,482	2,466	1,262	1,728	10,373	10.9	11,997	12,924	5,507	6,622	4,866	5,375
Czech	104	0.6	107	60	56	61	48	46	2,799	2.9	3,794	4,149	1,310	1,870	1,489	1,924
Slovak	110	0.7	81	44	59	44	51	37	571	0.6	724	380	299	425	272	299
Russian	373	2.2	871	148	218	554	155	317	3,974	4.2	5,365	1,035	2,209	3,185	1,765	2,180
Ruthenian	3	....	} 299	104	2 }	} 192	} 146	} 107	12	....	} 250	25	6 }	149	6 }	} 101
Ukrainian	323	1.0			177 }				220	0.2			119 }		101 }	
Slovenian	6	....	14	23	3	7	3	7	81	0.1	177	237	48	106	33	71
Croatian	1	....	5	2			1	5	53	0.1	62	99	38	43	15	19
Serbian			16	4		12	....	4	105	0.1	253	130	67	163	38	90
Bulgarian	1			8			1		19	....	20	42	14	23	5	6
Wendish									15				15			
Lithuanian	40	0.3	} 147	68	26 }	} 97	23 }	} 50	2,498	2.6	} 2,766	2,237	1,368 }	} 1,618	1,130 }	} 1,148
Lettish	8	....			6		2		71	0.1			41		30	
Unclassified:																
Yiddish	1,286	7.6	1,231	671	686	659	600	572	18,448	19.4	20,084	16,419	9,285	10,279	9,163	9,805
Magyar	122	0.7	218	158	60	116	62	102	793	0.8	1,065	707	410	571	383	494
Finnish	44	0.3	33	4	24	15	20	18	361	0.4	159	42	228	99	133	60
Estonian			8						35	....	14		28	10	7	4
Armenian	6	....	5	1	5	4	1	1	44	....	41	16	27	28	17	13
Arabic	9	0.1	10	12	8	9	1	1	86	0.1	87	75	57	61	29	26
Turkish	2	....	2	1	2	2	....		47	....	15	13	36	13	11	2
Albanian									8	....	2		6	2	2	
All other	1	....	3		1	3	....		9	....	3	2	8		1	1
Unknown	97	0.6	33	169	77	21	20	12	650	0.7	53	1,335	323	33	327	20

MOTHER TONGUE OF THE FOREIGN-BORN WHITE POPULATION　　363

TABLE 9.—MOTHER TONGUE OF THE FOREIGN-BORN WHITE POPULATION, BY SEX, BY DIVISIONS AND STATES: 1930, 1920, AND 1910—Continued

MOTHER TONGUE	TOTAL FOREIGN-BORN WHITE				MALE		FEMALE		TOTAL FOREIGN-BORN WHITE				MALE		FEMALE	
	1930		1920	1910	1930	1920	1930	1920	1930		1920	1910	1930	1920	1930	1920
	Number	Per cent							Number	Per cent						
	DISTRICT OF COLUMBIA								VIRGINIA							
Total	29,932	100.0	28,522	24,342	15,652	15,124	14,280	13,398	23,820	100.0	30,760	26,624	13,701	19,032	10,119	11,728
English and Celtic	8,973	30.0	9,925	9,816	3,971	4,285	5,002	5,640	7,316	30.7	9,005	8,867	3,880	5,073	3,436	3,932
Germanic:																
German	4,238	14.2	4,117	5,208	2,224	2,212	2,014	1,905	3,126	13.1	3,513	4,580	1,841	2,140	1,285	1,373
Dutch	150	0.5	140	75	90	90	60	50	261	1.1	354	102	165	231	96	123
Flemish	27	0.1	30	11	15	17	12	13	43	0.2	58	25	25	39	18	19
Scandinavian:																
Swedish	447	1.5	485	361	219	225	228	260	477	2.0	667	372	317	475	160	192
Norwegian	228	0.8	217	147	112	120	116	97	299	1.3	490	306	197	355	102	135
Danish	221	0.7	229	176	147	147	74	82	337	1.4	460	247	235	337	102	123
Icelandic	3			3	1		2	1	7		1		4		3	1
Latin and Greek:																
Italian	4,405	14.7	3,830	2,760	2,668	2,438	1,737	1,392	1,866	7.8	2,457	2,457	1,226	1,672	640	785
French	1,067	3.0	935	699	471	416	596	519	596	2.5	655	443	258	353	338	302
Spanish	463	1.5	338	145	282	213	181	125	240	1.0	425	100	158	364	82	61
Portuguese	38	0.1	14	4	21	8	17	6	75	0.3	116	65	49	93	26	23
Rumanian	56	0.2	56	35	31	37	25	19	61	0.3	85	61	34	51	27	34
Greek	1,473	4.9	1,292	350	1,000	995	473	297	1,466	6.2	1,801	821	1,084	1,573	382	288
Slavic and Lettic:																
Polish	621	2.1	479	508	355	299	266	180	753	3.2	837	1,437	449	530	304	307
Czech	114	0.4	123	59	59	77	55	46	555	2.3	685	548	283	367	272	318
Slovak	37	0.1	37	15	21	24	16	13	499	2.1	711	232	261	394	238	317
Russian	1,532	5.1	1,757	101	845	1,008	687	749	993	4.2	1,726	170	574	1,066	419	660
Ruthenian	13		} 11	6	7	} 5	6	} 6	9		} 16	24	3	} 9	6	} 7
Ukrainian	8				4		2		5				3		2	
Slovenian	12		14	4	6	7	6	7	16	0.1	83	155	10	55	6	28
Croatian	13		6		9	4	4	2	14	0.1	15	15	7	8	7	1
Serbian	19	0.1	29	16	18	21	1	8	15	0.1	67	25	14	44	1	23
Bulgarian	11		4	11	8	3	3	1	8		16	32	8	15		1
Lithuanian	48	0.2	} 45	74	37	} 34	11	} 11	95	0.4	} 93	122	66	} 78	29	} 15
Lettish	23	0.1			14		9		36	0.2			21		15	
Unclassified:																
Yiddish	4,825	16.1	3,775	2,333	2,531	2,040	2,294	1,735	3,085	13.0	4,061	2,419	1,606	2,224	1,479	1,887
Magyar	175	0.6	155	87	93	90	82	65	516	2.2	1,109	1,255	307	721	209	478
Finnish	54	0.2	89	21	32	58	22	31	55	0.2	228	50	35	176	20	52
Estonian	2				1		1		10		10		3	14	1	2
Armenian	109	0.4	60	7	68	50	41	10	212	0.9	163	97	120	123	92	40
Arabic	307	1.0	247	95	173	148	134	99	545	2.3	586	348	322	360	223	226
Turkish	40	0.1	16	1	29	10	11	6	35	0.1	46	5	26	37	9	9
Albanian	15	0.1	2		11	2	4		19	0.1	3	3	15	3	4	
All other	10		5	5	8	4	2	1	10		2	1	7	2	3	
Unknown	157	0.5	57	1,095	71	35	86	22	171	0.7	66	1,234	88	50	83	16
	WEST VIRGINIA								NORTH CAROLINA							
Total	51,520	100.0	61,864	57,067	32,864	41,875	18,656	19,989	8,788	100.0	7,092	5,940	5,089	4,337	3,699	2,755
English and Celtic	6,947	13.5	7,500	8,503	3,734	4,088	3,213	3,412	3,026	34.4	2,477	2,197	1,492	1,341	1,534	1,136
Germanic:																
German	4,855	9.4	5,619	7,441	2,744	3,230	2,111	2,389	1,137	12.0	821	1,150	666	499	471	322
Dutch	40	0.1	90	146	28	60	12	30	211	2.4	120	31	128	72	83	48
Flemish	74	0.1	554	78	45	296	29	258	10	0.1	7	2	4	2	6	5
Scandinavian:																
Swedish	303	0.6	333	283	206	242	97	91	162	1.8	164	113	103	116	59	48
Norwegian	52	0.1	48	36	32	29	20	19	90	1.0	68	89	55	41	35	27
Danish	71	0.1	119	76	44	73	27	46	62	0.7	68	36	46	48	16	25
Icelandic									1						1	
Latin and Greek:																
Italian	12,069	23.4	14,302	17,324	7,819	9,945	4,250	4,357	302	3.4	367	474	208	253	94	114
French	1,246	2.4	1,025	1,254	651	563	595	462	400	4.6	204	198	197	128	203	136
Spanish	1,534	3.0	1,581	460	1,134	1,101	400	480	79	0.9	67	21	49	40	30	27
Portuguese	58	0.1	15	8	53	11	5	4	11	0.1	11	4	8	11	3	
Rumanian	499	1.0	662	574	380	554	119	108	18	0.2	21	9	8	9	10	12
Greek	2,895	5.6	3,196	1,077	2,165	2,843	730	353	1,121	12.8	574	225	855	490	266	84
Slavic and Lettic:																
Polish	5,570	10.8	6,781	5,126	3,554	4,542	2,016	2,230	175	2.0	141	118	100	88	75	63
Czech	551	1.1	521	302	334	356	217	165	16	0.2	24	13	6	15	10	9
Slovak	2,353	4.6	2,962	2,160	1,460	1,968	893	994	15	0.2	58	33	8	33	7	25
Russian	1,786	3.5	2,357	270	1,364	1,800	422	557	330	3.8	385	18	214	257	116	128
Ruthenian	27	0.1	} 192	101	18	} 120	9	} 66	2		} 2	2	1		} 1	2
Ukrainian	176	0.3			111		65		3				1		2	
Slovenian	674	1.3	1,213	1,003	498	938	176	275	7		7	3		4		3
Croatian	1,179	2.3	1,654	1,387	843	1,258	336	306	4		3	1	1	3	1	
Serbian	602	1.2	726	87	452	636	150	90	26		26	2	8	14	1	12
Bulgarian	125	0.2	115	170	114	112	11	3	5	0.1	1	1	4	1	1	
Lithuanian	903	1.8	} 1,231	1,024	658	} 833	245	} 398	13	0.1	} 18	40	7	} 11	6	} 7
Lettish	25				21		4		4				3		1	
Unclassified:																
Yiddish	770	1.5	866	1,154	446	523	324	343	679	7.7	657	317	399	390	280	267
Magyar	4,088	7.9	6,390	3,903	2,643	4,497	1,445	1,893	62	0.7	53	16	36	33	26	20
Finnish	137	0.3	275	130	81	190	56	85	5	0.1	13	18	4	8	1	5
Estonian	14				12		2		1		1		1	1		
Armenian	32	0.1	44	17	24	35	8	9	13	0.1	10	9	5	4	6	6
Arabic	1,365	2.6	1,295	675	841	864	524	481	704	8.0	637	337	416	412	288	225
Turkish	75	0.1	104	31	61	102	14	2	9	0.1	3	8	7	3	2	
Albanian	44	0.1	3	8	43	3	1		5	0.1			5			
All other	8		2		7		1	2	4		6		3	5	1	1
Unknown	373	0.7	89	1,270	244	57	129	32	108	1.2	18	526	45	10	63	8

364

POPULATION

Table 9.—MOTHER TONGUE OF THE FOREIGN-BORN WHITE POPULATION, BY SEX, BY DIVISIONS AND STATES: 1930, 1920, AND 1910—Continued

SOUTH CAROLINA / GEORGIA

MOTHER TONGUE	SC Total 1930 Number	SC 1930 Per cent	SC 1920	SC 1910	SC Male 1930	SC Male 1920	SC Female 1930	SC Female 1920	GA Total 1930 Number	GA 1930 Per cent	GA 1920	GA 1910	GA Male 1930	GA Male 1920	GA Female 1930	GA Female 1920
Total	5,266	100.0	6,397	6,053	3,120	4,094	2,146	2,303	13,917	100.0	16,163	15,063	8,175	9,991	5,742	6,172
English and Celtic	1,237	23.5	1,422	1,666	640	806	597	622	3,814	27.4	4,387	4,598	2,038	2,411	1,776	1,976
Germanic:																
German	879	16.7	1,235	1,756	503	709	376	526	2,135	15.3	2,485	3,284	1,262	1,599	873	886
Dutch	23	0.4	44	30	17	29	6	15	63	0.5	98	53	53	74	10	24
Flemish	28	0.5	39	58	20	29	8	10	15	0.1	21	6	11	14	4	7
Scandinavian:																
Swedish	117	2.2	138	96	92	107	25	31	276	2.0	305	285	176	193	100	112
Norwegian	66	1.3	84	81	42	68	24	16	123	0.9	125	145	79	83	44	42
Danish	39	0.7	77	51	34	60	5	17	106	0.8	127	116	88	92	18	35
Icelandic																
Latin and Greek:																
Italian	185	3.5	345	316	130	273	55	72	620	4.5	704	555	447	516	173	188
French	135	2.6	117	122	67	67	68	50	421	3.0	445	325	188	220	233	225
Spanish	44	0.8	53	24	33	36	11	17	369	2.7	249	108	231	167	138	82
Portuguese	6	0.1	7	2	4	5	2	2	93	0.7	51	22	65	34	28	17
Rumanian	13	0.2	12	7	6	7	7	5	52	0.4	78	57	35	48	17	30
Greek	730	13.9	599	308	536	491	194	108	1,268	9.1	1,477	1,000	935	1,203	333	274
Slavic and Lettic:																
Polish	176	3.3	315	233	96	233	80	82	424	3.0	436	420	242	302	182	134
Czech	26	0.5	57	45	16	38	10	19	31	0.2	91	51	24	57	7	34
Slovak	9	0.2	12	4	5	8	4	4	20	0.1	43	23	16	34	4	9
Russian	269	5.1	518	43	152	332	117	186	892	6.4	1,682	175	509	950	383	732
Ruthenian			5		1	3	3	2	6		12	7	3	8	3	4
Ukrainian	4	0.1														
Slovenian	4	0.1	8		2	6	2	2	22	0.2	44	14	17	36	5	8
Croatian	8	0.2	5	1	5	5	3		24	0.2	35		19	27	5	8
Serbian	3	0.1	8		1	5	2	3	3		43	7	2	29	1	14
Bulgarian	1			1	1				8	0.1	7	4	8	7		
Lithuanian	9	0.2	14	7	6	14	3	2	32	0.2	42	54	21	36	11	6
Lettish	2								20	0.1			9		11	
Unclassified:																
Yiddish	730	13.9	772	270	404	452	326	320	2,297	16.5	2,385	2,338	1,244	1,366	1,053	1,019
Magyar	25	0.5	40	21	14	28	11	12	106	0.8	174	149	58	105	48	69
Finnish	22	0.4	41	42	12	32	10	9	94	0.7	28	69	58	21	36	7
Estonian									6		4		4		2	
Armenian			6	18		6			46	0.3	25	26	32	19	14	6
Arabic	407	7.7	417	247	244	247	163	170	396	2.8	506	246	233	300	163	206
Turkish	9	0.2	2	1	7		2	2	27	0.2	25	13	20	20	7	5
Albanian	2				2				2		3		2			3
All other	9	0.2			5		4		4				2		2	
Unknown	49	0.9	5	603	23	4	26	1	102	0.7	26	853	44	16	58	10

FLORIDA / KENTUCKY

MOTHER TONGUE	FL Total 1930 Number	FL 1930 Per cent	FL 1920	FL 1910	FL Male 1930	FL Male 1920	FL Female 1930	FL Female 1920	KY Total 1930 Number	KY 1930 Per cent	KY 1920	KY 1910	KY Male 1930	KY Male 1920	KY Female 1930	KY Female 1920
Total	59,057	100.0	42,949	33,798	32,152	24,572	26,905	18,377	21,840	100.0	30,707	40,041	12,292	17,426	9,548	13,281
English and Celtic	20,936	35.5	13,137	7,754	10,179	6,927	10,757	6,210	4,916	22.5	6,981	10,330	2,467	3,498	2,449	3,483
Germanic:																
German	7,061	12.0	4,389	2,460	3,981	2,614	3,080	1,775	9,231	42.3	13,415	21,473	4,885	6,965	4,346	6,450
Dutch	473	0.8	374	92	304	243	169	131	106	0.5	188	134	72	114	34	74
Flemish	114	0.2	87	6	67	51	47	36	18	0.1	47	29	10	28	8	19
Scandinavian:																
Swedish	2,194	3.7	1,457	732	1,237	826	957	631	167	0.8	215	191	93	145	74	70
Norwegian	838	1.4	599	303	536	384	302	215	40	0.2	62	53	24	42	16	20
Danish	926	1.6	579	303	619	420	307	159	73	0.3	84	88	52	67	21	17
Icelandic	1						1									
Latin and Greek:																
Italian	4,901	8.3	4,763	4,504	2,691	2,549	2,210	2,214	1,636	7.5	1,954	1,330	1,161	1,405	475	549
French	2,068	3.5	1,121	468	1,012	612	1,056	509	625	2.9	901	833	317	478	308	423
Spanish	10,692	18.1	10,974	13,215	6,146	6,374	4,546	4,600	142	0.7	154	51	111	110	31	44
Portuguese	145	0.2	229	26	106	164	39	65	33	0.2	7	3	31	5	2	2
Rumanian	302	0.7	208	230	214	162	178	136	101	0.5	193	227	78	136	23	57
Greek	2,081	3.5	1,436	1,617	1,596	1,218	485	218	490	2.2	425	343	415	390	75	35
Slavic and Lettic:																
Polish	673	1.1	360	114	375	215	298	145	514	2.4	748	615	322	551	192	197
Czech	295	0.5	215	35	170	115	125	100	56	0.3	114	189	28	82	28	32
Slovak	248	0.4	96	7	131	54	117	42	104	0.5	239	143	71	200	33	39
Russian	1,020	1.7	628	40	567	376	453	252	573	2.6	1,236	83	359	784	214	452
Ruthenian	5		10	12	3	7	2	3	2		29	3	1	21	1	8
Ukrainian	17				10		7		4				3		1	
Slovenian	43	0.1	32	4	27	23	16	9	44	0.2	86	28	37	63	7	23
Croatian	20		6		14	4	6	2	42	0.2	173	14	33	153	9	20
Serbian	25		56	3	16	37	9	19	68	0.3	101	122	54	85	14	16
Bulgarian	35	0.1	18	8	27	13	8	5	27	0.1	31	8	22	31	5	
Lithuanian	79	0.1	47	11	47	31	32	16	67	0.3	104	36	48	90	19	14
Lettish	40	0.1			28		12		12	0.1			10		2	
Unclassified:																
Yiddish	1,562	2.6	844	204	862	456	700	388	1,601	7.3	1,807	2,644	878	1,012	723	705
Magyar	538	0.9	249	18	270	131	268	118	499	2.3	957	232	323	663	176	294
Finnish	259	0.4	250	82	134	140	125	110	23	0.1	42	15	14	34	9	8
Estonian	21		11		13	7	8	4								
Armenian	70	0.1	43	8	49	31	21	12	17	0.1	22	20	12	17	5	5
Arabic	974	1.6	532	87	548	316	426	216	425	1.9	324	292	258	217	167	107
Turkish	27		11	10	21	9	6	2	17	0.1	13	6	13	9	4	4
Albanian	4		7		4	6		1	15	0.1	2		11	2	4	
All other	16		4		12	4	4		10				7		3	
Unknown	264	0.4	87	1,385	136	53	128	34	142	0.7	53	506	72	29	70	24

MOTHER TONGUE OF THE FOREIGN-BORN WHITE POPULATION   365

TABLE 9.—MOTHER TONGUE OF THE FOREIGN-BORN WHITE POPULATION, BY SEX, BY DIVISIONS AND STATES: 1930, 1920, AND 1910—Continued

TENNESSEE / ALABAMA

MOTHER TONGUE	TOTAL F-B WHITE 1930 Number	1930 Per cent	1920	1910	MALE 1930	MALE 1920	FEMALE 1930	FEMALE 1920	TOTAL F-B WHITE 1930 Number	1930 Per cent	1920	1910	MALE 1930	MALE 1920	FEMALE 1930	FEMALE 1920
Total	13,066	100.0	15,443	18,450	7,394	8,999	5,672	6,444	15,710	100.0	17,617	18,930	9,326	10,605	6,384	7,012
English and Celtic	3,473	26.6	4,563	6,155	1,818	2,537	1,655	2,026	4,367	27.8	4,909	5,610	2,349	2,753	2,018	2,156
Germanic: German	2,460	18.8	2,996	4,931	1,428	1,760	1,032	1,236	2,778	17.7	3,200	4,425	1,678	1,873	1,100	1,327
Dutch	58	0.4	77	80	42	47	16	30	92	0.6	114	143	66	75	26	39
Flemish	14	0.1	9	1	8	5	6	4	20	0.1	29	9	12	18	8	11
Scandinavian: Swedish	237	1.8	312	367	138	188	99	124	643	4.1	753	766	408	469	235	284
Norwegian	66	0.5	61	88	44	41	22	20	263	1.7	213	264	192	130	71	74
Danish	113	0.9	140	104	71	90	42	50	183	1.2	187	195	135	132	48	55
Icelandic	1						1		1			1			1	1
Latin and Greek: Italian	1,971	15.1	2,001	2,061	1,193	1,238	778	853	2,110	13.4	2,746	2,725	1,260	1,669	850	1,077
French	411	3.1	473	498	202	239	209	234	609	3.9	675	700	335	378	274	297
Spanish	87	0.7	171	60	41	106	46	65	242	1.5	222	174	142	125	100	97
Portuguese	7	0.1	18	3	3	10	4	8	8	0.1	5	3	6	4	2	1
Rumanian	45	0.3	50	61	31	32	14	18	64	0.4	71	79	36	42	28	29
Greek	546	4.2	502	400	420	425	126	77	1,013	6.4	924	720	783	762	230	162
Slavic and Lettic: Polish	456	3.5	473	582	246	283	210	190	241	1.5	294	520	137	177	104	117
Czech	86	0.7	101	93	48	50	38	42	357	2.3	99	92	204	65	153	34
Slovak	30	0.2	42	30	17	24	13	18	122	0.8	253	136	74	151	48	102
Russian	597	4.6	840	156	328	479	269	361	417	2.7	650	67	247	408	170	242
Ruthenian	2		3	14	1	2	1	1	2		2		3	1	4	1
Ukrainian	4				3		1		2				1		1	
Slovenian	11	0.1	10	28	8	12	3	7	37	0.2	101	153	25	78	12	23
Croatian	5		7	5	4	5	1	2	59	0.4	89	63	40	77	19	12
Serbian	2		19	22	2	16		3	8	0.1	38	58	8	25		13
Bulgarian	3		9	18	3	9			20	0.1	24	80	20	24		
Lithuanian	12	0.1	12	28	8	6	4	6	29	0.2	14	25	19	8	10	6
Lettish	5				4				5				2		3	
Unclassified: Yiddish	1,001	14.5	1,051	1,519	1,006	1,061	805	890	1,067	6.8	1,113	943	590	632	477	481
Magyar	152	1.2	238	217	78	139	74	99	201	1.3	170	205	113	94	88	85
Finnish	14	0.1	16	18	9	11	5	5	38	0.2	60	33	25	44	13	16
Estonian			1			1			5		3		5	2		1
Armenian	12	0.1	18	20	10	8	2	5	13	0.1	23	33	11	18	2	5
Arabic	123	0.9	147	93	91	104	32	43	519	3.3	501	307	299	282	220	219
Turkish	7	0.1	4	36	4	23	3		27	0.2	36	15	19	21	8	15
Albanian	35	0.3	23		26	23	9		1				1			
All other	2		2	1	1	1	1	1	4			1	4			1
Unknown	118	0.9	60	695	57	34	61	26	138	0.9	88	687	77	59	61	29

MISSISSIPPI / ARKANSAS

MOTHER TONGUE	TOTAL F-B WHITE 1930 Number	1930 Per cent	1920	1910	MALE 1930	MALE 1920	FEMALE 1930	FEMALE 1920	TOTAL F-B WHITE 1930 Number	1930 Per cent	1920	1910	MALE 1930	MALE 1920	FEMALE 1930	FEMALE 1920
Total	7,049	100.0	7,931	9,324	4,347	4,919	2,702	3,012	10,173	100.0	13,781	16,831	6,006	8,468	4,167	5,313
English and Celtic	1,252	17.8	1,628	2,118	754	1,001	498	627	2,252	22.1	3,157	4,091	1,306	1,944	946	1,213
Germanic: German	952	13.5	1,160	1,746	614	724	338	436	3,788	37.2	5,137	6,500	2,157	2,949	1,631	2,188
Dutch	39	0.6	51	34	33	39	6	12	70	0.8	155	133	56	91	23	64
Flemish	19	0.3	21	7	13	16	6	5	14	0.1	60	11	10	42	4	18
Scandinavian: Swedish	213	3.0	246	293	144	171	69	75	251	2.5	329	395	169	223	82	106
Norwegian	66	0.9	96	87	54	70	12	26	69	0.7	97	72	45	66	24	31
Danish	98	1.4	107	118	81	83	17	24	135	1.3	179	178	91	123	44	55
Icelandic																
Latin and Greek: Italian	1,620	23.0	1,833	2,161	921	1,026	699	807	967	9.5	1,332	1,746	574	853	393	479
French	242	3.4	289	352	140	183	102	106	467	4.6	539	720	249	314	218	225
Spanish	129	1.8	83	100	62	59	67	24	57	0.6	97	29	31	70	26	27
Portuguese	5	0.1	4	1	4	3	1	1	5		8		4	6	1	2
Rumanian	15	0.2	20	46	10	13	5	7	24	0.2	36	34	19	28	5	8
Greek	349	5.0	211	142	288	185	61	26	321	3.2	278	202	263	235	58	43
Slavic and Lettic: Polish	142	2.0	237	225	91	132	51	105	322	3.2	472	582	187	317	135	155
Czech	43	0.6	61	26	21	37	22	24	239	2.3	387	319	122	199	117	188
Slovak	13	0.2	45	22	9	37	4	8	154	1.5	310	188	79	186	75	124
Russian	259	3.7	397	78	154	254	105	143	145	1.4	341	28	99	240	46	101
Ruthenian	2			2	1		1		4		1	8	2	1	2	
Ukrainian	2				2											
Slovenian	177	2.5	183	147	106	112	71	71	94	0.9	55	330	61	39	33	16
Croatian	37	0.5	15	13	19	13	18	2	28	0.3	36	26	16	25	12	11
Serbian	5	0.1	21	1	4	11	1	10	10	0.1	21	12	8	16	2	5
Bulgarian	6	0.1		1	4		2		38	0.4	21	20	20	17	18	4
Lithuanian	10	0.1	7	21	4	5	6	2	30	0.3	46	62	20	37	10	9
Lettish	2				1		1		5				5			
Unclassified: Yiddish	461	6.5	482	219	292	312	169	170	283	2.8	334	235	169	204	114	130
Magyar	48	0.7	30	35	26	18	22	12	39	0.4	66	38	24	48	15	18
Finnish	44	0.6	60	90	30	41	14	19	4		10	12	2	10	2	
Estonian	1		1		1	1			1				1			
Armenian	5	0.1	2	27	4	2	1		5		5	7	5	3		2
Arabic	728	10.3	603	448	414	345	314	258	226	2.2	228	141	147	154	79	74
Turkish	2		8	8	2	6		2	5			4	4	1		
Albanian																
All other	1		4		1	2		2	3				3			
Unknown	62	0.9	26	756	43	18	19	8	109	1.1	44	648	58	28	51	16

POPULATION

Table 9.—MOTHER TONGUE OF THE FOREIGN-BORN WHITE POPULATION, BY SEX, BY DIVISIONS AND STATES: 1930, 1920, AND 1910—Continued

LOUISIANA and OKLAHOMA

Mother Tongue	LA Total 1930 Number	LA Per cent	LA Total 1920	LA Total 1910	LA Male 1930	LA Male 1920	LA Female 1930	LA Female 1920	OK Total 1930 Number	OK Per cent	OK Total 1920	OK Total 1910	OK Male 1930	OK Male 1920	OK Female 1930	OK Female 1920
Total	34,910	100.0	42,976	50,995	20,376	25,663	14,534	17,313	26,753	100.0	33,655	37,591	15,544	20,384	11,209	13,271
English and Celtic	4,394	12.6	5,006	7,446	2,393	3,386	2,001	2,520	6,184	23.1	7,962	8,850	3,454	4,718	2,730	3,244
Germanic:																
German	4,467	12.8	6,123	9,432	2,615	3,506	1,852	2,617	9,704	36.3	11,611	14,656	5,519	6,854	4,185	4,757
Dutch	241	0.7	293	108	197	238	44	55	239	0.9	246	260	161	169	78	77
Flemish	143	0.4	186	69	89	120	54	66	82	0.3	167	50	56	103	26	64
Scandinavian:																
Swedish	456	1.3	527	359	374	439	82	88	849	3.2	935	1,033	557	586	292	340
Norwegian	483	1.4	547	286	386	460	97	87	232	0.9	288	354	134	166	98	122
Danish	305	0.9	318	253	248	248	57	70	512	1.9	565	544	331	367	181	198
Icelandic	2		3		1	1	1	2								
Latin and Greek:																
Italian	13,576	38.9	16,291	20,290	7,707	9,179	5,869	7,112	1,181	4.4	2,186	2,640	746	1,382	435	804
French	3,263	9.3	4,425	5,828	1,722	2,405	1,541	2,020	1,074	4.0	1,198	1,186	608	691	466	507
Spanish	2,264	6.5	2,662	1,126	1,310	1,909	954	753	243	0.9	500	175	137	366	106	134
Portuguese	68	0.2	107	59	59	100	9	7	18	0.1	14	16	13	11	5	3
Rumanian	61	0.2	60	60	37	39	24	21	34	0.1	29	22	21	22	13	7
Greek	667	1.9	628	327	512	528	155	100	671	2.5	628	662	527	559	144	60
Slavic and Lettic:																
Polish	277	0.8	272	733	174	172	103	100	702	2.6	1,062	1,301	407	663	295	399
Czech	209	0.6	303	88	117	182	92	121	1,538	5.7	2,102	2,332	812	1,104	726	908
Slovak	86	0.2	143	63	52	101	34	42	242	0.9	217	85	127	139	115	78
Russian	492	1.4	1,103	102	289	670	203	433	669	2.5	1,281	143	395	736	274	545
Ruthenian	1		{1	5	{1	1	{—	—	10		{67	4	{7	42	{3	25
Ukrainian	5						{4		69	0.3			38		{31	
Slovenian	277	0.8	266	357	214	213	63	53	104	0.4	143	150	65	102	39	41
Croatian	76	0.2	70	109	51	57	25	13	18	0.1	51	90	13	50	5	1
Serbian	7		39	16	5	27	2	12	18	0.1	81	47	13	50	3	31
Bulgarian	28	0.1	47	26	20	38	8	9	116	0.4	104	103	99	88	17	16
Wendish									1				1			
Lithuanian	10		{28	26	{7	20	{3	8	127	0.5	{381	488	{77	236	{50	145
Lettish	8				8				6				4		2	
Unclassified:																
Yiddish	1,207	3.7	910	934	725	526	572	384	753	2.8	711	607	449	452	304	259
Magyar	379	1.1	324	232	207	177	172	147	130	0.5	217	183	74	136	56	81
Finnish	57	0.2	135	101	49	120	8	15	19	0.1	95	23	13	88	6	7
Estonian	8				8											
Armenian	14		26	57	8	16	6	10	15	0.1	21	45	11	14	4	7
Arabic	907	2.6	1,025	524	576	614	421	411	863	3.2	717	328	504	441	359	276
Turkish	24	0.1	33	93	20	25	4	8	4		5		4	5		
Albanian	7		2		7	2					1			1		
All other	20	0.1	5		17	5	3		15	0.1	3	5	8	1	7	2
Unknown	241	0.7	168	1,817	170	139	71	29	314	1.2	66	1,209	160	41	154	25

TEXAS and MONTANA

Mother Tongue	TX Total 1930 Number	TX Per cent	TX Total 1920	TX Total 1910	TX Male 1930	TX Male 1920	TX Female 1930	TX Female 1920	MT Total 1930 Number	MT Per cent	MT Total 1920	MT Total 1910	MT Male 1930	MT Male 1920	MT Female 1930	MT Female 1920
Total	98,396	100.0	117,784	119,189	55,394	68,574	43,002	49,210	72,961	100.0	93,420	91,589	44,899	58,062	28,062	35,358
English and Celtic	17,313	17.6	18,860	19,459	9,438	11,154	7,875	7,706	22,953	31.5	31,127	33,081	13,154	18,178	9,799	12,949
Germanic:																
German	31,657	32.2	38,239	48,032	17,452	21,268	14,205	16,971	12,786	17.5	15,424	11,641	7,645	9,272	5,141	6,152
Dutch	600	0.6	684	459	398	444	202	240	1,311	1.8	1,723	1,088	797	1,056	514	667
Flemish	242	0.2	274	187	136	168	106	106	353	0.5	551	81	226	357	127	194
Scandinavian:																
Swedish	4,058	4.1	4,580	4,747	2,435	2,748	1,623	1,832	5,908	8.1	7,497	6,712	3,766	4,713	2,142	2,784
Norwegian	1,471	1.5	1,687	1,763	941	1,044	530	643	9,004	12.3	10,022	7,176	5,857	6,241	3,147	3,781
Danish	1,336	1.4	1,504	1,314	922	1,037	414	467	2,544	3.5	2,973	1,987	1,695	1,987	849	986
Icelandic	8		2	1	5	1	3	1	14		27	4	5	9	9	18
Latin and Greek:																
Italian	6,591	6.7	8,112	7,315	4,007	5,007	2,584	3,105	2,930	4.0	3,992	6,930	1,943	2,842	987	1,150
French	2,497	2.5	2,893	2,434	1,297	1,640	1,200	1,253	2,793	3.8	3,285	3,659	1,642	1,992	1,151	1,293
Spanish	4,252	4.3	8,019	4,198	2,167	4,599	2,085	3,420	160	0.2	103	87	125	74	35	29
Portuguese	74	0.1	98	85	56	69	18	29	23		22	32	19	19	4	3
Rumanian	197	0.2	269	196	117	164	80	105	245	0.3	313	367	201	264	44	49
Greek	2,025	2.1	2,071	845	1,624	1,778	401	208	809	1.1	1,335	2,139	738	1,271	71	64
Slavic and Lettic:																
Polish	3,148	3.2	3,983	4,751	1,744	2,414	1,404	1,569	922	1.3	1,156	1,325	594	720	328	436
Czech	11,093	11.3	14,871	15,074	5,820	7,833	5,273	7,038	998	1.4	1,748	817	591	1,057	407	691
Slovak	867	0.9	405	179	480	276	387	129	682	0.9	936	398	409	580	273	356
Russian	1,835	1.9	2,651	177	1,110	1,665	725	986	751	1.0	1,722	167	493	1,034	258	688
Ruthenian	6		{29	17	{14	21	{13	8	30		{58	30	{10	32	{14	26
Ukrainian	27								120	0.2			67		53	
Slovenian	166	0.2	276	306	115	196	51	80	1,740	2.4	1,638	1,686	1,081	1,081	659	557
Croatian	103	0.1	151	271	75	116	28	35	1,360	1.9	1,867	2,445	878	1,303	482	554
Serbian	139	0.1	306	211	99	224	40	82	567	0.8	799	1,179	436	618	131	181
Bulgarian	60	0.1	68	124	49	61	11	7	260	0.4	389	1,608	220	383	31	6
Wendish	2		29	99	1	15	1	14								
Lithuanian	77	0.1	{136	171	{56	119	{21	17	150	0.2	{165	119	{111	125	{45	40
Lettish	24				17		7		12				8		4	
Unclassified:																
Yiddish	5,088	5.2	4,668	2,818	2,762	2,674	2,326	1,994	131	0.2	307	281	78	182	53	125
Magyar	492	0.5	653	384	294	419	198	234	222	0.3	348	358	134	213	88	135
Finnish	142	0.1	145	143	99	107	43	38	2,522	3.5	3,321	3,904	1,485	1,984	1,037	1,337
Estonian	10		5		7	4	3	1	40	0.1	48	1	28	31	12	17
Armenian	66	0.1	106	86	44	87	22	19	63	0.1	140	80	59	136	4	4
Arabic	1,823	1.9	1,727	946	1,097	1,056	726	671	166	0.2	206	137	109	139	57	67
Turkish	53	0.1	27	25	40	19	13	8	52	0.1	61	45	49	60	3	1
Albanian	11		6	2	9	6	2				34			25		1
All other	22		9		16	4	6	5	16		17		13	15	3	2
Unknown	821	0.8	241	2,370	448	142	373	99	293	0.4	76	2,025	193	61	100	15

MOTHER TONGUE OF THE FOREIGN-BORN WHITE POPULATION   367

TABLE 9.—MOTHER TONGUE OF THE FOREIGN-BORN WHITE POPULATION, BY SEX, BY DIVISIONS AND STATES: 1930, 1920, AND 1910—Continued

IDAHO / WYOMING

MOTHER TONGUE	IDAHO 1930 Number	1930 Per cent	1920	1910	Male 1930	Male 1920	Female 1930	Female 1920	WYOMING 1930 Number	1930 Per cent	1920	1910	Male 1930	Male 1920	Female 1930	Female 1920
Total	30,454	100.0	37,989	40,315	18,947	24,199	11,507	13,790	19,658	100.0	23,502	26,965	12,439	15,602	7,219	7,900
English and Celtic	9,535	31.3	12,302	13,239	5,464	7,324	4,071	4,978	5,553	28.2	6,592	7,824	3,179	3,921	2,374	2,671
Germanic:																
German	5,869	19.3	7,274	7,053	3,521	4,307	2,348	2,907	3,385	17.2	3,731	3,352	2,053	2,314	1,332	1,417
Dutch	336	1.1	449	290	209	277	127	172	114	0.6	146	89	78	110	36	36
Flemish	69	0.2	100	56	44	66	25	34	67	0.3	57	3	43	42	24	15
Scandinavian:																
Swedish	4,369	14.3	5,339	5,126	2,843	3,463	1,526	1,876	1,797	9.1	2,052	2,519	1,223	1,339	574	713
Norwegian	2,145	7.0	2,457	2,558	1,376	1,579	769	878	644	3.3	644	621	426	408	218	280
Danish	1,659	5.4	2,245	2,261	1,009	1,353	650	892	771	3.9	937	976	503	612	268	325
Icelandic	9	----	13	10	6	6	3	7	1	----			1			
Latin and Greek:																
Italian	1,217	4.0	1,375	2,115	833	998	384	377	1,667	8.5	2,038	2,571	1,088	1,450	579	588
French	1,059	3.5	1,082	1,239	660	675	399	407	566	2.9	515	538	345	325	221	190
Spanish	1,007	3.3	1,561	1,009	748	1,223	259	338	187	1.0	193	127	143	149	44	44
Portuguese	42	0.1	55	46	27	39	15	16	24	0.1	34	52	19	25	5	9
Rumanian	35	0.1	40	9	26	34	9	6	40	0.2	39	58	36	31	4	8
Greek	414	1.4	715	1,800	359	665	55	50	888	4.5	1,101	2,000	737	1,101	151	90
Slavic and Lettic:																
Polish	187	0.6	221	308	139	178	48	43	585	3.0	885	997	382	637	203	248
Czech	408	1.3	523	300	238	344	170	179	216	1.1	405	410	126	251	90	154
Slovak	112	0.4	91	53	80	67	32	24	324	1.0	519	285	192	343	132	176
Russian	315	1.0	377	44	202	247	113	130	342	1.7	315	70	211	202	131	113
Ruthenian	---	---	12	---	9	8		4	2	---	22	12	1	15	1	7
Ukrainian	9	----							4				3			
Slovenian	179	0.6	186	93	140	153	39	33	834	4.2	662	999	544	478	290	184
Croatian	170	0.6	252	267	134	221	36	31	201	1.0	262	508	146	219	55	43
Serbian	66	0.2	130	205	60	109	6	21	242	1.2	426	189	191	359	51	67
Bulgarian	40	0.1	51	413	38	49	2	2	69	0.4	112	322	57	107	12	5
Wendish			1					1								
Lithuanian	15	---	32	25	13	26	2	6	33	0.2	49	61	27	43	6	6
Lettish	3				2		1		2				2			
Unclassified:																
Yiddish	55	0.2	55	62	35	30	20	25	104	0.5	283	124	64	161	40	122
Magyar	81	0.3	106	80	49	62	32	44	165	0.8	330	248	102	226	63	104
Finnish	723	2.4	801	714	466	527	257	274	619	3.1	853	1,303	372	556	247	297
Estonian	11	---	10	---	7	7	4	3	13	0.1	20	---	6	11	7	9
Armenian	18	0.1	11	19	15	10	3	1	25	0.1	58	89	24	57	1	1
Arabic	46	0.2	58	50	32	37	14	21	51	0.3	82	57	35	64	16	18
Turkish	4	---	2	15	4	2	---	---	12	0.1	24	43	12	23	---	1
Albanian	1	---	41	---	---	41	---	---	6	---	10	---	6	10	---	---
All other	161	0.5	1	1	113	1	48	---	9	---	3	---	9	3	---	---
Unknown	85	0.3	21	565	45	11	40	10	96	0.5	13	398	53	10	43	3

COLORADO / NEW MEXICO

MOTHER TONGUE	COLORADO 1930 Number	1930 Per cent	1920	1910	Male 1930	Male 1920	Female 1930	Female 1920	NEW MEXICO 1930 Number	1930 Per cent	1920	1910	Male 1930	Male 1920	Female 1930	Female 1920
Total	85,406	100.0	108,259	124,355	48,004	61,560	37,402	44,630	7,797	100.0	10,013	11,240	4,755	6,369	3,042	3,644
English and Celtic	20,419	23.9	23,094	30,543	10,532	15,061	9,887	13,033	2,044	26.2	2,610	3,303	1,129	1,532	915	1,078
Germanic:																
German	21,776	25.5	27,143	27,996	11,837	15,300	9,939	11,843	1,307	16.8	1,556	2,200	733	943	574	613
Dutch	809	0.9	885	759	476	537	333	248	61	0.8	101	102	42	67	19	34
Flemish	224	0.3	285	121	149	183	75	102	21	0.3	48	15	18	31	3	17
Scandinavian:																
Swedish	8,539	10.0	10,389	12,855	4,709	5,760	3,830	4,629	275	3.5	316	374	172	108	103	118
Norwegian	1,219	1.4	1,505	1,750	633	810	531	695	114	1.5	126	151	81	82	33	44
Danish	2,362	2.8	2,800	2,810	1,437	1,695	925	1,105	101	1.3	113	117	62	70	39	48
Icelandic	3	---	5	1	2	3	1	2								
Latin and Greek:																
Italian	10,758	12.6	12,733	16,427	6,588	7,995	4,170	4,738	1,289	16.5	1,741	2,024	837	1,175	452	566
French	1,957	2.3	2,116	2,507	1,059	1,190	898	926	354	4.5	475	484	238	308	116	167
Spanish	597	0.7	565	242	400	385	197	180	550	7.1	991	612	310	572	240	419
Portuguese	28	---	32	45	19	19	9	13	7	0.1	18	4	6	15	1	3
Rumanian	180	0.2	182	89	110	109	70	73	13	0.2	7	6	11	7	2	---
Greek	1,286	1.5	1,788	2,473	1,102	1,044	184	144	300	3.8	234	171	264	257	36	27
Slavic and Lettic:																
Polish	1,231	1.4	1,430	2,498	710	882	521	548	83	1.1	140	133	52	89	31	51
Czech	701	0.8	1,126	1,703	377	660	324	406	86	1.1	133	93	47	77	39	56
Slovak	1,083	1.3	2,274	608	633	1,475	450	799	195	2.5	136	138	129	98	66	40
Russian	1,839	2.2	3,010	344	1,071	1,749	768	1,261	107	1.4	141	11	65	104	39	37
Ruthenian	11	---	46	24	6	30	5	16	1	---	2	---	1	2	---	---
Ukrainian	10				8		2		1				1			
Slovenian	2,888	3.4	2,053	3,593	1,784	1,317	1,104	736	194	2.5	229	132	114	165	80	64
Croatian	517	0.6	665	963	344	502	173	103	234	3.0	339	573	146	237	88	102
Serbian	222	0.3	381	570	180	265	42	116	16	0.2	35	146	10	26	6	9
Bulgarian	279	0.3	346	485	242	333	37	13	13	0.2	27	27	9	22	4	5
Lithuanian	166	0.2	185	216	121	135	45	50	10	0.1	14	19	6	10	4	4
Lettish	8				7		1		2				1		1	
Unclassified:																
Yiddish	4,207	5.0	4,443	4,621	2,309	2,419	1,988	2,024	49	0.6	68	30	33	46	16	22
Magyar	550	0.6	731	667	326	431	224	300	52	0.7	99	125	34	66	18	33
Finnish	355	0.4	570	907	204	353	151	217	31	0.4	41	17	26	31	5	10
Estonian	7	---	4	5	4	3	3	1	7	0.1	4	---	7	4	---	---
Armenian	42	---	33	44	35	27	7	6	1	---	2	18	1	2	---	---
Arabic	272	0.3	302	274	157	103	115	109	205	2.6	206	90	123	129	82	77
Turkish	22	---	23	18	19	22	3	1	2	---	---	5	2	---	---	---
Albanian	10	---	10	10	9	8	1	2	1	---	---	---	1	---	---	---
All other	8	---	11	1	6	6	2	5								
Unknown	751	0.9	94	2,007	394	59	357	35	71	0.9	6	111	41	6	30	---

368   POPULATION

TABLE 9.—MOTHER TONGUE OF THE FOREIGN-BORN WHITE POPULATION, BY SEX, BY DIVISIONS AND STATES: 1930, 1920, AND 1910—Continued

ARIZONA / UTAH

MOTHER TONGUE	ARIZONA 1930 Number	Per cent	1920	1910	Male 1930	Male 1920	Female 1930	Female 1920	UTAH 1930 Number	Per cent	1920	1910	Male 1930	Male 1920	Female 1930	Female 1920
Total	15,591	100.0	20,128	18,521	9,392	13,069	6,199	7,059	43,772	100.0	55,526	63,268	22,978	30,220	20,794	25,306
English and Celtic	6,125	39.3	7,078	7,607	3,468	4,278	2,657	2,800	15,840	36.2	21,570	26,141	7,761	10,771	8,079	10,799
Germanic:																
German	2,031	13.0	2,205	2,280	1,259	1,467	772	738	5,897	13.5	5,836	5,845	2,958	3,119	2,939	2,717
Dutch	99	0.6	83	44	76	68	23	15	2,330	5.3	2,000	1,425	1,106	902	1,224	1,038
Flemish	26	0.2	33	21	14	26	12	7	15		45	8	10	27	5	18
Scandinavian:																
Swedish	828	5.3	943	928	515	613	313	330	4,706	10.8	6,430	7,721	2,269	3,132	2,437	3,298
Norwegian	293	1.9	327	266	181	194	112	133	1,680	3.8	2,110	2,291	780	982	900	1,128
Danish	363	2.3	397	293	246	280	117	117	4,877	11.1	6,868	8,165	2,313	3,344	2,564	3,524
Icelandic	3		1		2		1	1	90	0.2	108	133	41	46	49	62
Latin and Greek:																
Italian	870	5.6	1,325	1,624	600	961	270	364	2,896	6.6	3,261	3,172	1,849	2,253	1,047	1,008
French	501	3.2	543	544	294	342	207	201	484	1.1	626	550	265	345	219	281
Spanish	1,441	9.2	3,262	1,958	728	2,017	713	1,245	378	0.9	365	27	273	295	105	70
Portuguese	21	0.1	34	20	14	28	7	6	6		7	8	6	7		
Rumanian	25	0.2	33	7	18	22	7	11	21		47	15	13	27	8	20
Greek	388	2.5	335	83	327	297	61	38	2,209	5.0	3,033	4,152	1,789	2,734	420	299
Slavic and Lettic:																
Polish	181	1.2	226	177	112	161	69	65	119	0.3	153	168	83	91	36	62
Czech	97	0.6	154	49	52	104	45	50	62	0.1	180	201	39	116	23	64
Slovak	98	0.6	97	153	62	77	36	20	49	0.1	188	30	30	136	19	52
Russian	337	2.2	622	20	208	373	129	249	177	0.4	327	28	117	212	60	115
Ruthenian			4	5	}	3	}	1	7		5		} 3		} 1	
Ukrainian	5		}		5		}		3		2					
Slovenian	204	1.3	221	284	145	170	59	51	586	1.3	410	610	403	292	183	118
Croatian	265	1.7	598	164	184	483	81	115	255	0.6	368	526	181	282	74	86
Serbian	299	1.9	487	562	223	368	76	119	93	0.2	215	303	69	155	24	60
Bulgarian	22	0.1	34	28	20	34	2		36	0.1	28	93	31	27	5	1
Lithuanian	38	0.2	43	17	27	} 35	11	} 8	23	0.1	38	7	21	} 30	2	} 8
Lettish	3				3				2				2			
Unclassified:																
Yiddish	222	1.4	222	111	127	138	95	84	280	0.6	404	198	166	235	114	109
Magyar	82	0.5	91	37	47	63	35	28	52	0.1	115	98	29	70	23	45
Finnish	245	1.6	310	484	145	191	100	119	221	0.5	448	650	137	296	84	152
Estonian	9	0.1	4		8	2	1	2	5				4		1	
Armenian	13	0.1	10	3	8	7	5	3	41	0.1	80	35	26	56	15	24
Arabic	313	2.0	356	123	185	230	128	126	144	0.3	162	118	85	101	59	61
Turkish	9	0.1	7	4	8	5	1	2	23	0.1	26	41	17	19	6	7
Albanian	9	0.1	4		9	4			23	0.1	47	19	17	45	6	2
All other	16	0.1	3		9	2	7	1	6				6			
Unknown	110	0.7	36	616	63	26	47	10	136	0.3	26	490	76	8	60	18

NEVADA / WASHINGTON

MOTHER TONGUE	NEVADA 1930 Number	Per cent	1920	1910	Male 1930	Male 1920	Female 1930	Female 1920	WASHINGTON 1930 Number	Per cent	1920	1910	Male 1930	Male 1920	Female 1930	Female 1920
Total	12,275	100.0	13,694	17,310	8,583	9,864	3,692	3,830	244,256	100.0	249,766	241,108	142,594	152,874	101,662	96,892
English and Celtic	2,889	23.5	3,843	5,786	1,755	2,447	1,134	1,396	80,482	32.9	80,549	73,468	42,477	45,475	38,005	35,074
Germanic:																
German	1,314	10.7	1,459	2,295	903	996	411	463	34,021	13.9	35,691	38,894	19,745	21,325	14,276	14,366
Dutch	48	0.4	38	47	32	26	16	12	3,664	1.5	3,240	2,325	2,159	1,075	1,505	1,265
Flemish	16	0.1	17	14	10	11	6	6	801	0.3	1,043	663	479	654	322	389
Scandinavian:																
Swedish	507	4.1	628	765	375	459	132	169	37,177	15.2	38,001	34,170	23,025	23,719	14,152	14,282
Norwegian	189	1.5	207	257	127	137	62	70	31,490	12.9	30,333	28,345	18,764	18,167	12,726	12,166
Danish	546	4.4	563	654	364	378	182	185	7,231	3.0	7,896	7,373	4,724	5,132	2,507	2,764
Icelandic	3				1		2		811	0.3	630	678	384	314	427	316
Latin and Greek:																
Italian	2,826	23.0	2,838	3,047	1,968	2,118	858	720	10,094	4.1	11,084	13,515	6,630	7,870	3,464	3,214
French	813	6.6	698	941	561	497	252	201	6,911	2.8	5,554	6,759	3,741	3,219	3,170	2,335
Spanish	996	8.1	1,278	834	783	1,076	213	202	1,150	0.5	1,174	545	723	823	427	351
Portuguese	242	2.0	250	338	175	193	67	57	139	0.1	187	185	100	130	39	57
Rumanian	13	0.1	6	9	10	5	3	1	238	0.1	248	283	176	176	62	72
Greek	515	4.2	623	1,070	463	586	52	37	3,038	1.2	4,012	4,528	2,694	3,812	344	200
Slavic and Lettic:																
Polish	56	0.5	58	89	42	42	14	16	3,219	1.3	3,634	3,780	1,990	2,370	1,229	1,258
Czech	33	0.3	88	47	23	62	10	26	980	0.4	1,750	1,409	555	1,055	425	695
Slovak	75	0.6	63	7	60	52	15	11	1,005	0.4	2,109	742	616	1,460	389	649
Russian	66	0.5	96	8	47	75	19	21	3,294	1.3	4,198	450	2,073	2,811	1,221	1,387
Ruthenian	1		}	1		}		}	41		135	78	25	97	16	} 38
Ukrainian	3				3				62				41		21	
Slovenian	173	1.4	194	209	145	149	28	45	2,157	0.9	1,833	2,700	1,482	1,311	675	522
Croatian	126	1.0	183	62	89	136	37	47	2,200	0.9	2,022	2,282	1,498	1,556	801	466
Serbian	211	1.7	205	354	167	229	44	66	854	0.1	718	1,294	302	616	52	102
Bulgarian	6		15	10	5	15	1		302	0.1	283	846	271	272	31	11
Lithuanian	5		10	13	4	} 8	1	} 2	746	0.3	931	707	506	652	240	279
Lettish	7	0.1			5		2		166	0.1			108		58	
Unclassified:																
Yiddish	60	0.5	62	57	41	39	19	23	2,007	0.8	2,066	2,545	1,082	1,176	925	890
Magyar	14	0.1	34	27	12	20	2	14	374	0.2	482	428	212	284	162	198
Finnish	97	0.8	95	122	71	66	26	29	8,450	3.5	8,877	7,584	4,985	5,597	3,465	3,280
Estonian	1		2			2	1		156	0.1	80	2	116	69	40	11
Armenian	28	0.2	9		27	9	1		142	0.1	246	81	114	192	28	54
Arabic	21	0.2	15	14	18	12	3	3	299	0.1	344	288	192	223	107	121
Turkish	27	0.2	16	8	24	14	3	2	70		109	136	59	81	20	28
Albanian	3				3				92		87	24	83	85	9	2
All other	304	2.5	1		243	1	61		32		17	1	25	13	7	4
Unknown	41	0.3	9	226	26	4	15	5	753	0.3	203	3,911	438	157	315	46

MOTHER TONGUE OF THE FOREIGN-BORN WHITE POPULATION 369

TABLE 9.—MOTHER TONGUE OF THE FOREIGN-BORN WHITE POPULATION, BY SEX, BY DIVISIONS AND STATES: 1930, 1920, AND 1910—Continued

MOTHER TONGUE	Total Foreign-Born White 1930 Number	1930 Per cent	1920	1910	Male 1930	Male 1920	Female 1930	Female 1920	Total Foreign-Born White 1930 Number	1930 Per cent	1920	1910	Male 1930	Male 1920	Female 1930	Female 1920
		OREGON								CALIFORNIA						
Total	105,475	100.0	101,648	102,830	62,078	61,895	43,397	39,753	810,034	100.0	599,543	485,540	454,027	353,894	356,007	245,649
English and Celtic	32,534	30.8	29,312	28,176	17,740	16,798	14,794	12,514	264,983	32.7	187,856	163,241	133,212	99,380	131,771	88,476
Germanic:																
German	24,852	23.6	24,790	25,908	14,173	14,410	10,679	10,380	117,733	14.5	94,806	93,985	66,192	55,534	51,541	39,272
Dutch	1,052	1.0	1,012	692	668	649	384	363	9,073	1.1	4,923	2,424	5,639	3,192	3,434	1,731
Flemish	475	0.5	557	326	292	360	183	197	1,512	0.2	1,153	530	872	733	640	420
Scandinavian:																
Swedish	12,104	11.5	11,475	10,982	7,664	7,178	4,440	4,297	44,016	5.4	33,577	27,980	24,444	18,969	19,572	14,608
Norwegian	7,396	7.0	6,940	6,774	4,509	4,211	2,887	2,729	17,363	2.1	11,374	9,893	10,054	6,741	7,309	4,633
Danish	3,537	3.4	3,601	3,251	2,243	2,289	1,294	1,312	23,284	2.9	18,990	15,112	14,402	11,974	8,882	7,016
Icelandic	43	----	31	14	20	16	23	15	237	----	32	17	125	20	112	12
Latin and Greek:																
Italian	4,758	4.5	4,419	5,666	3,127	2,982	1,631	1,437	115,650	14.3	94,527	70,235	72,705	61,545	42,945	32,982
French	2,770	2.6	2,226	2,605	1,492	1,275	1,278	951	31,249	3.9	24,461	22,595	16,126	13,555	15,123	10,906
Spanish	582	0.6	733	510	420	568	162	165	26,679	3.3	18,434	7,160	15,020	11,670	11,659	6,704
Portuguese	137	0.1	164	183	95	118	42	46	36,227	4.5	33,508	25,226	22,054	20,969	14,173	12,539
Rumanian	211	0.2	178	237	128	116	83	62	2,349	0.3	1,555	812	1,336	884	1,013	671
Greek	1,602	1.5	1,847	3,771	1,423	1,732	179	115	13,408	1.7	10,474	8,452	11,067	9,317	2,341	1,157
Slavic and Lettic:																
Polish	1,080	1.0	1,024	1,502	654	665	426	359	7,339	0.9	4,908	3,595	4,275	3,075	3,064	1,833
Czech	970	0.9	1,174	805	537	700	433	474	3,448	0.4	3,592	1,838	1,859	2,087	1,589	1,505
Slovak	411	0.4	431	106	283	300	128	71	1,837	0.2	1,653	404	1,147	1,191	690	462
Russian	1,037	1.6	2,121	209	954	1,313	683	808	22,317	2.8	14,034	1,121	12,337	8,326	9,980	5,708
Ruthenian	10	----	51 }	13	6 }	30 }	4 }	15 }	42	----	53 }	70	27 }	38 }	15 }	15 }
Ukrainian	60	0.1	}		45 }		24 }		145	----	}		93 }		52 }	
Slovenian	614	0.6	606	911	434	458	180	148	7,295	0.9	4,805	5,077	4,953	3,553	2,342	1,342
Croatian	589	0.6	540	781	432	458	157	82	3,755	0.5	2,108	1,554	2,565	1,577	1,190	531
Serbian	215	0.2	359	630	179	299	36	60	1,787	0.2	2,227	1,503	1,284	1,773	503	454
Bulgarian	231	0.2	278	873	197	272	34	6	454	0.1	244	290	359	217	95	27
Wendish	----	----	----	----	----	----	----	----	9	----	1	----	7	----	2	1
Lithuanian	245	0.2	318 }	182	156 }	214 }	89 }	104 }	833	0.1	684 }	443	560 }	488 }	273 }	196 }
Lettish	141	0.1	}		84 }	}	57 }	}	602	0.1	}		370 }	}	223 }	}
Unclassified:																
Yiddish	1,635	1.6	1,565	1,476	887	839	748	726	28,594	3.5	11,385	8,428	15,042	6,276	13,552	5,109
Magyar	253	0.2	315	423	144	193	109	122	5,560	0.7	3,663	1,830	3,016	2,059	2,544	1,604
Finnish	4,586	4.3	5,132	4,047	2,616	3,073	1,970	2,050	6,362	0.8	5,400	4,896	3,515	3,060	2,847	2,340
Estonian	107	0.1	58	23	65	43	42	15	361	----	145	37	254	104	107	41
Armenian	54	0.1	66	35	40	44	14	22	9,043	1.1	6,076	3,063	5,124	3,681	3,919	2,395
Arabic	194	0.2	101	178	114	128	80	63	3,055	0.4	1,940	783	1,869	1,306	1,186	643
Turkish	23	----	25	52	21	20	2	5	765	0.1	364	166	472	263	293	101
Albanian	12	----	15	----	11	15	1	----	93	----	44	66	79	37	14	7
All other	140	0.1	6	2	106	6	34	----	614	0.1	87	26	410	68	105	19
Unknown	206	0.2	88	1,397	119	57	87	31	1,961	0.2	361	2,688	1,144	232	817	129

CHAPTER 8

CITIZENSHIP OF THE FOREIGN BORN

CHAPTER 8.—CITIZENSHIP OF THE FOREIGN BORN

INTRODUCTION

The inquiry as to the citizenship of the foreign born has been made at each census beginning with 1890. In that year, however, no tabulation was made by color or race; and in 1890, 1900, and 1910 the returns related only to foreign-born males 21 years of age and over. At the census of 1920, which was the first census subsequent to the adoption of the 19th amendment to the Constitution of the United States, complete data as to citizenship were presented for foreign-born persons of both sexes; and the tabulations were extended to cover persons of all ages rather than being limited to those of voting age only.

The statistics here presented relate to the population of continental United States, the States, and those cities having 25,000 inhabitants or more. Citizenship data for the foreign-born white population 21 years old and over, by sex, are presented by counties and for cities and other urban places of 2,500 or more inhabitants in Volume III of the Reports on Population and in the Second Series State bulletins of which that volume is made up. Statistics for Alaska, Hawaii, Puerto Rico, Virgin Islands, and the Panama Canal Zone are given in the Fifteenth Census Report on Outlying Territories and Possessions.

The citizenship classification.—The classification in regard to citizenship embraces three specific groups, namely, naturalized, having first papers, and alien, the last comprising those persons who have taken no steps toward becoming naturalized. In addition, there is a fourth group, designated "Unknown," and made up of persons for whom the enumerator secured no report as to citizenship.

The "first papers" constitute the declaration of intention to become a citizen of the United States, which declaration may be made by any eligible alien 18 years of age or more at any time after arrival in the United States. The process of naturalization can not ordinarily be completed, however, until at least two years (but not more than seven years) have elapsed after the declaration of intention; nor until the applicant has resided at least five years continuously in the United States and at least six months continuously in the county in which his petition is filed. Following the World War the requirement of five years of residence was in some cases waived on account of military or naval service. Under the present naturalization law, an exception to the requirement of five years' residence is made in the case of an alien woman who married a citizen after September 22, 1922, or whose husband was naturalized after that date. Under these conditions, a woman may be naturalized without making a declaration of intention and after but one year's residence in the United States.

Under the provisions of the naturalization laws in force at the time the Fourteenth Census was taken in 1920, the citizenship status of a married woman was the same as that of her husband (but if the husband had taken out his first naturalization papers only, his wife was classified in the census returns as an alien); for an unmarried woman the process of naturalization was the same as for a man; a foreign-born widow or foreign-born divorced wife of a citizen of the United States retained the citizenship status of her former husband so long as she continued to reside in this country; a foreign-born widow or foreign-born divorced wife of an alien might become naturalized in the same manner as a man; and, in general, foreign-born minors had the same citizenship status as their parents.

By an act of Congress approved September 22, 1922, and effective from that date, it is provided that the citizenship status of a married woman shall no longer follow that of her husband, and that a married woman shall have the privilege of becoming naturalized on her own account. The status of single alien women is not changed by this law. The act referred to further provides that any woman citizen who marries an alien shall not cease to be a citizen unless she makes a formal renunciation of her citizenship, or unless she marries an alien ineligible to citizenship, in which case she shall cease to be a citizen; and that no married woman whose husband is not eligible to citizenship shall be naturalized during the continuance of the marital status. Under the present law the citizenship of legitimate minor children in general follows that of the father.

401

POPULATION

The citizenship data for the United States are summarized in Table 1, which gives the figures for the total foreign born, for the foreign-born white, and for the foreign-born white 21 years old and over.

TABLE 1.—FOREIGN-BORN POPULATION OF THE UNITED STATES BY CITIZENSHIP AND SEX: 1930 AND 1920

CITIZENSHIP	1930				1920	
	Number	Per cent	Male	Female	Number	Per cent
Total foreign born	14,204,149	100.0	7,647,090	6,557,059	13,920,692	100.0
Naturalized	7,919,536	55.8	4,365,403	3,554,133	6,489,883	46.6
Having first papers	1,266,419	8.9	955,942	310,477	1,222,553	8.8
Alien	4,518,341	31.8	2,081,710	2,436,631	5,406,780	38.8
Unknown	499,853	3.5	244,035	255,818	801,476	5.8
Total foreign-born white	13,366,407	100.0	7,153,709	6,212,698	113,255,394	100.0
Naturalized	7,859,193	58.8	4,332,288	3,526,905	6,457,665	48.7
Having first papers	1,246,521	9.3	941,985	304,536	1,216,285	9.2
Alien	3,787,086	28.3	1,650,313	2,136,773	4,809,076	36.3
Unknown	473,607	3.5	229,123	244,484	772,368	5.8
Foreign-born white, 21 years old and over	12,637,643	100.0	6,797,494	5,840,149	112,193,329	100.0
Naturalized	7,627,436	60.4	4,217,576	3,409,860	6,192,016	50.8
Having first papers	1,218,416	9.6	926,454	291,962	1,191,733	9.8
Alien	3,342,837	26.5	1,435,309	1,907,528	4,092,114	33.6
Unknown	448,054	3.6	218,155	230,799	717,466	5.9

[1] Adjusted for comparison with 1930 by subtracting from the 1920 foreign-born white population as reported the estimated number of persons who would have been counted as Mexican in 1930. (See Table 4.)

Since the foreign-born population of the United States consists mainly of white persons, the statistics in most of the tables relate to the foreign-born white alone. In Table 10, however, as well as in Table 1, citizenship figures are given for the total foreign-born population of all races; and in Table 4 a separate presentation is made for each of the several color or race classes eligible to citizenship.

Citizenship by naturalization is open only to "white persons" or "persons of African nativity or African descent." Mexicans are considered as white in the interpretation of the naturalization laws, and are therefore eligible to citizenship, though a relatively small proportion of them have become citizens.

Foreign-born Chinese and Japanese, and other nonwhite Asiatics of foreign birth, are not eligible to citizenship. A small number of Chinese may have been naturalized prior to 1882, in which year their legal ineligibility was made more explicit; and a few more Chinese and some Japanese may have been illegally admitted to citizenship prior to 1906, when measures were adopted for a stricter enforcement of the regulations. Small numbers of Chinese and Japanese were returned as naturalized and some were returned as having first papers, but since nearly all of these returns were obviously due either to a misunderstanding of the question or to deliberate misstatement, they have been entirely disregarded, and all foreign-born Chinese, Japanese, and other nonwhite Asiatics have been counted as aliens. Where comparative data are presented for earlier censuses, the figures have been revised in this respect, so far as possible, and placed on the same basis as those for 1930.

For most purposes where a figure representing the total alien population is required it would seem best to include not only the classes specifically designated as alien in the tables, but also those having first papers (since they had not become citizens at the time of the census) and those for whom no citizenship return was made (designated "unknown"). This last group doubtless contains a few persons who are naturalized, but it seems relatively unlikely that a person who had obtained his naturalization would fail to report that fact, or that it would be unknown to the members of the family in which he lived.

The sharp decline in the proportion of males 21 years old and over returned as naturalized which occurred between 1900 and 1910, as shown in Table 13, was undoubtedly due to the exceptionally heavy immigration between 1905 and 1910. This resulted in a foreign-born population in 1910 of which more than one-fifth were ineligible for full citizenship, because of less than five years' residence in the United States, as compared with less than one-tenth in 1900. In 1920 only about one-sixteenth of the foreign-born population had been in the United States less than five years, but naturalization laws had become more rigid since 1900 and changes had taken place in the national origins of the foreign-born population which made rapid assimilation somewhat more difficult. The stimulation of the loyalty of the immigrant to his native country which resulted from the war may also have caused many to delay making application for naturalization. By 1930 the influences adverse to the process of assimilation had been largely overcome and the proportion of the foreign born who had been naturalized reached a point considerably above that of 1900.

Citizenship by country of birth.—One of the most significant classifications of the citizenship data is that by country of birth. In general the foreign-born white from countries which contributed early to the population of the United States, like England, Germany, and the Scandinavian countries, show a relatively high percentage naturalized, while those from countries from which most of the immigrants have arrived within the past two or three decades show a much lower percentage. There are differences as between individual countries, however, which are based on factors other than the time of arrival in the United States.

The citizenship figures for the foreign-born white from the more important countries are summarized in Table 2.

CITIZENSHIP OF THE FOREIGN BORN

TABLE 2.—FOREIGN-BORN WHITE POPULATION OF THE UNITED STATES BY CITIZENSHIP AND COUNTRY OF BIRTH: 1930

COUNTRY OF BIRTH	Total foreign-born white	Naturalized	Having first papers	Alien	Unknown	Per cent naturalized
All countries	13,366,407	7,859,193	1,246,521	3,787,086	473,607	58.8
England	808,672	541,880	66,858	165,179	34,755	67.0
Scotland	354,323	189,538	44,221	107,555	13,009	53.5
Wales	60,205	44,403	4,054	8,965	2,783	73.8
Northern Ireland	178,832	121,748	14,114	34,424	8,546	68.1
Irish Free State	744,810	492,191	65,413	144,178	43,028	66.1
Norway	347,852	246,735	29,954	59,054	12,109	70.9
Sweden	595,250	432,411	50,886	93,682	18,271	72.6
Denmark	179,474	134,513	15,519	23,506	5,936	74.9
Netherlands	133,133	88,725	11,996	28,234	4,178	66.6
Belgium	64,194	41,881	6,986	13,204	2,033	65.2
Switzerland	113,010	76,142	10,462	21,536	4,870	67.4
France	135,232	85,283	9,869	34,004	6,076	63.1
Germany	1,608,814	1,133,730	158,689	252,576	63,810	70.5
Poland	1,268,583	640,490	142,571	458,338	27,184	50.5
Czechoslovakia	491,638	301,401	44,504	133,379	12,354	61.3
Austria	370,914	233,582	31,876	91,298	14,158	63.0
Hungary	274,450	152,759	30,306	83,589	7,796	55.7
Yugoslavia	211,416	97,880	29,444	79,932	4,160	46.3
Russia	1,153,624	717,906	91,956	309,335	34,367	62.2
Lithuania	193,606	91,875	22,736	74,547	4,448	47.5
Finland	142,478	72,700	15,754	50,489	3,526	51.0
Rumania	146,393	88,277	15,553	39,173	3,390	60.3
Greece	174,526	78,059	25,112	65,977	5,378	44.7
Italy	1,790,424	894,647	143,380	705,892	46,505	50.0
Spain	58,302	11,045	6,824	38,530	1,894	18.9
Portugal	69,074	13,062	4,875	49,094	2,043	18.7
Syria	57,227	29,133	5,889	20,454	1,751	50.9
Canada—French	370,852	173,938	29,797	154,002	13,115	46.9
Canada—Other	907,560	484,619	79,205	290,622	53,083	53.4
All other	360,030	148,502	37,658	155,330	19,071	41.2

Urban, rural-farm, and rural-nonfarm population.— Urban population, as defined by the Census Bureau, is in general that residing in cities and other incorporated places having 2,500 inhabitants or more, the remainder being classified as rural. In three of the New England States, New Hampshire, Massachusetts, and Rhode Island, towns (townships) are classified as urban if they have a population of 2,500 or more and certain urban characteristics; and a few large and densely populated townships in other States are likewise classified, even though not formally incorporated as municipalities.

In addition to the classification of the population as urban and rural, the rural population is subdivided into rural-farm and rural-nonfarm on the basis of the replies to a question reading "Does this family live on a farm?" The rural-farm population includes all persons living on farms in the rural areas. The rural-nonfarm or "village" population is made up largely of persons living in small towns or villages, both incorporated or unincorporated, though in many areas there are considerable numbers of families living in the open country but not on farms.

The citizenship data for the foreign-born white population in urban, rural-farm, and rural-nonfarm areas is summarized in Table 3.

TABLE 3.—CITIZENSHIP OF THE FOREIGN-BORN WHITE POPULATION IN THE URBAN, RURAL-FARM, AND RURAL-NONFARM AREAS OF THE UNITED STATES: 1930

CITIZENSHIP	URBAN		RURAL-FARM		RURAL-NONFARM	
	Number	Per cent	Number	Per cent	Number	Per cent
Foreign-born white	10,726,859	100.0	1,084,087	100.0	1,555,461	100.0
Naturalized	6,188,152	57.7	746,039	68.8	925,002	59.5
Having first papers	1,054,064	9.8	72,877	6.7	119,580	7.7
Alien	3,133,153	29.2	222,466	20.5	431,467	27.7
Unknown	351,490	3.3	42,705	3.9	79,412	5.1

POPULATION

404

CITIZENSHIP OF FOREIGN-BORN WHITE PERSONS 21 YEARS OLD AND OVER, BY COUNTRY OF BIRTH: 1930

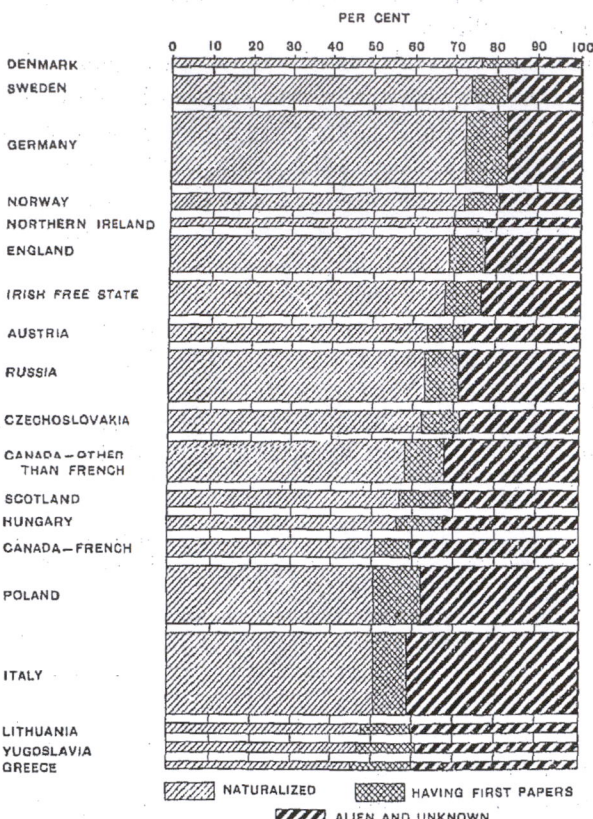

PERCENTAGE NATURALIZED IN THE FOREIGN-BORN WHITE POPULATION 21 YEARS OLD AND OVER, BY COUNTRY OF BIRTH AND SEX: 1930

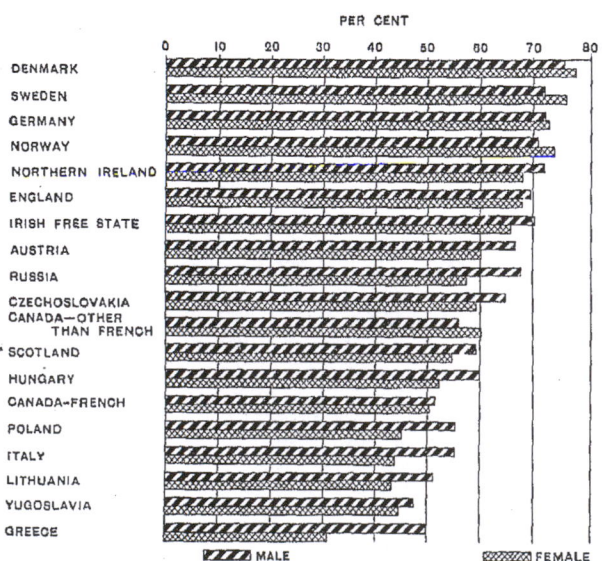

PERCENTAGE NATURALIZED IN THE FOREIGN-BORN WHITE POPULATION 21 YEARS OLD AND OVER, BY COUNTRY OF BIRTH: 1930 AND 1920

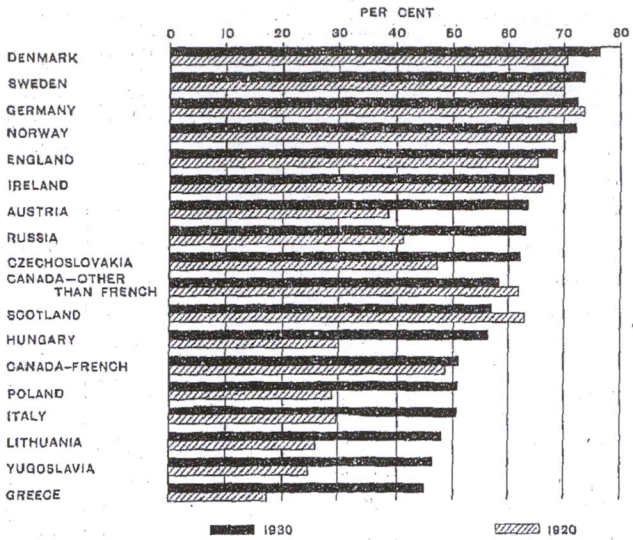

PERCENTAGE NATURALIZED IN THE FOREIGN-BORN WHITE POPULATION 21 YEARS OLD AND OVER, BY STATES: 1930

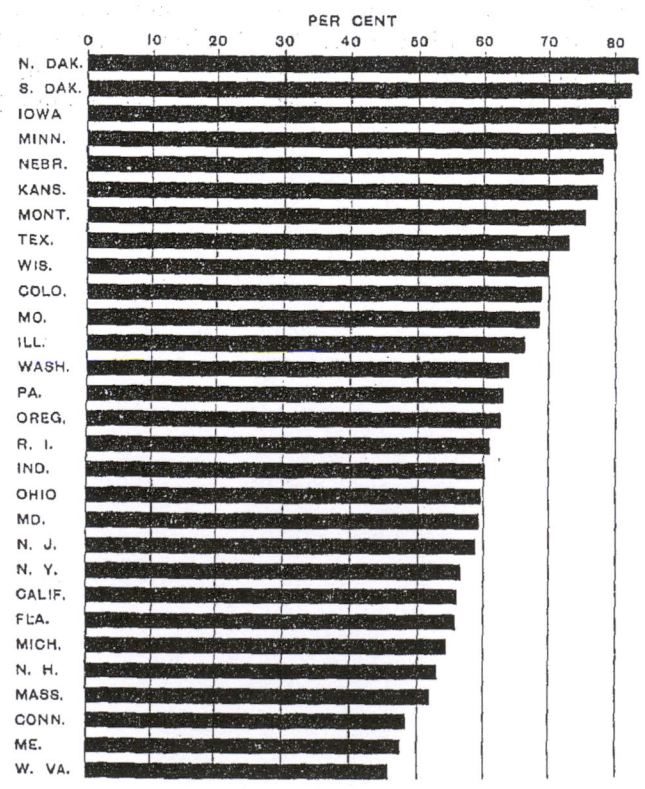

CITIZENSHIP OF THE FOREIGN BORN

405

TABLE 4.—CITIZENSHIP OF THE POPULATION, BY COLOR, NATIVITY, SEX, AND AGE, FOR THE UNITED STATES: 1890 TO 1930

[Figures for white population in 1920 and 1910 have been adjusted by deducting the estimated number of persons who would have been classified as Mexican in 1930]

CENSUS YEAR, SEX, AGE, AND COLOR OR RACE	Total population	Native population	FOREIGN-BORN POPULATION					PER CENT OF TOTAL FOREIGN BORN				CITIZENS, NATIVE OR NATURALIZED	
			Total	Naturalized	Having first papers	Alien	Unknown	Naturalized	Having first papers	Alien	Unknown	Number	Per cent of total population
1930													
Total, all ages	122,775,046	108,570,897	14,204,149	7,919,536	1,266,419	4,518,341	499,853	55.8	8.9	31.8	3.5	116,490,433	94.9
White	108,864,207	95,497,800	13,366,407	7,859,193	1,240,521	3,787,086	473,607	58.8	9.3	28.3	3.5	103,356,993	94.9
Negro	11,891,143	11,792,523	98,620	24,815	9,719	55,496	8,590	25.2	9.9	56.3	8.7	11,817,338	99.4
Mexican	1,422,533	805,535	616,998	35,529		10,179	553,635	5.8	1.6	89.9	2.9	841,063	59.1
All other	597,163	475,039	122,124				122,124			100.0		475,039	79.5
Males, all ages	62,137,080	54,489,990	7,647,090	4,365,403	955,942	2,081,710	244,035	57.1	12.5	27.2	3.2	58,855,393	94.7
White	55,163,854	48,010,145	7,153,709	4,332,288	941,985	1,650,313	229,123	60.6	13.2	23.1	3.2	52,342,433	94.9
Negro	5,855,660	5,801,588	54,081	15,024	6,773	27,401	4,883	27.8	12.5	50.7	9.0	427,983	99.3
Mexican	758,674	409,892	348,782	18,091	7,184	313,478	10,029	5.2	2.1	89.9	2.9	268,365	56.4
All other	358,883	268,365	90,518				90,518			100.0		268,365	74.8
Females, all ages	60,637,966	54,080,907	6,557,059	3,554,133	310,477	2,436,631	255,818	54.2	4.7	37.2	3.9	57,635,040	95.0
White	53,700,353	47,487,655	6,212,698	3,526,905	304,536	2,136,773	244,484	56.8	4.9	34.4	3.9	51,014,560	95.0
Negro	6,035,474	5,990,935	44,539	9,791	2,946	28,095	3,707	22.0	6.6	63.1	8.3	6,000,726	99.4
Mexican	663,850	395,643	268,216	17,437	2,995	240,157	7,627	6.5	1.1	89.5	2.8	413,080	62.3
All other	238,280	206,674	31,606				31,606			100.0		206,674	86.7
Total, 21 years and over	72,943,624	59,607,271	13,336,353	7,681,681	1,297,255	3,946,176	471,241	57.0	9.3	29.6	3.5	67,288,952	92.2
White	65,400,034	52,762,391	12,637,643	7,627,436	1,218,416	3,342,887	448,954	60.4	9.6	26.5	3.6	60,889,827	92.3
Negro	6,531,939	6,440,309	91,640	23,431	9,005	50,571	7,933	25.6	10.5	55.2	8.7	6,403,830	99.0
Mexican	687,440	195,858	491,582	30,814	9,234	437,180	14,354	0.3	1.9	88.9	2.9	226,672	33.0
All other	324,211	208,623	115,588				115,588			100.0		208,623	64.3
Males, 21 years and over	37,056,757	29,837,780	7,218,977	4,247,704	939,875	1,800,295	231,108	58.8	13.0	24.9	3.2	34,085,484	92.0
White	33,216,074	26,418,580	6,797,494	4,217,576	926,454	1,435,300	218,155	62.0	13.6	21.1	3.2	30,636,156	92.2
Negro	3,235,441	3,184,567	50,874	14,879	6,726	25,229	4,549	28.3	13.2	49.6	8.9	3,198,946	98.9
Mexican	389,595	104,048	284,947	15,740	6,695	254,104	8,399	5.5	2.3	89.2	2.9	120,307	30.9
All other	215,047	129,985	85,662				85,662			100.0		129,985	60.3
Females, 21 years and over	35,886,867	29,769,491	6,117,376	3,433,977	357,380	2,145,881	240,138	56.1	4.9	35.1	3.9	33,203,468	92.5
White	32,183,960	26,343,811	5,840,149	3,409,800	291,962	1,907,528	230,799	58.4	5.0	32.7	4.0	29,753,671	92.4
Negro	3,296,498	3,255,532	40,666	9,052	2,879	25,351	3,384	22.3	7.1	62.3	8.3	3,264,884	99.0
Mexican	297,845	91,210	206,635	15,065	2,539	183,076	5,955	7.3	1.2	88.6	2.9	106,275	35.7
All other	108,504	78,038	29,920				29,920			100.0		78,038	72.4
1920													
Total, all ages	105,710,620	91,789,928	13,920,692	6,489,883	1,222,553	5,406,780	801,476	46.6	8.8	38.8	5.8	98,279,811	93.0
White, as reported	94,820,915	81,108,161	13,712,754	6,470,159	1,219,057	5,223,715	790,823	47.2	8.9	38.1	5.8	87,587,320	92.4
Adjusted	94,120,374	80,864,980	13,255,394	6,457,665	1,216,285	4,809,076	772,368	48.7	9.2	36.3	5.8	87,522,845	92.8
Negro	10,463,131	10,389,328	73,803	10,724	3,496	49,128	10,053	14.5	4.7	66.8	14.4	10,400,052	99.4
Mexican (estimated)	700,541	243,181	457,360	21,494	2,772	414,639	18,455	4.7	0.6	90.7	4.0	264,675	37.8
All other	426,574	292,439	134,135				134,135			100.0		292,439	68.6
Males, all ages	53,900,431	46,224,996	7,675,435	3,446,547	1,187,021	2,695,042	308,825	44.9	14.8	35.1	5.1	49,674,543	92.2
White, as reported	48,430,655	40,902,333	7,528,322	3,443,968	1,183,727	2,502,917	387,710	45.7	15.1	34.0	5.2	44,346,301	91.6
Adjusted	48,049,193	40,780,002	7,269,191	3,435,948	1,181,273	2,325,504	376,576	47.3	15.6	32.0	5.2	44,215,960	92.0
Negro	5,209,436	5,160,795	42,641	5,570	3,204	27,053	6,115	13.1	7.7	64.0	14.3	5,172,374	99.3
Mexican (estimated)	381,462	122,331	259,131	8,020	2,454	237,523	11,134	3.1	0.9	91.7	4.3	130,351	34.2
All other	260,340	155,808	104,472				104,472			100.0		155,808	59.9
Females, all ages	51,810,189	45,564,932	6,245,257	3,040,336	85,532	2,711,738	407,651	48.7	1.4	43.4	6.5	48,605,208	93.8
White, as reported	46,390,260	40,205,828	6,184,432	3,035,191	85,330	2,720,798	403,113	49.1	1.4	43.0	6.5	43,241,019	93.2
Adjusted	46,071,181	40,084,578	5,986,603	3,021,717	85,012	2,483,682	396,702	50.5	1.4	41.5	6.6	43,106,885	93.6
Negro	5,253,695	5,222,533	31,162	5,145	202	21,277	4,538	16.5	0.6	68.3	14.6	5,227,678	99.5
Mexican (estimated)	319,079	120,850	198,229	13,474	318	177,116	7,321	6.8	0.2	89.5	3.7	134,324	42.1
All other	166,234	136,571	29,663				29,663			100.0		136,571	82.2
Total, 21 years and over	60,886,520	48,200,127	12,686,393	6,218,801	1,197,698	4,529,758	740,138	49.0	9.4	35.7	5.8	54,418,928	89.4
White, as reported	55,113,461	42,614,741	12,498,720	6,208,697	1,194,270	4,364,909	730,838	49.7	9.6	34.9	5.8	48,823,438	88.6
Adjusted	54,747,038	42,554,000	12,193,320	6,198,016	1,191,735	4,092,114	717,480	50.8	9.8	33.6	5.9	48,746,685	89.0
Negro	5,522,475	5,458,063	64,412	10,104	3,422	41,536	9,300	15.7	5.3	64.0	14.4	5,408,167	99.0
Mexican (estimated)	366,523	60,132	305,591	16,681	2,545	272,706	13,372	5.5	0.8	89.5	4.4	76,813	21.0
All other	250,584	127,323	123,201				123,201			100.0		127,323	50.8
Males, 21 years and over	31,403,370	24,339,776	7,063,594	3,320,226	1,119,962	2,259,310	364,076	47.0	15.9	32.0	5.2	27,660,002	88.1
White, as reported	28,442,400	21,513,948	6,928,452	3,314,910	1,116,744	2,138,237	358,561	47.8	16.1	30.9	5.2	24,828,858	87.3
Adjusted	28,220,777	21,488,385	6,747,304	3,308,924	1,114,452	1,973,918	350,120	49.0	16.5	29.3	5.2	24,759,088	87.8
Negro	2,792,006	2,753,772	38,234	5,316	3,238	24,165	5,515	13.9	8.5	63.2	14.4	87,551	17.7
Mexican (estimated)	212,623	31,565	181,058	5,986	2,512	164,319	8,441	3.3	1.3	90.8	4.7	72,056	42.6
All other	168,964	72,056	96,908				96,908			100.0		23,994,580	90.8
Females, 21 years and over	29,483,150	23,860,351	5,622,799	2,898,575	77,716	2,270,446	376,062	51.6	1.4	40.4	6.7	26,758,926	90.8
White, as reported	26,671,061	21,100,793	5,570,268	2,893,787	77,532	2,226,672	372,277	52.0	1.4	40.0	6.7	23,994,580	90.3
Adjusted	26,518,101	21,072,226	5,445,935	2,885,092	77,301	2,118,198	367,343	52.9	1.4	38.9	6.7	23,965,313	90.5
Negro	2,730,469	2,704,291	26,178	4,788	184	17,421	3,785	18.3	0.7	66.5	14.5	2,709,079	99.2
Mexican (estimated)	152,900	28,567	124,333	10,695	231	108,476	4,931	8.6	0.2	87.2	4.0	39,262	25.7
All other	81,620	55,267	26,353				26,353			100.0		55,267	67.7
1910[1]													
Males, 21 years and over	26,999,151	20,218,937	6,780,214	3,038,303	571,521	2,390,426	779,964	44.8	8.4	35.3	11.5	23,257,240	86.1
White, as reported	24,357,514	17,710,697	6,646,817	3,034,117	570,772	2,266,535	775,393	45.6	8.6	34.1	11.7	20,744,814	85.2
Adjusted	24,259,346	17,690,412	6,548,934	3,023,640	568,500	2,201,540	755,446	46.2	8.7	33.6	11.5	20,714,052	85.5
Negro	2,458,873	2,437,725	21,148	4,186	749	11,642	4,571	19.8	3.5	55.1	21.6	2,441,911	99.3
Mexican (estimated)	118,168	20,285	97,883	10,477	2,272	65,186	19,948	10.7	2.3	66.6	20.4	30,762	26.0
All other	182,764	70,515	112,249				112,249			100.0		70,515	38.6
1900[1]													
Males, 21 years and over	21,134,299	16,124,013	5,010,286	2,548,807	412,271	1,014,219	734,989	50.9	8.2	20.2	14.7	18,972,820	89.8
White	18,918,607	14,014,427	4,904,270	2,845,473	411,808	914,917	731,982	58.0	8.4	18.7	14.9	16,859,900	89.1
Negro	2,060,392	2,049,958	10,344	3,334		3,630	3,007	32.2		35.1	29.1	2,053,292	99.7
All other	155,300	59,628	95,672				95,672			100.0		59,628	38.4
1890[1]													
Males, 21 years and over	16,940,311	12,591,852	4,348,459	2,545,753	236,061	1,189,452	377,193	58.5	5.4	27.4	8.7	15,137,605	89.4

[1]Prior to 1920 the inquiry concerning citizenship was restricted to males 21 years old and over.

POPULATION

TABLE 5.—CITIZENSHIP OF THE FOREIGN-BORN WHITE POPULATION, BY SEX AND COUNTRY OF BIRTH, FOR THE UNITED STATES: 1930 AND 1920

[Figures for 1920 have been adjusted by deducting from the total and from persons born in Mexico the estimated number (total, 457,360; males, 259,131; females, 198,229) who would have been classified as Mexican in 1930]

CENSUS YEAR AND COUNTRY OF BIRTH	FOREIGN-BORN WHITE POPULATION						FOREIGN-BORN WHITE MALES						FOREIGN-BORN WHITE FEMALES					
	Total	Naturalized Number	Naturalized Per cent	Having first papers	Alien	Unknown	Total	Naturalized Number	Naturalized Per cent	Having first papers	Alien	Unknown	Total	Naturalized Number	Naturalized Per cent	Having first papers	Alien	Unknown
1930																		
All countries	13,366,407	7,859,193	58.8	1,246,521	3,787,086	473,607	7,153,709	4,332,288	60.6	941,985	1,650,313	229,123	6,212,698	3,526,905	56.8	304,536	2,136,773	244,484
Northwestern Europe:																		
England	808,672	541,880	67.0	66,858	165,179	34,755	412,065	279,379	67.8	47,206	68,621	16,859	396,607	262,501	66.2	19,652	96,558	17,896
Scotland	354,323	189,538	53.5	44,221	107,555	13,009	182,189	101,071	55.6	31,919	42,438	6,226	172,669	88,467	51.2	12,302	65,117	6,783
Wales	60,205	44,403	73.8	4,054	8,965	2,783	32,189	23,528	73.1	3,032	4,181	1,448	28,016	20,875	74.5	1,022	4,784	1,335
Northern Ireland	178,832	121,748	68.1	14,114	34,424	8,546	81,088	57,060	70.4	9,229	11,290	3,509	97,744	64,688	66.2	4,885	23,134	5,037
Irish Free State	744,810	492,191	66.1	65,413	144,178	43,028	324,841	224,198	69.0	40,541	43,212	16,890	267,993	109,843	63.8	24,872	100,966	26,138
Norway	347,852	246,735	70.9	29,954	50,054	12,109	196,349	136,892	69.7	23,581	29,487	6,439	151,503	109,843	72.5	6,373	20,617	5,670
Sweden	595,250	432,411	72.6	50,886	93,082	18,271	333,623	237,299	71.1	40,080	46,428	9,816	261,627	195,112	74.6	10,806	47,254	8,455
Denmark	179,474	134,513	74.9	15,519	23,500	5,936	109,975	81,753	74.3	12,453	12,254	3,515	69,499	52,760	75.9	3,066	11,252	2,421
Iceland	2,764	1,887	68.3	257	507	113	1,385	944	68.2	193	196	52	1,379	943	68.4	64	311	61
Netherlands	133,133	88,725	66.6	11,996	28,234	4,178	77,574	51,710	66.7	9,509	14,000	2,355	55,559	37,015	66.6	2,487	14,284	1,823
Belgium	64,194	41,881	65.2	6,986	13,294	2,033	35,265	23,697	67.2	5,016	5,476	1,076	28,929	18,184	62.9	1,970	7,818	957
Luxemburg	9,048	7,204	80.3	557	868	359	5,456	4,475	82.0	392	391	198	3,592	2,789	77.6	165	477	161
Switzerland	113,010	76,142	67.4	10,462	21,536	4,870	64,833	43,120	66.5	7,940	11,179	2,594	48,177	33,022	68.5	2,522	10,357	2,276
France	135,232	85,283	63.1	9,869	34,004	6,076	66,164	42,603	64.4	6,723	13,972	2,866	69,068	42,680	61.8	3,146	20,032	3,210
Central Europe:																		
Germany	1,608,814	1,133,739	70.5	158,089	252,576	63,810	843,136	593,752	70.4	110,679	108,766	29,930	765,678	539,987	70.5	48,010	143,810	33,871
Poland	1,268,583	640,490	50.5	142,571	458,338	27,184	681,425	375,673	55.1	111,553	181,232	12,967	587,158	264,817	45.1	31,018	277,106	14,217
Czechoslovakia	491,638	301,401	61.3	44,504	133,379	12,354	255,485	163,556	64.0	34,020	52,549	5,360	236,153	137,845	58.4	8,715	55,587	7,228
Austria	370,914	233,582	63.0	31,876	91,298	14,158	236,292	127,834	66.0	23,161	35,711	6,930	177,278	105,748	59.7	8,005	52,308	4,419
Hungary	274,450	152,759	55.7	30,306	83,589	7,796	139,828	82,929	59.3	22,301	31,221	3,377	134,622	69,830	51.9	8,005	52,308	4,419
Yugoslavia	211,416	97,880	46.3	29,444	79,932	4,100	131,351	62,274	47.4	24,848	41,846	2,883	80,065	35,606	44.5	4,596	38,086	1,777
Eastern Europe:																		
Russia	1,153,624	717,966	62.2	91,956	309,335	34,367	612,962	410,169	66.9	68,402	118,466	15,925	540,662	307,797	56.9	23,554	190,869	18,442
Latvia	20,673	12,590	60.9	2,178	5,405	500	11,061	7,300	66.0	1,577	1,951	233	9,612	5,290	55.0	601	3,454	267
Estonia	3,550	1,501	42.3	841	1,103	105	2,393	1,065	44.5	662	605	61	1,157	436	37.7	179	498	44
Lithuania	193,606	91,875	47.5	22,736	74,547	4,448	110,960	56,421	50.8	18,593	33,581	2,374	82,687	35,454	42.9	4,143	40,966	2,074
Finland	142,478	72,709	51.0	15,754	50,489	3,526	77,059	38,570	50.1	12,282	24,391	1,816	65,419	34,139	52.2	3,472	26,098	1,710
Rumania	146,393	88,277	60.3	15,553	39,173	3,390	78,685	50,879	64.7	11,882	14,421	1,503	67,708	37,398	55.2	3,671	24,752	1,887
Bulgaria	9,399	3,608	38.3	2,041	3,494	266	7,587	2,906	38.3	1,904	2,564	213	1,812	692	38.2	137	930	53
Turkey in Europe	2,257	1,018	45.1	294	879	66	1,269	690	54.4	235	311	33	988	328	33.2	59	568	33
Southern Europe:																		
Greece	174,526	78,059	44.7	25,112	65,977	5,378	129,101	63,969	49.5	22,857	38,409	3,866	45,425	14,090	31.0	2,255	27,568	1,512
Albania	8,814	2,797	31.7	1,510	4,315	192	6,549	2,338	35.7	1,402	2,667	142	2,265	459	20.3	108	1,648	50
Italy	1,790,424	894,647	50.0	143,380	705,892	46,505	1,042,621	569,100	54.6	120,645	328,884	23,992	747,803	325,547	43.5	22,735	377,008	22,513
Spain	58,302	11,045	18.9	6,824	38,539	1,894	41,976	7,800	18.6	6,145	26,768	1,263	16,326	3,245	19.9	679	11,771	631
Portugal	69,974	13,062	18.7	4,875	49,994	2,043	42,305	8,292	19.6	4,273	28,661	1,079	27,669	4,770	17.2	602	21,333	964
Other Europe	16,251	7,762	47.8	2,130	5,222	1,131	9,692	4,440	45.8	1,831	2,764	657	6,559	3,322	50.6	305	2,458	474
Asia:																		
Armenia	32,166	15,063	46.8	3,730	12,615	758	19,281	10,472	54.3	3,101	5,293	415	12,885	4,591	35.6	629	7,322	343
Palestine	6,135	3,469	56.5	638	1,781	247	3,634	2,147	59.1	503	847	137	2,501	1,322	52.9	135	934	110
Syria	57,227	29,133	50.9	5,889	20,054	1,751	32,510	18,635	57.3	4,778	8,210	887	24,717	10,498	42.5	1,111	12,244	864
Turkey in Asia	46,651	21,469	46.0	5,832	18,140	1,210	28,117	15,182	54.0	4,783	7,532	620	18,534	6,287	33.9	1,049	10,608	590
Other Asia	15,401	6,446	41.9	2,170	6,068	717	9,864	3,981	40.4	1,804	3,655	424	5,537	2,465	44.5	366	2,413	293
America:																		
Canada—French	370,852	173,938	46.9	29,797	154,002	13,115	187,523	89,258	47.6	22,725	69,354	6,186	183,329	84,680	46.2	7,072	84,648	6,929
Canada—Other	907,569	484,619	53.4	79,265	290,622	53,063	429,567	220,887	51.4	55,225	128,054	25,401	478,002	263,732	55.2	24,040	162,568	27,662
Newfoundland	23,971	9,299	38.8	3,155	10,378	1,139	11,520	4,514	39.2	2,297	4,236	473	12,451	4,785	38.4	858	6,142	666
Cuba	15,944	3,546	22.2	693	10,437	1,268	9,449	1,925	20.4	588	6,155	781	6,495	1,621	25.0	105	4,282	487
Other West Indies	15,482	7,091	45.8	1,432	5,076	1,283	7,678	3,856	50.2	951	2,330	541	7,804	3,235	41.5	481	3,346	742
Mexico	23,743	5,654	23.8	1,102	14,868	2,119	12,737	2,479	19.5	847	8,296	1,115	11,006	3,175	28.8	255	6,572	1,004
Central and South America	37,509	10,793	28.8	3,890	20,417	2,409	21,857	6,126	28.0	3,249	11,231	1,251	15,652	4,667	29.8	641	9,186	1,158
All other:																		
Africa	7,866	4,022	51.1	872	2,521	451	4,376	2,268	51.8	665	1,199	244	3,490	1,754	50.3	207	1,322	207
Australia	12,720	7,544	59.3	1,092	3,261	823	6,656	3,910	58.7	816	1,521	409	6,064	3,634	59.9	276	1,740	414
Azores	35,427	8,636	24.4	2,240	23,311	1,240	18,965	5,156	27.2	1,815	11,387	607	16,462	3,480	21.1	425	11,924	633
Other Atlantic Islands	4,052	1,408	34.7	392	2,009	243	2,385	820	34.4	327	1,106	132	1,667	588	35.3	65	903	111
Pacific Islands	4,364	2,364	54.2	444	1,259	297	2,350	1,249	53.1	322	620	159	2,014	1,115	55.4	122	639	138
Country not specified	1,485	481	32.4	73	359	572	926	282	30.5	55	209	380	559	199	35.6	18	150	192
Born at sea	4,958	2,860	57.7	89	446	1,563	2,763	1,455	52.7	68	235	1,005	2,195	1,405	64.0	21	211	558

CITIZENSHIP OF THE FOREIGN BORN 407

TABLE 5.—CITIZENSHIP OF THE FOREIGN-BORN WHITE POPULATION, BY SEX AND COUNTRY OF BIRTH, FOR THE UNITED STATES: 1930 AND 1920—Continued

CENSUS YEAR AND COUNTRY OF BIRTH	FOREIGN-BORN WHITE POPULATION						FOREIGN-BORN WHITE MALES						FOREIGN-BORN WHITE FEMALES					
	Total	Naturalized Number	Per cent	Having first papers	Alien	Unknown	Total	Naturalized Number	Per cent	Having first papers	Alien	Unknown	Total	Naturalized Number	Per cent	Having first papers	Alien	Unknown
1920																		
All countries	13,255,394	6,457,665	48.7	1,216,285	4,809,076	772,368	7,269,191	3,435,948	47.3	1,131,273	2,325,394	376,576	5,986,203	3,021,717	50.5	85,012	2,483,682	395,792
Northwestern Europe:																		
England	812,828	512,670	63.1	56,331	175,447	68,380	425,038	265,820	62.5	51,297	73,377	34,544	387,790	246,850	63.7	5,034	102,070	33,836
Scotland	254,567	154,981	60.9	20,268	58,824	20,544	133,955	82,425	61.5	18,464	22,827	10,239	120,612	72,556	60.1	1,804	35,997	10,305
Wales	67,066	48,897	72.9	3,264	8,271	6,634	36,184	26,152	72.3	3,009	3,574	3,449	30,882	22,745	73.7	255	4,697	3,185
Northern Ireland }Irish Free State	1,037,233	681,362	65.7	52,707	206,959	96,205	455,571	327,146	71.8	44,287	50,286	33,852	581,662	354,216	60.9	8,420	156,673	62,353
Norway	363,802	244,743	67.3	32,386	63,035	23,698	202,757	134,659	66.4	29,551	27,167	11,380	161,105	110,084	68.3	2,835	35,868	12,318
Sweden	625,580	431,556	69.0	53,007	105,445	35,572	344,933	236,614	68.6	48,173	42,369	17,777	280,647	194,942	69.5	4,834	63,076	17,795
Denmark }Iceland	180,154	130,826	69.2	16,882	28,987	12,479	114,063	78,036	68.4	15,671	13,175	7,187	75,091	52,796	70.3	1,191	15,812	5,292
Netherlands	131,766	73,773	56.0	13,405	36,550	7,978	75,510	41,383	54.8	12,567	17,216	4,344	56,256	32,390	57.6	898	19,334	3,634
Belgium	62,086	30,740	49.0	8,255	19,635	4,056	35,970	17,604	48.9	7,759	8,344	2,263	26,716	13,136	49.2	496	11,291	1,793
Luxemburg	12,585	9,124	72.5	969	1,507	985	7,671	5,543	72.3	605	695	538	4,914	3,581	72.9	74	812	447
Switzerland	118,659	76,957	64.9	8,756	22,635	10,311	67,830	43,332	63.9	7,983	11,194	5,321	50,829	33,625	66.2	773	11,441	4,990
France	152,890	86,740	56.7	11,205	41,229	13,716	79,351	45,875	57.8	10,010	16,945	6,521	73,539	40,865	55.6	1,195	24,284	7,195
Central Europe:																		
Germany	1,686,102	1,227,713	72.8	110,479	210,922	130,988	891,289	646,579	72.5	102,322	83,576	58,812	794,813	581,134	73.1	14,157	127,340	72,176
Poland	1,139,978	319,383	28.0	148,420	638,707	33,468	646,387	176,107	27.3	141,320	311,785	17,085	493,591	143,180	29.0	7,100	326,922	16,383
Czechoslovakia	362,436	165,997	45.8	49,244	132,176	15,019	196,251	85,444	43.5	46,110	57,565	7,132	166,185	80,553	48.5	3,134	74,611	7,887
Austria	575,025	210,908	37.7	67,913	262,660	28,054	323,451	115,481	35.7	64,227	129,325	14,388	252,174	101,487	40.2	3,686	133,335	13,666
Hungary	397,282	115,736	29.1	54,002	212,420	15,115	216,974	59,695	27.5	50,950	99,018	7,251	180,308	56,041	31.1	3,082	113,411	7,864
Yugoslavia	169,437	42,686	25.2	28,892	92,971	4,888	114,750	25,004	21.8	27,952	58,470	3,204	54,687	17,622	32.2	940	34,501	1,624
Eastern Europe:																		
Russia }Latvia }Estonia	1,400,489	562,930	40.2	139,149	644,966	53,444	774,013	310,284	40.1	130,870	305,841	27,018	626,476	252,646	40.3	8,279	339,125	26,426
Lithuania	135,008	34,627	25.6	16,890	80,428	3,123	82,806	20,891	25.2	16,304	43,860	1,802	52,202	13,736	26.3	586	36,559	1,321
Finland	149,824	61,902	41.3	18,797	63,000	6,125	85,287	33,065	38.8	17,601	31,449	3,112	64,537	28,837	44.7	1,130	31,551	3,013
Rumania	102,823	42,225	41.1	12,604	43,952	3,952	58,135	23,169	39.9	11,948	21,045	1,973	44,688	19,056	42.6	740	22,907	1,979
Bulgaria	10,477	1,268	12.1	1,710	7,023	470	9,508	994	10.5	1,096	6,395	423	969	274	28.3	20	628	47
Turkey in Europe	5,284	1,070	20.2	665	3,349	200	3,658	711	19.4	640	2,173	134	1,626	359	22.1	25	1,176	66
Southern Europe:																		
Greece	175,972	29,479	16.8	21,451	117,295	7,747	143,602	23,780	16.6	21,080	92,381	6,355	32,370	5,693	17.6	371	24,914	1,392
Albania	5,608	413	7.4	517	4,551	127	4,905	335	6.8	513	3,950	107	703	78	11.1	4	601	20
Italy	1,610,109	452,753	28.1	163,499	941,602	52,255	958,274	275,609	28.8	157,159	495,885	29,021	651,835	177,144	27.2	6,340	445,717	22,634
Spain	49,247	4,881	9.9	2,428	39,023	2,315	36,434	3,021	8.3	2,355	29,428	1,630	12,813	1,860	14.5	73	10,195	685
Portugal	67,453	11,049	16.4	2,481	51,590	2,333	39,372	6,319	16.0	2,337	29,332	1,384	28,081	4,730	16.8	144	22,258	949
Other Europe	5,001	2,835	48.0	675	1,821	570	3,665	1,560	42.6	631	1,172	302	2,236	1,275	57.0	44	649	208
Asia:																		
Armenia	36,626	10,574	28.9	4,630	20,125	1,297	25,351	6,948	27.4	4,472	13,055	876	11,275	3,626	32.2	158	7,070	421
Palestine	3,202	1,201	37.5	358	1,433	210	2,061	729	35.4	341	863	128	1,141	472	41.4	17	570	82
Syria	51,900	15,001	28.9	6,023	28,119	2,757	31,240	9,312	29.8	5,733	14,648	1,547	20,660	5,689	27.5	290	13,471	1,210
Turkey in Asia	11,014	2,768	25.1	1,148	6,511	587	8,039	1,868	23.2	1,108	4,089	374	2,975	900	30.3	35	1,822	213
Other Asia	7,708	2,815	36.5	838	3,379	676	5,082	1,642	32.3	803	2,193	444	2,626	1,173	44.7	35	1,186	232
America:																		
Canada—French	307,786	138,019	44.8	23,777	129,975	16,015	157,748	68,802	43.6	22,447	58,909	7,590	150,038	69,217	46.1	1,330	71,066	8,425
Canada—Other	810,002	460,284	57.9	48,987	215,582	70,289	389,600	212,570	54.6	43,972	94,586	38,472	420,483	250,705	61.1	4,965	120,996	37,817
Newfoundland	13,242	6,271	47.4	1,234	4,624	1,113	6,154	2,868	46.6	1,143	1,559	484	7,088	3,403	48.0	91	2,965	629
Cuba	12,843	2,712	21.1	263	8,363	1,505	7,030	1,350	19.2	243	4,553	884	5,813	1,362	23.4	20	3,810	621
Other West Indies	13,526	4,707	34.8	969	5,988	1,862	7,103	2,472	34.8	876	2,878	877	6,423	2,235	34.8	93	3,110	985
Mexico	21,023	1,238	5.9	217	18,389	1,179	12,433	507	4.1	204	10,996	726	8,590	731	8.5	18	7,393	453
Central and South America	20,929	5,046	24.1	1,232	12,413	2,238	12,624	2,592	20.5	1,131	7,575	1,326	8,305	2,454	29.5	101	4,838	912
All other:																		
Africa	5,222	2,276	43.6	405	2,087	454	2,981	1,228	41.2	373	1,114	266	2,241	1,048	46.8	32	973	188
Australia	10,801	5,345	49.5	916	3,415	1,125	5,935	2,613	44.0	837	1,814	671	4,866	2,732	56.1	79	1,601	454
Azores	33,788	6,987	20.7	1,130	24,767	904	18,062	3,983	22.1	1,078	12,499	502	15,726	3,004	19.1	52	12,268	402
Other Atlantic Islands	5,196	1,151	22.2	182	3,586	277	2,943	614	20.9	108	2,009	152	2,253	537	23.8	14	1,577	125
Pacific Islands	3,043	1,524	50.1	287	1,123	409	1,903	911	45.7	272	570	240	1,650	913	55.3	15	553	169
Country not specified	3,560	1,330	37.4	223	1,011	996	2,300	776	33.7	210	642	672	1,260	554	44.0	13	369	324
Born at sea	5,302	2,882	54.4	129	567	1,724	2,909	1,367	47.0	121	284	1,137	2,393	1,515	63.3	8	283	587

POPULATION

TABLE 6.—CITIZENSHIP OF THE FOREIGN-BORN WHITE POPULATION 21 YEARS OLD AND OVER, BY SEX AND COUNTRY OF BIRTH, FOR THE UNITED STATES: 1930 AND 1920

[Figures for 1920 have been adjusted by deducting from the total and from persons born in Mexico the estimated number of persons 21 years old and over (total, 305,391; males, 181,058; females, 124,333) who would have been classified as Mexican in 1930]

CENSUS YEAR AND COUNTRY OF BIRTH	FOREIGN-BORN WHITE POPULATION 21 YEARS OLD AND OVER						FOREIGN-BORN WHITE MALES 21 YEARS OLD AND OVER						FOREIGN-BORN WHITE FEMALES 21 YEARS OLD AND OVER					
	Total	Naturalized		Having first papers	Alien	Unknown	Total	Naturalized		Having first papers	Alien	Unknown	Total	Naturalized		Having first papers	Alien	Unknown
		Number	Per cent					Number	Per cent					Number	Per cent			
1930																		
All countries	12,637,643	7,627,436	60.4	1,218,416	3,342,837	448,954	6,797,494	4,217,576	62.0	926,454	1,435,309	218,155	5,840,149	3,409,860	58.4	291,962	1,907,528	230,799
Northwestern Europe:																		
England	768,201	528,108	68.7	65,178	141,379	33,536	391,838	272,566	69.6	46,307	56,671	16,294	376,363	255,542	67.9	18,871	84,708	17,242
Scotland	317,837	180,729	56.9	42,021	82,390	12,697	163,588	96,710	59.1	31,062	29,992	5,824	154,249	84,019	54.5	11,559	52,308	6,273
Wales	57,176	43,644	76.3	3,905	6,920	2,707	30,646	23,156	75.6	2,952	3,127	1,411	26,530	20,488	77.2	953	3,793	1,296
Northern Ireland	172,085	120,053	69.8	13,749	29,943	8,340	78,114	56,247	72.0	9,046	9,388	3,455	93,971	63,806	67.9	4,703	20,577	4,885
Irish Free State	721,246	488,740	67.8	63,185	127,556	41,765	316,731	222,642	70.3	39,530	38,017	16,542	404,515	266,098	65.8	23,655	89,539	25,223
Norway	338,268	243,912	72.1	29,532	52,987	11,837	191,248	135,482	70.8	23,298	26,173	6,295	147,020	108,430	73.8	6,234	26,814	5,542
Sweden	582,106	429,125	73.7	49,964	85,100	17,917	326,663	235,680	72.1	39,475	41,881	9,627	255,443	193,445	75.7	10,489	43,219	8,290
Denmark	174,583	132,807	76.1	15,242	20,755	5,779	107,423	80,911	75.3	12,267	10,808	3,437	67,160	51,896	77.3	2,975	9,947	2,342
Iceland	2,709	1,874	69.2	252	470	113	1,358	939	69.1	188	179	52	1,351	935	69.2	64	291	61
Netherlands	124,917	85,978	68.8	11,711	23,254	3,974	73,288	50,305	68.6	9,332	11,397	2,254	51,629	35,673	69.1	2,379	11,857	1,720
Belgium	60,147	40,056	66.6	6,741	11,414	1,936	33,260	22,789	68.5	4,877	4,509	1,025	26,887	17,267	64.2	1,864	6,845	911
Luxemburg	8,892	7,213	81.1	544	786	349	5,383	4,452	82.7	380	351	194	3,509	2,761	78.7	158	435	155
Switzerland	109,481	74,968	68.5	10,308	19,460	4,745	62,951	42,521	67.5	7,843	10,052	2,535	46,530	32,447	69.7	2,465	9,408	2,210
France	129,280	83,281	64.4	9,642	30,526	5,831	63,246	41,637	65.8	6,689	12,258	2,762	66,034	41,644	63.1	3,053	18,268	3,069
Central Europe:																		
Germany	1,548,253	1,122,702	72.5	154,135	209,390	62,026	813,294	588,295	72.3	108,098	87,696	29,205	734,959	534,407	72.7	46,037	121,694	32,821
Poland	1,216,630	616,349	50.7	140,835	433,503	25,853	656,348	363,922	55.4	110,597	169,496	12,333	560,282	252,427	45.1	30,238	264,097	13,520
Czechoslovakia	473,752	294,124	62.1	43,932	123,868	11,828	246,763	159,915	64.8	33,703	47,975	5,170	226,989	134,209	59.1	10,229	75,893	6,658
Austria	359,202	228,058	63.5	31,462	86,045	13,727	188,070	125,143	66.5	22,955	33,232	6,740	171,222	102,915	60.1	8,507	52,813	6,987
Hungary	261,877	147,150	56.2	29,813	77,472	7,442	133,697	80,138	59.9	22,025	28,284	3,250	128,180	67,012	52.3	7,788	49,188	4,192
Yugoslavia	202,438	93,981	46.4	29,104	75,419	3,934	126,732	60,234	47.5	24,640	39,562	2,296	75,706	33,747	44.6	4,464	35,857	1,638
Eastern Europe:																		
Russia	1,103,555	694,835	63.0	90,049	285,836	32,835	589,065	398,920	67.7	67,378	107,518	15,249	514,490	295,915	57.5	22,671	178,318	17,586
Latvia	19,874	12,264	61.7	2,143	4,987	480	10,687	7,132	66.7	1,559	1,773	223	9,187	5,132	55.9	584	3,214	257
Estonia	3,370	1,471	43.6	825	975	99	2,292	1,052	45.9	651	531	58	1,078	419	38.9	174	444	41
Lithuania	190,044	90,586	47.7	22,592	72,549	4,317	109,223	55,760	51.1	18,511	32,681	2,321	80,821	34,826	43.1	4,081	39,918	1,996
Finland	138,882	71,582	51.5	15,600	48,278	3,422	75,331	38,033	50.5	12,204	23,323	1,771	63,551	33,549	52.8	3,396	24,955	1,651
Rumania	139,299	65,130	51.1	15,307	35,038	3,224	75,241	49,298	65.5	11,751	12,767	1,425	64,058	35,832	55.9	3,556	22,871	1,799
Bulgaria	8,961	3,430	38.3	2,026	3,256	249	7,346	2,813	38.3	1,896	2,435	202	1,615	617	38.2	130	821	47
Turkey in Europe	2,053	948	46.2	288	760	57	1,179	655	55.6	234	260	30	874	293	33.5	54	500	27
Southern Europe:																		
Greece	167,336	75,474	45.1	24,859	61,865	5,138	125,619	62,649	49.9	22,701	36,516	3,753	41,717	12,825	30.7	2,158	25,349	1,385
Albania	8,059	2,587	32.1	1,484	3,806	182	6,146	2,227	36.2	1,386	2,396	137	1,913	360	18.8	98	1,410	45
Italy	1,679,708	848,843	50.5	141,931	646,306	43,528	986,531	545,729	55.3	119,191	299,015	22,596	693,177	303,114	43.7	21,840	347,291	20,932
Spain	54,965	10,540	19.2	6,747	35,924	1,754	40,250	7,554	18.8	6,098	25,408	1,190	14,715	2,986	20.3	649	10,516	564
Portugal	65,992	12,731	19.3	4,818	46,503	1,940	40,264	8,129	20.2	4,237	26,872	1,026	25,728	4,602	17.9	581	19,631	914
Other Europe	15,079	7,454	49.4	2,101	4,460	1,064	9,086	4,289	47.2	1,812	2,358	627	5,993	3,165	52.8	289	2,102	437
Asia:																		
Armenia	30,149	14,433	47.9	3,652	11,381	683	18,240	10,106	55.4	3,048	4,702	384	11,909	4,327	36.3	604	6,679	299
Palestine	5,087	2,990	58.8	612	1,280	205	3,106	1,907	61.4	488	596	115	1,981	1,083	54.7	124	684	90
Syria	54,125	27,873	51.5	5,780	18,805	1,658	30,994	17,997	58.1	4,707	7,449	841	23,131	9,876	42.7	1,082	11,356	817
Turkey in Asia	43,334	20,283	46.8	5,703	16,237	1,111	26,525	14,582	55.0	4,709	6,651	583	16,809	5,701	33.9	994	9,586	528
Other Asia	13,053	5,571	42.7	2,090	4,805	587	8,658	3,533	40.8	1,751	3,016	358	4,395	2,038	46.4	339	1,789	229
America:																		
Canada—French	329,153	167,196	50.8	28,842	121,142	11,973	167,493	86,019	51.4	22,209	53,572	5,693	161,660	81,177	50.2	6,633	67,570	6,280
Canada—Other	773,290	449,824	58.2	75,059	201,845	47,062	364,192	204,047	56.0	53,096	84,451	22,598	409,098	245,777	60.1	21,963	116,804	24,464
Newfoundland	21,091	8,743	41.5	3,088	8,263	997	10,177	4,239	41.7	2,250	2,828	414	10,914	4,504	41.3	832	4,995	583
Cuba	12,891	3,067	23.8	658	8,144	1,022	7,734	1,681	21.7	566	4,844	643	5,157	1,386	26.9	92	3,300	379
Other West Indies	14,013	6,666	47.6	1,390	4,804	1,153	6,971	3,642	52.2	932	1,916	481	7,042	3,024	42.9	458	2,888	672
Mexico	19,143	4,789	25.0	1,023	11,625	1,706	10,471	2,057	19.6	794	6,685	935	8,672	2,732	31.5	229	4,940	771
Central and South America	30,041	9,258	30.8	3,723	15,174	1,886	18,052	5,359	29.7	3,128	8,563	1,002	11,989	3,899	32.5	595	6,611	884
All other:																		
Africa	6,622	3,560	53.8	827	1,839	396	3,771	2,040	54.1	640	875	216	2,851	1,520	53.3	187	964	180
Australia	11,883	7,258	61.1	1,067	2,779	779	6,257	3,770	60.3	807	1,285	395	5,626	3,488	62.0	260	1,494	384
Azores	33,820	8,464	25.0	2,207	21,979	1,170	18,201	5,070	27.9	1,791	10,764	576	15,619	3,394	21.7	416	11,215	594
Other Atlantic Islands	3,780	1,351	35.7	386	1,818	225	2,241	789	35.2	324	1,005	123	1,539	562	36.5	62	813	102
Pacific Islands	3,899	2,235	57.3	419	976	269	2,104	1,179	56.0	310	468	147	1,795	1,056	58.8	109	508	122
Country not specified	1,400	467	33.4	73	327	533	875	276	31.5	55	187	357	525	191	36.4	18	140	176
Born at sea	4,522	2,681	59.3	83	244	1,514	2,531	1,359	53.7	64	123	985	1,991	1,322	66.4	19	121	529

CITIZENSHIP OF THE FOREIGN BORN

409

TABLE 6.—CITIZENSHIP OF THE FOREIGN-BORN WHITE POPULATION 21 YEARS OLD AND OVER, BY SEX AND COUNTRY OF BIRTH, FOR THE UNITED STATES: 1930 AND 1920—Continued

CENSUS YEAR AND COUNTRY OF BIRTH	FOREIGN-BORN WHITE POPULATION 21 YEARS OLD AND OVER						FOREIGN-BORN WHITE MALES 21 YEARS OLD AND OVER						FOREIGN-BORN WHITE FEMALES 21 YEARS OLD AND OVER					
	Total	Naturalized Number	Naturalized Per cent	Having first papers	Alien	Unknown	Total	Naturalized Number	Naturalized Per cent	Having first papers	Alien	Unknown	Total	Naturalized Number	Naturalized Per cent	Having first papers	Alien	Unknown
1920																		
All countries	12,193,329	6,102,016	50.8	1,191,733	4,092,114	717,466	6,747,394	3,308,924	49.0	1,114,432	1,973,918	350,120	5,445,935	2,883,092	52.9	77,301	2,118,196	367,346
Northwestern Europe:																		
England	745,398	487,639	65.4	54,838	138,449	64,472	392,116	253,937	64.8	50,338	55,148	32,693	353,282	233,702	66.2	4,500	83,301	31,779
Scotland	231,534	145,672	62.9	19,740	46,843	19,270	122,568	77,903	63.6	18,125	16,942	9,598	108,966	67,769	62.2	1,624	29,901	9,672
Wales	64,235	47,760	74.4	3,199	6,827	6,449	34,806	25,591	73.5	2,967	2,885	3,363	29,429	22,169	75.3	232	3,942	3,086
Northern Ireland	} 1,021,677	674,921	66.1	52,204	199,506	94,926	448,573	324,100	72.3	43,995	47,181	33,297	573,104	350,821	61.2	8,269	152,385	61,629
Irish Free State																		
Norway	348,885	238,032	68.2	31,907	56,223	22,723	195,101	131,322	67.3	20,223	23,640	10,916	153,784	106,710	69.4	2,684	32,583	11,807
Sweden	605,549	423,602	70.0	52,226	95,296	34,385	334,849	232,761	69.5	47,632	37,257	17,199	270,700	190,931	70.5	4,594	58,039	17,136
Denmark	} 180,798	127,530	70.5	16,552	24,749	11,958	109,754	76,412	69.6	15,447	10,978	6,917	71,044	51,127	72.0	1,105	13,771	5,041
Iceland																		
Netherlands	117,177	69,921	59.7	13,082	26,878	7,296	67,901	39,462	58.1	12,304	12,135	4,000	49,276	30,459	61.8	778	14,743	3,296
Belgium	54,342	27,990	51.5	8,028	14,778	3,546	31,811	16,260	51.1	7,612	5,913	2,026	22,531	11,730	52.1	416	8,865	1,520
Luxemburg	12,181	8,945	73.4	903	1,310	963	7,484	5,462	73.0	892	602	528	4,697	3,483	74.2	71	708	435
Switzerland	114,392	75,508	66.0	8,659	20,215	10,010	65,656	42,623	64.9	7,015	9,034	5,184	48,736	32,885	67.5	744	10,281	4,826
France	140,896	82,730	58.7	10,912	34,423	12,831	73,937	44,421	60.1	9,811	13,567	6,138	66,959	38,309	57.2	1,101	20,856	6,693
Central Europe:																		
Germany	1,648,884	1,213,451	73.6	115,195	191,755	128,483	873,231	639,843	73.3	101,473	74,277	57,638	775,653	573,608	74.0	13,722	117,478	70,845
Poland	1,048,050	302,635	28.9	146,008	580,411	20,996	602,918	168,354	27.9	139,759	279,386	15,419	445,132	134,281	30.2	6,339	290,025	14,487
Czechoslovakia	335,330	158,335	47.2	48,352	114,813	13,830	181,705	81,705	44.7	45,520	40,119	9,569	152,417	76,630	50.3	2,832	65,694	7,261
Austria	528,161	204,660	38.7	66,735	231,603	25,163	300,899	109,615	36.4	63,446	114,712	13,126	227,262	95,045	41.8	3,289	116,801	12,037
Hungary	353,792	106,183	30.0	52,860	181,761	12,988	196,093	55,188	28.1	50,215	84,406	6,284	157,699	50,995	32.3	2,645	97,355	6,704
Yugoslavia	155,950	38,816	24.9	28,523	84,210	4,398	107,974	23,140	21.4	27,687	54,134	3,013	47,982	15,676	32.7	836	30,085	1,385
Eastern Europe:																		
Russia	} 1,211,337	509,561	42.1	134,530	521,448	45,798	682,208	284,320	41.7	127,879	246,604	23,405	529,129	225,241	42.6	6,651	274,844	22,393
Latvia																		
Estonia																		
Lithuania	127,642	33,233	26.0	16,730	74,836	2,843	79,308	20,254	25.5	16,180	41,194	1,674	48,334	12,979	26.9	544	33,642	1,169
Finland	140,015	58,873	42.0	18,513	57,070	5,559	80,407	31,550	39.2	17,460	28,511	2,880	59,608	27,323	45.8	1,047	28,559	2,679
Rumania	92,117	38,880	42.2	12,336	37,465	3,436	52,979	21,602	40.8	11,718	17,949	1,710	39,138	17,278	44.1	618	19,516	1,726
Bulgaria	9,964	1,167	11.7	1,007	6,660	440	9,219	949	10.3	1,080	6,181	409	745	218	29.3	17	479	31
Turkey in Europe	4,601	968	21.0	655	2,805	173	3,311	656	19.8	630	1,902	123	1,290	312	24.2	25	903	50
Southern Europe:																		
Greece	161,515	28,129	17.4	21,044	105,353	6,989	135,207	23,093	17.1	20,736	85,459	5,919	26,308	5,036	19.1	308	19,894	1,070
Albania	5,090	370	7.3	507	4,100	113	4,543	308	6.8	504	3,632	99	547	62	11.3	3	468	14
Italy	1,408,933	419,713	29.8	159,086	784,927	44,607	858,111	259,547	30.2	154,380	418,583	25,651	550,822	160,166	29.1	5,356	366,344	18,956
Spain	41,436	4,450	10.7	2,347	32,716	1,923	31,540	2,814	8.9	2,285	25,061	1,380	9,896	1,636	16.5	62	7,655	543
Portugal	56,576	10,095	17.8	2,304	42,149	1,968	33,837	5,854	17.3	2,274	24,527	1,182	22,739	4,211	18.5	120	17,622	786
Other Europe	5,390	2,723	50.4	647	1,500	529	3,373	1,506	44.6	608	978	281	2,026	1,217	60.1	39	522	248
Asia:																		
Armenia	33,526	10,013	29.9	4,563	17,777	1,173	23,746	6,664	28.1	4,419	11,851	812	9,780	3,349	34.2	144	5,926	361
Palestine	2,539	973	38.3	343	1,058	165	1,703	610	35.8	327	655	111	836	363	43.4	16	403	54
Syria	46,575	14,057	30.2	5,872	24,251	2,395	28,478	8,821	31.0	5,610	12,683	1,364	18,097	5,236	28.9	262	11,568	1,031
Turkey in Asia	9,763	2,468	25.3	1,125	5,686	484	7,383	1,719	23.3	1,090	4,250	324	2,380	749	31.5	35	1,436	160
Other Asia	6,551	2,518	38.4	811	2,669	553	4,453	1,488	33.4	779	1,810	376	2,098	1,030	49.1	32	859	177
America:																		
Canada—French	274,176	132,081	48.5	23,176	103,573	14,446	141,514	66,579	47.0	21,997	46,094	6,844	132,662	66,402	50.1	1,179	57,479	7,602
Canada—Other	727,340	448,503	61.7	47,715	162,347	68,775	349,404	203,027	58.1	43,132	68,345	34,900	377,936	245,476	65.0	4,583	94,002	33,875
Newfoundland	12,260	6,074	49.5	1,213	3,050	1,023	5,689	2,767	48.6	1,125	1,345	452	6,571	3,307	50.3	88	2,005	571
Cuba	9,972	2,332	23.4	255	6,223	1,162	5,533	1,168	21.1	235	3,428	702	4,439	1,164	26.2	20	2,795	460
Other West Indies	11,687	4,340	37.2	940	4,777	1,621	6,157	2,293	37.2	853	2,245	766	5,530	2,056	37.2	87	2,532	855
Mexico	14,306	943	6.6	203	12,327	833	8,916	377	4.2	104	7,808	537	5,390	566	10.5	9	4,519	296
Central and South America	14,546	4,050	27.8	1,123	7,777	1,596	9,215	2,147	23.3	1,038	5,052	978	5,331	1,903	35.7	85	2,725	618
All other:																		
Africa	3,598	1,746	48.5	377	1,143	332	2,191	976	44.5	350	659	206	1,407	770	54.7	27	484	126
Australia	9,722	4,999	51.4	898	2,815	1,010	5,370	2,446	45.5	825	1,491	608	4,352	2,553	58.7	73	1,324	402
Azores	29,164	6,658	22.8	1,097	20,602	807	15,846	3,822	24.1	1,051	10,534	439	13,318	2,836	21.3	46	10,068	368
Other Atlantic Islands	4,393	1,073	24.4	174	2,896	250	2,547	573	22.5	162	1,675	137	1,846	500	27.1	12	1,221	113
Pacific Islands	3,197	1,721	53.8	274	854	348	1,761	849	48.2	263	435	214	1,436	872	60.7	11	419	134
Country not specified	3,333	1,286	38.6	220	919	908	2,180	756	34.7	207	594	623	1,153	530	46.0	13	325	285
Born at sea	4,819	2,711	56.3	126	322	1,660	2,681	1,290	48.1	118	167	1,106	2,138	1,421	66.5	8	155	554

POPULATION

410

TABLE 7.—CITIZENSHIP OF THE POPULATION, BY COLOR, NATIVITY, SEX, AND AGE, IN URBAN, RURAL-FARM, AND RURAL-NONFARM AREAS, FOR THE UNITED STATES: 1930

| CENSUS YEAR, SEX, AGE, AND COLOR OR RACE | Total population | Native population | FOREIGN-BORN POPULATION | | | | | PER CENT OF TOTAL FOREIGN BORN | | | | CITIZENS, NATIVE OR NATURALIZED | |
			Total	Naturalized	Having first papers	Alien	Unknown	Naturalized	Having first papers	Alien	Unknown	Number	Per cent of total population
URBAN													
Total, all ages	68,954,823	57,704,008	11,250,815	6,228,970	1,068,875	3,585,084	367,886	55.4	9.5	31.9	3.3	63,932,978	92.7
White	62,836,605	52,109,746	10,726,859	6,188,152	1,054,064	3,133,153	351,490	57.7	9.8	29.2	3.3	58,297,898	92.8
Negro	5,193,913	5,102,236	91,677	23,437	9,404	51,126	7,710	25.6	10.3	55.8	8.4	5,125,673	98.7
All other	924,305	492,026	432,279	17,381	5,407	400,805	8,086	4.0	1.3	92.7	2.0	509,407	55.1
Males, all ages	34,154,760	28,211,261	5,943,499	3,405,332	798,706	1,570,635	168,826	57.3	13.4	26.4	2.8	31,616,593	92.6
White	31,162,570	25,520,483	5,642,087	3,342,939	788,205	1,311,005	159,938	60.0	14.0	23.2	2.8	28,003,422	92.8
Negro	2,479,158	2,429,453	49,705	14,150	6,534	24,728	4,293	28.5	13.1	49.7	8.6	2,443,603	98.6
All other	513,032	261,325	251,707	8,243	3,967	234,902	4,595	3.3	1.6	93.3	1.8	269,508	52.5
Females, all ages	34,800,063	29,492,747	5,307,316	2,823,638	270,169	2,014,449	199,060	53.2	5.1	38.0	3.8	32,316,385	92.9
White	31,674,035	26,589,263	5,084,772	2,805,213	265,859	1,822,148	191,552	55.2	5.2	35.8	3.8	29,394,476	92.8
Negro	2,714,755	2,672,783	41,972	9,287	2,870	26,398	3,417	22.1	6.8	63.0	8.1	2,682,070	98.8
All other	411,273	230,701	180,572	9,138	1,440	165,903	4,091	5.1	0.8	91.9	2.3	230,839	58.3
Total, 21 years and over	43,896,714	33,348,301	10,548,413	6,026,721	1,043,578	3,132,123	345,991	57.1	9.9	29.7	3.3	39,375,022	89.7
White	40,069,960	29,962,589	10,107,371	5,980,350	1,029,266	2,756,909	331,846	59.3	10.2	27.3	3.3	35,951,930	89.7
Negro	3,335,060	3,250,012	85,048	22,104	9,294	46,554	7,096	26.0	10.9	54.7	8.3	3,272,116	98.1
All other	491,694	135,700	355,994	15,267	5,018	328,660	7,049	4.3	1.4	92.3	2.0	150,907	30.7
Males, 21 years and over	21,747,237	16,144,828	5,602,409	3,306,226	784,897	1,351,873	159,413	59.0	14.0	24.1	2.8	19,451,054	89.4
White	19,845,798	14,505,371	5,343,427	3,285,457	774,635	1,131,756	151,579	61.5	14.5	21.2	2.8	17,790,828	89.6
Negro	1,603,675	1,556,943	46,732	13,533	6,489	22,723	3,987	29.0	13.9	48.6	8.5	1,570,476	97.9
All other	294,764	82,514	212,250	7,236	3,773	197,394	3,847	3.4	1.8	93.0	1.8	89,750	30.4
Females, 21 years and over	22,149,477	17,203,473	4,946,004	2,720,495	258,681	1,780,250	186,578	55.0	5.2	36.0	3.8	19,923,968	90.0
White	20,221,162	15,457,218	4,763,944	2,703,893	254,631	1,625,153	180,267	56.8	5.3	34.1	3.8	18,161,111	89.8
Negro	1,731,385	1,693,069	38,316	8,571	2,805	23,831	3,109	22.4	7.3	62.2	8.1	1,701,640	98.3
All other	196,930	53,186	143,744	8,031	1,245	131,266	3,202	5.6	0.9	91.3	2.2	61,217	31.1
RURAL													
Total, all ages	53,820,223	50,866,889	2,953,334	1,690,566	197,544	933,257	131,967	57.2	6.7	31.6	4.5	52,557,455	97.7
White	46,027,602	43,388,054	2,639,548	1,671,041	192,457	653,933	122,117	63.3	7.3	24.8	4.6	45,059,095	97.9
Negro	6,697,230	6,690,287	6,943	1,378	315	4,370	880	19.8	4.5	62.9	12.7	6,691,665	99.9
All other	1,095,391	788,548	306,843	18,147	4,772	274,954	8,970	5.9	1.6	89.6	2.9	806,695	73.6
Males, all ages	27,982,320	26,278,729	1,703,591	960,071	157,236	511,075	75,209	56.4	9.2	30.0	4.4	27,238,800	97.3
White	24,001,284	22,489,662	1,511,622	940,849	153,780	339,308	69,185	62.8	10.2	22.4	4.6	23,430,011	97.7
Negro	3,376,511	3,372,135	4,376	874	239	2,673	590	20.0	5.5	61.1	13.5	3,373,009	99.9
All other	604,525	416,932	187,593	9,848	3,217	169,094	5,434	5.2	1.7	90.1	2.9	426,780	70.6
Females, all ages	25,837,903	24,588,160	1,249,743	730,495	40,308	422,182	56,758	58.5	3.2	33.8	4.5	25,318,655	98.0
White	22,026,318	20,898,392	1,127,926	721,692	38,677	314,625	52,932	64.0	3.4	27.9	4.7	21,620,084	98.2
Negro	3,320,719	3,318,152	2,567	504	76	1,697	290	19.6	3.0	66.1	11.3	3,318,656	99.9
All other	490,866	371,616	119,250	8,299	1,555	105,860	3,536	7.0	1.3	88.8	3.0	379,915	77.4
Total, 21 years and over	29,048,910	26,259,970	2,787,940	1,854,960	193,677	814,053	125,250	59.4	6.9	29.2	4.5	27,913,930	96.1
White	25,330,074	22,799,802	2,530,272	1,838,086	189,150	585,928	117,108	64.7	7.5	23.2	4.6	24,437,888	96.5
Negro	3,196,879	3,190,387	6,492	1,327	311	4,017	837	20.4	4.8	61.8	12.9	3,191,714	99.8
All other	519,957	268,781	251,176	15,547	4,216	224,108	7,305	6.2	1.7	89.2	2.9	284,328	54.7
Males, 21 years and over	15,309,520	13,692,952	1,616,568	941,478	164,978	448,422	71,690	58.2	9.6	27.7	4.4	14,634,430	95.6
White	13,367,276	11,913,209	1,454,067	932,119	151,819	303,553	66,576	64.1	10.4	20.9	4.6	12,845,328	96.1
Negro	1,631,766	1,627,624	4,142	846	237	2,497	562	20.4	5.7	60.3	13.6	1,628,470	99.8
All other	310,478	152,119	158,359	8,513	2,922	142,372	4,552	5.4	1.8	89.9	2.9	160,632	51.7
Females, 21 years and over	13,737,390	12,566,018	1,171,372	713,482	38,699	365,631	53,560	60.9	3.3	31.2	4.6	13,279,500	96.7
White	11,962,798	10,886,593	1,076,205	705,967	37,331	282,375	50,532	65.6	3.5	26.2	4.7	11,592,560	96.9
Negro	1,565,113	1,562,763	2,350	481	74	1,520	275	20.5	3.1	64.7	11.7	1,563,244	99.9
All other	209,479	116,662	92,817	7,034	1,294	81,736	2,753	7.6	1.4	88.1	3.0	123,696	59.0
RURAL-FARM													
Total, all ages:													
White	24,884,834	23,800,747	1,084,087	746,039	72,877	222,466	42,705	68.8	6.7	20.5	3.9	24,546,786	98.6
Negro	4,680,523	4,679,282	1,241	272	25	797	147	21.9	2.0	64.2	11.8	4,679,554	99.9
Males, all ages:													
White	13,186,577	12,555,408	631,169	430,826	58,860	116,762	24,721	68.3	9.3	18.5	3.9	12,986,234	98.5
Negro	2,354,445	2,353,623	822	168	21	524	109	20.4	2.6	63.7	13.3	2,353,791	99.9
Females, all ages:													
White	11,698,257	11,245,339	452,918	315,213	14,017	105,704	17,984	69.6	3.1	23.3	4.0	11,560,552	98.8
Negro	2,326,078	2,325,659	410	104	4	273	38	24.8	1.0	65.2	9.1	2,325,763	99.9
Total, 21 years and over:													
White	12,967,100	11,921,554	1,045,546	734,412	71,680	198,538	40,916	70.2	6.9	19.0	3.9	12,655,966	97.6
Negro	2,074,111	2,072,990	1,121	258	25	700	138	23.0	2.2	62.4	12.3	2,073,248	99.9
Males, 21 years and over:													
White	6,976,305	6,366,753	609,552	424,500	58,086	103,287	23,699	69.6	9.5	16.9	3.9	6,791,253	97.3
Negro	1,046,839	1,046,079	760	164	21	471	104	21.6	2.8	62.0	13.7	1,046,243	99.9
Females, 21 years and over:													
White	5,990,795	5,554,801	435,994	309,912	13,594	95,271	17,217	71.1	3.1	21.9	3.9	5,864,713	97.9
Negro	1,027,272	1,026,911	361	94	4	229	34	26.0	1.1	63.4	9.4	1,027,005	99.9
RURAL-NONFARM													
Total, all ages:													
White	21,142,768	19,587,307	1,555,461	925,002	119,580	431,467	79,412	59.5	7.7	27.7	5.1	20,512,309	97.0
Negro	2,016,707	2,011,005	5,702	1,106	290	3,573	733	19.4	5.1	62.7	12.9	2,012,111	99.8
Males, all ages:													
White	10,814,707	9,934,254	880,453	518,523	94,920	222,546	44,464	58.9	10.8	25.3	5.1	10,452,777	96.7
Negro	1,022,066	1,018,512	3,554	706	218	2,149	481	19.9	6.1	60.5	13.5	1,019,218	99.7
Females, all ages:													
White	10,328,061	9,653,053	675,008	406,479	24,660	208,921	34,948	60.2	3.7	31.0	5.2	10,059,532	97.4
Negro	994,641	992,403	2,148	400	72	1,424	252	18.6	3.4	66.3	11.7	992,893	99.8
Total, 21 years and over:													
White	12,362,974	10,878,248	1,484,726	903,674	117,470	387,390	76,192	60.9	7.9	26.1	5.1	11,781,922	95.3
Negro	1,122,768	1,117,397	5,371	1,069	286	3,317	699	19.9	5.3	61.8	13.0	1,118,466	99.6
Males, 21 years and over:													
White	6,390,971	5,546,456	844,515	507,619	93,733	200,286	42,877	60.1	11.1	23.7	5.1	6,054,075	94.7
Negro	584,027	581,545	3,382	682	216	2,020	458	20.2	6.4	59.9	13.5	582,227	99.5
Females, 21 years and over:													
White	5,972,003	5,331,792	640,211	396,055	23,737	187,104	33,315	61.9	3.7	29.2	5.2	5,727,847	95.9
Negro	537,841	535,852	1,980	387	70	1,291	241	19.5	3.5	64.9	12.1	536,239	99.7

CITIZENSHIP OF THE FOREIGN BORN

TABLE 8.—CITIZENSHIP OF THE FOREIGN-BORN WHITE POPULATION, BY COUNTRY OF BIRTH, IN URBAN, RURAL-FARM, AND RURAL-NONFARM AREAS, FOR THE UNITED STATES: 1930

[Per cent not shown where base is less than 100]

Country of birth	URBAN Total	Nat. Number	Nat. Per cent	Having first papers	Alien	Unknown	RURAL-FARM Total	Nat. Number	Nat. Per cent	Having first papers	Alien	Unknown	RURAL-NONFARM Total	Nat. Number	Nat. Per cent	Having first papers	Alien	Unknown
All countries	10,726,859	6,188,152	57.7	1,054,004	3,133,153	351,490	1,084,087	746,039	68.8	72,877	222,466	42,705	1,555,461	925,002	59.5	119,580	431,467	79,412
Northwestern Europe:																		
England	641,200	423,148	66.0	56,413	136,191	25,448	44,106	33,398	75.7	2,096	5,833	2,779	123,366	85,334	69.2	8,349	23,155	6,528
Scotland	205,541	151,907	51.4	39,468	94,187	9,999	13,871	10,104	72.8	797	2,196	774	44,911	27,527	61.3	3,956	11,192	2,236
Wales	45,968	33,421	72.7	3,386	7,275	1,886	4,008	3,200	80.1	167	376	256	10,220	7,778	76.0	501	1,314	641
Northern Ireland	150,782	101,880	67.6	12,566	29,496	6,840	8,207	6,169	75.2	383	1,113	542	19,843	13,699	69.0	1,165	3,815	1,164
Irish Free State	671,727	443,075	66.0	61,224	131,000	36,410	17,008	12,696	74.6	808	2,043	1,461	56,075	36,420	64.9	3,381	11,126	5,148
Norway	194,036	127,261	65.3	21,333	40,332	6,010	91,385	73,124	80.0	4,647	10,431	3,183	61,531	46,350	75.3	3,974	8,291	2,916
Sweden	408,032	285,516	70.0	30,672	71,440	11,395	98,589	81,693	82.9	4,850	9,217	2,829	88,629	65,202	73.6	6,364	13,016	4,047
Denmark	107,127	77,011	71.9	11,147	15,075	3,294	41,555	33,201	79.9	2,463	4,629	1,262	30,792	24,301	78.0	1,909	3,202	1,380
Iceland	1,348	817	60.6	171	297	63	772	613	70.4	28	105	26	644	457	71.0	58	105	24
Netherlands	80,466	54,386	67.6	7,870	15,079	2,231	31,408	20,191	64.3	2,446	7,876	895	21,259	14,148	66.6	1,680	4,379	1,052
Belgium	47,136	30,213	64.1	5,533	10,140	1,250	9,044	6,163	68.1	801	1,731	349	8,014	5,505	68.7	652	1,423	434
Luxemburg	5,693	4,475	78.6	399	592	227	1,955	1,615	82.6	98	169	73	1,400	1,174	83.9	60	107	59
Switzerland	67,918	46,369	68.3	6,621	12,111	2,817	25,887	16,783	64.8	2,157	6,004	943	19,205	12,990	67.6	1,684	3,421	1,110
France	104,865	65,495	62.5	7,956	26,895	4,519	10,345	6,906	66.8	647	2,242	550	20,022	12,882	64.3	1,266	4,867	1,007
Central Europe:																		
Germany	1,176,050	793,952	67.5	133,348	206,613	43,037	215,977	175,484	81.3	11,345	20,049	9,099	215,887	164,303	76.1	13,996	25,914	11,674
Poland	1,096,114	562,299	51.3	124,590	387,912	21,304	65,160	33,180	50.9	7,478	22,771	1,728	84,655	47,207	55.8	9,692	28,165	2,531
Czechoslovakia	348,261	212,219	60.9	33,171	94,692	8,179	58,722	41,915	71.4	4,641	10,522	1,044	40,455	20,820	51.5	3,417	12,002	3,217
Austria	308,482	198,512	64.4	26,581	73,203	10,096	21,977	14,241	64.8	1,878	5,013	845						
Hungary	228,642	131,415	57.5	24,603	66,472	9,002	14,801	7,464	50.4	2,056	4,845	446	31,007	13,890	44.8	3,557	12,272	1,288
Yugoslavia	154,501	71,765	46.4	22,657	57,264	2,815	12,055	6,803	53.8	1,567	3,953	332	44,260	19,312	43.6	5,220	18,715	1,013
Eastern Europe:																		
Russia	1,041,173	650,475	62.5	83,233	278,520	28,945	59,667	38,238	64.1	4,728	14,879	1,822	52,784	29,253	55.4	3,995	15,936	3,600
Latvia	18,744	11,490	61.3	1,926	4,881	438	672	362	53.9	81	209	20	1,257	729	58.0	171	315	42
Estonia	2,082	1,230	41.5	721	928	94	232	117	50.4	41	69	5	330	145	43.2	70	106	6
Lithuania	108,000	81,149	48.3	20,100	63,109	3,042	7,704	3,104	40.0	970	3,405	195	17,752	7,622	42.9	1,606	7,853	611
Finland	79,807	37,457	46.9	9,953	30,464	1,903	35,717	22,073	61.8	2,984	10,174	486	20,894	13,179	49.0	2,817	9,851	1,047
Rumania	131,465	79,937	60.8	13,767	34,785	2,976	6,469	4,072	62.9	709	1,564	124	8,459	4,208	50.5	1,077	2,824	290
Bulgaria	7,346	2,907	39.6	1,584	2,676	179	594	259	43.6	116	200	19	1,459	432	29.6	341	618	68
Turkey in Europe	2,158	965	44.7	284	844	65	31	14		8	14		68	39		7	21	1
Southern Europe:																		
Greece	159,370	72,498	45.5	22,609	59,448	4,761	2,458	900	36.6	444	1,038	76	12,602	4,601	36.7	1,099	5,491	541
Albania	8,179	2,638	32.3	1,382	3,981	63	59	12		19	26	2	576	147	25.5	109	308	12
Italy	1,573,003	790,244	50.2	125,510	617,728	39,521	49,283	21,645	43.9	4,593	21,615	1,430	168,138	82,758	49.2	13,277	66,549	5,554
Spain	46,181	9,194	19.9	5,813	29,791	1,383	3,908	630	16.1	304	2,817	157	8,213	1,221	14.9	707	5,931	354
Portugal	52,141	9,516	18.3	3,926	37,339	1,360	9,728	1,928	19.8	439	7,019	342	8,105	1,618	20.0	510	5,636	341
Other Europe	13,560	6,399	47.2	1,920	4,419	822	984	585	59.5	69	248	82	1,707	778	45.6	147	555	227
Asia:																		
Armenia	28,829	13,816	47.9	3,343	11,034	636	1,831	778	42.5	196	832	25	1,506	469	31.1	191	749	97
Palestine	5,875	3,328	56.6	602	1,716	220	63	41		8	11	3	197	100	50.8	28	54	15
Syria	51,482	25,875	50.3	5,335	18,812	1,460	1,081	649	60.0	104	279	49	4,604	2,609	55.9	450	1,303	242
Turkey in Asia	43,272	20,069	46.4	5,422	16,693	1,088	1,445	563	39.0	176	686	20	1,934	837	43.3	234	761	102
Other Asia	13,431	5,467	40.7	1,972	5,411	581	666	343	51.5	73	211	39	1,304	636	48.8	125	446	97
America:																		
Canada—French	292,564	137,728	47.1	24,789	120,260	9,787	22,068	10,941	48.3	1,425	9,339	963	55,620	25,269	45.4	3,583	24,403	2,365
Canada—Other	696,174	358,054	51.5	67,363	233,228	36,929	77,060	49,161	63.8	3,389	18,042	5,877	134,320	76,804	57.2	8,513	38,752	10,257
Newfoundland	22,021	8,497	38.6	2,900	9,641	983	228	127	55.7	16	72	13	1,722	675	39.2	239	665	143
Cuba	15,128	3,223	21.8	666	10,105	1,134	138	63	45.7	5	44	26	678	260	38.3	22	288	108
Other West Indies	13,960	6,283	45.0	1,336	5,220	1,121	242	155	64.0	16	57	14	1,280	653	51.0	80	399	148
Mexico	18,596	4,461	24.0	923	11,660	1,552	1,048	419	25.4	48	1,021	160	3,499	774	22.1	131	2,187	407
Central and South America	33,803	9,336	27.6	3,614	18,780	2,064	1,104	459	41.6	65	494	86	2,602	998	38.4	211	1,134	259
All other:																		
Africa	6,885	3,410	49.5	807	2,297	371	261	159	60.9	20	60	22	720	453	62.9	45	164	58
Australia	10,208	5,903	58.4	902	2,720	623	723	499	69.0	36	120	68	1,789	1,082	60.5	154	421	132
Azores	23,382	5,556	23.8	1,609	15,383	774	8,554	2,013	23.5	390	5,861	200	3,401	1,067	30.6	181	2,067	176
Other Atlantic Islands	3,427	1,173	34.2	345	1,718	191	207	86	41.5	11	96	14	418	149	35.6	36	195	38
Pacific Islands	3,395	1,787	52.6	363	1,019	226	376	232	61.7	28	88	28	593	345	58.2	53	152	43
Country not specified	1,164	875	32.2	53	208	468	83	38		6	22	17	238	68	28.6	14	69	87
Born at sea	3,309	1,808	57.4	64	322	1,025	696	423	60.8	12	46	215	953	530	56.6	13	78	323

119652—33——27

POPULATION

Table 9.—CITIZENSHIP OF THE FOREIGN-BORN WHITE POPULATION 21 YEARS OLD AND OVER, BY COUNTRY OF BIRTH AND SEX, IN URBAN, RURAL-FARM, AND RURAL-NONFARM AREAS, FOR THE UNITED STATES: 1930

[Per cent not shown where base is less than 100]

Sex and Country of Birth	URBAN Total	Naturalized Number	Per cent	Having first papers	Alien	Unknown	RURAL-FARM Total	Naturalized Number	Per cent	Having first papers	Alien	Unknown	RURAL-NONFARM Total	Naturalized Number	Per cent	Having first papers	Alien	Unknown
MALE																		
All countries	5,343,427	3,285,457	61.5	774,635	1,131,756	151,579	609,552	424,500	69.6	58,086	103,267	23,699	844,515	507,619	60.1	93,733	200,286	42,877
Northwestern Europe:																		
England	304,517	209,246	68.7	38,726	45,206	11,279	24,746	18,827	76.1	1,609	2,689	1,621	62,575	44,493	71.1	5,972	8,716	3,394
Scotland	134,032	76,560	57.1	27,655	25,574	4,243	7,670	5,698	74.3	607	932	433	21,880	14,452	66.0	2,800	3,486	1,148
Wales	22,785	17,013	74.7	2,435	2,445	892	2,382	1,905	80.0	132	177	168	5,479	4,238	77.3	385	505	351
Northern Ireland	64,689	46,340	71.6	8,004	7,729	2,616	4,435	3,355	75.6	286	466	328	8,990	6,552	72.9	756	1,171	511
Irish Free State	282,295	198,500	70.3	36,842	33,806	13,147	8,987	6,670	74.2	611	865	841	25,449	17,472	68.7	2,077	3,346	2,554
Norway	103,550	67,880	65.6	16,170	16,557	2,934	52,630	41,024	79.1	3,863	5,413	1,730	35,068	25,960	74.1	3,265	4,203	1,631
Sweden	215,839	150,072	69.5	30,175	29,930	5,662	58,874	48,404	82.2	4,013	4,817	1,640	51,950	37,204	71.6	5,287	7,134	2,325
Denmark	62,759	45,376	72.3	8,704	6,836	1,843	26,076	20,862	80.0	2,043	2,387	784	18,588	14,673	78.9	1,520	1,585	810
Iceland	668	403	60.3	126	110	29	380	310	81.6	22	35	13	310	226	72.9	40	34	10
Netherlands	43,877	30,448	69.4	6,054	6,208	1,167	17,689	11,829	66.9	1,952	3,408	500	11,722	8,028	68.5	1,326	1,781	587
Belgium	23,717	16,136	68.0	3,777	3,215	589	5,169	3,630	70.2	613	729	107	4,374	3,023	69.1	487	625	239
Luxemburg	3,205	2,611	81.5	260	220	114	1,295	1,090	84.2	81	79	45	883	751	85.1	45	52	35
Switzerland	35,730	24,655	69.0	4,731	5,098	1,336	16,232	10,382	64.0	1,823	3,463	564	10,989	7,484	68.1	1,289	1,581	635
France	46,851	30,727	65.6	5,165	9,094	1,865	6,263	4,134	66.0	517	1,270	342	10,132	6,776	66.9	907	1,894	555
Central Europe:																		
Germany	577,262	400,281	69.3	89,639	69,203	18,139	123,158	100,556	81.6	8,731	8,863	5,008	112,874	87,458	77.5	9,728	9,630	6,058
Poland	559,171	317,944	56.9	95,980	136,243	9,004	35,936	19,244	53.6	6,011	9,789	891	61,242	26,734	43.7	8,606	23,464	2,438
Czechoslovakia	170,819	111,276	65.1	24,777	31,606	3,160	31,205	22,897	73.4	3,554	3,925	829	44,739	25,742	57.5	5,372	12,444	1,181
Austria	152,661	105,415	69.1	18,741	24,164	4,341	12,057	7,933	65.8	1,468	2,213	443	23,352	11,795	50.5	2,746	6,855	1,956
Hungary	109,016	68,287	62.6	17,580	20,804	2,345	7,849	4,106	52.3	1,602	1,923	218	16,832	7,745	46.0	2,843	5,557	687
Yugoslavia	91,107	43,998	48.3	18,834	26,822	1,453	7,260	4,031	55.5	1,263	1,784	182	28,365	12,205	43.0	4,543	10,056	601
Eastern Europe:																		
Russia	526,016	361,626	68.7	60,542	91,633	12,215	32,169	20,787	64.0	3,658	6,777	947	30,880	16,507	53.5	3,178	9,108	2,087
Latvia	9,564	6,459	67.5	1,374	1,537	194	370	220	59.5	61	85	4	754	455	60.3	123	151	25
Estonia	1,927	880	45.7	558	437	52	138	77	55.8	30	30	1	227	95	41.9	63	64	5
Lithuania	93,523	48,965	52.4	10,293	26,475	1,790	4,660	1,926	41.3	813	1,818	103	11,039	4,867	44.1	1,406	4,338	428
Finland	40,131	18,915	47.1	7,496	12,798	922	19,284	11,741	60.9	2,399	4,899	245	15,916	7,377	46.3	2,309	5,626	604
Rumania	66,719	44,527	66.7	10,335	10,667	1,190	3,590	2,315	64.5	545	656	74	4,932	2,456	49.8	871	1,444	161
Bulgaria	5,609	2,242	40.0	1,465	1,774	128	455	197	43.3	104	138	16	1,282	374	29.2	327	523	58
Turkey in Europe	1,113	618	55.5	224	241	30	22	9	-----	3	10	-----	44	28	-----	7	9	-----
Southern Europe:																		
Greece	113,245	57,840	51.1	20,394	31,772	3,239	1,926	780	40.5	404	682	60	10,448	4,020	38.5	1,903	4,062	463
Albania	5,662	2,098	37.1	1,265	2,176	123	41	9	-----	15	15	2	443	120	27.1	106	205	12
Italy	857,321	480,063	56.0	103,878	254,912	18,468	29,186	13,356	45.8	3,881	11,124	825	100,024	52,310	52.3	11,432	32,979	3,303
Spain	31,809	6,310	19.8	5,177	19,452	870	2,752	414	15.0	277	1,940	121	5,689	830	14.6	644	4,016	199
Portugal	29,377	5,864	20.0	3,376	19,448	689	5,906	1,259	21.3	400	4,058	189	4,981	1,006	20.2	461	3,366	148
Other Europe	7,520	3,515	46.7	1,640	1,935	430	534	326	61.0	55	105	48	1,032	448	43.4	117	318	149
Asia:																		
Armenia	16,272	9,287	57.1	2,715	3,968	302	1,023	471	46.0	171	368	13	945	348	36.8	162	366	69
Palestine	2,939	1,814	61.7	459	564	102	41	26	-----	7	6	2	126	67	53.2	22	26	11
Syria	27,480	15,842	57.6	4,242	6,732	670	683	432	63.3	86	131	34	2,825	1,723	61.0	379	586	137
Turkey in Asia	24,357	13,593	55.8	4,351	5,920	493	838	374	44.6	149	303	12	1,830	615	46.2	209	428	78
Other Asia	7,577	3,017	39.8	1,603	2,674	283	343	166	48.4	56	102	19	738	350	47.4	92	240	56
America:																		
Canada—French	129,275	67,177	52.0	18,221	39,936	3,941	11,272	5,961	52.9	1,134	3,617	560	26,946	12,881	47.8	2,854	10,019	1,192
Canada—Other	269,494	146,317	54.3	44,448	64,095	14,634	35,949	23,600	65.6	2,490	6,779	3,080	58,749	34,130	58.1	6,158	13,577	4,884
Newfoundland	9,223	3,871	42.0	2,076	2,937	339	53	10	-----	7	23	5	866	315	36.4	173	308	70
Cuba	7,379	1,550	21.0	545	4,707	577	36	10	-----	3	13	10	819	121	37.9	18	124	56
Other West Indies	6,255	3,235	51.7	867	1,736	417	110	69	62.7	13	19	9	606	338	55.8	52	101	55
Mexico	7,865	1,573	20.0	689	4,983	620	819	183	22.3	31	515	90	1,787	301	16.8	74	1,187	225
Central and South America	16,220	4,657	28.7	2,890	7,803	870	514	216	42.0	54	214	30	1,311	481	36.7	183	546	101
All other:																		
Africa	3,275	1,718	52.5	592	790	175	125	73	58.4	14	24	14	371	249	67.1	34	61	27
Australia	4,926	2,937	59.6	655	1,056	278	400	285	69.7	26	56	42	922	548	59.4	126	173	75
Azores	11,104	3,169	28.5	1,267	6,375	293	5,187	1,252	24.1	358	3,401	176	1,910	649	34.0	166	988	107
Other Atlantic Islands	1,874	661	35.3	290	832	91	127	53	41.7	7	60	7	240	75	31.3	27	113	25
Pacific Islands	1,583	871	55.0	247	353	112	190	116	61.1	20	43	11	331	102	58.0	43	72	24
Country not specified	659	209	31.7	39	124	287	58	27	-----	6	13	12	158	40	25.3	10	50	58
Born at sea	1,578	851	53.9	47	74	606	415	230	55.4	8	16	161	545	283	51.9	10	33	219

CITIZENSHIP OF THE FOREIGN BORN

413

TABLE 9.—CITIZENSHIP OF THE FOREIGN-BORN WHITE POPULATION 21 YEARS OLD AND OVER, BY COUNTRY OF BIRTH AND SEX, IN URBAN, RURAL-FARM, AND RURAL-NONFARM AREAS, FOR THE UNITED STATES: 1930—Continued

SEX AND COUNTRY OF BIRTH	URBAN Total	Naturalized Number	Per cent	Having first papers	Alien	Unknown	RURAL-FARM Total	Naturalized Number	Per cent	Having first papers	Alien	Unknown	RURAL-NONFARM Total	Naturalized Number	Per cent	Having first papers	Alien	Unknown
FEMALE																		
All countries	4,763,944	2,703,893	56.8	254,631	1,625,153	180,267	435,994	309,912	71.1	13,594	95,271	17,217	640,211	396,055	61.9	23,737	187,104	33,315
Northwestern Europe:																		
England	302,450	202,260	66.9	16,180	70,795	13,215	18,428	14,246	77.3	458	2,632	1,002	55,477	39,036	70.4	2,224	11,281	2,936
Scotland	128,708	67,543	52.5	10,351	45,907	4,907	5,797	4,284	73.9	175	1,020	318	19,083	12,192	61.9	1,033	5,471	987
Wales	20,583	15,707	76.6	817	3,067	932	1,558	1,282	82.3	32	158	86	4,393	3,442	78.4	104	568	279
Northern Ireland	80,054	54,031	67.5	4,216	17,792	4,045	3,626	2,775	76.5	94	548	200	10,262	7,001	68.2	393	2,237	631
Irish Free State	367,381	241,383	65.7	22,200	81,630	22,108	7,704	5,966	76.8	182	1,008	608	29,366	18,746	63.8	1,213	6,901	2,506
Norway	84,246	57,330	68.1	4,818	19,215	2,883	37,411	31,049	83.0	748	4,210	1,404	25,363	20,051	79.1	668	3,389	1,255
Sweden	181,636	132,938	73.2	8,603	34,521	5,484	38,540	32,873	85.3	778	3,752	1,137	35,266	27,633	78.4	1,018	4,946	1,669
Denmark	40,970	30,480	74.4	2,232	6,904	1,354	14,575	11,093	82.3	379	1,753	450	11,615	9,423	81.1	364	1,290	538
Iceland	651	406	62.4	42	169	34	377	302	80.1	5	57	13	323	227	70.3	17	65	14
Netherlands	31,706	22,233	70.1	1,616	6,917	940	11,568	7,677	66.4	434	3,111	346	8,355	5,763	69.0	329	1,829	434
Belgium	20,128	12,616	62.7	1,532	5,391	589	3,382	2,300	68.0	170	700	143	3,972	2,351	60.7	153	680	179
Luxemburg	2,379	1,827	76.8	127	310	100	634	519	81.9	16	74	25	501	415	82.8	15	47	24
Switzerland	30,027	20,895	69.6	1,778	5,944	1,410	8,780	6,190	70.4	307	1,930	353	7,714	5,382	69.5	380	1,525	447
France	52,958	33,050	62.4	2,593	14,867	2,448	3,859	2,707	70.1	121	831	200	9,217	5,887	63.0	339	2,570	421
Central Europe:																		
Germany	548,168	384,768	70.2	39,736	100,263	23,411	89,040	74,031	83.1	2,385	8,674	3,950	97,751	75,618	77.4	3,916	12,757	5,460
Poland	488,525	221,455	45.3	27,017	228,897	11,156	28,005	13,531	48.3	1,417	12,282	775	43,752	17,441	39.9	1,804	22,918	1,589
Czechoslovakia	163,431	95,274	53.3	7,941	55,590	4,626	20,347	18,477	70.1	1,037	6,061	772	37,211	20,458	55.0	1,251	14,242	1,260
Austria	145,522	88,106	60.5	7,468	44,548	5,400	9,484	6,145	64.8	306	2,553	380	16,216	8,664	53.4	643	5,702	1,207
Hungary	108,621	58,081	53.5	6,677	40,445	3,418	6,521	3,182	48.8	431	2,687	221	13,038	5,749	44.1	680	6,056	553
Yugoslavia	56,205	24,629	43.8	3,545	26,840	1,191	4,091	2,607	52.2	282	1,977	125	14,510	6,511	44.9	637	7,040	322
Eastern Europe:																		
Russia	468,642	266,980	57.0	20,923	165,333	15,397	25,274	16,650	65.9	984	6,858	782	20,574	12,276	59.7	764	6,127	1,407
Latvia	8,439	4,738	56.1	519	2,955	227	281	134	47.7	18	115	14	474	260	54.9	47	151	16
Estonia	894	337	37.7	148	372	37	86	36		11	36	3	98	48		15	30	1
Lithuania	71,828	31,009	43.5	3,676	34,910	1,733	2,990	1,149	38.4	152	1,606	83	6,503	2,668	41.0	253	3,402	180
Finland	37,400	17,851	47.7	2,351	16,202	996	15,719	10,085	64.0	556	4,874	224	10,425	5,633	54.0	489	3,872	431
Rumania	58,123	32,448	55.8	3,208	20,832	1,635	2,667	1,674	63.0	148	701	44	3,278	1,710	52.2	200	1,248	120
Bulgaria	1,370	522	38.1	105	704	39	105	47	44.8	11	45	2	140	48	34.3	14	72	6
Turkey in Europe	846	278	32.9	54	488	26	7	5			2		21	10			10	1
Southern Europe:																		
Greece	39,370	12,187	31.0	2,029	23,837	1,317	468	108	23.1	39	309	12	1,889	530	28.1	90	1,203	66
Albania	1,803	340	18.9	92	1,326	45	15	3		3	9		95	17		3	75	
Italy	616,837	269,400	43.7	19,531	309,435	18,471	18,031	7,586	42.1	657	9,265	523	58,209	26,128	44.8	1,652	28,501	1,928
Spain	11,737	2,445	20.8	507	8,318	412	909	194	20.0	25	722	28	2,009	347	17.3	57	1,481	124
Portugal	19,580	3,393	17.3	498	15,095	603	3,407	636	18.7	39	2,591	141	2,732	573	21.0	44	1,945	170
Other Europe	4,938	2,597	52.6	245	1,757	339	433	253	58.4	14	135	31	621	314	50.6	30	210	67
Asia:																		
Armenia	10,715	3,931	36.7	558	5,961	265	745	291	39.1	24	418	12	450	106	23.6	22	300	22
Palestine	1,900	1,039	54.7	118	656	87	21	15		1	4	1	60	29		5	24	2
Syria	21,100	8,885	42.1	999	10,511	705	361	202	56.0	15	130	14	1,670	789	47.2	68	715	98
Turkey in Asia	15,752	5,343	33.9	950	8,957	502	551	174	31.6	20	345	6	506	184	36.4	18	284	20
Other Asia	8,808	1,726	44.6	293	1,656	103	227	126	55.5	17	72	12	342	186	54.4	20	103	24
America:																		
Canada—French	131,170	65,302	49.8	5,782	55,135	4,951	7,913	4,505	50.9	217	2,870	321	22,577	11,370	50.4	634	9,565	1,008
Canada—Other	321,741	185,849	57.8	19,352	98,390	18,141	29,954	22,070	73.7	608	5,122	2,055	57,361	37,849	66.0	1,013	13,331	4,208
Newfoundland	10,080	4,101	40.7	762	4,703	514	129	74	57.4	9	39	7	705	329	46.7	61	253	62
Cuba	4,018	1,252	25.5	88	3,234	344	52	20		2	10	11	187	105	56.1	2	56	24
Other West Indies	6,399	2,676	41.8	430	2,704	589	109	75	68.8	3	27	4	534	273	51.1	25	157	79
Mexico	9,960	2,174	31.2	189	3,987	610	565	184	32.6	13	316	52	1,147	374	32.6	27	637	109
Central and South America	10,749	3,305	30.7	584	6,118	762	376	195	51.9	7	140	34	804	399	46.2	24	353	88
All other:																		
Africa	2,499	1,291	51.7	174	887	147	97	70		3	17	7	255	159	62.4	10	60	26
Australia	4,598	2,793	60.7	230	1,261	314	275	196	71.3	6	50	23	753	499	66.3	24	183	47
Azores	11,139	2,282	20.5	373	8,053	431	3,020	708	23.4	30	2,186	96	1,460	404	27.7	13	976	67
Other Atlantic Islands	1,327	472	35.6	50	720	85	63	28		4	24	7	149	62	41.6	8	69	10
Pacific Islands	1,422	816	57.4	96	418	92	138	98	71.0	3	26	11	235	142	60.4	10	64	19
Country not specified	436	153	35.1	14	117	152	23	11			8	4	66	27		4	15	20
Born at sea	1,407	907	64.5	15	96	389	237	176	74.3	3	12	46	347	239	68.9	1	13	94

414

POPULATION

TABLE 10.—CITIZENSHIP OF THE FOREIGN-BORN AND THE FOREIGN-BORN WHITE POPULATION, BY DIVISIONS AND STATES: 1930

DIVISION AND STATE	FOREIGN-BORN POPULATION									FOREIGN-BORN WHITE POPULATION								
	Total	Naturalized		Having first papers		Alien		Unknown		Total	Naturalized		Having first papers		Alien		Unknown	
		Number	Per cent	Number	Per cent	Number	Per cent	Number	Per cent		Number	Per cent	Number	Per cent	Number	Per cent	Number	Per cent
United States	14,204,149	7,919,536	55.8	1,266,419	8.9	4,518,341	31.8	499,853	3.5	13,366,407	7,859,193	58.8	1,246,521	9.3	3,787,086	28.3	473,607	3.5
GEOGRAPHIC DIVS.:																		
New England	1,848,943	915,702	49.5	146,873	7.9	742,845	40.2	43,523	2.4	1,834,310	912,923	49.8	145,829	8.0	732,628	39.9	42,930	2.3
Middle Atlantic	5,352,731	3,015,190	56.3	475,769	8.9	1,676,423	31.3	185,349	3.5	5,269,042	2,998,696	56.9	467,961	8.9	1,022,701	30.8	179,084	3.4
E.N. Central	3,275,723	1,950,579	59.5	391,966	12.0	822,621	25.1	110,557	3.4	3,223,924	1,947,094	60.4	390,354	12.1	777,618	24.1	108,858	3.4
W.N. Central	1,084,153	823,620	76.0	62,874	5.8	155,820	14.4	41,839	3.9	1,050,277	822,280	77.6	62,582	5.9	133,862	12.6	40,544	3.8
South Atlantic	318,697	174,988	54.9	24,899	7.8	98,543	30.9	20,267	6.4	304,278	172,864	56.8	24,515	8.1	87,715	28.8	19,184	6.3
E.S. Central	59,364	38,802	65.4	3,547	6.0	11,446	19.3	5,569	9.4	57,665	38,545	66.8	3,509	6.1	10,238	17.8	5,373	9.3
W.S. Central	440,553	139,151	31.6	15,064	3.4	265,728	60.3	20,610	4.7	170,232	117,084	68.8	10,218	6.0	30,694	18.0	12,236	7.2
Mountain	384,323	204,471	53.2	21,528	5.6	142,083	37.0	16,241	4.2	287,914	198,764	69.0	20,376	7.1	55,205	19.2	13,569	4.7
Pacific	1,439,662	657,033	45.6	123,800	8.6	602,832	41.9	55,898	3.9	1,159,765	650,934	56.1	121,177	10.4	336,365	29.0	51,289	4.4
NEW ENGLAND:																		
Maine	100,728	44,619	44.3	6,318	6.3	45,000	44.7	4,791	4.8	100,368	44,541	44.4	6,299	6.3	44,745	44.6	4,783	4.8
New Hampshire	82,920	41,568	50.1	5,749	6.9	32,942	39.7	2,670	3.2	82,660	41,513	50.2	5,706	6.9	32,772	39.6	2,669	3.2
Vermont	43,101	21,452	49.8	3,094	7.2	17,938	41.6	617	1.4	43,061	21,446	49.8	3,094	7.2	17,906	41.6	615	1.4
Massachusetts	1,065,620	528,875	49.6	88,438	8.3	423,128	39.7	25,179	2.4	1,054,636	526,733	49.9	87,622	8.3	415,602	39.4	24,079	2.3
Rhode Island	171,929	100,532	58.5	11,646	6.8	57,879	33.7	1,872	1.1	170,714	100,311	58.8	11,562	6.8	56,986	33.4	1,855	1.1
Connecticut	384,636	178,656	46.4	31,628	8.2	165,958	43.1	8,394	2.2	382,871	178,379	46.6	31,546	8.2	164,617	43.0	8,329	2.2
MIDDLE ATLANTIC:																		
New York	3,262,278	1,764,753	54.1	313,037	9.6	1,065,974	32.7	118,514	3.6	3,191,549	1,750,939	54.9	305,873	9.6	1,020,782	32.0	113,955	3.6
New Jersey	850,038	484,793	57.0	74,876	8.8	262,434	30.9	27,935	3.3	844,442	483,497	57.3	74,523	8.8	258,991	30.7	27,431	3.2
Pennsylvania	1,240,415	765,644	61.7	87,856	7.1	348,015	28.1	38,900	3.1	1,233,051	764,260	62.0	87,565	7.1	342,928	27.8	38,298	3.1
E.N. CENTRAL:																		
Ohio	649,220	377,351	58.1	69,241	10.7	183,463	28.3	19,165	3.0	644,151	376,723	58.5	69,101	10.7	179,399	27.9	18,928	2.9
Indiana	142,999	79,852	55.8	16,399	11.5	39,559	27.7	7,189	5.0	135,134	79,641	58.9	16,262	12.0	32,245	23.9	6,986	5.2
Illinois	1,242,447	790,914	63.7	128,234	10.3	278,353	22.4	44,946	3.6	1,218,158	789,570	64.8	127,646	10.5	256,716	21.1	44,226	3.6
Michigan	852,758	436,566	51.2	142,524	16.7	251,269	29.5	22,399	2.6	840,268	435,358	51.8	141,828	16.9	241,152	28.7	21,930	2.6
Wisconsin	388,299	265,896	68.5	35,508	9.2	69,977	18.0	16,858	4.3	386,213	265,802	68.8	35,517	9.2	68,106	17.6	16,788	4.3
W.N. CENTRAL:																		
Minnesota	390,790	308,214	78.9	23,438	6.0	47,909	12.3	11,229	2.9	388,294	308,047	79.3	23,395	6.0	45,751	11.8	11,101	2.9
Iowa	168,250	131,548	78.2	7,763	4.6	22,826	13.6	6,113	3.6	165,735	131,444	79.3	7,729	4.7	20,561	12.4	6,001	3.6
Missouri	153,085	100,661	65.8	12,801	8.4	31,845	20.8	7,778	5.1	149,390	100,378	67.2	12,737	8.5	28,675	19.2	7,600	5.1
North Dakota	105,871	86,675	81.9	4,516	4.3	10,708	10.1	3,972	3.8	105,148	86,666	82.4	4,515	4.3	9,968	9.5	3,969	3.8
South Dakota	66,061	53,712	81.3	3,175	4.8	6,155	9.3	3,019	4.6	65,648	53,691	81.8	3,170	4.8	5,796	8.8	2,991	4.6
Nebraska	119,199	89,025	74.7	6,970	5.8	17,402	14.6	5,802	4.9	115,346	88,863	77.0	6,924	6.0	14,051	12.2	5,508	4.8
Kansas	80,897	53,785	66.5	4,211	5.2	18,975	23.5	3,926	4.9	69,716	53,200	76.3	4,112	5.9	9,030	13.0	3,374	4.8
SOUTH ATLANTIC:																		
Delaware	17,025	9,771	57.4	1,438	8.4	5,041	29.6	775	4.6	16,885	9,713	57.5	1,422	8.4	4,990	29.6	760	4.5
Maryland	96,330	55,339	57.4	8,193	8.5	25,971	27.0	6,827	7.1	95,093	55,059	57.9	8,100	8.5	25,340	26.6	6,594	6.9
Dist. of Columbia	30,733	19,204	62.5	2,382	7.8	6,693	21.8	2,454	8.0	29,932	19,039	63.6	2,342	7.8	6,232	20.8	2,319	7.7
Virginia	24,367	16,120	66.2	1,682	6.9	5,047	20.7	1,518	6.2	23,820	15,980	67.1	1,653	6.9	4,740	19.9	1,447	6.1
West Virginia	51,865	23,157	44.6	5,137	9.9	21,266	41.0	2,305	4.4	51,520	23,097	44.8	5,121	9.9	21,041	40.8	2,261	4.4
North Carolina	8,969	5,510	61.4	618	6.9	1,868	20.8	973	10.8	8,788	5,463	62.2	603	6.9	1,780	20.3	942	16.7
South Carolina	5,358	3,441	64.2	381	7.1	1,042	19.4	494	9.2	5,266	3,421	65.0	376	7.1	990	18.8	479	9.1
Georgia	14,303	9,454	66.1	867	6.1	2,813	19.7	1,169	8.2	13,917	9,391	67.5	854	6.1	2,569	18.5	1,103	7.9
Florida	69,747	32,992	47.3	4,201	6.0	28,802	41.3	3,752	5.4	59,057	31,701	53.7	4,044	6.8	20,033	33.9	3,279	5.6
E.S. CENTRAL:																		
Kentucky	22,007	15,489	70.4	1,259	5.7	3,403	15.5	1,856	8.4	21,840	15,444	70.7	1,255	5.7	3,306	15.1	1,835	8.4
Tennessee	13,251	8,309	62.7	751	5.7	2,680	20.2	1,511	11.4	13,066	8,272	63.3	748	5.7	2,571	19.7	1,475	11.3
Alabama	16,061	10,615	66.1	1,145	7.1	2,901	18.1	1,400	8.7	15,710	10,505	66.9	1,121	7.1	2,730	17.4	1,354	8.6
Mississippi	8,045	4,389	54.6	392	4.9	2,462	30.6	802	10.0	7,049	4,324	61.3	385	5.5	1,631	23.1	709	10.1
W.S. CENTRAL:																		
Arkansas	10,632	7,171	67.4	500	4.7	1,591	15.0	1,370	12.9	10,173	7,058	69.4	500	4.9	1,334	13.1	1,281	12.6
Louisiana	37,076	20,072	54.1	2,125	5.7	12,882	34.7	1,997	5.4	34,910	19,655	56.3	2,023	5.8	11,449	32.8	1,783	5.1
Oklahoma	30,558	19,962	65.3	1,645	5.4	6,068	19.9	2,883	9.4	26,753	19,665	73.5	1,595	6.0	3,144	11.8	2,349	8.8
Texas	362,287	91,946	25.4	10,794	3.0	245,187	67.7	14,360	4.0	98,396	70,706	71.9	6,100	6.2	14,767	15.0	6,823	6.9
MOUNTAIN:																		
Montana	75,903	54,281	71.5	4,388	5.8	13,823	18.2	3,411	4.5	72,961	54,215	74.3	4,366	6.0	11,086	15.2	3,294	4.5
Idaho	32,284	21,711	67.3	2,112	6.5	7,101	22.0	1,360	4.2	30,454	21,607	71.1	2,104	6.9	5,354	17.6	1,329	4.4
Wyoming	23,343	13,641	58.4	1,481	6.3	7,221	30.9	1,000	4.3	19,658	13,480	68.6	1,440	7.3	3,797	19.3	941	4.8
Colorado	99,875	58,221	58.3	6,024	6.0	30,342	30.4	5,288	5.3	85,406	57,678	67.5	5,923	6.9	17,018	19.9	4,787	5.6
New Mexico	24,052	6,365	26.5	913	3.8	15,741	65.4	1,033	4.3	7,797	4,878	62.6	657	8.4	1,780	22.8	482	6.2
Arizona	65,756	13,043	19.8	2,003	3.0	48,322	73.5	2,388	3.6	15,591	9,761	62.6	1,329	8.5	3,532	22.7	969	6.2
Utah	48,015	30,213	62.9	3,470	7.2	12,946	27.0	1,377	2.9	43,772	30,148	68.9	3,449	7.9	8,830	20.2	1,345	3.1
Nevada	15,095	6,996	46.3	1,128	7.5	6,587	43.6	384	2.5	12,275	6,937	56.5	1,108	9.0	3,868	31.5	362	2.9
PACIFIC:																		
Washington	255,258	150,658	59.0	27,368	10.7	64,778	25.4	12,454	4.9	244,256	150,547	61.6	27,323	11.2	53,977	22.1	12,409	5.1
Oregon	110,440	63,787	57.8	11,640	10.5	31,178	28.2	3,835	3.5	105,475	63,729	60.4	11,614	11.0	26,341	25.0	3,791	3.6
California	1,073,964	442,588	41.2	84,891	7.9	506,876	47.2	39,609	3.7	810,034	436,658	53.9	82,240	10.2	256,047	31.6	35,089	4.3

CHAPTER 9

YEAR OF IMMIGRATION OF
THE FOREIGN BORN

CHAPTER 9—YEAR OF IMMIGRATION OF THE FOREIGN BORN

INTRODUCTION

The inquiry as to the year of immigration of the foreign-born population has been made at each census beginning with that of 1910. Similar information was obtained in 1890 and 1900 through a question as to the number of years of residence in the United States, though the tabulation in 1890 was limited to alien (unnaturalized) males 21 years old and over. In 1910 the form of the inquiry on the census schedule was changed so as to obtain the actual calendar year of immigration into the United States. This form of inquiry has been retained in the censuses of 1920 and 1930. The statistics here presented relate to the foreign-born population of continental United States, and are presented by States and for cities of 25,000 or more. The year of immigration was not tabulated by counties nor for cities having less than 25,000 inhabitants. Statistics for Alaska, Hawaii, Puerto Rico, the Panama Canal Zone, and the Virgin Islands of the United States are given in the Fifteenth Census Report on Outlying Territories and Possessions.

The data on year of immigration for the total foreign-born and for the foreign-born white population are summarized in Table 1.

TABLE 1.—YEAR OF IMMIGRATION OF THE FOREIGN-BORN POPULATION OF THE UNITED STATES: 1930

YEAR OF IMMIGRATION	TOTAL FOREIGN-BORN POPULATION		FOREIGN-BORN WHITE POPULATION	
	Number	Per cent	Number	Per cent
Total	14, 204, 149	100. 0	13, 366, 407	100. 0
1925 to 1930	1, 085, 214	7. 6	960, 238	7. 2
1920 to 1924	1, 738, 185	12. 2	1, 552, 096	11. 6
1915 to 1919	730, 309	5. 1	553, 691	4. 1
1911 to 1914	1, 811, 637	12. 8	1, 712, 247	12. 8
1901 to 1910	3, 823, 694	26. 9	3, 681, 400	27. 5
1900 or earlier	4, 429, 494	31. 2	4, 366, 265	32. 7
Unknown	585, 616	4. 1	540, 470	4. 0

The tabulations for year of immigration have always been made for single years covering a period of four, five, or six years preceding the date of the census, and for groups of years for earlier dates. With this form of presentation, direct comparisons with the returns of preceding censuses are of little value. There is, for example, no significance in a comparison between the number of survivors in 1930 of the immigration of the five years 1920 to 1924 with the number of survivors in 1920 of the immigration of 1910 to 1914. Statistics from the censuses of 1920 and 1910

are therefore shown in Table 5, for the complete series of years as originally tabulated, only as a matter of record. In Table 6, however, the statistics from the censuses of 1930, 1920, and 1910 have been so arranged as to give a significant comparison for such groups of years as have been carried through two or more successive censuses. For example, this table shows, for the immigration of the 10 years from 1901 to 1910, the number of survivors in 1910, 1920, and 1930. The total foreign-born population as enumerated in 1900 has been included in this table to complete a comparison through four censuses of the foreign-born population which has survived from the immigration of the nineteenth century. In this table the foreign-born population for whom the year of arrival was not reported ("unknown") has been distributed on the assumption that the proportions arriving during each period of years were the same for the immigrants for whom the year was not reported as for those for whom the information was secured. This distribution, while arbitrary, is necessary for purposes of comparison, on account of the variation from census to census in the number for whom the year of immigration was not reported.

The decrease from one census to the next in the number returned as arriving in each group of years is due primarily to mortality, although it is affected to some extent by the emigration of foreign-born persons. It will be noted that the decrease in the number of persons arriving in 1900 and earlier is more rapid from census to census than the decrease for any other group of years. This is due to the fact that this group includes a large number of persons of advanced age among whom the death rate is high, while the immigrants who arrived after 1900 are for the most part still in middle life.

During the years 1914 to 1919 immigration to the United States was greatly reduced as a result of the World War, and from 1925 to 1930 immigration was restricted by law. Even in the years from 1920 to 1924 the number of immigrants was small as compared with that in any 5-year period between 1901 and 1914.

In 1930 the survivors of the immigration of the 14 years from 1901 to 1914 far outnumbered the survivors of the later immigration from 1915 to 1930. Under the present policy of immigration restriction, the net immigration in each year is not sufficient to replace the mortality in the foreign-born population.

495

POPULATION

Year of immigration by country of birth.—Statistics of year of immigration by country of birth, which have been tabulated for the first time from the returns of the Fifteenth Census, show clearly the changes which have taken place in 30 years in the nationality of the immigrants coming into the United States. Of the population living in the United States in 1930 who were born in Germany, Sweden, and Wales, more than 50 per cent had arrived in 1900 or earlier, while of the population born in Poland, Hungary, Yugoslavia, Italy, and Greece, less than 20 per cent had arrived in 1900 or earlier. Of the foreign born enumerated in 1930 who arrived in 1900 or earlier, 21.5 per cent were born in Germany, 11.6 per cent in Canada, 7.9 per cent in the Irish Free State, 7.6 per cent in England, and 7.1 per cent in Sweden. The heaviest immigration from Ireland was between 1840 and 1860 and many of the Irish born were already old in 1900 and subject to a high death rate. The German immigration was also early. Immigration from Canada and England was continuous from 1840 to 1890, while from Sweden the largest number of arrivals was between 1880 and

1890, and the average age of the survivors in 1900 must have been many years lower than that of the Irish-born population in that year.

The distribution by year of immigration is shown for the more important countries of birth in Table 2.

Urban, rural-farm, and rural-nonfarm population.—Urban population, as defined by the Census Bureau, is in general that residing in cities and other incorporated places having 2,500 inhabitants or more, the remainder being classified as rural. In three of the New England States, New Hampshire, Massachusetts, and Rhode Island, towns (townships) are classified as urban if they have a population of 2,500 or more and certain urban characteristics; and a few large and densely populated townships in other States are likewise classified, even though not formally incorporated as municipalities.

In addition to the classification of the population as urban and rural, the rural population is subdivided into rural-farm and rural-nonfarm, on the basis of the replies to a question reading "Does this family live on a farm?" The rural-farm population includes all persons living on farms in the rural areas. The rural-nonfarm or "village" population is made up largely of persons living in small towns or villages, both incorporated and unincorporated, though in many areas there are considerable numbers of families living in the open country but not on farms.

In general, the tendency of the earlier immigrants was to settle on farms, while that of the recent immigrants is to settle in the cities. Considerable significance therefore attaches to the data on year of immigration as presented in Table 3 for urban, rural-farm, and rural-nonfarm areas.

TABLE 2.—PER CENT DISTRIBUTION OF THE FOREIGN-BORN WHITE POPULATION OF THE UNITED STATES BY YEAR OF IMMIGRATION AND BY COUNTRY OF BIRTH: 1930

COUNTRY OF BIRTH	PER CENT OF TOTAL ARRIVING IN—						
	1925 to 1930	1920 to 1924	1915 to 1919	1911 to 1914	1901 to 1910	1900 or earlier	Unknown
All countries	7.2	11.6	4.1	12.8	27.5	32.7	4.0
England	8.9	12.9	4.5	9.2	20.6	41.0	4.9
Scotland	18.0	21.5	3.6	8.5	17.7	26.7	4.0
Wales	9.1	7.7	2.2	6.5	14.0	55.5	5.0
Northern Ireland	10.0	9.8	2.9	7.0	18.4	46.9	5.1
Irish Free State	12.3	7.8	2.9	6.4	18.1	46.4	6.2
Norway	6.7	7.1	3.1	5.9	26.0	47.1	4.2
Sweden	5.9	7.1	2.9	6.4	22.4	52.0	3.3
Denmark	5.9	7.8	4.0	8.5	21.6	48.3	3.9
Netherlands	6.4	10.8	5.5	12.7	24.3	36.8	3.4
Belgium	4.9	15.6	6.8	10.5	28.2	24.6	3.4
Switzerland	7.5	12.0	3.4	7.4	17.2	48.4	4.1
France	9.4	9.9	6.1	8.5	22.1	39.4	4.7
Germany	12.7	8.0	0.8	4.4	11.7	58.3	4.0
Poland	2.9	8.7	2.9	24.8	39.2	19.0	2.5
Czechoslovakia	3.5	9.8	1.7	14.9	37.2	30.1	2.8
Austria	2.6	10.4	2.3	15.5	38.1	26.7	4.2
Hungary	3.0	12.0	2.0	19.0	44.9	16.2	2.9
Yugoslavia	3.2	13.3	2.3	25.2	44.8	9.4	2.2
Russia	2.1	10.7	3.6	19.1	40.3	21.0	3.2
Lithuania	1.5	4.2	2.4	24.0	47.0	18.5	2.6
Finland	2.6	7.5	5.4	14.5	41.2	25.7	3.2
Rumania	3.5	14.4	3.1	18.6	42.5	15.5	2.5
Greece	5.0	15.9	14.4	23.0	32.5	4.6	3.6
Italy	4.6	14.8	6.2	17.2	36.4	17.8	3.0
Spain	7.7	26.7	19.1	15.6	18.2	5.3	7.4
Portugal	5.3	19.6	16.0	13.9	24.6	16.5	4.0
Syria	3.8	13.4	4.8	21.0	30.8	16.9	3.3
Canada—French	9.7	14.9	6.3	4.5	15.2	45.1	4.2
Canada—Other	13.5	16.7	7.0	4.5	13.1	37.3	7.9

TABLE 3.—YEAR OF IMMIGRATION OF THE FOREIGN-BORN WHITE POPULATION OF THE UNITED STATES, IN URBAN, RURAL-FARM, AND RURAL-NONFARM AREAS: 1930

YEAR OF IMMIGRATION	URBAN		RURAL-FARM		RURAL-NONFARM	
	Number	Per cent	Number	Per cent	Number	Per cent
Total foreign-born white	10,726,859	100.0	1,084,087	100.0	1,555,461	100.0
1925 to 1930	850,505	7.9	32,877	3.0	76,856	4.9
1920 to 1924	1,360,716	12.7	56,159	5.2	135,221	8.7
1915 to 1919	469,062	4.4	29,450	2.7	55,179	3.5
1911 to 1914	1,429,099	13.3	102,785	9.5	180,363	11.6
1901 to 1910	3,004,453	28.0	274,249	25.3	402,698	25.9
1900 or earlier	3,204,956	29.9	548,193	50.6	613,116	39.4
Unknown	408,068	3.8	40,374	3.7	92,028	5.9

YEAR OF IMMIGRATION

497

YEAR OF IMMIGRATION OF THE FOREIGN-BORN WHITE POPULATION, BY COUNTRY OF BIRTH: 1930

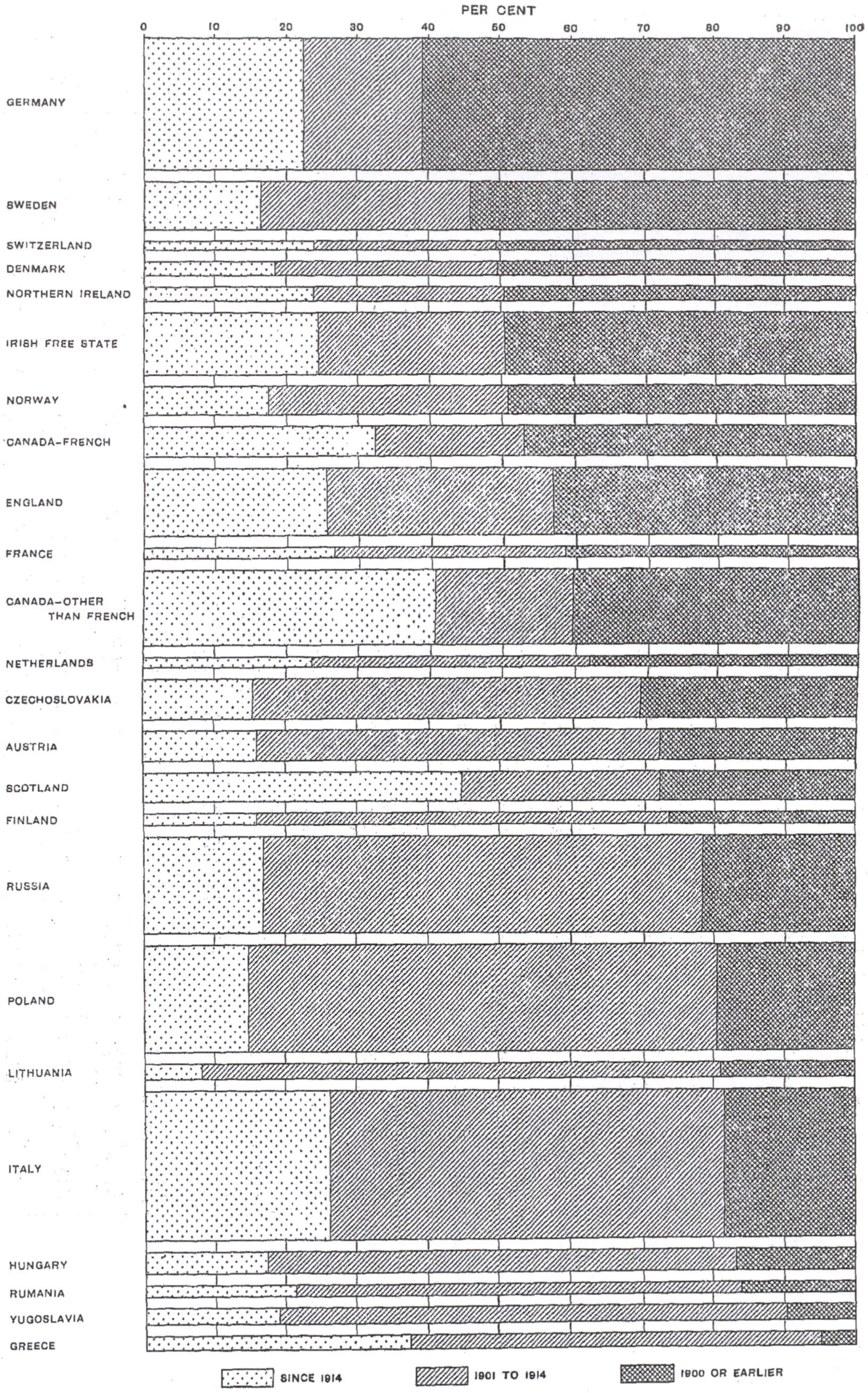
PER CENT
0
10
20
30
40
50
60
70
80
90
100
GERMANY
SWEDEN
SWITZERLAND
DENMARK
NORTHERN IRELAND
IRISH FREE STATE
NORWAY
CANADA-FRENCH
ENGLAND
FRANCE
CANADA-OTHER THAN FRENCH
NETHERLANDS
CZECHOSLOVAKIA
AUSTRIA
SCOTLAND
FINLAND
RUSSIA
POLAND
LITHUANIA
ITALY
HUNGARY
RUMANIA
YUGOSLAVIA
GREECE
SINCE 1914
1901 TO 1914
1900 OR EARLIER

POPULATION

TABLE 4.—YEAR OF IMMIGRATION OF THE FOREIGN-BORN POPULATION, BY COLOR OR RACE AND SEX, FOR THE UNITED STATES, URBAN AND RURAL: 1930

SEX, AREA, AND YEAR OF IMMIGRATION	ALL CLASSES		WHITE		NEGRO		MEXICAN		INDIAN		CHINESE		JAPANESE		ALL OTHER	
	Number	Per cent	Number	Per cent	Number	Per cent	Number	Per cent	Number	Per cent	Number	Per cent	Number	Per cent	Number	Per cent
Total	14,204,149	100.0	13,366,407	100.0	98,620	100.0	616,998	100.0	3,552	100.0	44,086	100.0	70,477	100.0	4,009	100.0
Year of immigration:																
1925 to 1930	1,035,214	7.6	960,238	7.2	7,582	7.7	108,704	17.6	445	12.5	5,413	12.3	2,490	3.5	342	8.5
1930, to April 1	46,456	0.3	42,347	0.3	302	0.3	3,263	0.5	28	0.8	323	0.7	176	0.2	17	0.4
1929	197,907	1.4	180,684	1.4	1,857	1.4	13,999	2.3	119	3.4	1,021	2.3	654	0.9	73	1.8
1928	197,990	1.4	173,162	1.3	1,173	1.2	21,865	3.5	81	2.3	1,146	2.6	492	0.7	71	1.8
1927	212,680	1.5	181,769	1.4	1,261	1.3	29,048	4.5	67	1.9	1,049	2.4	430	0.6	56	1.4
1925 and 1926	430,181	3.0	382,276	2.9	3,489	3.5	41,529	6.7	150	4.2	1,874	4.3	738	1.0	125	3.1
1920 to 1924	1,733,185	12.2	1,552,096	11.6	27,372	27.8	135,563	22.0	333	9.4	10,543	23.9	11,665	16.6	613	15.3
1915 to 1919	730,309	5.1	553,691	4.1	18,181	18.4	136,897	22.2	300	8.4	5,796	13.1	14,372	21.1	572	14.3
1911 to 1914	1,811,637	12.8	1,712,247	12.8	10,951	11.1	77,398	12.5	141	4.0	3,222	7.3	7,067	10.0	611	15.2
1901 to 1910	3,823,694	26.9	3,681,400	27.5	15,356	15.6	93,507	15.2	491	13.8	6,302	14.3	25,006	35.5	1,632	40.7
1900 or earlier	4,429,494	31.2	4,366,265	32.7	7,601	7.7	38,924	6.3	736	20.7	8,560	19.4	7,314	10.4	94	2.3
Unknown	585,616	4.1	540,470	4.0	11,577	11.7	26,005	4.2	1,106	31.1	4,250	9.6	2,063	2.9	145	3.6
Male	7,647,090	100.0	7,153,709	100.0	54,081	100.0	348,782	100.0	1,888	100.0	39,109	100.0	45,897	100.0	3,624	100.0
Year of immigration:																
1925 to 1930	554,145	7.2	477,544	6.7	3,806	7.0	66,137	19.0	225	11.9	4,579	11.7	1,548	3.4	306	8.4
1930, to April 1	23,845	0.3	20,980	0.3	142	0.3	2,291	0.7	14	0.7	275	0.7	126	0.3	17	0.5
1929	95,220	1.2	84,812	1.2	632	1.2	8,406	2.4	58	3.1	833	2.1	415	0.9	64	1.8
1928	98,526	1.3	83,252	1.2	558	1.0	13,350	3.8	41	2.2	955	2.4	305	0.7	65	1.8
1927	111,036	1.5	92,350	1.3	652	1.2	16,806	4.8	40	2.1	879	2.2	263	0.6	46	1.3
1925 and 1926	225,518	2.9	196,150	2.7	1,822	3.4	25,284	7.2	72	3.8	1,637	4.2	439	1.0	114	3.1
1920 to 1924	910,857	11.9	807,286	11.3	13,391	24.8	76,230	21.9	171	9.1	8,782	22.5	4,474	9.7	523	14.4
1915 to 1919	386,894	5.0	289,434	4.0	9,699	17.9	73,773	21.2	164	8.7	5,128	13.1	7,230	15.8	466	12.9
1911 to 1914	994,672	13.0	940,428	13.1	6,008	11.1	41,488	11.9	83	4.4	2,835	7.2	3,264	7.1	566	15.6
1901 to 1910	2,178,100	28.5	2,096,255	29.2	9,178	17.0	53,818	15.4	268	14.2	5,796	14.8	21,286	46.4	1,559	43.0
1900 or earlier	2,331,584	30.5	2,289,353	32.0	4,551	8.4	22,279	6.4	403	21.3	8,152	20.8	6,766	14.7	80	2.2
Unknown	291,778	3.8	263,409	3.7	7,448	13.8	15,057	4.3	574	30.4	3,837	9.8	1,329	2.9	124	3.4
Female	6,557,059	100.0	6,212,698	100.0	44,539	100.0	268,216	100.0	1,664	100.0	4,977	100.0	24,580	100.0	385	100.0
Year of immigration:																
1925 to 1930	531,069	8.1	482,694	7.8	3,776	8.5	42,567	15.9	220	13.2	834	16.8	942	3.8	36	9.4
1930, to April 1	22,611	0.3	21,367	0.3	160	0.4	972	0.4	14	0.8	48	1.0	50	0.2	----------	
1929	102,687	1.6	95,872	1.5	725	1.6	5,593	2.1	61	3.7	188	3.8	239	1.0	9	2.3
1928	99,464	1.5	89,910	1.4	615	1.4	8,515	3.2	40	2.4	191	3.8	187	0.8	6	1.6
1927	101,644	1.6	89,419	1.4	609	1.4	11,242	4.2	27	1.6	170	3.4	167	0.7	10	2.6
1925 and 1926	204,663	3.1	186,126	3.0	1,667	3.7	16,245	6.1	78	4.7	237	4.8	299	1.2	11	2.9
1920 to 1924	822,328	12.6	744,810	12.0	13,981	31.4	59,333	22.1	162	9.7	1,761	35.4	7,191	29.3	90	23.4
1915 to 1919	344,415	5.3	264,257	4.3	8,482	19.0	63,124	23.5	136	8.2	668	13.4	7,642	31.1	106	27.5
1911 to 1914	816,965	12.5	771,819	12.4	4,943	11.1	35,910	13.4	58	3.5	387	7.8	3,803	15.5	45	11.7
1901 to 1910	645,594	25.1	1,595,145	25.7	6,178	13.9	39,689	14.8	223	13.4	506	10.2	3,720	15.1	73	19.0
1900 or earlier	1,097,910	32.0	2,076,912	33.4	3,050	6.8	16,645	6.2	333	20.0	408	8.2	548	2.2	14	3.6
Unknown	2,293,838	4.5	277,061	4.5	4,129	9.3	10,948	4.1	532	32.0	413	8.3	734	3.0	21	5.5
Urban	11,250,815	100.0	10,726,859	100.0	91,677	100.0	350,132	100.0	1,001	100.0	38,377	100.0	40,695	100.0	2,074	100.0
Year of immigration:																
1925 to 1930	929,293	8.3	850,505	7.9	7,172	7.8	64,213	18.3	246	24.6	4,895	12.8	1,963	4.8	304	14.7
1930, to April 1	39,516	0.4	36,798	0.3	290	0.3	1,960	0.6	14	1.4	298	0.8	143	0.4	13	0.6
1929	171,551	1.5	160,266	1.5	1,282	1.4	8,420	2.4	63	6.3	918	2.4	538	1.3	64	3.1
1928	168,979	1.5	153,919	1.4	1,071	1.2	12,432	3.6	44	4.4	1,038	2.7	409	1.0	66	3.2
1927	180,664	1.6	161,519	1.5	1,205	1.3	16,558	4.7	35	3.5	948	2.5	349	0.9	50	2.4
1925 and 1926	368,588	3.3	338,003	3.2	3,324	3.6	24,843	7.1	90	9.0	1,693	4.4	524	1.3	111	5.4
1920 to 1924	1,480,790	13.2	1,360,716	12.7	26,209	28.6	76,519	21.9	163	16.3	9,483	24.7	7,218	17.7	482	23.2
1915 to 1919	579,806	5.2	469,062	4.4	17,257	18.8	79,234	22.6	130	13.0	5,203	13.6	8,531	21.0	389	18.8
1911 to 1914	1,492,121	13.3	1,420,099	13.3	10,071	11.0	45,835	13.1	52	5.2	2,823	7.4	4,041	9.9	200	9.6
1901 to 1910	3,090,856	27.5	3,004,453	28.0	13,944	15.2	52,571	15.0	99	9.9	5,450	14.2	13,797	33.9	542	26.1
1900 or earlier	3,242,309	28.8	3,204,956	29.9	6,560	7.2	19,962	5.7	146	14.6	6,733	17.5	3,892	9.6	60	2.9
Unknown	435,635	3.9	408,068	3.8	10,404	11.4	11,798	3.4	165	16.5	3,790	9.9	1,253	3.1	97	4.7
Rural	2,953,334	100.0	2,639,548	100.0	6,943	100.0	266,866	100.0	2,551	100.0	5,709	100.0	29,782	100.0	1,935	100.0
Year of immigration:																
1925 to 1930	155,916	5.3	109,733	4.2	410	5.9	44,491	16.7	199	7.8	518	9.1	527	1.8	38	2.0
1930, to April 1	6,940	0.2	5,549	0.2	12	0.2	1,303	0.5	14	0.5	25	0.4	33	0.1	4	0.2
1929	26,356	0.9	20,418	0.8	75	1.1	5,579	2.1	56	2.2	103	1.8	116	0.4	9	0.5
1928	29,011	1.0	19,243	0.7	102	1.5	9,433	3.5	37	1.5	108	1.9	83	0.3	5	0.3
1927	32,016	1.1	20,250	0.8	56	0.8	11,490	4.3	32	1.3	101	1.8	81	0.3	6	0.3
1925 and 1926	61,593	2.1	44,273	1.7	165	2.4	16,686	6.3	60	2.4	181	3.2	214	0.7	14	0.7
1920 to 1924	257,395	8.7	191,380	7.3	1,163	16.8	59,044	22.1	170	6.7	1,060	18.6	4,447	14.9	131	6.8
1915 to 1919	150,503	5.1	84,629	3.2	924	13.3	57,663	21.6	170	6.7	593	10.4	6,341	21.3	183	9.5
1911 to 1914	319,516	10.8	292,148	10.7	880	12.7	31,563	11.8	89	3.5	399	7.0	3,026	10.2	411	21.2
1901 to 1910	732,838	24.8	676,947	25.6	1,412	20.3	40,936	15.3	392	15.4	852	14.9	11,209	37.6	1,090	56.3
1900 or earlier	1,187,185	40.2	1,161,309	44.0	1,041	15.0	18,962	7.1	590	23.1	1,827	32.0	3,422	11.5	34	1.8
Unknown	149,981	5.1	132,402	5.0	1,113	16.0	14,207	5.3	941	36.9	460	8.1	810	2.7	48	2.5

YEAR OF IMMIGRATION

TABLE 5.—YEAR OF IMMIGRATION OF THE FOREIGN-BORN POPULATION, BY COLOR OR RACE AND SEX, FOR THE UNITED STATES: 1920 AND 1910

[Per cent not shown where base is less than 100]

CENSUS YEAR, SEX, AND YEAR OF IMMIGRATION	ALL CLASSES		WHITE [1]		NEGRO		INDIAN		CHINESE		JAPANESE		ALL OTHER	
	Number	Per cent	Number	Per cent	Number	Per cent	Number	Per cent	Number	Per cent	Number	Per cent	Number	Per cent
Total, 1920	13,920,692	100.0	13,712,754	100.0	73,803	100.0	6,299	100.0	43,107	100.0	81,338	100.0	3,391	100.0
Year of immigration:														
1919	214,123	1.5	201,280	1.5	5,938	8.0	644	10.2	1,141	2.6	5,027	6.2	93	2.7
1918	85,570	0.6	76,929	0.6	3,628	4.9	429	6.8	584	1.4	3,953	4.9	47	1.4
1917	116,222	0.8	106,059	0.8	4,537	6.1	435	6.9	952	2.2	4,120	5.1	119	3.5
1916	177,184	1.3	167,675	1.2	3,698	5.0	558	8.9	973	2.3	4,177	5.1	103	3.0
1915	203,098	1.5	193,684	1.4	3,213	4.4	374	5.9	1,299	3.0	4,396	5.4	132	3.9
1914	449,876	3.2	440,707	3.2	3,791	5.1	306	4.9	1,166	2.7	3,755	4.6	151	4.5
1911 to 1913	1,604,890	11.5	1,585,146	11.6	8,687	11.8	497	7.9	2,508	5.8	7,497	9.2	555	16.4
1906 to 1910	2,229,868	16.0	2,194,371	16.0	10,779	14.6	563	8.9	4,616	10.7	18,175	22.3	1,364	40.2
1901 to 1905	1,814,264	13.0	1,790,180	13.1	6,194	8.4	321	5.1	2,639	6.1	14,526	17.9	404	11.9
1900 or earlier	5,761,237	41.4	5,717,465	41.7	10,105	13.7	837	13.3	22,678	52.6	10,040	12.3	112	3.3
Unknown	1,264,360	9.1	1,239,258	9.0	13,233	17.9	1,335	21.2	4,551	10.6	5,672	7.0	311	9.2
Male, 1920	7,675,435	100.0	7,528,322	100.0	42,641	100.0	3,539	100.0	40,573	100.0	57,213	100.0	3,147	100.0
Year of immigration:														
1919	119,892	1.6	112,592	1.5	3,521	8.3	405	11.4	637	2.3	2,349	4.1	88	2.8
1918	47,320	0.6	42,723	0.6	1,953	4.6	237	6.7	460	1.1	1,908	3.3	39	1.2
1917	62,550	0.8	56,825	0.8	2,490	5.8	245	6.9	841	2.1	2,069	3.6	89	2.8
1916	96,056	1.3	90,676	1.2	2,004	4.7	305	8.6	859	2.1	2,123	3.7	89	2.8
1915	112,226	1.5	106,752	1.4	1,725	4.0	211	6.0	1,167	2.9	2,256	3.9	115	3.7
1914	256,216	3.3	250,808	3.3	2,136	5.0	181	5.1	1,052	2.6	1,904	3.3	135	4.3
1911 to 1913	933,333	12.2	921,758	12.2	4,796	11.2	295	8.3	2,222	5.5	3,733	6.5	529	16.8
1906 to 1910	1,288,152	16.8	1,261,115	16.8	6,326	14.8	331	9.4	4,269	10.5	14,783	25.8	1,328	42.2
1901 to 1905	1,057,498	13.8	1,037,602	13.8	3,883	9.1	178	5.0	2,492	6.1	12,914	22.6	369	11.7
1900 or earlier	3,168,590	41.3	3,130,503	41.6	6,208	14.6	479	13.5	22,075	54.4	9,224	16.1	101	3.2
Unknown	533,593	7.0	516,968	6.9	7,599	17.8	672	19.0	4,199	10.3	3,950	6.9	265	8.4
Female, 1920	6,245,257	100.0	6,184,432	100.0	31,162	100.0	2,760	100.0	2,534	100.0	24,125	100.0	244	100.0
Year of immigration:														
1919	94,231	1.5	88,688	1.4	2,417	7.8	239	8.7	204	8.1	2,678	11.1	5	2.0
1918	38,250	0.6	34,206	0.6	1,675	5.4	192	7.0	124	4.9	2,045	8.5	8	3.3
1917	53,663	0.9	49,234	0.8	2,047	6.6	190	6.9	111	4.4	2,051	8.5	30	12.3
1916	81,128	1.3	76,999	1.2	1,694	5.4	253	9.2	114	4.5	2,054	8.5	14	5.7
1915	90,872	1.5	86,932	1.4	1,488	4.8	163	5.9	132	5.2	2,140	8.9	17	7.0
1914	193,660	3.1	189,899	3.1	1,655	5.3	125	4.5	114	4.5	1,851	7.7	16	6.6
1911 to 1913	671,557	10.8	663,388	10.7	3,891	12.5	202	7.3	286	11.3	3,764	15.6	26	10.7
1906 to 1910	941,716	15.1	933,256	15.1	4,453	14.3	232	8.4	347	13.7	3,392	14.1	36	14.8
1901 to 1905	756,766	12.1	752,518	12.2	2,311	7.4	143	5.2	147	5.8	1,612	6.7	35	14.3
1900 or earlier	2,592,647	41.5	2,586,962	41.8	3,897	12.5	358	13.0	603	23.8	816	3.4	11	4.5
Unknown	730,767	11.7	722,350	11.7	5,634	18.1	663	24.0	352	13.9	1,722	7.1	46	18.9
Total, 1910	13,515,886	100.0	13,345,545	100.0	40,339	100.0	2,753	100.0	56,596	100.0	67,655	100.0	2,998	100.0
Year of immigration:														
1910, to April 15	233,852	1.7	231,606	1.7	707	1.8	140	5.1	357	0.6	448	0.7	504	16.8
1909	579,419	4.3	573,585	4.3	2,331	5.8	101	3.7	1,409	2.5	1,624	2.4	369	12.3
1908	412,683	3.1	405,631	3.0	2,093	5.2	41	1.5	1,297	2.3	3,354	5.0	267	8.9
1907	706,771	5.2	694,362	5.2	2,596	6.4	34	1.2	951	1.7	8,200	12.1	628	20.9
1906	637,308	4.7	623,647	4.7	2,545	6.3	55	2.0	653	1.2	10,115	15.0	383	12.8
1905	530,808	3.9	520,161	3.9	2,153	5.3	40	1.5	545	1.0	7,704	11.4	205	6.8
1901 to 1904	1,505,214	11.1	1,479,844	11.1	5,557	13.8	170	6.2	1,884	3.3	17,523	25.9	236	7.9
1896 to 1900	1,093,699	7.9	1,046,500	7.8	4,044	10.0	147	5.3	3,723	6.6	9,244	13.7	41	1.4
1891 to 1895	1,157,513	8.6	1,148,645	8.6	2,708	6.7	131	4.8	4,253	7.5	1,763	2.6	13	0.4
1890 or earlier	5,347,710	39.6	5,302,515	39.7	7,675	19.0	695	25.2	34,803	61.6	1,868	2.8	94	3.1
Unknown	1,340,819	9.9	1,318,959	9.9	7,930	19.7	1,199	43.6	6,661	11.8	5,812	8.6	258	8.6
Male, 1910	7,667,748	100.0	7,523,788	100.0	23,888	100.0	1,464	100.0	54,935	100.0	60,730	100.0	2,943	100.0
Year of immigration:														
1910, to April 15	172,170	2.2	170,459	2.3	487	2.0	126	8.6	340	0.6	254	0.4	504	17.1
1909	383,377	5.0	379,200	5.0	1,339	5.6	50	3.4	1,310	2.4	1,110	1.8	368	12.5
1908	256,638	3.3	251,148	3.3	1,214	5.1	21	1.4	1,235	2.2	2,754	4.5	266	9.0
1907	450,934	5.9	440,446	5.9	1,557	6.5	23	1.6	896	1.6	7,389	12.2	623	21.2
1906	394,289	5.1	382,537	5.1	1,532	6.4	30	2.0	612	1.1	9,202	15.2	376	12.8
1905	324,182	4.2	315,058	4.2	1,355	5.7	24	1.6	508	0.9	7,041	11.6	196	6.7
1901 to 1904	909,960	11.9	888,342	11.8	3,443	14.4	101	6.9	1,796	3.3	16,055	26.4	223	7.6
1896 to 1900	596,947	7.8	582,021	7.7	2,470	10.3	86	5.9	3,616	6.6	8,717	14.4	37	1.3
1891 to 1895	627,774	8.2	620,207	8.2	1,666	7.0	74	5.1	4,160	7.6	1,656	2.7	11	0.4
1890 or earlier	2,999,822	39.1	2,958,741	39.3	4,723	19.8	398	27.2	34,155	62.2	1,717	2.8	88	3.0
Unknown	551,655	7.2	535,629	7.1	4,102	17.2	531	36.3	6,307	11.5	4,835	8.0	251	8.5
Female, 1910	5,848,138	100.0	5,821,757	100.0	16,451	100.0	1,289	100.0	1,661	100.0	6,925	100.0	55	------
Year of immigration:														
1910, to April 15	61,682	1.1	61,237	1.1	220	1.3	14	1.1	17	1.0	194	2.8		------
1909	196,042	3.4	194,385	3.3	992	6.0	51	4.0	99	6.0	514	7.4	1	------
1908	156,045	2.7	154,483	2.7	879	5.3	20	1.6	62	3.7	600	8.7	1	------
1907	255,837	4.4	253,916	4.4	1,039	6.3	11	0.9	55	3.3	811	11.7	5	------
1906	243,109	4.2	241,110	4.1	1,013	6.2	25	1.9	41	2.5	913	13.2	7	------
1905	206,626	3.5	205,103	3.5	798	4.9	16	1.2	37	2.2	663	9.6	9	------
1901 to 1904	595,254	10.2	591,502	10.2	2,114	12.9	69	5.4	88	5.3	1,468	21.2	13	------
1896 to 1900	496,752	8.0	464,479	8.0	1,574	9.6	61	4.7	107	6.4	527	7.6	4	------
1891 to 1895	529,739	9.1	528,438	9.1	1,042	6.3	57	4.4	93	5.6	107	1.5	2	------
1890 or earlier	2,347,888	40.1	2,343,774	40.3	2,952	17.9	297	23.0	708	42.6	151	2.2	6	------
Unknown	789,164	13.5	783,330	13.5	3,828	23.3	668	51.8	354	21.3	977	14.1	7	------

[1] In 1920 and 1910 most of the persons who would have been classified as "Mexican" in 1930 were returned as white. The number of foreign-born Mexicans thus included has been estimated at 457,360 in 1920 (259,131 males and 198,229 females), and 211,233 in 1910 (129,866 males and 81,367 females), but there is no basis for distributing these estimates by year of immigration.

500

POPULATION

TABLE 6.—YEAR OF IMMIGRATION OF THE FOREIGN-BORN POPULATION OF THE UNITED STATES, BY COLOR OR RACE AND SEX, WITH "UNKNOWN" DISTRIBUTED: 1930, 1920, AND 1910

CENSUS YEAR, SEX, AND COLOR OR RACE	Total foreign born	1920 to 1930 Total	1925 to 1930	1920 to 1924	1911 to 1919 Total	1915 to 1918	1911 to 1914	1901 to 1910 Total	1906 to 1910	1901 to 1905	1900 or earlier
TOTAL											
All classes, 1930	14,204,149	2,947,641	1,132,654	1,814,987	2,652,491	763,367	1,889,124	3,985,827			4,618,190
White	13,366,407	2,618,749	1,001,025	1,617,724	2,361,318	577,091	1,784,227	3,835,611			4,550,729
Negro	98,620	39,515	8,576	30,939	33,012	20,597	12,415	17,453			8,640
Mexican	616,998	255,027	113,500	141,527	223,710	142,912	80,798	97,624			40,637
Indian	3,552	1,130	646	484	640	436	204	713			1,069
Chinese	44,086	17,644	5,987	11,657	9,979	6,414	3,565	6,979			9,484
Japanese	70,477	14,584	2,565	12,019	22,604	15,323	7,281	25,756			7,533
All other	4,009	992	355	637	1,228	594	634	1,091			98
All classes, 1920	13,920,692				3,136,743	878,380	2,258,363	4,443,964	2,450,805	1,993,159	6,339,985
White [1]	13,712,754				3,045,410	820,265	2,225,145	4,376,966	2,410,766	1,966,200	6,290,378
Negro	73,803				40,812	25,607	15,205	20,680	13,134	7,546	12,311
Indian	6,299				4,115	3,097	1,018	1,122	714	408	1,062
Chinese	43,107				9,668	5,551	4,117	8,116	5,165	2,951	25,323
Japanese	81,339				35,411	23,310	12,101	35,140	19,532	15,608	10,787
All other	3,891				1,327	550	777	1,040	1,494	446	124
All classes, 1910 [2]	13,515,886							5,098,111	2,841,238	2,256,873	8,417,775
White [1]	13,345,545							5,010,196	2,794,104	2,216,092	8,335,349
Negro [1]	40,339							22,386	12,798	9,588	17,953
Indian	2,753							1,016	643	373	1,737
Chinese	56,596							8,073	5,311	2,762	48,523
Japanese	67,655							53,605	26,030	27,575	14,050
All other	2,098							2,835	2,352	483	103
All classes, 1900 [3]	10,341,276										10,341,276
White	10,213,817										10,213,817
Negro	20,336										20,336
Indian	2,213										2,213
Chinese	80,853										80,853
Japanese	24,057										24,057
MALE											
All classes, 1930	7,647,090	1,525,125	576,646	948,479	1,436,615	402,699	1,033,916	2,263,247			2,422,103
White	7,153,700	1,333,948	405,800	928,148	1,276,879	300,499	976,380	2,106,010			2,376,872
Negro	54,081	19,944	4,414	15,530	18,215	11,248	6,967	10,644			5,278
Mexican	348,782	148,790	69,121	79,669	120,462	77,102	43,360	56,246			23,284
Indian	1,888	569	323	246	355	236	119	385			570
Chinese	39,109	14,814	5,077	9,737	8,829	5,686	3,143	6,427			9,039
Japanese	45,897	6,201	1,594	4,607	10,807	7,446	3,361	21,021			6,968
All other	3,624	859	317	542	1,068	482	586	1,614			83
All classes, 1920	7,675,435				1,750,905	472,438	1,278,467	2,520,449	1,384,286	1,136,163	3,404,081
White [1]	7,528,322				1,698,775	439,763	1,259,012	2,468,252	1,354,089	1,114,163	3,361,295
Negro	42,641				22,664	14,229	8,435	12,423	7,698	4,725	7,554
Indian	3,530				2,320	1,732	588	628	408	220	501
Chinese	40,573				8,408	4,756	3,652	7,542	4,762	2,780	24,623
Japanese	57,213				17,554	11,499	6,055	29,751	15,879	13,872	9,908
All other	3,147				1,184	459	725	1,853	1,450	403	110
All classes, 1910	7,667,748							3,115,623	1,785,841	1,329,782	4,552,125
White [1]	7,523,788							3,043,889	1,748,251	1,295,638	4,470,899
Negro	23,888							13,192	7,390	5,793	10,696
Indian	1,464							588	392	196	876
Chinese	54,935							7,566	4,963	2,603	47,360
Japanese	60,730							47,594	22,500	25,094	13,136
All other	2,943							2,704	2,336	458	149
All classes, 1900	5,630,190										5,630,190
White	5,515,285										5,515,285
Negro	11,820										11,820
Indian	1,207										1,207
Chinese	78,684										78,684
Japanese	23,185										23,185
FEMALE											
All classes, 1930	6,557,059	1,422,516	556,008	866,508	1,215,876	360,668	855,208	1,722,580			2,196,087
White	6,212,608	1,284,801	505,225	779,576	1,084,439	276,592	807,847	1,669,601			2,173,857
Negro	44,539	19,571	4,162	15,409	14,797	9,340	5,448	6,809			3,362
Mexican	268,216	106,237	44,379	61,858	103,248	65,810	37,438	41,378			17,353
Indian	1,664	561	323	238	285	200	85	328			499
Chinese	4,977	2,830	910	1,920	1,150	728	422	552			445
Japanese	24,580	8,383	971	7,412	11,797	7,877	3,920	3,835			505
All other	385	133	38	95	160	112	48	77			15
All classes, 1920	6,245,257				1,385,838	405,942	979,896	1,923,515	1,066,519	856,996	2,935,904
White [1]	6,184,432				1,346,635	380,502	966,133	1,908,714	1,056,677	852,037	2,920,083
Negro	31,162				18,148	11,378	6,770	8,257	5,436	2,821	4,757
Indian	2,760				1,795	1,365	430	494	306	188	471
Chinese	2,534				1,260	795	465	574	403	171	700
Japanese	24,125				17,857	11,811	6,046	5,389	3,653	1,736	879
All other	244				143	91	52	87	44	43	14
All classes, 1910	5,848,138							1,982,488	1,055,397	927,091	3,865,650
White [1]	5,821,757							1,966,307	1,045,853	920,454	3,855,450
Negro	16,451							9,194	5,399	3,795	7,257
Indian	1,289							428	251	177	861
Chinese	1,661							507	348	159	1,154
Japanese	6,925							6,011	3,530	2,481	914
All other	55							41	16	25	14
All classes, 1900	4,711,086										4,711,086
White	4,698,532										4,698,532
Negro	8,507										8,507
Indian	1,006										1,006
Chinese	2,169										2,169
Japanese	872										872

[1] See footnote on Table 5.

[2] Figures for periods ending with 1910 are "short" by approximately the net immigration between the census date, Apr. 15, and the end of the year. The total net immigration for 1910 was 817,619.

[3] Figures are "short" by approximately the net immigration from June 1 to Dec. 31, 1900. The total net immigration in 1900 was estimated at 320,000.

YEAR OF IMMIGRATION

501

TABLE 7.—YEAR OF IMMIGRATION OF THE FOREIGN-BORN WHITE POPULATION, BY SEX AND COUNTRY OF BIRTH, FOR THE UNITED STATES: 1930

SEX AND COUNTRY OF BIRTH	Total foreign-born white	1925 to 1930 Total	1930 (to Apr. 1)	1929	1928	1927	1925 and 1926	1920 to 1924	1915 to 1919	1911 to 1914	1901 to 1910	1900 or earlier	Unknown
TOTAL													
All countries	13,366,407	960,238	42,347	180,684	173,162	181,769	382,276	1,552,096	553,691	1,712,247	3,681,400	4,366,265	540,470
Northwestern Europe:													
England	808,672	55,424	3,516	11,074	8,152	9,331	23,351	104,248	36,600	74,052	166,553	331,906	39,280
Scotland	354,323	63,841	4,226	13,547	10,722	10,801	24,465	70,125	12,619	30,231	62,713	94,771	14,023
Wales	60,205	5,488	228	1,437	1,026	1,040	1,757	4,646	1,344	3,910	8,300	33,410	3,008
Northern Ireland	178,832	17,827	1,401	3,542	2,815	3,207	6,802	17,442	5,104	12,407	32,819	83,961	9,182
Irish Free State	744,810	91,795	3,123	14,690	16,595	18,646	38,741	57,000	21,327	47,847	134,508	345,411	45,893
Norway	347,852	23,250	662	4,146	4,741	4,580	9,121	24,555	10,663	20,304	90,489	163,846	14,865
Sweden	595,250	35,104	804	5,770	7,069	6,909	14,646	42,196	17,300	38,032	133,003	309,670	19,846
Denmark	179,474	10,638	300	1,902	2,129	1,985	4,322	14,055	7,133	15,224	38,787	86,675	6,962
Iceland	2,764	168	5	39	26	26	72	251	111	147	384	1,592	121
Netherlands	133,133	8,555	683	1,878	1,430	1,583	2,975	14,421	7,315	16,925	32,309	49,027	4,581
Belgium	64,194	3,154	250	603	580	483	1,172	10,013	4,308	10,611	18,121	15,774	2,153
Luxemburg	9,048	207	20	62	53	63	99	589	273	602	1,801	5,160	317
Switzerland	113,010	8,463	363	1,594	1,685	1,619	3,202	13,508	3,820	8,327	19,472	54,643	4,687
France	135,232	12,052	618	2,616	2,539	2,417	4,462	13,380	8,221	11,483	20,030	53,253	6,313
Central Europe:													
Germany	1,608,814	203,563	6,295	34,734	39,782	39,720	83,032	129,467	12,811	71,365	188,580	938,605	64,414
Poland	1,268,583	36,777	2,207	7,784	6,788	7,676	12,322	110,554	37,109	314,143	407,287	240,610	32,043
Czechoslovakia	491,638	17,187	1,044	3,915	3,388	3,151	5,689	48,325	8,215	73,347	182,670	148,182	13,712
Austria	370,914	9,741	580	2,000	1,772	1,831	3,558	38,668	8,674	57,574	141,306	99,200	15,742
Hungary	274,450	8,288	580	1,761	1,659	1,539	2,749	32,880	5,436	52,232	123,205	44,386	8,024
Yugoslavia	211,416	6,725	365	1,519	1,283	1,301	2,257	28,108	4,873	53,372	93,626	10,943	4,709
Eastern Europe:													
Russia	1,153,624	23,829	1,418	3,996	3,971	4,302	10,143	122,951	42,034	220,305	464,980	242,336	37,099
Latvia	20,673	836	64	178	185	128	281	2,830	730	2,776	8,544	4,300	648
Estonia	3,550	532	15	84	104	93	236	808	267	440	914	281	308
Lithuania	193,606	2,819	154	507	474	570	1,048	8,060	4,561	46,371	90,941	35,827	5,027
Finland	142,478	3,038	163	635	656	721	1,463	10,671	7,092	20,070	58,040	36,573	4,594
Rumania	146,393	5,059	291	1,275	982	930	1,581	21,043	4,521	27,238	62,153	22,609	3,686
Bulgaria	9,309	771	23	154	161	156	277	1,327	667	3,230	2,831	266	307
Turkey in Europe	2,257	175	6	34	40	47	48	777	187	522	410	120	66
Southern Europe:													
Greece	174,526	10,378	472	2,223	2,211	2,130	3,342	27,757	25,181	40,130	56,058	8,075	6,347
Albania	8,814	1,074	68	301	210	200	286	2,410	1,694	1,528	1,807	128	173
Italy	1,790,424	82,140	5,130	20,162	16,964	16,368	23,516	265,684	110,204	307,588	661,882	319,194	53,647
Spain	58,802	4,480	198	806	719	843	1,914	15,687	11,130	9,071	10,590	3,118	4,326
Portugal	60,974	3,711	179	677	687	776	1,392	13,691	11,224	9,753	17,246	11,584	2,815
Other Europe	16,251	1,964	107	515	399	336	637	2,863	897	1,789	3,761	3,570	1,407
Asia:													
Armenia	32,166	2,210	74	366	431	527	812	7,605	1,927	7,589	8,588	3,471	776
Palestine	6,135	1,037	59	295	228	192	263	1,471	582	1,022	1,215	537	271
Syria	57,227	2,156	109	386	398	458	805	7,686	2,719	12,030	21,039	9,693	1,904
Turkey in Asia	46,651	3,424	151	627	691	725	1,230	13,259	4,680	11,898	9,812	2,962	1,166
Other Asia	15,401	2,837	181	688	441	556	971	8,867	1,670	1,846	2,268	1,830	1,083
America:													
Canada—French	370,852	36,096	1,033	6,027	5,387	6,426	17,223	55,352	23,531	16,866	56,318	167,097	15,592
Canada—Other	907,560	122,896	3,819	19,624	18,254	21,257	59,942	151,663	63,840	40,488	118,539	338,469	71,674
Newfoundland	23,971	4,029	102	876	809	1,062	2,080	6,335	1,618	1,202	3,112	4,824	1,951
Cuba	15,044	4,886	170	1,384	828	825	1,170	2,263	1,404	880	2,727	2,820	1,404
Other West Indies	15,482	1,476	109	382	227	260	498	3,199	2,030	1,276	2,938	2,006	1,657
Mexico	23,743	4,802	170	817	901	1,131	1,774	4,447	4,025	2,522	3,195	2,038	2,714
Central America	7,454	2,517	119	601	519	548	730	1,710	1,144	337	472	802	972
South America	30,055	7,574	385	1,531	1,456	1,553	2,649	6,845	3,491	2,441	4,320	2,523	2,861
All other:													
Africa	7,806	1,230	59	267	241	219	444	1,393	724	1,019	1,837	1,060	603
Australia	12,720	949	70	227	168	144	340	1,572	1,120	1,098	3,314	3,526	1,132
Azores	35,427	533	34	99	83	94	223	3,882	3,097	4,721	11,895	9,472	1,227
Other Atlantic islands	4,052	144	9	30	25	24	56	630	603	546	958	796	375
Pacific islands	4,304	568	50	145	117	80	176	647	395	311	703	1,326	706
Country not specified	1,485	79	4	21	16	15	23	106	38	80	238	229	706
Born at sea	4,958	52	4	6	14	9	19	155	50	155	434	2,328	1,784
MALE													
All countries	7,153,709	477,544	20,980	84,812	83,252	92,350	196,150	807,286	289,434	940,428	2,086,255	2,289,353	263,409
Northwestern Europe:													
England	412,065	26,246	1,787	5,342	3,793	4,497	10,827	52,827	16,333	36,903	89,793	171,543	18,380
Scotland	181,654	29,415	2,157	6,211	4,895	5,270	10,882	41,510	5,676	14,207	34,707	49,431	6,702
Wales	32,189	3,057	128	798	588	581	962	2,567	654	2,143	4,947	17,340	3,522
Northern Ireland	81,088	8,067	747	1,703	1,310	1,016	3,291	8,892	2,243	5,855	15,747	36,382	3,522
Irish Free State	324,841	44,869	1,634	6,756	7,650	9,372	19,457	26,971	9,160	21,790	60,262	143,987	17,813
Norway	196,349	13,164	423	2,157	2,619	2,694	5,271	15,541	5,754	10,841	51,687	103,735	11,103
Sweden	333,623	22,176	503	3,585	4,421	4,572	9,095	27,996	10,395	22,151	76,007	163,785	11,103
Denmark	109,975	6,689	172	1,142	1,303	1,372	2,700	9,800	4,614	9,574	24,626	50,800	4,402
Iceland	1,385	98	4	24	13	16	41	116	69	63	190	782	67
Netherlands	77,574	5,015	458	1,084	815	807	1,761	8,727	4,574	9,774	19,461	27,390	2,633
Belgium	35,205	1,545	129	345	292	289	540	4,775	2,040	6,015	10,784	8,952	1,154
Luxemburg	5,456	153	12	33	26	36	46	252	128	351	1,100	3,205	177
Switzerland	64,833	5,008	235	897	1,001	954	1,921	8,290	2,101	4,964	11,780	30,107	2,523
France	66,104	6,369	348	1,321	1,284	1,233	2,183	5,205	2,570	5,640	15,393	28,166	2,815
Central Europe:													
Germany	843,136	108,342	2,307	17,471	20,052	22,386	45,126	69,607	7,410	41,724	104,330	480,593	31,130
Poland	681,425	16,233	1,046	3,138	3,152	3,444	5,453	48,473	19,712	169,205	231,088	130,848	15,286
Czechoslovakia	255,485	8,514	472	1,756	1,720	1,699	2,867	22,639	4,010	36,851	100,454	77,284	5,733
Austria	193,636	4,630	259	886	704	889	1,802	18,838	4,537	28,386	75,904	53,574	7,767
Hungary	139,828	3,743	249	747	710	603	1,335	15,348	2,076	24,168	67,109	23,198	3,526
Yugoslavia	181,351	3,132	146	616	584	615	1,171	12,610	3,269	32,558	63,478	13,598	2,709
Eastern Europe:													
Russia	612,962	10,382	650	1,586	1,723	1,884	4,539	56,886	22,996	120,970	251,680	132,808	17,290
Latvia	11,061	326	30	61	67	46	122	1,351	439	1,377	4,898	2,484	386
Estonia	2,393	246	4	37	51	35	119	517	221	293	649	203	264
Lithuania	110,909	1,090	68	181	178	243	420	3,190	2,652	24,839	54,128	22,204	2,776
Finland	77,059	1,519	74	265	266	291	623	4,825	4,045	10,704	32,048	20,702	2,615
Rumania	78,085	2,172	116	518	415	430	693	10,634	2,632	14,642	34,020	12,78	1,648
Bulgaria	7,587	399	10	63	90	79	157	740	600	2,872	2,524	2810	242
Turkey in Europe	1,200	37	1	9	3	12	12	323	123	361	302	83	40

POPULATION

TABLE 7.—YEAR OF IMMIGRATION OF THE FOREIGN-BORN WHITE POPULATION, BY SEX AND COUNTRY OF BIRTH, FOR THE UNITED STATES: 1930—Continued

SEX AND COUNTRY OF BIRTH	Total foreign-born white	1925 to 1930						1920 to 1924	1915 to 1919	1911 to 1914	1901 to 1910	1900 or earlier	Unknown
		Total	1930 (to Apr. 1)	1929	1928	1927	1925 and 1926						
MALE—Continued.													
Southern Europe:													
Greece	129,101	4,002	154	731	730	808	1,579	14,928	17,068	31,644	49,319	7,277	4,863
Albania	6,549	519	24	132	95	86	182	1,501	1,246	1,682	1,278	106	127
Italy	1,042,621	37,298	2,166	8,106	7,087	7,280	12,659	149,987	55,802	177,104	397,852	196,919	28,089
Spain	41,976	3,115	123	466	477	609	1,440	11,581	8,161	5,965	7,289	2,104	2,671
Portugal	42,305	2,658	101	404	508	610	1,035	9,314	6,339	5,676	9,734	6,822	1,702
Other Europe	9,692	1,183	130	318	166	200	369	1,907	641	981	2,160	1,879	851
Asia:													
Armenia	19,281	624	23	92	119	143	247	3,139	1,249	5,683	5,616	2,502	468
Palestine	3,634	524	37	120	102	109	147	847	357	670	762	334	140
Syria	32,510	800	45	135	140	177	312	3,686	1,546	6,920	12,520	6,110	960
Turkey in Asia	28,117	866	41	144	169	180	332	5,709	3,008	8,575	7,169	2,116	674
Other Asia	9,864	1,680	123	407	249	339	562	2,330	1,116	1,390	1,619	1,110	619
America:													
Canada—French	187,523	17,610	476	2,908	2,561	3,058	8,613	28,615	11,633	8,277	27,657	86,631	7,094
Canada—Other	429,567	57,215	1,665	8,612	8,067	9,351	29,520	76,794	29,144	18,217	53,322	163,784	31,091
Newfoundland	11,520	2,246	55	373	316	486	1,016	3,253	718	511	1,386	2,266	1,140
Cuba	9,449	2,056	127	939	560	552	778	1,413	831	503	1,412	1,434	900
Other West Indies	7,678	623	47	153	101	101	221	1,466	985	648	1,575	1,532	849
Mexico	12,737	2,763	88	449	504	659	1,063	2,546	2,155	1,252	1,711	907	1,343
Central America	3,805	1,200	52	287	242	262	357	866	662	182	240	154	501
South America	18,052	4,585	222	900	905	957	1,601	4,037	2,203	1,898	2,483	1,417	1,039
All other:													
Africa	4,376	670	31	144	130	120	245	751	412	554	1,016	623	350
Australia	6,656	407	28	100	72	57	150	756	564	605	1,884	1,842	598
Azores	18,965	263	19	44	47	47	106	2,094	1,816	2,371	6,307	5,516	598
Other Atlantic islands	2,385	85	5	15	13	18	34	343	320	344	584	478	231
Pacific islands	2,350	285	26	80	56	36	87	338	208	169	419	709	222
Country not specified	926	34	1	9	3	8	13	62	23	52	147	135	473
Born at sea	2,763	22	2	3	9	2	6	87	35	92	245	1,311	971
FEMALE													
All countries	6,212,698	482,694	21,367	95,872	89,910	89,419	186,126	744,810	264,257	771,819	1,595,145	2,076,912	277,061
Northwestern Europe:													
England	396,607	29,178	1,729	5,732	4,359	4,834	12,524	51,421	20,267	37,659	76,760	160,363	20,959
Scotland	172,669	34,420	2,060	7,386	5,827	5,621	13,573	34,609	6,943	16,024	28,006	45,340	7,321
Wales	28,016	2,431	100	639	438	459	795	2,079	690	1,767	3,452	10,070	1,527
Northern Ireland	97,744	9,160	654	1,830	1,505	1,651	3,511	8,750	2,861	6,042	17,072	47,599	5,660
Irish Free State	410,909	40,926	1,489	7,934	8,945	9,274	19,284	30,998	12,108	26,057	74,318	201,424	28,080
Norway	151,503	10,086	239	1,989	2,122	1,886	3,850	9,014	4,899	9,553	38,802	73,219	5,930
Sweden	261,627	12,926	301	2,191	2,648	2,337	5,451	14,200	6,014	15,881	57,086	145,935	8,883
Denmark	69,499	3,949	128	760	826	613	1,622	4,755	2,619	5,650	14,191	35,875	2,560
Iceland	1,379	70	1	15	13	10	31	135	42	84	194	800	54
Netherlands	55,559	3,540	225	794	621	686	1,214	5,694	2,741	7,151	12,848	21,637	1,948
Belgium	28,929	1,609	121	318	294	244	632	5,238	2,328	4,596	7,337	6,822	999
Luxemburg	3,592	144	8	29	27	27	53	337	145	251	611	1,904	140
Switzerland	48,177	3,395	128	697	634	665	1,221	5,308	1,719	3,363	7,602	24,536	2,164
France	69,068	6,283	270	1,295	1,255	1,184	2,279	8,175	5,651	5,837	14,537	25,087	3,498
Central Europe:													
Germany	765,678	95,221	2,988	17,263	19,730	17,334	37,906	59,860	5,401	29,641	84,250	458,012	33,284
Poland	587,153	20,544	1,161	4,646	3,636	4,232	6,869	62,081	17,457	144,938	215,619	109,762	10,757
Czechoslovakia	236,153	8,673	572	2,159	1,668	1,452	2,822	25,086	4,205	36,496	82,216	70,898	7,979
Austria	177,278	5,111	321	1,114	978	942	1,756	19,830	4,137	29,188	65,402	45,635	7,075
Hungary	134,622	4,545	331	1,014	940	846	1,414	17,532	2,760	28,064	56,086	21,187	4,498
Yugoslavia	80,065	3,593	219	903	699	686	1,086	15,558	1,604	20,814	30,148	6,345	2,003
Eastern Europe:													
Russia	540,662	13,447	768	2,409	2,248	2,418	5,604	66,065	19,038	99,425	213,350	109,528	19,809
Latvia	9,612	510	34	117	118	82	159	1,479	201	1,399	3,846	1,825	282
Estonia	1,157	236	11	47	53	58	117	291	46	147	265	78	44
Lithuania	82,637	1,729	86	386	296	333	628	4,870	1,909	21,532	30,813	13,533	2,251
Finland	65,410	2,119	89	370	390	430	840	5,840	3,647	9,966	25,992	15,870	1,979
Rumania	67,708	2,887	175	757	507	500	888	10,359	1,889	12,596	28,124	9,815	2,038
Bulgaria	1,812	372	13	91	71	77	120	587	67	358	307	56	65
Turkey in Europe	988	138	5	25	37	35	36	454	64	161	108	37	20
Southern Europe:													
Greece	45,425	6,376	318	1,492	1,481	1,322	1,763	12,829	8,113	8,486	7,339	798	1,484
Albania	2,265	555	44	169	124	114	104	819	448	250	125	22	46
Italy	747,803	44,842	2,964	12,056	9,877	9,088	10,857	115,697	54,932	130,419	254,030	122,275	25,008
Spain	16,326	1,365	75	340	242	234	474	4,006	2,969	3,106	3,301	924	655
Portugal	27,669	1,053	78	273	179	166	357	4,377	4,885	4,077	7,512	4,712	1,053
Other Europe	6,559	781	37	197	143	136	268	866	256	808	1,601	1,691	556
Asia:													
Armenia	12,885	1,586	51	274	312	384	565	4,466	678	1,906	2,972	969	308
Palestine	2,501	513	22	166	126	83	116	624	225	352	453	203	131
Syria	24,717	1,347	64	251	258	281	493	4,050	1,173	5,110	8,519	3,583	935
Turkey in Asia	18,534	2,558	110	483	522	545	898	7,550	1,622	2,823	2,643	846	492
Other Asia	5,537	1,157	53	281	192	217	409	1,537	554	456	649	720	464
America:													
Canada—French	183,329	18,480	557	3,119	2,826	3,368	8,610	26,737	11,898	8,580	28,661	80,466	8,498
Canada—Other	478,002	65,681	2,154	11,012	10,187	11,906	30,422	74,869	34,696	22,271	65,217	174,085	40,583
Newfoundland	12,451	2,683	47	503	493	576	1,064	3,082	900	691	1,726	2,558	811
Cuba	6,495	1,430	52	445	268	273	392	850	573	377	1,315	1,386	564
Other West Indies	7,804	853	62	229	126	159	277	1,733	1,045	628	1,363	1,374	808
Mexico	11,006	2,039	91	368	397	472	711	1,901	1,870	1,270	1,484	1,071	1,371
Central America	3,649	1,317	67	314	277	286	373	844	482	155	232	148	471
South America	12,003	2,989	163	681	551	596	1,048	2,808	1,288	1,053	1,837	1,106	922
All other:													
Africa	3,490	560	28	123	111	99	199	642	312	465	821	437	253
Australia	6,064	542	42	127	96	87	190	816	565	505	1,430	1,684	534
Azores	16,462	270	15	55	36	47	117	1,788	1,881	2,350	5,588	3,956	629
Other Atlantic islands	1,667	59	4	15	12	6	22	287	288	202	374	318	144
Pacific islands	2,014	283	24	65	61	44	89	309	177	142	284	617	202
Country not specified	559	45	3	12	13	7	10	44	15	37	91	94	238
Born at sea	2,195	30	2	3	5	7	13	68	15	63	189	1,017	813

YEAR OF IMMIGRATION

TABLE 8.—PER CENT DISTRIBUTION OF THE FOREIGN-BORN WHITE POPULATION, BY YEAR OF IMMIGRATION AND COUNTRY OF BIRTH, BY SEX, FOR THE UNITED STATES: 1930

[Per cent not shown where less than 0.1]

Sex and country of birth	PER CENT OF TOTAL ARRIVING IN— 1925 to 1930	1920 to 1924	1915 to 1919	1911 to 1914	1901 to 1910	1900 or earlier	Unknown	PER CENT DISTRIBUTION BY COUNTRY OF BIRTH OF THOSE ARRIVING IN— Total	1925 to 1930	1920 to 1924	1915 to 1919	1911 to 1914	1901 to 1910	1900 or earlier	Unknown
TOTAL															
All countries	7.2	11.6	4.1	12.8	27.5	32.7	4.0	100.0	100.0	100.0	100.0	100.0	100.0	100.0	100.0
Northwestern Europe:															
England	6.9	12.9	4.5	9.2	20.6	41.0	4.9	6.1	5.8	6.7	6.6	4.4	4.5	7.6	7.3
Scotland	18.0	21.5	3.6	8.5	17.7	26.7	4.0	2.7	6.6	4.9	2.3	1.8	1.7	2.2	2.6
Wales	9.1	7.7	2.2	6.5	14.0	55.5	5.0	0.5	0.6	0.3	0.2	0.2	0.2	0.8	0.6
Northern Ireland	10.0	9.8	2.9	7.0	18.4	46.9	5.1	1.3	1.9	1.1	0.9	0.7	0.9	1.9	1.7
Irish Free State	12.3	7.8	2.9	6.4	18.1	46.4	6.2	5.6	9.6	3.7	3.9	2.8	3.7	7.9	8.5
Norway	6.7	7.1	3.1	5.9	26.0	47.1	4.2	2.6	2.4	1.6	1.9	1.2	2.5	3.8	2.7
Sweden	5.0	7.1	2.9	6.4	22.4	52.0	3.3	4.5	3.7	2.7	3.1	2.2	3.0	7.1	3.7
Denmark	5.9	7.8	4.0	8.5	21.6	48.3	3.9	1.3	1.1	0.9	1.3	0.9	1.1	2.0	1.3
Iceland	6.1	9.1	4.0	5.3	13.9	57.2	4.4	-	-	-	-	-	-	-	-
Netherlands	6.4	10.8	5.5	12.7	24.3	36.8	3.4	1.0	0.9	0.9	1.3	1.0	0.9	1.1	0.8
Belgium	4.0	15.6	6.8	10.5	28.2	24.6	3.4	0.5	0.3	0.6	0.8	0.6	0.5	0.4	0.4
Luxemburg	3.3	6.5	3.0	6.7	19.9	57.1	3.5	0.1	-	-	-	-	-	0.1	0.1
Switzerland	7.5	12.0	3.4	7.4	17.2	48.4	4.1	0.8	0.9	0.9	0.7	0.5	0.5	1.3	0.9
France	9.4	9.9	6.1	8.5	22.1	39.4	4.7	1.0	1.3	0.9	1.5	0.7	0.8	1.2	1.2
Central Europe:															
Germany	12.7	8.0	0.8	4.4	11.7	58.8	4.0	12.0	21.2	8.3	2.3	4.2	5.1	21.5	11.9
Poland	2.9	8.7	2.9	24.8	39.2	19.0	2.5	9.5	3.8	7.1	6.7	18.3	13.5	5.5	5.9
Czechoslovakia	3.5	9.8	1.7	14.9	37.2	30.1	2.8	3.7	1.8	3.1	1.5	4.3	5.0	8.4	2.5
Austria	2.6	10.4	2.3	15.5	38.1	26.7	4.2	2.8	1.0	2.5	1.6	3.4	3.8	2.3	2.9
Hungary	3.0	12.0	2.0	19.0	44.9	16.2	2.0	2.1	0.9	2.1	1.0	3.1	3.3	1.0	1.5
Yugoslavia	3.2	13.3	2.3	25.2	44.3	9.4	2.2	1.0	0.7	1.8	0.9	3.1	2.5	0.5	0.9
Eastern Europe:															
Russia	2.1	10.7	3.6	19.1	40.3	21.0	3.2	8.6	2.5	7.9	7.6	12.9	12.0	5.6	6.9
Latvia	4.0	13.7	8.5	13.4	41.3	20.8	3.1	0.2	0.1	0.2	0.1	0.2	0.2	0.1	0.1
Estonia	15.0	22.8	7.5	12.4	25.7	7.9	8.7	-	0.1	0.1	-	-	-	-	0.1
Lithuania	1.5	4.2	2.4	24.0	47.0	18.5	2.6	1.4	0.3	0.5	0.8	2.7	2.5	0.8	0.9
Finland	2.6	7.5	5.4	14.5	41.2	25.7	3.2	1.1	0.4	0.7	1.4	1.2	1.6	0.8	0.9
Rumania	3.5	14.4	3.1	18.6	42.5	15.5	2.5	1.1	0.5	1.4	0.8	1.6	1.7	0.5	0.7
Bulgaria	8.2	14.1	7.1	34.4	30.1	2.8	3.3	0.1	0.1	0.1	0.1	0.2	0.1	-	0.1
Turkey in Europe	7.8	34.4	8.3	23.1	18.2	5.3	2.9	-	0.1	-	-	-	-	-	-
Southern Europe:															
Greece	5.9	15.9	14.4	23.0	32.5	4.6	3.6	1.3	1.1	1.8	4.5	2.3	1.5	0.2	1.2
Albania	12.2	27.3	19.2	17.3	20.5	1.5	2.0	0.1	0.1	0.2	0.3	0.1	-	-	0.1
Italy	4.6	14.8	6.2	17.2	36.4	17.8	3.0	13.4	8.6	17.1	19.9	18.0	17.7	7.3	9.9
Spain	7.7	26.7	19.1	15.6	18.2	5.3	7.4	0.4	0.5	1.0	2.0	0.5	0.3	0.1	0.8
Portugal	5.3	19.6	16.0	13.0	24.6	16.5	4.0	0.5	0.4	0.9	2.0	0.6	0.5	0.3	0.5
Other Europe	12.1	17.6	5.5	11.0	23.1	22.0	8.7	0.1	0.2	0.2	0.2	0.1	0.1	0.1	0.3
Asia:															
Armenia	6.9	23.6	6.0	23.6	26.7	10.8	2.4	0.2	0.2	0.5	0.8	0.4	0.2	0.1	0.1
Palestine	16.9	24.0	9.5	16.7	10.8	8.8	4.4	-	0.1	0.1	0.1	0.1	-	-	0.1
Syria	3.8	13.4	4.8	21.0	36.8	16.9	3.3	0.4	0.2	0.5	0.5	0.7	0.6	0.2	0.4
Turkey in Asia	7.3	28.4	9.9	24.4	21.0	0.3	2.5	0.3	0.4	0.9	0.8	0.7	0.3	0.1	0.2
Other Asia	18.4	25.1	10.8	12.0	14.7	11.9	7.0	0.1	0.3	0.2	0.3	0.1	0.1	-	0.2
America:															
Canada—French	9.7	14.9	6.3	4.5	15.2	45.1	4.2	2.8	3.8	3.6	4.2	1.0	1.5	3.8	2.9
Canada—Other	13.5	16.7	7.0	4.5	13.1	37.3	7.9	6.8	12.8	9.8	11.5	2.4	3.2	7.8	13.3
Newfoundland	20.6	26.4	6.7	5.0	13.0	20.1	8.1	0.2	0.5	0.4	0.3	0.1	0.1	0.1	0.4
Cuba	27.5	14.2	8.8	5.5	17.1	17.7	9.2	0.1	0.5	0.1	0.3	0.1	0.1	0.1	0.3
Other West Indies	9.5	20.7	13.1	8.2	10.0	18.8	10.7	0.1	0.2	0.2	0.4	0.1	0.1	0.1	0.3
Mexico	20.2	18.7	17.0	10.6	13.5	8.6	11.4	0.2	0.5	0.3	0.7	0.1	0.1	-	0.5
Central America	33.8	22.0	15.3	4.5	6.3	4.1	13.0	0.1	0.3	0.1	0.2	-	-	-	0.2
South America	25.2	22.8	11.6	8.1	14.4	8.4	9.5	0.2	0.8	0.4	0.6	0.1	0.1	0.1	0.5
All other:															
Africa	15.6	17.7	0.2	13.0	23.4	13.5	7.7	0.1	0.1	0.1	0.1	0.1	-	-	0.1
Australia	7.5	12.4	8.9	8.6	26.1	27.7	8.0	0.1	0.1	0.1	0.2	0.1	0.1	0.1	0.2
Azores	1.5	11.0	10.4	13.8	33.6	26.7	3.5	0.3	0.1	0.3	0.7	0.3	0.3	0.2	0.2
Other Atlantic islands	3.6	15.5	14.9	13.5	23.6	10.6	9.3	-	0.1	-	0.1	-	-	-	0.1
Pacific islands	13.0	14.8	8.8	7.1	16.1	30.4	9.7	-	0.1	0.1	-	-	-	-	0.1
Country not specified	5.3	7.1	2.6	6.0	16.0	15.4	47.5	-	-	-	-	-	-	-	0.1
Born at sea	1.0	3.1	1.0	3.1	8.8	47.0	36.0	-	-	-	-	-	-	0.1	0.3
MALE															
All countries	6.7	11.3	4.0	13.1	29.2	32.0	3.7	100.0	100.0	100.0	100.0	100.0	100.0	100.0	100.0
Northwestern Europe:															
England	6.4	12.8	4.0	9.0	21.8	41.6	4.4	5.8	5.5	6.5	5.6	3.9	4.3	7.5	7.0
Scotland	16.2	22.9	3.1	7.8	19.1	27.2	3.7	2.5	6.2	5.1	2.0	1.5	1.7	2.2	2.5
Wales	9.5	8.0	2.0	6.7	15.4	53.9	4.6	0.4	0.6	0.3	0.2	0.2	0.2	0.8	0.6
Northern Ireland	10.7	10.7	2.8	7.2	19.4	44.8	4.3	1.1	1.8	1.1	0.8	0.6	0.8	1.6	1.3
Irish Free State	13.8	8.3	2.8	6.7	18.5	44.3	5.5	4.5	9.4	3.3	3.2	2.3	2.9	6.3	6.8
Norway	6.7	7.9	2.9	5.5	26.3	46.2	4.4	2.7	2.8	1.0	2.0	1.2	2.5	4.0	3.3
Sweden	6.6	8.4	3.1	6.6	22.8	49.1	3.3	4.7	4.6	3.5	3.6	2.4	3.6	7.2	4.2
Denmark	6.1	8.5	4.2	8.7	22.4	46.2	4.0	1.5	1.4	1.2	1.6	1.0	1.2	2.2	1.7
Iceland	7.1	8.4	5.0	4.5	13.7	56.5	4.8	-	-	-	-	-	-	-	-
Netherlands	6.5	11.2	5.9	12.6	25.1	35.3	3.4	1.1	1.1	1.1	1.6	1.0	0.9	1.2	1.0
Belgium	4.4	13.5	5.8	17.1	30.6	25.4	3.3	0.5	0.3	0.6	0.7	0.6	0.5	0.4	0.4
Luxemburg	2.8	4.6	2.3	6.4	21.8	58.7	3.2	0.1	-	-	-	-	0.1	0.1	0.1
Switzerland	7.8	12.8	3.2	7.7	18.2	46.4	3.9	0.9	1.1	1.0	0.7	0.5	0.6	1.3	1.0
France	9.6	7.9	3.9	8.5	23.3	42.6	4.3	0.9	1.3	0.6	0.9	0.6	0.7	1.2	1.1
Central Europe:															
Germany	12.8	8.3	0.9	4.9	12.4	57.0	3.7	11.8	22.7	8.6	2.6	4.4	5.0	21.0	11.8
Poland	2.4	7.1	2.9	24.8	41.3	19.2	2.2	9.5	3.4	6.0	6.8	18.0	13.5	5.7	5.8
Czechoslovakia	3.3	8.9	1.6	14.4	39.3	30.2	2.2	3.6	1.8	2.8	1.4	3.9	4.8	8.4	2.2
Austria	2.4	9.7	2.3	14.7	39.2	27.7	4.0	2.7	1.0	2.3	1.6	3.0	3.6	2.3	2.9
Hungary	2.7	11.0	1.9	17.3	48.0	16.6	2.5	2.0	0.8	1.9	0.9	2.6	3.2	1.0	1.3
Yugoslavia	2.4	9.6	2.5	24.8	46.3	10.4	2.1	1.8	0.7	1.6	1.1	3.5	3.0	0.6	1.0
Eastern Europe:															
Russia	1.7	9.3	3.8	19.7	41.1	21.7	2.8	8.6	2.2	7.0	7.9	12.9	12.1	5.8	6.6
Latvia	2.9	12.2	4.0	12.4	42.5	22.5	3.5	0.2	0.1	0.2	0.2	0.1	0.2	0.1	0.1
Estonia	10.3	21.6	9.2	12.2	27.1	8.5	11.0	-	0.1	0.1	0.1	-	-	-	0.1
Lithuania	1.0	2.9	2.4	22.4	48.8	20.1	2.5	1.6	0.2	0.4	0.9	2.6	2.6	1.0	1.1
Finland	2.0	6.3	5.2	13.9	42.4	26.9	3.4	1.1	0.3	0.6	1.4	1.1	1.6	0.9	1.0
Rumania	2.8	13.6	3.3	18.6	43.2	16.4	2.1	1.1	0.5	1.3	0.9	1.6	1.6	0.6	0.6
Bulgaria	5.3	9.8	7.9	37.9	33.3	2.8	3.2	0.1	0.1	0.1	0.2	0.3	0.1	-	0.1
Turkey in Europe	2.9	25.5	9.7	28.4	23.8	6.5	3.2								

504

POPULATION

TABLE 8.—PER CENT DISTRIBUTION OF THE FOREIGN-BORN WHITE POPULATION, BY YEAR OF IMMIGRATION AND COUNTRY OF BIRTH, BY SEX, FOR THE UNITED STATES: 1930—Continued

SEX AND COUNTRY OF BIRTH	PER CENT OF TOTAL ARRIVING IN—							PER CENT DISTRIBUTION BY COUNTRY OF BIRTH OF THOSE ARRIVING IN—							
	1925 to 1930	1920 to 1924	1915 to 1919	1911 to 1914	1901 to 1910	1900 or earlier	Unknown	Total	1925 to 1930	1920 to 1924	1915 to 1919	1911 to 1914	1901 to 1910	1900 or earlier	Unknown
MALE—Continued															
Southern Europe:															
Greece	3.1	11.6	13.2	24.5	38.2	5.6	3.8	1.8	0.8	1.8	5.0	3.4	2.4	0.3	1.8
Albania	7.9	24.3	19.0	19.5	25.7	1.6	1.9	0.1	0.1	0.2	0.4	0.1	0.1	—	—
Italy	3.6	14.4	5.3	17.0	38.2	18.9	2.7	14.6	7.8	18.6	19.1	18.8	19.1	8.6	10.6
Spain	7.4	27.6	10.4	14.2	17.4	5.2	8.7	0.6	0.7	1.4	2.8	0.6	0.3	0.1	1.4
Portugal	6.3	22.0	15.0	13.4	23.0	16.1	4.2	0.6	0.6	1.2	2.2	0.6	0.5	0.3	0.7
Other Europe	12.2	20.6	6.6	10.1	22.3	19.4	8.8	0.1	0.2	0.2	0.2	0.1	0.1	0.1	0.3
Asia:															
Armenia	3.2	16.3	6.5	29.5	29.1	13.0	2.4	0.3	0.1	0.4	0.4	0.6	0.3	0.1	0.2
Palestine	14.4	23.3	9.8	18.4	21.0	9.2	3.9	0.1	0.1	0.1	0.1	0.1	—	—	0.1
Syria	2.5	11.2	4.8	21.3	38.5	18.8	3.0	0.5	0.2	0.5	0.5	0.7	0.6	0.3	0.4
Turkey in Asia	3.1	20.3	10.7	30.5	25.5	7.5	2.4	0.4	0.2	0.7	1.0	0.9	0.3	0.1	0.3
Other Asia	17.0	23.6	11.3	14.1	16.4	11.3	6.3	0.1	0.4	0.3	0.4	0.1	0.1	—	0.2
America:															
Canada—French	0.4	15.3	6.2	4.4	14.7	46.2	3.8	2.6	3.7	3.5	4.0	0.9	1.3	3.8	2.7
Canada—Other	13.3	17.9	6.8	4.2	12.4	38.1	7.2	6.0	12.0	9.5	10.1	1.9	2.6	7.2	11.8
Newfoundland	10.5	23.2	6.2	4.4	12.0	10.7	9.9	0.2	0.5	0.4	0.2	0.1	0.1	0.1	0.4
Cuba	31.3	15.0	8.8	5.3	14.9	15.2	9.5	0.1	0.6	0.2	0.3	0.1	0.1	0.1	0.3
Other West Indies	8.1	19.1	12.8	8.4	20.5	20.0	11.1	0.1	0.1	0.2	0.3	0.1	0.1	0.1	0.3
Mexico	21.7	20.0	16.9	9.8	13.4	7.6	10.5	0.2	0.6	0.3	0.7	0.1	0.1	—	0.5
Central America	31.5	22.8	17.4	4.8	6.3	4.0	13.2	0.1	0.3	0.1	0.2	—	—	—	0.2
South America	25.4	22.4	12.2	7.7	13.8	7.8	10.7	0.3	1.0	0.5	0.8	0.1	0.1	0.1	0.7
All other:															
Africa	15.3	17.2	9.4	12.7	23.2	14.2	8.0	0.1	0.1	0.1	0.1	0.1	—	—	0.1
Australia	6.1	11.4	8.5	9.1	28.3	27.7	9.0	0.1	0.1	0.1	0.2	0.1	0.1	0.1	0.2
Azores	1.4	11.0	9.6	12.5	33.3	29.1	3.2	0.3	0.1	0.3	0.6	0.3	0.3	0.2	0.2
Other Atlantic islands	3.6	14.4	13.4	14.4	24.5	20.0	9.7	—	—	—	0.1	—	—	—	0.1
Pacific islands	12.1	14.4	8.9	7.2	17.8	30.2	9.4	—	0.1	0.1	—	—	—	—	0.1
Country not specified	3.7	6.7	2.5	5.6	15.9	14.6	51.1	—	—	—	—	—	—	—	0.2
Born at sea	0.8	3.1	1.3	3.3	8.9	47.4	35.1	—	—	—	—	—	—	0.1	0.4
FEMALE															
All countries	7.8	12.0	4.3	12.4	25.7	33.4	4.5	100.0	100.0	100.0	100.0	100.0	100.0	100.0	100.0
Northwestern Europe:															
England	7.4	13.0	5.1	9.5	19.4	40.4	5.3	6.4	6.0	6.9	7.7	4.9	4.8	7.7	7.6
Scotland	19.9	20.0	4.0	9.3	16.2	26.3	4.2	2.8	7.1	4.6	2.6	2.1	1.8	2.2	2.6
Wales	8.7	7.4	2.5	6.3	12.3	57.4	5.5	0.5	0.5	0.3	0.3	0.2	0.2	0.8	0.6
Northern Ireland	9.4	9.0	2.9	6.8	17.5	48.7	5.8	1.6	1.9	1.2	1.1	0.9	1.1	2.3	2.0
Irish Free State	11.2	7.4	2.9	6.2	17.7	48.0	6.7	6.8	9.7	4.2	4.0	3.4	4.7	9.7	10.1
Norway	0.7	5.9	3.2	6.3	25.6	48.3	3.9	2.4	2.1	1.2	1.9	1.2	2.4	3.5	2.1
Sweden	4.9	5.4	2.6	6.1	21.8	55.8	3.3	4.2	2.7	1.9	2.6	2.1	3.6	7.0	3.1
Denmark	5.7	6.8	3.6	8.1	20.4	51.6	3.7	1.1	0.8	0.6	1.0	0.7	0.9	1.7	0.9
Iceland	5.1	9.8	3.0	6.1	14.1	58.0	3.9	—	—	—	—	—	—	—	—
Netherlands	6.4	10.2	4.9	12.9	23.1	38.9	3.5	0.9	0.7	0.8	1.0	0.9	0.8	1.0	0.7
Belgium	5.6	18.1	8.0	15.9	25.4	23.6	3.5	0.5	0.3	0.7	0.9	0.6	0.5	0.3	0.4
Luxemburg	4.0	0.4	4.0	7.0	17.0	54.7	3.9	0.1	—	—	0.1	—	—	0.1	0.1
Switzerland	7.0	11.0	3.6	7.0	16.0	50.9	4.5	0.8	0.7	0.7	0.7	0.4	0.5	1.2	0.8
France	9.1	11.8	8.2	8.5	21.0	36.3	5.1	1.1	1.3	1.1	2.1	0.8	0.9	1.2	1.3
Central Europe:															
Germany	12.4	7.8	0.7	3.9	11.0	59.8	4.3	12.3	19.7	8.0	2.0	3.8	5.3	22.1	12.0
Poland	3.5	10.6	3.0	24.7	36.7	18.7	3.0	9.5	4.3	8.3	6.6	18.8	13.5	5.3	6.0
Czechoslovakia	3.7	10.9	1.8	15.5	34.8	30.0	3.4	3.8	1.8	3.4	1.6	4.7	5.2	3.4	2.9
Austria	2.0	11.2	2.3	16.5	36.9	25.7	4.5	2.9	1.1	2.7	1.6	3.8	4.1	2.2	2.9
Hungary	3.4	13.0	2.1	20.8	41.6	15.7	3.3	2.2	0.9	2.4	1.0	3.6	3.5	1.0	1.6
Yugoslavia	4.5	19.4	2.0	20.0	37.7	7.9	2.5	1.3	0.7	2.1	0.6	2.7	1.9	0.3	0.7
Eastern Europe:															
Russia	2.5	12.2	3.5	18.4	39.5	20.3	3.7	8.7	2.8	8.0	7.2	12.9	13.4	5.2	7.1
Latvia	5.3	15.4	3.0	14.6	40.0	19.0	2.7	0.2	0.1	0.2	0.1	0.2	0.2	0.1	0.1
Estonia	24.7	25.2	4.0	12.7	22.9	6.7	3.8	0.1	0.1	—	—	—	—	—	—
Lithuania	2.1	5.9	2.3	26.1	44.5	16.4	2.7	1.3	0.4	0.7	0.7	2.8	2.3	0.7	0.8
Finland	3.2	8.9	5.6	15.2	39.7	24.3	3.0	1.1	0.4	0.8	1.4	1.3	1.6	0.8	0.7
Rumania	4.3	15.3	2.8	18.6	41.5	14.5	3.0	1.1	0.6	1.4	0.7	1.6	1.8	0.5	0.7
Bulgaria	20.5	32.4	3.7	10.8	16.9	3.1	3.6	0.1	0.1	0.1	—	—	—	—	—
Turkey in Europe	14.0	46.0	6.5	16.3	10.9	3.7	2.6	—	—	0.1	—	—	—	—	—
Southern Europe:															
Greece	14.0	28.2	17.9	18.7	16.2	1.8	3.3	0.7	1.3	1.7	3.1	1.1	0.5	—	0.5
Albania	24.5	36.2	10.8	11.0	5.5	1.0	2.0	0.1	0.1	0.1	—	—	—	—	—
Italy	6.0	15.5	7.3	17.4	34.0	16.4	3.4	12.0	9.3	15.5	20.8	16.9	15.9	5.9	9.2
Spain	8.4	24.5	18.2	19.0	20.2	5.7	4.0	0.3	0.3	0.5	1.1	0.4	0.2	—	0.2
Portugal	3.8	15.8	17.7	14.7	27.1	17.0	3.8	0.4	0.2	0.6	1.8	0.5	0.5	0.2	0.4
Other Europe	11.9	13.2	3.9	12.3	24.4	25.8	8.5	0.1	0.2	0.1	0.1	0.1	0.1	0.1	0.2
Asia:															
Armenia	12.3	34.7	5.3	14.8	23.1	7.5	2.4	0.2	0.3	0.6	0.3	0.2	0.2	—	0.1
Palestine	20.5	25.0	9.0	14.1	18.1	8.1	5.2	0.1	0.1	0.1	0.1	—	—	—	0.1
Syria	5.4	16.4	4.7	20.7	34.5	14.5	3.8	0.4	0.3	0.5	0.4	0.7	0.5	0.2	0.3
Turkey in Asia	13.8	40.7	8.8	15.2	14.3	4.6	2.7	0.3	0.5	1.0	0.6	0.4	0.2	—	0.2
Other Asia	20.9	27.8	10.0	8.2	11.7	13.0	8.4	0.1	0.2	0.2	0.2	0.1	—	—	0.2
America:															
Canada—French	10.1	14.6	6.5	4.7	15.6	43.9	4.6	3.0	3.8	3.6	4.5	1.1	1.8	3.9	3.1
Canada—Other	13.7	15.7	7.3	4.7	13.6	36.5	8.5	7.7	13.0	10.1	13.1	2.9	4.1	8.4	14.6
Newfoundland	21.5	24.8	7.2	5.5	13.9	20.5	6.5	0.2	0.6	0.4	0.3	0.1	0.1	0.1	0.3
Cuba	22.0	13.1	8.8	5.8	20.2	21.3	8.7	0.1	0.3	0.2	—	0.1	0.1	0.1	0.2
Other West Indies	10.9	22.2	13.4	8.0	17.5	17.6	10.4	0.1	0.2	0.4	0.1	0.1	0.1	0.1	0.3
Mexico	18.5	17.3	17.0	11.5	13.5	9.7	12.5	0.1	0.4	0.3	0.7	0.2	0.1	0.1	0.5
Central America	30.1	23.1	13.2	6.4	4.1	9.7	12.9	0.1	0.3	0.1	0.2	—	—	—	0.2
South America	24.9	23.4	10.7	8.8	15.3	9.2	7.7	0.2	0.6	0.4	0.5	0.1	0.1	0.1	0.3
All other:															
Africa	16.0	18.4	8.9	13.3	23.5	12.5	7.2	0.1	0.1	0.1	0.1	0.1	0.1	—	0.1
Australia	8.9	13.5	9.3	8.1	23.6	27.8	8.8	0.1	0.1	0.1	0.2	0.1	0.1	0.1	0.2
Azores	1.6	10.9	11.4	14.3	33.9	24.0	3.8	0.3	0.1	0.2	0.7	0.3	0.4	0.2	0.2
Other Atlantic islands	3.5	17.2	17.0	12.1	22.4	19.1	8.6	—	—	—	0.1	—	—	—	0.1
Pacific islands	14.1	15.3	8.8	7.1	14.1	30.6	10.0	—	0.1	0.1	—	—	—	—	0.1
Country not specified	8.1	7.9	2.7	6.6	16.3	16.8	41.7	—	—	—	—	—	—	—	0.1
Born at sea	1.4	3.1	0.7	2.9	8.6	46.3	37.0	—	—	—	—	—	—	—	0.3

TABLE 9.—YEAR OF IMMIGRATION OF THE FOREIGN-BORN WHITE POPULATION OF THE UNITED STATES, BY COUNTRY OF BIRTH, FOR URBAN, RURAL-FARM, AND RURAL-NONFARM AREAS: 1930

[Per cent not shown where base is less than 100]

COUNTRY OF BIRTH	Total foreign-born white	YEAR OF IMMIGRATION: 1925 to 1930: Total	1930 (to Apr. 1)	1929	1928	1927	1925 and 1926	1920 to 1924	1915 to 1919	1911 to 1914	1901 to 1910	1900 or earlier	Unknown	PER CENT OF TOTAL ARRIVING IN—: 1925 to 1930	1920 to 1924	1915 to 1919	1911 to 1914	1901 to 1910	1900 or earlier	Unknown
URBAN																				
All countries	10,726,859	850,505	36,798	160,266	153,919	161,519	338,003	1,360,716	469,062	1,429,099	3,004,453	3,204,956	408,068	7.9	12.7	4.4	13.3	28.0	29.9	3.8
Northwestern Europe:																				
England	641,200	48,306	3,030	9,768	7,209	8,181	20,118	88,265	30,130	59,849	134,122	250,876	29,652	7.5	13.8	4.7	9.3	20.9	39.1	4.6
Scotland	295,541	58,177	3,737	12,364	9,797	9,952	22,327	67,866	10,556	25,119	50,891	71,965	10,967	19.7	23.0	3.6	8.5	17.2	24.4	3.7
Wales	45,968	4,862	184	1,296	929	934	1,519	3,843	1,070	2,992	6,408	24,750	2,043	10.6	8.4	2.3	6.5	13.9	53.8	4.4
Northern Ireland	150,782	16,213	1,270	3,221	2,541	2,951	6,230	15,491	4,370	10,716	27,780	68,750	7,462	10.8	10.3	2.9	7.1	18.4	45.6	4.9
Irish Free State	671,727	86,604	2,923	13,874	15,658	17,551	36,598	54,126	19,581	43,903	122,785	306,504	38,224	12.9	8.1	2.9	6.5	18.3	45.6	5.7
Norway	194,936	18,605	387	3,157	3,813	3,692	7,556	19,957	7,826	13,013	53,607	72,794	9,134	9.5	10.2	4.0	6.7	27.5	37.3	4.7
Sweden	408,032	29,886	637	4,791	6,041	5,912	12,505	35,740	13,303	27,951	93,251	104,484	13,417	7.3	8.8	3.3	6.9	22.9	47.7	3.3
Denmark	107,127	8,080	203	1,418	1,590	1,484	3,385	10,597	5,002	9,245	22,981	46,731	4,491	7.5	9.9	4.7	8.6	21.5	43.6	4.2
Iceland	1,348	120	3	21	15	23	58	200	85	72	209	584	78	8.9	14.8	6.3	5.3	15.5	43.3	5.8
Netherlands	80,466	5,773	401	1,226	999	1,095	2,052	9,148	4,858	9,685	10,149	29,077	2,776	7.2	11.4	6.0	12.0	23.8	36.1	3.4
Belgium	47,136	2,736	227	549	510	441	1,009	8,512	3,515	7,873	12,905	10,000	1,445	5.8	18.1	7.5	16.7	27.6	21.3	3.1
Luxemburg	5,693	245	13	53	44	57	78	463	208	397	1,148	3,028	204	4.3	8.1	3.7	7.0	20.2	53.2	3.6
Switzerland	67,918	5,551	248	1,051	1,083	1,076	2,093	8,890	2,557	4,804	11,309	32,044	2,703	8.2	13.1	3.8	7.1	16.7	47.2	4.1
France	104,805	10,892	490	2,212	2,222	2,152	3,816	11,241	6,722	9,015	22,819	39,466	4,710	10.4	10.7	6.4	8.6	21.8	37.6	4.5
Central Europe:																				
Germany	1,176,950	182,029	5,409	31,356	36,020	35,851	73,303	108,934	10,400	54,457	139,571	636,556	45,003	15.5	9.3	0.9	4.6	11.9	54.1	3.8
Poland	1,096,114	34,586	2,007	7,418	6,433	7,239	11,489	105,121	33,125	274,245	424,576	199,181	25,280	3.2	9.6	3.0	25.0	38.7	18.2	2.3
Czechoslovakia	348,261	14,081	878	3,370	2,911	2,707	4,815	39,686	6,114	53,510	130,321	94,810	9,139	4.2	11.4	1.8	15.4	37.4	27.2	2.6
Austria	308,482	8,882	520	1,815	1,643	1,694	3,210	35,309	7,391	47,950	116,775	81,104	11,071	2.9	11.4	2.4	15.5	37.9	26.3	3.6
Hungary	228,642	7,607	540	1,612	1,519	1,439	2,497	29,766	4,554	42,904	99,816	37,850	6,145	3.3	13.0	2.0	18.8	43.7	16.6	2.7
Yugoslavia	154,501	5,639	320	1,295	1,092	1,051	1,875	22,976	3,805	39,997	66,080	12,745	3,253	3.6	14.0	2.5	25.9	42.8	8.2	2.1
Eastern Europe:																				
Russia	1,041,173	22,598	1,322	3,747	3,759	4,085	9,685	118,718	39,186	198,408	423,341	208,836	30,586	2.2	11.4	3.8	19.1	40.7	20.0	2.9
Latvia	18,744	786	64	108	167	123	264	2,688	647	2,493	7,621	3,918	591	4.2	14.3	3.5	13.3	40.7	20.9	3.2
Estonia	2,982	497	14	77	99	89	218	719	215	350	699	221	281	16.7	24.1	7.2	11.7	23.4	7.4	9.4
Lithuania	168,090	2,616	146	521	440	536	973	7,511	4,114	40,962	78,378	30,433	4,076	1.6	4.5	2.4	24.4	46.6	18.1	2.4
Finland	79,867	2,947	136	521	521	591	1,178	8,178	5,124	13,007	31,299	16,417	2,805	3.7	10.2	6.4	16.3	39.2	20.6	3.6
Rumania	131,405	4,811	279	1,213	945	892	1,482	19,961	4,187	23,950	54,852	20,560	3,144	3.7	15.2	3.2	18.2	41.7	15.0	2.4
Bulgaria	7,346	665	18	134	137	143	233	1,134	566	2,511	2,082	187	201	9.1	15.4	7.7	34.2	28.3	2.5	2.7
Turkey in Europe	2,158	169	6	34	38	45	46	755	180	505	374	110	65	7.8	35.0	8.3	23.4	17.3	5.1	3.1
Southern Europe:																				
Greece	159,376	9,855	435	2,110	2,120	2,023	3,167	26,083	23,387	36,295	50,770	7,441	5,536	6.2	16.4	14.7	22.8	31.9	4.7	3.5
Albania	8,179	1,022	63	286	211	185	277	2,261	1,552	1,384	1,689	114	157	12.5	27.6	19.0	16.9	20.7	1.4	1.9
Italy	1,573,003	74,549	4,639	18,375	15,404	14,722	21,409	238,342	99,411	267,816	568,401	278,999	45,485	4.7	15.2	6.3	17.0	36.1	17.7	2.9
Spain	46,181	3,890	177	706	622	723	1,662	12,940	8,767	6,379	7,885	2,509	3,811	8.4	28.0	19.0	13.8	17.1	5.4	8.3
Portugal	52,141	3,154	153	589	587	661	1,164	10,508	9,052	7,105	12,438	7,642	2,152	6.0	20.3	17.4	13.6	23.9	14.7	4.1
Other Europe	13,500	1,883	162	501	297	320	603	2,738	838	1,457	2,872	2,785	987	13.9	20.2	6.2	10.7	21.2	20.5	7.3
Asia:																				
Armenia	28,829	2,082	69	342	414	494	763	7,080	1,744	6,740	7,619	2,940	615	7.2	24.6	6.0	23.4	26.4	10.2	2.1
Palestine	5,875	1,021	58	291	223	192	257	1,439	563	976	1,140	492	244	17.4	24.5	9.6	16.6	19.4	8.4	4.2
Syria	51,482	1,993	105	354	372	417	745	7,220	2,515	11,045	18,725	8,400	1,584	3.9	14.0	4.9	21.5	36.4	16.3	3.1
Turkey in Asia	43,272	3,280	145	602	660	693	1,180	12,690	4,325	10,545	8,933	2,480	1,010	7.6	29.3	10.0	24.4	20.6	5.8	2.3
Other Asia	13,431	2,600	164	634	406	500	896	3,487	1,476	1,615	1,920	1,476	857	19.4	26.0	11.0	12.0	14.3	11.0	6.4
America:																				
Canada—French	292,564	28,794	746	4,587	4,102	5,010	14,349	45,025	17,996	13,073	45,593	130,473	11,610	9.8	15.4	6.2	4.5	15.6	44.6	4.0
Canada—Other	696,174	104,879	3,169	16,615	15,358	18,081	51,656	126,312	50,878	31,639	92,505	239,276	50,685	15.1	18.1	7.3	4.5	13.3	34.4	7.3
Newfoundland	22,021	4,682	97	840	764	1,021	1,960	5,973	1,491	1,108	2,836	4,370	1,561	21.3	27.1	6.8	5.0	12.9	19.8	7.1
Cuba	15,128	4,249	174	1,348	794	805	1,128	2,162	1,332	826	2,624	2,658	1,277	28.1	14.3	8.8	5.5	17.3	17.6	8.4
Other West Indies	13,960	1,387	107	357	219	248	456	2,995	1,857	1,136	2,622	2,534	1,429	9.9	21.5	13.3	8.1	18.8	18.2	10.2
Mexico	18,596	4,066	150	729	764	937	1,486	3,567	3,213	1,951	2,327	1,470	2,002	21.9	19.2	17.3	10.5	12.5	7.9	10.8
Central America	6,968	2,430	115	587	494	530	704	1,647	1,059	301	423	262	846	34.9	23.6	15.2	4.3	6.1	3.8	12.1
South America	26,836	7,093	356	1,423	1,373	1,461	2,480	6,297	3,206	2,072	3,541	2,056	2,570	26.4	23.5	11.9	7.7	13.2	7.7	9.6
All other:																				
Africa	6,885	1,146	59	253	223	198	413	1,256	637	905	1,618	828	495	16.6	18.2	9.3	13.1	23.5	12.0	7.2
Australia	10,208	819	62	209	139	133	276	1,343	948	873	2,665	2,680	874	8.0	13.2	9.3	8.6	26.1	26.3	8.6
Azores	23,382	328	23	61	40	68	136	2,157	2,547	3,094	8,212	6,238	806	1.4	9.2	10.9	13.2	35.1	26.7	3.4
Other Atlantic islands	3,427	122	9	26	21	20	46	551	518	460	801	671	304	3.6	16.1	15.1	13.4	23.4	19.6	8.0
Pacific islands	3,395	508	48	134	106	71	149	528	293	238	581	978	319	15.0	15.6	8.6	7.0	15.0	28.8	9.4
Country not specified	1,164	66	3	20	11	12	20	92	30	79	184	164	549	5.7	7.9	2.6	6.8	15.8	14.1	47.2
Born at sea	3,309	44	2	5	11	8	18	120	36	104	325	1,464	1,207	1.3	3.6	1.1	3.1	9.8	44.2	36.5
RURAL-FARM																				
All countries	1,084,087	32,877	1,904	6,153	5,896	5,974	12,950	56,159	29,450	102,785	274,249	548,193	40,374	3.0	5.2	2.7	9.5	25.3	50.6	3.7
Northwestern Europe:																				
England	44,106	1,164	69	258	172	204	461	2,509	1,389	3,413	7,580	25,557	2,494	2.6	5.7	3.1	7.7	17.2	57.9	5.7
Scotland	13,871	663	84	150	97	140	192	1,005	446	1,162	2,906	6,987	702	4.8	7.2	3.2	8.4	21.0	50.4	5.1
Wales	4,008	91	5	18	9	11	48	160	52	263	602	2,593	247	2.3	4.0	1.3	6.6	15.0	64.7	6.2
Northern Ireland	8,207	276	20	54	45	58	99	369	167	479	1,426	4,987	503	3.4	4.5	2.0	5.8	17.4	60.8	6.1
Irish Free State	17,008	768	41	137	134	164	292	638	311	747	2,623	10,603	1,318	4.5	3.8	1.8	4.4	15.4	62.3	7.7
Norway	91,385	2,272	220	549	423	421	659	1,986	1,543	4,413	22,941	55,775	2,455	2.5	2.2	1.7	4.8	25.1	61.0	2.7
Sweden	98,589	1,694	63	305	336	334	656	2,124	1,862	5,125	21,750	63,777	2,257	1.7	2.2	1.9	5.2	22.1	64.7	2.3
Denmark	41,555	1,481	63	297	310	304	507	1,897	1,174	3,740	9,933	22,209	1,121	3.6	4.6	2.8	9.0	23.9	53.4	2.7
Iceland	772	30	1	11	8	-------	10	20	14	48	90	559	11	3.9	2.6	1.8	6.2	11.7	72.4	1.4
Netherlands	31,408	1,508	170	329	238	287	484	3,339	1,485	4,688	8,248	11,265	875	4.8	10.6	4.7	14.9	26.3	35.9	2.8
Belgium	9,044	239	9	78	28	21	103	841	482	1,734	2,844	2,599	305	2.6	9.3	5.3	19.2	31.4	28.7	3.4
Luxemburg	1,955	28	3	9	4	4	8	67	40	135	434	1,186	65	1.4	3.4	2.0	6.9	22.2	60.7	3.3
Switzerland	25,887	1,847	73	352	398	333	691	2,691	706	2,182	4,969	12,663	829	7.1	10.4	2.7	8.4	19.2	48.9	3.2
France	10,345	560	64	131	90	81	194	566	405	754	2,356	5,223	481	5.4	5.5	3.9	7.3	22.8	50.5	4.6
Central Europe:																				
Germany	215,977	7,625	340	1,143	1,276	1,263	3,603	8,548	924	8,186	24,676	158,770	7,248	3.5	4.0	0.4	3.8	11.4	73.5	3.4
Poland	65,166	721	83	126	124	115	273	1,688	1,318	12,992	26,791	19,942	1,714	1.1	2.6	2.0	19.9	41.1	30.6	2.6
Czechoslovakia	58,722	555	40	107	105	77	226	2,074	784	7,110	20,247	26,358	1,594	0.9	3.5	1.3	12.1	34.5	44.9	2.7
Austria	21,977	247	23	43	44	39	98	885	383	2,935	8,518	8,203	806	1.1	4.0	1.7	13.4	38.8	37.3	3.7
Hungary	14,801	159	11	28	40	22	58	749	241	2,913	8,055	2,311	373	1.1	5.1	1.6	19.7	54.4	15.6	2.5
Yugoslavia	12,655	179	6	29	27	49	68	856	190	2,596	6,613	1,809	322	1.4	6.8	1.5	20.5	52.3	15.0	2.5

506

POPULATION

TABLE 9.—YEAR OF IMMIGRATION OF THE FOREIGN-BORN WHITE POPULATION OF THE UNITED STATES, BY COUNTRY OF BIRTH, FOR URBAN, RURAL-FARM, AND RURAL-NONFARM AREAS: 1930—Continued

COUNTRY OF BIRTH	Total foreign-born white	YEAR OF IMMIGRATION												PER CENT OF TOTAL ARRIVING IN—						
		1925 to 1930						1920 to 1924	1915 to 1919	1911 to 1914	1901 to 1910	1900 or earlier	Un-known	1925 to 1930	1920 to 1924	1915 to 1919	1911 to 1914	1901 to 1910	1900 or earlier	Un-known
		Total	1930 (to Apr.1)	1929	1928	1927	1925 and 1926													
RURAL-FARM—Con.																				
Eastern Europe:																				
Russia	59,667	515	46	114	83	89	183	1,709	1,220	11,287	24,160	18,962	1,814	0.9	2.9	2.0	18.9	40.5	31.8	3.0
Latvia	672	15		3	3	1	8	35	26	100	343	136	17	2.2	5.2	3.9	14.9	51.0	20.2	2.5
Estonia	232	8		2	1	1	4	23	12	38	117	27	7	3.4	9.9	5.2	16.4	50.4	11.6	3.0
Lithuania	7,764	50	4	9	6	10	21	158	141	1,638	3,939	1,643	195	0.6	2.0	1.8	21.1	50.7	21.2	2.5
Finland	35,717	166	8	30	24	31	73	991	1,244	3,979	16,116	12,681	540	0.5	2.8	3.5	11.1	45.1	35.5	1.5
Rumania	6,469	89	5	25	9	16	34	335	115	1,213	3,488	1,073	156	1.4	5.2	1.8	18.8	53.9	16.6	2.4
Bulgaria	594	31	5	7	3	2	14	62	22	178	263	24	24	5.2	10.4	3.7	30.0	42.6	4.0	4.0
Turkey in Europe	31	1			1			6	2	5	11	5	1							
Southern Europe:																				
Greece	2,458	80	9	13	6	18	34	212	238	587	1,126	139	76	3.3	8.6	9.7	23.9	45.8	5.7	3.1
Albania	59	1			1			12	11	19	14	1	1							
Italy	49,283	939	44	194	191	203	307	4,604	2,101	8,529	20,250	11,499	1,361	1.9	9.3	4.3	17.3	41.1	23.3	2.8
Spain	3,908	144	7	22	10	23	76	694	678	940	1,103	232	117	3.7	17.8	17.3	24.1	28.2	5.9	3.0
Portugal	9,728	203	7	37	31	36	92	1,552	1,167	1,488	2,876	2,155	277	2.1	16.0	12.0	15.3	29.6	22.3	2.8
Other Europe	984	17	1	2	1	2	11	21	19	110	353	366	98	1.7	2.1	1.9	11.2	35.9	37.2	10.0
Asia:																				
Armenia	1,831	28	2	6	6	2	12	263	98	422	609	375	36	1.5	14.4	5.4	23.0	33.3	20.5	2.0
Palestine	63	1		1				4	1	9	27	19	5							
Syria	1,081	29	1	11	2	6	9	40	54	175	422	310	51	2.7	3.7	5.0	16.2	39.0	28.7	4.7
Turkey in Asia	1,445	45	2	8	9	6	20	224	99	325	450	280	16	3.1	15.5	6.9	22.5	31.1	19.8	1.1
Other Asia	660	46	2	11	5	14	14	119	77	104	123	135	62	6.0	17.9	11.6	15.6	18.5	20.3	9.3
America:																				
Canada—French	22,668	2,322	92	461	513	465	791	2,746	2,120	1,120	2,536	10,714	1,104	10.2	12.1	9.4	5.0	11.2	47.3	4.9
Canada—Other	77,069	5,441	247	946	958	1,004	2,286	7,331	4,670	3,077	8,590	40,312	7,648	7.1	9.5	6.1	4.0	11.1	52.3	9.9
Newfoundland	228	28	1	5	8	7	7	23	18	8	44	87	20	12.3	10.1	7.9	3.5	19.3	38.2	8.8
Cuba	138	20	1	2	8	4	5	21	17	10	13	22	35	14.5	15.2	12.3	7.2	9.4	15.9	25.4
Other West Indies	242	9		1	1	2	5	14	21	25	49	104	20	3.7	5.8	8.7	10.3	20.2	43.0	8.3
Mexico	1,648	169	8	17	28	47	69	253	200	213	307	228	218	10.3	15.4	15.8	12.9	18.6	13.8	13.2
Central America	78	16	1	3	5	3	4	8	15	4	9	6	20							
South America	1,026	124	10	32	18	18	40	136	76	166	298	168	58	12.1	13.3	7.4	16.2	29.0	16.4	5.7
All other:																				
Africa	261	21		2	2	7	10	39	12	30	56	75	28	8.0	14.9	4.6	11.5	21.5	28.7	10.7
Australia	723	12			7	1	4	57	33	52	181	309	79	1.7	7.9	4.6	7.2	25.0	42.7	10.9
Azores	8,554	159	6	31	35	20	67	1,369	808	1,240	2,598	2,018	272	1.9	16.0	10.5	14.5	30.4	23.6	3.2
Other Atlantic Islands	207	8		2		1	5	24	32	22	56	46	19	3.9	11.6	15.5	10.6	27.1	22.2	9.2
Pacific Islands	376	27	2	1	5	6	14	50	30	22	54	152	41	7.2	13.3	8.0	5.9	14.4	40.4	10.9
Country not specified	83	3			2	1		6	3	5	21	16	29							
Born at sea	696	3		1	1		1	6	4	27	55	392	200	0.4	0.9	0.6	3.9	7.9	56.3	30.0
RURAL-NONFARM																				
All countries	1,555,461	76,856	3,645	14,265	13,347	14,276	31,323	135,221	55,179	180,363	402,698	613,116	92,028	4.9	8.7	3.5	11.6	25.9	39.4	5.9
Northwestern Europe:																				
England	123,366	5,954	417	1,048	771	946	2,772	13,474	5,081	11,390	24,851	55,473	7,143	4.8	10.9	4.1	9.2	20.1	45.0	5.8
Scotland	44,911	5,001	405	1,033	828	799	1,936	7,254	1,617	3,950	8,916	15,819	2,354	11.1	16.2	3.6	8.8	19.9	35.2	5.2
Wales	10,220	535	39	123	88	95	190	948	222	655	1,389	6,067	718	5.2	9.3	2.2	6.4	13.6	59.3	7.0
Northern Ireland	19,843	1,338	111	267	229	258	473	1,582	567	1,302	3,613	10,224	1,217	6.7	8.0	2.9	6.6	18.2	51.5	6.1
Irish Free State	56,075	4,423	159	679	803	931	1,851	3,205	1,435	3,197	9,160	28,304	6,351	7.9	5.7	2.6	5.7	16.3	50.5	11.3
Norway	61,531	2,373	55	440	505	467	906	2,612	1,284	2,968	13,941	35,277	3,076	3.9	4.2	2.1	4.8	22.7	57.3	5.0
Sweden	88,629	3,524	104	680	692	663	1,385	4,332	2,144	4,956	18,092	51,409	4,172	4.0	4.9	2.4	5.6	20.4	58.0	4.7
Denmark	30,792	1,077	34	187	229	197	430	1,561	957	2,239	5,873	17,735	1,350	3.5	5.1	3.1	7.3	19.1	57.6	4.4
Iceland	644	18	1	7	3	3	4	31	12	27	85	439	32	2.8	4.8	1.9	4.2	13.2	68.2	5.0
Netherlands	21,259	1,274	112	323	199	201	439	1,934	972	2,552	4,912	8,685	980	6.0	9.1	4.6	12.0	23.1	40.9	4.4
Belgium	8,014	179	14	36	39	21	69	660	371	1,004	2,282	3,115	403	2.2	8.2	4.6	12.5	28.5	38.9	5.0
Luxemburg	1,400	24	4		5	2	13	59	25	70	219	955	48	1.7	4.2	1.8	5.0	15.6	68.2	3.4
Switzerland	19,205	1,065	42	191	204	210	418	2,017	557	1,341	3,194	9,936	1,095	5.5	10.5	2.9	7.0	16.6	51.7	5.7
France	20,022	1,200	64	273	227	184	452	1,573	1,094	1,714	4,755	8,564	1,122	6.0	7.9	5.5	8.6	23.7	42.8	5.6
Central Europe:																				
Germany	215,887	13,909	456	2,235	2,486	2,600	6,126	11,985	1,487	8,722	24,342	143,279	12,163	6.4	5.6	0.7	4.0	11.3	66.4	5.6
Poland	107,303	1,470	117	240	231	322	560	3,745	2,726	26,006	45,920	21,487	5,049	1.4	3.5	2.5	25.1	42.8	20.0	4.7
Czechoslovakia	84,655	1,951	126	438	372	367	648	6,565	1,317	12,727	32,102	27,014	2,979	2.3	7.8	1.6	14.9	37.9	31.9	3.5
Austria	40,455	612	37	142	85	98	250	2,474	900	6,089	16,013	9,902	3,865	1.5	6.1	2.2	16.5	39.6	24.5	9.6
Hungary	31,007	522	29	121	100	78	194	2,365	641	6,415	15,334	4,224	1,506	1.7	7.6	2.1	20.7	49.5	13.6	4.9
Yugoslavia	44,260	907	33	195	164	201	314	4,336	878	10,779	20,927	5,299	1,134	2.0	9.8	2.0	24.4	47.3	12.0	2.6
Eastern Europe:																				
Russia	52,784	716	50	134	129	128	275	2,524	1,628	10,700	17,479	15,038	4,699	1.4	4.8	3.1	20.3	33.1	28.5	8.9
Latvia	1,257	35		7	15	4	9	107	57	183	580	255	40	2.8	8.5	4.5	14.6	46.1	20.3	3.2
Estonia	336	27	1	5	4	3	14	66	40	52	98	33	20	8.0	19.6	11.9	15.5	29.2	9.8	6.0
Lithuania	17,752	153	4	37	28	30	54	391	306	3,771	8,624	3,751	756	0.9	2.2	1.7	21.2	48.6	21.1	4.3
Finland	26,894	525	19	84	111	99	212	1,502	1,324	3,684	11,225	7,475	1,159	2.0	5.6	4.9	13.7	41.7	27.8	4.3
Rumania	8,459	159	7	37	28	22	65	747	219	2,075	3,813	1,060	386	1.9	8.8	2.6	24.5	45.1	12.5	4.6
Bulgaria	1,459	75		18	21	11	30	131	70	541	496	55	82	5.1	9.0	5.4	37.1	34.0	3.8	5.6
Turkey in Europe	68	5			1	2	2	16	5	12	25	5								
Southern Europe:																				
Greece	12,692	443	28	100	85	89	141	1,462	1,556	3,248	4,753	495	735	3.5	11.5	12.3	25.6	37.4	3.9	5.8
Albania	576	51	5	15	8	14	9	137	131	125	104	13	15	8.9	23.8	22.7	21.7	18.1	2.3	2.6
Italy	168,138	6,652	447	1,593	1,369	1,443	1,800	22,738	8,782	31,238	63,231	28,696	6,801	4.0	13.5	5.2	18.6	37.6	17.1	4.0
Spain	8,213	446	14	78	81	97	176	1,953	1,685	1,752	1,602	377	398	5.4	23.8	20.5	21.3	19.5	4.6	4.8
Portugal	8,105	354	19	51	69	79	136	1,541	1,005	1,160	1,932	1,727	386	4.4	19.0	12.4	14.3	23.8	21.3	4.8
Other Europe	1,707	64	4	12	11	14	23	104	40	222	536	419	322	3.7	6.1	2.3	13.0	31.4	24.5	18.9

YEAR OF IMMIGRATION

TABLE 9.—YEAR OF IMMIGRATION OF THE FOREIGN-BORN WHITE POPULATION OF THE UNITED STATES, BY COUNTRY OF BIRTH, FOR URBAN, RURAL-FARM, AND RURAL-NONFARM AREAS: 1930—Continued

COUNTRY OF BIRTH	Total foreign-born white	YEAR OF IMMIGRATION — 1925 to 1930 Total	1930 (to Apr. 1)	1929	1928	1927	1925 and 1926	1920 to 1924	1915 to 1919	1911 to 1914	1901 to 1910	1900 or earlier	Un-known	PER CENT OF TOTAL ARRIVING IN— 1925 to 1930	1920 to 1924	1915 to 1919	1911 to 1914	1901 to 1910	1900 or earlier	Unknown
RURAL-NONFARM— Continued																				
Asia:																				
Armenia	1,506	100	3	18	11	31	37	253	85	427	300	156	125	6.6	16.8	5.6	28.4	23.9	10.4	8.3
Palestine	197	15	1	3	5	------	6	28	18	40	48	26	22	7.6	14.2	9.1	20.3	24.4	13.2	11.2
Syria	4,664	134	3	21	24	35	51	420	150	810	1,802	983	269	2.9	9.1	3.2	17.4	40.6	21.1	5.8
Turkey in Asia	1,934	99	4	17	22	26	30	345	200	528	429	187	140	5.1	17.8	10.7	27.3	22.2	9.7	7.2
Other Asia	1,304	191	15	43	30	42	61	261	117	127	225	219	164	14.6	20.0	9.0	9.7	17.3	16.8	12.6
America:																				
Canada—French	55,620	4,980	195	979	772	951	2,083	7,581	3,415	2,067	8,180	25,010	2,878	9.0	13.6	6.1	4.8	14.7	46.6	5.2
Canada—Other	134,326	12,576	403	2,063	1,938	2,172	6,000	18,020	8,202	5,772	17,444	58,881	13,341	0.4	13.4	6.2	4.3	13.0	43.8	9.9
Newfoundland	1,722	219	4	31	37	34	113	339	109	80	232	367	370	12.7	19.7	6.3	5.0	13.5	21.3	21.5
Cuba	678	117	4	34	26	16	37	80	55	44	90	140	152	17.3	11.8	8.1	6.5	13.3	20.6	22.4
Other West Indies	1,280	80	2	24	7	10	37	190	152	115	287	208	208	6.3	14.8	11.9	9.0	20.9	20.9	16.3
Mexico	3,400	567	21	71	109	147	219	627	552	358	551	340	404	16.2	17.9	15.8	10.2	16.0	9.7	14.1
Central America	408	71	3	11	20	15	22	55	70	32	40	34	106	17.4	13.5	17.2	7.8	9.8	8.3	26.0
South America	2,194	357	13	76	65	74	129	412	200	203	481	209	233	16.3	18.8	9.5	9.3	21.9	13.0	10.6
All other:																				
Africa	720	63	------	12	16	14	21	98	75	84	163	157	80	8.7	13.6	10.4	11.7	22.6	21.8	11.1
Australia	1,780	118	8	18	22	10	60	172	148	173	408	531	170	6.6	9.6	8.3	9.7	26.2	20.7	10.0
Azores	3,491	40	5	7	8	6	20	356	252	387	1,085	1,210	149	1.3	10.2	7.2	11.1	31.1	34.8	4.3
Other Atlantic islands	418	14	------	2	4	3	5	55	53	64	101	79	52	3.3	13.2	12.7	15.3	24.2	18.9	12.4
Pacific islands	593	33	1	10	6	3	13	69	62	51	118	196	64	5.6	11.0	10.5	8.6	19.9	33.1	10.8
Country not specified	238	10	1	1	3	2	3	8	5	5	33	40	128	4.2	3.4	2.1	2.1	13.9	20.6	53.8
Born at sea	953	5	2	------	2	1	------	20	10	24	54	472	368	0.5	2.1	1.0	2.5	5.7	49.5	38.6

TABLE 10.—YEAR OF IMMIGRATION OF THE FOREIGN-BORN WHITE POPULATION OF THE UNITED STATES, BY SEX, FOR URBAN, RURAL-FARM, AND RURAL-NONFARM AREAS: 1930

YEAR OF IMMIGRATION	URBAN Male Number	Per cent	URBAN Female Number	Per cent	RURAL-FARM Male Number	Per cent	RURAL-FARM Female Number	Per cent	RURAL-NONFARM Male Number	Per cent	RURAL-NONFARM Female Number	Per cent
Total foreign-born white	5,642,087	100.0	5,084,772	100.0	631,169	100.0	452,918	100.0	880,453	100.0	675,008	100.0
Year of immigration:												
1925 to 1930	418,837	7.4	431,668	8.5	20,070	3.2	12,807	2.8	38,637	4.4	38,210	5.7
1930, to April 1	17,871	0.3	18,027	0.4	1,253	0.2	651	0.1	1,856	0.2	1,789	0.3
1929	74,033	1.3	86,233	1.7	3,860	0.6	2,284	0.5	6,910	0.8	7,355	1.1
1928	73,033	1.3	80,886	1.6	3,661	0.6	2,235	0.5	6,558	0.7	6,789	1.0
1927	81,377	1.4	80,142	1.6	3,600	0.6	2,305	0.5	7,364	0.8	6,912	1.0
1925 and 1926	172,523	3.1	105,480	3.3	7,678	1.2	5,272	1.2	15,949	1.8	15,374	2.3
1920 to 1924	704,224	12.5	656,492	12.9	30,810	4.9	25,349	5.6	72,252	8.2	62,969	9.3
1915 to 1919	244,228	4.3	224,834	4.4	15,571	2.5	13,879	3.1	20,035	3.4	25,544	3.8
1911 to 1914	777,045	13.8	652,054	12.8	58,034	9.2	44,751	9.9	105,349	12.0	75,014	11.1
1901 to 1910	1,679,688	29.8	1,324,770	26.1	161,609	25.6	112,640	24.9	244,963	27.8	157,735	23.4
1900 or earlier	1,625,173	28.8	1,579,783	31.1	324,728	51.4	223,405	49.3	339,452	38.6	273,664	40.5
Unknown	102,897	3.4	215,171	4.2	20,347	3.2	20,027	4.4	50,165	5.7	41,803	6.2

119652—33——33

508

POPULATION

TABLE 11.—YEAR OF IMMIGRATION OF THE TOTAL FOREIGN-BORN POPULATION, BY DIVISIONS AND STATES: 1930

DIVISION AND STATE	Total foreign born	YEAR OF IMMIGRATION												PER CENT OF TOTAL ARRIVING IN—						
		1925 to 1930						1920 to 1924	1915 to 1919	1911 to 1914	1901 to 1910	1900 or earlier	Un-known	1925 to 1930	1920 to 1924	1915 to 1919	1911 to 1914	1901 to 1910	1900 or earlier	Unknown
		Total	1930 (to Apr. 1)	1929	1928	1927	1925 and 1926													
United States...	14,204,149	1,085,214	46,456	197,907	197,990	212,680	430,181	1,738,185	730,309	1,811,637	3,823,694	4,429,494	585,616	7.6	12.2	5.1	12.8	26.9	31.2	4.1
GEOGRAPHIC DIVS.:																				
New England....	1,848,943	120,308	4,366	21,205	20,041	22,467	52,229	208,424	97,694	226,598	503,313	639,995	52,611	6.5	11.3	5.3	12.3	27.2	34.6	2.8
Middle Atlantic.	5,352,731	486,233	23,533	96,715	91,962	94,928	179,095	726,344	240,083	734,046	1,577,510	1,374,360	214,155	9.1	13.6	4.5	13.7	29.5	25.7	4.0
E. N. Central....	3,275,723	250,353	9,138	43,084	44,486	46,655	106,990	389,905	123,885	468,945	866,311	1,053,929	122,394	7.6	11.9	3.8	14.3	26.4	32.2	3.7
W. N. Central....	1,084,153	31,556	1,376	5,097	5,665	6,178	13,240	55,359	29,149	87,752	242,824	506,996	40,517	2.9	5.1	2.7	8.1	22.4	55.1	3.7
South Atlantic...	318,697	16,753	743	3,154	2,743	3,003	7,110	34,767	17,652	41,016	87,306	95,812	25,391	5.3	10.9	5.5	12.9	27.4	30.1	8.0
E. S. Central....	59,364	2,422	91	405	530	444	952	4,761	2,076	5,339	14,004	25,226	5,446	4.1	8.0	3.5	9.0	23.7	42.5	9.2
W. S. Central....	440,553	40,089	1,919	5,921	8,217	9,055	14,977	59,859	63,200	56,381	84,072	110,456	26,496	9.1	13.6	14.3	12.8	19.1	25.1	6.0
Mountain........	384,323	25,208	846	4,270	4,975	5,760	9,357	39,687	32,648	42,556	96,420	126,101	21,694	6.6	10.3	8.5	11.1	25.1	32.8	5.6
Pacific.........	1,439,662	112,292	4,444	18,056	19,371	24,190	46,231	219,078	123,922	149,004	351,835	406,619	76,912	7.8	15.2	8.6	10.3	24.4	28.2	5.3
NEW ENGLAND:																				
Maine..........	100,728	6,702	310	1,174	1,186	1,381	2,651	12,859	6,582	8,577	21,857	38,543	5,608	6.7	12.8	6.5	8.5	21.7	38.3	5.6
New Hampshire..	82,929	4,141	128	707	600	788	1,918	8,177	4,552	8,281	18,569	35,214	3,995	5.0	9.9	5.5	10.0	22.4	42.5	4.8
Vermont........	43,101	5,080	187	1,030	1,013	946	1,904	5,941	3,799	4,052	9,075	14,272	882	11.8	13.8	8.8	9.4	21.1	33.1	2.0
Massachusetts...	1,065,620	69,928	2,248	11,938	11,234	12,784	31,751	123,017	55,817	128,367	286,398	371,958	30,138	6.6	11.5	5.2	12.0	26.9	34.9	2.8
Rhode Island....	171,929	8,948	386	1,383	1,467	1,662	4,045	18,853	9,266	19,940	48,663	63,691	2,568	5.2	11.0	5.4	11.6	28.3	37.0	1.5
Connecticut.....	384,636	25,512	1,107	4,968	4,541	4,936	9,960	39,577	17,678	57,381	118,751	116,317	9,420	6.6	10.8	4.6	14.9	30.9	30.2	2.4
MIDDLE ATLANTIC:																				
New York.......	3,262,278	344,160	16,600	68,636	65,822	67,859	125,243	498,432	162,490	423,416	911,452	784,287	138,041	10.5	15.3	5.0	13.0	27.9	24.0	4.2
New Jersey......	850,038	74,061	3,733	15,232	13,901	13,966	27,229	101,391	35,150	117,834	256,148	232,193	33,261	8.7	11.9	4.1	13.9	30.1	27.3	3.9
Pennsylvania....	1,240,415	68,012	3,200	12,847	12,239	13,103	26,623	126,521	42,443	192,796	409,910	357,880	42,853	5.5	10.2	3.4	15.5	33.0	28.9	3.5
E. N. CENTRAL:																				
Ohio...........	649,220	38,412	1,633	7,085	6,819	7,242	15,633	75,400	24,776	109,697	196,401	182,751	21,783	5.9	11.6	3.8	16.9	30.3	28.1	3.4
Indiana.........	142,999	10,194	350	1,637	1,874	2,093	4,240	15,698	5,188	19,856	37,076	46,642	8,345	7.1	11.0	3.6	13.9	25.9	32.6	5.8
Illinois.........	1,242,447	89,002	3,040	15,050	16,510	17,359	37,043	140,310	41,737	174,590	355,021	393,486	48,301	7.2	11.3	3.4	14.1	28.6	31.7	3.9
Michigan........	852,758	94,257	3,438	16,279	16,117	16,421	42,002	133,423	45,222	125,000	192,507	235,809	25,934	11.1	15.6	5.3	14.7	22.6	27.7	3.0
Wisconsin.......	388,299	18,488	677	3,033	3,166	3,540	8,072	25,075	6,962	39,196	85,306	195,241	18,031	4.8	6.5	1.8	10.1	22.0	50.3	4.6
W. N. CENTRAL:																				
Minnesota.......	390,790	9,391	421	1,523	1,552	1,703	4,192	18,041	9,628	31,884	90,788	220,002	11,056	2.4	4.6	2.5	8.2	23.2	56.3	2.8
Iowa...........	168,250	4,802	266	784	876	914	1,962	8,682	3,975	13,453	29,148	102,519	5,671	2.9	5.2	2.4	8.0	17.3	60.9	3.4
Missouri........	153,085	6,697	214	1,041	1,196	1,260	2,986	12,723	5,009	14,714	39,732	66,646	7,565	4.4	8.3	3.3	9.6	26.0	43.5	4.9
North Dakota....	105,871	2,365	116	403	420	471	949	2,754	2,203	7,515	32,076	55,090	3,868	2.2	2.6	2.1	7.1	30.3	52.0	3.7
South Dakota....	66,061	1,402	91	272	231	213	595	2,226	1,371	4,514	14,546	38,836	3,106	2.1	3.4	2.1	6.8	22.0	58.8	4.8
Nebraska.......	119,199	3,079	110	431	534	700	1,304	6,202	3,088	10,412	22,581	68,747	5,030	2.6	5.3	2.6	8.7	18.9	57.7	4.2
Kansas.........	80,897	3,820	158	643	850	917	1,252	4,671	3,875	5,260	13,953	45,157	4,161	4.7	5.8	4.8	6.5	17.2	55.8	5.1
SOUTH ATLANTIC:																				
Delaware.......	17,025	951	47	235	174	156	339	1,511	759	2,454	4,923	5,025	1,402	5.6	8.9	4.5	14.4	28.9	29.5	8.2
Maryland.......	96,330	4,238	223	745	736	745	1,789	8,640	3,654	11,829	26,286	33,043	8,640	4.4	9.0	3.8	12.3	27.3	34.3	9.0
Dist. of Columbia.	30,733	2,219	110	454	378	436	841	3,785	1,469	3,281	7,718	8,955	3,306	7.2	12.3	4.7	10.7	25.1	29.1	10.8
Virginia........	24,367	1,112	57	259	170	205	412	2,259	1,316	2,841	6,616	8,290	1,933	4.6	9.3	5.4	11.7	27.2	34.0	7.9
West Virginia....	51,865	2,406	113	421	443	516	913	6,509	3,104	10,684	17,464	9,334	2,304	4.6	12.5	6.1	20.6	33.7	18.0	4.4
North Carolina...	8,969	599	20	145	97	97	240	1,162	559	1,064	2,117	2,527	941	6.7	13.0	6.2	11.9	23.6	28.2	10.5
South Carolina...	5,358	227	7	34	43	56	87	573	331	671	1,355	1,688	513	4.2	10.7	6.2	12.5	25.3	31.5	9.6
Georgia.........	14,303	706	22	167	125	156	236	1,480	749	1,586	3,898	4,741	1,143	4.9	10.3	5.2	11.1	27.3	33.1	8.0
Florida.........	69,747	4,295	144	694	568	636	2,253	8,848	5,051	6,606	16,929	22,209	5,200	6.2	12.7	8.1	9.5	24.3	31.8	7.5
E. S. CENTRAL:																				
Kentucky........	22,007	955	28	100	195	165	407	1,642	533	1,726	4,187	11,330	1,634	4.3	7.5	2.4	7.8	19.0	51.5	7.4
Tennessee.......	13,251	573	20	115	143	107	188	1,123	474	1,197	3,154	5,139	1,591	4.3	8.5	3.6	9.0	23.8	38.8	12.0
Alabama........	16,061	498	19	81	102	96	200	1,223	673	1,598	4,458	6,156	1,455	3.1	7.6	4.2	9.9	27.8	38.3	9.1
Mississippi......	8,045	396	24	49	90	76	157	773	396	818	2,295	2,601	766	4.9	9.6	4.9	10.2	28.5	32.3	9.5
W. S. CENTRAL:																				
Arkansas........	10,632	291	8	35	30	76	142	566	254	698	2,288	5,492	1,043	2.7	5.3	2.4	6.6	21.5	51.7	9.8
Louisiana.......	37,076	1,580	75	263	272	353	617	2,555	1,802	2,409	9,209	15,763	3,758	4.3	6.9	4.9	6.5	24.8	42.5	10.1
Oklahoma.......	30,558	1,267	77	164	200	244	522	1,868	1,345	2,122	6,021	14,296	3,639	4.1	6.1	4.4	6.9	19.7	46.8	11.9
Texas..........	362,287	36,951	1,759	5,459	7,655	8,382	13,606	54,870	59,799	51,152	66,554	74,905	18,056	10.2	15.1	16.5	14.1	18.4	20.7	5.0
MOUNTAIN:																				
Montana........	75,903	3,412	182	604	713	690	1,223	4,289	3,421	8,507	22,930	29,007	4,337	4.5	5.7	4.5	11.2	30.2	38.2	5.7
Idaho..........	32,284	1,422	50	269	228	302	573	2,380	1,562	2,931	7,057	14,130	1,902	4.4	7.4	4.8	9.1	24.6	43.8	5.9
Wyoming........	23,343	1,408	46	184	289	316	573	2,606	1,593	3,133	6,760	6,662	1,181	6.0	11.2	6.8	13.4	29.0	28.5	5.1
Colorado........	99,875	3,337	85	413	593	795	1,451	7,697	6,193	11,350	26,108	38,929	6,261	3.3	7.7	6.2	11.4	26.1	39.0	6.3
New Mexico......	24,052	1,912	37	221	405	459	790	4,159	3,911	3,116	4,802	4,409	1,683	7.9	17.3	16.3	13.0	20.2	18.3	7.0
Arizona........	65,758	9,103	249	1,641	1,841	2,357	3,015	12,651	12,181	6,806	11,746	9,276	3,993	13.8	19.2	18.5	10.4	17.9	14.1	6.1
Utah..........	48,015	3,315	122	603	664	699	1,227	4,068	2,050	4,839	11,782	19,607	1,754	6.9	8.5	5.5	10.1	24.5	40.8	3.7
Nevada.........	15,095	1,299	75	185	242	202	505	1,837	1,137	1,874	4,284	4,081	583	8.6	12.2	7.5	12.4	28.4	27.0	3.9
PACIFIC:																				
Washington......	255,258	15,361	790	2,918	2,604	2,928	6,121	26,587	14,414	23,079	68,716	90,314	16,787	6.0	10.4	5.6	9.0	26.9	35.4	6.6
Oregon.........	110,440	5,662	204	900	1,006	1,031	2,521	11,759	5,130	10,644	29,115	42,185	5,936	5.1	10.6	4.7	9.6	26.4	38.2	5.4
California.......	1,073,964	91,269	3,450	14,238	15,761	20,231	37,589	180,732	104,369	115,281	254,004	274,120	54,189	8.5	16.8	9.7	10.7	23.7	25.5	5.0

TABLE 12.—YEAR OF IMMIGRATION OF THE FOREIGN-BORN WHITE POPULATION, BY SEX, BY DIVISIONS AND STATES: 1930

DIVISION OR STATE AND SEX	Total foreign-born white	YEAR OF IMMIGRATION: 1925 to 1930: Total	1930 (to Apr. 1)	1929	1928	1927	1925 and 1926	1920 to 1924	1915 to 1919	1911 to 1914	1901 to 1910	1900 or earlier	Unknown	PER CENT OF TOTAL ARRIVING IN—: 1925 to 1930	1920 to 1924	1915 to 1919	1911 to 1914	1901 to 1910	1900 or earlier	Unknown
United States	13,366,407	960,238	42,347	180,684	173,162	181,769	382,276	1,552,096	553,691	1,712,247	3,681,400	4,366,265	540,470	7.2	11.6	4.1	12.8	27.5	32.7	4.0
Male	7,153,709	477,544	20,980	84,812	83,252	92,350	196,150	807,286	289,434	940,428	2,086,255	2,289,353	263,409	6.7	11.3	4.0	13.1	29.2	32.0	3.7
Female	6,212,698	482,694	21,367	95,872	89,910	89,419	186,126	744,810	264,257	771,819	1,595,145	2,076,912	277,061	7.8	12.0	4.3	12.4	25.7	33.4	4.5
New England	1,834,310	119,364	4,332	21,015	19,882	22,309	51,826	205,813	95,442	224,508	500,114	637,808	51,261	6.5	11.2	5.2	12.2	27.3	34.8	2.8
Male	904,742	53,261	2,028	9,037	8,483	9,876	23,837	99,816	44,679	115,302	260,074	307,895	23,115	5.9	11.0	4.9	12.7	28.8	34.0	2.6
Female	929,568	66,103	2,304	11,978	11,399	12,433	27,989	105,997	50,763	109,206	239,440	329,913	28,146	7.1	11.4	5.5	11.7	25.8	35.5	3.0
Middle Atlantic	5,269,042	476,252	23,135	95,010	90,288	93,048	174,771	699,909	223,657	725,996	1,566,552	1,370,435	206,241	9.0	13.3	4.2	13.8	29.7	26.0	3.9
Male	2,761,740	236,122	11,323	44,207	42,894	47,526	90,172	363,895	117,575	388,158	862,966	698,259	94,765	8.5	13.2	4.3	14.1	31.2	25.3	3.4
Female	2,507,302	240,130	11,812	50,803	47,394	45,522	84,599	336,014	106,082	337,838	703,586	672,176	111,476	9.6	13.4	4.2	13.5	28.1	26.8	4.4
East North Central	3,223,924	232,837	8,761	40,616	40,517	42,517	100,426	376,748	115,550	465,540	862,008	1,051,791	119,450	7.2	11.7	3.6	14.4	26.7	32.6	3.7
Male	1,766,458	119,364	4,409	19,444	20,197	22,216	53,098	200,300	63,107	263,927	508,455	552,756	58,549	6.8	11.3	3.6	14.9	28.8	31.3	3.3
Female	1,457,466	113,473	4,352	21,172	20,320	20,301	47,328	176,448	52,443	201,613	353,553	499,035	60,901	7.8	12.1	3.6	13.8	24.3	34.2	4.2
West North Central	1,059,277	26,110	1,111	4,365	4,476	4,647	11,511	50,138	23,350	85,358	239,745	596,066	38,510	2.5	4.7	2.2	8.1	22.6	56.3	3.6
Male	591,094	14,782	660	2,483	2,502	2,751	6,386	26,085	12,309	49,029	140,651	328,632	19,606	2.5	4.4	2.1	8.3	23.8	55.6	3.3
Female	468,183	11,328	451	1,882	1,974	1,896	5,125	24,053	11,041	36,329	99,094	267,434	18,904	2.4	5.1	2.4	7.8	21.2	57.1	4.0
South Atlantic	304,278	15,891	709	2,994	2,564	2,870	6,754	31,540	15,277	39,524	84,856	93,891	23,299	5.2	10.4	5.0	13.0	27.9	30.9	7.7
Male	170,300	7,595	353	1,394	1,189	1,349	3,310	16,210	8,675	23,482	50,547	51,076	12,715	4.5	9.5	5.1	13.8	29.7	30.0	7.5
Female	133,978	8,296	356	1,600	1,375	1,521	3,444	15,330	6,602	16,042	34,309	42,815	10,584	6.2	11.4	4.9	12.0	25.6	32.0	7.9
East South Central	57,665	2,153	87	374	440	385	867	4,471	1,876	5,174	13,842	25,000	5,149	3.7	7.8	3.3	9.0	24.0	43.4	8.9
Male	33,359	1,125	48	189	216	195	477	2,433	1,049	3,155	8,565	14,132	2,909	3.4	7.3	3.1	9.5	25.7	42.4	8.7
Female	24,306	1,028	39	185	224	190	390	2,038	827	2,019	5,277	10,868	2,240	4.2	8.4	3.4	8.3	21.7	44.7	9.3
West South Central	170,232	5,892	341	1,061	1,043	1,110	2,337	9,820	5,533	13,170	36,860	84,571	14,386	3.5	5.8	3.3	7.7	21.7	49.7	8.5
Male	97,320	2,916	168	459	495	558	1,236	5,091	3,131	7,709	22,047	47,995	8,431	3.0	5.2	3.2	7.9	22.7	49.3	8.7
Female	72,912	2,976	173	602	548	552	1,101	4,729	2,402	5,461	14,813	36,576	5,955	4.1	6.5	3.3	7.5	20.3	50.2	8.2
Mountain	287,914	10,624	523	2,228	1,903	1,812	4,158	18,328	11,028	32,455	80,927	118,646	15,906	3.7	6.4	3.8	11.3	28.1	41.2	5.5
Male	169,997	5,924	327	1,239	1,034	1,021	2,303	10,034	5,957	19,774	51,097	68,932	8,279	3.5	5.9	3.5	11.6	30.1	40.5	4.9
Female	117,917	4,700	196	989	869	791	1,855	8,294	5,071	12,681	29,830	49,714	7,627	4.0	7.0	4.3	10.8	25.3	42.2	6.5
Pacific	1,159,765	71,115	3,348	13,021	12,049	13,071	29,626	155,329	61,978	120,522	296,496	388,057	66,268	6.1	13.4	5.3	10.4	25.6	33.5	5.7
Male	658,699	36,455	1,664	6,360	6,242	6,858	15,331	83,422	32,952	69,892	181,253	219,676	35,049	5.5	12.7	5.0	10.6	27.5	33.3	5.3
Female	501,066	34,660	1,684	6,661	5,807	6,213	14,295	71,907	29,026	50,630	115,243	168,381	31,219	6.9	14.4	5.8	10.1	23.0	33.6	6.2
NEW ENGLAND																				
Maine	100,368	6,672	308	1,164	1,181	1,374	2,645	12,809	6,554	8,544	21,781	38,442	5,566	6.6	12.8	6.5	8.5	21.7	38.3	5.5
Male	50,299	3,087	154	535	524	638	1,236	6,228	3,083	4,459	11,362	19,609	2,471	6.1	12.4	6.1	8.9	22.6	39.0	4.9
Female	50,069	3,585	154	629	657	736	1,409	6,581	3,471	4,085	10,419	18,833	3,095	7.2	13.1	6.9	8.2	20.8	37.0	6.2
New Hampshire	82,660	4,123	128	698	596	785	1,916	8,160	4,544	8,265	18,552	35,198	3,818	5.0	9.9	5.5	10.0	22.4	42.6	4.6
Male	41,160	1,950	58	315	273	377	927	4,016	2,122	4,322	9,701	17,342	1,707	4.7	9.8	5.2	10.5	23.6	42.1	4.1
Female	41,500	2,173	70	383	323	408	989	4,144	2,422	3,943	8,851	17,856	2,111	5.2	10.0	5.8	9.5	21.3	43.0	5.1
Vermont	43,061	5,074	186	1,029	1,012	946	1,901	5,933	3,794	4,050	9,066	14,264	880	11.8	13.8	8.8	9.4	21.1	33.1	2.0
Male	22,824	2,683	116	553	534	476	1,004	3,193	2,027	2,193	4,895	7,412	421	11.8	14.0	8.9	9.6	21.4	32.5	1.8
Female	20,237	2,391	70	476	478	470	897	2,740	1,767	1,857	4,171	6,852	459	11.8	13.5	8.7	9.2	20.6	33.9	2.3
Massachusetts	1,054,636	69,205	2,224	11,803	11,115	12,635	31,428	121,055	54,173	126,851	283,918	370,291	29,143	6.6	11.5	5.1	12.0	26.9	35.1	2.8
Male	509,462	29,617	1,009	4,765	4,452	5,306	14,085	57,769	24,778	64,296	145,591	174,526	12,885	5.8	11.3	4.9	12.6	28.6	34.3	2.5
Female	545,174	39,588	1,215	7,038	6,663	7,329	17,343	63,286	29,395	62,555	138,327	195,765	16,258	7.3	11.6	5.4	11.5	25.4	35.9	3.0
Rhode Island	170,714	8,906	383	1,384	1,459	1,655	4,025	18,689	9,041	19,680	48,362	63,498	2,538	5.2	10.9	5.3	11.5	28.3	37.2	1.5
Male	83,151	3,773	167	603	609	705	1,689	8,917	4,122	9,968	24,828	30,398	1,145	4.5	10.7	5.0	12.0	29.9	36.6	1.4
Female	87,563	5,133	216	781	850	950	2,336	9,772	4,919	9,712	23,534	33,100	1,393	5.9	11.2	5.6	11.1	26.9	37.8	1.6
Connecticut	382,871	25,384	1,103	4,937	4,519	4,914	9,911	39,167	17,336	57,118	118,435	116,115	9,316	6.6	10.2	4.5	14.9	30.9	30.3	2.4
Male	197,846	12,151	524	2,266	2,091	2,374	4,896	19,693	8,547	30,064	64,297	58,608	4,486	6.1	10.0	4.3	15.2	32.5	29.6	2.3
Female	185,025	13,233	579	2,671	2,428	2,540	5,015	19,474	8,789	27,054	54,138	57,507	4,830	7.2	10.5	4.8	14.6	29.3	31.1	2.6
MIDDLE ATLANTIC																				
New York	3,191,549	335,952	16,248	67,160	64,449	66,400	121,695	474,984	148,178	416,563	902,493	781,762	131,622	10.5	14.9	4.6	13.1	28.3	24.5	4.1
Male	1,653,170	166,854	7,923	31,083	30,612	33,999	63,237	246,443	77,870	219,635	488,109	395,989	58,270	10.1	14.9	4.7	13.3	29.5	24.0	3.5
Female	1,538,379	169,098	8,325	36,077	33,837	32,401	58,458	228,541	70,308	196,928	414,384	385,773	73,352	11.0	14.9	4.6	12.8	26.9	25.1	4.8
New Jersey	844,442	73,541	3,715	15,145	13,808	13,842	27,031	100,084	34,223	117,261	255,198	231,601	32,534	8.7	11.9	4.1	13.9	30.2	27.4	3.9
Male	443,132	37,386	1,883	7,305	6,751	7,321	14,126	53,490	17,721	61,938	140,066	116,433	16,098	8.4	12.1	4.0	14.0	31.6	26.3	3.6
Female	401,310	36,155	1,832	7,840	7,057	6,521	12,905	46,594	16,502	55,323	115,132	115,168	16,436	9.0	11.6	4.1	13.8	28.7	28.7	4.1
Pennsylvania	1,233,051	66,759	3,172	12,705	12,031	12,806	26,045	124,841	41,261	192,172	408,861	357,072	42,085	5.4	10.1	3.3	15.6	33.2	29.0	3.4
Male	665,438	31,882	1,517	5,819	5,531	6,206	12,809	63,962	21,984	106,585	234,791	185,837	20,397	4.8	9.6	3.3	16.0	35.3	27.9	3.1
Female	567,613	34,877	1,655	6,886	6,500	6,600	13,236	60,879	19,277	85,587	174,070	171,235	21,688	6.1	10.7	3.4	15.1	30.7	30.2	3.8
E. N. CENTRAL																				
Ohio	644,151	37,036	1,614	6,893	6,503	6,920	15,106	74,175	24,069	109,350	195,827	182,314	21,380	5.7	11.5	3.7	17.0	30.4	28.3	3.3
Male	351,985	18,029	751	3,179	3,115	3,363	7,621	37,318	13,265	61,995	115,236	95,563	10,579	5.1	10.6	3.8	17.6	32.7	27.1	3.0
Female	292,166	19,007	863	3,714	3,388	3,557	7,485	36,857	10,804	47,355	80,591	86,751	10,801	6.5	12.6	3.7	16.2	27.6	29.7	3.7
Indiana	135,134	6,884	275	1,176	1,130	1,335	2,968	13,489	4,152	19,460	36,650	46,533	7,966	5.1	10.0	3.1	14.4	27.1	34.4	5.9
Male	76,957	3,630	153	571	581	725	1,600	7,191	2,446	11,444	22,883	25,077	4,286	4.7	9.3	3.2	14.9	29.7	32.6	5.6
Female	58,177	3,254	122	605	549	610	1,368	6,298	1,706	8,016	13,767	21,456	3,680	5.6	10.8	2.9	13.8	23.7	36.9	6.3
Illinois	1,218,158	80,801	2,854	13,895	14,720	15,364	33,968	134,267	37,471	173,020	353,003	392,654	46,942	6.6	11.0	3.1	14.2	29.0	32.2	3.9
Male	657,937	42,394	1,497	6,791	7,423	8,298	18,385	70,980	20,092	94,727	204,326	203,225	22,193	6.4	10.8	3.1	14.4	31.1	30.9	3.4
Female	560,221	38,407	1,357	7,104	7,297	7,066	15,583	63,287	17,379	78,293	148,677	189,429	24,749	6.9	11.3	3.1	14.0	26.5	33.8	4.4
Michigan	840,268	90,502	3,361	15,765	15,189	15,564	40,623	130,234	48,142	124,635	191,378	235,130	25,247	10.8	15.5	5.1	14.8	22.8	28.0	3.0
Male	464,902	45,515	1,648	7,389	7,457	7,913	21,108	71,750	28,597	73,133	114,777	123,465	12,665	9.8	15.4	5.1	15.7	24.7	26.6	2.7
Female	375,366	44,987	1,713	8,376	7,732	7,651	19,515	58,484	19,545	51,502	76,601	111,665	12,582	12.0	15.6	5.2	13.7	20.4	29.7	3.4
Wisconsin	386,213	17,614	657	2,887	2,975	3,334	7,761	24,583	6,716	39,075	85,150	195,160	17,915	4.6	6.4	1.7	10.1	22.0	50.5	4.6
Male	214,677	9,796	360	1,514	1,621	1,917	4,384	13,061	3,707	22,628	51,233	105,426	8,826	4.6	6.1	1.7	10.5	23.9	49.1	4.1
Female	171,536	7,818	297	1,373	1,354	1,417	3,377	11,522	3,009	16,447	33,917	89,734	9,089	4.6	6.7	1.8	9.6	19.8	52.3	5.3

POPULATION

TABLE 12.—YEAR OF IMMIGRATION OF THE FOREIGN-BORN WHITE POPULATION, BY SEX, BY DIVISIONS AND STATES: 1930—Continued

DIVISION OR STATE AND SEX	Total foreign-born white	YEAR OF IMMIGRATION												PER CENT OF TOTAL ARRIVING IN—						
		1925 to 1930						1920 to 1924	1915 to 1919	1911 to 1914	1901 to 1910	1900 or earlier	Unknown	1925 to 1930	1920 to 1924	1915 to 1919	1911 to 1914	1901 to 1910	1900 or earlier	Unknown
		Total	1930 (to Apr.1)	1929	1928	1927	1925 and 1926													
W. N. CENTRAL																				
Minnesota	388,294	8,764	348	1,453	1,426	1,560	3,977	17,540	9,239	31,624	90,478	219,833	10,815	2.3	4.5	2.4	8.1	23.3	56.6	2.8
Male	217,983	4,974	198	843	801	915	2,217	9,166	4,771	18,201	53,609	121,615	5,557	2.3	4.2	2.2	8.3	24.6	55.8	2.5
Female	170,311	3,790	150	610	625	645	1,760	8,374	4,468	13,423	36,780	98,218	5,258	2.2	4.9	2.6	7.9	21.6	57.7	3.1
Iowa	165,735	4,258	237	734	763	739	1,785	8,128	3,339	13,222	28,825	102,447	5,516	2.6	4.9	2.0	8.0	17.4	61.8	3.3
Male	92,129	2,608	166	466	471	461	1,044	4,415	1,817	7,849	17,175	55,374	2,891	2.8	4.8	2.0	8.5	18.6	60.1	3.1
Female	73,606	1,650	71	268	292	278	741	3,713	1,522	5,373	11,650	47,073	2,625	2.2	5.0	2.1	7.3	15.8	64.0	3.6
Missouri	149,390	5,960	201	941	1,054	1,061	2,703	11,998	4,125	14,297	39,227	66,438	7,345	4.0	8.0	2.8	9.6	26.3	44.5	4.9
Male	81,299	3,059	98	446	508	590	1,417	5,990	2,165	7,832	22,700	35,857	3,666	3.8	7.4	2.7	9.6	27.9	44.1	4.5
Female	68,091	2,901	103	495	546	471	1,286	6,008	1,960	6,465	16,527	30,581	3,649	4.3	8.8	2.9	9.5	24.3	44.9	5.4
North Dakota	105,146	2,173	100	392	398	409	875	2,657	2,153	7,479	31,982	54,698	3,771	2.1	2.5	2.0	7.1	30.4	52.2	3.6
Male	60,378	1,245	73	219	230	251	472	1,438	1,098	4,420	18,272	32,020	1,879	2.1	2.4	1.8	7.3	30.3	53.0	3.1
Female	44,770	928	36	163	168	158	403	1,219	1,055	3,059	13,710	22,907	1,892	2.1	2.7	2.4	6.8	30.6	51.2	4.2
South Dakota	65,648	1,337	82	263	220	200	572	2,134	1,296	4,489	14,500	38,792	3,100	2.0	3.3	2.0	6.8	22.1	59.1	4.7
Male	37,665	831	48	164	129	131	359	1,176	743	2,702	8,676	21,952	1,585	2.2	3.1	2.0	7.2	23.0	58.3	4.2
Female	27,983	506	34	99	91	69	213	958	553	1,787	5,824	16,840	1,515	1.8	3.4	2.0	6.4	20.8	60.2	5.4
Nebraska	115,346	2,400	96	381	401	449	1,073	5,301	2,176	10,000	22,080	68,590	4,819	2.1	4.6	1.9	8.7	19.1	59.5	4.2
Male	63,386	1,388	54	229	240	265	600	2,763	1,178	5,628	12,773	37,209	2,357	2.2	4.4	1.9	8.9	20.2	58.8	3.7
Female	51,960	1,012	42	152	161	184	473	2,538	998	4,372	9,287	31,291	2,462	1.9	4.9	1.9	8.4	17.9	60.2	4.7
Kansas	69,716	1,218	38	211	214	229	526	2,380	1,022	4,247	12,672	45,033	3,144	1.7	3.4	1.5	6.1	18.2	64.6	4.5
Male	38,254	677	23	116	123	138	277	1,137	537	2,397	7,356	24,509	1,641	1.8	3.0	1.4	6.3	19.2	64.1	4.3
Female	31,462	541	15	95	91	91	249	1,243	485	1,850	5,316	20,524	1,503	1.7	4.0	1.5	5.9	16.9	65.2	4.8
SOUTH ATLANTIC																				
Delaware	16,885	938	45	233	189	155	336	1,502	757	2,441	4,900	4,998	1,349	5.6	8.9	4.5	14.5	29.0	29.6	8.0
Male	9,281	465	28	107	80	83	167	740	387	1,349	2,785	2,576	979	5.0	8.0	4.2	14.5	30.0	27.8	10.5
Female	7,604	473	17	126	89	72	169	762	370	1,092	2,115	2,422	370	6.2	10.0	4.9	14.4	27.8	31.9	4.9
Maryland	95,093	4,147	219	728	718	728	1,754	8,483	3,542	11,751	26,108	32,882	8,170	4.4	8.9	3.7	12.4	27.5	34.6	8.6
Male	50,266	2,030	119	334	318	384	875	4,309	2,012	6,559	14,446	16,689	4,221	4.0	9.6	4.0	13.0	28.7	33.2	8.4
Female	44,827	2,117	100	394	400	344	879	4,174	1,530	5,192	11,662	16,203	3,949	4.7	9.3	3.4	11.6	26.0	36.1	8.8
Dist. of Columbia	29,932	2,100	99	422	352	413	814	3,642	1,389	3,213	7,618	8,870	3,100	7.0	12.2	4.6	10.7	25.5	29.6	10.4
Male	15,652	943	49	198	159	180	357	1,739	721	1,760	4,203	4,509	1,652	6.0	11.1	4.6	11.2	27.3	29.2	10.6
Female	14,280	1,157	50	224	193	233	457	1,903	668	1,453	3,350	4,301	1,448	8.1	13.3	4.7	10.2	23.5	30.1	10.1
Virginia	23,820	1,072	57	247	171	201	396	2,176	1,249	2,798	6,530	8,176	1,819	4.5	9.1	5.2	11.7	27.4	34.3	7.6
Male	13,701	509	22	116	77	86	208	1,110	701	1,691	3,899	4,092	1,099	3.7	8.1	5.1	12.3	28.5	34.2	8.0
Female	10,119	563	35	131	94	115	188	1,066	548	1,107	2,631	3,484	720	5.6	10.5	5.4	10.9	26.0	34.4	7.1
West Virginia	51,520	2,363	112	417	439	508	887	6,436	3,100	10,654	17,408	9,301	2,258	4.6	12.5	6.0	20.7	33.8	18.1	4.4
Male	32,864	1,173	48	184	220	248	473	3,651	2,018	7,076	11,972	5,702	1,272	3.6	11.1	6.1	21.5	36.4	17.4	3.9
Female	18,656	1,190	64	233	219	260	414	2,785	1,082	3,578	5,436	3,599	986	6.4	14.9	5.8	19.2	29.1	19.3	5.3
North Carolina	8,788	584	19	141	94	93	237	1,131	539	1,048	2,079	2,495	912	6.6	12.9	6.1	11.9	23.7	28.4	10.4
Male	5,089	283	6	74	51	42	110	544	315	683	1,307	1,466	491	5.6	10.7	6.2	13.4	25.7	28.8	9.6
Female	3,699	301	13	67	43	51	127	587	224	365	772	1,029	421	8.1	15.9	6.1	9.9	20.9	27.8	11.4
South Carolina	5,266	226	7	34	42	56	87	565	320	663	1,337	1,659	496	4.3	10.7	6.1	12.6	25.4	31.5	9.4
Male	3,120	101	4	15	17	23	42	282	188	427	855	1,015	252	3.2	9.0	6.0	13.7	27.4	32.5	8.1
Female	2,146	125	3	19	25	33	45	283	132	236	482	644	244	5.8	13.2	6.2	11.0	22.5	30.0	11.4
Georgia	13,917	674	21	162	118	148	225	1,414	715	1,546	3,839	4,652	1,077	4.8	10.2	5.1	11.1	27.6	33.4	7.7
Male	8,175	352	13	92	64	66	117	694	417	954	2,409	2,736	613	4.3	8.5	5.1	11.7	29.5	33.5	7.5
Female	5,742	322	8	70	54	82	108	720	298	592	1,430	1,916	464	5.6	12.5	5.2	10.3	24.9	33.4	8.1
Florida	59,057	3,787	130	610	461	568	2,018	6,191	3,666	5,410	15,037	20,848	4,118	6.4	10.5	6.2	9.2	25.5	35.3	7.0
Male	32,152	1,739	64	274	203	237	961	3,141	1,916	2,983	8,606	11,631	2,136	5.4	9.8	6.0	9.3	26.8	36.2	6.6
Female	26,905	2,048	66	336	258	331	1,057	3,050	1,750	2,427	6,431	9,217	1,982	7.6	11.3	6.5	9.0	23.9	34.3	7.4
E. S. CENTRAL																				
Kentucky	21,840	930	27	151	184	184	404	1,607	511	1,716	4,183	11,309	1,604	4.3	7.4	2.3	7.9	19.1	51.8	7.3
Male	12,292	504	13	75	93	91	232	908	304	1,110	2,636	5,044	886	4.1	7.4	2.5	9.0	21.4	48.4	7.2
Female	9,548	426	14	76	91	73	172	699	207	606	1,527	5,365	718	4.5	7.3	2.2	6.3	16.0	56.2	7.5
Tennessee	13,066	550	20	112	135	99	184	1,099	457	1,182	3,124	5,105	1,549	4.2	8.4	3.5	9.0	23.9	39.1	11.9
Male	7,394	282	13	60	64	53	92	584	248	682	1,874	2,031	793	3.8	7.9	3.4	9.2	25.3	39.6	10.7
Female	5,672	268	7	52	71	46	92	515	209	500	1,250	2,174	756	4.7	9.1	3.7	8.8	22.0	38.3	13.3
Alabama	15,710	471	19	73	95	92	192	1,183	629	1,572	4,399	6,090	1,366	3.0	7.5	4.0	10.0	28.0	38.8	8.7
Male	9,326	230	7	35	47	39	102	633	337	925	2,713	3,613	875	2.5	6.8	3.6	9.9	29.1	38.7	9.4
Female	6,384	241	12	38	48	53	90	550	292	647	1,686	2,477	491	3.8	8.6	4.6	10.1	26.4	38.8	7.7
Mississippi	7,049	202	21	38	28	30	87	582	279	704	2,156	2,496	630	2.9	8.3	4.0	10.0	30.6	35.4	8.9
Male	4,347	109	15	19	12	12	51	308	160	438	1,342	1,644	346	2.5	7.1	3.7	10.1	30.9	37.8	8.0
Female	2,702	93	6	19	14	18	36	274	119	266	814	852	284	3.4	10.1	4.4	9.8	30.1	31.5	10.5
W. S. CENTRAL																				
Arkansas	10,173	220	6	29	25	52	107	468	208	651	2,240	5,430	956	2.2	4.6	2.0	6.4	22.0	53.4	9.3
Male	6,006	105	3	10	12	26	54	217	101	374	1,360	3,272	568	1.7	3.6	1.7	6.2	22.8	54.5	9.5
Female	4,167	121	3	19	13	33	53	251	107	277	871	2,158	382	2.9	6.0	2.6	6.6	20.9	51.8	9.2
Louisiana	34,910	1,196	64	222	206	261	443	2,214	1,466	2,284	8,936	15,496	3,318	3.4	6.3	4.2	6.5	25.6	44.4	9.5
Male	20,376	577	35	101	88	136	217	1,194	871	1,373	5,305	8,918	2,238	2.8	5.9	4.3	6.7	26.0	43.8	11.0
Female	14,534	619	29	121	118	125	226	1,020	595	911	3,631	6,578	1,080	4.3	7.0	4.1	6.3	25.0	45.9	7.4

YEAR OF IMMIGRATION

TABLE 12.—YEAR OF IMMIGRATION OF THE FOREIGN-BORN WHITE POPULATION, BY SEX, BY DIVISIONS AND STATES: 1930—Continued

DIVISION OR STATE AND SEX	Total foreign-born white	YEAR OF IMMIGRATION												PER CENT OF TOTAL ARRIVING IN—						
		1925 to 1930						1920 to 1924	1915 to 1919	1911 to 1914	1901 to 1910	1900 or earlier	Unknown	1925 to 1930	1920 to 1924	1915 to 1919	1911 to 1914	1901 to 1910	1900 or earlier	Unknown
		Total	1930 (to Apr. 1)	1929	1928	1927	1925 and 1926													
W. S. CENTRAL—Continued																				
Oklahoma	26,753	690	54	101	124	118	293	1,363	672	1,839	5,511	14,061	2,617	2.6	5.1	2.5	6.9	20.6	52.6	9.8
Male	15,544	382	30	49	62	71	170	685	367	1,108	3,312	8,345	1,345	2.5	4.4	2.4	7.1	21.3	53.7	8.7
Female	11,209	308	24	52	62	47	123	678	305	731	2,199	5,716	1,272	2.7	6.0	2.7	6.5	19.6	51.0	11.3
Texas	98,396	3,780	217	709	688	672	1,494	5,775	3,187	8,396	20,173	49,584	7,501	3.8	5.9	3.2	8.5	20.5	50.4	7.6
Male	55,394	1,852	100	299	333	325	795	2,995	1,792	4,854	12,061	27,560	4,280	3.3	5.4	3.2	8.8	21.8	49.8	7.7
Female	43,002	1,928	117	410	355	347	699	2,780	1,395	3,542	8,112	22,024	3,221	4.5	6.5	3.2	8.2	18.9	51.2	7.5
MOUNTAIN																				
Montana	72,961	2,847	163	620	553	457	1,054	3,776	3,004	8,321	22,528	28,599	3,886	3.9	5.2	4.1	11.4	30.9	39.2	5.3
Male	44,899	1,739	116	383	326	293	621	2,110	1,584	5,183	14,046	17,535	2,102	3.9	4.7	3.5	11.5	32.6	39.1	4.7
Female	28,062	1,108	47	237	227	164	433	1,666	1,420	3,138	7,882	11,064	1,784	3.9	5.9	5.1	11.2	28.1	39.4	6.4
Idaho	30,454	1,200	46	250	180	227	497	2,010	1,202	2,769	7,597	13,907	1,763	3.9	6.6	4.0	9.1	24.9	45.7	5.8
Male	18,947	745	30	159	105	139	312	1,187	682	1,737	5,023	8,639	934	3.9	6.3	3.6	9.2	26.5	45.6	4.9
Female	11,507	455	16	91	75	88	185	823	520	1,032	2,574	5,268	829	4.0	7.2	4.6	9.0	22.4	45.8	7.2
Wyoming	19,658	699	30	147	138	112	272	1,658	810	2,778	6,161	6,497	1,055	3.6	8.4	4.1	14.1	31.3	33.1	5.4
Male	12,439	440	17	95	84	72	172	894	472	1,821	4,220	3,992	600	3.5	7.2	3.8	14.6	33.9	32.1	4.8
Female	7,219	259	13	52	54	40	100	764	338	957	1,941	2,505	455	3.6	10.6	4.7	13.3	26.9	34.7	6.3
Colorado	85,406	1,737	59	268	306	340	764	4,412	2,194	9,713	23,749	38,364	5,237	2.0	5.2	2.6	11.4	27.8	44.9	6.1
Male	48,004	943	40	148	161	184	410	2,329	1,184	5,588	14,006	21,439	2,515	2.0	4.9	2.5	11.6	29.2	44.7	5.2
Female	37,402	794	19	120	145	156	354	2,083	1,010	4,125	9,743	16,925	2,722	2.1	5.6	2.7	11.0	26.0	45.3	7.3
New Mexico	7,797	273	13	54	50	37	119	634	379	995	2,109	2,845	562	3.5	8.1	4.9	12.8	27.0	36.5	7.2
Male	4,755	134	8	29	25	18	54	356	219	634	1,373	1,732	307	2.8	7.5	4.6	13.3	28.9	36.4	6.5
Female	3,042	139	5	25	25	19	65	278	160	361	730	1,113	255	4.6	9.1	5.3	11.9	24.2	36.6	8.4
Arizona	15,591	746	41	184	125	117	279	1,369	871	1,767	4,269	5,273	1,296	4.8	8.8	5.6	11.3	27.4	33.8	8.3
Male	9,392	390	22	105	66	57	140	778	463	1,061	2,786	3,210	704	4.2	8.3	4.9	11.3	29.7	34.2	7.5
Female	6,199	356	19	79	59	60	139	591	408	706	1,483	2,063	592	5.7	9.5	6.6	11.4	23.9	33.3	9.5
Utah	43,772	2,509	112	582	458	428	929	3,295	1,851	4,487	10,724	19,279	1,627	5.7	7.5	4.2	10.3	24.5	44.0	3.7
Male	22,978	1,127	57	241	205	195	429	1,626	923	2,583	6,225	9,713	781	4.9	7.1	4.0	11.2	27.1	42.3	3.4
Female	20,794	1,382	55	341	253	233	500	1,669	928	1,904	4,499	9,566	846	6.6	8.0	4.5	9.2	21.6	46.0	4.1
Nevada	12,275	613	59	123	93	94	244	1,174	711	1,625	3,790	3,882	480	5.0	9.6	5.8	13.2	30.9	31.6	3.9
Male	8,583	406	37	79	62	63	165	754	430	1,167	2,818	2,672	336	4.7	8.8	5.0	13.6	32.8	31.1	3.9
Female	3,692	207	22	44	31	31	79	420	281	458	972	1,210	144	5.6	11.4	7.6	12.4	26.3	32.8	3.9
PACIFIC																				
Washington	244,256	14,731	710	2,783	2,503	2,794	5,941	24,747	12,421	21,951	65,095	89,013	16,298	6.0	10.1	5.1	9.0	26.7	36.4	6.7
Male	142,594	7,926	384	1,427	1,407	1,510	3,198	13,496	6,639	12,749	40,806	52,803	8,175	5.6	9.5	4.7	8.9	28.6	37.0	5.7
Female	101,662	6,805	326	1,356	1,096	1,284	2,743	11,251	5,782	9,202	24,289	36,210	8,123	6.7	11.1	5.7	9.1	23.9	35.6	8.0
Oregon	105,475	5,068	197	815	864	878	2,314	10,943	4,401	10,242	27,852	41,371	5,598	4.8	10.4	4.2	9.7	26.4	39.2	5.3
Male	62,078	2,764	116	426	484	483	1,255	5,867	2,363	6,108	17,639	24,254	3,083	4.5	9.5	3.8	9.8	28.4	39.1	5.0
Female	43,397	2,304	81	389	380	395	1,059	5,076	2,038	4,134	10,213	17,117	2,515	5.3	11.7	4.7	9.5	23.5	39.4	5.8
California	810,034	51,316	2,441	9,423	8,682	9,399	21,371	119,639	45,156	88,329	203,549	257,673	44,372	6.3	14.8	5.6	10.9	25.1	31.8	5.5
Male	454,027	25,765	1,164	4,507	4,351	4,865	10,878	64,059	23,950	51,035	122,808	142,619	23,791	5.7	14.1	5.3	11.2	27.0	31.4	5.2
Female	356,007	25,551	1,277	4,916	4,331	4,534	10,493	55,580	21,206	37,294	80,741	115,054	20,581	7.2	15.6	6.0	10.5	22.7	32.3	5.8

POPULATION

TABLE 13.—YEAR OF IMMIGRATION OF FOREIGN-BORN NEGROES, MEXICANS, CHINESE, AND JAPANESE, FOR SELECTED STATES: 1930

[The States for which figures are presented are those having 500 or more foreign born of the specified race]

COLOR OR RACE AND STATE	Total foreign born	YEAR OF IMMIGRATION — 1925 to 1930 Total	1930 (to Apr.1)	1929	1928	1927	1925 and 1926	1920 to 1924	1915 to 1919	1911 to 1914	1901 to 1910	1900 or earlier	Unknown	PER CENT 1925 to 1930	1920 to 1924	1915 to 1919	1911 to 1914	1901 to 1910	1900 or earlier	Unknown
NEGRO																				
United States	98,620	7,582	302	1,357	1,178	1,261	3,489	27,372	18,181	10,951	15,356	7,601	11,577	7.7	27.8	18.4	11.1	15.6	7.7	11.7
Massachusetts	8,934	411	12	53	49	56	241	1,465	1,433	1,391	2,162	1,335	737	4.6	16.4	16.0	15.6	24.2	14.9	8.2
Rhode Island	1,063	17	2	2	1	1	11	124	210	253	270	160	29	1.6	11.7	19.8	23.8	25.4	15.1	2.7
Connecticut	1,378	77	3	18	12	17	27	326	285	233	236	127	94	5.6	23.7	20.7	16.9	17.1	9.2	6.8
New York	57,895	5,508	237	1,027	836	909	2,499	19,797	11,869	6,094	7,439	1,647	5,541	9.5	34.2	20.5	10.5	12.8	2.8	9.6
New Jersey	3,719	288	10	39	41	55	93	815	574	467	609	348	578	6.4	21.9	15.4	12.6	18.8	9.4	15.5
Pennsylvania	2,951	158	2	17	21	29	89	484	475	319	574	408	533	5.4	16.4	16.1	10.8	19.5	13.8	18.1
Ohio	1,077	57	3	9	11	12	22	144	115	114	199	241	207	5.3	13.4	10.7	10.6	18.5	22.4	19.2
Illinois	1,566	100	1	17	15	21	46	269	183	141	276	296	301	6.4	17.2	11.7	9.0	17.6	18.9	19.2
Michigan	2,262	135	----	4	34	22	16	63	471	343	180	401	412	320	6.0	20.8	15.2	8.0	17.7	18.2	14.1
Maryland	872	40		2	4	10	20	71	76	57	137	89	402	4.6	8.1	8.7	6.5	15.7	10.2	46.1
Florida	10,347	480	13	81	102	68	216	2,598	1,940	1,162	1,805	1,291	1,071	4.6	25.1	18.7	11.2	17.4	12.5	10.4
Louisiana	809	45	----	3	7	4	31	127	133	45	102	107	250	5.6	15.7	16.4	5.6	12.6	13.2	30.9
California	1,652	122	8	20	14	24	56	305	205	160	325	226	309	7.4	18.5	12.4	9.7	19.7	13.7	18.7
All other States	4,095	194	7	35	38	39	75	376	340	335	731	914	1,205	4.7	9.2	8.3	8.2	17.9	22.3	29.4
MEXICAN																				
United States	616,998	108,704	3,263	13,999	21,865	28,048	41,529	135,563	136,897	77,398	93,507	38,924	26,005	17.6	22.0	22.2	12.5	15.2	6.3	4.2
New York	2,393	1,035	40	166	209	248	372	571	340	103	139	39	166	43.3	23.9	14.2	4.3	5.8	1.6	6.9
Pennsylvania	2,494	910	19	100	158	226	407	724	415	152	144	20	129	36.5	29.0	16.6	6.1	5.8	0.8	5.2
Ohio	2,037	1,159	12	148	265	272	462	831	401	146	191	36	113	39.5	28.3	15.7	5.0	6.5	1.2	3.8
Indiana	7,411	3,265	73	457	730	743	1,262	2,140	986	360	343	30	287	44.1	28.9	13.3	4.9	4.6	0.4	3.9
Illinois	20,069	7,747	172	1,070	1,684	1,916	2,905	5,186	3,707	1,161	1,201	137	930	38.6	25.8	18.5	5.8	6.0	0.7	4.6
Michigan	9,029	3,432	70	429	854	814	1,265	2,419	1,571	698	533	99	277	38.0	26.8	17.4	7.7	5.9	1.1	3.1
Wisconsin	1,767	832	16	140	170	199	298	440	206	91	100	19	79	47.1	24.9	11.7	5.1	5.7	1.1	4.5
Minnesota	1,986	567	70	58	113	129	197	414	349	208	223	43	182	28.5	20.8	17.6	10.5	11.2	2.2	9.2
Iowa	2,345	522	29	46	110	169	168	522	619	219	287	31	145	22.3	22.3	26.4	9.3	12.2	1.3	6.2
Missouri	3,019	681	13	93	129	190	256	614	805	361	303	47	148	22.6	20.3	26.7	12.0	12.0	1.6	4.9
Nebraska	3,411	664	14	47	133	245	225	897	841	384	381	67	177	19.5	26.3	24.7	11.3	11.2	2.0	5.2
Kansas	11,012	2,584	120	428	628	686	722	2,280	2,835	997	1,236	85	995	23.5	20.7	25.7	9.1	11.2	0.8	9.0
Mississippi	561	128			49	30	49	91	63	86	79	32	82	22.8	16.2	11.2	15.3	14.1	5.7	14.0
Louisiana	1,081	304	11	33	50	75	135	171	183	54	127	74	168	28.1	15.8	16.9	5.0	11.7	6.8	15.5
Oklahoma	3,496	565	19	60	135	123	228	478	639	268	400	156	930	16.2	13.7	18.3	7.7	13.2	4.5	26.6
Texas	262,672	33,041	1,537	4,720	6,930	7,690	12,164	48,941	56,416	42,658	46,120	25,113	10,383	12.6	18.6	21.5	16.2	17.6	9.6	4.0
Montana	1,687	521	19	66	152	138	146	415	337	119	126	34	135	30.9	24.6	20.0	7.1	7.5	2.0	8.0
Idaho	849	185	2	14	39	66	64	242	193	74	71	15	69	21.8	28.5	22.7	8.7	8.4	1.8	8.1
Wyoming	3,011	686	16	33	146	200	291	846	672	296	338	67	106	22.8	28.1	22.3	9.8	11.2	2.2	3.5
Colorado	12,816	1,564	25	133	284	453	669	3,124	3,658	1,478	1,714	348	930	12.2	24.4	28.5	11.5	13.4	2.7	7.3
New Mexico	15,983	1,628	24	165	352	420	667	3,487	3,509	2,093	2,686	1,503	1,077	10.2	21.8	22.0	13.1	16.8	9.4	6.7
Arizona	47,855	8,210	201	1,440	1,685	2,201	2,683	10,987	10,980	4,901	6,041	3,610	2,226	17.2	23.0	22.9	10.2	14.5	7.5	4.7
Utah	2,217	773	6	73	201	208	285	506	446	172	205	28	87	34.9	22.8	20.1	7.8	9.2	1.3	8.9
Nevada	2,078	657	16	58	141	194	248	551	332	184	231	45	78	31.6	26.5	16.0	8.9	11.1	2.2	3.8
Oregon	1,240	437	3	41	97	132	164	270	211	59	113	16	134	35.2	21.8	17.0	4.8	9.1	1.3	10.8
California	191,346	36,060	700	3,896	6,324	10,145	14,995	47,941	45,732	19,896	28,888	7,122	5,707	18.8	25.1	23.9	10.4	15.1	3.7	3.0
All other States	2,233	547	36	85	88	136	202	475	391	180	267	108	265	24.5	21.3	17.5	8.1	12.0	4.8	11.9
CHINESE																				
United States	44,086	5,413	323	1,021	1,146	1,049	1,874	10,543	5,796	3,222	6,302	8,560	4,250	12.3	23.9	13.1	7.3	14.3	19.4	9.6
Massachusetts	1,786	253	10	59	62	59	63	449	174	108	263	299	240	14.2	25.1	9.7	6.0	14.7	16.7	13.4
New York	7,301	980	18	135	161	180	486	2,412	1,599	471	799	608	432	13.4	33.0	21.9	6.5	10.9	8.3	5.9
New Jersey	1,109	122	2	19	25	27	49	203	181	64	156	205	88	11.0	26.4	16.3	5.8	14.1	18.5	7.9
Pennsylvania	1,593	162	5	19	27	40	71	414	224	121	273	320	79	10.2	26.0	14.1	7.6	17.1	20.1	5.0
Ohio	841	125	3	31	28	32	31	216	89	68	133	141	69	14.9	25.7	10.6	8.1	15.8	16.8	8.2
Illinois	2,008	259	11	45	64	45	104	507	285	220	377	346	94	12.8	24.2	13.6	10.5	18.0	16.5	4.5
Michigan	653	81	2	12	26	15	26	174	91	66	102	97	42	12.4	26.6	13.9	10.1	15.6	14.9	6.4
Arizona	618	79	6	13	19	18	23	133	72	41	63	140	90	12.8	21.5	11.7	6.6	10.2	22.7	14.6
Washington	1,287	208	52	20	35	37	58	273	112	94	146	358	96	16.2	21.2	8.7	7.3	11.3	27.8	7.5
Oregon	1,005	77	2	11	24	13	27	141	54	45	143	457	88	7.7	14.0	5.4	4.5	14.2	45.5	8.8
California	20,041	2,310	193	512	491	420	694	4,270	2,253	1,496	3,036	4,167	2,509	11.5	21.3	11.2	7.5	15.1	20.8	12.5
All other States	5,754	747	19	139	184	163	242	1,261	662	428	811	1,422	423	13.0	21.9	11.5	7.4	14.1	24.7	7.4
JAPANESE																				
United States	70,477	2,490	176	654	492	430	738	11,665	14,872	7,087	25,006	7,314	2,063	3.5	16.6	21.1	10.0	35.5	10.4	2.9
New York	2,238	432	43	103	115	82	89	425	387	145	502	202	145	19.3	19.0	17.3	6.5	22.4	9.0	6.5
Idaho	676	8			1	1	6	78	138	66	241	99	46	1.2	11.5	20.4	9.8	35.7	14.6	6.8
Wyoming	562	10		1	1		7	78	101	49	237	75	12	1.8	13.9	18.0	8.7	42.2	13.3	2.1
Colorado	1,386	16	1	1	5		10	133	315	137	576	148	61	1.2	9.6	22.7	9.9	41.6	10.7	4.4
Utah	1,730	26	3	8	5	8	7	224	324	149	777	204	26	1.5	12.9	18.7	8.6	44.9	11.8	1.5
Washington	8,919	320	23	79	54	74	90	1,473	1,775	964	3,281	859	247	3.6	16.5	19.9	10.8	36.8	9.6	2.8
Oregon	2,597	70	2	28	19	7	14	390	400	284	985	325	103	2.7	15.0	17.7	10.9	37.2	12.5	4.0
California	48,477	1,351	96	360	231	226	438	8,340	10,715	4,951	17,018	4,884	1,209	2.8	17.2	22.1	10.2	35.1	10.1	2.5
All other States	3,892	257	8	70	66	36	77	515	657	322	1,409	518	214	6.6	13.2	16.9	8.3	36.2	13.3	5.5

CHAPTER 10

AGE DISTRIBUTION

CHAPTER 10—AGE DISTRIBUTION

INTRODUCTION

At every census some attempt has been made to distribute the population by age. At the first census in 1790, white males 16 years old and over were shown separately from those under 16. In 1800 and 1810 white males and white females were distributed into five age groups—under 10, 10 to 15, 16 to 25, 26 to 44, and 45 and over. In 1820 the same distribution was maintained, and, in addition, white males 16 and 17 were shown as a separate subgroup. At this census the slave and free colored population were first distributed by age (four groups). In 1830 and 1840 the white population under 20 was shown by 5-year periods, and that 20 years old and over by 10-year periods, while the slave and the free colored population were distributed into six age groups. In 1850 the census returns were made on a new basis, the schedule providing a line for each person, in place of a line for each family; and the exact age of each person was reported. In 1850 and 1860, ages were tabulated for whites, slaves, and free colored in 5-year periods under age 20, with children under 1 shown as a separate group, and in 10-year periods from 20 years to 100 and over. In 1860 the Chinese and the civilized Indians were distributed in the same way. In 1870 the native, foreign-born, native white, foreign-born white, colored, Chinese, and civilized Indian populations were distributed by single years up to 4, then by 5-year periods. In addition, ages 18 and 19 were shown separately as one group, to make it possible to obtain the total of militia age (18 to 44), and the age group 20–24 was divided into age 20, and ages 21–24, thus making it possible for the first time to obtain the population 21 years old and over. In 1880, and at each subsequent census, the population, classified by color, nativity, and sex, has been tabulated by single years of age, though by reason of the limitations of space, publication of the figures for areas smaller than the United States as a whole (States, cities, etc.) has been limited rather largely to 5-year periods or broader age groups. Beginning with 1890, the same tabulation by age and sex was made for the native white population classified according to parentage. In 1930, for the first time, age data by single years, by color, nativity, parentage, and sex, are published for the urban, rural-farm, and rural-nonfarm population of the United States, and age statistics by 5-year periods are published for these three areas or types of population in each State.

For various uses to which census material is put, statistics in regard to age are of great importance. Mortality rates attain their full value only when the population can be distributed according to sex and age. Satisfactory birth rates and marriage rates can be computed only when statistics with regard to age, sex, and marital condition are available. The voting strength depends upon the age distribution, and the military strength on the distribution according to age and sex. The differences in the age distribution of the native and the foreign-born population are important in their bearing on the economic, social, and political effects of immigration. Statistics of school attendance and illiteracy would have much less value without the distribution by age. In fact, there are very few questions in vital statistics or sociology which can not be studied with greater profit when the age distribution of the population is taken into consideration.

The age classification is based on age at last birthday, that is, age in completed years.

The statistics of age distribution for continental United States are given in detail in this chapter by States and for cities of 25,000 or more. Age statistics for counties and smaller cities are published in Volume III of the Fifteenth Census Reports on Population, and in the Second Series State Bulletins which are consolidated to make up that volume. For the outlying possessions enumerated in the Fifteenth Census, the age data are presented in a series of bulletins giving population statistics for these areas and in the special report entitled "Outlying Territories and Possessions."

Distribution by single years of age.—In a population unaffected by immigration, the age distribution would be determined wholly by births and deaths. Such a population would be continually replenished by births and depleted by deaths, and the number of survivors at any age would normally be less than the number at any younger age, although some irregularities might result from unusual increases or decreases in the number of births from year to year, or from an excessive number of deaths among the persons born in any particular year or group of years. In the United States the native white population of native parentage most nearly approximates the age distribution of an isolated community. The extreme departure from the conditions of an isolated community is a foreign-born population which is replenished only by immigration. Since a large proportion of migrants are in the early years of adult life, in a foreign-born population the number of persons at any given age below a definite mode will tend to be greater than the number at any younger age, while above the mode the conditions will be reversed.

565

566   POPULATION

The age distribution of the population of the United States is that of a combination of native and foreign-born elements. Since approximately seven-eighths of the population is native, the distribution resembles that of a native population, but in the middle age periods the increase in the number of the foreign born at successive ages tends to balance the deaths among the native population. This condition results in a population with an age distribution abnormally weighted in the middle-age period, which includes not only the productive but the reproductive ages. This abnormality of age distribution has been further accentuated by the rapid fall in the birth rate in the past 30 years or more. Since there were relatively more births a generation ago than there are in the present generation, the number of survivors of those births is relatively high as compared with the expected survival from the births of the present generation. Since the middle years of life are not only the reproductive years but also years of relatively low death rates, the age distribution of the present population of the United States is favorable to a high birth rate and a low death rate. With the cessation of immigration the foreign-born population will be 10 years older in each decade and will soon pass the reproductive years and reach the years of high death rate. The inevitable result will be an increase in the (crude) death rate and a further decline in the birth rate. With no change in fertility or in health conditions, the aging of the population will in another generation bring about a balance of births and deaths, and in the absence of further immigration, a stationary or declining population.

Apart from the abnormalities in age distribution due to immigration, there are some irregularities in the age distribution by single years (see Table 21) which are due to errors in the census returns. Ages may be misstated, either intentionally or through ignorance of the true age on the part of the person giving the information. Where the age is not accurately known, there is a tendency to report it as a multiple of 2 or 5, or even, in the case of ages above 20, as a multiple of 10. There is also a tendency to concentrate on age 21 for men. In general, the degree of inaccuracy is greater for adults than for children. The errors at all ages are greatest for those classes of the population in which the proportion of illiterates is greatest. The returns also exaggerate the number of centenarians, particularly among Negroes and Indians.

At every census the enumeration of children under 5, and particularly of infants under 1, has been incomplete. This is evident from the fact that the number of children in the age group 10 to 14, in six out of the last eight censuses, was greater than the number in the age group under 5 years old at the census taken 10 years earlier. At the censuses of 1870 and 1910 the reverse was true, but in neither case was the difference great enough to allow for the deaths which must have occurred in the 10-year period. In the Negro population, it is probable that the underenumeration of children under 5 has usually amounted to 10 per cent or more. There is also a definite shortage in the enumeration of young children classed as native white of native parentage. On the other hand, the enumeration of native white children of foreign parentage appears to be practically complete. The underenumeration of children is not peculiar to the United States census. It has been noted by a comparison of ages as reported by the British census and in the census returns from some of the countries of continental Europe.

Tables 20 and 21, which relate to the United States as a whole, present the age distribution by single years up to 100, and Table 27 presents a similar distribution for the total population of each State. In Tables 28 and 34, the single-year distribution for persons under 30 is given for States and for cities of 500,000 or more. In Tables 29, 30, 35, and 36 the age distribution by single years is presented for persons 60 to 79 years of age. These tables, which are a new feature in the 1930 reports, are presented for the convenience of those who are studying the problem of old-age dependency.

Distribution by 5-year age periods.—In order to neutralize the effect of the concentration of multiples of 2 and 5, as well as to economize on space (or to make possible the presentation of age statistics for many classes of population in many areas), the age statistics are presented in most of the tables by 5-year periods. For many purposes these statistics are more useful, as well as more compact, because they avoid some of the irregularities of the single-year series and at the same time present the age distribution with a sufficient degree of detail to serve most purposes.

The distribution of the 1930 population of the United States by 5-year age periods is shown in Table 1, with percentages representing the distribution at each census from 1880 to 1930.

TABLE 1.—AGE BY 5-YEAR PERIODS FOR THE UNITED STATES, 1930, WITH PER CENT DISTRIBUTION BY AGE, 1880 TO 1930

AGE	Population, 1930	PER CENT DISTRIBUTION					
		1930	1920	1910	1900	1890	1880
All ages	122,775,046	100.0	100.0	100.0	100.0	100.0	100.0
Under 5 years	11,444,390	9.3	10.9	11.6	12.1	12.2	13.8
Under 1 year	2,190,701	1.8	2.1	2.4	2.5	2.5	2.9
5 to 9 years	12,607,609	10.3	10.8	10.6	11.7	12.1	12.9
10 to 14 years	12,004,877	9.8	10.1	9.9	10.6	11.2	11.4
15 to 19 years	11,552,115	9.4	8.9	9.9	9.9	10.5	10.0
20 to 24 years	10,870,378	8.9	8.8	9.8	9.7	9.9	10.1
25 to 29 years	9,833,608	8.0	8.6	8.9	8.6	8.3	8.1
30 to 34 years	9,120,421	7.4	7.6	7.6	7.3	7.3	6.7
35 to 39 years	9,208,645	7.5	7.4	7.0	6.5	6.2	6.0
40 to 44 years	7,990,195	6.5	6.0	5.7	5.6	5.1	4.9
45 to 49 years	7,042,279	5.7	5.5	4.9	4.5	4.4	4.2
50 to 54 years	5,975,804	4.9	4.5	4.2	3.9	3.7	3.7
55 to 59 years	4,645,677	3.8	3.4	3.0	2.9	2.7	2.5
60 to 64 years	3,751,221	3.1	2.8	2.5	2.4	2.3	2.2
65 to 69 years	2,770,605	2.3	2.0	1.8	1.7	1.6	1.4
70 to 74 years	1,950,004	1.6	1.3	1.2	1.2	1.1	1.0
75 to 79 years	1,106,390	0.9	0.8	0.7	0.7	0.6	0.6
80 to 84 years	534,676	0.4	0.4	0.3	0.3	0.3	0.3
85 years and over	272,130	0.2	0.2	0.2	0.2	0.2	0.1
Unknown	94,022	0.1	0.1	0.2	0.3	0.3	

AGE DISTRIBUTION

Age distribution by color and nativity.—Table 2 shows the per cent distribution by 5-year age periods for the 1930 population of the United States classified by color, nativity, and parentage. The population figures on which these percentages are based appear in Tables 8 and 9.

TABLE 2.—PER CENT DISTRIBUTION BY AGE FOR THE POPULA-
TION OF THE UNITED STATES, BY COLOR AND NATIVITY: 1930
[Per cent not shown where less than 0.1]

| AGE | Total population | NATIVE WHITE | | | | Foreign-born white | Negro | Other races |
		Total	Native parentage	Foreign parentage	Mixed parentage			
All ages	100.0	100.0	100.0	100.0	100.0	100.0	100.0	100.0
Under 5 years	9.3	10.4	11.3	6.6	10.0	0.2	10.3	14.2
5 to 9 years	10.3	11.3	11.9	9.5	10.7	0.9	11.5	14.0
10 to 14 years	9.8	10.9	10.7	11.8	10.4	1.1	10.5	10.3
15 to 19 years	9.4	10.2	9.9	11.9	9.9	2.4	10.5	9.4
20 to 24 years	8.0	9.2	9.1	9.9	9.1	5.0	10.1	10.0
25 to 29 years	8.0	7.9	7.9	7.9	8.3	7.6	9.0	9.3
30 to 34 years	7.4	7.2	7.0	7.6	7.9	9.3	7.3	7.2
35 to 39 years	7.5	6.9	6.7	7.3	7.6	12.2	7.5	6.6
40 to 44 years	6.5	5.8	5.6	5.0	6.5	12.7	5.8	5.2
45 to 49 years	5.7	5.0	4.9	4.0	5.6	11.7	5.3	4.4
50 to 54 years	4.9	4.3	4.2	4.5	4.6	9.9	4.2	3.1
55 to 59 years	3.8	3.4	3.3	4.0	3.4	7.7	2.6	2.1
60 to 64 years	3.1	2.7	2.6	3.2	2.4	6.8	2.0	1.6
65 to 69 years	2.3	2.0	1.9	2.4	1.6	5.3	1.3	1.0
70 to 74 years	1.6	1.4	1.5	1.6	1.0	3.4	0.8	0.6
75 to 79 years	0.9	0.8	0.9	0.7	0.5	2.0	0.5	0.4
80 to 84 years	0.4	.4	0.4	0.2	0.2	1.1	0.3	0.2
85 years and over	0.2	0.2	0.2	0.1	0.1	0.6	0.2	0.2
Unknown	0.1	0.1	0.1			0.1	0.1	0.1

The age distribution of the main color and nativity classes is shown graphically by sex in the eight diagrams on pages 572 and 573. The diagram representing the native white of native parentage is the most symmetrical and represents most nearly the age distribution in a stationary population. That for the foreign born not only shows the peculiarities of age characteristics of a group which is replenished only by immigration, but it shows also the predominance of males in the immigration of the years before 1914. The diagram for the native white of foreign parentage shows clearly the effect of successive variations in the volume of immigration. With the continuance of immigration restriction, the age distribution of this group will in time come to resemble that of the foreign born, but with the modal group from 25 to 30 years younger. The diagram for the native white of mixed parentage is more regular in form than that for the native born of foreign parentage. The apex is narrow because in the earlier years of heavy immigration there were comparatively few marriages between foreign born and natives. Such marriages probably did not become frequent until the native children of foreign parents reached maturity. The restriction of immigration has also begun to modify the age distribution of this class, but the modal age group is 35 years younger than the modal age group of the foreign born and 10 years younger than the modal group of the native white of foreign parentage.

The age distribution of Negroes, if ages were accurately reported, would approximate that of the native whites of native parentage, except that the younger groups would be relatively larger and the older groups smaller, because the life span of Negroes is shorter than that of whites. The age group under 5, as compared with that of 5 to 9, shows roughly the extent of the underenumeration of young Negro children, while the irregularities in older age groups are the result of the tendency to report ages in multiples of 10, 5, and 2. The irregularity of the diagram as between males and females is probably the result of understatement of age by Negro females.

Among the Indians (see Table 15) the proportion of children is larger and that of persons in the middle age groups is smaller than in the case of either the native whites or the Negroes. The chief, and perhaps the sole, explanation of this fact is to be found in the effect of intermixture of white and Indian blood. The children born of marriages between whites and Indians are all classified as Indians, while only one of the parents in each such marriage is thus classified. Since these intermarriages are becoming increasingly frequent, the number of persons of Indian-white mixed blood is increasing and is relatively greater among children than among older persons. The inclusion of these children with the Indian population, together with the exclusion of one parent in each case, increases the proportion of children and diminishes the proportion of adults in the Indian population.

Age distribution by sex.—The distribution of the 1930 population of the United States by sex and 5-year age periods is shown in Table 3, which gives also the sex ratio (the number of males per 100 females) for each age period.

TABLE 3.—AGE BY 5-YEAR PERIODS, BY SEX, FOR THE UNITED
STATES: 1930

| AGE | Total population | Male | Female | PER CENT DISTRIBUTION | | Males per 100 females |
				Male	Female	
All ages	122,775,046	62,137,080	60,637,966	100.0	100.0	102.5
Under 5 years	11,444,390	5,806,174	5,638,216	9.3	9.3	103.0
5 to 9 years	12,607,609	6,381,108	6,226,501	10.3	10.3	102.5
10 to 14 years	12,004,877	6,068,777	5,936,100	9.8	9.8	102.2
15 to 19 years	11,552,115	5,757,825	5,794,290	9.3	9.6	99.4
20 to 24 years	10,870,378	5,336,815	5,533,563	8.6	9.1	96.4
25 to 29 years	9,833,608	4,860,180	4,973,428	7.8	8.2	97.7
30 to 34 years	9,120,421	4,561,786	4,558,635	7.3	7.5	100.1
35 to 39 years	9,208,645	4,679,860	4,528,785	7.5	7.5	103.3
40 to 44 years	7,990,195	4,136,459	3,853,736	6.7	6.4	107.3
45 to 49 years	7,042,279	3,671,924	3,370,355	5.9	5.6	108.9
50 to 54 years	5,976,804	3,131,645	2,844,159	5.0	4.7	110.1
55 to 59 years	4,645,677	2,425,992	2,219,685	3.9	3.7	109.3
60 to 64 years	3,751,221	1,941,508	1,809,713	3.1	3.0	107.3
65 to 69 years	2,770,605	1,417,812	1,352,793	2.3	2.2	104.8
70 to 74 years	1,950,004	991,647	958,357	1.6	1.6	103.5
75 to 79 years	1,106,390	547,604	558,786	0.9	0.9	98.0
80 to 84 years	534,676	251,138	283,538	0.4	0.5	88.6
85 years and over	272,130	117,010	155,120	0.2	0.3	75.4
Unknown	94,022	51,816	42,206	0.1	0.1	122.8

Separate figures are given for each sex in most of the detailed tables in this chapter. In addition, the age distribution for each sex in the total population and in each class of the population is shown by 5-year periods in the diagrams on pages 572 and 573. In

568   POPULATION

order to permit ready comparison of the proportions of males and females in each age period, the percentages shown for the sexes in connection with each diagram are based on the total population in the group or class to which the diagram relates, and not on the totals for the sexes separately. For example, the diagram relating to the native white population of native parentage shows that men in the age period 25 to 29 formed 3.9 per cent of the total native white population of native parentage, of both sexes, whereas Table 8 shows that men in this age period formed 7.7 per cent of the total native white males of native parentage.

Differences in age distribution as between males and females in the total population of the country are to be expected, by reason of the fact that the foreign born, whose age distribution is abnormal, include many more males than females.

This condition explains in part the fact that in the total population a larger proportion of the males than of the females are in the ages 35 to 69, inclusive, while the proportion under 35 years of age is greater among females than among males. (See Table 7.)

This difference in age distribution as between the sexes in the total population, however, is not wholly attributable to the presence of the foreign born, there being also considerable differences among the native classes. Starting with a moderate excess of males over females in the three age periods under 15 years, the returns for the native whites of native parentage show a practical equality of the sexes in the 15 to 19 year period, an excess of females in the 20 to 29 year periods, an excess of males in the 30 to 74 year periods, and an excess of females in the periods above 74 years. Among the native whites of foreign parentage and of mixed parentage, however, the females outnumber the males in most of the age groups, especially in the foreign-parentage class. (See Table 8.)

In general, the age distribution for males is more symmetrical and appears to be more accurate than that for females. In each native population class the number of females in the age group 20 to 24 years is larger than the expected survivorship from the age group 10 to 14 years as returned in 1920. This excess is undoubtedly due to understatement of age, and is not at all peculiar to this census. Prior censuses and the censuses of other countries show similar age discrepancies that can only be accounted for by erroneous returns. The knowledge that these inaccuracies exist does not, however, destroy the value of the returns. On the whole, the returns present a reasonably accurate age distribution, and when greater accuracy is necessary, it is always possible to make adjustments for obvious inaccuracies.

Median age.—The median may be defined in a general way as that item which stands at the midpoint of a series arranged in order of size or value. The me-

dian age in a group of persons would be, therefore, the age of the person standing in the middle of the series if the whole number of persons were arranged in order of age. Or the median age may be defined as that age which divides the population into two equal groups, one-half being older, and one-half younger, than the median. Table 4 shows the median age of the population of the United States in 1930 and 1920 by color, nativity, and sex, disregarding persons of unknown age.

TABLE 4.—MEDIAN AGES BY COLOR, NATIVITY, AND SEX, FOR THE UNITED STATES: 1930 AND 1920

COLOR AND NATIVITY	TOTAL		MALE		FEMALE	
	1930	1920	1930	1920	1930	1920
All classes	26.4	25.2	26.7	25.8	26.1	24.7
White	26.9	25.6	27.2	26.1	26.7	25.1
Native white	23.8	22.4	23.7	22.4	23.9	22.3
Native parentage	23.3	22.7	23.4	22.8	23.3	22.5
Foreign parentage	25.2	21.6	24.9	21.4	25.4	21.7
Mixed parentage	24.9	21.8	24.3	21.3	25.5	22.2
Foreign-born white	44.4	40.0	44.6	40.1	44.0	39.9
Negro	23.4	22.3	23.7	22.8	23.2	22.0
Mexican	20.2	----	21.6	----	18.7	----
Indian	19.6	19.7	20.0	20.4	19.1	19.0
Chinese	32.3	40.2	35.1	42.7	17.3	19.4
Japanese	24.5	30.2	29.7	34.1	15.9	24.0

The difference between the median ages of the two sexes for all classes combined is due in part to the fact that among the foreign born, whose median age is much higher than that of the natives, the males are considerably in excess of the females.

The median ages of the total population and of the white population show uninterrupted increases since 1820. These increases have been due to two causes; first, an increase in average length of life; second, a reduction in the birth rate, which has resulted in a decrease in the proportion of young persons in the total population. Table 5 shows for the total population and for the white and colored population separately, disregarding persons of unknown age, the median age at each census from 1790 to 1930.

TABLE 5.—MEDIAN AGES, BY COLOR AND SEX, FOR THE UNITED STATES: 1790 TO 1930

CENSUS YEAR	ALL CLASSES			WHITE			NEGRO AND OTHER RACES [1]		
	Both sexes	Male	Female	Both sexes	Male	Female	Both sexes	Male	Female
1930	26.4	26.7	26.1	26.9	27.2	26.7	23.1	23.6	22.7
1920	25.2	25.8	24.7	25.6	26.1	25.1	22.5	23.0	21.9
1910	24.0	24.6	23.5	24.4	24.9	23.9	21.0	21.5	20.6
1900	22.9	23.3	22.4	23.4	23.8	22.9	19.7	20.0	19.5
1890	21.4	21.8	21.0	21.9	21.3	21.6	17.8	17.9	17.8
1880	20.9	21.1	20.6	21.3	21.6	21.0	18.0	18.0	18.0
1870	20.1	20.2	20.1	20.4	20.5	20.3	18.5	18.2	18.8
1860	19.4	19.7	19.0	19.7	20.1	19.3	17.7	17.8	17.5
1850	18.8	19.1	18.6	19.1	19.5	18.8	17.3	17.3	17.4
1840	17.8	17.8	17.7	17.9	17.9	17.8	17.3	17.0	17.5
1830	17.2	17.1	17.3	17.2	17.2	17.3	16.9	16.7	17.1
1820	16.7	16.6	16.7	16.5	16.5	16.6	17.2	16.9	17.4
1810	----	----	----	16.0	15.9	16.1	----	----	----
1800	----	----	----	16.0	15.7	16.3	----	----	----
1790	----	----	----	15.9	----	----	----	----	----

[1] For 1930 includes Mexicans, who were classified as white at earlier censuses.

AGE DISTRIBUTION

Divisions and States.—Very considerable differences exist among the nine geographic divisions of the country and among the individual States in regard to the age distribution of the total population and of specific classes of the population. The differences in regard to the total population are in part attributable to variations in the composition according to color, nativity, and parentage. Thus a large proportion foreign born tends to produce a relatively large proportion of adults in the total population.

The differences among the divisions and States with regard to the age distribution of specific classes of the population are due to various factors. Interstate migration has a great influence upon age distribution. Adults, particularly the younger adults, are relatively much more numerous among migrants than in the total population, and therefore a division or State which has lost extensively through interstate migration is likely to have a smaller proportion of persons in the younger and middle ages of adult life in its native population than one which has gained by such migration. The distribution of ages in the urban population is usually decidedly different from that in the rural population, partly by reason of migration from country to city, and consequently the age constitution of the total population of a given class in a State or division is much affected by the proportions urban and rural. Again, the age composition of the several native classes is affected by differences in birth rates and in death rates and by differences in the extent to which changes have taken place in these rates from one time to another. Finally, the age distribution of the foreign born and of the natives of foreign or mixed parentage in any given State or section of the country depends in considerable measure upon the period of time during which immigration to that State or section was most rapid.

Urban, rural-farm, and rural-nonfarm population.—Since there are important differences between urban and rural areas and between the farm and nonfarm population in rural areas, separate figures are given in considerable detail for these three classes or subdivisions of the population. Urban population, as defined by the Census Bureau, is in general that residing in cities and other incorporated places having 2,500 inhabitants or more, the remainder being classified as rural. In three of the New England States, New Hampshire, Massachusetts, and Rhode Island, conditions are exceptional in that the compactly built portions of the towns (townships) are not separately incorporated or politically distinct in any way from the rural territory within the same town; nor is it the usual practice to incorporate even the larger places as cities until they attain a population in excess of 10,000. Consequently, if only the cities were counted as urban the classification would be quite inadequate. In 1920

and 1910 all towns in these three States which had a population of 2,500 or more were classified as urban. This resulted in the inclusion of a considerable number of places that were mainly rural in their general characteristics. In 1930 the special rule for these New England States has been modified so as to place in the urban classification, in addition to the regularly incorporated cities, only those towns in which there is a village or thickly settled area having more than 2,500 inhabitants and comprising, either by itself or when combined with other villages in the same town, more than 50 per cent of the total population of the town.

One other modification has been made in the definition of urban population for use in connection with the 1930 census. This modification extends the classification so as to include townships and other political subdivisions (not incorporated as municipalities, nor containing any area so incorporated) which had a total population of 10,000 or more and a population density of 1,000 or more per square mile.

Since it has been found impracticable to go back and readjust to the new basis the 1920 urban and rural figures as they were tabulated by color, sex, age, etc., they are presented in all tables as established in 1920.

In addition to the classification of the population as urban and rural, which is based on the size and political status (municipal incorporation) of the geographic unit in which the persons live, the population, both urban and rural, is further classified as farm and nonfarm on the basis of a question reading "Does this family live on a farm?"

For the farm population living in urban territory, which forms less than 1 per cent of the total farm population, no detailed tabulations were made; hence the presentation of classified data for the farm population is limited to that part living in rural territory and designated as rural-farm population. This is done partly to simplify the classification (dividing the total population into three groups, namely, urban, rural-farm, and rural-nonfarm) and partly because it is felt that in general the farm families living within the corporate limits of cities or other incorporated places are living under conditions at least somewhat urban, rather than under typical farm conditions.

The rural-nonfarm, or "village," population is made up largely of persons living in small towns or villages, both incorporated and unincorporated, though in many areas there are considerable numbers of families living in the open country but not on farms.

The per cent distribution by 5-year age periods of the urban, rural-farm, and rural-nonfarm population is presented in Table 6, which shows also the number of males per 100 females for the three areas. The population figures on which these percentages and ratios are based appear in Table 16.

570

POPULATION

TABLE 6.—AGE DISTRIBUTION AND SEX RATIOS, FOR THE URBAN, RURAL-FARM, AND RURAL-NONFARM POPULATION OF THE UNITED STATES: 1930

[Per cent not shown where less than 0.1]

AGE	PER CENT DISTRIBUTION BY AGE			MALES PER 100 FEMALES		
	Urban	Rural-farm	Rural-nonfarm	Urban	Rural-farm	Rural-nonfarm
All ages	100.0	100.0	100.0	98.1	111.0	105.0
Under 5 years	8.2	11.1	10.5	103.0	102.9	102.9
5 to 9 years	9.0	12.5	11.1	101.5	103.9	102.8
10 to 14 years	8.6	12.4	9.8	99.7	106.9	101.6
15 to 19 years	8.7	11.3	8.9	91.9	115.1	97.8
20 to 24 years	9.3	8.1	8.5	89.4	116.4	97.9
25 to 29 years	9.0	6.0	7.8	94.5	105.3	101.7
30 to 34 years	8.4	5.5	7.1	98.5	99.4	106.2
35 to 39 years	8.4	5.9	7.0	102.2	100.4	110.9
40 to 44 years	7.2	5.5	6.0	106.2	105.6	113.7
45 to 49 years	6.1	5.2	5.3	105.8	112.9	115.1
50 to 54 years	5.1	4.6	4.6	103.2	125.1	115.1
55 to 59 years	3.9	3.7	3.7	99.5	133.0	113.0
60 to 64 years	3.1	2.9	3.1	95.4	140.5	109.0
65 to 69 years	2.2	2.1	2.5	91.1	145.3	105.8
70 to 74 years	1.5	1.5	1.9	87.7	146.5	106.5
75 to 79 years	0.8	0.9	1.2	81.3	136.7	105.0
80 to 84 years	0.4	0.4	0.6	73.4	116.6	98.9
85 years and over	0.2	0.2	0.3	64.1	87.5	88.4
Unknown	0.1		0.1	119.9	137.2	126.7

The pronounced differences between urban and rural communities and between rural-farm and rural-nonfarm communities in regard to the age distribution of their population are in part attributable to differences in the color or race, nativity, and parentage composition of their population, but there are also pronounced differences between them in regard to the age composition of any one population class. The opportunities to be found in urban communities have attracted large numbers of persons in the more active ages, and, because of the effect of this cityward migration on age distribution, it is impossible to draw directly from the statistics any trustworthy conclusions as to the relative fecundity or the relative longevity of the native whites of native parentage in urban and rural areas.

The age distribution of the foreign-born whites and of the native whites of foreign or mixed parentage in urban and in rural areas, respectively, has been influenced to a very considerable extent by the period—whether recent or remote—during which immigration into these areas has been most rapid. A large proportion of the earlier immigration went to the rural districts, but most of the recent immigration has gone to the cities.

The age distribution of the Negroes in urban and in rural areas is affected by the very considerable country-to-city migration of persons of this race in the active age periods, and probably also by differences in birth and death rates between the two classes of communities.

With respect to the sex distribution, it will be seen that females, particularly in the adult ages, form a much larger proportion of the population in the urban areas than in the rural areas, notwithstanding the fact that the foreign-born whites—a class in which males are considerably in the majority—are centered mainly in cities.

Age by country of origin.—The foreign-born white population has been classified for 1930 by age in combination with country of birth, and the native white population of foreign or mixed parentage has been classified by age in combination with country of birth of parents. Except for a tabulation of the foreign-born white by age and country of birth made in 1910 but not published,[1] this is the first attempt to show the age distribution of the population of foreign derivation by nationality or country of origin.

These figures are summarized for the United States, and for urban and rural areas, in Tables 40 and 41, and are presented by States and for the more important cities in Tables 42 and 43.

---

[1] It is planned to publish these 1910 figures, together with additional details tabulated for 1930, in a special bulletin on the age distribution of the foreign-born white population.

AGE DISTRIBUTION

571

DISTRIBUTION BY SINGLE YEARS OF AGE, FOR THE TOTAL POPULATION, BY SEX: 1930

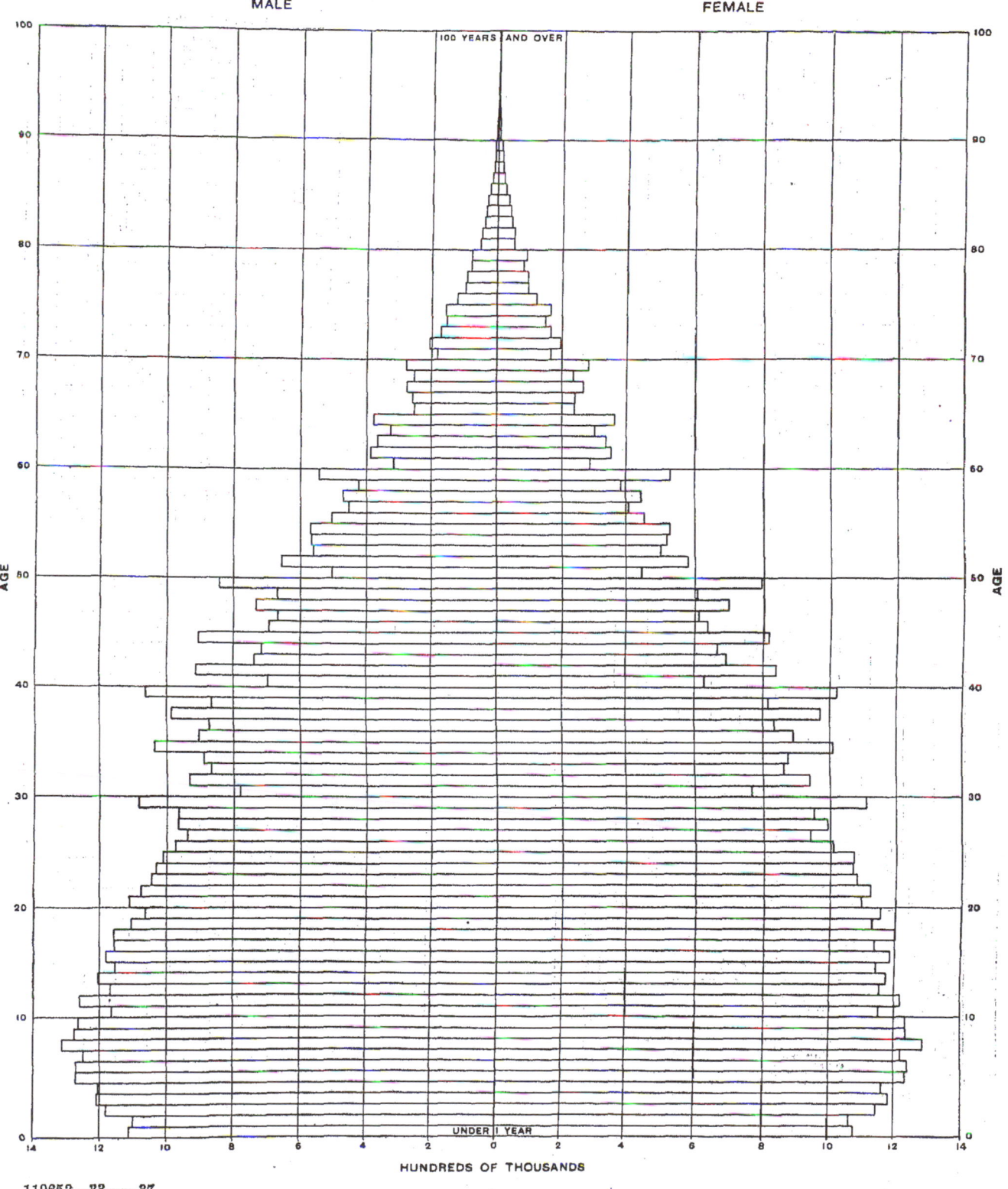

572

POPULATION

DISTRIBUTION BY AGE PERIODS, FOR THE TOTAL POPULATION AND

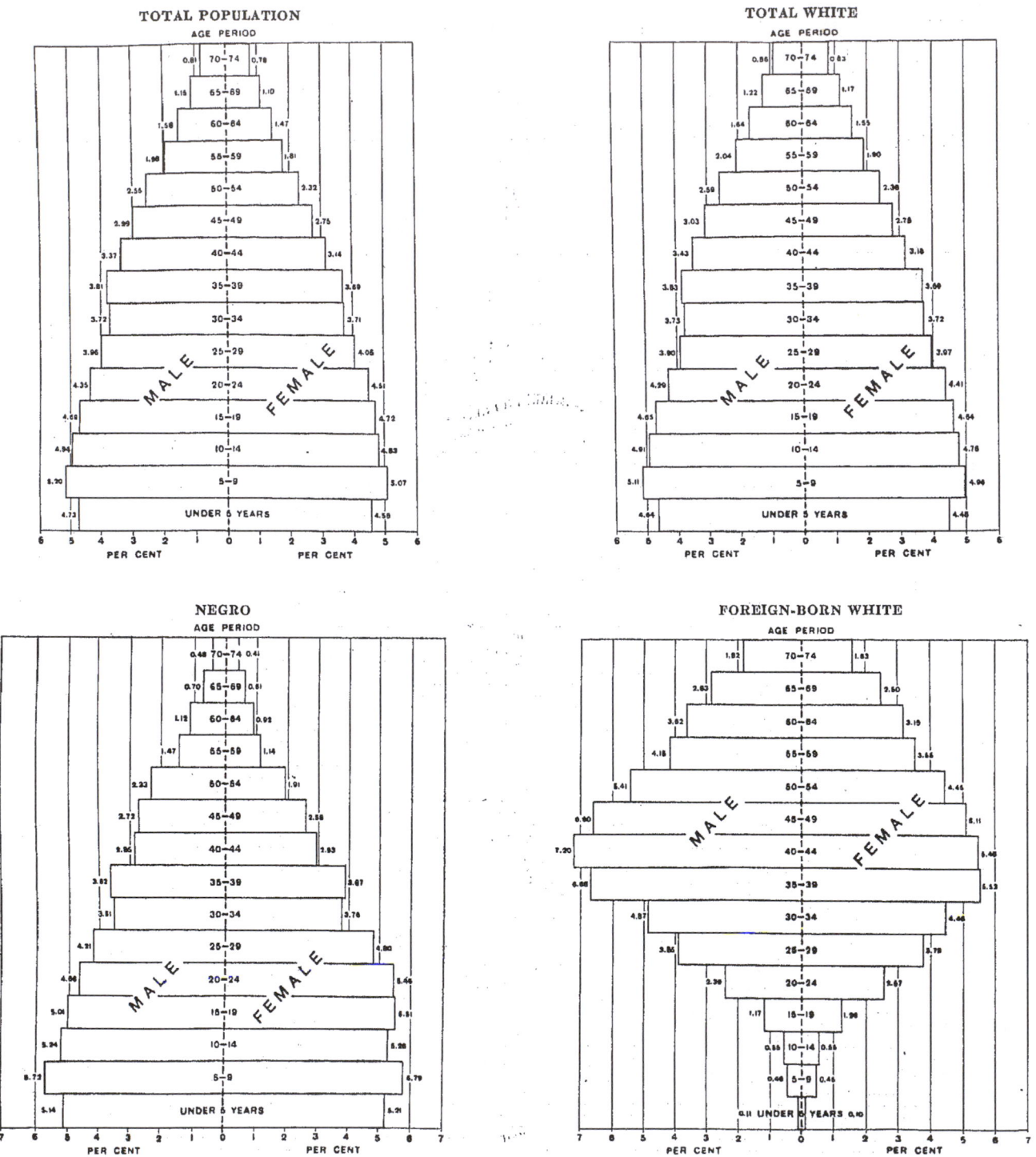

AGE DISTRIBUTION

573

FOR THE PRINCIPAL COLOR AND NATIVITY CLASSES, BY SEX: 1930

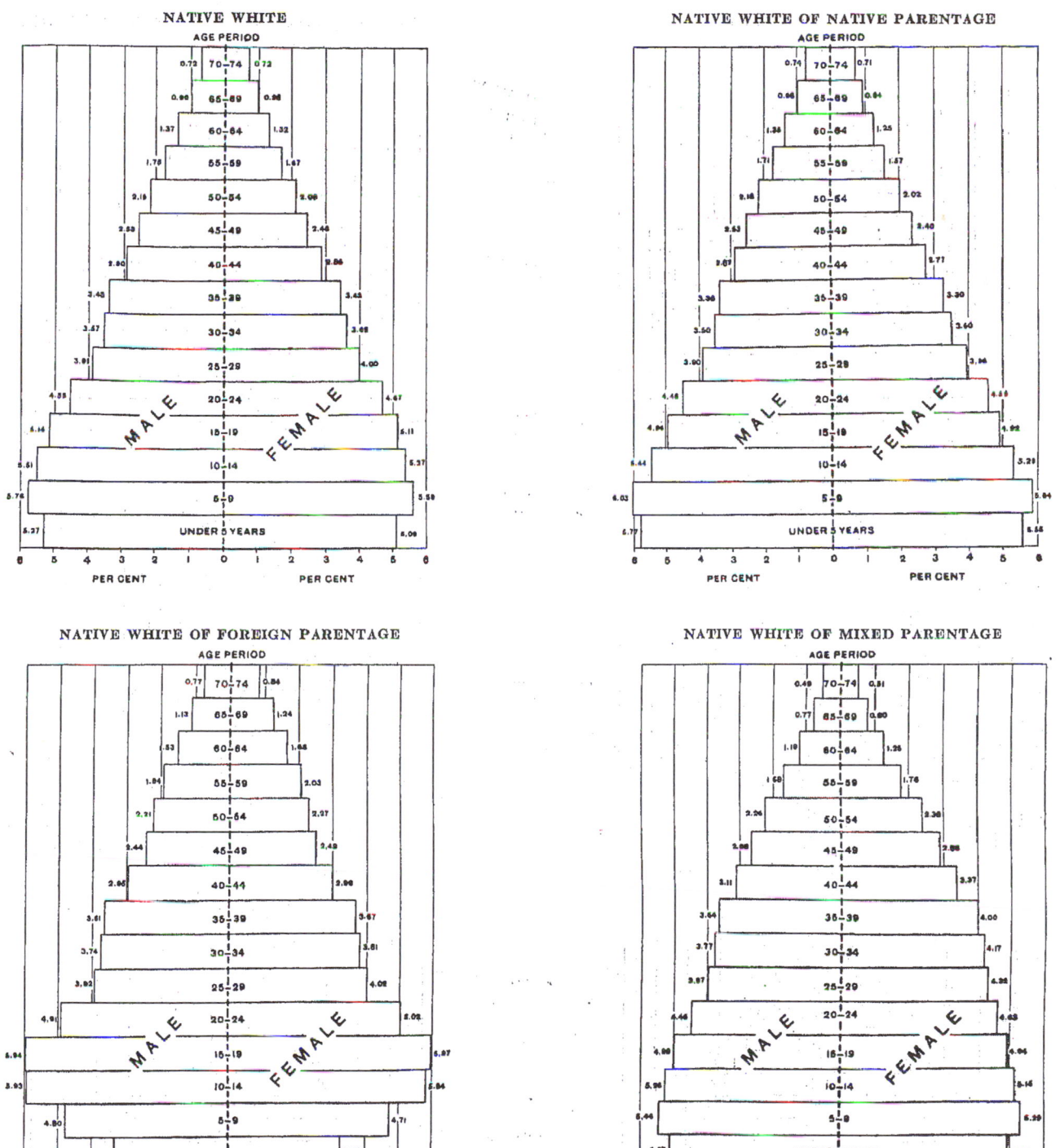

574

POPULATION

DISTRIBUTION BY AGE PERIODS, FOR THE PRINCIPAL COLOR AND NATIVITY

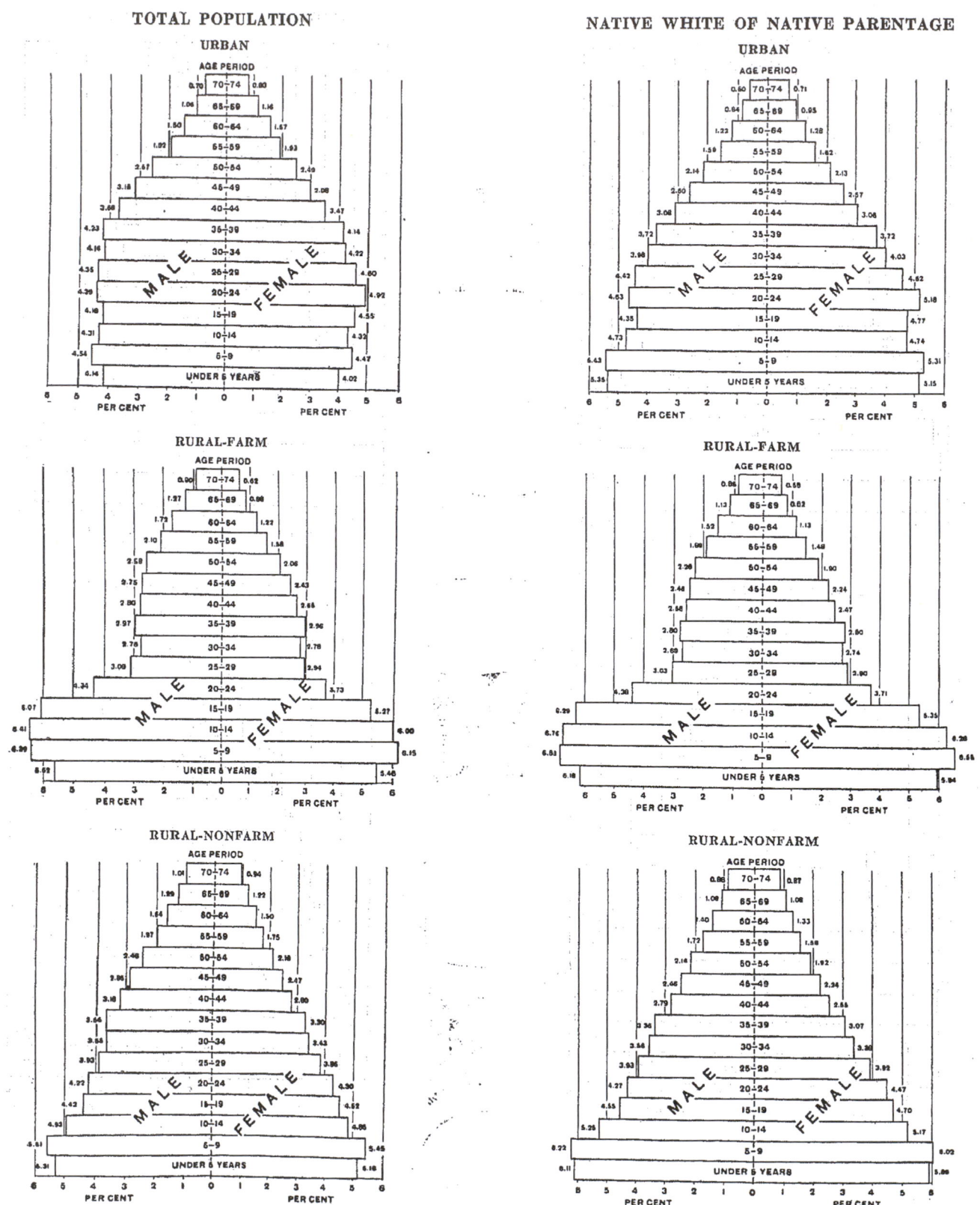

TOTAL POPULATION

NATIVE WHITE OF NATIVE PARENTAGE

AGE DISTRIBUTION

CLASSES, BY SEX, FOR URBAN, RURAL-FARM, AND RURAL-NONFARM AREAS: 1930

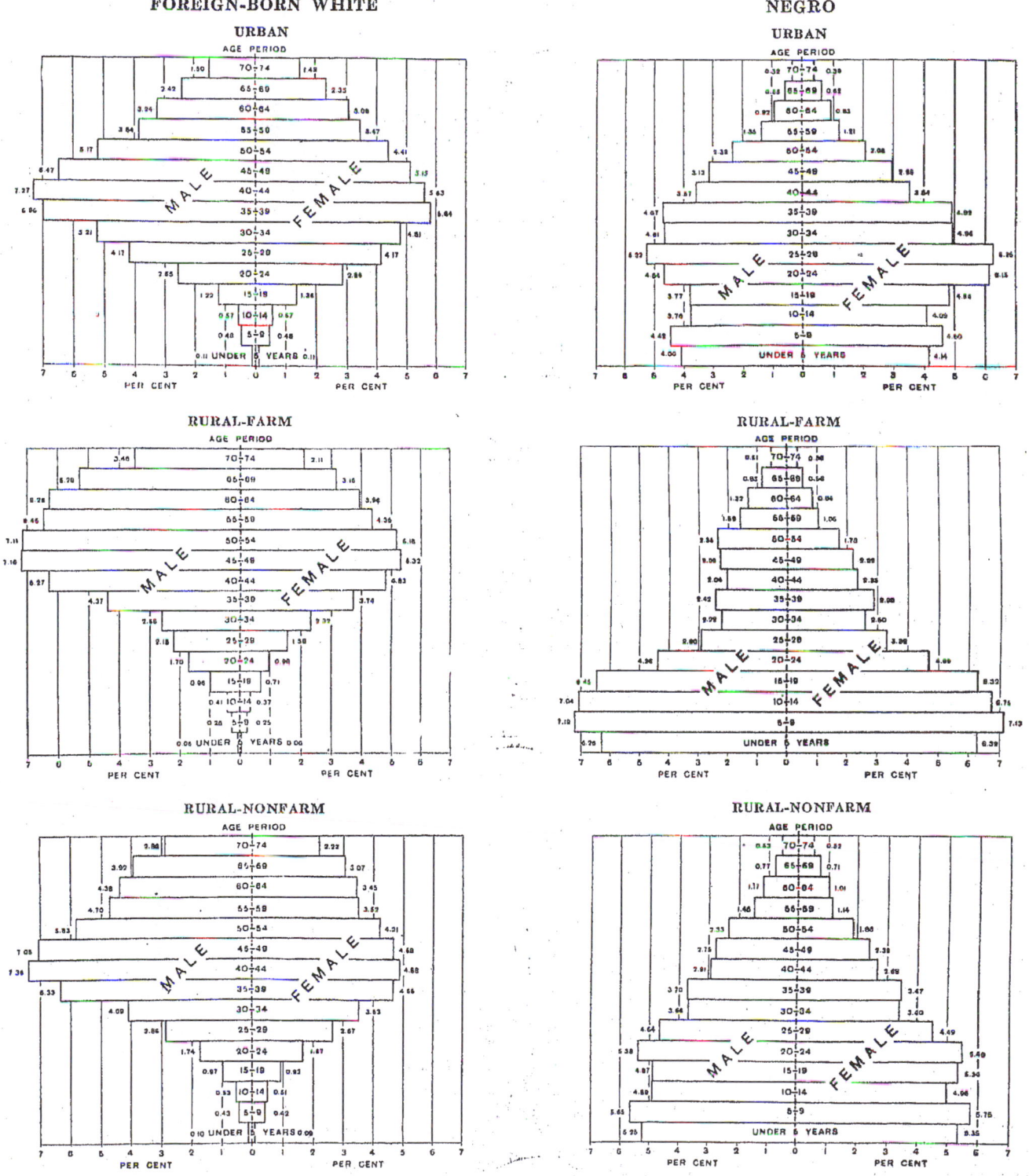

POPULATION

TABLE 7.—AGE BY 5-YEAR PERIODS, BY SEX, FOR THE UNITED STATES: 1850 TO 1930

[Per cent not shown where less than 0.1]

SEX AND AGE	POPULATION									PER CENT DISTRIBUTION								
	1930	1920	1910	1900	1890[1]	1880	1870	1860	1850	1930	1920	1910	1900	1890	1880	1870	1860	1850
TOTAL																		
All ages	122,775,046	105,710,620	91,972,266	75,994,575	62,622,250	50,155,783	38,558,371	31,443,321	23,191,876	100.0	100.0	100.0	100.0	100.0	100.0	100.0	100.0	100.0
Under 5 years	11,444,390	11,573,230	10,631,364	9,170,628	7,634,693	6,914,516	5,514,713	4,842,496	3,497,773	9.3	10.9	11.6	12.1	12.2	13.8	14.3	15.4	15.1
Under 1 year	2,190,791	2,257,255	2,217,342	1,916,892	1,566,734	1,447,983	1,100,475	934,583	629,446	1.8	2.1	2.4	2.5	2.5	2.9	2.9	3.0	2.7
1 year	2,164,565	2,300,605	1,976,472	1,768,078	1,077,008	1,256,956	1,078,803	3,907,913	2,808,327	1.8	2.2	2.1	2.3	1.7	2.5	2.8	12.4	12.4
2 years	2,326,016	2,331,110	2,166,492	1,830,332	1,729,817	1,427,086	1,143,139			1.9	2.2	2.4	2.4	2.8	2.8	3.0		
3 years	2,394,463	2,370,426	2,156,141	1,824,312	1,631,988	1,381,274	1,113,782			2.0	2.2	2.3	2.4	2.6	2.8	2.9		
4 years	2,368,555	2,313,834	2,114,917	1,831,014	1,629,146	1,401,217	1,078,514			1.9	2.2	2.3	2.4	2.6	2.8	2.8		
5 to 9 years	12,607,609	11,398,075	9,760,632	8,874,123	7,573,998	6,479,660	4,814,713	4,171,200	3,241,268	10.3	10.8	10.6	11.7	12.1	12.9	12.5	13.3	14.0
10 to 14 years	12,004,877	10,641,137	9,107,140	8,080,234	7,033,509	5,715,186	4,786,189	3,720,780	2,890,629	9.8	10.1	9.9	10.6	11.2	11.4	12.4	11.8	12.5
15 to 19 years	11,552,115	9,430,556	9,063,603	7,556,089	6,557,563	5,011,415	4,040,588	3,361,495	2,529,792	9.4	8.9	9.9	9.9	10.5	10.0	10.5	10.7	10.9
20 to 24 years	10,870,378	9,277,021	9,056,984	7,335,016	6,196,676	5,087,772	3,748,299	5,726,400	4,277,318	8.9	8.8	9.8	9.7	9.9	10.1	9.7	18.2	18.4
25 to 29 years	9,833,608	9,086,491	8,180,003	6,529,441	5,227,777	4,080,621	3,075,118			8.0	8.6	8.0	8.6	8.3	8.1	8.0		
30 to 34 years	9,120,421	8,071,193	6,972,185	5,556,039	4,578,630	3,368,943	2,562,829	4,021,248	2,825,819	7.4	7.6	7.6	7.3	7.3	6.7	6.6	12.8	12.2
35 to 39 years	9,208,645	7,775,281	6,396,100	4,964,781	3,866,161	3,000,419	2,314,976			7.5	7.4	7.0	6.5	6.2	6.0	6.0		
40 to 44 years	7,990,195	6,345,557	5,261,587	4,247,166	3,185,518	2,468,811	1,939,712	2,614,330	1,846,660	6.5	6.0	5.7	5.6	5.1	4.9	5.0	8.3	8.0
45 to 49 years	7,042,279	5,763,620	4,469,197	3,454,612	2,731,640	2,089,445	1,578,932			5.7	5.5	4.9	4.5	4.4	4.2	4.1		
50 to 54 years	5,975,804	4,734,873	3,900,791	2,942,829	2,326,262	1,839,883	1,367,969	1,585,879	1,109,540	4.9	4.5	4.2	3.9	3.7	3.7	3.5	5.0	4.8
55 to 59 years	4,645,677	3,549,124	2,786,951	2,211,172	1,672,336	1,271,434	876,552			3.8	3.4	3.0	2.9	2.7	2.5	2.3		
60 to 64 years	3,751,221	2,982,548	2,267,150	1,791,363	1,458,034	1,104,219	778,971	888,809	609,926	3.1	2.8	2.5	2.4	2.3	2.2	2.0	2.8	2.6
65 to 69 years	2,770,605	2,068,475	1,679,503	1,302,926	1,010,110	725,876	484,353			2.3	2.0	1.8	1.7	1.6	1.4	1.3		
70 to 74 years	1,950,004	1,395,036	1,113,728	883,841	701,751	495,442	344,358	348,890	257,234	1.6	1.3	1.2	1.2	1.1	1.0	0.9	1.1	1.1
75 to 79 years	1,106,390	856,560	667,302	519,857	393,062	281,065	175,686			0.9	0.8	0.7	0.7	0.6	0.6	0.5		
80 to 84 years	534,676	402,779	321,754	251,512	203,851	146,362	120,077	93,552	77,382	0.4	0.4	0.3	0.3	0.3	0.3	0.3	0.3	0.3
85 to 89 years	205,469	156,539	122,818	88,600	75,240	49,835				0.2	0.1	0.1	0.1	0.1	0.1			
90 to 94 years	51,664	39,980	33,473	23,992	23,045	16,100	16,653	13,778	11,695	-----	-----	-----	-----	-----	-----	-----	-----	0.1
95 to 99 years	11,033	9,579	7,391	6,266	5,648	4,763				-----	-----	-----	-----	-----	-----			
100 and over	3,964	4,267	3,555	3,504	3,981	4,016	3,522	2,953	2,555	-----	-----	-----	-----	-----	-----	-----	-----	-----
Age unknown	94,022	148,699	169,055	200,584	162,165	-----	5,161	51,511	14,285	0.1	0.1	0.2	0.3	0.3	-----	-----	0.2	0.1
MALE																		
All ages	62,137,080	53,900,431	47,332,277	38,816,448	32,067,880	25,518,820	19,493,565	16,085,204	11,837,660	100.0	100.0	100.0	100.0	100.0	100.0	100.0	100.0	100.0
Under 5 years	5,806,174	5,857,461	5,380,596	4,633,612	3,884,869	3,507,709	2,797,257	2,449,547	1,769,460	9.3	10.9	11.4	11.9	12.1	13.7	14.3	15.2	14.9
Under 1 year	1,112,171	1,141,939	1,123,409	969,257	799,373	734,024	557,617	471,804	318,226	1.8	2.1	2.4	2.5	2.5	2.9	2.9	2.9	2.7
1 year	1,099,641	1,165,937	1,001,392	893,263	549,646	638,032	548,058	1,977,743	1,451,234	1.8	2.2	2.1	2.3	1.7	2.5	2.8	12.3	12.3
2 years	1,179,615	1,180,051	1,098,266	925,260	881,406	726,038	581,290			1.9	2.2	2.3	2.4	2.7	2.8	3.0		
3 years	1,210,361	1,194,556	1,084,982	920,335	822,110	697,209	561,729			1.9	2.2	2.3	2.4	2.6	2.7	2.9		
4 years	1,204,386	1,174,978	1,072,547	925,497	832,244	712,406	548,563			1.9	2.2	2.3	2.4	2.6	2.8	2.8		
5 to 9 years	6,381,108	5,753,001	4,924,123	4,479,396	3,830,352	3,275,131	2,437,442	2,109,545	1,640,407	10.3	10.7	10.4	11.5	11.9	12.8	12.5	13.1	13.9
10 to 14 years	6,068,777	5,369,306	4,601,753	4,083,041	3,574,787	2,907,481	2,435,585	1,900,868	1,473,116	9.8	10.0	9.7	10.5	11.1	11.4	12.5	11.8	12.4
15 to 19 years	5,757,825	4,673,792	4,527,282	3,750,451	3,248,711	2,476,088	1,989,605	1,650,012	1,237,680	9.3	8.7	9.6	9.7	10.1	9.7	10.2	10.3	10.5
20 to 24 years	5,336,815	4,527,045	4,580,290	3,624,580	3,104,893	2,554,684	1,835,940	2,911,558	2,194,469	8.6	8.4	9.7	9.3	9.7	10.0	9.4	18.1	18.5
25 to 29 years	4,860,180	4,538,233	4,244,348	3,323,543	2,698,311	2,109,741	1,515,671			7.8	8.4	9.0	8.6	8.4	8.3	7.8		
30 to 34 years	4,561,786	4,130,783	3,656,768	2,901,321	2,425,664	1,744,308	1,273,633	2,129,017	1,490,135	7.3	7.7	7.7	7.5	7.6	6.8	6.5	13.2	12.6
35 to 39 years	4,679,860	4,074,361	3,367,016	2,616,865	2,051,044	1,527,159	1,179,366			7.5	7.6	7.1	6.7	6.4	6.0	6.1		
40 to 44 years	4,136,459	3,285,543	2,786,350	2,255,916	1,654,004	1,243,773	990,021	1,392,223	967,573	6.7	6.1	5.9	5.8	5.2	4.9	5.1	8.7	8.2
45 to 49 years	3,671,924	3,117,550	2,378,916	1,837,836	1,418,102	1,078,695	839,578			5.9	5.8	5.0	4.7	4.4	4.2	4.3		
50 to 54 years	3,131,645	2,535,545	2,110,013	1,564,622	1,208,922	966,702	740,360	835,350	575,685	5.0	4.7	4.5	4.0	3.8	3.8	3.8	5.2	4.9
55 to 59 years	2,425,992	1,880,065	1,488,437	1,145,257	871,063	674,927	469,495			3.9	3.5	3.1	3.0	2.7	2.6	2.4		
60 to 64 years	1,941,508	1,581,800	1,185,966	917,167	758,710	584,858	407,491	455,754	309,515	3.1	2.9	2.5	2.4	2.4	2.3	2.1	2.8	2.6
65 to 69 years	1,417,812	1,079,817	863,994	667,669	525,627	379,498	250,662			2.3	2.0	1.8	1.7	1.6	1.5	1.3		
70 to 74 years	991,647	706,301	561,644	449,609	303,642	250,001	173,036	172,563	127,460	1.6	1.3	1.2	1.2	1.1	1.0	0.9	1.1	1.1
75 to 79 years	547,604	419,965	331,280	261,579	199,093	138,601	86,282			0.9	0.8	0.7	0.7	0.6	0.5	0.4		
80 to 84 years	251,138	185,903	153,745	122,273	97,862	67,941	60,042	43,790	36,727	0.4	0.3	0.3	0.3	0.3	0.3	0.3	0.3	0.3
85 to 89 years	90,893	69,272	56,335	40,742	34,063	21,908				0.1	0.1	0.1	0.1	0.1	0.1			
90 to 94 years	20,431	16,383	14,553	9,858	9,848	6,351	6,922	5,854	5,183	-----	-----	-----	-----	-----	-----	-----	-----	-----
95 to 99 years	4,283	3,869	3,045	2,417	2,186	1,855				-----	-----	-----	-----	-----	-----			
100 and over	1,403	1,561	1,380	1,271	1,398	1,409	1,286	1,233	1,077	-----	-----	-----	-----	-----	-----	-----	-----	-----
Age unknown	51,816	92,875	114,443	127,423	103,529	-----	3,795	27,890	9,173	0.1	0.2	0.2	0.3	0.3	-----	-----	0.2	0.1
FEMALE																		
All ages	60,637,966	51,810,189	44,639,989	37,178,127	30,554,370	24,636,963	19,064,806	15,358,117	11,354,216	100.0	100.0	100.0	100.0	100.0	100.0	100.0	100.0	100.0
Under 5 years	5,638,216	5,715,769	5,250,768	4,537,016	3,749,824	3,406,807	2,717,456	2,392,949	1,728,313	9.3	11.0	11.8	12.2	12.3	13.8	14.3	15.6	15.2
Under 1 year	1,078,620	1,115,316	1,093,933	947,635	767,361	713,959	542,858	462,779	311,220	1.8	2.2	2.5	2.5	2.5	2.9	2.8	3.0	2.7
1 year	1,064,924	1,134,668	975,080	874,815	527,362	618,924	530,745	1,930,170	1,417,093	1.8	2.2	2.2	2.4	1.7	2.5	2.8	12.6	12.5
2 years	1,146,401	1,151,059	1,068,226	905,072	848,321	701,048	561,849			1.9	2.2	2.4	2.4	2.8	2.8	2.9		
3 years	1,184,102	1,175,870	1,071,159	903,977	809,878	684,065	552,053			2.0	2.3	2.4	2.4	2.7	2.8	2.9		
4 years	1,164,160	1,138,856	1,042,370	905,517	796,902	688,811	529,951			1.9	2.2	2.3	2.4	2.6	2.8	2.8		
5 to 9 years	6,226,501	5,645,074	4,836,509	4,394,727	3,743,646	3,204,529	2,377,271	2,061,655	1,600,861	10.3	10.9	10.8	11.8	12.3	13.0	12.5	13.4	14.1
10 to 14 years	5,936,100	5,271,831	4,505,387	3,997,193	3,458,722	2,807,705	2,350,604	1,819,912	1,417,513	9.8	10.2	10.1	10.8	11.3	11.4	12.3	11.8	12.5
15 to 19 years	5,794,290	4,756,764	4,536,321	3,805,638	3,308,852	2,535,327	2,050,893	1,711,483	1,292,112	9.6	9.2	10.2	10.2	10.8	10.3	10.8	11.1	11.4
20 to 24 years	5,533,563	4,749,976	4,476,694	3,710,436	3,091,783	2,533,088	1,912,353	2,814,842	2,082,849	9.1	9.2	10.0	10.0	10.1	10.3	10.0	18.3	18.3
25 to 29 years	4,973,428	4,548,258	3,935,655	3,205,898	2,529,466	1,970,880	1,559,447			8.2	8.8	8.8	8.6	8.3	8.0	8.2		
30 to 34 years	4,558,635	3,940,410	3,315,417	2,654,718	2,152,966	1,624,635	1,289,196	1,892,231	1,335,684	7.5	7.6	7.4	7.1	7.0	6.6	6.8	12.3	11.8
35 to 39 years	4,528,785	3,700,920	3,029,084	2,347,916	1,815,117	1,473,260	1,135,610			7.5	7.1	6.8	6.3	5.9	6.0	6.0		
40 to 44 years	3,853,736	3,060,014	2,475,237	1,991,250	1,530,914	1,225,038	949,691	1,222,107	879,087	6.4	5.9	5.5	5.4	5.0	5.0	5.0	8.0	7.7
45 to 49 years	3,370,355	2,646,070	2,090,281	1,616,776	1,313,538	1,010,750	739,354			5.6	5.1	4.7	4.3	4.3	4.1	3.9		
50 to 54 years	2,844,159	2,199,328	1,790,778	1,378,207	1,117,340	873,181	627,609	750,529	533,855	4.7	4.2	4.0	3.7	3.7	3.5	3.3	4.9	4.7
55 to 59 years	2,219,685	1,669,059	1,298,514	1,065,915	800,673	596,507	407,057			3.7	3.2	2.9	2.9	2.6	2.4	2.1		
60 to 64 years	1,809,713	1,400,748	1,081,184	874,196	699,324	519,361	371,480	433,055	300,411	3.0	2.7	2.4	2.4	2.3	2.1	1.9	2.8	2.6
65 to 69 years	1,352,793	988,658	815,509	635,257	484,483	346,378	233,691			2.2	1.9	1.8	1.7	1.6	1.4	1.2		
70 to 74 years	958,357	688,735	552,084	434,232	338,109	245,441	171,322	176,327	129,774	1.6	1.3	1.2	1.2	1.1	1.0	0.9	1.1	1.1
75 to 79 years	558,786	436,595	336,022	258,278	193,969	142,464	89,404			0.9	0.8	0.8	0.7	0.6	0.6	0.5		
80 to 84 years	283,538	216,876	168,009	129,239	105,989	78,421	69,035	49,762	40,655	0.5	0.4	0.4	0.3	0.3	0.3	0.4	0.3	0.4
85 to 89 years	114,576	87,267	66,483	47,858	41,177	27,927				0.2	0.2	0.1	0.1	0.1	0.1			
90 to 94 years	31,233	23,597	18,920	14,134	13,707	9,749	9,731	7,924	6,512	0.1	-----	-----	-----	-----	-----	0.1	0.1	0.1
95 to 99 years	6,750	5,710	4,340	3,849	3,402	2,908				-----	-----	-----	-----	-----	-----			
100 and over	2,561	2,706	2,175	2,233	2,583	2,607	2,236	1,720	1,478	-----	-----	-----	-----	-----	-----	-----	-----	-----
Age unknown	42,206	55,824	54,612	73,161	58,636	-----	1,366	23,621	5,112	0.1	0.1	0.1	0.2	0.2	-----	-----	0.2	-----

[1] Figures are exclusive of persons specially enumerated in 1890 in Indian Territory and on Indian reservations, for whom statistics of age are not available.

TABLE 8.—AGE BY 5-YEAR PERIODS, BY COLOR, NATIVITY, AND SEX, FOR THE UNITED STATES: 1930 AND 1920

[For total native white of foreign or mixed parentage, see Table 9. Per cent not shown where less than 0.1]

AGE	ALL CLASSES		NATIVE WHITE—NATIVE PARENTAGE		NATIVE WHITE—FOREIGN PARENTAGE		NATIVE WHITE—MIXED PARENTAGE		FOREIGN-BORN WHITE		NEGRO		OTHER RACES	
	1930	1920	1930	1920	1930	1920	1930	1920	1930	1920	1930	1920	1930	1920
All ages	122,775,046	105,710,620	70,136,614	58,421,957	16,999,221	15,694,539	8,361,965	6,991,665	13,366,407	13,712,754	11,891,143	10,463,131	2,019,696	426,574
Under 5 years	11,444,390	11,573,230	7,939,165	7,360,530	1,123,962	2,124,350	836,481	838,057	27,788	44,984	1,230,206	1,143,699	286,788	55,610
5 to 9 years	12,607,609	11,398,075	8,321,038	6,977,863	1,616,338	2,107,263	807,077	832,235	121,691	169,884	1,368,381	1,266,207	283,084	44,623
10 to 14 years	12,004,877	10,641,137	7,528,352	6,455,709	1,999,694	1,763,468	870,500	818,783	147,736	331,362	1,251,542	1,236,914	207,053	34,001
15 to 19 years	11,552,115	9,430,556	6,932,503	5,599,046	2,024,660	1,429,368	829,791	757,799	324,630	527,042	1,250,528	1,083,215	190,003	33,186
20 to 24 years	10,870,378	9,277,021	6,355,507	5,176,707	1,688,169	1,384,755	760,487	697,035	661,992	926,844	1,208,191	1,054,847	201,032	36,833
25 to 29 years	9,833,608	9,086,491	5,509,780	4,764,802	1,350,190	1,286,562	692,720	635,963	1,021,006	1,454,363	1,071,787	909,739	188,125	35,062
30 to 34 years	9,120,421	8,071,193	4,916,005	4,096,041	1,283,697	1,052,126	663,234	539,148	1,246,830	1,651,475	864,514	697,865	146,141	34,538
35 to 39 years	9,208,645	7,775,281	4,675,975	3,815,852	1,237,529	924,617	638,449	487,531	1,631,667	1,737,805	890,000	773,931	134,125	35,545
40 to 44 years	7,990,195	6,345,557	3,953,253	3,009,330	1,008,800	831,144	542,218	396,974	1,694,176	1,428,099	687,423	559,701	104,265	30,309
45 to 49 years	7,042,279	5,763,620	3,454,299	2,753,013	838,822	813,043	464,654	322,309	1,565,214	1,299,675	630,065	551,589	89,225	23,991
50 to 54 years	5,975,804	4,734,873	2,941,026	2,236,700	762,414	676,567	388,246	236,622	1,317,370	1,167,377	504,590	399,110	62,158	18,497
55 to 59 years	4,645,677	3,540,124	2,300,842	1,719,190	675,488	519,246	288,164	158,513	1,028,613	908,722	309,397	220,980	43,173	13,473
60 to 64 years	3,751,221	2,982,548	1,821,621	1,530,129	540,255	409,476	204,540	116,097	910,577	715,731	242,169	200,118	32,059	10,997
65 to 69 years	2,770,605	2,068,475	1,346,942	1,126,722	403,691	208,359	131,893	69,989	712,814	519,226	155,177	137,035	20,588	7,144
70 to 74 years	1,950,004	1,395,036	1,010,306	784,183	274,506	90,854	83,624	42,376	460,614	381,325	99,096	91,579	12,858	4,719
75 to 79 years	1,106,390	856,560	612,330	487,797	110,225	43,198	41,527	24,196	269,780	246,487	58,711	52,352	7,817	2,530
80 to 84 years	534,676	402,779	303,217	228,018	35,265	10,020	17,429	10,084	140,892	118,935	33,377	28,122	4,496	1,591
85 to 89 years	205,469	156,539	115,450	87,530	10,241	4,302	6,148	3,671	56,575	47,473	14,948	12,281	2,107	722
90 to 94 years	51,664	39,980	27,260	20,159	1,951	975	1,288	862	13,954	11,717	6,332	5,847	879	420
95 to 99 years	11,033	9,579	4,723	3,853	324	240	220	159	2,714	2,579	2,011	2,562	441	186
100 and over	3,964	4,267	659	614	44	37	27	32	450	485	2,467	2,985	317	164
Unknown	94,022	148,699	57,361	92,169	6,896	8,000	3,248	3,230	9,824	20,264	13,731	23,503	2,962	1,533
Per cent	100.0	100.0	100.0	100.0	100.0	100.0	100.0	100.0	100.0	100.0	100.0	100.0	100.0	100.0
Under 5 years	9.3	10.9	11.3	12.6	6.6	13.5	10.0	12.0	0.2	0.3	10.3	10.9	14.2	13.0
5 to 9 years	10.3	10.8	11.9	11.9	9.5	13.4	10.7	11.9	0.9	1.2	11.5	12.1	14.0	10.5
10 to 14 years	9.8	10.1	10.7	11.1	11.8	11.2	10.4	11.7	1.1	2.4	10.5	11.8	10.3	8.2
15 to 19 years	9.4	8.9	9.9	9.6	11.9	9.1	9.9	10.8	2.4	3.9	10.5	10.4	9.4	7.8
20 to 24 years	8.9	8.8	9.1	8.9	9.9	8.8	9.1	10.0	5.0	6.8	10.1	10.1	10.0	8.6
25 to 29 years	8.0	8.6	7.9	8.2	7.9	8.2	8.3	9.1	7.6	10.6	9.0	8.7	9.3	8.2
30 to 34 years	7.4	7.6	7.0	7.0	7.6	6.7	7.9	7.7	9.3	12.0	7.3	6.7	7.2	8.1
35 to 39 years	7.5	7.4	6.7	6.5	7.3	5.9	7.6	7.0	12.2	12.7	7.5	7.4	6.6	8.3
40 to 44 years	6.5	6.0	5.6	5.3	5.9	5.3	6.5	5.7	12.7	10.4	5.8	5.3	5.2	7.1
45 to 49 years	5.7	5.5	4.9	4.7	4.9	5.2	5.6	4.6	11.7	9.5	5.3	5.3	4.4	5.6
50 to 54 years	4.9	4.5	4.2	3.8	4.5	4.3	4.6	3.4	9.9	8.5	4.2	3.8	3.1	4.3
55 to 59 years	3.8	3.4	3.3	2.9	4.0	3.3	3.4	2.3	7.7	6.6	2.6	2.2	2.1	3.2
60 to 64 years	3.1	2.8	2.6	2.6	3.2	2.6	2.4	1.7	6.8	5.2	2.0	1.9	1.6	2.6
65 to 69 years	2.3	2.0	1.9	1.9	2.4	1.3	1.6	1.0	5.3	3.8	1.3	1.3	1.0	1.7
70 to 74 years	1.6	1.3	1.5	1.3	1.6	0.6	1.0	0.6	3.4	2.8	0.8	0.9	0.6	1.1
75 to 79 years	0.9	0.8	0.9	0.8	0.7	0.3	0.5	0.3	2.0	1.8	0.5	0.5	0.4	0.6
80 to 84 years	0.4	0.4	0.4	0.4	0.2	0.1	0.2	0.1	1.1	0.9	0.3	0.3	0.2	0.4
85 and over	0.2	0.2	0.2	0.2	0.1	----	0.1	0.1	0.6	0.5	0.2	0.2	0.2	0.3
Unknown	0.1	0.1	0.1	0.2	----	0.1	----	----	0.1	0.1	0.1	0.2	0.1	0.4
	Male 1930	Female 1930	Male 1930	Female 1930	Male 1930	Female 1930	Male 1930	Female 1930	Male 1930	Female 1930	Male 1930	Female 1930	Male 1930	Female 1930
All ages	62,137,080	60,637,966	35,460,001	34,676,613	8,438,676	8,560,545	4,111,468	4,250,497	7,153,709	6,212,698	5,855,669	6,035,474	1,117,557	902,139
Under 5 years	5,806,174	5,638,216	4,044,523	3,894,642	568,171	555,791	424,295	412,186	14,142	13,646	611,231	618,975	143,812	142,976
5 to 9 years	6,381,108	6,226,501	4,227,383	4,093,655	815,326	801,012	454,546	442,531	61,344	60,347	679,748	688,633	142,761	140,323
10 to 14 years	6,068,777	5,936,100	3,818,635	3,709,717	1,007,597	992,097	439,563	430,937	74,173	73,563	623,228	628,314	105,581	101,472
15 to 19 years	5,757,825	5,794,290	3,480,607	3,451,896	1,009,859	1,014,801	416,850	412,941	156,659	167,971	595,046	654,882	98,204	91,799
20 to 24 years	5,336,815	5,533,563	3,138,838	3,216,669	834,778	853,391	373,297	387,190	319,103	342,889	553,622	649,569	117,177	83,855
25 to 29 years	4,860,180	4,973,428	2,734,045	2,775,735	666,173	684,017	331,576	361,144	515,163	505,843	500,520	571,267	112,703	75,422
30 to 34 years	4,561,786	4,558,635	2,458,011	2,457,994	635,701	647,996	314,872	348,362	650,595	596,235	416,869	447,645	85,738	60,403
35 to 39 years	4,679,860	4,528,785	2,360,086	2,315,889	614,400	623,129	304,281	334,168	892,439	739,228	430,472	460,428	78,182	55,943
40 to 44 years	4,136,459	3,853,736	2,010,001	1,943,252	501,364	507,436	260,110	282,102	962,110	732,066	339,329	348,094	63,539	40,726
45 to 49 years	3,671,924	3,370,355	1,772,809	1,681,490	415,099	423,723	224,001	240,653	881,870	683,344	323,162	306,903	54,983	34,242
50 to 54 years	3,131,645	2,844,159	1,527,605	1,413,421	376,117	386,297	189,063	199,183	722,496	594,874	277,532	227,058	38,832	23,326
55 to 59 years	2,425,992	2,219,685	1,198,742	1,102,100	330,632	344,856	141,196	146,968	554,498	474,115	174,367	135,030	26,557	16,616
60 to 64 years	1,941,508	1,809,713	945,166	876,455	260,244	280,011	99,850	104,690	483,750	426,827	133,349	108,820	19,149	12,910
65 to 69 years	1,417,812	1,352,793	687,323	659,619	192,896	210,795	64,604	67,289	378,000	334,314	82,843	72,334	12,146	8,442
70 to 74 years	991,647	958,357	518,392	500,914	130,912	143,594	40,732	42,892	243,312	217,302	50,896	48,200	7,403	5,455
75 to 79 years	547,604	558,786	302,078	310,252	54,434	61,791	20,053	21,474	137,361	132,419	29,219	29,492	4,459	3,358
80 to 84 years	251,138	283,538	141,841	161,376	16,143	19,122	7,862	9,567	67,616	73,276	15,343	18,034	2,333	2,163
85 to 89 years	90,893	114,576	49,864	65,586	4,560	5,681	2,612	3,536	25,952	30,623	6,864	8,084	1,041	1,066
90 to 94 years	20,431	31,233	10,440	16,820	793	1,158	487	801	5,814	8,140	2,516	3,816	381	498
95 to 99 years	4,283	6,750	1,702	3,021	138	186	74	146	1,087	1,627	1,073	1,538	209	232
100 and over	1,403	2,561	260	399	22	22	16	11	205	245	776	1,691	124	193
Unknown	51,816	42,206	31,650	25,711	3,317	3,579	1,522	1,726	6,020	3,804	7,064	6,667	2,243	719
Per cent	100.0	100.0	100.0	100.0	100.0	100.0	100.0	100.0	100.0	100.0	100.0	100.0	100.0	100.0
Under 5 years	9.3	9.3	11.4	11.2	6.7	6.5	10.3	9.7	0.2	0.2	10.4	10.3	12.9	15.8
5 to 9 years	10.3	10.3	11.9	11.8	9.7	9.4	11.1	10.4	0.9	1.0	11.6	11.4	12.8	15.6
10 to 14 years	9.8	9.8	10.8	10.7	11.9	11.6	10.7	10.1	1.0	1.2	10.6	10.4	9.4	11.2
15 to 19 years	9.3	9.6	9.8	10.0	12.0	11.9	10.1	9.7	2.2	2.7	10.2	10.9	8.8	10.2
20 to 24 years	8.6	9.1	8.9	9.3	9.9	10.0	9.1	9.1	4.5	5.5	9.5	10.8	10.5	9.3
25 to 29 years	7.8	8.2	7.7	8.0	7.9	8.0	8.1	8.5	7.2	8.1	8.5	9.5	10.1	8.4
30 to 34 years	7.3	7.5	6.9	7.1	7.5	7.6	7.7	8.2	9.1	9.6	7.1	7.4	7.7	6.7
35 to 39 years	7.5	7.5	6.7	6.7	7.3	7.3	7.4	7.9	12.5	11.9	7.4	7.6	7.0	6.2
40 to 44 years	6.7	6.4	5.7	5.6	5.9	5.9	6.3	6.6	13.4	11.8	5.8	5.8	5.7	4.5
45 to 49 years	5.9	5.6	5.0	4.8	4.9	4.9	5.4	5.7	12.3	11.0	5.5	5.1	4.9	3.8
50 to 54 years	5.0	4.7	4.3	4.1	4.5	4.5	4.6	4.7	10.1	9.6	4.7	3.8	3.5	2.6
55 to 59 years	3.9	3.7	3.4	3.2	3.9	4.0	3.4	3.5	7.8	7.6	3.0	2.2	2.4	1.8
60 to 64 years	3.1	3.0	2.7	2.5	3.1	3.3	2.4	2.5	6.8	6.9	2.3	1.8	1.7	1.4
65 to 69 years	2.3	2.2	1.9	1.9	2.3	2.5	1.6	1.6	5.3	5.4	1.4	1.2	1.1	0.9
70 to 74 years	1.6	1.6	1.5	1.4	1.6	1.7	1.0	1.0	3.4	3.5	0.9	0.8	0.7	0.6
75 to 79 years	0.9	0.9	0.9	0.9	0.6	0.7	0.5	0.5	1.9	2.1	0.5	0.5	0.4	0.4
80 to 84 years	0.4	0.5	0.4	0.5	0.2	0.2	0.2	0.2	0.9	1.2	0.3	0.3	0.2	0.2
85 and over	0.2	0.3	0.2	0.2	0.1	0.1	0.1	0.1	0.5	0.7	0.2	0.3	0.2	0.2
Unknown	0.1	0.1	0.1	0.1	----	----	----	----	0.1	0.1	0.1	0.1	0.2	0.1

POPULATION

TABLE 9.—AGE BY 5-YEAR PERIODS, BY COLOR, NATIVITY, AND SEX, FOR THE UNITED STATES: 1880 TO 1930

[Corresponding figures for the total population of the United States by sex are given in Table 7]

SEX AND AGE	TOTAL WHITE						TOTAL NATIVE WHITE					
	1930	1920	1910	1900	1890 [1]	1880	1930	1920	1910	1900	1890 [1]	1880
TOTAL												
All ages	108,864,207	94,820,915	81,731,957	66,809,196	54,983,890	43,402,970	95,497,800	81,108,161	68,386,412	56,595,379	45,862,023	36,843,291
Under 5 years	9,927,396	10,373,921	9,322,914	7,919,952	6,579,648	5,800,151	9,899,608	10,328,937	9,220,407	7,867,583	6,493,019	5,737,780
Under 1 year	1,896,730	2,017,767	1,955,605	1,665,007	1,359,120	1,218,787	1,895,302	2,013,198	1,948,870	1,661,005	1,354,914	1,212,737
1 year	1,887,450	2,078,537	1,748,586	1,529,181	922,010	1,059,607	1,884,222	2,071,969	1,736,684	1,521,536	915,657	1,049,521
2 years	2,017,703	2,094,108	1,897,097	1,574,382	1,494,150	1,194,600	2,012,249	2,085,538	1,878,677	1,563,745	1,476,658	1,180,955
3 years	2,070,849	2,118,455	1,882,461	1,573,460	1,407,725	1,157,212	2,063,174	2,107,406	1,854,182	1,559,898	1,381,659	1,141,614
4 years	2,054,664	2,065,054	1,839,165	1,577,922	1,396,643	1,169,945	2,044,661	2,050,826	1,801,994	1,561,399	1,364,131	1,152,953
5 to 9 years	10,956,144	10,087,245	8,475,173	7,638,326	6,473,108	5,442,419	10,834,453	9,917,361	8,176,664	7,491,134	6,224,817	5,319,722
10 to 14 years	10,546,282	9,369,322	7,918,408	6,959,238	5,991,972	4,880,531	10,398,546	9,037,960	7,560,078	6,647,673	5,595,593	4,642,092
15 to 19 years	10,111,584	8,314,155	7,968,391	6,543,189	5,675,347	4,351,650	9,786,954	7,786,213	7,294,630	5,981,443	5,154,052	3,972,838
20 to 24 years	9,466,155	8,185,341	7,986,411	6,335,044	5,448,467	4,402,472	8,804,163	7,258,497	6,556,030	5,415,562	4,531,093	3,874,217
25 to 29 years	8,573,696	8,141,690	7,257,136	5,762,980	4,646,687	3,541,701	7,552,690	6,687,327	5,594,440	4,665,751	3,574,448	2,870,585
30 to 34 years	8,109,766	7,338,790	6,267,276	5,004,444	4,144,832	2,979,254	6,862,936	5,687,315	4,761,561	3,830,761	3,202,512	2,216,623
35 to 39 years	8,183,620	6,965,805	5,731,845	4,460,575	3,439,930	2,648,492	6,551,953	5,228,000	4,323,752	3,283,009	2,569,338	1,859,227
40 to 44 years	7,198,507	5,755,547	4,780,272	3,852,143	2,865,648	2,190,735	5,504,331	4,327,448	3,476,797	2,886,031	2,005,604	1,477,845
45 to 49 years	6,322,989	5,188,040	4,061,062	3,105,678	2,449,220	1,861,892	4,757,775	3,888,365	2,914,702	2,265,458	1,661,405	1,230,951
50 to 54 years	5,409,056	4,317,266	3,555,313	2,633,981	2,090,940	1,627,892	4,091,686	3,149,889	2,630,258	1,830,589	1,381,729	1,050,805
55 to 59 years	4,293,107	3,305,671	2,564,206	2,021,217	1,531,659	1,154,915	3,264,494	2,396,949	1,870,686	1,378,214	1,006,528	781,801
60 to 64 years	3,476,993	2,771,433	2,069,323	1,620,658	1,323,110	977,308	2,506,416	2,055,702	1,441,740	1,075,627	845,463	666,845
65 to 69 years	2,594,840	1,924,296	1,549,954	1,195,295	925,524	657,409	1,882,526	1,405,070	1,061,557	784,555	613,950	476,048
70 to 74 years	1,838,050	1,298,738	1,030,884	808,097	641,951	444,147	1,377,436	917,413	693,917	525,772	442,945	329,538
75 to 79 years	1,039,862	801,678	620,992	477,720	360,825	254,868	770,082	555,191	412,780	318,804	259,610	194,172
80 to 84 years	496,803	373,066	294,555	224,717	183,295	127,527	355,911	254,131	193,265	155,642	136,442	96,441
85 to 89 years	188,414	143,536	110,036	78,027	67,015	43,798	131,839	96,063	73,503	55,860	50,090	34,283
90 to 94 years	44,453	33,713	27,161	18,319	18,766	11,803	30,499	21,996	18,127	12,998	13,640	8,843
95 to 99 years	7,981	6,831	4,757	3,707	3,682	3,051	5,267	4,252	3,034	2,295	2,477	2,043
100 years and over	1,180	1,168	764	837	1,054	955	730	683	471	446	654	592
Unknown	77,329	123,663	134,224	145,052	121,141	----------	67,505	103,399	108,013	120,172	96,524	----------
MALE												
All ages	55,163,854	48,430,655	42,178,245	34,201,735	28,206,332	22,130,900	48,010,145	40,902,333	34,654,457	28,686,450	23,254,474	18,609,265
Under 5 years	5,051,131	5,260,714	4,728,650	4,011,455	3,351,104	2,949,449	5,036,989	5,237,857	4,676,710	3,984,888	3,307,064	2,918,193
Under 1 year	965,946	1,023,270	993,242	844,238	694,766	620,296	965,226	1,020,933	989,715	842,221	692,626	617,307
1 year	961,903	1,055,446	887,756	774,700	470,763	539,050	960,271	1,052,181	881,699	770,755	467,516	534,030
2 years	1,025,780	1,062,192	963,335	797,349	761,469	608,576	1,022,999	1,057,735	954,033	791,936	752,602	601,683
3 years	1,050,500	1,070,440	949,920	796,172	710,352	585,530	1,046,560	1,064,808	935,693	789,395	697,211	577,733
4 years	1,047,002	1,049,366	934,397	798,996	713,754	595,997	1,041,933	1,042,140	915,570	790,581	697,109	587,440
5 to 9 years	5,558,599	5,099,205	4,285,366	3,862,349	3,276,983	2,756,201	5,497,255	5,013,431	4,134,714	3,788,622	3,150,913	2,694,398
10 to 14 years	5,339,968	4,735,150	4,006,104	3,519,303	3,044,058	2,482,572	5,265,705	4,567,998	3,824,801	3,361,671	2,842,899	2,361,832
15 to 19 years	5,063,975	4,141,831	3,999,143	3,258,090	2,818,914	2,150,068	4,907,316	3,882,561	3,647,389	2,986,709	2,561,256	1,965,748
20 to 24 years	4,666,016	4,018,576	4,070,955	3,145,481	2,740,864	2,219,317	4,346,913	3,561,588	3,247,035	2,689,295	2,264,040	1,945,279
25 to 29 years	4,246,957	4,094,301	3,792,224	2,942,882	2,407,153	1,838,054	3,731,794	3,302,213	2,801,648	2,353,361	1,804,608	1,472,960
30 to 34 years	4,059,179	3,776,266	3,297,169	2,619,446	2,200,973	1,548,077	3,408,584	2,829,448	2,408,501	1,958,744	1,651,874	1,128,308
35 to 39 years	4,171,206	3,665,341	3,024,002	2,360,348	1,831,443	1,353,221	3,278,767	2,656,664	2,211,995	1,687,544	1,337,972	920,264
40 to 44 years	3,733,591	2,987,412	2,537,219	2,055,176	1,495,923	1,111,763	2,771,481	2,184,217	1,785,700	1,497,876	1,020,817	726,832
45 to 49 years	3,293,779	2,779,175	2,161,848	1,651,972	1,271,113	962,027	2,411,909	2,034,752	1,505,393	1,183,506	837,647	621,164
50 to 54 years	2,81[illegible],281	2,293,604	1,915,860	1,396,035	1,083,091	856,178	2,092,785	1,642,058	1,389,604	955,956	700,104	538,133
55 to 59 years	2,225,[illegible]68	1,740,661	1,363,821	1,040,235	793,301	610,080	1,670,570	1,236,872	983,711	694,994	514,816	403,260
60 to 64 years	1,789,[illegible]10	1,461,619	1,076,753	825,213	686,462	516,416	1,305,260	1,068,990	744,839	539,430	432,361	345,575
65 to 69 years	1,322,823	998,779	792,310	608,715	479,479	341,831	944,823	723,379	536,894	395,274	312,734	243,803
70 to 74 years	933,348	655,916	518,888	411,658	333,325	224,652	690,036	461,184	346,137	263,590	226,961	165,062
75 to 79 years	513,926	391,383	307,446	240,284	182,768	125,704	376,565	267,213	202,034	157,351	129,601	94,598
80 to 84 years	233,462	172,064	141,301	110,087	88,648	59,648	165,846	115,363	91,039	74,697	65,305	44,492
85 to 89 years	82,988	63,308	50,843	35,838	30,305	19,277	57,036	41,304	32,762	25,036	22,110	14,858
90 to 94 years	17,534	13,852	11,970	7,607	7,920	4,756	11,720	8,729	7,777	5,208	5,612	3,486
95 to 99 years	3,001	2,706	1,935	1,405	1,446	1,216	1,914	1,657	1,168	798	930	783
100 years and over	503	467	326	330	413	393	298	262	200	152	234	237
Unknown	42,509	78,325	94,112	97,826	80,646	----------	36,489	64,593	74,406	81,690	64,016	----------
FEMALE												
All ages	53,700,353	46,390,260	39,553,712	32,607,461	26,777,558	21,272,070	47,487,655	40,205,828	33,731,955	27,908,929	22,607,549	18,234,026
Under 5 years	4,876,265	5,113,207	4,594,264	3,908,497	3,228,544	2,850,702	4,862,619	5,091,080	4,543,697	3,882,695	3,185,955	2,819,587
Under 1 year	930,784	994,497	962,363	820,769	664,354	598,491	930,076	992,265	959,155	818,784	662,288	595,430
1 year	925,547	1,023,091	860,830	754,481	451,247	520,557	923,951	1,019,788	854,985	750,781	448,141	515,491
2 years	991,923	1,031,916	933,762	777,033	732,681	586,024	989,250	1,027,803	924,644	771,809	724,056	579,272
3 years	1,020,349	1,048,015	932,541	777,288	697,373	571,682	1,016,614	1,042,538	918,489	770,503	684,448	563,881
4 years	1,007,662	1,015,688	904,768	778,926	682,889	573,948	1,002,728	1,008,686	886,424	770,818	667,022	565,513
5 to 9 years	5,397,545	4,988,040	4,189,807	3,775,977	3,196,185	2,686,218	5,337,198	4,903,930	4,041,950	3,702,512	3,073,904	2,625,324
10 to 14 years	5,206,314	4,634,172	3,912,304	3,439,935	2,947,914	2,397,959	5,132,751	4,469,962	3,735,277	3,286,002	2,752,694	2,280,260
15 to 19 years	5,047,609	4,172,324	3,969,248	3,285,099	2,856,433	2,201,582	4,879,638	3,903,652	3,647,241	2,994,734	2,592,796	2,007,090
20 to 24 years	4,800,139	4,166,765	3,915,456	3,189,563	2,707,603	2,183,155	4,457,250	3,696,909	3,308,995	2,726,267	2,266,453	1,928,938
25 to 29 years	4,326,739	4,047,389	3,464,912	2,820,098	2,239,534	1,703,647	3,820,896	3,385,114	2,792,792	2,312,390	1,769,840	1,397,625
30 to 34 years	4,050,587	3,562,524	2,970,107	2,384,998	1,943,859	1,431,177	3,454,352	2,857,867	2,353,060	1,872,017	1,550,638	1,088,315
35 to 39 years	4,012,414	3,300,464	2,707,843	2,100,227	1,608,487	1,295,271	3,273,186	2,571,336	2,111,757	1,595,465	1,231,366	938,963
40 to 44 years	3,464,916	2,768,135	2,243,053	1,796,967	1,369,725	1,078,972	2,732,850	2,143,231	1,691,097	1,388,155	984,877	751,013
45 to 49 years	3,029,210	2,408,865	1,899,214	1,453,706	1,178,107	899,865	2,345,866	1,853,613	1,409,309	1,081,952	823,758	609,787
50 to 54 years	2,593,775	2,023,662	1,639,453	1,237,946	1,007,858	771,714	1,998,901	1,507,831	1,240,654	874,633	681,625	512,672
55 to 59 years	2,068,039	1,565,010	1,200,385	980,082	738,358	544,835	1,593,924	1,160,077	886,975	683,220	491,712	378,541
60 to 64 years	1,687,983	1,309,814	992,570	795,445	636,648	460,892	1,261,156	986,712	696,901	536,197	413,102	321,270
65 to 69 years	1,272,017	925,517	757,644	586,580	446,045	315,578	937,703	681,691	524,663	389,281	301,216	232,245
70 to 74 years	904,702	642,822	511,906	396,439	308,626	219,495	687,400	456,229	347,780	262,182	215,984	164,476
75 to 79 years	525,936	410,295	313,546	237,436	178,057	129,164	393,517	287,978	210,746	161,453	130,009	99,574
80 to 84 years	263,341	201,002	153,254	114,630	94,647	67,879	190,065	138,768	102,226	80,945	71,137	51,949
85 to 89 years	105,426	80,228	60,093	42,189	36,710	24,521	74,803	54,759	40,741	30,824	27,980	19,425
90 to 94 years	26,919	19,861	15,191	10,712	10,846	7,047	18,779	13,267	10,350	7,730	8,028	5,357
95 to 99 years	4,980	4,125	2,822	2,302	2,236	1,835	3,353	2,595	1,866	1,499	1,547	1,260
100 years and over	677	701	438	507	641	562	432	421	271	294	420	355
Unknown	34,820	45,338	40,112	47,226	40,495	----------	31,016	38,806	33,607	38,482	32,508	----------

[1] Figures are exclusive of persons specially enumerated in 1890 in Indian Territory and on Indian reservations, for whom statistics of age are not available.

AGE DISTRIBUTION

579

TABLE 9.—AGE BY 5-YEAR PERIODS, BY COLOR, NATIVITY, AND SEX, FOR THE UNITED STATES: 1880 TO 1930—Continued

SEX AND AGE	NATIVE WHITE—NATIVE PARENTAGE					NATIVE WHITE—FOREIGN OR MIXED PARENTAGE				
	1930	1920	1910	1900	1890 [1]	1930	1920	1910	1900	1890
TOTAL All ages	70,136,614	58,421,957	49,488,575	40,949,362	34,358,348	25,361,180	22,686,204	18,897,837	15,646,017	11,503,675
Under 5 years	7,930,165	7,366,530	6,546,282	5,464,881	4,550,682	1,960,443	2,962,407	2,674,125	2,402,702	1,942,337
Under 1 year	1,549,340	1,453,404	1,309,140	1,157,534	941,657	345,962	559,794	579,730	503,471	413,257
1 year	1,525,539	1,503,102	1,234,536	1,067,983	638,444	358,683	508,867	502,148	453,553	277,213
2 years	1,612,886	1,480,488	1,327,203	1,087,237	1,034,753	399,363	605,050	551,414	476,508	441,905
3 years	1,638,872	1,485,161	1,318,604	1,074,490	988,235	424,302	622,245	535,578	485,399	413,424
4 years	1,612,528	1,444,375	1,206,739	1,077,628	967,503	432,133	606,451	505,255	483,771	396,538
5 to 9 years	8,321,038	6,977,863	5,861,015	5,174,220	4,431,000	2,513,415	2,930,498	2,315,649	2,316,914	1,792,917
10 to 14 years	7,528,352	6,455,709	5,324,283	4,660,300	3,964,906	2,870,194	2,582,251	2,235,795	1,987,283	1,630,687
15 to 19 years	6,932,503	5,599,046	5,080,055	4,234,953	3,552,524	2,854,451	2,187,167	2,205,575	1,746,490	1,601,528
20 to 24 years	6,355,507	5,176,707	4,682,922	3,805,609	3,185,167	2,448,656	2,081,790	1,873,108	1,600,953	1,345,920
25 to 29 years	5,509,780	4,764,802	4,049,074	3,208,642	2,545,181	2,042,910	1,922,525	1,545,306	1,457,100	1,029,267
30 to 34 years	4,910,005	4,096,041	3,401,601	2,659,360	2,376,869	1,946,931	1,591,274	1,359,960	1,171,401	825,643
35 to 39 years	4,675,975	3,815,852	3,045,381	2,299,571	2,054,293	1,875,978	1,412,148	1,278,371	983,438	515,045
40 to 44 years	3,963,253	3,009,330	2,450,385	2,104,551	1,719,410	1,551,078	1,228,118	1,020,412	781,480	286,284
45 to 49 years	3,454,020	2,753,013	2,071,976	1,787,007	1,471,358	1,303,476	1,135,352	842,726	477,851	190,047
50 to 54 years	2,941,020	2,236,700	1,950,127	1,551,811	1,255,794	1,150,660	913,180	680,131	276,773	125,935
55 to 59 years	2,300,842	1,719,190	1,490,463	1,204,610	935,012	963,652	677,759	380,223	173,604	71,516
60 to 64 years	1,821,621	1,530,120	1,227,434	965,000	795,300	744,795	525,573	214,306	100,727	50,103
65 to 69 years	1,346,942	1,126,722	931,607	720,110	578,793	585,584	278,348	129,950	64,445	35,157
70 to 74 years	1,019,306	794,183	623,604	488,049	418,393	358,130	133,230	70,323	37,123	24,552
75 to 79 years	612,330	487,797	378,823	296,201	244,580	157,752	67,394	33,957	22,009	15,030
80 to 84 years	303,217	228,018	179,251	144,314	127,996	52,694	26,113	14,014	11,328	8,446
85 to 89 years	115,450	87,530	67,966	51,542	46,848	16,389	8,533	5,537	4,318	3,242
90 to 94 years	27,200	20,169	16,632	11,940	12,662	3,239	1,837	1,495	1,058	978
95 to 99 years	4,723	3,853	2,756	2,077	2,277	544	309	278	218	200
100 years and over	659	614	439	393	501	71	69	32	53	63
Unknown	57,301	92,169	97,500	112,031	87,812	10,144	11,230	10,504	8,141	8,712
MALE All ages	35,460,001	29,636,781	25,229,218	20,849,847	17,472,903	12,550,144	11,265,552	9,425,239	7,836,603	5,781,571
Under 5 years	4,044,523	3,741,194	3,326,237	2,773,201	2,323,933	992,406	1,496,663	1,350,473	1,211,687	983,131
Under 1 year	789,636	737,923	666,200	587,815	482,794	175,590	283,010	293,515	254,406	209,832
1 year	778,231	764,193	627,612	541,787	326,611	182,040	287,988	254,087	228,968	140,905
2 years	821,257	752,481	675,476	551,514	529,095	201,742	305,254	278,557	240,422	223,507
3 years	831,884	750,851	666,169	544,814	489,356	214,076	314,017	260,524	244,581	207,855
4 years	823,515	735,746	660,780	547,271	496,077	218,418	306,394	254,790	243,310	201,032
5 to 9 years	4,227,383	3,534,092	2,909,230	2,623,791	2,247,868	1,269,872	1,479,339	1,165,484	1,164,831	903,045
10 to 14 years	3,818,635	3,269,388	2,700,056	2,364,797	2,020,917	1,447,160	1,298,610	1,124,145	996,874	821,982
15 to 19 years	3,480,007	2,797,477	2,552,528	2,122,635	1,770,908	1,426,709	1,085,084	1,094,861	864,074	790,348
20 to 24 years	3,138,888	2,546,818	2,332,914	1,903,864	1,604,239	1,208,075	1,014,770	914,121	785,431	660,401
25 to 29 years	2,734,045	2,367,312	2,046,597	1,634,807	1,295,025	997,749	934,901	755,051	718,494	509,583
30 to 34 years	2,458,011	2,054,071	1,741,509	1,372,529	1,229,228	950,573	774,777	686,932	586,215	422,640
35 to 39 years	2,360,086	1,902,634	1,580,139	1,192,071	1,070,897	918,681	694,030	631,850	495,473	267,075
40 to 44 years	2,010,001	1,584,246	1,273,905	1,096,825	874,008	761,480	599,971	511,795	401,051	146,800
45 to 49 years	1,772,809	1,463,247	1,081,912	937,254	739,662	639,100	571,505	423,481	246,252	97,985
50 to 54 years	1,527,605	1,180,619	1,040,745	811,724	634,987	565,180	455,430	348,859	144,232	65,117
55 to 59 years	1,198,742	800,029	789,243	605,625	477,447	471,828	337,843	194,468	89,369	37,369
60 to 64 years	945,166	805,708	635,425	483,454	406,046	360,004	203,222	109,414	55,976	26,315
65 to 69 years	687,323	584,783	470,750	361,980	294,520	257,500	138,596	66,144	33,294	18,214
70 to 74 years	518,392	395,582	310,780	244,574	214,137	171,644	65,602	35,357	19,016	12,824
75 to 79 years	302,078	234,584	185,109	146,108	121,858	74,487	32,029	16,925	11,243	7,743
80 to 84 years	141,841	103,403	84,278	69,087	61,218	24,005	11,870	6,761	5,610	4,087
85 to 89 years	49,864	37,459	30,166	22,992	20,597	7,172	3,845	2,596	2,044	1,513
90 to 94 years	10,440	7,022	7,041	4,815	5,156	1,280	807	736	453	456
95 to 99 years	1,702	1,475	1,045	695	854	212	182	123	101	76
100 years and over	260	220	180	129	208	38	33	20	23	26
Unknown	31,650	58,759	68,769	76,830	50,190	4,830	5,834	5,637	4,860	4,826
FEMALE All ages	34,676,613	28,785,176	24,259,357	20,099,515	16,885,445	12,811,042	11,420,652	9,472,598	7,809,414	5,722,104
Under 5 years	3,894,642	3,625,336	3,220,045	2,691,680	2,226,749	967,977	1,465,744	1,323,652	1,191,015	959,206
Under 1 year	759,704	715,481	672,940	569,719	458,863	170,372	276,784	286,215	249,065	203,425
1 year	747,308	738,909	606,924	526,196	311,833	176,643	280,879	248,061	224,585	136,308
2 years	791,629	728,007	651,787	535,723	505,658	197,621	299,796	272,857	236,086	218,398
3 years	806,988	734,310	652,435	529,685	478,879	209,626	308,228	266,054	240,818	205,569
4 years	789,013	708,629	635,959	530,357	471,516	213,715	300,057	250,465	240,461	195,506
5 to 9 years	4,093,655	3,443,771	2,801,785	2,550,429	2,184,032	1,243,543	1,460,159	1,150,165	1,152,083	889,872
10 to 14 years	3,700,717	3,186,321	2,623,627	2,295,593	1,943,989	1,423,034	1,283,641	1,111,650	990,409	808,705
15 to 19 years	3,451,896	2,801,569	2,536,527	2,112,318	1,781,616	1,427,742	1,102,083	1,110,714	882,416	811,180
20 to 24 years	3,216,669	2,620,889	2,350,008	1,901,745	1,580,928	1,240,581	1,067,020	958,987	824,522	685,525
25 to 29 years	2,775,735	2,397,490	2,002,477	1,573,775	1,250,156	1,045,161	987,624	790,315	738,615	519,684
30 to 34 years	2,457,994	2,041,970	1,660,092	1,286,831	1,147,641	996,358	816,497	693,028	585,186	402,997
35 to 39 years	2,315,889	1,853,218	1,465,242	1,107,500	983,396	957,297	718,118	646,515	487,965	247,970
40 to 44 years	1,943,252	1,515,084	1,176,480	1,007,726	845,402	789,598	628,147	514,617	380,429	139,475
45 to 49 years	1,681,490	1,289,766	990,064	850,353	731,696	664,376	563,847	419,245	231,599	92,062
50 to 54 years	1,413,421	1,050,081	909,382	740,087	620,807	585,480	457,750	331,272	134,546	60,818
55 to 59 years	1,102,100	820,161	701,220	598,985	457,565	491,824	339,916	185,755	84,235	34,147
60 to 64 years	876,455	724,361	592,009	482,446	389,254	384,701	262,351	104,892	53,751	23,848
65 to 69 years	659,619	541,939	460,857	358,130	284,273	278,084	139,752	63,806	31,151	16,943
70 to 74 years	500,914	388,601	312,814	244,075	204,256	186,486	67,628	34,966	18,107	11,728
75 to 79 years	310,252	253,213	193,714	150,093	122,722	83,265	34,765	17,032	11,860	7,287
80 to 84 years	161,376	124,525	94,973	75,227	66,778	28,689	14,243	7,253	5,718	4,359
85 to 89 years	65,586	50,071	37,800	28,550	26,251	9,217	4,688	2,941	2,274	1,729
90 to 94 years	16,820	12,237	9,591	7,125	7,506	1,959	1,030	759	605	522
95 to 99 years	3,021	2,378	1,711	1,382	1,423	332	217	155	117	124
100 years and over	399	385	259	264	383	33	36	12	30	37
Unknown	25,711	33,410	28,740	35,201	28,622	5,305	5,396	4,867	3,281	3,886

[1] Figures are exclusive of persons specially enumerated in 1890 in Indian Territory and on Indian reservations, for whom statistics of age are not available.

119652—33——38

580

POPULATION

TABLE 9.—AGE BY 5-YEAR PERIODS, BY COLOR, NATIVITY, AND SEX, FOR THE UNITED STATES: 1880 TO 1930—Continued

SEX AND AGE	FOREIGN-BORN WHITE						NEGRO				
	1930	1920	1910	1900	1890	1880	1930	1920	1910	1900	1890 [1]
TOTAL											
All ages	13,366,407	13,712,754	13,345,545	10,213,817	9,121,867	6,559,679	11,891,143	10,463,131	9,827,763	8,833,994	7,470,040
Under 5 years	27,788	44,984	102,507	52,369	86,629	62,371	1,230,206	1,143,699	1,263,288	1,215,655	1,047,574
Under 1 year	1,428	4,569	6,735	4,206	4,206	6,050	232,378	227,660	252,386	244,510	
1 year	3,228	6,568	11,902	7,645	6,353	10,086	222,536	210,558	219,240	231,940	
2 years	5,454	8,570	18,420	10,637	17,492	13,645	252,585	225,939	260,037	248,922	
3 years	7,675	11,049	28,279	13,562	26,066	15,508	264,314	240,978	264,547	244,083	
4 years	10,003	14,228	37,171	16,523	32,512	16,992	258,393	238,564	267,078	246,200	
5 to 9 years	121,691	169,884	298,509	147,192	248,351	122,697	1,368,881	1,206,207	1,246,553	1,202,758	1,093,494
10 to 14 years	147,736	331,362	358,330	311,565	396,879	238,430	1,251,542	1,236,014	1,155,266	1,091,990	1,033,701
15 to 19 years	324,630	527,942	673,761	561,746	521,295	378,812	1,250,528	1,083,215	1,000,416	982,022	871,118
20 to 24 years	661,992	926,844	1,430,381	919,482	917,374	528,255	1,203,191	1,054,847	1,030,795	969,172	731,548
25 to 29 years	1,021,006	1,662,363	1,662,696	1,007,229	1,072,239	671,116	1,071,787	909,739	881,227	737,479	559,551
30 to 34 years	1,246,830	1,651,475	1,505,715	1,173,683	942,320	762,631	864,514	697,865	608,080	524,607	409,977
35 to 39 years	1,631,667	1,737,805	1,408,093	1,177,506	870,592	789,265	890,000	773,931	633,449	474,687	707,581
40 to 44 years	1,094,176	1,428,099	1,303,475	966,112	850,954	712,890	687,423	559,701	455,413	367,216	
45 to 49 years	1,565,214	1,299,075	1,146,360	840,220	787,815	630,941	630,065	551,589	385,900	326,384	
50 to 54 years	1,317,370	1,107,377	925,055	803,392	709,220	577,087	504,590	399,110	326,070	290,987	409,679
55 to 59 years	1,028,613	908,722	693,520	643,003	525,131	373,114	309,397	229,980	209,622	179,176	
60 to 64 years	910,577	715,731	627,583	545,031	477,047	310,463	242,169	200,118	186,502	161,687	268,320
65 to 69 years	712,314	519,226	488,397	410,740	311,574	181,361	155,177	137,035	123,550	102,671	
70 to 74 years	460,614	381,325	336,967	282,325	199,006	114,609	99,096	91,570	78,839	72,382	
75 to 79 years	269,780	246,487	208,212	158,916	101,215	60,696	58,711	52,352	44,018	40,420	211,684
80 to 84 years	140,892	118,935	101,290	69,075	46,853	31,086	33,377	28,122	25,570	25,527	
85 to 89 years	56,575	47,473	37,433	22,167	16,925	9,515	14,948	12,281	11,166	10,083	
90 to 94 years	13,954	11,717	9,034	5,321	5,126	2,960	6,332	5,847	5,850	5,293	
95 to 99 years	2,714	2,570	1,723	1,412	1,205	1,008	2,611	2,502	2,447	2,434	
100 years and over	450	485	293	391	400	363	2,467	2,935	2,675	2,553	
Unknown	9,824	20,264	26,211	24,880	24,617		13,731	23,503	31,040	48,811	35,813
MALE											
All ages	7,153,709	7,528,322	7,523,788	5,515,285	4,951,858	3,521,635	5,855,669	5,209,436	4,885,881	4,386,547	3,725,561
Under 5 years	14,142	22,857	51,940	26,567	44,040	31,256	611,231	568,633	629,320	604,487	529,085
Under 1 year	720	2,337	3,527	2,017	2,140	2,989	115,388	112,600	125,459	121,329	
1 year	1,632	3,265	6,057	3,945	3,247	5,020	110,284	104,064	109,357	115,102	
2 years	2,781	4,457	9,302	5,413	8,867	6,893	125,695	112,205	130,102	124,334	
3 years	3,940	5,572	14,227	6,777	13,141	7,797	130,378	118,573	130,526	120,671	
4 years	5,069	7,226	18,827	8,415	16,645	8,557	129,486	120,471	133,786	123,051	
5 to 9 years	61,344	85,774	150,652	73,727	126,070	61,803	679,748	631,341	619,175	600,410	549,405
10 to 14 years	74,173	167,152	181,303	157,632	201,159	120,740	623,228	616,251	578,074	548,642	526,450
15 to 19 years	156,659	259,270	351,754	271,381	267,658	184,320	595,646	513,416	507,945	473,750	422,258
20 to 24 years	319,103	456,988	823,920	450,186	476,224	274,038	553,022	487,169	482,157	458,921	350,392
25 to 29 years	515,163	792,088	990,576	589,521	602,545	365,094	500,520	424,352	421,805	360,597	272,044
30 to 34 years	650,595	946,818	828,668	660,702	549,099	419,769	416,869	331,579	332,163	262,130	203,361
35 to 39 years	892,430	1,008,677	812,007	672,804	493,471	432,957	430,472	383,587	320,450	233,371	348,858
40 to 44 years	962,110	803,195	751,519	557,300	475,106	384,931	339,329	275,926	229,680	170,090	
45 to 49 years	881,870	744,423	656,455	468,466	433,466	340,863	323,162	320,500	199,928	168,405	257,301
50 to 54 years	722,496	651,546	526,256	440,079	382,987	318,045	277,532	227,995	179,387	155,188	
55 to 59 years	554,498	503,789	380,110	345,241	278,485	206,820	174,307	129,153	115,090	97,323	
60 to 64 years	483,750	392,629	331,914	285,783	254,101	170,841	133,349	112,137	101,149	85,961	144,761
65 to 69 years	378,000	275,400	255,416	213,441	166,745	98,028	82,843	76,184	67,956	56,018	
70 to 74 years	243,312	194,732	172,751	148,068	106,364	59,590	50,806	47,411	40,584	36,235	
75 to 79 years	137,361	124,170	105,412	82,933	53,167	31,106	29,219	27,172	22,667	20,475	
80 to 84 years	67,016	56,701	50,262	35,390	23,343	15,156	15,343	13,049	11,696	11,655	107,31
85 to 89 years	25,952	22,004	18,081	10,802	8,195	4,419	6,864	5,620	5,164	4,713	
90 to 94 years	5,814	5,123	4,193	2,339	2,308	1,270	2,516	2,340	2,394	2,085	
95 to 99 years	1,087	1,049	767	609	516	433	1,073	1,087	1,017	958	
100 years and over	205	205	126	178	179	156	776	1,018	1,004	850	
Unknown	6,020	13,732	19,706	16,136	16,630		7,064	13,510	17,076	25,157	18,435
FEMALE											
All ages	6,212,698	6,184,432	5,821,757	4,698,532	4,170,009	3,038,044	6,035,474	5,253,695	4,941,882	4,447,447	3,744,479
Under 5 years	13,646	22,127	50,567	25,802	42,589	31,115	618,975	575,066	633,968	611,168	517,589
Under 1 year	708	2,232	3,208	1,985	2,066	3,061	116,990	115,000	126,927	123,181	
1 year	1,596	3,303	5,845	3,700	3,106	5,066	112,252	105,894	109,883	116,838	
2 years	2,673	4,113	9,118	5,224	8,625	6,752	126,890	113,674	129,845	124,588	
3 years	3,735	5,477	14,052	6,785	12,925	7,801	133,936	122,405	134,021	123,412	
4 years	4,934	7,002	18,344	8,108	15,867	8,435	128,907	118,093	133,292	123,149	
5 to 9 years	60,347	84,110	147,857	73,465	122,281	60,894	688,633	634,866	627,378	602,348	544,089
10 to 14 years	73,563	164,210	177,027	153,933	195,220	117,609	628,314	620,663	577,192	543,348	507,251
15 to 19 years	167,971	268,672	322,007	290,365	253,637	194,492	654,882	569,799	552,471	508,272	448,860
20 to 24 years	342,889	469,856	606,461	463,296	441,150	254,217	649,569	567,678	548,038	510,251	381,156
25 to 29 years	505,843	602,275	672,120	507,708	469,694	306,022	571,267	485,387	459,422	376,882	287,507
30 to 34 years	596,235	704,657	617,047	512,981	393,221	342,862	447,645	366,286	335,926	262,477	206,616
35 to 39 years	739,228	729,128	596,086	504,762	377,121	356,308	400,428	390,344	312,990	241,316	303,723
40 to 44 years	732,066	624,904	551,956	408,812	384,848	327,959	348,094	283,775	225,733	188,126	
45 to 49 years	683,344	555,252	489,905	371,754	354,349	290,078	306,903	231,083	185,981	157,889	242,378
50 to 54 years	594,874	515,831	398,799	363,313	326,233	259,042	227,058	171,115	146,683	135,799	
55 to 59 years	474,115	404,933	313,410	297,762	246,646	166,294	135,030	100,827	94,532	81,853	123,559
60 to 64 years	426,827	323,102	295,669	259,248	223,546	139,622	108,820	87,981	85,353	75,726	
65 to 69 years	334,314	243,826	232,981	197,299	144,829	83,333	72,334	60,851	55,594	46,653	
70 to 74 years	217,302	186,593	164,216	134,257	92,642	55,019	48,200	44,168	38,255	36,147	
75 to 79 years	132,419	122,317	102,800	75,983	48,048	29,590	29,492	25,180	21,351	19,945	
80 to 84 years	73,276	62,234	51,028	33,685	23,510	15,930	18,034	15,073	13,883	13,872	104,373
85 to 89 years	30,623	25,469	19,352	11,365	8,730	5,096	8,084	6,661	6,002	5,370	
90 to 94 years	8,140	6,594	4,841	2,982	2,818	1,690	3,816	3,507	3,456	3,208	
95 to 99 years	1,627	1,530	956	803	689	575	1,538	1,475	1,430	1,476	
100 years and over	245	280	167	213	221	207	1,691	1,917	1,671	1,667	
Unknown	3,804	6,532	6,505	8,744	7,987		6,667	9,993	13,964	23,654	17,378

[1] Figures are exclusive of persons specially enumerated in 1890 in Indian Territory and on Indian reservations, for whom statistics of age are not available.

AGE DISTRIBUTION

TABLE **10.**—PER CENT DISTRIBUTION BY 5-YEAR AGE PERIODS, BY COLOR, NATIVITY, AND SEX, FOR THE UNITED STATES: 1880 TO 1930

[Percentages for the total population by sex are shown in Table 7. Per cent not shown where less than 0.1]

SEX AND AGE	TOTAL WHITE						TOTAL NATIVE WHITE						NATIVE WHITE—NATIVE PARENTAGE				
	1930	1920	1910	1900	1890	1880	1930	1920	1910	1900	1890	1880	1930	1920	1910	1900	1890
TOTAL																	
All ages	100.0	100.0	100.0	100.0	100.0	100.0	100.0	100.0	100.0	100.0	100.0	100.0	100.0	100.0	100.0	100.0	100.0
Under 5 years	9.1	10.9	11.4	11.9	12.0	13.4	10.4	12.7	13.5	13.0	14.2	15.6	11.3	12.6	13.2	13.3	13.2
Under 1 year	1.7	2.1	2.4	2.5	2.5	2.8	2.0	2.5	2.9	2.9	3.0	3.3	2.2	2.5	2.8	2.8	2.7
1 year	1.7	2.2	2.1	2.3	1.7	2.4	2.0	2.6	2.5	2.7	2.0	2.8	2.2	2.6	2.5	2.6	1.9
2 years	1.9	2.2	2.3	2.4	2.7	2.8	2.1	2.6	2.7	2.8	3.2	3.2	2.3	2.5	2.7	2.7	3.0
3 years	1.9	2.2	2.3	2.4	2.6	2.7	2.2	2.6	2.7	2.8	3.0	3.1	2.3	2.5	2.7	2.6	2.8
4 years	1.9	2.2	2.3	2.4	2.5	2.7	2.1	2.5	2.6	2.8	3.0	3.1	2.3	2.5	2.6	2.6	2.8
5 to 9 years	10.1	10.6	10.4	11.4	11.8	12.5	11.3	12.2	12.0	13.2	13.6	14.4	11.9	11.9	11.8	12.6	12.9
10 to 14 years	9.7	9.0	9.7	10.4	10.9	11.2	10.9	11.1	11.1	11.7	12.2	12.6	10.7	11.1	10.8	11.4	11.5
15 to 19 years	9.3	8.8	9.7	9.8	10.3	10.0	10.2	9.6	10.7	10.6	11.2	10.8	9.9	9.6	10.3	10.3	10.3
20 to 24 years	8.7	8.6	9.8	9.5	9.9	10.1	9.2	8.9	9.6	9.6	9.9	10.5	9.1	8.9	9.5	9.3	9.3
25 to 29 years	7.9	8.6	8.9	8.6	8.5	8.2	7.9	8.2	8.2	8.2	7.8	7.8	7.9	8.2	8.2	7.8	7.4
30 to 34 years	7.4	7.7	7.7	7.5	7.5	6.9	7.2	7.0	7.0	6.8	7.0	6.0	7.0	7.0	6.9	6.5	6.9
35 to 39 years	7.5	7.3	7.0	6.7	6.3	6.1	6.9	6.4	6.3	5.8	5.6	5.0	6.7	6.5	6.2	5.6	6.0
40 to 44 years	6.0	6.1	5.8	5.8	5.2	5.0	5.8	5.3	5.1	5.1	4.4	4.0	5.6	5.3	5.0	5.1	5.0
45 to 49 years	5.8	5.5	5.0	4.6	4.5	4.3	5.0	4.8	4.3	4.0	3.6	3.3	4.9	4.7	4.2	4.4	4.3
50 to 54 years	5.0	4.6	4.3	3.9	3.8	3.8	4.3	3.9	3.8	3.2	3.0	2.9	4.2	3.8	3.9	3.8	3.7
55 to 59 years	3.9	3.5	3.1	3.0	2.8	2.7	3.4	3.0	2.7	2.4	2.2	2.1	3.3	2.9	3.0	2.9	2.7
60 to 64 years	3.2	2.9	2.5	2.4	2.4	2.3	2.7	2.5	2.1	1.9	1.8	1.8	2.6	2.6	2.5	2.4	2.3
65 to 69 years	2.4	2.0	1.9	1.8	1.7	1.5	2.0	1.7	1.6	1.4	1.3	1.3	1.9	1.9	1.9	1.8	1.7
70 to 74 years	1.7	1.4	1.3	1.2	1.2	1.0	1.4	1.1	1.0	0.9	1.0	0.9	1.5	1.3	1.3	1.2	1.2
75 to 79 years	1.0	0.8	0.8	0.7	0.7	0.6	0.8	0.7	0.6	0.6	0.6	0.5	0.9	0.8	0.8	0.7	0.7
80 to 84 years	0.5	0.4	0.4	0.3	0.3	0.3	0.4	0.3	0.3	0.3	0.3	0.3	0.4	0.4	0.4	0.4	0.4
85 years and over	0.2	0.2	0.2	0.2	0.2	0.1	0.2	0.2	0.1	0.1	0.1	0.1	0.2	0.2	0.2	0.2	0.2
Unknown	0.1	0.1	0.2	0.2	0.2		0.1	0.1	0.2	0.2	0.2		0.1	0.2	0.2	0.3	0.3
MALE																	
All ages	100.0	100.0	100.0	100.0	100.0	100.0	100.0	100.0	100.0	100.0	100.0	100.0	100.0	100.0	100.0	100.0	100.0
Under 5 years	9.2	10.9	11.2	11.7	11.9	13.3	10.5	12.8	13.5	13.9	14.2	15.7	11.4	12.6	13.2	13.3	13.3
Under 1 year	1.8	2.1	2.4	2.5	2.5	2.8	2.0	2.5	2.9	2.9	3.0	3.3	2.2	2.5	2.8	2.8	2.8
1 year	1.7	2.2	2.1	2.3	1.7	2.4	2.0	2.6	2.5	2.7	2.0	2.9	2.2	2.6	2.5	2.6	1.9
2 years	1.9	2.2	2.3	2.3	2.7	2.7	2.1	2.6	2.8	2.8	3.2	3.2	2.3	2.5	2.7	2.6	3.0
3 years	1.9	2.2	2.3	2.3	2.5	2.6	2.2	2.6	2.7	2.8	3.0	3.1	2.3	2.5	2.6	2.6	2.8
4 years	1.9	2.2	2.2	2.3	2.5	2.7	2.2	2.5	2.6	2.8	3.0	3.2	2.3	2.5	2.6	2.6	2.8
5 to 9 years	10.1	10.5	10.2	11.3	11.6	12.5	11.5	12.3	11.9	13.2	13.5	14.5	11.9	11.9	11.8	12.6	12.9
10 to 14 years	9.7	9.8	9.5	10.3	10.8	11.2	11.0	11.2	11.0	11.7	12.2	12.7	10.8	11.1	10.7	11.3	11.6
15 to 19 years	9.2	8.6	9.5	9.5	10.0	9.7	10.2	9.5	10.5	10.4	11.0	10.6	9.8	9.4	10.1	10.2	10.1
20 to 24 years	8.5	8.3	9.7	9.2	9.7	10.0	9.1	8.7	9.4	9.4	9.7	10.5	8.9	8.6	9.2	9.1	9.2
25 to 29 years	7.7	8.5	9.0	8.6	8.5	8.3	7.8	8.1	8.1	8.2	7.8	7.9	7.7	8.0	8.1	7.8	7.4
30 to 34 years	7.4	7.8	7.8	7.7	7.8	7.0	7.1	6.9	7.0	6.8	7.1	6.1	6.9	6.9	6.9	6.6	7.0
35 to 39 years	7.6	7.6	7.2	6.9	6.5	6.1	6.8	6.5	6.4	5.9	5.8	4.9	6.7	6.6	6.3	5.7	6.1
40 to 44 years	6.3	6.2	6.0	6.0	5.3	5.0	5.8	5.3	5.2	5.2	4.4	3.9	5.7	5.3	5.0	5.3	5.0
45 to 49 years	6.0	5.7	5.1	4.8	4.5	4.3	5.0	5.0	4.3	4.1	3.6	3.3	5.0	4.9	4.3	4.5	4.2
50 to 54 years	5.1	4.7	4.5	4.1	3.8	3.9	4.4	4.0	4.0	3.3	3.0	2.9	4.3	4.0	4.1	3.9	3.6
55 to 59 years	4.0	3.6	3.2	3.0	2.8	2.8	3.5	3.0	2.8	2.4	2.2	2.2	3.4	3.0	3.1	2.9	2.7
60 to 64 years	3.2	3.0	2.6	2.4	2.4	2.3	2.7	2.6	2.1	1.0	1.9	1.9	2.7	2.7	2.5	2.3	2.3
65 to 69 years	2.4	2.1	1.9	1.8	1.7	1.5	2.0	1.8	1.5	1.4	1.3	1.3	1.9	2.0	1.9	1.7	1.7
70 to 74 years	1.7	1.4	1.2	1.2	1.2	1.0	1.4	1.1	1.0	0.9	1.0	0.9	1.5	1.3	1.2	1.2	1.2
75 to 79 years	0.9	0.8	0.7	0.7	0.6	0.6	0.8	0.7	0.6	0.5	0.6	0.5	0.9	0.8	0.7	0.7	0.7
80 to 84 years	0.4	0.4	0.3	0.3	0.3	0.3	0.3	0.3	0.3	0.3	0.3	0.2	0.4	0.3	0.3	0.3	0.4
85 years and over	0.2	0.2	0.2	0.1	0.1	0.1	0.1	0.1	0.1	0.1	0.1	0.1	0.2	0.2	0.2	0.1	0.2
Unknown	0.1	0.2	0.2	0.3	0.3		0.1	0.2	0.2	0.3	0.3		0.1	0.2	0.3	0.4	0.3
FEMALE																	
All ages	100.0	100.0	100.0	100.0	100.0	100.0	100.0	100.0	100.0	100.0	100.0	100.0	100.0	100.0	100.0	100.0	100.0
Under 5 years	9.1	11.0	11.6	12.0	12.1	13.4	10.2	12.7	13.5	13.9	14.1	15.5	11.2	12.6	13.3	13.4	13.2
Under 1 year	1.7	2.1	2.4	2.5	2.5	2.8	2.0	2.5	2.8	2.9	2.9	3.3	2.2	2.5	2.8	2.8	2.7
1 year	1.7	2.2	2.2	2.3	1.7	2.4	1.9	2.5	2.5	2.7	2.0	2.8	2.2	2.6	2.5	2.6	1.8
2 years	1.8	2.2	2.4	2.4	2.7	2.8	2.1	2.6	2.7	2.8	3.2	3.2	2.3	2.5	2.7	2.7	3.0
3 years	1.9	2.3	2.4	2.4	2.6	2.7	2.1	2.6	2.7	2.8	3.0	3.1	2.3	2.6	2.7	2.6	2.8
4 years	1.9	2.2	2.3	2.4	2.6	2.7	2.1	2.5	2.6	2.8	3.0	3.1	2.3	2.5	2.6	2.6	2.8
5 to 9 years	10.1	10.8	10.6	11.6	11.9	12.6	11.2	12.2	12.0	13.3	13.6	14.4	11.8	12.0	11.9	12.7	12.9
10 to 14 years	9.7	10.0	9.9	10.5	11.0	11.3	10.8	11.1	11.1	11.8	12.2	12.5	10.7	11.1	10.8	11.4	11.5
15 to 19 years	9.4	9.0	10.0	10.1	10.7	10.3	10.3	9.7	10.8	10.7	11.5	11.0	10.0	9.7	10.5	10.5	10.6
20 to 24 years	8.9	9.0	9.9	9.8	10.1	10.3	9.4	9.2	9.8	9.8	10.0	10.6	9.3	9.1	9.7	9.5	9.4
25 to 29 years	8.1	8.7	8.8	8.6	8.4	8.0	8.0	8.4	8.3	8.3	7.8	7.7	8.0	8.3	8.3	7.8	7.4
30 to 34 years	7.5	7.7	7.5	7.3	7.3	6.7	7.3	7.1	7.0	6.7	6.9	6.0	7.1	7.1	6.8	6.4	6.8
35 to 39 years	7.5	7.1	6.8	6.4	6.0	6.1	6.9	6.4	6.3	5.7	5.4	5.1	6.7	6.4	6.0	5.5	5.8
40 to 44 years	5.5	6.0	5.7	5.5	5.1	5.1	5.8	5.3	5.0	5.0	4.4	4.1	5.6	5.3	4.8	5.0	5.0
45 to 49 years	5.6	5.2	4.8	4.5	4.4	4.2	4.9	4.6	4.2	3.9	3.6	3.3	4.8	4.5	4.1	4.2	4.3
50 to 54 years	4.8	4.4	4.1	3.8	3.8	3.6	4.2	3.8	3.7	3.1	3.0	2.8	4.1	3.6	3.7	3.7	3.7
55 to 59 years	3.9	3.4	3.0	3.0	2.8	2.6	3.4	2.9	2.6	2.4	2.2	2.1	3.2	2.8	2.9	3.0	2.7
60 to 64 years	3.1	2.8	2.5	2.4	2.4	2.2	2.7	2.5	2.1	1.9	1.8	1.8	2.5	2.5	2.4	2.4	2.3
65 to 69 years	2.4	2.0	1.9	1.8	1.7	1.5	2.0	1.7	1.6	1.4	1.3	1.3	1.9	1.9	1.9	1.8	1.7
70 to 74 years	1.7	1.4	1.3	1.2	1.2	1.0	1.4	1.1	1.0	0.9	1.0	0.9	1.4	1.4	1.3	1.2	1.2
75 to 79 years	1.0	0.9	0.8	0.7	0.7	0.6	0.8	0.7	0.6	0.6	0.6	0.5	0.9	0.9	0.8	0.7	0.7
80 to 84 years	0.5	0.4	0.4	0.4	0.4	0.3	0.4	0.3	0.3	0.3	0.3	0.3	0.5	0.4	0.4	0.4	0.4
85 years and over	0.3	0.2	0.2	0.2	0.2	0.2	0.2	0.2	0.2	0.1	0.2	0.1	0.2	0.2	0.2	0.2	0.2
Unknown	0.1	0.1	0.1	0.1	0.2		0.1	0.1	0.1	0.1	0.1		0.1	0.1	0.1	0.2	0.2

582

POPULATION

TABLE 10.—PER CENT DISTRIBUTION BY 5-YEAR AGE PERIODS, BY COLOR, NATIVITY, AND SEX, FOR THE UNITED STATES: 1880 TO 1930—Continued

SEX AND AGE	NATIVE WHITE—FOREIGN OR MIXED PARENTAGE					FOREIGN-BORN WHITE						NEGRO				
	1930	1920	1910	1900	1890	1930	1920	1910	1900	1890	1880	1930	1920	1910	1900	1890
TOTAL																
All ages	100.0	100.0	100.0	100.0	100.0	100.0	100.0	100.0	100.0	100.0	100.0	100.0	100.0	100.0	100.0	100.0
Under 5 years	7.7	13.1	14.2	15.4	16.9	0.2	0.3	0.8	0.5	0.9	1.0	10.3	10.9	12.9	13.8	14.0
Under 1 year	1.4	2.5	3.1	3.2	3.6		0.1				0.1	2.0	2.2	2.6	2.8	
1 year	1.4	2.5	2.7	2.9	2.4		0.1	0.1	0.1	0.2	0.2	1.9	2.0	2.2	2.6	
2 years	1.6	2.7	2.9	3.0	3.8		0.1	0.1	0.1	0.2	0.2	2.1	2.2	2.6	2.8	
3 years	1.7	2.7	2.8	3.1	3.6	0.1	0.1	0.2	0.1	0.3	0.2	2.2	2.3	2.7	2.8	
4 years	1.7	2.7	2.7	3.1	3.4	0.1	0.1	0.3	0.2	0.4	0.3	2.2	2.3	2.7	2.8	
5 to 9 years	9.9	13.0	12.3	14.8	15.6	0.9	1.2	2.2	1.4	2.7	1.9	11.5	12.1	12.7	13.6	14.6
10 to 14 years	11.3	11.4	11.8	12.7	14.2	1.1	2.4	2.7	3.1	4.3	3.6	10.5	11.8	11.8	12.4	13.8
15 to 19 years	11.3	9.6	11.7	11.2	13.9	2.4	3.9	5.0	5.5	5.7	5.8	10.5	10.4	10.8	11.1	11.7
20 to 24 years	9.7	9.2	9.9	10.3	11.7	5.0	6.6	9.0	9.0	10.1	8.1	10.1	10.1	10.5	11.0	9.8
25 to 29 years	8.1	8.5	8.2	9.3	8.9	7.6	10.6	12.5	10.7	11.8	10.2	9.0	8.7	9.0	8.3	7.5
30 to 34 years	7.7	7.0	7.2	7.5	7.2	9.3	12.0	11.3	11.5	10.3	11.6	7.3	6.7	6.8	5.9	5.5
35 to 39 years	7.4	6.2	6.8	6.3	4.5	12.2	12.7	10.6	11.5	9.5	12.0	7.5	7.4	6.4	5.4	
40 to 44 years	6.1	5.4	5.4	5.0	2.5	12.7	10.4	9.8	9.5	9.4	10.9	5.8	5.3	4.6	4.2	9.5
45 to 49 years	5.1	5.0	4.5	3.1	1.7	11.7	9.5	8.6	8.2	8.6	9.6	5.3	5.3	3.9	3.7	
50 to 54 years	4.5	4.0	3.6	1.8	1.1	9.9	8.5	6.9	7.9	7.8	8.8	4.2	3.8	3.3	3.3	6.7
55 to 59 years	3.8	3.0	2.0	1.1	0.6	7.7	6.6	5.2	6.3	5.8	5.7	2.6	2.2	2.1	2.0	
60 to 64 years	2.9	2.3	1.1	0.7	0.4	6.8	5.2	4.7	5.3	5.2	4.7	2.0	1.9	1.9	1.8	3.6
65 to 69 years	2.1	1.2	0.7	0.4	0.3	5.3	3.8	3.7	4.0	3.4	2.8	1.3	1.3	1.3	1.2	
70 to 74 years	1.4	0.6	0.4	0.2	0.2	3.4	2.8	2.5	2.8	2.2	1.7	0.8	0.9	0.8	0.8	
75 to 79 years	0.6	0.3	0.2	0.1	0.1	2.0	1.8	1.6	1.6	1.1	0.9	0.5	0.5	0.4	0.5	2.8
80 to 84 years	0.2	0.1	0.1	0.1	0.1	1.1	0.9	0.8	0.7	0.5	0.5	0.3	0.3	0.3	0.3	
85 years and over	0.1					0.6	0.5	0.4	0.3	0.3	0.2	0.2	0.2	0.2	0.2	
Unknown			0.1	0.1	0.1	0.1	0.1	0.2	0.2	0.3		0.1	0.2	0.3	0.6	0.5
MALE																
All ages	100.0	100.0	100.0	100.0	100.0	100.0	100.0	100.0	100.0	100.0	100.0	100.0	100.0	100.0	100.0	100.0
Under 5 years	7.9	13.3	14.3	15.5	17.0	0.2	0.3	0.7	0.5	0.9	0.9	10.4	10.9	12.9	13.8	14.2
Under 1 year	1.4	2.5	3.1	3.2	3.6						0.1	2.0	2.2	2.6	2.8	
1 year	1.5	2.6	2.7	2.9	2.4			0.1	0.1	0.1	0.1	1.9	2.0	2.2	2.6	
2 years	1.6	2.7	3.0	3.1	3.9		0.1	0.1	0.1	0.2	0.2	2.1	2.2	2.7	2.8	
3 years	1.7	2.8	2.9	3.1	3.6	0.1	0.1	0.2	0.1	0.3	0.2	2.2	2.3	2.7	2.8	
4 years	1.7	2.7	2.7	3.1	3.5	0.1	0.1	0.3	0.2	0.3	0.2	2.2	2.3	2.7	2.8	
5 to 9 years	10.1	13.1	12.4	14.9	15.6	0.9	1.1	2.0	1.3	2.5	1.8	11.6	12.1	12.7	13.7	14.7
10 to 14 years	11.5	11.5	11.9	12.7	14.2	1.0	2.2	2.4	2.9	4.1	3.4	10.6	11.8	11.8	12.5	14.1
15 to 19 years	11.4	9.6	11.6	11.0	13.7	2.2	3.4	4.7	4.9	5.2	5.2	10.2	9.9	10.4	10.8	11.3
20 to 24 years	9.6	9.0	9.7	10.0	11.4	4.5	6.1	8.3	8.3	9.6	7.8	9.5	9.4	9.9	10.5	9.4
25 to 29 years	8.0	8.3	8.0	9.2	8.8	7.2	10.5	13.2	10.7	12.2	10.4	8.5	8.1	8.6	8.2	7.3
30 to 34 years	7.6	6.9	7.1	7.5	7.3	9.1	12.0	11.8	12.0	11.1	11.9	7.1	6.4	6.8	6.0	5.5
35 to 39 years	7.3	6.2	6.7	6.3	4.6	12.5	13.4	10.8	12.2	10.0	12.3	7.4	7.4	6.6	5.3	
40 to 44 years	6.1	5.3	5.4	5.1	2.5	13.4	10.7	10.0	10.1	9.6	10.9	5.8	5.3	4.7	4.1	9.2
45 to 49 years	5.1	5.1	4.5	3.1	1.7	12.3	9.9	8.7	8.5	8.8	9.7	5.5	5.2	4.1	3.8	
50 to 54 years	4.5	4.0	3.7	1.8	1.1	10.1	8.7	7.0	8.0	7.7	9.0	4.7	4.4	3.7	3.5	6.9
55 to 59 years	3.8	3.0	2.1	1.1	0.6	7.8	6.7	5.1	6.3	5.6	5.9	3.0	2.5	2.4	2.2	
60 to 64 years	2.9	2.3	1.2	0.7	0.5	6.8	5.2	4.4	5.2	5.1	4.9	2.3	2.2	2.1	2.0	3.9
65 to 69 years	2.1	1.2	0.7	0.4	0.3	5.3	3.7	3.4	3.9	3.4	2.8	1.4	1.5	1.4	1.3	
70 to 74 years	1.4	0.6	0.4	0.2	0.2	3.4	2.6	2.3	2.7	2.1	1.7	0.9	0.9	0.8	0.8	
75 to 79 years	0.6	0.3	0.2	0.1	0.1	1.9	1.6	1.4	1.5	1.1	0.9	0.5	0.5	0.5	0.5	2.9
80 to 84 years	0.2	0.1	0.1	0.1	0.1	0.9	0.8	0.7	0.6	0.5	0.4	0.3	0.3	0.2	0.3	
85 years and over	0.1					0.5	0.4	0.3	0.3	0.2	0.2	0.2	0.2	0.2	0.2	
Unknown			0.1	0.1	0.1	0.1	0.2	0.3	0.3	0.3		0.1	0.3	0.3	0.6	0.5
FEMALE																
All ages	100.0	100.0	100.0	100.0	100.0	100.0	100.0	100.0	100.0	100.0	100.0	100.0	100.0	100.0	100.0	100.0
Under 5 years	7.6	12.8	14.0	15.3	16.8	0.2	0.4	0.9	0.5	1.0	1.0	10.3	10.9	12.8	13.7	13.8
Under 1 year	1.3	2.4	3.0	3.2	3.6		0.1				0.1	1.9	2.2	2.6	2.8	
1 year	1.4	2.5	2.6	2.9	2.4		0.1	0.1	0.1	0.1	0.2	1.9	2.0	2.2	2.6	
2 years	1.6	2.6	2.9	3.0	3.8		0.1	0.1	0.2	0.1	0.2	2.1	2.2	2.6	2.8	
3 years	1.6	2.7	2.8	3.1	3.6	0.1	0.1	0.2	0.1	0.3	0.3	2.2	2.3	2.6	2.8	
4 years	1.7	2.6	2.6	3.1	3.4	0.1	0.1	0.3	0.2	0.4	0.3	2.1	2.2	2.7	2.8	
5 to 9 years	9.7	12.8	12.1	14.8	15.6	1.0	1.4	2.5	1.6	2.9	2.0	11.4	12.1	12.7	13.5	14.5
10 to 14 years	11.1	11.2	11.7	12.7	14.1	1.2	2.7	3.0	3.3	4.7	3.9	10.4	11.8	11.7	12.2	13.5
15 to 19 years	11.1	9.6	11.7	11.3	14.2	2.7	4.3	5.5	6.2	6.3	6.4	10.9	10.8	11.2	11.4	12.0
20 to 24 years	9.7	9.3	10.1	10.6	12.0	5.5	7.6	10.4	9.9	10.6	8.4	10.8	10.8	11.1	11.5	10.2
25 to 29 years	8.2	8.6	8.3	9.5	9.1	8.1	10.7	11.5	10.8	11.3	10.1	9.5	9.2	9.3	8.5	7.7
30 to 34 years	7.8	7.1	7.3	7.5	7.0	9.6	11.4	10.6	10.9	9.4	11.3	7.4	7.0	6.8	5.9	5.5
35 to 39 years	7.5	6.3	6.8	6.2	4.3	11.9	11.8	10.2	10.7	9.0	11.7	7.6	7.4	6.3	5.4	
40 to 44 years	6.2	5.5	5.4	4.9	2.4	11.8	10.1	9.5	8.7	9.2	10.8	5.8	5.4	4.6	4.2	9.7
45 to 49 years	5.2	4.9	4.4	3.0	1.6	11.0	9.0	8.4	7.9	8.5	9.5	5.1	4.4	3.8	3.6	
50 to 54 years	4.6	4.0	3.5	1.7	1.1	9.6	8.3	6.9	7.7	7.8	8.5	3.8	3.3	3.0	3.1	6.5
55 to 59 years	3.8	3.0	2.0	1.1	0.6	7.6	6.5	5.4	6.3	5.9	5.5	2.2	1.9	1.9	1.8	
60 to 64 years	3.0	2.3	1.1	0.7	0.4	6.9	5.2	5.1	5.5	5.4	4.6	1.8	1.7	1.7	1.7	3.3
65 to 69 years	2.2	1.2	0.7	0.4	0.3	5.4	3.9	4.0	4.2	3.5	2.7	1.2	1.2	1.1	1.0	
70 to 74 years	1.5	0.6	0.4	0.2	0.2	3.5	3.0	2.8	2.9	2.2	1.8	0.8	0.8	0.8	0.8	
75 to 79 years	0.6	0.3	0.2	0.1	0.1	2.1	2.0	1.8	1.6	1.2	1.0	0.5	0.5	0.4	0.4	2.8
80 to 84 years	0.2	0.1	0.1	0.1	0.1	1.2	1.0	0.9	0.7	0.6	0.5	0.5	0.5	0.3	0.3	
85 years and over	0.1	0.1				0.7	0.5	0.4	0.3	0.3	0.2	0.3	0.3	0.3	0.3	
Unknown			0.1		0.1	0.1	0.1	0.1	0.1	0.2		0.1	0.2	0.3	0.5	0.5

AGE DISTRIBUTION   583

TABLE 11.—AGE BY 5-YEAR PERIODS, FOR THE NATIVE WHITE POPULATION OF FOREIGN PARENTAGE AND OF MIXED PARENTAGE, BY SEX, FOR THE UNITED STATES: 1930, 1920, AND 1910

[Per cent not shown where less than 0.1]

| NATIVITY AND AGE | NUMBER | | | | | | | | | PER CENT | | | | | | | | |
| | Total | | | Male | | | Female | | | Total | | | Male | | | Female | | |
	1930	1920	1910	1930	1920	1910	1930	1920	1910	1930	1920	1910	1930	1920	1910	1930	1920	1910
NATIVE WHITE—FOREIGN PARENTAGE																		
All ages	16,999,221	15,694,539	12,916,311	8,438,676	7,810,531	6,456,793	8,560,545	7,884,008	6,459,518	100.0	100.0	100.0	100.0	100.0	100.0	100.0	100.0	100.0
Under 5 years	1,123,962	2,124,350	1,819,847	568,171	1,072,885	917,613	555,791	1,051,465	902,234	6.6	13.5	14.1	6.7	13.7	14.2	6.5	13.3	14.0
5 to 9 years	1,616,338	2,107,263	1,493,496	815,326	1,058,618	750,355	801,012	1,048,745	743,141	9.5	13.4	11.6	9.7	13.6	11.6	9.4	13.3	11.5
10 to 14 years	1,999,694	1,763,468	1,450,618	1,007,597	886,217	729,047	992,097	877,251	721,571	11.8	11.2	11.2	11.9	11.3	11.3	11.6	11.1	11.2
15 to 19 years	2,024,660	1,429,368	1,450,608	1,009,859	707,722	719,111	1,014,801	721,646	731,587	11.9	9.1	11.2	12.0	9.1	11.1	11.9	9.2	11.3
20 to 24 years	1,688,169	1,384,755	1,240,411	834,778	676,135	607,469	853,391	708,620	632,942	9.9	8.8	9.6	9.9	8.7	9.4	10.0	9.0	9.8
25 to 29 years	1,350,190	1,286,562	1,028,610	666,173	631,349	508,410	684,017	655,213	520,200	7.9	8.2	8.0	7.9	8.1	7.9	8.0	8.3	8.1
30 to 34 years	1,283,697	1,052,120	934,608	635,701	518,974	463,060	647,996	533,152	471,548	7.6	6.7	7.2	7.5	6.6	7.2	7.6	6.8	7.3
35 to 39 years	1,237,529	924,617	929,755	614,400	459,056	462,196	623,129	465,561	467,550	7.3	5.9	7.2	7.3	5.9	7.2	7.3	5.9	7.2
40 to 44 years	1,008,860	831,144	770,049	501,364	407,919	384,726	507,496	423,225	385,323	5.9	5.3	6.0	5.9	5.2	6.0	5.9	5.4	6.0
45 to 49 years	838,822	813,043	655,789	415,099	409,412	329,853	423,723	403,631	325,936	4.9	5.2	5.1	4.9	5.2	5.1	4.9	5.1	5.0
50 to 54 years	762,414	676,567	536,299	376,117	336,564	275,073	386,297	340,003	261,226	4.5	4.3	4.2	4.5	4.3	4.3	4.5	4.3	4.0
55 to 59 years	675,488	519,246	268,653	330,632	257,752	147,437	344,856	261,494	141,216	4.0	3.3	2.2	3.9	3.3	2.3	4.0	3.3	2.2
60 to 64 years	540,255	409,476	150,294	260,244	204,438	77,123	280,011	205,038	73,171	3.2	2.6	1.2	3.1	2.6	1.2	3.3	2.6	1.1
65 to 69 years	403,691	208,359	85,721	192,896	103,405	43,982	210,795	104,954	41,739	2.4	1.3	0.7	2.3	1.3	0.7	2.5	1.3	0.6
70 to 74 years	274,506	90,854	43,904	130,912	44,781	22,214	143,594	46,073	21,690	1.6	0.6	0.3	1.6	0.6	0.3	1.7	0.6	0.3
75 to 79 years	116,225	43,198	19,157	54,434	21,058	9,700	61,791	22,140	9,457	0.7	0.3	0.1	0.6	0.3	0.2	0.7	0.3	0.1
80 to 84 years	35,265	16,029	7,029	16,143	7,333	3,467	19,122	8,696	3,562	0.2	0.1	0.1	0.2	0.1	0.1	0.2	0.1	0.1
85 to 89 years	10,241	4,862	2,834	4,560	2,230	1,368	5,681	2,632	1,466	0.1	—	—	0.1	—	—	0.1	—	—
90 to 94 years	1,951	975	787	793	440	410	1,158	535	377	—	—	—	—	—	—	—	—	—
95 to 99 years	324	240	148	138	110	71	186	130	77	—	—	—	—	—	—	—	—	—
100 years and over	44	37	10	22	18	12	22	19	7	—	—	—	—	—	—	—	—	—
Unknown	6,890	8,000	7,585	3,317	4,215	4,096	3,579	3,785	3,489		0.1	0.1		0.1	0.1			0.1
NATIVE WHITE—MIXED PARENTAGE																		
All ages	8,361,985	6,991,665	5,981,526	4,111,468	3,455,021	2,968,446	4,250,497	3,536,644	3,013,080	100.0	100.0	100.0	100.0	100.0	100.0	100.0	100.0	100.0
Under 5 years	836,481	838,057	854,278	424,295	423,778	432,860	412,180	414,270	421,418	10.0	12.0	14.3	10.3	12.3	14.6	9.7	11.7	14.0
5 to 9 years	897,077	832,235	822,153	454,540	420,821	415,129	442,531	411,414	407,024	10.7	11.9	13.7	11.1	12.2	14.0	10.4	11.6	13.5
10 to 14 years	870,500	818,783	785,177	439,563	412,393	395,098	430,937	406,390	390,079	10.4	11.7	13.1	10.7	11.9	13.3	10.1	11.5	12.9
15 to 19 years	829,791	757,799	754,877	416,850	377,362	375,750	412,941	380,437	379,127	9.9	10.8	12.6	10.1	10.9	12.7	9.7	10.8	12.6
20 to 24 years	760,487	697,035	632,697	373,297	338,635	306,652	387,190	358,400	326,045	9.1	10.0	10.6	9.1	9.8	10.3	9.1	10.1	10.8
25 to 29 years	692,720	635,963	516,756	331,576	303,552	246,641	361,144	332,411	270,115	8.3	9.1	8.6	8.1	8.8	8.3	8.5	9.4	9.0
30 to 34 years	663,234	539,148	425,352	314,872	255,803	203,872	348,362	283,345	221,480	7.9	7.7	7.1	7.7	7.4	6.9	8.2	8.0	7.4
35 to 39 years	638,449	487,531	348,616	304,281	234,074	169,660	334,168	252,557	178,956	7.6	7.0	5.8	7.4	6.8	5.7	7.9	7.1	5.9
40 to 44 years	542,218	396,974	256,303	260,116	192,052	127,060	282,102	204,022	129,294	6.5	5.7	4.3	6.3	5.6	4.3	6.6	5.8	4.3
45 to 49 years	464,654	322,309	186,937	224,001	162,093	93,628	240,653	160,216	93,309	5.6	4.6	3.1	5.4	4.7	3.2	5.7	4.5	3.1
50 to 54 years	388,246	230,622	143,832	189,063	118,875	73,786	199,183	117,747	70,046	4.6	3.4	2.4	4.6	3.4	2.5	4.7	3.3	2.3
55 to 59 years	288,164	158,513	91,570	141,196	80,001	47,031	146,968	78,422	44,539	3.4	2.3	1.5	3.4	2.3	1.6	3.5	2.2	1.5
60 to 64 years	204,540	116,097	64,012	99,850	58,784	32,291	104,690	57,319	31,721	2.4	1.7	1.1	2.4	1.7	1.1	2.5	1.6	1.1
65 to 69 years	131,893	69,989	44,229	64,604	35,191	22,162	67,289	34,798	22,067	1.6	1.0	0.7	1.6	1.0	0.7	1.6	1.0	0.7
70 to 74 years	83,024	42,370	26,419	40,732	20,821	13,143	42,892	21,555	13,276	1.0	0.6	0.4	1.0	0.6	0.4	1.0	0.6	0.4
75 to 79 years	41,527	24,196	14,800	20,053	11,571	7,225	21,474	12,625	7,575	0.5	0.3	0.2	0.5	0.3	0.2	0.5	0.4	0.3
80 to 84 years	17,429	10,084	6,985	7,862	4,537	3,294	9,567	5,547	3,691	0.2	0.1	0.1	0.2	0.1	0.1	0.2	0.2	0.1
85 to 89 years	6,148	3,671	2,703	2,612	1,615	1,228	3,536	2,056	1,475	0.1	0.1		0.1			0.1	0.1	
90 to 94 years	1,288	862	708	487	367	326	801	495	382	—	—	—	—	—	—	—	—	—
95 to 99 years	220	159	130	74	72	52	146	87	78	—	—	—	—	—	—	—	—	—
100 years and over	27	32	13	16	15	8	11	17	5	—	—	—	—	—	—	—	—	—
Unknown	3,248	3,230	2,919	1,522	1,019	1,541	1,726	1,011	1,378					0.1				

TABLE 12.—MALES PER 100 FEMALES BY 5-YEAR AGE PERIODS, BY COLOR AND NATIVITY, FOR THE UNITED STATES: 1930 AND 1920

[Ratio not shown where number of females is less than 100]

| AGE | ALL CLASSES | | TOTAL WHITE | | NATIVE WHITE—NATIVE PARENTAGE | | NATIVE WHITE—FOREIGN OR MIXED PARENTAGE | | | | | | FOREIGN-BORN WHITE | | NEGRO | | OTHER RACES | |
| | | | | | | | Total | | Foreign parentage | | Mixed parentage | | | | | | | |
	1930	1920	1930	1920	1930	1920	1930	1920	1930	1920	1930	1920	1930	1920	1930	1920	1930	1920
All ages	102.5	104.0	102.7	104.4	102.3	103.0	98.0	98.6	98.0	99.1	96.7	97.7	115.1	121.7	97.0	99.2	123.9	156.6
Under 5 years	103.0	102.5	103.6	102.9	103.8	103.2	102.5	102.1	102.2	102.0	102.9	102.3	103.6	103.3	98.7	98.9	100.6	102.2
5 to 9 years	102.5	101.9	103.0	102.2	103.3	102.6	102.1	101.3	101.8	100.9	102.7	102.3	101.7	102.0	98.7	99.4	101.7	101.3
10 to 14 years	102.2	101.8	102.6	102.2	102.9	102.6	101.7	101.2	101.6	101.0	102.0	101.5	100.8	101.8	99.2	99.3	104.0	105.8
15 to 19 years	99.4	98.3	100.3	99.3	100.8	99.9	99.9	98.5	99.5	98.1	100.9	99.2	93.3	96.5	91.0	90.1	107.0	126.7
20 to 24 years	96.4	95.3	97.2	96.3	97.6	96.8	97.4	95.1	97.8	95.4	96.4	94.1	93.1	97.8	85.2	85.8	139.7	137.1
25 to 29 years	97.7	99.8	98.2	101.2	98.5	98.7	95.5	94.7	95.4	94.0	91.8	91.8	101.8	119.6	87.6	87.4	149.4	126.5
30 to 34 years	100.1	104.8	100.2	106.0	100.7	100.7	95.4	94.9	98.1	97.3	90.4	90.5	109.1	134.4	93.1	90.5	141.9	197.7
35 to 39 years	103.3	110.1	104.0	111.1	101.9	105.9	96.0	96.6	98.6	98.0	91.1	93.0	120.7	138.3	93.5	98.3	139.8	251.5
40 to 44 years	107.3	107.4	107.8	107.9	103.4	104.6	96.4	95.5	98.8	96.4	92.2	93.7	131.4	128.5	97.5	97.2	156.0	274.0
45 to 49 years	108.9	117.8	108.7	115.4	105.4	113.5	96.2	101.4	98.0	101.4	93.1	94.9	132.3	134.1	105.3	133.7	160.6	291.9
50 to 54 years	110.1	115.3	108.5	113.3	108.1	113.0	95.5	99.5	97.4	99.0	94.9	101.0	121.5	126.8	122.2	133.2	166.5	306.4
55 to 59 years	109.3	112.6	107.6	111.2	108.8	109.6	95.9	99.4	95.9	98.6	96.1	102.1	117.0	124.4	129.1	128.1	159.8	318.2
60 to 64 years	107.3	112.9	106.0	111.6	107.8	111.2	93.6	100.3	92.9	99.7	95.4	102.6	113.3	121.5	122.5	127.5	148.3	272.4
65 to 69 years	104.8	109.2	104.0	107.9	104.2	107.9	92.6	98.5	92.5	98.0	96.0	101.1	113.1	112.0	114.5	125.2	143.9	212.0
70 to 74 years	103.5	102.6	103.2	102.0	103.5	101.8	92.0	97.0	91.2	97.2	95.0	96.6	112.0	104.4	105.6	107.3	135.7	170.4
75 to 79 years	98.0	96.2	97.7	95.4	97.4	92.6	88.1	95.1	88.0	93.9	93.4	91.7	103.7	101.5	99.1	107.9	132.8	125.9
80 to 84 years	88.6	85.7	88.7	85.6	87.9	83.1	83.7	83.3	83.4	84.3	82.2	81.8	92.3	91.1	85.1	86.6	107.9	98.6
85 to 89 years	79.3	79.4	78.7	78.9	76.0	74.8	77.8	82.0	80.3	84.7	73.9	78.6	84.7	86.4	84.9	84.4	97.7	91.0
90 to 94 years	65.4	69.4	65.1	69.7	62.1	64.7	65.3	78.8	66.5	82.2	60.8	74.1	71.4	77.7	65.9	66.7	76.5	83.4
95 to 99 years	63.5	67.8	60.3	65.6	56.3	62.0	63.9	83.9	74.2	84.6	50.7	—	66.8	65.6	69.8	73.7	90.1	69.1
100 years and over	54.8	57.7	74.3	66.6	65.2	59.5	—	—	—	—	—	—	83.7	73.2	45.6	53.1	64.2	—

CHAPTER 11

———

MARITAL CONDITION

CHAPTER 11.—MARITAL CONDITION

INTRODUCTION

This chapter presents statistics of the population classified according to marital condition as shown in the 1930 census, with comparative figures for each census back to 1890. Inquiry regarding marital condition was first made in the census of 1880, but the results were not tabulated; the earliest Federal census figures on marital condition therefore are those for 1890.

The terms "single," "married," "widowed," and "divorced," refer to the marital status at the time the census was taken. A person who has been widowed or divorced but has remarried is reported as married, so that the returns for widowed or divorced persons do not represent the total number of persons now living who have been widowed or divorced Since it is probable that some divorced persons are reported as single, married, or widowed, the census returns doubtless understate somewhat the actual number of divorced persons who have not remarried.

The number of persons under 15 years of age who are married, widowed, or divorced, is naturally very small, comprising, in 1930, 824 males and 4,506 females. In most of the tables, therefore, the statistics on marital condition are presented only for persons 15 years of age and over, since the total population in this age group forms a more logical base for the computation of percentages single, married, etc., than would the aggregate population of all ages.[1] Statistics of marital condition for the total population, including persons under 15 years of age, are presented for the United States in Table 5, and the data for persons under 15 years of age are given by States in Table 19.

For a small number of persons marital condition was not reported. When under 18 years old such persons were classified as single, otherwise as "Unknown." Where space will conveniently permit, the "unknown" are shown separately in the tables; from other tables they are omitted, since they have no particular significance, and form only two-tenths of 1 per cent of the total male population 15 years old and over, and one-tenth of 1 per cent of the female. They are always included in the totals on which the percentages single, married, widowed, and divorced are computed. The percentages would be practically the same, however, if they were based on the number of persons for whom marital condition was reported.

Statistics are presented in this chapter by States and for cities of 25,000 or more. Less detailed statistics are presented for counties and for incorporated places of 2,500 or more in Volume III of the Fifteenth Census Reports on Population; and statistics for the outlying areas enumerated at the Fifteenth Census are presented in the report on Outlying Territories and Possessions.

Marital condition and sex.—In the population 15 years old and over the excess of males over females amounted in 1930 to 1,043,872, or 2.4 per cent. Among single persons alone the males exceeded the females by 3,647,059, or 32.3 per cent. Aside from the excess of males over females in the total population, the principal reason for this disparity in the unmarried is found in the tendency of men to marry at later ages than women.

The excess of married men over married women in 1930 was 156,353, as compared with 530,333 in 1920. The excess of married men is due mainly to the fact that there is a large number of foreign-born married men present in the United States who have left their wives in their native countries. The rapid reduction of this excess is due to the restriction of immigration, and perhaps also to the fact that many of the wives came in as nonquota immigrants prior to the census of 1930.

The excess of widows over widowers is due primarily to the greater longevity of women than of men. This excess is made still greater by the fact that men usually marry at later ages than women, so that even aside from the greater longevity of women, the marriage is more likely to be broken by the death of the husband than by the death of the wife. The excess of widows over widowers is the natural correlative of the excess of single men over single women.

The marital condition of the population 15 years old and over in 1930 is shown in Table 1, with comparative figures for 1920 and 1910.

TABLE 1.—MARITAL CONDITION OF THE POPULATION OF THE UNITED STATES 15 YEARS OLD AND OVER, BY SEX: 1930, 1920, AND 1910

SEX AND MARITAL CONDITION	1930		1920		1910	
	Number	Per cent	Number	Per cent	Number	Per cent
Male	43,881,021	100.0	36,920,663	100.0	32,425,805	100.0
Single	14,963,712	34.1	12,967,565	35.1	12,550,129	38.7
Married	26,327,109	60.0	21,849,266	59.2	18,092,600	55.8
Widowed	2,025,036	4.6	1,758,308	4.8	1,471,390	4.5
Divorced	480,478	1.1	235,284	0.6	156,162	0.5
Unknown	85,686	0.2	110,240	0.3	155,524	0.5
Female	42,837,149	100.0	35,177,515	100.0	30,047,325	100.0
Single	11,300,653	26.4	9,616,902	27.3	8,933,170	29.7
Married	26,170,756	61.1	21,318,933	60.6	17,684,687	58.9
Widowed	4,734,207	11.1	3,917,625	11.1	3,176,228	10.6
Divorced	573,148	1.3	273,304	0.8	185,068	0.6
Unknown	52,385	0.1	5,751	0.1	68,172	0.2

[1] There would seem to be some argument in favor of using different basic age groups for males and females—perhaps 17 years and over for males, and 15 years and over for females—since the percentage married begins to be significant for females about two years earlier than for males. Because of the additional complications which this double set of age limits would bring into the statistics, however, it has not been adopted.

837

838　　POPULATION

Marital condition and age.—Age composition is an important factor in the statistics of marital condition. The prevailing age at marriage and the age distribution of the population govern, to a large extent, the proportion of the population who are or who have been married, because this proportion is smaller among the younger than among the older persons. In the early age groups, the ratio of married to single is larger for females than for males, but the excess of females gradually decreases with each advancing age period until in the older age periods the ratio is reversed and there are nearly twice as many married men as married women. Widows, on the other hand, outnumber widowers in all age groups. Single males greatly exceed single females in the earlier age groups, but in the older age periods, where the proportion single is approximately the same in both sexes, the excess of married males is counterbalanced by the excess of widows over widowers.

The marital condition of the population 15 years of age and over in specified age groups is given in Table 2.

TABLE 2.—MARITAL CONDITION OF THE POPULATION 15 YEARS OLD AND OVER, BY SEX AND AGE, FOR THE UNITED STATES: 1930

[Per cent not shown where less than 0.1]

SEX AND AGE	Total	Single	Married	Widowed	Divorced	Unknown
MALES:						
15 years and over	43,881,021	14,953,712	26,327,109	2,025,036	489,478	85,686
15 to 19 years	5,757,825	5,645,359	100,302	1,513	1,348	9,243
20 to 24 years	5,330,815	3,779,443	1,500,493	17,657	21,000	17,322
25 to 29 years	4,860,180	1,785,413	2,977,004	39,013	50,229	8,521
30 to 34 years	4,561,786	965,945	3,468,176	59,493	62,669	5,503
35 to 44 years	8,816,319	1,261,705	7,189,452	218,881	137,180	9,101
45 to 54 years	6,803,509	776,863	5,551,146	357,047	111,471	7,042
55 to 64 years	4,367,500	442,505	3,407,751	445,262	66,499	5,483
65 to 74 years	2,400,450	216,302	1,654,854	504,042	29,040	4,321
75 and over	915,752	64,315	461,683	379,638	7,431	2,685
PER CENT:						
15 years and over	100.0	34.1	60.0	4.6	1.1	0.2
15 to 19 years	100.0	98.0	1.7	---	---	0.2
20 to 24 years	100.0	70.8	28.1	0.3	0.4	0.3
25 to 29 years	100.0	36.7	61.3	0.8	1.0	0.2
30 to 34 years	100.0	21.2	76.0	1.3	1.4	0.1
35 to 44 years	100.0	14.3	81.5	2.5	1.6	0.1
45 to 54 years	100.0	11.4	81.6	5.2	1.6	0.1
55 to 64 years	100.0	10.1	78.0	10.2	1.5	0.1
65 to 74 years	100.0	9.0	68.7	20.9	1.2	0.2
75 and over	100.0	7.0	50.4	41.5	0.8	0.3
FEMALES:						
15 years and over	42,837,149	11,306,653	26,170,756	4,734,207	573,148	52,385
15 to 19 years	5,794,290	5,032,174	731,967	12,337	12,371	5,441
20 to 24 years	5,533,563	2,547,057	2,857,005	56,375	62,464	10,002
25 to 29 years	4,973,428	1,079,923	3,697,645	102,041	89,124	4,695
30 to 34 years	4,558,035	603,048	3,715,648	148,571	88,219	3,149
35 to 44 years	8,382,521	839,180	6,832,581	547,502	157,650	5,508
45 to 54 years	6,214,514	564,466	4,673,539	872,076	98,874	4,950
55 to 64 years	4,029,398	360,188	2,409,285	1,119,802	45,881	4,242
65 to 74 years	2,311,150	195,104	965,256	1,182,227	15,034	3,529
75 and over	997,444	73,312	181,944	736,807	2,859	2,522
PER CENT:						
15 years and over	100.0	26.4	61.1	11.1	1.3	0.1
15 to 19 years	100.0	86.8	12.6	0.2	0.2	0.1
20 to 24 years	100.0	46.0	51.6	1.0	1.1	0.2
25 to 29 years	100.0	21.7	74.3	2.1	1.8	0.1
30 to 34 years	100.0	13.2	81.5	3.3	1.9	0.1
35 to 44 years	100.0	10.0	81.5	6.5	1.9	0.1
45 to 54 years	100.0	9.1	75.2	14.0	1.6	0.1
55 to 64 years	100.0	8.9	62.0	27.8	1.1	0.1
65 to 74 years	100.0	8.4	41.8	49.0	0.7	0.2
75 and over	100.0	7.3	18.2	73.9	0.3	0.3

The changes in marital status from year to year of age are so rapid in the younger ages that 5-year groups do not show these changes adequately. In the 15 to 19 year group, for example, there are very few persons 15 or 16 years of age married, but the number married increases rapidly in ages 18 and 19. Marital condition is therefore shown by single years of age from 15 to 34 years in Tables 8, 9, and 11. Above the age of 35, changes are less rapid and the presentation by 5-year periods is adequate.

From the tabulation by single years, it is possible to arrive at an approximation of the median age at first marriage. The true median age at first marriage could only be computed from a tabulation of the records of all first marriages in a given period. In earlier years, however, nearly all marriages are first marriages, and the percentage of persons who are or have been married increases rapidly with every year of age. In these ages also there are comparatively few deaths of persons who are or have been married. It may be assumed, therefore, that the age at which exactly 50 per cent of the persons enumerated are or have been married, and at which 50 per cent remain single, will practically coincide with the median age at first marriage. The median age at first marriage calculated in this manner is presented in Table 3 for the population of the United States classified by sex, color, and nativity.

TABLE 3.—MEDIAN AGE AT MARRIAGE, BY SEX, COLOR, AND NATIVITY, FOR THE UNITED STATES: 1930

COLOR AND NATIVITY	Male	Female
All classes	25.8	22.4
Native white	25.6	22.6
Native parentage	25.0	22.0
Foreign or mixed parentage	27.3	23.9
Foreign-born white	27.6	23.4
Negro	23.3	20.5

Color, nativity, and parentage.—Statistics of marital condition are shown separately for the main population classes—native white of native parentage, native white of foreign or mixed parentage, foreign-born white, Negro, and "Other races." Each of these classes presents its own characteristics with respect to marital condition, especially when tabulated by age. The foreign-born population in particular differs widely from the native classes because of its abnormal age composition and its greater excess of males over females. In the foreign-born population the excess of single men over single women is large, and there is also a large excess of married men over married women.

In the native white population of foreign or mixed parentage there is a considerable excess of married women over married men. This probably results from the fact that many native women of foreign white stock marry foreign-born men, usually of the same nationality. Because of the fact that there is thus a considerable amount of intermarriage between one of the white classes and another, it should not be expected that there would be an approximate equality between the number of married men and the number of married women within any one class.

MARITAL CONDITION

In each class of the white population, and also among the Negroes, the number of widows is more than twice as large as the number of widowers for reasons already noted above; and in both white and Negro there is a considerable excess of divorced women over divorced men.

The relatively low proportion of married persons among the native white of foreign or mixed parentage—the children of immigrants—may be accounted for in part by the concentration of persons of this class in the lower age groups and by the large proportion that live in urban places (73.4 per cent in 1930), since the percentage of the population married is always smaller in urban than in rural communities.

Statistics on marital condition in the past have included Mexicans with the white population. Because of the large increase of Mexicans in certain States within the last 10 years, they were given a separate classification in the 1930 census and grouped in many of the tabulations with "Other races," which include also Indians, Chinese, Japanese, Filipinos, etc. The marital condition of the individual races is shown, for the United States in Table 7, for separate States in Table 16, and for the larger cities in Table 27.

Divisions, States, and cities.—Considerable differences in marital condition are found when one section of the country is compared with another, not only when the comparison is made with regard to the population as a whole, but also when particular classes are taken into consideration.

The marital condition of the total population or of any class may be affected by interstate migration, both directly, through differences between persons of different marital classes in regard to the disposition to migrate, and indirectly, through the influence of migration upon sex and age distribution. There are no statistics bearing specifically on this point, but it may be presumed that unattached persons—single men and women and widowed or divorced persons without children—are more likely to migrate than those with families. This being the case, and other things being equal, relatively fewer unmarried persons will be found in States and divisions which lose more than they gain through interstate migration than in those which gain more than they lose.

Another factor affecting marital condition in divisions and States as compared with one another is the relative importance of urban population. The sex and age distribution of the urban population differs from that of the rural population, and the proportion of unmarried persons is larger, as a rule, especially among women, in cities than in rural communities. A State in which the proportion of urban population is large is, therefore, likely to have a somewhat larger proportion of single persons in its adult population than a State which is predominantly rural.

Urban and rural population.—Urban population, as distinguished from rural, may in general be defined as that residing in cities or other incorporated places having 2,500 or more inhabitants, and the remainder of the country is classified as rural. In three of the New England States, New Hampshire, Massachusetts, and Rhode Island, conditions are exceptional in that compactly built portions of the towns (townships) are not separately incorporated or politically distinct in any way from the rural territory of the same town; nor is it the usual practice to incorporate even the larger places and cities until they attain a population in excess of 10,000. For these New England States, in 1930, the urban population included, in addition to regularly incorporated cities, those towns in which there is a village or thickly settled area having more than 2,500 inhabitants and comprising, either by itself or when combined with other villages in the same town, more than 50 per cent of the total population of the town. Furthermore, in other States, townships or other political subdivisions (not incorporated as municipalities nor containing any area so incorporated) which, in 1930, had a total population of 10,000 or more, and a population density of 1,000 or more per square mile, are classified as urban.

The rural population in 1930 is separated into the rural-farm and rural-nonfarm population. The *rural-farm* population comprises all persons in rural territory living on a farm, without regard to occupation. The *rural-nonfarm* population, sometimes termed the "village" population, includes in general all persons living outside of cities or other incorporated places having a population of 2,500 or more who do not live on farms. This rural-nonfarm population is not uniform in its make-up and varies in different parts of the country. In some sections it consists of inhabitants of small manufacturing villages or suburban areas which are not incorporated, in other parts it includes mining settlements, or in still other sections it is made up of inhabitants of small commercial centers who are mainly occupied in supplying the wants of the farm population.

Marital condition by country of origin.—The foreign-born white population has been classified for 1930 by marital condition in combination with country of birth; and the native white population of foreign or mixed parentage has been classified by marital condition in combination with country of birth of parents. This is the first attempt to show the marital condition of the population of foreign derivation by nationality or country of origin.

These figures are summarized for the United States, and for urban and rural areas, in Tables 31 and 32, and are presented by States and for the more important cities in Tables 33 and 34.

840

POPULATION

MARITAL CONDITION OF THE POPULATION 15 YEARS OLD AND OVER, BY SEX, COLOR, NATIVITY, AND AGE: 1930

1 ALL CLASSES	4 FOREIGN-BORN WHITE	SINGLE
2 NATIVE WHITE—NATIVE PARENTAGE	5 NEGRO	MARRIED
3 NATIVE WHITE—FOREIGN OR MIXED PARENTAGE		WIDOWED OR DIVORCED

MARITAL CONDITION

PER CENT MARRIED IN THE URBAN, RURAL-FARM, AND RURAL-NONFARM POPULATION 15 YEARS OLD AND OVER, BY SEX, COLOR, NATIVITY, AND AGE: 1930

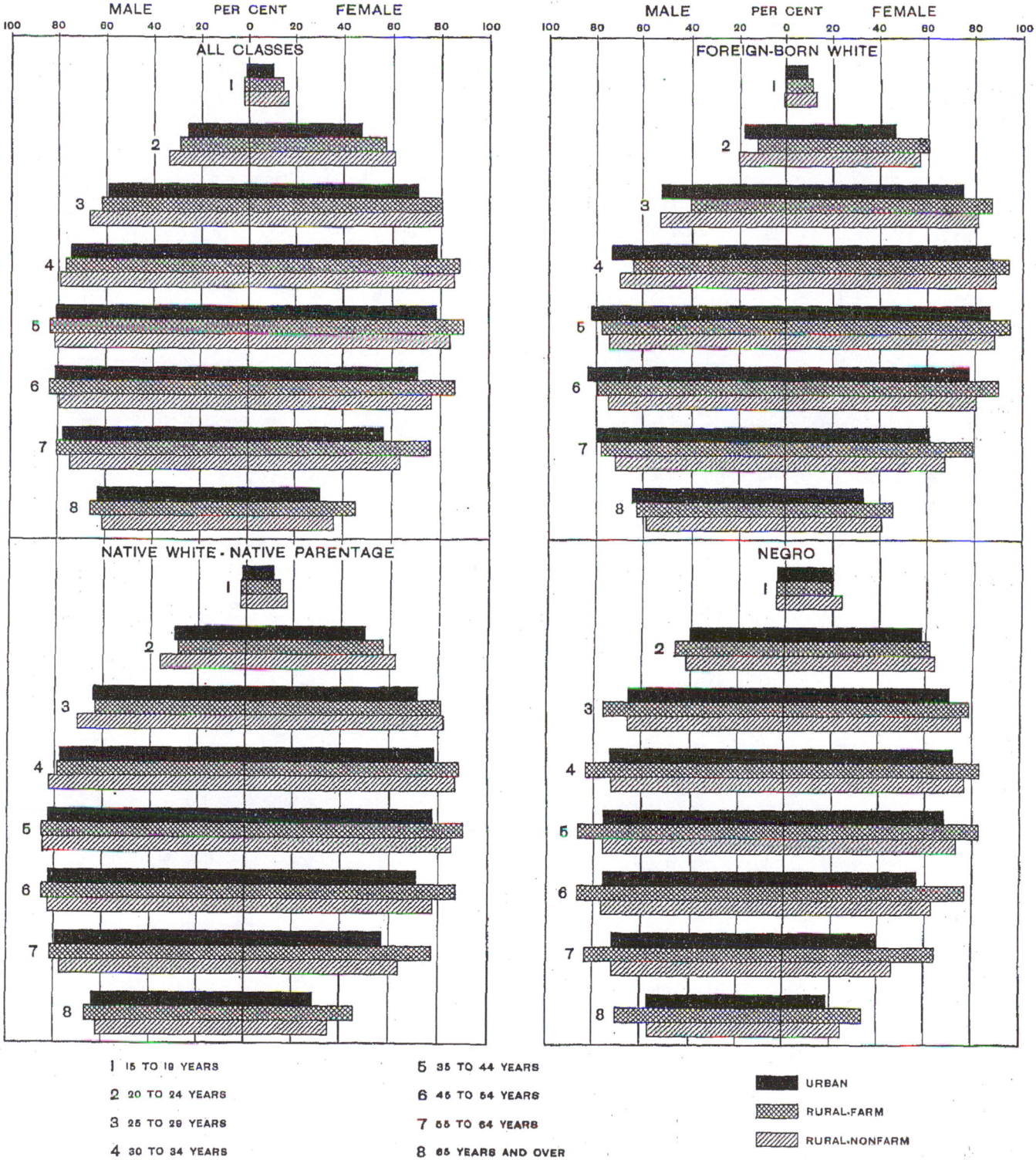

1 15 TO 19 YEARS	5 35 TO 44 YEARS
2 20 TO 24 YEARS	6 45 TO 54 YEARS
3 25 TO 29 YEARS	7 55 TO 64 YEARS
4 30 TO 34 YEARS	8 65 YEARS AND OVER

URBAN

RURAL-FARM

RURAL-NONFARM

TABLE 4.—MARITAL CONDITION OF THE POPULATION 15 YEARS OLD AND OVER, BY SEX, COLOR, AND NATIVITY, FOR THE UNITED STATES: 1890 TO 1930

[Per cent not shown where base is less than 100]

COLOR, NATIVITY, AND CENSUS YEAR	MALES 15 YEARS OLD AND OVER: Total	Single: Number	Single: Per cent	Married: Number	Married: Per cent	Widowed: Number	Widowed: Per cent	Divorced	Unknown	FEMALES 15 YEARS OLD AND OVER: Total	Single: Number	Single: Per cent	Married: Number	Married: Per cent	Widowed: Number	Widowed: Per cent	Divorced	Unknown
All classes:																		
1930	43,881,021	14,953,712	34.1	26,327,109	60.0	2,025,036	4.6	489,478	85,686	42,837,149	11,306,653	26.4	26,170,756	61.1	4,734,207	11.1	573,148	52,385
1920	36,920,663	12,967,565	35.1	21,849,266	59.2	1,758,308	4.8	235,284	110,240	35,177,515	9,616,902	27.3	21,318,933	60.6	3,917,625	11.1	273,304	50,751
1910	32,425,805	12,550,129	38.7	18,092,600	55.8	1,471,390	4.5	156,162	155,524	30,047,325	8,933,170	29.7	17,684,687	58.9	3,176,228	10.6	185,068	68,172
1900	25,620,399	10,297,940	40.2	13,955,650	54.5	1,177,976	4.6	84,230	104,603	24,249,191	7,566,530	31.2	13,810,057	57.0	2,717,715	11.2	114,647	40,242
1890[1]	20,777,872	8,655,711	41.7	11,205,205	53.9	815,437	3.9	49,100	52,419	19,602,178	6,233,316	31.8	11,124,785	56.8	2,154,598	11.0	71,883	17,596
White:																		
1930	39,214,156	13,364,509	34.1	23,603,312	60.2	1,745,213	4.5	428,073	73,049	38,220,229	10,229,306	26.8	23,444,243	61.3	4,023,372	10.5	477,624	45,684
1920	33,335,586	11,782,665	35.3	19,698,113	59.1	1,549,164	4.6	207,663	97,981	31,654,841	8,772,732	27.7	19,210,238	60.7	3,399,602	10.7	228,565	43,644
1910	29,158,125	11,360,282	39.0	16,253,940	55.7	1,274,388	4.4	135,203	134,312	26,857,337	8,091,249	30.1	15,852,011	59.0	2,705,990	10.1	150,801	57,286
1900	22,808,628	9,173,430	40.2	12,455,858	54.6	1,020,387	4.5	72,761	86,192	21,483,052	6,747,306	31.4	12,319,767	57.3	2,291,872	10.7	91,737	32,370
1890	18,534,187	7,732,832	41.7	9,992,910	53.9	721,971	3.9	43,829	42,645	17,404,915	5,575,143	32.0	9,924,785	57.0	1,831,772	10.5	61,125	12,090
Native white:																		
1930	32,210,106	11,858,592	36.8	18,042,713	57.9	1,282,341	4.0	365,243	61,217	32,155,087	9,459,175	29.4	19,200,906	59.7	3,030,472	9.4	425,682	38,852
1920	26,083,047	9,927,618	38.1	14,795,171	56.7	1,111,115	4.3	175,713	73,430	25,740,856	7,936,933	30.8	15,086,735	58.6	2,480,407	9.6	200,909	35,872
1910	22,018,232	9,091,366	41.3	11,821,805	53.7	889,662	4.0	112,144	103,255	21,411,031	7,097,139	33.1	12,228,008	57.1	1,905,878	8.9	130,259	49,747
1900	17,551,269	7,627,637	43.5	9,100,302	51.8	693,949	4.0	59,415	69,966	17,037,720	5,878,706	34.5	9,464,321	55.5	1,589,287	9.3	79,219	26,187
1890	13,953,598	6,262,921	44.9	7,142,105	51.2	483,646	3.5	34,722	30,204	13,594,906	4,787,006	35.2	7,489,739	55.1	1,256,918	9.2	52,146	8,287
Native white—Native par.:																		
1930	23,369,460	8,054,686	34.5	14,013,140	60.0	976,085	4.2	279,723	45,826	22,978,599	6,254,818	27.2	14,143,668	61.6	2,227,800	9.7	324,768	27,485
1920	19,092,107	6,776,518	35.5	11,244,289	58.9	874,821	4.6	134,789	61,690	18,529,748	5,268,490	28.4	11,195,865	60.4	1,885,000	10.2	152,743	27,650
1910	16,233,095	6,185,324	38.1	9,144,099	56.3	728,883	4.5	87,456	87,333	15,523,900	4,644,122	29.9	9,219,385	59.4	1,523,560	9.8	100,053	36,780
1900	13,088,058	5,195,263	39.7	7,193,922	55.0	587,894	4.5	47,993	62,986	12,561,813	3,893,417	31.0	7,251,375	57.7	1,332,334	10.6	62,585	22,102
1890	10,880,185	4,359,200	40.1	6,030,295	55.4	432,260	4.0	30,182	28,248	10,530,675	3,226,180	30.6	6,132,027	58.2	1,120,959	10.6	44,284	7,225
Native white—For. or mixed par.:																		
1930	8,840,646	3,803,906	43.0	4,629,573	52.4	306,256	3.5	85,520	15,391	9,176,488	3,204,357	34.9	5,057,238	55.1	802,012	8.7	100,914	11,307
1920	6,990,940	3,151,100	45.1	3,550,882	50.8	236,294	3.4	40,924	11,740	7,211,108	2,668,443	37.0	3,890,870	54.0	595,407	8.3	48,166	8,222
1910	5,785,137	2,906,042	50.2	2,677,706	46.3	160,779	2.8	24,688	15,922	5,887,131	2,453,017	41.7	3,008,623	51.1	382,318	6.5	30,206	12,907
1900	4,463,211	2,432,374	54.5	1,906,380	42.7	106,055	2.4	11,422	6,980	4,475,907	1,985,289	44.4	2,212,946	49.4	256,953	5.7	16,634	4,085
1890	3,073,413	1,903,721	61.9	1,111,810	36.2	51,386	1.7	4,540	1,956	3,064,321	1,561,726	51.0	1,357,712	44.3	135,959	4.4	7,862	1,002
Foreign-born white:																		
1930	7,004,050	1,505,917	21.5	4,960,599	70.8	462,872	6.6	62,830	11,832	6,065,142	770,131	12.7	4,243,337	70.0	992,900	16.4	51,942	6,832
1920	7,252,539	1,855,047	25.6	4,902,942	67.6	438,049	6.0	31,950	24,551	5,913,985	835,799	14.1	4,123,503	69.7	910,255	15.5	27,656	7,772
1910	7,139,893	2,268,916	31.8	4,432,135	62.1	384,726	5.4	23,059	31,057	5,446,306	994,110	18.3	3,624,003	66.5	800,112	14.7	20,542	7,539
1900	5,257,359	1,545,793	29.4	3,355,556	63.8	326,438	6.2	13,346	16,226	4,445,332	868,600	19.5	2,855,446	64.2	702,585	15.8	12,518	6,183
1890	4,580,589	1,469,911	32.1	2,850,805	62.2	238,325	5.2	9,107	12,441	3,809,919	787,237	20.7	2,435,046	63.9	574,854	15.1	8,979	3,803
Negro:																		
1930	3,941,462	1,270,950	32.2	2,357,821	59.8	247,595	6.3	55,713	9,383	4,099,552	953,806	23.3	2,398,144	58.5	652,063	15.9	88,868	6,071
1920	3,393,211	1,104,877	32.6	2,050,407	60.4	200,734	5.9	26,689	10,504	3,423,100	825,258	24.1	2,039,181	59.6	507,961	14.8	43,871	6,829
1910	3,059,312	1,083,472	35.4	1,749,228	57.2	189,970	6.2	20,146	16,496	3,103,344	823,996	26.6	1,775,949	57.2	459,831	14.8	33,286	10,282
1900	2,633,008	1,033,285	39.2	1,422,880	54.0	151,233	5.7	11,026	14,578	2,690,583	803,683	29.9	1,443,817	53.7	414,107	15.4	22,033	6,943
1890	2,110,721	842,764	39.8	1,175,513	55.5	91,683	4.3	5,212	4,549	2,175,550	652,314	30.0	1,187,434	54.6	320,194	14.7	10,088	4,920
Other races:																		
1930	725,403	318,253	43.9	365,976	50.5	32,228	4.4	5,692	3,254	517,368	123,541	23.9	328,369	63.5	58,172	11.2	6,656	630
1920	191,860	80,023	41.7	100,746	52.5	8,410	4.4	932	1,755	99,574	18,912	19.0	69,514	69.8	10,002	10.0	868	278
1910	208,368	106,375	51.1	89,432	42.9	7,032	3.4	813	4,716	86,644	17,925	20.7	56,727	65.5	10,407	12.0	981	604
1900	178,763	91,225	51.0	76,906	43.0	6,356	3.6	443	3,833	75,556	15,541	20.6	46,473	61.5	11,736	15.5	877	929
1890	123,964	80,115	64.6	36,782	29.7	1,783	1.4	59	5,225	21,713	5,859	27.0	12,566	57.9	2,632	12.1	70	586
Mexican:[2]																		
1930	472,575	198,936	42.1	247,592	52.4	21,453	4.5	3,299	1,205	381,524	93,302	24.5	238,077	62.4	45,661	11.8	4,587	407
Indian:																		
1930	103,441	38,021	36.8	56,382	54.5	7,173	6.9	1,646	219	96,084	23,335	24.3	59,168	61.6	11,541	12.0	1,876	164
1920	76,321	26,450	34.7	43,095	56.5	5,711	7.5	680	385	70,431	16,238	23.1	43,923	62.4	9,217	13.1	826	227
1910	80,383	27,391	34.1	46,154	57.4	5,319	6.6	679	840	76,982	16,324	21.2	49,095	63.8	10,071	13.1	959	533
1900	72,076	24,323	33.7	41,067	57.0	4,974	6.9	418	1,294	71,497	14,350	20.1	43,906	61.4	11,458	16.0	870	913
1890	19,011	7,990	40.1	9,863	49.5	1,241	6.2	45	772	18,412	4,717	25.6	10,543	57.3	2,541	13.8	67	544
Chinese:																		
1930	51,519	25,108	48.7	23,868	46.3	1,349	2.6	112	1,082	8,169	1,904	23.3	5,574	68.2	631	7.7	37	23
1920	49,818	23,096	46.4	24,782	49.7	1,355	2.7	66	519	4,407	962	21.8	3,046	69.1	371	8.4	15	13
1910	64,304	34,330	53.3	26,449	41.1	1,139	1.8	45	2,431	2,955	680	23.0	2,016	68.2	229	7.7	5	25
1900	83,633	48,997	58.6	31,794	38.0	1,310	1.6	19	1,513	3,204	778	24.3	2,157	67.3	259	8.1	3	7
1890	102,322	70,625	69.0	26,720	26.1	530	0.5	13	4,434	3,074	993	32.3	1,951	63.5	85	2.8	3	42
Japanese:																		
1930	52,799	21,059	39.9	29,401	55.7	1,756	3.3	403	180	20,411	4,475	15.2	23,930	81.4	853	2.9	123	30
1920	57,427	24,423	42.5	31,250	54.4	1,118	1.9	154	482	24,242	1,604	6.6	22,193	91.5	388	1.6	23	34
1910	60,636	42,688	70.5	15,918	26.3	495	0.8	86	1,349	6,648	908	13.7	5,581	84.0	96	1.4	17	46
1900	23,054	17,905	77.7	4,045	17.5	72	0.3	6	1,026	855	413	48.3	410	48.0	19	2.2	4	9
1890	1,731	1,500	86.7	199	11.5	12	0.7	1	19	227	149	65.6	72	31.7	6	2.6	-----	-----
Filipino:																		
1930	40,904	32,554	79.6	7,409	18.1	338	0.8	190	413	1,640	309	18.8	1,258	76.7	53	3.2	16	4
1920	5,077	4,177	82.3	589	11.6	49	1.0	21	241	231	61	26.4	164	71.0	4	1.7	2	-----
1910	132	96	72.7	25	18.9	5	3.8	1	5	9	4	-----	5	-----	-----	-----	-----	-----
All other:																		
1930	4,165	2,575	61.8	1,324	31.8	159	3.8	42	65	540	126	23.3	362	67.0	33	6.1	17	2
1920	3,223	1,877	58.2	1,030	32.0	177	5.5	11	128	263	47	17.9	188	71.5	22	8.4	2	4
1910	2,923	1,870	64.0	880	30.3	74	2.5	2	91	50	9	-----	30	-----	11	-----	-----	-----

[1] Figures for 1890 are exclusive of 325,464 persons (169,221 males and 156,243 females) specially enumerated in Indian Territory and on Indian reservations, for whom statistics of marital condition are not available.

[2] The Mexican classification was made for the first time in 1930. The total white population as classified in 1920 included 700,541 persons (estimated), comprising 243,181 natives of foreign or mixed parentage and 457,360 foreign born, who would have been counted as Mexican in 1930. It was not practicable to make further estimates, to distribute by age and marital condition. The earlier figures for the white population are therefore a little too large, and those for "other races" too small, for exact comparison with 1930; but it is not probable that the percentages single, married, widowed, or divorced are materially affected.

MARITAL CONDITION

843

TABLE 5.—MARITAL CONDITION OF THE TOTAL POPULATION, BY SEX, COLOR, NATIVITY, AND 5-YEAR AGE PERIODS, FOR THE UNITED STATES: 1930

COLOR, NATIVITY, AND AGE	MALES						FEMALES					
	Total	Single	Married	Widowed	Di-vorced	Un-known	Total	Single	Married	Widowed	Di-vorced	Un-known
All classes	62,137,080	33,203,947	26,327,870	2,025,078	489,499	85,686	60,637,966	29,102,964	26,174,997	4,734,374	573,246	52,385
Under 15 years old	18,256,059	18,255,235	761	42	21		17,800,817	17,796,311	4,241	167	98	
15 years old and over	43,881,021	14,953,712	26,327,109	2,025,036	489,478	85,686	42,837,149	11,306,653	26,170,756	4,734,207	573,148	52,385
15 to 19 years	5,757,825	5,645,359	100,362	1,513	1,348	9,243	5,794,200	5,032,174	731,907	12,337	12,371	5,441
20 to 24 years	5,336,815	3,779,443	1,500,493	17,657	21,000	17,322	5,533,563	2,547,057	2,857,665	56,375	62,464	10,002
25 to 29 years	4,860,180	1,785,413	2,977,004	39,013	50,229	8,521	4,973,428	1,070,923	3,697,645	102,041	89,124	4,695
30 to 34 years	4,501,786	965,945	3,468,176	59,493	62,669	5,503	4,558,635	603,048	3,715,648	148,571	88,219	3,140
35 to 39 years	4,679,860	718,306	3,792,614	93,204	70,765	4,881	4,528,785	472,058	3,725,680	240,604	87,533	2,915
40 to 44 years	4,130,450	543,309	3,396,838	125,677	66,415	4,220	3,863,736	367,077	3,106,901	306,958	70,117	2,683
45 to 49 years	3,071,924	435,252	3,013,521	158,561	60,850	3,740	3,370,355	303,864	2,616,213	391,342	56,446	2,400
50 to 54 years	3,131,645	341,611	2,537,625	198,486	50,621	8,302	2,844,150	260,602	2,057,326	481,334	42,428	2,469
55 to 59 years	2,425,992	251,017	1,929,201	204,742	38,220	2,812	2,210,685	199,500	1,469,931	520,158	27,808	2,129
60 to 64 years	1,941,508	191,486	1,478,550	240,520	28,279	2,671	1,800,713	160,619	1,029,354	590,644	17,983	2,113
65 to 69 years	1,417,812	131,451	1,013,226	252,072	18,783	2,280	1,352,793	114,186	630,203	596,224	10,204	1,886
70 to 74 years	901,647	84,851	641,028	251,070	11,157	2,041	958,857	80,918	334,963	536,003	4,830	1,643
75 years and over	915,752	64,315	461,683	379,038	7,431	2,685	997,444	73,312	181,944	736,807	2,859	2,522
Unknown	51,816	15,862	16,188	2,490	811	16,465	42,206	12,251	15,226	5,809	672	8,248
Native white	48,010,145	27,658,011	18,643,293	1,282,364	365,260	61,217	47,487,655	24,788,545	19,203,947	3,030,570	425,741	38,852
Under 15 years old	15,800,039	15,799,419	580	23	17		15,332,508	15,329,370	3,041	98	59	
15 years old and over	32,210,106	11,858,592	18,042,713	1,282,341	365,243	61,217	32,155,087	9,459,175	19,200,906	3,030,472	425,682	38,852
15 to 19 years	4,007,310	4,822,442	75,435	807	847	7,785	4,879,638	4,298,017	503,460	5,726	7,899	4,527
20 to 24 years	4,346,913	3,180,798	1,177,005	9,556	15,802	13,602	4,457,250	2,128,108	2,249,554	27,209	44,303	8,016
25 to 29 years	3,731,704	1,348,262	2,315,882	23,200	38,915	5,535	3,820,890	867,510	2,832,360	52,254	65,428	3,344
30 to 34 years	3,408,584	690,730	2,628,403	37,073	48,888	3,430	3,464,352	495,106	2,805,280	84,892	65,473	2,209
35 to 39 years	3,278,767	477,122	2,680,154	56,099	52,933	2,859	3,273,186	387,576	2,679,662	138,437	65,473	2,038
40 to 44 years	2,771,481	351,674	2,293,814	74,804	48,674	2,425	2,732,850	301,323	2,195,275	181,865	52,567	1,820
45 to 49 years	2,411,000	286,063	1,985,781	93,662	44,106	2,207	2,345,866	246,386	1,821,098	234,801	41,908	1,673
50 to 54 years	2,002,785	233,370	1,609,356	120,774	37,214	2,071	1,908,901	210,635	1,453,230	301,150	32,221	1,665
55 to 59 years	1,670,570	178,741	1,320,020	132,214	28,741	1,854	1,503,924	164,944	1,060,963	344,083	21,544	1,490
60 to 64 years	1,305,260	134,112	996,243	152,373	20,756	1,776	1,261,156	130,638	724,540	390,952	13,641	1,385
65 to 69 years	944,823	90,768	677,823	160,915	13,803	1,514	937,703	93,352	438,547	396,998	7,512	1,289
70 to 74 years	590,036	60,327	449,741	170,195	8,359	1,414	687,400	67,215	241,545	373,851	3,089	1,100
75 years and over	613,370	43,102	314,626	248,405	5,415	1,741	680,049	58,493	124,819	494,011	2,120	1,506
Unknown	36,489	10,991	10,370	1,574	610	12,944	31,016	9,812	10,564	3,348	482	6,810
Native white—Native parentage	35,460,001	20,144,711	14,013,623	976,103	279,738	45,826	34,676,613	17,949,828	14,146,538	2,227,944	324,818	27,485
Under 15 years old	12,090,541	12,090,025	483	18	15		22,978,599	11,605,010	2,870	84	50	
15 years old and over	23,369,460	8,054,686	14,013,140	976,085	279,723	45,826	22,978,599	6,254,818	14,143,668	2,227,860	324,768	27,485
15 to 19 years	3,480,607	3,405,820	68,783	748	773	4,474	3,451,896	2,955,561	481,596	5,322	7,018	2,399
20 to 24 years	3,188,838	2,138,640	969,747	8,513	13,680	8,258	3,216,609	1,402,570	1,749,322	23,268	36,870	4,039
25 to 29 years	2,734,045	880,375	1,790,507	18,972	31,543	3,648	2,775,735	563,273	2,116,789	42,076	51,485	2,112
30 to 34 years	2,458,011	441,034	1,948,325	28,577	37,564	2,511	2,467,094	318,020	2,028,131	64,432	50,323	1,479
35 to 39 years	2,360,086	302,813	1,972,514	42,677	39,803	2,180	2,315,889	241,969	1,921,072	102,347	48,461	1,440
40 to 44 years	2,010,001	222,665	1,692,794	56,176	36,442	1,924	1,943,252	185,835	1,584,541	132,605	38,052	1,319
45 to 49 years	1,772,809	181,062	1,485,982	70,517	33,515	1,733	1,681,490	148,700	1,320,722	170,762	31,090	1,216
50 to 54 years	1,527,605	144,439	1,264,076	89,545	27,846	1,699	1,418,421	123,392	1,050,970	218,875	23,944	1,231
55 to 59 years	1,198,742	107,037	972,470	95,693	21,100	1,473	1,102,100	93,827	752,531	238,803	15,780	1,099
60 to 64 years	945,106	82,737	734,414	110,960	15,636	1,419	876,455	75,018	517,006	272,060	10,137	1,034
65 to 69 years	687,323	57,034	501,262	117,492	10,327	1,208	669,610	55,205	317,333	280,413	5,720	948
70 to 74 years	518,302	40,045	342,743	127,955	6,453	1,196	500,914	44,901	181,413	272,869	2,825	847
75 years and over	506,185	32,530	260,649	200,901	4,430	1,585	557,454	44,001	103,158	406,330	1,769	1,296
Unknown	31,650	8,546	8,805	1,269	461	12,509	25,711	7,378	8,875	2,638	394	6,426
Native white—Foreign or mixed parentage	12,550,144	7,513,300	4,629,670	306,261	85,522	15,391	12,811,042	6,838,717	5,057,409	802,626	100,923	11,367
Under 15 years old	3,709,498	3,709,394	97	5	2		3,634,560	3,634,360	171	14	9	
15 years old and over	8,840,646	3,803,906	4,629,573	306,256	85,520	15,391	9,176,488	3,204,357	5,057,238	802,612	100,914	11,367
15 to 19 years	1,426,709	1,416,613	6,652	59	74	3,311	1,427,742	1,342,456	81,873	404	881	2,128
20 to 24 years	1,208,075	992,158	207,258	1,043	2,212	5,404	1,240,581	725,598	500,232	3,941	7,433	3,377
25 to 29 years	997,749	458,887	525,375	4,228	7,372	1,887	1,045,161	304,237	715,571	10,178	13,943	1,232
30 to 34 years	950,573	240,696	680,138	8,496	11,324	919	996,358	181,477	777,149	20,460	16,542	730
35 to 39 years	918,681	174,309	716,640	14,022	13,040	670	957,297	145,607	757,990	36,090	17,012	598
40 to 44 years	761,480	120,009	601,020	18,718	12,232	501	789,598	115,488	610,734	49,260	13,615	501
45 to 49 years	639,100	105,001	499,799	23,145	10,681	474	664,376	97,086	491,376	64,039	10,818	457
50 to 54 years	565,180	88,931	435,280	31,229	9,368	372	585,480	87,243	402,251	87,275	8,277	434
55 to 59 years	471,828	70,804	350,541	36,521	7,581	381	491,824	71,117	308,432	106,120	5,764	391
60 to 64 years	360,094	51,375	261,829	41,413	5,120	357	384,701	55,020	200,034	118,892	3,504	351
65 to 69 years	257,500	33,734	176,561	43,423	3,476	306	278,084	38,147	121,214	116,580	1,822	321
70 to 74 years	171,644	20,282	106,998	42,240	1,906	218	186,486	24,255	60,132	100,982	864	253
75 years and over	107,194	10,662	53,977	41,414	985	156	123,405	13,592	21,661	87,681	351	210
Unknown	4,839	2,445	1,505	305	149	435	5,305	2,434	1,089	710	88	384
Foreign-born white	7,153,709	1,655,548	4,960,626	462,875	62,830	11,832	6,212,698	917,683	4,243,388	992,907	51,943	6,832
Under 15 years old	149,059	149,029	27	3			147,556	147,502	46	7	1	
15 years old and over	7,004,050	1,505,017	4,960,599	462,872	62,830	11,832	6,065,142	770,131	4,243,337	992,900	51,942	6,832
15 to 19 years	156,659	155,061	1,030	26	14	528	107,971	151,308	16,035	106	129	303
20 to 24 years	319,103	259,044	57,718	320	495	1,520	342,889	176,381	162,714	1,178	1,628	988
25 to 29 years	515,103	244,388	265,281	1,845	2,363	1,286	505,843	111,872	383,873	4,921	4,540	631
30 to 34 years	650,595	169,131	470,602	5,173	4,703	926	596,235	59,347	518,186	12,197	6,113	392
35 to 39 years	892,430	162,758	708,103	12,574	7,931	1,013	730,228	49,828	652,236	20,113	7,680	371
40 to 44 years	902,110	139,901	737,965	23,362	9,921	961	732,086	43,907	631,316	48,472	7,961	410
45 to 49 years	881,870	111,880	726,707	32,665	9,768	850	688,344	42,030	561,244	72,100	7,484	417
50 to 54 years	722,496	82,578	588,016	42,201	8,369	782	594,874	38,871	451,905	97,715	5,936	447
55 to 59 years	554,408	57,764	443,722	46,041	6,380	611	426,327	25,143	251,236	146,932	3,013	503
60 to 64 years	483,750	47,650	360,470	60,085	5,342	603	334,314	17,825	162,451	151,669	1,916	453
65 to 69 years	378,000	34,792	269,722	69,135	3,763	588	217,302	11,601	79,384	125,079	840	398
70 to 74 years	243,312	21,062	155,344	64,254	2,176	476	246,330	12,288	46,278	186,518	501	745
75 years and over	288,035	17,453	114,186	104,171	1,493	732	3,804	990	1,684	779	57	294
Unknown	6,020	2,455	2,033	414	112	1,006						

Table 5.—MARITAL CONDITION OF THE TOTAL POPULATION, BY SEX, COLOR, NATIVITY, AND 5-YEAR AGE PERIODS, FOR THE UNITED STATES: 1930—Continued

COLOR, NATIVITY, AND AGE	MALES						FEMALES					
	Total	Single	Married	Widowed	Divorced	Unknown	Total	Single	Married	Widowed	Divorced	Unknown
Negro	5,855,669	3,185,005	2,357,954	247,610	55,717	9,383	6,035,474	2,888,607	2,399,171	652,721	88,904	6,071
Under 15 years old	1,914,207	1,914,055	133	15	4		1,935,922	1,934,801	1,027	58	36	
15 years old and over	3,941,462	1,270,950	2,357,821	247,595	55,713	9,383	4,099,552	953,806	2,398,144	652,663	88,868	6,071
15 to 19 years	595,646	571,834	22,017	651	441	703	654,882	510,064	134,241	6,145	3,998	434
20 to 24 years	553,622	302,556	237,172	7,214	5,013	1,667	649,569	214,897	392,074	26,471	15,250	877
25 to 29 years	500,520	138,788	339,869	12,597	8,020	1,246	571,267	90,632	419,858	42,345	17,778	654
30 to 34 years	416,869	79,215	313,274	15,272	8,237	871	447,645	44,205	340,397	48,262	14,263	518
35 to 39 years	430,472	60,682	338,705	21,263	9,050	772	460,428	31,702	346,217	68,496	13,544	469
40 to 44 years	339,329	30,703	267,772	24,088	7,119	647	348,094	20,061	247,700	70,935	8,971	427
45 to 49 years	328,162	28,760	259,149	28,402	6,300	551	306,903	14,142	208,459	77,347	6,584	371
50 to 54 years	277,532	19,891	220,934	31,733	4,586	388	227,058	10,167	136,804	75,792	3,976	319
55 to 59 years	174,367	11,078	137,017	23,200	2,803	269	135,030	5,341	74,453	52,964	2,055	217
60 to 64 years	133,349	7,335	99,687	24,187	1,965	225	108,820	4,393	47,569	55,455	1,200	203
65 to 69 years	82,843	4,304	57,881	19,371	1,000	137	72,334	2,716	26,001	42,825	651	141
70 to 74 years	50,896	2,454	32,278	15,500	553	111	48,200	1,916	12,411	33,478	261	134
75 years and over	55,791	2,677	28,757	23,728	459	170	62,655	2,281	9,311	50,614	212	237
Unknown	7,064	1,613	3,309	439	77	1,626	6,667	1,289	2,649	1,534	125	1,070
Other races	1,117,557	710,385	365,997	32,229	5,692	3,254	902,139	508,179	328,496	58,176	6,658	630
Under 15 years old	392,154	392,132	21	1			384,771	384,638	127	4	2	
15 years old and over	725,403	318,253	365,976	32,228	5,692	3,254	517,368	123,541	328,369	58,172	6,656	630
15 to 19 years	98,204	96,022	1,880	29	46	227	91,799	72,785	18,222	360	345	87
20 to 24 years	117,177	87,045	28,598	561	500	473	83,855	27,611	53,323	1,517	1,283	121
25 to 29 years	112,703	53,975	55,972	1,371	931	454	75,422	9,909	61,554	2,521	1,372	66
30 to 34 years	85,738	26,869	55,777	1,975	841	276	60,403	4,390	51,785	3,220	978	30
35 to 39 years	78,182	17,834	56,592	2,668	851	237	55,943	2,947	47,565	4,558	836	37
40 to 44 years	63,539	12,031	47,287	3,333	701	187	40,726	1,786	32,610	5,686	618	26
45 to 49 years	54,983	8,549	41,884	3,832	586	132	34,242	1,297	25,412	7,034	470	29
50 to 54 years	38,832	5,772	28,719	3,778	452	111	23,326	929	15,387	6,677	295	38
55 to 59 years	26,557	3,434	19,462	3,287	296	78	16,616	553	9,720	6,150	161	32
60 to 64 years	19,149	2,301	13,150	3,325	216	67	12,910	445	6,009	6,305	129	22
65 to 69 years	12,146	1,527	7,800	2,651	127	41	8,442	293	3,204	4,737	95	23
70 to 74 years	7,403	1,008	4,265	2,021	.69	40	5,455	186	1,623	3,595	40	11
75 years and over	8,547	993	4,114	3,334	64	42	7,510	250	1,536	5,664	26	34
Unknown	2,243	803	476	63	12	889	719	160	329	148	8	74

Table 6.—PER CENT DISTRIBUTION BY MARITAL CONDITION OF THE POPULATION 15 YEARS OLD AND OVER, BY SEX, COLOR, NATIVITY, AND 5-YEAR AGE PERIODS, FOR THE UNITED STATES: 1930

[Per cent not shown where less than 0.1]

COLOR, NATIVITY, AND AGE	MALES 15 YEARS OLD AND OVER				FEMALES 15 YEARS OLD AND OVER			
	Single	Married	Widowed	Divorced	Single	Married	Widowed	Divorced
All classes	34.1	60.0	4.6	1.1	26.4	61.1	11.1	1.3
15 to 19 years	98.0	1.7			86.8	12.6	0.2	0.2
20 to 24 years	70.8	28.1	0.3	0.4	46.0	51.6	1.0	1.1
25 to 29 years	36.7	61.3	0.8	1.0	21.7	74.3	2.1	1.8
30 to 34 years	21.2	76.0	1.3	1.4	13.2	81.5	3.3	1.9
35 to 39 years	15.4	81.0	2.0	1.5	10.4	82.3	5.3	1.9
40 to 44 years	13.1	82.1	3.0	1.6	9.5	80.6	8.0	1.8
45 to 49 years	11.9	82.1	4.3	1.7	9.0	77.6	11.6	1.7
50 to 54 years	10.9	81.0	6.3	1.6	9.2	72.3	16.9	1.5
55 to 59 years	10.3	79.5	8.4	1.6	9.0	66.2	23.4	1.3
60 to 64 years	9.9	76.2	12.4	1.5	8.9	56.9	33.1	1.0
65 to 69 years	9.3	71.5	17.8	1.3	8.4	46.6	44.1	0.8
70 to 74 years	8.6	64.7	25.4	1.1	8.4	35.0	55.9	0.5
75 years and over	7.0	50.4	41.5	0.8	7.3	18.2	73.9	0.3
Native white	36.8	57.9	4.0	1.1	29.4	59.7	9.4	1.3
15 to 19 years	98.3	1.5			88.1	11.5	0.1	0.2
20 to 24 years	72.0	27.1	0.2	0.4	47.7	50.5	0.6	1.0
25 to 29 years	36.1	62.1	0.6	1.0	22.7	74.1	1.4	1.7
30 to 34 years	20.3	77.1	1.1	1.4	14.3	81.2	2.5	1.9
35 to 39 years	14.6	82.0	1.7	1.6	11.8	81.9	4.2	2.0
40 to 44 years	12.7	82.8	2.7	1.8	11.0	80.3	6.7	1.9
45 to 49 years	11.9	82.3	3.9	1.8	10.5	77.6	10.0	1.8
50 to 54 years	11.2	81.2	5.8	1.8	10.5	72.7	15.1	1.6
55 to 59 years	10.7	79.6	7.9	1.7	10.3	66.6	21.6	1.4
60 to 64 years	10.3	76.3	11.7	1.6	10.4	57.5	31.0	1.1
65 to 69 years	9.6	71.7	17.0	1.5	10.0	46.8	42.3	0.8
70 to 74 years	8.7	65.2	24.7	1.2	9.8	35.1	54.4	0.5
75 years and over	7.0	51.3	40.5	0.9	8.6	18.3	72.5	0.3
Native white—Native parentage	34.5	60.0	4.2	1.2	27.2	61.6	9.7	1.4
15 to 19 years	97.9	2.0			85.6	14.0	0.2	0.2
20 to 24 years	68.1	30.9	0.3	0.4	43.6	54.4	0.7	1.1
25 to 29 years	32.5	65.5	0.7	1.2	20.3	76.3	1.5	1.9
30 to 34 years	17.9	79.3	1.2	1.5	12.8	82.5	2.6	2.0
35 to 39 years	12.8	83.6	1.8	1.7	10.4	83.0	4.4	2.1
40 to 44 years	11.1	84.2	2.8	1.8	9.6	81.5	6.8	2.0
45 to 49 years	10.2	83.8	4.0	1.9	8.8	79.1	10.2	1.8
50 to 54 years	9.5	82.7	5.9	1.8	8.7	74.4	15.1	1.7
55 to 59 years	9.0	81.1	8.0	1.8	8.5	68.3	21.7	1.4
60 to 64 years	8.8	77.7	11.7	1.7	8.6	59.1	31.0	1.2
65 to 69 years	8.3	72.9	17.1	1.5	8.4	48.1	42.5	0.9
70 to 74 years	7.7	66.1	24.7	1.2	8.6	36.2	54.5	0.6
75 years and over	6.4	51.5	40.9	0.9	8.1	18.5	72.9	0.3
Native white—Foreign or mixed parentage	43.0	52.4	3.5	1.0	34.9	55.1	8.7	1.1
15 to 19 years	99.3	0.5			94.0	5.7		0.1
20 to 24 years	82.1	17.2	0.1	0.2	58.5	40.3	0.3	0.6
25 to 29 years	46.0	52.7	0.4	0.7	29.1	68.5	1.0	1.3
30 to 34 years	26.3	71.6	0.9	1.2	18.2	78.0	2.1	1.7
35 to 39 years	19.0	78.0	1.5	1.4	15.2	79.2	3.8	1.8
40 to 44 years	16.9	78.9	2.5	1.6	14.6	77.3	6.2	1.7
Native white—Foreign or mixed parentage—Continued.								
45 to 49 years	16.4	78.2	3.6	1.7	14.7	74.0	9.6	1.6
50 to 54 years	15.7	77.0	5.5	1.7	14.9	68.7	14.9	1.4
55 to 59 years	15.0	75.6	7.7	1.6	14.5	62.7	21.6	1.2
60 to 64 years	14.3	72.7	11.5	1.4	14.3	53.8	30.9	0.9
65 to 69 years	13.1	68.6	16.9	1.3	13.7	43.6	41.9	0.7
70 to 74 years	11.8	62.3	24.6	1.1	13.0	32.2	54.1	0.5
75 years and over	9.9	50.4	38.6	0.9	11.0	17.5	71.0	0.3
Foreign-born white	21.5	70.8	6.6	0.9	12.7	70.0	16.4	0.9
15 to 19 years	99.0	0.7			90.1	9.5	0.1	0.1
20 to 24 years	81.2	18.1	0.1	0.2	51.4	47.5	0.3	0.5
25 to 29 years	47.4	51.5	0.4	0.5	22.1	75.9	1.0	0.9
30 to 34 years	26.0	72.3	0.8	0.7	10.0	86.9	2.0	1.0
35 to 39 years	18.2	79.4	1.4	0.9	6.7	88.2	3.9	1.0
40 to 44 years	14.5	81.9	2.4	1.0	6.0	86.2	6.6	1.1
45 to 49 years	12.7	82.4	3.7	1.1	6.2	82.1	10.6	1.1
50 to 54 years	11.4	81.5	5.8	1.2	6.5	76.0	16.4	1.0
55 to 59 years	10.4	80.0	8.3	1.2	6.1	68.5	24.5	0.9
60 to 64 years	9.9	76.4	12.5	1.1	5.9	58.9	34.4	0.7
65 to 69 years	9.2	71.4	18.3	1.0	5.3	48.6	45.4	0.6
70 to 74 years	8.7	63.8	26.4	0.9	5.3	36.5	57.6	0.4
75 years and over	7.3	48.0	43.8	0.6	5.0	18.8	75.7	0.2
Negro	32.2	59.8	6.3	1.4	23.3	58.5	15.9	2.2
15 to 19 years	96.0	3.7	0.1	0.1	77.9	20.5	0.9	0.6
20 to 24 years	54.7	42.8	1.3	0.9	33.1	60.4	4.1	2.3
25 to 29 years	27.7	67.9	2.5	1.6	15.9	73.5	7.4	3.1
30 to 34 years	19.0	75.1	3.7	2.0	9.9	76.0	10.8	3.2
35 to 39 years	14.1	78.7	4.9	2.1	6.9	75.2	14.9	2.9
40 to 44 years	11.7	78.9	7.1	2.1	5.8	71.2	20.4	2.6
45 to 49 years	8.9	80.2	8.8	1.9	4.6	67.9	25.2	2.1
50 to 54 years	7.2	79.6	11.4	1.7	4.5	60.3	33.4	1.8
55 to 59 years	6.4	78.6	13.3	1.6	4.0	55.1	39.2	1.5
60 to 64 years	5.5	74.8	18.1	1.5	4.0	43.7	51.0	1.1
65 to 69 years	5.3	69.9	23.4	1.3	3.8	35.9	59.2	0.9
70 to 74 years	4.8	63.4	30.5	1.1	4.0	25.7	69.5	0.5
75 years and over	4.8	51.5	42.5	0.8	3.6	14.9	80.8	0.3
Other races	43.9	50.5	4.4	0.8	23.9	63.5	11.2	1.3
15 to 19 years	97.8	1.9			79.3	19.8	0.4	0.4
20 to 24 years	74.3	24.4	0.5	0.4	32.9	63.6	1.8	1.5
25 to 29 years	47.9	49.7	1.2	0.8	13.1	81.6	3.3	1.8
30 to 34 years	31.3	65.1	2.3	1.0	7.3	85.7	5.3	1.6
35 to 39 years	22.8	72.4	3.4	1.1	5.3	85.0	8.1	1.5
40 to 44 years	18.9	74.4	5.2	1.1	4.4	80.1	14.0	1.5
45 to 49 years	15.5	76.2	7.0	1.1	3.8	74.2	20.5	1.4
50 to 54 years	14.9	74.0	9.7	1.2	4.0	66.0	28.6	1.3
55 to 59 years	12.9	73.3	12.4	1.1	3.3	58.5	37.0	1.0
60 to 64 years	12.5	68.7	17.4	1.1	3.4	46.5	48.8	1.0
65 to 69 years	12.6	64.2	21.8	1.0	3.5	39.0	56.1	1.1
70 to 74 years	13.6	57.6	27.3	0.9	3.4	29.8	65.9	0.7
75 years and over	11.6	48.1	39.0	0.7	3.3	20.5	75.4	0.3

MARITAL CONDITION

845

TABLE 7.—MARITAL CONDITION OF THE POPULATION OF MINOR RACES 15 YEARS OLD AND OVER, BY SEX AND RACE, FOR THE UNITED STATES, URBAN AND RURAL: 1930

[Per cent not shown where base is less than 100]

AREA AND RACE	MALES 15 YEARS OLD AND OVER									FEMALES 15 YEARS OLD AND OVER								
	Total	Single		Married		Widowed		Di-vorced	Un-known	Total	Single		Married		Widowed		Di-vorced	Un-known
		Number	Per cent	Number	Per cent	Num-ber	Per cent				Number	Per cent	Number	Per cent	Num-ber	Per cent		
Total	725,403	318,253	43.9	365,976	50.5	32,228	4.4	5,692	3,254	517,368	123,541	23.9	328,369	63.5	58,172	11.2	6,656	630
Mexican	472,575	198,930	42.1	247,592	52.4	21,453	4.5	3,299	1,295	381,524	93,392	24.5	238,077	62.4	45,061	11.8	4,587	407
Native	153,342	78,407	51.1	67,622	44.1	5,577	3.6	1,346	390	141,400	49,355	34.9	79,058	56.5	9,806	7.0	2,092	159
Foreign born	319,233	120,529	37.8	179,970	56.4	15,876	5.0	1,953	905	240,004	44,037	18.3	158,119	65.9	35,165	14.6	2,495	248
Indian	103,441	38,021	36.8	56,382	54.5	7,173	6.9	1,646	219	96,084	23,335	24.3	59,108	61.6	11,541	12.0	1,870	164
Chinese	51,519	25,108	48.7	23,868	46.3	1,349	2.6	112	1,082	8,169	1,904	23.3	5,574	68.2	631	7.7	37	23
Japanese	52,709	21,059	39.9	29,401	55.7	1,756	3.3	403	180	29,411	4,475	15.2	23,930	81.4	853	2.9	123	30
Filipino	40,904	32,554	79.6	7,409	18.1	338	0.8	100	413	1,640	309	18.8	1,258	76.7	53	3.2	16	4
Hindu	2,074	1,055	61.9	858	32.1	109	4.4	25	27	110	30	27.3	62	56.4	13	11.8	5	
Korean	935	532	56.9	348	37.2	41	4.4	8	6	322	77	23.9	226	70.2	14	4.3	3	2
All other	556	388	69.8	118	21.2	9	1.6	9	32	108	19	17.6	74	68.5	6	5.6	9	
Urban	346,122	156,219	45.1	171,908	49.7	13,088	3.8	2,838	2,079	245,684	60,392	24.6	148,771	60.6	32,203	13.1	4,003	275
Mexican	236,804	99,776	42.1	124,239	52.4	10,290	4.3	2,017	563	208,872	52,563	25.2	122,868	58.8	29,802	14.3	3,424	215
Native	64,200	33,749	52.5	27,480	42.7	2,107	3.3	787	167	63,744	23,273	36.5	33,603	52.7	5,344	8.4	1,443	81
Foreign born	172,604	66,027	38.4	96,759	56.1	8,192	4.7	1,230	396	145,128	29,290	20.2	89,255	61.5	24,458	16.9	1,981	134
Indian	10,481	4,029	38.4	5,675	54.1	474	4.5	268	35	10,805	3,007	27.6	6,286	57.7	1,184	10.9	406	12
Chinese	44,776	21,822	48.7	20,705	46.2	1,126	2.5	86	1,037	7,396	1,734	23.4	5,032	68.0	574	7.8	35	21
Japanese	30,340	12,422	40.9	16,598	54.7	915	3.0	286	119	16,941	2,740	16.2	13,494	79.7	574	3.4	111	22
Filipino	21,425	16,811	78.5	4,006	18.7	191	0.9	153	264	1,129	240	21.3	830	73.5	40	3.5	16	3
Hindu	1,006	670	61.1	342	31.2	45	4.1	14	25	84	24		47		10		3	
Korean	633	356	56.2	241	38.1	25	3.9	6	5	239	58	24.3	162	67.8	14	5.9	3	2
All other	477	333	69.8	97	20.3	8	1.7	8	31	78	16		52		5		5	
Rural	379,281	162,034	42.7	194,073	51.2	19,145	5.0	2,854	1,175	271,784	63,159	23.2	179,596	66.1	25,969	9.6	2,653	355
Mexican	235,681	99,160	42.1	123,353	52.3	11,154	4.7	1,282	732	172,652	40,829	23.6	115,209	66.7	15,259	8.8	1,163	192
Native	89,052	44,658	50.1	40,142	45.1	3,470	3.9	559	223	77,716	26,082	33.6	46,355	59.6	4,552	5.9	649	78
Foreign born	146,629	54,502	37.2	83,211	56.7	7,684	5.2	723	509	94,936	14,747	15.5	68,854	72.5	10,707	11.3	514	114
Indian	92,960	33,992	36.6	50,707	54.5	6,699	7.2	1,378	184	85,189	20,328	23.9	52,882	62.1	10,357	12.2	1,470	152
Chinese	6,743	3,286	48.7	3,163	46.9	223	3.3	26	45	773	170	22.0	542	70.1	57	7.4	2	2
Japanese	22,459	8,637	38.5	12,803	57.0	841	3.7	117	61	12,470	1,735	13.9	10,436	83.7	279	2.2	12	8
Filipino	19,479	15,743	80.8	3,403	17.5	147	0.8	37	149	511	69	13.5	428	83.8	13	2.5		1
Hindu	1,578	985	62.4	516	32.7	64	4.1	11	2	26	6		15		3		2	
Korean	302	176	58.3	107	35.4	16	5.3	2	1	83	19		64					
All other	79	55		21		1		1	1	30	3		22		1		4	

TABLE 8.—MARITAL CONDITION OF THE POPULATION 15 TO 34 YEARS OLD, BY SEX AND SINGLE YEARS OF AGE, FOR THE UNITED STATES: 1930, 1920, AND 1910

[Per cent not shown where less than 0.1]

CENSUS YEAR AND AGE	MALES									FEMALES								
	Total	Single		Married		Widowed		Di-vorced	Un-known	Total	Single		Married		Widowed		Di-vorced	Un-known
		Number	Per cent	Number	Per cent	Num-ber	Per cent				Number	Per cent	Number	Per cent	Num-ber	Per cent		
1930																		
15 years	1,154,648	1,153,745	99.9	849	0.1	36		18		1,141,051	1,125,673	98.7	14,798	1.3	337		243	
16 years	1,181,920	1,179,542	99.8	2,273	0.2	65		40		1,186,395	1,132,180	95.5	51,392	4.3	1,017	0.1	806	
17 years	1,157,150	1,149,419	99.3	7,431	0.6	180		120		1,138,672	1,021,707	89.7	113,234	9.9	1,930	0.2	1,821	
18 years	1,157,703	1,126,939	97.3	25,837	2.2	399		367	4,161	1,200,131	960,024	80.0	229,042	19.2	3,848	0.3	3,812	2,505
19 years	1,106,404	1,035,714	93.6	63,972	5.8	833	0.1	803	5,082	1,129,041	792,590	70.2	322,621	28.6	5,205	0.5	5,680	2,936
20 years	1,066,439	934,936	87.7	128,563	11.6	1,631	0.2	1,715	4,502	1,155,992	699,019	60.5	436,595	37.8	8,026	0.7	8,091	2,761
21 years	1,112,453	884,031	79.5	219,211	19.7	2,461	0.2	2,819	3,931	1,098,578	581,205	52.9	496,255	45.2	8,726	0.8	10,200	2,192
22 years	1,078,834	763,070	70.7	304,141	28.2	3,616	0.3	4,408	3,599	1,123,697	505,801	45.0	591,659	52.7	11,837	1.0	12,770	2,031
23 years	1,046,165	644,223	61.6	389,052	37.2	4,440	0.4	5,600	2,760	1,084,626	412,776	38.1	642,438	59.2	13,059	1.2	14,719	1,634
24 years	1,082,924	553,181	53.6	464,526	45.0	5,509	0.5	7,268	2,440	1,070,670	347,266	32.4	690,718	64.5	15,227	1.4	16,075	1,384
25 years	1,012,298	476,734	47.1	518,344	51.2	6,512	0.6	8,492	2,216	1,074,117	304,029	28.3	733,009	68.2	18,198	1.7	17,514	1,307
26 years	975,485	402,160	41.2	555,305	56.9	6,870	0.7	9,270	1,880	1,010,472	244,122	24.2	729,840	72.2	17,843	1.8	17,608	1,059
27 years	939,345	337,071	35.9	583,588	62.1	7,395	0.8	9,690	1,601	943,097	196,616	20.8	710,086	75.3	18,681	2.0	16,903	811
28 years	966,962	309,755	32.0	635,657	65.7	8,971	0.9	11,061	1,518	992,323	186,418	18.8	762,727	76.9	23,422	2.4	18,921	835
29 years	966,090	259,693	26.9	684,110	70.8	9,265	1.0	11,716	1,306	953,419	148,738	15.6	761,923	79.9	23,897	2.5	18,178	683
30 years	1,086,289	289,925	26.7	766,419	70.6	13,698	1.3	14,679	1,568	1,110,841	187,656	16.9	863,785	77.8	35,871	3.2	22,587	942
31 years	782,464	164,884	21.1	598,273	76.5	8,382	1.1	10,024	901	766,411	97,813	12.8	634,069	82.7	19,997	2.6	14,020	503
32 years	933,929	198,373	21.2	708,574	75.9	12,597	1.3	13,206	1,179	941,294	123,198	13.1	767,774	81.6	31,189	3.3	18,524	659
33 years	868,097	159,738	18.4	683,648	78.8	11,750	1.4	12,048	913	863,031	96,218	11.1	721,090	83.6	20,036	3.4	16,153	534
34 years	891,007	153,025	17.2	711,202	79.8	13,060	1.5	12,712	942	877,058	98,163	11.2	728,930	83.1	32,528	3.7	16,926	511
1920																		
15 years	925,679	923,997	99.8	1,600	0.2	69		13		935,766	922,433	98.6	12,834	1.4	367		132	
16 years	976,834	973,468	99.7	3,222	0.3	116		28		996,124	953,230	95.7	41,626	4.2	860	0.1	408	
17 years	926,033	918,008	99.1	7,699	0.8	199		67		929,140	835,418	89.9	90,930	9.8	1,864	0.2	928	
18 years	938,646	909,332	96.9	24,944	2.7	546	0.1	224	3,600	971,400	776,931	80.0	186,645	19.2	3,727	0.4	1,827	2,270
19 years	906,600	842,905	93.0	58,909	6.5	900	0.1	427	3,459	924,334	649,638	70.3	264,507	28.6	5,421	0.6	2,722	2,046
20 years	843,501	732,213	86.8	105,369	12.5	1,600	0.2	826	3,493	937,601	562,965	60.0	360,112	38.4	8,388	0.9	3,997	2,139
21 years	920,779	719,816	78.2	193,663	21.0	2,743	0.3	1,425	3,132	900,938	473,019	52.5	412,285	45.8	9,479	1.1	4,541	1,659
22 years	918,849	648,916	70.6	260,530	28.4	4,169	0.5	2,008	3,136	968,431	434,966	44.9	512,587	52.9	13,368	1.4	5,773	1,737
23 years	911,705	574,761	63.0	326,245	35.8	5,313	0.6	2,503	2,793	969,884	371,616	38.3	574,133	59.2	16,026	1.7	6,700	1,409
24 years	932,211	524,917	56.3	394,511	42.3	6,686	0.7	3,338	2,759	973,127	321,485	33.0	624,630	64.2	18,153	1.9	7,571	1,288

POPULATION

TABLE 8.—MARITAL CONDITION OF THE POPULATION 15 TO 34 YEARS OLD, BY SEX AND SINGLE YEARS OF AGE, FOR THE UNITED STATES: 1930, 1920, AND 1910—Continued

CENSUS YEAR AND AGE	MALES Total	Single Number	Per cent	Married Number	Per cent	Widowed Number	Per cent	Divorced	Unknown	FEMALES Total	Single Number	Per cent	Married Number	Per cent	Widowed Number	Per cent	Divorced	Unknown
1920—Contd.																		
25 years	932,333	462,811	49.6	454,791	48.8	8,309	0.9	3,901	2,521	990,861	287,842	29.0	672,240	67.8	21,525	2.2	8,016	1,238
26 years	915,495	403,477	44.1	495,955	54.2	9,180	1.0	4,255	2,628	937,840	236,899	25.3	669,638	71.4	22,069	2.4	8,128	1,106
27 years	910,809	349,753	38.4	543,508	59.7	10,417	1.1	4,662	2,469	880,836	194,201	22.0	655,125	74.4	22,458	2.5	8,152	900
28 years	943,654	326,809	34.6	596,913	63.3	12,186	1.3	5,216	2,470	942,759	190,285	20.2	715,183	75.0	27,184	2.9	9,191	916
29 years	835,942	246,811	29.5	570,957	68.3	11,378	1.4	4,822	1,974	795,962	139,058	17.5	624,315	78.4	24,151	3.0	7,756	682
30 years	956,587	277,588	29.0	654,280	68.4	16,232	1.7	6,012	2,455	995,298	184,062	18.5	762,156	76.6	37,799	3.8	10,234	1,047
31 years	724,643	178,608	24.7	528,367	72.9	11,308	1.6	4,707	1,563	681,985	98,907	14.5	552,079	81.1	22,760	3.3	6,757	522
32 years	826,738	201,562	24.4	602,328	72.9	15,203	1.8	5,810	1,775	812,005	119,743	14.7	651,391	80.2	31,801	3.9	8,401	669
33 years	795,555	171,147	21.5	602,050	75.7	15,102	1.9	5,576	1,611	726,524	92,550	12.7	597,208	82.2	28,986	4.0	7,211	509
34 years	827,280	166,874	20.2	630,323	76.9	16,489	2.0	5,975	1,619	724,598	92,707	12.8	592,120	81.7	31,547	4.4	7,585	549
1910																		
15 years	862,475	858,522	99.5	531	0.1	49	------	11	3,362	858,750	844,134	98.3	10,201	1.2	322	------	111	3,802
16 years	925,246	918,028	99.2	993	0.1	81	------	15	6,129	939,405	897,449	95.5	34,829	3.7	703	0.1	260	6,134
17 years	900,649	891,324	99.0	3,466	0.4	122	------	44	5,693	885,591	801,681	90.5	76,683	8.7	1,582	0.2	496	5,149
18 years	940,876	920,457	98.0	13,321	1.4	287	------	106	5,705	978,490	802,804	82.1	166,460	17.0	3,273	0.3	1,153	4,710
19 years	889,036	840,736	95.6	33,506	3.8	571	0.1	171	4,992	874,025	639,606	73.2	224,976	25.7	4,291	0.5	1,030	3,522
20 years	899,372	814,735	90.6	77,658	8.6	1,432	0.2	456	5,091	955,250	595,869	62.4	345,340	36.2	7,699	0.8	2,911	3,431
21 years	937,420	776,575	82.8	152,208	16.2	2,453	0.3	983	5,161	851,984	467,705	54.9	370,534	43.5	7,079	0.9	3,133	2,543
22 years	925,234	695,600	75.2	219,949	23.8	3,790	0.4	1,373	4,522	900,826	430,332	47.3	461,618	50.7	11,301	1.2	4,195	2,380
23 years	906,182	603,256	66.6	292,308	32.3	4,864	0.5	1,810	3,944	885,814	359,344	40.6	506,478	57.2	13,276	1.4	4,847	1,869
24 years	912,082	541,995	59.4	357,880	39.2	6,276	0.7	2,160	3,771	873,820	310,343	35.5	541,302	62.0	15,099	1.7	5,284	1,792
25 years	918,733	480,148	52.0	418,325	45.5	7,047	0.9	2,736	3,577	893,542	280,278	31.4	587,126	65.7	18,494	2.1	5,995	1,649
26 years	860,196	411,521	47.3	443,475	51.0	8,202	0.9	2,862	3,136	819,189	222,280	27.1	572,559	69.9	17,320	2.1	5,760	1,255
27 years	818,862	341,528	41.7	463,158	56.6	8,538	1.0	3,031	2,607	736,589	175,380	23.8	537,207	72.9	17,567	2.4	5,434	1,001
28 years	901,975	348,254	38.1	540,990	60.0	11,143	1.2	3,729	2,859	827,788	181,024	21.9	616,240	74.4	22,995	2.8	6,555	974
29 years	735,582	233,086	31.8	487,577	66.3	9,202	1.3	3,145	1,912	658,547	122,585	18.6	510,803	77.6	19,009	2.9	5,403	747
30 years	973,592	310,707	31.9	638,582	65.6	16,448	1.7	4,602	3,253	881,016	170,536	20.4	658,339	74.7	34,358	3.9	7,660	1,123
31 years	600,222	155,515	25.9	431,291	71.9	9,056	1.5	2,883	1,477	538,778	81,972	15.2	434,760	80.7	17,335	3.2	4,201	450
32 years	745,653	194,918	26.1	531,582	71.3	13,337	1.8	3,989	1,827	685,815	108,369	15.8	544,654	79.4	26,315	3.8	5,840	628
33 years	663,778	147,525	22.2	498,557	75.1	12,660	1.9	3,715	1,315	600,469	81,461	13.6	480,324	81.5	24,112	4.0	5,073	499
34 years	673,523	143,155	21.3	511,232	75.9	13,832	2.1	3,879	1,425	609,330	83,832	13.8	492,882	80.9	26,822	4.4	5,206	587

TABLE 9.—MARITAL CONDITION OF THE POPULATION 15 TO 34 YEARS OLD, BY SEX, COLOR, NATIVITY, AND SINGLE YEARS OF AGE, FOR THE UNITED STATES: 1930

[Per cent not shown where less than 0.1]

COLOR, NATIVITY, AND AGE	MALES Total	Single Number	Per cent	Married Number	Per cent	Widowed Number	Per cent	Divorced	Unknown	FEMALES Total	Single Number	Per cent	Married Number	Per cent	Widowed Number	Per cent	Divorced	Unknown
Native white:																		
15 years	999,893	999,280	99.9	626	0.1	22	------	15	------	980,573	969,454	98.9	10,810	1.1	168	------	141	------
16 years	1,013,638	1,011,921	99.8	1,648	0.2	43	------	26	------	1,006,607	967,298	96.1	38,474	3.8	462	------	403	------
17 years	985,776	980,188	99.4	5,414	0.5	105	------	69	------	963,681	874,832	90.8	86,841	9.0	872	0.1	1,130	------
18 years	974,894	951,062	97.6	18,994	1.9	196	------	238	3,509	992,798	811,827	81.8	174,703	17.6	1,807	0.2	2,863	2,008
19 years	933,115	879,141	94.2	48,753	5.2	441	------	504	4,276	985,889	674,606	72.1	252,641	27.0	2,417	0.3	3,796	2,420
20 years	884,210	784,036	88.7	94,473	10.7	814	0.1	1,106	3,781	931,638	584,463	62.7	335,710	36.0	3,484	0.4	5,674	2,298
21 years	920,616	744,428	80.9	169,741	18.4	1,280	0.1	1,972	3,189	910,616	496,577	54.5	400,365	44.0	4,510	0.5	7,384	1,771
22 years	876,455	631,591	72.1	237,058	27.0	1,884	0.2	3,100	2,822	905,201	422,003	46.6	467,175	51.6	5,416	0.6	8,903	1,614
23 years	844,735	527,960	62.5	307,977	36.5	2,444	0.3	4,247	2,107	866,375	341,867	39.5	506,324	58.4	6,343	0.7	10,553	1,288
24 years	820,807	442,783	53.9	367,756	44.8	3,128	0.4	5,467	1,763	843,420	283,258	33.6	539,071	64.0	7,447	0.9	11,699	1,045
25 years	781,933	367,329	47.0	403,202	51.6	3,585	0.5	6,351	1,466	827,793	242,773	29.3	563,166	68.0	8,422	1.0	12,506	926
26 years	762,674	310,507	40.7	439,440	57.6	4,148	0.5	7,302	1,277	788,008	197,833	25.1	567,233	72.0	9,208	1.2	12,072	702
27 years	724,949	254,391	35.1	457,435	63.1	4,509	0.6	7,592	1,022	730,372	159,450	21.8	547,911	75.0	9,790	1.3	12,027	594
28 years	728,291	225,982	31.0	487,555	66.9	5,305	0.7	8,494	955	747,246	147,224	19.7	573,525	76.8	12,111	1.6	13,815	571
29 years	733,047	190,053	25.9	528,250	72.0	5,653	0.8	9,176	815	727,387	120,230	16.5	580,525	79.8	12,663	1.7	13,508	461
30 years	782,486	200,664	25.6	562,429	71.9	7,432	0.9	11,024	937	810,442	147,321	18.2	620,349	77.7	17,161	2.1	16,015	596
31 years	614,829	123,855	20.1	476,749	77.5	5,532	0.9	8,110	583	611,250	82,900	13.6	504,310	82.5	12,510	2.0	11,158	372
32 years	698,019	142,379	20.4	536,535	76.9	7,976	1.1	10,391	738	711,004	101,677	14.3	577,232	81.2	17,608	2.5	14,015	472
33 years	651,817	114,908	17.6	519,195	79.7	7,635	1.2	9,479	600	657,801	80,804	12.3	546,512	83.1	17,538	2.7	12,560	387
34 years	661,483	108,924	16.5	533,555	80.7	8,498	1.3	9,884	572	663,765	82,404	12.4	547,877	82.5	19,985	3.0	13,117	382
Native white—Native parentage:																		
15 years	704,157	703,618	99.9	509	0.1	18	------	12	------	688,760	678,246	98.5	10,222	1.5	159	------	133	------
16 years	718,684	717,104	99.8	1,480	0.2	36	------	24	------	709,811	673,516	94.9	35,421	5.0	443	0.1	431	------
17 years	701,581	696,422	99.3	5,002	0.7	92	------	65	------	681,343	602,145	88.4	77,341	11.4	827	0.1	1,030	------
18 years	692,100	672,186	97.1	17,536	2.5	183	------	211	1,984	704,958	550,616	78.1	149,473	21.2	1,683	0.2	2,108	1,078
19 years	664,085	616,409	92.8	44,300	6.7	419	------	461	2,490	687,024	451,038	67.6	209,139	31.4	2,210	0.3	3,316	1,321
20 years	630,916	543,470	86.1	83,411	13.2	750	0.1	1,018	2,258	667,874	387,791	58.1	270,806	40.5	3,107	0.4	4,907	1,203
21 years	663,246	513,205	77.4	145,104	21.9	1,163	0.2	1,753	1,981	654,272	327,362	50.0	315,715	48.3	3,939	0.6	6,225	1,031
22 years	629,853	427,466	67.9	198,320	31.2	1,697	0.3	2,679	1,682	650,476	276,019	42.4	361,329	55.5	4,074	0.7	7,539	915
23 years	613,504	359,142	58.1	250,299	40.8	2,150	0.4	3,629	1,275	628,388	224,745	35.8	388,846	61.9	5,342	0.9	8,679	776
24 years	601,319	298,207	49.6	294,004	49.0	2,735	0.5	4,601	1,112	615,659	186,653	30.3	412,626	67.0	6,206	1.0	9,520	654

MARITAL CONDITION

847

TABLE 9.—MARITAL CONDITION OF THE POPULATION 15 TO 34 YEARS OLD, BY SEX, COLOR, NATIVITY, AND SINGLE YEARS OF AGE, FOR THE UNITED STATES: 1930—Continued

| | MALES | | | | | | | | | FEMALES | | | | | | | | |
COLOR, NATIVITY, AND AGE	Total	Single Number	Single Per cent	Married Number	Married Per cent	Widowed Number	Widowed Per cent	Divorced	Unknown	Total	Single Number	Single Per cent	Married Number	Married Per cent	Widowed Number	Widowed Per cent	Divorced	Unknown
Native white—Native parentage—Contd.																		
25 years	572,974	245,591	42.9	318,116	55.5	3,032	0.5	5,311	924	603,580	158,873	26.3	427,123	70.8	6,973	1.2	10,042	578
26 years	558,496	205,401	36.8	342,640	61.4	3,436	0.6	5,987	832	573,976	128,976	22.5	426,016	74.3	7,570	1.3	10,317	488
27 years	530,927	167,086	31.5	353,299	66.5	3,684	0.7	6,195	663	529,751	103,278	19.5	408,331	77.1	7,859	1.5	9,900	383
28 years	535,435	148,292	27.7	375,353	70.1	4,346	0.8	6,795	649	542,881	94,766	17.5	427,320	78.7	9,636	1.8	10,801	358
29 years	530,213	123,005	22.9	400,899	74.8	4,474	0.8	7,255	580	525,538	77,380	14.7	427,399	81.3	10,029	1.9	10,425	305
30 years	571,442	131,165	23.0	424,955	74.4	5,955	1.0	8,692	675	581,018	94,949	16.3	460,105	79.2	13,358	2.3	12,215	391
31 years	443,125	78,868	17.8	353,301	79.7	4,258	1.0	6,258	440	436,054	52,831	12.1	365,000	83.7	9,516	2.2	8,446	261
32 years	503,315	90,606	18.0	398,007	79.1	6,152	1.2	8,023	527	505,709	63,859	12.6	417,527	82.6	13,466	2.7	10,531	326
33 years	466,145	71,953	15.4	380,823	81.7	5,750	1.2	7,171	448	464,984	50,490	10.9	391,744	84.2	13,125	2.8	9,372	253
34 years	473,984	68,442	14.4	391,239	82.5	6,462	1.4	7,420	421	470,220	51,500	11.0	393,755	83.7	14,967	3.2	9,759	248
Native white—Foreign or mixed parentage:																		
15 years	295,736	295,612	100.0	117		4		3		291,813	291,208	99.8	588	0.2	9		8	
16 years	204,954	204,727	99.9	218	0.1	7		2		296,886	293,782	99.0	3,053	1.0	10		32	
17 years	284,195	283,766	99.8	412	0.1	13		4		282,338	272,687	96.6	9,500	3.4	45		106	1,020
18 years	282,794	279,776	98.9	1,458	0.5	13		22	1,525	287,840	261,211	90.7	25,230	8.8	124		255	1,108
19 years	280,030	262,732	97.7	4,447	1.7	22		43	1,780	268,805	223,568	83.2	43,502	16.2	207	0.1	480	1,108
20 years	253,294	240,566	95.0	11,062	4.4	55		88	1,523	263,704	196,672	74.6	64,913	24.6	377	0.1	767	1,035
21 years	257,370	231,133	89.8	24,037	9.6	123		210	1,268	256,344	169,215	66.0	84,650	33.0	580	0.2	1,159	740
22 years	246,602	204,125	82.8	40,729	16.5	187	0.1	421	1,140	254,725	145,984	57.3	105,846	41.6	742	0.3	1,454	699
23 years	231,231	171,818	74.3	57,678	24.9	285	0.1	618	832	237,087	117,122	49.2	117,478	49.4	1,001	0.4	1,874	512
24 years	219,578	144,516	65.8	73,152	33.3	393	0.2	866	651	227,701	96,605	42.4	127,345	55.9	1,241	0.5	2,179	391
25 years	208,959	121,738	58.3	85,086	40.7	553	0.3	1,040	542	224,204	83,900	37.4	136,043	60.7	1,449	0.6	2,464	348
26 years	204,178	105,106	51.5	96,600	47.3	712	0.3	1,315	445	214,122	68,857	32.2	140,617	65.7	1,689	0.8	2,655	304
27 years	194,022	87,305	45.0	104,136	53.7	825	0.4	1,397	359	200,621	56,172	28.0	139,580	69.6	1,931	1.0	2,727	211
28 years	192,856	77,690	40.3	112,202	58.2	959	0.5	1,690	306	204,365	52,458	25.7	146,205	71.5	2,475	1.2	3,014	213
29 years	197,734	67,048	33.9	127,351	64.4	1,179	0.6	1,921	235	201,849	42,850	21.2	153,126	75.9	2,634	1.3	3,083	150
30 years	211,044	69,490	32.9	137,474	65.1	1,477	0.7	2,332	262	220,424	52,372	22.8	160,244	73.8	3,803	1.7	3,800	205
31 years	171,704	44,987	26.2	123,448	71.9	1,274	0.7	1,852	143	175,196	30,069	17.2	130,310	79.5	2,994	1.7	2,712	111
32 years	194,704	51,773	26.6	138,528	71.1	1,824	0.9	2,308	211	205,385	37,818	18.4	159,705	77.8	4,232	2.1	3,484	146
33 years	185,672	42,955	23.1	138,372	74.5	1,885	1.0	2,308	152	192,817	30,314	15.7	154,788	80.3	4,413	2.3	3,188	134
34 years	187,449	40,482	21.6	142,316	75.9	2,036	1.1	2,464	151	198,530	30,904	16.0	154,122	79.6	5,018	2.6	3,358	134
Foreign-born white:																		
15 years	19,390	19,361	99.9	24	0.1	5				19,034	18,957	99.8	71	0.4	5		1	
16 years	25,025	24,986	99.8	36	0.1	1		2		26,052	25,643	98.4	397	1.5	8		4	
17 years	31,829	31,752	99.8	70	0.2	7				33,441	31,764	95.0	1,645	4.9	13		19	
18 years	37,784	37,344	98.8	211	0.6	3		4	222	42,302	37,303	88.3	4,720	11.2	30	0.1	35	154
19 years	42,631	41,618	97.6	689	1.6	10		8	306	47,142	37,581	79.7	9,202	19.5	50	0.1	70	239
20 years	49,897	47,424	95.0	2,119	4.2	17		17	320	57,022	40,000	70.3	16,467	28.9	121	0.2	145	239
21 years	57,058	51,723	90.6	4,945	8.7	22		50	318	59,452	36,061	60.7	22,779	38.3	180	0.3	217	215
22 years	61,695	52,021	84.3	9,192	14.9	61	0.1	86	335	67,280	35,555	52.8	31,000	46.2	174	0.3	302	192
23 years	69,707	53,005	75.9	16,317	23.4	83	0.1	132	200	74,324	32,806	44.2	40,508	54.6	301	0.4	412	177
24 years	80,656	54,871	68.0	25,145	31.2	143	0.2	210	287	84,802	31,830	37.5	51,844	61.1	402	0.5	552	165
25 years	92,608	56,371	60.8	35,503	38.3	211	0.2	314	209	95,636	30,608	32.0	63,529	66.4	651	0.7	671	177
26 years	97,640	52,335	53.6	44,388	45.5	287	0.3	339	291	96,428	24,934	25.9	69,776	72.4	748	0.8	832	138
27 years	101,506	47,900	47.0	52,793	52.0	359	0.4	446	248	96,869	20,035	20.7	74,902	77.3	928	1.0	909	97
28 years	111,107	47,973	43.2	61,852	55.7	442	0.4	599	241	110,060	21,194	19.3	86,402	78.6	1,231	1.1	1,051	122
29 years	112,212	40,049	35.7	70,745	63.0	546	0.5	665	207	106,850	15,101	14.1	89,204	83.5	1,365	1.3	1,083	97
30 years	140,105	48,787	34.8	89,333	63.8	840	0.6	863	273	134,291	19,713	14.7	110,936	82.6	2,117	1.6	1,400	125
31 years	98,034	25,908	26.4	70,686	72.1	644	0.7	662	134	88,340	8,831	10.0	77,148	87.3	1,446	1.6	865	59
32 years	133,648	34,933	26.1	96,498	72.2	1,069	0.8	949	199	125,272	12,094	9.7	109,203	87.2	2,542	2.0	1,354	79
33 years	134,543	29,891	22.2	102,261	76.0	1,217	0.9	1,017	157	121,680	9,181	7.5	108,484	89.2	2,741	2.3	1,204	70
34 years	144,265	29,612	20.5	111,884	77.6	1,394	1.0	1,212	163	126,643	9,528	7.5	112,415	88.8	3,351	2.6	1,290	59
Negro:																		
15 years	117,062	116,867	99.8	183	0.2	9		3		123,375	119,630	97.0	3,483	2.8	159	0.1	94	
16 years	123,800	123,333	99.6	531	0.4	17		9		133,835	121,941	91.1	11,070	8.3	519	0.4	305	
17 years	120,994	119,078	98.4	1,805	1.5	63	0.1	48		123,991	100,744	81.3	21,667	17.5	983	0.8	597	
18 years	123,927	117,147	94.5	6,186	5.0	193	0.2	116	305	145,204	97,183	66.9	44,600	30.7	1,899	1.3	1,314	208
19 years	109,773	95,409	86.9	13,332	12.1	369	0.3	265	398	128,477	70,557	54.9	53,421	41.6	2,585	2.0	1,688	226
20 years	110,375	84,044	76.1	24,652	22.3	756	0.7	541	382	148,172	66,705	45.0	74,463	50.3	4,188	2.8	2,625	191
21 years	113,774	70,804	62.2	40,823	35.9	1,077	0.9	733	337	114,530	43,088	37.6	65,036	56.8	3,814	3.3	2,406	186
22 years	115,651	60,592	52.4	52,045	45.0	1,561	1.3	1,107	346	133,740	42,720	31.9	82,200	61.5	5,427	4.1	3,201	192
23 years	107,118	46,804	43.7	57,080	53.3	1,745	1.6	1,183	304	127,376	33,721	26.5	83,045	65.9	6,079	4.8	3,477	154
24 years	106,706	40,312	37.8	62,572	58.6	2,075	1.9	1,449	298	125,751	28,663	22.8	86,430	68.7	6,963	5.5	3,541	154
25 years	112,485	38,720	34.4	69,310	61.6	2,473	2.2	1,650	332	133,762	27,692	20.7	93,220	69.7	8,654	6.5	4,013	183
26 years	92,974	27,862	30.0	61,205	65.8	2,218	2.4	1,466	223	110,637	19,051	17.2	80,597	72.8	7,366	6.7	3,511	112
27 years	92,341	25,246	27.3	63,106	68.3	2,275	2.5	1,466	248	102,581	15,497	15.1	76,305	74.4	7,525	7.3	3,138	116
28 years	105,189	25,907	24.6	74,340	70.7	2,914	2.8	1,768	251	119,635	16,315	13.6	80,892	75.1	9,508	7.9	3,700	130
29 years	97,531	21,053	21.6	71,899	73.7	2,717	2.8	1,670	192	104,652	12,077	11.5	79,844	76.3	9,292	8.9	3,326	113
30 years	135,112	30,207	22.4	97,250	72.0	4,852	3.6	2,538	265	146,634	18,908	12.9	107,044	73.0	15,626	10.7	4,845	211
31 years	57,438	11,117	19.4	43,147	75.1	1,923	3.3	1,123	128	59,006	5,506	9.3	45,861	77.4	5,680	9.6	1,881	69
32 years	85,060	15,738	18.5	64,301	75.6	3,149	3.7	1,688	189	92,580	8,563	9.2	70,744	76.4	10,210	11.0	2,902	101
33 years	67,484	11,162	16.5	52,262	77.4	2,539	3.8	1,400	121	73,106	5,602	7.7	57,032	78.0	8,178	11.2	2,224	70
34 years	71,775	10,991	15.3	56,314	78.5	2,809	3.9	1,493	168	76,319	5,626	7.4	59,716	78.2	8,550	11.2	2,351	67

TABLE 10.—MARITAL CONDITION OF THE URBAN, RURAL-FARM, AND RURAL-NONFARM POPULATION 15 YEARS OLD AND OVER, BY SEX, COLOR, NATIVITY, AND 5-YEAR AGE PERIODS, FOR THE UNITED STATES: 1930

[Per cent not shown where less than 0.1]

AREA, COLOR, NATIVITY, AND AGE	MALES 15 YEARS OLD AND OVER									FEMALES 15 YEARS OLD AND OVER								
	Total	Single		Married		Widowed		Divorced	Unknown	Total	Single		Married		Widowed		Divorced	Unknown
		Number	Per cent	Number	Per cent	Number	Per cent				Number	Per cent	Number	Per cent	Number	Per cent		
ALL CLASSES																		
Urban	25,201,037	8,501,813	33.7	15,242,615	60.5	1,086,856	4.3	316,383	53,370	25,966,592	7,228,694	27.8	15,199,397	58.5	3,076,806	11.8	426,658	35,037
15 to 19 years	2,881,288	2,837,190	98.5	37,234	1.3	461	------	588	5,815	3,134,123	2,800,250	89.3	318,528	10.2	4,738	0.2	6,698	3,909
20 to 24 years	3,030,032	2,217,261	73.2	782,241	25.8	7,092	0.2	12,624	10,814	3,390,276	1,714,078	50.6	1,597,197	47.1	29,508	0.9	42,234	7,199
25 to 29 years	2,998,048	1,162,218	38.8	1,776,769	59.3	20,159	0.7	33,596	5,306	3,173,903	787,689	24.8	2,250,301	70.9	64,617	2.0	68,035	3,261
30 to 34 years	2,865,528	637,901	22.3	2,145,358	74.9	34,499	1.2	44,425	3,345	2,907,948	449,111	15.4	2,285,829	78.6	101,203	3.5	69,607	2,198
35 to 39 years	2,918,120	470,048	16.1	2,339,088	80.2	55,539	1.9	50,442	3,003	2,855,644	354,237	12.4	2,261,922	79.2	168,258	5.9	69,224	2,003
40 to 44 years	2,539,994	341,868	13.5	2,073,844	81.6	75,360	3.0	46,402	2,520	2,392,392	270,783	11.3	1,850,665	77.4	214,985	9.0	54,169	1,790
45 to 49 years	2,170,686	261,063	12.0	1,774,541	81.8	92,413	4.3	40,460	2,209	2,052,143	221,749	10.8	1,513,293	73.7	272,762	13.3	42,709	1,630
50 to 54 years	1,773,324	195,593	11.0	1,431,486	80.7	112,736	6.4	31,648	1,861	1,717,933	189,049	11.0	1,164,425	67.8	331,949	19.3	30,874	1,636
55 to 59 years	1,324,757	135,946	10.3	1,051,850	79.4	113,138	8.5	22,250	1,573	1,331,659	142,679	10.7	812,019	61.0	356,051	26.7	19,015	1,295
60 to 64 years	1,035,328	99,730	9.6	786,472	76.0	132,103	12.8	15,527	1,496	1,084,932	112,852	10.4	557,796	51.4	400,890	37.0	12,099	1,295
65 to 69 years	728,128	64,823	8.9	518,252	71.2	134,392	18.5	9,435	1,226	799,596	78,497	9.8	328,125	41.0	385,367	48.2	6,475	1,132
70 to 74 years	481,805	39,658	8.2	307,920	63.9	127,971	26.6	5,195	1,061	549,427	53,861	9.8	164,196	29.9	327,578	59.6	2,849	943
75 years and over	417,995	27,813	6.7	206,354	49.4	179,518	42.9	3,166	1,144	546,584	44,990	8.2	84,057	15.4	414,688	75.9	1,510	1,339
Unknown	36,004	10,701	29.7	11,206	31.1	1,475	4.1	625	11,997	30,032	8,869	29.5	11,044	36.8	4,152	13.8	560	5,407
Rural-farm	10,310,705	3,765,451	36.5	5,967,324	57.9	492,797	4.8	74,230	10,903	8,984,743	2,263,065	25.2	5,929,564	66.0	729,074	8.1	57,182	5,858
15 to 19 years	1,830,526	1,786,670	97.6	40,686	2.2	739	------	490	1,941	1,590,443	1,347,575	84.7	234,064	14.7	4,850	0.3	3,174	780
20 to 24 years	1,309,335	912,340	69.7	382,088	29.2	6,870	0.5	4,917	3,120	1,124,906	457,265	40.6	640,946	57.0	15,530	1.4	9,889	1,276
25 to 29 years	932,992	335,930	36.0	577,895	61.9	10,825	1.2	7,261	1,081	886,086	146,284	16.5	711,573	80.3	18,852	2.1	8,854	523
30 to 34 years	833,180	171,683	20.6	640,378	76.9	13,226	1.6	7,286	607	838,326	74,471	8.9	734,827	87.7	21,689	2.6	7,019	320
35 to 39 years	895,665	124,787	13.9	743,081	83.0	19,394	2.2	7,941	462	892,317	53,604	6.0	799,587	89.6	32,391	3.6	6,378	297
40 to 44 years	844,484	99,540	11.8	710,872	84.2	25,977	3.1	7,681	414	799,738	42,380	5.3	710,901	88.9	40,676	5.1	5,490	291
45 to 49 years	827,932	87,265	10.5	696,882	84.2	34,901	4.2	8,467	417	733,459	34,508	4.7	641,072	87.4	52,884	7.2	4,723	272
50 to 54 years	776,855	74,214	9.6	647,865	83.4	46,173	5.9	8,186	417	621,134	29,306	4.7	520,937	83.9	66,567	10.7	4,031	293
55 to 59 years	634,462	57,751	9.1	520,151	82.0	49,051	7.7	7,165	344	475,048	22,584	4.8	378,688	79.7	70,603	14.9	2,022	251
60 to 64 years	518,615	45,817	8.8	408,430	78.8	58,045	11.2	5,946	377	369,239	18,816	5.1	262,954	71.2	85,114	23.1	2,077	278
65 to 69 years	383,662	32,092	8.4	284,872	74.3	62,004	16.2	4,357	337	264,003	13,549	5.1	159,963	60.6	88,883	33.7	1,353	255
70 to 74 years	271,900	20,604	7.6	183,895	67.6	64,433	23.7	2,670	202	185,608	10,396	5.6	86,138	46.4	88,060	47.4	722	202
75 years and over	246,025	14,684	6.0	128,354	52.2	100,749	41.0	1,790	448	200,739	11,010	5.5	46,309	23.1	142,422	70.9	518	480
Unknown	5,072	2,074	40.9	1,875	37.0	410	8.1	67	646	3,697	1,257	34.0	1,605	43.4	553	15.0	32	250
Rural-nonfarm	8,369,279	2,686,448	32.1	5,117,170	61.1	445,383	5.3	98,865	21,413	7,885,814	1,814,894	23.0	5,041,795	63.9	928,327	11.8	89,308	11,490
15 to 19 years	1,046,011	1,021,409	97.7	22,442	2.1	313	------	270	1,487	1,060,724	884,349	82.7	179,375	16.8	2,749	0.3	2,499	752
20 to 24 years	997,448	649,842	65.2	336,164	33.7	3,695	0.4	4,359	3,388	1,018,381	375,714	36.9	619,522	60.8	11,277	1.1	10,341	1,527
25 to 29 years	929,140	287,265	30.9	622,340	67.0	8,029	0.9	9,372	2,134	913,439	145,950	16.0	735,771	80.5	18,572	2.0	12,235	911
30 to 34 years	863,078	156,361	18.1	682,440	79.1	11,768	1.4	10,958	1,551	812,361	79,466	9.8	694,992	85.6	25,679	3.2	11,593	631
35 to 39 years	866,075	123,561	14.3	710,445	82.0	18,271	2.1	12,382	1,416	780,824	64,152	8.2	664,171	85.1	39,955	5.1	11,931	615
40 to 44 years	751,981	101,901	13.6	612,122	81.4	24,340	3.2	12,332	1,286	661,606	53,914	8.1	545,335	82.4	51,297	7.8	10,458	602
45 to 49 years	673,306	86,924	12.9	542,098	80.5	31,247	4.6	11,923	1,114	584,753	47,607	8.1	461,848	79.0	65,696	11.2	9,014	588
50 to 54 years	581,466	71,804	12.3	458,274	78.8	39,577	6.8	10,787	1,024	505,092	42,247	8.4	371,964	73.6	82,818	16.4	7,523	540
55 to 59 years	466,773	57,320	12.3	357,200	76.5	42,553	9.1	8,805	895	412,078	34,306	8.3	279,224	67.6	93,504	22.6	5,361	583
60 to 64 years	387,565	45,941	11.9	283,648	73.2	50,372	13.0	6,806	798	355,542	28,951	8.1	208,604	58.7	113,640	32.0	3,807	540
65 to 69 years	306,022	34,536	11.3	210,102	68.7	55,676	18.2	4,991	717	289,194	22,140	7.7	142,205	49.2	121,974	42.2	2,370	499
70 to 74 years	237,942	24,580	10.3	149,813	63.0	59,566	25.0	3,286	688	223,322	16,661	7.5	84,629	37.9	120,365	53.9	1,259	408
75 years and over	251,732	21,818	8.7	126,975	50.4	99,371	39.5	2,475	1,093	250,121	17,312	6.9	51,578	20.6	179,697	71.8	831	703
Unknown	10,740	3,087	28.7	3,107	28.9	605	5.6	119	3,822	8,477	2,125	25.1	2,577	30.4	1,104	13.0	80	2,591
NATIVE WHITE—NATIVE PAR.																		
Urban	11,322,687	3,843,634	33.9	6,850,950	60.5	429,680	3.8	172,211	26,212	11,888,265	3,473,117	29.2	6,908,864	58.1	1,252,402	10.5	237,642	16,240
15 to 19 years	1,457,276	1,430,374	98.2	24,073	1.7	206	------	355	2,268	1,596,602	1,400,438	87.7	188,887	11.8	1,901	0.1	3,936	1,440
20 to 24 years	1,552,487	1,071,406	69.0	465,635	30.0	3,122	0.2	7,996	4,328	1,735,039	832,603	48.0	863,052	49.7	11,120	0.6	25,348	2,856
25 to 29 years	1,479,052	499,529	33.8	947,778	64.1	8,846	0.6	20,840	2,059	1,548,402	369,078	23.8	1,114,806	72.0	24,124	1.6	39,171	1,283
30 to 34 years	1,332,462	251,559	18.9	1,039,308	78.0	14,444	1.1	25,765	1,386	1,351,540	212,827	15.7	1,058,841	78.3	39,737	2.9	39,206	929
35 to 39 years	1,244,616	170,456	13.7	1,024,026	82.3	21,674	1.7	27,258	1,202	1,245,685	166,340	13.4	975,450	78.3	65,288	5.2	37,701	906
40 to 44 years	1,031,767	120,546	11.7	857,607	83.1	28,440	2.8	24,135	1,039	1,024,104	124,525	12.2	785,051	76.7	84,217	8.2	29,512	799
45 to 49 years	871,122	92,461	10.6	722,300	82.9	34,401	3.9	21,037	923	862,324	97,236	11.3	634,888	73.6	106,542	12.4	22,038	720
50 to 54 years	715,847	69,283	9.7	587,216	82.0	42,223	5.9	16,287	838	713,015	79,095	11.1	486,128	68.2	130,242	18.3	16,834	716
55 to 59 years	534,233	48,089	9.0	430,786	80.6	43,265	8.1	11,360	733	543,422	58,341	10.7	333,651	61.4	140,299	25.8	10,544	587
60 to 64 years	407,831	35,098	8.6	315,022	77.2	49,261	12.1	7,763	687	429,614	45,916	10.7	222,065	51.7	154,711	36.0	6,396	526
65 to 69 years	280,636	22,780	8.1	203,049	72.4	49,609	17.7	4,646	552	317,533	32,581	10.3	129,436	40.8	151,699	47.8	3,353	404
70 to 74 years	201,261	15,111	7.5	131,071	65.1	51,789	25.7	2,745	545	238,422	24,693	10.4	70,700	29.7	141,126	59.2	1,512	391
75 years and over	192,684	11,688	6.1	97,021	50.4	81,740	42.4	1,671	564	264,990	24,336	9.2	39,508	14.9	199,631	75.3	860	565
Unknown	21,413	5,254	24.5	6,058	28.3	660	3.1	353	9,088	17,513	5,048	28.8	6,311	36.0	1,765	10.1	331	4,058
Rural-farm	6,694,278	2,522,526	37.7	3,828,217	57.2	291,325	4.4	45,271	6,939	5,896,362	1,554,257	26.4	3,889,321	66.0	418,795	7.1	30,316	3,673
15 to 19 years	1,288,531	1,258,863	97.7	27,747	2.2	303	------	246	1,312	1,096,865	932,757	85.0	160,045	14.6	2,042	0.2	1,526	495
20 to 24 years	897,762	633,548	70.6	255,077	28.5	3,410	0.4	2,763	2,064	760,111	312,388	41.1	435,310	57.3	6,587	0.9	4,989	837
25 to 29 years	620,420	216,416	34.9	393,225	63.4	5,758	0.9	4,376	645	593,676	98,624	16.6	481,631	81.1	8,493	1.4	4,610	318
30 to 34 years	551,358	103,784	18.8	435,101	78.9	7,518	1.4	4,589	366	561,426	50,588	9.0	496,243	88.4	10,667	1.9	3,741	187
35 to 39 years	573,783	71,202	12.4	486,378	84.8	11,077	1.9	4,888	238	573,809	36,146	6.3	518,582	90.4	15,601	2.7	3,302	178
40 to 44 years	528,165	54,355	10.3	454,035	86.0	14,804	2.8	4,723	248	506,677	28,416	5.6	455,017	89.8	20,258	4.0	2,830	156
45 to 49 years	504,450	47,650	9.4	431,822	85.6	19,584	3.9	5,160	234	458,191	22,759	5.0	405,327	88.5	27,464	6.0	2,480	101
50 to 54 years	466,409	40,357	8.7	395,213	84.7	25,661	5.5	4,934	244	389,787	19,292	4.9	332,119	85.2	35,937	9.2	2,261	178
55 to 59 years	386,436	31,551	8.2	321,822	83.3	28,480	7.4	4,392	191	302,947	14,970	4.9	244,164	80.6	41,932	13.8	1,724	157
60 to 64 years	310,550	25,057	8.1	248,137	79.9	33,454	10.8	3,676	226	231,901	12,392	5.3	168,487	72.7	49,626	21.4	1,223	173
65 to 69 years	231,589	17,406	7.5	174,644	75.4	36,608	15.8	2,662	209	167,437	9,225	5.5	102,837	61.4	54,399	32.5	812	164
70 to 74 years	174,419	12,007	6.9	119,945	68.8	40,584	23.3	1,689	194	121,733	7,427	6.1	57,915	47.6	55,729	45.8	471	101
75 years and over	157,208	8,972	5.7	83,178	52.9	63,688	40.5	1,138	292	129,545	8,408	6.5	30,714	23.7	89,798	69.3	337	288
Unknown	3,138	1,358	43.3	993	31.6	276	8.8	35	476	2,257	865	38.3	930	41.2	262	11.6	10	190
Rural-nonfarm	5,352,495	1,688,526	31.5	3,333,973	62.3	255,080	4.8	62,241	12,675	5,193,972	1,227,444	23.6	3,345,483	64.4	556,663	10.7	56,810	7,572
15 to 19 years	734,800	716,592	97.5	16,963	2.3	179	------	172	894	758,429	622,366	82.1	132,664	17.5	1,379	0.2	1,556	464
20 to 24 years	688,589	433,686	63.0	248,135	36.0	1,981	0.3	2,921	1,866	721,519	257,519	35.7	450,960	62.5	5,561	0.8	6,533	946
25 to 29 years	634,573	173,430	27.3	449,504	70.8	4,368	0.7	6,327	944	633,597	95,571	15.1	520,352	82.1	9,459	1.5	7,704	511
30 to 34 years	574,191	85,691	14.9	473,916	82.5	6,615	1.2	7,210	759	545,028	50,214	9.2	473,047	86.8	14,028	2.6	7,376	363
35 to 39 years	541,687	61,155	11.3	462,110	85.3	9,926	1.8	7,747	749	496,395	39,483	8.0	427,640	86.1	21,458	4.3	7,458	356
40 to 44 years	450,069	47,764	10.6	381,152	84.7	12,932	2.9	7,584	637	412,471	32,894	8.0	344,473	83.5	28,130	6.8	6,610	364
45 to 49 years	397,237	40,951	10.3	331,860	83.5	16,532	4.2	7,318	576	360,975	28,705	8.0	289,507	80.2	36,756	10.2	5,672	335
50 to 54 years	345,349	34,799	10.1	281,647	81.6	21,661	6.3	6,625	617	310,619	25,005	8.1	232,732	74.9	47,096	15.4	4,849	337
55 to 59 years	278,073	28,297	10.2	219,871	79.1	23,948	8.6	5,408	549	255,731	20,516	8.0	174,716	68.3	56,632	22.1	3,512	355
60 to 64 years	226,785	22,582	10.0	171,255	75.5	28,245	12.5	4,197	506	214,940	17,310	8.1	127,054	59.1	67,723	31.5	2,518	335
65 to 69 years	175,098	16,848	9.6	123,569	70.6	31,215	17.8	3,019	447	174,649	13,399	7.7	85,060	48.7	74,815	42.6	1,555	320
70 to 74 years	142,712	12,927	9.1	91,727	64.3	35,582	24.9	2,019	457	140,759	10,840	7.7	52,798	37.5	76,014	54.0	842	265
75 years and over	156,238	11,870	7.6	80,450	51.5	61,563	39.4	1,621	729	162,919	12,157	7.5	32,846	20.2	116,901	71.8	572	443
Unknown	7,099	1,934	27.2	1,814	25.6	333	4.7	73	2,945	5,941	1,465	24.7	1,634	27.5	611	10.3	53	2,178

TABLE 10.—MARITAL CONDITION OF THE URBAN, RURAL-FARM, AND RURAL-NONFARM POPULATION 15 YEARS OLD AND OVER, BY SEX, COLOR, NATIVITY, AND 5-YEAR AGE PERIODS, FOR THE UNITED STATES: 1930—Continued

AREA, COLOR, NATIVITY, AND AGE	MALES 15 YEARS OLD AND OVER: Total	Single: Number	Single: Per cent	Married: Number	Married: Per cent	Widowed: Number	Widowed: Per cent	Divorced	Unknown	FEMALES 15 YEARS OLD AND OVER: Total	Single: Number	Single: Per cent	Married: Number	Married: Per cent	Widowed: Number	Widowed: Per cent	Divorced	Unknown
NATIVE WHITE—FOR. OR MIXED PAR.																		
Urban	6,173,365	2,748,154	44.5	3,154,845	51.1	195,869	3.2	62,597	11,900	6,824,165	2,560,477	37.5	3,555,597	52.1	613,842	9.0	84,050	9,299
15 to 19 years	1,055,733	1,048,085	99.3	4,835	0.5	40	------	52	2,721	1,100,424	1,038,217	94.3	59,409	5.4	291	------	680	1,827
20 to 24 years	907,702	743,333	81.9	157,528	17.4	702	0.1	1,709	4,340	989,689	594,792	60.1	382,675	38.7	3,070	0.3	6,267	2,885
25 to 29 years	742,958	338,927	45.6	393,571	53.0	3,099	0.4	5,923	1,438	814,885	252,274	31.0	541,281	66.4	8,205	1.0	12,130	989
30 to 34 years	690,546	178,372	25.8	496,052	71.8	6,275	0.9	9,156	691	752,677	150,667	20.0	570,411	75.8	16,546	2.2	14,458	595
35 to 39 years	644,468	119,827	18.6	503,747	78.2	10,100	1.6	10,329	465	700,423	120,301	17.2	535,675	76.5	29,117	4.2	14,794	476
40 to 44 years	511,346	84,452	16.5	404,268	79.1	12,848	2.5	9,425	353	560,752	94,015	16.8	415,165	74.0	39,689	7.1	11,498	385
45 to 49 years	416,732	66,842	16.0	326,335	78.3	15,444	3.7	7,784	327	465,548	78,543	16.9	326,685	70.2	51,061	11.0	8,903	356
50 to 54 years	364,657	56,062	15.4	281,001	77.1	20,870	5.7	6,460	264	412,651	70,547	17.1	265,705	64.4	69,364	16.8	6,684	351
55 to 59 years	297,487	42,982	14.4	225,847	75.9	23,466	7.9	4,933	259	345,288	56,890	16.5	200,386	58.0	83,185	24.1	4,540	287
60 to 64 years	224,025	30,830	13.8	163,157	72.8	26,572	11.9	3,218	248	271,281	43,487	16.0	132,813	49.0	92,026	33.9	2,695	260
65 to 69 years	154,274	19,423	12.6	105,596	68.4	27,042	17.5	1,997	216	194,047	29,774	15.3	75,234	38.8	87,456	45.1	1,343	240
70 to 74 years	100,372	11,494	11.5	62,087	61.9	25,664	25.6	990	137	129,128	18,761	14.5	36,279	28.1	73,276	56.7	637	175
75 years and over	59,444	5,676	9.5	29,736	50.0	23,457	39.5	495	80	83,044	10,141	12.2	12,563	15.1	59,972	72.2	237	131
Unknown	3,621	1,849	51.1	1,085	30.0	200	5.5	126	361	4,328	2,008	46.4	1,316	30.4	584	13.5	78	342
Rural-farm	1,400,369	574,915	41.1	762,039	54.4	53,002	3.8	8,637	1,776	1,114,787	295,397	26.5	748,191	67.1	65,934	5.9	4,533	732
15 to 19 years	196,275	195,170	99.4	780	0.4	11	------	10	304	160,118	150,821	94.2	9,066	5.7	36	------	69	126
20 to 24 years	157,580	136,310	86.5	20,446	13.0	116	0.1	171	546	110,986	61,428	55.3	48,659	43.8	343	0.3	370	186
25 to 29 years	127,573	68,038	53.3	58,292	45.7	510	0.4	510	223	100,497	22,831	22.7	76,335	76.0	688	0.7	549	94
30 to 34 years	130,754	41,448	31.7	87,441	66.9	1,038	0.8	710	117	114,150	13,291	11.6	98,945	86.7	1,301	1.1	575	44
35 to 39 years	143,399	31,879	22.2	108,575	75.7	1,882	1.3	938	125	127,781	10,234	8.0	114,676	89.7	2,254	1.8	585	32
40 to 44 years	137,029	25,443	18.6	107,525	78.5	2,990	2.2	997	74	119,172	8,470	7.1	106,830	89.6	3,275	2.7	555	36
45 to 49 years	124,448	21,228	17.1	98,091	78.8	3,933	3.2	1,110	86	103,908	7,387	7.1	91,185	87.8	4,762	4.6	546	28
50 to 54 years	110,821	17,659	15.9	86,740	78.3	5,220	4.7	1,147	55	87,294	6,102	7.0	74,262	85.1	6,466	7.4	436	28
55 to 59 years	94,683	14,359	15.2	72,714	76.8	6,492	6.9	1,065	53	70,975	5,118	7.2	57,051	80.4	8,421	11.9	353	32
60 to 64 years	71,704	10,355	14.4	53,222	74.2	7,274	10.1	804	49	50,272	4,128	8.2	36,492	72.6	9,379	18.7	245	28
65 to 69 years	51,913	6,950	13.4	36,449	70.2	7,850	15.1	625	39	33,758	2,719	8.1	20,955	62.1	9,918	29.4	142	24
70 to 74 years	33,506	3,949	11.8	21,334	63.7	7,834	23.4	352	37	21,460	1,738	8.1	10,106	47.1	9,519	44.4	67	30
75 years and over	20,166	1,875	9.3	10,259	50.9	7,818	38.8	188	20	14,096	1,010	7.2	3,486	24.7	9,532	67.6	38	30
Unknown	509	252	49.5	171	33.6	34	6.7	10	42	314	114	36.3	143	45.5	40	12.7	3	14
Rural-nonfarm	1,266,912	480,837	38.0	712,689	56.3	57,385	4.5	14,286	1,715	1,237,536	348,483	28.2	753,450	60.9	122,836	9.9	11,431	1,336
15 to 19 years	174,701	173,358	99.2	1,037	0.6	8	------	12	286	167,200	153,418	91.8	13,398	8.0	77	------	132	175
20 to 24 years	142,784	112,515	78.8	29,284	20.5	135	0.1	332	518	139,906	69,378	49.6	68,898	49.2	528	0.4	796	306
25 to 29 years	127,218	51,922	40.8	73,512	57.8	619	0.5	939	226	129,779	29,132	22.4	97,955	75.5	1,285	1.0	1,258	149
30 to 34 years	129,273	29,876	23.1	96,645	74.8	1,183	0.9	1,458	111	129,525	17,519	13.5	107,793	83.2	2,613	2.0	1,509	91
35 to 39 years	130,814	22,603	17.3	104,318	79.7	2,040	1.6	1,773	80	129,093	15,012	11.6	107,639	83.4	4,719	3.7	1,633	90
40 to 44 years	113,105	19,114	16.9	89,227	78.9	2,880	2.5	1,810	74	109,674	12,997	11.9	88,739	80.9	6,296	5.7	1,562	80
45 to 49 years	97,920	16,931	17.3	75,373	77.0	3,768	3.8	1,787	61	94,920	11,756	12.4	73,506	77.4	8,216	8.7	1,369	73
50 to 54 years	89,702	15,210	17.0	67,539	75.3	5,139	5.7	1,761	53	85,535	10,594	12.4	62,284	72.8	11,445	13.4	1,157	55
55 to 59 years	79,658	13,463	16.9	57,980	72.8	6,563	8.2	1,583	69	75,561	9,109	12.1	50,995	67.5	14,514	19.2	871	72
60 to 64 years	64,365	10,190	15.8	45,450	70.6	7,567	11.8	1,098	60	63,148	7,405	11.7	37,629	59.6	17,487	27.7	564	63
65 to 69 years	51,313	7,361	14.3	34,516	67.3	8,531	16.6	854	51	50,279	5,654	11.2	25,025	49.8	19,206	38.2	337	57
70 to 74 years	37,766	4,839	12.8	23,577	62.4	8,742	23.1	564	44	35,808	3,756	10.5	13,747	38.3	18,187	50.7	100	48
75 years and over	27,584	3,111	11.3	13,982	50.7	10,139	36.8	302	50	26,355	2,441	9.3	5,612	21.3	18,177	69.0	76	49
Unknown	709	344	48.5	249	35.1	71	10.0	13	32	663	312	47.1	230	34.7	86	13.0	7	28
FOREIGN-BORN WHITE																		
Urban	5,516,834	1,177,692	21.3	3,952,186	71.6	329,770	6.0	47,928	9,258	4,960,475	680,083	13.7	3,427,303	69.1	802,028	16.2	45,273	5,728
15 to 19 years	131,156	129,840	99.0	823	0.6	23	------	12	458	145,746	131,971	90.5	13,213	9.1	86	0.1	111	365
20 to 24 years	273,513	221,631	81.0	49,813	18.2	273	0.1	437	1,359	306,277	161,322	52.7	141,571	46.2	1,004	0.3	1,464	916
25 to 29 years	446,991	209,926	47.0	232,345	52.0	1,560	0.3	2,018	1,142	447,239	102,884	23.0	335,271	75.0	4,312	1.0	4,199	573
30 to 34 years	558,966	141,062	25.2	408,719	73.1	4,369	0.8	4,016	809	516,202	53,582	10.4	445,723	86.3	10,915	2.1	5,630	352
35 to 39 years	746,535	128,862	17.3	599,858	80.4	10,314	1.4	6,670	831	626,282	44,278	7.1	548,810	87.6	25,852	4.1	7,021	321
40 to 44 years	779,622	103,912	13.3	648,207	83.2	18,552	2.4	8,008	763	603,770	38,090	6.3	515,757	85.4	42,456	7.0	7,105	353
45 to 49 years	694,549	78,731	11.3	582,142	83.8	25,318	3.6	7,723	635	552,774	36,028	6.5	447,452	80.9	62,433	11.3	6,528	333
50 to 54 years	554,737	55,515	10.0	460,157	83.0	32,231	5.8	6,304	530	473,159	32,790	6.9	351,014	74.2	83,958	17.7	5,015	382
55 to 59 years	411,537	36,954	9.0	335,406	81.5	34,237	8.3	4,512	428	372,130	23,995	6.4	246,164	66.1	98,286	26.4	3,387	304
60 to 64 years	347,684	28,870	8.3	270,042	77.7	44,695	12.9	3,652	425	330,181	20,873	6.3	184,778	56.0	121,734	36.9	2,400	306
65 to 69 years	259,857	19,819	7.6	188,503	72.5	48,832	18.8	2,322	381	252,366	14,550	5.8	114,066	45.2	121,962	48.3	1,441	347
70 to 74 years	160,840	11,542	7.2	103,846	64.6	43,894	27.3	1,243	315	159,801	9,406	5.9	53,239	33.3	96,263	60.2	590	303
75 years and over	146,037	9,020	6.2	70,582	48.3	65,169	44.6	825	441	171,330	9,461	5.5	28,891	16.9	132,110	77.1	329	539
Unknown	4,810	2,008	41.7	1,653	34.4	312	6.5	96	741	3,212	844	26.3	1,414	44.0	657	20.5	53	244
Rural-farm	623,216	125,177	20.1	433,520	69.6	58,609	9.4	5,235	675	445,624	23,726	5.3	348,745	78.3	71,039	15.9	1,855	259
15 to 19 years	10,355	10,249	99.0	76	0.7	------	------	1	29	7,695	6,774	88.0	898	11.7	8	0.1	5	10
20 to 24 years	18,454	16,033	86.9	2,307	12.5	24	0.1	10	80	10,640	4,115	38.7	6,437	60.5	37	0.3	40	17
25 to 29 years	23,658	13,896	58.7	9,543	40.3	88	0.4	78	53	17,007	1,989	11.6	14,887	87.1	142	0.8	74	5
30 to 34 years	27,950	9,731	34.8	17,777	63.6	253	0.9	155	34	25,153	1,106	4.4	23,683	94.2	256	1.0	105	3
35 to 39 years	47,382	10,565	22.3	35,769	75.5	684	1.4	326	38	40,536	1,030	2.5	38,571	95.2	799	2.0	130	6
40 to 44 years	67,978	12,009	17.7	53,894	79.3	1,533	2.3	515	27	52,350	1,195	2.3	49,307	94.2	1,629	3.1	213	6
45 to 49 years	77,500	12,133	15.6	62,110	80.0	2,666	3.4	641	40	57,727	1,407	2.4	53,077	91.9	2,963	5.1	268	12
50 to 54 years	77,033	10,977	14.2	61,176	79.4	4,049	5.3	778	53	56,159	1,554	2.8	49,595	88.3	4,723	8.4	275	12
55 to 59 years	69,886	8,666	12.4	55,272	79.1	5,157	7.4	730	52	47,259	1,214	2.6	39,467	83.5	6,317	13.4	244	17
60 to 64 years	67,869	8,038	11.8	51,789	76.3	7,297	10.8	696	49	42,930	1,097	2.6	32,442	75.6	9,170	21.4	193	28
65 to 69 years	57,190	6,221	10.9	40,959	71.6	9,330	16.3	627	53	34,269	834	2.4	22,171	64.7	11,067	32.3	168	29
70 to 74 years	37,695	3,734	9.9	24,242	64.3	9,286	24.6	395	38	22,912	606	2.6	11,164	48.7	11,027	48.1	86	29
75 years and over	39,908	2,826	7.1	18,508	46.4	18,222	45.7	270	82	30,775	796	2.6	6,982	22.7	22,869	74.3	51	77
Unknown	268	99	36.9	98	36.6	20	7.5	4	47	116	9	7.8	64	55.2	32	27.6	3	8
Rural-nonfarm	864,000	203,048	23.5	574,893	66.5	74,493	8.6	9,667	1,899	659,043	66,322	10.1	467,229	70.9	119,833	18.2	4,814	845
15 to 19 years	15,148	14,972	98.8	131	0.9	3	------	1	41	14,530	12,563	86.5	1,924	13.2	12	0.1	13	18
20 to 24 years	27,136	21,380	78.8	5,598	20.6	29	0.1	48	81	25,966	10,944	42.1	14,706	56.6	137	0.5	124	55
25 to 29 years	44,514	20,566	46.2	23,393	52.6	197	0.4	267	91	41,507	6,999	16.9	33,715	81.2	467	1.1	273	53
30 to 34 years	63,679	18,338	28.8	44,166	69.4	560	0.9	532	83	54,880	4,659	8.5	48,780	88.9	1,026	1.9	378	37
35 to 39 years	98,522	23,331	23.7	72,536	73.6	1,576	1.6	935	144	72,410	4,520	6.2	64,855	89.6	2,462	3.4	529	44
40 to 44 years	114,510	23,980	20.9	85,774	74.9	3,277	2.9	1,308	171	75,946	4,613	6.1	66,252	87.2	4,387	5.8	643	51
45 to 49 years	109,731	21,016	19.2	82,455	75.1	4,681	4.3	1,404	175	72,843	4,604	6.3	60,715	83.4	6,764	9.3	688	72
50 to 54 years	90,726	16,086	17.7	67,283	74.2	5,921	6.5	1,287	149	65,550	4,527	6.9	51,296	78.2	9,034	13.8	640	53
55 to 59 years	73,075	12,144	16.6	53,024	72.6	6,647	9.1	1,129	131	54,720	3,522	6.4	39,164	71.6	11,458	20.9	507	69
60 to 64 years	68,197	10,742	15.8	47,630	69.9	8,693	12.7	904	129	53,716	3,173	5.9	34,016	63.3	16,028	29.8	420	79
65 to 69 years	60,953	8,752	14.4	40,260	66.1	10,973	18.0	814	154	47,079	2,441	5.1	26,214	55.6	18,640	39.6	307	77
70 to 74 years	44,777	5,786	12.9	27,256	60.9	11,074	24.7	538	123	34,589	1,589	4.6	14,981	43.3	17,789	51.4	164	66
75 years and over	52,090	5,607	10.8	25,096	48.2	20,780	39.9	398	209	44,225	2,031	4.6	10,405	23.5	31,539	71.3	121	129
Unknown	942	348	36.9	282	29.9	82	8.7	12	218	470	137	28.8	206	43.3	90	18.9	1	42

850

POPULATION

TABLE 10.—MARITAL CONDITION OF THE URBAN, RURAL-FARM, AND RURAL-NONFARM POPULATION 15 YEARS OLD AND OVER, BY SEX, COLOR, NATIVITY, AND 5-YEAR AGE PERIODS, FOR THE UNITED STATES: 1930—Continued

AREA, COLOR, NATIVITY, AND AGE	MALES 15 YEARS OLD AND OVER									FEMALES 15 YEARS OLD AND OVER								
	Total	Single Number	Per cent	Married Number	Per cent	Widowed Number	Per cent	Divorced	Unknown	Total	Single Number	Per cent	Married Number	Per cent	Widowed Number	Per cent	Divorced	Unknown
NEGRO																		
Urban	1,842,029	576,114	31.3	1,112,781	60.4	118,454	6.4	30,809	3,921	2,048,053	454,635	22.2	1,158,802	56.6	376,331	18.4	54,790	3,495
15 to 19 years	195,723	188,308	96.2	6,759	3.5	170	0.1	151	260	251,432	197,431	78.5	49,054	19.7	2,320	0.9	1,783	244
20 to 24 years	240,821	138,750	57.6	96,638	40.1	2,084	1.1	2,208	541	310,304	111,111	34.8	185,760	58.2	13,661	4.3	8,367	405
25 to 29 years	271,191	84,425	31.1	175,977	64.9	6,071	2.2	4,318	400	325,239	57,645	17.7	229,027	70.4	26,518	8.2	11,667	382
30 to 34 years	239,226	51,863	21.7	173,521	72.5	8,527	3.6	5,029	286	257,246	29,356	11.4	185,860	72.2	32,059	12.5	9,666	305
35 to 39 years	242,537	40,903	16.9	183,380	75.6	12,201	5.0	5,713	331	255,528	21,399	8.4	179,590	70.3	45,077	17.6	9,179	283
40 to 44 years	185,421	26,320	14.2	140,480	75.8	13,984	7.5	4,383	254	184,008	13,008	7.1	110,937	65.2	45,143	24.5	5,676	244
45 to 49 years	162,055	18,564	11.5	124,057	76.6	15,567	9.6	3,632	235	154,535	9,075	5.9	92,940	60.1	48,255	31.2	4,059	206
50 to 54 years	120,482	11,868	9.9	90,190	74.9	15,804	13.2	2,398	162	108,074	6,014	5.6	55,367	51.2	44,340	41.0	2,182	171
55 to 59 years	69,921	6,208	8.9	51,390	73.5	10,889	15.0	1,330	104	63,019	3,103	4.9	28,100	44.6	30,639	48.6	1,072	105
60 to 64 years	47,738	3,702	7.8	32,855	68.8	10,265	21.5	813	93	48,046	2,317	4.8	16,053	33.4	29,011	60.4	560	105
65 to 69 years	28,505	2,037	7.1	18,084	63.4	7,899	27.7	432	53	32,028	1,431	4.5	8,398	26.2	21,821	68.1	306	72
70 to 74 years	16,563	1,022	6.2	9,413	56.8	5,888	35.5	197	43	20,087	908	4.5	3,565	17.7	15,446	76.9	99	69
75 years and over	17,173	1,001	5.8	7,791	45.4	8,168	47.6	103	64	24,752	943	3.8	2,685	10.8	20,953	84.7	77	94
Unknown	4,673	1,083	23.2	2,177	46.6	268	5.7	42	1,103	4,665	894	19.2	1,866	40.0	1,088	23.3	97	720
Rural-farm	1,395,651	460,114	33.0	841,149	60.3	79,452	5.7	13,800	1,136	1,380,749	352,961	25.6	845,806	61.3	161,530	11.7	19,421	1,031
15 to 19 years	301,727	280,513	96.0	11,402	3.8	358	0.1	219	235	295,851	233,308	78.9	58,286	19.7	2,637	0.9	1,500	120
20 to 24 years	204,272	103,864	50.8	95,078	46.5	3,135	1.5	1,875	325	219,391	71,302	32.5	135,507	61.8	8,114	3.7	4,274	194
25 to 29 years	135,841	26,710	19.7	102,804	75.7	4,040	3.0	2,095	102	155,559	20,483	13.2	122,559	78.8	9,000	5.8	3,414	94
30 to 34 years	103,852	11,694	11.3	86,560	83.4	3,872	3.7	1,664	56	121,827	8,609	7.1	101,703	83.5	8,964	7.4	2,470	81
35 to 39 years	113,332	8,008	7.1	98,550	87.0	5,082	4.5	1,045	47	134,987	5,737	4.3	113,856	84.3	13,058	9.7	2,201	75
40 to 44 years	95,265	5,465	5.7	82,778	86.9	5,682	6.0	1,203	47	110,080	3,976	3.6	90,652	81.4	14,507	13.2	1,807	87
45 to 49 years	105,737	4,276	4.0	92,429	87.4	7,577	7.2	1,412	43	104,141	2,767	2.7	83,329	80.0	16,622	16.0	1,301	62
50 to 54 years	110,150	3,690	3.3	95,246	86.5	9,953	9.0	1,209	52	81,094	2,221	2.7	59,500	73.4	18,244	22.5	1,001	68
55 to 59 years	74,602	2,251	3.0	63,072	85.3	7,762	10.4	881	36	49,002	1,195	2.4	34,366	70.1	12,837	26.2	569	35
60 to 64 years	61,992	1,772	2.9	50,555	81.6	8,920	14.4	701	44	40,465	1,131	2.8	23,248	57.5	15,601	38.7	381	44
65 to 69 years	38,742	1,148	3.0	29,905	77.2	7,254	18.7	405	30	26,007	719	2.8	12,044	46.6	12,408	47.7	204	32
70 to 74 years	23,700	704	3.0	16,752	70.7	6,014	25.4	213	17	17,700	575	3.2	6,249	35.3	10,755	60.8	83	38
75 years and over	25,572	802	3.1	14,818	57.9	9,740	38.1	172	40	23,822	722	3.0	4,467	18.8	18,478	77.6	83	72
Unknown	867	217	25.0	509	58.7	63	7.3	16	62	814	216	26.5	380	46.7	176	21.6	13	29
Rural-nonfarm	703,782	234,722	33.4	403,941	57.4	49,689	7.1	11,104	4,326	670,750	146,210	21.8	393,536	58.7	114,802	17.1	14,657	1,545
15 to 19 years	98,196	93,953	95.7	3,856	3.9	114	0.1	71	202	107,599	79,325	73.7	26,301	24.4	1,188	1.1	715	70
20 to 24 years	108,529	59,942	55.2	45,461	41.9	1,305	1.3	930	801	110,784	32,484	29.3	70,807	63.9	4,606	4.2	2,009	188
25 to 29 years	93,488	27,653	29.6	60,998	65.2	2,486	2.7	1,007	744	90,469	12,504	13.8	68,272	75.5	6,818	7.5	2,607	178
30 to 34 years	73,791	15,658	21.2	53,187	72.1	2,873	3.9	1,544	529	68,572	6,240	9.1	52,834	77.0	7,230	10.6	2,127	132
35 to 39 years	74,603	11,771	15.8	56,766	76.1	3,980	5.3	1,692	394	60,913	4,566	6.5	52,771	75.5	10,361	14.8	2,104	111
40 to 44 years	58,643	7,918	13.5	44,514	75.9	4,422	7.5	1,443	346	53,907	3,077	5.7	38,111	70.6	11,225	20.8	1,488	96
45 to 49 years	55,370	5,920	10.7	42,663	77.1	5,258	9.5	1,256	273	48,227	2,300	4.8	32,190	66.7	12,470	25.9	1,164	103
50 to 54 years	46,900	4,333	9.2	35,498	75.7	5,016	12.6	979	174	37,890	1,932	5.1	21,877	57.7	13,208	34.9	703	80
55 to 59 years	29,844	2,619	8.8	21,955	73.6	4,549	15.2	592	129	23,009	1,043	4.5	11,987	52.1	9,488	41.2	414	77
60 to 64 years	23,619	1,861	7.9	16,207	68.0	4,952	21.0	451	88	20,309	945	4.7	8,208	40.7	10,783	53.1	250	54
65 to 69 years	15,596	1,170	7.6	9,892	63.4	4,218	27.0	253	54	14,299	566	4.0	4,959	34.7	8,596	60.1	141	37
70 to 74 years	10,633	728	6.8	6,113	57.5	3,598	33.9	143	51	10,413	433	4.2	2,597	24.9	7,277	69.0	79	27
75 years and over	13,046	874	6.7	6,148	47.1	5,820	44.6	124	80	14,081	616	4.4	2,159	15.3	11,183	79.4	52	71
Unknown	1,524	313	20.5	623	40.9	108	7.1	19	461	1,188	179	15.1	403	33.9	270	22.7	15	321

MARITAL CONDITION

851

TABLE 11.—MARITAL CONDITION OF THE URBAN, RURAL-FARM, AND RURAL-NONFARM POPULATION 15 TO 34 YEARS OLD, BY SEX AND SINGLE YEARS OF AGE, FOR THE UNITED STATES: 1930

[Per cent not shown where less than 0.1]

AREA AND AGE	MALES Total	Single Number	Single Per cent	Married Number	Married Per cent	Widowed Number	Widowed Per cent	Divorced	Unknown	FEMALES Total	Single Number	Single Per cent	Married Number	Married Per cent	Widowed Number	Widowed Per cent	Divorced	Unknown
Urban:																		
15 years	508,459	508,082	99.9	352	0.1	15		10		585,109	581,005	99.3	3,914	0.7	92		98	
16 years	577,633	576,824	99.9	770	0.1	22		17		613,668	596,407	97.2	16,590	2.7	323	0.1	348	
17 years	571,370	569,044	99.6	2,224	0.4	58		44		610,612	565,528	92.6	43,509	7.1	659	0.1	916	
18 years	584,795	573,146	98.0	8,788	1.5	116		146	2,599	667,260	562,609	84.3	99,397	14.9	1,455	0.2	1,004	1,795
19 years	579,031	550,094	95.0	25,100	4.3	250		371	3,216	657,484	494,701	75.2	155,118	23.6	2,200	0.3	3,342	2,114
20 years	572,512	514,054	89.9	53,335	9.3	514	0.1	857	2,852	682,992	450,658	66.0	221,361	32.4	3,649	0.5	5,335	1,989
21 years	617,399	508,603	82.4	103,985	16.8	886	0.1	1,491	2,434	669,739	388,615	58.0	268,529	40.1	4,387	0.7	6,638	1,570
22 years	613,643	453,141	73.8	154,378	25.2	1,405	0.2	2,448	2,271	689,617	343,719	49.8	330,216	47.9	5,704	0.8	8,522	1,456
23 years	611,609	394,720	64.5	200,055	34.3	1,822	0.3	3,375	1,737	670,060	286,705	42.4	371,417	54.0	7,159	1.1	10,193	1,186
24 years	614,869	345,843	56.2	260,588	42.4	2,465	0.4	4,453	1,520	671,268	244,381	36.4	405,674	60.4	8,609	1.3	11,546	998
25 years	615,096	300,218	48.8	299,047	48.6	3,088	0.5	5,374	1,369	680,397	219,321	32.2	436,630	64.2	10,651	1.6	12,883	912
26 years	597,441	259,387	43.4	327,434	54.8	3,400	0.6	6,036	1,184	642,866	176,402	27.4	441,649	68.7	10,874	1.7	13,216	725
27 years	582,070	220,834	37.9	349,960	60.1	3,814	0.7	6,472	996	603,302	143,531	23.8	434,310	72.0	11,017	2.0	12,983	561
28 years	601,753	204,716	34.0	383,815	63.8	4,715	0.8	7,571	936	635,479	138,606	21.8	466,560	73.4	15,112	2.4	14,614	587
29 years	601,682	171,063	28.4	416,513	69.2	5,142	0.9	8,143	821	611,859	109,820	18.0	471,152	77.0	16,063	2.6	14,339	470
30 years	679,028	193,124	28.4	467,355	68.8	7,503	1.1	10,049	997	715,105	141,065	19.7	532,232	74.4	23,646	3.3	17,403	609
31 years	492,121	108,080	22.0	371,309	75.5	4,969	1.0	7,213	550	487,550	71,862	14.7	390,063	80.1	13,547	2.8	11,145	342
32 years	500,505	112,046	22.4	373,867	74.7	7,367	1.2	9,391	710	602,583	92,012	15.3	473,874	78.6	21,537	3.6	14,702	458
33 years	546,456	105,100	19.2	425,070	77.8	7,040	1.3	8,670	567	547,607	71,424	13.0	442,078	80.9	19,068	3.6	12,861	376
34 years	557,358	99,551	17.9	440,573	79.0	7,020	1.4	9,003	521	555,004	72,748	13.1	446,082	80.4	22,505	4.1	13,406	353
Rural-farm:																		
15 years	373,928	373,502	99.9	347	0.1	16		3		341,092	333,806	97.9	7,040	2.1	151		95	
16 years	388,643	387,563	99.7	1,037	0.3	29		14		348,839	326,852	93.7	21,244	6.1	461	0.1	282	
17 years	378,020	374,269	99.0	3,612	1.0	84		55		316,508	274,733	86.8	40,461	12.8	799	0.3	515	
18 years	363,793	351,035	96.5	11,508	3.2	206	0.1	138	906	315,970	238,087	75.4	74,901	23.7	1,570	0.5	1,046	366
19 years	326,142	300,242	92.1	24,182	7.4	404	0.1	280	1,034	208,034	174,097	65.0	90,418	33.7	1,869	0.7	1,236	414
20 years	300,286	256,345	85.4	41,715	13.9	770	0.3	516	940	204,670	143,900	54.4	115,903	43.8	2,696	1.0	1,797	388
21 years	289,851	222,180	76.7	65,080	22.5	1,055	0.4	779	757	228,375	106,927	46.8	110,921	51.2	2,517	1.1	1,725	285
22 years	262,856	178,650	68.0	81,023	30.8	1,476	0.6	1,083	624	227,232	88,013	38.7	133,511	58.8	3,306	1.5	2,149	253
23 years	235,734	140,379	59.5	92,113	39.1	1,685	0.7	1,179	428	205,224	65,332	31.8	134,161	65.4	3,307	1.6	2,157	207
24 years	220,608	114,786	52.0	102,167	46.3	1,934	0.9	1,360	371	199,390	53,093	26.6	140,450	70.4	3,644	1.8	2,061	148
25 years	206,263	93,377	45.3	109,084	52.9	2,081	1.0	1,422	299	197,085	43,393	22.0	147,353	74.8	4,108	2.1	2,075	156
26 years	192,012	77,896	40.6	110,340	57.5	2,083	1.1	1,443	250	180,889	34,372	19.0	140,871	77.9	3,652	2.0	1,870	124
27 years	177,418	62,357	35.1	111,391	62.8	2,050	1.2	1,412	208	166,142	26,176	15.8	134,839	81.2	3,353	2.0	1,677	97
28 years	180,910	55,955	30.9	120,850	66.8	2,307	1.3	1,544	170	176,540	23,500	13.3	147,056	83.3	4,094	2.3	1,743	87
29 years	176,383	46,345	26.3	126,229	71.6	2,215	1.3	1,440	154	165,430	18,783	11.4	141,454	85.5	3,645	2.2	1,480	59
30 years	203,049	51,360	25.3	146,103	72.0	3,425	1.7	1,990	171	202,233	23,509	11.7	170,345	84.2	6,038	3.0	2,179	102
31 years	140,049	29,857	21.3	107,261	76.6	1,793	1.3	1,057	91	137,369	12,218	8.9	121,267	88.3	2,850	2.1	987	47
32 years	167,758	34,973	20.8	128,363	76.5	2,734	1.6	1,555	133	171,320	15,106	8.8	150,333	87.7	4,387	2.6	1,433	61
33 years	157,683	28,254	17.9	125,573	79.6	2,436	1.5	1,320	100	161,091	11,699	7.3	144,221	89.5	3,973	2.5	1,146	52
34 years	164,641	27,239	16.5	133,088	80.8	2,838	1.7	1,304	112	166,313	11,879	7.1	148,661	89.4	4,441	2.7	1,274	58
Rural-nonfarm:																		
15 years	212,261	212,101	99.9	150	0.1	5		5		214,850	210,862	98.1	3,844	1.8	94		50	
16 years	215,644	215,155	99.8	466	0.2	14		9		222,888	208,921	93.7	13,558	6.1	238	0.1	170	
17 years	207,760	206,106	99.2	1,595	0.8	38		21		211,552	181,446	85.8	29,244	13.8	472	0.2	390	
18 years	209,115	202,758	97.0	5,541	2.6	77		83	656	210,911	159,328	73.5	55,644	25.7	823	0.4	772	344
19 years	201,281	185,379	92.1	14,690	7.3	170	0.1	152	831	208,523	123,792	60.8	77,085	37.9	1,127	0.6	1,111	408
20 years	193,641	163,639	84.5	28,513	14.7	347	0.2	342	800	208,321	105,361	50.6	99,331	47.7	1,681	0.8	1,559	389
21 years	205,203	153,248	74.7	50,146	24.4	520	0.3	549	740	200,464	85,663	42.7	110,805	55.3	1,822	0.9	1,887	337
22 years	202,335	131,279	64.9	68,740	34.0	735	0.4	877	704	206,848	74,150	35.9	127,932	61.8	2,327	1.1	2,108	322
23 years	198,822	109,124	54.9	86,984	43.7	983	0.5	1,136	595	202,742	60,789	30.0	136,800	67.5	2,533	1.2	2,369	241
24 years	197,447	92,552	46.9	101,781	51.5	1,110	0.6	1,455	549	200,006	49,792	24.9	144,594	72.3	2,914	1.5	2,468	238
25 years	190,939	77,130	40.4	110,218	57.7	1,343	0.7	1,696	548	190,635	41,315	21.0	149,086	75.8	3,439	1.7	2,556	239
26 years	186,032	64,877	34.9	117,531	63.2	1,387	0.7	1,791	446	186,717	33,848	17.0	147,820	78.9	3,817	1.8	2,522	210
27 years	179,851	53,880	30.0	122,237	68.0	1,531	0.9	1,806	397	178,053	26,909	15.5	140,037	81.2	4,411	2.0	2,243	153
28 years	184,293	49,084	26.6	130,992	71.1	1,859	1.0	1,946	412	180,304	24,252	13.3	149,111	82.7	4,216	2.3	2,564	161
29 years	188,025	42,285	22.5	141,367	75.2	1,909	1.0	2,133	331	176,130	20,126	11.4	149,317	84.8	4,189	2.4	2,350	148
30 years	204,212	45,441	22.3	152,961	74.9	2,770	1.4	2,640	400	198,503	23,022	11.0	161,208	83.3	6,187	3.2	2,915	171
31 years	150,294	26,947	17.9	119,713	79.7	1,620	1.1	1,754	260	141,483	13,733	9.7	122,139	86.3	3,600	2.5	1,897	114
32 years	175,600	31,354	17.9	139,160	79.2	2,496	1.4	2,260	336	167,391	16,080	9.6	143,567	85.8	5,215	3.1	2,389	140
33 years	163,058	26,384	16.1	133,005	81.1	2,274	1.4	2,049	246	154,833	13,095	8.5	133,891	86.5	5,095	3.3	2,146	106
34 years	169,008	26,235	15.5	137,601	81.4	2,608	1.5	2,255	309	155,651	13,536	8.7	134,187	86.2	5,582	3.6	2,246	100

852

POPULATION

TABLE 12.—MARITAL CONDITION OF THE POPULATION 15 YEARS OLD AND OVER, BY SEX, BY DIVISIONS AND STATES: 1930

DIVISION AND STATE	MALES 15 YEARS OLD AND OVER						FEMALES 15 YEARS OLD AND OVER					
	Total	Single	Married	Widowed	Di-vorced	Un-known	Total	Single	Married	Widowed	Di-vorced	Un-known
United States	43,881,021	14,953,712	26,327,109	2,025,036	489,478	85,686	42,837,149	11,306,653	26,170,756	4,734,207	573,148	52,385
GEOGRAPHIC DIVISIONS:												
New England	2,901,430	1,024,340	1,701,884	146,012	24,588	4,606	3,044,692	972,313	1,697,691	340,898	30,705	3,085
Middle Atlantic	9,580,982	3,413,672	5,673,131	421,004	50,541	22,634	9,547,467	2,804,829	5,622,781	1,038,636	64,634	16,587
East North Central	9,378,073	3,100,837	5,701,796	435,523	126,309	13,608	8,961,107	2,246,305	5,640,326	934,140	132,226	8,170
West North Central	4,844,547	1,673,552	2,876,764	227,980	58,184	8,067	4,632,669	1,225,894	2,865,534	475,523	61,008	3,810
South Atlantic	5,167,443	1,757,614	3,129,089	233,004	36,338	10,798	5,246,825	1,414,211	3,145,495	626,831	53,461	6,827
East South Central	3,214,755	1,005,370	2,016,400	156,157	31,127	5,701	3,263,427	787,502	2,020,880	393,040	48,053	3,802
West South Central	4,144,135	1,325,261	2,565,026	195,546	53,534	4,768	3,906,245	917,077	2,558,815	445,917	71,142	3,294
Mountain	1,354,047	489,101	775,861	62,515	24,269	2,301	1,173,018	274,065	761,361	116,611	19,968	1,013
Pacific	3,295,609	1,163,905	1,886,558	147,295	84,588	13,203	2,981,639	664,397	1,857,873	362,611	91,051	5,707
NEW ENGLAND:												
Maine	285,114	90,569	172,525	17,444	4,102	474	283,484	72,768	172,270	33,899	4,211	336
New Hampshire	168,465	54,460	100,586	10,680	2,545	185	171,907	48,174	99,922	21,148	2,534	129
Vermont	131,484	44,303	77,076	8,232	1,779	94	126,417	32,274	76,472	16,004	1,582	85
Massachusetts	1,501,904	545,566	870,510	72,410	10,610	2,808	1,620,410	551,892	869,725	181,875	15,020	1,898
Rhode Island	238,074	84,434	140,310	11,568	2,070	202	256,835	85,282	140,578	27,821	3,056	98
Connecticut	575,789	204,099	340,877	25,678	3,482	753	585,639	181,923	338,724	60,151	4,302	539
MIDDLE ATLANTIC:												
New York	4,714,608	1,718,371	2,761,908	197,157	22,117	15,055	4,721,139	1,417,657	2,738,973	522,983	30,596	10,930
New Jersey	1,476,159	512,215	892,349	62,415	7,137	2,043	1,470,247	416,041	884,506	158,585	9,678	1,437
Pennsylvania	3,390,215	1,183,086	2,018,874	161,432	21,287	5,536	3,356,081	971,131	1,999,302	357,068	24,360	4,220
EAST NORTH CENTRAL:												
Ohio	2,436,685	769,282	1,514,131	117,191	33,696	2,385	2,384,808	594,443	1,496,574	255,108	37,165	1,518
Indiana	1,185,534	351,910	750,884	62,775	18,076	1,889	1,155,964	262,586	744,990	128,917	18,458	1,013
Illinois	2,869,347	985,343	1,715,640	127,762	35,562	5,040	2,780,510	735,489	1,701,801	299,551	40,186	3,393
Michigan	1,806,530	601,745	1,095,563	78,849	28,161	2,212	1,629,915	373,677	1,075,586	164,241	25,259	1,152
Wisconsin	1,079,977	392,557	625,578	48,946	10,814	2,082	1,009,970	280,110	621,285	96,323	11,158	1,094
WEST NORTH CENTRAL:												
Minnesota	939,795	367,844	520,870	41,981	8,135	965	882,618	270,487	519,131	83,104	9,283	613
Iowa	899,826	298,856	545,117	43,180	11,758	915	872,053	226,333	543,432	89,464	12,224	600
Missouri	1,330,551	415,233	825,917	68,248	18,442	2,711	1,328,769	323,109	825,087	158,222	21,102	1,179
North Dakota	241,350	104,297	125,670	9,269	1,611	503	205,764	65,124	124,632	14,292	1,474	242
South Dakota	249,409	97,168	138,870	10,447	2,314	610	218,763	61,087	138,030	17,363	2,021	262
Nebraska	498,502	172,548	297,725	21,694	5,645	890	471,298	123,988	296,670	44,080	6,072	479
Kansas	685,114	217,606	422,595	33,161	10,279	1,473	653,414	155,766	418,552	68,980	9,072	435
SOUTH ATLANTIC:												
Delaware	88,886	30,508	52,604	4,712	661	251	85,276	22,203	52,344	9,037	731	61
Maryland	588,895	205,202	348,003	28,854	4,869	1,907	582,733	158,968	346,675	69,352	5,853	1,885
District of Columbia	181,673	63,695	107,418	8,113	1,808	639	204,556	61,700	109,427	29,766	2,902	662
Virginia	802,623	284,780	473,870	35,948	5,801	2,224	800,589	224,421	475,428	92,050	7,765	925
West Virginia	575,638	195,006	352,122	22,899	5,183	428	532,849	133,496	346,568	46,874	5,000	311
North Carolina	968,308	336,359	589,236	37,605	3,815	1,293	1,001,408	293,855	596,027	103,850	6,704	972
South Carolina	516,766	180,416	312,653	21,918	1,418	361	553,365	160,775	318,837	70,604	2,667	392
Georgia	926,871	304,704	569,512	45,205	6,341	1,109	972,461	250,859	573,377	135,213	12,271	741
Florida	517,783	156,884	324,121	27,750	6,442	2,586	513,588	107,925	326,812	69,095	8,878	878
EAST SOUTH CENTRAL:												
Kentucky	870,198	270,339	546,342	43,573	9,005	939	855,056	204,684	543,928	95,357	10,411	676
Tennessee	864,634	270,671	541,796	41,673	8,269	2,225	883,297	218,534	543,405	106,237	13,026	2,095
Alabama	835,246	266,977	521,268	38,946	7,307	748	861,967	214,039	524,158	110,080	13,019	671
Mississippi	644,677	197,383	406,994	31,965	6,546	1,789	653,107	150,305	409,389	81,366	11,597	450
WEST SOUTH CENTRAL:												
Arkansas	613,805	183,707	389,325	33,197	7,057	519	595,127	126,357	388,783	70,231	9,421	335
Louisiana	662,160	230,262	422,503	32,460	6,121	814	703,077	178,203	424,774	89,141	10,142	817
Oklahoma	823,058	254,549	517,512	37,583	12,548	866	764,569	162,964	513,982	72,782	14,397	444
Texas	2,015,112	656,743	1,235,686	92,306	27,808	2,569	1,933,472	449,553	1,231,276	213,763	37,182	1,608
MOUNTAIN:												
Montana	211,910	86,283	111,496	9,397	4,388	396	166,045	40,153	109,514	14,503	2,659	116
Idaho	163,154	59,889	93,455	6,990	3,020	300	135,154	31,359	91,745	10,927	1,995	128
Wyoming	89,966	35,726	48,671	3,715	1,611	243	67,257	14,139	46,831	5,155	1,057	75
Colorado	379,165	125,015	227,494	18,895	6,938	823	357,236	83,456	226,078	40,337	7,013	352
New Mexico	141,079	47,817	83,537	7,938	1,678	109	126,945	29,828	82,557	12,852	1,628	80
Arizona	158,621	57,232	90,370	7,785	2,957	277	133,547	28,613	87,791	14,650	2,348	145
Utah	168,237	59,334	100,785	5,842	2,153	123	158,726	41,808	99,613	15,338	2,357	110
Nevada	41,915	18,305	20,053	1,953	1,574	30	27,108	5,109	18,232	2,849	911	7
PACIFIC:												
Washington	628,346	224,798	357,702	28,951	14,876	2,019	545,790	122,694	352,466	56,054	13,701	875
Oregon	381,529	130,768	221,806	18,332	10,126	497	339,219	74,867	218,946	36,489	8,783	134
California	2,285,734	808,399	1,307,050	100,012	59,586	10,687	2,096,630	466,836	1,286,461	270,068	68,567	4,698

MARITAL CONDITION

TABLE 13.—PER CENT DISTRIBUTION BY MARITAL CONDITION OF THE MALE POPULATION 15 YEARS OLD AND OVER, BY DIVISIONS AND STATES: 1890 TO 1930

DIVISION AND STATE	PER CENT SINGLE					PER CENT MARRIED					PER CENT WIDOWED					PER CENT DIVORCED				
	1930	1920	1910	1900	1890	1930	1920	1910	1900	1890	1930	1920	1910	1900	1890	1930	1920	1910	1900	1890
United States	34.1	35.1	38.7	40.2	41.7	60.0	59.2	55.8	54.5	53.9	4.6	4.8	4.5	4.6	3.9	1.1	0.6	0.5	0.3	0.2
GEOGRAPHIC DIVISIONS:																				
New England	35.3	35.8	38.6	39.2	40.1	58.7	58.2	55.5	54.6	54.6	5.0	5.3	5.1	5.3	4.7	0.8	0.6	0.5	0.4	0.3
Middle Atlantic	35.6	35.5	39.0	39.7	40.7	59.2	59.2	56.1	55.3	54.9	4.4	4.7	4.3	4.6	4.1	0.5	0.3	0.2	0.2	0.1
East North Central	33.1	34.5	37.5	38.9	40.5	60.8	59.8	57.0	55.8	55.2	4.6	4.7	4.5	4.5	3.9	1.3	0.8	0.6	0.4	0.3
West North Central	34.5	36.4	40.5	41.8	43.0	59.4	58.0	54.1	53.3	53.0	4.7	4.6	4.3	4.2	3.6	1.2	0.7	0.5	0.4	0.3
South Atlantic	34.0	34.5	36.9	39.7	40.5	60.6	60.2	57.9	55.3	55.6	4.5	4.6	4.6	4.4	3.7	0.7	0.4	0.3	0.2	0.1
East South Central	31.3	31.9	34.9	38.6	39.6	62.7	62.2	59.2	56.0	56.1	4.9	5.1	5.1	4.8	4.0	1.0	0.5	0.5	0.3	0.2
West South Central	32.0	34.0	36.5	39.2	40.5	61.9	60.1	57.5	55.1	54.7	4.7	4.9	4.9	4.9	4.1	1.3	0.7	0.5	0.3	0.2
Mountain	36.1	38.0	45.1	47.3	54.5	57.3	55.6	49.5	47.0	41.2	4.6	4.6	3.8	4.1	3.2	1.8	1.1	0.8	0.6	0.4
Pacific	35.3	38.1	46.9	49.0	54.3	57.2	55.0	46.7	44.7	40.5	4.5	4.7	4.2	4.6	3.5	2.0	1.6	1.0	0.7	0.5
NEW ENGLAND:																				
Maine	31.5	32.9	34.6	36.0	36.9	60.5	59.5	57.8	56.5	57.3	6.1	6.5	6.4	6.3	5.0	1.4	0.9	1.0	0.7	0.5
New Hampshire	32.3	33.8	35.7	36.5	37.4	59.7	58.5	56.9	55.9	56.4	6.3	6.4	6.1	6.3	5.5	1.5	1.1	1.0	0.8	0.6
Vermont	33.7	32.8	34.3	35.1	36.1	58.6	59.7	58.5	57.4	57.7	6.3	6.5	6.2	6.3	5.6	1.4	0.9	0.9	0.6	0.5
Massachusetts	36.3	36.9	40.0	40.4	41.7	58.0	57.6	54.7	53.8	53.4	4.8	5.0	4.7	4.9	4.5	0.7	0.4	0.4	0.2	0.2
Rhode Island	35.4	36.7	40.1	40.5	41.0	58.8	57.6	54.0	53.5	54.0	4.8	5.1	5.0	5.1	4.6	0.9	0.6	0.6	0.5	0.3
Connecticut	35.6	35.6	39.3	40.4	41.2	59.2	59.2	55.3	54.1	53.9	4.5	4.6	4.8	5.0	4.3	0.6	0.4	0.3	0.3	0.3
MIDDLE ATLANTIC:																				
New York	36.4	36.2	39.8	39.7	40.5	58.6	58.5	55.2	55.1	54.9	4.2	4.6	4.4	4.8	4.3	0.5	0.3	0.2	0.2	0.1
New Jersey	34.7	34.4	37.0	38.2	39.5	60.5	60.6	57.3	56.7	56.2	4.2	4.6	4.4	4.7	4.1	0.5	0.2	0.2	0.1	0.1
Pennsylvania	34.9	35.0	38.4	40.0	41.3	59.6	59.7	56.8	55.1	54.5	4.8	4.8	4.3	4.3	3.9	0.6	0.4	0.3	0.2	0.1
EAST NORTH CENTRAL:																				
Ohio	31.6	33.5	36.1	38.3	39.9	62.1	60.7	58.2	56.4	55.7	4.8	4.8	4.8	4.7	4.0	1.4	0.8	0.6	0.4	0.3
Indiana	29.7	30.9	34.0	36.5	38.9	63.3	62.6	59.8	57.7	56.5	5.3	5.2	5.1	4.9	4.1	1.5	1.0	0.8	0.6	0.4
Illinois	34.3	35.4	39.3	40.7	42.5	59.8	59.1	55.2	54.2	53.4	4.5	4.6	4.2	4.3	3.7	1.2	0.7	0.5	0.4	0.3
Michigan	33.3	34.6	36.1	37.2	38.7	60.6	59.8	58.3	57.4	56.9	4.4	4.6	4.6	4.6	3.9	1.6	0.9	0.7	0.5	0.4
Wisconsin	36.3	38.3	41.4	41.1	41.5	57.0	56.5	53.6	53.0	54.0	4.5	4.4	4.2	4.3	4.0	1.0	0.6	0.5	0.4	0.3
WEST NORTH CENTRAL:																				
Minnesota	39.1	42.1	46.8	46.1	46.2	55.4	53.0	48.3	49.4	49.9	4.5	4.1	3.8	3.9	3.3	0.9	0.5	0.4	0.3	0.2
Iowa	33.2	35.1	38.6	40.1	41.7	60.6	59.2	55.9	54.9	54.2	4.8	4.7	4.4	4.3	3.6	1.3	0.8	0.6	0.4	0.3
Missouri	31.2	33.4	37.2	40.2	42.3	62.1	60.3	56.9	54.4	53.3	5.1	5.2	4.8	4.7	3.9	1.4	0.8	0.6	0.3	0.3
North Dakota	43.2	41.1	46.9	49.0	48.0	52.1	54.3	48.6	46.8	48.5	3.8	3.6	2.9	3.4	3.1	0.7	0.4	0.3	0.3	0.2
South Dakota	39.0	39.7	44.6	43.9	44.3	55.7	55.1	50.4	51.5	51.8	4.2	4.0	3.6	3.7	3.3	0.9	0.6	0.6	0.4	0.4
Nebraska	34.6	36.7	40.9	42.9	44.5	59.7	57.9	54.2	52.7	51.9	4.4	4.3	3.8	3.7	3.0	1.1	0.7	0.6	0.4	0.4
Kansas	31.8	33.3	37.4	39.5	40.6	61.7	60.7	56.8	55.3	55.3	4.8	4.9	4.5	4.3	3.6	1.5	0.8	0.6	0.4	0.4
SOUTH ATLANTIC:																				
Delaware	34.4	34.1	37.0	39.7	41.9	59.3	59.0	56.1	54.4	54.0	5.3	5.2	5.1	5.1	4.0	0.7	0.4	0.2	0.1	0.1
Maryland	34.8	36.0	38.7	40.9	42.1	59.1	58.1	55.8	53.6	53.3	4.9	5.2	5.0	4.8	4.2	0.8	0.5	0.3	0.2	0.1
District of Columbia	35.1	38.3	40.2	43.1	43.9	59.1	55.8	53.8	51.1	51.2	4.5	4.8	5.2	5.3	4.4	1.0	0.6	0.4	0.3	0.2
Virginia	35.5	36.6	38.5	41.6	42.7	59.0	58.3	56.1	53.1	53.0	4.5	4.6	4.9	4.8	4.1	0.7	0.4	0.3	0.2	0.1
West Virginia	33.9	35.5	38.9	41.0	41.2	61.2	59.7	56.7	54.5	55.1	4.0	4.0	3.7	3.7	3.2	0.9	0.5	0.3	0.2	0.2
North Carolina	34.7	34.1	36.3	39.0	39.1	60.0	61.3	59.1	56.5	56.6	3.9	4.2	4.1	4.1	3.4	0.4	0.2	0.2	0.1	0.1
South Carolina	34.9	34.2	35.5	38.2	37.6	60.5	61.1	59.7	57.3	58.8	4.2	4.4	4.4	4.2	3.4	0.3	0.1	0.1	0.1	0.1
Georgia	32.9	32.0	34.2	37.3	38.8	61.4	62.7	60.4	57.6	57.7	4.9	4.8	4.8	4.4	3.3	0.7	0.4	0.3	0.2	0.1
Florida	30.3	32.2	36.4	40.6	40.3	62.6	61.0	56.3	53.6	55.3	5.4	5.8	5.2	4.8	3.9	1.2	0.6	0.6	0.4	0.3
EAST SOUTH CENTRAL:																				
Kentucky	31.1	32.7	35.6	38.8	40.6	62.8	61.3	58.4	55.8	54.9	5.0	5.2	5.1	4.8	4.1	1.0	0.6	0.5	0.3	0.2
Tennessee	31.3	31.6	35.0	38.9	39.7	62.7	62.5	59.1	55.6	55.7	4.8	5.2	5.2	4.9	4.1	1.0	0.5	0.4	0.3	0.2
Alabama	32.0	31.9	34.5	38.2	38.6	62.4	62.5	60.0	56.7	57.6	4.7	4.8	4.9	4.6	3.5	0.9	0.5	0.4	0.3	0.2
Mississippi	30.6	31.3	34.3	38.3	39.0	63.1	62.8	59.5	56.2	56.6	5.0	5.1	5.2	5.0	4.1	1.0	0.5	0.5	0.3	0.2
WEST SOUTH CENTRAL:																				
Arkansas	29.9	30.8	34.3	37.6	38.7	63.4	62.8	58.9	56.1	56.4	5.4	5.5	5.9	5.6	4.4	1.1	0.7	0.5	0.3	0.3
Louisiana	33.3	35.0	37.9	39.8	39.7	61.0	59.4	56.1	54.6	55.6	4.7	4.7	5.0	5.1	4.2	0.9	0.4	0.3	0.3	0.2
Oklahoma	30.9	32.6	35.7	38.4	41.0	62.9	61.4	58.2	55.6	53.9	4.6	4.8	4.8	4.9	4.5	1.5	0.8	0.6	0.4	0.4
Texas	32.6	35.3	37.2	39.9	41.8	61.3	58.8	57.2	54.7	53.5	4.6	4.8	4.6	4.6	4.0	1.4	0.7	0.5	0.4	0.2
MOUNTAIN:																				
Montana	40.7	40.1	52.4	56.9	64.3	52.6	54.0	42.5	37.9	31.9	4.4	4.1	3.0	3.6	2.4	2.0	1.1	0.7	0.6	0.4
Idaho	36.4	38.3	45.9	49.2	55.9	57.3	56.3	49.2	45.7	40.2	4.3	4.1	3.4	4.0	3.1	1.9	1.1	0.7	0.7	0.5
Wyoming	39.7	41.8	56.3	58.2	61.7	54.1	52.2	39.7	37.1	33.9	4.1	4.0	2.8	3.5	2.8	1.8	1.2	0.7	0.5	0.5
Colorado	33.0	35.2	41.2	44.0	54.7	60.0	57.2	53.2	49.7	40.7	5.0	5.0	4.3	4.2	3.3	1.8	1.2	0.9	0.6	0.4
New Mexico	33.9	36.9	38.2	36.9	40.5	59.2	56.0	55.7	50.6	54.5	5.6	6.2	5.2	5.6	4.6	1.2	0.8	0.7	0.7	0.4
Arizona	36.1	40.4	45.8	45.9	60.3	57.0	53.3	47.7	43.6	35.7	4.9	4.9	4.4	5.1	3.4	1.9	0.9	0.8	0.7	0.4
Utah	35.3	36.4	41.0	41.0	46.2	59.9	59.1	54.2	54.8	50.2	3.5	3.5	2.9	3.3	2.7	1.3	0.9	0.6	0.4	0.3
Nevada	43.7	40.2	51.3	53.1	60.4	47.8	45.9	41.4	40.1	34.4	4.7	4.3	4.6	5.1	3.3	3.8	2.0	1.4	0.9	0.7
PACIFIC:																				
Washington	35.8	38.8	48.6	50.4	57.2	56.9	54.8	45.7	43.0	38.5	4.6	4.4	3.6	3.9	3.1	2.4	1.6	0.9	0.7	0.5
Oregon	34.3	36.4	47.5	47.8	51.5	58.1	56.9	46.6	46.1	43.3	4.8	4.7	4.3	4.8	3.7	2.7	1.8	1.2	0.8	0.6
California	35.4	38.2	45.8	48.8	54.1	57.2	54.6	47.3	44.9	40.5	4.4	4.8	4.4	4.7	3.6	2.6	1.5	1.0	0.7	0.5

854

POPULATION

TABLE 14.—PER CENT DISTRIBUTION BY MARITAL CONDITION OF THE FEMALE POPULATION 15 YEARS OLD AND OVER, BY DIVISIONS AND STATES: 1890 TO 1930

DIVISION AND STATE	PER CENT SINGLE					PER CENT MARRIED					PER CENT WIDOWED					PER CENT DIVORCED				
	1930	1920	1910	1900	1890	1930	1920	1910	1900	1890	1930	1920	1910	1900	1890	1930	1920	1910	1900	1890
United States	26.4	27.3	29.7	31.2	31.8	61.1	60.6	58.9	57.0	56.8	11.1	11.1	10.6	11.2	11.0	1.3	0.8	0.6	0.5	0.4
GEOGRAPHIC DIVISIONS:																				
New England	31.9	32.1	34.2	34.7	35.1	55.8	55.4	53.6	52.3	51.8	11.2	11.8	11.5	12.3	12.5	1.0	0.7	0.6	0.5	0.4
Middle Atlantic	29.4	29.8	32.6	33.3	34.1	58.9	58.2	56.1	54.7	54.1	10.9	11.5	10.8	11.6	11.5	0.7	0.4	0.3	0.2	0.2
East North Central	25.1	26.2	29.1	30.1	30.9	62.9	62.1	59.8	58.7	58.7	10.4	10.7	10.1	10.4	9.9	1.5	0.9	0.7	0.6	0.5
West North Central	26.5	27.7	29.7	30.3	30.0	61.9	61.4	60.4	60.0	61.3	10.3	9.9	9.0	9.0	8.2	1.3	0.8	0.7	0.5	0.4
South Atlantic	27.0	27.7	29.6	32.5	33.1	60.0	60.0	58.4	54.9	54.4	11.9	11.6	11.3	12.1	12.1	1.0	0.5	0.4	0.3	0.2
East South Central	24.2	25.3	26.8	29.9	30.6	62.1	61.7	60.3	56.7	56.2	12.1	12.0	11.8	12.7	12.7	1.5	0.9	0.8	0.6	0.4
West South Central	22.9	24.5	25.3	27.0	26.8	64.0	63.5	63.1	60.1	60.0	11.2	10.8	10.6	12.1	12.7	1.8	1.0	0.7	0.6	0.4
Mountain	23.4	23.4	25.2	25.2	25.7	64.0	65.4	64.5	64.0	64.3	9.9	9.8	9.0	9.8	9.2	1.7	1.2	1.0	0.8	0.7
Pacific	22.3	23.5	27.4	29.7	30.0	62.3	62.4	60.5	58.1	59.6	12.2	12.1	10.6	11.0	9.5	3.1	1.9	1.3	0.9	0.7
NEW ENGLAND:																				
Maine	25.7	26.6	27.4	28.8	29.0	60.8	59.8	59.2	57.5	57.3	12.0	12.5	12.3	12.8	12.5	1.5	1.0	0.9	0.7	0.6
New Hampshire	28.0	28.7	29.7	30.4	31.3	58.1	57.3	56.6	55.3	54.7	12.3	12.7	12.6	13.3	13.2	1.5	1.1	1.0	0.9	0.8
Vermont	25.5	26.1	26.4	26.9	27.0	60.5	60.1	60.6	59.6	59.2	12.7	12.9	12.2	12.6	12.2	1.3	0.8	0.8	0.7	0.6
Massachusetts	34.1	34.4	36.9	37.4	38.0	53.7	53.2	51.2	49.8	49.2	11.2	11.7	11.4	12.2	12.5	0.9	0.6	0.5	0.4	0.3
Rhode Island	33.2	33.8	35.8	36.9	37.5	54.7	54.1	52.2	50.6	49.9	10.8	11.2	10.9	11.7	12.0	1.2	0.8	0.8	0.7	0.6
Connecticut	31.1	30.4	33.6	34.1	35.0	57.8	58.0	54.6	53.0	51.8	10.3	11.0	11.2	12.3	12.6	0.7	0.4	0.4	0.4	0.5
MIDDLE ATLANTIC:																				
New York	30.0	30.9	33.7	33.7	34.3	58.0	56.7	54.5	53.6	53.2	11.1	11.9	11.3	12.4	12.3	0.8	0.4	0.3	0.2	0.2
New Jersey	28.3	28.5	31.6	32.3	33.5	60.2	59.8	57.3	55.7	54.9	10.8	11.3	10.7	11.6	11.5	0.7	0.3	0.2	0.2	0.1
Pennsylvania	28.9	28.8	31.4	33.2	34.1	59.6	59.7	57.9	55.9	55.1	10.6	10.9	10.2	10.5	10.5	0.7	0.4	0.3	0.3	0.2
EAST NORTH CENTRAL:																				
Ohio	24.9	25.5	28.9	31.1	32.4	62.8	62.4	59.5	57.2	56.5	10.7	11.1	10.7	11.0	10.6	1.6	0.9	0.7	0.5	0.5
Indiana	22.7	23.9	26.2	28.0	29.9	64.4	63.6	62.3	60.4	59.2	11.2	11.2	10.4	10.7	10.2	1.6	1.0	0.9	0.8	0.7
Illinois	26.5	27.6	30.4	31.0	31.9	61.2	60.3	58.6	57.7	57.8	10.8	11.1	10.1	10.6	9.9	1.4	0.9	0.7	0.5	0.4
Michigan	22.9	23.8	27.1	28.0	27.3	66.0	65.3	62.2	61.6	63.2	9.5	9.9	9.8	9.7	9.0	1.5	0.9	0.8	0.6	0.5
Wisconsin	27.7	30.1	32.6	31.6	31.0	61.5	59.6	57.7	58.5	59.7	9.5	9.5	9.0	9.3	8.8	1.1	0.7	0.6	0.5	0.4
WEST NORTH CENTRAL:																				
Minnesota	30.6	32.1	35.0	32.6	31.9	58.8	58.2	56.2	58.9	60.3	9.4	8.9	8.0	8.0	7.4	1.1	0.6	0.5	0.4	0.3
Iowa	26.0	27.4	29.8	30.7	31.0	62.3	61.6	60.0	59.9	60.4	10.3	9.9	9.1	8.6	8.1	1.4	0.9	0.7	0.6	0.5
Missouri	24.3	26.0	28.0	30.3	30.9	62.1	61.1	60.1	58.2	58.3	11.9	11.8	10.8	10.9	10.3	1.6	1.0	0.8	0.5	0.4
North Dakota	31.6	30.1	30.2	28.8	26.0	60.6	62.7	63.4	64.3	66.8	6.9	6.4	5.2	6.3	6.0	0.7	0.4	0.4	0.3	0.2
South Dakota	27.0	28.2	29.3	28.7	26.0	63.1	63.6	63.0	63.7	67.7	7.9	7.3	6.6	7.0	5.9	0.9	0.6	0.6	0.5	0.4
Nebraska	26.3	27.2	29.4	29.6	28.1	62.9	63.0	61.9	62.4	65.1	9.4	8.0	7.8	7.3	6.2	1.3	0.8	0.6	0.5	0.5
Kansas	23.8	25.0	26.6	28.4	27.7	64.1	64.0	63.7	62.1	64.4	10.6	10.0	8.7	8.6	7.3	1.5	0.9	0.7	0.6	0.5
SOUTH ATLANTIC:																				
Delaware	26.0	25.9	29.4	31.6	32.8	61.4	61.6	58.6	56.5	56.0	11.7	11.8	11.4	11.4	11.1	0.9	0.5	0.3	0.2	0.1
Maryland	27.3	29.1	33.1	35.0	35.9	59.5	58.0	54.8	52.4	51.6	11.9	12.3	11.5	12.1	12.2	1.0	0.5	0.4	0.3	0.2
Dist. of Columbia	30.2	37.3	34.5	38.2	38.8	53.5	47.0	48.8	45.2	45.0	14.6	14.7	15.7	16.0	15.8	1.5	0.7	0.6	0.5	0.4
Virginia	28.0	28.9	31.6	35.0	36.2	59.4	59.2	56.5	52.6	51.1	11.5	11.8	11.3	12.0	12.3	1.0	0.5	0.4	0.3	0.2
West Virginia	25.1	25.5	28.0	31.6	33.3	65.0	65.1	63.3	59.4	58.0	8.8	8.6	7.9	8.5	8.4	1.1	0.6	0.5	0.4	0.3
North Carolina	29.3	29.3	31.2	34.1	34.0	59.5	59.9	58.0	54.4	53.9	10.4	10.3	10.3	11.1	11.9	0.7	0.3	0.3	0.3	0.2
South Carolina	29.1	28.5	29.0	31.4	30.5	57.6	59.2	58.4	55.8	56.7	12.8	11.9	12.1	12.5	12.5	0.5	0.3	0.2	0.2	0.1
Georgia	25.8	25.1	26.5	29.1	29.5	59.0	61.3	60.2	56.7	56.9	13.9	12.9	12.5	13.4	13.0	1.3	0.7	0.5	0.5	0.3
Florida	21.0	22.2	23.5	25.9	27.2	63.6	63.9	63.8	60.3	60.0	13.5	13.0	11.2	12.9	12.1	1.7	0.8	0.8	0.7	0.5
EAST SOUTH CENTRAL:																				
Kentucky	23.9	25.3	27.0	30.2	31.6	63.6	62.4	60.3	57.4	56.3	11.2	11.3	10.9	11.7	11.5	1.2	0.8	0.8	0.6	0.4
Tennessee	24.7	25.4	27.3	30.5	31.0	61.5	61.7	60.0	56.2	55.8	12.0	11.9	11.7	12.5	12.6	1.5	0.9	0.8	0.6	0.5
Alabama	24.8	25.3	26.3	29.7	29.9	60.8	61.1	60.3	56.2	56.4	12.8	12.5	12.4	13.5	13.3	1.5	0.9	0.9	0.6	0.3
Mississippi	23.0	25.0	25.6	29.0	29.2	62.7	61.7	60.7	56.6	56.5	12.5	12.2	12.5	13.6	13.7	1.8	0.9	0.9	0.6	0.3
WEST SOUTH CENTRAL:																				
Arkansas	21.2	22.1	23.7	26.0	25.2	65.3	65.5	64.0	60.8	62.4	11.8	11.2	11.3	12.5	11.9	1.6	1.0	0.8	0.6	0.4
Louisiana	25.3	27.2	28.3	29.6	29.5	60.4	59.3	57.6	55.0	54.7	12.7	12.5	13.2	14.7	15.3	1.4	0.8	0.8	0.6	0.4
Oklahoma	21.3	22.3	21.9	22.3	21.5	67.2	67.7	69.3	68.2	72.3	9.5	8.7	7.9	8.4	5.9	1.9	1.0	0.6	0.6	0.3
Texas	23.3	25.1	26.0	27.3	26.3	63.7	62.7	62.7	60.4	61.4	11.1	10.9	10.2	11.5	11.8	1.9	1.1	0.8	0.7	0.4
MOUNTAIN:																				
Montana	24.2	23.1	26.3	24.6	25.4	65.4	67.3	65.1	66.6	66.8	8.7	8.3	7.5	7.8	6.8	1.6	1.1	0.8	0.9	0.8
Idaho	23.0	22.8	24.7	23.7	22.3	67.4	68.6	67.8	68.1	70.6	8.0	7.6	6.4	7.4	6.5	1.5	0.9	0.7	0.8	0.6
Wyoming	21.0	20.5	23.5	24.7	24.8	69.6	70.5	69.1	68.2	67.9	7.7	7.5	6.2	6.4	6.4	1.6	1.2	1.0	0.6	0.8
Colorado	23.4	23.8	25.8	26.2	27.2	63.3	63.5	62.8	62.7	62.3	11.3	11.1	10.1	9.9	8.8	2.0	1.3	1.2	0.8	0.7
New Mexico	23.5	24.1	23.3	19.8	21.1	65.0	64.3	66.2	67.8	66.9	10.1	10.5	9.6	11.3	11.3	1.3	0.9	0.9	1.0	0.7
Arizona	21.4	21.1	22.2	21.0	23.3	65.7	66.6	65.7	64.8	64.5	11.0	11.3	10.5	12.6	11.7	1.8	0.9	1.0	1.0	0.5
Utah	26.0	26.3	27.9	29.5	27.7	62.8	62.6	61.3	59.3	61.1	9.7	9.9	9.2	10.2	10.3	1.5	1.1	0.8	0.9	0.9
Nevada	18.8	19.3	21.0	26.6	29.8	67.3	66.6	67.1	59.6	57.9	10.5	11.1	10.1	12.0	9.7	3.4	2.3	1.3	0.9	1.2
PACIFIC:																				
Washington	22.5	22.9	26.5	25.5	24.0	64.6	65.7	64.1	65.5	69.2	10.3	9.6	7.9	7.8	6.1	2.5	1.8	1.2	0.9	0.5
Oregon	22.1	23.0	27.1	28.9	28.2	64.5	64.9	63.0	61.4	63.9	10.8	10.1	8.6	8.6	7.2	2.6	1.9	1.1	0.9	0.7
California	22.3	23.9	27.9	31.1	31.9	61.4	60.6	58.4	55.2	56.3	12.9	13.5	12.2	12.5	10.9	3.3	1.9	1.3	0.9	0.7

CHAPTER 12

———

SCHOOL ATTENDANCE

CHAPTER 12.—SCHOOL ATTENDANCE

INTRODUCTION

The statistics of school attendance obtained in the census of 1930 are based upon the answer to a question on the Population Schedule as to whether the person enumerated had attended school or college at any time between September 1, 1929, and the census date, April 1, 1930. If the person had attended any kind of school, college, or other educational institution at any time within the period in question, an affirmative answer was to be made. The total number of persons returned as attending school is therefore larger than the number who were in attendance at any one time between September 1, 1929, and April 1, 1930.

In 1920 the question was asked in practically the same form, though since the census date was January 1 (instead of April 1) the period covered was somewhat less and the returns may have been somewhat smaller than they would have been if the inquiry had been made in April. It is believed, however, that the difference is very small and that the figures for 1930 are fairly comparable with those for 1920 and for the earlier censuses, except possibly those of 1890 and 1900. At these two censuses the enumerators were required to ascertain not only the fact of school attendance, but also the number of months of attendance. In some instances the person from whom the enumerator obtained his information would not know the number of months of school attendance, even though he knew the child had attended school. In a few of these cases the enumerator, since he could not make a complete report, probably made no report at all with respect to school attendance. The returns for 1890 and 1900 are therefore doubtless less nearly complete than those for the subsequent censuses and perhaps less nearly complete than those for the earlier censuses. In the censuses prior to 1890, and also in 1910, as well as 1920, the general form of the inquiry on school attendance was the same as in 1930.

Statistics on school attendance for continental United States are presented in this chapter by States and for cities of 25,000 or more. Less detailed statistics are presented for counties and for incorporated places of 10,000 or more in Volume III of the Fifteenth Census Reports on Population; and statistics for the outlying territories and possessions enumerated at the Fifteenth Census are presented in the Report on Outlying Territories and Possessions.

110652—33——70

School attendance by age.—The ages of compulsory school attendance vary from State to State, beginning at 6 years in 2 States, 7 years in 29 States and the District of Columbia, and at 8 years in 17 States. The main body of pupils attending the elementary schools (grades 1 to 8) are included in the group 7 to 13 years of age, for which statistics are presented in somewhat more detail in the accompanying tables than for the other age groups. Very significant changes have taken place, however, in the percentage of school attendance in those higher age groups representing pupils in secondary schools. The school attendance figures are summarized by single years of age from 5 to 20 in Table 1.

TABLE 1.—SCHOOL ATTENDANCE BY SEX AND AGE, FOR THE UNITED STATES: 1930 AND 1920

	1930			1920		
SEX AND AGE	Total number	Attending school		Total number	Attending school	
		Number	Per cent		Number	Per cent
TOTAL						
5 to 20 years	38, 387, 032	26, 849, 639	69. 9	33, 250, 870	21, 373, 976	64. 3
5 and 6 years	5, 020, 535	2, 168, 220	43. 2	4, 686, 154	1, 922, 125	41. 0
5 years	2, 505, 250	500, 734	20. 0	2, 347, 839	441, 411	18. 8
6 years	2, 515, 285	1, 667, 486	66. 3	2, 338, 315	1, 480, 714	63. 3
7 to 13 years	17, 209, 566	16, 398, 400	95. 3	15, 300, 793	13, 869, 010	90. 6
7 years	2, 470, 150	2, 207, 331	89. 4	2, 287, 609	1, 905, 404	83. 3
8 years	2, 604, 215	2, 451, 048	94. 1	2, 273, 280	2, 010, 894	88. 5
9 years	2, 512, 760	2, 401, 356	95. 6	2, 151, 032	1, 944, 314	90. 4
10 years	2, 500, 648	2, 427, 254	97. 1	2, 233, 704	2, 077, 965	93. 0
11 years	2, 319, 394	2, 260, 735	97. 5	2, 097, 782	1, 970, 255	93. 9
12 years	2, 480, 123	2, 408, 623	97. 1	2, 234, 759	2, 082, 749	93. 2
13 years	2, 322, 327	2, 242, 053	96. 5	2, 028, 627	1, 877, 429	92. 5
14 and 15 years	4, 678, 084	4, 156, 378	88. 8	3, 907, 710	3, 124, 129	79. 9
14 years	2, 382, 385	2, 212, 825	92. 9	2, 046, 265	1, 766, 784	86. 3
15 years	2, 295, 699	1, 943, 553	84. 7	1, 861, 445	1, 357, 345	72. 9
16 and 17 years	4, 663, 137	2, 669, 857	57. 3	3, 828, 131	1, 644, 061	42. 9
16 years	2, 367, 315	1, 569, 839	66. 3	1, 972, 958	1, 001, 701	50. 8
17 years	2, 295, 822	1, 100, 018	47. 9	1, 855, 173	642, 360	34. 6
18 to 20 years	6, 815, 710	1, 456, 784	21. 4	5, 522, 082	814, 651	14. 8
18 years	2, 357, 834	723, 524	30. 7	1, 910, 046	413, 619	21. 7
19 years	2, 235, 445	441, 814	19. 8	1, 830, 934	252, 680	13. 8
20 years	2, 222, 431	291, 446	13. 1	1, 781, 102	148, 352	8. 3
MALE						
5 to 20 years	19, 274, 149	13, 521, 768	70. 2	16, 639, 600	10, 663, 547	64. 1
5 and 6 years	2, 543, 553	1, 079, 827	42. 5	2, 365, 772	956, 746	40. 4
7 to 13 years	8, 699, 846	8, 274, 754	95. 1	7, 723, 238	6, 984, 902	90. 4
14 and 15 years	2, 361, 134	2, 099, 723	88. 9	1, 958, 976	1, 556, 519	79. 5
16 and 17 years	2, 339, 070	1, 322, 324	56. 5	1, 902, 867	767, 533	40. 3
18 to 20 years	3, 330, 546	745, 140	22. 4	2, 688, 747	397, 847	14. 8
FEMALE						
5 to 20 years	19, 112, 883	13, 327, 871	69. 7	16, 611, 270	10, 710, 429	64. 5
5 and 6 years	2, 476, 982	1, 088, 393	43. 9	2, 320, 382	965, 379	41. 6
7 to 13 years	8, 509, 720	8, 123, 646	95. 5	7, 583, 555	6, 884, 108	90. 8
14 and 15 years	2, 316, 950	2, 056, 655	88. 8	1, 948, 734	1, 567, 610	80. 4
16 and 17 years	2, 324, 067	1, 347, 533	58. 0	1, 925, 264	876, 528	45. 5
18 to 20 years	3, 485, 164	711, 644	20. 4	2, 833, 335	416, 804	14. 7

POPULATION

Color and nativity.—The differences in the proportion attending school as between one and another of the color and nativity classes for which census statistics are presented are due in part to the extent to which these classes are found in urban and rural communities—or on farms and elsewhere. The foreign-born white and the native white of foreign or mixed parentage are found largely in urban communities, in which school attendance begins, and in general ends, at somewhat earlier ages than in rural communities. The native white of native parentage and the Negro population, on the other hand, are found more largely in the rural areas.

The United States totals for school attendance are presented by color and nativity in Table 2.

TABLE 2.—SCHOOL ATTENDANCE BY COLOR AND NATIVITY, FOR THE UNITED STATES: 1930

| COLOR AND NATIVITY | PERSONS 5 TO 20 YEARS OLD | | | PERSONS 7 TO 13 YEARS OLD | | |
| | Total number | Attending school | | Total number | Attending school | |
		Number	Per cent		Number	Per cent
All classes	38,387,032	26,849,639	69.9	17,209,566	16,398,400	95.3
White	33,536,777	23,969,129	71.5	15,065,790	14,547,737	96.6
Native	32,835,801	23,579,380	71.8	14,850,438	14,343,660	96.5
Native parentage	24,080,683	17,288,107	71.8	11,029,603	10,594,986	96.1
Foreign or mixed parentage	8,755,118	6,291,273	71.9	3,826,835	3,748,674	98.0
Foreign born	700,976	389,749	55.6	209,352	204,077	97.5
Negro	4,128,998	2,477,311	60.0	1,811,015	1,580,624	87.3
Other races	721,257	403,199	55.9	332,761	270,039	81.2

Urban, rural-farm, and rural-nonfarm population.—Because of the marked differences between urban and rural communities in regard to school facilities and also in the composition of their population, statistics for school attendance are presented for these three population groups in several of the tables.

Urban population, as defined by the Census Bureau, is in general that residing in cities and other incorporated places having 2,500 inhabitants or more, the remainder being classified as rural. In three of the New England States, New Hampshire, Massachusetts, and Rhode Island, towns (townships) are classified as urban if they have a population of 2,500 or more and certain urban characteristics; and a few large and densely populated townships in other States are likewise classified, even though not formally incorporated as municipalities.

In addition to the classification of the population as urban and rural, the rural population is further subdivided into rural-farm and rural-nonfarm, on the basis of the replies to a question reading "Does this family live on a farm?" The rural-farm population includes all persons living on farms in the rural areas. The rural-nonfarm or "village" population is made up largely of persons living in small towns or villages, both incorporated and unincorporated, though in many areas there are considerable numbers of families living in the open country but not on farms.

The school-attendance figures for these urban and rural areas are summarized in Table 3.

TABLE 3.—SCHOOL ATTENDANCE BY COLOR AND NATIVITY, FOR THE URBAN, RURAL-FARM, AND RURAL-NONFARM POPULATION OF THE UNITED STATES: 1930

| AREA, COLOR, AND NATIVITY | PERSONS 5 TO 20 YEARS OLD | | | PERSONS 7 TO 13 YEARS OLD | | |
| | Total number | Attending school | | Total number | Attending school | |
		Number	Per cent		Number	Per cent
URBAN						
All classes	19,431,749	14,044,180	72.3	8,524,852	8,297,704	97.3
White	17,692,214	12,931,146	73.1	7,775,884	7,596,965	97.7
Native	17,096,331	12,599,623	73.7	7,600,102	7,425,570	97.7
Native parentage	10,459,942	7,777,689	74.4	4,702,846	4,584,689	97.5
Foreign or mixed parentage	6,636,389	4,821,934	72.7	2,897,256	2,840,881	98.1
Foreign born	595,883	331,523	55.6	175,782	171,395	97.5
Negro	1,431,246	916,727	64.1	607,212	571,918	94.2
Other races	308,289	196,307	63.7	141,756	128,821	90.9
RURAL-FARM						
All classes	11,506,573	7,640,734	66.4	5,264,346	4,849,965	92.1
White	9,252,720	6,358,791	68.7	4,246,606	4,024,060	94.8
Native	9,215,455	6,339,935	68.8	4,235,926	4,013,701	94.8
Native parentage	8,189,696	5,653,757	69.0	3,797,505	3,586,160	94.4
Foreign or mixed parentage	1,025,759	686,178	66.9	438,421	427,535	97.5
Foreign born	37,274	18,856	50.6	10,680	10,359	97.0
Negro	2,017,586	1,174,826	58.2	909,108	753,583	82.9
Other races	236,278	107,117	45.3	108,632	72,222	66.5
RURAL-NONFARM						
All classes	7,448,710	5,164,725	69.3	3,420,368	3,250,831	95.0
White	6,591,834	4,679,192	71.0	3,043,300	2,926,712	96.2
Native	6,524,015	4,639,822	71.0	3,020,410	2,904,389	96.2
Native parentage	5,431,045	3,856,661	71.0	2,529,252	2,424,131	95.8
Foreign or mixed parentage	1,092,970	783,161	71.7	491,158	480,258	97.8
Foreign born	67,819	39,370	58.1	22,890	22,323	97.5
Negro	680,186	385,758	56.7	294,699	255,123	86.6
Other races	176,690	99,775	56.5	82,373	68,996	83.8

Gainful employment and school attendance.—For persons from 10 to 24 years of age a tabulation of school attendance in combination with occupational status has been made; that is, the school attendance data have been tabulated separately for persons returned as gainfully occupied and for those not gainfully occupied. One of the main objects of this tabulation is to show the number of young persons past the compulsory school attendance age who are neither attending school nor engaged in a gainful occupation. The total number of persons 19 years of age in this group, for example, is made up rather largely of young men and young women seeking their first jobs. The data are especially significant, therefore, in connection with the statistics of unemployment. In the tabulations for females separate figures are presented for those married and for those not married, since a young married woman could hardly be counted as a probable first-job seeker, even though she were not attending school. Another significant figure is that representing the number of persons both following a gainful occupation and attending school.

The results of this special tabulation are presented in detail, by age, in Tables 29 to 34.

SCHOOL ATTENDANCE

SCHOOL ATTENDANCE OF THE POPULATION 5 TO 20 YEARS OLD: 1930

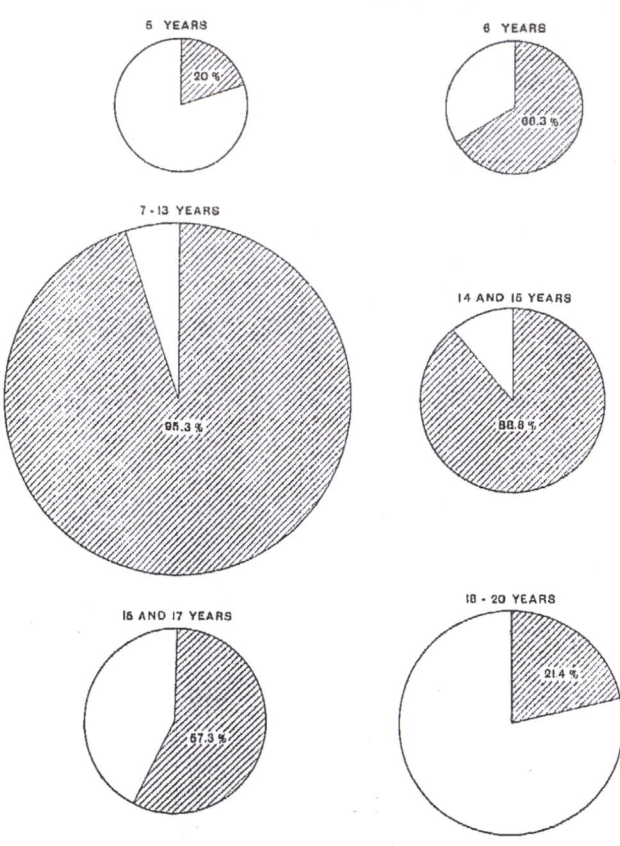

SCHOOL ATTENDANCE BY SINGLE YEARS OF AGE FROM 5 TO 20, BY COLOR AND NATIVITY: 1930

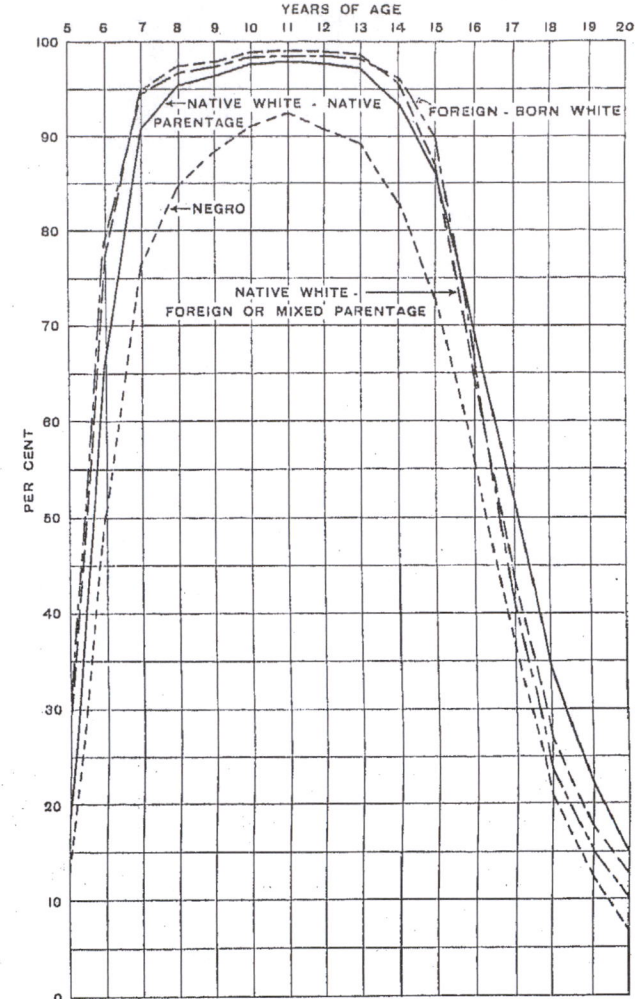

SCHOOL ATTENDANCE BY SINGLE YEARS OF AGE: 1930 AND 1920

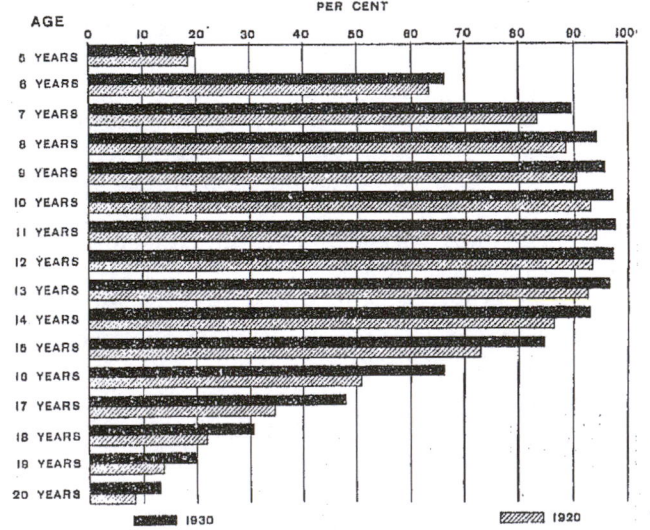

SCHOOL ATTENDANCE OF THE POPULATION 7 TO 13 YEARS OLD, BY COLOR AND NATIVITY: 1930 AND 1920

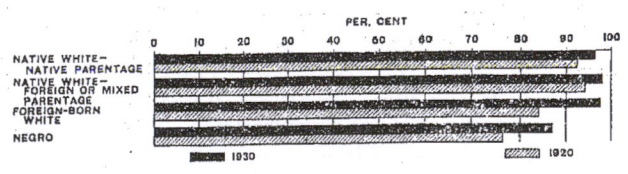

1094

POPULATION

TABLE 4.—SCHOOL ATTENDANCE OF THE POPULATION 5 TO 20 YEARS OLD, BY COLOR, NATIVITY, AND SEX, FOR THE UNITED STATES: 1890 TO 1930

[Per cent not shown where base is less than 100]

CENSUS YEAR AND COLOR AND NATIVITY	POPULATION 5 TO 20 YEARS OLD								
	Total			Male			Female		
	Total number	Attending school		Total number	Attending school		Total number	Attending school	
		Number	Per cent		Number	Per cent		Number	Per cent
1930									
All classes	38,387,032	26,849,639	69.9	19,274,149	13,521,768	70.2	19,112,883	13,327,871	69.7
White	33,536,777	23,989,129	71.5	16,896,649	12,120,553	71.7	16,640,128	11,848,576	71.2
Native	32,835,801	23,579,380	71.8	16,554,576	11,919,976	72.0	16,281,225	11,659,404	71.6
Native parentage	24,080,683	17,288,107	71.8	12,157,541	8,722,736	71.7	11,923,142	8,565,371	71.8
Foreign or mixed parentage	8,755,118	6,291,273	71.9	4,397,035	3,197,240	72.7	4,358,083	3,094,033	71.0
Foreign born	700,976	389,749	55.6	342,073	200,577	58.6	358,903	189,172	52.7
Negro	4,128,998	2,477,311	60.0	2,008,997	1,193,775	59.4	2,120,001	1,283,536	60.5
Other races	721,257	403,199	55.9	368,503	207,440	56.3	352,754	195,759	55.5
Mexican	520,320	270,854	52.1	261,771	138,418	52.9	258,549	132,436	51.2
Indian	129,145	77,806	60.2	64,945	39,084	60.2	64,200	38,722	60.3
Chinese	15,286	11,549	75.6	9,573	7,058	73.7	5,713	4,496	78.7
Japanese	47,825	40,156	84.0	24,836	20,942	84.3	22,989	19,214	83.6
Filipino	7,807	2,180	27.9	6,929	1,624	23.4	878	556	63.3
Hindu	216	151	69.9	124	79	63.7	92	72	
Korean	525	435	82.9	248	210	84.7	277	225	81.2
All other	133	68	51.1	77	30		56	38	
1920 [1]									
All classes	33,250,870	21,373,976	64.3	16,639,600	10,663,547	64.1	16,611,270	10,710,429	64.5
White	29,333,533	19,278,528	65.7	14,727,541	9,660,402	65.6	14,605,992	9,618,126	65.9
Native	28,164,483	18,761,366	66.6	14,150,528	9,396,070	66.4	14,013,955	9,365,296	66.8
Native parentage	20,048,170	13,418,814	66.9	10,090,524	6,716,784	66.6	9,957,646	6,702,030	67.3
Foreign or mixed parentage	8,116,313	5,342,552	65.8	4,060,004	2,679,286	66.0	4,056,309	2,663,266	65.7
Foreign born	1,169,050	517,162	44.2	577,013	264,332	45.8	592,037	252,830	42.7
Negro	3,790,957	2,030,269	53.5	1,848,797	969,066	52.4	1,948,160	1,061,203	54.0
Other races	120,380	65,179	54.1	63,292	34,079	53.9	57,118	31,100	54.4
Indian	94,605	50,709	53.8	47,248	25,360	53.7	47,357	25,579	54.0
Chinese	8,116	5,100	62.8	5,432	3,226	59.4	2,684	1,874	69.8
Japanese	16,254	8,506	52.0	9,443	5,111	54.1	6,811	3,485	51.2
Filipino	1,085	345	31.8	956	277	29.0	129	68	52.7
Hindu	83	38		59	26		24	12	
Korean	192	129	67.2	96	60		96	69	
All other	45	32		28	19		17	13	
1910 [1]									
All classes	29,785,997	17,646,877	59.2	14,952,530	8,833,533	59.1	14,833,467	8,813,344	59.4
White	25,992,293	15,945,412	61.3	13,092,081	8,031,599	61.3	12,900,212	7,913,813	61.3
Native	24,403,180	15,330,814	62.8	12,267,050	7,715,983	62.9	12,136,130	7,614,831	62.7
Native parentage	17,246,081	10,802,753	63.2	8,691,250	5,488,627	63.2	8,554,831	5,404,126	63.2
Foreign or mixed parentage	7,157,099	4,438,061	62.0	3,575,800	2,227,356	62.3	3,581,299	2,210,705	61.7
Foreign born	1,589,113	614,598	38.7	825,031	315,616	38.3	764,082	298,982	39.1
Negro	3,677,860	1,644,759	44.7	1,797,688	771,587	42.9	1,880,172	873,172	46.4
Other races	115,844	56,706	49.0	62,761	30,347	48.4	53,083	26,359	49.7
Indian	102,163	51,877	50.8	51,964	26,820	51.6	50,199	25,057	49.9
Chinese	7,286	3,314	45.5	5,716	2,447	42.8	1,570	867	55.2
Japanese	6,039	1,459	24.2	4,743	1,032	21.8	1,296	427	32.9
Filipino	43	8		37	8		6		
Hindu	240	9	3.8	234	6	2.6	6	3	
Korean	72	39		66	34		6	5	
All other	1			1					
1900									
All classes	26,041,940	13,100,900	50.5	13,048,537	6,544,412	50.2	12,993,403	6,616,488	50.9
White	22,441,947	12,039,594	53.6	11,271,583	6,021,453	53.4	11,170,364	6,018,141	53.9
Native	21,248,914	11,668,616	54.9	10,687,135	5,833,538	54.6	10,561,779	5,835,078	55.2
Native parentage	14,876,715	8,112,850	54.5	7,506,903	4,061,193	54.1	7,369,812	4,051,657	55.0
Foreign or mixed parentage	6,372,199	3,555,766	55.8	3,180,232	1,772,345	55.7	3,191,967	1,783,421	55.9
Foreign born	1,193,033	370,978	31.1	584,448	187,915	32.2	608,585	183,063	30.1
Negro	3,499,187	1,083,516	31.0	1,721,758	503,099	29.2	1,777,429	580,417	32.7
Other races	100,806	37,790	37.5	55,196	19,860	36.0	45,610	17,930	39.3
Indian	89,632	36,243	40.4	45,440	18,688	41.1	44,192	17,555	39.7
Chinese	4,927	1,250	25.4	3,707	915	24.7	1,220	335	27.5
Japanese	6,247	297	4.8	6,049	257	4.2	198	40	20.2
1890 [2]									
All classes	21,165,070	11,488,543	54.3	10,653,850	5,831,033	54.7	10,511,220	5,657,510	53.8
White	18,140,487	10,493,946	57.8	9,139,955	5,348,825	58.5	9,000,532	5,145,121	57.2
Native	16,974,462	9,990,251	58.9	8,555,068	5,088,262	59.5	8,419,394	4,901,989	58.2
Native parentage	11,949,330	7,072,083	59.2	6,039,693	3,607,054	59.7	5,909,637	3,465,029	58.6
Foreign or mixed parentage	5,025,132	2,918,168	58.1	2,515,375	1,481,208	58.9	2,509,757	1,436,960	57.3
Foreign born	1,166,025	503,695	43.2	584,887	260,563	44.5	581,138	243,132	41.8
Negro	2,998,313	986,873	32.9	1,498,113	477,968	31.0	1,500,200	508,905	33.9
Other races	26,270	7,724	29.4	15,782	4,240	26.9	10,488	3,484	33.2

[1] Mexicans classified separately for the first time in 1930; included for the most part with whites of foreign birth or parentage in 1920 and 1910.

[2] All figures for 1890 are based upon population and school attendance for the age group 5 to 19 instead of 5 to 20, as the number of persons 20 years old attending school is not available. It is estimated that the percentage attending school for all classes would be reduced from 54.3 to 52.0 if figures for age 20 could be included.

SCHOOL ATTENDANCE

TABLE 5.—SCHOOL ATTENDANCE BY SEX, FOR WHITE, NEGRO, AND OTHER RACES, FOR THE UNITED STATES: 1850 TO 1880

CENSUS YEAR AND CLASS	POPULATION 5 TO 19 YEARS OLD, INCLUSIVE			PERSONS ATTENDING SCHOOL					
				Number (all ages)			Per cent of population 5 to 19		
	Total	Male	Female	Total	Male	Female	Total	Male	Female
1880									
All classes	17,206,261	8,658,700	8,547,561	9,951,608	5,123,507	4,828,101	57.8	59.2	56.5
White	14,674,600	7,388,841	7,285,759	9,095,485	4,690,093	4,405,392	62.0	63.5	60.5
Negro	} 2,531,661	1,269,859	1,261,802	856,123	433,414	422,709	33.8	34.1	33.5
Other races									
1870									
All classes	13,641,490	6,862,722	6,778,768	6,596,466	3,416,153	3,180,313	48.4	49.8	46.9
White	11,799,212	5,938,426	5,860,786	6,414,740	3,326,797	3,087,943	54.4	56.0	52.7
Negro	1,825,692	912,956	912,736	180,372	88,594	91,778	9.9	9.7	10.1
Other races	16,586	11,340	5,246	1,354	762	592	8.2	6.7	11.3
1860									
All classes	11,253,475	5,660,425	5,593,050	5,692,954	2,978,292	2,714,662	50.6	52.6	48.5
White	9,494,432	4,779,719	4,714,713	5,660,325	2,961,698	2,698,627	59.6	62.0	57.2
Negro	1,741,046	870,477	870,569	32,629	16,594	16,035	1.9	1.9	1.8
Other races	17,907	10,229	7,768						
1850									
All classes	8,661,689	4,351,203	4,310,486	4,089,507	2,160,296	1,929,211	47.2	49.6	44.8
White	7,234,973	3,639,129	3,595,844	4,063,046	2,146,432	1,916,614	56.2	59.0	53.3
Negro	1,426,716	712,074	714,642	26,461	13,864	12,597	1.9	1.9	1.8

TABLE 6.—SCHOOL ATTENDANCE BY COLOR, NATIVITY, SEX, AND AGE PERIODS, FOR THE UNITED STATES: 1930

COLOR, NATIVITY, AND SEX	Total number of persons attending school	PERSONS 7 TO 13 YEARS OLD			PERSONS 14 AND 15 YEARS OLD			PERSONS 16 AND 17 YEARS OLD			PERSONS 18 TO 20 YEARS OLD			OTHERS ATTENDING SCHOOL			
		Total number	Attending school		Total number	Attending school		Total number	Attending school		Total number	Attending school		Under 5 years old	5 years old	6 years old	21 years old and over
			Number	Per cent		Number	Per cent		Number	Per cent		Number	Per cent				
All classes	27,947,009	17,209,566	16,398,400	95.3	4,678,084	4,156,378	88.8	4,663,137	2,669,857	57.3	6,815,710	1,456,784	21.4	62,588	500,734	1,667,486	1,034,782
Male	14,136,079	8,699,846	8,274,754	95.1	2,361,134	2,099,723	88.9	2,339,070	1,322,324	56.5	3,330,546	745,140	22.4	30,422	247,739	832,088	583,889
Female	13,810,930	8,509,720	8,123,646	95.5	2,316,950	2,056,655	88.8	2,324,067	1,347,533	58.0	3,485,164	711,644	20.4	32,166	252,995	835,398	450,893
White	24,973,932	15,065,790	14,547,737	96.6	4,110,385	3,716,963	90.4	4,086,139	2,405,061	58.9	5,929,322	1,338,189	22.0	56,374	458,620	1,502,550	948,429
Male	12,686,114	7,629,109	7,358,438	96.5	2,081,579	1,889,255	90.8	2,056,268	1,200,525	58.4	2,922,531	691,605	23.7	27,483	227,830	752,900	538,078
Female	12,287,818	7,436,681	7,189,299	96.7	2,028,806	1,827,708	90.1	2,029,871	1,204,536	59.3	3,006,791	646,584	21.5	28,891	230,799	749,650	410,351
Native	24,460,860	14,856,438	14,343,660	96.5	4,040,695	3,652,398	90.4	3,999,792	2,344,248	59.1	5,652,544	1,294,953	22.0	55,917	454,953	1,489,170	825,563
Male	12,408,008	7,523,946	7,255,939	96.4	2,046,511	1,856,458	90.7	1,999,414	1,168,968	58.5	2,792,219	666,534	23.9	27,260	225,977	746,102	460,772
Female	12,052,852	7,332,492	7,087,721	96.7	1,994,184	1,795,940	90.1	1,970,378	1,175,280	59.6	2,860,325	628,419	22.0	28,657	228,976	743,068	364,791
Native par.	17,918,875	11,029,603	10,594,986	96.1	2,856,696	2,570,821	90.0	2,811,419	1,714,588	61.0	4,026,957	980,896	24.4	36,666	315,322	1,111,494	594,102
Male	9,066,611	5,594,306	5,366,028	95.9	1,449,477	1,304,279	90.0	1,420,265	846,410	59.6	1,987,101	493,194	24.8	17,824	156,272	556,553	326,051
Female	8,852,264	5,435,297	5,228,958	96.2	1,407,219	1,266,542	90.0	1,391,154	868,178	62.4	2,039,856	487,702	23.9	18,842	159,050	554,941	268,051
For. or mixed par.	6,541,985	3,826,835	3,748,674	98.0	1,183,999	1,081,577	91.3	1,188,373	629,658	54.4	1,625,587	314,057	19.3	19,251	139,631	377,676	231,461
Male	3,341,397	1,929,640	1,889,911	98.1	597,034	552,179	92.5	579,149	322,556	55.7	805,118	173,340	21.5	9,436	69,705	189,549	134,721
Female	3,200,588	1,897,195	1,858,763	98.0	586,965	529,398	90.2	579,224	307,102	53.0	820,469	140,717	17.2	9,815	69,926	188,127	96,740
Foreign born	513,072	209,352	204,077	97.5	69,690	64,565	92.6	116,347	60,815	52.3	276,778	43,236	15.6	457	3,676	13,380	122,866
Male	278,106	105,163	102,499	97.5	35,008	32,797	93.5	56,854	31,559	55.5	130,312	25,071	19.2	223	1,853	6,708	77,306
Female	234,966	104,189	101,578	97.5	34,622	31,768	91.7	59,493	29,256	49.2	146,466	18,165	12.4	234	1,823	6,582	45,560
Negro	2,553,151	1,811,015	1,580,624	87.3	493,897	385,502	78.1	502,710	232,648	46.3	765,928	102,038	13.3	4,813	34,748	141,751	71,027
Male	1,230,618	901,969	778,809	86.4	242,357	182,559	75.3	244,884	104,500	42.7	344,075	43,748	12.7	2,312	16,274	67,735	34,531
Female	1,322,533	909,046	801,725	88.2	251,540	202,943	80.7	257,826	128,088	49.7	421,853	58,290	13.8	2,501	18,474	74,016	36,496
Other races	419,926	332,761	270,039	81.2	73,802	53,913	73.1	74,288	32,148	43.3	120,460	16,557	13.7	1,401	7,357	23,185	15,326
Male	219,347	168,768	137,417	81.4	37,198	27,909	75.0	37,918	17,230	45.5	63,940	9,787	15.3	627	3,635	11,453	11,280
Female	200,579	163,993	132,622	80.9	36,604	26,004	71.0	36,370	14,909	41.0	56,520	6,770	12.0	774	3,722	11,732	4,046

1096

POPULATION

TABLE 7.—SCHOOL ATTENDANCE OF THE POPULATION 7 TO 20 YEARS OLD, BY COLOR, NATIVITY, AGE, AND SEX, FOR THE UNITED STATES: 1930, 1920, AND 1910

[Some part of the increase from 1920 to 1930 in the percentages at school, shown by whites of foreign birth or parentage, is doubtless due to the separate classification in 1930 of Mexicans who were included for the most part with these two white classes in 1920 and 1910]

| COLOR, NATIVITY, AND AGE | TOTAL | | | | | | MALE | | | | | | FEMALE | | | | | |
| | Number attending school | | | Per cent | | | Number attending school | | | Per cent | | | Number attending school | | | Per cent | | |
	1930	1920	1910	1930	1920	1910	1930	1920	1910	1930	1920	1910	1930	1920	1910	1930	1920	1910
All classes	24,681,419	19,451,851	16,240,851	74.0	68.1	63.2	12,441,941	9,706,801	8,132,602	74.4	68.0	63.0	12,239,478	9,745,050	8,108,249	73.6	68.2	63.3
7 to 13 years	16,398,400	13,869,010	11,146,173	95.3	90.6	86.1	8,274,754	6,984,902	5,608,062	95.1	90.4	85.8	8,123,646	6,884,108	5,538,111	95.5	90.8	86.4
14 and 15 years	4,156,378	3,124,129	2,676,465	88.8	79.9	75.0	2,099,723	1,556,519	1,337,710	88.9	79.5	74.4	2,056,655	1,567,610	1,338,755	88.8	80.4	75.6
16 and 17 years	2,669,857	1,644,061	1,573,377	57.3	42.9	43.1	1,322,324	767,533	762,029	56.5	40.3	41.7	1,347,533	876,528	811,348	58.0	45.5	44.5
18 to 20 years	1,456,784	814,651	844,836	21.4	14.8	15.2	745,140	397,847	424,801	22.4	14.8	15.5	711,644	416,804	420,035	20.4	14.7	15.0
White	22,007,050	17,504,580	14,646,040	75.4	69.5	65.2	11,139,823	8,774,646	7,381,188	75.8	69.5	65.3	10,868,127	8,729,043	7,264,861	74.9	69.5	65.1
7 to 13 years	14,547,737	12,499,436	10,057,883	96.6	92.5	89.4	7,358,438	6,309,623	5,079,331	96.5	92.4	89.3	7,189,299	6,189,813	4,978,552	96.7	92.6	89.5
14 and 15 years	3,716,963	2,797,409	2,409,311	90.4	81.5	77.4	1,889,255	1,405,367	1,216,478	90.8	81.4	77.4	1,827,708	1,392,042	1,192,833	90.1	81.6	77.4
16 and 17 years	2,405,061	1,468,476	1,414,376	58.9	43.4	44.1	1,200,525	693,491	694,896	58.4	41.0	43.1	1,204,536	774,985	719,480	59.3	45.7	45.0
18 to 20 years	1,338,189	739,268	764,479	22.6	15.2	15.7	691,605	366,165	390,483	23.7	15.4	16.1	646,584	373,103	373,996	21.5	15.1	15.3
Native white	21,635,257	17,004,957	14,072,549	75.9	70.7	67.1	10,947,897	8,519,220	7,086,452	76.2	70.6	67.3	10,687,360	8,485,737	6,986,097	75.5	70.8	66.9
7 to 13 years	14,343,660	12,181,396	9,640,513	96.5	92.7	89.5	7,255,939	6,148,896	4,867,727	96.4	92.7	89.3	7,087,721	6,032,500	4,772,786	96.7	92.8	89.6
14 and 15 years	3,652,398	2,690,787	2,321,048	90.4	82.2	78.3	1,856,458	1,351,089	1,170,305	90.7	82.0	78.1	1,795,940	1,339,698	1,150,743	90.1	82.4	78.5
16 and 17 years	2,344,246	1,420,296	1,376,133	59.1	44.7	46.0	1,168,906	668,716	674,701	58.5	42.1	44.9	1,175,280	751,580	701,432	59.6	47.2	47.1
18 to 20 years	1,294,953	712,478	734,855	22.9	15.9	17.3	666,534	350,519	373,719	23.9	15.9	17.9	628,419	361,959	361,136	22.0	16.0	16.7
Native par	15,861,291	12,241,234	10,055,770	76.5	71.3	68.0	8,009,911	6,129,476	5,070,421	76.0	71.0	68.1	7,851,380	6,111,758	4,985,349	76.4	71.6	67.9
7 to 13 years	10,594,986	8,584,079	6,744,539	96.1	92.2	88.2	5,366,028	4,338,518	3,409,430	95.9	92.0	88.0	5,228,958	4,246,161	3,335,109	96.2	92.3	88.4
14 and 15 years	2,570,821	1,982,664	1,664,279	90.0	83.9	80.3	1,304,279	994,541	838,613	90.0	83.4	79.8	1,266,542	988,123	825,666	90.0	84.4	80.9
16 and 17 years	1,714,588	1,111,569	1,060,244	61.0	48.7	51.1	846,410	522,656	520,842	59.6	45.7	49.9	868,178	588,913	539,402	62.4	51.6	52.4
18 to 20 years	980,896	562,322	586,708	24.4	17.5	19.6	493,194	273,761	301,530	24.8	17.3	20.5	487,702	288,561	285,172	23.9	17.7	18.8
For. or mixed par	5,773,966	4,763,723	4,016,779	74.1	69.2	64.9	2,937,986	2,389,744	2,016,031	75.1	69.4	65.3	2,835,980	2,373,979	2,000,748	73.0	68.9	64.5
7 to 13 years	3,748,674	3,596,717	2,895,974	98.0	94.1	92.6	1,889,911	1,810,378	1,458,297	98.1	94.2	92.7	1,858,763	1,786,339	1,437,677	98.0	94.1	92.5
14 and 15 years	1,081,577	708,123	656,769	91.3	77.9	73.6	552,179	356,548	331,692	92.5	78.5	74.3	529,398	351,575	325,077	90.2	77.3	72.9
16 and 17 years	629,658	308,727	315,889	54.4	34.5	34.5	322,556	146,060	153,859	55.7	32.8	33.6	307,102	162,667	162,030	53.0	36.1	35.3
18 to 20 years	314,057	150,156	148,147	19.3	11.9	11.8	173,340	76,758	72,183	21.5	12.4	11.8	140,717	73,398	75,964	17.2	11.4	11.8
Foreign-born white	372,693	499,632	573,500	55.4	44.5	38.6	191,926	255,426	294,736	58.6	46.1	38.1	180,767	244,206	278,764	52.4	42.9	39.1
7 to 13 years	204,077	318,040	417,370	97.5	84.1	87.1	102,499	160,727	211,604	97.5	84.2	87.4	101,578	157,313	205,766	97.5	84.0	86.8
14 and 15 yrs	64,565	106,622	88,263	92.0	66.7	58.9	32,797	54,278	46,173	93.5	68.3	61.7	31,768	52,344	42,090	91.7	65.0	56.1
16 and 17 yrs	60,815	48,180	38,243	52.3	23.5	17.5	31,559	24,775	20,195	55.5	24.5	18.4	29,256	23,405	18,048	49.1	22.6	16.5
18 to 20 yrs	43,236	26,790	29,624	15.0	7.0	4.6	25,071	15,046	16,764	19.2	8.6	4.8	18,165	11,744	12,860	12.4	5.6	4.4
Negro	2,300,812	1,887,282	1,541,575	64.4	57.5	48.8	1,109,766	900,638	722,762	64.0	56.6	46.9	1,191,046	986,644	818,813	64.7	58.4	50.6
7 to 13 years	1,580,624	1,331,043	1,056,791	87.3	76.5	64.1	778,899	655,699	512,609	86.4	75.5	62.2	801,725	675,344	544,182	88.2	77.6	66.0
14 and 15 years	395,502	317,355	257,894	78.1	68.7	53.3	182,550	146,225	116,209	75.3	65.0	53.2	202,043	171,130	141,685	80.7	72.3	63.4
16 and 17 years	232,048	168,760	152,145	46.3	39.2	35.5	104,560	70,365	63,327	42.7	34.1	30.6	128,088	98,395	88,818	49.7	43.8	40.1
18 to 20 years	102,038	70,124	74,745	13.8	10.8	11.7	43,748	28,349	30,617	12.7	9.7	10.5	58,290	41,775	44,128	13.8	11.7	12.7
Other races [1]	372,657	59,980	53,227	62.0	59.7	53.6	102,352	31,517	28,652	62.5	59.1	52.7	180,305	28,463	24,575	61.4	60.3	54.8
7 to 13 years	270,039	38,531	31,499	81.2	72.9	64.0	137,417	19,580	16,122	81.4	72.9	64.4	132,622	18,951	15,377	80.9	72.9	64.8
14 and 15 years	53,913	9,365	9,260	73.1	71.8	69.4	27,909	4,927	5,023	75.0	71.5	69.3	26,004	4,438	4,237	71.0	72.2	69.6
16 and 17 years	32,148	6,825	6,856	43.3	53.4	52.8	17,239	3,677	3,806	45.5	52.5	52.5	14,909	3,148	3,050	41.0	54.5	53.2
18 to 20 years	16,557	5,259	5,612	13.7	24.1	23.3	9,787	3,333	3,701	15.3	26.6	24.0	6,770	1,926	1,911	12.0	20.8	20.7

[1] Mexicans are included with "Other races" in the figures for 1930 and with the white population in 1920 and 1910.

557

SCHOOL ATTENDANCE

TABLE 8.—SCHOOL ATTENDANCE BY SINGLE YEARS OF AGE FROM 5 TO 20, BY COLOR, NATIVITY, AND SEX, FOR THE UNITED STATES: 1930

SEX AND AGE	ALL CLASSES			NATIVE WHITE—NATIVE PARENTAGE			NATIVE WHITE—FOREIGN OR MIXED PARENTAGE			FOREIGN-BORN WHITE			NEGRO			OTHER RACES	
	Total number	Attending school		Total number	Attending school		Total number	Attending school		Total number	Attending school		Total number	Attending school		Total number	Number attending school
		Number	Per cent		Number	Per cent		Number	Per cent		Number	Per cent		Number	Per cent		
Total	38,387,032	26,849,639	69.9	24,080,683	17,288,107	71.8	8,755,118	6,291,273	71.9	700,976	389,749	55.6	4,128,998	2,477,311	60.0	721,257	403,199
5 years	2,505,250	500,734	20.0	1,687,508	315,322	18.7	471,768	139,631	29.6	11,880	3,676	30.9	273,732	34,748	12.7	60,362	7,357
6 years	2,515,285	1,667,486	66.3	1,668,500	1,111,494	66.6	488,556	377,676	77.3	16,929	13,380	79.0	281,716	141,751	50.3	59,584	23,185
7 years	2,470,159	2,207,331	89.4	1,622,790	1,471,166	90.7	495,066	469,129	94.8	24,940	23,551	94.4	271,228	207,248	76.4	56,135	30,237
8 years	2,604,215	2,451,048	94.1	1,703,412	1,621,077	95.2	532,039	517,566	97.3	31,431	30,371	96.6	281,481	238,002	84.6	55,852	44,032
9 years	2,512,700	2,401,356	95.6	1,638,828	1,578,883	96.3	525,986	514,493	97.8	36,511	35,501	97.2	260,224	229,466	88.2	51,151	43,013
10 years	2,500,648	2,427,254	97.1	1,585,544	1,550,673	97.8	551,901	545,814	98.9	36,408	35,836	98.4	276,104	251,219	91.0	50,691	43,712
11 years	2,319,394	2,260,735	97.5	1,495,375	1,464,935	98.0	536,050	530,496	99.0	26,569	26,166	98.5	221,884	204,479	92.2	39,516	34,659
12 years	2,480,123	2,408,623	97.1	1,509,586	1,544,300	97.8	602,645	596,180	98.9	26,529	26,133	98.5	263,679	239,453	90.8	42,970	37,271
13 years	2,322,327	2,242,053	96.5	1,439,354	1,398,666	97.2	583,148	574,996	98.6	26,964	26,519	98.3	236,415	210,757	89.1	36,446	31,115
14 years	2,382,385	2,212,825	92.9	1,463,779	1,371,880	93.7	596,450	571,111	95.8	31,266	30,103	96.3	253,400	210,308	83.0	37,430	29,411
15 years	2,205,699	1,043,553	84.7	1,392,917	1,198,932	86.1	587,549	510,466	86.9	38,424	34,459	89.7	240,437	175,194	72.9	36,372	24,502
16 years	2,367,315	1,569,830	66.3	1,428,495	990,725	69.4	591,840	383,107	64.7	51,077	33,832	66.2	244,985	89,994	36.7	36,110	12,627
17 years	2,295,822	1,100,018	47.9	1,382,024	723,863	52.3	566,533	246,551	43.5	65,270	26,983	41.3	244,985	89,994	36.7	36,110	12,627
18 years	2,357,834	723,524	30.7	1,397,058	486,646	34.8	570,634	153,763	26.9	80,086	18,807	23.5	269,131	55,931	20.8	40,925	8,377
19 years	2,235,445	441,814	19.8	1,331,109	298,810	22.4	537,805	95,281	17.7	89,773	13,582	15.1	238,250	29,168	12.2	38,418	4,973
20 years	2,222,431	291,446	13.1	1,298,790	195,440	15.0	517,058	65,013	12.6	106,919	10,847	10.1	258,547	16,939	6.6	41,117	3,207
Male	19,274,149	13,521,768	70.2	12,157,641	8,722,736	71.7	4,397,035	3,197,240	72.7	342,073	200,577	58.6	2,008,997	1,193,775	59.4	368,503	207,440
5 years	1,272,424	247,739	19.5	859,650	156,272	18.2	239,522	69,705	29.1	6,024	1,853	30.8	136,447	16,274	11.9	30,781	3,635
6 years	1,271,129	832,088	65.5	846,742	556,553	65.7	246,572	189,549	76.9	8,652	6,798	78.6	139,265	67,735	48.6	29,898	11,453
7 years	1,248,494	1,111,729	80.0	823,659	744,065	90.3	249,604	236,456	94.7	12,560	11,847	94.3	134,403	101,153	75.3	28,178	18,208
8 years	1,313,852	1,234,410	94.0	802,376	819,454	95.0	267,773	260,373	97.2	15,722	15,203	96.7	139,759	117,194	83.9	28,222	22,186
9 years	1,275,209	1,217,161	95.4	834,956	803,661	96.3	266,311	260,376	97.8	18,380	17,863	97.2	129,874	113,588	87.5	25,682	21,673
10 years	1,265,368	1,226,457	96.9	803,939	785,365	97.7	278,349	275,244	98.9	18,143	17,852	98.4	138,953	125,543	90.3	25,984	22,453
11 years	1,167,181	1,136,412	97.4	754,470	738,571	97.9	268,959	266,121	98.9	13,459	13,252	98.5	110,329	100,879	91.4	19,964	17,589
12 years	1,261,035	1,222,203	96.9	788,410	769,638	97.6	304,729	301,440	98.9	13,388	13,196	98.6	132,232	118,545	89.6	22,276	19,384
13 years	1,168,707	1,126,382	96.4	726,496	705,274	97.1	293,825	289,901	98.7	13,505	13,286	98.4	116,419	101,997	87.6	18,462	15,924
14 years	1,206,486	1,120,653	92.9	745,320	698,761	93.8	301,208	290,518	96.4	15,678	15,167	96.7	125,205	101,039	80.6	18,895	15,168
15 years	1,154,648	970,070	84.8	704,157	605,518	86.0	295,736	261,661	88.5	19,390	17,630	90.9	117,062	81,520	69.6	18,303	12,741
16 years	1,181,920	777,585	65.8	718,684	490,488	68.2	294,054	195,466	66.3	25,025	17,224	68.8	123,890	64,056	51.7	19,367	10,351
17 years	1,157,150	544,730	47.1	701,581	355,022	50.7	284,195	127,090	44.7	31,820	14,335	45.0	120,994	40,504	33.5	18,551	6,888
18 years	1,157,703	359,527	31.1	692,100	239,121	34.6	282,794	81,602	28.9	37,784	10,440	27.6	123,927	23,771	19.2	21,098	4,503
19 years	1,106,404	229,809	20.8	664,085	152,277	22.9	269,030	53,717	20.0	42,631	8,024	18.8	109,773	12,793	11.7	20,885	3,088
20 years	1,066,439	155,714	14.6	630,916	101,796	16.1	253,294	38,021	15.0	49,897	6,607	13.2	110,375	7,184	6.5	21,957	2,106
Female	19,112,883	13,327,871	69.7	11,923,142	8,565,371	71.8	4,358,083	3,094,033	71.0	358,903	189,172	52.7	2,120,001	1,283,536	60.5	352,754	195,759
5 years	1,232,826	252,995	20.5	827,858	159,050	19.2	232,246	69,926	30.1	5,856	1,823	31.1	137,285	18,474	13.5	29,581	3,722
6 years	1,244,156	835,398	67.1	821,758	554,941	67.5	241,984	188,127	77.7	8,277	6,582	79.5	142,451	74,016	52.0	29,686	11,732
7 years	1,221,665	1,095,602	89.7	799,131	727,101	91.0	245,372	232,673	94.8	12,380	11,704	94.5	136,825	106,095	77.5	27,957	18,029
8 years	1,290,363	1,216,638	94.3	841,036	801,623	95.3	264,266	257,193	97.3	15,709	15,168	96.6	141,722	120,808	85.2	27,630	21,846
9 years	1,237,491	1,184,195	95.7	803,872	775,222	96.4	259,675	254,117	97.9	18,125	17,638	97.3	130,350	115,878	88.9	25,469	21,340
10 years	1,235,280	1,200,797	97.2	781,605	765,308	97.9	273,552	270,570	98.9	18,265	17,984	98.5	137,151	125,676	91.6	24,707	21,259
11 years	1,152,213	1,124,323	97.6	740,905	726,364	98.0	267,091	264,375	99.0	13,110	12,914	98.5	111,555	103,600	92.9	19,552	17,070
12 years	1,219,088	1,186,420	97.3	755,890	739,948	97.9	297,916	294,740	98.9	13,141	12,937	98.4	131,447	120,908	92.0	20,694	17,887
13 years	1,153,620	1,115,671	96.7	712,858	693,392	97.3	289,323	285,095	98.5	13,459	13,233	98.3	119,996	108,760	90.6	17,984	15,191
14 years	1,175,899	1,092,172	92.9	718,459	673,128	93.7	295,152	280,593	95.1	15,588	14,939	95.8	128,165	109,269	85.3	18,535	14,243
15 years	1,141,051	964,483	84.5	688,760	593,414	86.2	291,813	248,805	85.3	19,034	16,829	88.4	123,375	93,674	75.9	18,069	11,761
16 years	1,185,395	792,254	66.8	709,811	500,237	70.5	296,886	187,641	63.2	26,052	16,608	63.7	133,835	78,598	58.7	17,559	5,739
17 years	1,138,672	555,279	48.8	681,343	367,941	54.0	282,338	119,461	42.3	33,441	12,648	37.8	123,991	49,400	39.9	19,827	3,784
18 years	1,200,131	363,997	30.3	704,958	247,525	35.1	287,840	72,161	25.1	42,302	8,307	19.8	145,204	32,160	22.1	19,827	3,874
19 years	1,129,041	211,915	18.8	667,024	146,533	22.0	268,865	41,564	15.5	47,142	5,558	11.8	128,477	16,375	12.7	17,533	1,885
20 years	1,155,992	135,732	11.7	667,874	93,644	14.0	263,764	26,992	10.2	57,022	4,240	7.4	148,172	9,755	6.6	19,160	1,101

POPULATION

TABLE 9.—SCHOOL ATTENDANCE BY SINGLE YEARS OF AGE FROM 5 TO 20, BY COLOR, NATIVITY, AND SEX, FOR THE UNITED STATES: 1930, 1920, AND 1910

COLOR, NATIVITY, AND AGE	TOTAL						MALE						FEMALE					
	Number attending school			Per cent			Number attending school			Per cent			Number attending school			Per cent		
	1930	1920	1910	1930	1920	1910	1930	1920	1910	1930	1920	1910	1930	1920	1910	1930	1920	1910
All classes:																		
5 years	500,734	441,411	346,673	20.0	18.8	17.0	247,730	217,446	171,687	19.5	18.3	16.7	252,995	223,965	174,986	20.5	19.3	17.4
6 years	1,667,486	1,480,714	1,059,353	66.3	63.3	52.1	832,088	739,300	529,244	65.5	62.8	51.7	835,398	741,414	530,109	67.1	63.9	52.4
7 years	2,207,331	1,905,404	1,464,730	89.4	83.3	75.0	1,111,729	959,128	737,137	89.0	83.1	74.7	1,095,602	946,276	727,593	89.7	83.5	75.2
8 years	2,451,048	2,010,894	1,586,572	94.1	88.5	82.7	1,234,410	1,011,506	797,445	94.0	88.3	82.5	1,216,638	999,388	789,127	94.3	88.6	82.8
9 years	2,401,356	1,944,314	1,567,665	95.6	90.4	86.2	1,217,161	982,227	792,754	95.4	90.3	86.1	1,184,195	962,087	774,911	95.7	90.5	86.3
10 years	2,427,254	2,077,965	1,681,342	97.1	93.0	90.0	1,226,457	1,048,389	848,141	96.9	92.9	89.6	1,200,797	1,029,576	833,201	97.2	93.2	90.4
11 years	2,260,735	1,970,255	1,555,301	97.5	93.9	91.2	1,136,412	989,744	779,675	97.4	93.8	90.9	1,124,323	980,511	775,626	97.6	94.1	91.5
12 years	2,408,623	2,082,749	1,716,310	97.1	93.2	89.8	1,222,203	1,052,583	864,709	96.9	93.0	89.2	1,186,420	1,030,166	851,511	97.3	93.4	90.3
13 years	2,242,053	1,877,429	1,574,253	96.5	92.5	88.8	1,126,382	941,325	788,111	96.4	92.4	88.3	1,115,671	936,104	786,142	96.7	92.7	89.3
14 years	2,212,825	1,766,784	1,501,456	92.9	86.3	81.2	1,120,653	890,571	755,379	92.9	86.2	80.7	1,092,172	876,213	746,077	92.9	86.5	81.8
15 years	1,943,553	1,357,345	1,175,009	84.7	72.9	68.3	979,070	665,948	582,331	84.8	71.9	67.5	964,483	691,397	592,678	84.5	73.9	69.0
16 years	1,569,839	1,001,701	943,511	66.3	50.8	50.6	777,585	470,433	456,081	65.8	48.2	49.3	792,254	531,268	487,430	66.8	53.3	51.9
17 years	1,100,018	642,360	629,866	47.9	34.6	35.3	544,739	297,100	305,948	47.1	32.1	34.0	555,279	345,260	323,918	48.8	37.2	36.6
18 years	723,524	413,619	434,864	30.7	21.7	22.6	359,527	192,481	209,687	31.1	20.5	22.1	363,997	221,138	225,177	30.3	22.8	23.0
19 years	441,814	252,680	254,421	19.8	13.8	14.4	229,899	127,011	131,514	20.8	14.0	14.8	211,915	125,669	122,907	18.8	13.6	14.1
20 years	291,446	148,352	155,551	13.1	8.3	8.4	155,714	78,355	83,600	14.6	9.3	9.3	135,732	69,997	71,951	11.7	7.5	7.5
Native white—Native parentage:																		
5 years	315,322	255,041	191,562	18.7	17.6	15.5	156,272	125,461	94,883	18.2	17.1	15.1	159,050	129,580	96,679	19.2	18.2	15.8
6 years	1,111,494	922,539	645,421	66.6	64.5	52.6	556,553	461,847	323,323	65.7	63.9	52.2	554,941	460,692	322,098	67.5	65.3	53.0
7 years	1,471,166	1,188,435	902,676	90.7	84.9	77.2	744,065	599,742	455,622	90.3	84.7	76.9	727,101	588,693	447,054	91.0	85.2	77.4
8 years	1,621,077	1,250,685	972,457	95.2	90.2	85.2	819,454	631,393	491,955	95.0	90.0	85.0	801,623	619,292	480,502	95.3	90.3	85.3
9 years	1,578,883	1,206,836	957,403	96.3	91.8	88.3	803,661	611,500	486,151	96.3	91.7	88.2	775,222	595,336	471,252	96.4	91.8	88.4
10 years	1,550,673	1,281,469	1,009,228	97.8	94.7	92.2	785,365	648,691	511,385	97.7	94.5	92.0	765,308	632,778	497,843	97.9	94.8	92.5
11 years	1,464,935	1,230,869	946,079	98.0	95.2	92.9	738,571	620,380	475,668	97.9	95.1	92.6	726,364	610,489	470,411	98.0	95.3	93.1
12 years	1,509,586	1,208,532	1,017,758	97.8	94.9	92.0	769,638	644,264	516,120	97.6	94.7	91.7	739,948	624,268	501,638	97.9	95.0	92.4
13 years	1,398,666	1,157,853	938,938	97.2	94.2	90.9	705,274	582,548	472,529	97.1	94.1	90.6	693,392	575,305	466,409	97.3	94.3	91.3
14 years	1,371,889	1,110,160	915,468	93.7	89.3	85.3	698,761	563,367	463,852	93.8	89.2	84.8	673,128	546,793	451,616	93.7	89.5	85.8
15 years	1,198,932	872,504	748,811	86.1	77.8	75.0	605,518	431,174	374,761	86.0	76.8	74.3	593,414	441,330	374,050	86.2	78.8	75.7
16 years	990,725	668,973	625,529	69.4	56.8	58.9	490,488	317,034	306,164	68.2	53.9	57.7	500,237	351,939	319,365	70.5	59.6	60.2
17 years	723,863	442,596	434,715	52.3	40.1	42.9	355,922	205,622	214,678	50.7	37.1	41.8	367,941	236,974	220,037	54.0	43.1	44.1
18 years	486,646	286,403	302,474	34.8	25.6	28.6	239,121	133,360	149,276	34.6	24.0	28.6	247,525	153,043	153,198	35.1	27.1	28.5
19 years	298,810	174,455	177,065	22.4	16.2	18.5	152,277	87,139	93,432	22.9	16.2	19.4	146,533	87,316	83,633	22.0	16.3	17.6
20 years	195,440	101,464	107,169	15.0	10.0	11.0	101,796	53,262	58,828	16.1	10.9	12.5	93,644	48,202	48,341	14.0	9.2	9.6
Native white—For. or mixed par.:																		
5 years	139,631	151,892	118,983	29.6	24.5	24.5	69,705	75,456	59,456	29.1	24.1	24.3	69,926	76,436	59,527	30.1	24.9	24.7
6 years	377,676	426,937	302,299	77.3	70.1	62.9	189,549	214,086	151,869	76.9	70.1	62.9	188,127	212,851	150,430	77.7	70.1	62.9
7 years	469,129	518,886	390,416	94.8	88.4	84.3	236,456	261,646	197,280	94.7	88.5	84.6	232,673	257,240	193,136	94.8	88.4	84.0
8 years	517,566	531,888	407,343	97.3	92.4	90.5	260,373	266,754	204,390	97.2	92.5	90.5	257,193	265,134	202,953	97.3	92.4	90.4
9 years	514,493	513,597	403,016	97.8	93.6	92.4	260,376	258,949	203,601	97.8	93.6	92.5	254,117	254,648	199,415	97.9	93.6	92.4
10 years	545,814	529,185	430,364	98.9	96.2	95.7	275,244	265,811	216,462	98.9	96.3	95.6	270,570	263,374	213,902	98.9	96.2	95.8
11 years	530,496	504,519	402,931	99.0	96.6	96.1	266,121	252,989	202,444	98.9	96.6	96.1	264,375	251,530	200,487	99.0	96.6	96.0
12 years	596,180	528,442	442,229	98.9	96.5	95.6	301,440	266,578	222,950	98.9	96.5	95.6	294,740	261,864	219,279	98.9	96.5	95.6
13 years	574,996	470,200	419,675	98.6	95.7	94.3	289,901	237,651	211,170	98.7	95.9	94.7	285,095	232,549	208,505	98.5	95.5	93.9
14 years	571,111	410,102	381,445	95.8	87.0	83.1	290,518	208,310	193,817	96.4	88.0	83.9	280,593	201,792	187,628	95.1	86.1	82.3
15 years	510,466	298,021	275,324	86.9	68.0	63.5	261,661	148,238	137,875	88.5	68.1	64.0	248,805	149,783	137,449	85.3	68.0	63.0
16 years	383,107	192,374	197,293	64.7	41.7	41.8	195,466	91,717	96,655	66.3	40.0	41.2	187,641	100,657	100,638	63.2	43.3	42.4
17 years	246,551	116,353	118,596	43.5	26.8	26.7	127,090	54,343	57,204	44.7	25.1	25.7	119,461	62,010	61,392	42.3	28.4	27.7
18 years	153,763	73,030	75,931	26.9	16.9	16.9	81,602	35,146	35,535	28.9	16.5	16.2	72,161	37,884	40,396	25.1	17.2	17.6
19 years	95,281	47,382	44,949	17.7	11.3	11.1	53,717	24,964	22,433	20.0	12.0	11.1	41,564	22,418	22,516	15.5	10.6	11.1
20 years	65,013	29,744	27,267	12.6	7.3	6.8	38,021	16,648	14,215	15.0	8.5	7.4	26,992	13,096	13,052	10.2	6.2	6.3
Foreign-born white:																		
5 years	3,676	3,489	10,151	30.9	18.8	21.6	1,853	1,769	5,128	30.8	18.6	21.5	1,823	1,720	5,023	31.1	18.9	21.6
6 years	13,380	14,041	30,947	79.0	53.1	55.5	6,798	7,137	15,752	78.6	53.3	55.7	6,582	6,904	15,195	79.5	52.8	55.3
7 years	23,551	26,371	47,744	94.4	72.9	76.9	11,847	13,246	24,121	94.3	73.0	77.2	11,704	13,125	23,623	94.5	72.8	76.6
8 years	30,371	33,605	56,284	96.6	79.8	84.2	15,203	16,914	28,335	96.7	79.8	84.5	15,168	16,691	27,949	96.6	79.8	83.8
9 years	35,501	38,673	58,341	97.2	83.1	87.5	17,863	19,506	29,558	97.2	82.9	87.5	17,638	19,167	28,783	97.3	83.3	87.4
10 years	35,836	50,496	67,578	98.4	86.3	90.3	17,852	25,568	34,147	98.4	86.3	90.3	17,984	24,928	33,431	98.5	86.3	90.3
11 years	26,166	50,987	60,332	98.5	87.8	91.4	13,252	25,614	30,586	98.5	88.0	91.7	12,914	25,373	29,746	98.5	87.5	91.1
12 years	26,133	58,738	67,858	98.5	86.6	90.2	13,196	29,897	34,454	98.6	86.6	90.5	12,937	28,841	33,404	98.4	86.6	89.9
13 years	26,519	59,170	59,233	98.3	85.9	87.7	13,286	29,982	30,403	98.4	86.3	88.7	13,233	29,188	28,830	98.3	85.4	86.8
14 years	30,106	59,700	53,491	96.3	76.5	71.6	15,167	30,532	28,001	96.7	77.9	74.1	14,939	29,168	25,490	95.8	75.1	69.0
15 years	34,459	46,922	34,772	89.7	57.3	46.2	17,630	23,746	18,172	90.9	59.0	49.0	16,829	23,176	16,600	88.4	55.7	43.6
16 years	33,832	30,408	23,665	66.2	30.2	23.7	17,224	15,405	12,489	68.8	31.0	25.3	16,608	15,003	11,176	63.7	29.5	22.1
17 years	26,983	17,712	14,578	41.3	17.0	12.2	14,335	9,370	7,706	45.0	18.2	12.8	12,648	8,342	6,872	37.8	15.9	11.7
18 years	18,807	12,135	12,406	23.5	10.1	6.8	10,440	6,790	6,669	27.6	11.6	6.9	8,367	5,345	5,737	19.8	8.7	6.7
19 years	13,582	8,501	9,502	15.1	7.0	4.8	8,024	5,123	5,482	18.8	8.6	5.0	5,558	3,378	4,020	11.8	5.4	4.5
20 years	10,847	6,154	7,716	10.1	4.4	3.0	6,607	3,733	4,613	13.2	5.8	3.3	4,240	2,421	3,103	7.4	3.2	2.6
Negro:																		
5 years	34,748	29,760	25,060	12.7	11.8	9.8	16,274	14,122	11,774	11.9	11.2	9.3	18,474	15,638	13,286	13.5	12.3	10.3
6 years	141,751	113,227	78,124	50.3	42.9	29.7	67,735	54,306	37,051	48.6	41.7	28.5	74,016	58,921	41,073	52.0	44.1	30.9
7 years	207,248	166,457	120,104	76.4	64.9	47.7	101,153	81,807	58,270	75.3	64.0	46.3	106,095	84,650	61,834	77.5	65.9	49.2
8 years	238,002	188,743	146,186	84.6	72.7	57.9	117,194	93,447	70,609	83.9	72.1	56.5	120,808	95,296	75,577	85.2	73.3	59.3
9 years	229,466	179,845	144,540	88.2	77.0	64.6	113,588	89,558	71,232	87.5	76.4	63.7	115,878	90,287	73,308	88.9	77.7	65.4
10 years	251,219	210,888	169,155	91.0	80.0	69.8	125,543	105,328	83,575	90.3	79.1	68.0	125,676	105,560	85,580	91.6	80.9	71.5
11 years	204,479	178,834	141,723	92.2	82.1	72.7	100,879	88,166	68,730	91.4	81.0	70.8	103,600	90,668	72,993	92.9	83.2	74.5
12 years	239,453	221,168	183,267	90.8	80.6	70.1	118,545	108,801	88,619	89.6	79.0	67.5	120,908	112,367	94,648	92.0	82.1	72.8
13 years	210,757	185,108	151,816	89.1	79.3	68.4	101,997	88,592	71,574	87.6	77.3	64.9	108,760	96,516	80,242	90.6	81.3	71.9
14 years	210,308	181,761	146,034	83.0	73.4	62.3	101,039	85,701	66,988	80.6	70.2	57.4	109,269	96,060	79,046	85.3	76.5	67.0
15 years	175,194	135,594	111,860	72.9	63.3	53.9	81,520	60,524	49,221	69.6	58.7	48.3	93,674	75,070	62,639	75.9	67.6	59.3
16 years	142,654	106,045	93,055	55.4	47.1	41.5	64,056	44,260	38,600	51.7	41.7	36.2	78,598	61,785	54,455	58.7	51.9	46.3
17 years	89,994	62,715	59,090	36.7	30.5	29.0	40,504	26,105	24,727	33.5	26.1	24.7	49,490	36,610	34,363	39.9	34.6	33.1
18 years	55,931	39,748	41,507	20.8	17.3	17.9	23,771	15,842	16,613	19.2	14.8	15.3	32,160	23,906	24,894	22.1	19.6	20.2
19 years	29,168	20,615	21,110	12.2	9.9	10.9	12,793	8,631	8,964	11.7	8.9	9.9	16,375	11,984	12,146	12.7	10.7	11.9
20 years	16,939	9,761	12,128	6.6	4.6	5.6	7,184	3,876	5,040	6.5	4.4	5.4	9,755	5,885	7,088	6.0	4.8	5.8
Other races:																		
5 years	7,357	1,229	917	12.2	12.3	11.1	3,635	638	446	11.8	12.7	10.6	3,722	591	471	12.6	11.9	11.6
6 years	23,185	3,970	2,562	38.9	40.1	30.7	11,453	1,924	1,249	38.3	38.9	30.1	11,732	2,046	1,313	39.5	41.4	31.3
7 years	36,237	5,255	3,790	64.6	60.5	48.4	18,208	2,687	1,844	64.6	61.0	46.7	18,029	2,568	1,946	64.5	60.1	50.2
8 years	44,032	5,973	4,302	78.8	68.1	56.3	22,186	2,998	2,156	78.6	67.9	56.0	21,846	2,975	2,146	79.1	68.3	56.7
9 years	43,013	5,363	4,365	84.1	73.6	64.0	21,673	2,714	2,212	84.4	73.8	64.3	21,340	2,649	2,153	83.8	73.4	63.6
10 years	43,712	5,927	5,017	86.2	75.1	68.3	22,453	2,991	2,572	86.4	74.8	68.5	21,259	2,936	2,445	86.0	75.4	68.2
11 years	34,659	5,046	4,236	87.7	80.7	73.7	17,589	2,595	2,247	88.1	80.7	74.6	17,070	2,451	1,989	87.3	80.7	72.6
12 years	37,271	5,869	5,198	86.7	77.4	72.0	19,384	3,043	2,656	87.0	77.5	70.8	17,887	2,826	2,542	86.4	77.2	73.3
13 years	31,115	5,098	4,591	85.4	79.8	74.2	15,924	2,552	2,435	86.3	79.2	73.9	15,191	2,546	2,156	84.5	80.5	74.7
14 years	29,411	5,061	5,018	78.6	74.6	72.0	15,168	2,661	2,721	80.3	75.1	72.3	14,243	2,400	2,297	76.8	74.0	71.5
15 years	24,502	4,304	4,242	67.4	68.8	66.5	12,741	2,266	2,302	69.6	67.6	66.0	11,761	2,038	1,940	65.1	70.1	67.2
16 years	19,521	3,841	3,969	51.1	58.5	57.6	10,351	2,017	2,173	53.4	57.3	57.2	9,170	1,824	1,796	48.7	59.9	58.2
17 years	12,627	2,984	2,887	35.0	48.0	47.3	6,888	1,660	1,633	37.1	47.6	47.3	5,739	1,324	1,254	32.7	48.6	47.3
18 years	8,377	2,303	2,546	20.5	31.9	32.4	4,593	1,343	1,594	21.8	33.4	34.3	3,784	960	952	19.1	30.0	29.6
19 years	4,973	1,727	1,795	12.9	24.9	23.7	3,088	1,154	1,203	14.8	27.7	25.0	1,885	573	592	10.8	20.7	21.4
20 years	3,207	1,229	1,271	7.8	16.0	14.6	2,106	836	904	9.6	19.2	16.7	1,101	393	367	5.7	11.9	11.2

SCHOOL ATTENDANCE

1101

TABLE 12.—TOTAL NUMBER OF PERSONS ATTENDING SCHOOL, BY AGE PERIODS, BY DIVISIONS AND STATES: 1930, 1920, AND 1910

DIVISION AND STATE	TOTAL NUMBER OF PERSONS ATTENDING SCHOOL			PERSONS 7 TO 20 YEARS OLD								
				1930			1920			1910		
				Total number	Attending school		Total number	Attending school		Total number	Attending school	
	1930	1920	1910		Number	Per cent		Number	Per cent		Number	Per cent
United States	27,947,009	21,763,275	18,009,891	33,366,497	24,681,419	74.0	28,564,716	19,451,851	68.1	25,716,765	16,240,851	63.2
GEOGRAPHIC DIVISIONS:												
New England	1,834,790	1,424,088	1,222,228	2,077,611	1,576,870	75.9	1,708,290	1,223,023	69.2	1,610,552	1,051,485	65.3
Middle Atlantic	5,749,361	4,260,677	3,531,373	6,760,204	5,022,091	74.3	5,527,757	3,746,560	67.8	4,979,935	3,131,190	62.9
East North Central	5,600,622	4,236,641	3,576,003	6,444,059	4,942,087	76.7	5,350,637	3,728,706	69.7	4,870,108	3,197,292	65.7
West North Central	3,118,367	2,741,410	2,530,591	3,568,032	2,717,324	76.2	3,393,143	2,420,920	71.3	3,318,977	2,271,448	68.4
South Atlantic	3,708,882	3,080,686	2,418,444	4,894,885	3,375,291	69.0	4,323,620	2,818,406	65.2	3,815,749	2,226,901	58.4
East South Central	2,351,486	2,018,295	1,730,191	3,055,113	2,146,173	70.2	2,818,595	1,858,650	65.9	2,665,236	1,589,551	59.6
West South Central	2,833,557	2,247,456	1,795,100	3,677,539	2,593,428	70.5	3,259,000	2,097,596	64.4	2,815,947	1,673,480	59.4
Mountain	915,230	732,593	505,191	1,046,707	815,642	77.9	896,406	656,638	73.3	684,190	460,193	67.3
Pacific	1,774,705	1,021,429	700,770	1,842,347	1,491,913	81.0	1,227,268	900,734	73.4	956,011	639,311	66.9
NEW ENGLAND:												
Maine	180,885	154,163	140,831	203,336	157,245	77.3	188,822	134,299	71.1	181,632	122,218	67.3
New Hampshire	98,406	81,850	77,550	114,709	87,738	76.5	104,581	73,063	69.9	104,082	68,048	65.4
Vermont	76,447	68,745	70,531	92,142	69,492	75.4	87,302	62,544	71.6	88,177	62,064	70.4
Massachusetts	962,698	741,029	630,119	1,058,699	818,467	77.3	907,212	633,124	69.8	820,931	530,615	65.7
Rhode Island	149,791	110,838	96,242	179,871	129,431	72.0	149,774	95,499	63.8	138,015	83,312	60.4
Connecticut	366,563	267,403	206,955	428,854	314,497	73.3	330,599	225,094	68.1	277,715	176,228	63.5
MIDDLE ATLANTIC:												
New York	2,637,172	1,900,039	1,650,863	3,029,331	2,270,691	75.0	2,461,306	1,656,905	67.3	2,289,201	1,452,179	63.4
New Jersey	906,804	613,575	469,272	1,051,043	771,838	73.4	786,040	525,979	66.9	658,328	405,496	61.6
Pennsylvania	2,205,385	1,747,063	1,411,238	2,679,830	1,979,562	73.9	2,280,411	1,563,676	68.6	2,032,406	1,273,515	62.7
EAST NORTH CENTRAL:												
Ohio	1,497,330	1,125,097	808,098	1,687,607	1,323,018	78.4	1,386,799	989,417	71.3	1,223,240	810,136	66.2
Indiana	708,392	572,310	529,742	824,768	636,701	77.2	745,281	515,237	69.1	723,663	482,697	66.7
Illinois	1,623,242	1,251,189	1,004,346	1,903,015	1,421,472	74.7	1,619,847	1,108,216	68.4	1,502,604	955,869	63.6
Michigan	1,134,710	723,639	508,926	1,245,278	963,601	77.4	893,744	626,165	70.1	739,692	500,305	67.6
Wisconsin	696,930	564,406	514,901	783,391	597,895	76.3	704,966	489,671	69.5	680,969	448,385	65.8
WEST NORTH CENTRAL:												
Minnesota	617,379	510,238	462,867	694,706	532,741	76.7	643,287	451,096	70.1	603,310	417,496	69.2
Iowa	590,151	526,864	490,272	649,630	504,479	77.7	627,248	454,078	72.4	628,492	434,117	69.1
Missouri	757,941	699,809	665,972	918,692	666,414	72.5	901,604	624,395	69.2	922,695	608,226	65.9
North Dakota	181,127	161,221	121,640	216,305	164,587	76.1	198,020	146,280	73.9	168,166	110,459	65.7
South Dakota	176,934	146,950	126,903	204,944	159,430	77.8	181,271	131,943	72.8	170,033	115,692	68.0
Nebraska	346,302	298,619	275,829	379,501	293,434	77.3	358,143	256,961	71.7	347,607	242,625	69.8
Kansas	449,533	397,703	378,099	504,245	396,230	78.6	483,480	356,167	73.7	478,674	342,933	71.6
SOUTH ATLANTIC:												
Delaware	50,326	41,713	36,330	61,633	45,480	73.8	54,739	37,759	69.0	53,004	33,302	61.8
Maryland	335,315	270,908	234,628	425,455	298,830	70.2	381,106	246,056	64.6	360,808	213,622	59.2
Dist. of Columbia	96,004	70,886	54,688	98,904	75,326	76.2	89,931	58,005	64.5	73,055	47,062	64.4
Virginia	554,396	495,674	401,696	746,541	516,094	69.1	709,980	400,037	64.8	646,000	381,532	59.1
West Virginia	426,245	324,747	207,411	530,591	387,124	73.0	437,703	297,044	67.9	365,700	244,996	67.0
North Carolina	811,680	620,981	495,196	1,062,026	749,529	70.6	830,574	576,239	68.6	721,114	455,109	63.1
South Carolina	443,585	427,962	300,350	617,242	404,078	65.6	576,564	393,077	68.2	518,817	277,210	53.4
Georgia	678,785	624,776	404,781	952,959	615,474	64.6	953,304	570,386	59.8	851,147	452,234	53.1
Florida	312,546	196,979	133,855	399,534	282,756	70.8	280,719	179,803	64.1	224,154	121,174	54.1
EAST SOUTH CENTRAL:												
Kentucky	596,205	524,342	473,481	770,776	543,841	70.6	717,667	480,526	67.0	698,446	437,863	62.7
Tennessee	607,071	528,993	451,190	792,314	557,849	70.4	724,688	488,543	67.4	681,513	417,862	61.3
Alabama	625,436	527,595	396,845	849,871	581,859	68.5	774,048	499,888	64.6	691,822	371,850	53.7
Mississippi	522,774	437,365	408,675	642,152	462,624	72.0	602,192	389,702	64.7	593,455	361,976	61.0
WEST SOUTH CENTRAL:												
Arkansas	459,757	410,853	333,795	585,613	420,479	71.8	569,870	375,115	65.8	506,549	304,909	60.2
Louisiana	488,820	356,690	257,027	636,241	431,092	67.8	574,202	327,546	57.0	529,497	235,204	44.4
Oklahoma	612,509	487,013	394,201	729,957	549,144	75.2	647,939	444,247	68.6	519,327	361,376	69.6
Texas	1,272,471	992,900	810,077	1,725,728	1,192,713	69.1	1,466,989	950,688	64.8	1,260,574	771,931	61.2
MOUNTAIN:												
Montana	130,743	115,367	62,755	148,833	118,724	79.8	135,886	102,621	75.5	86,625	56,076	65.8
Idaho	118,138	104,456	68,603	132,695	108,113	81.5	122,278	95,027	77.7	89,215	63,613	71.3
Wyoming	53,424	38,827	23,745	60,369	47,581	78.8	47,474	34,387	72.4	33,042	21,475	65.0
Colorado	244,039	108,060	153,412	275,166	212,797	77.3	239,926	175,745	73.2	200,022	138,467	69.2
New Mexico	105,051	83,370	66,717	129,911	93,689	72.1	109,738	75,119	68.5	96,859	60,704	62.7
Arizona	93,465	60,688	31,346	120,656	86,717	71.9	89,464	54,387	60.8	52,248	28,753	55.0
Utah	147,460	118,934	88,056	159,052	132,122	83.1	136,039	107,908	79.3	111,284	80,725	72.5
Nevada	17,919	12,891	10,557	20,025	15,899	79.4	15,601	11,444	73.4	14,895	9,480	63.6
PACIFIC:												
Washington	350,090	265,051	201,695	386,482	312,833	80.9	321,410	238,012	74.1	272,793	185,795	68.1
Oregon	210,813	157,552	121,409	232,558	185,970	80.0	187,704	141,613	75.4	163,739	111,597	68.2
California	1,213,802	598,826	377,666	1,223,307	993,110	81.2	718,154	521,109	72.6	519,479	341,919	65.8

1102

POPULATION

TABLE 12.—TOTAL NUMBER OF PERSONS ATTENDING SCHOOL, BY AGE PERIODS, BY DIVISIONS AND STATES: 1930, 1920, AND 1910—Continued

DIVISION AND STATE	PERSONS UNDER 7 YEARS OLD ATTENDING SCHOOL												PERSONS 21 YEARS OLD AND OVER ATTENDING SCHOOL		
	Total			Under 5 years old			5 years old			6 years old					
	1930	1920	1910	1930	1920	1910	1930	1920	1910	1930	1920	1910	1930	1920	1910
United States	2,230,808	1,966,635	1,455,784	62,588	44,510	49,758	500,734	441,411	346,673	1,667,486	1,480,714	1,059,353	1,034,782	344,789	313,256
GEOGRAPHIC DIVISIONS:															
New England	186,003	174,175	149,077	8,598	6,862	7,203	53,104	53,019	50,091	124,301	114,294	91,783	71,917	26,290	21,666
Middle Atlantic	513,913	447,445	339,050	17,838	12,829	14,199	125,501	107,721	85,829	370,574	326,895	239,628	213,357	66,072	60,527
East North Central	497,476	427,749	315,207	13,527	9,208	10,321	120,363	94,395	70,556	363,586	324,146	234,330	220,459	80,186	63,504
West North Central	292,778	270,428	209,562	4,580	4,160	5,576	80,313	69,064	50,020	207,885	197,204	153,966	108,265	50,053	49,581
South Atlantic	228,809	225,573	154,223	4,385	3,288	4,080	26,867	34,091	29,593	197,557	188,194	120,550	104,782	36,707	37,320
East South Central	147,033	141,808	114,204	3,046	2,291	2,795	24,124	31,145	27,757	119,863	108,372	83,712	58,280	17,828	26,376
West South Central	151,097	125,955	94,808	3,467	2,408	2,944	20,216	21,787	18,337	127,414	101,760	73,527	80,032	23,905	26,812
Mountain	65,420	63,174	35,122	1,261	1,220	1,028	11,079	11,321	6,340	53,080	50,633	27,754	34,177	12,781	9,876
Pacific	148,279	90,328	43,855	5,896	2,244	1,612	39,167	18,868	8,150	103,226	69,216	34,103	134,513	30,367	17,594
NEW ENGLAND:															
Maine	19,735	17,622	16,257	631	524	804	6,116	5,952	5,580	12,988	11,146	9,864	3,905	2,242	2,356
New Hampshire	7,915	7,298	8,374	399	234	364	1,709	1,635	2,571	5,807	5,429	5,439	2,753	1,489	1,128
Vermont	5,212	5,264	7,540	87	52	265	720	803	2,503	4,405	4,399	4,781	1,743	947	918
Massachusetts	97,202	91,931	78,259	5,187	3,729	3,769	27,096	27,419	26,076	64,919	60,783	48,414	47,020	15,074	12,245
Rhode Island	15,182	13,822	10,877	580	504	515	3,951	4,037	3,346	10,651	9,281	7,016	5,178	1,517	2,053
Connecticut	40,757	38,248	27,761	1,714	1,819	1,486	13,512	13,173	10,006	25,531	23,256	16,269	11,309	4,121	2,966
MIDDLE ATLANTIC:															
New York	249,415	206,238	166,068	9,160	6,883	7,651	69,676	57,668	48,122	170,579	141,687	111,195	117,066	36,896	31,716
New Jersey	104,542	80,202	56,840	4,848	3,038	3,189	35,589	26,038	18,244	64,105	51,126	35,407	30,424	7,304	6,936
Pennsylvania	159,956	161,005	115,848	3,830	2,908	3,359	20,236	24,015	19,463	135,890	134,082	93,026	65,867	22,382	21,875
EAST NORTH CENTRAL:															
Ohio	114,075	107,461	72,575	1,662	1,301	1,573	18,363	18,418	12,560	94,050	87,742	58,442	60,246	28,210	15,377
Indiana	49,004	48,908	36,416	800	712	701	7,244	6,878	4,689	41,950	41,408	31,026	21,097	8,075	10,729
Illinois	130,628	120,945	88,269	4,099	2,560	2,911	25,137	21,504	16,174	101,392	96,881	69,184	71,142	22,028	20,208
Michigan	129,980	85,894	59,416	2,827	1,718	1,595	47,112	27,117	18,387	80,041	57,059	39,434	41,129	11,580	9,205
Wisconsin	72,799	64,451	58,531	4,139	2,917	3,541	22,507	20,478	18,746	46,153	41,056	36,244	26,245	10,284	7,985
WEST NORTH CENTRAL:															
Minnesota	57,773	47,778	35,728	907	736	1,147	16,866	11,531	8,316	40,000	35,511	26,265	26,865	11,364	9,643
Iowa	67,808	62,457	54,961	1,059	919	1,625	23,632	21,480	17,675	43,117	40,058	35,661	17,864	10,329	10,104
Missouri	65,533	65,014	46,280	1,093	910	997	14,637	14,345	6,643	49,803	49,759	38,640	25,994	10,400	11,466
North Dakota	11,506	12,162	8,793	155	192	246	1,194	1,484	1,553	10,157	10,486	6,994	5,034	2,770	2,307
South Dakota	12,572	12,601	8,840	177	193	215	1,506	1,855	1,575	10,889	10,643	7,050	4,023	2,329	2,471
Nebraska	40,248	36,505	27,671	737	779	703	14,445	12,692	8,374	25,066	23,004	18,594	11,620	5,093	5,533
Kansas	37,338	33,781	27,289	452	431	643	8,033	5,677	5,884	28,853	27,653	20,762	15,905	7,775	7,877
SOUTH ATLANTIC:															
Delaware	3,229	3,391	2,409	70	69	68	244	355	399	2,915	2,967	1,942	1,617	563	559
Maryland	23,791	20,730	16,967	480	257	466	3,175	2,878	3,099	20,136	17,595	13,402	12,694	4,182	4,039
Dist. of Columbia	8,602	6,704	4,726	227	234	264	2,675	2,037	1,205	5,700	4,433	3,197	12,076	6,177	2,300
Virginia	25,025	29,746	14,868	436	464	413	2,882	5,341	3,488	21,707	23,941	10,967	13,277	5,891	5,296
West Virginia	26,897	24,439	18,519	440	292	365	2,860	3,503	3,179	23,597	20,644	14,975	12,224	3,264	3,896
North Carolina	47,609	44,817	32,032	712	570	613	3,004	5,396	5,078	43,893	38,851	26,341	14,542	5,925	8,055
South Carolina	24,938	31,070	18,663	466	407	585	2,362	4,303	3,981	22,110	26,360	14,097	13,969	3,815	4,486
Georgia	46,435	49,264	36,007	945	625	833	6,424	7,478	7,030	39,066	41,161	28,144	16,876	5,126	6,540
Florida	22,283	15,412	10,032	609	370	473	3,241	2,800	2,074	18,433	12,242	7,485	7,507	1,764	2,149
EAST SOUTH CENTRAL:															
Kentucky	35,208	39,203	28,520	779	636	678	3,934	6,167	4,510	30,495	32,400	23,332	17,156	4,613	7,098
Tennessee	33,056	35,533	26,004	639	376	545	3,427	5,560	4,864	28,990	29,597	20,685	16,166	4,917	7,234
Alabama	29,260	23,270	18,641	590	400	522	2,443	4,496	4,520	26,227	18,374	13,599	14,317	4,437	6,354
Mississippi	49,509	43,802	41,009	1,038	879	1,050	14,320	14,922	13,863	34,151	28,001	26,096	10,641	3,861	5,690
WEST SOUTH CENTRAL:															
Arkansas	29,114	31,911	23,450	476	299	448	2,449	5,550	3,876	26,189	26,062	19,126	10,164	3,827	5,436
Louisiana	34,929	25,884	18,124	957	736	624	5,860	5,051	4,344	28,112	20,097	13,156	22,700	3,260	3,639
Oklahoma	44,540	37,546	27,689	763	540	746	5,949	5,626	4,503	37,828	31,380	22,440	18,825	5,220	5,136
Texas	42,514	30,614	25,545	1,271	833	1,126	5,958	5,560	5,614	35,285	24,221	18,805	37,244	11,598	12,601
MOUNTAIN:															
Montana	8,054	10,975	4,638	121	177	146	814	1,977	790	7,119	8,821	3,702	3,965	1,771	1,141
Idaho	6,340	7,976	3,798	71	77	120	290	807	512	5,970	7,092	3,166	3,685	1,453	1,192
Wyoming	4,141	3,793	1,842	51	74	47	630	617	250	3,460	3,102	1,545	1,702	647	428
Colorado	19,386	18,176	11,642	455	439	330	4,038	3,802	2,153	14,893	13,935	9,159	11,856	4,139	3,303
New Mexico	8,823	7,171	5,201	244	123	97	1,014	1,789	1,466	6,565	5,259	3,638	2,539	1,080	812
Arizona	7,893	5,271	2,092	190	162	84	1,846	1,083	406	5,857	4,026	1,602	3,855	1,030	501
Utah	9,385	8,615	5,052	108	138	175	1,275	999	596	8,002	7,478	4,281	5,953	2,411	2,279
Nevada	1,398	1,197	857	21	30	29	272	247	167	1,105	920	661	622	250	220
PACIFIC:															
Washington	19,116	19,568	11,320	305	248	343	1,758	2,131	1,522	17,053	17,189	9,464	18,141	7,471	4,571
Oregon	11,932	10,778	6,590	183	116	182	952	1,102	927	10,797	9,560	5,481	12,911	5,161	3,222
California	117,231	59,982	25,946	5,398	1,880	1,087	36,457	15,635	5,701	75,376	42,467	19,158	103,461	17,735	9,801

SCHOOL ATTENDANCE 1103

TABLE 13.—SCHOOL ATTENDANCE OF THE POPULATION 7 TO 20 YEARS OLD, BY SEX, BY DIVISIONS AND STATES: 1930, 1920, AND 1910

DIVISION AND STATE	MALES 7 TO 20 YEARS OLD							FEMALES 7 TO 20 YEARS OLD						
	1930			1920, attending school		1910, attending school		1930			1920, attending school		1910, attending school	
	Total number	Attending school						Total number	Attending school					
		Number	Per cent	Number	Per cent	Number	Per cent		Number	Per cent	Number	Per cent	Number	Per cent
United States	16,780,596	12,441,941	74.4	9,706,801	68.0	8,132,602	63.0	16,635,901	12,239,478	73.6	9,745,050	68.2	8,108,249	63.3
GEOGRAPHIC DIVISIONS:														
New England	1,038,756	795,930	76.6	608,434	69.3	523,899	65.2	1,038,855	780,940	75.2	615,189	69.1	527,586	65.4
Middle Atlantic	3,382,566	2,554,663	75.5	1,879,234	68.4	1,566,531	63.2	3,377,038	2,467,428	73.1	1,867,326	67.2	1,564,650	62.5
East North Central	3,236,013	2,507,431	77.5	1,860,629	69.6	1,610,601	65.6	3,208,046	2,435,256	75.9	1,850,077	60.8	1,586,691	65.6
West North Central	1,801,093	1,364,848	75.8	1,208,596	71.0	1,144,488	68.2	1,766,939	1,352,476	76.5	1,212,333	71.7	1,126,960	68.7
South Atlantic	2,443,013	1,672,960	68.5	1,395,324	64.8	1,101,477	57.0	2,451,872	1,702,331	69.4	1,423,082	65.5	1,125,424	58.8
East South Central	1,529,576	1,077,201	70.4	925,257	65.9	793,545	59.5	1,525,537	1,068,972	70.1	933,402	66.0	796,000	59.8
West South Central	1,839,661	1,303,028	70.8	1,040,793	63.9	839,147	59.4	1,837,878	1,290,400	70.2	1,056,803	64.8	834,333	59.5
Mountain	529,842	411,632	77.7	328,957	72.6	232,044	66.2	516,865	404,010	78.2	327,081	73.9	227,549	68.4
Pacific	930,076	754,248	81.1	450,577	72.6	320,270	64.9	912,271	737,605	80.9	450,157	74.2	319,041	68.9
NEW ENGLAND:														
Maine	102,525	78,966	77.0	66,239	70.2	60,941	66.7	100,811	78,270	77.6	68,060	72.0	61,277	67.9
New Hampshire	57,502	44,270	76.9	36,128	69.5	33,805	64.4	57,117	43,468	76.1	36,035	70.2	34,243	66.4
Vermont	46,955	34,901	74.3	31,206	70.8	31,030	68.9	45,187	34,591	76.6	31,278	72.5	31,034	71.9
Massachusetts	527,678	413,032	78.3	314,027	70.1	267,791	65.8	531,021	405,435	76.4	318,197	69.4	271,824	65.6
Rhode Island	89,653	65,220	72.7	47,336	63.4	42,580	61.2	90,218	64,211	71.2	48,163	64.1	40,723	59.5
Connecticut	214,353	159,541	74.4	112,538	68.6	87,743	63.4	214,501	154,956	72.2	112,556	67.6	88,485	63.5
MIDDLE ATLANTIC:														
New York	1,515,134	1,157,442	76.4	832,157	68.2	723,463	64.2	1,514,107	1,113,240	73.5	824,748	66.4	728,716	62.7
New Jersey	526,602	394,229	74.9	263,928	67.5	203,327	62.3	524,351	377,609	72.0	262,051	66.3	202,169	60.0
Pennsylvania	1,340,740	1,002,992	74.8	783,149	68.9	639,741	62.5	1,339,000	976,570	72.9	780,527	68.3	633,774	62.8
EAST NORTH CENTRAL:														
Ohio	845,338	670,778	79.4	494,510	71.0	409,085	66.5	842,209	652,240	77.4	494,808	71.7	401,051	66.0
Indiana	414,932	323,293	77.9	259,245	60.2	243,500	66.6	409,836	313,408	76.5	255,002	60.1	239,097	66.8
Illinois	952,923	724,819	76.1	557,008	68.8	480,520	64.0	950,092	696,653	73.3	551,208	68.0	475,343	63.3
Michigan	626,720	488,734	78.0	314,030	60.5	251,550	67.2	618,558	474,867	76.8	311,535	70.6	248,755	68.1
Wisconsin	396,100	299,807	75.7	244,227	60.0	225,940	65.7	387,291	298,088	77.0	245,444	60.9	222,445	66.0
WEST NORTH CENTRAL:														
Minnesota	350,078	265,891	76.0	225,043	69.7	210,343	69.0	344,628	266,850	77.4	226,053	70.6	207,153	69.5
Iowa	328,813	253,162	77.0	226,167	71.8	218,044	68.6	320,826	251,317	78.3	227,911	72.9	216,073	69.5
Missouri	461,183	337,588	73.2	312,806	60.6	305,552	66.3	457,509	328,826	71.9	311,529	68.9	302,674	65.6
North Dakota	109,837	81,696	74.4	73,083	73.6	56,380	65.0	106,468	82,891	77.9	73,206	74.2	54,079	66.4
South Dakota	104,201	79,329	76.1	66,151	71.8	59,038	67.4	100,743	80,110	79.5	65,792	73.8	56,554	68.7
Nebraska	192,007	147,332	76.7	128,304	71.0	122,544	69.5	187,494	146,102	77.9	128,657	72.9	120,081	70.1
Kansas	254,974	199,850	78.4	176,982	73.0	172,587	70.9	249,271	196,380	78.8	179,185	74.3	170,346	72.4
SOUTH ATLANTIC:														
Delaware	31,085	23,003	74.0	18,957	69.4	17,144	62.2	30,548	22,477	73.6	18,802	68.5	16,218	61.3
Maryland	214,645	151,263	70.5	124,602	64.9	107,311	59.9	210,810	147,507	70.0	121,454	64.2	106,311	58.5
Dist. of Columbia	47,533	37,247	78.4	28,720	67.3	23,135	65.0	51,371	38,070	74.1	29,285	61.9	24,527	64.0
Virginia	376,372	255,444	67.9	226,508	63.3	188,141	58.2	370,169	260,650	70.4	233,529	66.3	193,391	60.0
West Virginia	267,232	195,716	73.2	148,588	67.3	124,086	66.3	263,350	191,408	72.7	148,456	68.5	120,310	67.1
North Carolina	530,270	371,609	70.1	286,398	68.5	227,744	63.2	531,756	377,920	71.1	289,841	68.7	227,365	63.0
South Carolina	305,865	196,730	64.3	193,276	68.0	134,767	52.5	311,377	207,048	66.8	199,801	68.3	142,443	54.4
Georgia	473,390	302,077	63.8	270,458	59.4	219,420	52.3	479,500	313,397	65.3	290,928	60.3	232,814	54.0
Florida	196,621	139,871	71.1	88,817	64.1	59,129	53.0	202,913	142,885	70.4	90,986	64.0	62,045	55.1
EAST SOUTH CENTRAL:														
Kentucky	380,903	273,942	70.3	239,915	66.4	220,640	62.8	380,873	269,899	70.9	240,611	67.6	217,223	62.6
Tennessee	397,831	280,021	70.4	244,777	67.6	209,798	61.2	394,483	277,828	70.4	243,766	67.2	208,064	61.5
Alabama	422,155	291,208	69.0	248,315	65.0	184,397	53.6	427,710	290,651	68.0	251,573	64.2	187,453	53.9
Mississippi	319,687	232,030	72.6	192,250	64.5	178,710	60.6	322,405	230,594	71.5	197,452	64.9	183,266	61.4
WEST SOUTH CENTRAL:														
Arkansas	293,146	211,591	72.2	187,438	66.1	152,402	60.2	292,467	208,888	71.4	187,677	65.6	152,507	60.2
Louisiana	314,361	213,718	68.0	159,544	56.5	114,896	43.9	321,880	217,374	67.5	168,002	57.6	120,368	44.0
Oklahoma	367,681	277,844	75.6	222,124	68.1	185,149	70.0	362,276	271,300	74.9	222,123	69.0	176,227	69.2
Texas	864,473	599,875	69.4	471,687	64.0	386,700	71.0	861,255	592,838	68.8	479,001	65.6	385,231	61.5
MOUNTAIN:														
Montana	75,828	59,226	78.1	51,244	74.6	28,409	62.8	73,005	59,498	81.5	51,377	76.5	28,507	69.0
Idaho	67,877	54,599	80.4	47,975	76.8	32,610	70.1	64,818	53,514	82.6	47,052	78.7	30,997	72.6
Wyoming	31,230	24,028	76.9	17,274	70.1	10,813	60.7	29,130	23,553	80.9	17,113	74.9	10,062	70.0
Colorado	138,325	106,893	77.3	87,277	72.4	69,139	68.2	136,841	105,890	77.4	88,468	74.1	69,328	70.2
New Mexico	65,090	47,518	73.0	37,662	68.5	31,391	63.8	64,821	46,171	71.2	37,457	68.4	29,313	61.5
Arizona	61,036	44,238	72.5	27,363	60.3	14,633	54.1	59,620	42,479	71.2	27,024	61.3	14,120	56.0
Utah	80,143	67,009	83.6	54,429	79.8	40,858	72.7	78,909	65,113	82.5	53,479	78.8	39,867	72.4
Nevada	10,304	8,116	78.8	5,733	71.0	4,785	59.8	9,721	7,783	80.1	5,711	75.9	4,695	68.1
PACIFIC:														
Washington	195,932	157,537	80.4	118,386	73.1	93,199	66.1	190,550	155,296	81.5	119,626	75.0	92,596	70.2
Oregon	117,202	93,199	79.5	70,622	75.0	56,570	66.8	115,356	92,771	80.4	70,991	75.9	55,027	69.6
California	616,942	503,512	81.6	261,569	71.8	170,501	63.8	606,365	480,598	80.7	259,540	73.4	171,418	68.0

CHAPTER 13

———

ILLITERACY

CHAPTER 13—ILLITERACY

INTRODUCTION

The Census Bureau defines as illiterate any person 10 years of age or over who is not able to read and write, either in English or in some other language. The classification is based on the answers given to the enumerator in response to the question "Whether able to read and write." No specific test of ability to read and write was prescribed, but the enumerators were instructed *not* to return the answer "Yes" (which would classify the person as literate) simply because the person was able to write his or her name.

Statistics of illiteracy were first obtained for the entire population 10 years old and over in 1870. In the several censuses prior to 1930, two questions have been asked, namely, "Whether able to read" and "Whether able to write," and illiteracy has been defined as inability to write, "regardless of ability to read." As a matter of fact, the figures for illiterates presented in most of the tables in the Reports of the 1920 Census, for example, represent persons who were unable both to read and to write, since every person tabulated as able to write was also counted as able to read. The earlier statistics are therefore strictly comparable with the 1930 figures obtained through the use of the consolidated question.

It should be noted that ability to read and write can not be defined so precisely as to cover all cases with certainty. A person may know the alphabet and a small number of printed words and yet not be able to read in a true sense; or he may be able to write his name or other disconnected words, but wholly unable to express his thoughts in writing in any satisfactory fashion. In general, the illiterate population as shown by the census may be assumed to comprise only those persons who have had no education whatever.

Statistics of illiteracy in connection with ability to speak English are presented in Chapter 14, Inability to Speak English. From these tables may be obtained approximately the numbers of persons who are unable to read and write English, including those who can read their native language.

Statistics of illiteracy for continental United States are presented in this chapter by States and for cities of 25,000 or more. Less detailed statistics are presented for counties and for incorporated places of 2,500 or more in Volume III of the Fifteenth Census Reports on Population; and statistics of illiteracy in the outlying territories and possessions enumerated at

the Fifteenth Census are presented in the volume containing the 1930 census reports for those areas.

Color and nativity.—The variations in the proportion of illiterates in the several color and nativity classes reflect the educational opportunities, past and present, which have been open to them in the different sections of the United States, and in the case of the foreign born, in the countries from which they have come.

The decidedly higher percentage of illiteracy for the native whites of native parentage than for the native whites of foreign or mixed parentage results mainly from the fact that a much larger proportion of the former class are found in the rural communities, where school attendance has been less general than in the cities. Further, most of the rural native whites of foreign or mixed parentage live in States where educational facilities, even in the country, are relatively good. In order to make a fair comparison between these two elements of the population, therefore, in regard to illiteracy, the statistics for individual cities and for urban and rural areas in individual States, should be examined. (See Tables 18 to 22.)

The statistics of illiteracy for the United States are presented, by color and nativity, in Table 1.

TABLE 1.—ILLITERACY IN THE POPULATION 10 YEARS OLD AND OVER, BY COLOR AND NATIVITY, FOR THE UNITED STATES: 1930 AND 1920

COLOR AND NATIVITY	1930 [1]			1920 [1]		
	Total number	Illiterate		Total number	Illiterate	
		Number	Per cent		Number	Per cent
All classes	98,723,047	4,283,753	4.3	82,739,315	4,931,905	6.0
White	87,980,667	2,407,218	2.7	74,359,749	3,006,312	4.0
Native	74,763,739	1,103,134	1.5	60,861,863	1,242,572	2.0
Native parentage	53,876,411	986,469	1.8	44,077,504	1,109,875	2.5
For. or mixed par.	20,887,328	116,665	0.6	16,784,299	132,697	0.8
Foreign born	13,216,928	1,304,084	9.9	13,497,886	1,763,740	13.1
Negro	9,292,556	1,513,892	16.3	8,063,225	1,842,161	22.9
Other races	1,449,824	362,643	25.0	326,341	83,432	25.6

[1] Mexicans, with a relatively high percentage of illiteracy (27.5 in 1930), are included with "Other races" in the figures for 1930 and with the white population in 1920.

Illiteracy by age.—The results of the extension of educational opportunities from decade to decade are brought out clearly by the statistics of illiteracy for the various age periods. The illiteracy shown for persons in each age period measures the lack of educational advantages during the childhood and youth of

1220 POPULATION

that age group. If school facilities should make no further growth from now on, there would nevertheless be a gradual reduction in illiteracy for several decades to come, as the older and more illiterate population died out; and the general level of illiteracy would gradually approach that found at present in the younger age groups. The improvement in educational facilities since 1890 can be studied by making a comparison of the percentages of illiteracy for the age groups 10 to 14 and 15 to 19 as shown by the census figures for 1900, 1910, 1920, and 1930. (See Tables 2 and 7.)

The statistics of illiteracy for the several age periods are summarized for the United States in Table 2.

TABLE 2.—ILLITERACY IN THE POPULATION 10 YEARS OLD AND OVER, BY AGE, FOR THE UNITED STATES: 1930 AND 1920

	1930			1920		
		Illiterate			Illiterate	
AGE	Total number	Number	Per cent	Total number	Number	Per cent
10 years and over____	98,723,047	4,283,753	4.3	82,739,315	4,931,905	6.0
10 to 14 years_____	12,004,877	140,440	1.2	10,641,137	246,360	2.3
15 to 19 years_____	11,552,115	221,942	1.9	9,430,556	283,316	3.0
20 to 24 years_____	10,870,378	294,360	2.7	9,277,021	392,858	4.2
25 to 34 years_____	18,954,029	618,266	3.3	17,157,684	961,200	5.6
35 to 44 years_____	17,198,840	887,955	5.2	14,120,838	988,961	7.0
45 to 54 years_____	13,018,083	864,433	6.6	10,408,493	857,776	8.2
55 to 64 years_____	8,396,898	606,811	7.2	6,531,672	594,573	9.1
65 years and over_____	6,633,805	642,966	9.7	4,933,215	591,385	12.0
Unknown_____	94,022	6,580	7.0	148,699	15,481	10.4

In many of the tables statistics of illiteracy are presented for the population 10 years old and over, without further age classification. In such cases the group includes persons with age unknown. Age 21 and over likewise includes age unknown.

Urban, rural-farm, and rural-nonfarm population.— Because of the marked differences between urban and rural communities in regard to school facilities and also in the composition of their population, statistics for illiteracy are presented for these three population groups in several of the tables.

Urban population, as defined by the Census Bureau, is in general that residing in cities and other incorporated places having 2,500 inhabitants or more, the remainder being classified as rural. In three of the New England States, New Hampshire, Massachusetts, and Rhode Island, towns (townships) are classified as urban if they have a population of 2,500 or more and certain urban characteristics; and a few large and densely populated townships in other States are likewise classified, even though not formally incorporated as municipalities.

In addition to the classification of the population as urban and rural, the rural population is further subdivided into rural-farm and rural-nonfarm, on the basis of the replies to a question reading "Does this family live on a farm?" The rural-farm population includes all persons living on farms in the rural areas. The rural-nonfarm or "village" population is made up largely of persons living in small towns or villages, both incorporated and unincorporated, though in many areas there are considerable numbers of families living in the open country but not on farms.

The statistics of illiteracy for these urban and rural areas are summarized in Table 3.

TABLE 3.—ILLITERACY IN THE URBAN, RURAL-FARM, AND RURAL-NONFARM POPULATION 10 YEARS OLD AND OVER, BY COLOR AND NATIVITY, FOR THE UNITED STATES: 1930

[For population on which percentages are based, see Table 8]

COLOR AND NATIVITY	URBAN POPULATION		RURAL-FARM POPULATION		RURAL-NON-FARM POPULATION	
	Number illiterate	Per cent	Number illiterate	Per cent	Number illiterate	Per cent
All classes_____	1,800,604	3.2	1,583,030	8.9	900,119	4.8
White_____	1,282,441	2.5	644,101	3.4	480,676	2.9
Native_____	223,596	0.5	559,624	3.1	319,914	2.1
Native parentage_____	163,227	0.6	533,412	3.5	289,830	2.4
Foreign or mixed par____	60,369	0.4	26,212	0.9	30,084	1.0
Foreign born_____	1,058,845	10.0	84,477	7.8	160,702	10.4
Negro_____	395,849	9.2	704,866	23.2	323,177	20.5
Other races_____	122,314	18.0	144,063	34.8	96,266	26.0

Illiteracy by country of origin.—Illiteracy in the foreign-born white population has been classified for 1930 by age in combination with country of birth; and for the native white of foreign or mixed parentage has been classified by age in combination with country of birth of parents. This is the first attempt to show illiteracy in the population of foreign derivation by nationality or country of origin.

These figures are summarized for the United States, and for urban and rural areas, in Tables 26 to 29, and are presented by States and for the more important cities in Tables 30 and 31.

ILLITERACY

PERCENTAGE OF ILLITERACY IN THE UNITED STATES: 1880 TO 1930

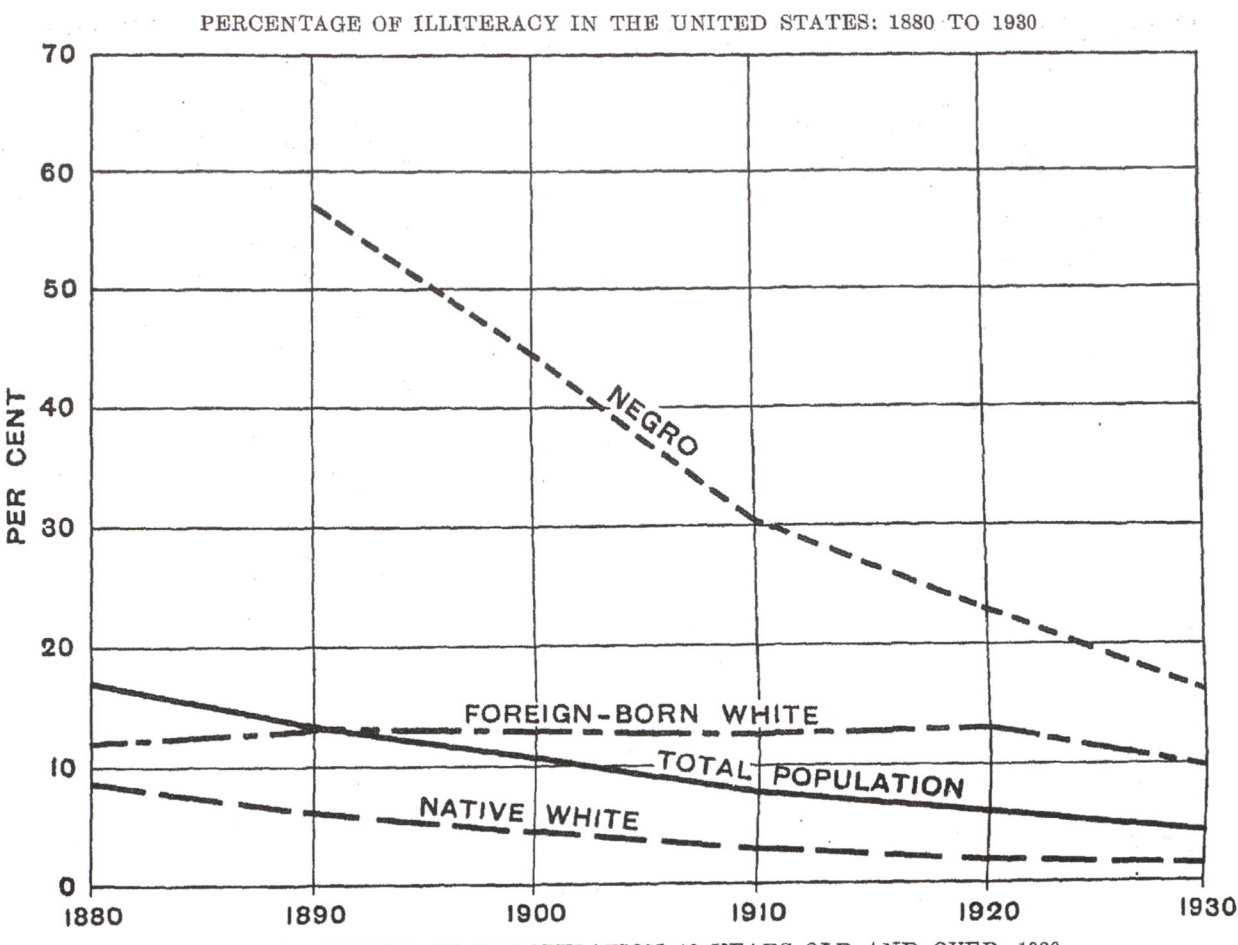

PER CENT ILLITERATE IN POPULATION 10 YEARS OLD AND OVER: 1930

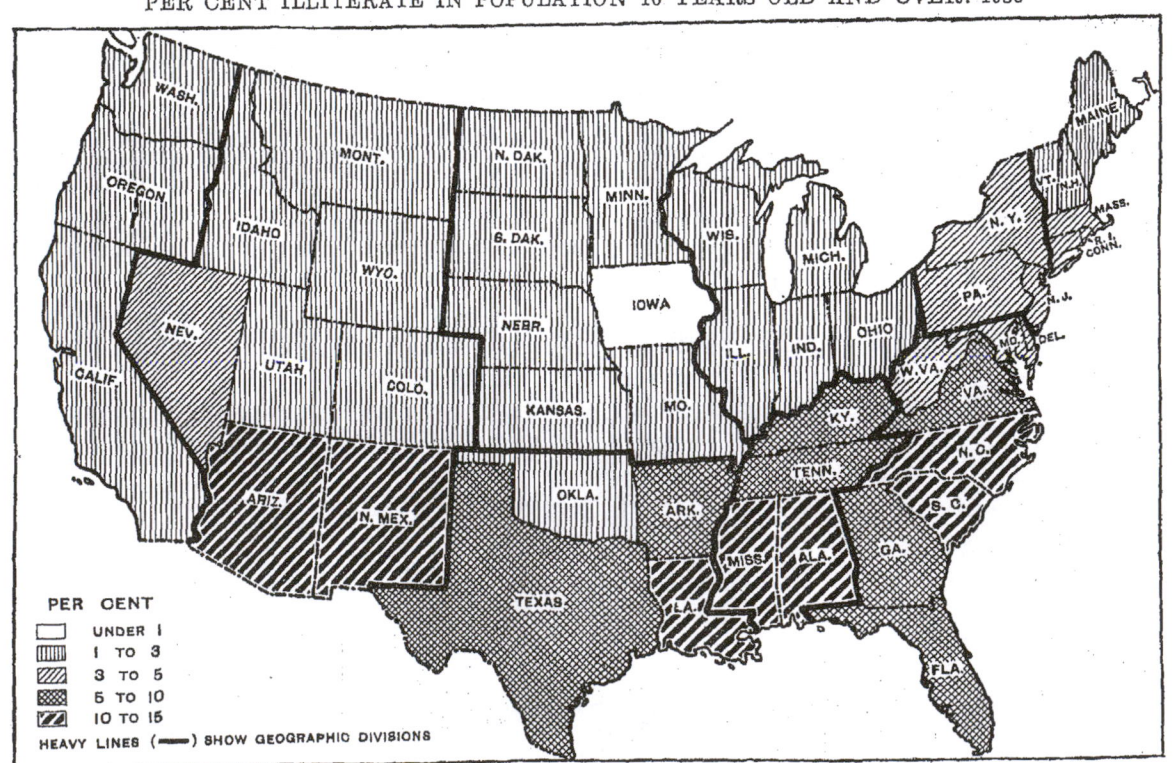

PER CENT
- UNDER 1
- 1 TO 3
- 3 TO 5
- 5 TO 10
- 10 TO 15

HEAVY LINES (———) SHOW GEOGRAPHIC DIVISIONS

POPULATION

1222

PER CENT ILLITERATE IN POPULATION 10 YEARS OLD AND OVER, BY COLOR AND NATIVITY, BY STATES: 1930 AND 1920

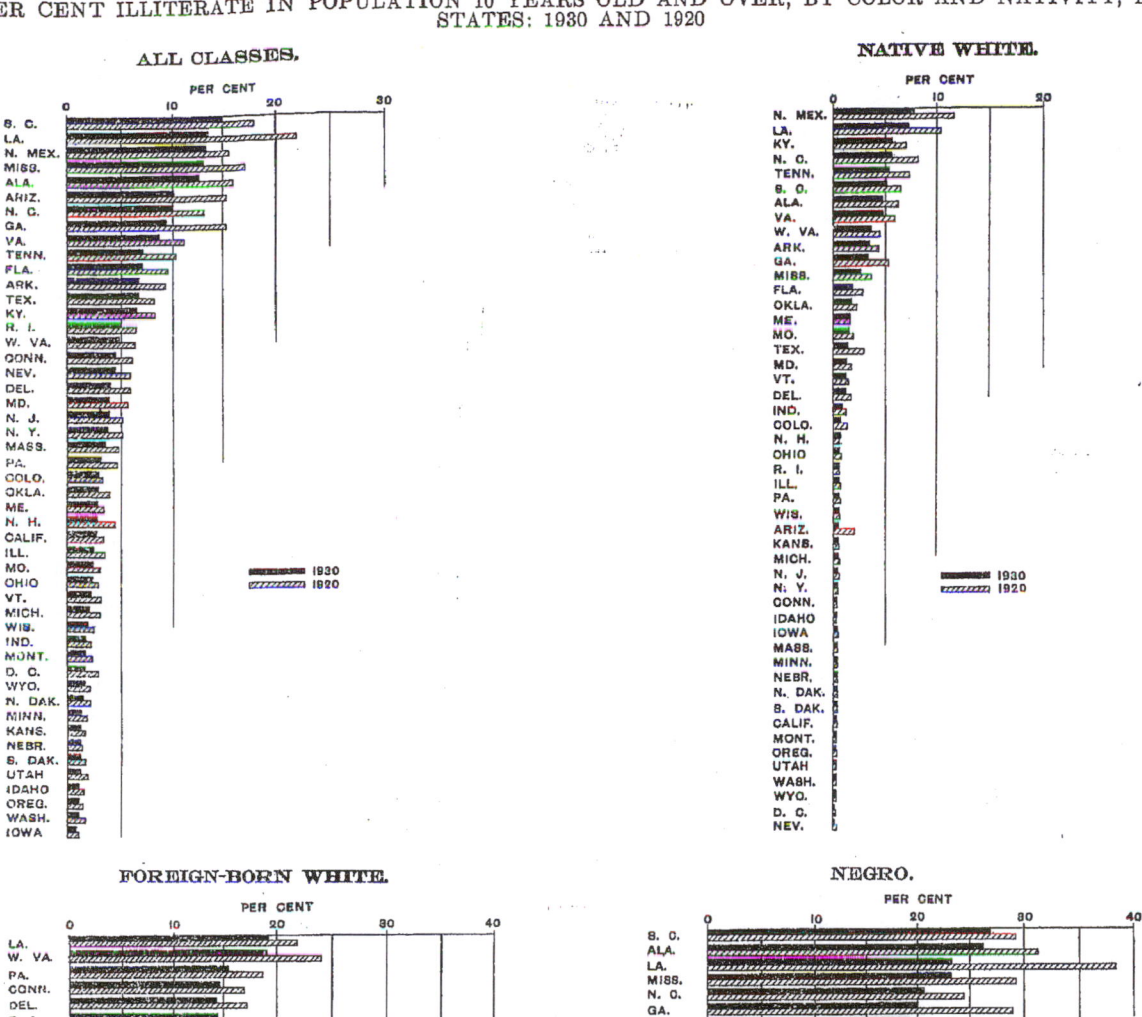

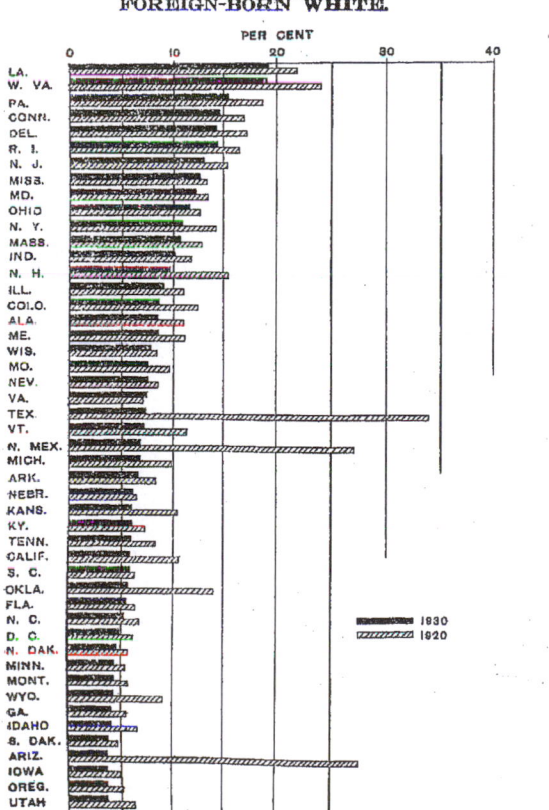

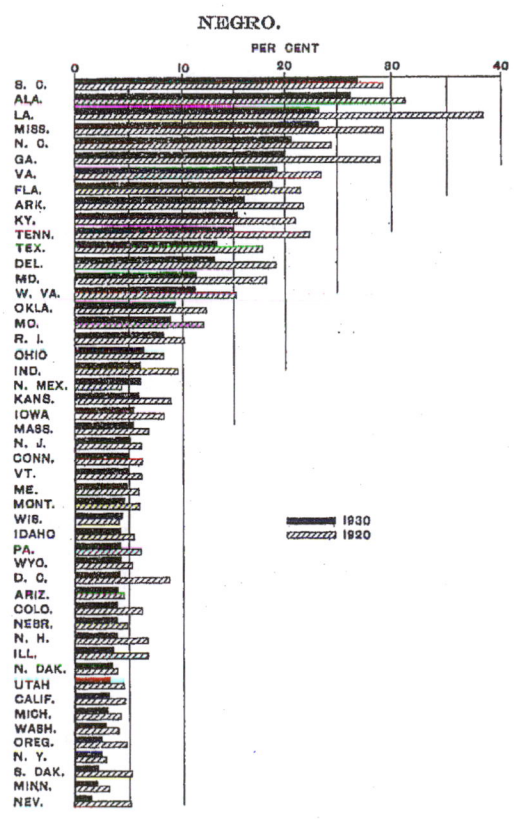

ILLITERACY

1223

TABLE 4.—ILLITERACY IN THE POPULATION 10 YEARS OLD AND OVER, BY COLOR, NATIVITY, AND SEX, FOR THE UNITED STATES: 1870 TO 1930

[Per cent not shown where base is less than 100]

CENSUS YEAR, COLOR, AND NATIVITY	TOTAL 10 YEARS OLD AND OVER			MALE			FEMALE		
	Total number	Illiterate Number	Illiterate Per cent	Total number	Illiterate Number	Illiterate Per cent	Total number	Illiterate Number	Illiterate Per cent
1930									
All classes	98,723,047	4,283,753	4.3	49,949,798	2,198,293	4.4	48,773,249	2,085,460	4.3
White	87,980,667	2,407,218	2.7	44,554,124	1,214,025	2.7	43,426,543	1,193,193	2.7
Native	74,763,739	1,103,134	1.5	37,475,901	640,048	1.7	37,287,838	463,086	1.2
Native parentage	53,876,411	986,469	1.8	27,188,095	577,312	2.1	26,688,316	409,157	1.5
Foreign or mixed parentage	20,887,328	116,665	0.6	10,287,806	62,736	0.6	10,599,522	53,929	0.5
Foreign born	13,216,928	1,304,084	9.9	7,078,223	573,977	8.1	6,138,705	730,107	11.9
Negro	9,292,556	1,513,892	16.3	4,564,690	801,949	17.6	4,727,866	711,943	15.1
Other races	1,449,824	362,643	25.0	830,984	182,319	21.9	618,840	180,324	29.1
Mexican	1,002,241	275,470	27.5	547,863	134,234	24.5	454,378	141,236	31.1
Indian	238,981	61,517	25.7	123,469	29,630	24.0	115,512	31,887	27.6
Chinese	63,392	12,912	20.4	53,650	10,735	20.0	9,742	2,177	22.3
Japanese	97,273	8,932	9.2	60,580	4,231	7.0	36,693	4,701	12.8
Filipino	42,904	2,834	6.6	41,128	2,589	6.3	1,836	245	13.3
Hindu	2,833	753	26.6	2,697	741	27.5	136	12	8.8
Korean	1,446	184	12.7	1,029	120	11.7	417	64	15.3
All other	694	41	5.9	568	39	6.9	126	2	1.6
1920 [1]									
All classes	82,739,315	4,931,905	6.0	42,289,969	2,540,209	6.0	40,449,346	2,391,696	5.9
White	74,350,749	3,006,312	4.0	38,070,736	1,551,529	4.1	36,280,013	1,454,783	4.0
Native	60,861,863	1,242,572	2.0	30,651,045	684,707	2.2	30,210,818	557,865	1.8
Native parentage	44,077,564	1,109,875	2.5	22,361,495	614,612	2.7	21,716,069	495,263	2.3
Foreign or mixed parentage	16,784,299	132,697	0.8	8,289,550	70,095	0.8	8,494,749	62,602	0.7
Foreign born	13,497,886	1,763,740	13.1	7,419,691	866,822	11.7	6,078,195	896,918	14.8
Negro	8,053,225	1,842,161	22.9	4,009,462	942,368	23.5	4,043,763	899,793	22.3
Other races	326,341	83,432	25.6	209,771	46,312	22.1	116,570	37,120	31.8
Indian	176,925	61,730	34.9	91,546	30,010	32.8	85,379	31,720	37.2
Chinese	56,230	11,262	20.0	51,041	10,064	19.7	5,189	1,198	23.1
Japanese	84,238	9,276	11.0	58,806	5,145	8.7	25,432	4,131	16.2
Filipino	5,380	288	5.4	5,110	254	5.0	270	34	12.6
Hindu	2,460	701	32.2	2,382	785	33.0	78	6	-------
Korean	973	79	8.1	787	51	6.5	186	28	15.1
All other	135	6	4.4	99	3	-------	36	3	-------
1910 [1]									
All classes	71,580,270	5,516,163	7.7	37,027,558	2,814,950	7.6	34,552,712	2,701,213	7.8
White	63,933,870	3,184,633	5.0	33,104,229	1,662,505	5.0	30,760,641	1,522,128	4.9
Native	50,989,341	1,534,272	3.0	25,843,033	796,055	3.1	25,146,308	738,217	2.9
Native parentage	37,081,278	1,378,884	3.7	18,933,751	715,928	3.8	18,147,527	662,956	3.7
Foreign or mixed parentage	13,908,063	155,388	1.1	6,909,282	80,129	1.2	6,998,781	75,259	1.1
Foreign born	12,944,529	1,650,361	12.7	7,321,196	866,450	11.8	5,623,333	783,911	13.9
Negro	7,317,922	2,227,731	30.4	3,637,386	1,096,000	30.1	3,680,536	1,131,731	30.7
Other races	328,478	103,799	31.6	225,943	56,445	25.0	102,535	47,354	46.2
Indian	188,758	85,445	45.3	96,582	40,104	41.5	92,176	45,341	49.2
Chinese	68,924	10,891	15.8	65,479	9,849	15.0	3,445	1,042	30.2
Japanese	67,661	6,213	9.2	60,809	5,247	8.6	6,852	966	14.1
Filipino	145	52	35.9	136	51	37.5	9	1	-------
Hindu	2,540	1,142	45.0	2,523	1,141	45.2	17	1	-------
Korean	443	56	12.6	411	53	12.9	32	3	-------
All other	7	-------	-------	3	-------	-------	4		
1900									
All classes	57,949,824	6,180,069	10.7	29,703,440	3,011,224	10.1	28,246,384	3,168,845	11.2
White	51,250,918	3,200,746	6.2	26,327,931	1,567,153	6.0	24,922,987	1,633,593	6.6
Native	41,236,662	1,913,611	4.6	20,912,940	955,517	4.6	20,323,722	958,094	4.7
Native parentage	30,310,261	1,734,764	5.7	15,452,855	862,175	5.6	14,857,406	872,589	5.9
Foreign or mixed parentage	10,926,401	178,847	1.6	5,460,085	93,342	1.7	5,466,316	85,505	1.6
Foreign born	10,014,256	1,287,135	12.9	5,414,991	611,636	11.3	4,599,265	675,499	14.7
Negro	6,415,581	2,853,194	44.5	3,181,650	1,371,432	43.1	3,233,931	1,481,762	45.8
Other races	283,325	126,129	44.5	193,859	72,630	37.5	89,466	53,499	59.8
Indian	171,552	96,347	56.2	86,504	45,376	52.5	85,048	50,971	59.9
Chinese	87,682	25,396	29.0	84,141	23,052	27.4	3,541	2,344	66.2
Japanese	24,001	4,386	18.2	23,214	4,211	18.1	877	175	20.0
1890 [2]									
All classes	47,413,559	6,324,702	13.3	24,352,659	3,008,222	12.4	23,060,900	3,316,480	14.4
White	41,931,074	3,212,574	7.7	21,578,245	1,517,722	7.0	20,352,829	1,694,852	8.3
Native	33,144,187	2,065,003	6.2	16,796,497	978,408	5.8	16,347,690	1,086,595	6.6
Native parentage	25,375,766	1,890,723	7.5	12,901,102	888,415	6.9	12,474,664	1,002,308	8.0
Foreign or mixed parentage	7,768,421	174,280	2.2	3,895,395	89,993	2.3	3,873,026	84,287	2.2
Foreign born	8,786,887	1,147,571	13.1	4,781,748	539,314	11.3	4,005,139	608,257	15.2
Negro	5,328,972	3,042,668	57.1	2,646,171	1,438,923	54.4	2,682,801	1,603,745	59.8
Other races	153,513	69,460	45.2	128,243	51,577	40.2	25,270	17,883	70.8
1880									
All classes	36,761,607	6,239,958	17.0	18,735,980	2,966,421	15.8	18,025,627	3,273,537	18.2
White	32,160,400	3,019,080	9.4	16,425,250	1,410,805	8.6	15,735,150	1,608,275	10.2
Native	25,785,789	2,255,460	8.7	-------	-------	-------	-------	-------	-------
Foreign born	6,374,611	763,620	12.0	-------	-------	-------	-------	-------	-------
Negro and other races	4,601,207	3,220,878	70.0	2,310,730	1,555,616	67.3	2,290,477	1,665,262	72.7
1870									
All classes	28,228,945	5,658,144	20.0	14,258,866	2,603,888	18.3	13,970,079	3,054,256	21.9
White	24,717,870	2,851,911	11.5	12,526,487	1,250,970	10.0	12,191,383	1,600,941	13.1
Negro	3,428,757	2,780,689	81.4	1,664,656	1,342,347	80.6	1,764,101	1,447,342	82.0
Other races	82,318	16,544	20.1	67,723	10,571	15.6	14,595	5,973	40.9

[1] Mexicans classified separately for the first time in 1930; included for the most part with whites of foreign birth or parentage in 1920 and 1910.
[2] Figures for 1890 are exclusive of persons in Indian Territory and on Indian reservations, areas specially enumerated, but for which illiteracy statistics are not available.

1224

POPULATION

TABLE 5.—ILLITERACY IN THE POPULATION 21 YEARS OLD AND OVER, BY COLOR, NATIVITY, AND SEX, FOR THE UNITED STATES: 1900 TO 1930

CENSUS YEAR, COLOR, AND NATIVITY	TOTAL 21 YEARS OLD AND OVER			MALE			FEMALE		
	Total number	Illiterate		Total number	Illiterate		Total number	Illiterate	
		Number	Per cent		Number	Per cent		Number	Per cent
1930									
All classes	72,943,624	3,863,215	5.3	37,056,757	1,942,729	5.2	35,886,867	1,920,486	5.4
White	65,400,034	2,251,470	3.4	33,216,074	1,116,497	3.4	32,183,960	1,134,973	3.5
Native	52,762,391	954,968	1.8	26,418,580	545,849	2.1	26,343,811	409,119	1.6
Native parentage	38,116,766	855,318	2.2	19,257,937	492,322	2.6	18,858,829	362,996	1.9
Foreign or mixed parentage	14,645,625	99,650	0.7	7,160,643	53,527	0.7	7,484,982	46,123	0.6
Foreign born	12,637,643	1,296,502	10.3	6,797,494	570,648	8.4	5,840,149	725,854	12.4
Negro	6,531,939	1,306,650	20.0	3,235,441	672,234	20.8	3,296,498	634,416	19.2
Other races [1]	1,011,651	305,095	30.2	605,242	153,998	25.4	406,409	151,097	37.2
1920 [2]									
All classes	60,886,520	4,333,111	7.1	31,403,370	2,192,368	7.0	29,483,150	2,140,743	7.3
White	55,113,461	2,747,814	5.0	28,442,400	1,403,609	4.9	26,671,061	1,344,205	5.0
Native	42,614,741	1,040,669	2.4	21,513,948	563,546	2.6	21,100,793	477,123	2.3
Native parentage	31,007,257	938,311	3.0	15,805,063	509,343	3.2	15,202,194	428,968	2.8
Foreign or mixed parentage	11,607,484	102,358	0.9	5,708,885	54,203	0.9	5,898,599	48,155	0.8
Foreign born	12,498,720	1,707,145	13.7	6,928,452	840,063	12.1	5,570,268	867,082	15.6
Negro	5,522,475	1,512,987	27.4	2,792,006	748,229	26.8	2,730,469	764,758	28.0
Other races	250,584	72,310	28.9	168,964	40,530	24.0	81,620	31,780	38.9
1910 [2]									
All classes	51,554,905	4,570,017	8.9	26,999,151	2,273,603	8.4	24,555,754	2,296,414	9.4
White	46,416,750	2,739,838	5.9	24,357,514	1,406,364	5.8	22,059,236	1,333,474	6.0
Native	34,762,825	1,232,345	3.5	17,710,697	617,733	3.5	17,052,128	614,612	3.6
Native parentage	25,696,212	1,113,427	4.3	13,211,731	557,042	4.2	12,484,481	556,385	4.5
Foreign or mixed parentage	9,066,613	118,918	1.3	4,498,966	60,691	1.3	4,567,647	58,227	1.3
Foreign born	11,653,925	1,507,493	12.9	6,646,817	788,631	11.9	5,007,108	718,862	14.4
Negro	4,886,615	1,742,648	35.7	2,458,873	819,135	33.3	2,427,742	923,513	38.0
Other races	251,540	87,531	34.8	182,764	48,104	26.3	68,776	39,427	57.3
1900									
All classes	40,782,007	4,881,026	12.0	21,134,299	2,288,470	10.8	19,647,708	2,592,556	13.2
White	36,447,297	2,644,240	7.3	18,918,697	1,249,897	6.6	17,528,600	1,394,343	8.0
Native	27,478,882	1,455,083	5.3	14,014,427	687,581	4.9	13,464,455	767,502	5.7
Native parentage	20,607,766	1,318,529	6.4	10,569,743	618,606	5.9	10,038,023	699,923	7.0
Foreign or mixed parentage	6,871,116	136,554	2.0	3,444,684	68,975	2.0	3,426,432	67,579	2.0
Foreign born	8,968,415	1,189,157	13.3	4,904,270	562,316	11.5	4,064,145	626,841	15.4
Negro	4,119,152	2,131,028	51.7	2,060,302	976,610	47.4	2,058,850	1,154,418	56.1
Other races	215,558	105,758	49.1	155,300	61,963	39.9	60,258	43,795	72.7

[1] Includes Mexicans who were classified for the most part with whites of foreign birth or parentage in 1920 and 1910.
[2] Mexicans included with the white population in 1920 and 1910.

ILLITERACY

1225

TABLE 6.—ILLITERACY IN THE POPULATION 10 YEARS OLD AND OVER, BY COLOR, NATIVITY, SEX, AND AGE, FOR THE UNITED STATES: 1930

COLOR, NATIVITY, AND SEX	POPULATION 10 YEARS OLD AND OVER [1] Total number	Illiterate Number	Per cent	10 TO 14 YEARS Total number	Illiterate Number	Per cent	15 TO 19 YEARS Total number	Illiterate Number	Per cent	20 TO 24 YEARS Total number	Illiterate Number	Per cent	25 TO 34 YEARS Total number	Illiterate Number	Per cent
All classes	98,723,047	4,283,753	4.3	12,004,877	140,440	1.2	11,552,115	221,942	1.9	10,870,378	294,360	2.7	18,954,029	618,266	3.3
Male	49,949,798	2,198,293	4.4	6,068,777	82,030	1.4	5,757,825	140,632	2.4	5,336,815	173,019	3.2	9,421,966	323,919	3.4
Female	48,773,249	2,085,460	4.3	5,936,100	58,410	1.0	5,794,290	81,310	1.4	5,533,563	121,341	2.2	9,532,063	294,347	3.1
White	87,980,667	2,407,218	2.7	10,546,282	53,693	0.5	10,111,584	81,995	0.8	9,466,155	107,533	1.1	16,683,462	287,948	1.7
Male	44,554,124	1,214,025	2.7	5,339,968	32,060	0.6	5,063,975	53,337	1.1	4,666,016	64,571	1.4	8,306,136	144,057	1.7
Female	43,426,543	1,193,193	2.7	5,206,314	21,633	0.4	5,047,609	28,658	0.6	4,800,139	42,962	0.9	8,377,326	143,891	1.7
Native	74,763,739	1,103,134	1.5	10,398,546	53,323	0.5	9,786,954	77,337	0.8	8,804,103	89,993	1.0	14,415,626	159,068	1.1
Male	37,475,901	640,048	1.7	5,265,795	31,874	0.6	4,907,316	51,242	1.0	4,346,913	57,771	1.3	7,140,378	96,804	1.4
Female	37,287,838	463,086	1.2	5,132,751	21,449	0.4	4,879,638	26,095	0.5	4,457,250	32,222	0.7	7,275,248	62,264	0.9
Native parentage	53,876,411	986,469	1.8	7,528,352	47,636	0.6	6,932,503	68,100	1.0	6,355,507	79,204	1.2	10,425,785	141,276	1.4
Male	27,188,095	577,312	2.1	3,818,635	28,769	0.8	3,480,607	46,230	1.3	3,138,838	52,108	1.7	5,192,056	87,793	1.7
Female	26,688,316	409,157	1.5	3,709,717	18,867	0.5	3,451,896	21,870	0.6	3,216,669	27,180	0.8	5,233,729	53,483	1.0
Foreign or mixed par.	20,887,328	116,665	0.6	2,870,194	5,687	0.2	2,854,451	9,237	0.3	2,448,656	10,699	0.4	3,989,841	17,792	0.4
Male	10,287,806	62,736	0.6	1,447,160	3,105	0.2	1,426,700	5,012	0.4	1,208,075	5,663	0.5	1,948,322	9,011	0.5
Female	10,599,522	53,929	0.5	1,423,034	2,582	0.2	1,427,742	4,225	0.3	1,240,581	5,036	0.4	2,041,519	8,781	0.4
Foreign born	13,216,928	1,304,084	9.9	147,736	370	0.3	324,630	4,658	1.4	661,992	17,540	2.6	2,267,836	128,880	5.7
Male	7,078,223	573,977	8.1	74,173	186	0.3	156,659	2,095	1.3	319,103	6,800	2.1	1,165,758	47,253	4.1
Female	6,138,705	730,107	11.9	73,563	184	0.3	167,971	2,563	1.5	342,889	10,740	3.1	1,102,078	81,627	7.4
Negro	9,292,556	1,513,892	16.3	1,251,542	66,238	5.3	1,250,528	111,111	8.9	1,203,191	146,350	12.2	1,930,301	251,026	13.0
Male	4,564,690	801,949	17.6	623,228	39,766	6.4	595,646	72,986	12.3	553,622	87,580	15.8	917,389	140,221	15.3
Female	4,727,866	711,943	15.1	628,314	26,472	4.2	654,882	38,125	5.8	649,569	58,770	9.0	1,018,912	110,805	10.9
Other races	1,449,824	362,643	25.0	207,053	20,509	9.9	190,003	28,836	15.2	201,032	40,477	20.1	334,266	79,292	23.7
Male	830,984	182,319	21.9	105,581	10,204	9.7	98,204	14,300	14.6	117,177	20,808	17.8	198,441	39,641	20.0
Female	618,840	180,324	29.1	101,472	10,305	10.2	91,799	14,527	15.8	83,855	19,669	23.4	135,825	39,651	29.2

COLOR, NATIVITY, AND SEX	35 TO 44 YEARS Total number	Illiterate Number	Per cent	45 TO 54 YEARS Total number	Illiterate Number	Per cent	55 TO 64 YEARS Total number	Illiterate Number	Per cent	65 YEARS AND OVER Total number	Illiterate Number	Per cent	21 YEARS AND OVER [1] Total number	Illiterate Number	Per cent
All classes	17,198,840	887,955	5.2	13,018,083	864,439	6.6	8,896,898	606,811	7.2	6,633,805	642,966	9.7	72,943,624	3,863,215	5.3
Male	8,816,319	433,510	4.9	6,803,569	441,883	6.5	4,367,590	303,907	7.0	3,325,211	296,105	8.9	37,056,757	1,942,729	5.2
Female	8,382,521	454,445	5.4	6,214,514	422,556	6.8	4,029,308	302,904	7.5	3,308,594	346,861	10.5	35,886,867	1,920,486	5.4
White	15,382,127	551,464	3.6	11,732,045	534,738	4.6	7,770,100	382,047	4.9	6,211,583	404,534	6.5	65,400,034	2,251,470	3.4
Male	7,904,797	265,087	3.4	6,109,060	274,578	4.5	4,014,078	190,710	4.8	3,107,585	187,856	6.0	33,216,074	1,116,497	3.4
Female	7,477,330	286,377	3.8	5,622,985	260,160	4.6	3,756,022	191,337	5.1	3,103,998	216,678	7.0	32,183,960	1,134,973	3.5
Native	12,056,284	176,926	1.5	8,849,461	185,902	2.1	5,830,910	157,254	2.7	4,554,290	201,198	4.4	52,762,301	954,968	1.8
Male	6,050,248	102,750	1.7	4,504,694	108,750	2.4	2,975,830	88,384	3.0	2,248,238	101,325	4.5	26,418,580	545,849	2.1
Female	6,006,036	74,176	1.2	4,344,767	77,152	1.8	2,855,080	68,870	2.4	2,306,052	99,873	4.3	26,343,811	409,119	1.6
Native parentage	8,629,228	158,088	1.8	6,395,325	169,110	2.6	4,122,463	141,150	3.4	3,429,887	179,932	5.2	38,116,766	855,318	2.2
Male	4,370,087	92,736	2.1	3,300,414	98,944	3.0	2,143,908	79,267	3.7	1,711,900	90,440	5.3	19,257,937	492,322	2.6
Female	4,259,141	65,352	1.5	3,094,911	70,166	2.3	1,978,555	61,883	3.1	1,717,987	89,492	5.2	18,858,829	362,996	1.9
Foreign or mixed par.	3,427,056	18,838	0.5	2,454,136	16,792	0.7	1,708,447	16,104	0.9	1,124,403	21,266	1.9	14,645,625	99,650	0.7
Male	1,680,161	10,014	0.6	1,204,280	9,806	0.8	831,922	9,117	1.1	536,338	10,885	2.0	7,160,643	53,527	0.7
Female	1,746,895	8,824	0.5	1,249,856	6,986	0.6	876,525	6,987	0.8	588,065	10,381	1.8	7,484,982	46,123	0.6
Foreign born	3,325,843	374,538	11.3	2,882,584	348,836	12.1	1,939,190	224,793	11.6	1,657,293	203,336	12.3	12,637,643	1,296,502	10.3
Male	1,854,549	162,337	8.8	1,604,366	165,828	10.3	1,038,248	102,326	9.9	859,347	86,531	10.1	6,797,494	570,648	8.4
Female	1,471,294	212,201	14.4	1,278,218	183,008	14.3	900,942	122,467	13.6	797,946	116,805	14.6	5,840,149	725,854	12.4
Negro	1,578,323	264,541	16.8	1,134,655	274,642	24.2	551,566	189,929	34.4	372,719	207,506	55.7	6,531,939	1,306,650	20.0
Male	769,801	133,047	17.3	600,694	139,161	23.2	307,716	95,468	31.0	180,530	92,630	48.9	3,235,441	672,234	20.8
Female	808,522	131,494	16.3	533,961	135,481	25.4	243,850	94,461	38.7	183,189	114,876	62.7	3,296,498	634,416	19.2
Other races	238,390	71,950	30.2	151,383	55,053	36.4	75,232	34,835	46.3	49,503	30,926	62.5	1,011,651	305,095	30.2
Male	141,721	35,376	25.0	93,815	28,144	30.0	45,706	17,729	38.8	28,096	15,619	55.6	605,242	153,908	25.4
Female	96,669	36,574	37.8	57,508	26,909	46.7	29,526	17,106	57.9	21,407	15,307	71.5	406,409	151,097	37.2

[1] Includes persons of unknown age.

TABLE 7.—ILLITERACY IN THE POPULATION 10 YEARS OLD AND OVER, BY COLOR, NATIVITY, SEX, AND AGE, FOR THE UNITED STATES: 1900 TO 1930

[Some part of the decrease from 1920 to 1930 in the percentage illiterate, shown by whites of foreign birth or parentage, is doubtless due to the separate classification in 1930 of Mexicans who were included for the most part with these white classes in 1920 and 1910.]

COLOR, NATIVITY, AND AGE	TOTAL								MALE						FEMALE					
	Number illiterate				Per cent				Number illiterate			Per cent			Number illiterate			Per cent		
	1930	1920	1910	1900	1930	1920	1910	1900	1930	1920	1910	1930	1920	1910	1930	1920	1910	1930	1920	1910
All classes	4,283,753	4,931,905	5,516,163	6,180,069	4.3	6.0	7.7	10.7	2,198,293	2,540,209	2,814,950	4.4	6.0	7.6	2,085,460	2,391,696	2,701,213	4.3	5.9	7.8
10 to 14 years	140,440	246,360	370,136	577,649	1.2	2.3	4.1	7.1	82,030	141,576	211,763	1.4	2.6	4.6	58,410	104,784	158,373	1.0	2.0	3.5
15 to 19 years	221,942	283,316	448,414	576,978	1.9	3.0	4.9	7.6	140,632	171,489	262,770	2.4	3.7	5.8	81,310	111,827	185,644	1.4	2.4	4.1
20 to 24 years	294,360	392,853	622,073	644,273	2.7	4.2	6.9	8.8	173,019	203,773	343,450	3.2	4.5	7.5	121,341	189,080	278,623	2.2	4.0	6.2
25 to 34 years	618,266	961,200	1,102,384	1,103,478	3.3	5.6	7.3	9.1	323,919	486,217	597,657	3.4	5.6	7.6	294,347	474,983	504,727	3.1	5.6	7.0
35 to 44 years	887,955	988,961	940,510	1,033,591	5.2	7.0	8.1	11.2	433,510	509,107	466,287	4.9	6.9	7.6	454,445	479,854	474,223	5.4	7.1	8.6
45 to 54 years	864,433	857,776	829,153	943,607	6.6	8.2	9.9	14.7	441,883	453,950	389,608	6.5	8.0	8.7	422,550	403,826	439,545	6.8	8.3	11.3
55 to 64 years	606,811	594,573	607,754	642,257	7.2	9.1	12.0	16.0	303,907	292,511	283,076	7.0	8.4	10.6	302,904	302,062	324,678	7.5	9.8	13.6
65 and over	642,966	591,385	573,799	611,446	9.7	12.0	14.5	19.8	296,105	273,000	248,875	8.9	11.0	12.5	346,861	318,385	324,924	10.5	13.0	16.5
Unknown	6,580	15,481	21,940	46,790	7.0	10.4	13.0	23.3	3,288	8,586	11,464	6.3	9.2	10.0	3,292	6,895	10,476	7.8	12.4	19.2
White	2,407,218	3,006,312	3,184,633	3,200,746	2.7	4.0	5.0	6.2	1,214,025	1,551,529	1,602,505	2.7	4.1	5.0	1,193,193	1,454,783	1,582,128	2.7	4.0	4.9
10 to 14 years	53,693	100,643	144,675	240,580	0.5	1.1	1.8	3.5	32,060	57,150	82,569	0.6	1.2	2.1	21,633	43,493	62,106	0.4	0.9	1.6
15 to 19 years	81,995	125,495	226,432	255,707	0.8	1.5	2.8	3.9	53,337	74,455	132,616	1.1	1.8	3.3	28,658	51,040	93,816	0.6	1.2	2.4
20 to 24 years	107,533	207,649	367,669	292,468	1.1	2.5	4.6	4.0	64,571	103,958	211,861	1.4	2.6	5.2	42,962	103,691	155,808	0.9	2.5	4.0
25 to 34 years	287,948	660,706	702,962	583,293	1.7	4.3	5.2	5.4	144,057	336,106	403,285	1.7	4.3	5.7	143,891	324,600	299,677	1.7	4.3	4.7
35 to 44 years	551,464	662,629	569,403	569,819	3.6	5.2	5.4	6.0	265,087	355,103	303,719	3.4	5.3	5.5	286,377	307,526	265,684	3.8	5.1	5.4
45 to 54 years	534,738	518,918	477,080	501,571	4.6	5.5	6.3	8.7	274,578	279,937	232,165	4.5	5.5	5.7	260,160	238,981	244,915	4.6	5.4	6.9
55 to 64 years	382,047	370,421	344,877	362,297	4.9	6.1	7.4	9.9	190,710	181,988	155,476	4.8	5.7	6.4	191,337	188,433	189,401	5.1	6.6	8.6
65 and over	404,534	352,525	342,420	378,071	6.5	7.7	9.4	13.5	187,856	158,298	135,102	6.0	6.9	7.4	216,678	194,227	207,318	7.0	8.5	11.4
Unknown	3,266	7,326	9,115	16,040	4.2	5.9	6.8	11.7	1,769	4,534	5,712	4.2	5.8	6.1	1,497	2,792	3,403	4.3	6.2	8.5
Native white	1,103,134	1,242,572	1,534,272	1,913,611	1.5	2.0	3.0	4.6	640,048	684,707	796,055	1.7	2.2	3.1	463,086	557,865	738,217	1.2	1.8	2.9
10 to 14 years	53,323	85,856	131,991	223,208	0.5	0.9	1.7	3.4	31,874	49,650	76,359	0.6	1.1	2.0	21,449	36,206	55,632	0.4	0.8	1.5
15 to 19 years	77,337	97,013	140,323	196,393	0.8	1.2	1.9	3.3	51,242	60,731	85,510	1.0	1.6	2.3	26,095	36,282	54,813	0.5	0.9	1.5
20 to 24 years	89,993	98,938	148,541	185,966	1.0	1.4	2.3	3.4	57,771	57,040	84,586	1.3	1.6	2.6	32,222	41,898	63,955	0.7	1.1	1.9
25 to 34 years	159,068	190,913	247,774	307,899	1.1	1.5	2.4	3.6	96,804	108,587	136,583	1.4	1.8	2.6	62,264	82,326	111,191	0.9	1.3	2.2
35 to 44 years	176,926	201,739	235,489	314,959	1.5	2.1	3.0	5.1	102,750	112,982	120,488	1.7	2.3	3.0	74,176	88,757	115,001	1.2	1.9	3.0
45 to 54 years	185,902	202,196	248,900	292,643	2.1	2.9	4.5	7.1	108,750	113,275	122,110	2.4	3.1	4.2	77,152	88,921	126,790	1.8	2.6	4.8
55 to 64 years	157,254	177,515	197,955	187,727	2.7	4.0	6.0	7.7	88,384	92,008	95,273	3.0	4.0	5.5	68,870	85,507	102,682	2.4	4.0	6.5
65 and over	201,198	185,133	179,219	194,713	4.4	5.7	7.3	10.5	101,325	88,662	73,035	4.5	5.5	6.0	99,873	96,471	106,184	4.3	5.9	8.6
Unknown	2,133	3,269	4,080	10,103	3.2	3.2	3.8	8.4	1,148	1,772	2,111	3.1	2.7	2.8	985	1,497	1,969	3.2	3.9	5.9
Native parentage	986,469	1,109,875	1,378,884	1,734,764	1.8	2.5	3.7	5.7	577,312	614,612	715,926	2.1	2.7	3.8	409,157	495,263	662,958	1.5	2.3	3.7
10 to 14 years	47,636	71,845	117,973	205,735	0.6	1.1	2.2	4.4	28,769	42,349	69,087	0.8	1.3	2.6	18,867	29,496	48,886	0.5	0.9	1.9
15 to 19 years	68,100	83,303	121,878	175,505	1.0	1.5	2.4	4.1	46,230	53,406	75,394	1.3	1.9	3.0	21,870	29,897	46,484	0.6	1.1	1.8
20 to 24 years	79,294	86,669	130,991	166,884	1.2	1.7	2.8	4.4	52,108	50,891	75,193	1.7	2.0	3.2	27,186	35,778	55,798	0.8	1.4	2.4
25 to 34 years	141,276	168,484	220,797	272,557	1.4	1.9	3.0	4.6	87,793	97,189	121,983	1.7	2.2	3.2	53,483	71,295	98,814	1.0	1.6	2.7
35 to 44 years	158,088	182,269	210,694	280,246	1.8	2.6	3.8	6.4	92,736	102,180	107,355	2.1	2.9	3.8	65,352	80,089	103,339	1.5	2.4	3.9
45 to 54 years	169,110	183,398	224,421	266,889	2.6	3.7	5.6	8.0	98,944	102,506	109,758	3.0	3.9	5.2	70,166	80,892	114,663	2.3	3.5	6.0
55 to 64 years	141,150	160,362	181,363	174,089	3.4	4.9	6.7	8.0	79,267	82,986	87,500	3.7	4.9	6.1	61,883	77,376	93,863	3.1	5.0	7.3
65 and over	179,932	170,603	167,099	183,428	5.2	6.2	7.6	10.7	90,440	81,498	67,752	5.3	6.0	6.2	89,492	89,105	99,347	5.2	6.5	8.9
Unknown	1,883	2,942	3,668	9,431	3.3	3.2	3.8	8.4	1,025	1,607	1,904	3.2	2.7	2.8	858	1,335	1,764	3.3	4.0	6.1
For. or mixed par.	116,665	132,697	155,388	178,847	0.6	0.8	1.1	1.6	62,736	70,095	80,129	0.6	0.8	1.2	53,929	62,602	75,259	0.5	0.7	1.1
10 to 14 years	5,687	14,011	14,018	17,473	0.2	0.5	0.6	0.9	3,105	7,301	7,272	0.2	0.6	0.6	2,582	6,710	6,746	0.2	0.5	0.6
15 to 19 years	9,237	13,710	18,445	20,888	0.3	0.6	0.8	1.2	5,012	7,325	10,116	0.4	0.7	0.9	4,225	6,385	8,329	0.3	0.6	0.7
20 to 24 years	10,699	12,269	17,550	19,082	0.4	0.6	0.9	1.2	5,663	6,149	9,393	0.5	0.6	1.0	5,036	6,120	8,157	0.4	0.6	0.9
25 to 34 years	17,792	22,429	26,977	35,342	0.4	0.6	0.9	1.3	9,011	11,398	14,600	0.5	0.7	1.0	8,781	11,031	12,377	0.4	0.6	0.8
35 to 44 years	18,838	19,470	24,795	34,713	0.5	0.7	1.1	2.0	10,014	10,802	13,133	0.6	0.8	1.1	8,824	8,668	11,662	0.5	0.6	1.0
45 to 54 years	16,792	18,798	24,479	25,754	0.7	0.9	1.6	3.4	9,806	10,769	12,352	0.8	1.0	1.6	6,986	8,029	12,127	0.6	0.8	1.6
55 to 64 years	16,104	17,153	16,592	13,638	0.9	1.4	2.8	4.8	9,117	9,022	7,773	1.1	1.5	2.6	6,987	8,131	8,819	0.8	1.4	3.0
65 and over	21,266	14,530	12,120	11,285	1.9	2.8	4.7	8.0	10,885	7,164	5,283	2.0	2.8	4.1	10,381	7,366	6,837	1.8	2.8	5.4
Unknown	250	327	412	672	2.5	2.9	3.9	8.3	123	165	207	2.5	2.8	3.7	127	162	205	2.4	3.0	4.2
For.-born white	1,304,084	1,763,740	1,650,361	1,287,135	9.9	13.1	12.7	12.9	573,977	866,822	866,450	8.1	11.7	11.8	730,107	896,918	783,911	11.9	14.8	13.9
10 to 14 years	370	14,787	12,684	17,372	0.3	4.5	3.5	5.6	186	7,500	6,210	0.3	4.5	3.4	184	7,287	6,474	0.3	4.4	3.7
15 to 19 years	4,658	28,482	86,109	59,314	1.4	5.4	12.8	10.6	2,095	13,724	47,106	1.3	5.3	13.4	2,563	14,758	39,003	1.5	5.5	12.1
20 to 24 years	17,540	108,711	219,128	106,502	2.6	11.7	15.3	11.6	6,800	46,918	127,275	2.1	10.3	15.4	10,740	61,793	91,853	3.1	13.2	15.1
25 to 34 years	128,880	469,793	455,188	275,304	5.7	15.1	14.4	12.1	47,253	227,519	266,702	4.1	13.1	14.2	81,627	242,274	188,486	7.4	17.7	14.6
35 to 44 years	374,538	460,890	333,914	254,860	11.3	14.6	12.3	11.9	162,337	242,121	183,231	8.8	13.4	11.7	212,201	218,769	150,683	14.4	16.2	13.1
45 to 54 years	348,836	316,722	228,180	208,928	12.1	12.8	11.0	12.7	165,828	166,662	110,055	10.3	11.9	9.3	183,008	150,060	118,125	14.3	14.0	13.3
55 to 64 years	224,793	192,906	146,922	174,570	11.6	11.9	11.1	14.7	102,326	89,980	60,203	9.9	10.0	8.5	122,467	102,926	86,719	13.6	14.1	14.2
65 and over	203,336	167,392	163,201	183,358	12.3	12.6	13.8	19.3	86,531	69,636	62,067	10.1	10.2	10.2	116,805	97,756	101,134	14.6	15.1	17.5
Unknown	1,133	4,057	5,035	6,837	11.5	20.0	19.2	27.5	621	2,762	3,601	10.3	20.1	18.3	512	1,295	1,434	13.5	19.8	22.0
Negro	1,513,892	1,842,161	2,227,731	2,853,194	16.3	22.9	30.4	44.5	801,949	942,368	1,096,000	17.6	23.5	30.1	711,943	899,793	1,131,731	15.1	22.3	30.7
10 to 14 years	66,238	140,892	218,555	328,992	5.3	11.4	18.9	30.1	39,766	81,944	125,616	6.4	13.3	21.7	26,472	58,948	92,939	4.2	9.5	16.1
15 to 19 years	111,111	152,998	214,860	312,094	8.9	14.1	20.3	31.8	72,986	94,455	126,459	12.3	18.4	24.9	38,125	58,543	88,401	5.8	10.3	16.0
20 to 24 years	146,350	179,124	245,860	340,516	12.2	17.0	23.9	35.1	87,580	96,895	126,970	15.8	19.9	26.3	58,770	82,229	118,890	9.0	14.5	21.7
25 to 34 years	251,026	287,063	380,742	496,180	13.0	17.9	24.6	39.3	140,221	143,515	183,993	15.3	19.0	24.4	110,805	143,548	196,749	10.9	16.9	24.7
35 to 44 years	264,541	310,538	351,858	437,503	16.8	23.3	32.3	52.0	133,047	144,961	152,132	17.3	22.0	27.7	131,494	165,577	199,726	16.3	24.6	37.1
45 to 54 years	274,642	323,924	334,930	420,438	24.2	34.1	47.0	68.1	139,161	164,954	147,542	23.2	30.1	38.9	135,481	158,970	187,388	25.4	38.5	56.3
55 to 64 years	189,929	212,682	246,584	267,312	34.4	40.4	63.0	78.4	95,468	103,407	126,046	31.0	42.9	55.5	94,461	109,275	120,538	38.7	57.9	72.0
65 and over	207,506	227,310	219,255	223,124	55.7	68.3	74.5	85.4	92,630	108,473	107,877	48.9	62.4	70.7	114,876	118,837	111,378	62.7	74.8	78.6
Unknown	2,540	7,630	12,087	27,035	18.6	32.5	38.9	55.4	1,090	3,764	5,365	15.4	27.9	31.4	1,450	3,866	6,722	21.0	38.7	48.1
Other races [1]	362,643	83,432	103,799	126,129	25.0	25.6	31.6	44.5	182,319	46,312	56,445	21.9	22.1	25.0	180,324	37,120	47,354	29.1	31.8	46.2
10 to 14 years	20,509	4,825	6,906	8,077	9.9	13.8	20.6	27.8	10,204	2,482	3,578	9.7	13.9	20.4	10,305	2,343	3,328	10.2	13.8	20.9
15 to 19 years	28,836	4,823	7,122	9,177	15.2	14.5	20.5	29.7	14,309	2,579	3,695	14.6	13.9	18.3	14,527	2,244	3,427	15.8	15.3	23.5
20 to 24 years	40,477	6,080	8,544	11,289	20.1	16.5	21.5	36.7	20,868	2,920	4,619	17.8	13.7	17.0	19,609	3,160	3,925	23.4	20.3	31.2
25 to 34 years	79,292	13,431	18,680	24,005	23.7	19.3	23.8	42.9	39,641	6,596	10,379	20.0	15.5	18.0	39,651	6,835	8,301	29.2	25.2	40.1
35 to 44 years	71,950	15,794	19,249	26,269	30.2	24.0	33.9	45.8	35,376	9,043	10,436	25.0	19.0	24.8	36,574	6,751	8,813	37.8	37.1	60.0
45 to 54 years	55,053	14,934	17,143	21,598	36.4	35.1	41.2	53.4	28,144	9,059	9,901	30.0	28.5	31.0	26,909	5,875	7,242	46.7	55.0	74.4
55 to 64 years	34,835	11,470	13,293	12,648	46.3	46.9	54.4	63.9	17,729	7,116	7,554	38.8	38.9	42.9	17,106	4,354	5,739	57.9	70.5	83.7
65 and over	30,926	11,550	12,124	10,251	62.5	66.1	78.7	82.6	15,619	6,229	5,896	55.6	58.1	69.6	15,307	5,321	6,228	71.5	78.7	90.0
Unknown	765	525	738	2,815	25.8	34.2	19.5	41.9	429	288	387	19.1	27.7	11.9	336	237	351	46.7	48.1	65.5

[1] Mexicans, with a relatively high percentage of illiteracy (27.5 in 1930), are included with "Other races" in the figures for 1930 and with the white population in 1920 and 1910.

TABLE 8.—ILLITERACY IN THE URBAN, RURAL-FARM, AND RURAL-NONFARM POPULATION 10 YEARS OLD AND OVER, BY COLOR, NATIVITY, SEX, AND AGE, FOR THE UNITED STATES: 1930

AREA, SEX, AND AGE	ALL CLASSES			NATIVE WHITE—NATIVE PARENTAGE			NATIVE WHITE—FOREIGN OR MIXED PARENTAGE			FOREIGN-BORN WHITE			NEGRO			OTHER RACES		
	Total number	Illiterate: Number	Illiterate: Per cent	Total number	Illiterate: Number	Illiterate: Per cent	Total number	Illiterate: Number	Illiterate: Per cent	Total number	Illiterate: Number	Illiterate: Per cent	Total number	Illiterate: Number	Illiterate: Per cent	Total number	Illiterate: Number	Illiterate: Per cent
URBAN																		
Total, 10 and over	57,117,322	1,800,604	3.2	26,382,359	163,227	0.6	15,158,412	60,369	0.4	10,600,298	1,058,845	10.0	4,297,949	395,849	9.2	678,304	122,314	18.0
10 to 14 years	5,949,693	16,047	0.3	3,171,407	5,820	0.2	2,160,882	3,083	0.1	122,989	248	0.2	407,867	4,746	1.2	86,548	2,144	2.5
15 to 19 years	6,015,411	37,046	0.6	3,053,878	8,864	0.3	2,156,157	5,322	0.2	276,902	3,892	1.4	447,155	13,027	2.9	81,319	5,941	7.3
20 to 24 years	6,420,308	75,690	1.2	3,287,526	12,496	0.4	1,897,391	6,643	0.4	579,790	15,025	2.6	560,215	29,151	5.2	95,386	12,375	13.0
25 to 34 years	11,945,427	249,194	2.1	5,711,516	25,237	0.4	3,001,066	10,402	0.3	1,969,398	110,505	5.6	1,092,902	72,899	6.7	170,545	30,151	17.7
35 to 44 years	10,706,150	460,269	4.3	4,546,172	28,119	0.6	2,416,989	10,219	0.4	2,756,209	310,727	11.3	867,494	82,453	9.5	119,286	28,751	24.1
45 to 54 years	7,714,086	421,570	5.5	3,162,308	28,707	0.9	1,650,588	7,871	0.5	2,275,219	283,694	12.5	545,146	80,223	14.7	71,825	21,075	29.3
55 to 64 years	4,776,676	276,466	5.8	1,915,100	23,203	1.2	1,138,081	7,320	0.6	1,461,538	181,066	12.4	228,724	52,488	22.9	33,233	12,389	37.3
65 and over	3,523,535	260,971	7.4	1,495,520	30,100	2.0	720,309	9,319	1.3	1,150,231	152,836	13.3	130,108	59,555	42.8	18,361	9,161	49.9
Males, 10 and over	28,171,056	806,974	2.9	12,906,981	86,039	0.7	7,258,811	29,064	0.4	5,578,243	448,253	8.0	2,037,334	184,530	9.1	389,687	59,088	15.2
10 to 14 years	2,970,019	8,809	0.3	1,584,294	3,240	0.2	1,085,446	1,663	0.2	61,409	110	0.2	195,305	2,789	1.4	43,565	992	2.3
15 to 19 years	2,881,288	19,541	0.7	1,457,276	5,132	0.4	1,055,733	2,709	0.3	131,156	1,618	1.2	195,723	7,292	3.7	41,400	2,790	6.7
20 to 24 years	3,030,032	37,237	1.2	1,552,487	7,199	0.5	907,702	3,296	0.4	273,513	5,402	2.0	240,821	15,114	6.3	55,509	6,226	11.2
25 to 34 years	5,863,576	110,638	1.9	2,811,514	14,154	0.5	1,433,504	4,765	0.3	1,005,957	39,064	3.9	510,417	37,731	7.4	102,184	14,924	14.6
35 to 44 years	5,458,114	205,310	3.8	2,276,383	15,301	0.7	1,155,814	4,849	0.4	1,526,157	131,306	8.6	427,958	39,975	9.3	71,802	13,879	19.3
45 to 54 years	3,944,010	196,978	5.0	1,586,969	15,376	1.0	781,389	4,080	0.5	1,249,286	130,307	10.4	282,537	37,139	13.1	43,829	10,076	23.0
55 to 64 years	2,360,085	121,984	5.2	942,064	11,810	1.3	521,512	3,652	0.7	759,221	78,530	10.3	117,659	22,324	19.0	19,629	5,668	28.9
65 and over	1,627,928	104,928	6.4	674,581	13,503	2.0	314,090	3,956	1.3	566,734	61,473	10.8	62,241	21,670	34.8	10,282	4,326	42.1
Females, 10 and over	28,946,266	993,630	3.4	13,475,378	77,188	0.6	7,899,601	31,305	0.4	5,022,055	610,592	12.2	2,260,615	211,319	9.3	288,617	63,226	21.9
10 to 14 years	2,979,674	7,238	0.2	1,587,113	2,580	0.2	1,075,436	1,420	0.1	61,580	120	0.2	212,562	1,957	0.9	42,983	1,152	2.7
15 to 19 years	3,134,123	17,505	0.6	1,596,602	3,732	0.2	1,100,424	2,613	0.2	145,746	2,274	1.6	251,432	5,735	2.3	39,919	3,151	7.9
20 to 24 years	3,390,276	38,453	1.1	1,735,039	5,297	0.3	989,689	3,347	0.3	306,277	9,623	3.1	319,394	14,037	4.4	39,877	6,149	15.4
25 to 34 years	6,081,851	138,556	2.3	2,900,002	11,083	0.4	1,567,562	5,637	0.4	963,441	71,441	7.4	582,485	35,168	6.0	68,361	15,227	22.3
35 to 44 years	5,248,036	254,959	4.9	2,269,789	12,818	0.6	1,261,175	5,370	0.4	1,230,052	179,421	14.6	439,536	42,478	9.7	47,484	14,872	31.3
45 to 54 years	3,770,076	224,592	6.0	1,575,339	13,331	0.8	878,199	3,791	0.4	1,025,933	153,387	15.0	262,609	43,084	16.4	27,996	10,999	39.3
55 to 64 years	2,416,591	154,482	6.4	973,036	11,393	1.2	616,569	3,668	0.6	702,317	102,536	14.6	111,065	30,164	27.2	13,604	6,721	49.4
65 and over	1,895,607	156,043	8.2	820,945	16,597	2.0	406,219	5,363	1.3	583,497	91,363	15.7	76,867	37,885	49.3	8,079	4,835	59.8
Total, 21 and over	43,896,714	1,734,741	4.0	19,520,107	146,171	0.7	10,442,482	50,708	0.5	10,107,371	1,052,520	10.4	3,335,060	373,293	11.2	491,694	112,049	22.8
Male	21,747,237	772,592	3.6	9,576,541	76,377	0.8	4,928,830	24,068	0.5	5,343,427	445,687	8.3	1,603,675	172,093	10.7	294,764	54,367	18.4
Female	22,149,477	962,149	4.3	9,943,566	69,794	0.7	5,513,652	26,640	0.5	4,763,944	606,833	12.7	1,731,385	201,200	11.6	196,930	57,682	29.3
RURAL-FARM																		
Total, 10 and over	23,036,395	1,583,030	6.9	15,264,565	533,412	3.5	2,859,002	26,212	0.9	1,077,347	84,477	7.8	3,421,512	794,866	23.2	413,969	144,063	34.8
10 to 14 years	3,740,947	94,206	2.5	2,673,925	28,640	1.1	343,840	781	0.2	8,507	39	0.5	645,112	50,157	7.8	69,557	14,589	21.0
15 to 19 years	3,420,969	135,733	4.0	2,385,396	40,381	1.7	356,393	1,370	0.4	18,050	273	1.5	597,578	77,218	12.9	63,552	16,491	25.9
20 to 24 years	2,434,241	144,239	5.9	1,657,873	41,808	2.5	208,575	1,562	0.6	29,100	952	3.3	423,663	82,819	19.5	55,030	17,008	31.1
25 to 34 years	3,490,584	225,561	6.5	2,326,880	70,345	3.0	472,980	3,182	0.7	93,858	5,275	5.6	517,079	119,881	23.2	79,787	26,878	33.7
35 to 44 years	3,432,204	254,599	7.4	2,182,434	83,064	3.8	527,381	4,267	0.8	208,246	18,710	9.0	453,673	124,903	27.5	60,470	23,655	39.1
45 to 54 years	2,959,380	279,504	9.4	1,818,837	94,131	5.2	426,471	4,786	1.1	268,509	21,962	8.2	401,122	138,833	34.6	44,441	19,702	44.5
55 to 64 years	1,997,364	213,323	10.7	1,231,834	79,038	6.4	287,634	4,670	1.6	227,944	16,556	7.3	226,061	99,749	44.1	23,891	13,310	55.7
65 and over	1,551,937	234,665	15.1	981,991	95,630	9.7	174,899	5,578	3.2	222,749	20,660	9.3	155,543	100,747	64.8	16,755	12,044	71.9
Males, 10 and over	12,243,404	902,858	7.4	8,080,592	328,237	4.1	1,576,865	16,773	1.1	627,706	42,329	6.7	1,724,997	442,402	25.6	233,244	73,117	31.3
10 to 14 years	1,932,699	55,729	2.9	1,386,314	17,705	1.3	176,496	412	0.2	4,490	22	0.5	329,346	30,194	9.2	36,053	7,336	20.3
15 to 19 years	1,830,526	91,050	5.0	1,288,531	29,263	2.3	196,275	860	0.4	10,355	194	1.9	301,727	52,301	17.3	33,638	8,432	25.1
20 to 24 years	1,309,335	90,815	6.9	897,702	29,314	3.3	157,589	983	0.6	18,454	658	3.6	204,272	51,286	25.1	31,258	8,574	27.4
25 to 34 years	1,766,172	131,005	7.4	1,171,778	45,930	3.9	258,327	1,954	0.8	51,608	2,517	4.9	239,693	67,725	28.3	44,766	12,873	28.8
35 to 44 years	1,740,149	135,002	7.8	1,101,948	50,535	4.6	280,428	2,747	1.0	115,360	8,286	7.2	208,597	62,206	29.8	33,816	11,228	33.2
45 to 54 years	1,604,787	156,172	9.7	970,859	57,568	5.9	235,209	3,252	1.4	154,623	11,341	7.3	215,887	73,423	34.0	28,149	10,588	37.6
55 to 64 years	1,153,077	121,207	10.5	696,986	46,987	6.7	166,387	3,087	1.9	137,755	8,916	6.5	136,504	54,716	40.1	15,355	7,501	48.9
65 and over	901,587	121,260	13.4	563,276	50,653	9.0	105,585	3,468	3.3	134,793	10,367	7.7	88,014	50,288	57.1	9,919	6,484	65.4
Females, 10 and over	10,792,991	680,172	6.3	7,183,973	205,175	2.9	1,282,137	9,439	0.7	449,641	42,148	9.4	1,696,515	352,464	20.8	180,725	70,946	39.3
10 to 14 years	1,808,248	38,477	2.1	1,287,611	10,875	0.8	167,350	369	0.2	4,017	17	0.4	315,766	19,963	6.3	33,504	7,253	21.6
15 to 19 years	1,590,443	44,683	2.8	1,096,865	11,118	1.0	160,118	510	0.3	7,695	79	1.0	295,851	24,917	8.4	29,914	8,059	26.9
20 to 24 years	1,124,906	53,424	4.7	760,111	12,494	1.6	110,986	579	0.5	10,646	294	2.8	219,391	31,533	14.4	23,772	8,524	35.9
25 to 34 years	1,724,412	94,556	5.5	1,155,102	24,409	2.1	214,653	1,228	0.6	42,250	2,758	6.5	277,386	52,156	18.8	35,021	14,005	40.0
35 to 44 years	1,692,055	119,597	7.1	1,080,486	32,529	3.0	246,953	1,520	0.6	92,886	10,424	11.2	245,076	62,697	25.6	26,654	12,427	46.6
45 to 54 years	1,354,593	123,332	9.1	847,978	36,563	4.3	191,202	1,534	0.8	113,886	10,621	9.3	185,235	65,410	35.3	16,292	9,204	56.5
55 to 64 years	844,287	92,116	10.9	534,848	32,051	6.0	121,247	1,583	1.3	90,189	7,640	8.5	89,467	45,033	50.3	8,536	5,809	68.1
65 and over	650,350	113,405	17.4	418,715	44,977	10.7	69,314	2,110	3.0	87,956	10,299	11.7	67,529	50,459	74.7	6,836	5,560	81.3
Total, 21 and over	15,309,514	1,321,592	8.6	9,822,423	455,954	4.6	2,099,131	23,756	1.1	1,045,546	84,015	8.0	2,074,111	648,851	31.3	268,303	109,016	40.6
Male	8,179,893	737,103	9.0	5,197,422	275,335	5.3	1,169,331	15,328	1.3	609,552	42,004	6.9	1,046,839	349,027	33.3	156,749	55,409	35.3
Female	7,129,621	584,489	8.2	4,625,001	180,619	3.9	929,800	8,428	0.9	435,994	42,011	9.6	1,027,272	299,824	29.2	111,554	53,607	48.1
RURAL-NONFARM																		
Total, 10 and over	18,569,330	900,119	4.8	12,229,487	289,830	2.4	2,869,914	30,084	1.0	1,539,283	160,762	10.4	1,573,095	323,177	20.5	357,551	96,266	26.9
10 to 14 years	2,314,237	30,187	1.3	1,683,020	13,170	0.8	365,466	1,823	0.5	16,240	83	0.5	198,563	11,335	5.7	50,948	3,776	7.4
15 to 19 years	2,115,735	49,163	2.3	1,493,229	18,855	1.3	341,901	2,545	0.7	29,678	493	1.7	205,705	20,866	10.1	45,132	6,404	14.2
20 to 24 years	2,015,829	74,431	3.7	1,410,108	24,990	1.8	282,690	2,494	0.9	53,102	1,563	2.9	219,313	34,380	15.7	50,616	11,004	21.7
25 to 34 years	3,518,018	143,511	4.1	2,387,389	45,694	1.9	515,705	4,208	0.8	204,580	13,100	6.4	326,320	58,246	17.8	83,934	22,263	26.5
35 to 44 years	3,060,486	173,087	5.7	1,900,622	46,905	2.5	482,686	4,352	0.9	361,388	45,101	12.5	257,156	57,185	22.2	58,634	19,544	33.3
45 to 54 years	2,344,617	163,359	7.0	1,414,180	46,272	3.3	368,077	4,135	1.1	338,850	43,180	12.7	188,387	55,586	29.5	35,117	14,186	40.4
55 to 64 years	1,622,858	117,022	7.2	975,529	38,909	4.0	282,732	4,114	1.5	249,708	27,171	10.9	96,781	37,692	38.9	18,108	9,136	50.5
65 and over	1,558,333	147,330	9.5	952,370	54,202	5.7	229,195	6,369	2.8	284,313	29,834	10.5	78,068	47,204	60.5	14,387	9,721	67.6
Males, 10 and over	9,535,338	488,461	5.1	6,200,522	163,036	2.6	1,452,130	16,899	1.2	872,274	83,395	9.6	802,359	175,017	21.8	208,053	50,114	24.1
10 to 14 years	1,166,059	17,492	1.5	848,027	7,758	0.9	185,218	1,030	0.6	8,274	45	0.5	98,577	6,783	6.9	25,963	1,876	7.2
15 to 19 years	1,046,011	30,041	2.9	734,800	11,835	1.6	174,701	1,443	0.8	15,148	283	1.9	98,196	13,393	13.6	23,166	3,087	13.3
20 to 24 years	997,448	44,967	4.5	688,589	15,595	2.3	142,784	1,384	1.0	27,136	740	2.7	108,529	21,180	19.5	30,410	6,068	20.0
25 to 34 years	1,792,218	82,276	4.6	1,208,764	27,703	2.3	256,491	2,292	0.9	108,193	5,672	5.2	167,279	34,765	20.8	51,491	11,844	23.0
35 to 44 years	1,618,056	93,198	5.8	991,756	26,900	2.7	243,919	2,418	1.0	213,032	22,745	10.7	133,246	30,866	23.2	36,103	10,269	28.4
45 to 54 years	1,254,772	88,733	7.1	742,586	26,000	3.5	187,622	2,474	1.3	200,457	24,180	12.1	102,270	28,599	28.0	21,837	7,480	34.3
55 to 64 years	854,338	60,716	7.1	504,858	20,470	4.1	144,023	2,378	1.7	141,272	14,880	10.5	53,463	18,428	34.5	10,722	4,560	42.5
65 and over	795,696	69,017	8.8	474,043	26,284	5.5	116,663	3,461	3.0	157,820	14,691	9.3	39,275	20,672	52.6	7,895	4,809	60.9
Females, 10 and over	9,033,992	411,658	4.6	6,028,965	126,794	2.1	1,417,784	13,185	0.9	667,009	77,307	11.6	770,736	148,160	19.2	149,498	46,152	30.9
10 to 14 years	1,148,178	12,695	1.1	834,993	5,412	0.6	180,248	793	0.4	7,966	38	0.5	99,986	4,552	4.6	24,985	1,900	7.6
15 to 19 years	1,069,724	19,122	1.8	758,429	7,020	0.9	167,200	1,102	0.7	14,530	210	1.4	107,599	7,473	6.9	21,966	3,317	15.1
20 to 24 years	1,018,381	29,464	2.9	721,519	9,395	1.3	139,900	1,110	0.8	25,966	823	3.2	110,784	13,200	11.9	20,206	4,936	24.4
25 to 34 years	1,725,800	61,235	3.5	1,178,625	17,991	1.5	259,304	1,916	0.7	96,387	7,428	7.7	159,041	23,481	14.8	32,443	10,419	32.1
35 to 44 years	1,442,430	79,889	5.5	908,866	20,005	2.2	238,767	1,934	0.8	148,356	22,356	15.1	123,910	26,319	21.2	22,531	9,275	41.2
45 to 54 years	1,089,845	74,626	6.8	671,594	20,272	3.0	180,455	1,661	0.9	138,399	19,000	13.7	86,117	26,987	31.3	13,280	6,706	50.5
55 to 64 years	768,520	56,306	7.3	470,671	18,439	3.9	138,709	1,736	1.3	108,436	12,291	11.3	43,318	19,264	44.5	7,386	4,576	62.0
65 and over	762,637	77,413	10.2	478,327	27,918	5.8	112,532	2,908	2.6	126,493	15,143	12.0	38,793	26,532	68.4	6,492	4,912	75.7
Total, 21 and over	13,737,396	806,882	5.9	8,774,236	253,193	2.9	2,104,012	25,186	1.2	1,484,726	159,967	10.8	1,122,768	284,506	25.3	251,654	84,030	33.4
Male	7,129,627	433,034	6.1	4,483,974	140,610	3.1	1,062,482	14,131	1.3	844,515	82,957	9.8	584,927	151,114	25.8	153,729	44,222	28.8
Female	6,607,769	373,848	5.7	4,290,262	112,583	2.6	1,041,530	11,055	1.1	640,211	77,010	12.0	537,841	133,392	24.8	97,925	39,808	40.7

1228

POPULATION

TABLE 9.—ILLITERACY IN THE POPULATION OF MINOR RACES, 10 YEARS OLD AND OVER AND 21 YEARS OLD AND OVER, FOR THE UNITED STATES, URBAN AND RURAL: 1930

[Per cent not shown where base is less than 100]

AREA AND RACE	10 YEARS OLD AND OVER									21 YEARS OLD AND OVER								
	Total			Male			Female			Total			Male			Female		
	Total number	Illiterate Number	Per cent	Total number	Number	Per cent	Total number	Number	Per cent	Total number	Illiterate Number	Per cent	Total number	Number	Per cent	Total number	Illiterate Number	Per cent
Total	1,449,824	362,643	25.0	830,984	182,319	21.9	618,840	180,324	29.1	1,011,651	305,095	30.2	605,242	153,998	25.4	406,409	151,097	37.2
Mexican	1,002,241	275,470	27.5	547,863	134,234	24.5	454,378	141,236	31.1	687,440	228,370	33.2	389,595	111,334	28.6	297,845	117,036	39.3
Native	412,146	89,853	21.8	212,699	42,627	20.0	199,447	47,226	23.7	195,858	57,956	29.6	104,648	26,948	25.8	91,210	31,008	34.0
Foreign born	590,095	185,617	31.5	335,164	91,607	27.3	254,931	94,010	36.9	491,582	170,414	34.7	284,947	84,386	20.6	206,635	86,028	41.6
Indian	238,981	61,517	25.7	123,469	29,630	24.0	115,512	31,887	27.6	156,572	51,807	33.1	81,958	24,894	30.4	74,614	27,003	36.2
Chinese	63,392	12,912	20.4	53,650	10,735	20.0	9,742	2,177	22.3	53,887	12,573	23.3	47,182	10,441	22.1	6,705	2,132	31.8
Japanese	97,273	8,932	9.2	60,580	4,231	7.0	36,693	4,701	12.8	73,310	8,785	12.0	47,858	4,161	8.7	25,452	4,624	18.2
Filipino	42,964	2,834	6.6	41,128	2,589	6.3	1,836	245	13.3	35,978	2,498	6.9	34,623	2,272	6.6	1,355	226	16.7
Hindu	2,833	753	26.6	2,697	741	27.5	136	12	8.8	2,740	750	27.4	2,644	738	27.9	96	12	-----
Korean	1,446	184	12.7	1,029	120	11.7	417	64	15.3	1,130	181	16.0	877	119	13.6	253	62	24.5
All other	694	41	5.9	568	39	6.9	126	2	1.6	594	41	6.9	505	39	7.7	89	2	-----
Urban	678,304	122,314	18.0	389,687	59,088	15.2	288,617	63,226	21.9	491,694	112,049	22.8	294,764	54,367	18.4	196,930	57,682	29.3
Mexican	517,815	105,607	20.4	272,979	47,225	17.3	244,836	58,382	23.8	363,572	95,874	26.4	197,155	42,915	21.8	166,417	52,959	31.8
Native	182,726	21,699	11.9	91,471	9,207	10.1	91,255	12,492	13.7	84,460	16,532	19.6	43,576	6,938	15.9	40,884	9,594	23.5
Foreign born	335,089	83,908	25.0	181,508	38,018	20.9	153,581	45,890	29.9	279,112	79,342	28.4	153,579	35,977	23.4	125,533	43,365	34.5
Indian	24,952	1,157	4.6	12,213	541	4.4	12,739	616	4.8	17,037	1,084	6.4	8,554	504	5.9	8,483	580	6.8
Chinese	55,472	10,681	19.3	46,669	8,795	18.8	8,803	1,886	21.4	47,013	10,880	22.1	40,939	8,538	20.9	6,074	1,851	30.5
Japanese	54,458	3,770	6.9	33,972	1,599	4.7	20,486	2,171	10.6	42,357	3,697	8.7	27,653	1,563	5.7	14,704	2,134	14.5
Filipino	22,820	764	3.3	21,563	638	3.0	1,257	126	10.0	19,298	675	3.5	18,371	560	3.0	927	115	12.4
Hindu	1,205	205	17.0	1,106	199	18.0	99	6	-----	1,151	203	17.6	1,076	197	18.3	75	6	-----
Korean	1,000	92	9.2	698	54	7.7	302	38	12.6	776	89	11.5	589	53	9.0	187	36	19.3
All other	582	38	6.5	487	37	7.6	95	1	-----	490	38	7.8	427	37	8.7	63	1	-----
Rural	771,520	240,329	31.2	441,297	123,231	27.9	330,223	117,098	35.5	519,957	193,046	37.1	310,478	99,631	32.1	209,479	93,415	44.6
Mexican	484,426	169,863	35.1	274,884	87,009	31.7	209,542	82,854	39.5	323,868	132,496	40.9	192,440	68,419	35.6	131,428	64,077	48.8
Native	229,420	68,154	29.7	121,228	33,420	27.6	108,192	34,734	32.1	111,398	41,424	37.2	61,072	20,010	32.8	50,326	21,414	42.6
Foreign born	255,006	101,709	39.9	153,656	53,580	34.9	101,350	48,120	47.5	212,470	91,072	42.9	131,368	48,409	36.8	81,102	42,663	52.6
Indian	214,029	60,360	28.2	111,256	29,089	26.1	102,773	31,271	30.4	139,535	50,813	36.4	73,404	24,390	33.2	66,131	26,423	40.0
Chinese	7,920	2,231	28.2	6,981	1,940	27.8	939	291	31.0	6,874	2,184	31.8	6,243	1,903	30.5	631	281	44.5
Japanese	42,815	5,162	12.1	26,608	2,632	9.9	16,207	2,530	15.6	30,953	5,088	16.4	20,205	2,598	12.9	10,748	2,490	23.2
Filipino	20,144	2,070	10.3	19,565	1,951	10.0	579	119	20.6	16,680	1,823	10.9	16,252	1,712	10.5	428	111	25.9
Hindu	1,628	548	33.7	1,591	542	34.1	37	6	-----	1,589	547	34.4	1,568	541	34.5	21	6	-----
Korean	446	92	20.6	331	66	19.9	115	26	22.6	354	92	26.0	288	66	22.9	66	26	-----
All other	112	3	2.7	81	2	-----	31	1	-----	104	3	2.9	78	2	-----	26	1	-----

ILLITERACY

1229

TABLE 10.—ILLITERACY IN THE POPULATION 10 YEARS OLD AND OVER, BY COLOR AND NATIVITY, BY DIVISIONS AND STATES: 1930

DIVISION AND STATE	ALL CLASSES, 10 YEARS OLD AND OVER			NATIVE WHITE—NATIVE PARENTAGE			NATIVE WHITE—FOREIGN OR MIXED PARENTAGE			FOREIGN-BORN WHITE			NEGRO		
	Total number	Illiterate Number	Per cent	Total number	Illiterate Number	Per cent	Total number	Illiterate Number	Per cent	Total number	Illiterate Number	Per cent	Total number	Illiterate Number	Per cent
United States	98,723,047	4,283,753	4.3	53,876,411	986,469	1.8	20,887,328	116,665	0.6	13,216,928	1,304,084	9.9	9,292,556	1,513,892	16.3
GEOGRAPHIC DIVISIONS:															
New England	6,707,717	245,270	3.7	2,426,051	14,080	0.6	2,388,014	16,049	0.7	1,811,951	210,046	11.6	75,710	4,187	5.5
Middle Atlantic	21,575,741	757,228	3.5	8,882,572	52,050	0.6	6,588,731	30,693	0.5	5,206,049	636,470	12.2	867,875	32,223	3.7
East North Central	20,674,201	442,064	2.1	11,127,295	79,697	0.7	5,523,505	30,587	0.6	3,183,971	281,645	8.8	771,626	36,454	4.7
West North Central	10,764,533	156,068	1.4	6,443,049	53,276	0.8	2,923,444	15,562	0.5	1,054,651	51,982	4.9	278,865	21,170	7.6
South Atlantic	12,171,045	1,012,523	8.3	7,070,015	310,381	3.9	520,335	4,202	0.8	301,423	31,328	10.4	3,363,864	662,055	19.7
East South Central	7,500,382	727,861	9.6	5,270,886	268,052	5.1	176,022	2,078	1.2	57,287	4,238	7.4	2,052,951	452,082	22.0
West South Central	9,436,457	675,791	7.2	6,412,454	172,286	2.7	514,513	10,181	2.0	160,236	15,958	9.4	1,777,935	302,280	17.0
Mountain	2,900,044	120,866	4.2	1,727,104	26,730	1.5	612,674	2,316	0.4	285,935	15,962	5.6	25,092	1,070	4.1
Pacific	6,922,427	146,082	2.1	3,016,985	9,917	0.3	1,640,090	4,997	0.3	1,146,425	56,446	4.9	77,729	2,371	3.1
NEW ENGLAND:															
Maine	642,659	17,172	2.7	405,763	5,745	1.4	130,817	2,872	2.1	98,310	8,393	8.5	900	43	4.8
New Hampshire	382,400	10,231	2.7	188,364	1,155	0.6	111,717	1,211	1.1	81,496	7,820	9.6	607	27	3.9
Vermont	291,614	6,299	2.2	184,029	1,921	1.0	65,382	1,340	2.0	41,695	3,005	7.2	445	22	4.9
Massachusetts	3,509,317	124,158	3.5	1,081,327	3,247	0.3	1,330,077	6,405	0.5	1,042,880	111,508	10.7	42,356	2,303	5.4
Rhode Island	560,253	27,536	4.9	155,058	741	0.5	227,909	1,991	0.9	168,975	24,124	14.3	7,836	635	8.1
Connecticut	1,321,474	59,874	4.5	411,510	1,271	0.3	567,112	2,230	0.4	378,580	55,136	14.6	23,485	1,157	4.9
MIDDLE ATLANTIC:															
New York	10,513,933	388,883	3.7	3,487,903	19,712	0.6	3,506,583	14,942	0.4	3,150,593	341,345	10.8	347,381	8,604	2.5
New Jersey	3,330,748	128,022	3.8	1,215,349	6,336	0.5	1,109,003	5,236	0.5	833,727	107,102	12.9	160,214	8,711	5.1
Pennsylvania	7,731,060	240,323	3.1	4,179,320	26,002	0.6	1,972,545	10,515	0.5	1,221,729	187,942	15.4	351,280	14,908	4.2
EAST NORTH CENTRAL:															
Ohio	5,434,261	123,804	2.3	3,409,567	26,588	0.8	1,120,731	5,799	0.5	637,535	74,131	11.6	252,500	16,213	6.4
Indiana	2,638,556	43,721	1.7	2,074,526	19,074	1.0	320,041	2,530	0.8	133,889	13,536	10.1	92,873	5,605	6.0
Illinois	6,333,046	153,507	2.4	2,894,330	20,559	0.7	1,027,218	7,725	0.4	1,206,806	108,084	10.0	277,834	10,044	3.6
Michigan	3,891,914	76,800	2.0	1,749,814	8,102	0.5	1,103,116	6,088	0.6	822,302	55,034	6.7	139,490	4,201	3.0
Wisconsin	2,376,424	44,232	1.9	999,058	4,474	0.4	974,399	7,830	0.8	383,340	20,900	7.8	8,929	391	4.4
WEST NORTH CENTRAL:															
Minnesota	2,076,201	26,302	1.3	749,956	2,489	0.3	920,427	4,755	0.5	386,654	16,759	4.3	8,155	160	2.0
Iowa	2,007,609	15,870	0.8	1,287,834	5,805	0.5	536,041	2,372	0.4	165,045	5,932	3.6	14,420	777	5.4
Missouri	2,984,368	67,905	2.3	2,207,328	35,824	1.6	435,029	3,428	0.8	148,460	11,183	7.5	188,664	16,532	8.8
North Dakota	527,000	7,814	1.5	162,873	477	0.3	252,612	1,286	0.5	104,703	4,049	4.4	326	11	3.4
South Dakota	543,564	6,763	1.2	260,453	706	0.3	200,633	933	0.5	65,422	2,422	3.7	546	12	2.2
Nebraska	1,106,139	12,725	1.2	644,021	2,362	0.4	328,392	1,400	0.4	114,896	6,924	6.0	11,605	450	3.9
Kansas	1,519,562	18,080	1.2	1,130,584	5,613	0.5	249,410	1,388	0.6	69,471	4,113	5.9	55,143	3,228	5.9
SOUTH ATLANTIC:															
Delaware	196,776	7,805	4.0	126,685	1,775	1.4	26,686	121	0.5	16,701	2,392	14.3	26,567	3,496	13.2
Maryland	1,324,241	49,910	3.8	823,262	11,561	1.4	185,935	1,641	0.9	94,302	11,539	12.2	219,800	25,073	11.4
District of Columbia	418,941	6,611	1.6	223,849	439	0.2	53,445	94	0.2	29,650	1,411	4.8	111,224	4,591	4.1
Virginia	1,872,838	162,588	8.7	1,308,282	65,114	5.0	45,514	368	0.8	23,017	1,738	7.4	494,429	95,148	19.2
West Virginia	1,301,752	62,492	4.8	1,088,214	41,657	3.8	72,313	819	1.1	51,007	9,788	19.2	89,921	10,173	11.3
North Carolina	2,352,014	236,261	10.0	1,644,224	93,205	5.7	14,028	167	1.2	8,663	450	5.2	673,800	139,105	20.6
South Carolina	1,292,939	192,878	14.9	694,683	36,148	5.2	11,188	103	0.9	5,239	207	5.7	581,085	156,065	26.9
Georgia	2,238,192	210,736	9.4	1,376,840	46,707	3.4	26,100	191	0.7	13,822	554	4.0	821,083	163,237	19.9
Florida	1,174,252	83,242	7.1	683,976	13,780	2.0	85,117	698	0.8	58,263	3,159	5.4	345,937	65,167	18.8
EAST SOUTH CENTRAL:															
Kentucky	2,005,492	131,545	6.6	1,707,149	100,763	5.9	90,846	932	1.0	21,722	1,267	5.8	185,629	28,553	15.4
Tennessee	2,028,100	145,460	7.2	1,597,782	87,025	5.4	34,174	381	1.1	12,945	754	5.8	382,974	57,251	14.9
Alabama	2,000,653	251,095	12.6	1,232,304	60,512	4.9	32,974	447	1.4	15,615	1,335	8.5	719,290	188,673	26.2
Mississippi	1,526,128	199,761	13.1	733,651	19,752	2.7	18,028	318	1.8	7,005	882	12.6	765,058	177,605	23.2
WEST SOUTH CENTRAL:															
Arkansas	1,419,945	96,818	6.8	1,003,629	35,280	3.5	32,092	610	1.9	10,118	666	6.6	373,273	60,102	16.1
Louisiana	1,622,808	219,750	13.5	887,914	69,288	7.8	96,876	2,615	2.7	34,712	6,677	19.2	598,258	139,393	23.3
Oklahoma	1,845,657	51,102	2.8	1,519,969	26,941	1.8	93,072	855	0.9	26,642	1,479	5.6	135,500	12,560	9.3
Texas	4,547,987	308,121	6.8	3,000,942	40,777	1.4	292,473	6,101	2.1	97,764	7,136	7.3	671,335	90,225	13.4
MOUNTAIN:															
Montana	434,351	7,303	1.7	211,971	536	0.3	134,993	396	0.3	72,405	3,085	4.3	1,128	52	4.6
Idaho	349,148	3,743	1.1	236,823	873	0.4	76,389	278	0.4	30,188	1,198	4.0	599	25	4.2
Wyoming	178,973	2,895	1.6	112,565	283	0.3	38,382	98	0.3	19,536	811	4.2	1,118	47	4.2
Colorado	835,341	23,141	2.8	520,669	5,095	1.0	177,009	712	0.4	85,092	7,331	8.6	10,280	403	3.9
New Mexico	314,370	41,845	13.3	225,095	18,468	8.2	17,540	265	1.5	7,755	530	6.8	2,328	140	6.0
Arizona	335,029	33,960	10.1	164,848	785	0.5	33,009	175	0.5	15,410	551	3.6	9,125	366	4.0
Utah	386,347	4,640	1.2	217,325	608	0.3	116,954	344	0.3	43,348	1,547	3.6	942	30	3.2
Nevada	76,085	3,330	4.4	37,808	82	0.2	18,398	48	0.3	12,201	909	7.5	472	7	1.5
PACIFIC:															
Washington	1,312,529	13,458	1.0	693,200	2,020	0.3	345,929	1,011	0.3	240,846	7,108	2.9	5,992	174	2.9
Oregon	803,408	7,814	1.0	508,895	1,505	0.3	176,999	538	0.3	104,276	3,743	3.6	2,600	49	2.5
California	4,806,490	124,810	2.6	2,414,890	6,392	0.3	1,117,162	3,448	0.3	801,303	45,600	5.7	69,737	2,148	3.1

1230

POPULATION

TABLE 11.—ILLITERACY IN THE POPULATION 21 YEARS OLD AND OVER, BY COLOR AND NATIVITY, BY DIVISIONS AND STATES: 1930

DIVISION AND STATE	ALL CLASSES, 21 YEARS OLD AND OVER			NATIVE WHITE—NATIVE PARENTAGE			NATIVE WHITE—FOREIGN OR MIXED PARENTAGE			FOREIGN-BORN WHITE			NEGRO		
	Total number	Illiterate Number	Per cent	Total number	Illiterate Number	Per cent	Total number	Illiterate Number	Per cent	Total number	Illiterate Number	Per cent	Total number	Illiterate Number	Per cent
United States	72,943,624	3,863,215	5.3	38,116,766	855,318	2.2	14,645,625	99,650	0.7	12,637,643	1,296,502	10.3	6,531,939	1,306,650	20.0
GEOGRAPHIC DIVISIONS:															
New England	5,095,074	239,810	4.7	1,802,649	12,146	0.7	1,506,908	13,634	0.9	1,721,714	209,046	12.1	58,770	4,104	7.0
Middle Atlantic	16,311,742	738,166	4.5	6,496,649	45,486	0.7	4,131,762	23,978	0.6	4,960,316	632,172	12.7	696,317	30,948	4.4
East North Central	15,685,265	428,457	2.7	7,931,955	72,273	0.9	4,020,715	27,282	0.7	3,047,877	280,308	9.2	621,236	35,075	5.7
West North Central	8,000,433	146,207	1.8	4,390,768	47,065	1.1	2,311,444	13,990	0.6	1,031,527	51,760	5.0	221,775	20,325	9.2
South Atlantic	8,415,339	859,341	10.2	5,527,515	208,476	4.9	377,996	3,710	1.0	289,259	31,148	10.8	2,210,041	552,521	25.0
East South Central	5,220,526	628,891	12.0	3,611,664	220,226	6.3	148,981	1,941	1.3	55,577	4,220	7.6	1,402,055	392,519	28.0
West South Central	6,611,094	574,632	8.7	4,428,219	146,284	3.3	413,124	9,031	2.2	164,630	15,867	9.6	1,235,976	267,218	21.6
Mountain	2,108,221	107,404	5.1	1,176,650	24,028	2.0	459,557	1,962	0.4	276,304	15,869	5.7	21,431	1,019	4.8
Pacific	5,495,930	140,217	2.6	2,750,697	8,384	0.3	1,266,138	4,113	0.3	1,090,349	56,112	5.1	64,338	2,321	3.6
NEW ENGLAND:															
Maine	487,125	16,092	3.3	305,668	4,978	1.6	89,222	2,646	3.0	90,891	8,316	9.1	713	40	5.6
New Hampshire	294,055	9,928	3.4	143,751	1,016	0.7	72,671	1,080	1.5	76,960	7,782	10.1	566	24	4.2
Vermont	220,428	6,013	2.7	135,869	1,741	1.3	46,802	1,278	2.7	37,387	2,904	7.9	319	19	6.0
Massachusetts	2,686,487	121,925	4.5	799,584	2,697	0.3	856,456	5,173	0.6	994,411	111,174	11.2	32,898	2,263	6.9
Rhode Island	421,197	26,989	6.4	111,803	625	0.6	142,588	1,702	1.2	160,448	23,993	15.0	5,952	626	10.5
Connecticut	985,782	58,863	6.0	305,974	1,089	0.4	299,100	1,746	0.6	361,608	54,817	15.2	18,322	1,132	6.2
MIDDLE ATLANTIC:															
New York	8,142,851	379,180	4.7	2,590,409	16,770	0.6	2,256,655	11,629	0.5	2,990,101	338,529	11.3	287,066	8,113	2.8
New Jersey	2,512,112	124,932	5.0	892,354	5,652	0.6	688,766	3,919	0.6	796,522	106,464	13.4	131,896	8,369	6.3
Pennsylvania	5,656,779	234,054	4.1	3,013,886	23,064	0.8	1,186,341	8,430	0.7	1,173,693	187,179	15.9	277,355	14,466	5.2
EAST NORTH CENTRAL:															
Ohio	4,132,251	119,732	2.9	2,508,593	24,160	1.0	800,635	4,907	0.6	610,549	73,789	12.1	199,291	15,857	8.0
Indiana	2,003,019	42,047	2.1	1,530,279	18,663	1.2	262,895	2,421	0.9	129,034	13,475	10.4	73,642	5,504	7.5
Illinois	4,841,768	149,504	3.1	2,052,821	18,871	0.9	1,377,258	6,600	0.5	1,162,700	108,418	9.3	226,602	9,818	4.3
Michigan	2,939,409	74,573	2.5	1,230,274	7,048	0.6	808,846	6,023	0.7	772,426	54,776	7.1	114,346	4,118	3.6
Wisconsin	1,768,818	42,601	2.4	609,988	3,531	0.6	771,081	7,331	1.0	373,168	29,850	8.0	7,265	383	5.3
WEST NORTH CENTRAL:															
Minnesota	1,537,983	24,971	1.6	443,190	1,923	0.4	702,263	4,206	0.6	378,450	16,702	4.4	6,805	158	2.3
Iowa	1,506,129	14,790	1.0	870,401	5,014	0.6	451,209	2,206	0.5	161,712	5,886	3.6	11,330	757	6.7
Missouri	2,269,657	63,575	2.8	1,599,699	32,504	2.0	371,677	3,283	0.9	144,076	11,183	7.7	150,457	15,763	10.5
North Dakota	358,182	7,160	2.0	88,418	303	0.3	162,953	966	0.6	102,308	4,629	4.5	278	10	3.6
South Dakota	385,808	6,316	1.6	157,113	513	0.3	162,903	817	0.5	64,174	2,413	3.8	420	12	2.0
Nebraska	812,450	11,996	1.5	424,077	1,948	0.5	261,382	1,222	0.5	112,444	6,804	6.1	9,521	442	4.6
Kansas	1,130,224	17,489	1.5	798,870	4,860	0.6	200,057	1,290	0.6	68,363	4,103	6.0	42,964	3,183	7.4
SOUTH ATLANTIC:															
Delaware	148,792	7,520	5.1	95,074	1,660	1.7	17,011	98	0.6	16,097	2,382	14.8	19,939	3,359	16.8
Maryland	996,928	46,912	4.7	603,308	10,547	1.7	138,180	1,478	1.1	91,178	11,488	12.6	163,464	23,311	14.3
District of Columbia	341,465	6,450	1.9	180,871	405	0.2	43,065	86	0.2	28,405	1,403	4.9	88,388	4,480	5.1
Virginia	1,300,893	140,450	10.8	914,297	55,555	6.1	33,910	308	0.9	22,745	1,730	7.6	329,220	82,893	25.2
West Virginia	900,987	56,853	6.3	742,035	36,675	4.9	42,858	702	1.6	48,688	9,725	20.0	67,155	9,697	14.4
North Carolina	1,542,125	202,223	13.1	1,097,596	82,865	7.5	10,613	158	1.5	8,290	443	5.3	418,075	116,220	27.7
South Carolina	819,384	152,312	18.6	461,513	30,458	6.6	8,582	93	1.1	5,022	295	5.9	343,788	121,270	35.3
Georgia	1,498,567	175,072	11.7	936,386	38,898	4.2	20,508	184	0.9	13,324	552	4.1	528,087	135,392	25.6
Florida	866,198	71,543	8.3	495,775	11,613	2.3	63,269	612	1.0	55,420	3,135	5.7	251,025	55,884	22.3
EAST SOUTH CENTRAL:															
Kentucky	1,422,434	114,905	8.1	1,178,736	85,653	7.3	81,878	900	1.1	21,196	1,250	5.9	140,503	27,065	19.3
Tennessee	1,418,144	126,924	9.0	1,105,162	74,454	6.7	28,329	366	1.3	12,496	752	6.0	271,974	51,310	18.9
Alabama	1,348,401	213,924	15.9	828,303	52,186	6.3	24,725	410	1.7	15,135	1,335	8.8	470,950	159,900	33.3
Mississippi	1,031,547	173,138	16.8	499,463	16,933	3.4	14,049	265	1.9	6,750	874	12.9	509,628	154,235	30.3
WEST SOUTH CENTRAL:															
Arkansas	968,231	84,197	8.7	674,293	29,474	4.4	26,265	571	2.2	9,951	664	6.7	257,130	53,357	20.8
Louisiana	1,184,852	191,249	16.9	606,427	60,459	10.0	76,158	2,286	3.0	33,771	6,603	19.7	415,047	120,469	20.0
Oklahoma	1,287,131	45,087	3.5	1,045,674	23,246	2.2	76,971	797	1.0	26,030	1,471	5.7	94,162	11,552	12.3
Texas	3,220,880	254,099	7.9	2,101,825	35,055	1.7	233,730	5,377	2.3	94,878	7,009	7.5	469,637	81,840	17.4
MOUNTAIN:															
Montana	318,611	6,980	2.2	143,251	459	0.3	95,017	321	0.3	69,056	3,066	4.4	961	51	5.3
Idaho	246,770	3,520	1.4	153,673	730	0.5	59,487	244	0.4	29,184	1,104	4.1	518	24	4.6
Wyoming	132,954	2,643	2.0	79,195	214	0.3	28,353	81	0.3	18,845	795	4.2	962	47	4.9
Colorado	623,523	21,008	3.5	373,373	4,617	1.2	130,916	601	0.5	82,760	7,310	8.8	8,570	303	4.6
New Mexico	216,956	36,306	16.7	154,415	16,820	10.9	13,278	240	1.8	7,530	528	7.0	1,768	123	7.0
Arizona	244,115	28,992	11.9	120,568	669	0.6	26,122	149	0.6	14,795	541	3.7	7,407	344	4.6
Utah	204,498	4,155	1.6	123,783	451	0.4	92,080	285	0.3	41,716	1,535	3.7	806	30	3.7
Nevada	60,794	3,191	5.2	28,402	62	0.2	14,304	41	0.3	11,899	900	7.6	439	7	1.6
PACIFIC:															
Washington	1,010,167	12,634	1.3	500,774	1,508	0.3	256,610	792	0.3	228,263	7,064	3.1	5,061	169	3.3
Oregon	621,375	7,371	1.2	373,570	1,223	0.3	138,177	445	0.3	99,264	3,717	3.7	1,717	48	2.8
California	3,864,388	120,212	3.1	1,876,353	5,593	0.3	871,351	2,876	0.3	762,822	45,331	5.9	57,560	2,104	3.7

ILLITERACY

1231

TABLE 12.—PER CENT ILLITERATE IN THE POPULATION 10 YEARS OLD AND OVER, BY SEX, AND BY COLOR AND NATIVITY, BY DIVISIONS AND STATES: 1900 TO 1930

[A part of the decreases from 1920 to 1930 in the percentage illiterate, shown by whites of foreign birth or parentage in some States, is doubtless due to the separate classification in 1930 of Mexicans who were included for the most part with these white classes in 1920 and 1910]

| DIVISION AND STATE | ALL CLASSES, 10 YEARS OLD AND OVER | | | | | | | | | | NATIVE WHITE— NATIVE PARENTAGE | | | NATIVE WHITE— FOREIGN OR MIXED PARENTAGE | | | FOREIGN-BORN WHITE | | | NEGRO | | |
| | Total | | | | Male | | | Female | | | | | | | | | | | | | | |
	1930	1920	1910	1900	1930	1920	1910	1930	1920	1910	1930	1920	1910	1930	1920	1910	1930	1920	1910	1930	1920	1910
United States	4.3	6.0	7.7	10.7	4.4	6.0	7.6	4.3	5.9	7.8	1.8	2.5	3.7	0.6	0.8	1.1	9.9	13.1	12.7	16.3	22.9	30.4
GEOGRAPHIC DIVISIONS:																						
New England	3.7	4.9	5.3	6.0	3.4	4.8	5.3	3.9	5.0	5.2	0.6	0.6	0.7	0.7	0.8	1.3	11.6	14.0	13.8	5.5	7.1	7.8
Middle Atlantic	3.5	4.9	5.7	5.8	3.1	4.7	5.6	3.9	5.1	5.7	0.6	0.7	1.2	0.5	0.5	0.8	12.2	15.7	15.8	3.7	5.0	7.9
East North Central	2.1	2.9	3.4	4.3	2.1	3.0	3.5	2.2	2.8	3.3	0.7	1.0	1.7	0.6	0.6	0.9	8.8	10.8	10.1	4.7	7.3	11.0
West North Central	1.4	2.0	2.9	4.1	1.5	2.0	2.9	1.4	1.9	2.9	0.8	1.1	1.7	0.5	0.5	0.7	4.9	6.4	7.6	7.6	10.5	14.9
South Atlantic	8.3	11.5	16.0	23.9	9.2	12.1	16.0	7.5	11.0	16.1	3.9	5.4	8.0	0.8	0.9	1.2	10.4	12.8	13.5	19.7	25.2	32.5
East South Central	9.6	12.7	17.4	24.9	10.8	13.3	17.4	8.5	12.0	17.3	5.1	6.0	9.6	1.2	1.5	1.7	7.4	9.1	9.3	22.0	27.0	34.8
West South Central	7.2	10.0	13.2	20.5	7.3	10.0	12.7	7.0	10.0	13.8	2.7	3.9	5.6	2.0	6.6	7.7	9.4	29.0	25.6	17.0	26.3	33.1
Mountain	4.2	5.2	6.9	9.6	3.7	4.7	6.3	4.6	5.7	7.5	1.5	2.4	3.0	0.4	1.0	1.2	5.6	12.7	12.5	4.1	5.3	8.0
Pacific	2.1	2.7	3.0	4.2	2.1	2.8	3.3	2.1	2.5	2.5	0.3	0.4	0.4	0.3	0.4	0.5	4.9	8.6	8.0	3.1	4.6	6.3
NEW ENGLAND:																						
Maine	2.7	3.3	4.1	5.1	3.2	3.9	4.9	2.1	2.5	3.2	1.4	1.3	1.4	2.1	2.9	4.5	8.5	11.1	13.7	4.8	5.9	8.0
New Hampshire	2.7	4.4	4.6	6.2	2.8	4.5	5.2	2.5	4.2	4.1	0.6	0.6	0.8	1.1	1.1	2.1	9.6	15.4	14.5	3.9	6.7	10.6
Vermont	2.2	3.0	3.7	5.8	2.6	3.6	4.4	1.7	2.4	3.1	1.0	1.1	1.2	2.0	2.8	4.0	7.2	11.3	13.1	4.9	6.2	4.8
Massachusetts	3.5	4.7	5.2	5.9	3.1	4.5	5.0	3.9	4.9	5.3	0.3	0.3	0.4	0.5	0.5	0.7	10.7	12.8	12.7	5.4	6.8	8.1
Rhode Island	4.9	6.5	7.7	8.4	4.4	6.0	7.4	5.4	7.0	8.0	0.5	0.5	0.7	0.9	0.9	1.8	14.3	16.5	17.3	8.1	10.2	9.5
Connecticut	4.5	6.2	6.0	5.9	3.9	5.8	5.7	5.1	6.6	6.3	0.3	0.4	0.5	0.4	0.4	0.8	14.6	17.0	15.4	4.9	6.2	6.3
MIDDLE ATLANTIC:																						
New York	3.7	5.1	5.5	5.5	3.1	4.5	5.0	4.3	5.6	5.9	0.6	0.6	0.8	0.4	0.5	0.7	10.8	14.2	13.7	2.5	2.9	5.0
New Jersey	3.8	5.1	5.6	5.9	3.5	4.9	5.5	4.2	5.3	5.7	0.5	0.7	1.1	0.5	0.4	0.7	12.9	15.3	14.7	5.1	6.1	9.0
Pennsylvania	3.1	4.6	5.9	6.1	2.9	4.7	6.4	3.3	4.5	5.4	0.6	0.8	1.4	0.5	0.6	1.1	15.4	18.9	20.1	4.2	6.1	9.1
EAST NORTH CENTRAL:																						
Ohio	2.3	2.8	3.2	4.0	2.3	3.0	3.5	2.2	2.6	3.0	0.8	1.0	1.7	0.5	0.6	0.9	11.6	12.6	11.5	6.4	8.1	11.1
Indiana	1.7	2.2	3.1	4.6	1.8	2.4	3.2	1.5	2.0	2.9	1.0	1.4	2.2	0.8	1.0	1.4	10.1	11.8	11.7	6.0	9.5	13.7
Illinois	2.4	3.4	3.7	4.2	2.3	3.3	3.7	2.6	3.4	3.8	0.7	1.1	1.7	0.4	0.4	0.6	9.0	11.0	10.1	3.6	6.7	10.5
Michigan	2.0	3.0	3.3	4.2	1.9	3.1	3.6	2.1	2.9	3.1	0.5	0.6	1.0	0.6	0.7	1.2	6.7	9.9	9.3	3.0	4.2	5.7
Wisconsin	1.9	2.4	3.2	4.7	1.8	2.5	3.1	1.9	2.4	3.2	0.4	0.5	0.9	0.8	0.8	1.0	7.8	8.4	8.7	4.4	4.1	4.5
WEST NORTH CENTRAL:																						
Minnesota	1.3	1.8	3.0	4.1	1.2	1.8	2.9	1.3	1.9	3.1	0.3	0.4	0.4	0.5	0.5	0.6	4.3	5.4	7.6	2.0	3.1	3.4
Iowa	0.8	1.1	1.7	2.3	0.8	1.2	1.7	0.7	1.0	1.7	0.5	0.5	0.9	0.4	0.4	0.6	3.6	4.9	6.3	5.4	8.1	10.3
Missouri	2.3	3.0	4.3	6.4	2.6	3.3	4.4	2.0	2.8	4.2	1.6	2.2	3.4	0.8	0.9	1.2	7.5	9.6	10.1	8.8	12.1	17.4
North Dakota	1.5	2.1	3.1	5.6	1.4	1.9	2.8	1.6	2.4	3.5	0.3	0.3	0.3	0.5	0.5	0.7	4.4	5.6	6.3	3.4	4.0	4.8
South Dakota	1.2	1.7	2.9	5.0	1.1	1.6	2.5	1.4	1.9	3.3	0.3	0.3	0.3	0.5	0.5	0.4	3.7	4.7	5.0	2.2	5.2	5.5
Nebraska	1.2	1.4	1.9	2.3	1.1	1.3	1.9	1.2	1.4	2.0	0.4	0.4	0.6	0.4	0.4	0.5	6.0	6.4	7.1	3.9	4.8	7.2
Kansas	1.2	1.6	2.2	2.9	1.3	1.7	2.3	1.2	1.6	2.1	0.5	0.6	0.8	0.6	0.5	0.8	5.9	10.5	10.5	5.9	8.8	12.0
SOUTH ATLANTIC:																						
Delaware	4.0	5.9	8.1	12.0	4.2	6.2	8.4	3.8	5.5	7.8	1.4	2.0	3.3	0.5	0.6	0.9	14.3	17.3	19.8	13.2	19.1	25.6
Maryland	3.8	5.6	7.2	11.1	4.1	5.7	7.2	3.5	5.4	7.1	1.4	2.0	3.0	0.9	0.9	1.0	12.2	13.4	11.9	11.4	18.2	23.4
District of Columbia	1.6	2.8	4.9	8.6	1.4	2.5	4.1	1.7	3.0	5.7	0.2	0.3	0.6	0.2	0.2	0.4	4.8	6.1	8.2	4.1	8.6	13.5
Virginia	8.7	11.2	15.2	22.9	10.0	12.1	15.7	7.4	10.2	14.6	5.0	6.1	8.2	0.8	1.0	1.2	7.4	7.1	9.2	19.2	23.5	30.0
West Virginia	6.4	8.3	11.4	17.0	5.5	7.2	8.8	4.1	5.6	7.3	3.8	4.8	6.7	1.1	1.5	2.0	19.2	24.0	23.9	11.3	15.3	20.3
North Carolina	10.0	13.1	18.5	28.7	11.2	13.7	18.2	8.9	12.5	18.7	5.7	8.2	12.3	1.2	1.9	3.0	5.2	6.8	8.3	20.6	24.5	31.9
South Carolina	14.9	18.1	25.7	35.9	15.8	18.3	25.0	14.1	17.9	26.3	5.2	6.6	10.5	0.9	1.0	1.4	5.7	6.2	6.8	26.9	29.3	38.7
Georgia	9.4	15.3	20.7	30.5	10.6	16.2	20.9	8.3	14.4	20.5	3.4	5.5	8.0	0.7	1.1	1.6	4.0	5.4	6.0	19.9	29.1	36.5
Florida	7.1	9.6	13.8	21.9	7.7	9.6	13.2	6.5	9.5	14.4	2.0	3.1	5.2	0.8	1.1	2.2	5.4	6.3	10.5	18.8	21.5	25.5
EAST SOUTH CENTRAL:																						
Kentucky	6.6	8.4	12.1	16.5	7.7	9.3	12.6	5.4	7.6	11.6	5.9	7.3	10.7	1.0	1.3	1.5	5.8	7.3	8.3	15.4	21.0	27.6
Tennessee	7.2	10.3	13.6	20.7	8.4	11.2	13.8	6.0	9.5	13.4	5.4	7.4	9.9	1.1	1.5	1.8	5.8	8.3	8.3	14.9	22.4	27.3
Alabama	12.6	16.1	22.9	34.0	13.5	16.4	22.5	11.6	15.8	23.3	4.9	6.4	10.1	1.4	1.7	2.3	8.5	10.9	11.3	26.2	31.3	40.1
Mississippi	13.1	17.2	22.4	32.0	14.4	18.1	22.4	11.8	16.3	22.5	2.7	3.6	5.3	1.8	2.3	2.2	12.6	13.3	15.1	23.2	29.3	35.6
WEST SOUTH CENTRAL:																						
Arkansas	6.8	9.4	12.6	20.4	7.4	9.6	12.1	6.2	9.1	13.1	3.5	4.6	7.1	1.9	2.0	2.8	6.6	8.3	8.9	16.1	21.8	26.4
Louisiana	13.5	21.9	29.0	38.5	13.6	21.6	28.0	13.5	22.2	30.1	7.8	11.4	15.0	2.7	3.5	3.6	19.2	21.0	24.0	23.3	38.5	48.4
Oklahoma [1]	2.8	3.8	5.6	12.1	3.2	4.1	5.5	2.4	3.4	5.8	1.8	2.4	3.5	0.9	1.2	1.3	5.6	14.0	9.8	9.3	12.4	17.7
Texas	6.8	8.3	9.9	14.5	6.8	8.5	9.8	6.8	8.2	10.1	1.4	2.2	3.3	2.1	9.4	11.6	7.3	33.8	30.0	13.4	17.8	24.6
MOUNTAIN:																						
Montana	1.7	2.3	4.8	6.1	1.7	2.3	5.2	1.7	2.3	4.0	0.3	0.3	0.3	0.3	0.3	0.4	4.3	5.6	9.4	4.6	6.0	7.0
Idaho	1.1	1.5	2.2	4.6	1.2	1.7	2.6	1.0	1.3	1.5	0.4	0.3	0.4	0.4	0.3	0.3	4.0	0.5	6.9	4.2	5.4	6.4
Wyoming	1.6	2.1	3.3	4.0	1.7	2.5	3.7	1.6	1.5	2.5	0.3	0.4	0.8	0.3	0.4	0.4	4.2	9.0	9.7	4.2	5.3	5.0
Colorado	2.8	3.2	3.7	4.2	2.5	2.9	3.6	3.1	3.6	3.8	1.0	1.7	2.0	0.4	0.6	0.5	8.6	12.4	11.3	3.9	6.2	8.6
New Mexico	13.3	15.6	20.2	33.2	11.2	12.7	15.9	15.7	18.9	25.4	8.2	11.9	15.5	1.5	8.2	8.9	6.8	27.1	31.0	6.0	4.3	14.2
Arizona	10.1	15.3	20.9	29.0	9.0	13.9	19.2	11.4	17.1	23.5	0.5	1.3	2.3	0.5	4.6	8.4	3.6	27.5	31.5	4.0	4.6	7.2
Utah	1.2	1.9	2.5	3.1	1.3	2.1	2.7	1.1	1.6	2.2	0.3	0.3	0.4	0.3	0.4	0.4	3.6	6.3	5.9	3.2	4.6	4.8
Nevada	4.4	5.9	6.7	13.3	4.3	5.8	6.1	4.5	6.2	8.0	0.2	0.4	0.4	0.3	0.2	0.5	7.5	8.5	7.6	1.5	5.1	5.5
PACIFIC:																						
Washington	1.0	1.7	2.0	3.1	1.0	1.7	2.1	1.0	1.6	1.8	0.3	0.3	0.3	0.3	0.3	0.3	2.9	4.7	4.8	2.9	4.0	4.3
Oregon	1.0	1.5	1.9	3.3	1.0	1.6	2.2	0.9	1.3	1.4	0.3	0.4	0.4	0.3	0.3	0.4	3.6	5.1	6.1	2.5	4.7	3.4
California	2.6	3.3	3.7	4.8	2.6	3.5	4.2	2.6	3.1	3.1	0.3	0.4	0.5	0.3	0.5	0.6	5.7	10.5	10.0	3.1	4.7	7.1

[1] Includes Indian Territory for 1900.

1232   POPULATION

TABLE 13.—PER CENT ILLITERATE IN THE POPULATION 21 YEARS OLD AND OVER, BY SEX, AND BY COLOR AND NATIVITY, BY DIVISIONS AND STATES: 1900 TO 1930

[A part of the decreases from 1920 to 1930 in the percentage illiterate, shown by whites of foreign birth or parentage, in some States, is doubtless due to the separate classification in 1930 of Mexicans who were included for the most part with these white classes in 1920 and 1910]

DIVISION AND STATE	Total 1930	1920	1910	1900	Male 1930	1920	1910	Female 1930	1920	1910	NW—Native Par. 1930	1920	1910	NW—For/Mixed Par. 1930	1920	1910	For.-Born White 1930	1920	1910	Negro 1930	1920	1910
United States	5.3	7.1	8.9	12.0	5.2	7.0	8.4	5.4	7.3	9.4	2.2	3.0	4.3	0.7	0.9	1.3	10.3	13.7	12.9	20.0	27.4	35.7
GEOGRAPHIC DIVISIONS:																						
New England	4.7	6.1	6.3	7.1	4.3	6.0	6.3	5.1	6.2	6.3	0.7	0.6	0.8	0.9	1.1	1.8	12.1	14.8	14.3	7.0	8.5	9.4
Middle Atlantic	4.5	6.3	6.9	7.1	4.0	5.9	6.8	5.1	6.6	7.0	0.7	0.9	1.5	0.6	0.6	1.1	12.7	16.7	16.4	4.4	6.0	9.4
East North Central	2.7	3.7	4.3	5.6	2.7	3.7	4.3	2.8	3.6	4.2	0.9	1.3	2.2	0.7	0.8	1.2	9.2	11.4	10.3	5.7	8.7	13.0
West North Central	1.8	2.5	3.7	5.3	1.9	2.5	3.5	1.8	2.5	3.9	1.1	1.4	2.2	0.6	0.6	0.9	5.0	6.5	7.7	9.2	12.5	18.3
South Atlantic	10.2	14.0	18.6	26.9	10.9	14.0	17.6	9.5	13.9	19.6	4.9	6.6	9.3	1.0	1.1	1.4	10.8	13.5	13.6	25.0	31.5	39.1
East South Central	12.0	15.5	20.4	28.5	13.1	15.7	19.4	11.0	15.2	21.4	6.3	8.4	11.3	1.3	1.6	1.9	7.6	9.3	8.4	28.0	34.1	41.4
West South Central	8.7	11.7	15.0	23.0	8.7	11.3	13.7	8.7	12.1	16.5	3.3	4.6	6.4	2.2	5.2	6.4	9.6	20.1	24.4	21.0	30.5	38.5
Mountain	5.1	6.0	7.7	10.8	4.5	5.4	6.9	5.8	6.8	8.9	2.0	3.0	4.3	0.4	1.0	1.3	5.7	12.7	12.2	4.8	5.8	9.1
Pacific	2.6	3.2	3.4	5.1	2.5	3.3	3.7	2.6	3.0	3.1	0.3	0.4	0.5	0.3	0.4	0.6	5.1	8.8	7.9	3.6	5.4	7.3
NEW ENGLAND:																						
Maine	3.3	3.9	4.7	5.7	3.9	4.7	5.5	2.7	3.1	3.8	1.6	1.3	1.5	3.0	4.1	6.3	9.1	12.0	14.5	5.6	6.8	10.3
New Hampshire	3.4	5.4	5.5	6.9	3.5	5.6	6.2	3.2	5.2	4.8	0.7	0.6	0.9	1.5	1.6	3.1	10.1	10.4	15.4	4.2	7.7	13.3
Vermont	2.7	3.8	4.6	7.0	3.2	4.5	5.3	2.2	3.0	3.8	1.3	1.3	1.5	2.7	3.8	5.3	7.9	12.5	14.1	0.0	8.2	5.0
Massachusetts	4.5	5.9	6.2	7.0	4.0	5.7	6.1	5.0	6.1	6.3	0.3	0.3	0.4	0.6	0.6	1.0	11.2	13.5	13.1	6.0	8.2	9.7
Rhode Island	6.4	8.2	9.2	9.8	5.8	7.6	8.8	7.0	8.8	9.6	0.6	0.6	0.9	1.2	1.3	2.4	15.0	17.5	18.1	10.5	12.5	11.4
Connecticut	6.0	7.8	7.2	7.0	5.2	7.4	6.8	6.8	8.4	7.5	0.4	0.4	0.6	0.6	0.6	1.1	15.2	18.1	16.0	6.2	7.5	7.8
MIDDLE ATLANTIC:																						
New York	4.7	6.4	6.6	6.6	3.9	5.7	6.0	5.4	7.1	7.2	0.6	0.7	1.1	0.5	0.6	0.9	11.3	15.2	14.3	2.8	3.4	5.8
New Jersey	5.0	6.6	6.7	7.1	4.4	6.3	6.6	5.5	6.9	6.8	0.6	0.9	1.4	0.6	0.5	0.8	13.4	16.3	14.8	6.3	7.5	11.9
Pennsylvania	4.1	6.0	7.3	7.7	3.9	6.2	7.8	4.4	5.9	6.8	0.8	1.0	1.8	0.7	0.8	1.4	15.0	20.1	20.8	5.2	7.3	11.0
EAST NORTH CENTRAL:																						
Ohio	2.9	3.6	4.0	5.2	2.9	3.8	4.2	2.9	3.3	3.8	1.0	1.2	2.2	0.6	0.7	1.1	12.0	13.4	11.8	8.0	9.7	13.0
Indiana	2.1	2.8	3.9	6.1	2.3	3.0	4.1	1.9	2.6	3.8	1.2	1.8	3.0	0.9	1.1	1.7	10.4	12.4	11.8	7.5	11.7	17.5
Illinois	3.1	4.3	4.7	5.4	2.9	4.1	4.6	3.3	4.4	4.8	0.9	1.4	2.2	0.5	0.5	0.8	9.3	11.7	10.3	4.3	7.9	12.4
Michigan	2.5	3.9	4.2	5.4	2.4	3.9	4.4	2.7	3.8	4.0	0.6	0.8	1.3	0.7	0.9	1.6	7.1	10.5	9.6	3.6	4.9	6.9
Wisconsin	2.4	3.2	4.2	6.3	2.4	3.2	4.0	2.5	3.2	4.4	0.6	0.6	0.9	1.0	1.0	1.3	8.0	8.8	8.9	5.3	4.8	5.3
WEST NORTH CENTRAL:																						
Minnesota	1.6	2.4	4.0	5.4	1.6	2.3	3.7	1.7	2.6	4.4	0.4	0.4	0.5	0.6	0.6	0.9	4.4	5.6	7.7	2.3	3.5	3.9
Iowa	1.0	1.4	2.2	3.1	1.0	1.4	3.1	0.9	1.3	2.2	0.6	0.7	1.2	0.5	0.5	0.8	3.6	5.0	6.3	0.7	9.9	12.8
Missouri	2.8	3.8	5.4	7.9	3.1	4.0	5.3	2.5	3.6	5.5	2.0	2.8	4.3	0.9	1.0	1.4	7.7	10.0	10.2	10.5	14.3	21.1
North Dakota	2.0	2.9	3.7	6.8	1.8	2.5	3.1	2.3	3.5	4.5	0.3	0.3	0.4	0.6	0.6	0.6	4.5	5.9	6.2	3.6	4.8	5.3
South Dakota	1.6	2.2	3.7	6.0	1.4	1.9	3.1	1.9	2.6	4.6	0.3	0.4	0.4	0.6	0.6	0.6	3.8	4.9	5.0	2.0	0.7	0.8
Nebraska	1.5	1.8	2.5	3.1	1.4	1.7	2.4	1.6	1.9	2.7	0.5	0.5	0.8	0.5	0.4	0.7	6.1	6.6	7.1	4.6	5.7	8.5
Kansas	1.5	2.0	2.8	3.9	1.6	2.1	2.9	1.5	2.0	2.8	0.6	0.7	1.1	0.6	0.6	1.0	6.0	10.2	10.3	7.4	11.2	15.9
SOUTH ATLANTIC:																						
Delaware	5.1	7.4	10.0	14.5	5.2	7.7	10.1	4.9	7.0	9.8	1.7	2.6	4.2	0.6	0.7	1.0	14.8	18.2	19.7	16.8	24.6	32.9
Maryland	4.7	6.8	8.7	13.3	5.0	6.9	8.5	4.4	6.7	8.9	1.7	2.5	3.7	1.1	1.1	1.1	12.6	14.3	12.3	14.3	22.2	28.6
District of Columbia	1.9	3.3	6.0	10.4	1.7	3.0	4.9	2.1	3.6	7.0	0.2	0.3	0.7	0.2	0.2	0.5	4.9	6.4	8.3	5.1	10.7	16.8
Virginia	10.8	13.5	17.9	26.4	12.1	14.1	17.7	9.5	12.7	18.0	6.1	7.1	9.4	0.9	1.1	1.5	7.6	7.5	9.3	25.2	29.3	37.1
West Virginia	6.3	8.2	10.2	13.9	7.0	8.9	10.4	5.5	7.3	10.0	4.9	6.1	8.4	1.6	1.7	2.3	20.0	25.4	23.9	14.4	18.0	24.2
North Carolina	13.1	16.9	22.6	32.8	14.2	17.0	21.3	12.0	16.8	24.0	7.5	10.7	15.0	1.5	2.4	4.0	5.3	7.0	8.1	27.7	32.4	40.4
South Carolina	18.6	23.0	29.0	39.3	18.8	22.8	27.1	18.4	23.8	32.0	6.6	8.5	11.4	1.1	1.2	1.4	5.9	6.5	6.5	35.3	38.7	40.0
Georgia	11.7	18.4	24.1	34.6	12.5	18.4	22.8	10.9	18.4	25.5	4.2	6.7	9.2	0.9	1.3	1.8	4.1	5.6	5.9	25.6	35.8	43.8
Florida	8.3	10.9	15.5	25.3	8.7	10.0	14.0	7.8	11.3	17.3	2.3	3.7	5.7	1.0	1.1	1.9	5.7	6.0	10.5	22.3	24.8	28.8
EAST SOUTH CENTRAL:																						
Kentucky	8.1	10.6	14.5	20.0	9.3	11.3	14.5	6.8	9.8	14.6	7.3	9.2	12.8	1.1	1.4	1.7	5.9	7.5	8.2	19.3	26.4	34.7
Tennessee	9.0	12.6	16.3	24.0	10.3	13.2	15.7	7.7	12.0	17.0	6.7	9.2	11.9	1.3	1.8	2.1	6.0	8.7	8.2	18.9	26.6	33.3
Alabama	15.9	20.0	26.2	37.4	16.6	19.5	24.3	15.2	20.5	28.2	6.3	8.3	11.5	1.7	1.9	2.7	8.8	11.3	11.1	33.3	38.8	46.4
Mississippi	16.8	20.8	26.8	37.2	18.0	20.9	25.3	15.6	20.7	28.4	3.4	4.4	6.2	1.9	2.4	2.3	12.9	13.4	13.6	30.3	35.9	43.2
WEST SOUTH CENTRAL:																						
Arkansas	8.7	11.5	15.1	23.5	9.2	11.1	13.5	8.2	11.8	16.9	4.4	5.7	8.5	2.2	2.3	3.2	6.7	8.3	8.2	20.8	26.5	32.0
Louisiana	16.9	24.9	31.1	40.9	16.5	23.6	28.6	17.2	26.2	33.7	10.0	13.5	16.8	3.0	2.6	2.7	19.7	22.6	23.2	29.0	43.8	52.2
Oklahoma ¹	3.5	4.7	6.9	12.2	3.9	4.9	6.4	3.1	4.5	7.6	2.2	2.9	4.2	1.0	1.3	1.6	5.7	13.4	9.7	12.3	16.4	22.7
Texas	7.9	9.6	11.6	17.3	7.8	9.6	10.9	8.0	9.7	12.4	1.7	2.5	3.7	2.3	7.5	10.0	33.3	28.8	17.4	17.4	23.4	31.4
MOUNTAIN:																						
Montana	2.2	2.8	5.5	7.0	2.1	2.7	5.7	2.3	2.9	5.1	0.3	0.4	0.4	0.3	0.4	0.5	4.4	6.0	9.2	5.3	6.7	8.0
Idaho	1.4	1.9	2.7	5.8	1.5	2.1	3.1	1.3	1.6	2.2	0.5	0.4	0.4	0.3	0.4	0.5	4.1	6.6	6.6	4.6	5.9	6.8
Wyoming	2.0	2.5	3.8	4.7	2.0	2.9	4.1	2.0	1.9	3.2	0.3	0.4	0.4	0.3	0.3	0.4	4.2	9.2	9.5	4.9	6.1	5.3
Colorado	3.5	3.9	4.4	4.8	3.1	3.5	4.2	3.9	4.4	4.7	1.2	2.0	2.4	0.5	0.7	0.6	8.8	12.8	11.3	4.6	7.4	10.0
New Mexico	16.7	18.9	23.4	38.1	13.6	14.7	17.6	20.3	24.1	30.8	24.1	15.2	18.8	10.9	15.2	18.8	8.8	12.8	11.3	4.6	7.4	10.0
Arizona	11.9	16.3	21.0	30.4	10.4	14.5	19.5	13.7	18.8	25.6	0.6	1.4	0.7	1.8	8.3	9.0	7.0	28.6	31.2	7.0	4.4	15.9
Utah	1.6	2.5	3.1	4.3	1.7	2.8	3.3	1.4	2.2	2.9	0.4	0.5	0.4	0.6	4.5	0.7	3.7	28.7	31.4	4.6	4.8	8.4
Nevada	5.2	6.7	6.8	14.4	5.0	6.4	6.0	5.6	7.3	8.7	0.2	0.5	0.3	0.3	0.2	0.5	7.6	8.5	7.0	3.7	5.0	5.3
PACIFIC:																						
Washington	1.3	2.1	2.3	3.8	1.2	2.1	2.4	1.3	2.1	2.2	0.3	0.3	0.3	0.3	0.3	0.3	3.1	5.0	4.7	3.3	4.6	4.8
Oregon	1.2	1.8	2.2	4.2	1.3	2.0	2.5	1.1	1.6	1.8	0.3	0.5	0.5	0.3	0.4	0.5	3.7	5.4	5.9	2.8	5.5	3.7
California	3.1	3.9	4.3	6.7	3.0	4.0	4.6	3.2	3.6	3.7	0.3	0.4	0.6	0.3	0.5	0.7	5.9	10.7	9.8	3.7	5.6	8.4

¹ Includes Indian Territory for 1900.

ILLITERACY

TABLE 14.—ILLITERACY IN THE POPULATION 10 TO 15 YEARS OLD, BY COLOR AND NATIVITY, BY DIVISIONS AND STATES: 1930 AND 1920

[Per cent not shown where base is less than 100]

Division and State	All classes, 10 to 15 years old — Total number 1930	Illiterate Number 1930	Per cent 1930	Per cent 1920	Native white—native parentage — Total number 1930	Illiterate Number 1930	Per cent 1930	Per cent 1920	Native white—foreign or mixed parentage — Total number 1930	Illiterate Number 1930	Per cent 1930	Per cent 1920	Foreign-born white — Total number 1930	Illiterate Number 1930	Per cent 1930	Per cent 1920	Negro — Total number 1930	Illiterate Number 1930	Per cent 1930	Per cent 1920
United States	14,300,576	173,434	1.2	2.3	8,921,269	58,430	0.7	1.1	3,457,743	7,028	0.2	0.6	186,160	512	0.3	4.4	1,491,979	82,266	5.5	11.5
GEOG. DIVS.:																				
New England	900,425	1,823	0.2	0.3	365,797	780	0.2	0.3	498,936	938	0.2	0.2	31,549	75	0.2	0.9	9,686	24	0.2	0.4
Mid. Atlantic	2,916,623	6,247	0.2	0.3	1,364,837	2,975	0.2	0.2	1,390,002	2,757	0.2	0.2	71,717	235	0.3	1.0	87,561	264	0.3	0.5
E. N. Central	2,783,510	5,312	0.2	0.2	1,823,672	3,441	0.2	0.2	829,388	1,424	0.2	0.2	44,427	80	0.2	0.6	79,058	229	0.3	0.5
W. N. Central	1,534,302	4,156	0.3	0.4	1,172,852	2,824	0.2	0.3	313,151	683	0.2	0.2	8,843	17	0.2	2.2	30,156	291	1.0	2.5
S. Atlantic	2,088,758	63,320	3.0	5.1	1,370,110	18,493	1.3	2.2	79,662	196	0.2	0.4	3,968	15	0.4	1.6	631,742	44,106	7.0	10.9
E. S. Central	1,297,950	40,576	3.1	6.1	930,784	17,216	1.8	2.7	14,106	64	0.5	0.8	553	4	0.7	3.1	352,005	23,070	6.6	14.3
W. S. Central	1,547,462	44,654	2.9	6.0	1,097,468	10,884	1.0	2.3	51,086	410	0.8	10.6	1,357	28	2.1	34.1	202,336	14,252	4.9	13.7
Mountain	453,531	5,039	1.2	2.3	316,918	1,032	0.3	0.8	83,298	165	0.2	0.9	2,887	9	0.3	10.7	2,370	13	0.5	1.3
Pacific	771,955	1,698	0.2	0.4	478,831	785	0.2	0.2	197,524	391	0.2	0.3	22,859	40	0.2	3.2	7,065	17	0.2	0.6
NEW ENGLAND:																				
Maine	88,153	325	0.4	0.8	57,969	232	0.4	0.8	26,713	79	0.3	0.6	3,227	9	0.3	1.2	113	1	0.9	0.9
N. Hampshire	49,920	98	0.2	0.3	25,995	62	0.2	0.3	22,022	33	0.1	0.2	1,838	3	0.2	0.8	62	1	......	......
Vermont	40,045	118	0.3	0.3	27,496	77	0.3	0.2	10,406	30	0.3	0.3	2,015	4	0.2	0.5	62	1	......	......
Massachusetts	461,412	811	0.2	0.2	166,752	263	0.2	0.2	272,406	406	0.2	0.3	16,454	38	0.2	0.8	5,550	12	0.2	0.5
Rhode Island	76,873	186	0.2	0.3	25,422	63	0.2	0.2	47,393	116	0.2	0.2	2,927	6	0.2	1.4	1,103	1	0.1	0.3
Connecticut	190,013	285	0.1	0.3	62,163	83	0.1	0.4	110,936	178	0.1	0.1	5,088	15	0.3	0.9	2,796	9	0.3	0.3
MID. ATLANTIC:																				
New York	1,287,915	2,907	0.2	0.2	512,025	1,223	0.2	0.2	697,842	1,450	0.2	0.2	46,662	140	0.3	0.9	29,044	85	0.3	0.4
New Jersey	456,727	983	0.2	0.3	187,191	352	0.2	0.2	238,160	505	0.2	0.2	11,642	45	0.4	1.2	19,601	80	0.4	0.5
Pennsylvania	1,171,981	2,357	0.2	0.3	664,721	1,400	0.2	0.3	454,600	802	0.2	0.2	13,413	50	0.4	1.3	38,916	99	0.3	0.6
E. N. CENTRAL:																				
Ohio	729,487	1,699	0.2	0.3	509,660	1,146	0.2	0.3	183,251	416	0.2	0.2	7,675	27	0.4	0.6	28,525	103	0.4	0.5
Indiana	353,909	683	0.2	0.2	304,458	602	0.2	0.2	37,324	44	0.1	0.2	1,503	1	0.1	0.5	10,078	28	0.3	0.5
Illinois	816,191	1,355	0.2	0.2	477,422	755	0.2	0.2	207,839	468	0.2	0.2	12,587	27	0.2	0.7	26,201	64	0.2	0.5
Michigan	540,890	799	0.1	0.2	301,803	446	0.1	0.2	204,063	256	0.1	0.2	19,681	23	0.1	0.5	13,365	32	0.2	0.2
Wisconsin	343,033	776	0.2	0.2	230,329	492	0.2	0.2	196,911	240	0.2	0.2	2,981	11	0.4	0.6	889	2	0.2	0.2
W. N. CENTRAL:																				
Minnesota	303,083	619	0.2	0.3	185,112	307	0.2	0.3	112,525	245	0.2	0.2	2,614	6	0.2	0.5	729	......	......	0.2
Iowa	281,116	508	0.2	0.2	234,097	406	0.2	0.2	43,750	75	0.2	0.2	988	2	0.2	1.0	1,686	10	0.6	0.5
Missouri	388,470	1,660	0.4	0.7	335,271	1,328	0.4	0.6	31,580	55	0.2	0.2	1,175	5	0.4	2.3	19,840	266	1.3	3.6
North Dakota	95,179	326	0.3	0.3	45,398	99	0.2	0.1	24,515	51	0.2	0.3	742	2	0.3	1.0	66	1	......	......
South Dakota	89,353	226	0.3	0.3	61,301	102	0.2	0.2	33,355	68	0.2	0.3	610	1	0.2	1.8	1,102	2	0.2	0.3
Nebraska	162,370	320	0.2	0.2	126,005	221	0.2	0.2	19,733	40	0.2	0.3	326	1	0.3	11.1	6,713	12	0.2	0.5
Kansas	214,785	488	0.2	0.4	185,668	361	0.2	0.2	......	......	......	......	388	......	......	......	......	......	......	......
S. ATLANTIC:																				
Delaware	26,720	87	0.3	0.5	17,415	50	0.3	0.3	5,606	9	0.2	0.2	152	1	0.7	1.2	3,547	27	0.8	1.9
Maryland	181,066	1,030	0.6	1.5	124,023	462	0.4	0.5	25,823	74	0.3	0.2	868	5	0.6	0.9	30,312	480	1.6	6.1
Dist. of Columbia	39,115	45	0.1	0.2	21,883	18	0.1	0.1	5,400	5	0.1	0.1	366	......	......	0.6	11,307	22	0.2	0.5
Virginia	320,069	9,499	3.0	5.4	219,694	4,321	2.0	3.4	6,073	18	0.3	0.8	291	......	......	1.9	93,856	5,128	5.5	10.0
West Virginia	227,675	2,406	1.1	1.8	196,441	2,170	1.1	1.9	18,157	45	0.2	0.8	719	5	0.7	2.7	12,334	186	1.5	2.3
North Carolina	454,572	12,440	2.7	4.2	309,246	3,907	1.3	2.2	1,983	4	0.2	0.7	141	1	0.7	2.1	140,518	8,148	5.8	8.3
South Carolina	264,587	17,222	6.5	6.1	130,680	2,632	2.0	1.7	1,459	7	0.5	0.2	64	......	......	1.3	132,230	14,545	11.0	9.6
Georgia	404,777	15,438	3.8	8.3	244,184	3,862	1.6	2.8	2,974	4	0.1	0.2	156	1	0.6	1.4	157,420	11,570	7.3	15.4
Florida	170,177	5,162	3.0	5.7	106,544	1,071	1.0	1.7	12,078	30	0.2	0.7	1,211	2	0.2	1.4	50,209	3,991	7.9	13.2
E. S. CENTRAL:																				
Kentucky	331,210	7,795	2.4	2.8	302,278	7,158	2.4	2.7	4,527	18	0.4	0.8	177	3	1.7	2.8	24,217	616	2.5	4.1
Tennessee	332,584	7,342	2.2	5.1	271,586	5,090	1.9	3.2	3,018	4	0.1	0.4	159	......	......	1.0	57,800	2,245	3.9	13.2
Alabama	362,158	16,136	4.5	7.6	226,794	3,670	1.6	2.4	4,406	16	0.4	1.0	145	......	......	2.8	130,720	12,420	9.5	15.6
Mississippi	271,998	9,303	3.4	9.3	130,126	1,298	1.0	2.0	2,155	26	1.2	2.4	72	1	......	8.1	139,268	7,780	5.6	15.5
W. S. CENTRAL:																				
Arkansas	251,825	5,741	2.3	5.2	185,568	2,952	1.6	2.4	3,020	16	0.5	0.9	47	......	......	4.0	63,072	2,760	4.4	12.8
Louisiana	270,507	11,984	4.4	14.1	157,827	3,680	2.3	6.3	10,750	107	1.0	6.2	321	6	1.9	9.9	100,674	8,017	8.0	25.6
Oklahoma	307,299	2,766	0.9	1.8	262,108	1,730	0.7	1.3	7,967	24	0.3	0.9	173	1	0.6	17.3	21,835	443	2.0	4.8
Texas	717,831	24,163	3.4	4.9	491,965	2,533	0.5	1.4	20,349	263	0.9	14.0	816	21	2.6	35.7	106,755	3,032	2.8	4.6
MOUNTAIN:																				
Montana	66,889	157	0.2	0.4	41,248	52	0.1	0.2	22,323	35	0.2	0.3	815	2	0.2	0.8	100	1	1.0	1.9
Idaho	58,900	105	0.2	0.4	48,560	74	0.2	0.1	9,132	11	0.1	0.2	394	1	0.3	4.4	43	......	......	......
Wyoming	25,684	94	0.4	0.3	18,836	35	0.2	0.2	5,552	5	0.1	0.2	171	4	2.3	2.5	84	......	......	......
Colorado	117,683	519	0.4	0.8	83,412	180	0.2	0.5	24,392	48	0.2	0.4	529	1	0.2	6.8	886	4	0.5	1.1
New Mexico	54,834	2,302	4.2	5.9	39,678	540	1.4	3.5	2,415	15	0.6	6.5	65	......	......	15.5	292	3	1.0	2.6
Arizona	50,697	2,176	4.3	11.5	24,694	57	0.2	0.5	3,785	14	0.4	4.4	207	......	......	19.9	856	5	0.6	0.6
Utah	70,375	233	0.3	0.4	55,235	84	0.2	0.1	13,405	32	0.2	0.3	601	1	0.2	1.4	94	......	......	......
Nevada	8,469	53	0.6	1.6	5,255	10	0.2	0.3	2,294	5	0.2	0.4	105	......	......	5.9	16	......	......	......
PACIFIC:																				
Washington	165,994	418	0.3	0.2	108,963	252	0.2	0.1	47,088	116	0.2	0.2	5,525	7	0.1	0.4	497	3	0.6	0.2
Oregon	99,134	200	0.2	0.2	75,303	146	0.2	0.2	20,024	40	0.2	0.2	2,169	5	0.2	0.5	144	1	0.7	......
California	506,827	1,080	0.2	0.6	294,565	387	0.1	0.2	130,412	235	0.2	0.3	15,165	28	0.2	4.3	6,424	13	0.2	0.6

1234

POPULATION

TABLE 15.—ILLITERACY IN THE POPULATION 16 TO 20 YEARS OLD, BY COLOR AND NATIVITY, BY DIVISIONS AND STATES: 1930 AND 1920

[Per cent not shown where base is less than 100]

DIVISION AND STATE	ALL CLASSES, 16 TO 20 YEARS OLD Total number, 1930	Illiterate Number, 1930	Per cent 1930	Per cent 1920	NATIVE WHITE—NATIVE PARENTAGE Total number, 1930	Illiterate Number, 1930	Per cent 1930	Per cent 1920	NATIVE WHITE—FOREIGN OR MIXED PARENTAGE Total number, 1930	Illiterate Number, 1930	Per cent 1930	Per cent 1920	FOREIGN-BORN WHITE Total number, 1930	Illiterate Number, 1930	Per cent 1930	Per cent 1920	NEGRO Total number, 1930	Illiterate Number, 1930	Per cent 1930	Per cent 1920
United States	11,478,947	247,104	2.2	3.3	6,838,376	72,721	1.1	1.6	2,783,960	9,987	0.4	0.6	393,125	7,070	1.8	6.6	1,268,638	124,976	9.9	15.1
GEOG. DIVS:																				
New England	706,218	3,637	0.5	1.1	257,605	1,154	0.4	0.5	382,170	1,477	0.4	0.4	58,688	925	1.6	5.0	7,263	59	0.8	1.8
Mid. Atlantic	2,347,376	12,815	0.5	0.8	1,021,086	3,589	0.4	0.3	1,066,367	3,953	0.4	0.3	174,016	4,072	2.3	4.1	83,907	1,011	1.2	1.6
E. N. Central	2,205,426	8,295	0.4	0.5	1,371,668	3,983	0.3	0.4	664,402	1,881	0.3	0.3	91,067	1,248	1.4	2.7	71,832	550	0.8	1.9
W. N. Central	1,229,738	5,615	0.5	0.6	870,429	3,387	0.4	0.5	298,849	880	0.3	0.4	16,281	205	1.3	4.0	26,084	554	2.1	3.0
S. Atlantic	1,687,848	89,853	5.4	7.9	1,072,390	23,412	2.2	3.4	62,687	287	0.5	0.7	8,196	165	2.0	5.6	522,081	65,428	12.5	16.8
E. S. Central	1,041,906	58,394	5.6	7.6	728,438	21,610	3.0	3.7	12,935	73	0.6	0.8	1,157	14	1.2	6.7	298,801	36,403	12.2	16.9
W. S. Central	1,277,001	56,505	4.4	7.3	886,767	13,168	1.5	2.7	50,303	740	1.5	9.0	3,249	63	1.9	38.6	249,623	20,810	8.3	16.6
Mountain	347,802	7,823	2.2	3.7	233,536	1,670	0.7	1.7	69,819	189	0.3	1.1	6,654	84	1.3	15.0	2,191	38	1.7	2.3
Pacific	654,542	4,167	0.6	1.2	387,457	748	0.2	0.2	170,428	493	0.3	0.4	33,217	294	0.9	7.7	6,326	33	0.5	0.9
NEW ENGLAND:																				
Maine	67,381	755	1.1	1.6	42,126	535	1.3	1.3	20,882	147	0.7	1.4	4,192	68	1.6	4.1	74	2	------	2.0
N. Hampshire	38,416	205	0.5	1.1	18,618	77	0.4	0.4	17,024	89	0.5	0.4	2,699	35	1.3	6.4	69	3	------	------
Vermont	31,141	168	0.5	0.8	20,664	103	0.5	0.6	8,114	26	0.3	0.8	2,293	37	1.6	2.4	64	2	------	------
Massachusetts	361,418	1,422	0.4	1.0	114,991	287	0.2	0.3	210,215	736	0.4	0.3	32,024	356	1.1	4.8	3,908	28	0.7	1.7
Rhode Island	62,183	361	0.6	1.5	17,833	53	0.3	0.2	37,928	173	0.5	0.5	5,000	126	2.2	7.1	781	8	1.0	2.0
Connecticut	145,679	726	0.5	1.0	43,373	99	0.2	0.4	88,007	306	0.3	0.2	11,890	304	2.6	4.9	2,367	16	0.7	2.1
MID. ATLANTIC:																				
New York	1,083,167	6,796	0.6	0.9	384,569	1,719	0.4	0.4	552,080	1,863	0.3	0.3	113,830	2,676	2.4	3.6	31,271	406	1.3	1.1
New Jersey	361,909	2,107	0.6	0.9	135,804	332	0.2	0.4	182,677	812	0.4	0.3	25,563	683	2.7	4.5	17,717	262	1.5	1.9
Pennsylvania	902,300	3,912	0.4	0.8	500,713	1,538	0.3	0.4	331,604	1,283	0.4	0.4	34,623	713	2.1	4.9	35,000	343	1.0	1.9
E. N. CENTRAL:																				
Ohio	572,523	2,373	0.4	0.6	391,314	1,282	0.3	0.4	136,845	476	0.3	0.3	19,311	315	1.6	3.1	24,684	253	1.0	2.1
Indiana	281,628	991	0.4	0.5	239,789	709	0.3	0.4	28,822	71	0.2	0.4	3,352	60	1.8	2.8	9,153	73	0.8	1.5
Illinois	675,087	2,648	0.4	0.6	364,087	933	0.3	0.4	252,121	657	0.3	0.3	31,609	539	1.7	2.9	24,041	162	0.6	1.8
Michigan	411,615	1,428	0.3	0.5	217,737	608	0.3	0.3	150,207	409	0.3	0.3	30,195	235	0.8	2.4	11,779	56	0.5	1.7
Wisconsin	264,573	855	0.3	0.4	158,741	451	0.3	0.3	96,407	268	0.3	0.4	7,200	99	1.4	1.5	775	6	0.8	1.5
W. N. CENTRAL:																				
Minnesota	235,135	712	0.3	0.4	121,654	259	0.2	0.3	105,639	304	0.3	0.2	5,590	51	0.9	1.3	621	2	0.3	1.1
Iowa	220,454	581	0.3	0.3	174,336	385	0.2	0.2	41,982	91	0.2	0.3	2,345	44	1.9	4.1	1,410	10	0.7	1.6
Missouri	326,241	2,670	0.8	1.1	272,358	1,992	0.7	0.9	31,772	90	0.3	0.3	3,209	45	1.4	4.6	18,367	503	2.7	4.0
North Dakota	73,039	328	0.4	0.5	29,057	75	0.3	0.2	41,966	171	0.4	0.4	1,653	18	1.1	1.7	28	------	------	------
South Dakota	68,403	221	0.3	0.4	42,039	91	0.2	0.2	23,215	65	0.3	0.3	800	9	1.0	1.7	60	------	------	------
Nebraska	131,913	400	0.3	0.4	93,939	193	0.2	0.3	33,655	110	0.3	0.3	1,842	20	1.0	3.8	982	6	0.6	1.5
Kansas	174,553	703	0.4	0.7	146,046	392	0.3	0.3	20,620	58	0.3	0.4	782	9	1.2	15.7	5,466	33	0.6	1.0
S. ATLANTIC:																				
Delaware	21,264	198	0.9	1.6	13,596	65	0.5	0.5	4,069	14	0.3	0.4	512	9	1.8	5.1	3,081	110	3.6	6.2
Maryland	146,247	1,908	1.3	2.4	95,871	552	0.6	0.9	21,932	80	0.4	0.6	2,340	51	2.2	3.2	26,033	1,273	4.9	8.8
Dist. Columbia	38,861	110	0.3	0.7	21,005	11	0.1	0.1	4,881	3	0.1	0.1	798	8	1.0	2.0	11,529	80	0.7	1.7
Virginia	251,876	12,639	5.0	6.9	174,291	5,488	3.1	4.1	5,531	42	0.8	0.5	581	8	1.4	3.0	71,353	7,127	10.0	13.5
West Virginia	173,090	3,233	1.9	3.2	149,738	2,812	1.9	2.7	11,298	72	0.6	1.0	1,600	68	3.6	14.5	10,432	290	2.8	7.5
North Carolina	355,317	21,598	6.1	8.2	237,382	6,433	2.7	4.8	1,432	5	0.3	0.6	232	6	2.6	5.6	114,316	14,731	12.9	15.2
South Carolina	208,968	23,344	11.2	14.1	102,490	3,053	3.0	4.7	1,147	3	0.3	0.6	153	2	1.3	1.7	105,058	20,250	19.3	21.0
Georgia	334,848	20,226	6.0	10.7	196,270	3,947	2.0	3.5	2,627	3	0.1	0.4	342	1	0.3	2.1	135,576	16,275	12.0	19.8
Florida	137,877	6,537	4.7	6.9	81,657	1,096	1.3	2.1	9,770	56	0.6	1.6	1,632	22	1.3	4.6	44,703	5,292	11.8	14.7
E. S. CENTRAL:																				
Kentucky	251,848	8,845	3.5	4.4	226,135	7,952	3.5	4.2	4,441	14	0.3	0.3	349	5	1.4	4.5	20,909	872	4.2	7.0
Tennessee	277,381	11,194	4.0	5.6	221,034	7,481	3.4	4.1	2,827	11	0.4	0.7	290	2	0.7	3.3	53,200	3,696	6.9	11.6
Alabama	290,094	21,035	7.3	9.6	177,207	4,656	2.6	3.6	3,843	21	0.5	1.4	335	------	------	7.1	108,620	16,335	15.0	18.0
Mississippi	222,583	17,320	7.8	11.7	104,062	1,521	1.5	2.1	1,824	27	1.5	1.6	183	7	3.8	15.9	116,102	15,590	13.4	16.6
W. S. CENTRAL:																				
Arkansas	199,880	6,880	3.4	5.1	143,768	2,854	2.0	2.4	2,807	23	0.8	1.0	120	2	1.7	11.2	53,071	3,985	7.5	11.7
Louisiana	217,500	16,517	7.6	17.9	128,660	5,169	4.2	9.0	9,968	222	2.2	2.4	620	8	1.3	14.0	82,537	10,007	13.2	31.1
Oklahoma	251,227	3,249	1.3	1.8	212,187	1,956	0.9	1.2	8,134	34	0.4	0.6	439	7	1.6	22.6	19,072	565	3.0	4.0
Texas	609,276	29,859	4.9	6.3	407,152	3,180	0.8	1.7	29,394	461	1.6	11.8	2,070	46	2.2	35.6	94,943	5,353	5.6	9.0
MOUNTAIN:																				
Montana	48,851	157	0.3	0.6	27,472	25	0.1	0.2	17,653	40	0.2	0.3	1,994	17	0.9	1.7	67	------	------	------
Idaho	43,478	118	0.3	0.6	34,690	63	0.2	0.2	7,770	23	0.3	0.2	610	3	0.5	6.5	38	1	------	------
Wyoming	20,335	158	0.8	1.0	14,544	34	0.2	0.3	4,477	12	0.3	0.4	520	12	2.3	10.2	72	------	------	0.0
Colorado	94,135	1,014	1.1	1.6	63,884	298	0.5	1.2	21,701	63	0.3	0.5	1,803	20	1.1	10.2	825	6	0.7	1.2
New Mexico	42,580	3,237	7.6	11.2	31,002	1,108	3.6	7.7	1,847	10	0.5	10.1	151	2	1.3	24.4	208	14	5.2	2.8
Arizona	40,217	2,801	7.0	14.0	19,586	59	0.3	1.2	3,102	12	0.4	5.5	408	10	2.5	25.8	802	17	2.0	4.0
Utah	51,474	252	0.5	0.7	38,807	73	0.2	0.3	11,469	27	0.2	0.3	1,031	11	1.1	3.6	42	------	------	------
Nevada	6,822	86	1.3	3.6	4,151	10	0.2	0.3	1,800	2	0.1	0.2	197	9	4.6	9.3	17	------	------	------
PACIFIC:																				
Washington	136,368	406	0.3	0.4	83,403	200	0.2	0.2	42,231	108	0.2	0.3	7,058	32	0.5	1.4	434	2	0.5	0.8
Oregon	82,899	243	0.3	0.4	60,022	136	0.2	0.2	18,798	53	0.3	0.2	2,843	21	0.7	1.9	139	------	------	------
California	435,275	3,518	0.8	1.7	243,972	412	0.2	0.3	115,399	337	0.3	0.4	23,316	241	1.0	10.1	5,753	31	0.5	1.0

CHAPTER 14

INABILITY TO SPEAK
ENGLISH

CHAPTER 14.—INABILITY TO SPEAK ENGLISH

INTRODUCTION

The inquiry as to ability to speak English has been made at each of the last five censuses, beginning with that of 1890. The determination of this ability has been left to the judgment of the enumerator, and no specific tests of the knowledge of the English language have been prescribed. The standards may therefore be subject to some variation in different parts of the country, but on the whole the replies are believed to indicate the ability or inability to use the English language in ordinary daily activities. The inquiry was made only with respect to persons 10 years old and over. The statistics here presented cover continental United States, the States, and cities having 25,000 or more inhabitants. No tabulation of inability to speak English was made for counties or for the smaller cities. Statistics for Alaska, Hawaii, Puerto Rico, Guam, American Samoa, the Panama Canal Zone, and the Virgin Islands of the United States are presented in the Fifteenth Census Report on Outlying Territories and Possessions.

Color and nativity.—The statistics of inability to speak English were tabulated in 1930 for the foreign-born population only, and except for Tables 1, 5, and 11, the tables shown in this chapter relate to the foreign-born white population alone. The 1930 figures for inability to speak English are summarized for the several color or race groups in Table 1.

TABLE 1.—INABILITY TO SPEAK ENGLISH IN THE FOREIGN-BORN POPULATION OF THE UNITED STATES 10 YEARS OLD AND OVER, BY COLOR OR RACE: 1930

COLOR OR RACE	Total 10 years old and over	UNABLE TO SPEAK ENGLISH		PER CENT UNABLE TO SPEAK ENGLISH, BY SEX	
		Number	Per cent	Male	Female
Total foreign born	14,025,800	1,224,995	8.7	6.1	11.8
Foreign-born white	13,216,928	869,865	6.6	4.1	9.5
Foreign-born Negro	97,702	1,859	1.9	1.6	2.2
Foreign-born Mexican	590,095	324,359	55.0	46.5	66.0
Foreign-born Indian	3,380	1,104	32.7	29.6	36.2
Foreign-born Chinese	43,682	12,144	27.8	25.6	45.1
Foreign-born Japanese	69,923	15,125	21.6	12.2	39.4
Other foreign born	4,000	539	13.5	13.0	17.9

The United States totals for the various classes of population covered by the inquiry on ability to speak English at the several censuses are presented in Table 5, while Table 11 gives the 1930 statistics by divisions and states for all of the important nonwhite races. At the census of 1890 statistics were compiled for the native white classes, and at the census of 1900 for the native white of foreign or mixed parentage, as well as for the foreign-born white. In 1910 and 1920 the statistics of inability to speak English were presented for the foreign-born white population, and for Negroes,

Indians, Chinese, and Japanese, without regard to nativity.

There are still in parts of the United States some tens of thousands of persons of native birth who are unable to speak English, but their number is rapidly diminishing, and in the total population it is negligible. In the States of New Mexico, Arizona, and Texas, there are considerable numbers of natives of Mexican origin who speak only Spanish; and in Louisiana many parishes contain a relatively large number of native persons, both white and Negro, who speak only French. There are also a few thousand Indians on reservations who still maintain tribal relations and who have never learned English. In the native white population of States other than Louisiana the few persons who do not speak English are mainly persons of advanced age living in isolated communities.

Country of birth.—Inability to speak English has been tabulated in 1930 for the first time by country of birth. The results of this tabulation taken in connection with the data on year of immigration afford material for a study of the rates at which the foreign born from the different European countries are being assimilated into our American population. In the presentation of these statistics by country of birth only the more important non-English-speaking countries are shown. The totals for the United States are summarized in Table 2.

TABLE 2.—INABILITY TO SPEAK ENGLISH IN THE FOREIGN-BORN WHITE POPULATION OF THE UNITED STATES 10 YEARS OLD AND OVER, BY COUNTRY OF BIRTH AND SEX: 1930

COUNTRY OF BIRTH	Foreign-born white, 10 years old and over	UNABLE TO SPEAK ENGLISH		PER CENT UNABLE TO SPEAK ENGLISH, BY SEX	
		Number	Per cent	Male	Female
All countries	13,216,928	869,865	6.6	4.1	9.5
Denmark	178,212	1,584	0.9	0.5	1.6
Sweden	592,291	9,116	1.5	1.0	2.2
Norway	345,231	8,012	2.3	1.2	3.8
Switzerland	112,240	2,865	2.6	2.0	3.3
Germany	1,589,240	45,694	2.9	1.8	4.1
Netherlands	131,430	4,168	3.2	2.1	4.7
Belgium	63,577	2,088	3.3	2.0	4.8
France	133,857	5,275	3.9	3.3	4.5
Austria	369,192	20,228	5.5	3.5	7.6
Rumania	145,037	9,033	6.2	3.9	9.0
Russia	1,150,441	72,800	6.3	3.7	9.3
Hungary	272,977	21,616	7.9	5.5	10.4
Canada—French	300,724	31,701	8.8	4.4	13.3
Yugoslavia	210,141	19,363	9.2	5.6	15.1
Syria	56,870	5,244	9.2	4.2	15.8
Greece	173,531	17,426	10.0	4.1	27.0
Czechoslovakia	487,794	52,230	10.7	5.9	15.9
Lithuania	193,196	20,936	10.8	6.3	16.9
Finland	142,060	15,411	10.8	5.9	16.7
Poland	1,282,892	161,731	12.8	7.7	18.7
Italy	1,769,705	277,010	15.7	8.9	25.1
Spain	57,957	11,305	16.5	15.5	29.8
Portugal	69,535	16,114	23.2	17.0	32.6
All other countries	3,348,790	38,930	1.2	0.9	1.4

POPULATION

Inability to speak English and literacy.—Another new combination made in the 1930 tabulation involves a cross classification between inability to speak English and literacy. One of the most important of the classes obtained from this combination is that made up of persons able to read and write but not able to speak English. There has been a considerable demand for statistics of literacy in English. The number of persons unable to read and write in English can be approximated by adding to the number of illiterate persons (persons not able to read and write in any language) the number of literate persons who are unable to speak English. Further, the number of persons able to read and write only in some foreign language will doubtless be of significance as indicating the probable number of readers of the foreign language press—or at least of persons whose reading must be limited to publications in foreign languages.

The more important data obtained for the United States through the combination of illiteracy with ability to speak English are presented in Table 3. Similar data, classified also by country of birth, may be found in Tables 6, 7, and 8.

TABLE 3.—INABILITY TO SPEAK ENGLISH IN THE FOREIGN-BORN WHITE POPULATION OF THE UNITED STATES 10 YEARS OLD AND OVER, BY SEX AND LITERACY: 1930

CLASS	Total	Male	Female
Foreign-born white population 10 years old and over	13,216,928	7,078,223	6,138,705
Unable to speak English:			
Number	869,865	287,282	582,583
Per cent of total	6.6	4.1	9.5
Literate—			
Number	392,732	135,552	257,180
Per cent of total	3.0	1.9	4.2
Illiterate—			
Number	477,133	151,730	325,403
Per cent of total	3.6	2.1	5.3
Per cent of those unable to speak English	54.9	52.8	55.9
Able to speak English:			
Number	12,347,063	6,790,941	5,556,122
Per cent of total	93.4	95.9	90.5
Literate—			
Number	11,520,112	6,368,694	5,151,418
Per cent of total	87.2	90.0	83.9
Illiterate—			
Number	826,951	422,247	404,704
Per cent of total	6.3	6.0	6.6
Per cent of those able to speak English	6.7	6.2	7.3
Total literate	11,912,844	6,504,246	5,408,598
Unable to speak English [1]	392,732	135,552	257,180
Per cent of total literate	3.3	2.1	4.8
Total illiterate	1,304,084	573,977	730,107
Unable to speak English	477,133	151,730	325,403
Per cent of total illiterate	36.6	26.4	44.6

[1] Persons able to read and write in their native language but not able even to speak English.

Age.—In order to add still further to the material available for the study of our foreign-born population, the tabulation of inability to speak English in combination with illiteracy and country of birth has been subdivided into broad age groups. In general it would appear that the younger persons in the foreign-born white population were learning to speak English more rapidly than did the older ones, many of whom arrived in periods when immigration was very rapid and the formation of foreign-language settlements more likely to take place. Data on inability to speak English, by age and sex, are presented in Table 4. Similar figures, classified also by country of birth, may be found in Table 7.

TABLE 4.—INABILITY TO SPEAK ENGLISH IN THE FOREIGN-BORN WHITE POPULATION OF THE UNITED STATES 10 YEARS OLD AND OVER, BY AGE AND SEX: 1930

AGE	Total	UNABLE TO SPEAK ENGLISH		PER CENT UNABLE TO SPEAK ENGLISH, BY SEX	
		Number	Per cent	Male	Female
Total 10 years old and over	13,216,928	869,865	6.6	4.1	9.5
10 to 24	1,134,358	41,418	3.7	3.2	4.1
25 to 44	5,593,679	329,473	5.9	3.4	8.9
45 to 64	4,821,774	341,891	7.1	4.5	10.2
65 years and over	1,657,293	156,351	9.4	5.7	13.4
Unknown	9,824	732	7.5	6.0	9.7

Urban and rural areas.—Urban population, as defined by the Census Bureau, is in general that residing in cities and other incorporated places having 2,500 inhabitants or more, the remainder being classified as rural. In three of the New England States—New Hampshire, Massachusetts, and Rhode Island—towns (townships) are classified as urban if they have a population of 2,500 or more and certain urban characteristics; and a few large and densely populated townships in other States are likewise classified, even though not formally incorporated as municipalities.

In addition to the classification of the population as urban and rural, the rural population is subdivided into rural-farm and rural-nonfarm, on the basis of the replies to a question reading "Does this family live on a farm?" The rural-farm population includes all persons living on farms in the rural areas. The rural-nonfarm or "village" population is made up largely of persons living in small towns or villages, both incorporated and unincorporated, though in many areas there are considerable numbers of families living in the open country but not on farms.

Statistics of inability to speak English for urban, rural-farm, and rural-nonfarm areas are presented in Tables 8, 12, and 13.

INABILITY TO SPEAK ENGLISH   1349

TABLE 5.—INABILITY TO SPEAK ENGLISH IN THE FOREIGN-BORN POPULATION 10 YEARS OLD AND OVER, BY COLOR OR RACE AND SEX, FOR THE UNITED STATES: 1890 TO 1930

[Figures for foreign-born nonwhite classes not available prior to 1930]

CENSUS YEAR AND COLOR OR RACE	TOTAL 10 YEARS OLD AND OVER			MALE			FEMALE		
	Total number	Unable to speak English		Total number	Unable to speak English		Total number	Unable to speak English	
		Number	Per cent		Number	Per cent		Number	Per cent
1930									
Total foreign born	14,025,800	1,224,995	8.7	7,556,957	460,661	6.1	6,468,843	764,334	11.8
Foreign-born white	13,216,928	869,865	6.6	7,078,223	287,282	4.1	6,138,705	582,583	9.5
Foreign-born Negro	97,792	1,859	1.9	53,701	877	1.6	44,091	982	2.2
Foreign-born Mexican	590,005	324,359	55.0	335,104	155,995	46.5	254,931	168,364	66.0
Foreign-born Indian	3,380	1,104	32.7	1,795	531	29.6	1,585	573	36.2
Foreign-born Chinese	43,682	12,144	27.8	38,826	9,955	25.6	4,856	2,189	45.1
Foreign-born Japanese	69,923	15,125	21.6	45,627	5,550	12.2	24,296	9,575	39.4
Other foreign born	4,000	539	13.5	3,621	471	13.0	379	68	17.9
1920									
Foreign-born white [1]	13,497,886	1,488,948	11.0	7,419,691	680,033	9.2	6,078,195	808,915	13.3
Total Negro	8,053,225	14,644	0.2	4,009,462	7,207	0.2	4,043,763	7,437	0.2
Total Indian	176,925	36,752	20.8	91,546	17,469	19.1	85,379	19,283	22.6
Total Chinese	56,230	10,020	17.8	51,041	8,903	17.4	5,189	1,117	21.5
Total Japanese	84,238	19,008	22.6	58,806	8,709	14.8	25,432	10,359	40.7
1910									
Foreign-born white [1]	12,944,529	2,953,011	22.8	7,321,196	1,683,949	23.0	5,623,333	1,269,062	22.6
Total Negro	7,317,922	22,110	0.3	3,637,386	10,870	0.3	3,680,536	11,240	0.3
Total Indian	188,758	59,055	31.3	96,582	26,705	27.7	92,176	32,350	35.1
Total Chinese	68,924	28,370	41.2	65,479	26,632	40.7	3,445	1,738	50.4
Total Japanese	67,661	26,564	39.3	60,809	22,848	37.6	6,852	3,710	54.2
1900									
Foreign-born white	10,014,256	1,217,280	12.2	5,414,991	563,982	10.4	4,599,265	653,298	14.2
Total Indian	171,552	72,583	42.3	86,504	32,309	37.3	85,048	40,274	47.4
Total Chinese	87,682	33,498	38.2	84,141	31,191	37.1	3,541	2,307	65.2
Total Japanese	24,091	14,843	61.6	23,214	14,448	62.2	877	395	45.0
1890									
Foreign-born white	8,780,887	1,371,044	15.6	4,781,748	666,496	13.9	4,005,139	704,548	17.6
Total colored	5,482,485	109,427	2.0	2,774,414	85,860	3.1	2,708,071	23,567	0.9

[1] Includes those persons of Mexican birth who in 1930 would have been classified as Mexican.

FOREIGN-BORN WHITE POPULATION 10 YEARS OLD AND OVER, BY SEX AND ABILITY TO SPEAK ENGLISH, FOR THE UNITED STATES: 1930

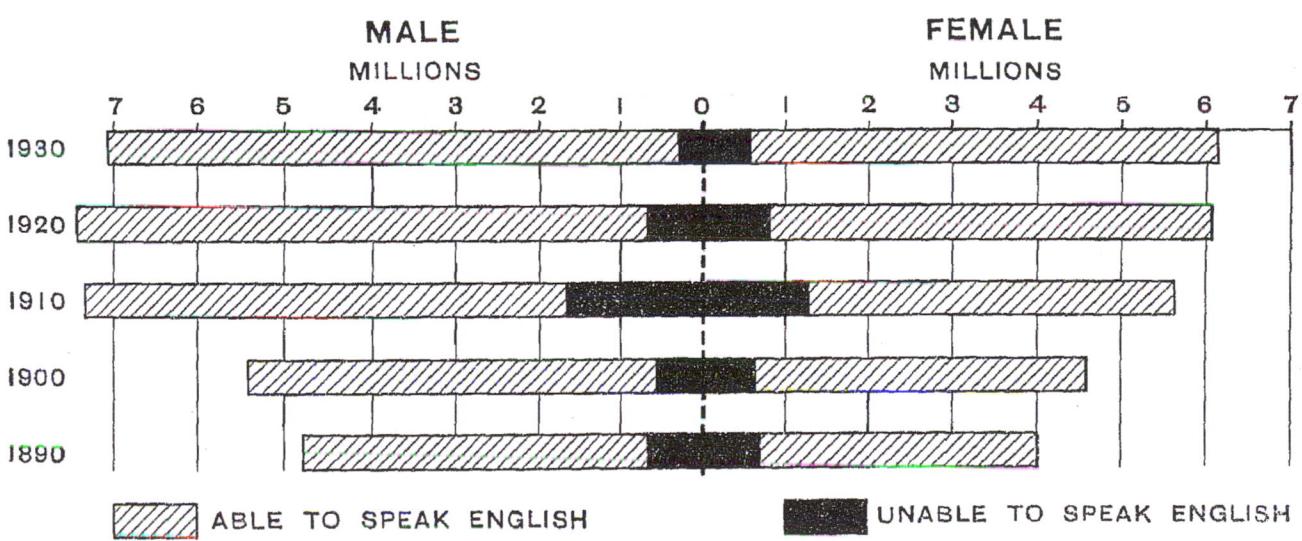

1350

POPULATION

ILLITERACY AND INABILITY TO SPEAK ENGLISH IN THE FOREIGN-BORN WHITE POPULATION 10
YEARS OLD AND OVER, BY COUNTRY OF BIRTH: 1930

POPULATION

1360

TABLE 10.—INABILITY TO SPEAK ENGLISH IN THE FOREIGN-BORN WHITE POPULATION 10 YEARS OLD AND OVER, BY SEX, BY DIVISIONS AND STATES: 1900 TO 1920

[The high percentages of inability to speak English shown in some States are doubtless due to the inclusion of persons of Mexican birth who were separately classified in 1930; see Table 11]

DIVISION AND STATE	1920 Total number	1920 Unable to speak English Number	1920 Per cent	1910 Total number	1910 Unable to speak English Number	1910 Per cent	1900 Total number	1900 Unable to speak English Number	1900 Per cent	1920 Male	1920 Female	1910 Male	1910 Female	1900 Male	1900 Female
United States	13,497,886	1,486,948	11.0	12,544,529	2,953,011	22.8	10,014,256	1,217,280	12.2	9.2	13.3	23.0	22.6	10.4	14.2
GEOGRAPHIC DIVISIONS:															
New England	1,843,028	180,851	9.8	1,757,244	326,890	18.6	1,392,969	155,429	11.2	7.5	12.1	18.3	18.9	9.0	12.3
Middle Atlantic	4,853,256	525,849	10.8	4,661,990	1,217,608	26.1	3,227,687	430,188	13.3	8.9	13.0	27.2	24.8	13.2	13.4
East North Central	3,183,790	328,981	10.3	2,985,823	693,961	23.2	2,583,594	302,531	11.7	8.5	12.7	23.4	23.1	9.0	15.0
West North Central	1,358,323	85,259	6.3	1,570,694	274,620	17.4	1,511,527	168,887	11.2	4.6	8.5	15.9	19.5	7.4	16.1
South Atlantic	311,385	32,042	10.3	280,387	71,389	25.5	205,209	19,518	9.5	9.7	11.1	28.5	20.9	9.4	9.6
East South Central	71,211	2,363	3.3	84,898	9,983	11.8	88,774	3,618	4.1	2.7	4.3	12.0	11.5	3.3	5.1
West South Central	430,053	181,790	42.3	330,431	148,028	44.8	254,168	82,043	32.3	37.0	48.1	40.9	50.3	27.0	38.6
Mountain	436,304	71,096	16.3	423,008	96,637	22.8	283,167	30,359	10.7	14.2	19.5	24.3	20.0	9.2	12.0
Pacific	1,010,536	80,708	8.0	840,999	113,805	13.5	407,161	24,707	5.3	6.8	9.7	14.3	12.1	4.4	6.8
NEW ENGLAND:															
Maine	104,585	10,333	9.9	105,336	19,589	18.6	88,796	13,919	15.7	6.4	13.6	16.1	21.4	11.7	20.0
New Hampshire	89,472	11,339	12.7	92,976	26,783	28.8	83,542	17,107	20.5	9.5	16.1	27.4	30.3	16.0	25.0
Vermont	42,701	3,065	7.2	47,654	8,342	17.5	43,105	3,921	9.1	5.9	8.6	18.0	16.9	8.4	10.0
Massachusetts	1,063,572	96,426	9.1	1,020,594	171,014	16.8	816,808	76,637	9.4	7.1	11.0	16.9	16.7	8.5	10.2
Rhode Island	171,032	21,620	12.6	171,904	36,961	21.5	128,901	17,029	13.2	9.4	15.8	19.8	23.2	11.1	15.2
Connecticut	371,666	38,068	10.2	318,780	64,201	20.1	231,817	26,816	11.6	7.8	13.0	20.1	20.1	11.3	11.8
MIDDLE ATLANTIC:															
New York	2,752,055	290,200	10.5	2,634,578	597,012	22.7	1,844,333	220,306	11.9	8.7	12.6	22.1	23.3	10.3	13.6
New Jersey	729,799	73,409	10.1	636,848	153,861	24.2	420,765	48,709	11.6	8.2	12.2	25.0	23.2	11.4	11.8
Pennsylvania	1,371,402	162,240	11.8	1,390,564	466,825	33.6	962,589	161,173	16.7	9.8	14.4	36.6	29.0	19.0	13.9
EAST NORTH CENTRAL:															
Ohio	669,924	81,161	12.1	570,274	163,722	28.3	452,120	51,752	11.4	10.8	13.9	30.6	25.0	10.1	13.0
Indiana	149,239	13,289	8.9	155,596	40,731	26.2	140,402	11,339	8.1	7.5	10.0	29.6	20.7	6.4	10.2
Illinois	1,194,979	121,995	10.2	1,108,559	266,557	22.8	951,701	103,301	10.9	8.2	12.6	22.7	23.0	8.4	13.6
Michigan	713,228	68,105	9.5	579,803	102,286	17.6	529,731	49,342	9.3	8.0	11.7	17.8	17.4	7.4	11.6
Wisconsin	456,420	44,481	9.7	502,591	120,665	24.0	509,640	86,797	17.0	7.1	13.2	20.7	28.3	11.1	24.2
WEST NORTH CENTRAL:															
Minnesota	482,230	28,311	5.9	538,915	89,850	16.8	498,960	68,804	13.8	3.9	8.5	14.6	20.1	9.1	20.1
Iowa	223,782	9,559	4.3	269,246	37,109	13.8	303,226	25,544	8.4	3.4	5.4	13.3	14.4	5.3	12.4
Missouri	184,894	11,126	6.0	223,578	37,747	16.9	214,001	14,511	6.8	4.9	7.4	17.3	16.3	4.8	9.2
North Dakota	129,051	10,189	7.8	150,451	33,491	22.3	108,107	18,082	16.7	4.7	12.0	17.8	28.8	12.2	23.3
South Dakota	81,781	4,861	5.9	98,334	18,486	18.8	86,770	13,104	15.1	3.7	9.0	15.2	24.0	9.5	22.7
Nebraska	148,209	9,186	6.2	172,497	29,519	17.1	175,262	17,908	10.2	4.6	8.2	16.0	18.6	6.6	14.9
Kansas	108,006	12,027	11.1	131,673	28,358	21.5	125,145	10,844	8.7	9.9	12.7	22.3	20.4	5.4	13.1
SOUTH ATLANTIC:															
Delaware	19,541	2,733	14.0	16,940	4,824	28.5	13,524	1,529	11.3	12.7	15.7	32.8	22.7	13.9	8.2
Maryland	101,155	7,765	7.7	100,951	17,544	17.4	91,609	7,520	8.2	6.3	9.3	17.5	17.3	6.7	9.7
District of Columbia	28,292	779	2.8	23,755	1,349	5.7	19,309	254	1.3	2.2	3.4	5.6	5.7	0.8	1.8
Virginia	30,325	1,135	3.7	25,680	3,983	15.5	18,742	827	4.4	3.1	4.8	17.4	12.4	4.4	4.5
West Virginia	60,679	11,121	18.3	54,646	27,461	50.3	22,025	3,612	16.4	18.5	17.9	55.2	36.8	21.0	8.3
North Carolina	6,981	190	2.7	5,734	779	13.6	4,314	128	2.0	2.0	3.8	14.0	12.9	2.2	3.0
South Carolina	6,327	116	1.8	5,911	447	7.6	5,320	52	1.0	1.6	2.2	7.8	7.1	0.8	1.3
Georgia	16,028	285	1.8	14,656	953	6.5	11,829	177	1.5	1.4	2.4	6.3	6.0	1.1	2.1
Florida	42,057	7,918	18.8	32,155	14,049	43.7	18,537	5,424	29.3	16.0	21.4	42.8	45.2	26.0	33.9
EAST SOUTH CENTRAL:															
Kentucky	30,603	688	2.2	39,571	3,816	9.6	49,860	1,850	3.7	2.0	2.6	10.7	8.4	2.7	4.8
Tennessee	15,297	506	3.3	17,985	1,648	9.2	17,339	675	3.9	2.6	4.3	8.6	10.0	3.4	4.6
Alabama	17,393	724	4.2	18,291	3,028	16.6	14,060	759	5.4	3.0	5.9	16.1	17.3	4.5	6.8
Mississippi	7,918	445	5.6	9,046	1,491	16.5	7,515	334	4.4	4.4	7.7	14.9	19.3	3.8	5.6
WEST SOUTH CENTRAL:															
Arkansas	13,834	697	5.0	16,454	2,741	16.7	13,971	877	6.3	3.6	7.4	14.8	19.8	4.8	8.8
Louisiana	44,244	3,683	8.3	50,333	11,547	22.9	50,132	7,817	15.6	6.3	11.4	20.9	25.7	14.3	17.3
Oklahoma	39,020	5,362	13.7	39,064	7,975	20.4	20,029	1,718	8.6	13.7	13.8	20.3	20.7	5.5	13.7
Texas	332,955	172,057	51.7	224,580	125,765	56.0	170,036	71,631	42.1	47.2	57.4	51.5	62.0	36.4	49.8
MOUNTAIN:															
Montana	91,729	3,098	3.4	89,456	13,718	15.3	61,306	3,100	5.1	2.4	5.0	17.4	10.2	4.6	6.2
Idaho	38,379	1,956	5.1	39,619	5,805	14.7	21,638	921	4.3	4.8	5.5	17.2	8.9	3.7	5.3
Wyoming	24,762	2,003	8.1	26,381	5,970	22.6	16,374	1,962	12.0	7.8	8.7	24.9	15.8	13.6	8.2
Colorado	114,285	10,050	9.3	123,026	22,610	18.4	89,158	6,429	7.2	7.5	12.0	19.0	17.0	7.2	7.8
New Mexico	26,786	13,225	49.4	21,235	11,770	55.5	12,620	5,478	43.4	44.8	55.0	54.4	57.5	38.8	51.2
Arizona	70,053	36,352	51.9	43,724	25,072	57.3	21,379	9,775	45.7	47.0	58.6	54.1	63.8	38.7	58.3
Utah	55,724	2,303	4.1	61,840	8,129	13.1	52,148	2,208	4.2	4.4	3.8	17.0	8.0	3.4	5.1
Nevada	14,586	1,509	10.3	17,787	3,557	20.0	8,544	477	5.6	9.7	12.2	22.2	12.5	6.3	3.9
PACIFIC:															
Washington	244,881	7,796	3.2	234,928	25,568	10.9	100,482	3,815	3.8	2.5	4.3	11.7	9.2	2.9	5.6
Oregon	100,672	3,342	3.3	100,759	13,531	13.4	53,309	2,087	3.9	2.9	4.0	15.3	9.4	2.7	6.0
California	664,983	69,570	10.5	505,312	74,706	14.8	313,370	18,805	6.0	9.1	12.4	15.4	13.8	5.2	7.2

BIBLIOGRAPHY

CODE (Leave blank)	Citizenship of the foreign born	IN WHAT PLACE DID THIS PERSON LIVE ON APRIL 1, 1935? City, town, or village having 2,500 or more inhabitants. Enter "R" for all other places.	COUNTY	STATE (or Territory or foreign country)	On a farm? (Yes or No)	CODE (leave blank)	Was this person AT WORK for pay or profit in private or nonemergency Govt. work during week of March 24-30? (Yes or No)	If not, was he at work on, or assigned to, public EMERGENCY WORK (WPA, NYA, CCC, etc.) during week of March 24-30? (Yes or No)	If neither at work nor assigned to public emergency work. ("No" in Cols. 21 and 22)			For persons answering "No" to quest. 21, 22, 23, and 24	CODE	If at private or nonemergency Government work. ("Yes" in Col. 21)	If seeking work or assigned to public emergency work. ("Yes" in Col. 24)	OCCUPATION
									Was this person SEEKING WORK? (Yes or No)	If not seeking work, did he HAVE A JOB, business, etc.? (Yes or No)	Indicate whether engaged in home housework, in school, unable to work, etc.			Number of hours worked week of March 24-30, 1940	Duration of unemployment up to March 30, 1940—in weeks	
C	16	17	18	19	20	D	21	22	23	24	25	E		26	27	28
		Same House			No		Yes	—	—	—	—		1	40	-	Foreman
		Same House			No		No	No	No	No	H			-	-	
		Same House			No		No	No	No	No	S					
		Same House			No		Yes	—	—	—	—		1			Laborer

General

Alchon, Guy. *The Invisible Hand of Planning; Capitalism, Social Science, and the State in the 1920s.* Princeton, NJ: Princeton University Press, 1985.

Allen, Frederick Lewis. *Only Yesterday: An Informal History of the 1920s.* 1931; reprint, New York: Harper Perennial Classics, 2000.

The American Heritage History of the 1920s & 1930s, ed. by the editors of American Heritage; Ralph K. Andrist, editor in charge. 1970; reprint, New York: American Heritage/Bonanza Books, 1987.

Banta, Martha. *Taylored Lives: Narrative Productions in the Age of Taylor, Veblen, and Ford.* Chicago: University of Chicago Press, 1993.

Best, Gary Dean. *The Dollar Decade: Mammon and the Machine in 1920s America.* Westport, CT: Praeger, 2003.

Borus, Daniel H., ed. *These United States: Portraits of America from the 1920s.* Ithaca, NY: Cornell University Press, 1992.

Braeman, John, et al., eds. *Change and Continuity in Twentieth Century America: The 1920's.* Columbus: Ohio State University Press, 1968.

Broer, Lawrence R., and John D. Walther, eds. *Dancing Fools and Weary Blues: The Great Escape of the Twenties.* Bowling Green, OH: Bowling Green State University Popular Press, 1990.

Brown, Dorothy M. *Setting a Course: American Women in the 1920s.* Boston: Twayne, 1987.

Bryson, Bill. *One Summer; America, 1927.* New York: Doubleday, 2013.

Carter, Paul A. *Another Part of the Twenties.* New York: Columbia University Press, 1977.

Cashman, Sean Dennis. *America in the Twenties and Thirties; The Olympian Age of Franklin Delano Roosevelt.* New York: New York University Press, 1989.

Currell, Susan. *American Culture in the 1920s.* Edinburgh: Edinburgh University Press, 2009.

Davis, Ronald L., ed. *The Social and Cultural Life of the 1920s.* New York: Holt, 1972.

Dinnerstein, Leonard, and David M. Reimers. *Ethnic Americans: A History of Immigration and Assimilation*, 2d ed. New York: Harper & Row, 1982.

Drowne, Kathleen, and Patrick Huber. *The 1920s.* Westport, CT: Greenwood Press, 2004.

Dumenil, Lynn. *The Modern Temper: American Culture and Society in the 1920s.* Eric Foner, consulting ed. New York: Hill and Wang, 1995.

Flink, James J. *The Automobile Age.* Cambridge, MA: MIT Press, 1988.

Furnas, J. C. *Great Times; An Informal Social History of the United States, 1914-1929.* New York: Putnam, 1974.

Goldberg, David J. *Discontented America: The United States in the 1920s.* Baltimore: Johns Hopkins University Press, 1999.

Goodman, Paul, and Frank Otto Gatell. *America in the Twenties: The Beginnings of Contemporary America.* New York: Holt, 1971.

Gusfield, Joseph R. *Symbolic Crusade: Status Politics and the American Temperance Movement.* 1963; reprint, Urbana, IL: Illini Books, 1986.

Hawley, Ellis W. *The Great War and the Search for a Modern Order; A History of the American People and Their Institutions, 1917-1933.* 2d ed. New York: St. Martin's Press, 1992.

Hoffmann, Frederick J. *The Twenties: American Writers in the Post-War Decade,* new ed. New York: Collier, 1962.

The Jazz Age; The 20s, ed. by the editors of Time-Life Books. Alexandria, VA: Time-Life Books, 1998.

Kirschner, Don S. *City and Country: Rural Responses to Urbanization in the 1920s.* Westport, CT: Greenwood Press, 1970.

Kobler, John. *Ardent Spirits; The Rise and Fall of Prohibition.* 1973; reprint, New York: Da Capo Press, 1993.

Kyvig, David E. *Daily Life in the United States, 1920-1940: How Americans Lived through the Roaring Twenties and the Great Depression.* Westport, CT: Greenwood Press, 2001.

Leighton, Isabel, ed. *The Aspirin Age: 1919-1941: The Essential Events of American Life in the Chaotic Years between the Two World Wars.* 1949; reprint, New York: Simon & Schuster, 1963.

Leuchtenberg, William E. *The Perils of Prosperity, 1914-1932,* 2d ed. Chicago: University of Chicago Press, 1993.

Lynd, Robert S., and Helen Merrell Lynd. *Middletown: A Study in Modern American Culture.* 1929; reprint, New York: Harcourt Brace, 1954.

Mecklin, John Moffatt. *The Ku-Klux Klan: A Study of the American Mind.* 1924; reprint, Whitefish, MT: Kessinger, 2006. [Facsimile reprint of the 1963 Russell and Russell edition.]

Mencken, H. L. *The American Language,* 2d ed., rev. and enl. New York: Knopf, 1921. [Preface: "The discussion of foreign languages in the United States, scarcely more than a footnote in the first edition, is now enlarged and put into an appendix."]

Miller, Donald L. *Supreme City: How Jazz Age Manhattan Gave Birth to Modern America.* New York: Simon & Schuster, 2014.

Miller, Nathan. *New World Coming: The 1920s and the Making of Modern America.* New York: Scribner, 2003.

Moore, Lucy. *Anything Goes: A Biography of the Roaring Twenties.* New York: Overlook, 2010.

Moskowitz, Marina. *Standard of Living: The Measure of the Middle Class in Modern America.* Baltimore: Johns Hopkins University Press, 2004.

Murphy, Paul V. *The New Era: American Thought and Culture in the 1920s.* Lanham, MD: Rowman & Littlefield, 2012.

Nash, Roderick. *The Nervous Generation; American Thought, 1917-1930*. Chicago: Elephant Paperbacks, 1990.

Olson, James S. *Historical Dictionary of the 1920s: From World War I to the New Deal, 1919-1933*. Westport, CT: Greenwood Press, 1988.

O'Neal, Michael. *America in the 1920s*. New York: Facts on File, 2006.

Parker, Alison M. *Purifying America: Women, Cultural Reform, and Pro-Censorship Activism, 1873-1933*. Urbana: University of Illinois Press, 1997.

Paschen, Stephen H., and Leonard Schlup, eds. *The United States in the 1920s as Observed in Contemporary Documents: The Ballyhoo Years*. Lewiston, NY: Edwin Mellen Press, 2007.

Schlesinger, Arthur M., Jr. *The Crisis of the Old Order: The Age of Roosevelt, 1919-1933*. 1957; reprint, Boston: Houghton Mifflin, 2003.

Sklar, Martin J. *The United States as a Developing Country: Studies in U.S. History in the Progressive Era and the 1920s*. New York: Cambridge University Press, 1992.

Sklar, Robert, ed. *The Plastic Age (1917-1930)*. New York: G. Braziller, 1970.

Smith, Page. *Redeeming the Time: A People's History of the 1920s and the New Deal*. New York: McGraw-Hill, 1987.

Strauss, Anselm. *Images of the American City*. 1961; reprint, New Brunswick, NJ: Transaction, 2014.

Susman, Warren I. *Culture as History: The Transformation of American Society in the Twentieth Century*. New York: Pantheon, 1984.

Touring America Seventy-Five Years Ago: How the Automobile and the Railroad Changed the Nation; Chronicles from National Geographic. Arthur M. Schlesinger, Jr., senior consulting ed.; Fred L. Israel, gen. ed. Philadelphia: Chelsea House, 1999.

Welky, David, ed. *America between the Wars, 1919-1941; A Documentary Reader*. Malden, MA: Wiley-Blackwell, 2012.

Wilson, Edmund. *The American Earthquake; A Documentary of the Twenties and Thirties*. 1958; reprint, New York: Octagon, 1971.

African Americans and the Harlem Renaissance

Abel, Elizabeth. *Signs of the Times: The Visual Politics of Jim Crow*. Berkeley: University of California Press, 2010.

Anderson, Jervis. *This Was Harlem: A Cultural Portrait, 1900-1950*. New York: Farrar, Straus & Giroux, 1982.

Aycock, Colleen, and Mark Scott, eds. *The First Black Boxing Champions: Essays on Fighters from the 1800s to the 1920s*. Jefferson, NC: McFarland, 2010.

Bone, Robert. *Down Home: A History of Afro-American Short Fiction from Its Beginnings to the End of the Harlem Renaissance*. New York: Putnam, 1975.

Bontemps, Arna., ed. *The Harlem Renaissance Remembered: Essays Edited with a Memoir by Arna Bontemps*. New York: Dodd, Mead, 1972.

Brundage, W. Fitzhugh, ed. *Beyond Blackface: African American and the Creation of American Popular Culture, 1890-1930*. Chapel Hill: University of North Carolina Press, 2011.

Candaele, Kerry. *Bound for Glory: From the Great Migration to the Harlem Renaissance, 1910-1930*. New York: Chelsea House, 1996.

Carney, Court. *Cuttin' Up: How Early Jazz Got America's Ear*. Lawrence: University Press of Kansas, 2009.

Chapman, Erin D. *Prove It on Me: New Negroes, Sex, and Popular Culture in the 1920s*. New York: Oxford University Press, 2012.

Douglas, Ann. *Terrible Honesty: Mongrel Manhattan in the 1920s*. New York: Farrar, Straus & Giroux, 1995.

Du Bois, W. E. B. *Selections from* The Crisis, ed. by Herbert Aptheker. Millwood, NY: Kraus-Thompson, 1983.

Ewing, Adam. *The Age of Garvey: How a Jamaican Activist Created a Mass Movement and Changed Global Black Politics*. Princeton, NJ: Princeton University Press, 2014.

Favor, J. Martin. *Authentic Blackness: The Folk in the New Negro Renaissance*. Durham, NC: Duke University Press, 1999.

Floyd, Samuel A. Jr., ed. *Black Music in the Harlem Renaissance: A Collection of Essays*. New York: Greenwood Press, 1990.

Foner, Philip S., and James S. Allen, eds. *American Communism and Black Americans: A Documentary History, 1919-1929*. Philadelphia: Temple University Press, 1987.

Francis, Jacqueline. *Making Race: Modernism and "Racial Art" in America*. Seattle: University of Washington Press, 2012.

Gates, Henry Louis, Jr., and Gene Andrew Jarrett, eds. *The New Negro: Readings on Race, Representation, and African American Culture, 1892-1938*. Princeton, NJ: Princeton University Press, 2007.

Harlem Renaissance: Art of Black America, essays by David Driskell, David Levering Lewis, and Deborah Willis Ryan. New York: The Studio Museum in Harlem/Harry N. Abrams, 1987.

Harrison, Daphne Duval. *Black Pearls: Blues Queens of the 1920s*. New Brunswick, NJ: Rutgers University Press, 1988.

Huggins, Nathan I. *Harlem Renaissance*. New York: Oxford University Press, 1971.

Hutchinson, George. *The Harlem Renaissance in Black and White*. Cambridge, MA: Belknap Press of Harvard University Press, 1995.

Johnson, James Weldon. *Black Manhattan*. 1930; reprint, New York: Da Capo Press, 1991.

Lewis, David Levering. *When Harlem Was In Vogue*. New York: Oxford University Press, 1979.

Locke, Alain, ed. *The New Negro*. 1925; reprint, New York: Maxwell Macmillan, 1992. [New introduction by Arnold Rampersad.]

Lutz, Tom, and Susanna Ashton, eds. *These "Colored" United States: African American Essays from the 1920s*. New Brunswick, NJ: Rutgers University Press, 1996.

Marks, Carole, and Diana Edkins. *The Power of Pride: Stylemakers and Rulebreakers of the Harlem Renaissance*. New York: Crown, 1999.

Packard, Jerrold. *American Nightmare: The History of Jim Crow*. New York: St. Martin's Press, 2002.

Perry, Margaret. *The Harlem Renaissance: An Annotated Bibliography and Commentary*. New York: Garland Press, 1982.

Perry, Margaret. *Silence to the Drums: A Survey of the Literature of the Harlem Renaissance*. Westport, CT: Greenwood Press, 1976.

Rhapsodies in Black: Art of the Harlem Renaissance. Richard J. Powell and David A. Bailey, comps. London: Hayward Gallery/Berkeley, CA: University of California Press, 1997.

Schatzberg, Rufus and Kelly, Robert J. *African American Organized Crime: A Social History*. New Brunswick, NJ: Rutgers University Press, 1997.

Springer, Robert, ed. *Nobody Knows Where the Blues Come From; Lyrics and History*. Jackson: University Press of Mississippi, 2006.

Trotter, Joe William Jr., ed. *The Great Migration in Historical Perspective: New Dimensions of Race, Class, and Gender*. Bloomington: Indiana University Press, 1991.

Vincent, Theodore G. *Voices of a Black Nation: Political Journalism in the Harlem Renaissance*. San Francisco: Ramparts Press, 1973.

Wilkerson, Isabel, *The Warmth of Other Suns: The Epic Story of America's Great Migration*. New York: Random House, 2010.

Wintz, Cary D., series ed. *The Harlem Renaissance, 1920-1940*, 7 vols. New York: Garland, 1996. [vol. 1: *The Emergence of the Harlem Renaissance*; vol. 2: *The Politics and Aesthetics of "New Negro" Literature*; vol. 3: *Black Writers Interpret the Harlem Renaissance*; vol. 4: *The Critics and the Harlem Renaissance*; vol. 5: *Remembering the*

Harlem Renaissance; vol. 6: *Analysis and Assessment, 1940-1979*; vol. 7: *Analysis and Assessment, 1980-1994.*]

Woodward, C. Vann. *The Strange Career of Jim Crow*, commemorative edition with a new afterword by William F. McFeely. New York: Oxford University Press, 2002. [First edition, 1955.]

Wormser, Richard. *The Rise and Fall of Jim Crow.* New York: St. Martin's Press, 2003.

Art and Design

B. Altman Company. *1920s Fashions from B. Altman & Company.* Mineola, NY: Dover, 1999.

Bayer, Patricia. *Art Deco Architecture: Design, Decoration, and Detail from the Twenties and Thirties.* New York: H. Abrams, 1992.

Bayer, Patricia. *Art Deco Interiors: Decoration and Design Classics of the 1920s and 1930s.* New York: Thames and Hudson, 1998.

Blaszczyk, Regina Lee. *Imagining Consumers: Design and Innovation from Wedgwood to Corning.* Baltimore: Johns Hopkins University Press, 2000.

Deepwell, Katy, ed. *Women Artists and Modernism.* New York: Manchester University Press, 1998.

Foglesong, Richard F. *Planning the Capitalist City: The Colonial Era to the 1920s.* Princeton, NJ: Princeton University Press, 1986.

Francis, Jacqueline. *Making Race: Modernism and "Racial Art" in America.* Seattle: University of Washington Press, 2012.

Galassi, Peter. *Walker Evans & Company.* New York: Museum of Modern Art, 2000.

Gorman, Carma R. *The Industrial Design Reader.* New York: Allworth, 2003.

Harlem Renaissance: Art of Black America, essays by David Driskell, David Levering Lewis, and Deborah Willis Ryan. New York: The Studio Museum in Harlem/Harry N. Abrams, 1987.

Jakle, John A., and Keith A. Sculle. *The Garage: Automobility and Building Innovation in America's Early Auto Age.* Knoxville: University of Tennessee Press, 2013.

Loeb, Carolyn S. *Entrepreneurial Vernacular: Developers' Subdivisions in the 1920s.* Baltimore: Johns Hopkins University Press 2001.

Maloney, Alison: *Bright Young Things: A Modern Guide to the Roaring Twenties.* 2012; reprint, New York: Potter Style, 2013.

Morningstar, Connie. *Flapper Furniture and Interiors of the 1920s.* Des Moines: Wallace-Homestead, 1971.

Power, Ethel B. *Smaller Houses of the 1920s: 55 Examples.* Mineola, NY: Dover, 2007.

Rhapsodies in Black: Art of the Harlem Renaissance. Richard J. Powell and David A. Bailey, comps. London: Hayward Gallery/Berkeley, CA: University of California Press, 1997.

Saab, A. Joan. *For the Millions: American Art and Culture between the Wars.* Philadelphia: University of Pennsylvania Press, 2004.

Seleshanko, Kristina. *Vintage Fashions for Women, 1920s-1940s.* Atglen, PA: Schiffer, 1996.

Smith, Terry. *Making the Modern: Industry, Art, and Design in America.* Chicago: University of Chicago Press, 1993.

Swedberg, Robert W., and Harriett Swedberg. *Furniture of the Depression Era: Furniture and Accessories of the 1920s, 1930s, and 1940s.* Paducah, KY: Collector Books, 1987.

Tartsinis, Ann Marguerite. *An American Style: Global Sources for New York Textile and*

Fashion Design, 1915-1928. New York: Bard Graduate Center, 2013.

Tiffin Glass Collectors Club. *U.S. Glass Co.; Decorated Satin Glass and Lamps of the 1920s.* Atglen, PA: Schiffer, 2004.

Warner, Patricia Campbell. *When the Girls Came Out to Play: The Birth of American Sportswear.* Amherst, MA: University of Massachusetts Press, 2006.

Business and Economy

Alchon, Guy. *The Invisible Hand of Planning: Capitalism, Social Science, and the State in the 1920s.* Princeton, NJ: Princeton University Press, 1985.

Bartoletti, Susan Campbell. *Growing Up in Coal Country.* Boston: Houghton Mifflin, 1996.

Benson, Susan Porter. *Counter Cultures: Saleswomen, Managers, and Customers in American Department Stores, 1890-1940.* Urbana: University of Illinois Press, 1986.

Best, Gary Dean. *The Dollar Decade: Mammon and the Machine in 1920s America.* Westport, CT: Praeger, 2003.

Blatz, Perry K. *Democratic Miners: Work and Labor Relations in the Anthracite Coal Industry, 1875-1925.* Albany: State University of New York Press, 1994.

Calder, Lendol Glen. *Financing the American Dream: A Cultural History of Consumer Credit.* Princeton, NJ: Princeton University Press, 1999.

Chandler, Alfred D., Jr. *The Visible Hand: The Managerial Revolution in American Business.* Cambridge, MA: Belknap Press of Harvard University Press, 1993.

Cohen, Lisabeth. *Making a New Deal: Industrial Workers in Chicago, 1919-1939,* 2nd ed. New York: Cambridge University Press, 2008.

Conference on Unemployment, Washington, D.C., 1921. *Recent Economic Changes in the United States; Report of the Committee on Recent Economic Changes, of the President's Conference on Unemployment, Herbert Hoover, Chairman, Including the Reports of a Special Staff of the National Bureau of Economic Research.* 2 vols. New York: McGraw Hill, 1929.

Cook, Daniel Thomas. *The Commodification of Childhood: The Children's Clothing Industry and the Rise of the Child Consumer.* Durham, NC: Duke University Press, 2004.

Crawford, M. *Building the Workingman's Paradise: The Design of American Company Towns.* London: Verso, 1995.

Foner, Philip S. *The T. U. E. L., 1925-1929,* vol. 10 of *History of the Labor Movement in the United States,* 2d ed. 1975-1988; reprint, New York: International Publishers, 1991.

Foner, Philip S. *The T. U. E. L. to the End of the Gompers Era,* vol. 9 of *History of the Labor Movement in the United States,* 2d ed. 1975-1988; reprint, New York: International Publishers, 1991.

Francaviglia, R., *Hard Places: Reading the Landscape of America's Historic Mining Districts.* Iowa City: University of Iowa Press, 1991.

Gage, Beverly. *The Day Wall Street Exploded; A Story of America in Its First Age of Terror.* New York: Oxford University Press, 2009.

Garbade, Kenneth D. *Birth of a Market: The U.S. Treasury Securities Market from the Great War to the Great Depression.* Cambridge, MA: MIT Press, 2012.

Gidlow, Liette. *The Big Vote: Gender, Consumer Culture, and the Politics of Exclusion, 1890s-1920s.* Baltimore: Johns Hopkins University Press, 2004.

Hawley, Ellis W., ed. *Herbert Hoover as Secretary of Commerce: Studies in New Era Thought and Practice.* Iowa City: University of Iowa Press, 1981.

Heitmann, John A. *The Automobile and American Life.* Jefferson, NC: McFarland, 2009.

Horowitz, Daniel. *The Morality of Spending: Attitudes toward the Consumer Society in America, 1875-1940.* 1985; reprint, Ivan Dee, 1992.

Hounshell, David A. *From the American System to Mass Production, 1800-1932: The Development of Manufacturing Technology in the United States.* Baltimore: Johns Hopkins University Press, 1984.

Jablonsky, Thomas J. *Pride in the Jungle: Community and Everyday Life in Back of the Yards Chicago.* Baltimore: Johns Hopkins University Press, 1993.

Jacobson, Lisa. *Raising Consumers: Children and the American Mass Market in the Early Twentieth Century.* New York: Columbia University Press, 2004.

Knapp, Joseph G. The Advance of American Cooperative Enterprise, 2 vols. Danville, IL: Interstate, 1973.

Kobrin, Rebecca, ed. *Chosen Capital: The Jewish Encounter with American Capitalism.* New Brunswick, NJ: Rutgers University Press, 2012.

Leach, William. *Land of Desire: Merchants, Power, and the Rise of a New American Culture.* New York: Pantheon Books, 1993.

Leary, William M., ed. *Aviation's Golden Age: Portraits from the 1920s and 1930s.* Iowa City: University of Iowa Press, 1989.

Lundén, Rolf. *Business and Religion in the American 1920s.* New York: Greenwood Press 1988.

Michrina, Barry P. *Pennsylvania Mining Families: The Search for Dignity in the Coal Fields.* Lexington: University Press of Kentucky, 1993.

Moskowitz, Marina. *Standard of Living: The Measure of the Middle Class in Modern America.* Baltimore: Johns Hopkins University Press, 2004.

Olney, Martha E. *Buy Now, Pay Later: Advertising, Credit, and Consumer Durables in the 1920s.* Chapel Hill: University of North Carolina Press, 1991.

Rutherford, Janice Williams. *Selling Mrs. Consumer: Christine Frederick and the Rise of Household Efficiency.* Athens, University of Georgia Press, 2002.

Salay, David L. *Hard Coal, Hard Times; Ethnicity and Labor in the Anthracite Region.* Scranton: Anthracite Museum Press, 1984.

Schwartz, Michael. *Broadway and Corporate Capitalism; The Rise of the Professional-Managerial Class, 1900-1920.* New York: Palgrave Macmillan, 2009.

Seltzer, Curtis. *Fire in the Hole: Miners and Managers in the American Coal Industry.* Lexington: University Press of Kentucky, 1985.

Sobel, Robert. *The Great Bull Market: Wall Street in the 1920s.* New York: W. W. Norton, 1968.

Thomas, W. Donald. *Lindbergh and Commercial Aviation: A Pictorial Review of Colonel Lindbergh's Association with TAT, TWA, and PAA as Technical Advisor.* Dunedin, FL: D. Thomas, 1988.

Walker, Susannah. *Style and Status: Selling Beauty to African American Women, 1920-1975.* Lexington: University Press of Kentucky, 2007.

Crime and Criminals

Albanese, Jay S. *Organized Crime in America,* 3d ed. Cincinnati: Anderson, 1995.

Allsop, Kenneth. *The Bootleggers: The Story of Chicago's Prohibition Era.* New Rochelle, NY: Arlington House, 1968.

Asbury, Herbert. *Gem of the Prairie: An Informal History of the Chicago Underworld.* 1940; reprint, New York: Knopf, 1986.

Fox, Stephen R. *Blood and Power; Organized Crime in Twentieth Century America.* New York: Penguin, 1990.

Helmer, William J., with Rick Mattix. *Public Enemies: America's Criminal Past, 1919-1940.* New York: Facts on File, 1998.

Helmer, William J., and Arthur J. Bilek. *The St. Valentine's Day Massacre: The Untold Story of the Gangland Bloodbath that Brought Down Al Capone.* Nashville, TN: Cumberland House, 2004.

LaCerra. Charles. *Franklin Delano Roosevelt and Tammany Hall of New York.* Lanham, MD: University Press of America, 1997.

Landesco, John. *Organized Crime in Chicago.* 1929; Chicago: University of Chicago Press, 1968. [First published as Part III of the Illinois

crime survey issued in 1929 by the Illinois Association for Criminal Justice.]

Mappen, Marc. *Prohibition Gangsters: The Rise and Fall of a Bad Generation.* New Brunswick, NJ: Rutgers University Press, 2013.

Schatzberg, Rufus. *Black Organized Crime in Harlem, 1920-1930.* New York: Garland, 1993.

Schatzberg, Rufus, and Robert J. Kelly. *African American Organized Crime: A Social History.* New Brunswick, NJ: Rutgers University Press, 1997.

Sullivan, Edward D. *Rattling the Cup on Chicago Crime.* 1929; reprint, Freeport, NY: Books for Libraries Press, 1971.

Vyhnanek, Louis. *Unorganized Crime: New Orleans in the 1920s.* Lafayette: Center for Louisiana Studies, University of Southwestern Louisiana, 1998.

Woodiwiss, Michael. *Crime, Crusades, and Corruption: Prohibitions in the United States, 1900-1987.* Totowa, NJ: Barnes & Noble, 1988.

Woodiwiss, Michael. *Organized Crime and American Power: A History.* Toronto: University of Toronto Press, 2001.

Film, Music, and Popular Culture

Anderson, Mark Lynn. *Twilight of the Idols: Hollywood and the Human Sciences in 1920s America.* Berkeley: University of California Press, 2011.

B. Altman Company. *1920s Fashions from B. Altman & Company.* Mineola, NY: Dover, 1999.

Bak, Richard. *The Big Jump: Lindbergh and the Great Atlantic Air Race.* Hoboken, NJ: John Wiley, 2011.

Barnouw, Erik. *A Tower in Babel: A History of Broadcasting in the United States,* 2 vols. New York: Oxford University Press, 1966. [Vol. 1: To 1933.]

Barnouw, Erik. *Tube of Plenty: The Evolution of American Television,* 2d ed. New York: Oxford University Press, 1990.

Basinger, Jeanine. *Silent Stars.* New York: Knopf, 1999.

Best, Gary Dean. *The Dollar Decade: Mammon and the Machine in 1920s America.* Westport, CT: Praeger, 2003.

Bianchi, William. *Schools of the Air: A History of Instructional Programs on Radio in the United States.* Jefferson, NC: McFarland, 2008.

Bilton, Alan. *Silent Film Comedy and American Culture.* New York: Palgrave Macmillan, 2013.

Blake, Angela M. *How New York Became American, 1890-1924.* Baltimore: Johns Hopkins University Press, 2006.

Blaszczyk, Regina Lee. *Imagining Consumers: Design and Innovation from Wedgwood to Corning.* Baltimore: Johns Hopkins University Press, 2000.

Bohn, Michael K. *Heroes and Ballyhoo: How the Golden Age of the 1920s Transformed American Sports.* Washington, DC: Potomac Books, 2009.

Boyer, Paul S. *Purity in Print: Book Censorship in America from the Gilded Age to the Computer Age,* 2d ed. Madison: University of Wisconsin Press, 2002.

Brown, Elspeth H. The Corporate Eye: Photography and the Rationalization of American Commercial Culture, 1884-1929. Baltimore: Johns Hopkins University Press, 2005.

Browning, Reed. *Baseball's Greatest Season, 1924.* Amherst: University of Massachusetts Press, 2003.

Brundage, W. Fitzhugh, ed. *Beyond Blackface: African Americans and the Creation of American Popular Culture, 1890-1930.* Chapel Hill: University of North Carolina Press, 2011.

Bryson, Bill. *One Summer; America, 1927.* New York: Doubleday, 2013.

Calder, Lendol Glen. *Financing the American Dream: A Cultural History of Consumer Credit.* Princeton, NJ: Princeton University Press, 1999.

Carney, Court. *Cuttin' Up: How Early Jazz Got America's Ear.* Lawrence: University Press of Kansas, 2009.

Chapman, Erin D. *Prove It on Me: New Negroes, Sex, and Popular Culture in the 1920s.* New York: Oxford University Press, 2012.

Coben, Stanley. *Rebellion against Victorianism; The Impulse for Cultural Change in 1920s America.* New York: Oxford University Press, 1991.

Cook, Daniel Thomas. *The Commodification of Childhood: The Children's Clothing Industry and the Rise of the Child Consumer.* Durham, NC: Duke University Press, 2004.

Cooke, Bob, ed. *Wake Up the Echoes: From the Sports Pages of the* New York Herald Tribune. Garden City, NY: Hanover House, 1956.

Cox, Jim. *Music Radio: The Great Performers and Programs of the 1920s through Early 1960s.* Jefferson, NC: McFarland, 2005.

Crafton, Donald. *Before Mickey: The Animated Film, 1898-1928.* Chicago: University of Chicago Press, 1993.

Currell, Susan. *American Culture in the 1920s.* Edinburgh: Edinburgh University Press, 2009.

Davis, Simone Weil. *Living Up to the Ads; Gender Fictions of the 1920s.* Durham, NC: Duke University Press, 2000.

DesRochers, Rick. *The New Humor in the Progressive Era; Americanization and the Vaudeville Comedian.* New York: Palgrave Macmillan, 2014.

Dulles, Foster Rhea. *A History of Recreation; America Learns to Play,* 2d ed. New York: Appleton Century Crofts, 1965.

Dumenil, Lynn. *The Modern Temper: American Culture and Society in the 1920s.* Eric Foner, consulting ed. New York: Hill and Wang, 1995.

Dunning, John. *On The Air: The Encyclopedia of Old-Time Radio.* New York : Oxford University Press, 1997.

Eyman, Scott. *The Speed of Sound: Hollywood and the Talkie Revolution, 1926-1930.* New York: Simon & Schuster, 1997.

Fass, Paula F. *The Damned and the Beautiful: American Youth in the 1920s.* New York: Oxford University Press, 1977.

Finnegan, Margaret Mary. *Selling Suffrage: Consumer Culture and Votes for Women.* New York: Columbia University Press, 1999.

Fischer, Lucy, ed. *American Cinema of the 1920s: Themes and Variations.* New Brunswick, NJ: Rutgers University Press, 2009.

Floyd, Samuel A. Jr., ed. *Black Music in the Harlem Renaissance: A Collection of Essays.* New York: Greenwood Press, 1990.

Fox, Craig. *Everyday Klanfolk: White Protestant Life and the KKK in 1920s Michigan.* Lansing: Michigan State University Press, 2011.

Francaviglia, R., *Hard Places: Reading the Landscape of America's Historic Mining Districts.* Iowa City: University of Iowa Press, 1991.

George, Jennifer, et al. The art of Rube Goldberg: a) Inventive b) Cartoon c) Genius, ed. by Paul Tumey. New York: Abrams ComicArts, 2013.

Gewirtz, Arthur, and James J. Kolb, eds. *Art, Glitter, and Glitz: Mainstream Playwrights and Popular Theatre in 1920s America.* Westport, CT: Praeger, 2003.

Gidlow, Liette. *The Big Vote: Gender, Consumer Culture, and the Politics of Exclusion, 1890s-1920s.* Baltimore: Johns Hopkins University Press, 2004.

Giordano, Ralph G. *Satan in the Dance Hall: Rev. John Roach Straton, Social Dancing, and Morality in 1920s.* New York City. Lanham, MD: Scarecrow Press, 2008.

Goldberg, David J., *Discontented America: The United States in the 1920s.* Baltimore: Johns Hopkins University Press, 1999.

Golden, Eve. *Golden Images: Forty-One Essays on Silent Film Stars.* Jefferson, NC: McFarland, 2001.

Gordon, Ian. *Comic Strips and Consumer Culture, 1890-1945.* Washington, DC: Smithsonian Institution Press, 1998.

Gray, Susan M. *Charles A. Lindbergh and the American Dilemma: The Conflict of Technology and Human Values.* Bowling Green, OH: Bowling Green State University Popular Press, 1988.

Gusfield, Joseph R. *Symbolic Crusade: Status Politics and the American Temperance Movement.* 1963; reprint, Urbana, IL: Illini Books, 1986.

Hansen, Miriam. *Babel and Babylon: Spectatorship in American Silent Film.* 1991; reprint, Cambridge, MA: Harvard University Press, 1994.

Harrison, Daphne Duval. *Black Pearls: Blues Queens of the 1920s.* New Brunswick, NJ: Rutgers University Press, 1988.

Horowitz, Daniel. *The Morality of Spending: Attitudes toward the Consumer Society in America, 1875-1940.* 1985; reprint, Ivan Dee, 1992.

Jacobs, Lea. *The Decline of Sentiment: American Film in the 1920s.* Berkeley: University of California Press, 2008.

Jacobs, Lewis. *The Rise of the American Film: A Critical History.* 1939; reprint, New York: Teachers College Press, 1968.

Jacobson, Lisa. *Raising Consumers: Children and the American Mass Market in the Early Twentieth Century.* New York: Columbia University Press, 2004.

Jakle, John A., and Keith A. Sculle. *The Garage: Automobility and Building Innovation in America's Early Auto Age.* Knoxville: University of Tennessee Press, 2013.

Koritz, Amy. *Culture Makers: Urban Performance and Literature in the 1920s.* Urbana: University of Illinois Press, 2009.

Latham, Angela J. *Posing a Threat: Flappers, Chorus Girls, and Other Brazen Performers of the American 1920s.* Hanover, NH: University Press of New England/Wesleyan University Press, 2000.

Leary, William M., ed. *Aviation's Golden Age: Portraits from the 1920s and 1930s.* Iowa City: University of Iowa Press, 1989.

Leff, Leonard J. and Jerold L. Simmons. *The Dame in the Kimono: Hollywood, Censorship, and the Production Code from the 1920s to the 1960s.* New York: Grove Weidenfeld, 1990.

Lewinnek, Elaine. *The Working Man's Reward: Chicago's Early Suburbs and the Roots of American Sprawl.* New York: Oxford University Press, 2014.

Lieberman, Philip A. *Radio's Morning Show Personalities: Early Hour Broadcasters and Deejays from the 1920s to the 1990s.* Jefferson, NC: McFarland, 1996.

Madison, Nathan Vernon. *Anti-Foreign Imagery in American Pulps and Comic Books, 1920-1960.* Jefferson, NC: McFarland, 2013.

Maloney, Alison: *Bright Young Things: A Modern Guide to the Roaring Twenties.* 2012; reprint, New York: Potter Style, 2013.

Marchand, Roland. *Advertising the American Dream: Making Way for Modernity, 1920-1940.* Berkeley: University of California Press, 1985.

Marks, Carole, and Diana Edkins. *The Power of Pride: Stylemakers and Rulebreakers of the Harlem Renaissance.* New York: Crown, 1999.

Martin, Carol. *Dance Marathons: Performing American Culture of the 1920s and 1930s.* Jackson: University Press of Mississippi, 1994.

May, Lary. *Screening Out the Past: The Birth of Mass Culture and the Motion Picture Industry.* Oxford: Oxford University Press, 1980.

McCann, Richard Dyer, comp. *Films of the 1920s.* Lanham, MD: Scarecrow Press/Iowa City, IA: In Association with Image and Idea, 1996.

Nasaw, David. *Going Out: The Rise and Fall of Public Amusements.* Cambridge, MA: Harvard University Press, 1999.

Newton, James D. *Uncommon Friends: Life with Thomas Edison, Henry Ford, Harvey Firestone, Alexis Carrel and Charles Lindbergh.* San Diego, CA: Harcourt Brace Jovanovich, 1987.

Olney, Martha E. *Buy Now, Pay Later: Advertising, Credit, and Consumer Durables in the 1920s.* Chapel Hill: University of North Carolina Press, 1991.

Pegram, Thomas R. *One Hundred Percent American: The Rebirth and Decline of the Ku Klux Klan in the 1920s.* Chicago: Ivan Dee, 2011.

Petro, Patrice, ed. *Idols of Modernity: Movie Stars of the 1920s.* New Brunswick, NJ: Rutgers University Press, 2010.

Ritter, Lawrence S. *The Glory of Their Times: The Story of the Early Days of Baseball Told by the Men Who Played It,* new enl. ed. New York: Morrow, 1984.

Rose, Kenneth D. *American Women and the Repeal of Prohibition.* New York: New York University Press, 1996.

Rubin, Joan Shelley. *The Making of Middlebrow Culture.* Chapel Hill: University of North Carolina Press, 1992.

Rutherford, Janice Williams. *Selling Mrs. Consumer: Christine Frederick and the Rise of Household Efficiency.* Athens: University of Georgia Press, 2002.

Schrum, Kelly. *Some Wore Bobby Sox: The Emergence of Teen Girl Culture, 1920-1945.* New York: Palgrave Macmillan, 2004.

Schweitzer, Marlis. *When Broadway Was the Runway: Theater, Fashion, and American Culture.* Philadelphia: University of Pennsylvania Press, 2009.

Seleshanko, Kristina. *Vintage Fashions for Women, 1920s-1940s.* Atglen, PA: Schiffer, 1996.

Seymour, Harold. *Baseball: The Golden Age,* vol. 2 of *Baseball,* 3 vols. 1960-1971; reprint, New York: Oxford University Press, 1989-1990.

Sies, Luther F. *Encyclopedia of American Radio, 1920-1960.* Jefferson, NC: McFarland, 2000.

Slotten, Hugh Richard. *Radio's Hidden Voice: The Origins of Public Broadcasting in the United States.* Urbana: University of Illinois Press, 2009.

Slowik, Michael. *After the Silents: Hollywood Film Music in the Early Sound Era, 1926-1934.* New York: Columbia University Press, 2014.

Smith, Page. *Redeeming the Time: A People's History of the 1920s and the New Deal.* New York: McGraw-Hill, 1987.

Smulyan, Susan. *Selling Radio: The Commercialization of American Broadcasting, 1920-1934.* Washington, DC: Smithsonian Institution Press, 1994.

Solomon, Barbara H., ed. *Ain't We Got Fun?: Essays, Lyrics, and Stories of the Twenties.* New York: New American Library, 1980.

Springer, Robert, ed. *Nobody Knows Where the Blues Come From; Lyrics and History.* Jackson: University Press of Mississippi, 2006.

Standard Homes Company. *Best Homes of the 1920s.* Mineola, NY: Dover, 2008.

Strasser, Susan. *Never Done; A History of American Housework.* 1982; reprint, New York: Holt, 2013.

Touring America Seventy-Five Years Ago: How the Automobile and the Railroad Changed the Nation; Chronicles from National Geographic. Arthur M. Schlesinger, Jr., senior consulting ed.; Fred L. Israel, gen. ed. Philadelphia: Chelsea House, 1999.

Tyler, Bruce M. *From Harlem to Hollywood: The Struggle for Racial and Cultural Democracy, 1920-1943.* New York: Garland, 1992.

Valgemae, Mardi. *Accelerated Grimace: Expressionism in the American Drama of the 1920s.* Carbondale: Southern Illinois University Press, 1972.

Warner, Patricia Campbell. *When the Girls Came Out to Play: The Birth of American Sportswear.* Amherst, MA: University of Massachusetts Press, 2006.

Wheeler, Lesley. *Voicing American Poetry: Sound and Performance from the 1920s to the Present.* Ithaca, NY: Cornell University Press, 2008.

Immigration

Avrich, Paul. *Sacco and Vanzetti: The Anarchist Background.* Princeton, NJ: Princeton University Press, 1991.

Chermayeff, Ivan, Fred Wasserman, and Mary J. Shapiro. *Ellis Island: An Illustrated History of the Immigrant Experience.* New York: Macmillan, 1991.

Dinnerstein, Leonard, and David M. Reimers. *Ethnic Americans: A History of Immigration and Assimilation,* 2d ed. New York: Harper & Row, 1982.

Ewen, Elizabeth. *Immigrant Women in the Land of Dollars: Life and Culture on the Lower East Side, 1890-1925.* New York: Monthly Review Press, 1985.

Fleegler, Robert L. *Ellis Island Nation: Immigration Policy and American Identity in the Twentieth Century.* Philadelphia: University of Pennsylvania Press, 2013.

Garland, Libby. *After They Closed the Gates; Jewish Illegal Immigration to the United States, 1921-1965.* Chicago: University of Chicago Press, 2014.

Higham, John. *Strangers in the Land: Patterns of American Nativism, 1865-1925.* 1955; reprint, New Brunswock, NJ: Rutgers University Press, 2002.

Hoerder, Dirk. *American Labor and Immigration History, 1877-1920s; Recent European Research.* Urbana: University of Illinois Press, 1983.

Irving, Katrina. *Immigrant Mothers: Narratives of Race and Maternity, 1890-1925.* Urbana: University of Illinois Press, 2000.

Knobel, Dale T. *America for the Americans: The Nativist Movement in the United States.* New York: Twayne Publishers/London: Prentice Hall International, 1996.

Lee, Erika. *At America's Gates; Chinese Immigration during the Exclusion Era, 1882-1943.* Chapel Hill: University of North Carolina Press, 2003.

Madison, Nathan Vernon. *Anti-Foreign Imagery in American Pulps and Comic Books, 1920-1960.* Jefferson, NC: McFarland, 2013.

Moreno, Barry. *Encyclopedia of Ellis Island.* Westport, CT: Greenwood Press, 2004.

Murray, Robert K. *Red Scare: A Study in National Hysteria, 1919-1920.* Minneapolis: University of Minnesota Press, 1955.

Ngai, Mae M. *Impossible Subjects: Illegal Aliens and the Making of Modern America.* 2004; reprint, Princeton, NJ: Princeton University Press, 2014.

Preston, William, Jr. *Aliens and Dissenters: Federal Suppression of Radicals, 1903-1933.* 1963; reprint, Urbana: University of Illinois Press, 1994.

Ramirez, Bruno, with Yves Otis. *Crossing the 49th Parallel; Migration from Canada to the United States, 1900-1930.* Ithaca, NY: Cornell University Press, 2001.

Reimers, David M. *Unwelcome Strangers: American Identity and the Turn against Immigration.* New York: Columbia University Press, 1998.

Van Nuys, Frank. *Americanizing the West: Race, Immigrants, and Citizenship, 1890-1930.* Lawrence: University Press of Kansas, 2002.

Veverka, Fayette Breaux. *For God and Country; Catholic Schooling in the 1920s.* New York: Garland, 1988.

Wan, Amy J. *Producing Good Citizens; Literacy Training in Anxious Times.* Pittsburgh, PA: University of Pittsburgh Press, 2014.

Weiss, Bernard J., ed. *American Education and the European Immigrant, 1840-1940.* Urbana: University of Illinois Press, 1982.

Wilson, Sarah. *Melting-Pot Modernism.* Ithaca, NY: Cornell University Press, 2010.

Labor

Altenbaugh, Richard J. *Education for Struggle: The American Labor Colleges of the 1920s and 1930s*. Philadelphia: Temple University Press, 1990.

Bernstein, Irving. *The Lean Years: A History of the American Worker, 1920-1933*. 1960; reprint, Chicago: Haymarket Books, 2010.

Corbin, David Alan, ed. *Gun Thugs, Rednecks, and Radicals: A Documentary History of the West Virginia Mine Wars*. Oakland, CA: PM Press, 2011.

Foner, Philip S. *The Boshevik Revolution, Its Impact on American Radicals, Liberals, and Labor; A Documentary Study*. New York: International Publishers, 1967.

Foner, Philip S., and James S. Allen, eds. *American Communism and Black Americans: A Documentary History, 1919-1929*. Philadelphia: Temple University Press, 1987.

Hoerder, Dirk. *American Labor and Immigration History, 1877-1920s; Recent European Research*. Urbana: University of Illinois Press, 1983.

Jacoby, Sanford M. *Employing Bureaucracy: Managers, Unions, and the Transformation of Work in the Twentieth Century*. Mahwah, NJ: Lawrence Erlbaum, 2004.

McCartin, Joseph A. *Labor's Great War: The Struggle for Industrial Democracy and the Origins of Modern American Labor Relations, 1912-1921*. Chapel Hill: University of North Carolina Press, 1997.

Nelson, Daniel, ed. *A Mental Revolution: Scientific Management since Taylor*. Columbus: Ohio State University Press, 1992.

Quirke, Carol. *Eyes on Labor: News Photography and America's Working Class*. New York: Oxford University Press, 2012.

Savage, Lon. *Thunder in the Mountains: The West Virginia Mine War, 1920-21*. 1985; reprint, Pittsburgh: University of Pittsburgh Press, 1990.

Schmidt, James D. *Industrial Violence and the Legal Origins of Child Labor*. New York: Cambridge University Press, 2010.

Zeitlin, Maurice, ed. *How Mighty a Force? Studies of Workers' Consciousness and Organization in the United States*. Los Angeles: Institute of Industrial Relations, University of California at Los Angeles, 1983.

Literature and Drama

Aaron, Daniel. *Writers on the Left; Episodes in American Literary Communism*. 1961; reprint, New York: Columbia University Press, 1992.

Banta, Martha. *Taylored Lives: Narrative Productions in the Age of Taylor, Veblen, and Ford*. Chicago: University of Chicago Press, 1993.

Bone, Robert. *Down Home: A History of Afro-American Short Fiction from Its Beginnings to the End of the Harlem Renaissance*. New York: Putnam, 1975.

Botshon, Lisa, and Meredith Goldsmith, eds. *Middlebrow Moderns: Popular Women Writers of the 1920s*. Boston: Northeastern University Press, 2003.

Boyer, Paul S. *Purity in Print: Book Censorship in America from the Gilded Age to the Computer Age*, 2d ed. Madison: University of Wisconsin Press, 2002.

Childs, Peter. *Modernist Literature: A Guide for the Perplexed*. New York: Continuum, 2011.

Cowley, Malcolm. *Exile's Return: A Literary Odyssey of the 1920s*. 1969; reprint, New York: Penguin, 1976.

Gewirtz, Arthur, and James J. Kolb, eds. *Art, Glitter, and Glitz: Mainstream Playwrights and Popular Theatre in 1920s America*. Westport, CT: Praeger, 2003.

Gewirtz, Arthur, and James J. Kolb, eds. *Experimenters, Rebels, and Disparate Voices; The Theatre of the 1920s Celebrates American Diversity*. Westport, CT: Praeger, 2003.

Hutner, Gordon. *What America Read: Taste, Class, and the Novel, 1920-1960*. Chapel Hill: University of North Carolina Press, 2009.

Inabinett, Mark. *Grantland Rice and His Heroes: The Sportswriter as Mythmaker in the 1920s*. Knoxville: University of Tennessee Press, 1994.

Koritz, Amy. *Culture Makers: Urban Performance and Literature in the 1920s*. Urbana: University of Illinois Press, 2009.

Marcus, Leonard S. *Minders of Make-Believe: Idealists, Entrepreneurs, and the Shaping of American Children's Literature*. Boston, Houghton Mifflin, 2008.

Perry, Margaret. *The Harlem Renaissance: An Annotated Bibliography and Commentary*. New York: Garland Press, 1982.

Perry, Margaret. *Silence to the Drums: A Survey of the Literature of the Harlem Renaissance*. Westport, CT: Greenwood Press, 1976.

Scott, Bonnie Kime, ed. *Gender in Modernism: New Geographies, Complex Intersections*. Urbana: University of Illinois Press, 2007.

Scruggs, Charles. *The Sage in Harlem: H. L. Mencken and the Black Writers of the 1920s*. Baltimore: Johns Hopkins University Press, 1984.

Stratton, Matthew. *The Politics of Irony in American Modernism*. New York: Fordham University Press, 2014.

Valgemae, Mardi. *Accelerated Grimace: Expressionism in the American Drama of the 1920s*. Carbondale: Southern Illinois University Press, 1972.

Van Dover, J. Kenneth. *Making the Detective Story American: Biggers, Van Dine and Hammett and the Turning Point of the Genre, 1925-1930*. Jefferson, NC: McFarland, 2010.

Vincent, Theodore G. *Voices of a Black Nation: Political Journalism in the Harlem Renaissance*. San Francisco: Ramparts Press, 1973.

Wheeler, Lesley. *Voicing American Poetry: Sound and Performance from the 1920s to the Present*. Ithaca, NY: Cornell University Press, 2008.

Wilson, Sarah. *Melting-Pot Modernism*. Ithaca, NY: Cornell University Press, 2010.

Wintz, Cary D., series ed. *The Harlem Renaissance, 1920-1940*, 7 vols. New York: Garland, 1996. [vol. 1: *The Emergence of the Harlem Renaissance*; vol. 2: *The Politics and Aesthetics of "New Negro" Literature*; vol. 3: *Black Writers Interpret the Harlem Renaissance*; vol. 4: *The Critics and the Harlem Renaissance*; vol. 5: *Remembering the Harlem Renaissance*; vol. 6: *Analysis and Assessment, 1940-1979*; vol. 7: *Analysis and Assessment, 1980-1994*.]

Politics and the Presidency

Avrich, Paul. *Sacco and Vanzetti: The Anarchist Background*. Princeton, NJ: Princeton University Press, 1991.

Clements, Kendrick A. *Imperfect Visionary, 1918-1928*, vol. 4 of *The Life of Herbert Hoover*. New York: Palgrave Macmillan, 2010.

Coolidge, Calvin. *The Autobiography of Calvin Coolidge*. 1929; reprint, Rutland, VT: Academy Books, 1984.

Eagles, Charles W. *Democracy Delayed: Congressional Reapportionment and Urban-Rural Conflict in the 1920s*. Athens: University of Georgia Press, 1990.

Ferrell, Robert H. *The Presidency of Calvin Coolidge*. Lawrence: University Press of Kansas, 1998.

Ferrell, Robert H. *The Strange Deaths of President Harding*. Columbia: University of Missouri Press, 1996.

Flanagan, Maureen A. *America Reformed: Progressives and Progressivisms, 1890s-1920s*. New York: Oxford University Press, 2007.

Foner, Philip S., and James S. Allen, eds. *American Communism and Black Americans: A Documentary History, 1919-1929.* Philadelphia: Temple University Press, 1987.

Goldstein, Robert Justin, ed. *Little "Red Scares": Anti-Communism and Political Repression in the United States, 1921-1946.* Farnham, Surrey, England: Ashgate, 2013.

Hawley, Ellis W., ed. *Herbert Hoover as Secretary of Commerce: Studies in New Era Thought and Practice.* Iowa City: University of Iowa Press, 1981.

Haynes, John Earl, ed., *Calvin Coolidge and the Coolidge Era: Essays on the History of the 1920s.* Washington, DC: Library of Congress, 1998.

Jeansonne, Glen, *Fighting Quaker, 1928-1933,* vol. 5 of *The Life of Herbert Hoover.* New York, Palgrave Macmillan, 2013.

McCoy, Donald R. *Calvin Coolidge: The Quiet President.* 1967; reprint, Lawrence: University Press of Kansas, 1988.

Murphy, Paul L. *World War I and the Origin of Civil Liberties in the United States.* New York: W. W. Norton, 1979.

Murray, Robert K. *The Harding Era; Warren G. Harding and His Administration.* 1969; reprint, Newtown, CT: American Political Biography Press, June 2000.

Murray, Robert K. *The Politics of Normalcy: Governmental Theory and Practice in the Harding-Coolidge Era.* New York: W. W. Norton, 1973.

Nash, George H., *The Engineer, 1874-1914,* vol. 1 of *The Life of Herbert Hoover.* New York: W. W. Norton, 1983.

Nash, George H., *The Humanitarian, 1914-1917,* vol. 2 of *The Life of Herbert Hoover.* New York: W. W. Norton, 1988.

Nash, George H., *The Master of Emergencies, 1917-1918,* vol. 3 of *The Life of Herbert Hoover.* New York: W. W. Norton, 1996.

Quint, Howard H., and Robert H. Ferrell, eds. *The Talkative President; The Off-the-Record Press Conferences of Calvin Coolidge.* Amherst: University of Massachusetts Press, 1964.

Rusco, Elmer R. *A Fateful Time: The Background and Legislative History of the Indian Reorganization Act.* Reno: University of Nevada Press, 2000.

Sibley, Katherine A. S., ed. *A Companion to Warren G. Harding, Calvin Coolidge, and Herbert Hoover.* Hoboken, NJ: John Wiley, 2014.

Silver, Thomas B. *Coolidge and the Historians.* Durham, NC: Academic Press, for the Claremont Institute, 1982.

Vincent, Theodore G. *Voices of a Black Nation: Political Journalism in the Harlem Renaissance.* San Francisco: Ramparts Press, 1973.

Wan, Amy J. *Producing Good Citizens; Literacy Training in Anxious Times.* Pittsburgh, PA: University of Pittsburgh Press, 2014.

Religion

Anderson, Robert Mapes. *Vision of the Disinherited; The Making of American Pentecostalism.* New York: Oxford University Press, 1979.

Bailey, Kenneth K. *Southern White Protestantism in the Twentieth Century.* 1964; reprint, Gloucester, MA: Peter Smith, 1988.

Baker, Kelly G. *Gospel according to the Klan: The KKK's Appeal to Protestant America, 1915-1930.* Lawrence: University Press of Kansas, 2011.

Braeman, John, et al., eds. *Change and Continuity in Twentieth Century America: The 1920's.* Columbus, OH: Ohio State University Press, 1968.

Carter, Paul A. *The Decline and Revival of Social Gospel: Social and Political Liberalism in American Protestant Churches, 1920-1940.* Ithaca, NY: Cornell University Press, 1956.

Curtis, Susan. *Consuming Faith: The Social Gospel and Modern American Culture.* Baltimore: Johns Hopkins University Press, 1991.

Feingold, Henry L. *A Time for Searching: Entering the Mainstream, 1920-1945,* vol. 4 of *The Jewish People in America.* Baltimore: Johns Hopkins University Press, 1992.

Fox, Craig. *Everyday Klanfolk: White Protestant Life and the KKK in 1920s Michigan.* Lansing: Michigan State University Press, 2011.

Furniss, Norman K. *The Fundamentalist Controversy, 1918-1931.* 1954; reprint, Hamden, CT: Archon, 1963.

Giordano, Ralph G. *Satan in the Dance Hall; Rev. John Roach Straton, Social Dancing, and Morality in 1920s New York City.* Lanham, MD: Scarecrow Press, 2008.

Halsey, William M. *The Survival of American Innocence; Catholicism in an Era of Disillusionment, 1920-1940.* Notre Dame, IN: University of Notre Dame Press, 1980.

Handy, Robert T. *The American Religious Depression, 1925-1935.* Philadelphia: Fortress Press, 1968. [Reprint from *Church History,* v. 29, 1960.]

Hutchinson, William R. *The Modernist Impulse in American Protestantism.* 1976; reprint, Durham, NC: Duke University Press, 1992.

Lundén, Rolf. *Business and Religion in the American 1920s.* New York: Greenwood Press, 1988.

Marsden, George M. *Fundamentalism and American Culture,* 2d ed. New York: Oxford University Press, 2006.

Mecklin, John Moffatt. *The Ku-Klux Klan: A Study of the American Mind.* 1924; reprint, Kessinger, 2006. [Facsimile reprint of the 1963 Russell and Russell edition.]

Raphael, Marc Lee, ed. *Columbia History of Jews and Judaism in America.* New York: Columbia University Press, 2008.

Robinson, Thomas A., and Lanette R. Ruff. *Out of the Mouths of Babes: Girl Evangelists in the Flapper Era.* New York: Oxford University Press, 2011.

Slawson, Douglas J. *The Department of Education Battle, 1918-1932; Public Schools, Catholic Schools, and the Social Order.* Notre Dame, IN: University of Notre Dame Press, 2005.

Smith, Christian, ed. *The Secular Revolution: Power, Interests, and Conflict in the Secularization of American Public Life.* Berkeley: University of California Press, 2003.

Synan, Vinson. *The Holiness-Pentecostal Tradition; Charismatic Movements in the Twentieth Century,* 2d. ed. Grand Rapids, MI: W. B. Eerdmans, 1997.

Veverka, Fayette Breaux. *For God and Country; Catholic Schooling in the 1920s.* New York: Garland, 1988.

Wacker, Grant. *Heaven Below: Early Pentecostals and American Culture.* Cambridge, MA: Harvard University Press, 2001.

Weissbach, Lee Shai. *Jewish Life in Small-Town America: A History* (New Haven: Yale University Press, 2005.

Wenger, Tisa. *We Have a Religion: The 1920s Pueblo Indian Dance Controversy and American Religious Freedom.* Chapel Hill: William P. Clements Center for Southwest Studies, Southern Methodist University/ University of North Carolina Press, 2009.

Sports

Aycock, Colleen, and Mark Scott, eds. *The First Black Boxing Champions: Essays on Fighters from the 1800s to the 1920s.* Jefferson, NC: McFarland, 2010.

Boddy, Kasia. *Boxing: A Cultural History.* London: Reaktion Books, 2008.

Bodner, Allen. *When Boxing Was a Jewish Sport.* Westport, CT: Praeger, 1997.

Bohn, Michael K. *Heroes and Ballyhoo: How the Golden Age of the 1920s Transformed American Sports.* Washington, DC: Potomac Books, 2009.

Browning, Reed. *Baseball's Greatest Season, 1924.* Amherst: University of Massachusetts Press, 2003.

Bryson, Bill. *One Summer; America, 1927.* New York: Doubleday, 2013.

Cooke, Bob, ed. *Wake Up the Echoes: From the Sports Pages of the* New York Herald Tribune. Garden City, NY: Hanover House, 1956.

Dulles, Foster Rhea. *A History of Recreation; America Learns to Play,* 2d ed. New York: Appleton Century Crofts, 1965.

Inabinett, Mark. *Grantland Rice and His Heroes: The Sportswriter as Mythmaker in the 1920s.* Knoxville: University of Tennessee Press, 1994.

Jerris, Rand, et al. *Golf's Golden Age: Robert T. Jones, Jr. and the Legendary Players of the '10s, '20s, and '30s.* Photographs by George S. Pietzcker. Far Hills, NJ: U.S. Golf Association/Washington, DC: National Geographic, 2005.

Kaye, Ivan N. *Good Clean Violence: A History of College Football.* Philadelphia, Lippincott, 1973.

Lang, Arne K. *Prizefighting: An American History.* Jefferson, NC: McFarland, 2008.

Peterson, Robert W. *Pigskin: The Early Years of Pro Football.* New York: Oxford University Press, 1997.

Riess, Steven A. *City Games: The Evolution of American Urban Society and the Rise of Sports.* 1989; reprint, Urbana, IL: Illini Books, 1991.

Riess, Steven A. *Touching Base: Professional Baseball and American Culture in the Progressive Era,* rev. ed. Urbana: University of Illinois Press, 1999.

Ritter, Lawrence S. *The Glory of Their Times: The Story of the Early Days of Baseball Told by the Men Who Played It,* new enl. ed. New York: Morrow, 1984.

Seymour, Harold. *Baseball: The Golden Age,* vol. 2 of *Baseball,* 3 vols. 1960-1990; reprint, New York: Oxford University Press, 1989-1991.

Shackelford, Geoff. *The Golden Age of Golf Design.* Chelsea, MI: Sleeping Bear Press, 1999.

Streible, Dan. *Fight Pictures: A History of Boxing in Early Cinema.* Berkeley: University of California Press, 2008.

Tygiel, Jules. *Past Time: Baseball as History.* New York: Oxford University Press, 2000.

Warner, Patricia Campbell. *When the Girls Came Out to Play: The Birth of American Sportswear.* Amherst: University of Massachusetts Press, 2006.

Youngs, Larry R. "Creating America's Winter Golfing Mecca at Pinehurst, North Carolina: National Marketing and Local Control," in vol. 2 of *Sport in America: From Colonial Leisure to Celebrity Figures and Globalization,* ed. David K. Wiggins Champaign, IL: Human Kinetics, 2010.

Waltzer, Jim. *The Battle of the Century: Dempsey, Carpentier, and the Birth of Modern Promotion.* Santa Barbara, CA: Praeger, 2011.

Ziemba, Joe. *When Football Was Football: The Chicago Cardinals and the Birth of the NFL.* Chicago: Triumph Books, 1999.

Women's History

Andersen, Kristi. *After Suffrage: Women in Partisan and Electoral Politics before the New Deal.* Chicago: University of Chicago Press, 1996.

Brown, Dorothy M. *Setting a Course: American Women in the 1920s.* Boston: Twayne, 1987.

Cott, Nancy F. *The Grounding of Modern Feminism.* (New Haven: Yale University Press, 1987.

Davis, Simone Weil. *Living Up to the Ads; Gender Fictions of the 1920s.* Durham, NC: Duke University Press, 2000.

Deepwell, Katy, ed. *Women Artists and Modernism.* New York: Manchester University Press, 1998.

Ewen, Elizabeth. *Immigrant Women in the Land of Dollars: Life and Culture on the Lower East Side, 1890-1925. New York: Monthly Review Press,* 1985.

Finnegan, Margaret Mary. *Selling Suffrage: Consumer Culture and Votes for Women.* New York: Columbia University Press, 1999.

Foster, Catherine. *Women for All Seasons: The Story of the Women's International League for Peace and Freedom.* Athens: University of Georgia Press, 1989.

Gidlow, Liette. *The Big Vote: Gender, Consumer Culture, and the Politics of Exclusion, 1890s-1920s.* Baltimore: Johns Hopkins University Press, 2004.

Latham, Angela J. *Posing a Threat: Flappers, Chorus Girls, and Other Brazen Performers of the American 1920s.* Hanover, NH: University Press of New England/Wesleyan University Press, 2000.

Lemons, J. Stanley. *The Woman Citizen: Social Feminism in the 1920's.* Urbana: University of Illinois Press, 1973.

Marshall, Susan E. *Splintered Sisterhood: Gender and Class in the Campaign against Woman Suffrage.* Madison: University of Wisconsin Press, 1997.

Mencken, H. L. "The Flapper" (*Smart Set,* 1915)," in *The American New Woman Revisited: A Reader, 1894-1930,* ed. by Martha H. Patterson. New Brunswick, NJ: Rutgers University Press, 2008.

Parker, Alison M. *Purifying America: Women, Cultural Reform, and Pro-Censorship Activism, 1873-1933.* Urbana: University of Illinois Press, 1997.

Robinson, Thomas A., and Lanette R. Ruff. *Out of the Mouths of Babes: Girl Evangelists in the Flapper Era.* New York: Oxford University Press, 2011.

Rose, Kenneth D. *American Women and the Repeal of Prohibition.* New York: New York University Press, 1996.

Scharf, Lois, and Joan M. Jensen, eds. *Decades of Discontent: The Women's Movement, 1920-1940.* Westport, CT: Greenwood Press, 1983.

Scott, Bonnie Kime, ed. *Gender in Modernism: New Geographies, Complex Intersections.* Urbana: University of Illinois Press, 2007.

Walker, Susannah. *Style & Status; Selling Beauty to African American Women, 1920-1975.* Lexington: University Press of Kentucky, 2007.

Zeitz, Joshua. *Flapper: A Madcap Story of Sex, Style, Celebrity, and the Women Who Made America Modern.* New York: Crown, 2006.

CITIZENSHIP		RESIDENCE, APRIL 1, 1935												PERSONS 14 YEARS OLD AND O...
CODE (Leave blank)	Citizenship of the foreign born	IN WHAT PLACE DID THIS PERSON LIVE ON APRIL 1, 1935?	COUNTY	STATE (or Territory or foreign country)	On a farm? (Yes or No)	CODE (Leave blank)	Was this person AT WORK for pay or profit...	If not, was he at work on, or assigned to Public EMERGENCY WORK...	Was this person SEEKING WORK? (Yes or No)	If not seeking work, did he HAVE A JOB, business, etc.?	Indicate whether engaged in home housework (H), in school (S), unable to work (U), other (Ot)	CODE	Number of hours worked during week of March 24-30, 1940	If seeking work or assigned to public emergency work...	OCCUP...
C	16	17	18	19	20	D	21	22	23	24	25	E	26	27	28
53		Same House			No		Yes	–	–	–		1	40	–	Foreman
56		Same House			No		No	No	No	No	H	5	–	–	
56		Same House			No		No	No	No	No	S	6	–	–	
		Same House			No		Yes	–	–	–		1	–	–	Laborer

General Reference

America's College Museums
American Environmental Leaders: From Colonial Times to the Present
An African Biographical Dictionary
An Encyclopedia of Human Rights in the United States
Constitutional Amendments
Encyclopedia of African-American Writing
Encyclopedia of the Continental Congress
Encyclopedia of Gun Control & Gun Rights
Encyclopedia of Invasions & Conquests
Encyclopedia of Prisoners of War & Internment
Encyclopedia of Religion & Law in America
Encyclopedia of Rural America
Encyclopedia of the United States Cabinet, 1789-2010
Encyclopedia of War Journalism
Encyclopedia of Warrior Peoples & Fighting Groups
From Suffrage to the Senate: America's Political Women
Nations of the World
Political Corruption in America
Speakers of the House of Representatives, 1789-2009
The Environmental Debate: A Documentary History
The Evolution Wars: A Guide to the Debates
The Religious Right: A Reference Handbook
The Value of a Dollar: 1860-2009
The Value of a Dollar: Colonial Era
This is Who We Were: A Companion to the 1940 Census
This is Who We Were: The 1920s
This is Who We Were: The 1950s
This is Who We Were: The 1960s
US Land & Natural Resource Policy
Working Americans 1770-1869 Vol. IX: Revolutionary War to the Civil War
Working Americans 1880-1999 Vol. I: The Working Class
Working Americans 1880-1999 Vol. II: The Middle Class
Working Americans 1880-1999 Vol. III: The Upper Class
Working Americans 1880-1999 Vol. IV: Their Children
Working Americans 1880-2003 Vol. V: At War
Working Americans 1880-2005 Vol. VI: Women at Work
Working Americans 1880-2006 Vol. VII: Social Movements
Working Americans 1880-2007 Vol. VIII: Immigrants
Working Americans 1880-2009 Vol. X: Sports & Recreation
Working Americans 1880-2010 Vol. XI: Inventors & Entrepreneurs
Working Americans 1880-2011 Vol. XII: Our History through Music
Working Americans 1880-2012 Vol. XIII: Education & Educators
World Cultural Leaders of the 20th & 21st Centuries

Business Information

Complete Television, Radio & Cable Industry Directory
Directory of Business Information Resources
Directory of Mail Order Catalogs
Directory of Venture Capital & Private Equity Firms
Environmental Resource Handbook
Food & Beverage Market Place
Grey House Homeland Security Directory
Grey House Performing Arts Directory
Hudson's Washington News Media Contacts Directory
New York State Directory
Sports Market Place Directory

Education Information

Charter School Movement
Comparative Guide to American Elementary & Secondary Schools
Complete Learning Disabilities Directory
Educators Resource Directory
Special Education

Health Information

Comparative Guide to American Hospitals
Complete Directory for Pediatric Disorders
Complete Directory for People with Chronic Illness
Complete Directory for People with Disabilities
Complete Mental Health Directory
Diabetes in America: A Geographic & Demographic Analysis
Directory of Health Care Group Purchasing Organizations
Directory of Hospital Personnel
HMO/PPO Directory
Medical Device Register
Older Americans Information Directory

Statistics & Demographics

America's Top-Rated Cities
America's Top-Rated Small Towns & Cities
America's Top-Rated Smaller Cities
American Tally
Ancestry & Ethnicity in America
Comparative Guide to American Hospitals
Comparative Guide to American Suburbs
Profiles of America
Profiles of... Series – State Handbooks
The Hispanic Databook
Weather America

Financial Ratings Series

TheStreet.com Ratings Guide to Bond & Money Market Mutual Funds
TheStreet.com Ratings Guide to Common Stocks
TheStreet.com Ratings Guide to Exchange-Traded Funds
TheStreet.com Ratings Guide to Stock Mutual Funds
TheStreet.com Ratings Ultimate Guided Tour of Stock Investing
Weiss Ratings Consumer Guides
Weiss Ratings Guide to Banks & Thrifts
Weiss Ratings Guide to Credit Unions
Weiss Ratings Guide to Health Insurers
Weiss Ratings Guide to Life & Annuity Insurers
Weiss Ratings Guide to Property & Casualty Insurers

Bowker's Books In Print®Titles

Books In Print®
Books In Print® Supplement
American Book Publishing Record® Annual
American Book Publishing Record® Monthly
Books Out Loud™
Bowker's Complete Video Directory™
Children's Books In Print®
El-Hi Textbooks & Serials In Print®
Forthcoming Books®
Law Books & Serials In Print™
Medical & Health Care Books In Print™
Publishers, Distributors & Wholesalers of the US™
Subject Guide to Books In Print®
Subject Guide to Children's Books In Print®

Canadian General Reference

Associations Canada
Canadian Almanac & Directory
Canadian Environmental Resource Guide
Canadian Parliamentary Guide
Financial Services Canada
Governments Canada
Health Services Canada
Libraries Canada
Major Canadian Cities
The History of Canada

Grey House Publishing | Salem Press | H.W. Wilson
4919 Route, 22 PO Box 56, Amenia NY 12501-0056

2014 Title List

Visit **www.SalemPress.com** for Product Information, Table of Contents and Sample Pages

Literature

American Ethnic Writers
Critical Insights: Authors
Critical Insights: New Literary Collection Bundles
Critical Insights: Themes
Critical Insights: Works
Critical Survey of Drama
Critical Survey of Graphic Novels: Heroes & Super Heroes
Critical Survey of Graphic Novels: History, Theme & Technique
Critical Survey of Graphic Novels: Independents & Underground Classics
Critical Survey of Graphic Novels: Manga
Critical Survey of Long Fiction
Critical Survey of Mystery & Detective Fiction
Critical Survey of Mythology and Folklore: Heroes and Heroines
Critical Survey of Mythology and Folklore: Love, Sexuality & Desire
Critical Survey of Mythology and Folklore: World Mythology
Critical Survey of Poetry
Critical Survey of Poetry: American Poetry
Critical Survey of Poetry: British, Irish & Commonwealth Poets
Critical Survey of Poetry: European Poets
Critical Survey of Poetry: European Poets
Critical Survey of Poetry: Topical Essays
Critical Survey of Poetry: World Poets
Critical Survey of Science Fiction & Fantasy Literature
Critical Survey of Shakespeare's Sonnets
Critical Survey of Short Fiction
Critical Survey of Short Fiction: American Writers
Critical Survey of Short Fiction: British, Irish & Commonwealth Poets
Critical Survey of Short Fiction: European Writers
Critical Survey of Short Fiction: Topical Essays
Critical Survey of Short Fiction: World Writers
Cyclopedia of Literary Characters
Introduction to Literary Context: American Post-Modernist Novels
Introduction to Literary Context: American Short Fiction
Introduction to Literary Context: English Literature
Introduction to Literary Context: World Literature
Magill's Literary Annual 2014
Magill's Survey of American Literature
Magill's Survey of World Literature
Masterplots
Masterplots II: African American Literature
Masterplots II: Christian Literature
Masterplots II: Drama Series
Masterplots II: Short Story Series
Notable African American Writers
Notable American Novelists
Notable Playwrights
Short Story Writers

Science, Careers & Mathematics

Applied Science
Applied Science: Engineering & Mathematics
Applied Science: Science & Medicine
Applied Science: Technology
Biomes and Ecosystems
Careers in Chemistry
Careers in Communications & Media
Careers in Healthcare
Careers in Hospitality & Tourism
Careers in Law & Criminology
Careers in Physics
Computer Technology Inventors
Contemporary Biographies in Chemistry
Contemporary Biographies in Communications & Media
Contemporary Biographies in Healthcare
Contemporary Biographies in Hospitality & Tourism
Contemporary Biographies in Law & Criminology
Contemporary Biographies in Physics
Earth Science
Earth Science: Earth Materials & Resources
Earth Science: Earth's Surface and History
Earth Science: Physics & Chemistry of the Earth
Earth Science: Weather, Water & Atmosphere
Encyclopedia of Energy
Encyclopedia of Environmental Issues
Encyclopedia of Global Resources
Encyclopedia of Global Warming
Encyclopedia of Mathematics and Society
Encyclopedia of the Ancient World
Forensic Science
Internet Innovators
Introduction to Chemistry
Magill's Encyclopedia of Science: Animal Life
Magill's Encyclopedia of Science: Plant life
Magill's Medical Guide
Notable Natural Disasters
Solar System

Health

Addictions & Substance Abuse
Cancer
Complementary & Alternative Medicine
Genetics & Inherited Conditions
Infectious Diseases & Conditions
Magill's Medical Guide
Psychology & Mental Health
Psychology Basics

Grey House Publishing | Salem Press | H.W. Wilson
4919 Route, 22 PO Box 56, Amenia NY 12501-0056

2014 Title List

Visit **www.SalemPress.com** for Product Information, Table of Contents and Sample Pages

History and Social Science

A 2000s in America
50 States
African American History
Agriculture in History (check)
American First Ladies
American Heroes
American Indian Tribes
American Presidents
American Villains
Ancient Greece
Bill of Rights, The
Cold War, The
Defining Documents: American Revolution 1754-1805
Defining Documents: Civil War 1860-1865
Defining Documents: Emergence of Modern America, 1868-1918
Defining Documents: Exploration & Colonial America 1492-1755
Defining Documents: Manifest Destiny 1803-1860
Defining Documents: Reconstruction, 1865-1880
Defining Documents: The 1920s
Defining Documents: The 1930s
Defining Documents: World War I
Eighties in America
Encyclopedia of American Immigration
Fifties in America
Forties in America
Great Athletes
Great Events from History: 17th Century
Great Events from History: 18th Century
Great Events from History: 19th Century
Great Events from History: 20th Century, 1901-1940
Great Events from History: 20th Century, 1941-1970
Great Events from History: 20th Century, 1971-200
Great Events from History: Ancient World
Great Events from History: Middle Ages
Great Events from History: Modern Scandals
Great Events from History: Renaissance & Early Modern Era
Great Lives from History: 17th Century
Great Lives from History: 18th Century
Great Lives from History: 19th Century
Great Lives from History: 20th Century
Great Lives from History: African Americans
Great Lives from History: Ancient World
Great Lives from History: Asian & Pacific Islander Americans
Great Lives from History: Incredibly Wealthy
Great Lives from History: Inventors & Inventions
Great Lives from History: Jewish Americans
Great Lives from History: Latinos
Great Lives from History: Middle Ages
Great Lives from History: Notorious Lives
Great Lives from History: Renaissance & Early Modern Era
Great Lives from History: Scientists & Science
Historical Encyclopedia of American Business
Immigration in U.S. History
Magill's Guide to Military History
Milestone Documents in African American History
Milestone Documents in American History
Milestone Documents in World History
Milestone Documents of American Leaders
Milestone Documents of World Religions
Musicians & Composers 20th Century
Nineties in America
Seventies in America

Sixties in America
Survey of American Industry and Careers
Thirties in America
Twenties in America
U.S. Court Cases
U.S. Laws, Acts, and Treaties
U.S. Legal System
U.S. Supreme Court
United States at War
USA in Space
Weapons and Warfare
World Conflicts: Asia and the Middle East

Grey House Publishing | Salem Press | H.W. Wilson
4919 Route, 22 PO Box 56, Amenia NY 12501-0056

2014 Title List

Visit **www.HwWilsonInPrint.com** for Product Information, Table of Contents and Sample Pages

Current Biography

Current Biography Cumulative Index 1946-2013
Current Biography Magazine
Current Biography Yearbook-2004
Current Biography Yearbook-2005
Current Biography Yearbook-2006
Current Biography Yearbook-2007
Current Biography Yearbook-2008
Current Biography Yearbook-2009
Current Biography Yearbook-2010
Current Biography Yearbook-2011
Current Biography Yearbook-2012
Current Biography Yearbook-2013
Current Biography Yearbook-2014

Core Collections

Senior High Core Collection
Middle & Junior High School Core
Children's Core Collection
Fiction Core Collection
Public Library Core Collection: Nonfiction

Sears List

Sears List of Subject Headings
Sears: Lista de Encabezamientos de Materia

The Reference Shelf

Aging in America
Revisiting Gender
The U.S. National Debate Topic, 2014/2015
Embracing New Paradigms in education
Marijuana Reform
Representative American Speeches 2013-2014
Reality Television
The Business of Food
The Future of U.S. Economic Relations: Mexico, Cuba, and Venezuela
Sports in America
Global Climate Change
Representative American Speeches, 2012-2013
Conspiracy Theories
The Arab Spring
U.S. National Debate Topic: Transportation Infrastructure
Families: Traditional and New Structures
Faith & Science
Representative American Speeches 2011-2012
Social Networking
Dinosaurs
Space Exploration & Development
U.S. Infrastructure
Politics of the Ocean
Representative American Speeches 2010-2011
Robotics
The News and its Future
American Military Presence Overseas
Russia
Graphic Novels and Comic Books
Representative American Speeches 2009-2010

Readers' Guide

Readers Guide to Periodicals Literature
Abridged Readers' Guide to Periodical Literature
Short Story Index

Indexes

Short Story Index
Index to Legal Periodicals & Books

Facts About Series

Facts About the Presidents, Eighth Edition
Facts About China
Facts About the 20th Century
Facts About American Immigration
Facts About World's Languages

Nobel Prize Winners

Nobel Prize Winners, 2002-2013

World Authors

World Authors 2000-2005
World Authors 2006-2013

Famous First Facts

Famous First Facts, Seventh Edition
Famous First Facts About American Politics
Famous First Facts About Sports
Famous First Facts About the Environment
Famous First Facts, International Edition

American Book of Days

The American Book of Days, Fifth Edition
The International Book of Days

Junior Authors & Illustrators

Tenth Book of Junior Authors & Illustrations

Monographs

The Barnhart Dictionary of Etymology
Celebrate the World
Indexing from A to Z
Radical Change: Books for Youth in a Digital Age
The Poetry Break
Guide to the Ancient World

Wilson Chronology

Wilson Chronology of Asia and the Pacific
Wilson Chronology of Human Rights
Wilson Chronology of Ideas
Wilson Chronology of the Arts
Wilson Chronology of the World's Religions
Wilson Chronology of Women's Achievements

Book Review Digest

Book Review Digest, 2014

Grey House Publishing | Salem Press | H.W. Wilson
4919 Route, 22 PO Box 56, Amenia NY 12501-0056